Caring for Your Baby and Young Child

This invaluable volume was prepared under the editorial direction of distinguished pediatricians Steven P. Shelov, MD, MS, FAAP, and Tanya Remer Altmann, MD, FAAP, and draws on the contributions and practical wisdom of more than 100 pediatric experts and an editorial review board. Written in a warm, accessible style and illustrated with more than 350 helpful drawings and diagrams, this book gives you the information you need to safeguard your child's most precious asset: his or her health.

In *Caring for Your Baby and Young Child* you'll find:

- A month-by-month guide to your baby's first year that lets you know what to expect in terms of growth, behavior, and development
- A yearly guide to ages one through five, with practical advice for dealing with sleeping, toilet training, and temper tantrums
- "Health Watch" features that alert you to potential medical problems at each stage
- "Safety Check" reminders for home, outdoors, and car travel
- A discussion of family issues—from grandparents and siblings to single parenting and stepfamilies

Plus reliable information on:

- All common infectious diseases, from chickenpox and measles to flu and ear infections
- Developmental disabilities, such as congenital abnormalities, cerebral palsy, hearing loss, autism, and intellectual disability
- Skin problems, from birthmarks to head lice and sunburn
- Emergencies, including bites, poisoning, choking, and CPR
- Feeding and nutrition
- Car safety seats

The sixth edition of this book includes current AAP policy information, updated content on developmental disabilities, early brain development, breastfeeding and nutrition, obesity, and safety standards, as well as a new chapter on the effects of media and technology on children.

Additional Parenting Books from the American Academy of Pediatrics

COMMON CONDITIONS

ADHD: What Every Parent Needs to Know

Allergies and Asthma: What Every Parent Needs to Know

Autism Spectrum Disorders: What Every Parent Needs to Know

The Big Book of Symptoms: A–Z Guide to Your Child's Health

My Child Is Sick! Expert Advice for Managing Common Illnesses and Injuries

Sleep: What Every Parent Needs to Know

Waking Up Dry: A Guide to Help Children Overcome Bedwetting

DEVELOPMENTAL, BEHAVIORAL, AND PSYCHOSOCIAL INFORMATION

CyberSafe: Protecting and Empowering Kids in the Digital World of Texting, Gaming, and Social Media

Mama Doc Medicine: Finding Calm and Confidence in Parenting, Child Health, and Work-Life Balance

Mental Health, Naturally: The Family Guide to Holistic Care for a Healthy Mind and Body

NEWBORNS, INFANTS, AND TODDLERS

Baby & Child Health: The Essential Guide From Birth to 11 Years

Dad to Dad: Parenting Like a Pro

Guide to Toilet Training*

Heading Home With Your Newborn: From Birth to Reality

Mommy Calls: Dr. Tanya Answers Parents' Top 101 Questions About Babies and Toddlers

New Mother's Guide to Breastfeeding*

Newborn Intensive Care: What Every Parent Needs to Know

Raising Twins: Parenting Multiples From Pregnancy Through the School Years

Your Baby's First Year*

NUTRITION AND FITNESS

Food Fights: Winning the Nutritional Challenges of Parenthood Armed With Insight, Humor, and a Bottle of Ketchup

A Parent's Guide to Childhood Obesity: A Road Map to Health

Nutrition: What Every Parent Needs to Know

Sports Success R_x! Your Child's Prescription for the Best Experience

SCHOOL-AGE CHILDREN AND ADOLESCENTS

Caring for Your School-Age Child: Ages 5 to 12

Caring for Your Teenager

**FOR MORE INFORMATION, PLEASE VISIT THE
OFFICIAL AAP WEBSITE FOR PARENTS,
WWW.HEALTHYCHILDREN.ORG/BOOKSTORE**

*This book is also available in Spanish.

Caring for Your Baby and Young Child

Steven P. Shelov, MD, MS, FAAP

EDITOR-IN-CHIEF

Associate Dean, Undergraduate Medical Education
Winthrop University Hospital, Mineola, New York

Professor of Pediatrics, Stony Brook School of Medicine
Stony Brook, New York

Tanya Remer Altmann, MD, FAAP

ASSOCIATE MEDICAL EDITOR

Community Pediatrics Medical Group, Westlake Village, California

Clinical Instructor, Mattel Children's Hospital at UCLA

Robert E. Hannemann, MD, FAAP

ASSOCIATE MEDICAL EDITOR, EMERITUS

Visiting Professor, Child Psychology, Biomedical and Chemical Engineering
Purdue University

Richard Trubo

Writer

BANTAM BOOKS
New York

A note about revisions: Every effort is made to keep CARING FOR YOUR BABY AND YOUNG CHILD consistent with the most recent advice and information available from the American Academy of Pediatrics. In addition to major revisions identified as "Revised Editions" and "Sixth Edition," the text has been updated as necessary for each additional printing listed below.

2014 Bantam Books Trade Paperback Edition

Published in the United States by Bantam Books, an imprint of Random House, a division of Random House LLC, a Penguin Random House Company, New York.

Originally published in the United States in hardcover in 1991 and in revised paperback editions in 1993, 1998, 2004 and 2009 by Bantam Books, an imprint of Random House, a division of Random House LLC.

LIBRARY OF CONGRESS CATALOGING-IN-PUBLICATION DATA
Caring for your baby and young child : birth to age 5 / Steven P. Shelov, M.D., M.S., FAAP, editor-in-chief. ; Tanya Remer Altmann, M.D., FAAP, associate medical editor ; Robert E. Hannemann, M.D., FAAP, associate medical editor.—6th edition.
pages cm
ISBN 978-0-553-39382-8
1. Infants—Care. 2. Child care. 3. Child development.
I. Shelov, Steven P., editor of compilation. II. Remer Altmann, Tanya III. Hannemann, Robert E.
RJ61.C329 2014
618.92'01—dc23   2014013096

Printed in the United States of America on acid-free paper

www.bantamdell.com

2 4 6 8 9 7 5 3 1

Book design by Donna Mugavero

Reviewers and Contributors

Editor-in-Chief
Steven P. Shelov, MD, MS, FAAP

Associate Medical Editor
Tanya Remer Altmann, MD, FAAP

Associate Editor Emeritus
Robert E. Hannemann, MD, FAAP

AAP Board of Directors Reviewer
Jane Foy, MD, FAAP

*American Academy of Pediatrics
Executive Director*
Errol R. Alden, MD, FAAP

Associate Executive Director
Roger F. Suchyta, MD, FAAP

*Director, Department of Marketing
and Publications*
Maureen DeRosa, MPA

*Director, Division of Product
Development*
Mark T. Grimes

*Manager, Consumer Publishing,
Division of Product Development*
Kathryn Sparks

*Project Coordinator, Division of
Product Development*
Holly L. Kaminsk

Contributors
Steven Abrams, MD, FAAP
Henry Adams, MD, FAAP
Phyllis F. Agran, MD, MPH, FAAP
Lisa Albers, MD, FAAP
Susan Aronson, MD, FAAP
Diane L. Atkins, MD, FAAP
Richard G. Azizkhan, MD, FAAP
Susan S. Baker, MD, PhD, FAAP

Miriam Bar-On, MD, FAAP
Robert Beekman III, MD, FAAP
Roger L. Berkow, MD, FAAP
Henry H. Bernstein, DO, MHCM, FAAP
Dana Best, MD, MPH, FAAP
Jatinder J. S. Bhatia, MD, FAAP
Carol Jean Blaisdell, MD, FAAP
David A. Bloom, MD, FAAP
Thomas Bojko, MD, MS, FAAP
Suzanne C. Boulter, MD, FAAP
Charles M. Bower, MD, FAAP
Geoffrey E. Bradford, MS, MD, FAAP
Michael Thomas Brady, MD, FAAP
Ari Brown, MD, FAAP
Lawrence W. Brown, MD, FAAP
Marilyn Bull, MD, FAAP
Robert Thomas Burke, MD, MPH,
  FAAP
Susan Buttross, MD, FAAP
Anthony J. Casale, MD, FAAP
Earl Y. Cheng, MD, FAAP
William J. Cochran, MD, MPH, FAAP
Bernard Cohen, MD, FAAP
George J. Cohen, MD, FAAP
William L. Coleman, MD, FAAP
Donald E. Cook, MD, FAAP
Mark R. Corkins, MD, FAAP
James J. Corrigan, MD, FAAP
David Howard Darrow, MD, DDS, FAAP
Beth Ellen Davis, MD, MPH, FAAP
Catherine DeAngelis, MD, FAAP
Larry Desch, MD, FAAP
Ellen Sue Deutsch, MD, FAAP
Douglas Diekema, MD, MPH, FAAP
William H. Dietz, MD, PhD, FAAP
Elaine Donoghue, MD, FAAP
Joanna Douglass, BDS, DDS
John C. Duby, MD, FAAP
Paul Dworkin, MD, FAAP
Roselyn Epps, MD, FAAP
Maria Escolar, MD, FAAP
Stephen A. Feig, MD, FAAP
Lori Feldman-Winter, MD, MPH, FAAP
Margaret Fisher, MD, FAAP

Irene N. Sills, MD, FAAP
Janet Silverstein, MD, FAAP
Deborah Mulligan Smith, MD, FAAP
Gary Smith, MD, FAAP
Gayle Smith, MD, FAAP
Michael Smith, MD, FAAP
Vincent C. Smith, MD, MPH, FAAP
Edward P. Southern, MD, FAAP
Adam J. Spanier, MD, PhD, MPH, FAAP
Sarah H. Springer, MD, FAAP
Martin Stein, MD, FAAP
John Stirling, Jr., MD, FAAP
Janice E. Sullivan, MD, FAAP
Jack T. Swanson, MD, FAAP

David E. Tunkel, MD, FAAP
Renee M. Turchi, MD, MPH, FAAP
Dennis L. Vickers, MD, FAAP
Sunita Vohra, MD, FAAP
Robert Gerard Voigt, MD, FAAP
Robert Walker, MD, FAAP
Richard Walls, MD, PhD, FAAP
Jeffrey C. Weiss, MD, FAAP
Marc Weissbluth, MD, FAAP
Mark Widome, MD, FAAP
Catherine Wilfert, MD, FAAP
Modena Hoover Wilson, MD, MPH, FAAP
Theoklis E. Zaoutis, MD, FAAP

Acknowledgments

Writer:
Richard Trubo

Writer, first edition:
Aimee Liu

Illustrators:
Wendy Wray/Morgan Gaynin Inc.
Alex Grey

Additional Assistance:
Laura Aird
Lynn Colegrove, MBA
Carolyn Kolbaba
Bonnie Kozial
Stephanie Mucha, MPH
Regina Shaefer, MPH

Designer:
Donna Mugavero

Deep appreciation to Kenneth R. Ginsburg, MD, MSEd, FAAP, for granting permission to reference his "Seven Crucial C's" for resilience from *Building Resilience in Children and Teens: Giving Kids Roots and Wings.*

Please Note

The information contained in this book is intended to complement, not substitute for, the advice of your child's pediatrician. Before starting any medical treatment or medical program, you should consult with your child's pediatrician, who can discuss your child's individual needs and counsel you about symptoms and treatment. If you have questions regarding how the information in this book applies to your child, speak to your child's pediatrician.

Products mentioned in this book are for informational purposes only. Inclusion in this publication does not constitute or imply a guarantee or an endorsement by the American Academy of Pediatrics.

The information and advice in this book apply equally to children of both sexes (except where noted). To indicate this, we have chosen to alternate between masculine and feminine pronouns throughout the book.

~ ~ ~

The American Academy of Pediatrics constantly monitors new scientific evidence and makes appropriate adjustments in its recommendations. For example, future research and the development of new childhood vaccines may alter the regimen for the administration of existing vaccines. Therefore, the schedule for immunizations outlined in this book is subject to change. These and other potential situations serve to emphasize the importance of always checking with your child's pediatrician for the latest information concerning the health of your child. For additional information on caring for your child, their health and well-being, visit HealthyChildren.org.

This book is dedicated to
all the people who recognize that children are our greatest inspiration
in the present and our greatest hope for the future.

We also appreciate the contributions of the late
Leonard P. Rome, MD, FAAP, to the original publication of this book.

Contents

Foreword xxi

Introduction: The Gifts of
Parenthood xxiii
Your Child's Gifts to You xxiv
The Gifts You Give Your Child xxv
How to Make Giving a Part of Your Daily
   Family Life xxviii

PART 1

1 Preparing for a New Baby 3
Giving Your Baby a Healthy Start 4
Getting the Best Prenatal Care 9
   Nutrition 10
   Eating for Two 10
   Exercise 10
   Tests During Pregnancy 11
Preparing for Delivery 14
Choosing a Pediatrician 17
   A Pediatrician's Training 18
   Finding a Pediatrician 19
Issues to Discuss with
   Your Pediatrician 22
   When Should the Baby Leave the
      Hospital? 24
   Should the Baby Be Circumcised? 24
   The Importance of Breastfeeding 25
   Should I Store My Newborn's
      Cord Blood? 27
Preparing Your Home and Family for the
   Baby's Arrival 28
   Choosing Baby Clothing and
      Accessories 28
   Buying Furniture and Baby
      Equipment 29
   Preparing Your Other Children for the
      Baby's Arrival 34
   Finally—Delivery Day! 38

2 Birth and the
First Moments After 43
Routine Vaginal Delivery 44
Delivery by Cesarean Section 46
Delivery Room Procedures Following
   a Normal Vaginal Birth 48
Leaving the Delivery Area 51
If Your Baby Is Premature 52
Reflecting on Your Baby's Arrival 56

3 Basic Infant Care 57
Day to Day 58
   Responding to Your Baby's Cries 58
   Helping Your Baby Sleep 61
   Positioning for Sleep 61
   Diapers 63
   Urination 67
   Bowel Movements 67
   Bathing 69
   Skin and Nail Care 72
   Clothing 75
Your Baby's Basic Health Care 78
   Taking a Rectal Temperature 78
   Visiting the Pediatrician 79
   Immunizations 81

4 Feeding Your Baby 83
Breastfeeding 85
   Getting Started: Preparing for
      Lactation 88
   Letting Down and Latching On 89
   When Your Milk Supply Increases 96
   How Often and How Long? 100
   What About Bottles? 104
   Milk Expression and Storage 105
   Possible Nursing Concerns and
      Questions 109
Bottle-Feeding 115
   Why Formula Instead of Cow's
      Milk? 116

Choosing a Formula......................116
Preparing, Sterilizing, and Storing
    Formula................................119
The Feeding Process....................122
Amount and Schedule of Formula
    Feedings..............................124
Supplementation for Breastfed and
Bottle-Fed Infants.........................125
Vitamin Supplements..................125
Iron Supplements.......................126
Water and Juice.........................126
Fluoride Supplements..................127
Burping, Hiccups, and Spitting Up...........128
Burping.................................128
Hiccups.................................128
Spitting Up.............................128

5 Your Baby's First Days.................133
Your Newborn's First Days................134
How Your Newborn Looks................134
Your Baby's Birth Weight and
    Measurements.........................140
How Your Newborn Behaves..............142
Going Home.............................143
Parenting Issues.........................144
Mother's Feelings......................144
Father's Feelings......................148
Sibling's Feelings.....................149
Health Watch............................150
Your Newborn's First Physical Exams......155

6 The First Month........................157
Growth and Development..................157
Physical Appearance and Growth.........157
Reflexes...............................159
States of Consciousness................165
Crying and Colic.......................166
The First Smile........................169
Movement...............................169
Vision.................................171
Hearing................................173
Smell and Touch........................174
Temperament............................174
Basic Care..............................176
Feeding and Nutrition..................176

Carrying Your Baby......................180
Pacifiers...............................180
Going Outside...........................182
Finding Help at Home....................183
Traveling with Your Baby................185
The Family...............................186
A Special Message to Mothers...........186
A Special Message to Fathers...........187
A Special Message to Grandparents......189
Health Watch............................192
Safety Check.............................198
Car Safety Seats.......................198
Bathing................................198
Changing Table.........................199
Suffocation Prevention.................199
Fire and Burn Prevention...............199
Supervision............................200
Necklaces and Cords....................200
Jiggling...............................200

7 Age One Month Through
Three Months.............................201
Growth and Development..................202
Physical Appearance and Growth.........202
Movement...............................203
Vision.................................206
Hearing and Making Sounds..............208
Emotional and Social Development.......210
Basic Care..............................215
Feeding................................215
Sleeping...............................216
Siblings...............................217
Health Watch............................219
Immunization Update.....................224
Safety Check.............................225
Falls..................................225
Burns..................................225
Choking................................225

8 Age Four Months Through
Seven Months.............................227
Growth and Development..................229
Physical Appearance and Growth.........229
Movement...............................229
Vision.................................233

Language Development.............................235
Cognitive Development............................236
Emotional Development...........................238
Basic Care...241
  Introducing Solid Foods.........................241
  Dietary Supplements...............................244
  Sleeping..245
  Teething..246
  Swings and Playpens..............................246
Behavior..248
  Discipline..248
  Siblings...252
Health Watch...253
Immunization Update.............................255
Safety Check..256
  Car Safety Seats......................................256
  Drowning..256
  Falls...257
  Burns...257
  Choking...257

9 Age Eight Months Through Twelve Months...................................259
Growth and Development.......................260
  Physical Appearance and Growth........260
  Movement...261
  Hand and Finger Skills............................266
  Language Development...........................267
  Cognitive Development...........................270
  Brain Development..................................272
  Emotional Development..........................274
Basic Care...280
  Feeding...280
  Weaning from Breast to Bottle..............284
  Weaning to a Cup....................................285
  Sleeping..287
Behavior..288
  Discipline..288
  Siblings...290
  Grandparents...291
Immunization Update.............................292
Safety Check..293
  Car Safety Seats......................................293
  Falls...293
  Burns...294

Drowning..294
Poisoning and Choking..........................294

10 Your One-Year-Old........................295
Growth and Development.......................296
  Physical Appearance and Growth........296
  Movement...297
  Hand and Finger Skills............................299
  Language Development...........................300
  Cognitive Development...........................302
  Social Development.................................304
  Emotional Development..........................307
Basic Care...309
  Feeding and Nutrition............................309
  Getting Ready for Toilet Training...........321
  Sleeping..322
Behavior..323
  Discipline..323
  Coping with Temper Tantrums...............326
  Family Relationships..............................330
Immunization Update.............................331
Safety Check..332
  Sleeping Safety.......................................332
  Toy Safety..332
  Water Safety..334
  Auto Safety..334
  Home Safety..335
  Outdoor Safety.......................................335

11 Your Two-Year-Old........................337
Growth and Development.......................338
  Physical Appearance and Growth........338
  Movement...339
  Hand and Finger Skills............................341
  Language Development...........................342
  Cognitive Development...........................343
  Social Development.................................345
  Emotional Development..........................349
Basic Care...352
  Feeding and Nutrition............................352
  Teething and Dental Hygiene.................354
  Toilet Training..356
  Sleeping..359
  Discipline..364
Family Relationships...............................365

A New Baby.................................365
Hero Worship..............................367
Visit to the Pediatrician......................370
Immunization Update 370
Safety Check..................................371
Falls...371
Burns...371
Poisoning...................................371
Car Safety..................................372

12 Your Three-Year-Old....................373

Growth and Development....................374
Physical Appearance and Growth.........374
Movement...................................375
Hand and Finger Skills....................377
Language Development...................379
Cognitive Development..................382
Social Development.......................384
Emotional Development................387
Basic Care.......................................389
Feeding and Nutrition...................389
Beyond Toilet Training...................390
Bed-Wetting................................392
Sleeping.....................................393
Discipline...................................394
Preparing for School.....................395
Traveling with Your Preschooler.........398
Visit to the Pediatrician......................399
Immunization Update 400
Safety Check....................................401
Falls...401
Burns...401
Car Safety..................................401
Drowning...................................402

13 Your Four- and
Five-Year-Old.............................403

Development 404
Movement...................................404
Hand and Finger Skills....................405
Language Development...................406
Cognitive Development..................409
Social Development.......................410
Emotional Development................412

Basic Care.......................................415
Healthy Lifestyle..........................415
Feeding and Nutrition...................418
Sleeping.....................................421
Discipline...................................424
Preparing for Kindergarten.............425
Visit to the Pediatrician......................429
Safety Check....................................429
Traveling with Your Child...................430

14 Early Education and
Child Care.................................435

What to Look for in a Care Provider:
Guidelines for the Toddler and
Preschool Child............................436
Choices in Care................................438
In-Home Care/Nanny....................439
Family Child Care.........................442
Child Care Centers.......................445
Making a Final Selection....................447
Building a Relationship with Your Child's
Care Providers.............................452
Resolving Conflicts...........................455
What to Do When Your Child Is Sick......456
Controlling Infectious Diseases............458
Colds and Flu..............................459
Cytomegalovirus (CMV) and Parvovirus
Infection.................................459
Diarrheal Diseases........................460
Eye and Skin Infections..................460
Head Lice...................................460
Hepatitis A Virus..........................461
Hepatitis B Virus..........................461
Human Immunodeficiency Virus (HIV)/
AIDS.....................................461
Ringworm...................................462
Preventing Injuries and Promoting Car
Safety.......................................462
Care for Children with Special Needs.....464

15 Keeping Your Child Safe...........471

Why Children Get Injured...................472
Safety Inside Your Home 475
Room to Room.............................475

Nursery 475
Kitchen 479
Bathroom 480
Garage and Basement 481
All Rooms 482
Baby Equipment 485
High Chairs 485
Infant Seats 486
Playpens 487
Walkers 488
Pacifiers 488
Toy Boxes and Toy Chests 489
Toys 489
Safety Outside the Home 491
Car Safety Seats 491
Choosing a Car Safety Seat 492
Types of Car Safety Seats 494
Installing a Car Safety Seat 495
Using the Car Safety Seat 497
Air Bag Safety 499
Kids Around Cars 501
Baby Carriers—Backpacks, Front Packs,
    and Slings 502
Strollers 503
Shopping Cart Safety 504
Bicycles and Tricycles 505
Playgrounds 506
Your Backyard 508
Water Safety 509
Safety Around Animals 512
In the Community and
    Neighborhood 513

PART 2

16 Abdominal/
Gastrointestinal Tract 521
Abdominal Pain 521
Abdominal Pain in Infants 522
Abdominal Pain in Older Children 523
Appendicitis 525
Celiac Disease 526
Constipation 528

Diarrhea 530
Food Poisoning and
    Food Contamination 537
Hepatitis 542
Inguinal Hernia 545
Communicating Hydrocele 546
Malabsorption 547
Reye Syndrome 549
Vomiting 549

17 Allergies 553
Asthma 553
Eczema 560
Food Allergy 562
Milk Allergy 566
Hay Fever/Nasal Allergy 567
Hives 570
Insect Bites and Stings 571

18 Behavior 575
Anger, Aggression, and Biting 575
Coping with Disasters and Terrorism 580
If a Loved One Dies 582
Hyperactivity and the
    Distractible Child 583
Temper Tantrums 587
Thumb and Finger Sucking 591
Tics 592

19 Chest and Lungs 595
Bronchiolitis 595
Cough 598
Croup 600
Flu/Influenza 602
Pneumonia 605
Tuberculosis 607
Whooping Cough (Pertussis) 609

20 Chronic Conditions and
Diseases 613
Coping with Chronic (Long-Term) Health
    Problems 613
Anemia 621
Sickle Cell Disease 623

Cystic Fibrosis.....................................626
Diabetes Mellitus...............................627
HIV Infection and AIDS....................630

21 Developmental Disabilities....635
Autism Spectrum Disorder..........................636
Cerebral Palsy.....................................642
Associated Problems.......................644
Congenital Abnormalities.............646
When Your Child Has a Congenital
    Disorder..647
Congenital Conditions.....................647
Hearing Loss.......................................652
Intellectual Disability......................656

22 Ears, Nose, and Throat...........659
Colds/Upper Respiratory Infection..........659
Middle Ear Infections.......................662
Sinusitis..668
Epiglottitis...669
Herpes Simplex.................................670
Nosebleeds...671
Sore Throat (Strep Throat, Tonsillitis)....673
Tonsils and Adenoid.........................675
Swimmer's Ear (External Otitis).......677
Swollen Glands..................................680

23 Emergencies..............................683
Bites..686
Burns..688
Cardiopulmonary Resuscitation
    (CPR) and Mouth-to-Mouth
    Resuscitation................................691
Choking..691
Cuts and Scrapes...............................692
Drowning...696
Electric Shock.....................................697
Fingertip Injuries..............................698
Fractures/Broken Bones..................699
Head Injury/Concussion..................702
Poisoning..703

24 Environmental Health...............709
Air Pollution and Secondhand Smoke....709

Asbestos..711
Carbon Monoxide..............................712
Contaminated Fish............................712
Drinking Water...................................713
Lead Poisoning...................................716
Pesticides/Herbicides......................720
Radon...722

25 Eyes...723
Amblyopia...726
Cataracts...727
Eye Infections....................................728
Eye Injuries..728
Eyelid Problems.................................730
Glaucoma..731
Strabismus..732
Tear (or Lacrimal) Production
    Problems..733
Vision Difficulties Requiring Corrective
    Lenses...734

26 Family Issues..............................737
Adoption..737
Child Abuse and Neglect.................739
Divorce...743
Grief Reactions..................................748
Sibling Rivalry...................................751
Single-Parent Families....................754
Stepfamilies.......................................756
Multiples...758

27 Fever..763

28 Genital and Urinary
Systems..771
Blood in the Urine (Hematuria)..............771
Proteinuria...772
Circumcision......................................773
Hypospadias.......................................774
Meatal Stenosis.................................774
Labial Adhesions...............................775
Undescended Testicles
    (Cryptorchidism)..........................776
Urethral Valves..................................777

Urinary Tract Infections 778
Wetting Problems or Enuresis 780

29 Head, Neck, and Nervous System 785
Meningitis 785
Motion Sickness 788
Mumps 789
Seizures, Convulsions, and Epilepsy 790
Head Tilt (Torticollis) 792

30 Heart 796
Arrhythmias 796
Heart Murmur 797
Hypertension/High Blood Pressure 799
Kawasaki Disease 802

31 Immunizations 805
Important and Safe 806
What Shots Does Your Child Need? 808

32 Media 813
Early Years 813
Ages Two and Three 814
Ages Four and Five 816
Guidelines for Media Use 817
A Message to Parents 818

33 Musculoskeletal Problems 819
Arthritis 819
Bowlegs and Knock-Knees 823
Elbow Injuries 824
Flat Feet/Fallen Arches 825
Limp 826
Pigeon Toes (Intoeing) 828
Sprains 829

34 Skin 831
Birthmarks and Hemangiomas 831
Chickenpox 834
Cradle Cap and Seborrheic Dermatitis 836
Fifth Disease (Erythema Infectiosum) 837
Hair Loss (Alopecia) 838
Head Lice 839
Impetigo 841
Measles 841
MRSA Infections 843
Pinworms 844
Poison Ivy, Poison Oak, and Poison Sumac 845
Ringworm 846
Roseola Infantum 847
Rubella (German Measles) 848
Scabies 849
Scarlet Fever 851
Sunburn 851
Warts 853
West Nile Virus 854

35 Your Child's Sleep 857
Getting Sleep in Sync 859
Sleep Routines and Dealing with Crying 860
Sharing the Bedtime Routine 861
Parent Sleep Deprivation 861
Daytime Nap Evolution 864
Getting the Most Out of Sleep ...866
Dealing with Other Sleep Concerns 869
Putting Sleep in Perspective 869

Appendix 871

Index 891

Foreword

This sixth edition of *Caring for Your Baby and Young Child: Birth to Age 5* offers parents updated information on raising and caring for their child with the contributions and wisdom from more than one hundred pediatric specialists. As one of our top-selling parenting guides, this book has shaped the health and well-being of children for more than twenty years. The American Academy of Pediatrics (AAP) also has published books for parents on topics ranging from breastfeeding, nutrition, and toilet training to sleep, allergies and asthma, and attention-deficit/hyperactivity disorder.

The AAP is an organization of 62,000 primary-care pediatricians, pediatric medical subspecialists, and pediatric surgical specialists dedicated to the health, safety, and well-being of all infants, children, adolescents, and young adults. This book is part of the ongoing educational efforts of the Academy to provide parents and caregivers with high-quality information on a broad spectrum of children's health issues.

What distinguishes this book from the many others in bookstores and on library shelves is that it has been developed and extensively reviewed by physician members of the American Academy of Pediatrics. A six-member editorial board developed the initial material with the assistance of more than one hundred contributors and reviewers. Because medical information is constantly changing, every effort has been made to ensure that this book contains the most up-to-date findings. Readers can visit the AAP's official website for parents at www.healthychildren.org to keep current on the latest information related to child health and guidance on parenting.

It is the Academy's hope that this book will become an invaluable resource and reference guide for parents and caregivers. We believe it is the best comprehensive source of information on matters of children's health and well-being. We are confident that parents and caregivers will find the book extremely valuable and encourage its use along with the advice and counsel of our readers' own pediatricians, who will provide individual guidance and assistance related to the health of children.

Errol R. Alden, MD, FAAP
Executive Director
American Academy of Pediatrics

Introduction:
The Gifts of Parenthood

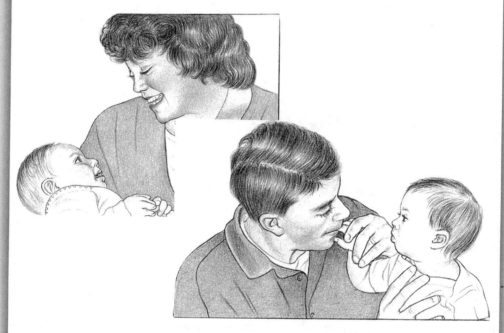

YOUR CHILD IS THE GREATEST GIFT you will ever receive. From the moment you first hold this miracle of life in your arms, your world will be broader and richer. You will experience a flood of feelings, some of wonder and joy and others of confusion and of being overwhelmed and wondering whether you can ever measure up to the needs of your new baby. These are feelings you could barely imagine before—feelings that no one can truly experience without having a child.

Even describing them can be difficult because the bond between parent and child is so intensely personal. Why do tears come to your eyes the first time your baby smiles or reaches for you? Why are you so proud of her first words? Why does your heart suddenly start to pound the first time you watch her stumble and fall? The answer lies in the unique two-way giving relationship between you and your child.

Your Child's Gifts to You

- Unqualified love

- Absolute trust

- The thrill of discovery

- The heights of emotion

Your Child's Gifts to You

Although simple, your child's gifts to you are powerful enough to change your life positively.

UNQUALIFIED LOVE. From birth, you are the center of your child's universe. He gives you his love without question and without demand. As he gets older, he will show this love in countless ways, from showering you with his first smiles to giving you his handmade valentines. His love is filled with admiration, affection, loyalty, and an intense desire to please you.

ABSOLUTE TRUST. Your child believes in you. In her eyes, you are strong, capable, powerful, and wise. Over time, she will demonstrate this trust by relaxing when you are near, coming to you with problems, and proudly pointing you out to others. Sometimes she also will lean on you for protection from things that frighten her, including her own sensitivities. For example, in your presence she may try out new skills that she would never dare to try alone or with a stranger. She trusts you to keep her safe.

THE THRILL OF DISCOVERY. Having a child gives you a unique chance to rediscover the pleasure and excitement of childhood. Although you cannot relive your life through your child, you can share in his delight as he explores the world. In the process, you probably will discover abilities and talents you never dreamed you possessed. Feelings of empathy mixed with growing self-awareness will help shape your ability to play and interact with your growing child. Discovering things together, whether they are new skills or words or ways to overcome obstacles, will add to your experience and confidence as a parent and will better prepare you for new challenges that you never even envisioned.

THE HEIGHTS OF EMOTION. Through your child, you will experience new heights of joy, love, pride, and excitement. You probably also will experience anxiety, anger, and frustration. For all those delicious moments when you hold your baby close and feel her loving arms around your neck, there are bound to be times when you feel you cannot communicate. The extremes sometimes become sharper as your child gets older and seeks to establish her independence. The same child who at three dances across the room with you may at four have a rebellious and active period that surprises you. The extremes are not contradictions, but simply a reality of growing up. For you as a parent, the challenge is to accept and appreciate all the feelings with which your child expresses himself and arouses in you, and to use them in giving him steady guidance.

The Gifts You Give Your Child

As his parent, you have many vital gifts to offer your child in return. Some are subtle, but all are very powerful. Giving them will make you a good parent. Receiving them will help your child become a healthy, happy, capable individual.

UNCONDITIONAL LOVE. Love lies at the core of your relationship with your child. It needs to flow freely in both directions. Just as she loves you without question, you must give her your love and acceptance absolutely. Your love shouldn't depend on the way she looks or behaves. It shouldn't be used as a reward or withheld as a threat. Your love for your child is constant and indisputable, and it's up to you to convey that, especially when she misbehaves and

The Gifts You Give Your Child

- Unconditional love
- Self-esteem
- Values and traditions
- Joy in life
- Good health
- Secure surroundings
- Skills and abilities

needs to have limits set or behavior corrected. Love must be held separate and above any fleeting feelings of anger or frustration over her conduct. Never confuse the actions with the child. The more secure she feels in your love, the more self-assurance she will have as she grows up.

SELF-ESTEEM. One of your most important gifts as a parent is to help your child develop self-esteem. It's not an easy or quick process. Self-respect, confidence, and belief in oneself, which are the building blocks of self-esteem, take years to become firmly established. Your child needs your steady support and encouragement to discover his strengths. He needs you to believe in him as he learns to believe in himself. Loving him, spending time with him, listening to him, and praising his accomplishments are all part of this process. On other occasions, helping him modify his troubling behaviors in ways that aren't punitive or hurtful, but constructive, is just as important to building a firm self-esteem. If he is confident of your love, admiration, and respect, it will be easier for him to develop the solid self-esteem he needs to grow up happy and emotionally healthy.

VALUES AND TRADITIONS. Regardless of whether you actively try to pass on your values and beliefs to your child, she is bound to absorb some of them just by living with you. She'll notice how disciplined you are in your work, how deeply you hold your beliefs, and whether you practice what you preach. She'll participate in family rituals and traditions and think about their significance. You can't expect or demand that your child subscribe to all your opinions, but you can present your beliefs honestly, clearly, and thoughtfully, in keeping with the child's age and maturity level. Give her guidance and encouragement, not only commands. Encourage questions and discussions, when age and language permit, instead of trying to force your values on your child. If your beliefs are well reasoned and if you are true to them, she probably will adopt many of them. If there are inconsistencies in your actions—something we all live with— often your child will make that clear to you, either subtly by his behavior or, when he is older, more directly by disagreeing with you. The road to developing values is not straight and unerring. It demands flexibility built on firm foundations. Self-awareness, a willingness to listen to your child and change when appropriate, and, above all, a demonstration of your commitment to traditions will best serve your relationship with your child. While the choice of values and principles ultimately will be hers to make, she depends on you to give her the foundation through your thoughts, shared ideas, and, most of all, your actions and deeds.

JOY IN LIFE. Your baby doesn't need to be taught to be joyful, but he does need your encouragement and support to let his natural enthusiasm fly free. The more joyful you are, particularly when you are with him, the more delightful life will seem to him and the more eagerly he will embrace it. When he hears music, he'll dance. When the sun shines, he'll turn his face skyward. When he feels happy, he'll laugh. This exuberance often is expressed through his being attentive and curious, willing to explore new places and things, and eager to take in the world around him and incorporate the new images, objects, and people into his own growing experience. Remember, different babies have different temperaments—some are more apparently exuberant than others, some are more noisily rambunctious, some are more playful, some are more reserved and quiet. Still others are more even-keeled, mixtures of the two extremes. But all babies demonstrate their joy in life in their own ways, and you as the parent will discover what those ways are and will nurture your child's joy.

GOOD HEALTH. Your child's health depends significantly on the care and guidance you offer her during these early years. You begin during pregnancy by taking good care of yourself and by arranging for obstetric and pediatric care. By taking your child to the doctor regularly for checkups and consultations, keeping her safe from injuries, providing a nutritious diet, and encouraging exercise throughout childhood, you help protect and strengthen her body. You'll also need to maintain good health habits yourself, while avoiding unhealthy ones, such as smoking, excessive drinking, drug use, and lack of adequate physical activity. In this way, you'll give your child a healthy example to follow as she grows up.

SECURE SURROUNDINGS. You naturally want to give your child a safe, comfortable home. This means more than a warm place to sleep and a collection of toys. As important as it is to provide shelter that is physically safe and secure, it is even more important to create a home that is emotionally secure with a minimum of stress and a maximum of consistency and love. Your child can sense problems between other family members and may be very troubled by them, so it's important that all family problems, even minor conflicts, be dealt with directly and resolved as quickly as possible through cooperation. This may entail seeking advice, but remember, your family's well-being helps maintain an environment that promotes your child's development and will allow him to achieve his potential. The family's dealing effectively with conflicts or differences ultimately will help him feel secure in his ability to manage conflicts and disagreements and will provide him with a positive example for resolving his own challenges.

SKILLS AND ABILITIES. As your child grows up, she'll spend most of her time developing and polishing a variety of skills and abilities in all areas of her life. You should help her as much as possible by encouraging her and providing the equipment and instruction she needs. Books, magazines, play groups, and pre-school will quickly take on a central role as your toddler becomes a preschooler. But it's important not to forget some of the most critical learning tools: Your child will learn best when she feels secure, confident, and loved; she will learn best when information is presented in a way that she will respond to positively. Some information is best presented through play—the language of children. Young children learn a tremendous amount through play, especially when with parents or playmates. Other information is best learned or incorporated through actual experience. This may mean learning through exposure to diverse places, people, activities, and experiences. Other things are learned through stories, picture books, magazines, and activity books. Still other things are learned by watching—sometimes just watching you, sometimes watching other children or adults. Preschool experiences also promote socialization.

If you enjoy learning and making discovery fun for your child, she soon will recognize that achievement can be a source of personal satisfaction as well as a way to please you. The secret is to give her the opportunities and let her learn as best fits her style and at her own rate.

How to Make Giving a Part of Your Daily Family Life

The back-and-forth sharing of these gifts between you and your child will foster your relationship and nurture your child's development. Much like learning a new dance, working out the actual steps in giving is not always going to be easy. But it will happen with time and patience, and with your own commitment to strengthen the parent-child relationship.

Giving your child the guidance and support that he needs to grow up healthy involves all the skills of parenthood: nurturing, guiding, protecting, sharing, and serving as an example or model. Like other skills, these must be learned and perfected through practice. Some will be easier for you than others. Some will seem easier on certain days than on others. These variations are a normal part of raising a child, but they do make the job challenging. The following suggestions will help you make the most of your natural parenting skills so you can give your child the best possible start.

ENJOY YOUR CHILD AS AN INDIVIDUAL. Recognize that your child is unique—different from everyone else—and appreciate her special qualities. Discover her special needs and strengths, her moods and vulnerabilities, and especially her sense of humor, which starts to show itself early in infancy. Let her show you the joy of play. The more you enjoy your child and appreciate her individuality, the more successful you'll be in helping her develop a sense of trust, security, and self-esteem. You'll also have a lot more fun being a parent!

EDUCATE YOURSELF. You probably know much more than you think you do about being a parent. You spent years observing your own parents and other families. Perhaps you've cared for other children. And you have many instinctive responses that will help make you a giving parent. In other times, this probably would have been all the preparation you needed to raise a child. However, our society is extremely complex and is constantly changing. In order to guide their children in this new world, parents often benefit from some extra education. Talk to your pediatrician and other parents, and ask questions. Get to know other families with children the same age, and watch how these parents raise their children (for example, when are they protective and when do they let go, and how much responsibility do they expect of their children at various ages?). Also, read about issues and problems that affect your family. Contact your local religious organizations, school systems and PTAs, child care programs, parent education classes, and other groups that specialize in child-related concerns. Often these groups serve as networks for concerned and interested parents. These networks will help you feel more comfortable and secure when issues seem puzzling or frustrating.

As you gather advice, sift through it for information that is right for you and your child. Much of what you receive will be very valuable, but not all of it. Because child rearing is such a personal process, there is bound to be disagreement. You are not obligated to believe everything you hear or read. In fact, one of the purposes of educating yourself is to protect your child from advice that does not fit your family. The more you know, the better equipped you'll be to decide what works best for your family.

BE A GOOD EXAMPLE. One of the ways your child shows her love for you is by imitating you. This is also one of the ways she learns how to behave, develop new skills, and take care of herself. From her earliest moments, she watches you closely and patterns her own behavior and beliefs after yours. Your examples become permanent images, which will shape her attitudes and actions for the rest of her life. Setting a good example for your child means being responsible, loving, and consistent not only with her but with all members of the family. Show your affection and nurture your relationships. If your child sees her parents communicating openly, cooperating, and sharing household responsibilities, she'll bring these skills to her own future relationships.

Setting good examples also means taking care of yourself. As an eager, well-meaning parent, it's easy to concentrate so hard on your family that you lose sight of your own needs. That's a big mistake. Your child depends on you to be physically and emotionally healthy, and she looks to you to show her how to keep herself healthy. By taking care of yourself, you demonstrate your self-esteem, which is important for both you and your child. Getting a sitter and resting when you're overtired or ill teaches your child that you respect yourself and your needs. Setting aside time and energy for your own work or hobbies teaches your child that you value certain skills and interests and are willing to pursue them. By giving yourself some personal time (at least once a week), the easier it will be for you and your child to develop your own identities. That needs to occur as she grows older. She also will benefit from getting to know other trusted grown-ups by having them babysit, and at times involving your entire family in group activities with other families. Ultimately she will pattern some of her own habits after yours, so the healthier and happier you keep yourself, the better it will be for both of you.

You can set an example in still another important area, too, and that's in demonstrating tolerance and acceptance in an increasingly multicultural society. As the United States has become a melting pot of nationalities and cultures, it is more important than ever to teach tolerance to your child when relating to people of other racial, ethnic, and religious groups and alternate lifestyles. Make an effort to help your child understand and even celebrate diversity. No boy or girl is born prejudiced, but it can be learned at a very young age. By four years old, children are aware of differences among people. The way you relate to people in your life will provide a foundation for how your child will treat her peers and others throughout her childhood and adulthood. Let your child know that there are many similarities among people and make an effort to dispel stereotypes that she is exposed to, replacing them with the belief that all people deserve to be respected and valued.

SHOW YOUR LOVE. Giving love means more than just saying "I love you." Your child can't understand what the words mean unless you also treat him with love. Be spontaneous, relaxed, and affectionate with him. Give him plenty of physical contact through hugging, kissing, rocking, and playing. Take the time to talk, sing, and read with him every day. Listen and watch as he responds to you. By paying attention and freely showing your affection, you make him feel special and secure and lay a firm foundation for his self-esteem.

COMMUNICATE HONESTLY AND OPENLY. One of the most important skills you teach your child is communication. The lessons begin when she is a tiny baby gazing into your eyes and listening to your soothing voice. They continue as she watches and listens to you talking with other members of the family and, later, as you help her sort out her concerns, problems, and confusions. She needs you to be understanding, patient, honest, and clear with her. Good communication within a family is not always easy. It can be especially difficult when both parents are working, overextended, or under a great deal of stress, or when one person is depressed, ill, or angry. Preventing a communications breakdown requires commitment, cooperation among family members, and a willingness to recognize problems as they arise. Express your own feelings, and encourage your child to be equally open with you. Look for changes in her behavior—such as frequent or constant crying, irritability, sleep problems, or appetite loss—that may signal sadness, fear, frustration, or worry, and show her that you're aware of and understand these emotions. Ask questions, listen to the responses, and offer constructive suggestions.

Listen to yourself, as well, and consider what you say to your child before the words leave your mouth. It's sometimes easy to make harsh, even cruel, statements in anger or frustration that you don't really mean but that your child may never forget. Thoughtless comments or jokes that seem incidental to you may be hurtful to your child. Phrases like "That's a dumb question" or "Don't bother me" make your child feel worthless and unwanted and may seriously damage her self-esteem. If you constantly criticize or put her off, she also may back away from you. Instead of looking to you for guidance, she may hesitate to ask questions and may mistrust your advice. Like everyone else, children need encouragement to ask questions and speak their minds. The more sensitive, attentive, and honest you are, the more comfortable she'll feel being honest with you.

SPEND TIME TOGETHER. You cannot give your child all that he needs if you spend only a few minutes a day with him. In order to know you and feel confident of your love, he has to spend a great deal of time with you, both physically and emotionally. Spending this time together is possible even if you have outside commitments. You can work full-time and still spend some intimate time with your child every day. The important thing is that it be time devoted just to him, meeting his needs and your needs together. Is there any fixed amount? No one can really say. One hour of quality time is worth more than a day of being in the same house but in different rooms. You can be at home full-time and never give him the undivided attention he requires. It's up to you to shape your schedule and direct your attention so that you meet his needs.

It may help to set aside a specific block of time for your child each day and devote it to activities he enjoys. Also make an effort to include him in all family activities—meal preparation, mealtimes, and so forth. Use these times to talk about each other's problems (do be attentive, however, to overburdening your child with adult problems; kids don't need to shoulder your anxieties), personal concerns, and the day's events.

If you're a working parent, your attentiveness to your child when you're together will help ensure that he is well adjusted and well loved. If your child is well taken care of when you're at work, he will thrive regardless of your hours spent away on the job.

NURTURE GROWTH AND CHANGE. When your child is a newborn, it may be difficult for you to imagine her ever growing up, and yet your main purpose as a parent is to encourage, guide, and support her growth. She depends on you to provide the food, protection, and health care her body needs to grow properly, as well as the guidance her mind and spirit need to make her a healthy, mature individual. Instead of resisting change in your child, your job is to welcome and nurture it.

Guiding your child's growth involves a significant amount of discipline, both for you and for your child. As she becomes increasingly independent, she needs rules and guidelines to help her find what she can do and grow from there. You need to provide this framework for her, establishing rules that are appropriate for each stage of development and adjusting them as your child changes so they encourage growth instead of stifling it.

Confusion and conflict do not help your child to mature. Consistency does. Make sure that everyone who cares for her understands and agrees on the way she is being raised and the rules she's expected to follow. Establish policies for all her care providers to observe when she misbehaves, and adjust these policies along with the rules as she becomes more responsible.

You also should create an environment that encourages the healthy brain development of your child. His world—including where he lives and plays and whom he interacts with—will affect how his brain grows. Your child's environment and experiences need to be nurtured constantly, with warm and loving care providers who give him the freedom to explore and learn safely. (Throughout this book, you'll find guidelines on ensuring the optimal development of your child's brain.)

MINIMIZE FRUSTRATIONS AND MAXIMIZE SUCCESS. One of the ways your child develops self-esteem is by succeeding. The process starts in the crib with his very first attempts to communicate and use his body. If he achieves his goals and receives approval, he soon begins to feel good about himself and eager to take on greater challenges. If, instead, he's prevented from succeeding and his efforts are ignored, eventually he may become so discouraged that he quits trying and either withdraws or becomes angry and even more frustrated.

As a parent, you must try to expose your child to challenges that will help him discover his abilities and achieve successes while simultaneously preventing him from encountering obstacles or tasks likely to lead to too great a series of frustrations and defeats. This does not mean doing his work for him or keeping him from tasks you know will challenge him. Success is meaningless unless it involves a certain amount of struggle. However, too much frustration in the face of challenges that really are beyond your child's current abilities can be self-defeating and perpetuate a negative self-image. The key is to moderate the challenges so they're within your child's reach while asking him to stretch a bit. For example, try to have toys that are appropriate for his age level, neither too basic for him nor too difficult for him to handle. See if you can find a variety of playmates, some older and some younger. Invite your child to help you around the house and have him do chores as he gets older, but don't expect more of him than he realistically can manage.

As you raise your child, it's easy to get carried away by your hopes and dreams for him. You naturally want him to have the best education, all possible opportunities, and eventually a successful career and lifestyle. But be careful not to confuse your own wishes with his choices. In our highly competitive society, a great deal of pressure is placed on children to perform. Some preschools have entrance requirements. In some professions and sports, children are considered out of the running if they haven't begun training by age ten. In this atmosphere, the popularity of programs that promise to turn "ordinary babies" into "super babies" is understandable. Many well-meaning parents want desperately to give their children a head start on lifetime success. Unfortunately, this is rarely in the children's best interests. In fact, there is a lack of evidence that these rigorous, early training programs can actually produce "super babies." Achieving a balanced, moderate approach is the key to meeting expectations and avoiding frustration and disappointment for both you and your child.

Children who are pressured to perform early in life do not learn better or achieve higher skills over the long run than do other children. On the contrary, the effects of psychological and emotional pressures may be so negative that the child develops learning or behavioral problems. If a child is truly gifted, he might be able to handle the early learning barrage and develop normally, but most gifted children require less pressure, not more. If their parents push them, they may feel overloaded and become anxious. If they don't live up to their parents' expectations, they may feel like failures and worry that they'll lose their parents' love. This kind of chronic stress and so-called adverse childhood experiences (see page xxxiv) can even have a negative impact on brain development and keep children from reaching their own innate potential.

Your child needs understanding, security, and opportunity geared to his own special gifts, needs, and developmental timetable. These things cannot be packaged in a program and they don't guarantee the future, but they will make him a success on his own terms.

OFFER COPING STRATEGIES. Some disappointment and failure are inevitable, so your child needs to learn constructive ways to handle anger, conflict, and frustration. Much of what she sees in movies and on television teaches her that violence is the way to solve disputes. Her personal inclination may be either to erupt or to withdraw when she's upset. She may not be able to distinguish the important issues from the insignificant ones. She needs your help to sort out

Building Resilience

As a parent, one of your greatest challenges is to protect your child from danger and discomfort throughout her younger years and beyond. But no matter how skilled and conscientious you are, you can't shield your child from all of the misfortunes she'll encounter during childhood. As she goes out into the world—spending time in preschool and in the homes of playmates and care providers—she'll encounter stresses and setbacks that are simply part of life. She may also experience a divorce, a serious family illness, or a death, any of which can have a profound effect on her.

So how should you react? Can you insulate your child from every misfortune, from being teased or bullied to being excluded from a group activity? And even if you could protect her, should you always do so?

Most pediatricians agree that it may not be a good idea to protect her from every negative experience that the world puts in her path. So, within the safe and supportive environment of your family, you need to nurture in her the resilience that can help her bounce back from the upsets and disappointments that are part of life.

By definition, resilience is the capacity to rebound from setbacks. It is the opposite of vulnerability, or the risk of being temporarily or permanently scarred by those same setbacks. Researchers have focused considerable attention on the home environment and the powerful impact it can have on how children develop emotionally. Studies have shown that by two to three years old, a child's early life experiences are already shaping her level of resilience or vulnerability to adverse life events. Of course, some life experiences are much tougher to deal with than others, and unfortunately, many of these traumatic experiences are more common in American homes than most of us would like to acknowledge. These traumatic home and family experiences have been described by researchers as "adverse childhood experiences (ACEs)." ACEs include abuse (emotional, physical, or sexual abuse), neglect (emotional or physical), and several different types of family or "household dysfunction" (domestic violence, criminal activity, parental substance abuse or mental illness, or childhood neglect). A study of more than 17,000 HMO (health maintenance organization) members found that these types of early childhood traumas can be life-changing. In fact, the ACE study showed that a number of life experiences pose major risks for the leading causes of illness and death as they progress through adolescence and into adulthood. These events can negatively affect their quality of life and put them at greater risk, not only for problems such as depression, substance abuse, sexual promiscuity, unintended pregnancies, and suicide attempts, but also for illnesses such as diabetes, high blood pressure, and heart disease. (See also *Child Abuse and Neglect*, page 739.)

Every child is born with some ability to cope with stress and setbacks, but all children can increase their resilience with help from their parents. A resilient child is confident that she will receive what she needs to get through a stressful situation. She knows that others will be there to protect and assist her, and that she also has the tools to solve problems in life.

The body's response to stress can be life-saving if the stressful situation is socially and emotionally buffered, brief, or infrequent. However, if a stress response is prolonged and frequent, the body's reaction to stress can be toxic, altering the way the brain works and changing the way an individual's genetic blueprint is read.

Some children may need more support than others to confront and deal with the pressures they encounter. To help strengthen your child's resilience, she needs your nurturing beginning at birth and continuing throughout childhood. She needs to know that there are parents and other adults in her life who believe in her and love her unconditionally. Provide her with a secure environment at home. Tell her how proud you are of her, particularly when she tries her best or handles disappointments well. At the same time, be aware of outside circumstances that can negatively affect her mental health. Your presence and guidance will provide a buffer against the most serious stressful times, dampening the stress response and making stress less toxic. Remember that each challenge is also an educational opportunity to teach skills that your child can use with the next challenge. Even when an uncontrollable event like a major family illness takes place, try keeping your child's life as predictable as you can, and make her feel secure and protected.

There are many ways to help build and maintain your child's resilience, which have been studied by a number of researchers. Kenneth R. Ginsburg, MD, MSEd, FAAP, believes the ingredients of resilience are the seven crucial C's. Although they may be most applicable to older children, not newborns, keep them in mind because these skills need to be built over time.

■ *Competence.* Encourage your youngster to focus on her strengths, and point out how she has managed life situations effectively in the past and can continue to do so. While you want to protect your child from the most serious stresses, don't communicate the message that you don't think she can handle things without your help. At the same time, do not push her beyond the point where she can realistically manage events on her own. Over time, children build their ability to cope, particularly when you reinforce it with statements such as "I know you will do this differently next time."

■ *Confidence.* Boost her confidence by drawing attention to her best qualities. Tell her when she has done something well. Provide praise for the things she achieves at school and at home. Focus on the effort, which will help your child build her sense of control ("I can do it if I try"), and is healthier than "I am/am not good at this."

■ *Connection.* To build secure feelings, strengthen the ties your child has to family members and people in the community. This is very important for newborns and young children as these connections allow youngsters to turn off stress responses that are potentially toxic. Your own home should be a place of physical safety and emotional security. Schedule quality family time that can foster healthy relationships that your child can always rely on, no matter what the circumstances. Create family rituals like having meals together as a family, reading bedtime stories, and developing family hobbies. Make in-person "face-time" a priority and limit screen time (e.g., TV, videos, movies) to less than 2 hours per day. (See also *Guidelines for Media Use,* page 817.)

■ *Character.* From the earliest ages, instill a set of values and morals that will help your child learn right from wrong, and show a caring attitude toward others. Remind her that her own behaviors can affect others, either positively or negatively. Let her know how pleased you are when she responds to situations with kindness and fairness, and the importance of caring for others. This type of behavior needs to be modeled by you and your spouse since actions speak louder than words.

■ *Contribution.* Tell your child that the world is a better place because she's in it, and that she can make a difference in the lives of others. As early as possible, become a good example for treating other people with compassion and generosity. This teaching usually begins with siblings and family members. Later, you can create ways in which she can contribute to others in the community (perhaps by accompanying you in bringing food to homeless shelters or holiday gifts to less fortunate children). When she realizes that she can make a difference in other people's lives as well as in her own, it will give her more confidence to rebound from experiences that haven't gone well.

- *Coping.* Give your child encouragement and tools for dealing with stress, and become a positive role model for coping effectively. Communication is an essential coping tool. Create an environment where she feels safe and comfortable talking about what's on her mind and the events in her life. Let her know that to help her cope and adjust, she can always express her feelings and bring her concerns to you, especially during tough times. Another critical tool is to help her identify what her passions are and the activities, hobbies, and sports that she truly enjoys. These healthy distractions also help to turn off potentially toxic stress. If her coping "toolbox" is full of healthy distractions, she will be less likely to adopt unhealthy distractions (screen time, eating, drinking, smoking, promiscuity) as she gets older.

- *Control.* Let your child know that the decisions she makes and the actions she takes can affect what happens in her life. Remind her that she is capable of bouncing back from events that upset her.

The American Academy of Pediatrics is strongly committed to having children grow up with caring adults and in safe places. But if you're feeling overloaded with the stresses in your own life—from work-related anxieties to financial or marital concerns—it can rub off on your child. So don't hesitate to ask your doctor for a referral to a therapist for yourself. Family stresses and changes can influence your child's psychological well-being, and major problems such as domestic violence or parental depression need prompt attention for your child's resilience to thrive during difficult times. If you're feeling depressed and isolated, your child might respond by withdrawing, clinging, becoming aggressive, or having difficulty adapting in preschool or child care settings.

Research by psychologist and educator Martin E. P. Seligman indicates that optimism is learned. Your child can learn to change her outlook in the direction of being more positive and hopeful. In Seligman's book *The Optimistic Child,* he describes skills that older children in particular can be taught to minimize negative thinking and depression by providing guidance such as "I know you will do this differently next time."

these confusing messages and find healthy, constructive ways to express her negative feelings.

Begin by handling your own anger and unhappiness in a mature fashion so that she learns from your example. Encourage her to come to you with problems she can't solve herself, and help her work through them and understand them. Set clear limits for her so that she understands that violence is not permissible, but at the same time let her know it's normal and OK to feel sad, angry, hurt, or frustrated.

RECOGNIZE PROBLEMS AND GET HELP WHEN NECESSARY. Although it is an enormous challenge, parenthood can be more rewarding and enjoyable than any other part of your life. Sometimes, though, problems are bound to arise, and occasionally you may not be able to handle them alone. There is no reason to feel guilty or embarrassed about this. Healthy families accept the fact and confront difficulties directly. They also respect the danger signals and get help promptly when it's needed.

Sometimes all you need is a friend. If you're fortunate enough to have parents and relatives living nearby, your family may provide a source of support. If not, you could feel isolated unless you create your own network of neighbors, friends, and other parents. One way to build such a network is by joining organized parent-child groups at your local YM/YWCA, religious center, or community center. The other parents in these groups can be a valuable source of advice and support. Allow yourself to use this support when you need it.

Occasionally you may need expert help in dealing with a specific crisis or ongoing problem. Your personal physician and pediatrician are sources of support and referral to other health professionals, including family and marriage counselors. Don't hesitate to discuss family problems with your pediatrician. If not resolved, eventually many of these problems can adversely affect your family's health. Your pediatrician should know about them and be interested in helping you resolve them.

If your child has special needs, you and your family may face particularly difficult challenges. Families whose children have chronic illnesses or disabilities often deal with and conquer everyday obstacles in order to ensure that their children have access to optimal care to support their well-being and proper development. In such situations, one of your immediate goals is to find a pediatrician who is accessible and knowledgeable, can coordinate your child's treatment with other health care providers, and can help you navigate the conflicting advice that you may encounter. The term *medical home* often is used to describe care that is accessible, family-centered, continuous, comprehensive, coordinated, compassionate, and culturally effective. This is the optimal system of medical care for all children, particularly those with special health care needs. Creating a medical home is a partnership between pediatric health care professionals, parents, and child care providers, and is a goal you should strive for in helping your child lead a fulfilling life that is as normal and healthy as possible.

Your journey with your child is about to begin. It will be a wondrous time filled with many ups and downs, times of unbridled joy and times of sadness or frustration. The chapters that follow provide a measure of knowledge intended to make fulfilling the responsibilities of parenthood a little easier and, it is hoped, a lot more fun.

~ PART 1 ~

~ 1 ~

Preparing for a New Baby

PREGNANCY IS A TIME of anticipation, excitement, preparation, and, for many new parents, uncertainty. You dream of a baby who will be strong, healthy, and bright—and you make plans to provide her with everything she needs to grow and thrive. You probably also have fears and questions, especially if this is your first child, or if there have been problems with this or a previous pregnancy. What if something goes wrong during the course of your pregnancy, or what if labor and delivery are difficult? What if being a parent isn't everything you've always dreamed it would be? These are perfectly normal feelings and fears to have. Fortunately, most of these worries are needless. The nine months of pregnancy will give you time to have your questions answered, calm your fears, and prepare yourself for the realities of parenthood.

Some of your initial concerns may have been raised and addressed if you had difficulty becoming pregnant, particularly if you sought treatment for an infertility problem. But now that you're pregnant, preparations for your new baby can begin. The best way to help your baby develop is to take good care of yourself, since medical attention and good nutrition will directly benefit your baby's health. Getting plenty of rest and exercising moderately will help you feel better and ease the physical stresses of pregnancy. Talk to your physician about prenatal vitamins, and avoid smoking, alcohol, and eating fish containing high levels of mercury.

As pregnancy progresses, you're confronted with a long list of related decisions, from planning for the delivery to decorating the nursery. You probably have made many of these decisions already. Perhaps you've postponed some others because your baby doesn't yet seem "real" to you. However, the more actively you prepare for your baby's arrival, the more real that child will seem, and the faster your pregnancy will appear to pass.

Eventually it may seem as if your entire life revolves around this baby-to-be. This increasing preoccupation is perfectly normal and healthy and actually may help prepare you emotionally for the challenge of parenthood. After all, you'll be making decisions about your child for the next two decades—at least! Now is a perfect time to start.

Here are some guidelines to help you with the most important of these preparations.

Giving Your Baby a Healthy Start

Virtually everything you consume or inhale while pregnant will be passed through to the fetus. This process begins as soon as you conceive. In fact, the embryo is most vulnerable during the first two months, when the major body parts (arms, legs, hands, feet, liver, heart, genitalia, eyes, and brain) are just starting to form. Chemical substances such as those in cigarettes, alcohol, illegal drugs, and certain medications can interfere with the developmental process and with later development, and some can even cause congenital abnormalities.

Take smoking, for instance. If you smoke cigarettes during pregnancy, your baby's birth weight may be significantly decreased. Even inhaling smoke from the cigarettes of others (passive smoking) can affect your baby. Stay away from smoking areas and ask smokers not to light up around you. If you smoked before you got pregnant and still do, this is the time to stop—not just until you give birth, but forever. Children who grow up in a home where a parent smokes have more ear infections and more respiratory problems during infancy and early childhood. They also have been shown to be more likely to smoke when they grow up.

There's just as much concern about alcohol consumption. Alcohol intake during pregnancy increases the risk for a condition called fetal alcohol syndrome (FAS), which is responsible for birth defects and below-average intelligence. A baby with fetal alcohol syndrome may have heart defects, malformed limbs (e.g., clubfoot), a curved spine, a small head, abnormal facial characteristics, small body size, and low birth weight. Fetal alcohol syndrome is also the leading cause of intellectual disability in newborns. Alcohol consumption during pregnancy increases the likelihood of a miscarriage or preterm delivery, as well.

There is evidence that the more alcohol you drink during pregnancy, the greater the risk to the fetus. It is safest not to drink any alcoholic beverages during pregnancy.

You also should avoid all medications and supplements except those your physician has specifically recommended for use during pregnancy. This includes not only prescription drugs that you may have already been taking, but also non-prescription or over-the-counter products such as aspirin, cold medications, and antihistamines. Even vitamins can be dangerous if taken in high doses. (For example, excessive amounts of vitamin A have been known to cause congenital [existing from birth] abnormalities.) Consult with your physician before taking drugs or supplements of any kind during pregnancy, even those labeled "natural."

Fish and shellfish contain high-quality protein and other essential nutrients, are low in saturated fat, and contain fatty acids called omega-3s. They can be an essential part of a balanced diet for pregnant women.

At the same time, you should be aware of the possible health risks from eating fish while you're pregnant. You should avoid raw fish during pregnancy because it may contain parasites such as flukes or worms. Cooking and freezing are the most effective ways to kill the parasite larvae found in fish. For safety reasons, the US Food and Drug Administration (FDA) recommends cooking fish at 140 degrees Fahrenheit (60 degrees Celsius). The fish should appear opaque and flaky when done. Certain types of cooked sushi such as eel and California rolls are safe to eat when pregnant.

The most worrisome contaminant in both freshwater and ocean fish is mercury (or more specifically, a form of mercury called methyl mercury). Mercury in a pregnant woman's diet has been shown to be damaging to the development of the brain and nervous system of the fetus. The FDA advises pregnant women, women who may become pregnant, nursing mothers, and young children to avoid eating shark, swordfish, king mackerel, and title fish due to high levels of mercury in these fish. According to the FDA, pregnant women can safely eat an average of 12 ounces (two average meals) of other types of cooked fish each week. Five of the most commonly eaten fish that are low in mercury are shrimp, canned light tuna, salmon, pollock, and catfish. Albacore tuna tends to be high in mercury, so canned chunk light tuna is a better choice. If local health agencies have not issued any advisories about the safety of fish caught in your area, you can eat up to 6 ounces (one average meal) per week of fish you catch from local waters, but don't consume any other fish during that week.

While no adverse effects from minimal caffeine intake (one cup of caffeinated coffee per day) have yet been proven, you may want to limit or avoid caffeine when you are pregnant. Remember, caffeine is also found in many soft drinks and foods such as chocolate.

Another cause of congenital abnormalities is illness during pregnancy. You should take precautions against these dangerous diseases:

German measles (rubella) can cause intellectual disability, heart abnormalities, cataracts, and deafness, with the highest risk of these problems occurring in the first twenty weeks of pregnancy. Fortunately, this illness now can be prevented by immunization, *although you must not get immunized against rubella during pregnancy.* If you're not sure whether you're immune, ask your obstetrician to order a blood test for you. In the unlikely event that the test shows you're not immune, you must do your best to avoid sick children, especially during the first three months of your pregnancy. It is then recommended that you receive this immunization after giving birth to prevent this same concern in the future.

Chickenpox is particularly dangerous if contracted shortly before delivery. If you have not already had chickenpox, avoid anyone with the disease or anyone recently exposed to the disease. You also should receive the preventive vaccine when you are not pregnant.

Herpes is an infection that newborns can get at the time of birth. Most often, it occurs as the infant moves through the birth canal of a mother infected with genital herpes. Babies who get a herpes viral infection may develop fluid-filled blisters on the skin that can break and then crust over. A more serious form of the disease can progress into a severe and potentially fatal inflammation of the brain called encephalitis. When a herpes infection occurs, it is often treated with an antiviral medication called acyclovir. For the last month of pregnancy, your doctor may advise taking a recommended dose of acyclovir or valacyclovir to reduce the risk of an outbreak close to the time of delivery. If you have an outbreak or feel symptoms of one coming on during your delivery time, a Cesarean section (or C-section) may be recommended to decrease the risk of exposure to the baby.

Toxoplasmosis may be a danger for cat owners. This illness is caused by a parasitic infection common in cats, but much more often it is found in un-cooked meat and fish. Take care that meat is cooked thoroughly prior to consumption, and avoid tasting meat (even while seasoning) before cooking. Wash all cutting boards and knives thoroughly with hot soapy water after each use. Wash and/or peel all fruits and vegetables before eating them. When it comes to infected animals, outdoor cats are far more likely to contract toxoplasmosis. These cats excrete a form of the toxoplasmosis parasite in their stools, and people who come in contact with the infected stools could become infected themselves. To guard against this disease, have someone who is healthy and not pregnant change your cat's litter box daily; if this is not possible, wear gloves and clean the litter box every day. Wash your hands well with soap and water afterward. Also, wash your hands with soap and water after *any* exposure to soil, sand, raw meat, or unwashed vegetables. There have been no documented cases of animal-transmitted toxoplasmosis in the US in recent years.

Tdap/DTaP Vaccine: Protection for You (Tdap) and Baby (DTaP)

In their first four to six months, babies are more prone to infections because their immune systems are not fully developed. That is why it is important that moms are protected against many things, including tetanus, diphtheria, and pertussis. The vaccine for these three serious diseases is known as Tdap or DTaP and it stands for:

- **D**iphtheria—a severe throat infection caused by a germ that makes it difficult to breathe. This can affect the heart and nervous system and lead to death.

- **T**etanus—also called lockjaw, a painful tightening of the muscles, including the jaw, which gets "locked" shut, making it impossible to open the mouth or swallow. This can lead to death.

- **P**ertussis—also called whooping cough, causes severe coughing, vomiting, and may cause trouble sleeping for months in adults. In infants this infection can be much more serious and cause severe cough and trouble breathing that lasts for months and can even lead to brain damage or death. There has been a recent rise in the cases of pertussis in the US, as well as infant deaths due to pertussis. For this reason, it is recommended that everyone (parents and children) make sure they are current on pertussis vaccines.

Bacteria cause all these diseases, and infection can be prevented with vaccines. Diphtheria and pertussis are spread from person to person. Tetanus enters the body through cuts, scratches, or wounds.

Since newborns haven't gotten their first few doses of the vaccine that protects them from these diseases, moms who were never immunized or moms who may have lost their own immunity from earlier immunizations could pick up these diseases and pass them on to their babies.

Tdap is recommended for every pregnant woman and during each and every pregnancy to protect herself and her baby against pertussis (whooping cough). After a pregnant woman is immunized, she passes her protection across the placenta to her baby before the baby is born. This helps protect the baby from pertussis until he or she is old enough to get vaccinated. The ideal time for a pregnant mom to receive the vaccine and protect her unborn child is between twenty-seven and thirty-six weeks of gestation. If the vaccine is not given during pregnancy, it should be given to the mom immediately after delivery. It is recommended that anyone who will be in close contact with your baby should be vaccinated against pertussis as well, and they should ask their doctor if Tdap or DTaP vaccine is needed. This includes dads, grandparents, other relatives, and child care providers, regardless of age. Other children in the family should be sure their tetanus, diphtheria, and pertussis immunizations are up-to-date also.

WHERE WE STAND

DRINKING ALCOHOL DURING pregnancy is one of the leading preventable causes of birth defects, intellectual disability, and other developmental disorders in newborns. There is no known safe amount of alcohol consumption during pregnancy. For that reason, the American Academy of Pediatrics recommends that women who are pregnant, or who are planning to become pregnant, abstain from drinking alcoholic beverages of any kind.

Getting the Best Prenatal Care

Throughout your pregnancy, you should work closely with your obstetrician to make sure that you stay as healthy as possible. Regular doctor's visits up until the birth of your baby can significantly improve your likelihood of having a healthy newborn. During each doctor's visit, you will be weighed, your blood

WHERE WE STAND

THE AMERICAN ACADEMY OF PEDIATRICS' message is clear—don't smoke when pregnant, and protect yourself and your children from secondhand tobacco smoke. Many studies have shown that if a woman smokes or is exposed to secondhand smoke during pregnancy, her child may be born too early (prematurely) or be smaller than normal. Other effects caused by smoking during pregnancy may include sudden infant death syndrome (SIDS), depressed breathing movements while in the uterus, learning problems, respiratory disorders, and heart disease as an adult.

After birth, children exposed to secondhand tobacco smoke have more respiratory infections, bronchitis, pneumonia, poor lung function, and asthma than children who aren't exposed. Smoke exposure is most dangerous for younger children because they spend more time in close proximity to parents or other smokers, and they have immature lungs.

If you smoke, quit. Ask your child's pediatrician or your primary care doctor for free help, or call 1-800-QUIT-NOW. If you can't quit, don't expose your child to smoke—make your home and car completely smoke-free. The Academy supports legislation that would prohibit smoking in public places, including outdoor public places that children frequent. The Academy also supports banning tobacco advertising, harsher warning labels on cigarette packages, attaching an "R" rating to movies depicting tobacco use, FDA regulation of nicotine, insurance coverage for smoking-cessation counseling, and increases in cigarette excise taxes. For more information, visit www.aap.org/richmondcenter.

pressure will be checked, and the size of your uterus will be estimated to evaluate the size of your growing fetus.

Here are some areas that deserve attention during your pregnancy.

Nutrition

Follow your obstetrician's advice regarding your use of prenatal vitamins. As mentioned, you should take vitamins only in the doses recommended by your doctor. Perhaps more than any other single vitamin, make sure you have an adequate intake (generally, 400 mcg a day) of folic acid, a B vitamin that can reduce the risk of certain birth defects, such as spina bifida. Your obstetrician may recommend a daily prenatal vitamin pill, which includes not only folic acid and other vitamins, but also iron, calcium, and other minerals, and the fatty acids docosahexaenoic acid (DHA) and arachidonic acid (ARA). Fatty acids are "good" fats, and DHA in particular accumulates in the brain and eyes of the fetus, especially during the last trimester of pregnancy. These fatty acids are also found in the fat of human breast milk. Make sure your doctor knows about any other supplements you may be taking, including herbal remedies.

Eating for Two

When it comes to your diet, do some planning to ensure that you're consuming balanced meals. Make sure that they contain protein, carbohydrates, fats, vitamins, and minerals. This is no time for fad or low-calorie dieting. In fact, as a general rule, you need to consume about 300 more calories per day than you did before you became pregnant. You need these extra calories and nutrients so your baby can grow normally.

Exercise

Physical activity is just as important when you're pregnant as at any other time of life. Discuss a fitness program with your doctor, including fitness DVDs or videotapes that you've found of interest. Particularly if you haven't been exercising regularly, your doctor may suggest a moderate walking or swimming regimen, or perhaps prenatal yoga or Pilates classes. Don't overdo it. Take it particularly slowly during the first few workouts—even just five to ten minutes a day is beneficial and a good place to start. Drink plenty of water while working out, and avoid activity with jumping or jarring movements.

Tests During Pregnancy

Whether your pregnancy is progressing normally or concerns are present, your obstetrician may recommend some of the following tests.

- An *ultrasound* exam is a safe procedure and one of the most common tests given to pregnant women. It monitors your fetus's growth and the well-being of his internal organs by taking sonograms (images made from sound waves) of him. It can ensure that your baby is developing normally and will help determine any problems or fetal abnormality. It also can be used close to the time of delivery if your doctor suspects that your baby is in the breech position. Although most babies are in a head-down position in the uterus at the time of delivery, breech babies are positioned so that their buttocks or feet will move first through the birth canal, before the baby's head. Because of the risk of head entrapment, breech deliveries are not advised in "first world" countries like the US except in very rare circumstances. Even when a new mother is fully di-lated, if the baby is found to be breech, the recently revised recommendations are to always perform a C-section. (For further discussion of breech babies and Cesarean births, see *Delivery by Cesarean Section* in Chapter 2, pages 46–48.)

- A *nonstress* test electronically monitors the fetus's heart rate and movements. In this test, a belt is positioned around your abdomen. It is called a "nonstress" test because medications are not used to stimulate movement in your unborn baby or trigger contractions of the uterus.

- A *contraction stress test* is another means of checking the fetus's heart rate, but in this case it is measured and recorded in response to mild contractions of the uterus that are induced during the test. For example, an infusion of the hormone oxytocin may be used to cause these contractions. By monitoring your baby's heart rate during the contractions, your doctor may be able to determine how your baby will react to contractions during the actual delivery; if your baby is not responding favorably during these contractions, the delivery of your baby (perhaps by Cesarean section) might be scheduled prior to your due date.

- A *biophysical profile* uses both a nonstress test and an ultrasound. It evaluates the movement and breathing of the unborn baby, as well as the volume of amniotic fluid. Scores are given for each component of the profile, and the collective score will help determine whether there is a need for an early delivery.

Other tests may be recommended, depending on your own physical health and personal and family history. For example, particularly for women with a family history of genetic problems or for those who are age thirty-five or older, your obstetrician may advise tests that can detect genetic disorders. The most common genetic tests are *amniocentesis* and *chorionic villus sampling*, which are described in the box *Detecting Genetic Abnormalities* below.

Many states have standard programs to screen for chromosomal abnormalities (such as Down syndrome) and other birth defects.

Screening tests for other birth defects are also available, such as:

■ *Neural tube defects* (an incomplete closure for the fetal spine)

■ *Abdominal wall defects*

■ *Heart defects* (in which the chambers of the heart are not well developed)

■ *Trisomy 18* (a chromosomal defect that causes intellectual disability)

Also see *Detecting Genetic Abnormalities* below.

Detecting Genetic Abnormalities

Some tests can detect genetic abnormalities before birth. By learning about these problems before birth, you can help plan your child's health care in advance, and in some cases even treat the disorder while the baby is still in the womb.

■ With *amniocentesis,* the doctor inserts a thin needle through the pregnant woman's abdominal wall and into the uterus, where a small sample of amniotic fluid is withdrawn from the sac surrounding the fetus. When the fluid is analyzed in the laboratory, it can indicate (or rule out) serious genetic and chromosomal disorders, including Down syndrome and some cases of spina bifida. Amniocentesis is usually performed during the second trimester (between the fifteenth and twentieth weeks of pregnancy), although it may be done later (typically after the thirty-sixth week) to test whether the baby's lungs are developed enough for birth. Results of most amniocentesis tests are available within about two weeks.

■ With *chorionic villus sampling (CVS),* a long, slender needle is inserted through the abdomen to remove a small sample of cells (called chorionic villi) from the placenta. Or a catheter (a thin plastic tube) is placed into the vagina and then inserted through the cervix to withdraw cells from the placenta. This sample is then analyzed in the laboratory. CVS is usually performed earlier during the pregnancy than amniocentesis, most often between the tenth and twelfth week of pregnancy, and the test results are available within one to two weeks. It can be used to detect various genetic and chromosomal conditions, including Down syndrome, Tay-Sachs disease, and (especially in African American families) so-called hemoglobinopathies such as sickle cell disease and thalassemia (see pages 622 and 623).

Both amniocentesis and CVS are considered accurate and safe procedures for prenatal diagnosis, although they pose a small risk of miscarriage and other complications. You should discuss both the benefits and the risks with your doctor and, in some cases, with a genetic counselor.

Your doctor may recommend other screening tests. For example:

■ *Glucose screening* can check for high blood sugar levels, which could be an indication of gestational diabetes, a form of diabetes that can develop during pregnancy. To conduct the test, which is usually performed between the twenty-fourth and twenty-eighth week of pregnancy, you'll be asked to drink a sugar solution and then a sample of your blood will be collected after one hour. If a high level of glucose (a type of sugar used for energy) is in the blood, then additional testing should be done. This will determine if you do have gestational diabetes, which is associated with an increased likelihood of pregnancy complications.

■ *Group B streptococcus (GBS) screening,* which will determine whether a type of bacteria is present that can cause a serious infection (such as meningitis or a blood infection) in your baby. While GBS bacteria are common and may be found in the mother's vagina or rectum—and are harmless in healthy adults—they can cause illness if they're passed to a newborn during childbirth. If GBS is detected in a pregnant woman, the doctor will prescribe antibiotics to be given intravenously in the hospital during the birthing process; once the baby is born, she may be observed for a longer time in the hospital nursery. The GBS screening test is usually performed between the thirty-fifth and thirty-seventh week of pregnancy.

■ *HIV (or human immunodeficiency virus) testing* is now commonly done in pregnant women, preferably early in their pregnancy. HIV is the virus that causes AIDS, and when a pregnant woman is infected with the virus, it can be passed to her baby during pregnancy, during delivery of her baby, or during breastfeeding.

Preparing for Delivery

As the weeks and months pass leading up to your delivery date, you're probably eagerly planning for the new addition to your family, and adjusting to what is going on in your own body. During the third trimester, you'll notice many changes that may affect how you feel:

■ You'll gain weight, typically at a rate averaging about 1 pound a week during the last trimester.

■ As your baby grows in size and places pressure on nearby organs, you may experience episodes of shortness of breath and back pain.

■ You may urinate more frequently as pressure is placed on your bladder, and you might have episodes of incontinence.

■ You may find it harder to get comfortable, and sleep may become more difficult. You may prefer to sleep on your side.

■ You could experience more fatigue than usual.

■ You may have heartburn, swelling in your feet and ankles, back pain, and hemorrhoids.

■ You may have "false labor" contractions known as Braxton-Hicks contractions. These Braxton-Hicks contractions begin to soften and thin the cervix, preparing it for the delivery of the baby. But unlike true labor contractions, they are irregular, do not occur more often as time passes, and do not become stronger or more intense.

While you're pregnant, you and your spouse/partner may be participating in childbirth education classes, which will give you information about labor and birth, provide the chance to meet other parents-to-be, and help you prepare for the birth. Several types of classes are available in many communities. The Lamaze method, for example, uses approaches such as focused breathing, massage, and labor support that can be used during the actual childbirth process. The Bradley method emphasizes natural childbirth, and relies heavily on deep-breathing techniques. Many childbirth education classes discuss a combination of these as well as other methods to teach expectant parents about the birth process and ways to make the delivery successful, comfortable, and enjoyable.

Whatever class you're considering, ask in advance about the topics and methods of childbirth that will be emphasized, and whether the classes are primarily lectures or also involve your active participation. What is the instructor's philosophy about pregnancy and birth? Is he or she certified? Will you learn proper methods for breathing and relaxation? What will the classes cost? Is there a limit on class size?

At the same time, consider signing up for other classes that can help prepare you for the parenting challenges ahead. Ask your doctor for referrals to breastfeeding classes, infant care programs, or instructional courses on cardiopulmonary resuscitation (CPR).

Some education classes encourage their participants to develop a "birth plan," and may provide guidance in helping you do so. The birth plan is usually a written document for both you and your doctor in which you'll record your own preferences for labor and delivery. For example:

- Where will you be delivering your baby?

- Based on your doctor's instructions, do you plan to go directly to the hospital when labor begins, or will you call the office first? What arrangements have you made for transportation to the hospital or birthing center? Do you have a doula or want to participate in a doula program? (A doula provides various forms of nonmedical support in the childbirth process.)

- Who would you like to deliver your baby (an obstetrician or a nurse midwife)?

- Who do you want to be present to support you during the childbirth experience?

- What position would you prefer to be in during delivery?

■ What are your preferences for pain medication (if any is going to be used)?

■ What options would you consider if unexpected circumstances develop (e.g., the need for an episiotomy or a Cesarean section)?

■ If you deliver prematurely, does the facility have adequate resources to take care of your prematurely born infant?

Not only should you talk about and share this document with your doctor, but also let your family members and friends know of your decisions. (Also see the *Last-Minute Activities* checklist below for other ideas of what to include in your "birth plan.")

Last-Minute Activities

If you do have the time, consider these activities before delivery. For example:

■ Make a list of people who will receive birth announcements. If you're ordering print announcements, select the announcement style, and address the envelopes in advance. Likewise, gather e-mail addresses or phone numbers for announcing your baby's arrival.

■ Cook a number of meals and freeze them.

■ Look for child care and/or housekeeping help if you can afford it, and interview candidates in advance. (See *Finding Help at Home*, page 183.) You can also take advantage of friends and family members who are available to help. Even if you don't think you'll need extra help, you should have a list of names to call in case the situation changes.

Before your ninth month, make last-minute preparations for delivery. Your checklist should include the following:

■ Name, address, and phone number of the hospital.

■ Name, address, and phone number of the doctor or nurse-midwife who will deliver your baby and of the person who covers the practice when your doctor is not available.

■ The quickest and easiest route to the hospital or birthing center.

- The location of the hospital entrance you should use when labor begins.

- The phone number of an ambulance service, in case you need such assistance in an emergency.

- The phone number of the person who will take you to the hospital (if that individual does not live with you).

- A bag packed with essentials for labor and for the rest of your hospital stay, including toiletries, clothing, addresses and phone numbers of friends and relatives, reading material, and a receiving blanket and clothes for the baby to wear home.

- A car safety seat for the vehicle so you can take your baby home safely. Make sure the seat is approved for use by a baby at typical newborn weights, or for babies less than 5 pounds if you are having multiples or anticipate an early birth. The lower and upper weight limits can be found on the label and in the manual. Read and follow the manufacturer's instructions carefully. Install it in the backseat, facing the rear. (*Never* place a rear-facing car safety seat in front of an air bag.) **All infants and toddlers should ride in a rear-facing car safety seat until they are at least two years of age or until they reach the highest weight or height allowed by their car safety seat's manufacturer.**

- Don't forget to have your car safety seat checked by a trained professional. Proper use and installation is key to protecting your little one during a crash. (See *Car Safety Seats,* page 491, for complete details.)

- If you have other children, arrange for their care during the time you will be at the hospital.

Choosing a Pediatrician

Sometime in the last trimester of pregnancy, you will choose a care provider for your baby. It is important to know that infants and young children have many more visits to the doctor's office than most adults.

The person you choose to be your child's health care provider may be a pediatrician, family physician, or a nurse practitioner. This is a personal decision for families, and you should consider what factors are most important to your family before choosing your baby's doctor.

- **Pediatricians** focus their care on infants, children, and teenagers. Children have different health care needs from adults—both medical and emotional. Pediatricians are specially trained to prevent and manage these health concerns. Older patients trust their pediatrician because they have known each other for many years. (For more information, see *A Pediatrician's Training,* below.) Family physicians have broad experience in caring for patients of all ages, and they are able to treat the entire family.

- **A nurse practitioner** is a nurse with advanced training that allows her/him to provide health care services similar to a doctor's. Nurse practitioners focus on wellness, disease prevention, health education, and counseling. They can also provide acute care.

- **A physician assistant (PA)** is a specialist who has earned a certificate or degree from an accredited master's-level educational program that includes didactic education and clinical rotations in pediatrics. He or she must also pass the national certifying examination administered by the National Commission on Certification of Physician Assistants (NCCPA). PAs provide medical care specifically under the direction and supervision of a physician, and support the concept of physician-directed, team-based care.

In selecting a doctor, here are some specific considerations to help you make your choice.

A Pediatrician's Training

Pediatricians graduate from medical school and then take special courses solely in pediatrics for three or more years. This is called residency. Under supervised conditions, the pediatrician-in-training acquires the knowledge and skills necessary to treat a broad range of conditions, from the mildest childhood illnesses to the most serious diseases.

After completing residency training, the pediatrician is eligible to take a written exam given by the American Board of Pediatrics. Once she passes this exam, a certificate is issued, which you probably will see hanging on the pediatrician's office wall. If you see the initials "FAAP" after a pediatrician's name, it means she has passed her board exam and is now a full Fellow of the American Academy of Pediatrics. Only board-certified pediatricians can add the designation "FAAP" after their names, which means they have reached the highest status of membership in this professional organization.

Following their residency, some pediatricians elect an additional one to three years of training in a subspecialty, such as neonatology (the care of sick and premature newborns) or pediatric cardiology (the diagnosis and treatment of heart problems in children). These pediatric subspecialists may be called on to consult with general pediatricians when a patient develops uncommon or special problems. If a subspecialist is ever needed to treat your child, your regular pediatrician will help you find the right one for your child's problem.

Finding a Pediatrician

The best way to start looking for a pediatrician is by asking other parents you know and trust. They are likely to know you, your style, and your needs. You also should consider asking your obstetrician for advice. She will know local pediatricians who are competent and respected within the medical community. If you're new to the community, you may decide to contact a nearby hospital, medical school, or county medical society for a list of local pediatricians. If you are a member of a managed care plan, you probably will be required to choose a pediatrician from among their approved network of doctors. (For more information about managed care, see *Managed Care Plans: Getting Good Care for Your Child* on pages 23–24.)

Once you have the names of several pediatricians you wish to consider, start by contacting and arranging a personal interview with each of them during the final months of your pregnancy. Many pediatricians are happy to fit such preliminary interviews into their busy schedules. Before meeting with the pediatrician, the office staff should be able to answer some of your more basic questions:

- Is the pediatrician accepting new patients with my insurance or managed care plan?

- What are the office hours?

- What is the best time to call with routine questions?

- How does the office handle billing and insurance claims? Is payment due at the time of the visit?

Both parents should attend the interviews with pediatricians, if possible, to be sure you both agree with the pediatrician's policies and philosophy about child rearing. Don't be afraid or embarrassed to ask any questions. Here are a few suggestions to get you started.

■ *How soon after birth will the pediatrician see your baby?*

Most hospitals ask for the name of your pediatrician when you're admitted to deliver your baby. The delivery nurse will then phone that pediatrician or her associate on call as soon as your baby is born. If you had any complications during either your pregnancy or the delivery, your baby should be examined at birth, although this exam may be conducted by a staff pediatrician or neonatologist at the hospital if your pediatrician is not there at the time of delivery. Otherwise, the routine newborn examination can take place anytime during the first twenty-four hours of life. Ask the pediatrician if you can be present during that initial examination. This will give you an opportunity to learn more about your baby and get answers to any questions you may have. Your baby will undergo routine newborn tests that will screen for hearing and jaundice levels as well as congenital heart disease and thyroid and other metabolic disorders.

Other tests may need to be done if your baby develops any problems after birth or to follow up on any unusual findings on your prenatal sonograms.

■ *When will your baby's next exams take place?*

Pediatricians routinely examine newborns and talk with parents before the babies are discharged from the hospital. Many pediatricians will check the baby every day that the newborn is in the hospital, and then will conduct a thorough exam on the day of discharge. During these exams, the doctor can identify any problems that may have come up, while also giving parents a chance to ask questions that occurred to them during the hospital stay. Your pediatrician also will let you know when to schedule the first office visit for your baby and how to reach her if a medical problem develops before then.

All babies also should begin their immunizations before leaving the hospital. The first and most important "immunization" is starting to breastfeed your baby as soon as possible after the baby is born. This provides some early disease protection for your baby. The second recommended immunization is the first dose of the hepatitis B vaccine, which is given as a shot in the baby's thigh. The second dose of hepatitis B can be given at least four weeks after the first. Your baby will receive the next series of vaccinations when he is six to eight weeks old. (The American Academy of Pediatrics' immunization schedule appears in the Appendix on page 872.)

■ *When is the doctor available by phone? E-mail?*

Some pediatricians have a specific call-in period each day when you can phone with questions, while others will return calls as they come in throughout the day. If members of the office staff routinely answer these calls, consider asking what their training is. Also ask your pediatrician for guidelines to help you determine which questions can be resolved with a phone call and which require an office visit. Some pediatricians prefer using e-mail, which you both may find a more convenient way to communicate and help foster your relationship with the doctor.

- *What hospital does the doctor prefer to use?*

Ask the pediatrician where to go if your child becomes seriously ill or is injured. If the hospital is a teaching hospital with interns and residents, find out who would actually care for your child if he were admitted.

- *What happens if there is an after-hours (nighttime or weekend) concern or emergency?*

Find out if the pediatrician takes her own emergency calls at night. If not, how are such calls handled? Also, ask if the pediatrician sees patients in the office after regular hours, or if you must take your child to an emergency department or urgent care center. When possible, it's easier and more efficient to see the doctor in her office, because hospitals often require lengthy paperwork and extended waits before your child receives attention. However, serious medical problems usually are better handled at the hospital, where staff and medical equipment are always available.

- *Who "covers" the practice when your pediatrician is unavailable?*

If your physician is in a group practice, it's wise to meet the other doctors in the practice, since they may treat your child in your pediatrician's absence. If your pediatrician practices alone, she probably will have an arrangement for coverage with other doctors in the community. Usually your pediatrician's answering service will refer you to the doctor on call automatically, but it's still a good idea to ask for the names and phone numbers of all the doctors who take these calls—just in case you have trouble getting through to your own physician.

If your child is seen by another doctor at night or on the weekend, you should check in by phone with your own pediatrician the next morning (or first thing Monday, after the weekend). Your doctor probably will already know what has taken place, but this phone call will give you a chance to bring her up-to-date and reassure you that everything is being handled as she would recommend.

- *How often will the pediatrician see your baby for checkups and immunizations?*

The American Academy of Pediatrics recommends a checkup within forty-eight to seventy-two hours after your newborn is discharged from the hospital. This is especially important in breastfed babies to evaluate feeding, weight gain, and any yellow discoloration of skin (jaundice). Your pediatrician may adjust this schedule, particularly in the first weeks of life, depending on how your newborn is doing.

During your baby's first year of life, additional visits to your doctor's office should take place at about two to four weeks of age, and then at two, four, six, nine, and twelve months of age as well. During your baby's second year of life, she should be seen by your pediatrician at ages fifteen, eighteen, and twenty-four months, followed by annual visits from two to five years of age. If the doctor routinely schedules examinations more or less frequently than the Academy's guidelines, discuss the differences with her. Additional appointments can be scheduled anytime that you have a concern or if your child is ill.

■ *What are the costs of care?*

Your pediatrician should have a standard fee structure for hospital and office visits as well as after-hours visits and home visits (if she makes them). Find out if the charges for routine visits include immunizations. Be sure to familiarize yourself with the scope of your insurance coverage before you actually need services.

After these interviews, ask yourself if you are comfortable with the pediatrician's philosophy, policies, and practice. You must feel that you can trust her and that your questions will be answered and your concerns handled compassionately. You also should feel comfortable with the staff and the general atmosphere of the office.

Once your baby arrives, the most important test of the pediatrician you have selected is how she cares for your child and responds to your concerns. If you are unhappy with any aspect of the treatment you and your child are receiving, you should talk to the pediatrician directly about the problem. If the response does not address your concerns, or if the problem simply cannot be resolved, seek out another physician.

Issues to Discuss with Your Pediatrician

Once you have found a pediatrician with whom you feel comfortable, let her help you plan for your child's basic care and feeding. Certain decisions and preparations should be made before the baby arrives. Your pediatrician can advise you on such issues as the following.

Managed Care Plans:
Getting Good Care for Your Child

Many Americans receive their health care in managed care plans. These plans, typically offered by employers and state Medicaid programs, provide services through health maintenance organizations (HMOs) or preferred provider organizations (PPOs). The plans have their own networks of pediatricians and other physicians, and if you or your employer change from one managed care plan to another, you may find that the pediatrician you've been using and whom you like is not part of the new network. Once you have a pediatrician whom you like, ask what plans she is in, and see if you can join one of them if there's a need to switch from one HMO or PPO to another.

Managed care plans attempt to reduce their costs by having doctors control patient access to certain health care services. Your pediatrician may act as a "gatekeeper," needing to give approval before your child can be seen by a pediatric medical subspecialist or surgical specialist. Without this approval, you'll have to pay for part or all of these services out of pocket.

To help you maneuver effectively through your managed care plan, here are some points to keep in mind:

- To determine what care is provided in your managed care plan, carefully read the materials provided by the plan (often called a certificate of coverage). If you have questions, talk to a plan representative or your employer's benefits manager. All plans limit some services (e.g., mental health care, home health care), so find out what's covered and what's not.

- When you're part of a managed care plan, primary and preventive care visits usually will be covered, including well-child checkups, treatment for illnesses or injuries, and immunizations. In many plans, you'll have to pay a portion of the primary care services that your family receives, called a copayment, for each doctor's visit.

- Once you've chosen a pediatrician, it's best to stay with her. But if you feel the need to switch, all plans allow you to select another doctor from among those who are part of their network. The plan administrator can give you information on how to make this change; some plans allow you to switch only during certain time periods called "open enrollment."

■ If you feel that your child needs to see a pediatric subspecialist, work with your pediatrician to find one who is part of your plan, and obtain approval to schedule an appointment with her. Check your plan contract for details about whether your insurer will pay at least a portion of these costs. Also, if hospital care is needed, use your pediatrician's guidance in selecting a hospital in your plan that specializes in the care of children. (Most hospital procedures and surgeries require prior approval.)

■ Know in advance what emergency services are covered since you won't always have time to contact your pediatrician. Most managed care plans will pay for emergency room care in a true emergency, so in a life-threatening situation, go immediately to the nearest hospital. In general, follow-up care (e.g., removing stitches) should be done in your pediatrician's office.

■ To file a complaint—for example, if coverage of certain procedures is denied—start by expressing your concern to your pediatrician. If she is unable to resolve the problem, contact your plan's member service representative or employee benefits manager about filing a complaint. If a claim has been denied, you typically have fifteen to thirty days to file an appeal, and you should receive a decision about the appeal within thirty to ninety days of the request. If you still are dissatisfied, you may decide to seek help from the office of your state insurance commissioner, or you can take legal action.

When Should the Baby Leave the Hospital?

Each mother and baby should be evaluated individually to determine the best time of discharge. The timing of the discharge should be the decision of you and the physician caring for the infant, not the insurance company.

Should the Baby Be Circumcised?

If you have a boy, you'll need to decide whether to have him circumcised. Unless you are sure you're having a girl, it's a good idea to make a decision about circumcision ahead of time, so you don't have to struggle with it amid the fatigue and excitement following delivery.

Circumcision has been practiced as a religious rite for thousands of years. In the United States, most boys are circumcised for religious or social reasons.

Circumcision

At birth, most boys have skin that completely covers, or almost covers, the end of the penis. Circumcision removes some of this foreskin so that the tip of the penis (glans) and the opening of the urethra, through which the baby urinates, are exposed to air. Routine circumcisions are performed in the hospital within a few days of birth. When done by an experienced physician, circumcision takes only a few minutes and is rarely complicated. After consultation with you, your doctor will provide local anesthesia to reduce the pain the baby experiences during the procedure; the doctor should inform you in advance about the type of anesthesia she recommends.

Studies have concluded that circumcised infants have a slightly lower risk of urinary tract infections, although these are not common in boys and occur less often in circumcised boys mostly in the first year of life. Neonatal circumcision also provides some protection from penile cancer, a very rare condition. (See also *Circumcision,* above.)

Some research also suggests a reduced likelihood of developing sexually transmitted diseases and HIV infections in circumcised men, and possibly a reduced risk for cervical cancer in female partners of circumcised men. However, while there are potential medical benefits, these data are not sufficient to recommend routine neonatal circumcision. (See *Where We Stand* box, page 26.)

Circumcision does, however, pose certain risks, such as infection and bleeding. Although the evidence also is clear that infants experience pain, there are several safe and effective ways to reduce the pain. If the baby is born prematurely, has an illness at birth, or has congenital abnormalities or blood problems, he should not be circumcised immediately. For example, if a condition called *hypospadias* (see page 774) is present, in which the infant's urinary opening has not formed normally, your doctor will probably recommend that your baby boy not be circumcised at birth. In fact, circumcision should be performed only on stable, healthy infants.

The Importance of Breastfeeding

The American Academy of Pediatrics advocates breastfeeding as the optimal form of infant feeding. Even though formula-feeding is not identical to breastfeeding, formulas do provide appropriate nutrition. Both approaches are safe and healthy for your baby, and each has its advantages.

WHERE WE STAND

THE AMERICAN ACADEMY OF PEDIATRICS believes that circumcision has potential medical benefits and advantages, as well as risks. Evaluation of current evidence indicates that the health benefits of newborn male circumcision outweigh the risks and that the procedure's benefits justify access to this procedure for families who choose it; however, existing scientific evidence is not sufficient to recommend routine circumcision. Therefore, because the procedure is not essential to a child's current well-being, we recommend that the decision to circumcise is one best made by parents in consultation with their pediatrician, taking into account what is in the best interests of the child, including medical, religious, cultural, and ethnic traditions. Your pediatrician (or your obstetrician if he or she would be performing the circumcision) should discuss the benefits and risks of circumcision with you and the forms of analgesia that are available.

The most practical benefits of breastfeeding are convenience and cost, but there are some real medical benefits, too. Breast milk provides your baby with natural antibodies that help her resist some types of infections (including ear, respiratory, and intestinal infections). Breastfed babies also are less likely to suffer from allergies that occasionally occur in babies fed cow's milk formulas. Breastfed infants also may be less likely to develop asthma and diabetes, or become overweight, than those who are bottle-fed (see also Chapter 4).

Mothers who nurse their babies feel there are many emotional rewards.

The American Academy of Pediatrics advocates breastfeeding as the optimal form of infant feeding.

Once the milk supply is established and the baby is nursing well, both mother and child experience a tremendous sense of closeness and comfort, a bond that continues throughout infancy. The first week or two can be challenging for some, but most pediatricians can offer guidance or refer you to a certified lactation consultant for assistance if needed.

If there is a medical reason you cannot breastfeed or you choose not to do so, you still can achieve similar feelings of closeness during bottle-feedings. Rocking, cuddling, stroking, and gazing into your baby's eyes will enhance the experience for both of you, regardless of the milk source.

Chapter 4 more thoroughly explains the advantages and disadvantages of breastfeeding and bottle-feeding so that you are aware of all the options available to you. Remember, there are breastfeeding classes available in many communities to help you plan for breastfeeding and get your questions about it answered. Ask your doctor for a referral.

Should I Store My Newborn's Cord Blood?

Umbilical cord blood has been used successfully to treat a number of genetic, blood, and cancer conditions in children such as leukemia and immune disorders. Some parents are choosing to store their baby's cord blood for possible future use. However, there are no accurate statistics on the likelihood of children someday needing their own stored cells. In response, the American Academy of Pediatrics discourages storing cord blood at private banks for later personal or family use as a general "insurance policy." Rather, they encourage families to donate their newborn's cord blood, which is normally discarded at birth, to cord blood banks (if accessible in their area) for other individuals in need. (You should be aware, though, that your baby's donated cord blood would not be available as a stem cell source if your child developed leukemia later in life.)

Storing your child's cord blood is certainly an issue that you should discuss with your obstetrician and/or pediatrician before your baby is born, not during the emotionally stressful time of delivery. She may refer you to cord blood banks in your community. You will need to register ahead of time so that the appropriate collection kit can be sent to you or your obstetrician to be used at your delivery. Many states now mandate that obstetricians/pediatricians discuss cord blood collection with their patients. An informed consent form must be signed prior to the onset of active labor and before the cord blood collection.

Keep in mind that because cord blood is collected after the baby is born and the umbilical cord is clamped and cut, it does not affect the baby or the birth experience. The cord blood stem cell collection process should not alter the routine practice for the timing of umbilical cord clamping.

Once the cord blood is collected, it is typed, and screened for infectious diseases and hereditary hematologic diseases. If the donation meets all the required standards, it will be cryogenically stored for potential transplantation if a match is found, or it might be used for quality improvement and research.

Preparing Your Home and Family for the Baby's Arrival

Choosing Baby Clothing and Accessories

As your due date nears, you'll need the basic collection of baby clothes and accessories that will get your newborn through his first few weeks. A suggested starting list includes:

- 3 or 4 pajama sets (with feet)
- 6 to 8 T-shirts
- 3 newborn sleep sacks
- 2 sweaters
- 2 bonnets/hats
- 4 pairs of socks or booties
- 4 to 6 receiving/swaddle blankets
- 1 set of baby washcloths and towels (look for towels with hoods)
- 3 to 4 dozen newborn-size diapers
- 3 to 4 onesies/T-shirts with snaps between legs

For more information to help you make your selections for the rest of the items you need, see *Guidelines on Clothing Choices* on page 30.

Buying Furniture and Baby Equipment

Walk into any baby store and you probably will be overwhelmed by the selection of equipment available. A few items are essential, but most things, while enticing, are not necessary. In fact, some are not even useful. To help you sort through the options, here is a list of the basic necessities you should have on hand when your baby arrives.

- **A crib that** meets the current safety standard (see *Safety Alert: Cribs,* page 31). New cribs sold today must meet this standard, but if you're looking at used cribs, check them carefully to make sure they were originally sold after June 28, 2011, and have not been recalled. Cribs purchased before June 2011 probably do not meet the current safety standard and are illegal to sell, even privately. Unless you have money to spare, don't bother with a bassinet. Your baby will outgrow it in just a few weeks.

- **Bedding for the crib,** including a cotton flannel waterproof mattress cover and snug, fitted sheets. No other bedding products should be used in the crib. This means there should be no pillows, loose blankets, quilts, comforters, pillowlike toys, positioning devices, or bumper pads in the crib.

- **A changing table** that meets all safety specifications (see *Changing Tables,* page 477). It should be placed on a carpet or padded mat and against a wall, not a window, so there is no danger of your child falling out the window. Put shelves or tables to hold diapers, wipes, and other changing equipment within immediate reach (but away from the baby's reach), so you will not have to step away from the table—even for a second—to get anything.

- **A diaper pail.** Keep the pail securely closed. If you are going to wash your own diapers, you'll need a second pail so you can separate wet diapers from "soiled" ones.

- **A large plastic washtub** for bathing the baby. As an alternative to the washtub, you can use the kitchen sink to bathe your newborn, provided the faucet swings out of the way and the dishwasher is off. (The water from the dishwasher could dump into the sink, resulting in scalding.) After the first month, it's safer to switch to a separate tub, because the baby will be able to reach and turn on the faucet from the sink. Always make sure the bathing area is very clean before bathing your baby. Also, be sure the hottest temperature at the faucet is no more than 120 degrees Fahrenheit (48.9 degrees Celsius) to avoid burns. In most cases, you can adjust your water heater.

Everything in the nursery should be kept clean and dust-free. (See Chapter 15 for safety specifications.) All surfaces, including window and floor coverings, should be washable. So should all toys that are left out. Although stuffed

Guidelines on Clothing Choices

Here are some suggestions to keep in mind when selecting clothing for your newborn:

- Buy big. Unless your baby is born prematurely or is very small, she probably will outgrow "newborn" sizes in a matter of days—if she ever fits into them at all! Even three-month sizes may be outgrown within the first month. You'll want a couple of garments that your child can wear in the very beginning, but concentrate on larger sizes for the rest of the wardrobe. Your baby won't mind if her clothes are slightly large for a while, or if she wears the same outfit every day.

- To avoid injury from a garment that catches fire, all children should wear flame-retardant sleepwear and clothing. Make sure the label indicates this. These garments should be washed in laundry detergents, not soap, because soap will wash out the flame retardant. Check garment labels and product information to determine which detergents to use.

- Make sure the crotch opens easily for diaper changes.

- Avoid any clothing that pulls tightly around the neck, arms, or legs or has ties or cords. These clothes are not only safety hazards, but are also uncomfortable.

- Check washing instructions. Clothing for children of all ages should be washable and require little or no ironing.

- Do *not* put shoes on a newborn's feet. Shoes are not necessary until after she starts to walk. Worn earlier, they can interfere with the growth of her feet. The same is true of socks and footed pajamas if they're too small and worn for a prolonged period of time.

Safety Alert: Cribs

Your baby usually will be unattended when in her crib, so this should be a totally safe environment. The AAP recommends that new babies sleep in close proximity to their parents, with the baby on a separate sleep surface, such as a safety-approved bassinet. You can prevent the most serious injuries by using a safe crib with no soft objects or loose bedding, placing it away from windows, and keeping cords and other objects well out of reach. Falls can be prevented by lowering the crib mattress as your baby grows; it should be in its lowest position before the baby can stand. Remember that the safest position for a baby to sleep in is on her back (see *Positioning for Sleep*, page 61).

A new mandatory crib safety standard was implemented in 2011. This new standard prohibits the manufacture or sale of cribs with a drop-side rail and implements many requirements for stronger parts, hardware, and safety testing. It is strongly recommended to use a crib that meets the current safety standard. All cribs sold since June 28, 2011, must meet this standard. If you must use an older crib, check with the manufacturer to see if they offer hardware to keep the drop side from moving. Do not use something from the hardware store as a substitute for original parts. Check to see if the crib has been recalled at www.cpsc.gov.

All cribs should be inspected carefully for the following features:

- Slats should be no more than $2^3/_8$ inches (6 cm) apart so a child's head cannot become trapped between them.

- There should be no cutouts in the headboard or footboard, as your child's head could become trapped in them.

- Corner posts should be flush with the end panels or very, very tall (such as posts on a canopy bed). Loose clothing can become snagged on these and choke your baby.

You can prevent other crib hazards by observing the following guidelines:

1. If you purchase a new mattress, remove and destroy all plastic wrapping material that comes with it, because it can suffocate a child. The mattress should be firm, not soft.

2. As soon as your baby can sit, lower the crib mattress to the level where she cannot fall out either by leaning against the side or by pulling herself

over it. Set the mattress at its lowest position before your child learns to stand (typically between ages six and nine months). The most common falls occur when a baby tries to climb out, so move your child to another bed when she is 35 inches (88.9 cm) tall, or the height of the side rail is at or below her nipple line while standing.

3. The top of the crib's side rail should be at least 4 inches (10.16 cm) above the mattress, even when the mattress is set at its highest position. If the crib has a drop side or a drop gate, be sure it has a sturdy locking latch that can't be released by your child. Always leave the side up when your child is in the crib.

4. The mattress should fit snugly so your child cannot slip into the crack between it and the crib side. If you can insert two fingers between the mattress and the sides or ends of the crib, replace the mattress with one that fits snugly.

5. Periodically check the crib to be sure all hardware is tight, there are no rough edges or sharp points on the metal parts, and there are no splinters or cracks in the wood.

6. Bumper pads and other products that attach to crib slats are not recommended. There is no evidence that they prevent injuries and there is the potential for suffocation, entrapment, and strangulation.

7. Remove all soft objects and loose bedding from the crib. This includes pillows, quilts, comforters, sheepskins, and stuffed toys. Consider dressing your baby in a wearable blanket or warm sleeper as an alternative to a blanket.

8. If you use a mobile or crib gym, be sure it is securely attached to the side rails. Hang it high enough so your baby cannot reach it to pull it down, and remove it when he starts to push up on his hands and knees or when he reaches five months, whichever comes first. Even before pushing up, some infants roll on their side and reach up to grab the mobile and pull it down.

9. Keep baby monitors and other products well out of reach. Your baby may be able to reach the cord before you realize it, which can lead to strangulation. Cords from window coverings should be far out of reach as well; it is best to use cordless window products, if possible.

10. To prevent the most serious falls, don't place a crib—or any other child's bed—beside a window. Do not hang pictures or shelves above the child's bed; they can fall onto your child in the event of an earthquake.

Safety Alert: Bassinets and Cradles

Many parents prefer to use a bassinet or cradle for the first few weeks, because it's portable and allows the newborn to sleep in the parents' room. But remember that infants grow very quickly, so a cradle that is sturdy enough one month may be outgrown the next. To get the longest and safest possible use from your baby's first bed, check the following before buying:

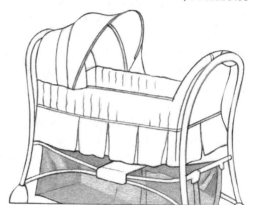

1. The bassinet should meet the current safety standard. A new, stronger standard became effective on April 23, 2014.

2. The bottom of the cradle or bassinet should be well supported so it cannot possibly collapse.

3. The bassinet or cradle should have a wide base so it cannot tip over even if someone bumps against it. If the bassinet or cradle has folding legs, they should be locked straight whenever the bed is in use. Your baby should graduate to a crib around the end of the first month or by the time she weighs 10 pounds (4.5 kg).

A "side car" arrangement—the crib placed next to the parents' bed—may be more comfortable and will be safer than bed sharing. For most families, a crib in the parents' room allows plenty of togetherness with fewer interruptions to sleep. While the AAP recommends that new babies sleep in close proximity to their parents, the baby should be on a separate sleep surface, such as a bassinet.

animals look cute around newborns (they seem to be a favorite shower gift), they tend to collect dust and may contribute to stuffy noses. Since your baby won't actively play with them for many months, you might consider storing them until she's ready for them.

If the air in the nursery is extremely dry, your pediatrician may recommend using a cool mist humidifier or vaporizer. This also may help clear your child's stuffy nose when she has a cold. If you do use a humidifier or vaporizer, clean it frequently as directed in the package instructions and empty it when not in use. Otherwise, bacteria and molds may grow in the still water.

One object that your baby is sure to enjoy is a mobile. Look for one with bright colors (the first color she'll see is red) and varied shapes. Some also play music. When shopping for a mobile, look at it from below so that you'll know how it appears from your baby's point of view. Avoid the models that look good only from the side or above—they were designed more for your enjoyment than for the infant's. Make sure you remove the mobile at five months of age or as soon as your baby can sit up, because that's when she'll be able to pull it down and risk injury.

Other useful additions to the nursery may include a rocking chair or glider, a music box or musical toy, and a music player. The rocking motion of the chair will increase the soothing effect your baby feels when you hold her. Playing soft music or white noise for your baby will comfort her when you're not nearby and will help her fall asleep.

You will want to keep the lights in the nursery soft once your newborn has arrived and leave a night-light on after dark. The night-light will allow you to check on the baby more easily, and as she gets older, it will reassure her when she awakens at night. Make sure all lights and cords are kept safely out of the baby's reach.

Preparing Your Other Children for the Baby's Arrival

If you have other children, you'll need to plan carefully how and when to tell them about the new baby. A child who is four or older should be told as soon as you start telling friends and relatives. She should have a basic sense of how she is related to her new brother or sister. Fables about storks and such may seem cute, but they won't help your youngster understand and accept the situation. Using one of the picture books published on the subject may help you to explain "where babies come from." Too much detail can be scary for her. It's usually enough to say: "Like you, this baby was made from a little bit of Mommy and a little bit of Daddy."

If your child is younger than four when you become pregnant, you can wait awhile before telling her. When she's this young, she's still very self-centered

Take advantage of any questions your child may ask about Mom's growing "stomach" to explain what's happening.

and may have difficulty understanding an abstract concept like an unborn baby. But once you start furnishing the nursery, bringing her crib back into the house, and making or buying baby clothes, she should be told what's going on. Also take advantage of any questions she may ask about Mom's growing "stomach" to explain what's happening. Picture books about babies or about becoming a big sister or brother can be useful with very young children, too. Sharing ultrasound pictures with her can be helpful, as well. Even if she doesn't ask any

Picture books can be helpful with very young children.

questions, start talking to your older child about the baby by the last few months of pregnancy. If your hospital offers a sibling preparation class, take her so that she can see where the baby will be born and where she can visit you. Point out other newborns and their older siblings, and tell her how she's going to be a big sister soon.

Don't promise that things will be the same after the baby comes, because they won't be, no matter how hard you try. But reassure your child that you will love her just as much, and help her understand the positive side of having a baby sibling.

Breaking the news is most difficult if your child is between two and three. At this age, she's still extremely attached to you and doesn't yet understand the concept of sharing time, possessions, or your affection with anyone else. She's also very sensitive to changes going on around her and may feel threatened by the idea of a new family member. The best way to minimize her jealousy is to include her as much as possible in the preparations for the new baby. Let her shop with you for baby clothing and nursery equipment. Show her pictures of herself as a newborn, and if you're recycling some of her old baby equipment, let her play with it a bit before you get it in order for the newcomer.

Any major changes in your preschooler's routine, such as toilet training, switching from a crib to a bed, changing bedrooms, or starting preschool, should be completed before the baby arrives. If that's not possible, put them off until after the baby is settled in at home. Otherwise, your child may feel overwhelmed when the upheaval caused by the baby's arrival is added to the stress of her own adjustments.

Make sure you reserve some special time each day just for you and your older child.

Don't be alarmed if news that a baby is coming—or, later, the baby's arrival—prompts your older child's behavior to regress a little. She may demand a bottle, ask to wear diapers again, cry for no apparent reason, or refuse to leave your side. This is her way of demanding your love and attention and reassuring herself that she still has it. Instead of protesting or telling her to act her age, simply grant her requests, and don't get upset about it. A three-year-old toilet-trained child who demands a diaper for a few days, or the five-year-old who wants her outgrown (you thought long-forgotten) security blanket for a week, will soon return to her normal routine when she realizes that she now has just as important a place in the family as her new sibling. Similarly, an older sibling who wants to try nursing again will quickly lose interest.

However busy or preoccupied you may be with your new arrival, make sure you reserve some special time each day just for you and your older child. Read, play games, listen to music, or simply talk together. Show her that you're interested in what she's doing, thinking, and feeling—not only in relation to the baby, but about everything else in her life. It takes only five or ten minutes a day of protected time—time when the baby is asleep or being cared for by another adult—to make your older child feel special.

Preparing Dad for Delivery

If you're the father-to-be, remember that having a baby is a family event. You can help with the tasks and preparations for the baby's arrival described above. At the same time, you'll be making your own adjustments, which are challenging, too. Of course, your role during the nine-month pregnancy has been quite different, but you still have had adjustments to make. At times you've felt excited and elated; other times, fearful, exhausted, and perhaps just tired of waiting for the baby to arrive. There probably have been times when you've been an emotional anchor for your wife or partner during some of the more difficult moments of pregnancy, from periods of extreme fatigue to morning sickness.

When you attend prenatal visits to the obstetrician, discuss what role you'll play in the delivery room. Be sure to get all your questions answered about what will take place and how you can be most supportive. If you can do any advance planning in order to take off a few days or weeks from work once the baby arrives, make those arrangements now. And, of course, be ready to play a very active role in your child's life, not only in the first few days after her birth, but for the rest of your lives together. (For a further discussion about the unique role of fathers—and grandparents—in the birth of their baby, see Chapter 6, pages 187–192.)

For both parents, once your baby finally arrives, all the waiting and discomforts of pregnancy will seem like minor inconveniences. Suddenly you'll get to meet this new person who's been so close and yet so mysterious all these months. The rest of this book is about the child she will become and the job that awaits you as a parent.

There's only so much preparation you can do before you start any journey. We have discussed a lot of the supplies you will need as well as many of the dos and don'ts. Ultimately, the way you assume your role as a parent will be determined more by the way you prepare yourself spiritually and emotionally than by what color you choose for the nursery wallpaper or the style of crib you buy. Only you know how you respond to stress and change. Try to prepare yourself for parenthood in a way that feels most comfortable to you. Some parents find support groups helpful; others prefer to meditate, sketch, or write.

Preparing yourself might be more difficult for some soon-to-be parents than others, especially if you are the kind of person who likes spontaneity more than figuring everything out in advance, but preparation is important, since it gives rise to greater confidence. It takes a stunning amount of confidence for a child to begin to walk. Similarly, you will need that type of confidence to take your own first steps into parenting.

Finally—Delivery Day!

The duration of most pregnancies is between thirty-seven and forty-two weeks. Labor contractions are the clearest indication that your body is getting ready to deliver your baby. When labor starts, your cervix (the lower end of the uterus) will open, and the uterus will begin contracting or squeezing. The cervix must be effaced (or thinned out) in order for the baby's head to move into the birth canal. Each time a contraction occurs, your uterus and abdomen will become tighter and firmer. Between contractions, the uterus will soften, and you can relax for a short time while awaiting the next contraction.

Although most women know when they are nearing labor or when labor has started, it isn't always easy to tell for sure when this process has begun. That's because "false labor" can occur, in which contractions are sporadic and relatively weak. Even so, don't be embarrassed to call your doctor or go to the hospital if you're uncertain whether this is the real thing!

With actual labor, you will experience:

- Repeated contractions, cramps, and increases in pain levels corresponding to the opening up (dilating) of your cervix and the baby's descent through the birth canal.

- A slightly bloody, pink, or clear vaginal discharge that is the mucus plug at the cervix.

- A breaking of your water, which is really a rupture in the amniotic sac that contains watery fluid that surrounds and protects your baby.

As labor progresses, the contractions will become stronger, they'll occur more often, and they'll continue for about 30 to 70 seconds each. The pain of the contractions will tend to start in your back, and then move forward to the lower abdomen.

When should you call your doctor or go to the hospital? Hopefully, you've already discussed this with your doctor. In general, you should head for the hospital or phone your doctor if your water breaks (even if you aren't having contractions yet), you're experiencing vaginal bleeding, or the pain is severe and persistent even between contractions.

The doctor may induce labor before you go into labor on your own. This

What About the Pain?

Pain levels during delivery vary from one woman to another. For some, the process can be very painful, but women can often turn to relaxation and breathing techniques (taught in their childbirth classes) to help them deal with the discomfort. Massage on the lower back by a spouse or other labor coach often eases discomfort as well, as does taking a bath or shower (if allowed) or applying ice packs to the back.

If an episiotomy (surgical incision in vaginal area) is needed to ease the baby's head through the birth canal, a local anesthetic is injected ahead of time to make the area numb. Local anesthetics given in this manner almost never have any negative effects upon the baby.

As labor progresses, many women decide to have medication to ease the pain of the contractions. These include:

1. *Narcotic (opioid) medications given as a shot or through an intravenous catheter.* These medications make the labor pains more tolerable but can slow the baby's breathing if given very close to delivery.

2. *Numbing medicines given in the spinal region to reduce the intensity of the contractions.* This is generally referred to as epidural analgesia or an epidural block. A small tube called a catheter is placed into the epidural space, an area just outside of the spinal cord region. Medicines are then

given through this catheter to decrease the feeling in your abdomen and make the contractions less painful. Pain relief generally begins within ten to twenty minutes. Most of the time these medications are given in small enough doses so that you are still alert, aware of the contractions (though they are not as painful), and still have enough strength to push the baby down the birth canal. Side effects or complications are rare, but may include headaches or a drop in your blood pressure.

If your doctor decides that a Cesarean section is necessary, there are three options for pain relief/anesthesia:

1. *Additional numbing medicine can be given through an epidural catheter to make your entire lower body numb (from below your rib cage to your toes).* If you already had an epidural catheter placed to ease the labor pain, then extra medicine can be given through this catheter to make you numb enough for surgery. The advantage of this type of anesthesia is that the baby will not be as sleepy and you can be awake when the baby is born.

2. *If you are having a scheduled Cesarean section, your doctor may recommend a spinal block.* This is a single injection into the fluid surrounding the spinal cord. Spinal blocks are very quick and easy to perform and generally make you even more numb than an epidural block. Pain relief begins immediately. One difference between a spinal and an epidural block is that a spinal is a one-time shot of pain medication that wears off on its own in several hours, instead of being administered continuously through a catheter. Side effects or complications are rare, but are similar to an epidural.

3. *If the surgery needs to be performed as an emergency or you have a medical issue that would make an epidural or spinal block dangerous for you, medicines can be given that will make you lose consciousness or "go to sleep" (general anesthesia).* This can make the baby very sleepy when he is born and affect the baby's breathing. When general anesthesia is given, the baby must be delivered very quickly in order to decrease these effects, so epidural or spinal blocks are preferred when possible.

For more detailed information about routine vaginal deliveries and Cesarean sections, including procedures in hospital delivery rooms upon the birth of your baby, see Chapter 2, *Birth and the First Moments After*, pages 43–56.

induction may be chosen if your doctor determines that your health or the health of your baby is being threatened. Perhaps you have a chronic disease such as diabetes or high blood pressure that may pose risks to you or your child. Or your doctor may recommend inducing labor if tests indicate that your baby's growth is unusual. With certain medications (such as oxytocin or prostaglandin drugs that may be given intravenously in the hospital), the mother will have contractions and her cervix will start to open and efface. The doctor can also intentionally rupture the membranes that surround the fetus or use other means to get labor started.

~ 2 ~

Birth and the First Moments After

GIVING BIRTH IS one of the most extraordinary experiences of a woman's life. Yet after all the months of careful preparation and anticipation, the moment of birth is almost never what you had expected. Labor may be easier or more physically demanding than you had imagined. You may end up in a delivery room instead of the birthing room you'd wanted, or you could have a Cesarean section instead of a vaginal delivery. Your health, the condition of the fetus, and the policies of the hospital will all help determine what actually happens. But fortunately, despite what you may have thought when you were pregnant, these are not the issues that will make your child's birth a "success." What counts is the baby, here at last and healthy.

Routine Vaginal Delivery

In the days and weeks leading up to the birth of your baby, you'll probably feel a bit of apprehension along with your excitement, wondering when this much-anticipated event finally will happen. Then, usually between the thirty-seventh and forty-second week of your pregnancy, you'll go into labor. Although no one knows for certain what triggers this process, shifts in hormone levels appear to play a role. Your amniotic sac may seem to begin the process by rupturing, commonly referred to as "breaking your water." As you proceed through labor, your uterus will contract rhythmically, or squeeze, which will move your baby down the birth canal. At the same time, these contractions will fully open, or dilate, your cervix to an opening of about 10 centimeters (4 in.) so the baby can make his appearance through the vagina.

In a routine vaginal delivery, your first view of your child may be the top, or crown, of his head, seen with the help of a mirror. After the head is delivered, the obstetrician will suction the nose and mouth and your baby will take her first breath. She doesn't need to be slapped or spanked to begin breathing, nor will she necessarily cry; many newborns take their first breath quietly.

With the most difficult part of the birth now over, there is usually one last pause before the push that sends the rest of your child's body, which is smaller than his head, gliding smoothly into the doctor's or nurse midwife's waiting arms. After another, more thorough suctioning of his nose and mouth, your child may be handed to you to hold—and behold.

Even if you've seen pictures of newborns, you're bound to be amazed by the first sight of your own infant. When she opens her eyes, they will meet yours with curiosity. All the activity of birth may make her very alert and responsive to your touch, voice, and warmth. Take advantage of this attentiveness, which may last for the first few hours. Stroke her, talk to her, and look closely at this child you've created. The obstetrician or nurse midwife may place the baby on your abdomen or lower chest in those first few moments. Watch how the baby moves up toward your breast, seeking that first feeding. Those moments are magical for you and the baby. Those moments should not be hindered; they should be allowed to happen. The natural wonder of your baby looking at you, looking at your breasts and wriggling upward, will make you realize just how exciting those important first few minutes are. Attendants should not wash you, nor should they wash the baby or interfere. The smell and feel of the moment will guide the baby to her first feeding. As with many moms, you may find that putting your baby to your breast creates an intense emotional bond between you and your newborn.

Fresh from birth, your child may be covered with a white cheesy substance called vernix. This protective coating is produced toward the end of pregnancy by the sebaceous (oil-producing) glands in her skin. She'll also be wet with am-

Nursing After Delivery

We recommend that you plan to breastfeed your baby. Ask ahead of time about the hospital's policies on nursing in the delivery area. Today, most hospitals encourage immediate breastfeeding following routine delivery unless the baby's scores on the Apgar test are low or she's breathing very rapidly, in which case nursing may need to be delayed temporarily. (See page 48 for detailed information on these tests.)

Breastfeeding right away benefits the mother by causing the uterus to contract, thus reducing the amount of uterine bleeding. (The same hormone that stimulates the milk ejection reflex, or let-down response, triggers the uterine contractions.)

The first hour or so after birth is a good time to begin breastfeeding, because your baby is very alert and eager. When put to the breast she may first lick it. Then, with a little help, she'll grasp and latch on to the areola, not the nipple, and suck vigorously for several minutes. If you wait until later, she may be sleepier and have more difficulty holding the nipple effectively.

For the first two to five days after delivery, your body produces colostrum, a thin, yellowish fluid that contains protein and antibodies to protect her from infection. Colostrum provides all the nutrients and fluids your baby needs in the first few days of life. (For a complete discussion of breastfeeding, see Chapter 4.)

niotic fluid. If there was an episiotomy (surgical cutting) or tearing of tissue in the vaginal area, she may have some of your own blood on her. Her skin, especially on the face, may be quite wrinkled from the wetness and pressure of birth.

Your baby's shape and size also may surprise you, especially if this is your first child. On one hand, it's hard to believe that a human being can be so tiny; on the other, it's incredible that this "enormous" creature could possibly have fit inside your body. The size and shape of her head in particular may alarm you. How could the head possibly have made it through the birth canal? The answer lies in its slightly elongated shape. The head was able to adapt to the contours of the passageway as it was pushed through, squeezing to fit. Now free, it may take up to several days to revert to its normal oval shape. Your baby's skin color may be a little blue at first, but gradually will turn pinker as her breathing becomes regular. Her hands and feet may be slightly blue and feel cool, and may remain so, on and off, for several weeks until her body is better able to adjust to the temperature around her.

You also may notice that your newborn's breathing is irregular and very rapid. While you normally take twelve to fourteen breaths per minute, your newborn may take as many as forty to sixty breaths per minute. An occasional deep breath may alternate with bursts of short, shallow breaths followed by pauses. Don't let this make you anxious. It's normal for the initial days after birth.

Delivery by Cesarean Section

About one mother in three gives birth by Cesarean section in the US (it is also called C-section or, simply, section). In a C-section, surgery is performed, with an incision made in the mother's abdomen and uterus, so the baby can be taken directly from the uterus instead of traveling through the birth canal.

Cesarean sections are done most often when:

- The mother has had a previous baby by Cesarean delivery

- The baby is in a breech or "head-up" position

- The cervix does not adequately dilate to the 10 centimeters necessary to start pushing or the baby does not descend through the birth canal despite an adequate pushing effort

- The obstetrician feels that the baby's health might suffer if born vaginally

- The fetus's heartbeat slows abnormally or becomes irregular (in which case the obstetrician will perform an emergency C-section instead of taking the chance of allowing labor to progress)

While most babies are in a head-down position in the mother's uterus, about three in one hundred newborns have their buttocks, feet, or both positioned to come out first during birth (a breech presentation). If your baby has assumed a breech position, your obstetrician will recommend a Cesarean section as the best means of delivery. The reason is because breech babies are more difficult to deliver vaginally, and complications are more likely to occur with a vaginally delivered breech baby. A doctor can determine the baby's position by feeling the mother's lower abdomen at particular points; the physician may decide to confirm the breech position by ordering an ultrasound or other tests.

The birth experience with a C-section is very different from that of a vaginal delivery. For one thing, the whole operation ordinarily takes no more than an hour, and—depending on the circumstances—you may not experience any

labor at all. Another important difference is the need to use medication that affects the mother and may affect the baby. If given a choice of anesthetic, most women prefer to have a regional anesthesia—an injection in the back that blocks pain by numbing the spinal nerves—such as an epidural or a spinal. Administration of a regional anesthesia numbs the body from the waist down, has relatively few side effects, and allows you to witness the delivery. But sometimes, especially for an emergency C-section, a general anesthetic must be used, in which case you are not conscious at all. Your obstetrician and the anesthesiologist in attendance will advise you which approach they think is best, based on the medical circumstances at the time.

Because of the effects of the anesthesia and the way the baby is delivered, babies born by C-section sometimes have difficulty breathing in the beginning and need extra help. A pediatrician or other person skilled in newborn problems usually is present during a Cesarean section to examine and assist the baby's breathing, if necessary, immediately after birth.

If you were awake during the operation, you may be able to see your baby as soon as she's been examined and proclaimed healthy. She may then be taken to the nursery to spend several hours in a temperature-controlled crib or isolette. This allows the hospital staff to observe her while the anesthesia wears off and she adjusts to her new surroundings.

If general anesthesia was used during the delivery, you may not wake up for a few hours. When you do, you may feel groggy and confused. You'll probably also experience some pain where the incision was made. But you'll soon be able to hold your baby, and you'll quickly make up for lost time.

Don't be surprised if your baby is still affected by the anesthesia for six to twelve hours after delivery and appears a little sleepy. If you're going to breast-feed, try to nurse her as soon as you feel well enough. Even if she's drowsy, her first feeding should provide a reason for her to wake up and meet her new world—and you. It will also help stimulate your breast milk production.

As mentioned, many obstetricians believe that once a woman has a C-section, her subsequent babies should be delivered the same way because of higher rates of complications with vaginal deliveries after previously having a C-section. However, many women are candidates for a vaginal birth after Cesarean section (VBAC). But a decision to do this will depend on a number of factors and should be made together with your doctor.

If you're the father-to-be, discuss your role and presence in the delivery room and ways you can best support your partner during the birth.

Delivery Room Procedures Following a Normal Vaginal Birth

As your baby lies with you following a routine delivery, her umbilical cord still will be attached to the placenta. The cord may continue to pulsate for several minutes, supplying the baby with oxygen while she establishes her own breath-

Apgar Scores

As soon as your baby is born, a delivery nurse will set one timer for one minute and another for five minutes. When each of these time periods is up, a nurse or physician will give your baby her first "tests," called Apgars.

This scoring system (named after its creator, Virginia Apgar) helps the physician estimate your baby's general condition at birth. The test measures your baby's heart rate, breathing, muscle tone, reflex response, and color. It cannot predict how healthy she will be as she grows up or how she will develop; nor does it indicate how bright she is or what her personality is like. But it does alert the hospital staff if she is sleepier or slower to respond than normal and may need assistance as she adapts to her new world outside the womb.

Each characteristic is given an individual score, two points for each of the five categories if all is completely well; then all scores are totaled. For example, let's say your baby has a heart rate of more than 100, cries lustily, moves actively, grimaces and coughs in response to the syringe, but is blue; her one-minute Apgar score would be 8—two points off because she is blue and not pink. Most newborn infants have Apgar scores greater than 7. Because their hands and feet remain blue until they are quite warm, few score a perfect 10.

If your baby's Apgar scores are between 5 and 7 at one minute, she may have experienced some problems during birth that lowered the oxygen in her blood. In this case, individuals (e.g., doctors, nurses, respiratory therapists) specially trained in evaluation and resuscitation of newborns will evaluate and treat the baby. This may include drying her vigorously with a towel while oxygen is held under her nose. This should start her breathing deeply and improve her oxygen supply so that her five-minute Apgar scores total between 8 and 10.

A small percentage of newborns have Apgar scores of less than 5. For example, babies born prematurely or delivered by emergency C-section are more likely to have low scores than infants with normal births. These scores may reflect difficulties the baby experienced during labor or problems with her heart or respiratory system.

If your baby's Apgar scores are very low, a mask may be placed over her face to provide oxygen and help with breathing. If she's not breathing on her own within a few minutes, a tube can be placed into her windpipe, and fluids and medications may be administered through one of the blood vessels in her umbilical cord to strengthen her heartbeat. If her Apgar scores are still low after these treatments, she may be taken to the special-care nursery for observation or more intensive medical attention.

APGAR SCORING SYSTEM

Score	0	1	2
Heart Rate	Absent	Less than 100 beats per minute	More than 100 beats per minute
Respiration	Absent	Slow, irregular; weak cry	Good; strong cry
Muscle Tone	Limp	Some flexing of arms and legs	Active motion
Reflex*	Absent	Grimace	Grimace and cough or sneeze
Color	Blue or pale	Body pink; hands and feet blue	Completely pink

*Reflex judged by placing a catheter or bulb syringe in the infant's nose and watching her response.

ing. Once the pulsing stops, the cord will be clamped and cut. (Because there are no nerves in the cord, the baby feels no pain during this procedure.) The clamp will remain in place for twenty-four to forty-eight hours, or until the cord is dry and no longer bleeds. The stump that remains after the clamp is removed will fall off sometime between one and three weeks after birth.

Once you've had a few moments to get acquainted with your baby, she will be dried to keep her from getting too cold, and a doctor or nurse will examine her briefly to make sure there are no obvious problems or abnormalities. She will be given Apgar scores (see pages 48–49), which measure her overall responsiveness. Then she will be wrapped in a blanket and given back to you.

Depending on the hospital's routine, your baby also may be weighed and

Bonding

If you have a delivery without complications, you'll be able to spend the first hour or so after birth holding, stroking, and looking at your baby. Because babies are usually alert and very responsive during this time, researchers have labeled this the sensitive period.

The first exchanges of eye contact, sounds, and touches between the two of you are all part of a process called bonding, which helps lay the foundation for your relationship as parent and child. Although it will take months to learn your child's basic temperament and personality, many of the core emotions you feel for her may begin to develop during this brief period immediately after birth. As you gaze at her and she looks back, following your movements and perhaps even mirroring some of your expressions, you may feel a surge of protectiveness, awe, and love. This is part of the attachment process.

It's also quite normal if you do *not* immediately have tremendously warm feelings for your baby. Labor is a demanding experience, and your first reaction to the birth may well be a sense of relief that at last it's over. If you're exhausted and emotionally drained, you may simply want to rest. That's perfectly normal. Give yourself until the strain of labor fades and then request your baby. Bonding has no time limit.

Also, if your baby must be taken to the nursery right away for medical attention, or if you are sedated during the delivery, don't despair. You needn't worry that your relationship will be harmed because you didn't "bond" during this first hour. You can and will love your baby just as much, even if you weren't able to watch her birth or hold her immediately afterward. Your baby also will be fine, just as loving of you and connected to you.

measured, and receive medication before leaving the delivery room. She will receive a dose of vitamin K as well, since all newborns have slightly low levels of this vitamin (which is needed for normal blood clotting). You should feel comfortable to suggest that all of these steps wait 30 minutes to an hour while you hold your new baby and allow her to move successfully to your breast for her first feeding. Once successful, and once your baby appears to be resting on your skin, then those other steps, including the vitamin K injection, can be performed. The most important thing is to maximize the skin-to-skin contact between you and your baby as much as possible in those first minutes.

Because bacteria in the birth canal can infect a baby's eyes, your baby will be given antibiotic or antiseptic eye drops or ointment (erythromycin ointment is commonly used), either immediately after delivery or later in the nursery, to prevent an eye infection.

At least one other important procedure must be done before either you or your newborn leave the delivery room: Both of you (and the baby's father) will receive matching labels bearing your name and other identifying details. After you verify the accuracy of these labels, each will be attached to your wrist and to the father's, while the other will be placed on your baby's wrist (and often to her ankle as well). Each time the child is taken from or returned to you while in the hospital, the nurse will check these bracelets to make sure they match. Many hospitals also footprint newborns as an added precaution and attach a small security device to the baby's ankle.

Leaving the Delivery Area

If you've given birth in a birthing room or alternative birth center, you probably won't be moved right away. But if you've delivered in a conventional delivery room, you'll be taken to a recovery area where you can be watched for problems such as excessive bleeding. Once again, insist that this separation from your baby wait until the baby has been with you for a while, at least an hour. Your baby may then be taken to the nursery at that time, or she may receive her first physical examination by your side.

This exam will measure her vital signs: temperature, respiration, and pulse rate. The pediatrician or nurse will check your baby from head to toe, paying specific attention to her color, activity level, and breathing pattern. If she didn't receive her vitamin K and eye drops earlier, they will be administered now. And once she's warm, she'll be given her first bath, and the stump of her cord may be painted with a blue antibacterial dye or other medication to prevent infection. Then she'll be wrapped in a blanket and, if you wish, returned to you.

If Your Baby Is Premature

Premature birth occurs in about 11 to 13 percent of pregnancies in the US. Almost 60 percent of twins, triplets, and other multiple deliveries result in preterm births. A birth is considered "preterm" when a child is born before thirty-seven weeks of pregnancy have been completed. Other categories of preterm birth include late preterm (thirty-four to thirty-six weeks), moderately preterm (thirty-two to thirty-six weeks), and very preterm (less than thirty-two weeks).

It is important to recognize that preterm deliveries, even if late preterm, should never be done for the convenience of the mother or obstetrician. Research has shown that late-preterm babies have significantly greater risk for negative outcomes, and all efforts should be made to have babies reach full term.

If your baby is born prematurely, she may neither look nor behave like a full-term infant. While the average full-term baby weighs about 7 pounds (3.17 kg) at birth, a premature newborn might weigh 5 pounds (2.26 kg) or even considerably less. But thanks to medical advances, children born after twenty-eight weeks of pregnancy, and weighing more than 2 pounds 3 ounces (1 kg), have almost a full chance of survival; eight out of ten of those born after the thirtieth week have minimal long-term health or developmental problems, while those preterm babies born before twenty-eight weeks have more complications, and require intensive treatment and support in a neonatal intensive care unit.

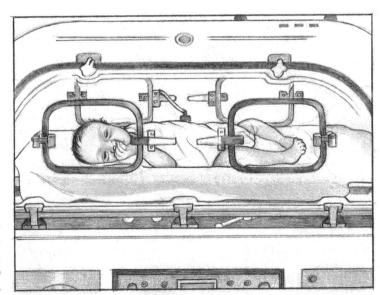

Your premature baby will be placed immediately after birth in an enclosed bed to keep her warm.

The earlier your baby arrives, the smaller she will be, the larger her head will seem in relation to the rest of her body, and the less fat she will have. With so little fat, her skin will seem thinner and more transparent, allowing you actually to see the blood vessels beneath it. She also may have fine hair, called lanugo, on her back and shoulders. Her features will appear sharper and less rounded than they would at term, and she probably won't have any of the white, cheesy vernix protecting her at birth, because it isn't produced until late in pregnancy. Don't worry, however; in time she'll begin to look like a typical newborn.

Because she has no protective fat, your premature baby will get cold in normal room temperatures. For that reason, she'll be placed immediately after birth in an incubator (often called an isolette) or under a special heating device called a radiant warmer. Here the temperature can be adjusted to keep her warm. After a quick examination in the delivery room, she'll probably be moved to a special-care nursery (often called a neonatal intensive care unit [NICU]).

You also may notice that your premature baby will cry only softly, if at all, and may have trouble breathing. This is because her respiratory system is still immature. If she's more than two months early, her breathing difficulties can cause serious health problems, because the other immature organs in her body may not get enough oxygen. To make sure this doesn't happen, doctors will keep her under close observation, watching her breathing and heart rate with equipment called a cardio-respiratory monitor. If she needs help breathing, she may be given extra oxygen, or special equipment such as a ventilator; or another breathing assistance technique called CPAP (continued positive airway pressure) may be used temporarily to support her breathing. As important as this care is for your baby's survival, her move to the special-care nursery may be wrenching for you. On top of all the worry about her health, you may miss the experience of holding, breastfeeding, and bonding with her right after delivery. You won't be able to hold or touch her whenever you want, and you can't have her with you in your room.

To deal with the stress of this experience, ask to see your baby as soon as possible after delivery, and become as active as you can in caring for her. Spend as much time with her in the special-care nursery as your condition—and hers—permit. Even if you can't hold her yet (until she's stable), touch her often. Many intensive care units allow parents to do "skin-to-skin" for their babies once the infants don't require major support to their organ systems.

You can also feed her as soon as your doctor says it's OK. The nurses will instruct you on either breast- or bottle-feeding techniques, whichever is appropriate for the baby's needs and your desires. Some premature babies may initially require fluids given intravenously or through a feeding tube that passes through the mouth or nose into the stomach. But your breast milk is the best possible nutrition, and provides antibodies and other substances that enhance her immune response and help her resist infection. In some cases, if it's too difficult for your premature baby to nurse at the breast, you can pump breast milk for feeding through a tube or bottle. Once you are able to start breastfeeding directly, your baby should nurse frequently to increase your milk supply. Even so, mothers of premature babies sometimes find it necessary to continue using a breast pump in addition to feeding frequently to maintain a good milk supply.

You may be ready to return home before your newborn is, which can be very difficult, but remember that your baby is in good hands, and you can visit her as often as you'd like. You can use your time away from the hospital to get some needed rest and prepare your home and family for your baby's homecoming, and read a book or two for parents on caring for preterm babies. Even after you've returned home, if you participate in your infant's recovery and have plenty of contact with her during this time, the better you'll feel about the situation and the easier it will be for you to care for her when she leaves the special-care nursery. As soon as your doctor says it's OK, gently touch, hold, and cradle your newborn.

Your own pediatrician may participate in, or at least will be informed about, your infant's immediate care. Because of this, he will be able to answer most of your questions. Your baby will be ready to come home once she's breathing on her own, able to maintain her body temperature, able to be fed by breast or bottle, and gaining weight steadily.

For more resources and information on premature birth, contact the March of Dimes (www.marchofdimes.org; 1-914-997-4488) or the American College of Obstetricians and Gynecologists (www.acog.org; 1-202-638-5577).

Health Issues of Premature Babies

Because premature babies are born before they are physically ready to leave the womb, they often have health problems. These newborns have higher rates of disabilities (such as cerebral palsy) and even death. African Americans and Native Americans have the highest neonatal death rate associated with prematurity.

Because of these health concerns, premature babies are given extra medical attention and assistance immediately after delivery. Depending on how early the baby has arrived, your pediatrician or obstetrician may call in a neonatologist (a pediatrician who specializes in the care of premature or very ill babies) to help determine what, if any, special treatment the infant needs. Here are some of the most common conditions that occur in premature infants:

- *Respiratory distress syndrome* is a breathing disorder related to the baby's immature lungs. It occurs because the lungs of preterm babies often lack surfactant, a liquid substance that allows the lungs to remain expanded. Artificial surfactants can be used to treat these babies, along with a ventilator or CPAP machine to help them breathe better and maintain adequate oxygen levels in their blood. Sometimes, extremely preterm babies may need long-term oxygen treatment and occasionally may go home on supportive oxygen therapy.

- *Bronchopulmonary dysplasia,* or chronic lung disease, is a term used to describe babies who require oxygen for several weeks or months. They tend to outgrow this uncommon condition, which varies in severity, as their lungs grow and mature.

- *Apnea* is a temporary pause (more than fifteen seconds) in breathing that is common in preterm infants. It often is associated with a decline in the heart rate, called bradycardia. A drop in oxygen saturation as measured by a machine called *pulse oximetry* is called desaturation. Most infants outgrow the condition by the time they leave the hospital for home.

- *Retinopathy of prematurity (ROP)* is an eye disease in which the retina is not fully developed. Most cases resolve without treatment, although serious cases may need treatment, including laser surgery in the most severe instances. Your infant may be examined by a pediatric ophthalmologist or retina specialist to diagnose and, if needed, recommend treatment for this condition.

- *Jaundice* happens when a chemical called bilirubin builds up in the baby's blood. As a result, the skin may develop a yellowish color. Jaundice can occur in babies of any race or color. Treating it involves placing the undressed baby under special lights (while her eyes are covered to protect them). For additional information about jaundice, see pages 151–153.

- Other conditions sometimes seen in preterm babies include *anemia of prematurity* (a low red blood cell count) and *heart murmurs.* For additional information on heart murmurs, see pages 797–799.

Newborn Screening Tests

Shortly after birth, and before you and your baby are discharged from the hospital to return home, she'll be given a number of screening tests to detect a variety of congenital conditions. These tests are designed to detect problems early in order to treat them promptly, prevent disabilities, and save lives. However, while laws mandate some tests, the tests required in one state are often different from those required in another (and they change periodically). Before your baby is born, talk to your pediatrician about which screening tests your baby will undergo, including their benefits and any risks, and ask if it is necessary for you to consent to this testing. Ask when you can find out the test results, and what they mean if your newborn is found to be out of the normal range (this may not necessarily mean that your baby actually has a congenital or genetic condition, so inquire about whether and when retesting would be done). Also, double-check to make certain the tests are actually performed before your baby leaves the hospital.

Reflecting on Your Baby's Arrival

After all this activity during her first few hours of life, your baby probably will fall into a deep sleep, giving you time to rest and think back over the exciting things that have happened since labor began. If you have your baby with you, you may stare at her in wonder that you could possibly have produced such a miracle. Such emotions may wipe away your physical exhaustion temporarily, but don't fool yourself. You need to relax, sleep, and gather your strength. You have a very big job ahead of you—you're a parent now!

~ 3 ~

Basic Infant Care

WHEN YOUR BABY first arrives, you may feel a bit overwhelmed by the job of caring for her. Even such routine tasks as diapering and dressing her can fill you with anxiety—especially if you've never spent much time around babies before. But it doesn't take long to develop the confidence and calm of an experienced parent, and you'll have help. While you are in the hospital, the nursery staff and your pediatrician will give you instructions and support your needs. Later, family and friends can be helpful; don't be bashful about asking for their assistance. But your baby will give you the most important information—how she likes to be treated, talked to, held, and comforted. She'll bring out parental instincts that will guide you automatically to many of the right responses, almost as soon as she's born.

The following sections address the most common questions and concerns that arise during the first months of life.

Day to Day

Responding to Your Baby's Cries

Crying serves several useful purposes for your baby. It gives her a way to call for help when she's hungry or uncomfortable. It helps her shut out sights, sounds, and other sensations that are too intense to suit her. And it helps her release tension.

You may notice that your baby has fussy periods throughout the day, even though she's not hungry, uncomfortable, or tired. Nothing you do at these times will console her, but right after these spells, she may seem more alert than before, and shortly thereafter she may sleep more deeply than usual. This kind of fussy crying seems to help babies get rid of excess energy so they can return to a more contented state.

Pay close attention to your baby's different cries. You'll soon be able to tell when she needs to be picked up, consoled, or tended to, and when she is better off left alone. You may even be able to identify her specific needs by the way she cries. For instance, a hungry cry is usually short and low-pitched, and it rises and falls. An angry cry tends to be more turbulent. A cry of pain or distress generally comes on suddenly and loudly with a long, high-pitched shriek followed by a long pause and then a flat wail. The "leave-me-alone" cry is usually similar to a hunger cry. It won't take long before you have a pretty good idea of what your baby's cries are trying to tell you.

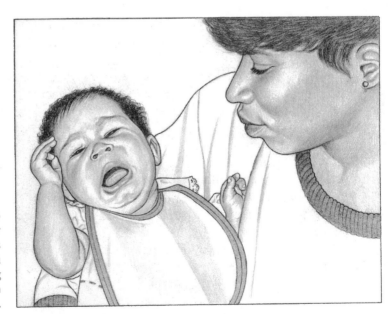

Respond promptly to your infant whenever he cries during his first few months. You cannot spoil a young baby by giving him attention.

Sometimes different types of cries overlap. For example, newborns generally wake up hungry and crying for food. If you're not quick to respond, your baby's hunger cry may give way to a wail of rage. You'll hear the difference. As your baby matures, her cries will become stronger, louder, and more insistent. They'll also begin to vary more, as if to convey different needs and desires.

The best way to handle crying is to respond promptly to your infant whenever she cries during her first few months. You cannot spoil a young baby by giving her attention, and if you answer her calls for help, she'll cry less overall.

When responding to your child's cries, try to meet her most pressing need first. If she's cold and hungry and her diaper is wet, warm her up, change her diaper, and then feed her. If there's a shrieking or panicked quality to the cry, consider the possibility that a piece of clothing or something else is making her uncomfortable. Perhaps a strand of hair is caught around a finger or toe. If she's warm, dry, and well fed but nothing is working to stop the crying, try the following consoling techniques to find the ones that work best for your baby:

- Rocking, either in a rocking chair or in your arms as you sway from side to side

- Gently stroking her head or patting her back or chest

- Swaddling (wrapping her snugly in a receiving blanket)

- Singing or talking

- Playing soft music

- Walking her in your arms, a stroller, or a carriage

- Rhythmic white noise and vibration

- Burping her to relieve any trapped gas bubbles

- Warm baths (*Most* babies like this, but not all.)

Sometimes, if all else fails, the best approach is simply to leave the baby alone. Many babies cannot fall asleep without crying, and will go to sleep more quickly if left to cry for a while. The crying shouldn't

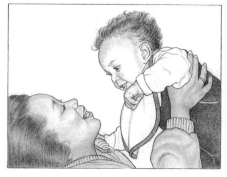

Enjoy all those wondrous moments with your child.

last long if the child is truly tired. If your baby is inconsolable no matter what you do, she may be sick. Check her temperature (see *Taking a Rectal Temperature*, page 78). If you take it rectally and it is 100.4 degrees Fahrenheit (38 degrees Celsius) or higher, she could have an infection. Contact your pediatrician.

The more relaxed you remain, the easier it will be to console your child. Even very young babies are sensitive to tension around them and react to it by crying. Listening to a wailing newborn can be agonizing, but letting your frustration turn to anger or panic will only intensify your infant's screams. If you

How Your Baby Sleeps

Even before birth your baby's days were divided between periods of sleep and wakefulness. By the eighth month of pregnancy or earlier, her sleep periods consisted of the same two distinct phases that we all experience:

1. **Rapid eye movement (or REM) sleep,** the times during which she does her active dreaming. During these periods, her eyes will move beneath her closed lids, almost as if she were watching a dream take place. She also may seem to startle, twitch her face, and make jerking motions with her hands and feet. All are normal signs of REM sleep.

2. **Non-REM sleep,** which consists of four phases: drowsiness, light sleep, deep sleep, and very deep sleep. During the progression from drowsiness to deepest sleep, your baby becomes less and less active, and her breathing slows and becomes very quiet, so that in deepest sleep she is virtually motionless. Very little, if any, dreaming occurs during non-REM sleep.

At first your newborn probably will sleep about sixteen hours a day, divided into three- or four-hour naps evenly spaced between feedings.

Each of these sleep periods will include relatively equal amounts of REM and non-REM sleep, organized in this order: drowsiness, REM sleep, light sleep, deep sleep, and very deep sleep.

After about two to three months the order will change, so that as she grows older, she will cycle through all the non-REM phases before entering REM sleep. This pattern will last into and through adulthood. As she grows older, the amount of REM sleep decreases, and her sleep generally will become calmer. By the age of three, children spend one-third or less of total sleep time in REM sleep.

start to feel that you can't handle the situation, get help from another family member or a friend. Not only will this give you needed relief, but a new face sometimes can calm your baby when all your own tricks are spent. No matter how impatient or angry you feel, *do not* shake the baby. Shaking an infant hard can cause blindness, brain damage, or even death. Also, make sure to share this information on crying with other caretakers of your baby, including your spouse or partner.

Above all, don't take your newborn's crying personally. She's not crying because you're a bad parent or because she doesn't like you. All babies cry, often without any apparent cause. Newborns routinely cry a total of one to four hours a day. It's part of adjusting to this strange new life outside the womb.

No mother can console her child *every* time she cries, so don't expect to be a miracle worker with your baby. Instead, take a realistic approach to the situation, line up some help, get plenty of rest, and enjoy all those wondrous moments with your child.

Helping Your Baby Sleep

Initially your infant doesn't know the difference between day and night. Her stomach holds only enough to satisfy her for three or four hours, regardless of the time, so there's no escaping round-the-clock waking and feeding for the first few weeks. But even at this age, you can begin to teach her that nighttime is for sleeping and daytime is for play. Do this by keeping nighttime feedings as subdued as possible. Don't turn up the lights or prolong late-night diaper changes. Instead of playing, put her right back down after feeding and changing her. If she's napping longer than three or four hours, particularly in the late afternoon, wake her up and play with her. This will train her to save her extra sleeping for nighttime. Also begin to develop a routine before bedtime. Repeatedly experiencing a strong sensation (like a sponge bath), followed by soothing time (like applying a bit of moisturizing lotion and reading or singing) and then a final feeding in the evening followed by a short bedtime story, can help signal to your baby that the "longer nap" is coming.

Positioning for Sleep

The American Academy of Pediatrics recommends that healthy infants be placed on their backs for sleep, as this is the safest position for an infant to sleep. Putting your baby to sleep on his back decreases his chance of *sudden infant death syndrome (SIDS), which is responsible for more infant deaths in the United States than any other cause during the first year of life (beyond the newborn period).*

In addition, recent findings suggest that certain regions of the brain may be underdeveloped in babies who die from SIDS. When these sleeping babies encounter a situation challenging to their well-being, they may fail to wake up to remove themselves from danger. Since it is impossible to identify which babies may not arouse normally, and because the relationship between SIDS and sleep position is so strong, the Academy recommends that all infants be placed to sleep on their backs. Some doctors once thought that sleeping on the side might be a reasonable alternative to back positioning, but recent evidence has shown that side sleeping also should be avoided for safety reasons. (Please note that there are a few exceptions to this recommendation, including babies with certain medical conditions, which your pediatrician can discuss with you.)

This recommendation of putting the baby down on her back applies to infants throughout the first year of life. However, it is particularly important during the first six months, when the incidence of SIDS is the highest.

Even when you are sure your baby is lying on her back when going to sleep, it is also important to avoid placing her on soft, porous surfaces such as pillows, quilts, comforters, sheepskins, or bean bags—even soft materials used for stuffed toys—which may block her airway if she burrows her face in them. Also avoid having her sleep on waterbeds, sofas, or soft mattresses. A firm crib mattress covered by a sheet is the safest bedding. Keep all soft toys and stuffed animals out of your child's crib throughout infancy. Keep the temperature in your baby's room comfortable and do not place her near air-conditioning or heating vents, open windows, or other sources of drafts. Use sleep clothing (such as a one-piece sleeper) with no other covering, as an alternative to blankets. For an extra layer, a wearable blanket sleeper or sleep sack is a safe alternative.

Pacifiers also may help reduce the risk of SIDS. However, if your baby doesn't want the pacifier or if it falls out of her mouth, don't force it. If you are breastfeeding, wait until breastfeeding is well established, usually around three or four weeks of age, before using a pacifier.

While sleeping on the back is important, your baby also should spend some time on her stomach *when she is awake and being observed*. This will help to develop her shoulder muscles and her head control, and avoid the development of flat spots on the back of her head.

As she gets older and her stomach grows, your baby will be able to go longer between feedings. In fact, you'll be encouraged to know that more than 90 percent of babies sleep through the night (six to eight hours without waking) by three months. Most infants are able to last this long between feedings when they reach 12 or 13 pounds (5.44–5.89 kg), so if yours is a very large baby, she may begin sleeping through the night even earlier than three months. As encouraging as this sounds, don't expect the sleep struggle to end all at once. Most children swing back and forth, sleeping beautifully for a few weeks, or even months, then returning abruptly to a late-night wake-up schedule. This may have to do with growth spurts increasing the need for food, or, later, it may be related to teething or developmental changes.

From time to time, you will need to help your baby fall asleep or go back to sleep. Especially as a newborn, she probably will doze off most easily if given gentle continuous stimulation. Some infants are helped by rocking, by walking, by patting on the back, or by a pacifier in the mouth. For others, music from a radio or a CD player can be very soothing if played at moderate volume. Certain stimulation, however, is irritating to any baby—for example, ringing telephones, barking dogs, and roaring vacuum cleaners.

There is no reason to restrict your baby's sleeping to her crib. If, for any reason, you want her closer to you while she sleeps, use her bassinet as a temporary crib and move it around the house with you.

Diapers

Since disposable diapers were introduced about forty years ago, these modern diapers are meeting the needs and expectations of most parents; however, diaper choice is a decision that every new parent faces. Ideally, you should make the choice between cloth and disposable diapers before the baby arrives, so you can stock up or make delivery arrangements ahead of time. In order to plan ahead, you should know that most newborns go through about ten diapers a day.

WHERE WE STAND

BASED ON AN evaluation of current sudden infant death syndrome (SIDS) data, the American Academy of Pediatrics recommends that healthy infants always be placed for sleep—whether it be nap time or nighttime—on their backs. Despite common beliefs, there is no evidence that choking is more frequent among infants lying on their backs (the supine position) when compared to other positions, nor is there evidence that sleeping on the back is harmful to healthy babies. Babies with gastroesophageal reflux should still be placed on their backs. In some very rare circumstances (for instance, if your baby has just had back surgery), your infant may need to be on the stomach for sleep. Discuss your individual circumstances with your pediatrician.

Since 1992, when the American Academy of Pediatrics began recommending this sleep position, the annual SIDS rate has declined more than 50 percent.

How to Diaper Your Baby

Before you start to change your baby, make sure you have all the necessary supplies within arm's reach. Never leave your baby alone on the changing table—not even for a second. Babies wiggle and squirm and can easily fall off a changing table. In addition, it won't be long before she will be able to turn over, and if she does it when your attention is diverted, a serious injury could result.

When changing a newborn, you will need:

- **a clean diaper (plus fasteners if a cloth diaper is used)**

- **a small basin (or a mug or bowl) with lukewarm water and a wash-cloth, soft paper towels, or cotton balls (commercial diaper wipes also can be used, although some babies are sensitive to them; if any irritation occurs, discontinue use)**

- **diaper ointment or petroleum jelly**

This is how you proceed:

1. Remove the dirty diaper and use the lukewarm water and cotton ball, soft paper towel, or unscented diaper wipe to gently wipe your baby clean. (Remember to wipe front to back on female infants.)

2. Use the damp washcloth, soft paper towel, or unscented diaper wipe to wipe the diaper area.

3. Use the diaper rash preparation recommended by your pediatrician if needed.

DISPOSABLE DIAPERS. Most disposable diapers today consist of an inner liner next to the baby to help keep wetness away from the skin, an absorbent core, and an outer waterproof covering. Over the years, disposable diapers have become thinner and lighter, while continuing to meet the needs for containment, comfort, ease of use, and skin care. When changing a soiled diaper, dump loose stool into a toilet. Do not flush the diaper, because it can block your plumbing. Wrap the diaper in its outer cover, and discard in a waste receptacle.

CLOTH DIAPERS. Like disposable diapers, reusable cloth diapers have improved in recent years, and are available in a variety of absorbencies and textures. If

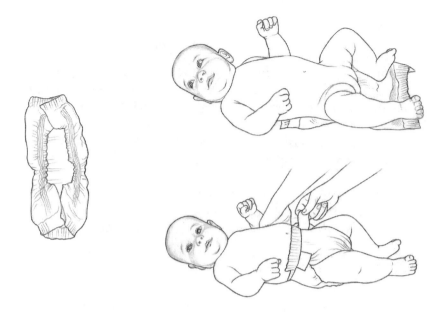

you want to use a diaper service, shop around; ideally, a diaper service should pick up dirty diapers and drop off clean ones twice a week. If you choose to wash diapers yourself, keep them separate from other clothes. After you dump stool into the toilet, rinse the diapers in cold water, then soak them in a mild detergent solution with bleach. Wring them out, then wash in hot water with a mild detergent.

DIAPER CHOICE. Diaper choice has been complicated in recent years by the debate on the environmental effects of diapers, mostly centered on the effects of disposable diapers on landfill space. Actually, a number of scientific studies have found that both cloth and disposable diapers have environmental effects, including raw material and energy usage, air and water pollution, and waste disposal. Disposable diapers add 1 to 2 percent to municipal solid waste, while cloth diapers use more energy and water in laundering and contribute to air and water pollution. In the end, it is up to individuals to make their own decisions about diaper type based on their own concerns and needs.

There are some health aspects to consider as well. Excessively wet skin and contact with urine and stool can cause diaper rash. Because cloth diapers can't keep wetness away from your baby's skin as effectively as disposables, it's especially important to change cloth diapers quickly after they become wet or soiled.

Diaper Rash

Diaper rash is the term used to describe a rash or irritation in the area covered by the diaper. The first sign of diaper rash is usually redness or small bumps on the lower abdomen, buttocks, genitals, and thigh folds—surfaces that have been in direct contact with the wet or soiled diaper. This type of diaper rash is rarely serious and usually clears in three or four days with appropriate care. The most common causes of diaper rash include:

1. Leaving a wet diaper on too long. The moisture makes the skin more susceptible to chafing. Over time, the urine in the diaper decomposes, forming chemicals that can further irritate the skin.

2. Leaving a stool-soiled diaper on too long. Digestive agents in the stool then attack the skin, making it more susceptible to a rash.

Regardless of how the rash begins, once the surface of the skin is damaged, it becomes even more vulnerable to further irritation by contact with urine and stool and to subsequent infection with bacteria or yeast. Yeast infections are common in this area and often appear as a rash on the thighs, genitals, and lower abdomen, but they almost never appear on the buttocks.

Although most babies develop diaper rash at some point during infancy, it happens less often in babies who are breastfed (for reasons we still do not know). Diaper rash occurs more often at particular ages and under certain conditions:

- **Among babies eight to ten months old**

- **If babies are not kept clean and dry**

- **When babies have diarrhea**

- **When a baby starts to eat solid food (probably due to changes in the digestive process caused by the new variety of foods)**

- **When a baby is taking antibiotics (because these drugs encourage the growth of yeast organisms that can infect the skin)**

To reduce your baby's risk of diaper rash, make these steps part of your diapering routine:

1. Change the diaper as soon as possible after a bowel movement. Cleanse the diaper area with a soft cloth and water after each bowel movement.

2. Change wet diapers frequently to reduce skin exposure to moisture.

3. Expose the baby's bottom to air whenever feasible. When using plastic pants or disposable diapers with tight gathers around the abdomen and legs, make sure air can circulate inside the diaper.

If a diaper rash develops in spite of your efforts, begin using a diaper rash ointment as a barrier to prevent further irritation from the urine or stool. The rash should improve noticeably within forty-eight to seventy-two hours. If it doesn't, consult your pediatrician.

Urination

Your baby may urinate as often as every one to three hours or as infrequently as four to six times a day. If she's ill or feverish, or when the weather is extremely hot, her usual output of urine may drop by half and still be normal. Urination should never be painful. If you notice any signs of distress while your infant is urinating, notify your pediatrician, as this could be a sign of infection or some other problem in the urinary tract.

In a healthy child, urine is light to dark yellow in color. (The darker the color, the more concentrated the urine; the urine will be more concentrated when your child is not drinking a lot of liquid.) Sometimes you'll see a pink stain on the diaper that you may mistake for blood. In fact, this stain is usually a sign of highly concentrated urine, which has a pinkish color. As long as the baby is wetting at least four diapers a day, there probably is no cause for concern, but if the pinkish staining persists, consult your pediatrician.

The presence of actual blood in the urine or a bloody spot on the diaper is never normal, and your pediatrician should be notified. It may be due to nothing more serious than a small sore caused by diaper rash, but it also could be a sign of a more serious problem. If this bleeding is accompanied by other symptoms, such as abdominal pain or bleeding in other areas, seek medical attention for your baby immediately.

Bowel Movements

Beginning with the first day of life and lasting for a few days, your baby will have her first bowel movements, which are often referred to as meconium. This thick black or dark-green substance filled her intestines before birth, and once the meconium is passed, the stools will turn yellow-green.

If your baby is breastfed, her stools soon should resemble light mustard with seedlike particles. Until she starts to eat solid foods, the consistency of the stools may range from very soft to loose and runny. If she's formula-fed, her stools usually will be tan or yellow in color. They will be firmer than in a baby who is breastfed, but no firmer than peanut butter.

Whether your baby is breastfed or bottle-fed, hard or very dry stools may be a sign that she is not getting enough fluid or that she is losing too much fluid due to illness, fever, or heat. Once she has started solids, hard stools might indicate that she's eating too many constipating foods, such as cereal or cow's milk, before her system can handle them. (Whole cow's milk is not recommended for babies under twelve months.)

Here are some other important points to keep in mind about bowel movements:

- **Occasional variations in** color and consistency of the stools are normal. For example, if the digestive process slows down because the baby has had a particularly large amount of cereal that day or foods requiring more effort to digest, the stools may become green; or if the baby is given supplemental iron, the stools may turn dark brown. If there is a minor irritation of the anus, streaks of blood may appear on the outside of the stools. However, if there are large amounts of blood, mucus, or water in the stool, call your pediatrician immediately. These symptoms may indicate an intestinal condition that warrants attention from your doctor.

- **Because an infant's** stools are normally soft and a little runny, it's not always easy to tell when a young baby has mild diarrhea. The telltale signs are a sudden increase in frequency (to more than one bowel movement per feeding) and unusually high liquid content in the stool. Diarrhea may be a sign of intestinal infection, or it may be caused by a change in the baby's diet. If the baby is breastfeeding, she can even develop diarrhea because of a change in the mother's diet.

- **The main concern** with diarrhea is the possibility that dehydration can develop. If fever is also present and your infant is less than two months old, call your pediatrician. If your baby is over two months and the fever lasts more than a day, check her urine output and rectal temperature; then report your findings to your doctor so he can determine what needs to be done. Make sure your baby continues to feed frequently. As much as anything else, if she simply looks sick, let your doctor know.

The frequency of bowel movements varies widely from one baby to another. Many pass a stool soon after each feeding. This is a result of the gastrocolic reflex, which causes the digestive system to become active whenever the stomach is filled with food.

By three to six weeks of age, some breastfed babies have only one bowel movement a week and still are normal. This happens because breast milk leaves very little solid waste to be eliminated from the child's digestive system. Thus, infrequent stools are not a sign of constipation and should not be considered a problem as long as the stools are soft (no firmer than peanut butter), and your infant is otherwise normal, gaining weight steadily, and nursing regularly.

If your baby is formula-fed, she should have at least one bowel movement a day. If she has fewer than this and appears to be straining because of hard stools, she may be constipated. Check with your pediatrician for advice on how to handle this problem. (See *Constipation,* page 528.)

Bathing

Your infant doesn't need much bathing if you wash the diaper area thoroughly during diaper changes. Three times a week during her first year may be enough. Bathing her more frequently may dry out her skin, particularly if soaps are used or moisture is allowed to evaporate from the skin. Patting her dry and applying a fragrance-free, hypoallergenic moisturizer immediately after bathing can help prevent the skin condition called eczema (see page 560).

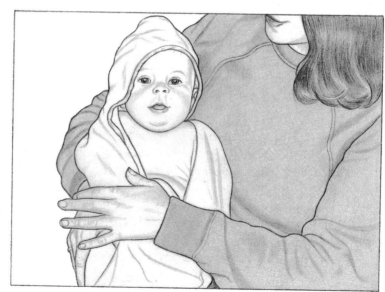

Baby towels with built-in hoods are a very effective way to keep your baby's head warm when she's wet.

Bathing Your Baby

Once you've undressed your baby, place her in the water immediately so she doesn't get chilled. Use one of your hands to support her head and the other to guide her in, feet first. Speak to her encouragingly, and gently lower the rest of her body until she's in the tub. Most of her body and face should be well above the water level for safety, so you'll need to pour warm water over her body frequently to keep her warm.

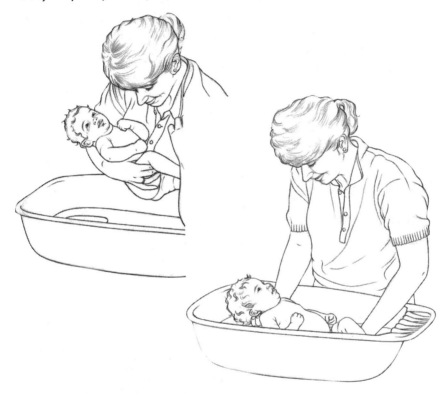

Use a soft cloth to wash her face and hair, shampooing once or twice a week. Massage her entire scalp gently, including the area over her fontanelles (soft spots). When you rinse the soap or shampoo from her head, cup your hand across her forehead so the suds run toward the sides, not into her eyes. Should you get some soap in her eyes, and she cries out in protest, simply take the wet washcloth and liberally wipe her eyes with plain, lukewarm water until any remains of the soap are gone, and she will open her eyes again. Wash the rest of her body from the top down.

During her first week or two, until the stump of the umbilical cord falls off, your newborn should have only sponge baths. In a warm room, lay the baby anywhere that's flat and comfortable for both of you—a changing table, bed, floor, or counter next to the sink will do. Pad hard surfaces with a blanket or fluffy towel. If the baby is on a surface above the floor, use a safety strap or keep one hand on her *at all times* to make sure she doesn't fall.

Have a basin of water, a damp, double-rinsed washcloth (so there is no soap residue in it), and a supply of mild baby soap within reach before you begin. Keep your baby wrapped in a towel, and expose only the parts of her body you are actively washing. Use the dampened cloth first without soap to wash her face, so you don't get soap into her eyes or mouth. Then dip it in the basin of soapy water before washing the remainder of her body and, finally, the diaper area. Pay special attention to creases under the arms, behind the ears, around the neck, and, especially with a girl, in the genital area.

Once the umbilical area is healed, you can try placing your baby directly in the water. Her first baths should be as gentle and brief as possible. She probably will protest a little; if she seems miserable, go back to sponge baths for a week or two, then try the bath again. She will make it clear when she's ready.

Most parents find it easiest to bathe a newborn in a bathinette, sink, or plastic tub lined with a clean towel. Fill the basin with 2 inches (5.08 cm) of water that feels warm—not hot—to the inside of your wrist or elbow. If you're filling the basin from the tap, turn the cold water on first (and off last) to avoid scalding yourself or your child. The hottest temperature at the faucet should be no more than 120 degrees Fahrenheit (48.9 degrees Celsius) to avoid burns. In many cases you can adjust your water heater.

Make sure that supplies are at hand and the room is warm before undressing the baby. You'll need the same supplies that you used for sponge bathing, but also a cup for rinsing with clear water. When your child has hair, you'll need baby shampoo, too.

If you've forgotten something or need to answer the phone or door during the bath, *you must take the baby with you*, so keep a dry towel within reach. *Never leave a baby alone in the bath, even for an instant.*

If your baby enjoys her bath, give her some extra time to splash and explore the water. The more fun your child has in the bath, the less she'll be afraid of the water. As she gets older, the length of the bath will extend until most of it is taken up with play. Bathing should be a very relaxing and soothing experience, so don't rush unless she's unhappy.

Bath toys are not really needed for very young babies, as the stimulation of the water and washing is exciting enough. Once a baby is old enough for the bathtub, however, toys become invaluable. Containers, floating toys, even waterproof books make wonderful distractions as you cleanse your baby.

When your infant comes out of the bath, baby towels with built-in hoods are the most effective way to keep her head warm when she's wet. Bathing a baby of any age is wet work, so you may want to wear a terry-cloth robe or hang a towel over your shoulder to keep you dry.

The bath is a relaxing way to prepare her for sleep and should be given at a time that's convenient for you.

Skin and Nail Care

Your newborn's skin may be susceptible to irritation from chemicals in new clothing and from soap or detergent residue on clothes that have been washed. To avoid problems, double-rinse all baby clothes, bedding, blankets, and other washable items before exposing the child to them. For the first few months, do your infant's wash separately from the rest of the family's.

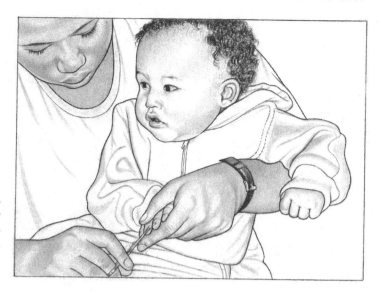

In the early weeks, your baby's fingers are so small and his nails grow so quickly you may have to trim them twice a week.

Contrary to what you may read in ads for baby products, your infant does not ordinarily need any lotions, oils, or powders. If her skin is very dry, you can apply a small amount of nonperfumed baby moisturizer sparingly to the dry areas; the massage involved in applying the moisturizer will make your baby feel good. Never use any skin-care products that are not specifically made for babies, because they generally contain perfumes and other chemicals that can irritate an infant's skin. Also avoid baby oil, which does not penetrate or lubricate as well as baby lotion or cream. If the dryness persists, you may be bathing your child too often. Give her a bath just once a week for a while and see if the dryness stops. If not, consult your pediatrician.

The only care your child's nails require is trimming. You can use a soft emery board, baby nail clippers, or blunt-nosed toenail scissors, but be very careful when using clippers or scissors because accidentally cutting the tip of your baby's finger will cause pain and bleeding. A good time to trim nails is after a bath if your baby will lie quietly, but you may find it easiest to do when she's asleep. Keep her fingernails as short and smoothly trimmed as possible so she can't scratch herself (or you). In the early weeks, her fingers are so small and her nails grow so quickly you may have to trim them twice a week. Some parents bite their child's nails as a way of trimming them, which they should avoid doing to prevent the risk of infection.

By contrast, your baby's toenails grow much more slowly and are usually very soft and pliable. They needn't be kept as short as the fingernails, so you may have to trim them only once or twice a month. Because they are so soft, they sometimes look as if they're ingrown, but there's no cause for concern unless the skin alongside the nail gets red, inflamed, or hard. As your baby gets older, his toenails will become harder and better defined.

Dressing and Undressing Your Baby

When dressing your baby, support her on your lap, stretch the garment neckline and pull it over your baby's head. Use your fingers to keep it from catching on her face or ears.

Don't try to push your baby's arm through the sleeve. Instead, put your hand into the sleeve from the outside, grasp your baby's hand, and pull it through.

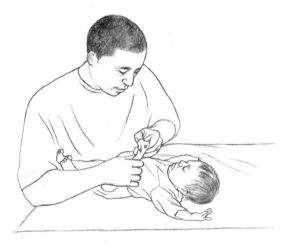

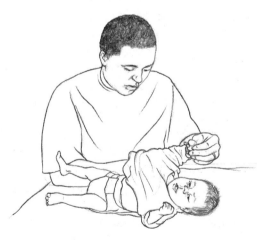

When undressing, take off the sleeves one at a time while you support your baby's back and head.

Then stretch the neckline, lifting it free of your baby's chin and face as you gently slip it off.

Clothing

Unless the temperature is hot (over 75 degrees Fahrenheit [23.88 degrees Celsius]), your newborn will need several layers of clothing to keep her warm. It's generally best to dress her in an undershirt and diapers, covered by pajamas or a dressing gown, and then wrap her in a receiving blanket. If your baby is premature, she may need still another layer of clothing until her weight reaches that of a full-term baby and her body is better able to adjust to changes in temperature. In hot weather you can reduce her clothing to a single layer. A good rule of thumb is to dress the baby in one more layer of clothing than you are wearing to be comfortable in the same environment.

Swaddling

During the first few weeks, your baby will spend most of her time wrapped in a receiving blanket. Not only does this keep her warm, but the slight pressure around the body seems to give most newborns a sense of security. To swaddle, spread the blanket out flat, with one corner folded over. Lay the baby face-up on the blanket, with her head at the folded corner.

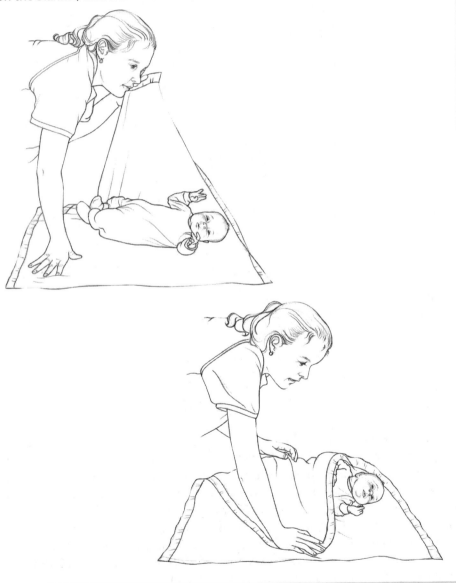

Wrap the left corner over her body and tuck it beneath her. Bring the bottom corner up over her feet, and then wrap the right corner around her, leaving only her head and neck exposed. It is most important that the hips and legs are allowed to move freely within the blanket. Tight swaddling of the hips could lead to dysplasia or even dislocation. For more information on swaddling, visit HealthyChildren.org/swaddling.

If you've never taken care of a newborn baby before, the first few times you change her clothes can be quite frustrating. Not only is it a struggle to get that tiny little arm through the sleeve, but your infant may shriek in protest through the whole process. She doesn't like the rush of air against her skin, nor does she enjoy being pushed and pulled through garments. It may make things easier for both of you if you hold her on your lap while changing the upper half of her body, then lay her on a bed or changing table while doing the lower half. When you're dressing her in one-piece pajamas, pull them over her legs before putting on the sleeves. Pull T-shirts over her head first, then put one arm at a time through the sleeves. Use this opportunity to ask, "Where's the baby's hand?" As she gets older this will turn into a game, with her pushing her arm through just to hear you say, "*There's* the baby's hand!"

Certain clothing features can make dressing much easier. Look for garments that

■ Snap or zip all the way down the front, instead of the back

■ Snap or zip down both legs to make diaper changes easier

■ Have loose-fitting sleeves so your hand fits to gently pull the baby's arm through

■ Have no ribbons or strings to knot up, unravel, or wrap around the neck (which could cause choking)

■ Are made of soft stretchy fabric (avoid tight bindings around arms, legs, or neck)

Your Baby's Basic Health Care
Taking a Rectal Temperature

Very few babies get through infancy without having a fever, which can be a sign of infection somewhere in the body. A fever often indicates that the immune system is actively fighting viruses or bacteria, so—in this respect—it is a positive sign that the body is protecting itself. Because young babies have very few signs that they are ill, any child three months (twelve weeks) or younger with a fever needs an urgent evaluation by a physician to determine the cause of the fever; if it is due to a minor viral infection, it will usually resolve on its own, while a bacterial infection or more serious viral infection (e.g., herpes) will usually require immediate treatment with antibiotics or antiviral medications and frequently, in infants under two months of age, will require hospitalization.

An infant or toddler cannot hold a thermometer steady in her mouth for you to take an oral temperature, and "fever strips" that are placed on the child's forehead are not accurate. The best way to measure fever in a young child is by taking a rectal temperature. Once you know how to take a rectal temperature, it is really quite simple; but it's best to learn the procedures in advance so you're not nervous about them the first time your child is actually sick. For a complete description of taking a rectal temperature properly, or other means of properly taking temperatures in infants and children, see Chapter 27, *Fever*.

Visiting the Pediatrician

You probably will see more of your pediatrician in your baby's first year than at any other time. The baby's first examination will take place immediately after birth. The schedules on pages 872 and 873 list the minimum routine checkups from infancy through adolescence. Your pediatrician may want to see your baby more often.

Ideally, both parents should attend these early visits to the doctor. These appointments give you and your pediatrician a chance to get to know each other and exchange questions and answers. Don't restrict yourself to medical questions; your pediatrician is also an expert on general child care issues and a valuable resource if you're looking for child care help, parent support groups, or other outside assistance. Many pediatricians hand out information sheets that cover the most common concerns, but it is a good idea to make a list of questions before each visit so you don't forget any important ones.

If only one parent can attend, try to get a friend or a relative to join the parent who does. It's much easier to concentrate on your discussions with the doctor if you have a little help dressing and undressing the baby and gathering all of her things. While you're getting used to outings with your newborn, an extra adult also can help carry the diaper bag and hold doors. Grandparents can fulfill this role quite well if they live nearby. (For additional information about the role of grandparents in your baby's life, see pages 189, 214, 249, 291, 333, 368, 400, 432, 441, and 514 in Chapters 6 through 15.)

The purpose of these early checkups is to make sure your child is growing and developing properly and has no serious abnormalities. Specifically, the doctor will check the following areas.

GROWTH. You will be asked to undress your baby, and then she'll be weighed on an infant scale. Her length may be measured lying on a flat table with her legs stretched straight. A special tape is used to measure the size of her head. All of these measurements should be plotted on a graph in order to determine her growth curve from one visit to the next. (You can plot your baby's growth curve in the same way using the charts on pages 878–881.) This is the most reliable way to judge whether she's growing normally, and will show you her position on the growth curve in relation to other children her age.

HEAD. The soft spots (fontanelles) should be open (normal skin-covered openings in the skull) and flat for the first few months. By two to three months of age, the spot at the back should be closed. The front soft spot should close before your child's second birthday (around eighteen months of age).

EARS. The doctor will look inside both ears with an otoscope, an instrument that provides a view of the ear canal and eardrum. This tells him whether there is any evidence of fluid or infection in the ear. You'll also be asked if the child responds normally to sounds. Formal hearing tests are done in the newborn nursery and later if there is suspicion that a problem exists.

EYES. The doctor will use a bright object or flashlight to catch your baby's attention and track her eye movements. He also may look inside the baby's eyes with a lighted instrument called an ophthalmoscope—repeating the internal eye examination that was first done in the hospital nursery. This is particularly helpful in detecting cataracts (clouding of the lens of the eye). (See *Cataracts*, page 727.)

MOUTH. The mouth is checked for signs of infection and, later, for teething progress.

HEART AND LUNGS. The pediatrician will use a stethoscope on the front and back of the chest to listen to your child's heart and lungs. This examination determines whether there are any abnormal heart rhythms, sounds, or breathing difficulties.

ABDOMEN. By placing his hand on the child's abdomen and gently pressing, the doctor makes sure that none of the organs are enlarged and there are no unusual masses or tenderness.

GENITALIA. The genitalia are examined at each visit for any unusual lumps, tenderness, or signs of infection. In the first exam or two, the doctor pays special attention to a circumcised boy's penis to make sure it's healing properly. Pediatricians also check all baby boys to make certain both testes are down in the scrotum.

HIPS AND LEGS. The pediatrician will move your baby's legs to check for problems with the hip joints. The movements your pediatrician will perform with your baby's legs are designed to detect dislocation or dysplasia of the hip joint. It is important to look for this early in life as early detection can lead to proper referral and correction. Later, after the baby starts to walk, the doctor will watch her take a few steps to make sure the legs and feet are properly aligned and move normally.

DEVELOPMENTAL MILESTONES. The pediatrician also will ask about the baby's general development. Among other things, he'll observe and discuss when the baby starts to smile, roll over, sit up, and walk, and how she uses her hands and arms. During the exam, the pediatrician will test reflexes and general muscle tone. (See Appendix and Chapters 5 through 13 for details of normal development.)

Immunizations

Your child should receive most of his childhood immunizations before his second birthday. These will protect him against thirteen major diseases: hepatitis B, diphtheria, tetanus, pertussis (whooping cough), polio, *Haemophilus* (Hib) infections, pneumococcal infections, rotavirus, measles, mumps, rubella, chickenpox, and hepatitis A. In addition, after six months of age your baby will receive a yearly flu vaccine. (See Chapter 31, *Immunizations,* for more information on each of these diseases as well as the Appendix for the immunization schedule recommended by the American Academy of Pediatrics.)

This chapter has dealt in a general way with the topic of infant care. Your baby is a unique individual, however, so you will have some questions specific to her and her alone. These are best answered by your own pediatrician.

~ 4 ~

Feeding Your Baby

YOUR BABY'S NUTRITIONAL needs during the rapid-growth period of infancy are greater than at any other time in his life. He will approximately triple his birth weight during his first year.

Feeding your infant provides more than just good nutrition. It also gives you a chance to hold your newborn close, cuddle him, and make eye contact. These are relaxing and enjoyable moments for you both, and they bring you closer together emotionally.

Before your baby arrives, you should consider how you are going to feed him. All major medical groups worldwide agree that breast-feeding is best for mother and baby. This chapter will provide the basic information you need to learn more about infant feeding and to feel comfortable with your feeding decision.

Because of its nutritional composition, human milk is the ideal food for human infants. Babies who are not breastfed are at an increased risk of acquiring ear infections, eczema, asthma, and gastrointestinal infections that cause vomiting and diarrhea, and of developing allergic reactions. Furthermore, formula-fed babies are 25 percent more likely to need hospitalization for respiratory problems. Recent information indicates that breastfeeding plays a significant role in the prevention of overweight and diabetes, both in childhood and in later years. In addition, there is some evidence that for mothers, breastfeeding helps to return to pre-pregnancy weight, prevents cardiovascular diseases and diabetes, and reduces the incidence of certain types of cancers later in life. As a result, most pediatricians urge expectant and new mothers to breastfeed.

Many women are uncertain about breastfeeding for various reasons. Try to get more information from your prenatal care provider. Be sure someone knowledgeable discusses your specific concerns, doubts, or fears with you. If for some reason you are unable to breastfeed, infant formula is an acceptable and nutritious alternative to human milk. But you should thoughtfully weigh the many benefits of breastfeeding for yourself and your baby before making the choice to formula-feed. It's important that you give it serious consideration before your baby arrives, because starting with formula and then switching to breast milk can be difficult if you wait too long. The production of milk by the breast (the process is called lactation) is most successful if breastfeeding begins immediately after delivery.

WHERE WE STAND

THE AMERICAN ACADEMY OF PEDIATRICS believes that breastfeeding is the optimal source of nutrition through the first year of life. We recommend exclusively breastfeeding for about the first six months of a baby's life, and then gradually adding solid foods while continuing breastfeeding until at least the baby's first birthday. Thereafter, breastfeeding can be continued for as long as both mother and baby desire it.

Breastfeeding should begin as soon as possible after birth, usually within the first hour. Newborns should be nursed whenever they show signs of hunger—approximately eight to twelve times every twenty-four hours. The amount of time for each feeding and the frequency of feeding vary widely for each mother-baby pair. It is important to recognize signs that the baby is getting milk, particularly after the first few days of life. These signs include four to eight wet diapers and three to four loose, seedy stools per day.

The American Academy of Pediatrics, the World Health Organization (WHO), and many other experts encourage women to breastfeed as long as possible, one year or longer, with a recommendation of six months of exclusive breastfeeding (see *Where We Stand* on page 84). That's because breast milk provides optimal nutrition and protection against infections. One recent survey found that 80 to 90 percent of pregnant women wanted to breastfeed. Of infants born in 2010, 77 percent were breastfed at birth and 49 percent were being breastfed at six months of age (see CDC 2013 breastfeeding report card at http://www.cdc.gov/breastfeeding/data/reportcard.htm). Because most women want to breastfeed, and actually start out breastfeeding, national efforts have shifted to building a better breastfeeding support system for maintenance of breastfeeding. We know that the longer your baby is breastfed, the greater the benefits.

Breastfeeding

As we've already mentioned, human milk is the best possible food for any infant. Its major ingredients are sugar (lactose), easily digestible protein (whey and casein), and fat (digestible fatty acids)—all properly balanced to suit your baby and protect against such conditions as ear infections (otitis media), allergies, vomiting, diarrhea, pneumonia, wheezing, bronchiolitis, and meningitis. In addition, breast milk contains numerous minerals and vitamins, as well as enzymes that aid the digestive and absorptive process. Formulas only approximate this combination of nutrients and don't provide all of the enzymes, as well as all the antibodies, growth-promoting factors, and many other valuable ingredients of breast milk.

There are many practical reasons to breastfeed, or nurse, your baby. Human milk is relatively low in cost. While maintaining a balanced diet yourself, you should slightly increase your own caloric intake, but that costs only a small percentage of what you would spend for formula. Also, human milk needs no preparation and is instantly available at any time, wherever you may be. As an added advantage to the nursing mother, breastfeeding may make it easier for some women to get back into shape physically after giving birth, by using about 500 calories a day to produce the milk. Breastfeeding also helps the uterus tighten up and return more quickly to its normal size.

The psychological and emotional advantages of breastfeeding are just as compelling, for both mother and child. Nursing provides direct skin-to-skin contact, which is soothing for your baby and pleasant for you. The same hormones that stimulate milk production and milk release also may promote feelings that enhance mothering. Almost all nursing mothers find that the experience of breastfeeding makes them feel more attached and protective toward their babies and more confident about their own abilities to nurture and care for

THE HEALTH BENEFITS OF BREASTFEEDING

Studies show that there are numerous health benefits for breastfed babies. Compared to formula-fed babies, those who are breastfed have lower rates of:

- **Ear infections**
- **Gastrointestinal infections that cause vomiting and diarrhea**
- **Eczema, asthma, and food allergies**
- **Respiratory diseases, including pneumonia**
- **Diabetes (types 1 and 2)**
- **Obesity in adolescence and adulthood**
- **Childhood leukemia and lymphoma**
- **Sudden infant death syndrome (SIDS)**

Adapted from American Academy of Pediatrics, *New Mother's Guide to Breastfeeding*, ed. J. Y. Meek. 2nd ed. (New York: Bantam Books, 2011).

their children. When breastfeeding is going well, it has no known disadvantages for the baby. The breastfeeding mother may feel that there is some increased demand on her time. Actually, studies show that breastfeeding and formula-feeding take about the same total amount of time, but in breastfeeding all the time is spent with the baby. In bottle-feeding, more time is spent shopping and cleaning feeding utensils. Time spent with the baby is an important component of infant nurturing and development and is pleasurable to mothers. Other family members can assist by assuming the responsibility for household tasks, especially during the first few weeks after delivery when the mother needs extra rest and the baby needs frequent feeding.

Keep in mind that other family members can actively share in all aspects of caring for the baby even though they do not directly feed milk to her. Remain sensitive to the needs of fathers and siblings. In fact, other members of the family can hold the baby during burping or change the diaper before or after feeding, for example. For the father of the breastfed infant, nonnutritive cuddling plays an important role. A father is invaluable when comforting is necessary for baby and mother. He can hold, diaper, bathe, and walk with the baby. As the baby gets older, and breastfeeding is well established (about three to four weeks of age), the father may feed a bottle of expressed milk.

Considering Special Circumstances

In rare medical circumstances, breastfeeding may not be recommended. A mother who is extremely ill may not have the energy or stamina to breastfeed without interfering with her own recovery. She also may be taking certain medications that would pass into her milk and be dangerous to her infant, although most medications are safe for breastfeeding. If you are taking medications for any reason (prescription drugs or over-the-counter medications), let your pediatrician know before you start breastfeeding. She can advise you whether any of these drugs can pass through breast milk and cause problems for your baby. Sometimes medicines can be switched to safer ones for your baby while you are nursing.

The best protection against miscommunication about matters surrounding feeding is for parents to discuss these issues openly and make sure both mother and father understand and support the choice before the baby arrives. Many parents and care providers want their children to receive the best possible nutrition from the start, and without question, that is mother's milk. Once breastfeeding is well established (usually between three and four weeks of age), if the mother is away from the baby for a period of time (to return to work, for example, or to go out with family or friends), she can continue to provide her milk to the baby by pumping and collecting breast milk for feeding from a bottle by the father, other family members, or child care providers.

Some mothers may experience mild discomfort in the early days of breastfeeding. But significant discomfort is *not* normal. If you are experiencing pain, having difficulty getting the baby to latch on and feed well, or would like further support with nursing, seek help early in the first week from an experienced health professional (pediatrician, nurse, or lactation specialist). All babies should be seen by their pediatrician, nurse, or lactation consultant within two to three days of hospital discharge to check on how breastfeeding is going.

Self-confidence is an important part of breastfeeding, but common problems do arise. Seeking help from an expert early is a good way to overcome these problems and maintain the confidence necessary to continue breastfeeding. Occasionally some mothers have breastfeeding problems that lead to untimely weaning from the breast (before the mother had intended). Most women feel disappointed and sad when breastfeeding does not work out as they had planned. Still, you should not feel that you have failed. Sometimes, despite the best attempts and with all available support, it just doesn't work. (Also see *Bottle-Feeding* on page 115.)

Getting Started: Preparing for Lactation

Your body starts preparing to breastfeed as soon as you become pregnant. The area surrounding the nipples—the areola—becomes darker. The breasts themselves enlarge as the cells that will manufacture the milk multiply, and the ducts that will carry the milk to the nipple develop. This increase in breast size is normal and is a sign that your breasts are preparing to produce milk for your baby. Meanwhile, your body starts storing excess fat in other areas to provide the extra energy needed for pregnancy and lactation.

As early as the sixteenth week of pregnancy, the breasts are ready to produce milk as soon as the infant is born. Early milk, called colostrum, is a rich, somewhat thick-appearing, orange-yellow substance that is produced for several days after delivery. Colostrum contains more protein, salt, antibodies, and other protective properties than later breast milk, but less fat and calories. Colostrum helps your baby establish his immune system. Your body will produce colostrum for several days after delivery, as it gradually changes into mature milk. Colostrum is a form of milk, even though people commonly say that the "milk comes in" two to five days after delivery. At this time, colostrum increases rapidly in volume, becomes milklike in color and thinner in consistency, and continues to adjust to the baby's needs for the rest of the time that you breastfeed. The nutritional qualities of breast milk change to match the changing needs of your growing infant. This is a characteristic that infant formula cannot duplicate.

As your body naturally prepares for breastfeeding, there is very little that you need to do. Your nipples do not need to be "toughened up" to withstand your baby's sucking. Tactics such as stretching, pulling, rolling, or buffing the nipples may interfere with normal lactation by harming the tiny glands in the areola that secrete a milky fluid that lubricates the nipples in preparation for breastfeeding. In short, it could make your nipples more likely to develop soreness and irritation.

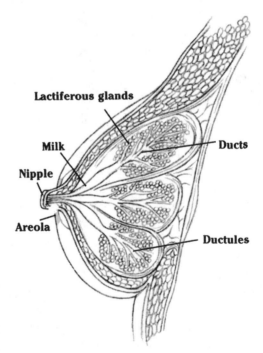

Milk is produced by the lactiferous glands. The milk then passes through the ductules into the ducts and out the nipple.

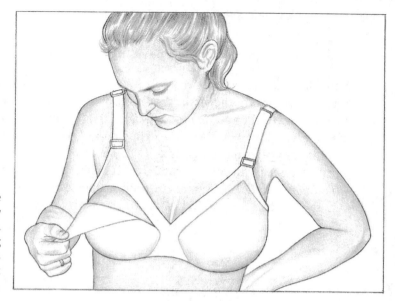

Nursing bras have flaps that allow easy access to the breast. If you wear a nursing bra, make sure it fits properly and is not constricting.

Normal bathing and gentle drying is the best way to care for your breasts during pregnancy. Although many women rub lotions and ointments on their breasts to soften them, these are not necessary and may even clog the skin pores. Salves, particularly those containing vitamins or hormones, are unnecessary and could cause problems for your baby if used while breastfeeding. On the other hand, some women find that applying lanolin is helpful in soothing sore or irritated nipples.

Some women start wearing nursing bras during pregnancy. They are more adjustable and roomier than normal bras, and are more comfortable as the breast size increases. Nursing bras also have flaps that can be opened for breast-feeding or expressing milk.

Letting Down and Latching On

By the time your baby is born, your breasts are already producing colostrum. As he nurses, your infant's actions will let your body know when to start and stop the flow of milk. The process of the baby going to the breast begins in those first moments after birth in the delivery room. The placement of the baby on your upper abdomen in the first moments after birth will allow your new baby to move up your chest and latch on during the first thirty minutes after birth. The process begins with the baby getting a good grip on the areola, *not* just on the nipple, and starting to suck. He will do this "latching on" instinctively as soon as he feels the breast against his mouth.

Preparing Inverted Nipples for Breastfeeding

Normally, when you press the areola (the darkened area around your nipple) between two fingers, the nipple should protrude and become erect. If the nipple seems to pull inward and disappear instead, it is said to be "inverted" or "tied." Inverted nipples are a normal variation. They may begin to move out more as the pregnancy progresses. If you have questions about your nipples, discuss the issue with your prenatal professional or with a lactation specialist.

At times, inverted nipples may be noticed only at the time of delivery. In this case, the postpartum staff will assist you with early feedings.

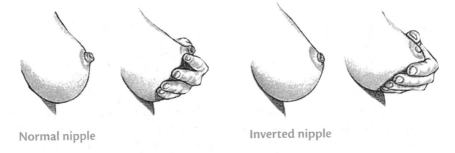

Normal nipple   Inverted nipple

Once the baby is born, the baby should be placed on your chest or abdomen for "skin-to-skin" contact. This should happen after all routine vaginal deliveries and after nonurgent Cesarean sections. If you are having a planned Cesarean delivery, you will need to talk to your prenatal health care provider to ask about "skin-to-skin" contact and breastfeeding immediately after birth. While on your chest or abdomen in the delivery room, your baby will begin to move toward your breast and will latch on to one of your breasts. If you have had complications with the delivery, or if your newborn needs immediate medical attention, you may have to wait a few hours. If the first feeding takes place within the first day or two, you should have no physical difficulty nursing. If nursing must be delayed beyond the first few hours of life, the nursing staff will assist you with pumping or hand expression.

When you begin to breastfeed in the first few days, you may start by reclining in a chair or bed and again placing your baby on your chest between your breasts without your bra on. Just like in the delivery room, your baby will begin moving down toward one of your breasts and will latch on to the breast. You may also start by holding your baby so that he squarely faces the breast and then stroking his lower lip or cheek with the nipple or touching his chin to your breast. Doing this stimulates the reflex that causes him to search for the nipple with his mouth (the rooting reflex). It will result in the infant opening the mouth widely; at that moment, the baby should be moved toward the breast. Using the hand to express a few drops of milk will also help your baby to root and attach to your breast, as the smell and taste of milk will stimulate the reflex to latch on.

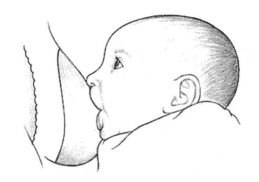

The baby has latched on to the breast correctly. The nose, lips, and chin are all close to the breast, allowing for effective breastfeeding.

As your baby takes the breast into his mouth, his jaws should close around the areola, *not* the nipple. His lips will separate and the gums will encircle the areola. His tongue will form a trough around the nipple and, in a wave-like motion, compress the milk reservoirs and empty the milk ducts. Putting your baby to the breast in the first hour after delivery will establish good breastfeeding patterns at a time when infants are usually alert and vigorous. Later in the first day he may get sleepy, but if he began nursing in the first hour, he is more likely to be a successful breastfeeder.

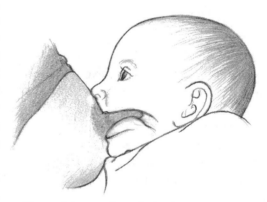

Most of the areola and nipple are in his mouth.

When your baby suckles effectively at the breast, his movements will stimulate the nerve fibers in the nipple. Breast stimulation also starts milk flowing through the milk ducts in what is known as the let-down reflex, which is associated with the release of another pituitary hormone, oxytocin. In turn, the release of the hormone prolactin from the pituitary gland and the removal of milk from the breast cause the breasts to make more milk.

Oxytocin causes many wonderful things to happen for you. It gives a feeling of euphoria and diminishes the sense of pain immediately after the birth. Some also say it enhances the feeling of love between you and your baby. It also causes the muscles of the uterus to contract. So, in the first days or weeks after delivery, you may feel "after pains," or cramping of the uterus, each time you nurse. Although this may be annoying and occasionally painful, it helps the uterus return quickly to its normal size and condition and reduces postpartum blood loss. It also is a good sign that your baby is feeding effectively. Use some

Cradle or Madonna hold

deep-breathing techniques or pain medication (ibuprofen is commonly prescribed after delivery) to ease the pain.

Once lactation has begun, it usually takes just a brief period of sucking before the milk lets down (begins to flow). Just hearing your baby cry actually may be enough to trigger milk flow. The signs that let-down is occurring vary from woman to woman and change with the volume of milk the baby demands. Some women feel a subtle tingling sensation, while others experience a buildup of pressure that feels as if their breasts are swelling and overfull—sensations that are quickly relieved as the milk starts to flow. Some women never feel these sensations, even though they are nursing successfully and the infant is getting plenty of milk. The way the milk flows also varies widely. It may spray, gush, trickle, or flow. Some women have leakage of milk with let-down or between feedings and others don't; either case can be normal. Flow or leakage also may be quite different in each breast—perhaps gushing on one side and trickling on the other. This is due to slight differences in the ducts on either side and is no cause for concern, as long as the baby is getting adequate milk and growing well.

When you nurse in the first couple of days after birth, you might find it most comfortable to lie on your side, with the baby lying facing you, opposite the breast. If you'd rather sit up, use pillows to help support your arms and cradle the baby slightly below breast level, making sure his entire body, not just his head, is facing your body.

Following a Cesarean delivery, the most comfortable position may be a side hold, or what's also called a football hold, in which you sit up and the baby

Football or clutch hold

lies at your side facing you. Curl your arm underneath him and support and hold his head at your breast. This position keeps the baby's weight off your abdomen, but the infant must squarely face the breast for the proper grasp.

If you stroke your newborn's lower lip with the nipple, he'll instinctively open his mouth wide, latch on, and begin to suck. He's been practicing this for some time by sucking his hand, fingers, and possibly even his feet in utero. (Some babies actually are born with blisters on their fingers

Whichever position you choose, make sure his entire body, not just his head, is facing your body.

caused by this sucking in the uterus, or womb.) It takes little encouragement to get him to nurse, but you may need to help him properly grasp the areola. You can hold the breast with your thumb above the areola and your fingers and palm underneath it. Some gentle compression may be helpful to form a surface for latch-on. Then, when the baby opens his mouth very wide, pull him onto the breast. It is important to keep fingers behind the areola and be sure the nipple is level or pointed slightly up. No matter which technique you try, you need to keep your fingers clear of the areola so the baby can grasp it. Be sure your fingers are no closer than 2 inches from the base of the nipple. Let your baby nurse at the first side as long as he wishes, then put him on the other side if he is still interested in feeding. It is more important to complete a feeding on

If you stroke your newborn's cheek or lower lip with your finger or with the nipple, he'll instinctively turn, latch on, and begin to suck. You may need to help him properly grasp the areola.

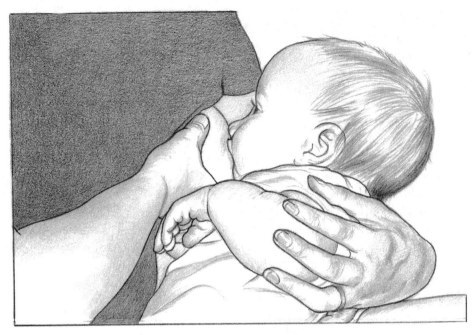

You may continue to provide some breast support while the baby is feeding, especially if the breasts are large.

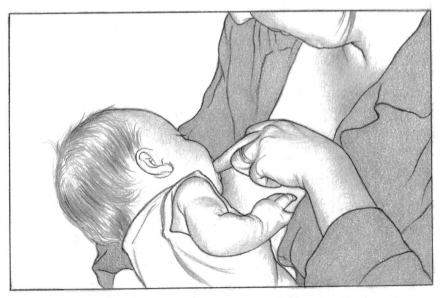

You can slide your finger into the corner of your baby's mouth if you need to interrupt the feeding before the baby is finished.

one breast than to have brief feedings from both breasts. The longer your baby feeds, the more fat and calories he will consume. Let-down, uterine cramping, swallowing sounds, and return to sound sleep by the baby are all signs of successful breastfeeding. In the beginning, it may take one to two minutes for let-down to occur. Within a week or so, let-down will take place much more rapidly and your milk supply will increase dramatically.

If you are not sure you are experiencing a let-down sensation, just watch your baby. Following a let-down, he should be swallowing after every few sucks at the start of the feeding. After five or ten minutes, he may switch to what's called nonnutritive sucking—a more relaxed sucking that provides emotional comfort along with small amounts of creamier, fat-rich *hindmilk*. Other signs of let-down vary from woman to woman and already have been discussed: uterine cramps the first few days after delivery; sensations of let-down; leakage of milk from the opposite breast during breastfeeding; the breast feeling full before and soft after feeding; or the appearance of milk in or around the baby's mouth after feeding. The more relaxed and confident you feel, the quicker your milk will let down.

The first feedings may be difficult because of excitement or, perhaps, your uncertainty about what to do. Breastfeeding should not cause sustained pain in the nipple, areola, or breast. If there is pain for more than a few moments at the beginning, ask the doctor, nurse, or lactation specialist to evaluate the breastfeeding and suggest changes. Ask the hospital staff for help; they are usually very experienced at assisting nursing mothers and babies. In some cases an infant will have trouble latching on. This occurs most often in newborns that have been given bottles or pacifiers. Suckling from the breast is different from sucking the nipple on a bottle or pacifier, and some infants are very sensitive to the difference. These babies may simply lick, nibble, or chew with their jaws instead of using the tongue. Others may show frustration by pulling away or crying. There is now good evidence to show that starting artificial nipples early on is associated with decreased exclusive breastfeeding and decreased duration of breastfeeding. Researchers are still uncertain if the artificial nipples are the cause of breastfeeding problems or are just a response to a breastfeeding problem that already existed. *Experts recommend that you avoid bottles and pacifiers for the first several weeks until you feel that breastfeeding is going well.* During that time, if the baby seems to need more sucking, offer the breast again, or help him to find his own hand or fingers to soothe himself. If your baby has trouble latching on when you are home, you should call your baby's doctor for help or for a referral if needed.

Once you are back home, try the following suggestions to help the let-down reflex.

■ Apply moist heat (e.g., warm, wet washcloths) to the breast several minutes before starting the feeding.

- Sit in a comfortable chair, with good support for your back and arms. (Many nursing mothers recommend rocking chairs or gliders, while others do best in a straight-back chair using propping pillows.)

- Make sure the baby is positioned so he squarely faces the breast and is well latched on, as described earlier.

- Use some relaxation techniques, such as deep breathing or visual imagery.

- Listen to soothing music and sip a nutritious drink during feedings.

- If your household is very busy, find a quiet corner or room where you won't be disturbed during feedings.

- Do not smoke, and avoid secondhand smoke. Do not consume alcohol, or use illegal drugs (e.g., marijuana, cocaine, heroin, ecstasy, etc.), as all contain substances that can interfere with let-down, affect the content of breast milk, and be harmful to the baby. Check with your obstetrician or pediatrician about any prescription or nonprescription drugs, as well as any herbal supplements, you may be taking.

If you still are not letting down after trying these suggestions, contact your pediatrician for additional help. If you continue to have difficulties, ask to be referred to a lactation expert.

When Your Milk Supply Increases

For the first few days after delivery, your breasts will be soft to the touch; but as the blood supply increases and milk-producing cells start to function more efficiently, the breasts will become firmer. By the second to fifth day following delivery, your breasts should be producing transitional milk (the milk that follows colostrum) and may feel very full. At the end of the baby's first week, you will see creamy white breast milk; after ten to fourteen days, your milk may initially look like skimmed milk, but as the feeding continues, the amount of fat in the milk will increase and the milk will look creamier. This is normal and does not mean there is anything wrong with your milk. Nursing your baby frequently and massaging your breasts prior to and during feeding may help minimize the fullness.

Engorgement occurs when the breasts become overfilled with milk and excess body fluids. This can be very uncomfortable and at times painful. The best

Is Your Baby Nursing Correctly?
A Breastfeeding Checklist

SIGNS OF CORRECT NURSING

■ Your baby's mouth is open wide with lips turned out.

■ His chin and nose are resting against the breast.

■ He is suckling rhythmically and deeply, in short bursts separated by pauses.

■ You can hear him swallowing regularly.

■ Your nipple is comfortable after the first few suckles.

SIGNS OF INCORRECT NURSING

■ Your baby's head is not in line with his body.

■ He is sucking on the nipple only, instead of suckling on the areola with the nipple far back in his mouth.

■ He is sucking in a light, quick, fluttery manner rather than taking deep, regular sucks.

■ His cheeks are puckered inward or you hear clicking noises.

■ You don't hear him swallow regularly after your milk production has increased.

■ You experience pain throughout the feed or have signs of nipple damage (such as cracking or bleeding).

From American Academy of Pediatrics, *New Mother's Guide to Breastfeeding,* ed. J. Y. Meek. 2nd ed. (New York: Bantam Books, 2011).

solution to this problem is to nurse your baby whenever she is hungry, feeding at both breasts about every two hours or before your breasts get swollen, firm, or painful. Sometimes the breasts are so engorged that the baby has trouble latching on. If that happens, you can apply moist heat to soften the breasts, and if necessary, manually express some milk or use a mechanical breast pump before you start to nurse. Doing this may help the baby get a better grasp and nurse more efficiently. (See page 105 regarding milk expression.) You also can try several techniques to ease the pain of engorgement, such as the following.

■ Soak a cloth in warm water and put it on your breasts. Or take a warm shower. These techniques, when used just before breastfeeding or expressing milk, will encourage milk flow.

■ Warmth may not help cases of severe engorgement. In this case, you may want to use cool compresses in between or just after feeding.

■ Express milk or pump just enough milk for comfort's sake.

■ Try feeding your baby in more than one position. Begin by sitting up, then lying down. This changes the segments of the breast that are drained most optimally at each feeding.

What About Vitamins for Breastfed Babies?

Your breast milk provides your baby with all the vitamins he needs, except for vitamin D. Even though human milk provides small amounts of vitamin D, it is not enough to prevent rickets (softening of the bones). The American Academy of Pediatrics advises that all breastfed babies consume 400 IU of oral vitamin D drops per day, beginning in the first few days of life, and continuing until they are drinking other vitamin D–fortified fluids. The current Academy recommendation is that all infants and children should have a minimum intake of 400 IU (International Units) of vitamin D per day beginning soon after birth with 600 units/day in children over age one. Prepared formula has vitamin D added to it, so if your baby is drinking formula, vitamin D supplementation is not needed, but breastfed babies will require a vitamin D supplement.

Once your baby is one year old and on vitamin D milk, extra vitamins with vitamin D are no longer needed. Your baby also may need vitamin supplements if he was born prematurely or has certain other medical problems. Discuss the need for supplements of vitamins or minerals with your doctor.

If you are a vegan (a diet that excludes all foods of animal origin), talk about your nutritional needs with your pediatrician. A vegan diet lacks not only vitamin D but also vitamin B_{12}, and a deficiency in B_{12} in babies can lead to anemia and nervous system abnormalities.

For more information about vitamin D and other supplements, see pages 125–128.

Breastfeeding Twins

Twins present a unique challenge to the nursing mother. At first it may be easier to feed them one at a time, but after lactation is established, often it's more convenient to feed them simultaneously in order to save time. Feeding them together can also help to increase your milk supply. You can do this using the "football hold" to position one at each side, or cradle them both in front of you with their bodies crossing each other. Books and support groups for parents of twins can provide further information.

For more information about raising multiples, see the book *Raising Twins: Parenting Multiples From Pregnancy Through the School Years* by Shelly Vaziri Flais, MD, FAAP, published by the American Academy of Pediatrics (2015).

- Gently massage your breasts from under the arm and down the nipple. This will help reduce soreness and ease milk flow.

- The use of ibuprofen has been shown to be safe and effective for the treatment of engorgement. Take the dosage recommended by your doctor. Do not take any other medications without your doctor's approval.

Engorgement lasts only a few days while lactation is getting established. However, your breasts can still get firm or overfilled anytime feedings are skipped and the breasts are not emptied frequently.

The volume of milk produced by the breasts increases dramatically over the first week. Your baby may take as little as 1 teaspoon (5 ml) at each feeding in the first couple of days. But by the fourth or fifth day, the volume may be up to 1 ounce (30 ml), and by the end of the week—depending on the size and appetite of the baby and the length of feedings—you may be producing 2 to 6 ounces (60–180 ml) at each feeding. At the end of your baby's first month, she should be receiving an average of 24 ounces (720 ml) of milk a day. See page 103 for information on how to tell if your baby is getting enough.

How Often and How Long?

Breastfed babies vary greatly in their feeding behaviors. They generally eat more frequently than formula-fed infants. Breastfed newborns typically feed eight to twelve or more times per twenty-four hours. As they get older, some may be able to go longer between feedings, because their stomach capacity enlarges and their mothers' milk production increases. Others continue to prefer frequent, smaller feeds.

What's the best feeding schedule for a breastfed baby? It's the one she designs herself. Your baby lets you know when she's hungry by waking and looking alert, putting hands toward her mouth, making sucking motions, whimpering and flexing arms and hands, moving fists to her mouth, becoming more active, and nuzzling against your breast. (She can smell its location even through your clothing.) It is best to start nursing the baby before crying starts. Crying is a late sign of hunger. Whenever possible, use these signals rather than the clock to decide when to nurse her. This way, you'll ensure that she's hungry when she eats. In the process, she'll stimulate the breast more efficiently to produce milk.

As stated earlier, breastfeeding for the healthy mother and

The baby will generally feed for about ten to fifteen minutes on the first breast. Then the baby can be burped and offered the other breast.

infant is generally most successful when you start nursing immediately after delivery (in the first hour). Keep the baby with you as much as possible (rooming in with her in the hospital), and respond promptly to cues of hunger (a practice called *demand feeding*). A sleepy baby should be awakened to feed after every three to four hours during the first few weeks of life (or until she has regained her birth weight and your pediatrician says it's OK to let her sleep at night), so that she has a minimum of eight feedings in twenty-four hours.

Allow your baby to continue nursing on the first breast as long as desired. When she spontaneously stops for a prolonged period or withdraws from the breast, burp her. If your baby seems sleepy after the first breast, you may want to wake her up a bit by changing her diaper or playing with her a little before switching her to the second side. Since your infant sucks more efficiently on the first breast she uses, you should alternate from feeding to feeding the one she uses first. You might consider placing a safety pin or an extra nursing pad on the side

where the baby last nursed as a reminder to start first on the other side at the next feeding. Or you can start on the breast that feels more full.

Initially your newborn probably will nurse every couple of hours, regardless of whether it's day or night. By six to eight weeks of age, many newborns have one sleep period of four to five hours. Establish nighttime sleep patterns by keeping the room dark, warm, and quiet. Don't turn on a bright light for the nighttime feeding. If soiled or wet, change her diaper quickly and without fanfare before this feeding and put her right back to sleep afterward. By four months, many—but not all—babies are sleeping six hours or more at a stretch without awakening during the night. However, some breastfed babies may continue to awaken more frequently for feedings at night. (See *Helping Your Baby Sleep,* page 61.)

Getting to Know Your Baby's Feeding Patterns

Each baby has a particular style of eating. Years ago researchers at Yale University playfully attached names to five common eating patterns. See if you recognize your baby's dining behavior among them:

Barracudas get right down to business. As soon as they're put to the breast, they grasp the areola and suck energetically for ten to twenty minutes. They usually become less eager as time goes on.

Excited Ineffectives become frantic at the sight of the breast. In a frenzied cycle they grasp it, lose it, and start screaming in frustration. They must be calmed down several times during each feeding. The key to nourishing this type of baby is to feed him as soon as he wakes up, before he gets desperately hungry. Also, if the milk tends to spray from the breast as the baby struggles, it may help to manually express a few drops first to slow the stream.

Procrastinators can't be bothered with nursing until the milk supply increases, commonly referred to as "coming in." These babies shouldn't be given bottles of water or formula. Feeding them bottles may make it more difficult to get them to nurse at the breast. You should continue to put them to the breast regularly, whenever they appear alert or make mouthing movements. Reluctant nursers sometimes benefit from being placed naked on the reclining mother's bare abdomen and chest for a period of time. They may spontaneously move toward the breast, or they can be placed on the breast after a time. You may find advice on improved positioning and attachment from a lactation specialist helpful. For a baby who resists nursing for the first few days, you can use an electric pump between feedings to stimulate milk production. (See pages 105–109.) Just don't give up! Contact your pediatrician's office for assistance or referral to a lactation specialist.

Gourmets or *Mouthers* insist on playing with the nipple, tasting the milk first and smacking their lips before digging in. If hurried or prodded, they become furious and scream in protest. The best solution is tolerance. After a few minutes of playing, they do settle down and nurse well. Just be sure the lips and gums are on the areola and not on the nipple.

Resters prefer to nurse for a few minutes, rest a few minutes, and resume nursing. Some fall asleep on the breast, nap for half an hour or so, and then awaken ready for dessert. This pattern can be confusing, but these babies cannot be hurried. The solution? It's best just to schedule extra time for feedings and remain as flexible as possible.

Learning your own baby's eating patterns is one of your biggest challenges in the first few weeks after delivery. Once you understand his patterns, you'll find it much easier to determine when he's hungry, when he's had enough, how often he needs to eat, and how much time is required for feedings. It is generally best to initiate a feeding at the earliest signs of hunger and before the baby cries. Babies also have unique positions that they prefer and will even show preference for one breast over the other.

You'll also find that your infant may require long feedings at certain times of the day and be satisfied quickly at others. She'll let you know when she's finished by letting go or drifting off to sleep between spurts of nonnutritive sucking. A few babies want to nurse around the clock. If your baby falls into this category, check with your pediatrician's office. You may be referred to a lactation specialist. There are several reasons why infants behave this way, and the sooner the situation is evaluated, the easier it is to address the cause. Once evaluated, if breastfeeding is going smoothly, your milk supply is well established, and the baby is gaining weight, you may decide to provide a pacifier for extra sucking. But be aware that the early introduction of pacifiers is associated with a shorter duration of breastfeeding.

Is Your Baby Eating Enough?

Your baby's diapers will provide clues about whether he is getting enough to eat. During the first month, after your milk supply increases and if his diet is adequate, he should wet six or more times a day and generally have three to four or more bowel movements daily (often one little one after each feeding). Later he may have less frequent bowel movements, and there may even be a day or more between them. If the bowel movements are soft, and your baby is otherwise thriving, this is quite normal. Another clue about intake is whether you can hear your baby swallow, usually after several sucks in a row. Appearing satisfied for a couple of hours right after a feeding is also a sign that he is getting enough. On the other hand, a baby who is not getting enough to eat over several days may become very sleepy and seem "easy" to care for. In the early weeks, a baby who regularly sleeps for four hours or more at a time should be seen by the pediatrician to make sure he is gaining weight as expected.

One of the most accurate ways to judge your baby's intake over time is by checking her weight gain. We now recommend that babies be examined by a health care provider at the third to fifth day of life, which provides an opportunity to check her weight, feeding, and head circumference. During the first week of life, babies can lose up to 10 percent of birth weight (that's about 10 ounces [340 g] in an approximately 7½-lb. [3.4 kg] full-term baby), but after that she should gain fairly steadily. By the end of her second week, she ought to be back to her birth weight. If you've breastfed other children, lactation probably will get established more quickly this time around, so the new baby may lose little weight and return to her birth weight within days.

Once your milk supply is established, your baby should gain between ½ and 1 ounce (14–28 g) a day during his first three months. Between three and six months, his weight gain will taper off to about ½ ounce (14 g) a day, and after six months, the amount your baby gains each day will be even less. Your pediatrician typically will weigh the baby at every visit. If you have concerns between visits, call to schedule an appointment to have the baby weighed; don't depend on a home scale, which is not very reliable for young infants.

What About Bottles?

It is usually best to try to breastfeed your newborn around the clock, which can be made easier by having your baby "rooming in" with you in your hospital room as much as possible. You might be tempted to have your baby sleep in the nursery for one night so you can get an uninterrupted night's sleep. But most hospitals now provide mother-infant care so you can sleep while your newborn is being safely cared for by his nurse in the same room. Research shows that mothers actually sleep better when their newborns are cared for in the same room as opposed to being cared for in a nursery setting. Hospitals are shifting away from the traditional nursery model and using the old nurseries for procedures and sick newborns. Furthermore, if your newborn is rooming in, you can respond to early feeding cues and avoid any unnecessary water or formula supplementation, which may interfere with your ability to have a successful breastfeeding experience.

If circumstances keep you away from your baby, you will need to express breast milk, manually or mechanically, in order to stimulate continued milk production. The hospital staff will work with you and your baby to feed your milk in a way that minimizes any problem transitioning back to the breast, including using feeding techniques that avoid bottles and teats. These techniques may include syringe or cup feeding, or feeding through a supplemented nursing system. Only rarely are there serious situations where mother's milk may not be used. If you use bottles of formula when you are away, your baby receives less breast milk and fewer benefits of breastfeeding. Avoiding formula may be particularly important in babies from families with a history of allergy. Always check with your pediatrician or other expert before you stop giving your milk to your baby.

Once breastfeeding is going well and the milk supply is established, usually three or four weeks after delivery, you may decide to use an occasional bottle so you can be away during some feedings. But you won't need to substitute formula: If you express breast milk in advance and store it, your baby can continue to receive the benefits of your milk by bottle. In addition, using expressed breast milk will maintain your body's full milk production for your baby. An occasional bottle at this stage probably won't interfere with your baby's nursing habits, but it may cause another problem: Your breasts may become engorged, and they can leak milk. You can relieve the engorgement by expressing milk to drain the breasts; store this milk to replace the breast milk that was used while you were away. Wearing nursing pads will help you manage the problem of leakage. (Some women wear nursing pads constantly during the first month or two of lactation to avoid milk stains on their clothing.) It is important to either breastfeed or express your milk regularly throughout the day to avoid engorgement and potential problems from milk stasis which may lead to a decrease in milk production.

Milk Expression and Storage

Milk can be expressed either by hand or by pump. In either case, you must have the let-down reflex in order to get the milk out of the breast. Manual or hand expression is easier to learn if someone shows you or by watching a video, rather than just reading about it. Manual expression can be quick and effective once it is learned, but it requires practice. Many hospitals teach mothers hand expression before leaving the hospital. Initially breast pumps seem easier to use than learning hand expression, but the quality of pumps varies widely. A poor-quality breast pump will not remove milk effectively, resulting in engorgement or a gradually lower milk supply over time. Poor-quality breast pumps also may irritate the nipples or be quite painful.

If you choose to use hand expression, wash your hands and use a clean container to collect the milk. Place your thumb on the breast, above the areola, and your fingers underneath. Gently but firmly roll the thumb and fingers toward each other while compressing the breast tissue and pushing toward the chest wall. Do not slide your fingers toward your nipple as this can cause soreness. Transfer the milk into a clean bottle, rigid plastic container, or specially made plastic bag for storage in the freezer. (See page 107.) If your baby is hos-

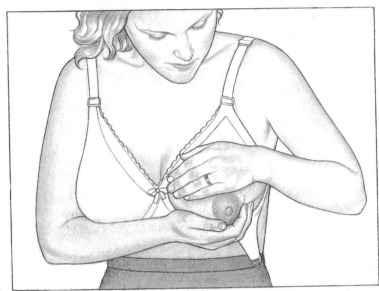

Expressing milk is easier if you stimulate the breast first by massaging it gently.

pitalized, the hospital may give you more specific and detailed information about milk collection and storage, and may loan you a hospital-grade breast pump to express milk for your baby.

While hand pumps are available, good-quality electric pumps are a wonderful option and can stimulate the breast more effectively than manual expression. These pumps have regulated pressures and are self-cycling for efficient milk removal. They are used primarily to induce or maintain lactation when a mother is unable to feed her infant directly for several days or more, or when the mother returns to work or school. Electric pumps are efficient but can be costly—ranging in price from $150 to $300 and up. If you will need the pump for only a limited period, it's often much more economical to rent one from a medical supply store, hospital, or lactation rental agency. If you have a hospitalized newborn or return to work shortly after your baby is born and want to continue breastfeeding, obtaining a breast pump is essential.

When shopping for an electric pump to buy or rent, make sure it creates a steady milking action with variable pressure and is not simply a suction device. You also may want to consider a pump that expresses both breasts at the same time; such a pump will increase your milk volume as well as save time. Make sure that all parts of the pump that come in contact with the skin or milk can be removed for proper cleaning. Sterilization is not required for pumps and containers for a healthy baby; simply washing them well with hot soapy water is fine, as is running them through the dishwasher. Talk to your pediatrician or a lactation consultant for advice about which type of pump may be best for

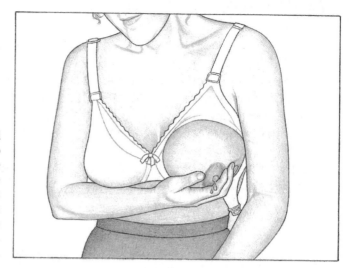

To use hand expression, hold the breast with the thumb and index finger at the edge of the areola on opposite sides of the breast, then press toward the chest wall with a rhythmic motion. Rotate position of fingers so all parts of the breast are emptied.

you. And remember, whenever you use a pump, wash your hands immediately before pumping.

As with breast milk that is expressed manually, milk that is pumped should be stored in clean containers, preferably glass or rigid plastic containers or special plastic bags. Baby bottle insert bags are not sufficiently strong or thick to protect the milk from contamination. Expressed breast milk can be stored safely at room temperature for three to four hours and in the refrigerator for up to three days or in a freezer for up to six months. Store frozen breast milk in the back of the freezer. It is important to place a label with the date on each container so you can use the oldest milk first. It's useful to freeze milk in quantities of about 3 to 4 ounces (90–120 ml)—the amount of a single feeding. You also can freeze some 1- to 2-ounce portions (30–60 ml); these will come in handy if the baby wants a little extra at any feeding.

When it's time to use this stored milk, keep in mind that your baby is accustomed to breast milk at body temperature, so the baby may prefer that the milk be heated to at least room

Hand pumps are available at most drug and baby stores.

"Is My Baby Getting Enough Nourishment?"

If your baby is breastfeeding, the thought has probably crossed your mind as to whether he is getting enough to eat. After all, there's really no way to determine exactly how much breast milk he's getting.

If that becomes one of your concerns, here are some guidelines that can help ensure that your baby is getting the nourishment he needs. These tips are adapted from the American Academy of Pediatrics' book *New Mother's Guide to Breastfeeding*, edited by Joan Younger Meek, MD, MS, RD, FAAP, IBCLC (Bantam, 2nd edition, 2011).

Your well-fed newborn should:

- Lose no more than 10 percent of his birth weight in the first few days after birth before he starts to gain weight again.

- Have one or two bowel movements per day on days one and two, with blackish, tarry stools, and at least two stools that are starting to appear greenish to yellow in days three and four. By days five to seven, his stools should be yellow and loose, with small curds, and should number at least three to four per day. When your milk production increases, your baby will often have a bowel movement with each feeding during the first month of life.

- Have six or more wet diapers per day, with urine that is nearly colorless or pale yellow, by days five to seven.

- Appear content and happy for an average of one to three hours between feedings.

- Nurse at least eight to twelve times during every twenty-four-hour period.

temperature (68–72 degrees Fahrenheit [20–22 degrees Celsius]) for feeding. Frozen milk may be thawed in the refrigerator, or the container of frozen milk may be held under warm running water, or placed in a container of warm water. Once milk is thawed, its fat may separate, but that does not affect its quality. You may swirl the container gently until the milk returns to a uniform consistency. Stored human milk may have an altered smell or taste due to breakdown of fat into fatty acids by an enzyme in the milk. This is not harmful to the baby. Thawed milk should be used within twenty-four hours. Never refreeze it. If the infant does not finish all the thawed breast milk in the bottle, it should be consumed within one to two hours or discarded.

Do not heat breast milk, formula, or bottles in a microwave oven. Microwaving overheats the milk in the center of the container. Even if the bottle feels comfortably warm to your touch, the superheated milk in the center can scald your baby's mouth. Also, the bottle itself can explode if left in the microwave too long. Bear in mind that heat also can destroy some of the anti-infectious, nutritious, and protective properties of breast milk.

Not all breastfed babies react to the bottle the same way. Some accept it easily, regardless of when it is first introduced. Others are willing to take an occasional bottle, but not from the mother or when the mother is in the house. You can increase the likelihood that your baby will accept a bottle the first few times if someone other than the mother offers it, and she is out of sight at the time. Once familiar with the bottle, he may be willing to take it in his mother's presence, possibly even from the mother herself. If your breastfed baby refuses a bottle, try using a cup or "sippy cup" instead. Even premature newborns are able to cup feed. Some breastfed babies go from breast to cup without ever using a bottle.

Possible Nursing Concerns and Questions

For some babies and mothers, nursing goes well from the start and there are never any problems. But breastfeeding can have its ups and downs, especially in the beginning. Fortunately, many of the most common difficulties can be prevented with proper positioning and latch-on, along with frequent feedings. Once problems crop up, many may resolve quickly if you seek advice right away. Don't hesitate to ask your pediatrician or his office nurse for help with the following problems.

SORE AND CRACKED NIPPLES. Breastfeeding may produce some initial mild soreness, especially with latch-on in the first week or so. But breastfeeding should not cause sustained pain, discomfort, or open cracks. Proper latch-on is the most important factor in preventing sore and cracked nipples. If your nipple or other areas of the breast are painful, you should seek advice from your lactation expert.

During your bath or shower, wash your breasts only with water, not soap. Creams, lotions, and more vigorous rubbing actually may aggravate the problem. Also, try varying the baby's position at each feeding.

In humid climates, the best treatments for cracked nipples are sunlight, heat, and keeping the area dry. Don't wear plastic breast shields or plastic-lined nursing pads, which hold in moisture; instead, expose your breasts to the air as much as possible. Also, after nursing, express a little milk from your breasts and let it dry on the nipples. This dried milk will leave a protective coating that may help the healing process. As we pointed out earlier in this chapter (see page 89), you might want to apply purified hypoallergenic lanolin in a dry climate. If these measures do not solve the problem, consult your doctor for further advice; you might have a yeast or bacterial infection of the nipple.

ENGORGEMENT. As we've already mentioned, your breasts can become severely engorged if your baby doesn't nurse often or efficiently during the first few days after your milk comes in. While some engorgement is to be expected when you start lactation, extreme engorgement causes swelling of the milk ducts in the breasts and of blood vessels across the entire chest area. The best treatment is to feed your baby frequently; express milk between feedings, either manually or with a pump; and make sure the baby nurses at both breasts at every feeding. Since warmth encourages milk flow, standing in a warm shower as you manually express the milk may help, or use warm compresses. You also may get some relief with the use of warm compresses during nursing and cool compresses between nursing.

MASTITIS. Mastitis is an infection of the breast tissue caused by bacteria. Mastitis causes flulike symptoms of fever, chills, headache, nausea, dizziness, and lack of energy. These general symptoms occur along with local breast symptoms of redness, tenderness, swelling, heat, and pain. If you experience any of these symptoms, call your doctor at once. The infection is treated with milk removal (by feeding or pumping), rest, fluids, antibiotics, and pain medicine if needed. Your doctor will prescribe an antibiotic that is safe during breastfeeding. Be sure to take all the antibiotics even if you feel better. Do not stop nursing; doing so will worsen the mastitis and cause increased pain. The milk itself is *not* infected. Your baby will not be harmed by nursing during mastitis, and mastitis and the antibiotics will not cause changes in the composition of your milk.

Mastitis may be a sign that your body's immune defenses are down. Bed rest, sleep, and decreased activity will help you recover your stamina. Rarely, you may find that it's too painful to have the baby nurse on the infected breast; in that case, open up both sides of your bra and let the milk flow from that breast onto a towel or absorbent cloth such as a clean diaper, relieving the pressure as you feed the baby on the opposite side. Then she can finish the feeding on the infected side with less discomfort. Some women with severe pain find that it is more comfortable to pump the breast than it is to feed the baby. The pumped milk can be stored or can be fed to the baby.

A mother's return to work is a peak time for the development of mastitis. It is important to express milk regularly, approximately on the same sched-

Supplemental Nurser (Infant Feeding Device)

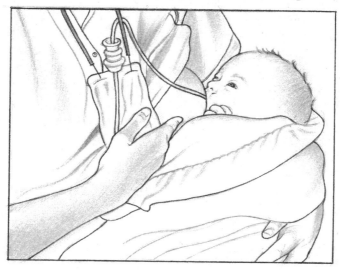

The amount of milk your breasts produce depends on the amount of milk that is removed from them. If you miss too many feedings, your body automatically will decrease milk production. This can occur even if you express milk during missed feedings, since pumps do not stimulate or empty the breasts nearly as efficiently as your baby's sucking.

If your milk supply is not meeting the needs of your baby, if you miss a number of feedings because of illness, or if your baby is unable to nurse for some reason, you may be able to reestablish your milk supply by nursing your baby more frequently such as every hour for 24 hours or with the help of a device called a supplemental nurser (also known as a supplementer tube, infant feeding device, or nursing trainer). Unlike a bottle, which trains the baby away from the breast, this device provides supplemental formula while the infant is at the breast.

The supplemental nurser also is used for premature infants or to train babies with feeding problems. It even can help stimulate lactation in adoptive mothers, or in mothers who have stopped breastfeeding for a prolonged period and wish to start again.

The device consists of a small plastic container that holds formula or expressed breast milk and hangs from a cord around your neck. The container has a thin flexible tube that is held or taped along the breast with its tip adjacent to the nipple and placed in the corner of the baby's mouth as she sucks.

Her suction draws the formula from the container into her mouth, so that even if you aren't producing much milk, she still will be getting a full feeding. This process reinforces her desire to nurse at the breast. At the same time, her sucking stimulates your body to step up milk production.

Supplemental nursers are available from lactation specialists, medical supply stores, some pharmacies, or via mail order. If possible, purchase the device from someone who can help you use it for the first time and show you how to clean it. Most mothers and babies need a few days of practice to get comfortable with the device. Using a supplemental nurser requires commitment and dedication, as it may take weeks or months to rebuild the milk supply and the breastfeeding relationship.

ule with which the baby would feed, to try to prevent the infection from occurring.

INFANT FUSSINESS. There are a number of reasons for a breastfed baby to be unusually fussy. These range from normal variations in personality to a serious illness. Although most "fussy babies" do not have a serious medical problem, their constant crying can become extremely difficult for parents. The fussy baby wears on Mom and Dad's energy, time, and enjoyment of their young infant. Here are some general causes for excessive crying in the breastfed baby and suggestions for working with your pediatrician to pinpoint and treat the problem.

- **Hunger:** If your newborn infant feeds constantly and is never satisfied after coming off the breast, your breastfeeding needs to be evaluated by an experienced health care provider. He will weigh and examine your baby, examine your breast and nipples, and observe an entire breastfeeding session. The solution may be as simple as improving the baby's positioning and latch-on. It may be more complicated, however, particularly if the baby has lost too much weight or is not gaining well.

- **Growth spurt:** A rapid growth phase often happens at two to three weeks of age, again around six weeks, and once more at about three months. During these growth spurts, babies will want to nurse *constantly*. Many women think this is because the baby is not getting enough to eat (which is correct) and are tempted to give supplemental bottles at this time. However the baby is doing what is right. By nursing constantly or every hour or so, for several days, your breasts will respond to this frequent nursing and make more milk. Remember, this is normal, and it is only temporary; keep breastfeeding very often, and do not give other liquids. If this frequent feeding does not return to a more regular pattern after four to five days, or if you are tempted to start your baby on bottles, call your pediatrician's office for assistance. He should see the baby, check her weight, and evaluate the feeding process (or refer you to a lactation specialist if needed).

- **Hyperalert or high-needs infants:** These babies require more of everything, except sleep. They cry seemingly around the clock. They are not very regular in their eating, sleeping, or reactions to others. They need lots of holding, carrying, and usually motion, such as rocking. Sometimes swaddling in a blanket helps them, but at other times it makes them worse. They tend to "snack" at the breast frequently and sleep in catnaps, brief fifteen- to thirty-minute naps while someone is holding or carrying them. Slings or other baby carriers, as well as swings, are good to try to help calm these babies. In spite of their fussiness, they should be gaining weight normally.

- **Colic:** Colic begins after four weeks of age. Colicky babies generally have at least one period of time each day when they appear to be in pain with their legs drawn up, crying hard, and turning red. They may act hungry during these times, but then pull back and refuse the breast. Your baby's doctor can provide suggestions for managing colic. (See Chapter 6, page 166.)

- **Oversupply or overactive let-down of breast milk:** This could begin at almost any time in the first month. Your breasts will feel very full, and you may experience lots of leaking and spraying. Your baby will be gulping down milk very fast, sometimes pulling away to catch his breath or coughing or sputtering milk. This rapid drinking causes the baby to swallow lots of air and milk. Later, gas bubbles will form, causing plenty of discomfort and tummy rumbling. Your pediatrician may guide you to a lactation consultant to assist with this problem. (Also see *Engorgement*, page 110.)

- **Reflux (also called gastroesophageal reflux):** Most newborns spit up after feeding. When spitting up results in problems for the baby, such as fussiness, or becomes more like vomiting (much larger amount), he should be evaluated by your pediatrician. (See page 220.)

- **Food sensitivities:** Occasionally a particular food (including caffeinated beverages) that you're eating may cause problems in your breastfed baby.

If you think this might be the case, avoid that food for one week to see if the symptoms go away. Then you may try the food again carefully to see if the symptoms return.

- **Allergies:** Although infant crying often is blamed on food allergies, such allergies are less common than some other reasons for fussiness. Allergies occur more often in babies from families where mother, father, or siblings are affected by asthma, eczema, or other allergic diseases. In the breastfed baby, the mother's diet may be the source of these allergies. It can be difficult to pinpoint the precise food, however, and allergic symptoms can linger for more than a week after the food has been removed from the mother's diet. Food allergies can be very serious, with blood in the stools, wheezing, hives, or shock (collapse). True food allergies definitely require the attention of your pediatrician.

- Other serious illnesses may not be related to feeding and may cause babies to cry endlessly, unable to be comforted. If this occurs suddenly or seems unusually severe, call your pediatrician or seek emergency care immediately.

THE CANCER QUESTION. Most studies indicate that breastfeeding offers some protection against breast cancer, perhaps because nursing lowers the total number of menstrual cycles during a woman's lifetime (see www.cancer.org). One large study in the United Kingdom found a 4.3 percent reduction in the risk of breast cancer for every year of breastfeeding. If a woman has been diagnosed with cancer or has had a malignant tumor removed, but is no longer getting chemotherapy or radiation treatment, breastfeeding should be acceptable. (Check with your physician.) Breastfeeding is safe after a woman has had a benign (noncancerous) lump or cyst removed.

BREASTFEEDING AFTER PLASTIC SURGERY ON THE BREASTS. Plastic surgery to enlarge the breasts should not interfere with breastfeeding—provided that the breasts were normal to begin with and that the nipples have not been moved and no ducts have been cut. (It is a good sign if there are no surgical scars close to the nipple or areola.) Saline implants pose no risk to the baby. Women with silicone implants may worry about leakage of silicone causing problems for their baby. But most authorities recommend breastfeeding even after implant surgery and feel that it does not pose any dangers to the baby.

The course of breastfeeding after breast reduction surgery is highly individual. Plastic surgery to reduce the size of the breasts typically involves at least some disruption of normal breast tissue and often movement of the entire nipple and areola. Each mother-baby pair must be helped and followed individually. Your baby's weight should be checked at least twice a week for the first few weeks, until the baby is gaining well. Even if you don't have a full supply, you can still breastfeed and supplement with formula. This will provide your baby with some of the benefits of receiving breast milk.

Make sure you discuss all your concerns with your doctor. Your baby's pediatrician needs to be aware of previous breast surgery that you've had so your infant can be followed closely.

For additional difficulties such as jaundice and worries about milk supply, refer to pages 151 and 108, respectively.

Bottle-Feeding

While recognizing the benefits of breastfeeding, mothers—and fathers, too—may feel that bottle-feeding gives the mother more freedom and time for duties other than those involving baby care. Dad, grandparents, sitters, and even older siblings can feed an infant breast milk or formula in a bottle. This may give some mothers more flexibility.

There are other reasons why some parents feel more comfortable with bottle-feeding. They know exactly how much food the baby is getting, and there's no need to worry about the mother's diet or medications that might affect the milk.

Even so, formula manufacturers have not yet found a way to reproduce the components that make human milk so unique. Although formula does provide the basic nutrients an infant needs, it lacks the antibodies and many of the other components that only mother's milk contains.

Formula-feeding is also costly and may be inconvenient for some families. The formula must be bought and prepared (unless you use the more expensive, ready-to-use types). This means trips to the kitchen in the middle of the night, as well as extra bottles, nipples, and other equipment. Unintended contamination of formula also must be considered a potential risk.

If you have decided to bottle-feed your baby, you'll have to start by selecting a formula. Your pediatrician will help you pick one based on your baby's needs. The American Academy of Pediatrics does not recommend homemade baby formulas, since they tend to be deficient in vitamins and other important nutrients. Today there are several varieties and brands of commercial formulas from which to choose.

Why Formula Instead of Cow's Milk?

Many parents ask why they can't just feed their baby regular cow's milk. The answer is simple: Young infants cannot digest cow's milk as completely or easily as they digest formula. Also, cow's milk contains high concentrations of protein and minerals, which can stress a newborn's immature kidneys and cause severe illness at times of heat stress, fever, or diarrhea. In addition, cow's milk lacks the proper amounts of iron, vitamin C, and other nutrients that infants need. It may even cause iron-deficiency anemia in some babies, since cow's milk protein can irritate the lining of the stomach and intestine, leading to loss of blood into the stools. Cow's milk also does not contain the healthiest types of fat for growing babies. For these reasons, your baby should not receive any regular cow's milk for the first twelve months of life.

Once your baby is past one year old, you may give him whole cow's milk or reduced-fat (2 percent) milk, provided he has a balanced diet of solid foods (cereals, vegetables, fruits, and meats). But limit his intake of milk to 1 quart (about 32–36 oz.) per day. More than this can provide too many calories and may decrease his appetite for the other foods he needs. If your baby is not yet eating a broad range of solid foods, talk to your pediatrician about the best nutrition for him.

At this age, children still need a higher fat content, which is why whole vitamin D milk is recommended for most infants after one year of age. If your child is overweight or at risk for being overweight, or if there is a family history of obesity, high blood pressure, or heart disease, your pediatrician may recommend 2 percent milk (reduced-fat) instead. Do not give your baby 1 percent (low-fat) or nonfat (skimmed) milk before his second birthday. Also, nonfat, or skimmed, milk provides too high a concentration of protein and minerals and should not be given to infants or toddlers under age two. After two years of age, you should discuss your child's nutritional needs, including choice of low-fat or nonfat milk products, with your pediatrician.

Choosing a Formula

To maintain safety standards for infant health in this country, an act of Congress governs the contents of infant formula, and the Food and Drug Administration monitors all formulas. When shopping for infant formula, you'll find several basic types.

Cow's milk–based formulas account for about 80 percent of the formula sold today. Although cow's milk is the basis for such formulas, the milk has been changed dramatically to make it safe for infants. It is treated by heating and other methods to make the protein more digestible. More milk sugar (lactose) is added to make the concentration equal to that of breast milk, and the fat (butterfat) is removed and replaced with vegetable oils and other fats that infants can more easily digest and are better for infant growth.

Cow's milk formulas have additional iron added. These iron-fortified formulas have dramatically reduced the rate of iron-deficiency anemia in infancy in recent decades. Some infants do not have enough natural reserves of iron, a mineral necessary for normal human growth and development, to meet their needs. For that reason, the American Academy of Pediatrics currently recommends that iron-fortified formula be used for all infants who are not breastfed, or who are only partially breastfed, from birth to one year of age. Additional iron is available in many baby foods, especially in meats, egg yolks, and iron-fortified cereals. Low-iron formulas should not be used, since they do not provide enough iron to optimally support your baby's growth and development. Some mothers worry about the iron in infant formula causing constipation, but the amount of iron provided in infant formula does not contribute to constipation in babies. Most formulas also have docosahexaenoic acid (DHA) and arachidonic acid (ARA) added to them, which are fatty acids, believed to be important for the development of a baby's brain and eyes.

Some formulas also are fortified with probiotics, which are types of "friendly" bacteria. Others are now fortified with prebiotics, in the form of manufactured oligosaccharides, in an attempt to mimic the natural human milk oligosaccharides, which are substances that promote healthy intestinal lining. For more information, see page 119.

Another type of formula is *hydrolyzed formulas*. They often are called "predigested," meaning that their protein content has already been broken down into smaller proteins that can be digested more easily. In infants who have a high risk of developing allergies (because of family history, for example) and who have not been breastfed exclusively for four to six months, there is some evidence that skin conditions like eczema or atopic dermatitis can be prevented or delayed by feeding them either extensively or partially hydrolyzed (hypoallergenic) formulas. Ask your pediatrician to recommend a brand of hypoallergenic formula, which can reduce the risk of allergic reactions. However, these hydrolyzed formulas tend to be costlier than regular formulas. Your pediatrician can advise you on whether your child is a candidate for hydrolyzed formulas.

The hypoallergenic formulas will help at least 90 percent of babies who have food allergies, which can cause symptoms such as hives, a runny nose, and intestinal problems. In these types of situations, breastfeeding is particularly desirable because—when there is a strong family history of allergies—it could help avoid some infant food allergies, especially when the child is exclusively breastfed for about six months.

Soy formulas contain a protein (soy) and carbohydrate (either glucose or sucrose) different from milk-based formulas. They are sometimes recommended for babies unable to digest lactose, the main carbohydrate in cow's milk formula, although simple lactose-free cow milk–based formula is also available. Many infants have brief periods when they cannot digest lactose, particularly following bouts of diarrhea, which can damage the digestive enzymes in the lining of the intestines. But this is usually only a temporary problem and does not require a change in your baby's diet. It is rare for babies to have a significant problem digesting and absorbing lactose (although it tends to occur in older children and adults). If your pediatrician suggests a lactose-free formula, know that it provides your baby with everything that she needs to grow and develop just as a lactose-containing formula does.

When a true milk allergy is present, causing colic, failure to thrive, and even bloody diarrhea, the allergy is to the protein in the cow's milk formula. In this case soy formulas, with soy as the protein, might seem like a good alternative. However, as many as half the infants who have milk allergy are also sensitive to soy protein, and thus they must be given a specialized formula (such as amino-based or elemental) or breast milk.

Some strict vegetarian parents choose to use soy formula because it contains no animal products. Remember that breastfeeding is the best option for vegetarian families. Also, although some parents believe that a soy formula might prevent or ease the symptoms of colic or fussiness, there is no evidence to support its effectiveness for this purpose.

The American Academy of Pediatrics believes that there are few circumstances in which soy formula should be chosen instead of cow milk–based formula in term infants. One of these situations is in infants with a rare disorder called galactosemia; children with this condition have an intolerance to galactose, one of the two sugars that make up lactose, and they cannot tolerate breast milk and must be fed a formula free of lactose. Most states include a test for galactosemia in routine newborn screening, which involves performing a blood test on all newborns after birth.

Specialized formulas are manufactured for infants with specific disorders or diseases. There are also formulas made specifically for premature babies. If your pediatrician recommends a specialized formula for your infant, follow his guidance about feeding requirements (amounts, scheduling, special preparations), since these may be quite different from regular formulas.

BPA (bisphenol A) is a chemical used in many containers and bottles, including baby bottles, and you need to be aware of its possible harmful effects. Breastfeeding is an obvious way to protect your child from BPA exposure (for more, see Chapter 24, *Environmental Health*, p. 714).

Probiotics in Formulas

Probiotics (meaning "for life") is a word that you may run across when shopping for infant formula for your baby. Some formulas are fortified with these probiotics, which are types of live bacteria. They are "good" or "friendly" bacteria that are already present at high levels in the digestive system of breastfed babies. In formula-fed babies, the introduction of probiotics to formulas is designed to promote a balance of bacteria in your baby's intestines, and offset the growth of "unfriendly" organisms that could cause infections and inflammation.

The most common types of probiotics are strains of tiny organisms called *Bifidobacterium* and *Lactobacillus*. Some research has shown that these probiotics may prevent or treat disorders such as infectious diarrhea and atopic dermatitis (eczema) in children (see pages 530 and 560). Other possible health benefits are being studied as well, including whether probiotics can lower your child's risk of food-related allergies and asthma, prevent urinary tract infections, or improve the symptoms of infant colic.

With many of these health conditions, the evidence confirming any positive effects of probiotic use is limited and more research is needed. At this time, any benefits appear to occur only as long as the probiotics are being taken. Once your baby stops consuming probiotic-fortified formula, the bacteria in the intestines will return to their previous levels.

Before giving your child infant formula that is fortified with probiotics, discuss the issue with your pediatrician. (For more information about probiotics, see page 536.)

Preparing, Sterilizing, and Storing Formula

Most infant formulas are available in ready-to-feed liquid forms, concentrates, and powders. Although ready-to-feed formulas are very convenient, they are also the most expensive. Formula made from concentrate is prepared by mixing equal amounts of concentrate and water. If the entire can is not used, the remaining concentrate may be covered and left in the refrigerator for no more than forty-eight hours. Powder, the least expensive form, comes either in premeasured packets or in a can with a measuring scoop. To prepare most powdered formula, you'll add one level scoop of powder for every 2 ounces (60 ml) of water, and then mix thoroughly to make sure there are no clumps of undissolved powder in the bottle. The solution will mix more easily and the

Preparing Formula from Concentrate
(One Bottle at a Time)

Wash hands and measure concentrate.

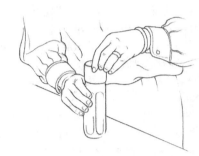

Pour in an equal amount of water. Shake and use promptly. If the entire can is not used, the remaining concentrate may be covered and left in the refrigerator for no more than forty-eight hours.

lumps will dissolve faster if you use room-temperature water. Always read the label to make sure you are mixing the formula properly.

Aside from the price, one advantage of the powder is its light weight and portability. The powder will not spoil, even if it stays in the bottle several days before you add water. If you choose a formula that requires preparation, be sure to follow the manufacturer's directions exactly. If you add too much water, your baby won't get the calories and nutrients she needs for proper growth; and if you add too little water, the high concentration of formula could cause diarrhea or dehydration and will give your infant more calories than she needs.

If you use well water or are concerned about the safety of your tap water, boil it for approximately one minute before you add it to the formula. (If there is any concern, it may be a good idea to have your well water tested for bacteria or other contaminants.) You also can use bottled water.

Powdered infant formula is not commercially sterile and has been associated with a severe illness attributed to *Cronobacter* bacteria. However, the illness is very rare and the World Health Organization (WHO) has issued guidelines to improve the safety of powdered infant formula. For more information, visit www.cdc.gov/features/cronobacter.

Make sure all bottles, nipples, and other utensils you use to prepare formula—or to feed your baby—are clean. If the water in your home is chlorinated,

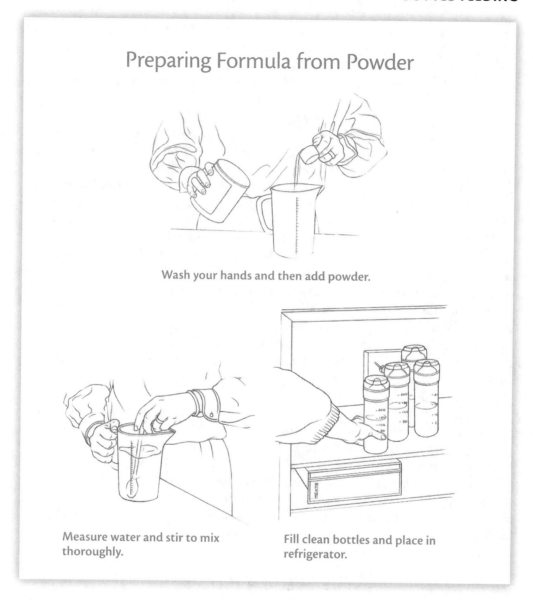

Preparing Formula from Powder

Wash your hands and then add powder.

Measure water and stir to mix thoroughly.

Fill clean bottles and place in refrigerator.

you can simply use your dishwasher or wash the utensils in hot tap water with dishwashing detergent and then rinse them in hot tap water. For nonchlorinated water, place the utensils in boiling water for five to ten minutes.

Store any formula you prepare in advance in the refrigerator to discourage bacterial growth. If you don't use refrigerated formula within twenty-four hours, discard it. Refrigerated formula doesn't necessarily have to be warmed for your baby, but most infants prefer it at least at room temperature. You can either leave the bottle out for an hour so it can reach room temperature, or

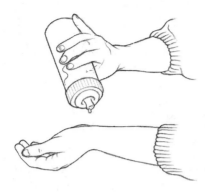

Be sure to test the temperature of warmed milk before feeding it to your child.

warm it in a pan of hot water. (Again, do not use a microwave.) If you warm it, test it in advance to make sure it's not too hot for your child. The easiest way to test the temperature is to shake a few drops on the inside of your wrist.

The bottles you use may be glass, plastic, or plastic with a soft plastic liner. These inner liners are convenient to use and may help limit the amount of air your baby swallows when she sucks, but they are also more expensive. As your baby gets older and begins holding the bottle herself, avoid using breakable glass bottles. Also, bottles that are designed to promote self-feeding are not recommended, as they may contribute to nursing-bottle tooth decay by promoting constant feeding and exposure of the teeth to sugars throughout the day and night. When milk collects behind the teeth, bacterial growth occurs. Also, self-feeding in a supine position (lying down on the back) has been shown to contribute occasionally to ear infections. (See *Middle Ear Infections,* page 662.) Infants and older children should not receive a bottle to suck on during the night. If you give your baby a feeding at bedtime, take away the bottle before she falls asleep.

In selecting bottles, you may need to try several nipples before finding the one your baby prefers. You can choose from among the standard rubber nipples, orthodontic ones, and special designs for premature infants and babies with cleft palates. Whichever type you use, always check the size of the hole. If it's too small, your baby may suck so hard that she swallows too much air; if it's too big, the formula may flow so fast that she chokes. Ideally, formula should flow at a rate of one drop per second when you first turn the bottle upside down. (It should stop dripping after a few seconds.)

The Feeding Process

Feeding times should be relaxing, comforting, and enjoyable for both you and your baby. They provide opportunities to show your love and to get to know each other. If you are calm and content, your infant will respond in kind. If you are nervous or uninterested, he may pick up these negative feelings and a feeding problem can result.

You probably will be most comfortable in a chair with arms or in one with pillows that let you prop up your own arms as you feed your infant. Cradle him in a semi-upright position and support his head. Don't feed him

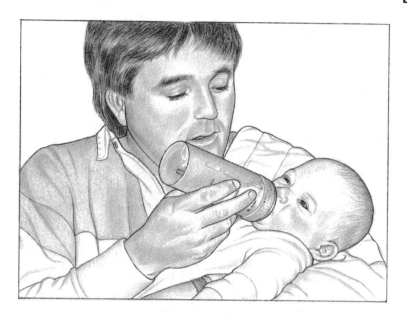

when he's lying down totally flat, because this will increase the risk of choking; it also may cause formula to flow into the middle ear, where it can lead to an infection.

Hold the bottle so that formula fills the neck of the bottle and covers the nipple. This will prevent your baby from swallowing air as he sucks. To get him to open his mouth and grasp the nipple, stimulate his rooting reflex by stroking the nipple against the lower lip or cheek. Once the nipple is in his mouth, he will begin to suck and swallow naturally.

Amount and Schedule of Formula Feedings

After the first few days, your formula-fed newborn will take from 2 to 3 ounces (60–90 ml) of formula per feeding and will eat every three to four hours on average during her first few weeks. (Breastfed infants usually take smaller, more frequent feedings than formula-fed infants.) During the first few weeks, if your baby sleeps longer than four to five hours and starts missing feedings, wake her up and offer a bottle. By the end of her first month, she'll be up to at least 4 ounces (120 ml) per feeding, with a fairly predictable schedule of feedings about every four hours. By six months, your baby will consume 6 to 8 ounces (180–240 ml) at each of four or five feedings in twenty-four hours.

On average, your baby should take in about 2½ ounces (75 ml) of formula a day for every pound (453 g) of body weight. But he probably will regulate his intake from day to day to meet his own specific needs. So instead of going by fixed amounts, let him tell you when he's had enough. If he becomes fidgety or easily distracted during a feeding, he's probably finished. If he drains the bottle and still continues smacking his lips, he might still be hungry. There are high and low limits, however. Most babies are satisfied with 3 to 4 ounces (90–120 ml) per feeding during the first month and increase that amount by 1 ounce (30 ml) per month until they reach a maximum of about 7 to 8 ounces (210–240 ml). If your baby consistently seems to want more or less than this, discuss it with your pediatrician. Your baby should drink no more than 32 ounces (960

WHERE WE STAND

THE AMERICAN ACADEMY OF PEDIATRICS believes that healthy children receiving a normal, well-balanced diet do not need vitamin supplementation over and above the recommended dietary allowances, which includes 400 IU (International Units) of vitamin D a day in infants less than one year of age and 600 units/day for children over one year of age. Megadoses of vitamins—for example, large amounts of vitamins A, C, or D—can produce toxic symptoms, ranging from nausea to rashes to headaches and sometimes to even more severe adverse effects. Talk with your pediatrician before giving vitamin supplements to your child.

ml) of formula in twenty-four hours. Some babies have higher needs for sucking and may just want to suck on a pacifier after feeding.

Initially it is best to feed your formula-fed newborn on demand, or whenever he cries because he's hungry. As time passes, he'll begin to develop a fairly regular timetable of his own. As you become familiar with his signals and needs, you'll be able to schedule his feedings around his routine.

Between two and four months of age (or when the baby weighs more than 12 lb. [5.4 kg]), most formula-fed babies no longer need a middle-of-the-night feeding, because they're consuming more during the day and their sleeping patterns have become more regular (although this varies considerably from baby to baby). Their stomach capacity has increased, too, which means they may go longer between daytime feedings—occasionally up to four or five hours at a time. If your baby still seems to feed very frequently or consume larger amounts, try distracting him with play or with a pacifier. Sometimes patterns of obesity begin during infancy, so it is important not to overfeed your baby.

The most important thing to remember, whether you breastfeed or bottle-feed, is that your baby's feeding needs are unique. No book can tell you precisely how much or how often he needs to be fed or exactly how you should handle him during feedings. You will discover these things for yourself as you and your baby get to know each other.

Supplementation for Breastfed and Bottle-Fed Infants

Vitamin Supplements

Human milk contains a natural balance of vitamins, especially C, E, and the B vitamins, so if you and your baby are both healthy, and you are well nourished, your child may not require any supplements of these vitamins.

Breastfed infants need supplemental vitamin D. This vitamin is naturally manufactured by the skin when it is exposed to sunlight. However, the American Academy of Pediatrics feels strongly that all children should be kept out of the direct sun as much as possible and wear sunscreen while in the sun to avoid long-term risk of sun exposure, which may contribute to skin cancer. Sunscreen keeps the skin from manufacturing vitamin D. For that reason, talk to your pediatrician about the need for supplemental vitamin D drops. The current Academy recommendation is that all infants and children should have a minimum intake of 400 IU (International Units) of vitamin D per day beginning soon after birth with 600 units/day in children over age one. Prepared formula has vitamin D added to it; so if your baby is drinking formula, vitamin D supplementation is not needed. In addition, once your baby is one year old and on vitamin D milk, extra vitamins with vitamin D are no longer needed. Your baby also may need vitamin supplements if he was born prematurely or has certain other medical problems. Discuss the need for supplements of vitamins or minerals with your doctor.

A regular, well-balanced diet should provide all the vitamins necessary for both nursing mothers and their babies. However, pediatricians recommend that mothers continue taking a daily prenatal vitamin supplement to ensure the proper nutritional balance. If you are on a strict vegetarian diet, you need to take an extra B-complex supplement, since certain B vitamins are available only from meat, poultry, or fish products. If your baby is on infant formula, he generally will receive adequate vitamins because formula has added vitamins.

Iron Supplements

Most babies are born with sufficient reserves of iron that will protect them from anemia. If your baby is breastfed, there is sufficient, well-absorbed iron to give her an adequate supply so that no additional supplement is necessary. When she is about six months old, you should be starting your breastfed infant on baby foods that contain supplemental iron (cereals, meats, green vegetables), which should further guarantee sufficient iron for proper growth. The best way to prevent iron deficiency during infancy is to allow the umbilical cord time to pulsate after birth for at least 1–1½ minutes before clamping and cutting. You should speak with your obstetrician about this practice before delivery.

If you are bottle-feeding your baby, it is now recommended that you use iron-fortified formula (containing from 4 to 12 mg of iron) from birth through the entire first year of life. Premature babies have fewer iron stores, so they often need additional iron beyond what they receive from breast milk or formula.

Water and Juice

Until your baby starts eating solid foods, he'll get all the water he needs from breast milk or formula. In the first six months, additional water or juice is not needed for breastfed or bottle-fed infants. After a baby is six months old, you may offer him a small amount of water in a cup, but don't force it on him or worry if he rejects it. He may prefer to get the extra liquid from more frequent feedings. Juice is not recommended for babies in the first year of life. It is much healthier for infants to eat fruit and drink water instead of drinking juice.

Once your baby is eating solid foods, his need for liquid will increase. Getting your infant used to the taste of plain water is a healthy habit that will last

WHERE WE STAND

THE AMERICAN ACADEMY OF PEDIATRICS recommends that fruit juice not be given to infants under six months of age since it offers no nutritional benefit to babies in this age group. After six months of age, infants may have limited amounts of juice each day. For children older than six months, fruit juice offers no nutritional benefits over whole fruit. Whole fruits also provide fiber and other nutrients. Infants should not be given fruit juice at bedtime, nor as a treatment of dehydration or management of diarrhea. For children ages one to six years old, limit fruit juice consumption to 4 to 6 ounces (120–180 ml) each day.

a lifetime. Juice is not recommended. Getting infants used to drinking juice instead of water may cause them to want only sweet drinks as they get older, which has been associated with overweight and obesity.

Your baby may need extra fluids when he's ill, especially when he has a fever or experiences vomiting and diarrhea. The best fluid for a breastfed infant who is ill is breast milk. Ask your pediatrician what liquids are best and how much to give at these times.

Fluoride Supplements

Babies should not receive fluoride supplementation during the first six months of life, whether they are breastfed or formula-fed. After that time, breastfed and formula-fed infants need appropriate fluoride supplementation if local drinking water contains less than 0.3 parts per million (ppm) of fluoride. If your home is supplied by its own well, have the well tested to determine the amount of natural fluoride in the water. If your baby consumes bottled water instead or your home is connected to a municipal water supply, check to see if the water is fluoridated. If your family prefers to use bottled water rather than tap water, you should consider purchasing water marketed for babies with specific amounts of fluoride added; sometimes called "nursery water," it is available in the baby food aisle in grocery stores, and can be used when mixing formula.

Your pediatrician or pediatric dentist can advise you on whether there is a need for fluoride drops for your baby and prescribe the appropriate dosage. Formula-fed infants receive some fluoride from their formula if the drinking water is fluoridated in their community or if it is made with bottled or well water containing fluoride. The American Academy of Pediatrics recommends that you check with your pediatrician or pediatric dentist to find out if any additional fluoride supplements are necessary, or whether your child is already receiving the right amount.

Remember, appropriate fluoride supplementation is based on each child's unique needs. A supplement should be considered by you and your doctor until all of a child's permanent teeth are present in the mouth.

Burping, Hiccups, and Spitting Up

Burping

Young babies naturally fuss and get cranky when they swallow air during feedings. Although this occurs in both breastfed and bottle-fed infants, it's seen more often with the bottle. When it happens, it may be helpful to stop the feeding rather than letting your infant fuss and nurse at the same time. This continued fussing will cause her to swallow even more air, which will only increase her discomfort and may make her spit up.

A much better strategy is to burp her frequently, even if she shows no discomfort. The pause and the change of position alone will slow her gulping and reduce the amount of air she takes in. If she's bottle-feeding, burp her after every 2 to 3 ounces (60–90 ml). If she's nursing, burp her when she switches breasts. Some breastfed babies don't swallow very much air, and therefore they may not need to burp.

Hiccups

Most babies hiccup from time to time. Usually this bothers parents more than the infant, but if hiccups occur during a feeding, change his position, try to get him to burp, or help him relax. Wait until the hiccups are gone to resume feeding. If they don't disappear on their own in five to ten minutes, try to resume feeding for a few minutes. Doing this usually stops them. If your baby gets hiccups often, try to feed him when he's calm and before he's extremely hungry. This will usually reduce the likelihood of hiccups occurring during the feeding.

Spitting Up

Spitting up is another common occurrence during infancy. Sometimes spitting up means the baby has eaten more than her stomach can hold; sometimes she spits up while burping or drooling. Although it may be a bit messy, it's usually

How Do You Burp a Baby?

Here are a few tried-and-true techniques. After a little experimentation, you'll find which ones work best for your child.

1. Hold the baby upright with his head on your shoulder, supporting his head and back while you gently pat his back with your other hand.

2. Sit the baby on your lap, supporting his chest and head with one hand while patting his back with your other hand.

3. Lay the baby on your lap with his back up. Support his head so it is higher than his chest, and gently pat or rotate your hand on his back.

If he still hasn't burped after several minutes, continue feeding him and don't worry; no baby burps every time. When he's finished, burp him again and keep him in an upright position for ten to fifteen minutes so he doesn't spit up.

no cause for concern. It almost never involves choking, coughing, discomfort, or danger to your child, even if it occurs while she's sleeping.

Some babies spit up more than others, but most are out of this phase by the time they are sitting. A few "heavy spitters" will continue until they start to walk or are weaned to a cup. Some may continue throughout their first year.

It is important to know the difference between normal spitting up and true vomiting. Unlike spitting up, which most babies don't even seem to notice, vomiting is forceful and usually causes great distress and discomfort for your child. It generally occurs soon after a meal and produces a much greater volume than spitting up. If your baby vomits on a regular basis (one or more times a day) or if you notice blood or a bright green color in your baby's vomit, consult your pediatrician. (See *Vomiting*, pages 197 and 549.)

While it is practically impossible to prevent all spitting up, the following steps will help you decrease the frequency of these episodes and the amount spit up.

1. Make each feeding calm, quiet, and leisurely.

2. Avoid interruptions, sudden noises, bright lights, and other distractions during feedings.

3. Burp your bottle-fed baby at least every three to five minutes during feedings.

4. Avoid feeding while your infant is lying down.

5. Hold the baby in an upright position for twenty to thirty minutes after each feeding.

6. Do not jostle or play vigorously with the baby immediately after feeding.

7. Try to feed her before she gets frantically hungry.

8. If bottle-feeding, make sure the hole in the nipple is neither too big (which lets the formula flow too fast) nor too small (which frustrates your baby and causes her to gulp air). If the hole is the proper size, a few drops should come out when you invert the bottle, and then stop.

Developing the Right Attitude

You can do it! This should be your attitude about breastfeeding from the beginning. There's plenty of help available, and you should take advantage of the expert advice, counseling, classes, and group meetings that are available. For example, you can:

- Talk to your obstetrician and pediatrician. They can provide not only medical information but also encouragement and support when you need it most.

- Talk to your prenatal instructors and attend a breastfeeding class.

- Talk to women who have breastfed or are breastfeeding successfully and ask their advice. Sisters-in-law, cousins, office mates, yoga instructors, and fellow congregants at your place of worship are precious resources.

- Talk to members of La Leche League or other mother-to-mother support groups in your community. La Leche League is a worldwide organization dedicated to helping families learn about and enjoy the experience of breastfeeding. Information and support for parents is available at www.llli.org.

- Read about breastfeeding. A recommended book is the American Academy of Pediatrics' *New Mother's Guide to Breastfeeding*, edited by Joan Younger Meek, MD, MS, RD, FAAP, IBCLC (Bantam, 2nd edition, 2011); and the booklet "Breastfeeding Your Baby: Answers to Common Questions" available at www.aap.org.

For more information on breastfeeding, visit www.healthychildren.org.

As you can tell from the length and detail of this chapter, feeding your baby is one of the most important and, at times, confusing challenges you'll face as a parent. The recommendations in this section apply to infants in general. Please remember that your child is unique and may have special needs. If you have questions that these pages have not answered to your satisfaction, ask your pediatrician to help you find the answers that apply specifically to you and your infant.

~ 5 ~

Your Baby's First Days

AFTER ALL THE months of pregnancy, you may believe that you already know your baby. You've felt his kicks, monitored his quiet and active periods during the day, and run your hands over your abdomen as he nestled in the womb. Although all of this does bring you closer to him, nothing can prepare you for the sight of his face and the grip of his fingers around yours.

For the first few days after his birth, you may not be able to take your eyes off him. Watching him, you may see hints of yourself or other members of the family reflected in his features. But despite any distinct resemblance, he is uniquely special—unlike anyone else. And he'll have a definite personality all his own that may start making itself known immediately. As he turns and stretches, only he knows what he wants and feels.

Some babies waste no time protesting wet or messy diapers from the day they are born and complain loudly until they are changed, fed, and rocked back to sleep. Infants who behave like this not only tend to spend more time awake than other babies, but they also may cry and eat more. Other newborns won't seem to notice when their diapers are dirty and may be more likely to object to having their bottoms exposed to the cold air during changes. These babies tend to sleep a lot and eat less frequently than their more sensitive counterparts. These kinds of individual differences are both normal and can serve as early hints of your child's future personality.

Some mothers say that after so many months of the baby being in their wombs, it becomes difficult to view their baby as a separate human being, with thoughts, emotions, and desires of his own. Making this adjustment and respecting their baby's individuality, however, are important parts of being a parent. If parents can welcome their child's uniqueness from the time he is born, they'll have a much easier time accepting the person the baby will become in the years ahead.

Your Newborn's First Days

How Your Newborn Looks

As you relax with your baby in your own room, unwrap his blankets and examine him from head to toe. You'll notice many details that may have escaped

you in the first moments after birth. For instance, when your baby opens his eyes, you'll see their color. While many Caucasian newborns have blue eyes, the color may actually change over the first year. If a baby's eyes are going to turn brown, they'll probably become "muddy"-looking during the first six months; if they're still blue at that time, they'll probably remain so. In contrast, infants with dark-skinned heritage generally have brown eyes at birth, and they tend to remain that color throughout life.

You may notice a bloodred spot in the white area of one or both of your newborn's eyes. This spot, as well as the general puffiness of a newborn's face, are most commonly caused by pressures exerted during labor. Although you might find them a bit worrisome at first, fortunately both tend to fade in a few days. If your baby was delivered by C-section, he won't have this puffiness and the whites of his eyes should not have any red spots right from the start.

Bathed and dry, your baby's skin will seem very delicate. If he was born after his due date, it may peel and appear wrinkled as a result of having lost the vernix (a whitish, creamy substance covering the skin). If he was born on time or early, he may still peel a little as a newborn because of his skin's sudden exposure to air after the vernix is washed away. Either way, peeling skin is a normal newborn process and requires no treatment. All babies, including those with a dark-skinned heritage, have lighter-appearing skin at birth. This gradually darkens as they become older.

As you examine your baby's shoulders and back, you also may notice some fine hair, called lanugo. This hair is produced toward the end of pregnancy; however, it's usually shed before birth or soon thereafter. If your baby was born before his due date, he is more likely to still have this hair, and it may take a couple of weeks to disappear.

You also may notice a lot of pink spots and marks on your baby's skin. Some, like those that appear around the edges of his diaper, may simply be due to pressure. Mottled or blotchy-looking patches are commonly caused by exposure to cool air and will disappear quickly if you cover him again. If you find scratches, particularly on your baby's face, it serves as a good reminder that it's time to trim his fingernails. This will help prevent him from continuing to scratch himself as he randomly moves his hands and arms. For some new parents, this can seem like a monumental and nerve-racking task, so don't hesitate to ask for advice from the nurse at the hospital nursery, or at your pediatrician's office, or from anyone else with experience on how to clip an infant's nails. Your baby also may develop other newborn rashes and have some birthmarks. Most will fade or resolve on their own without treatment (although some birthmarks may be permanent).

The following are the most common newborn rashes and birthmarks:

SALMON PATCHES OR "STORK BITES." So-called because they are distributed over the areas that a stork would supposedly carry a baby in its beak, in reality "stork bites" are simply patches, light to deep pink in color, and most commonly located on the bridge of the nose, lower forehead, upper eyelids, back of the head, and/or on the neck. They are the most common birthmark, especially in light-skinned babies. They also may be referred to as "angel kisses," and typically disappear over the first few months.

MONGOLIAN SPOTS. These birthmarks can vary considerably in size but are all flat areas of skin that contain extra pigment, which causes them to appear brown, gray, or even blue (like a bruise). Most often located on the back or buttocks, Mongolian spots are very common, especially in dark-skinned babies. They usually disappear before school age and are of no medical significance.

PUSTULAR MELANOSIS. Small blisters that typically appear at birth, they peel open and dry up within a couple of days. They leave dark spots like freckles that usually disappear over several weeks. Some newborns may have only the spots, indicating that they had the rash before birth. While pustular melanosis is common (particularly in babies with darker skin) and is a harmless newborn rash, it is always important to have all blisterlike rashes evaluated by your baby's doctor to make sure they aren't due to an infection.

MILIA. These tiny white bumps or yellow spots are found on the cheeks, chin, or across the tip of the nose, and are caused by skin-gland secretion. This common newborn rash generally disappears on its own within the first two to three weeks of life.

MILIARIA. Often referred to as a "heat rash" or "prickly heat," miliaria most often occurs in hot, humid climates or when babies are over-bundled. The rash can contain tiny sweat blisters and/or small red bumps. It shows up most often in skin folds and covered areas, and usually goes away within a few days.

ERYTHEMA TOXICUM. Often called "E tox" for short, this rash is very common and usually appears within the first few days after birth. It consists of multiple red splotches with yellowish-white bumps in the center, and goes away within a week or so. It generally resolves if it's left completely alone.

CAPILLARY HEMANGIOMAS. These raised red spots are caused by a strawberrylike collection of blood vessels in the skin. For the first week or so, they may appear white or pale, then turn red later. While they often enlarge during the first year, most shrink and almost disappear by the time a child reaches school age usually without requiring treatment.

PORT WINE STAIN. Large, flat, and irregularly shaped dark red or purple areas. Caused by extra blood vessels under the skin, port wine stains are usually located on the face or neck but, unlike hemangiomas, don't disappear without treatment. These birthmarks can be treated, sometimes with laser surgery by either a plastic surgeon or a pediatric dermatologist. (See also *Birthmarks and Hemangiomas,* page 831.)

If your baby was born vaginally, in addition to the elongated shape of his head, there also may be some scalp swelling in the area that was pushed out first during birth. If you press gently on this area, your finger may even leave a small indentation. This swelling (called *caput*) is not serious and should disappear in a few days.

Sometimes there may be swelling under a newborn's scalp that is present on only one side of the head, and will seem to spring right back after it is gently pressed. This type of swelling is likely to be what is called a *cephalohematoma,* and it, too, is caused by the intense pressure on the head during labor. While not serious, it typically represents some bleeding in the scalp (but outside the skull bones—not inside the brain) and usually takes six to ten weeks to disappear. Parents should be careful not to injure this area with their long nails or a sharp-toothed comb, since this swelling may get infected.

All babies have two soft spots, or *fontanelles,* on the top of the head. These are the areas where the immature bones of the skull are still growing together. The larger opening is on the top of the head toward the front; a smaller one is at the back. Parents needn't be afraid to touch these areas gently, as there is a thick, durable membrane that protects the brain.

All infants are born with hair but the amount, texture, and color vary from one newborn to another. Most, if not all, of this "baby hair" falls out during the first six months of life and is replaced by mature hair. The color and texture of the mature hair may be quite different from the hair the baby was born with.

In the weeks following their birth, babies can be affected by the large amount of their mother's hormones that they were exposed to during pregnancy. As a result, babies' breasts may be enlarged temporarily and they might even secrete a few drops of milk. It is equally likely to occur in boy and girl babies, and normally lasts less than a week, although it can last several weeks. It is best not to press on or squeeze a baby's breasts, since this won't reduce the swelling and could cause an infection. In infant girls, there could be a discharge from the vagina. Although disconcerting to some new parents, this so-called pseudomenses is actually quite harmless.

As you examine your baby's abdomen, it will seem prominent, and you may even notice an area that seems to bulge during crying spells. These small hernias are most commonly seen around the umbilical cord/belly button, but may also appear in a line down the center of the abdomen. (For more information, see *Umbilical Hernia* on page 154 of this chapter.)

The genitals of newborn babies can be somewhat reddish and seem quite large for bodies so small. The scrotum of a baby boy may be smooth and barely big enough to hold the testicles, or it might be large and wrinkled. The testicles can seem to move in and out of the scrotum. Sometimes they will move as far up in the scrotum as the base of the penis or even to the crease at the top of the thigh/belly. As long as a baby boy's testicles are located in the scrotum most of the time, the fact that they move around is normal.

Some boys have a buildup of fluid in a sac called a hydrocele (see page 546) inside the scrotum. This buildup will shrink gradually without treatment over several months as the fluid is reabsorbed by the body. If the scrotum swells up suddenly or gets larger when the baby cries, notify your pediatrician; this could be a sign of what is called an *inguinal* hernia, which requires treatment.

At birth, a baby boy's foreskin is attached to the head, or glans, of the penis, and it cannot be pushed back as it can in older boys and men. There is a small opening at the tip through which urine flows. If you have your son circumcised, the connections between the foreskin and the glans are artificially separated and the foreskin is removed, leaving the head of the penis visible. Without a circumcision, the foreskin will separate from the glans naturally during the first few years. (For a detailed description of circumcision, see *Should the Baby Be Circumcised?* on page 24.)

While you're still in the hospital, the staff will watch carefully for your baby's first urination and bowel movement to make sure he has no problem with-

Care of the Penis

Caring for the Circumcised Penis. If you chose to have your son circumcised, the procedure probably has been performed in the hospital on the second or third day after birth, but may be done after discharge during the first week of life (see *Should the Baby Be Circumcised?* on page 24). Ritual circumcisions for religious reasons are usually performed in the second week of life. Afterward, a light dressing such as gauze with petroleum jelly will have been placed over the head of the penis. The next time the baby urinates, this dressing usually will come off. Some pediatricians recommend keeping a clean dressing on until the penis is fully healed, while others advise leaving it off. The important thing is to keep the area as clean as possible. If particles of stool get on the penis, wipe it gently with soap and water during diaper changes.

The tip of the penis may look quite red for the first few days, and you may notice a yellow secretion. Both indicate that the area is healing normally. The redness and secretion should disappear gradually within a week. If the redness persists or there is swelling or crusted yellow sores that contain cloudy fluid, there may be an infection. This does not happen very often, but if you suspect that infection is present, consult your pediatrician.

Usually, after the circumcision has healed, the penis requires no additional care. Occasionally a small piece of the foreskin remains. You should pull back this skin gently each time the child is bathed. Examine the groove around the head of the penis and make sure it's clean.

If circumcision is not performed within the baby's first two weeks (perhaps for medical reasons), it is usually put off for several weeks or months. The follow-up care is the same whenever it is done. Should circumcision become necessary after the newborn period, general anesthesia is often used and requires a more formal surgical procedure necessitating control of bleeding and suturing of skin edges.

Caring for the Uncircumcised Penis. In the first few months, you should simply clean and bathe your baby's uncircumcised penis with soap and water, like the rest of the diaper area. Initially, the foreskin is connected by tissue to the glans, or head, of the penis, so you shouldn't try to retract it. No cleansing of the penis with cotton swabs or antiseptics is necessary, but you should watch your baby urinate occasionally to make sure that the hole in the foreskin is large enough to permit a normal stream. If the stream consistently is no more than a trickle, or if your baby seems to have some discomfort while urinating, consult your pediatrician.

The doctor will tell you when the foreskin has separated and can be retracted safely. This will not be for several months or years, and should never be forced; if you were to force the foreskin to retract before it is ready, you could cause painful bleeding and tears in the skin. After this separation occurs, retract the foreskin occasionally to gently cleanse the end of the penis underneath.

As your son gets older, you'll need to teach him what he must do in order to urinate and wash his penis. Teach him to clean his foreskin by:

- **Gently pulling it back away from the head of the penis.**

- **Rinsing the head of the penis and inside fold of the foreskin with soap and warm water.**

- **Pulling the foreskin back over the head of the penis.**

these important tasks. They may occur right after birth or up to a day later. The first bowel movement or two will be dark black-green and very slimy. It contains meconium, a substance that fills the infant's intestines before he is born. If meconium is not passed within the baby's first forty-eight hours, further evaluation is required to make sure that no problems exist in the lower bowel.

On occasion, newborns have a little blood in their bowel movements. Especially if it occurs during the first few days, it generally means that the infant swallowed some blood during birth or while breastfeeding. Both causes are harmless, but even so, let your pediatrician know about any signs of blood in order to make sure this is really the reason behind it, since there are other causes of blood in the stool that require further evaluation and treatment.

Your Baby's Birth Weight and Measurements

What makes a baby big or small? The following are some of the most common causes:

Large Babies: An infant can be born large when the parents are large or the mother is overweight. There is also a greater likelihood of a large newborn due to factors such as:

- The pregnancy lasting longer than forty-two weeks

- The fetus's growth overstimulated in the uterus

- Fetal chromosomal abnormalities

- Weight gain during pregnancy

- The mother's ethnicity

- The mother having diabetes before or during pregnancy

- The mother having given birth to other children

- Having a boy

Large infants may have metabolic abnormalities (such as low blood sugar and calcium), traumatic birth injuries, higher hemoglobin levels, jaundice, or various congenital abnormalities. Almost one-third of large babies initially have feeding difficulties. Your pediatrician will keep a close watch on these issues.

Small Babies: A baby may be born small for a number of reasons, including:

- Being born early (preterm)

- Being born to small parents

- The mother's ethnicity

- Fetal chromosomal abnormalities

- The mother's chronic diseases such as high blood pressure, or heart or kidney disease

- Malnutrition

- The mother's substance abuse during pregnancy

- The mother's alcohol use and smoking

A small baby may need to have his temperature, glucose, and hemoglobin level closely monitored. After birth, the pediatrician will thoroughly evaluate a small infant and decide when he is ready to go home.

To determine how your baby's measurements compare with those of other babies born after the same length of pregnancy, your pediatrician will refer to one of the growth charts (see Appendix).

The first two growth charts examine length and weight in boys and girls, from birth to thirty-six months. They are followed by body mass index for age charts for boys and girls, ages two to twenty years. (Body mass index, or BMI, is a measure of weight in relation to height.)

As illustrated in the first two charts, eighty out of every one hundred babies born at forty weeks of pregnancy, or full term, weigh between 5 pounds 11½ ounces (2.6 kg) and 8 pounds 5¾ ounces (3.8 kg). This is a healthy average. Those above the ninetieth percentile on the chart are considered large, and those below the tenth percentile are regarded as small. Keep in mind that these early weight designations (large or small) do not predict whether a child will be above or below average when he grows up, but they do help the hospital staff determine whether he needs extra attention during the first few days after birth.

At every physical exam, beginning with the first one after birth, the pediatrician will routinely measure the baby's length, weight, and head circumference (the distance around his head) and will plot them on growth charts similar to the ones in the Appendix. In a healthy, well-nourished infant, these three important measurements should increase at a predictable rate. Any interrup-

tion in this rate can help the doctor better detect and address any feeding, developmental, or medical issues.

How Your Newborn Behaves

Lying in your arms or in the crib beside you, your newborn makes a tight little bundle. Just as he did in the womb, he'll keep his arms and legs bent up close to his body and his fingers tightly clenched, although you should be able to straighten them gently with your hands. His feet will naturally curve inward. It may take several weeks for his body to unfold from this preferred fetal position.

You'll have to wait even longer for him to make the cooing or babbling sounds we generally think of as "baby talk." However, from the beginning he'll be very noisy. Besides crying when something is wrong, he'll have a wide variety of grunts, squeaks, sighs, sneezes, and hiccups. (You may even remember the hiccups from pregnancy!) Most of these sounds, just like his sudden movements, are reactions to disturbances around him; a shrill sound or a strong odor may be all it takes for him to jump or cry.

These reactions, as well as more subtle ones, are signs of how well your baby's senses are functioning at birth. After all those months in the womb, he'll quickly recognize his mother's voice (and possibly his father's, as well). If you play soothing music, he may become quiet as he listens or he'll move gently in time with it.

By using the senses of smell and taste, your newborn is able to distinguish breast milk from any other liquid. Born with a sweet tooth, he'll prefer sugar water to plain water and will wrinkle his nose at sour or bitter scents and tastes.

Your baby's vision will be best within an 8- to 12-inch (20.3–30.5 cm) range, which means he can see your face perfectly as you hold and feed him. But when you are farther away, his eyes may wander, giving him a cross-eyed appearance. During the first couple of months of his life, don't worry about this. As his eye muscles mature and his vision improves, both eyes will remain focused on the same thing at the same time. This usually occurs between two and three months of age. If it does not, bring it to the attention of your baby's pediatrician.

While your infant will be able to distinguish light from dark at birth, he will not yet see the full range of colors. While young infants who are shown a pattern of black and white or sharply contrasting colors may study them with interest, they are not likely to respond at all when shown a picture with lots of closely related colors.

Perhaps the newborn's most important sense is touch. After months of being bathed in warm fluid in the womb, your baby will now be exposed to all sorts of new sensations—some harsh, some wonderfully comforting. While he may cringe at a sudden gust of cold air, he'll love the feel of a soft blanket and the warmth of your arms around him. Holding your baby will give him as much pleasure as it does you. It will give him a sense of security and comfort, and it will tell him he is loved. Research shows that close emotional bonding actually will promote his growth and development.

Going Home

Most hospitals will discharge you and your baby within forty-eight hours if you have delivered vaginally. However, if you undergo a Cesarean section, you may stay at the facility for four to five days. If your baby is born in an alternative birthing center, you may be able to go home within twenty-four hours. Nevertheless, just because a full-term, healthy infant *could* be discharged from the hospital in less than forty-eight hours doesn't mean it should necessarily occur. The American Academy of Pediatrics believes that the health and well-being of the mother and her child are paramount. Since every child is different, the decision to discharge a newborn should be made on a case-by-case basis. If a newborn does leave the hospital early, he or she should be seen by a doctor twenty-four to forty-eight hours after discharge.

Prior to making the decision about when to go home, you and your doctor need to weigh the advantages and disadvantages carefully. From an emotional and physical standpoint, there are arguments for both a short (one to two days) and a longer (three-plus days) stay. Some women simply dislike being in the hospital and feel more comfortable and relaxed at home; as soon as they and their baby are proclaimed healthy and able to travel, they're eager to leave. By keeping the hospital stay short, they'll certainly save themselves—or their insurance company—money. However, many new mothers often cannot get as much rest at home as in the hospital—especially if there are older children clamoring for attention. Nor are they likely to have access to the valuable support that trained nurses can offer in the hospital during the first days of breastfeeding and baby care.

If a newborn does leave the hospital early, he should have received all the appropriate newborn tests such as a hearing screen (see *Newborn Screening Tests,* page 56), and he also should be seen by the pediatrician twenty-four to forty-eight hours *after* discharge. Of course, the doctor should be called immediately whenever a newborn appears listless or is feverish, is vomiting, has difficulty feeding, or develops a yellow color to his skin (jaundice).

Before you do leave the hospital, your home and car should be equipped with at least the bare essentials. Make sure you have a federally approved car safety seat that is appropriate for your baby's size, and that you have correctly installed rear-facing in the backseat of your vehicle. It is extremely important to follow the car seat manufacturer's instructions on installation and proper use carefully, and if possible, it is helpful to get your car seat installation checked by a certified child passenger safety technician to ensure that you've gotten it right. (For more information on the choice and proper use of car safety seats, see pages 492–499.)

At home you'll need a safe place for the baby to sleep, plenty of diapers, and enough clothing and blankets to keep him warm and protected.

WHERE WE STAND

THE TIMING OF newborn discharge from the hospital should be a mutual decision between the parents and the physician caring for the infant. The American Academy of Pediatrics believes that the health and well-being of the mother and her baby should take precedence over financial considerations. Academy policy has established minimum criteria for early discharge of a mother and her baby, which include term delivery, appropriate growth, and normal physical examination, and states that it is unlikely that all of its criteria can be met in less than forty-eight hours. The Academy supports state and federal legislation based on AAP guidelines as long as physicians, in consultation with parents, have the final authority in determining when to discharge the patient.

Parenting Issues

Mother's Feelings

If you find your first few days with your baby to be a mixture of delight, pain, utter exhaustion, and—especially if this is your first child—some apprehension about your capabilities as a parent—take comfort in knowing you are not alone.

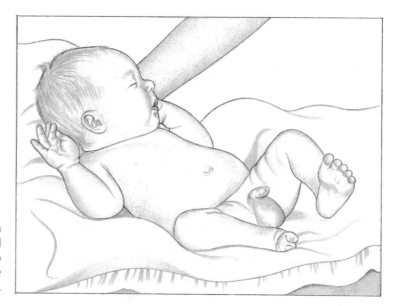

You have just given birth to a wonderful new being, but also to a new awesome responsibility.

If you're like many other women, you're so excited about your new arrival that you may not even notice how tired and sore you are. In spite of the fatigue, it still may be difficult to relax enough to fall asleep. Your own rooming-in arrangements may add to the problem; however, if you imagine that every crying baby you hear is your own, having your baby sleep in the nursery may not give you the peace you thought it would. You can solve these problems by letting him sleep in his hospital-supplied bassinet next to you, so you can sleep when he does and hold him when he awakens.

On the other hand, particularly if you had a long, hard labor or a Cesarean section, you simply may not have the strength to keep the baby with you full-time, and that's understandable. After having a C-section, you may initially find it painful to lift your baby and are likely to find it more comfortable to try positions for both holding and nursing him that put less strain on your stitches. These obstacles may make you feel that you're not bonding with your baby as you imagined you would, and you may feel especially disappointed if you had planned for a problem-free, natural delivery. Fortunately, your child's major preoccupation during these first few days also will be sleeping and recuperating, and he won't much care where he does it as long as he's warm, dry, and fed when he's hungry. So for the moment, the hospital nursery will suit him fine. You will have plenty of time to form a secure bond with each other after your physical recoveries are complete.

In general, instead of worrying while in the hospital, it is best to take advantage of your time in the hospital to rest, learn from the trained professionals around you, and let your body recover. If and when your anxiety levels peak, it can admittedly be difficult to believe that you'll ever be an expert on baby care. But rest assured. Once new parents have had a few days to get used to routine baby care and get home, things start to fall into place for most of them. If they don't, be sure to enlist the help of your pediatrician, friends, and family. (For more information about postpartum blues and depression, see the description on pages 147–148.)

If this is not your first child, there may be some questions on your mind, such as:

■ **Will this new baby come between you and an older child?**

This needn't happen, especially if you make a point of including your older child(ren) in your new routine. Toddlers are usually quite happy to go retrieve a clean diaper, and older children often take great pride in being put in charge of checking for hazards (e.g., stray toys) and making sure that all visitors wash their hands before touching the new baby. As you become more comfortable with your daily routine, be sure to include special times with your older child.

■ **Will you be able to give the same intensity of love to the new child?**

In fact, each child is special and will draw out different responses and feelings from you. Even the birth order of your children may influence the way you relate to each of them. It is often helpful to keep in mind that "new" isn't "better" or "worse," but usually just . . . different. This concept is an important one for both you and your child(ren) to remember.

■ **How can you avoid comparing one to another?**

It's only natural to compare. You may even find yourself thinking that the new baby is not as beautiful or as alert as another child was right after birth, or you may worry because he's more attractive and attentive. In the beginning, these comparisons are inevitable, but as the new baby's own unique qualities begin to emerge, you'll become as proud of your children's differences as you are of their similarities.

On a more practical note, the prospect of taking care of two or more young children may worry you. This only makes sense, but as greater time demands and fears of sibling rivalry loom before you, don't let yourself get overwhelmed. Given time and patience, all of you will adjust and learn to be a family.

If the newness, fatigue, and seemingly unanswerable questions push you to tears, don't feel bad. You won't be the first new mother to cry—or the last. The hormonal changes you went through as an adolescent or experienced during your menstrual cycles are minor compared to the hormonal shifts associated with giving birth. So blame it on the hormones!

In addition to the hormonal effects, significant emotional changes are taking place. You have just given birth not only to a wonderful new human being, but also to a new and awesome responsibility. There are sure to be significant changes taking place in your family life. It is normal to think about these things and easy to attach too much importance to them.

The emotional changes of this time can sometimes lead mothers to feel sadness, fear, irritability, or anxiety—or even anger toward their baby—feelings doctors call the postpartum blues or baby blues. About three out of four new mothers experience these baby blues a few days after birth. Fortunately, these feelings tend to subside on their own as quickly as they develop, typically lasting no more than several days.

Some new mothers, however, have such severe feelings of sadness, emptiness, apathy, and even despair that doctors categorize them as having *postpartum depression*. They also may experience feelings of inadequacy, and they may begin to withdraw from family and friends. These feelings may develop a few weeks after the baby is born and affect about one out of ten new mothers. The symptoms can last for many months (or even for more than a year), worsen with time, and become so intense that these mothers may feel helpless and incapable of caring for their baby and their other children. If they don't receive care for their postpartum depression, the condition may worsen with time, and in some cases they may worry about harming themselves or their baby.

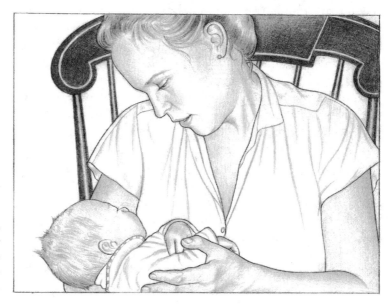

Do not be afraid to ask for help if your concerns seem too great for you to handle.

You should discuss your feelings with the baby's father, your extended family, and close friends. Allow them to give you brief breaks from being the primary caregiver, and try to reduce your stress and anxiety by getting some exercise and as much rest as possible. If this doesn't help and these feelings are severe and haven't subsided in about two weeks, talk to your obstetrician or pediatrician, or seek help from a mental health professional; counseling and/or antidepressant medications may be recommended (check in with your pediatrician if you're breastfeeding). Do not be afraid to ask for help from professionals if your concerns seem too great for you to handle, or if you feel increasingly depressed. Although a certain amount of post-delivery depression may be normal, it should not be overwhelming or last more than a few days.

Father's Feelings

As a new dad, your new role is no less complicated than the mother's. No, you didn't have to carry the baby for nine months, but you did have to make adjustments physically and emotionally as the due date approached and the preparations for the baby became all-important. On one hand, you may have felt as if you had nothing to do with this birth; but on the other, this is very much your baby, too.

When the baby finally arrived, you may have been tremendously relieved as well as excited and somewhat awed. In witnessing your baby's birth, feelings of commitment and love may have surfaced that you had worried you might never feel for this child. You also may have experienced a greater admiration and love for your wife than you ever felt before. At the same time, contemplating the responsibility of caring for this child for the next twenty years may have been more than a little unnerving.

Depending on the hospital and your own schedule, you may have been able to room in with mother and/or child until it was time to take the baby home. This helps you feel less like a bystander and more like a key participant, allowing you to get to know your baby right from the start. It also allows you to share an intense emotional experience with Mom.

If you continue to feel conflicting emotions, how should you deal with them? The best approach is to become as actively involved in fathering as possible. Once the entire family is home, you can—and should—help feed (if bottle-fed), diaper, bathe, and comfort your baby. Contrary to old-fashioned stereotypes, these jobs are not exclusively "woman's work." They are the best way for you to bond with your child, and they are wonderful opportunities for the entire family—mother, father, and even older siblings—to get to know, love, and welcome this new member home.

Sibling's Feelings

Older children may greet a new baby with either open arms or closed minds. Their reaction will depend largely on their age and developmental level. Consider a toddler, for instance. There's little you can do to prepare him in advance for the changes that will come with a new sibling. To begin with, he may have been confused by the sudden disappearance of his parents when the baby was born. Upon visiting the hospital, he may have been frightened by the sight of his mother in bed, perhaps attached to intravenous tubing.

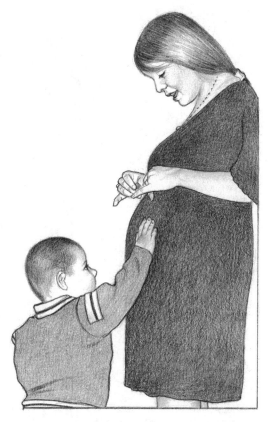

He also may be jealous that his parents are holding someone else instead of him, and he may misbehave or begin acting younger—for example, by insisting on wearing diapers or suddenly having accidents several months after being toilet trained. These are normal responses to stress and change, and don't deserve discipline. Instead of punishing him or insisting that he share your love for the new baby, give him extra love and reassurance. Also, try very hard to catch him "being good," so he'll get lots of attention for appropriate behaviors. Praise him for acting "like the big brother," letting him know that he, too, has an important new role to play. Tell him that there's plenty of room in your heart to love both him and the new baby. Over time, his attachment to the baby will build, gradually and naturally.

If your older child is a preschooler, he'll be better able to understand what's happening. If you prepared him during the pregnancy, you may have helped ease his confusion, if not his jealousy. He would have been able to understand the basic facts of the situation ("The baby is in Mommy's tummy"; "The baby will sleep in your old crib"), and he probably became very curious about this mysterious person.

If your older child is of school age, he'll still need to adapt to a new role. At the same time, he was probably fascinated by the process of pregnancy and childbirth and eager to meet the new baby. Once the infant arrived, he may have become very proud and protective. Let him help take care of the little one at times, but don't forget that he still needs time and attention himself.

Let the older siblings know frequently that there's enough room and love in your heart for both children.

(If you're the grandparent of a newborn, see pages 189–192 for some thoughts about your new role now that your new grandson or granddaughter has arrived.)

Health Watch

Some physical conditions are especially common during the first couple of weeks after birth. If you notice any of the following in your baby, contact your pediatrician.

ABDOMINAL DISTENSION. Most babies' bellies normally stick out, especially after a large feeding. Between feedings, however, they should feel quite soft. If your child's abdomen feels swollen and hard, and if he has not had a bowel movement for more than one or two days or is vomiting, call your pediatrician. Most likely the problem is due to gas or constipation, but it also could signal a more serious intestinal problem.

BIRTH INJURIES. It is possible for babies to be injured during birth, especially if labor is particularly long or difficult, or when babies are very large. While newborns recover quickly from some of these injuries, others persist longer term. Quite often the injury is a broken collarbone, which will heal quickly if the arm on that side is kept relatively motionless. Incidentally, after a few weeks a small lump may form at the site of the fracture, but don't be alarmed; this is a positive sign that new bone is forming to mend the injury.

Muscle weakness is another common birth injury, caused during labor by pressure or stretching of the nerves attached to the muscles. These muscles, usually weakened on one side of the face or one shoulder or arm, generally return to normal after several weeks. In the meantime, ask your pediatrician to show you how to nurse and hold the baby to promote healing.

BLUE BABY. Babies may have mildly blue hands and feet, but this may not be a cause for concern. If their hands and feet turn a bit blue from cold, they should return to pink as soon as they are warm. Occasionally, the face, tongue, and lips may turn a little blue when the newborn is crying hard, but once he becomes calm, his color in these parts of the body should quickly return to normal. However, persistently blue skin coloring, especially with breathing difficulties and feeding difficulties, is a sign that the heart or lungs are not operating properly, and the baby is not getting enough oxygen in the blood. Immediate medical attention is essential.

COUGHING. If the baby drinks very fast or tries to drink water for the first time, he may cough and sputter a bit; but this type of coughing should stop as soon as he adjusts to a familiar feeding routine. This may also be related to how strong or fast a breastfeeding mom's milk comes down. If he coughs persistently or routinely gags during feedings, consult the pediatrician. These symptoms could indicate an underlying problem in the lungs or digestive tract.

EXCESSIVE CRYING. All newborns cry, often for no apparent reason. If you've made sure that your baby is fed, burped, warm, and dressed in a clean diaper, the best tactic is probably to hold him and talk or sing to him until he stops. You cannot "spoil" a baby this age by giving him too much attention. If this doesn't work, wrap him snugly in a blanket or try some of the approaches listed on pages 167–168.

You'll become accustomed to your baby's normal pattern of crying. If it ever sounds peculiar—for example, like shrieks of pain—or if it persists for an unusual length of time, it could mean a medical problem. Call the pediatrician and ask for advice.

FORCEPS MARKS. When forceps are used to help during a delivery, they can leave red marks or even superficial scrapes on a newborn's face and head where the metal pressed against the skin. These generally disappear within a few days. Sometimes a firm, flat lump develops in one of these areas because of minor damage to the tissue under the skin, but this, too, usually will go away within two months.

JAUNDICE. Many normal, healthy newborns have a yellowish tinge to their skin, which is known as jaundice. It is caused by a buildup of a chemical

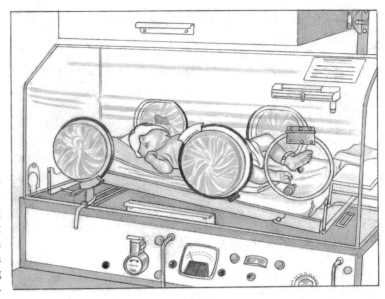

Phototherapy—or light treatment—can be delivered through different light sources or by a blanket that has a special lighting source.

called bilirubin in the child's blood. This occurs most often when the immature liver has not yet begun to efficiently do its job of removing bilirubin from the bloodstream (bilirubin is formed from the body's normal breakdown of red blood cells). While babies often have a mild case of jaundice, which is harmless, it can become a serious condition when bilirubin reaches what the pediatrician considers to be a very high level. Although jaundice is quite treatable, if the bilirubin level is very high and is not treated effectively, it can even lead to nervous system or brain damage in some cases, which is why the condition must be checked for and appropriately treated. Jaundice tends to be more common in newborns who are breastfeeding, most often in those who are not nursing well; breastfeeding mothers should nurse at least eight to twelve times per day, which will help produce enough milk and help keep bilirubin levels low.

Jaundice appears first on the face, then on the chest and abdomen, and finally on the arms and legs in some instances. The whites of the eyes may also be yellow. The pediatrician will examine the baby for jaundice, and if she suspects that it may be present—based not only on the amount of yellow in the skin, but also on the baby's age and other factors—she may order a skin or blood test to definitively diagnose the condition. If jaundice develops before the baby is twenty-four hours old, a bilirubin test is *always* needed to make an accurate diagnosis. At three to five days old, newborns should be checked by a doctor or nurse, since this is the time when the bilirubin level is highest; for that reason, if an infant is discharged before he is seventy-two hours old, he should be seen by the pediatrician within two days of that discharge. Some newborns need to be seen even sooner, including:

- Those with a high bilirubin level before leaving the hospital

- Those born early (more than two weeks before the due date)

- Those whose jaundice is present in the first twenty-four hours after birth

- Those who are not breastfeeding well

- Those with considerable bruising and bleeding under the scalp, associated with labor and delivery

- Those who have a parent or sibling who had high bilirubin levels and underwent treatment for it

When the doctor determines that jaundice is present and needs to be treated, the bilirubin level can be reduced by placing the infant under special lights when he is undressed—either in the hospital or at home. His eyes will be covered to protect them during the light therapy. This kind of treatment can prevent the harmful effects of jaundice. In infants who are breastfed, jaundice may last for more than two to three weeks; in those who are formula-fed, most cases of jaundice go away by two weeks of age.

LETHARGY AND SLEEPINESS. Every newborn spends most of his time sleeping. As long as he wakes up every few hours, eats well, seems content, and is alert part of the day, it's perfectly normal for him to sleep the rest of the time. But if he's rarely alert, does not wake up on his own for feedings, or seems too tired or uninterested to eat, you should consult your pediatrician. This lethargy—especially if it's a sudden change in his usual pattern—may be a symptom of a serious illness.

RESPIRATORY DISTRESS. It may take your baby a few hours after birth to form a normal pattern of breathing, but then he should have no further difficulties. If he seems to be breathing in an unusual manner, it is most often from blockage of the nasal passages. The use of saline nasal drops, followed by the use of a bulb syringe, are what may be needed to fix the problem; both are available over the counter at all pharmacies.

However, if your newborn shows any of the following warning signs, notify your pediatrician immediately:

- Fast breathing (more than sixty breaths in one minute), although keep in mind that babies normally breathe more rapidly than adults

- Retractions (sucking in the muscles between the ribs with each breath, so that her ribs stick out)

- Flaring of her nose

- Grunting while breathing

- Persistent blue skin coloring

UMBILICAL CORD. You'll need to keep the stump of the umbilical cord clean and dry as it shrivels and eventually falls off. To keep the cord dry, sponge bathe your baby rather than submersing him in a tub of water. Also keep the diaper folded below the cord to keep urine from soaking it. You may notice a few drops of blood on the diaper around the time the stump falls off; this is normal. But if the cord does actively bleed, call your baby's doctor immediately. If the stump becomes infected, however, it will require medical treatment. Although an infection is quite uncommon, contact your doctor if any of these signs is present:

- Foul-smelling yellowish discharge from the cord

- Red skin around the base of the cord

- Crying when you touch the cord or the skin next to it

The umbilical cord stump should dry up and fall off by the time your baby is eight weeks old. If it remains beyond that time, there may be other issues at play. See the baby's doctor if the cord has not dried up and fallen off by the time the baby is two months old.

UMBILICAL GRANULOMA. Sometimes instead of completely drying, the cord will form a granuloma or a small reddened mass of scar tissue that stays on the belly button after the umbilical cord has fallen off. This granuloma will drain a light-yellowish fluid. This condition will usually go away in about a week, but if not, your pediatrician may need to burn off (cauterize) the granulomatous tissue.

UMBILICAL HERNIA. If your baby's umbilical cord area seems to push outward when he cries, he may have an umbilical hernia—a small hole in the muscular part of the abdominal wall that allows tissue to bulge out when there's pressure inside the abdomen (e.g., when the baby cries). This is not a serious condition, and it usually heals by itself in the first twelve to eighteen months. (For unknown reasons it takes longer to heal in African American babies.) In the unlikely event that it doesn't heal, the hole may need to be surgically closed. Taping this area or putting a "taped coin" over this area may be harmful.

Your Newborn's First Physical Exams

Your baby should have one thorough physical examination within his first twenty-four hours and a follow-up at some point before you and the baby leave the hospital. If you take your baby home early (less than twenty-four hours after delivery), your pediatrician should see the baby again in her office twenty-four to forty-eight hours after discharge for follow-up. The purpose of this visit is to assess your baby's general health, such as weight; discuss important topics such as your baby's stool and urine patterns, and sleep habits; review feeding techniques, including those associated with breastfeeding (adequate position, latch-on, and swallowing); and evaluate for jaundice, besides identifying any new questions or concerns you may have. The American Academy of Pediatrics also recommends that you and your baby schedule a doctor's visit when he's age two to four weeks. As we described in Chapter 3 on pages 79–81, your doctor will physically examine your baby and take measurements such as his length, weight, and head circumference. She'll listen to your baby's heart and lungs to ensure that they are normal; look into his eyes, ears, and mouth; feel his abdomen for tenderness; evaluate how his belly button is healing and check a baby boy's circumcision; check his reflexes; and examine other parts of the body from head to toe, including the hips. If there is a persistent "clunking" sound of the hip, especially in a girl born breech, your pediatrician may request that an orthopedist do an ultrasound and/or a repeat physical exam at four to eight weeks of age.

These early visits to the pediatrician are also opportunities to ask questions about baby care and relieve any worries you may have. Don't hesitate to ask questions; the goal is for you to get valuable information and leave confident and reassured.

~ 6 ~

The First Month

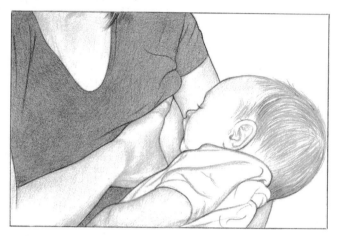

Growth and Development

IN THE VERY beginning, it may seem that your baby does nothing but eat, sleep, cry, and fill her diapers. By the end of the first month, she'll be much more alert and responsive. Gradually she'll begin moving her body more smoothly and with much greater coordination—especially in getting her hand to her mouth. You'll realize that she listens when you speak, watches you as you hold her, and occasionally moves her own body to respond to you or attract your attention. But before we explore her expanding capabilities, let's look at the changes in her physical appearance during the first month.

Physical Appearance and Growth

When your baby was born, her birth weight included excess body fluid, which she lost during her first few days. Most babies lose about one-tenth of their birth weight during the first five days, then regain it over the next five, so that by about day ten they usually are back to their original birth weight. You can plot your own infant's growth on the charts in the Appendix.

Most babies grow very rapidly after regaining their birth weight, especially during growth spurts, which occur around seven to ten days and again between three and six weeks. The average newborn gains weight at a rate of ⅔ of an ounce (20–30 g) per day and by one month weighs about 10 pounds (4.5 kg). She grows between 1½ and 2 inches (4.5–5 cm) during this month. Boys tend to weigh slightly more than girls (by less than 1 lb., or approximately 350 g). They also tend to be slightly longer than girls at this age (by about ½ in., or 1.25 cm).

Your pediatrician will pay particular attention to your child's head growth, because it reflects the growth of her brain. The bones in your baby's skull are still growing together, and the skull is growing faster during the first four months than at any other time in her life. The average newborn's head circumference measures about 13¾ inches (35 cm), growing to about 15 inches (38 cm) by one month. Because boys tend to be slightly larger than girls, their heads are larger, though the average difference is less than ½ inch (1 cm).

During these first weeks your baby's body gradually will straighten from the tightly curled position she held inside the uterus during the final months of pregnancy. She'll begin to stretch her arms and legs and may arch her back from time to time. Her legs and feet may continue to rotate inward, giving her a bowlegged look. This condition usually will correct itself gradually over the first year of life. If the bowlegged appearance is particularly severe or associated with pronounced curving of the front part of the foot, your pediatrician may suggest a splint or a cast to correct it, but in most instances these circumstances are extremely unusual. (See *Bowlegs and Knock-Knees,* page 823; *Pigeon Toes [Intoeing],* page 828.)

If your baby was born vaginally and her skull appeared misshapen at birth, it soon should resume its normal shape. Any bruising of the scalp or swelling of the eyelids that occurred during birth will be gone by the end of the first week or two. Any red spots in the eyes will disappear in about three weeks.

To your dismay, you may discover that the fine hair that covered your child's head when she was born soon begins falling out. If she rubs the back of her head on her sleep surface, she may develop a temporary bald spot there, even if the rest of her hair remains. This loss is not medically significant. The bare spots will be covered with new hair in a few months.

Another normal development is baby acne—pimples that break out on the face, usually during the fourth or fifth week of life. They are thought to be due to stimulation of oil glands in the skin by hormones passed across the placenta during pregnancy. This condition may be made worse if the baby lies in sheets laundered in harsh detergents or soiled by milk that she's spit up. If your baby does have baby acne, place a soft, clean receiving blanket under her head while she's awake and wash her face gently once a day with a mild baby soap to remove milk or detergent residue.

Your newborn's skin also may look blotchy, ranging in color from pink to blue. Her hands and feet in particular may be colder and bluer than the rest of her body. The blood vessels leading to these areas are more sensitive to temperature changes and tend to shrink in response to cold. As a result, less blood gets to the exposed skin, causing it to look pale or bluish. If you move her arms and legs, however, you should notice that they quickly turn pink again.

Your baby's internal "thermostat," which causes her to sweat when she's too hot or shiver when she's too cold, won't be working properly for some time. Also, in these early weeks, she'll lack the insulating layer of fat that will protect her from sudden temperature shifts later on. For these reasons, it's important for you to dress her properly—warmly in cool weather and lightly when it's hot. A general rule of thumb is to dress her in one more layer of clothing than you would wear in the same weather conditions. Don't automatically bundle her up just because she's a baby.

Between ten days and three weeks after birth, the stump from the umbilical cord should have dried and fallen off, leaving behind a clean, well-healed area. Occasionally a raw spot is left after the stump is gone. It may even ooze a little blood-tinged fluid. Just keep it dry and clean (using a cotton ball dipped in rubbing alcohol) and it will heal by itself. If it is not completely healed and dry in two weeks, consult your pediatrician.

Reflexes

Much of your baby's activity in her first weeks of life is reflexive. For instance, when you put your finger in her mouth, she doesn't think about what to do, but sucks by reflex. When confronted by a bright light, she will tightly shut her eyes, because that's what her reflexes make her do. She's born with many of these automatic responses, some of which remain with her for months, while others vanish in weeks.

In some cases, reflexes change into voluntary behavior. For example, your baby is born with a "rooting" reflex that prompts her to turn her head toward your hand if you stroke her cheek or mouth. This helps her find the nipple at feeding time. At first she'll root from side to side, turning her head toward the nipple and then away in decreasing arcs. But by about three weeks she'll simply turn her head and move her mouth into position to suck.

Sucking is another survival reflex present even before birth. If you had an ultrasound test done during pregnancy, you may have seen your baby sucking her thumb. After birth, when a nipple is placed in your baby's mouth and touches the roof of her mouth, she automatically begins to suck. This motion actually takes place in two stages: First, she places her lips around the areola (the circular area of pigmented skin surrounding the nipple) and squeezes the nipple between her tongue and palate. (Called "expression," this action forces out the milk.) Then comes the second phase, or the milking action, in which the tongue moves from the areola to the nipple. This whole process is helped by the negative pressure, or suction, that secures the breast in the baby's mouth.

Coordinating these rhythmic sucking movements with breathing and swallowing is a relatively complicated task for a newborn. So even though this is a reflexive action, not all babies suck efficiently at first. With practice, however, the reflex becomes a skill that they all manage well.

As rooting, sucking, and bringing her hand to her mouth become less reflexive and more directed, your infant will start to use these movements to console herself. She also may be comforted when you give her a pacifier or when you help her find her thumb or her fingers.

Another, more dramatic reflex during these first few weeks is called the Moro reflex. If your baby's head shifts positions abruptly or falls backward, or she is startled by something loud or abrupt, she will react by throwing out her arms and legs and extending her neck, then rapidly bringing her arms together and she may cry loudly. The Moro reflex, which may be present in varying

Moro reflex

degrees in different babies, peaks during the first month and then disappears after two months.

One of the more interesting automatic responses is the tonic neck reflex, otherwise known as the fencing posture. You may notice that when your baby's head turns to one side, her arm on that side will straighten, with the opposite

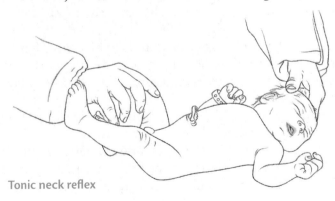

Tonic neck reflex

Newborn Reflexes

The following are some of the normal inborn reflexes you will see your baby perform during her first weeks. Not all infants acquire and lose these reflexes at exactly the same time, but this table will give you a general idea of what to expect.

Reflex	Age When Reflex Appears	Age When Reflex Disappears
Moro reflex	Birth	2 months
Walking/stepping	Birth	2 months
Rooting	Birth	4 months
Tonic neck reflex	Birth	5–7 months
Palmar grasp	Birth	5–6 months
Plantar grasp	Birth	9–12 months

arm bent as if she's fencing. Do not be surprised if you don't see this response, however. It is subtle, and if your baby is disturbed or crying, she may not perform it. It disappears at five to seven months of age.

You'll see still another reflex when you stroke the palm of your baby's hand and watch her immediately grip your finger. Or stroke the sole of her foot, and watch it flex as the toes curl tightly. In the first few days after birth, your baby's grasp will be so strong that it may seem she can hold her own weight—but don't try it. She has no control over this response and may let go suddenly.

Aside from her strength, your baby's other special talent is stepping. She can't support her own weight, of course, but if you hold her under the arms (being careful to support her head, as well) and let her soles touch a flat surface, she'll place one foot in front of the other and "walk." This reflex will disappear after two months, then recur as the learned voluntary behavior of walking toward the end of the first year.

Although you may think of babies as utterly defenseless, they actually have several protective reflexes. For instance, if an object comes straight toward her, she'll turn her head and try to squirm out of its way. (Amazingly, if the object is on a path that would make it a near miss instead of a collision, she will calmly watch it approach without flinching.) Yes, she's very dependent on her mother and father at this age, but she's not totally defenseless.

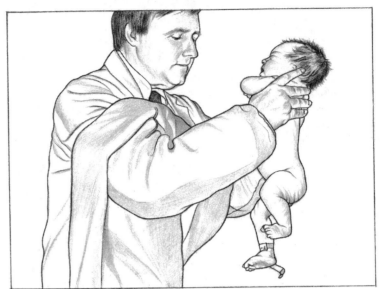

Walking/stepping reflex

Early Brain Development

As a parent, you know that your actions affect your child. You laugh, she laughs. You frown at her misbehavior, she saddens. At six to eight weeks of age, she begins demonstrating social smiles. You are at the center of your child's universe, and as your connection and bond with her intensify, her language and even the effects of discipline increase.

Research shows that during the first three years of a baby's life, the brain grows and develops significantly and patterns of thinking and responding are established. What does this mean for you as a parent? It means that you have a very special opportunity to help your baby develop appropriately and thrive socially, physically, and cognitively throughout her life. The first years last forever.

For years, people have mistakenly believed that the baby's brain is an exact replica of the genetic codes of her parents. For example, if the mother is a good artist, then the baby has more potential to possess the same artistic skills when she grows up. While genetics does play a role in determining your child's skills and abilities, new research highlights the equally significant role that environment plays. Recently, neuroscientists realized that the experiences that fill a baby's first days, months, and years have a great impact on how the brain develops. Both nature and nurture work hand in hand in the development of young children.

Studies have shown that children need certain elements in the early stages of life to grow and develop to their full potential:

- A child needs to feel special, loved, and valued.

- She needs to feel safe.

- She needs to feel confident about what to expect from her environment.

- She needs guidance.

- She needs a balanced experience of freedom and limits.

- She needs to be exposed to a diverse environment filled with language, play, exploration, books, music, and appropriate toys.

While it may seem that what goes on in a baby's brain would be relatively simple compared to an adult's, in fact, a baby's brain is twice as active as an adult's brain. Seven hundred new connections or synapses form every second. Neuroscientists are focusing especially on the first three years of a baby's life because they have identified these as times of special importance. During these years, the human brain has the greatest potential for learning. Not only is learning occurring rapidly, but basic ways of thinking, responding, and solving problems are established. For example, notice how easy it is for a child to pick up words from a foreign language. How difficult is that same task for an adult?

What does this mean for you as a parent? It means that you and the environment that you create for your baby will influence the way she deals with her emotions, the way she interacts with people, the way she thinks, and the way she grows physically. By creating an appropriate environment for your child, you are allowing normal brain development to take place. You may wonder what is considered an "appropriate" environment. It's one that is "child-centered" and provides opportunities for learning that are geared to your child's development, interests, and personality. Fortunately, the components of a good environment include basic things that many parents want to provide for their children: proper nutrition; a warm, responsive, and loving family as well as other providers; fun playtime; consistent positive reinforcement; engaging conversation; good books to read and to listen to; music to stimulate brain activities; and the freedom to explore and learn from their surroundings.

Review the following elements of children's health and how each one contributes to a child's brain development:

- *Language.* Direct face-to-face communication between parents and other caregivers and their young children supports language development, as does reading to them beginning in early infancy.

- *Early identification of developmental problems.* Many developmental and medical problems can be treated if detected early. Children with disabilities and other special health care needs also can greatly benefit from close monitoring of early brain development.

- *Positive parenting.* Raising a child in a loving, supportive, and respectful environment enhances self-esteem and self-confidence, and has a great impact on the child's development. Your parental nurturing and your responsiveness to your infant will play a critical role in shaping your baby's future.

- *Stimulating environment.* Exploring and problem solving in a variety of safe places promotes learning.

More and more behavioral researchers are discovering how much the environment plays a role in shaping a baby's life. This new science helps us understand exactly how significant our role is in the development of the child's brain.

To build a positive environment for your baby in your home and in your community, follow these suggestions:

- **Get good prenatal care.** Since brain development begins in the womb, good prenatal care can help ensure the healthy development of your child's brain. Start prenatal care early, see your doctor regularly, and be sure to follow her instructions. Eating a balanced, healthy diet, taking prenatal vitamins, and avoiding drugs, alcohol, and tobacco are just a few steps you can take to contribute to your child's future health.

- **Try to create a "village" around you.** Since it's hard to raise a child on your own, seek support from your family, friends, and community. Talk to your pediatrician about parent-support groups and activities.

- **Interact with your child as much as possible.** Talk with your child, read, listen to music, draw pictures, and play together. These kinds of activities allow you to spend time focused on your child's thoughts and interests. This, in turn, can make your child feel special and important.

You also can teach the language of communication that your child will use to form healthy relationships over a lifetime.

- **Give your child plenty of love and attention.** A warm and loving environment helps children feel safe, competent, and cared for, as well as helping them feel concern for others. Such attention cannot "spoil" a child.

- **Provide consistent guidelines.** Be sure you and other care providers are working with the same routines. Also, be sure your own guidelines are consistent while taking into account your child's growing competency. Consistency helps children feel confident about what to expect from their environment.

States of Consciousness

As you get to know your baby, you'll soon realize that there are times when she's very alert and active, times when she's watchful but rather passive, and times when she's tired and irritable. You may even try to schedule your daily activities to capitalize on her "up" times and avoid overextending her during the "down" periods. Don't count on this schedule, however. These so-called states of consciousness will change dramatically in this first month.

There are actually six states of consciousness through which your baby cycles several times a day. Two are sleep states; the others are waking states.

State 1 is deep sleep, when the baby lies quietly without moving and is relatively unresponsive. If you shake a rattle loudly in her ear, she may stir a little, but not much. During lighter, more active sleep (State 2), the same noise will startle her and may awaken her. During this light sleep, you also can see the rapid movements of her eyes beneath her closed eyelids. She will alternate between these two sleep states, cycling through both of them within a given hour. Sometimes she'll retreat into these sleep states when she's overstimulated, as well as when she's physically tired.

As your baby wakes up or starts to fall asleep, she'll go through State 3. Her eyes will roll back under drooping eyelids and she may stretch, yawn, or jerk her arms and legs. Once awake, she'll move into one of the three remaining states. She may be wide awake, happy, and alert but relatively motionless (State 4). Or she may be alert, happy, and very active (State 5). Or she may cry and flail about (State 6).

If you shake a rattle by your baby's ear when she's happy and alert (States 4 and 5), she'll probably become quiet and turn her face to look for the source

Your Baby's States of Consciousness

State	Description	What Your Baby Does
State 1	Deep sleep	Lies quietly without moving
State 2	Light sleep	Moves while sleeping; startles at noises
State 3	Drowsiness	Eyes start to close; may doze
State 4	Quiet alert	Eyes open wide; face is bright; body is quiet
State 5	Active alert	Face and body move actively
State 6	Crying	Cries, perhaps screams; body moves in very disorganized ways

of this strange sound. This is the time when she'll appear most responsive to you and the activity around her, and be most attentive and involved in play.

In general, it's a mistake to expect much attention from a baby who is crying. At these times, she's not receptive to new information or sensations; what she wants instead is to be comforted. The same rattle that enchanted her when she was happy five minutes earlier will only irritate her and make her more upset when she's crying. As she gets older, sometimes you may be able to distract her with an attractive object or sound so that she stops crying, but at this young age, the best way to comfort her usually is to pick her up and hold her. (See *Responding to Your Baby's Cries,* page 58.)

As your baby's nervous system becomes more developed, she'll begin to settle into a pattern of crying, sleeping, eating, and playing that matches your own daily schedule. She still may need to eat every three to four hours, but by the end of the month she'll be awake for longer periods during the day and be more alert and responsive at those times.

Crying and Colic

Beginning at about two weeks of age, normal infants cry. Some parents hesitate to pick up a crying baby, often on the belief that they'll spoil the infant. But babies can't be spoiled, and their needs should be met as best as you can.

There are great variations in the crying patterns and temperaments of babies. Sometimes babies just cry for no apparent reason, and it can be difficult to figure out what's behind the tears. But as the crying persists, parents can understandably become upset and stressed out.

Does your infant have a regular fussy period each day when it seems you can do nothing to comfort her? In fact, this is quite common, particularly between 6:00 p.m. and midnight—just when you, too, are feeling tired from the day's trials and tribulations. These periods of crankiness may feel like torture, especially if you have other demanding children or work to do, but fortunately they don't last long. The length of this fussing usually peaks at about three hours a day by six weeks and then declines to one or two hours a day by three to four months. As long as the baby calms within a few hours and is relatively peaceful the rest of the day, there's no reason for alarm.

If the crying does not stop, but intensifies and persists throughout the day or night, it may be caused by colic. About one-fifth of all babies develop colic, usually between the second and fourth weeks. It may occur even after you change your baby's diaper, feed her, and soothe her by cuddling, rocking, or walking with her. Colicky children cry inconsolably, often screaming, extending or pulling up their legs, and passing gas. Their stomachs may be enlarged or distended with gas. The crying spells can occur around the clock, although they often become worse in the early evening.

Unfortunately, there is no definite explanation for why this happens. Most often, colic means simply that the child is unusually sensitive to stimulation or cannot "self-console" or regulate her nervous system (also known as an immature nervous system). As she matures, this inability to self-console—marked by constant crying—will improve. Generally this "colicky crying" will stop by three to four months, but it can last until six months of age. Sometimes, in breastfeeding babies, colic is a sign of sensitivity to a food in the mother's diet. The discomfort is caused only rarely by sensitivity to milk protein in formula. Colicky behavior also may signal a medical problem, such as a hernia or some type of illness.

Although you simply may have to wait it out, several things might be worth trying. First, of course, consult your pediatrician to make sure that the crying is not related to any serious medical condition that may require treatment. Then ask him which of the following would be most helpful.

- **If you're nursing,** you can try to eliminate milk products, caffeine, onions, cabbage, and any other potentially irritating foods from your own diet. If you're feeding formula to your baby, talk with your pediatrician about a protein hydrolysate formula. If food sensitivity is causing the discomfort, the colic should decrease within a few days of these changes.

- **Do not overfeed** your baby, which could make her uncomfortable. In general, try to wait at least two to two and a half hours from the start of one feeding to the start of the next one.

■ **Walk your baby** in a baby carrier to soothe her. The motion and body contact will reassure her, even if her discomfort persists.

■ **Rock her,** run the vacuum in the next room, or place her where she can hear the clothes dryer, a fan, or a white-noise machine. Steady rhythmic motion and a calming sound may help her fall asleep. However, be sure to never place your child *on top* of the washer/dryer.

■ **Introduce a pacifier.** While some breastfed babies will actively refuse it, it will provide instant relief for others. (See page 180.)

■ **Lay your baby** tummy-down across your knees and gently rub her back. The pressure against her belly may help comfort her.

■ **Swaddle her** in a large, thin blanket so that she feels secure and warm.

■ **When you're feeling** tense and anxious, have a family member or a friend look after the baby—and get out of the house. Even an hour or two away will help you maintain a positive attitude. No matter how impatient or angry you become, a baby should *never* be shaken. Shaking an infant hard can cause blindness, brain damage, or even death (see text box *Abusive Head Trauma: Shaken Baby Syndrome,* below). Let your own doctor know if you are depressed or are having trouble dealing with your emotions, as she can recommend ways to help.

Abusive Head Trauma: Shaken Baby Syndrome

Shaking a baby is a serious form of child abuse that occurs mostly in infants in the first year of life. The act of severely or violently shaking a baby—which may also include striking the baby's head—is often the result of a parent's or caregiver's frustration or anger in response to a baby's or toddler's constant crying or irritability. Shaking or striking a baby's head can cause serious physical and mental damage, even death.

Serious injuries associated with abusive head trauma may include blindness or eye injuries, brain damage, damage to the spinal cord, and delay in normal development. Signs and symptoms may include irritability, lethargy (difficulty staying awake), tremors (shakiness), vomiting, seizures, difficulty breathing, and coma.

The American Academy of Pediatrics feels strongly that it is *never* OK to shake your baby. If you suspect that a care provider has shaken or hurt your baby—or if you or your spouse have done so in a moment of frustration—take your baby to the pediatrician or an emergency room immediately. Any brain damage that might have occurred will only get worse without treatment. Don't let embarrassment or fear keep you from getting treatment for your baby.

If you feel as if you might lose control when caring for your baby:

- **Take a deep breath and count to ten.**

- **Put your baby in her crib or another safe place, leave the room, and let her cry alone.**

- **Call a friend or relative for emotional support.**

- **Give your pediatrician a call. Perhaps there's a medical reason why your baby is crying.**

The First Smile

A few of the most important developments during this month are your baby's first smiles and giggles. These start during sleep, for reasons that are not understood. They may be a signal that the baby feels aroused in some way or is responding to some internal impulse. While it's great fun to watch a newborn smile her way through a nap, the real joy comes near the end of this month when she begins to grin back at you during her alert periods.

Those first loving smiles will help you tune in even more closely to each other, and you'll soon discover that you can predict when your baby will smile, look at you, make sounds, and, equally important, pause for time-out from play. Gradually you'll recognize each other's patterns of responsiveness so that your play together becomes a kind of dance in which you take turns leading and following. By identifying and responding to your child's subtle signals, even at this young age, you are telling her that her thoughts and feelings are important and that she can affect the world around her. These messages are vital to her developing self-esteem and sense of fun.

Movement

For the first week or two, your baby's movements will be very jerky. Her chin may quiver and her hands may tremble. She'll startle easily when moved sud-

denly or when she hears a loud sound, and the startling may lead to crying. If she appears overly sensitive to stimulation, she may be comforted if you hold her close to your body or swaddle her tightly in a blanket. There are even special blankets for swaddling small babies who are particularly difficult to console. But by the end of the first month, as her nervous system matures and her muscle control improves, these shakes and quivers will give way to much smoother arm and leg movements that look almost as if she's riding a bicycle. Lay her on her stomach now and she will make crawling motions with her legs and may even push up on her arms.

Movement Milestones for Your One-Month-Old

- **Makes jerky, quivering arm thrusts**
- **Brings hands within range of eyes and mouth**
- **Moves head from side to side while lying on stomach**
- **Head flops backward if unsupported**
- **Keeps hands in tight fists**
- **Strong reflex movements**

Your baby's neck muscles also will develop rapidly, giving her much more control over her head movements by the end of this month. Lying on her stomach, she may lift her head and turn it from one side to the other. However, she won't be able to hold her head independently until about three months, so make sure you support it whenever you're holding her.

Your baby's hands, a source of endless fascination throughout much of this first year, will probably catch her eyes during these weeks. Her finger movements are limited, since her hands are likely to be clenched in tight fists most of the time. But she can flex her arms and bring her hands to her mouth and into her line of vision. While she can't control her hands precisely, she'll watch them closely as long as they're in view.

Vision

Your baby's vision will go through many changes this first month. She was born with peripheral vision (the ability to see to the sides), and she'll gradually acquire the ability to focus closely on a single point in the center of her visual field. She likes to look at objects held about 8 to 15 inches (20.3–38.1 cm) in front of her, but by one month she'll focus briefly on things as far away as 3 feet (91.4 cm).

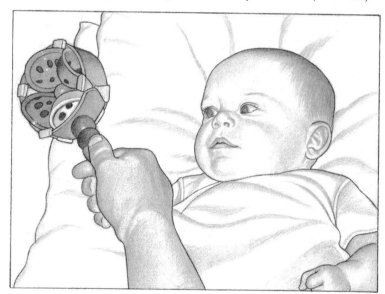

Your baby likes to look at objects held about 8 to 15 inches (20.3 to 38.1 cm) in front of her.

At the same time, she'll learn to follow, or track, moving objects. To help her practice this skill, you can play tracking games with her. For example, move your head slowly from side to side as you hold her facing you; or pass a patterned object up and down or side to side in front of her (making sure it's within her range of focus). At first she may only be able to follow large objects moving slowly through an extremely limited range, but soon she'll be tracking even small, speedy movements.

She is most attentive to black-and-white pictures or high-contrast patterns, such as sharply contrasting stripes, bull's-eyes, checks, and very simple faces.

At birth your baby was extremely sensitive to bright light, and her pupils were constricted (small) to limit the amount of light that entered her eyes. At two weeks of age, her pupils will begin to enlarge, allowing her to experience a broader range of shades of light and dark. As her retina (the light-sensitive tissue inside the eyeball) develops, her ability to see and recognize patterns also will improve.

The more contrast there is in a pattern, the more it will attract her attention, which is why she is most attentive to black-and-white pictures or high-contrast patterns, such as sharply contrasting stripes, bull's-eyes, checks, and very simple faces.

If you show your infant three identical toys—one blue, one yellow, and one red—she probably will look longest at the red one, although no one yet understands why. Is it the color red itself? Or is it the brightness of this color that

Visual Milestones for Your One-Month-Old

- Focuses 8 to 12 inches (20.3–30.4 cm) away

- Eyes wander and occasionally cross

- Prefers black-and-white or high-contrast patterns

- Prefers the human face to all other patterns

attracts newborn babies? We do know that color vision doesn't fully mature before about four months, so if you show your baby two related colors, such as green and turquoise, she probably can't tell the difference at this age.

Hearing

Your baby may have had a hearing test shortly after birth; in fact, the American Academy of Pediatrics recommends that newborn hearing screenings occur prior to every baby's discharge from the hospital, and parents should ask their pediatrician for the results. (See *Hearing Loss,* pages 652–656.)

Infants born with normal hearing abilities will pay close attention to human voices during the first month, especially high-pitched ones speaking "baby talk." When you talk to her, she'll turn her head to search for you and listen closely as you sound out different syllables and words. Watch carefully and you may even see her make subtle movements of her arms and legs in time with your speech.

Your infant also will be sensitive to noise levels. If you make a loud clicking sound in her ear or bring her into a noisy, crowded room, she may "shut down," becoming as unresponsive as if she had heard nothing. Or she may be so sensitive that she startles, erupts into crying, and turns her entire body away from the noise. (Extremely sensitive babies also will cry when exposed to a very bright light.) Substitute the sound of a soft rattle or quiet music and she'll become alert and turn her head and eyes to locate the source of this interesting sound.

Not only does your baby hear well, but even at this age, she'll remember some of the sounds she hears. Some mothers who repeatedly read a story aloud late in their pregnancy have found—and some research supports—that their babies seemed to recognize the story when it was read to them again after birth—the babies became quiet and looked more attentive. Try reading your favorite children's story aloud for several days in a row at times when your baby is alert and attentive. Then wait a day or two and read it again. Does she seem to recognize it?

Hearing Milestones for Your One-Month-Old

- **Hearing is fully mature**
- **Recognizes some sounds**
- **May turn toward familiar sounds and voices**

Smell and Touch

Just as babies prefer certain patterns and sounds, they are typically very particular about tastes and smells. They will breathe deeply to catch a whiff of milk, vanilla, banana, or sugar, but will turn up their nose at the smell of alcohol or vinegar. By the end of their first week, if they're nursing, they'll turn toward their mother's breast pad but will ignore the pads of other nursing mothers. This radarlike system helps direct them at feeding times and warn them away from substances that could harm them.

Babies are equally sensitive to touch and the way you handle them. They'll nestle into a soft piece of flannel or satin, but pull away from scratchy burlap or coarse sandpaper. When they are stroked gently with a palm, they'll relax and become quiet. If they're picked up roughly, they'll probably take offense and start to cry. If they're picked up gently and rocked slowly, they'll become quiet and attentive. Holding, stroking, rocking, and cuddling will calm them when they're upset and make them more alert when they're drowsy. It also sends a clear message of a parent's love and affection. Long before they understand a word that parents say, they'll understand parental moods and feelings from the way they are touched.

Smell and Touch Milestones for Your One-Month-Old

- **Prefers sweet smells**
- **Avoids bitter or acidic smells**
- **Recognizes the scent of her own mother's breast milk**
- **Prefers soft to coarse sensations**
- **Dislikes rough or abrupt handling**

Temperament

Consider these two babies, both from the same family, both girls:

- **The first infant** is calm and quiet, happy to play by herself. She watches everything that happens around her, but rarely demands attention herself. Left on her own, she sleeps for long periods and eats infrequently.

■ **The second baby** is fussy and startles easily. She thrashes her arms and legs, moving almost constantly whether awake or asleep. While most newborns sleep fourteen hours a day, she sleeps only ten, and wakens whenever there's the slightest activity nearby. She seems in a hurry to do everything at once and even eats in a rush, gulping her feedings and swallowing so much air that she needs frequent burping.

Both these babies are absolutely normal and healthy. One is no "better" than the other, but because their personalities are so far apart, the two will be treated very differently, right from birth.

Like these babies, your infant will demonstrate many unique personality traits from the earliest weeks of life. Discovering these traits is one of the most exciting parts of having a new baby. Is she very active and intense, or relatively slow-going? Is she timid when faced with a new situation, such as the first bath, or does she enjoy it? You'll find clues to her personality in everything she does, from falling asleep to crying. The more you pay attention to these signals and learn to respond appropriately to her unique personality, the calmer and more predictable your life will be in the months to come.

While most of these early character traits are built into the newborn's hereditary makeup, their appearance may be delayed if your baby is born quite prematurely. Premature babies don't express their needs—such as hunger, fatigue, or discomfort—as clearly as other newborns. They may be extra sensitive to light, sound, and touch for several months. Even playful conversation may be too intense for them and cause them to become fussy and look away.

Developmental Health Watch

If during the second, third, or fourth weeks of your baby's life she shows any of the following signs of developmental delay, notify your pediatrician.

- ■ Sucks poorly and feeds slowly
- ■ Doesn't blink when shown a bright light
- ■ Doesn't focus and follow a nearby object moving side to side
- ■ Rarely moves arms and legs; seems stiff
- ■ Seems excessively loose in the limbs or floppy
- ■ Lower jaw trembles constantly, even when not crying or excited
- ■ Doesn't respond to loud sounds

Toys Appropriate for Your One-Month-Old

- Mobile with highly contrasting colors and patterns
- Unbreakable mirror attached securely to inside of crib
- Music players with soft music
- Soft, brightly colored and patterned toys that make gentle sounds

When this happens, it's up to the parent to stop and wait until the baby is alert and ready for more attention. Eventually most of these early reactions will fade away, and the baby's own natural character traits will become more evident.

Babies who are less than 5.5 pounds or 2.5 kilograms at birth (low birth weight), even if they're full term, also may be less responsive than other newborns. At first they may be very sleepy and not seem very alert. After a few weeks they seem to wake up, eating eagerly but still remaining irritable and hypersensitive to stimulation between feedings. This irritability may last until they grow and mature further.

From the very beginning, your baby's temperamental traits will influence the way you treat her and feel about her. If you had specific ideas about child rearing before she was born, reevaluate them now to see if they're really in tune with her character. The same goes for expert advice—from books, articles, and especially from well-meaning relatives and friends—about the "right way" to raise a child. The truth is, there is no right way that works for every child. You have to create your own guidelines based on your child's unique personality, your own beliefs, and the circumstances of your family life. The important thing is to remain responsive to your baby's individuality. Don't try to box her in to some previously set mold or pattern. Your baby's uniqueness is her strength, and respecting that strength from the start will help lay the best possible foundation for her high self-esteem and for loving relationships with others.

Basic Care

Feeding and Nutrition

(See Chapter 4 for additional information.)

Breast milk should be your child's sole nutritional source for the first six months, and the major source of nutrition throughout the first twelve months with continued breastfeeding after one year as long as the mother and baby desire.

During this time, you and your pediatrician will need to pay attention to her pattern of feedings and make sure that she's getting enough for growth. Regular checkups and monitoring of growth is the best way to ensure this.

Here are some important points to keep in mind about feeding:

- **Establishing a pattern** of feedings does not mean setting a rigid timetable and insisting that your baby breastfeed for a set amount of time or eat a full 4 ounces (120 ml) at each feeding. It's much more important to pay attention to your baby's signals and work around her needs. Crying at the end of the feed does not necessarily mean she is not getting enough to eat. Some babies are fussy and simply need to suckle for comfort. If she is bottle-fed, you will know the exact amount of the feed, but bottle-feeding infants commonly overfeed, which may lead to obesity. On the other hand, breastfeeding at the breast does not permit you to know the exact amount of the feed, and crying at the end of a feed does not necessarily mean the feed was not enough as long as she is gaining weight and producing enough urine and stools. If she is getting an adequate amount in the first ten minutes, she may stop and fall asleep, and this may be normal. Getting to know your baby's feeding patterns and behaviors will help to reassure you of what is normal for your baby.

- **During the first** month, breastfed babies indicate interest in feeding when they begin to root (reflexively turn toward the breast) or place their fist in their mouth and start sucking. Crying is a late sign of hunger. It is easier to get the baby to latch on and feed when she is showing the early signs of rooting or lip smacking.

- **Your baby should** be fed at least eight times in a twenty-four–hour period, but may feed irregularly over the day, with varying amounts of time between feeds. During the first month, your baby should be feeding through the day and night. In fact, it may be troubling if your baby is sleeping contentedly through the night (more than six to seven hours); she may not be getting enough to eat. Tallying feeds over the course of the day, as opposed to timing the intervals, will help you keep track of the minimum recommended feeds per day.

- **Generally, your baby** will feed adequately in about ten to twenty minutes, but these times vary for each baby. By this time, she will frequently begin to look drowsy or fall asleep. If she still acts hungry after feeding well on the first breast or wakes up during a diaper change, offer the other breast. Very long feedings may indicate that there is little milk being transferred from you to the baby, and this may be due to a latch problem, a milk transfer problem, or a milk production problem. Alternatively, some babies spend a lot of time at the breast comfort suckling, but not ingesting enough milk to become full or satiated. Adjusting the position and latch or hand expression during a feed can help when there is a problem with milk transfer.

■ **Your newborn does** not need vitamin supplements, except for vitamin D. The American Academy of Pediatrics recommends that all breastfed babies be given 400 IU of oral vitamin D drops per day. (Also see page 98 in Chapter 4.)

Growth spurts can occur at different times for different babies. At the beginning of the second week and again between three and six weeks, your baby may go through growth spurts that may make her hungrier than usual. Even if you don't notice any outward growth, her body is changing in important ways and needs extra calories during these times. Be prepared to feed her more often if she's breastfed; more frequent breastfeeding will stimulate more milk production by the mother's body. If your baby is bottle-fed, try giving her slightly more at each feeding, or feeding her more often.

If your baby has a nutritional problem, she's likely to start losing weight or not gain adequately. There are some signals that may help you detect such a problem. It is normal for your breasts to become quite full from two to five days after giving birth. After this time, you should notice that your breasts feel full and somewhat firm before feeding and soften after feeding. While your baby nurses on one breast, you may notice some milk dripping or spraying from the other breast.

If you fail to notice fullness in your breasts after five days or you don't see milk dripping from your breast at the start of each feeding, you may not have an adequate milk supply or the baby may not be providing enough stimulation when she sucks. These also may be signs of medical problems that are unrelated to your baby's nutrition, so call your pediatrician if they persist. Every infant should have a checkup within three to five days after birth and forty-eight hours after hospital discharge to help detect any problems.

Most babies in the first month of life begin to spit up occasionally after feedings. That's because the muscular valve between the esophagus (the passage between throat and stomach) and the stomach is small and immature. Instead of closing tightly, it remains open enough to allow the contents of the stomach to come back up and gently spill out of the mouth. This could be normal, may not harm your baby, and will resolve as your baby grows, usually by one year of age. If your baby is gaining weight appropriately and does not have

Signs of Feeding Difficulties

The following are some possible warning signs of feeding problems, and should be discussed with your pediatrician.

TOO MUCH FEEDING:

■ If bottle-fed, the baby is consuming more than 4 to 6 ounces (120 to 180 ml) per feeding.

■ She vomits most or all the food after a complete feeding.

■ Her stools are loose and very watery, eight or more times a day. (Keep in mind that breastfed babies normally tend to have much more frequent and looser stools.)

TOO LITTLE FEEDING:

■ If breastfed, the baby stops feeding after ten minutes or less, and does not seem satisfied.

■ She wets fewer than four diapers per day; particularly if she has begun sleeping through the night, she may be feeding inadequately (since most babies feed at least once during the night), and may urinate less often and become mildly dehydrated.

■ She has infrequent or very hard stools in the first month.

■ She appears hungry, searching for something to suck shortly after feedings.

■ She becomes more yellow, instead of less, during the first week.

■ She seems excessively sleepy or lethargic.

FEEDING ALLERGY OR DIGESTIVE DISTURBANCE:

■ Your baby vomits most or all food after a complete feeding.

■ She produces loose and very watery stools eight or more times a day or has blood in the stools.

■ She has a severe skin rash.

any other problems, it should reassure you. But if spitting up occurs frequently or is associated with diarrhea, rash, or failure to gain weight, this may indicate a food allergy or problem with the gastrointestinal tract and your physician should be contacted.

You also do not necessarily need to be concerned if your newborn has a bowel movement every time she feeds—or only once a week. These bowel movements should be soft and mushy. However, two exceptions exist: (1) If your baby is having bowel movements that are hard marbles or rocks, your baby should be checked by her pediatrician; (2) If a breastfed infant who is less than one month of age does not have at least four bowel movements a day, it can be a sign that your baby is not getting enough breast milk, so again call your baby's pediatrician for a weight check. If your infant is otherwise feeding normally, there is a wide range of acceptable bowel patterns. (Other warning signs of feeding problems appear in the box *Signs of Feeding Difficulties* on page 179.)

Carrying Your Baby

A newborn or very young infant who has not developed head control needs to be carried in a way that keeps her head from flopping from side to side or snapping from front to back. This is done by cradling the head when carrying the baby in a lying position and supporting the head and neck with your hand when carrying the baby upright.

Pacifiers

Many babies soothe themselves by sucking. If your baby wants to suck beyond nursing or bottle-feeding, a pacifier can satisfy that need.

A pacifier is meant to satisfy your baby's noneating sucking needs, not to replace or delay meals. So offer a pacifier to your baby only after or between feedings, when you are sure she is not hungry. If she is hungry, and you offer a pacifier as a substitute, she may become so angry that it interferes with feeding or she may not get enough to eat. Remember, the pacifier is for your baby's benefit, not your convenience, so let her decide whether and when to use it.

Still, offering a pacifier when your baby is going to sleep may help reduce the risk of SIDS (sudden infant death syndrome), although doctors do not know the reason for this. If you are breastfeeding, wait until your baby is one month old before using a pacifier. However, if your baby doesn't want it or if it falls out of her mouth, don't force it because it may interfere with breastfeeding.

A very young infant who has not developed head control needs to be carried in a way that keeps her head from flopping from side to side or snapping from front to back.

If your baby does use a pacifier to fall asleep, she may wake up when it falls out of her mouth. When she's younger, she may cry for you to put it back for her. Babies who suck their fingers or hands have a real advantage here, because their hands are always readily available. Once your baby is older and has the hand coordination to find and replace it, there should be no problem.

When shopping for a pacifier, look for a model that is age-appropriate for your baby, and that has a soft nipple without any pieces that can break off and become a choking hazard. (Some models can break into two pieces and should be avoided.) It should be dishwasher-safe so you can either boil it or run it through the dishwasher before your baby uses it. You should clean the pacifier this way frequently, so she's not exposed to any increased risk of infection, as her immune system is still maturing. After that, the likelihood of her picking up an infection in that way is minimal, so you can just wash it with soap and rinse it in clear water.

Pacifiers are available in a variety of shapes and sizes. Once you decide which your baby prefers, buy some extras. Pacifiers have a way of disappearing or falling on the floor or street when you need them most. However, never try to solve this problem by fastening the pacifier with a cord around your baby's neck. Babies can choke or strangle on the cords, strings, ribbons, and fasteners attached to pacifiers, whether or not they go around the child's neck. Also, for safety reasons, it's never a good idea to make pacifiers out of a bottle nipple.

Babies have pulled the nipple out of such homemade pacifiers and choked on them. Babies also can choke on a pacifier that's not the right size for their age, so again, be sure that the one you choose is age-appropriate, following the recommended age range on the packaging.

Going Outside

Fresh air and a change of surroundings are good for both you and your baby, even in her first month, so take her out for walks when the weather is nice. Be sure to dress her properly for these outings, however. Her internal temperature control isn't fully mature until the end of her first year. This makes it difficult for her to regulate her body temperature when she's exposed to excessive heat or cold. Her clothing must do some of this work for her by keeping heat in when she is in a cold location and letting heat escape when she's in a very warm place. In general, she should wear one more layer than you do.

Here are a few suggestions for those outings with your baby:

- **Your infant's skin** also is extremely susceptible to sunburn during the first six months, so it's important to keep her out of direct and reflected sunlight (e.g., off of water, sand, or concrete) as much as possible. If you must take her out in the sun, dress her in lightweight and light-colored clothing, with a bonnet or hat to shade her face. If she is lying or sitting in one place, make sure it is shady, and adjust her position to keep her in the shade as the sun moves. Sunscreen can be used on exposed areas of your baby if protective clothing, hats, and shade are not available. Apply it only on small areas of the body such as the face and the backs of the hands as needed. Test it out ahead of time on a small patch on her back to make sure she isn't sensitive to it. Although sunscreen can be applied to all areas of the body that the sun can reach, be careful to avoid the eyes.

- **Another warning for** the hot-weather months: Do not let baby equipment (such as car safety seats and strollers) sit in the sun for a long period of time. When that happens, the plastic and metal parts can get hot enough to burn your child. Check the surface temperature of any such equipment before you allow your baby to come in contact with it.

- **In uncomfortably cold** or rainy weather, keep your baby inside as much as possible. If you have to go out, bundle her up and use a warm hat to cover her head and ears. You can shield her face from the cold with a blanket when you're outside.

■ **To check whether** she's clothed appropriately, feel her hands and feet and the skin on her chest. Her hands and feet should be slightly cooler than her body, but not cold. Her chest should feel warm. If her hands, feet, and chest feel cold, take her to a warm room, unwrap her, and feed her something warm or hold her close so the heat from your body warms her. Until her temperature is back to normal, extra layers of clothing will just trap the cold, so use these other methods to warm her body before wrapping her in additional blankets or clothing.

Finding Help at Home

Most families need some in-house help when they bring a new baby home. If your partner is able to take a few days off from work during the first week or two, this will help a lot. If this isn't an option, the next best choice is to ask a close relative or friend. If relatives are not available, hiring a baby nurse is sometimes a good option. If you think you'll need the extra help, especially if it is going to be a baby nurse, it is wise to make these arrangements in advance rather than waiting until after the delivery to seek it.

Some communities have a visiting nurse or homemaking service. This will not solve your middle-of-the-night problems, but it will provide an hour or two during the day to catch up on work or simply rest a little. These arrangements, too, should be made in advance.

Be selective about the help you seek. Look for assistance from those who will really support you. Your goal is to reduce the stress level in your home, not add to it.

Before you start interviewing or asking friends or family for assistance, decide exactly what kind of help will work best for you. Ask yourself the following questions:

■ Do you want someone who can help you tend to the baby, or do the housework, or cook meals—or a little bit of everything?

■ During what hours do you want help?

■ Do you need someone who can drive (to pick up other children at school, shop for groceries, run errands, and the like)?

Once you know what you need, make sure the person you choose to help out understands and agrees to meet those needs. Explain your expectations clearly to her, and if this is an employment situation, put those expectations in writing. She should be someone you trust. If employing help, be certain that a background check has been performed and the person has basic life-support training. If she will be driving, her driving record should be checked. Regardless of whether this is a relative, friend, or employee, ask her to notify you if she is ill so she doesn't pass any infections to your baby.

YOUR BABY'S FIRST SITTER. Sometime in the first month or two, you may need to leave your baby for the first time, often to take a break or run an errand. The more confidence you have in your babysitter, the easier this experience will be for you. Therefore, you may want to have your first sitter be someone very close and trusted—a grandparent, close friend, or relative who's familiar with both you and the child.

After your first separation, you may want to look for a regular babysitter. You can ask your friends, neighbors, and coworkers for recommendations, or see if your pediatrician or nurse practitioner can refer you to someone. Local child care agencies or referral services are great resources and should be one of the first places to look. If that still doesn't yield any names, contact the placement services at local colleges for a listing of child development or early education students who babysit. You also can find the names of sitters in community newspapers, telephone directories, and church and grocery store bulletin boards, but remember that no one screens the people in these listings. *It is absolutely essential that you check references—inquiring about the sitter's responsibility, maturity, and ability to adhere to instructions—particularly for someone you've only recently met or don't know well.*

Interview every candidate in person and with your baby present. You should be looking for someone who is affectionate, capable, and supports your views about child care. If you feel comfortable with the individual after you've talked awhile, let her hold the baby so you can see how she handles the infant. Ask if she's had experience caring for babies. Although experience, references, and good health are very important, the best way to judge a babysitter is by giving her a trial run while you're home. It will give your baby and the babysitter a chance to get to know each other before they're alone together and it will give you an opportunity to make sure you feel comfortable with the sitter.

Whenever you leave your child with a sitter, give her a list of all emergency phone numbers, including those where you or other close family members can be contacted if problems arise; she should know where you'll be and how to reach you at all times. Establish clear guidelines about what to do in an emergency, and remind her about calling 911 for emergency help. Show her where all exits to your home are located, as well as smoke detectors and fire extinguishers. Make sure your sitter has taken an approved CPR class (from the American Red Cross, for example), and has learned how to respond when a child is choking or not breathing. (See *Cardiopulmonary Resuscitation and*

Mouth-to-Mouth Resuscitation, page 691; *Choking*, page 691); in fact, some local YMCAs or American Red Cross chapters can provide a list of babysitters who have taken CPR or babysitting safety courses. Give your sitter any other guidelines that you feel are important (e.g., she should never open the door to strangers, including delivery people). Ask the sitter to jot down any notes or questions she has about your child. Let friends and neighbors know about your arrangement so they can help if there's an emergency, and ask them to tell you if they suspect any problems in your absence.

Traveling with Your Baby

The key to traveling with your baby during this time is to maintain her normal patterns as much as possible. Long trips involving a change of time zones can disturb your baby's sleep schedule. (See *Traveling by Plane*, page 398.) So do your best to plan your activities according to the schedule your child is on and allow several days for her to adjust to a time change if possible. If she awakens very early in the morning, plan to start your own activities earlier. Be ready to stop earlier, too, because your little one might be getting tired and cranky long before the clock says it's time to go to bed. Always remember to perform a safety inspection of any cribs when checking into a hotel. (See *Cribs*, page 475.)

If you're going to remain in a new time zone for more than two or three days, your baby's internal time clock gradually will shift to coincide with the time zone you're in. You'll have to adjust mealtimes to match the times when her body is telling her she's hungry. Mom and Dad—and even older children—may be able to postpone meals to fit the new time zone, but a baby isn't able to make those adjustments as easily.

Here are some other suggestions when traveling:

- **Your baby will** adapt to her new environment more quickly if you bring some familiar things from home. A favorite rattle and toy will provide some comfort and reassurance. Use her regular soap, a familiar towel, and bring along one of her tub toys to make her more at ease during baths.

- **When packing for** a trip with your baby, it's usually best to use a separate bag for her things. This makes it easier to find items quickly when you want them and reduces the chance that you'll forget an important one. You'll also need a large diaper bag for bottles, formula if formula-feeding, pacifier, a changing pad, diapers, diaper ointment, and baby wipes. Keep this bag with you at all times.

■ **When traveling by** car, make sure your child is safely strapped into her safety seat. For more information on car safety seats, see page 491. The backseat is the safest place for children to ride. Rear-facing seats should never be placed in the front seat of a car with a passenger-side airbag. At this age a baby always should ride in the rear-facing position. The same car seat safety rules apply in rental cars, taxis, and any vehicle your baby rides in.

■ **Always use a** car safety seat on planes and trains, instead of holding her on your lap. If you're not sure how to secure your baby safely on a plane or train, ask a flight attendant or a conductor to help you. It is best that all children should travel with proper restraints on an aircraft. Again, this would mean that your baby needs her own seat on the plane. Some airlines offer discounted fares for children younger than two years old.

■ **If your baby** is bottle-fed, bring not only enough formula for the expected travel time, but plenty extra in case any unexpected delays occur. If you're nursing and are concerned about privacy on a plane or train, bring a nursing cover or ask for some blankets you can use as a screen.

■ **A bottle** (or pacifier) may have other benefits when traveling with a baby by plane. The rapid changes in air pressure associated with air travel can cause discomfort in the baby's middle ear. Babies cannot intentionally "pop" their ears as adults can (by swallowing or yawning), but this relief within the ear may occur when they suck on a bottle or pacifier. To reduce the risk of pain, feed your baby during takeoff and landing.

The Family

A Special Message to Mothers

One reason why this first month can be especially difficult is that you are still recovering physically from the stress of pregnancy and delivery. It may take weeks before your body is back to normal, your incisions (if you had an episiotomy or C-section) have healed, and you're able to resume everyday activities. You also may experience strong mood swings due to changes in the amount of hormones in your body. These changes can prompt sudden crying episodes for no apparent reason or feelings of mild depression for the first few weeks. These emotions may be intensified by the exhaustion that comes with waking up every two or three hours at night to feed and change the baby.

If you experience these so-called postpartum blues, they may make you feel a little "crazy," embarrassed, or even that you're a "bad mother." Difficult as it may be, try to keep these emotions in perspective by reminding yourself that they're normal after pregnancy and delivery. Even fathers sometimes feel sad and unusually emotional after a new baby arrives (possibly a response to the psychological intensity of the experience). To keep the blues from dominating your life—and your enjoyment of your new baby—avoid isolating yourself in these early weeks. Try to nap when your baby does, so you don't get overtired. If these feelings persist past a few weeks or become severe, consult your pediatrician or your own physician about getting extra help. (For more information about the postpartum blues, see also Chapter 5, pages 147–148.)

Visitors often can help you combat the blues by celebrating the baby's arrival with you. They may bring welcome gifts for the baby or—even better during these early weeks—offer food or household help. But they also can be exhausting for you and overwhelming for the baby, and may expose her to infection. It is wise to strictly limit the number of visitors during the first couple of weeks, and keep anyone with a cough, cold, or contagious disease away from your newborn. Ask all visitors to call in advance, wash their hands before holding the baby, and keep their visits brief until you're back to a regular schedule. If the baby seems unsettled by all the attention, don't let anyone outside the family hold or come close to her.

If you become overwhelmed with phone calls, consider leaving a message on your voice mail with information you may want to share about your new baby such as sex, name, birth date, time, weight, and length. State that you are spending time with your family and you will return the call when you have a moment. Then turn off your ringer. This way you can return the calls on your schedule without feeling stressed or guilty every time the phone rings. With a new baby, constant visitors, an aching body, unpredictable mood swings, and, in some cases, other siblings demanding attention, it's no wonder many routine activities in your home will get neglected. Resign yourself ahead of time to knowing that this will happen. What's important is to concentrate on recuperating and enjoying your new baby. If need be, allow extended family and friends to lend a hand with all the other tasks now and then. This is not a sign of weakness; it shows that your priorities are in the right place. And it also allows loved ones to both care for you and feel like they, too, are a part of this new child's life.

A Special Message to Fathers

While this time can be challenging for new fathers, it can also be uniquely rewarding. Just as mothers occasionally need to readjust their priorities, fathers

Become as involved as possible in caring for and playing with your new baby. You'll get just as emotionally attached to her as her mother will.

now have a golden opportunity to show more of their nurturing side by caring for Mom, the baby, and possibly other siblings. Although not all fathers have the option of paternity leave from work, those who do and take advantage of it may find it priceless. If Mom was the center of a sibling's universe and Dad was only an afterthought, Dad may suddenly be more "cool" once a newborn comes home. By adjusting his priorities (at home and at work) and "rising to the occasion," Dad can strengthen an already strong bond with Mom as well as with the new child. By working as a team, parenting couples may be amazed at how well they can adapt to their new, stressful circumstances.

Of course, balancing the seemingly constant demands of the baby, the needs of other children, and the household chores is not always easy. Nights spent feeding, diapering, and walking the floor with a crying baby can quickly take their toll in fatigue for both parents. But by working as a team to relieve each other for naps, for exercise, and for "downtime," parenting couples might find that even though they share less "quality time" together, they may actually feel closer than ever. Sometimes there may be conflict and jealous feelings. These are normal, and thankfully, temporary. Life soon settles into a fairly regular routine that will once again give you some time to yourselves and restore your sex life and social activities to normal. Meanwhile, make an effort for just the two of you to spend some time together each day enjoying each other's company while the baby is sleeping or somebody else is caring for her.

Remember, you're entitled to hold, hug, cuddle, and kiss each other as well as the baby.

A positive way for men to deal with these issues is to become as involved as possible in caring for and playing with the new baby. When you spend this extra time with your child, you'll get just as emotionally attached to her as her mother will.

This is not to say that moms and dads play with babies the same way. In general, fathers play to arouse and excite their babies, while mothers generally concentrate on more low-key stimulation such as gentle rocking, quiet interactive games, singing, and soothing activities. From the baby's viewpoint, both play styles are equally valuable and complement each other beautifully, which is another reason why it's so important to have both of you involved in the care of the baby.

For a unique perspective on fatherhood, see the book *Dad to Dad: Parenting Like a Pro*, by pediatrician David L. Hill, MD, FAAP, published by the American Academy of Pediatrics.

A Special Message to Grandparents

The first time you gaze into the eyes of your new grandchild, you probably will be overwhelmed by many feelings: love, wonder, amazement, and joy, among many other emotions. You might find yourself reflecting back on when your own children were born and feel enormous pride now that your own adult child is raising a family of her own.

Depending on your other responsibilities and how close you live to your grandchild, you can and should play as active a role as possible in the life of the new baby. Research shows that children who have grandparents participating

in their lives fare better throughout childhood and later in life. You have plenty of love and lots of hugs to give, and they can make a difference. As you spend time with your grandchild, you'll form and strengthen a lasting bond and become an invaluable source of nurturing and guidance.

If you live in the same city as your new grandchild, make frequent visits at times deemed appropriate by your adult child. (Don't show up uninvited on the doorstep, and of course know when to leave.) At the same time, also encourage their family to visit you at your home. (Make sure that your home is child-proofed in the ways recommended in this book.) Minimize the advice and certainly the criticism you offer the new parents; instead, give them support, respect their opinions, and be patient. They may have approaches to child rearing that are somewhat different from yours, but remember that they're the parents now. If they should ask, "Mom, what do you think I should do about . . . ?", then of course provide some input. Share your point of view, but don't try to impose your beliefs on them.

Remember, it's been a while since you were raising your own babies, and although much may be the same, much has changed, as well. Ask how you can support the new parents in the child-rearing process, and take your lead from them on how, when, and how often to get involved. For example, you might focus on basic baby care, including feeding and changing diapers, but don't try to take over. Also, offer them a break from time to time by giving them a night out (or, at some point, perhaps a weekend away). No matter how often you visit, however, make regular phone calls, not only during your grandchild's infancy, but also in the upcoming years when you're actually able to have a conversation with her.

Later, as your grandchild grows, tell her stories of what her own mother or father was like during childhood. (Sharing the family history and teaching family values are important contributions you can make as your grandchild becomes older.) In the meantime, consider keeping your own scrapbook of photos and other mementos of your grandchild that you can share with her someday; as part of that scrapbook, create a family tree that the entire family can contribute to. Make it a priority to get together on holidays, attend birthday parties, and, later on, go to as many soccer matches, Little League games, and piano recitals as possible.

If you live hundreds of miles away, and thus can't be as much of a presence in your grandchild's life as you'd like, you still can be an excellent long-distance grandparent. One option: E-mail is a wonderful way to stay in touch. If the new parents have a digital camera, ask them to e-mail photographs of your grandchild to you that you can view on your computer or on a digital photo frame. Maybe they can make and share videos of your grandchild, as well. Make some videos of you and your spouse that your children can share with your grandchild when she is older. If you and the parents have the computer or

Keeping Siblings Happy

Once your new baby arrives, you can expect your older child to be very proud and protective.

With all the excitement over the new baby's arrival, siblings might feel somewhat neglected. They still may be a little upset over their mother's hospitalization, especially if this was their first prolonged separation from her. Even after Mom returns home, they may have trouble understanding that she's tired and cannot play with them as much as they're used to. Compound this with the attention she's now devoting to the baby—attention that just a couple of weeks ago belonged to them!—and it's no wonder that they may feel jealous and left out. It's up to both parents to find ways to reassure the siblings that they're still very much loved and valued, and to help them come to terms with their new "competition."

Here are some suggestions to help soothe your older children and make them feel more involved during the first month home with your new baby.

1. If possible, have the siblings visit mother and baby in the hospital.

2. When Mom comes home from the hospital, bring each sibling a special gift to celebrate.

3. Set aside a special time to spend alone with each sibling every day. Make sure that both Mom and Dad have time with each child, individually and together.

4. While you're taking pictures of the new baby, take some of the older children—alone and with the baby.

5. Ask the grandparents or other close relatives to take the older children on a special outing—to the zoo, a movie, or just dinner. This special attention may help them through moments when they feel abandoned.

6. Have some small gifts for the older child and present them when friends come with gifts for the baby.

7. Especially during the first month, when the baby needs to eat so often, older children can get very jealous of the intimacy you have with the baby during feedings. Show them that you can share this intimacy by turning feeding times into story times. Reading stories that specifically deal with issues of jealousy encourages a toddler or preschooler to voice her feelings so that you can help her become more accepting.

smartphone technology to videoconference, you can interact with the baby at convenient times for everyone.

Health Watch

The following medical problems are of particular concern to parents during the first month. (For problems that occur generally throughout childhood, check the listings in Part II.)

BREATHING DIFFICULTIES. Normally, your baby should take from twenty to forty breaths per minute. This pattern is most regular when she is asleep and healthy. When awake, occasionally she may breathe rapidly for a short period, then take a brief pause (less than ten seconds) before returning to normal breathing. This is called periodic breathing. A runny nose may interfere with breathing because your baby's nasal passages are narrow and fill easily. This condition can be eased by using a cool-mist humidifier and gently suctioning the nose with a rubber aspirating bulb (ordinarily given to you by the hospital; for its use, see page 223). Occasionally, mild salt-solution nose drops are used to help thin the mucus and clear the nasal passages. If she has a fever, notify your pediatrician right away. Her breathing may become faster, increasing by about two breaths per minute for each degree of temperature elevation. When the number of breaths exceeds sixty per minute, or the baby's chest muscles are retracting, her nose is flaring, or she is coughing a lot, be sure to contact your pediatrician. A fever with a temperature higher than 100.4 degrees Fahrenheit (38 degrees Celsius) in a one-month-old baby may be serious and you should call the doctor.

DIARRHEA. A baby has diarrhea if she produces loose, very watery stools more than six to eight times a day. Diarrhea usually is caused by a viral infection. The danger, especially at this young age, is of losing too much fluid and becoming dehydrated. The first signs of dehydration are a dry mouth and a significant decrease in the number of wet diapers. But don't wait for dehydration to occur. Call your pediatrician if the stools are very loose or occur more often than after each feeding (six to eight per day).

CONSTIPATION. The first week a baby should be producing a stool at least once a day. If not, call your pediatrician as your infant may have a condition that makes it difficult for the stool to pass. Or it may be a sign that your baby isn't getting enough to eat. Once your baby has demonstrated that he is eating and pooping well, at a few weeks of age his pattern will become more predictable.

EXCESSIVE SLEEPINESS. Since each infant requires a different amount of sleep, it's difficult to tell when a baby is excessively drowsy. If your infant starts sleeping much more than usual, it might indicate the presence of an infection, so notify your pediatrician. Also, if you are nursing and your baby sleeps more than five hours without a feeding in the first month, you must consider the possibility that she is not getting enough milk or perhaps is being affected, through the breast milk, by a medication that you are taking. Bottle-fed babies may also be sleepy from inadequate feeding or any herbal medication administered by parents.

EYE INFECTIONS/TEAR PRODUCTION PROBLEMS. Some babies are born with one or both tear ducts partially or totally blocked. They typically open by about two weeks, when tear production begins. If they don't, the blockage may cause a watery or mucous tearing. In this case, the tears will back up and flow over the eyelids instead of draining through the nose. This is not harmful, and the ducts generally will open without treatment, usually by nine months of age. You also may help open them by gently massaging the inner corner of the eye and down the side of the nose. However, do this only at the direction of your pediatrician.

If the ducts remain blocked, it will keep the tears from draining properly. Although this will produce pus, it does not mean your baby has an infection, or "pinkeye" (see page 194). You may see a greenish-yellow or white discharge in the corner of the eye, and the eyelashes may become sticky and may dry together at night so the eyelid can't open when your baby wakes up in the morning. But since this discharge does not indicate an infection, it usually is not treated with an antibiotic (see *Tear Production Problems,* page 733).

On the other hand, if your doctor believes that this does represent a true infection, it will usually be treated with special drops or an ointment that he will prescribe after examining the eye. But in many cases, all that's needed is a gentle cleansing with sterile water. When the lashes are sticky, dip a cotton ball in sterile water, and use it to gently wipe from the part of the lid nearest the nose to the outside. Use each cotton ball just once, moving in one clean motion from inside to outside (avoid going back and forth), then discard it. Use as many cotton balls as you need to clean the eye thoroughly.

Although this type of mild discharge may recur several times during your baby's first months, it will not damage the eye and she probably will outgrow it, even without more intensive treatment. Only rarely does this tear-duct blockage require surgical care.

If the eye itself is bloodshot or pinkish, your infant could have conjunctivitis or "pinkeye," and you should notify your pediatrician (see *Eye Infections,* page 728).

FEVER. Whenever your child is unusually cranky or feels warm, take her temperature. (See *Taking a Rectal Temperature,* page 78.) If her rectal temperature reads 100.4 degrees Fahrenheit (38 degrees Celsius) or higher on two separate readings, and she's not overly bundled up, call your pediatrician at once. Fever in these first few weeks can signal an infection, and babies this age can become seriously ill quickly.

FLOPPINESS. Newborn infants all seem somewhat floppy because their muscles are still developing, but if your baby feels exceptionally loose or floppy, it could be a sign of a more serious problem, such as an infection. Consult your pediatrician immediately.

HEARING. Pay attention to the way your baby responds to sounds even if she passed her newborn hearing screening. Does she startle at loud or sudden noises? Does she become quiet or turn toward you when you talk to her? If she does not respond normally to sounds around her, ask your pediatrician about formal hearing testing. (See *Hearing Loss,* pages 652–656.) This testing might be particularly appropriate if your infant was extremely premature, if she was deprived of oxygen or had a severe infection at birth, or if your family has a history of hearing loss in early childhood. If there is any suspicion of hearing loss, your infant should be tested as early as possible, as a delay in diagnosis and treatment is likely to interfere with normal language development.

Sudden Infant Death Syndrome (SIDS) and Other Sleep-Related Infant Deaths

Approximately one newborn out of every two thousand dies in her sleep, for no apparent reason, usually between two and four months. These babies generally are well cared for and show no obvious symptoms of illness. Their autopsies turn up no identifiable cause of death, so the term *sudden infant death syndrome (SIDS)* is used.

The risk factor most clearly associated with SIDS is stomach-sleeping. Therefore, unless your pediatrician has advised otherwise, **your baby should be placed for sleep on her back.** Babies of mothers who smoke and those who sleep in adult beds with other family members (including their parents) also are at increased risk. Soft or loose bedding, pillows, bumper pads, and stuffed toys are also risk factors and should be kept out of the baby's sleeping environment. Babies who sleep in their own bassinet or crib, particularly when the crib is in the parents' room, breastfed babies, and those who use a pacifier when going to sleep have a lower incidence of SIDS.

There are many theories about the cause of SIDS. Infection, milk allergy, pneumonia, and immunizations all have been disproven as causes. The most plausible theory at this time is that there is a delay in the maturation of the arousal centers in the brains of certain babies, which predisposes them to stop breathing under certain conditions.

Following safe sleep recommendations will not only protect your baby from SIDS, but will also decrease your baby's chance of an accidental death from suffocation or strangulation. So keep your baby on his back, in a bare crib (no pillows, blankets, or bumper pads) next to your bed. If you are worried that your baby may be cold, put another layer of clothing on him. Many manufacturers make sleep clothing for babies that will keep them warm without blankets.

Along with the normal feelings of grief and depression, many parents who lose a child to SIDS feel guilty and become extremely protective of older siblings or any babies born afterward. Help for parents is available through local groups or through the national First Candle organization (www.firstcandle .org; 1-800-221-7437). Ask your pediatrician about other resources in your area.

Can SIDS Be Prevented?

At this time, the best measure you can take to prevent SIDS is to place your baby to sleep on her back. Since 1992, the American Academy of Pediatrics has recommended that babies always be placed in this sleep position. Before this recommendation was made, more than 5,000 babies died from SIDS every year in the US. But today, with the decrease in the number of babies sleeping on their stomach, the deaths from SIDS have declined to about 2,300 per year. Each of these deaths is tragic, and campaigns are continuing to promote a back-to-sleep message to parents and others who care for young children. Between the ages of four and seven months, however, you may notice that your infant begins rolling over when placed to sleep on her back. Fortunately, SIDS decreases markedly after an infant is over six months of age and rolling over is a sign that she has some head and neck control. So while it is important to continue to place your infant to sleep on her back, you should not stay up all night constantly flipping her onto her back. Still, this situation has not been scientifically studied so a definitive answer on how best to handle it cannot be given.

JAUNDICE. Jaundice, the yellow color that often appears in the skin shortly after birth, sometimes lasts for more than two to three weeks in a baby who is breastfed. In formula-fed babies, most jaundice goes away within two weeks. If your baby is jaundiced for more than three weeks or the jaundice seems to be increasing, see your pediatrician. If you are having trouble breastfeeding, ask your pediatrician or nurse or lactation specialist for help, as breast milk is the ideal food for your baby. (For additional information about jaundice, see Chapter 5, page 151.)

JITTERS. Many newborns have quivery chins and shaky hands, but if your baby's whole body seems to be shaking, it could be a sign of low blood sugar or calcium levels, or some type of seizure disorder. Notify your pediatrician so he can determine the cause.

RASHES AND INFECTIONS. Common newborn rashes include the following:

■ **Cradle cap (seborrheic dermatitis)** appears as scaly patches on the scalp. Washing the hair and brushing out the scales daily helps control this condition. It usually disappears on its own within the first few months, but may have to be treated with a special shampoo. (See *Cradle Cap and Seborrheic Dermatitis*, page 836.)

- **Fingernail or toenail infections** will appear as redness around the edge of the toenail or fingernail, which may seem to hurt when touched. These infections may respond to warm compresses, but at this age they should be taken seriously and be examined by a doctor, as they may require medication.

- **Umbilical infections** are rare, but if one occurs it often appears as redness around the umbilical stump. There's usually pus and often tenderness. These infections should be examined by your pediatrician. If your baby is also running a fever, see your pediatrician right away as she may need antibiotics or hospitalization. It is normal, though, to have a small amount of clear oozing, drops of blood, and a scab around the umbilical stump without any redness or fever. If this is the case, watch it for a few days and if it doesn't heal on its own, see your pediatrician.

- **Diaper rash.** See instructions for handling this problem on pages 66–67.

THRUSH. White patches in the mouth may indicate that your baby has thrush, a common yeast infection. This condition is treated with an oral antifungal medication prescribed by your pediatrician.

VISION. Watch how your baby looks at you when she is alert. When you're about 8 to 15 inches (20.3 to 38.1 cm) from her face, do her eyes follow you? Will she follow a light or small toy passing before her at the same distance? At this age, the eyes may appear crossed, or one eye occasionally may drift inward or outward. This is because the muscles controlling eye movement are still developing. Both eyes should be able to move equally and together in all directions, however, and she should be able to track slowly moving objects at close range. If she can't, or if she was born premature (less than thirty-two weeks into the pregnancy), or if she needed oxygen as a newborn, your pediatrician may refer you to an eye specialist for further examination.

VOMITING. If your baby starts forcefully vomiting (shooting out several inches rather than dribbling from the mouth), contact your pediatrician at once to make sure she does not have an obstruction of the valve between the stomach and the small intestine (pyloric stenosis; see page 221). Any vomiting that persists for more than eight hours or two to three feedings, or is accompanied by diarrhea or fever, also should be evaluated by your pediatrician.

WEIGHT GAIN. Your baby should be gaining weight rapidly (½–1 oz. per day [14–28 g]) by the middle of this month. If she isn't, your pediatrician will want to make sure that she's getting adequate calories in her feedings and that she is absorbing them properly. Be prepared to answer these questions.

- How often does the baby eat?

- How much does she eat at a feeding, if bottle-feeding? How long does she nurse, if breastfeeding?

- How many bowel movements does the baby have each day?

- What is the amount and thinness or thickness of the stools?

- How often does the baby urinate?

If your baby is eating well and the contents of her diapers are normal in amount and consistency, there is probably no cause for alarm. Your baby may just be getting off to a slow start, or her weight could even have been inaccurately measured. Your pediatrician may want to schedule another office visit in two or three days to reevaluate the situation.

Safety Check

Car Safety Seats

- Your baby should ride in a properly installed, federally approved car safety seat *every time* she is in the car during travel. Do not use it as a place for her to nap in the house. At this age, she should ride in the rear-facing position, in the backseat. Never place a baby in the front seat of a car with a passenger-side air bag.

Bathing

- If you are bathing your baby in the sink, seat her on a washcloth or bath mat to prevent slipping, and hold her under the arms. Never run the dishwasher at the same time that your baby is being bathed in the sink; otherwise, you may risk scald burns from the dishwasher's hot water. Also, don't run the faucet while your baby is in the sink; instead, fill it first, test the temperature, and then put the baby in the water.

■ Adjust the maximum temperature of your water heater to 120 degrees Fahrenheit (48.9 degrees Celsius) or lower so hot water can't scald her.

Changing Table

■ Never leave your baby unattended on any surface above the floor. Even at this young age, she can suddenly extend her body and flip over the edge.

Suffocation Prevention

■ Do not use baby or talcum powders on the baby. If inhaled, talc-containing powders can cause severe lung damage and breathing problems in babies.

■ Keep the crib free of all small objects (safety pins, small parts of toys, etc.) that she could swallow.

■ Never leave plastic bags or wrappings where your baby can reach them.

■ Don't have your baby sleep in your own bed next to you. Keep her in her crib.

■ Instead of using loose blankets that your baby could get tangled in, dress her in appropriate-weight sleepwear (like a wearable blanket or sleep sack).

■ Don't allow your baby to sleep on her stomach, nor should she sleep on a soft comforter or pillow. Place her to sleep only on her back.

Fire and Burn Prevention

■ Do not carry your baby and hot liquids like coffee, tea, or soup at the same time. Even a small splash could scald your baby.

■ Install smoke detectors in the proper places throughout your home.

Supervision

■ Never leave your baby unattended in the house, yard, or car.

Necklaces and Cords

■ Don't let strings or cords dangle in or anywhere near the crib.

■ Don't attach pacifiers, medallions, or other objects to the crib or body with a cord.

■ Don't place a string or necklace around the baby's neck.

■ Don't use clothing with drawstrings.

Jiggling

■ Be careful not to jiggle or shake the baby's head too vigorously.

■ Always support the baby's head and neck when moving her body.

~ 7 ~

Age One Month
Through Three Months

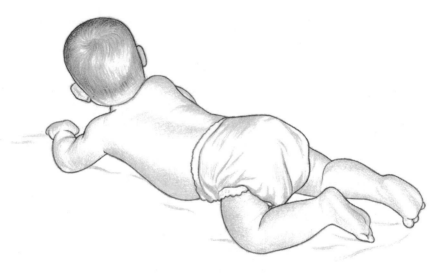

BY THE BEGINNING of your baby's second month, much of the awe, exhaustion, and uncertainty that you may have felt immediately after his birth is likely to give way to self-confidence. You hopefully have settled into a fairly routine (if still demanding) schedule around his feedings and naps. You've adjusted to having a new member of the family and are beginning to understand his general temperament. And you probably already have received the crowning reward that makes all the sacrifice worthwhile: his first true smile. This smile is just a glimmer of the delights in store over the next three months.

You may also find yourself returning to work and needing to find infant-centered day care for your baby. Chapter 14 will help you select the proper type of child care for you depending on your circumstances. The need to be back at work might create a sense of sadness or separation from your infant. This is totally normal, and quite expected. Try to find a setting that allows you frequent visits to check in, but in ways that are not intrusive on the child care providers you have chosen. Establishing their sense of attachment and commitment to your child is important and any sense that your presence is questioning their ability needs to be avoided.

Between one and four months, your baby will undergo a dramatic transformation from a totally dependent newborn to an active and responsive infant. He'll lose many of his newborn reflexes while acquiring more voluntary control of his body. You'll find him inspecting his hands and watching their movements. He'll also become increasingly interested in his surroundings, especially the people close to him. He'll often smile when he sees or hears you. Sometime during his second or third month, he'll even begin "talking" back to you in gentle but intentional coos and gurgles. With each of his new discoveries or achievements, you'll see a new part of your child's personality emerging.

Occasionally there will be moments in which your baby's development seems to lag, usually followed by a spurt in progress. For example, he may seem to be stretching out his nighttime feedings for several weeks and then begin waking up again to feed more frequently. What should you make of this? It's probably a sign that he's about to take a major developmental leap forward. In a week or two (although the time frame varies from one child to another), he'll probably be sleeping longer stretches at night again and maybe take fewer naps, although each nap may be for a longer period of time. In addition, he'll have longer periods during the day where he will be considerably more alert and responsive to people and events around him. Many other types of developmental progress, including physical growth, may occur in spurts and pauses, with periods where there even seems to be a slight setback or lag. As challenging as this may be at first, you'll soon learn to read the signals, anticipate, and appreciate these periods of change.

Growth and Development

Physical Appearance and Growth

From months one through four, your baby will continue growing at the same rate he established during his first few weeks of life. In general, babies gain between 1½ and 2 pounds (0.7–0.9 kg) and grow 1 to 1½ inches (2.5–4 cm). Their head size will increase in circumference by about ½ inch (1.25 cm) each month. These figures are only averages, however, so keep track of your child's development to see if it matches one of the normal curves on the growth charts in the Appendix on pages 878–881.

At two months, the soft spots on your baby's head should still be open and flat, but by two to three months, the soft spot at the back should be closed. Also, his head is more likely to be proportionately larger as compared to his body because it is growing faster. This is quite normal; his body will soon catch up.

At two months, your baby will look round and chubby, but as he starts using his arms and legs more actively, muscles will develop. His bones also will grow rapidly, and as his arms and legs loosen up, his body and limbs will seem to stretch out, making him appear taller and leaner.

Movement

Many of your baby's movements still will be reflexive at the beginning of this period. For example, he may assume a "fencing" position every time his head turns (tonic neck reflex; see page 160) and throw out his arms if he hears a loud noise or feels that he's falling (Moro reflex, page 160). But as we've mentioned, most of these common newborn reflexes will begin to fade by the second or third month. He may temporarily seem less active after the reflexes have diminished, but now his movements, however subtle, are intentional ones and will build steadily toward mature activity.

One of the most important developments of these early months will be your baby's increasing neck strength. Try placing him on his stomach and see what happens. Before two months, he'll struggle to raise his head to look around. Even if he succeeds for only a second or two, that will allow him to turn for a slightly different view of the world. These momentary exercises also will strengthen the muscles in the back of his neck so that, by sometime around his four-month birthday, he'll be able to hold up his head and chest as he supports himself on his elbows. This is a major accomplishment, giving him the freedom and control to look all around at will, instead of just staring at his crib or the mobile directly overhead.

For you, it's also a welcome development because you no longer have to support his head quite so much when carrying him (although sudden move-

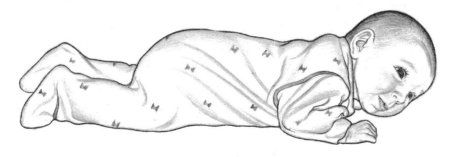

By four months, your baby will be able to hold up her head and chest as she supports herself on her elbows.

ments or force will still require some head support). If you use a front or back carrier, he'll now be able to hold his own head up and look around as you walk.

A baby's control over the front neck muscles and abdominal muscles develops more gradually, so it will take a little longer for your baby to be able to raise his head when lying on his back. At one month, if you gently pull your baby by the arms to a sitting position, his head will flop backward; by four months, however, he'll be able to hold it steady in all directions.

Your child's legs also will become stronger and more active. During the second month, they'll start to straighten from their inward-curving newborn position. Although his kicks will remain mostly reflexive for some time, they'll quickly gather force, and by the end of the third month, he might even kick himself over from front to back. (He probably won't roll from back to front until he's about six months old.) Since you cannot predict when he'll begin rolling over, you'll need to be especially careful and pay close attention whenever he's on the changing table or any other surface above floor level.

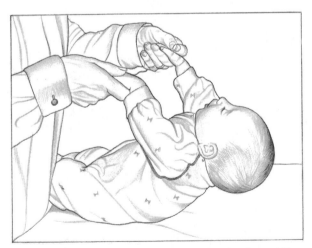

At one month, your baby's head will flop backward if you gently pull her to a sitting position (so always support your baby's head when picking her up).

Another newborn reflex—the stepping reflex (described in Chapter 6, page 161)—will allow him to take steps when you hold him under his arms, while his feet touch the floor. But this reflex will disappear at about six weeks, and you may not see your baby step again until he's ready to walk. By three or four months, however, he'll be able to flex and straighten his legs at will. Lift him upright with his feet on the floor and he'll push down and straighten his legs so that he's virtually standing by himself (except for the balance you're providing). Then he'll try bending his knees and discover that he can bounce himself. Although parents are often concerned about whether this kind of bouncing is harmful to the baby's legs, it is perfectly healthy and safe.

Your baby's hand and arm movements also will develop rapidly during these three months. In the beginning, his hands will be tightly clenched with his thumb

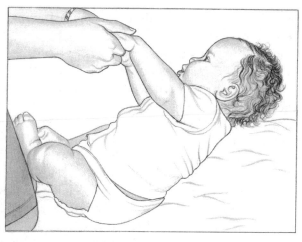

By four months, however, she will be able to hold her head steady in all directions.

curled inside his fingers; if you uncoil the fingers and place a rattle in his palm, he'll grasp it automatically, yet he won't be able to shake it or bring it to his

Movement Milestones for Your One- to Three-Month-Old

- **Raises head and chest when lying on stomach**

- **Supports upper body with arms when lying on stomach**

- **Stretches legs out and kicks when lying on stomach or back**

- **Opens and shuts hands**

- **Pushes down on legs when feet are placed on a firm surface**

- **Brings hands to mouth**

- **Takes swipes at dangling objects with hands**

- **Grasps and shakes hand toys**

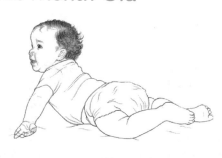

mouth. He'll gaze at his hands with interest when they come into view by chance or because of reflexive movements, but he probably won't be able to bring them to his face on his own.

However, many changes will occur within just a month or two. Suddenly your baby's hands will seem to relax and his arms will open outward. During the third month, his hands will be half-open most of the time, and you'll notice him carefully opening and shutting them. Try placing a rattle in his palm and he'll grip it, perhaps bring it to his mouth, and then drop it only after he's explored it fully. (The more lightweight the toy, the better he'll be able to control it.) He'll never seem to grow bored with his hands themselves; just staring at his fingers will amuse him for long stretches of time.

Your baby's attempts to bring his hands to his mouth will be persistent, but mostly in vain at first. Even if his fingers occasionally reach their destination, they'll quickly fall away. By four months, however, he'll probably have finally mastered this game (which is also an important developmental skill) and be able to get his thumb to his mouth and keep it there whenever he wishes. Put a rattle in his palm now and he'll clench it tightly, shake it, mouth it, and maybe even transfer it from hand to hand.

Your baby also will be able to reach accurately and quickly—not only with both hands but with his entire body. Hang a toy overhead and he'll reach up eagerly with arms and legs to bat at it and grab for it. His face will tense in concentration, and he may even lift his head toward his target. It's as if every part of his body shares in his excitement as he masters these new skills.

Vision

At one month your baby still can't see very clearly beyond 12 inches (30.4 cm) or so, but he'll closely study anything within this range: the corner of his crib or the shapes of his mobile dangling above the crib. The human face is his favorite image, however. As you hold him in your arms, his attention is drawn automatically to your face, particularly your eyes. Often the mere sight of your eyes will make him smile. Gradually his visual span will broaden so that he can take in your whole face instead of just a single feature like your eyes. As this happens he'll be much more responsive to facial expressions involving your mouth, jaw, and cheeks. He'll also love flirting with himself in the mirror.

In his early weeks, your baby will have a hard time following an object that is moving in front of his face. If you wave a ball or toy quickly in front of him, he'll seem to stare through it, or if you shake your head, he'll lose his focus on your eyes. But this will change dramatically by two months, when his eyes are more coordinated and can work together to move and focus at the same time. Soon he'll be able to track an object moving through an entire half-circle in

By two months your baby's eyes are more coordinated and can work together to move and focus at the same time.

front of him. This increased visual coordination will give him the depth perception he needs to track objects as they move toward and away from him. By three months, he'll also have the arm and hand control needed to bat at objects as they move above or in front of him; his aim won't be very good for a long time to come, but the practice will help him develop his hand-to-eye coordination. However, if you think your baby's eyes may not be tracking together by three months of age, talk with your pediatrician.

Your baby's distance vision also is developing at this time. You may notice at three months that he's smiling at you halfway across the room, or studying a toy several feet away. By four months, you'll catch him staring at the distant

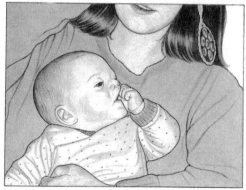

Soon he'll be able to track an object moving through an entire half-circle in front of him.

Visual Milestones for Your One- to Three-Month-Old

- **Watches faces intently**
- **Follows moving objects**
- **Recognizes familiar objects and people at a distance**
- **Starts using hands and eyes in coordination**

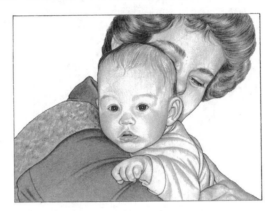

wall hanging or looking out the window. These are clues that his distance vision is developing properly.

Your infant's color vision will mature at about the same rate. At one month, he'll be quite sensitive to the brightness or intensity of color; consequently, he'll prefer to look at bold patterns in sharply contrasting colors or in black-and-white. Young infants do not appreciate the soothing pastels we usually associate with a newborn's nursery because of the babies' limited color vision. By about four months, your baby finally will be responsive to the full range of colors and their many shades.

As his eyesight develops, your infant naturally will seek out more stimulating things to see. Around one month, his favorite patterns will be simple patterns with straight lines such as big stripes or a checkerboard. By three months, he'll be much more interested in circular patterns (bull's-eyes, spirals). This is one reason why faces, which are full of circles and curves, are so appealing to him.

Hearing and Making Sounds

Just as your baby naturally prefers the human face over any other visual pattern, he also prefers the human voice to other sounds. His mother's voice is his absolute favorite, because he associates it with warmth, food, and comfort. Babies like the high-pitched voices of women in general—a fact that most adults

Hearing and Speech Milestones for Your One- to Three-Month-Old

- Smiles at the sound of your voice
- Begins to babble
- Begins to imitate some sounds
- Turns head toward direction of sound

seem to understand intuitively and respond to accordingly, without even realizing it.

Just listen to yourself the next time you talk to your baby. You'll probably notice that you raise the pitch of your voice, slow your rate of speech, exaggerate certain syllables, and widen your eyes and mouth more than normal. This dramatic approach is guaranteed to capture almost any baby's attention—and usually make him smile.

By listening to you and others talk to him, your baby will discover the importance of speech long before he understands or repeats any specific words himself. By one month, he'll be able to identify you by voice, even if you're in another room, and as you talk to him, he'll be reassured, comforted, and entertained. When he smiles and gurgles back at you, he'll see the delight on your face and realize that talk is a two-way process. These first conversations will teach him many of the subtle rules of communication, such as turn-taking, vocal tone, imitation and pacing, and speed of verbal interaction.

At about two months, you may begin to hear your infant cooing and repeating some vowel sounds (ah-ah-ah, ooh-ooh-ooh). Go ahead and imitate his cooing, while also adding simple words and phrases to your "conversations" over the first four to six months. Along the way, it's easy to fall into a habit of baby talk, but you should try to mix your conversations with adult language and eventually phase out the baby talk. During early infancy, you also should read to your baby, even though you may not think he comprehends what you're reading.

By four months, your infant will babble routinely, often amusing himself for long periods by producing strange new sounds (muh-muh, bah-bah). He'll also be more sensitive to your tone of voice and the emphasis you put on certain words or phrases. As you move through each day together, he'll learn from your voice when you're going to feed him, change his diapers, go out for a walk, or put him down to sleep. The way you talk will tell him a great deal about your mood and personality, and the way he responds will tell you a lot about him. If you speak in an upbeat or comforting way, he may smile or coo. Yell or talk angrily, and he'll probably startle or cry.

Emotional and Social Development

By the second month, your baby will spend much of each day watching and listening to the people around him. He learns that they will entertain and soothe him, feed him, and make him comfortable. He feels good when they smile at him, and he seems to know instinctively that he can smile, too. Even during his first month, he'll experiment with primitive grins and grimaces. Then, during the second month, these movements will turn to genuine signals of pleasure and friendliness.

Have you experienced his first true smile yet? It's a major turning point for both you and your infant. In case there was any doubt in your mind, all the sleepless nights and erratic days of these first weeks suddenly seem worthwhile at the sight of that first grin, and you'll do everything in your power to keep those smiles coming. For his part, your baby suddenly will discover that just by moving his lips he can have two-way "conversations" with you, as his grins bring him even more attention than usual and make him feel good. Smiling also will give him another way besides crying to express his needs and exert some control over what happens to him. The more engaged he is with you and your smiles, and eventually with the rest of this great big world around him, not only will his brain development advance, but the more he'll be distracted from internal sensations (hunger, gas, fatigue) that once strongly influenced much of his behavior. His increasing socialization is further proof that he enjoys and appreciates these new experiences. Expanding his world with these experiences is not only fun for both of you but also important to his overall development.

At first your baby actually may seem to smile past you without meeting your gaze, but don't let this disturb you. Looking away from you gives him some control and protects him from being overwhelmed by you. It's his way of taking in the total picture without being "caught" by your eyes. In this way, he can pay equal attention to your facial expressions, the sound of your voice, the warmth of your body, and the way you're holding him. As you get to know each other, he'll gradually hold your gaze

Emotional/Social Milestones for Your One- to Three-Month-Old

- Begins to develop a social smile
- Enjoys playing with other people and may cry when playing stops
- Becomes more communicative and expressive with face and body
- Imitates some movements and facial expressions

for longer and longer periods, and you'll find ways to increase his "tolerance"—perhaps by holding him at a certain distance, adjusting the level of your voice, or modifying your expressions.

By three months, your baby will be a master of "smile talk." Sometimes he'll start a "conversation" by aiming a broad smile at you and gurgling to catch your attention. At other times he'll lie in wait, watching your face until you give the first smile and then beaming back his enthusiastic response. His whole body will participate in these dialogues. His hands will open wide, one or both arms will lift up, and his arms and legs will move in time with the rhythms of your speech. His facial movements also may mirror yours. As you talk he may open his mouth and widen his eyes, and if you stick out your tongue, he may do the same!

Of course, your baby probably won't act this friendly with everyone. Like adults, your infant will prefer certain people to others. And his favorites, naturally, will be his parents. Then, at about three or four months, he'll become intrigued by other children. If he has brothers or sisters, you'll see him beaming as soon as they start talking to him. If he hears children's voices down the street or on television, he may turn to find them. This fascination with children will increase as he gets older.

Grandparents or familiar sitters may receive a hesitant smile at first, followed by coos and body talk once they've played with your baby awhile. By contrast, strangers may receive no more than a curious stare or a fleeting smile. This selective behavior tells you that even at this young age, he's starting to sort out who's who in his life. Although the signals are subtle, there's no doubt that he's becoming very attached to the people closest to him.

This unspoken give-and-take may seem like no more than a game, but these early exchanges play an important part in his social and emotional development. By responding quickly and enthusiastically to his smiles and engaging him often in these "conversations," you'll let him know that he's important to you, that he can trust you, and that he has a certain amount of control in his life. By recognizing his cues and not interrupting or looking away when he's "talking," you'll also show him that you are interested in him and value him. This contributes to his developing self-esteem.

As your baby grows, the way the two of you communicate will vary with his needs and desires. On a day-to-day basis you'll find that he has three general levels of need, each of which shows a different side of his personality:

1.   When his needs are urgent—when he's very hungry or in pain, for instance— he'll let you know in his own special way, perhaps by screaming, whimpering, or using desperate body language. In time you'll learn to recognize these signals so quickly that you usually can satisfy him almost before he himself knows what he wants.

2. While your baby is peacefully asleep, or when he's alert and entertaining himself, you'll feel reassured that you've met all his needs for the moment. This will give you a welcome opportunity to rest or take care of other business. The times when he's playing by himself provide you with wonderful opportunities to observe—from a distance—how he is developing important new skills such as learning to play by himself, reaching, tracking objects, or manipulating his hands. These activities set the stage for learning to self-soothe, which will help him settle down and ultimately sleep through the night. These are especially important skills for more colicky or difficult-to-console babies to learn.

3.   Each day there will be periods when your baby's obvious needs are met but he's still fussy or fitful. He may let you know this with a whine, agitated move-ments, or spurts of aimless activity between moments of calm. He probably won't even know what he wants, and any of several responses might help calm him. Playing, talking, singing, rocking, and walking may work sometimes; on other occasions, simply repositioning him or letting him "fuss it out" may be the most successful strategy. You also may find that while a particular response calms him down momentarily, he'll soon become even fussier and demand more attention. This cycle may not break until you either let him cry a few minutes or distract him by doing something different—for example, taking him outside or feeding him. As trying as these spells can be, you'll both learn a lot about each other because of them. You'll discover how your baby likes to be rocked, what funny faces or voices he most enjoys, and what he most likes to look at. He'll find out what he has to do to get you to respond, how hard you'll try to please him, and where your limits of tolerance lie.

There may be times, however, where you feel very frustrated, even angry, when your baby simply will not stop crying. The best thing to do here is gently place him back in the crib and take a little "break" for yourself. It is most im-

Developmental Health Watch

Although each baby develops in his own individual way and at his own rate, failure to reach certain milestones may signal medical or developmental problems requiring special attention. If you notice any of the following warning signs in your infant at this age, discuss them with your pediatrician.

- **Still has Moro reflex after four months**

- **Doesn't seem to respond to loud sounds**

- **Doesn't notice his hands by two months**

- **Doesn't smile at the sound of your voice by two months**

- **Doesn't follow moving objects with his eyes by two to three months**

- **Doesn't grasp and hold objects by three months**

- **Doesn't smile at people by three months**

- **Cannot support his head well at three months**

- **Doesn't reach for and grasp toys by three to four months**

- **Doesn't babble by three to four months**

- **Doesn't bring objects to his mouth by four months**

- **Begins babbling, but doesn't try to imitate any of your sounds by four months**

- **Doesn't push down with his legs when his feet are placed on a firm surface by four months**

- **Has trouble moving one or both eyes in all directions**

- **Crosses his eyes most of the time (Occasional crossing of the eyes is normal in these first months.)**

- **Doesn't pay attention to new faces, or seems very frightened by new faces or surroundings**

- **Still has the tonic neck reflex at four to five months**

portant that you resist any temptation to shake or strike your baby in any way. The danger from shaking your baby is that such shaking can cause serious damage to your baby. This "shaken baby" situation is one form of child abuse

For the Grandparents

As a grandparent, your role can be especially important in the lives of not only your newborn grandchild and his parents, but also the other children in the family. Make sure you pay plenty of attention to the older youngsters, who might feel a little neglected with all the attention showered on the baby. You can serve as a "pinch hitter" when the new parents are adjusting to their infant by planning some special activities just for you and the baby's older brother(s) or sister(s). For example, make time for the sibling(s) with:

- **Trips to the store or other activities**

- **Car rides**

- **Appropriate stimulating times with music or reading stories**

- **Sleepovers at Grandma's house**

As we've suggested elsewhere in the book (see pages 189, 291, and 514), you can play other important roles to help your daughter or son adjust to the new addition to their family. Help them with cleaning, shopping, and other errands. At the same time, without being overly intrusive, pass along some of your own wisdom and reassurances about baby care—perhaps explaining the "normalness" of crying, the color of bowel movements, the little rashes or other changes in skin color, and a host of other occurrences in the early months. For example, there will be times of frustration for the new parents, such as when the baby is crying excessively and is difficult to console. Provide support and encouragement for the parents—and give them a breather, if possible, by taking the baby out for a stroll in the carriage. The insights and assistance of both grandfathers and grandmothers can have a calming and "life-saving" effect on new parents.

that continues to be a problem around the world. If the difficulties with crying remain an issue, discuss this in detail with your pediatrician who will give you other ideas as to how to get through these episodes. Be sure you share these new techniques for quieting your infant with your child care provider who no doubt will be feeling similar frustrations with inconsolable crying.

Over time your baby's periods of acute need will decrease, and he'll be able to entertain himself for longer stretches. In part, this is because you're learning to anticipate and care for many of his problems before he's uncomfortable. But also, his nervous system will be maturing, and, as a result, he'll be better able to cope with everyday stresses by himself. With greater control over his body, he'll be able to do more things to amuse and console himself and he'll experience fewer frustrations. The periods when he seems most difficult to satisfy probably won't disappear entirely for a few years, but as he becomes more active, it will be easier to distract him. Ultimately he should learn to overcome these spells on his own.

During these early months, don't worry about spoiling your baby with too much attention. Observe him closely and respond promptly when he needs you. You may not be able to calm him down every time, but it never hurts to show him how much you care. In fact, the more promptly and consistently you comfort your baby's fussing in the first six months, the less demanding he's likely to be when he's older. At this age, he needs frequent reassurance in order to feel secure about himself and about you. By helping him establish this sense of security now, you're laying a foundation for the confidence and trust that will allow him gradually to separate from you and become a strong, independent person.

Basic Care

Feeding

Ideally, your baby will continue on his exclusive diet of breast milk until four to six months of age. The best way to monitor whether your baby is getting enough is by making sure his growth is appropriate. Your doctor will measure his weight, length, and head at each visit. Most breastfed babies will continue to request feedings on demand throughout the day and night. The average amount he consumes at a feeding will increase gradually from about 4 or 5 ounces (120 to 150 ml) during the second month, to 5 or 6 ounces (150 to 180 ml) by four months, but these amounts vary from baby to baby and from feeding to feeding. His daily intake should range from about 25 to 30 ounces (750 to 900 ml) by four months. Ordinarily, this amount will supply all his nutritional needs at this age.

But if your baby seems persistently hungry after what you think are adequate feedings, consult your pediatrician for advice. When a breastfeeding infant is not gaining weight, your milk supply may have decreased. If the milk supply had once been adequate but has recently declined, this decrease could be associated with Mom's return to work without adequate pumping, or increased stress for the mother, longer sleep intervals in the baby, or a variety of other factors. Several techniques can be used to increase the milk supply and the baby's intake of it. Try increasing the frequency of feedings, and use a breast pump to increase milk production. If you continue to be concerned about your milk supply, however, mention it again to your doctor, and/or see a certified lactation consultant.

Generally, you should avoid introducing solid foods before six months of age, and certainly not before four months. When you do give him solids, feed him from a spoon. However, placing a spoon in the baby's mouth before four months will cause the baby to thrust out his tongue, which is normal at this stage, even though parents or care providers may mistake this behavior for refusing or disliking the food. At four to five months old, this tongue thrusting will go away and by six months the baby will be able to move a small amount of pureed solid food from the front of the mouth to the back of the mouth and swallow it. But if your baby seems resistant to solid foods, avoid the solid foods for one to two weeks and try again. If the problem persists, talk to your pediatrician to ensure that his resistance is not the sign of any problem. (For more information about introducing solids, see pages 241–244 in Chapter 8.)

Even without any additions to your baby's diet, you'll probably notice a change in his bowel movements during these months. His intestines can hold more now and absorb a greater amount of nutrients from the milk, so his stools may be more solid. The gastrocolic reflex (see *Bowel Movements,* page 67) is also diminishing, so he should no longer have a bowel movement after each feeding. In fact, between two and three months, the frequency of stools in both breastfed and formula-fed babies may decrease dramatically; some breastfed babies have only one bowel movement every three or four days, and a few perfectly healthy breastfed infants have just one a week. As long as your baby is eating well, gaining weight, and his stools are not too hard or dry, there's no reason to be alarmed by this drop in frequency.

Sleeping

By two months, your baby will be more alert and social and will spend more time awake during the day. Meanwhile, his stomach capacity will be growing, so that he'll need less frequent feedings; as a result, he may start skipping one middle-of-the-night feeding. Around three months, most (but not all) infants consistently sleep through the night (six to eight hours without disruption).

Your child should be placed on his back when going to sleep.

Remember, at this age, your child should be placed to sleep on his back (but be sure to give him some "tummy time" during his waking hours, which is good for his normal physical development). See Chapter 35 (pages 857–870) for detailed information on sleep.

Siblings

By the second month, although you may be used to having a new baby in the house, your older children still may be having a hard time adjusting. Especially if the baby is your second child, your first probably may be saddened by not being the primary focus of the family.

Sometimes your older child might display his frustration by talking back, doing something he knows is forbidden, or literally shouting for attention. He also might regress, suddenly wetting his bed or having daytime accidents even though he's been toilet trained for months. Remember, there is no such thing as "negative" attention. He would rather be punished for bad behavior than feel like he is being ignored. But this can quickly escalate into a vicious cycle of more and more inappropriate behavior associated with more and more attention. One important way to reverse this frustrating cycle is to actively "catch him being good." Giving him praise for playing by himself or reading a book makes those activities more likely to occur the next time he's looking for attention. Having each

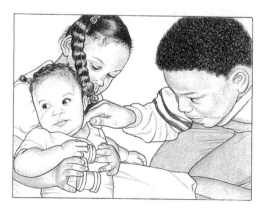

Invite older siblings to play with the baby.

Set clear and consistent rules, such as never picking up the baby without permission.

parent take time with him alone each day may also help. Also, you may need to pick your battles. If you suspect that your child is doing something to get your attention that is not harmful or dangerous (whining, for example), if you ignore that behavior, he will likely find some other way to get your attention.

However, if your older child takes out his frustration on the baby—pulling away his bottle or even hitting him—you'll need to take more direct action. Sit down and talk with him, and be prepared to hear things such as "I wish that baby had never come here." Try to keep these and his other feelings in mind as you confront him. Reassure him that you still love him very much, but explain firmly that he must not hurt the baby. Make an extra effort to include him in all family activities, and encourage him to interact with the newborn. Make him feel like an important "big kid" by giving him specific baby-related jobs, such as carrying the diaper bag, putting away toys, helping dress the baby, or being the one in charge of making sure that visitors and other people wash their hands before they get to hold "his" baby. At the same time, set clear and consistent rules, such as never picking up the baby without permission.

Toys and Activities Appropriate for Your One- to Three-Month-Old

- **Images or books with high-contrast patterns**
- **Bright, varied mobile**
- **Rattles**
- **Singing to your baby**
- **Playing varied music from music boxes, MP3s, CDs, records, or tapes**

Stimulating Infant Brain Growth: Age One Month Through Three Months

- Provide healthful nutrition as your baby grows; have periodic checkups and timely immunizations from a regular source of medical care.

- Give consistent, warm, physical contact—hugging, skin-to-skin, body-to-body contact—to establish your infant's sense of security and well-being. Talk or sing to your baby during dressing, bathing, feeding, playing, walking, and driving. Use simple, lively phrases and address your baby by name. Respond to his gestures, as well as to the faces and the sounds he makes.

- Be attentive to your baby's rhythms and moods. Learn to read his cues and respond to him when he is upset as well as when he is happy. Babies cannot be spoiled.

- Provide colorful objects of different shapes, sizes, and textures that he can play with. Show him children's picture books and family photographs.

- Your face is by far the most interesting visual object at this age. Play peekaboo with your baby.

- If you speak a foreign language, use it at home.

- Avoid subjecting your baby to stressful or traumatic experiences, physical or psychological.

- Make sure other people who provide care and supervision for your baby understand the importance of forming a loving and comforting relationship with your child and also provide consistent care.

Health Watch

A newborn can get very sick very quickly, so if your infant is under three months of age and has a temperature of 100.4 degrees Fahrenheit (38 degrees Celsius) or higher, call your pediatrician. The following medical problems are particularly common between the ages of two and four months. If you are concerned that your baby has any of these conditions while younger than two months of age, contact your pediatrician. Check Part II of this book for other illnesses and conditions that occur throughout childhood.

DIARRHEA (see also *Diarrhea*, page 530). If your baby has a vomiting spell followed a day or two later by diarrhea, he probably has a viral infection in his intestinal tract. If you're breastfeeding, your pediatrician probably will suggest that you continue nursing him as usual. If you're formula-feeding, in most cases you can continue to do so. You may be advised to use a "reduced" lactose formula for a few days before returning to the original formula if diarrhea persists. In some instances your pediatrician may advise you to limit your baby's intake to a special solution containing electrolytes (e.g., salt and potassium) and sugar. This is because diarrhea can sometimes "wash out" the enzymes needed to properly and effectively digest the sugar in cow's milk–based formulas.

EAR INFECTIONS (see also *Middle Ear Infections,* page 662). Although ear infections are more common in older babies, occasionally they occur in infants under three months. Babies are prone to ear infections because the tube that connects the nasal passages to the middle ear is very short, making it easy for a virus that causes a cold in the nasal passages to spread to the ear. The virus infection in the middle ear can then have an added bacterial infection. When this occurs, your pediatrician will examine your baby and diagnose a true middle ear infection.

The first sign of an ear infection is usually irritability, especially at night. The infection may also produce a fever. If your pediatrician's ear examination confirms that an infection is present, the doctor may recommend giving liquid acetaminophen to your baby in an appropriate dose. (Do *not* give him aspirin; it can cause a serious brain disorder called Reye syndrome; see page 549.) Your pediatrician also may prescribe a course of antibiotics, although if your child does not have a fever or is not severely ill, antibiotics may not be necessary. While ear infections can be caused by bacteria or viruses, antibiotics treat only bacterial infections, and thus your pediatrician may not recommend them if he isn't convinced that a bacterial infection is present.

EYE INFECTIONS (see *Eye Infections,* page 728). Any signs of eye infection such as eye swelling, redness, or discharge during the first few weeks of life can be potentially serious, but that's certainly not always the case. For example, there can be discharge and tearing—but generally without redness—if a tear duct is blocked, which can set the stage for subsequent eye infection.

SPITTING UP (GASTROESOPHAGEAL REFLUX) (see page 550). This condition occurs when contents from the stomach make their way back into the esophagus (the tube through which food and liquids are transported from the throat to the stomach). This so-called reflux takes place when the sphincter (the muscle responsible for keeping the stomach contents from coming back up into the esophagus) relaxes at the wrong time or, less commonly, is too weak, allowing food and/or liquid to flow upward in the direction from which it came. Because of this immaturity of the sphincter, all babies reflux to some degree, although the level decreases over time with most children. In some cases, however, it becomes a problem that may require the advice of your pediatrician.

Recent research shows that chronic gastroesophageal reflux is more common in children than was once believed, and can begin as early as infancy. Not long after eating, an infant with this condition may vomit, have periods of coughing, become irritable, have difficulty swallowing, arch his back, and may be underweight. Spitting/vomiting in infancy is common in about half of the infants less than six months of age who vomit and about 5 percent of infants at twelve months of age. To minimize the problem, stop to burp your baby several times during a feed, as well as afterward. Because the condition can worsen when your infant is lying flat, try keeping him in an upright position for about half an hour following each feeding. Because of concerns about SIDS (sudden infant death syndrome) when babies sleep, do not place them in a prone position (on stomach) for sleep or to help their reflux symptoms, unless recommended by a specialist for babies with very severe reflux. The safest way for your baby to sleep is always on his back. Remember . . . "back to sleep."

A baby with gastroesophageal reflux should be evaluated by a pediatrician or pediatric gastroenterologist. In some cases, your doctor may recommend thickening your baby's formula or breast milk to help reduce the amount of reflux. In some cases, he might suggest switching to a protein hydrolysate formula (ask your doctor what kind to buy), and then see if symptoms improve in the next week or two. If your infant has an allergy to cow's milk, this switch in formulas may help. In cases where your baby isn't keeping enough down to gain weight properly, or if she is very uncomfortable, medications may be prescribed as well.

Some cases of vomiting in the first few months of age may be caused by *pyloric stenosis,* a condition in which there is a narrowing of the opening connecting the stomach to the small intestine, causing forceful vomiting and a change in bowel movement patterns. If your pediatrician is concerned that your baby may have pyloric stenosis, he will order an ultrasound and, if needed, refer you for further treatment. (See also *Vomiting, Pyloric Stenosis* pages 549–552.)

RASHES AND SKIN CONDITIONS. Many of the rashes seen in the first month may persist through the second or third month of life. In addition, eczema may occur anytime after one month. Eczema, or atopic dermatitis (see also *Eczema,* page 560), is a skin condition that can result in dry, scaly skin, and often red patches, usually on the face, in the bends of the elbows, and behind the knees. In young infants, elbows and knees are the most common locations. The patches can range from small and mild to extremely itchy, which may make a baby irritable. Ask your pediatrician to recommend treatment, which may vary depending on the severity of the condition, and could include either over-the-counter or prescription lotions, creams, or ointments (only use the over-the-counter or OTC products if your doctor specifically recommends them, since he can guide you toward those products that are most effective). For babies who have only occasional and mild eczema (small patches), he may feel no treatment is necessary.

To prevent a recurrence of this condition, make sure you use only the mildest unscented soaps to wash your baby and his clothes, and dress him only in soft clothing (no wool or rough weaves). Bathe him no more than three times a week, since frequent baths may further dry his skin. (If your doctor believes that certain foods may be triggering your child's eczema, particularly once he's feeding on solid foods, he may recommend avoiding these foods.) For more information about eczema, see pages 560–562.

RESPIRATORY SYNCYTIAL VIRUS (RSV) INFECTIONS (see *Bronchiolitis,* page 595). RSV is the most common cause of lower respiratory tract infections in infants and young children, and is one of many viruses that causes colds in children. Infecting the lungs and breathing passages, it is frequently responsible for bronchiolitis and pneumonia in children under age one. In fact, the highest incidence of RSV illness occurs in infants from two months to eight months of age. RSV is also the most common reason that infants under one year of age are hospitalized.

RSV is a highly contagious infection, occurring most often during the months from fall through spring. It causes symptoms such as a runny or stuffy nose with or without an accompanying sore throat, a mild cough, and sometimes a fever. The infection can remain in the nose or involve the ears and it can spread to the lower respiratory tract causing bronchiolitis. The symptoms of bronchiolitis include abnormally rapid breathing and wheezing.

If your baby was born prematurely, or has chronic lung disease, he has a higher risk of having a serious RSV infection. Premature babies frequently have underdeveloped lungs, and may not have received enough antibodies from their mother to help them combat RSV if they encounter it.

You can reduce your infant's chances of developing a more serious RSV infection by:

- Having people wash their hands with warm water and soap before picking up and holding your baby

- Reducing close contact with people who have runny noses or other sicknesses. Continue to breastfeed when you have a cold, however, since doing so will supply the baby with nourishment and protective antibodies

- As much as possible, limiting your baby's siblings from spending time with your infant when they have a cold (and make sure they wash their hands frequently)

- Keeping your baby away from crowded areas, such as shopping malls and elevators, where he'll have close contact with people who may be sick

- Avoiding smoking around your baby, since secondhand smoke could increase his susceptibility to a serious RSV infection

If your pediatrician determines that your baby has developed bronchiolitis or another RSV infection, she may recommend symptomatic treatment, such as easing nasal stuffiness with a nasal aspirator or mild salt-solution nasal drops. Severe pneumonia or bronchiolitis may require hospitalization in order to administer humidified oxygen and medications to help your child breathe more easily. (For more information about RSV infections, see *Bronchiolitis,* page 595.)

UPPER RESPIRATORY INFECTIONS (URI) (see also *Colds/Upper Respiratory Infection,* page 659). Many babies have their first cold during these months. Breastfeeding provides some immunity, but it is not complete protection by any means, especially if another member of the family has a respiratory illness. The infection can spread easily through respiratory droplets in the air or by hand contact. (Exposure to cold temperatures or drafts, on the other hand—contrary to popular opinion—does not cause colds.) Washing hands, covering mouths while sneezing or coughing, and refraining from kissing when you have a cold will decrease spreading viruses to others; at the same time, keep in mind that you won't be able to avoid the spread of all colds, since people can spread most viruses even before they develop symptoms.

Most respiratory infections in young babies are mild, producing a cough, runny nose, and slightly elevated temperature, but rarely a high fever. A runny nose, however, can be troublesome for an infant. He cannot blow his nose, so the mucus blocks the nasal passages. Before three or four months of age, an infant doesn't breathe well through his mouth, so this blockage of his nose causes more discomfort for him than for older children. A congested nose also often disturbs sleep and causes babies to wake up when they're not able to breathe well. It can interfere with feeding, too, since infants must interrupt sucking in order to breathe through their mouth.

If congestion does occur and is interfering with your baby's ability to drink and breathe comfortably, try using a bulb syringe to suction the mucus from his nose, especially before feedings and when it's obviously blocked. Put a few drops of normal saline (prescribed by your pediatrician) into his nose first to thin the mucus, making it easier to suction. Squeeze the bulb first; then insert the tip **gently** into the nostril and slowly release the bulb. (Caution: Too vigorous or frequent suctioning may cause increased swelling of delicate nasal tissues.) Although acetaminophen will lower an elevated temperature and calm him if he's irritable, you should give it to a baby in this young age group *only* on your pediatrician's advice. *Do not use aspirin.* (See *Reye Syndrome*, page 549; *Medication*, page 768.) Fortunately, in the case of most common colds and upper respiratory infections, babies don't need to see the doctor. You should call, however, if any of the following occurs:

- A persistent cough

- Loss of appetite and refuses several feedings

- Fever: *Contact your pediatrician anytime a baby under three months of age has a rectal temperature of 100.4 degrees Fahrenheit (38 degrees Celsius) or higher*

- Excessive irritability

- Unusual sleepiness or hard to awaken

Immunization Update

Your baby should receive the hepatitis B vaccine soon after birth and before he is discharged from the hospital, and again at least four weeks after the first dose. At two months, and again at four months, your baby should receive:

- DTaP vaccine

- Inactivated polio vaccine

- Hib vaccine

- Pneumococcal vaccine

- Rotavirus vaccine

(For detailed information, see page 81 and Chapter 31, *Immunizations*.)

Safety Check

Falls

- Never place the baby in an infant seat on a table, chair, or any other surface above floor level.

- Never leave your baby unattended on a bed, couch, changing table, or chair. When purchasing a changing table, look for one with two-inch (or higher) guardrails. To avoid a serious fall, don't place it near a window. (For more information about changing tables, see pages 477–478.)

- On all kinds of gear, always use their safety straps or bars.

Burns

- Never hold your baby while smoking, drinking a hot liquid, or cooking by a hot stove or oven.

- Never allow anyone to smoke around your baby.

- Before placing your baby in the bath, always test the water temperature with the inside of your wrist or forearm. Also, fill up the bathing tub (or sink) with water—and then test its temperature—before placing your baby in the water. To prevent scalding, the hottest temperature at the faucet should be no more than 120 degrees Fahrenheit (48.9 degrees Celsius).

- Never heat your baby's milk (or, later on, food) in a microwave oven. Mix it well and test the temperature before serving.

Choking

- Routinely check all toys for small parts that could be pulled or broken off. Also look for sharp edges, which can pose a danger, too.

- For this age group, do not attach a toy to the crib since the baby could pull it down or become entangled in it.

~ 8 ~

Age Four Months Through Seven Months

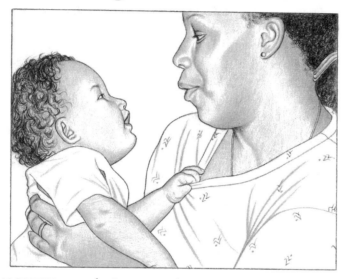

THESE MONTHS ARE glorious ones for you and your baby. As her personality emerges, her laughter, giggles, and the joy of being with you and all she sees are a wonder every day. For her each day has new surprises, new accomplishments, and for you there is a growing sense of just how special the experience is.

By your infant's four-month birthday, you'll probably have a daily routine for her feeding, napping, bathing, and going to sleep at night. This routine will provide a predictability that will help your baby feel secure while allowing you to budget your time and activities. The schedule should be flexible, however, to allow for spur-of-the-moment fun. Short strolls when the sun finally appears on a dreary day, an unexpected lunch visit from grandparents, or a family excursion to the zoo or park are all wonderful excuses to break the routine. Being open to impulse will make your life together more enjoyable and help your baby learn to adapt to all the changes facing her in her life ahead.

For the time being, the most important changes are taking place within her. This is the period when she'll learn to coordinate her emerging perceptive abilities (the use of senses like vision, touch, and hearing) and her increasing motor abilities to develop skills like grasping, rolling over, sitting up, and possibly even crawling. The control that's evident in her budding motor skills will extend to every part of her life. Instead of reacting primarily by reflex, as she did during her earlier months, she'll now choose what she will and won't do. For example, as a newborn, she sucked on almost anything placed in her mouth, but now she has definite favorites. Although in the past she merely looked at a strange new toy, now she mouths, manipulates, and explores every one of its qualities.

Your baby will be better able to communicate her emotions and desires now, and she'll voice them frequently. For example, she'll cry not only when she's hungry or uncomfortable, but also when she wants a different toy or a change in activity.

You may find that your five- or six-month-old also occasionally cries when you leave the room or when she's suddenly confronted by a stranger. This is because she's developing a strong attachment for you and the other people who regularly care for her. She now associates you with her own well-being and can distinguish you from other people. Even if she doesn't cry out for you, she will signal this new awareness by curiously and carefully studying a stranger's face. By eight or nine months, she may openly object to strangers who come too close. This signals the start of a normal developmental stage known as stranger anxiety.

During these months before stranger anxiety hits full force, however, your child probably will go through a period of delightful showmanship, smiling and playing with everyone she meets. Her personality will be coming out in full bloom, and even people meeting her for the first time will notice many of her unique character traits. Take advantage of her sociability to acquaint her with people who will help care for her in the future, such as babysitters, relatives, or child care workers. This won't guarantee clear sailing through the stranger-anxiety period, but it may help smooth the waters.

You'll also learn during these months, if you haven't before, that there is no formula for raising an ideal child. You and your baby are each unique, and the relationship between the two of you is unique, as well. So what works for one baby may not for another. You have to discover what succeeds for you through trial and error. While your neighbor's child may fall asleep easily and sleep through the night, your baby may need some extra holding and cuddling to settle her down at bedtime and again in the middle of the night. While your first child might have needed a great deal of hugging and comforting, your second might prefer more time alone. These individual differences don't necessarily indicate that your parenting is "right" or "wrong"; they just mean that each baby is unique.

Over these first months and years, you will get to know your child's individual traits and you'll develop patterns of activity and interaction that are designed especially for her. If you remain flexible and open to her special traits, she'll help steer your actions as a parent in the right direction. (Also see the discussion of *temperament* on page 238 of this chapter.)

Growth and Development

Physical Appearance and Growth

Between four and seven months, your baby will continue to gain approximately 1 to 1¼ pounds (0.45–0.56 kg) a month. By the time she reaches her eighth-month birthday, she probably will weigh about two and a half times what she did at birth. Her bones also will continue to grow at a rapid rate. As a result, during these months her length will increase by about 2 inches (5 cm) and her head circumference by about 1 inch (2.5 cm).

Your child's specific weight and height are not as important as her rate of growth. By now you should have established her position on the growth curve in the Appendix. Continue to plot her measurements at regular intervals to make sure she keeps growing at the same rate. If you find that she's beginning to follow a different curve or gaining weight or height unusually slowly, discuss it with your pediatrician.

Movement

In her first four months, your baby established the muscle control she needed to move both her eyes and her head so she could follow interesting objects. Now she'll take on an even greater challenge: sitting up. She'll accomplish this in small steps as her back and neck muscles gradually strengthen and she develops better balance in her trunk, head, and neck. First she'll learn to raise her head and hold it up while lying on her stomach. You can encourage this by placing her on her stomach and extending her arms forward; then hold a rattle or other attractive toy in front of her to get her attention and coax her to hold her head up and look at you. This also is a good way to check her hearing and vision.

Once she's able to lift her head, your baby will start pushing up on her arms and arching her back to lift her chest. This strengthens her upper body so she

can remain steady and upright when sitting. At the same time she may rock on her stomach, kick her legs, and "swim" with her arms. These abilities, which usually appear at about five months, are necessary for rolling over and crawling. By the end of this period, she'll probably be able to roll over in both directions, although babies normally vary in the age when they're able to do so. Most children roll first from the stomach to the back and later in the opposite direction, although doing it in the opposite sequence is perfectly normal.

Once your baby is strong enough to raise her chest, you can help her practice sitting up. Hold her up or support her back with pillows or a couch corner as she learns to balance herself. Soon she'll learn to "tripod," leaning forward as she extends her arms to balance her upper body. Bright, interesting toys placed in front of her will give her something to focus on as she gains her balance. It will be some time before she can maneuver herself into a sitting posture without your assistance, but by six to eight months, if you position her upright, she'll be able to remain sitting without leaning forward on her arms. Then she can discover all the wonderful things that can be done with her hands as she views the world from this new vantage point.

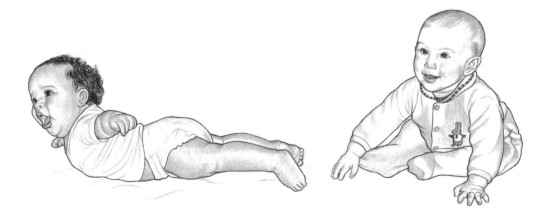

By the fourth month, your baby can easily bring interesting objects to her mouth. During her next four months, she'll begin to use her fingers and thumbs together in a mitten or clawlike grip or raking motion, and she'll manage to pick up many things. She won't develop the pincer grasp using her index finger and thumb until she's about nine months old, but by the sixth to eighth month, she'll learn how to transfer objects from hand to hand, turn them from side to side, and twist them upside down.

Movement Milestones for Your Four- to Seven-Month-Old

- **Rolls both ways (front to back, back to front)**
- **Sits with, and then without, support of her hands**
- **Supports her whole weight on her legs**
- **Reaches with one hand**
- **Transfers object from hand to hand**
- **Uses raking grasp (not pincer)**

As her physical coordination improves, your baby will discover parts of her body that she never knew existed. Lying on her back, she can now grab her feet and toes and bring them to her mouth. While being diapered, she may reach down to touch her genitals. When sitting up, she may slap her knee or thigh. Through these explorations she'll discover many new and interesting sensations. She'll also start to understand the function of

Toys Appropriate for a Four- to Seven-Month-Old

- Unbreakable mirror
- Soft balls, including some that make soft, pleasant sounds
- Textured toys that make sounds
- Toys that have fingerholds
- Musical toys, such as bells, maracas, tambourines (Make sure none of the parts can become loose.)
- See-through rattles that show the pieces making the noise
- Old magazines with bright pictures for you to show her
- Baby books with board, cloth, or vinyl pages

each body part. For example, when you place her newly found feet on the floor, she may first curl her toes and stroke the carpet or wood surface, but soon she'll discover she can use her feet and legs to practice "walking" or just to bounce up and down. Watch out! These are all preparations for the next major milestones: crawling and standing.

Vision

As your baby works on her important motor skills, have you noticed how closely she watches everything she's doing? The concentration with which she reaches for a toy may remind you of a scientist engrossed in research. It's obvious that her good vision is playing a key role in her early motor and cognitive development. Conveniently, her eyes become fully functional just when she needs them most.

Although your baby was able to see at birth, her total visual ability has taken months to develop fully. Only now can she distinguish subtle shades of reds, blues, and yellows. Don't be surprised if you notice that she prefers red or blue to other colors; these seem to be favorites among many infants this age. Most babies also like increasingly complex patterns and shapes as they get older—something to keep in mind when you're shopping for picture books or posters for your child's nursery.

By four months, your baby's range of vision has increased to several feet (meters) or more, and it will continue to expand until, at about seven months, her eyesight will be more nearly mature. At the same time, she'll learn to follow faster and faster movements with her eyes. In the early months, when you rolled

By four months, your baby will begin noticing not only the way you talk but the individual sounds you make.

a ball across the room, she couldn't coordinate her eyes well enough to track it, but now she'll follow the path of moving objects easily. As her hand-to-eye coordination improves, she'll be able to grab these objects as well.

A mobile hung over the crib or in front of an infant's "bouncy" seat is an ideal way to stimulate a young baby's vision. However, by about five months, your baby will quickly get bored and search for other things to watch. Also by this age, she may be sitting up and might pull down or tangle herself in a mobile. *For this reason, remove mobiles from cribs or playpens as soon as your baby is able to pull or hold herself upright.* Still another way to hold your baby's visual interest is to keep her moving—around your home, down the block, to the store, or out on special excursions. Help her find things to look at that she's never seen before, and name each one out loud for her.

A mirror is another source of endless fascination for babies this age. The reflected image is constantly changing, and, even more important, it responds directly to your child's own movements. This is her clue that the person in the mirror is actually herself. It may take your baby a while to come to this realization, but it probably will register during this period.

In general, then, your child's visual awareness should clearly increase during these four months. Watch how she responds as you introduce her to new shapes,

Vision Milestones for Your Four- to Seven-Month-Old

- **Develops full color vision**
- **Distance vision matures**
- **Ability to track moving objects improves**

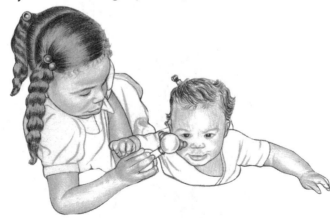

colors, and objects. If she doesn't seem to be interested in looking at new things, or if one or both eyes turn in or out, inform your pediatrician. (See also Chapter 25, *Eyes*.)

Language Development

Your baby learns language in stages. From birth, she receives information about language by hearing people make sounds and watching how they communicate with one another. At first she is most interested in the pitch and level of your voice. When you talk to her in a soothing way, she'll stop crying because she hears that you want to comfort her. By contrast, if you shout out in anger, she probably will cry, because your voice is telling her something is wrong. By four months, she'll begin noticing not only the way you talk but the individual sounds you make. She'll listen to the vowels and consonants and begin to notice the way these combine into syllables, words, and sentences.

Besides receiving sounds, your baby also has been producing them from the very beginning, first in the form of cries and then as coos. At about four months, she'll start to babble, using many of the rhythms and characteristics of her native language. Although it may sound like gibberish, if you listen closely, you'll hear her raise and drop her voice as if she were making a statement or asking a question. Encourage her by talking to her throughout the day. When she says a recognizable syllable, repeat it back to her and then say some simple words that contain that sound. For example, if her sound of the day is "bah," introduce her to "bottle," "box," "bonnet," and "Baa, Baa, Black Sheep."

Your participation in your child's language development will become even more important after six or seven months, when she begins actively imitating the sounds of speech. Up to that point, she might repeat one sound for a whole day or even several days at a stretch before trying another. But now she'll become much more responsive to the sounds she hears you make, and she'll try to follow your lead. So introduce her to simple syllables and words such as "baby," "cat," "dog," "go," "hot," "cold," and "walk," as well as "Mama" and "Dada." Although it may be as much as a year or more before you can interpret any of her babbling, your baby can understand many of your words well before her first birthday.

If she doesn't babble or imitate any sounds by her seventh month, it could mean a problem with her hearing or speech development. A baby with a partial hearing loss still can be startled by loud noises or will turn her head in their direction, and she may even respond to your voice. But she will have difficulty imitating speech. If your child does not babble or produce a variety of sounds, alert your pediatrician. If she has had frequent ear infections, she might have some fluid remaining in her inner ear, and this could interfere with her hearing.

Language Milestones for Your Four- to Seven-Month-Old

- **Responds to own name**
- **Begins to respond to "no"**
- **Distinguishes emotions by tone of voice**
- **Responds to sound by making sounds**
- **Uses voice to express joy and displeasure**
- **Babbles chains of consonants**

Special equipment is used to check a very young baby's hearing. All newborns should be tested for hearing loss. Your observations are the early warning system that tells whether further testing is needed. If you suspect a problem, you might ask your pediatrician for a referral to a children's hearing specialist.

Cognitive Development

During your baby's first four months, did you have doubts that she really understood much that was happening around her? This parental reaction is not surprising. After all, although you knew when she was comfortable and uncomfortable, she probably showed few signs of actually thinking. But studies show that from the minute your baby is born, she is learning about the world around her, even though it may not be apparent to you or others. Now, as her memory and attention span increase, you'll start to see evidence that she's not only absorbing information but also applying it to her day-to-day activities.

During this period, one of the most important concepts she'll refine is the principle of cause and effect. She'll probably stumble on this notion by accident somewhere between four and five months. Perhaps while kicking her mattress, she'll notice the crib shaking. Or maybe she'll realize that her rattle makes a noise when she hits or waves it. Once she understands that she can cause these interesting reactions, she'll continue to experiment with other ways to make things happen.

Your baby will quickly discover that some things, such as bells and keys, make interesting sounds when moved or shaken. When she bangs certain things

When she bangs certain things on the table or drops them on the floor, she'll start a chain of responses from her audience.

on the table or drops them on the floor, she'll start a chain of responses from her audience, including funny faces, groans, and other reactions that may lead to the reappearance—or disappearance—of the object. Before long, she'll begin dropping things intentionally to see you pick them up. As annoying as this may be at times, it's one important way for her to learn about cause and effect and her personal ability to influence her environment.

It's important that you give your child the objects she needs for these experiments and encourage her to test her "theories." But make sure that everything you give her to play with is unbreakable, lightweight, and large enough that she can't possibly swallow it. If you run out of the usual toys or she loses interest in them, plastic or wooden spoons, unbreakable cups, and jar or bowl lids and boxes are endlessly entertaining and inexpensive.

Another major discovery that your baby will make toward the end of this period is that objects continue to exist when they're out of her sight—a principle called object permanence. During her first few months, she assumed that the world consisted only of things that she could see. When you left her room, she assumed you vanished; when you returned, you were a whole new person to her. In much the same way, when you hid a toy under a cloth or a box, she thought it was gone for good and wouldn't bother looking for it. But sometime after four months, she'll begin to realize that the world is more permanent than she thought. You're the same person who greets her every morning. Her teddy bear on the floor is the same one that was in bed with her the night before. The block that you hid under the can did not actually vanish after all. By playing hiding games like peekaboo and observing the comings and goings of people and things around her, your baby will continue to learn about object permanence for many months to come.

Cognitive Milestones for Your Four- to Seven-Month-Old

- **Finds partially hidden objects**
- **Explores with hands and mouth**
- **Struggles to get objects that are out of reach**

Emotional Development

Between four and seven months, your baby may undergo a dramatic change in personality. At the beginning of this period, she may seem relatively passive and preoccupied with getting enough food, sleep, and affection. But as she learns to sit up, use her hands, and move about, she's likely to become increasingly assertive and more attentive to the world outside. She'll be eager to reach out and touch everything she sees, and if she can't manage on her own, she'll demand your help by yelling, banging, or dropping the nearest object at hand. Once you've come to her rescue, she'll probably forget what she was doing and concentrate on you—smiling, laughing, babbling, and imitating you for many minutes at a stretch. While she'll quickly get bored with even the most engaging toy, she'll never tire of your attention.

The more subtle aspects of your baby's personality are determined largely by her constitutional makeup or temperament. Is she rambunctious or gentle? Easygoing or easily upset? Headstrong or compliant? To a large extent, these are inborn character traits. Just as infants come in different sizes and shapes, their temperaments differ as well. Their unique character traits include their activity levels, their persistence, and their adaptability to the world around them—and these traits will become increasingly apparent during these months. You won't necessarily find all of their personal characteristics enjoyable all the time—especially not when your determined six-month-old is screaming in frustration as she lunges for the family cat. But in the long run, adapting to her natural personality is best for both of you. And because your baby's temperament is real and directly affects you and the rest of the family, it's important to understand her as completely as possible.

Your child's "behavioral style" even affects how you parent and how you feel about yourself. An agreeable, even-tempered child, for example, is more likely to make you feel competent as a parent than one who is constantly irritable.

As you've probably discovered already, some infants of this age are "easy," calm and predictable, while others are much more difficult. Strong-willed and high-strung babies require an extra dose of patience and gentle guidance. They often don't adapt to changing surroundings as easily as calmer babies, and will become increasingly upset if pushed to move or perform before they're ready. To a large degree, you'll fare better not by trying to change your child's temperament, but by accommodating it. You can reduce the stresses of rearing an infant by recognizing and acknowledging her temperament rather than resisting or working against it.

Language and cuddling sometimes will do wonders to calm the nerves of an irritable child. Distracting her can help refocus her energy. For instance, if she screams because you won't retrieve the toy she dropped for the tenth time, move her to the floor so she can reach the toy herself.

The shy or "sensitive" child also requires special attention, particularly if you have more boisterous children in the household who overshadow her. When a baby is quiet and undemanding, it's easy to assume she's content, or if she doesn't laugh or smile a lot, you may lose interest in playing with her. But a baby like this often needs personal contact even more than other children. She may be overwhelmed easily and needs you to show her how to be assertive and become involved in the activities around her. How should you do this? Give her plenty of time to warm up to any situation, and make sure that other people approach her slowly. Let her sit on the sidelines before attempting to involve her directly with other children. Once she feels secure, gradually she'll become more responsive to the people around her.

Developmental Health Watch

Because each baby develops in her own particular manner, it's impossible to tell exactly when or how your child will perfect a given skill. The developmental milestones listed in this book will give you a general idea of the changes you can expect, but don't be alarmed if your own baby's development takes a slightly different course. Alert your pediatrician, however, if your baby displays any of the following signs of possible developmental delay for this age range.

- **Seems very stiff, with tight muscles**

- **Seems very floppy, like a rag doll**

- **Head still flops back when body is pulled up to a sitting position**

- **Reaches with one hand only**

- Refuses to cuddle
- Shows no affection for the person who cares for her
- Doesn't seem to enjoy being around people
- One or both eyes consistently turn in or out
- Persistent tearing, eye drainage, or sensitivity to light
- Does not respond to sounds around her
- Has difficulty getting objects to her mouth
- Does not turn her head to locate sounds by four months
- Doesn't roll over in either direction (front to back or back to front) by five to seven months
- Seems inconsolable at night after five months
- Doesn't smile spontaneously by five months
- Cannot sit with help by six months
- Does not laugh or make squealing sounds by six months
- Does not actively reach for objects by six to seven months
- Doesn't follow objects with both eyes at near (1 ft.) [30 cm] and far (6 ft.) [180 cm] ranges by seven months
- Does not bear some weight on legs by seven months
- Does not try to attract attention through actions by seven months
- Does not babble by eight months
- Shows no interest in games of peekaboo by eight months

Also let your pediatrician know if you have any concerns about your baby's emotional development. Your pediatrician can help if she knows there are problems, but such concerns can often be difficult to detect in a routine office visit. That's why it's important for you to call the doctor's attention to your concerns and describe your day-to-day observations. Write them down so you don't forget them. And take comfort in the fact that with time and patience, some of her personality traits that you wish you could change will evolve. In the meantime, enjoy her as she is.

Social/Emotional Milestones for
Your Four- to Seven-Month-Old

- **Enjoys social play**

- **Interested in mirror images**

- **Responds to other people's expressions of emotion and appears joyful often**

Basic Care

Introducing Solid Foods

Exclusive breastfeeding is recommended until six months of age. At around six months, you can begin adding solid foods. Babies are born with a tongue thrust reflex. Because of this reflex, the young infant will push her tongue against a spoon or anything else inserted into her mouth, including food. Most babies lose this reflex at about four to five months, so waiting until this reflex goes away is a time to begin taking solid food. Talk with your pediatrician at the four-month checkup to see when she feels your infant should begin eating solid food.

Once you decide to begin, you may start solid food at whichever feedings during the day are most acceptable to you and your baby. However, remember that as she gets older, she will want to eat with the other family members. To minimize the chances of choking, make sure your baby is sitting upright when you introduce solids. If she cries or turns away when you try to feed her, don't force the issue. It's more important that you both enjoy her mealtimes than for her to start these foods by a specific date. Go back to nursing or bottle-feeding exclusively for a week or two, then try again.

Always use a spoon to feed your baby solids unless, at your pediatrician's recommendation, you are thickening the formula because your infant has gastroesophageal reflux (spitting up stomach contents). Some parents try putting solid foods in a bottle or infant feeder with a nipple, but feeding a baby this way can drastically increase the amount of food she takes in at each feeding and lead to excessive weight gain. Besides, it's important for your baby to get used to the process of eating—sitting up, taking bites from a spoon, resting between bites, and stopping when she's full. This early experience will help lay the foundation for good eating habits throughout her life.

Even standard baby spoons may be too wide for a child this young, but a small coffee spoon will work well; use of a rubber-coated baby spoon is also a good choice and can avoid injury. Start with half a spoonful or less, and talk your baby through the process ("Mmm, see how good this is"). She probably won't know what to do the first time or two. She may look confused, wrinkle her nose, and roll the food around her mouth or reject it entirely. This is an understandable reaction, considering how different her feedings have been up to this point.

One way to ease the transition to solids is to give your infant a little breast milk first, then switch to very small half-spoonfuls of food, and finally finish off with more breast milk. This will prevent her from being overly frustrated when she's very hungry, and it will link the satisfaction of nursing with this new experience of spoon-feeding.

No matter what you do, most of the first few solid-food feedings are sure to wind up outside her mouth on her face and bib, so increase the size of her feedings very gradually, starting with just a teaspoonful or two, until she gets the idea of swallowing solids.

What foods should you feed her? By tradition, single-grain cereals have usually been introduced first. However, there is no medical evidence that introducing solid foods in any particular order has an advantage for your infant. Though many pediatricians recommend starting vegetables before fruits, there is no research indicating that your infant will develop a dislike for vegetables or an allergy if vegetables follow the introduction of fruit.

Many babies enjoy eating cereals. You may use premixed baby cereals in a jar or dry varieties to which you add formula, breast milk, or water. The prepared cereals are convenient, but the dry ones are richer in iron and can be varied in consistency to suit your baby. Whichever you choose, make sure that it's made for babies. This assures you that it contains the extra nutrients your child needs at this age and not additional salt, etc.

If your infant has been mostly breastfeeding, she may benefit from pureed baby meats, which contain iron and zinc. These nutrients are easily absorbed, and are needed by six months of age.

Give your baby just one new food at a time, and wait at least three to five days before starting another. After each new food, watch for responses such as diarrhea, rash, or vomiting. If any of these occur, eliminate the suspect food from her diet until you've consulted your pediatrician. Within two or three months, your baby's daily diet should include breast milk, cereal, vegetables, meats, eggs, and fruits, distributed among three meals. It's also important to note that because canned adult-type foods generally contain added salt and preservatives, they should not be fed to babies.

Once your baby sits up independently, you can begin to give her finger foods to help her learn to feed herself. Most infants can begin learning to self-feed around eight months of age. Make sure anything you give her is soft, easy to swallow, and breaks down into small pieces that she can't possibly choke on. Well-cooked cut-up yams, sweet potatoes, green beans, peas, diced chicken or meat and small pieces of bread, or whole-grain crackers are good examples. Don't give her any food that requires chewing at this age, even if she already has teeth.

When feeding your baby solid foods, do not feed directly from the jar but rather from a small dish into which a portion of the jar of food has been placed. This will prevent the jar of food from becoming contaminated from the introduction of bacteria from the baby's mouth. The portion left in the dish also should be discarded, not saved.

What if you want your baby to have fresh food instead of canned or dehydrated? In that case, use a blender or food processor, or just mash softer foods with a fork. Everything should be soft, unsalted, well cooked, and unseasoned. Cooked fresh vegetables and stewed fruits are the easiest to prepare. Although you can feed your baby mashed raw bananas, all other fruits should be cooked until soft. Refrigerate any food you don't use immediately, and then inspect it carefully for signs of spoilage before giving it to your baby. Unlike commercial foods, your own are not bacteria-free, so they will spoil more quickly.

The healthiest option for drinking other than breast milk or formula is water. The American Academy of Pediatrics recommends that fruit juice not be given to infants under six months of age since it offers no nutritional benefit to babies in this age group. After this age, infants may have limited amounts of juice, but it does not offer nutritional benefits over whole fruit. Infants should not be given juice as a treatment for dehydration or management of diarrhea. Giving fruit juice to infants and young children may get them used to drinking sweet beverages and can lead to excessive weight gain.

If your infant seems to be thirsty between feedings, put her to the breast or, after six months, offer her small sips of extra water. Getting a child used to the taste of plain water is a healthy habit for life. During the hot months when your child is losing fluid through sweat, offer water two or more times a day. If you live in an area where the water is fluoridated, these feedings also will help prevent future tooth decay.

By the time your baby is six or seven months old, she'll probably sit up well enough to use a high chair during mealtime. To ensure her comfort, the seat of the chair should be covered with a pad that's removable and washable, so you can clean out the food that probably will accumulate there. Also, when shopping for a high chair, look for one with a detachable tray with raised rims. (See page 485 for safety recommendations.) The rims will help keep dishes and food from sliding off during your baby's more rambunctious feeding sessions. The detachable tray can be carried straight to the sink for cleaning, a feature you're bound to appreciate in the months to come. (There still may be days when the only solution is to put the entire chair in the shower for a complete wipe-down!)

As your child's diet expands and she begins feeding herself more regularly, discuss her personal nutritional needs with your pediatrician. Poor eating habits established in infancy can lead to health problems later on.

Your pediatrician will help you determine whether your baby is overfed, not eating enough, or eating too many of the wrong kinds of foods. By familiarizing yourself with the caloric and nutritional contents of what she eats, you can make sure she's eating a proper diet. Be aware of the food habits of others in your family. As your baby eats more and more "table foods" (this usually starts at eight to ten months in quantities similar to those used for baby foods), she'll imitate the way you eat—including using the saltshaker and nibbling on salty snacks and processed foods. For her sake as well as your own, cut your salt use to a minimum, and eat a healthy, nutrient-rich diet.

What if you're concerned that your baby is *already* overweight? Even when infants are young, some parents are already worried that their babies are gaining too much weight. On one hand, there is a rise in childhood obesity and all of its potential complications (such as diabetes), and thus it's wise to be sensitive to the problem, no matter what age your child is. Some evidence indicates that bottle-fed infants gain weight more rapidly than breastfed babies, perhaps because some parents encourage their infant to finish a bottle. **However, *don't let any anxiety over obesity lead you to underfeed your infant during the first year.* **Get your pediatrician's advice before making any dietary adjustments. During these months of rapid growth, your infant needs the proper balance of fat, carbohydrates, and protein. As soon as you start giving your child solid foods, her stools will become more solid and variable in color. Due to the added sugars and fats, they'll also have a much stronger odor. Peas and other green vegetables may turn the stool deep green; beets may make it red. (Beets sometimes make urine red, as well.) If her meals aren't strained, her stools may contain undigested particles of food, especially hulls of peas or corn, and the skin of tomatoes or other vegetables. All of this is perfectly normal. If the stools are extremely loose, watery, or full of mucus, however, it may mean her digestive tract is irritated. In this case, consult your pediatrician to determine if your infant or child has a digestive problem.

Dietary Supplements

Although the American Academy of Pediatrics recommends breastfeeding your baby for the first twelve months of her life, human milk does not contain sufficient vitamin D to prevent a deficiency of this vitamin, which can produce diseases such as rickets (the severe form of vitamin D deficiency characterized by the softening of bones). Even though sunlight stimulates the skin to manufacture vitamin D, all children should wear sunscreen, hats, and protective clothing when they're outdoors, and this prevents the skin from making vitamin D.

As a result, the American Academy of Pediatrics recommends that breastfed babies and some formula-fed babies receive supplemental vitamin D, beginning soon after birth. Vitamin D supplements of 400 IU (International Units) (contained in a combination multivitamin or a vitamin that contains vitamins A, C, and D or vitamin D alone) per day are recommended. Discuss with your pediatrician how much vitamin D your baby needs.

What about iron? For the first four to six months, your breastfed baby needs no additional iron. The iron she had in her body at birth was enough to see her through her initial growth. But now the reserves will be running low and her need for iron will increase as her growth speeds up. If there were complications with your pregnancy such as diabetes, or at birth such as low birth weight, or if your baby is small for her gestational age, there may be an additional need to supplement with iron drops; ask your pediatrician for advice. The American Academy of Pediatrics believes that babies who are not breastfed or are only partially breastfed should receive an iron-fortified formula from birth through twelve months of age. We discourage the use of low-iron infant formulas as they do not contain enough iron to support an infant's proper growth and development. Fortunately, once you start your baby on solid foods, she'll also receive iron from meats, iron-fortified baby cereals, and green vegetables. For example, four level tablespoons of fortified cereal, diluted with breast milk or formula, provides a good source of iron; meat is another very good source of iron. (See also *Supplementation for Breastfed and Bottle-Fed Infants,* page 125.)

Sleeping

Most babies this age still need at least two naps a day, one at mid-morning and the other midday. Some babies may nap a third time later in the afternoon. In general, it's best to let your baby sleep as long as she wants, unless she has trouble falling asleep at her normal nightly bedtime. If this becomes a problem, wake her up earlier from her afternoon nap.

Because your child is more alert and active now, she may have trouble winding down at the end of the day. A consistent bedtime routine will help. Experiment to see what works best, taking into consideration both the activities in the rest of the household and your baby's temperament. A warm bath, a massage, rocking, a story or lullaby, and a breast- or bottle-feeding will all help relax her and put her in a bedtime mood. *Remember to begin these activities before your baby becomes overtired.* Eventually she'll associate these activities with going to sleep, and that will help relax and soothe her.

Settle your baby in her crib while she's still awake so she learns to fall asleep on her own. Gently put her down, whisper your good-night, and leave the room. If she cries, check on her and offer a few comforting words and then leave the room. As the days pass, gradually give her less attention at night.

If parents are consistent, most babies will cry less each night and will be more likely to learn self-soothing. See Chapter 35 for more information on sleep.

Teething

Teething usually starts during these months. The two front teeth (central incisors), either upper or lower, usually appear first, followed by the opposite front teeth. The first molars come in next, followed by the canines or eyeteeth.

There is great variability in the timing of teething. If your child doesn't show any teeth until later than this age period, don't worry. The timing may be determined by heredity, and it doesn't mean that anything is wrong.

Teething *occasionally* may cause mild irritability, crying, a low-grade temperature (but not over 101 degrees Fahrenheit or 38.3 degrees Celsius), excessive drooling, and a desire to chew on something hard. More often, the gums around the new teeth will swell and be tender. To ease your baby's discomfort, try gently rubbing or massaging the gums with one of your fingers. Teething rings are helpful, too, but they should be made of firm rubber. (The teethers that you freeze tend to get too hard and can cause more harm than good.) Pain relievers and medications that you rub on the gums are not necessary or useful since they wash out of the baby's mouth within minutes. Some medication you rub on your child's gums can even be harmful if too much is used and the child swallows an excessive amount. If your child seems particularly miserable or has a fever higher than 101 degrees Fahrenheit (38.3 degrees Celsius), it's probably not because she's teething, and you should consult your pediatrician.

How should you clean the new teeth? Simply brush them with a soft child's toothbrush when you first start seeing her teeth. To prevent cavities, never let your baby fall asleep with a bottle, either at nap time or at night. By avoiding this situation, you'll keep milk from pooling around the teeth and creating a breeding ground for decay.

Swings and Playpens

Many parents find that mechanical swings, especially those with cradle attachments, can calm a crying baby when nothing else seems to work. If you use one

Stimulating Infant Brain Growth: Age Four Months Through Seven Months

Many connections are being made in your baby's brain during this time in her young life, reflected in her behaviors, such as showing strong attachments to you and others who regularly take care of her, crying when you leave the room or when she is approached suddenly by a stranger, or crying when she wants a particular toy or a change in activity. She is becoming more interested in the world around her and is better able to communicate her emotions and desires—all the while developing new skills such as grasping, rolling over, and sitting up.

Without overstimulating your baby, try these activities to help strengthen the connections in her developing brain:

- **Provide a stimulating, safe environment where your baby can begin to explore and roam freely.**

- **Give consistent, warm, physical contact—hugging, skin-to-skin, body-to-body contact—to establish your infant's sense of security and well-being.**

- **Be attentive to your baby's rhythms and moods. Respond to her when she is upset as well as when she is happy.**

- **Talk and sing to your baby during dressing, bathing, feeding, playing, walking, and driving. She may not yet understand the language, but as she hears it all the time, her language skills will develop. Check with your pediatrician if your baby doesn't seem to hear sounds or doesn't imitate your words.**

- **Engage your child in face-to-face talk. Mimic her sounds to show interest.**

- **Read books to your baby every day. She'll love the sound of your voice, and before long she'll enjoy looking at the pictures and "reading" on her own.**

- **If you speak a foreign language, use it at home.**

- **Engage in rhythmic movement with your child, such as dancing together with music.**

- **Avoid subjecting your baby to stressful or traumatic experiences, physical or psychological.**

- Introduce your child to other children and parents; this is a very special period for infants. Be sensitive to cues indicating that she is ready to meet new people.

- Encourage your child to reach for toys. Give her baby blocks and soft toys that can stimulate her eye-hand coordination and her fine motor skills.

- Make sure other people who provide care and supervision for your baby understand the importance of forming a loving and comforting relationship with your child.

- Encourage your child to begin to sleep for extended periods at night; if you need advice about this important step in your infant's development, ask your pediatrician.

- Spend time on the floor playing with your child every day.

- If your child will be cared for by others, choose quality child care that is affectionate, responsive, educational, and safe. Visit your child care provider frequently and share your ideas about positive caregiving.

of these devices, check the weight limit or age recommendations on the device. Use only swings that stand firmly on the floor, not the ones that hang suspended from door frames. Also, don't use a swing more than half an hour twice a day; while it may quiet your baby, it is no substitute for your attention. Secure your baby properly with the safety harness at all times.

Once your baby starts to move about, you may need to start using a playpen (also called a portable play yard). But even before she crawls or walks, a playpen offers a protected place where she can lie or sit outdoors as well as in rooms where you have no crib or bassinet. (See *Playpens*, page 487, for specific recommendations.) Be sure the playpen or swing that you're considering buying has not been recalled. Check the Consumer Product Safety Commission website (www.cpsc.gov) for recalled products.

Behavior

Discipline

As your baby becomes more mobile and inquisitive, she'll naturally become more assertive, as well. This is wonderful for her self-esteem and should be encouraged as much as possible. When she wants to do something that's dangerous or disrupts the rest of the family, however, you'll need to take charge.

For the first six months or so, the best way to deal with such conflicts is to distract her with an alternative toy or activity. Standard discipline won't work until her memory span increases around the end of her seventh month. Only then can you use a variety of techniques to discourage undesired behavior.

When you finally begin to discipline your child, it should never be harsh. Remember that discipline means to teach or instruct, not necessarily to punish. Often the most successful approach is simply to reward desired behavior and withhold rewards when she does not behave as desired. For example, if she cries for no apparent reason, make sure there's nothing wrong physically; then when she stops, reward her with extra attention, kind words, and hugs. If she starts up again, wait a little longer before turning your attention to her, and use a firm tone of voice as you talk to her. This time, don't reward her with extra attention or hugs.

The main goal of discipline is to teach limits to the child, so try to help her understand exactly what she's doing wrong when she breaks a rule. If you notice her doing something that's not allowed, such as pulling your hair, let her know that it's wrong by calmly saying "no," stopping her, and redirecting her attention to an acceptable activity.

A Word for Grandparents

As a grandparent, you thoroughly love watching your grandchild develop. During this time of her life (ages four to seven months), she's continuing to discover the world around her and has more physical skills and cognitive abilities to engage and enjoy her environment.

As sights and sounds take on more meaning for your grandchild, and as laughter abounds, these are great months for both of you. Smiles, interactive play, and recognition of familiar objects, sounds, people, and names will become part of these discovery months. Her vision is better, her hand transfer is more efficient, and her curiosity is unstoppable. Be sure to reinforce these early learning milestones that are occurring along the way.

Your grandchild also is beginning to move during this time. Although it is a wondrous period of life, you need to be particularly vigilant as she begins to sit. While she will be upright more frequently, she is also likely to tip over.

You have an important role to play as a grandparent, and can make the most of it—enjoying your time with her and stimulating her development—by taking these steps:

- Follow your own child's lead with respect to activities to do with your grandchild, adding some special things of your own when appropriate. Special names you share ("Nana," "Grandpa Stan"), places that the two of you go, and books or music that you share can be unique to her experiences with you. Also consider inviting other grandparents and their grandchildren to join you from time to time, which can be a special treat for your own grandchild.

- When buying gifts for your grandchild, choose age-appropriate books, as well as toys that encourage creative play.

- Make yourself available as a babysitter as often as possible when your son or daughter requests it. These times spent alone with your grandchild will be special moments that you'll always treasure. Take her on field trips (to the park or the zoo), and as the years pass, help her develop hobbies that you can do together.

- You will get a better idea of your grandchild's temperament as she moves through this time of life. Inevitably, you will make comparisons as to whom she really resembles in the family. Some of her own likes and dislikes will start to emerge, and it is best to respect them. If your grandchild is particularly boisterous and active, you may need extra patience at times to fully enjoy her company. Give her some space, let her be the person she is—but rein her in if she gets too far out of bounds. The same with a shy child; don't expect her to break free of her bashfulness the moment you show up. Enjoy her for who she is.

- Diaper changing is often an exercise in controlling the "wiggly worm," and you may need all of your strength just to keep the baby from rolling onto the floor. Switching from the changing table to the bed or floor is often a good idea; remember to keep all of the diapering supplies close by and within reach.

- When it comes to discipline, discuss it with the baby's parents, and make sure your own approach is consistent with their wishes.

- Consider investing in a grandchild-appropriate crib and other furniture for your home. A high chair certainly will come in handy if she occasionally (or frequently) eats meals at your home. A stroller and a car safety seat may be very useful, as well. And keep some everyday medications at your home (for a fever, diaper rash, etc.), and a few toys that she can enjoy.

- Your grandchild's eating has become more regular, and by the end of this time period, she will be on solid foods (e.g., infant cereal and pureed vegetables, fruits, and meats). When you're caring for your grandchild, again follow the guidance of her parents on what and when to feed her. If they're on her menu, let her explore your own versions of "junior foods," such as fruit, pureed vegetables, and meats. Stay away from adult-type canned foods. Avoid giving her food chunks that are too large and could cause choking. If your grandchild is still being breastfed, keep some frozen breast milk in your freezer.

- Your grandchild should be sleeping through the night, so "overnighters" will be more enjoyable and less disruptive of your own schedule. When she spends the night at your home, you and your spouse can take turns on who's going to take the early morning shift if the baby awakens before you normally would.

- Make your home a safe environment for your grandchild. Follow the guidelines in Chapter 15 to baby-proof your home, from placing all medications out of sight and reach to ensuring that matches are nowhere where the baby can reach them.

- At times, having your grandchild and her siblings staying at your home at the same time may be too much for you to handle. Try caring for one youngster at a time, especially at first. Doing this will allow you to tailor-make the activities you do, while still providing much-needed relief to your own child, who can then focus her energies on the child(ren) she has remaining at her home. Your continued, valued role in assisting your child to become the most effective parent possible remains the core purpose for all that you do.

- You can promote your grandchild's development now and in the future by taking family pictures and movies, creating photo albums, and putting family stories down on paper (accompanied by old and new photos).

If your child is touching or trying to put something in her mouth that she shouldn't, gently pull her hand away as you tell her this particular object is off-limits. But since you do want to encourage her to touch *other* things, avoid saying "Don't touch." More pointed phrases, such as "Don't eat the flowers" or "No eating leaves," will convey the message without confusing her.

Never rely on discipline to keep your child safe. All household chemicals (e.g., soaps, detergents) should be stored out of reach of children, either high up or in locked cabinets. Household water temperature should be checked at the tap. The hottest water temperature at the faucet should be no higher than 120 degrees Fahrenheit (48.9 degrees Celsius) to prevent scalding. In many cases, you can adjust your water heater to prevent exceeding this temperature. Special care should be taken while cooking, ironing clothes, or using any other heating sources.

Because it's still relatively easy to modify her behavior at this age, this is a good time to establish your authority and a sense of consistency. Be careful not to overreact, however. She's still not old enough to misbehave intentionally and won't understand if you punish her or raise your voice. She may be confused and even become startled when told that she shouldn't be doing or touching something. Instead, remain calm, firm, consistent, and loving in your approach. If she learns now that you have the final word, it may make life much more comfortable for both of you later on, when she naturally becomes more head-strong. Remember that it may take many, many repetitions of the same actions for an infant to learn what is expected!

Siblings

If your baby has a big brother or sister, you may start to see increasing signs of rivalry at about this time, particularly if there are less than two years separating their ages. Earlier, the baby was more dependent, slept a lot, and didn't require your constant attention. But now that she's becoming more demanding, you'll need to ration your time and energy so you have enough for each child individually as well as all of them together.

Your older child may still be experiencing jealousy over having to share your attention with the baby. One way to give some extra attention to your older child is to set aside special "big brother" or "big sister" chores that don't involve the baby. Doing this allows you to spend some time together and get the housework done. Be sure to show the child how much you appreciate this help.

You also might help sibling relations by including the older child in activities with the baby. If the two of you sing a song or read a story, the baby will enjoy listening. The older child also can help take care of the baby to some extent, assisting you at bathtime or changing time. But unless the child is at least twelve years old, don't leave him alone with the baby, even if he's trying to be helpful. Younger children can easily drop or injure an infant without realizing what they're doing.

For more information, see the section entitled *Siblings* in Chapter 7 (*Age One Month Through Three Months*). Many of the same issues and guidelines described there also apply to children ages four through seven months.

Health Watch

Don't be surprised if your baby catches her first cold or ear infection soon after her four-month birthday. Now that she can actively reach for objects, she'll come into physical contact with many more things and people, so she'll be much more likely to contract contagious diseases.

The first line of defense is to keep your child away from anyone you know is sick. Be especially careful of infectious diseases such as influenza (the flu), RSV, chickenpox, or measles (see *Chickenpox*, page 834; *Measles*, page 841). If someone in your play group has caught one of these diseases, keep your child out of the group until you're sure no one else is infected. But remember that children and adults are contagious a day or so before they have symptoms, so it is impossible to prevent some exposures.

Your Child and Antibiotics

Antibiotics are among the most powerful and important medicines known. When used properly, they can save lives, but when used improperly, antibiotics actually can harm your child.

Two main types of germs—viruses and bacteria—cause most infections. Viruses cause all colds and most coughs. There are no medicines that are effective against the common cold. Antibiotics never cure common viral infections. Your child recovers from these common viral infections when the illness has run its course. *Antibiotics should not be used to treat viral infections.*

Antibiotics can be used to treat bacterial infections, but some strains of bacteria have become resistant to certain antibiotics. If your child is infected with resistant bacteria, she might need a different antibiotic or even need to be treated in the hospital with more powerful medicines given by vein (intravenously [by IV]). A few new strains of bacteria are already untreatable. To protect your child from antibiotic-resistant bacteria, use antibiotics only when your pediatrician has determined that they might be effective, since repeated or improper use of antibiotics contributes to the increase in resistant bacteria and viruses.

- When are antibiotics needed? When are they not needed?

  These complicated questions are best answered by your pediatrician, as the answer depends on the specific diagnosis. If you think your child might need treatment, contact your pediatrician.

- *Ear infections:* Sometimes require antibiotics.

- *Sinus infections:* These are very uncommon at this age, in large part because the sinuses themselves are so small. Just because your child's mucus is yellow or green does not mean that she has a bacterial infection. It is normal for the mucus to get thick and change color during a viral cold.

- *Bronchitis:* Children rarely need antibiotics for bronchitis.

- *Colds:* Colds are caused by viruses and sometimes can last for two weeks or more. Antibacterial antibiotics have no effect on colds. Your pediatrician may have suggestions for comfort measures while the cold runs its course.

- *Influenza:* Once your child reaches six months old, she will be old enough for her own seasonal flu shot. Until then, other family members— parents and older siblings—should receive theirs to protect the baby. There are antiviral medications for this infection, but not all are appropriate for newborns and very young children.

Viral infections sometimes may lead to bacterial infections. Keep your pediatrician informed if the illness gets worse or lasts a long time, so that proper treatment can be given as needed.

If an antibiotic is prescribed, make sure your child takes the entire course, even if she's feeling better before all of the pills or liquid are gone. Never save antibiotics for later use or let other family members use a prescription that wasn't intended for them.

No matter how you try to protect your baby, of course, there will be times when she gets sick. This is an inevitable part of growing up, and will happen more frequently as she has more direct contact with other children. It's not always easy to tell when a baby is ill, but there are some signs that will tip you off. Does she look pale or have dark circles under her eyes? Is she acting less energetic or more irritable than usual? If she has an infectious disease, she'll probably have a fever (see Chapter 27, *Fever*), and she may be losing weight due to loss of appetite, diarrhea, or vomiting. Some difficult-to-detect infections of the kidneys or lungs also can prevent weight gain in babies. At this age, weight loss could mean that the baby has some digestive problem, such as an allergy to wheat or milk protein (see *Celiac Disease,* page 526; *Milk Allergy,* page 566), or lacks the digestive enzymes needed to digest certain solid foods. If you suspect that your child may be ill but can't identify the exact problem, or if you have any concerns about what is happening, call your pediatrician and describe the symptoms that worry you.

The following illnesses are the most common ones that occur at this age. (All are described in Part II of this book.)

Bronchiolitis
(see page 595)

Colds (URIs)
(see page 659)

Conjunctivitis (pinkeye)
(see page 728)

Croup
(see page 600)

Diarrhea
(see page 530)

Earache/Ear Infection
(see page 662)

Fever
(see page 763)

Pneumonia
(see page 605)

Sore Throat
(see page 673)

Vomiting
(see page 549)

Immunization Update

At four months, your baby should receive:

- Second DTaP vaccine

- Second polio vaccine

- Second Hib (*Haemophilus influenzae* type b) vaccine

- Second pneumococcal vaccine

- Second hepatitis B vaccine (may be given between one and four months)

- Second rotavirus vaccine (may be given as early as four weeks after the first dose)

And at six months:

- First dose of influenza vaccine if during flu season; second dose given one month later

- Third DTaP vaccine

- Third polio vaccine (which can be given between six and eighteen months)

- Third pneumococcal vaccine

- Third Hib vaccine (depending on vaccine type given for doses one and two)

- Third hepatitis B vaccine (may be given between six and eighteen months)

- Third rotavirus vaccine (depending on vaccine type; one requires two doses and the other three)

Safety Check
Car Safety Seats

- Buckle your baby into an approved, properly installed infant car safety seat before you start the car. It should be equipped with a five-point harness. When your child reaches the top weight or height allowed by her rear-facing-only car safety seat (check the labels or instructions to find these limits), she will need to use a convertible car safety seat, which can accommodate children rear-facing. You may choose to use a convertible car safety seat rear-facing from birth; this is safe as long as the seat fits your baby properly.

- The backseat is the safest place for all children to ride. Never place a rear-facing car safety seat in the front seat of a car that has a passenger-side air bag.

Drowning

- Never leave a baby alone even for a moment in a bath or near a pool of water, no matter how shallow it is. Infants can drown in just a few inches of water. Baby bath seats or supporting rings are not a substitute for adult supervision. Practice touch supervision by staying within arm's reach anytime your baby is in or near water.

Falls

■ Never leave the baby unattended in high places, such as on a tabletop, changing table, or near stairs. If she does fall and seems to be acting abnormally in any way, call the pediatrician immediately.

Burns

■ Never smoke or eat, drink, or carry anything hot while holding a baby.

■ Keep all hot liquids, like coffee and tea, out of baby's reach.

■ Prevent scalding by making sure the hottest temperature at the faucet is no more than 120 degrees Fahrenheit (48.9 degrees Celsius).

Choking

■ Never give a baby any food or small object that could cause choking. All foods should be mashed, ground, or soft enough to swallow without chewing.

~ 9 ~

Age Eight Months Through Twelve Months

DURING THESE MONTHS, your baby is becoming increasingly mobile, a development that will thrill and challenge both of you. Being able to move from place to place gives your child a delicious sense of power and control—her first real taste of physical independence. And while this is quite exhilarating for her, it's also frightening, since it comes at the time when she may be upset by separation from you. So as eager as she is to move out on her own and explore the farthest reaches of her domain, she may wail if she wanders out of your sight or you move too far from her.

From your point of view, your baby's mobility is a source of considerable concern as well as great pride. Crawling and walking are signals that she's developing right on target, but these achievements also mean that you'll have your hands full keeping her safe. If you haven't already fully childproofed your home, do it now. (See Chapter 15, on safety.) At this age, your baby has no concept of danger and only a limited memory for your warnings. The only way to protect her from the hundreds of hazards in your home is to secure cupboards and drawers, place dangerous and precious objects out of her reach, and make perilous rooms such as the bathroom inaccessible unless she's supervised.

By childproofing your home, you'll also give your baby a greater sense of freedom. After all, fewer areas will be off-limits, and thus you can let her make her own discoveries without your intervention or assistance. These personal accomplishments will promote her emerging self-esteem; you might even think of ways of facilitating them—for example:

1. Fill a low kitchen cupboard or drawer with safe objects and let your baby discover it herself.

2. Pad edges of a coffee table or sofa or consider a soft-edged ottoman and allow her to learn to pull up and cruise.

3. Equip your home with cushions of assorted shapes and sizes and let her experiment with the different ways she can move over and around them.

Knowing when to guide a child and when to let her do things for herself is part of the art of parenting. At this age, your child is extremely expressive and will give you the cues you need to decide when to intervene. When she's acting frustrated rather than challenged, for instance, don't let her struggle alone. If she's crying because her ball is wedged under the sofa out of her reach, if she's pulled to a standing position and can't get down, she needs your help. At other times, however, it's important to let her solve her own problems. Don't let your own impatience cause you to intervene any more than absolutely necessary. You may be tempted to feed your nine-month-old, for instance, because it's faster and less messy than letting her feed herself. However, that also deprives her of a chance to learn a valuable new skill. The more opportunities you can give her to discover, test, and strengthen her new capabilities, the more confident and adventurous she'll be.

Growth and Development

Physical Appearance and Growth

Your baby will continue to grow rapidly during these months. The typical eight-month-old boy weighs between 17.5 and 22 pounds (8–10 kg). Girls tend to weigh half a pound less. By his first birthday, the average child has tripled his birth weight and is 28 to 32 inches (71–81 cm) tall. Head growth between eight and twelve months slows down a bit from the first six months. Typical head size at eight months is 17½ inches (44.5 cm) in circumference; by one year, it's 18 inches (46 cm). Each baby grows at his own rate, however, so you should check your child's height and weight curves on the growth charts in the Appendix to make sure he's following the pattern established in his first eight months.

When your child first stands, you may be surprised by his posture. His belly will protrude, his rear end will stick out, and his back will have a forward sway to it. It may look unusual, but this stance is perfectly normal from the time he starts to stand until he develops a confident sense of balance sometime in the second year.

Your child's feet also may look a little odd to you. When he lies on his back, his toes may turn inward so that he appears pigeon-toed. This common condition usually disappears by eighteen months. If it persists, your pediatrician may show you some foot or leg exercises to do with your baby. If the problem is severe, your pediatrician may refer you to a pediatric orthopedist. (See *Pigeon Toes,* page 828.)

When your child takes his first teetering steps, you may notice quite a different appearance—his feet may turn outward. This occurs because the ligaments of his hips are still so loose that his legs naturally rotate outward. During the first six months of his second year, the ligaments will tighten and then his feet should point nearly straight.

At this age, your child's feet will seem flat because the arch is hidden by a pad of fat. In two to three years, this fat will disappear and his arch will be evident.

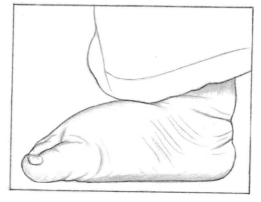

At this age, your child's feet will seem flat because the arch is hidden by a pad of fat. In two to three years, this fat will disappear and his arch will be evident.

Movement

At eight months, your baby probably will be sitting without support. Although she may topple over from time to time, she'll usually catch herself with her arms. As the muscles in her trunk grow stronger, she'll also start leaning over to pick up toys. Eventually she'll figure out how to roll down onto her stomach and get back up to a sitting position.

When she's lying on a flat surface, your baby is now in constant motion. When on her stomach, she'll arch her neck so she can look around, and when on her back, she'll grab her feet (or anything else nearby) and pull them to her mouth. But she won't be content to stay on her back for long. She can turn over at will now and flip without a moment's notice. This can be especially dangerous during diaper changes, so you may want to retire her changing table, using instead the floor or a bed from which she's less likely to fall. Never leave her alone for an instant at any time.

All this activity strengthens muscles for crawling, a skill that usually is mastered between seven and ten months. For a while she simply may rock on her hands and knees. Since her arm muscles are better developed than her legs, she may even push herself backward instead of forward. But with time and practice she'll discover that, by digging with her knees and pushing off, she can propel herself forward across the room toward the target of her choice.

A few children never do crawl. Instead, they use alternative movement methods, such as scooting on their bottoms or slithering on their stomachs. As long as your baby is learning to coordinate each side of her body and is using each arm and leg equally, there's no cause for concern. The important thing is that she's able to explore her surroundings on her own and is strengthening her body in preparation for walking. If you feel your child is not moving normally, discuss your concern with the pediatrician.

How can you encourage your child to crawl? Try presenting her with intriguing objects placed just beyond her reach. As she becomes more agile, create miniature obstacle courses using pillows, boxes, and sofa cushions for her to crawl over and between. Join in the game by hiding behind one of the obstacles and surprising her with a "peekaboo!" Don't ever leave your baby unsupervised among these props, though. If she falls between pillows or under a box, she might not be able to pull herself out. This is bound to frighten her, and she could even smother.

Stairs are another ready-made—but potentially dangerous—obstacle course. Although your baby needs to learn how to go up and down stairs, you should not allow her to play on them alone during this time. If you have a staircase in your home, she'll probably head straight for it every chance she gets, so place sturdy gates at both the top and the bottom of your staircase to close off her access. (To see a safe, horizontal-type gate, see page 485.)

As a substitute for real stairs, let your baby practice climbing up and down steps constructed of heavy-duty foam blocks or sturdy cardboard cartons covered in fabric. At about a year of age, when your baby has become a competent crawler, teach her to go down real stairs backward. She may take a few tumbles before she understands the logic of going feet first instead of headfirst, so practice on carpeted steps and let her climb only the first few. If your home doesn't have carpeted stairs, let her perfect this skill when you visit a home that does.

Although crawling makes a huge difference in how your baby sees the

Soon he will manage to keep himself up and moving until you catch him several steps later.

world and what she can do in it, don't expect her to be content with that for long. She'll see everyone else around her walking, and that's what she'll want to do, too. In preparation for this big step, she'll pull herself to a standing position every chance she gets—although when she first starts, she may not know how to get down. If she cries for your help, physically show her how to bend her knees so she can lower herself to the floor without falling. Teaching her this skill will save you many extra trips to her room at night when she's standing in her crib and crying because she doesn't know how to sit down.

Once your baby feels secure standing, she'll try some tentative steps while holding on to a support. For instance, when your hands aren't available, she'll "cruise" alongside furniture. Just make sure that whatever she uses for support has no sharp edges and is properly weighted or securely attached to the floor so it won't fall on her.

As her balance improves, occasionally she may let go, only to grab for support when she feels herself totter. The first time she continues forth on her own, her steps will be shaky. At first, she may take only one step before dropping, in either surprise or relief. Soon, however, she'll manage to keep herself up and moving until you catch her several steps later. As miraculous as it may seem, most children advance from these first steps to quite confident walking in a matter of days.

Although both of you will feel excited over this dramatic development, you'll also find yourself unnerved at times, especially when she stumbles and falls. But even if you take pains to provide a safe and soft environment, it's almost impossible to avoid bumps and bruises. Just be matter-of-fact about these accidents. Offer a quick hug or a reassuring word and send your little one on her way again. She won't be unduly upset by these falls if you're not.

At this stage, or even earlier, many parents start using a baby walker. Contrary to what the name suggests, these devices do not help the process of learning to walk. They actually eliminate the desire to walk. To make matters worse, they present a serious safety hazard because they can tip over easily when the child bumps into an obstacle, such as a small toy or a throw rug. Children in walkers also are more likely to fall down stairs and get into dangerous places that would otherwise be beyond their reach. For these reasons, **the American Academy of Pediatrics strongly urges parents not to use baby walkers.**

A stationary walker or activity center is a better choice. These do not have wheels, but seats that rotate and bounce. You may also want to consider a sturdy wagon or a "kiddie push car." Be sure the toy has a bar she can push and that it's weighted so it won't tip over when she pulls herself up on it.

As your child begins to walk outside, she'll need shoes to protect her feet. They should be closed toe, comfortable, and flexible with nonskid soles to avoid slips and provide room to grow; sneakers are a great choice. Your child

Movement Milestones for Your Eight- to Twelve-Month-Old

- Gets to sitting position without assistance
- Crawls forward on belly by pulling with arms and pushing with legs
- Assumes hands-and-knees position
- Creeps on hands and knees supporting trunk on hands and knees
- Gets from sitting to crawling or prone (lying on stomach) position
- Pulls self up to stand
- Walks holding on to furniture
- Stands momentarily without support
- May walk two or three steps without support

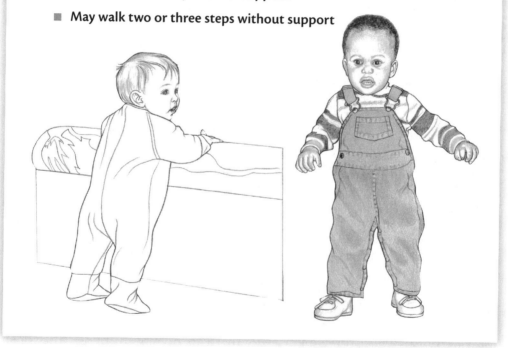

does not need wedges, inserts, high backs, reinforced heels, special arches, and other features designed to shape and support the feet as they have no proven benefit for the average child. Her feet will grow rapidly during these months, and her shoes will have to keep pace. Her first pair of shoes probably will last two to three months, but you should check the fit of her shoes as often as monthly during this formative period. It's often best to have your infant's shoes fit by a professional trained in a child's specific foot needs.

Many babies' first steps are taken around their first birthday, although it's perfectly normal for children to start walking a little earlier or later. At first, your child will walk with her feet wide apart to improve her shaky sense of balance. During those initial days and weeks, she accidentally may get going too fast and fall when she tries to stop. As she becomes more confident, she'll learn how to stop and change directions. Before long, she'll be able to squat to pick something up and then stand again. When she reaches this level of accomplishment, she'll get enormous pleasure from push-pull toys—the noisier the better.

Hand and Finger Skills

Your baby's mastery of crawling, standing, and walking are bound to be his most dramatic accomplishments during these months, but don't overlook all the wonderful things he's learning to do with his hands. At the beginning of this period, he'll still clumsily "rake" things toward himself, but by the end, he'll grasp accurately with his thumb and first or second finger. You'll find him practicing this pincer movement on any small object, from dust balls to cereal, and he may even try to snap his fingers if you show him how.

As your baby learns to open his fingers at will, he'll delight in dropping and throwing things. If you leave small toys on the tray of his high chair or in his playpen, he'll fling them down and then call loudly for someone to retrieve them so he can do it again. If he throws hard objects such as blocks, he might do some damage and probably will increase the noise level in your household considerably. Your life will be a little calmer if you redirect him toward softer objects, such as balls of various sizes, colors, and textures. (Include some with beads or chimes inside so they make a sound as they roll.) One activity that not only is fun but also allows you to observe your child's developing skills is to sit on the floor and roll a large ball toward him. At first, he'll slap randomly at it, but eventually he'll learn to swat it so it rolls back in your direction.

With his improved coordination, your baby can now investigate the objects he encounters more thoroughly. He'll pick them up, shake them, bang them, and pass them from hand to hand. He'll be particularly intrigued by toys with moving parts—wheels that spin, levers that can be moved, hinges that open and close. Holes also are fascinating because he can poke his fingers in them and, when he becomes a little more skilled, drop things through them.

Blocks are another favorite toy at this age. In fact, nothing motivates a baby to crawl quite as much as a tower waiting to be toppled. Toward the end of this period, your child may even start to build towers of his own by stacking one block on top of another.

Milestones in Hand and Finger Skills for Your Eight- to Twelve-Month-Old

- Uses pincer grasp
- Bangs two cubes together
- Puts objects into container
- Takes objects out of container
- Lets objects go voluntarily
- Pokes with index finger
- Tries to imitate scribbling

Language Development

Toward the end of the first year, your baby will begin to communicate what she wants by pointing, crawling, or gesturing toward her target. She'll also imitate many of the gestures she sees adults make as they talk. This nonverbal communication is only a temporary measure, however, while she learns how to phrase her messages in words.

Do you notice the coos, gurgles, and screeches of earlier months now giving way to recognizable syllables, such as "ba," "da," "ga," and "ma"? Your child may even stumble on words such as "mama" and "bye-bye" quite accidentally, and when you get excited she'll realize she's said something meaningful. Before long she'll start using "mama" to summon you or attract your attention. At this age, she may also say "mama" throughout the day just to practice saying the word. Ultimately, however, she'll use words only when she wants to communicate their meanings.

Even though you've been talking to your baby from birth, she now understands more language, and thus your conversations will take on new significance. Before she can say many, if any, words, she'll probably comprehend more than you suspect. For example, watch how she responds when you mention a favorite toy across the room. If she looks toward it, she's telling you she understands. To help her increase her understanding, keep talking to her as much as possible. Tell her what's happening around her, particularly as you bathe, change, and feed her. Make your language simple and specific: "I'm drying you with the big blue towel. How soft it feels!" Verbally label familiar toys and objects for her, and try to be as consistent as possible—that is, if you call the family pet a cat today, don't call it a kitty tomorrow.

Picture books can enhance this entire process by reinforcing her budding

Bilingual Babies

If you speak a second language in your home, don't be concerned that your child is going to become confused by hearing two languages. Millions of American families speak not only English but also another language in their daily lives. Research and parental experience show that when children are exposed to two (or even more) languages at a very young age, particularly when they hear both of them consistently, they are able to learn both languages simultaneously. Yes, during the child's normal language development, he may be more proficient in one or the other language, and at times he may interject words from one language when speaking the other. But with time, the two languages will become distinct and separate, and he should be able to communicate in both. (Some studies suggest that while he may be able to understand both languages, he will speak one of them better than the other for a time.)

Certainly you should encourage your child to become bilingual. It's an asset and a skill that will benefit him for the rest of his life. In general, the younger he is when both languages are introduced, the more proficiently he'll learn them; by contrast, he may have a little more difficulty learning the second language if he is introduced to it during the preschool years only after learning and speaking the first language exclusively.

understanding that everything has a name. Choose books with large board, cloth, or vinyl pages that she can turn herself. Also look for simple but colorful illustrations of things your child will recognize.

Whether you're reading or talking to her, give her plenty of opportunities to join in. Ask questions and wait for a response. Or let her take the lead. If she says "Gaagaagaa," repeat it back and see what she does. Yes, these exchanges may seem meaningless, but they tell your baby that communication is two-way and that she's a welcome participant. Paying attention to what she says also will help you identify the words she understands and make it more likely that you'll recognize her first spoken words.

These first words, incidentally, often aren't proper English. For your child, a "word" is any sound that consistently refers to the same person, object, or event. So if she says "mog" every time she wants milk, you should treat "mog" with all the respect of a legitimate word. When you speak back to her, however, use "milk," and eventually she'll make the correction herself.

There's a tremendous variance in the age at which children begin to say recognizable words. Some have a vocabulary of two to three words by their first birthday. More likely, your baby's speech at twelve months will consist of a sort of gibberish that has the tones and variations of intelligible speech. As long as she's experimenting with sounds that vary in intensity, pitch, and quality, she's getting ready to talk. The more you respond to her as if she were speaking, the more you'll stimulate her urge to communicate.

Language Milestones for Your Eight- to Twelve-Month-Old

- **Pays increasing attention to speech**
- **Responds to simple verbal requests**
- **Responds to "no"**
- **Uses simple gestures, such as shaking head for "no"**
- **Babbles with inflection**
- **Says "dada" and "mama"**
- **Uses exclamations, such as "oh-oh!"**
- **Tries to imitate words**

Cognitive Development

An eight-month-old is curious about everything, but he also has a very short attention span and will move rapidly from one activity to the next. Two to three minutes is the most he'll spend with a single toy, and then he'll turn to something new. By twelve months, he may be willing to sit for as long as fifteen minutes with a particularly interesting plaything, but most of the time he'll still be a body in motion, and you shouldn't expect him to be any different.

Ironically, although toy stores are brimming with one expensive plaything after another, the toys that fascinate children most at this age are ordinary household objects such as wooden spoons, egg cartons, and plastic containers of all shapes and sizes. Your baby will be especially interested in things that differ just a bit from what he already knows, so if he's bored with the oatmeal box he's been playing with, you can renew his interest by putting a ball inside or turning it into a pull toy by tying a short string to it. These small changes will help him learn to detect small differences between the familiar and the unfamiliar. Also, when you choose playthings, remember that objects too much like what he's seen before will be given a quick once-over and dismissed, while things that are too foreign may be confusing or frightening. Look instead for objects and toys that gradually help him expand his horizons.

Often your baby won't need your help to discover objects that fall into this middle ground of newness. In fact, as soon as he can crawl, he'll be off in search of new things to conquer. He'll rummage through your drawers, empty out wastebaskets, ransack kitchen cabinets, and conduct elaborate experiments on everything he finds. (Make sure there's nothing that can hurt him in those containers, and keep an eye on him whenever he's into these things.) He'll never tire of dropping, rolling, throwing, submerging, or waving objects to find out how they behave. This may look like random play to you, but it's your child's way of finding out how the world works. Like any good scientist, he's observing the properties of objects, and from his observations, he'll develop ideas about shapes (some things roll and others don't), textures (things can be scratchy, soft, or smooth), and sizes (some things fit inside each other). He'll even begin to understand that some things are edible and others aren't, although he'll still put everything into his mouth just to be sure. (Again, make sure there's nothing dangerous lying around that he can put in his mouth.)

His continuing observations during these months also will help him understand that objects exist even when they're out of his sight. This concept is called object permanence. At eight months, when you hide a toy under a scarf, he'll pick up the scarf and search for the toy underneath—a response that wouldn't have occurred three months earlier. Try hiding the toy under the scarf and then removing it when he's not looking, however, and your eight-month-old will be

Variations of Peekaboo

The possible variations of peekaboo are almost endless. As your child becomes more mobile and alert, create games that let her take the lead. Here are some suggestions.

1. Drape a soft cloth over her head and ask, "Where's the baby?" Once she understands the game, she'll pull the cloth away and pop up grinning.

2. With baby on her back facing toward you, lift both her legs together—"Up, up, up"—until they conceal your face from her. Then open them wide: "Peekaboo!" As she gets the idea, she'll move her legs herself. (This is a great game at diaper-changing time.)

3. Hide behind a door or a piece of furniture, leaving a foot or arm in her view as a clue. She'll be delighted to come find you.

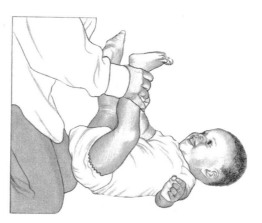

4. Take turns with your baby "hiding" your head under a large towel and letting her pull the towel off and then putting it over her head and pulling it off.

puzzled. By ten months, he'll be so certain that the toy still exists that he'll continue looking for it. To help your baby learn object permanence, play peekaboo with him. By switching from one variation of this game to another, you'll maintain his interest almost indefinitely.

As he approaches his first birthday, your child will become increasingly conscious not only that things have names but that they also have particular functions. You'll see this new awareness weave itself into his play as a very early form of fantasy. For example, instead of treating a toy telephone as an interesting object to be chewed, poked, and banged, he'll put the receiver to his ear just as he's seen you do. You can encourage important developmental activities like this by offering him suggestive props—a hairbrush, toothbrush, cup, or spoon—and by being an enthusiastic audience for his performances.

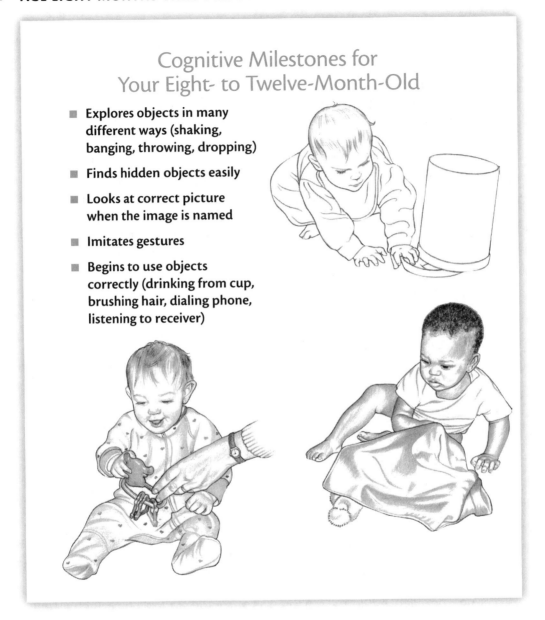

Cognitive Milestones for Your Eight- to Twelve-Month-Old

- Explores objects in many different ways (shaking, banging, throwing, dropping)
- Finds hidden objects easily
- Looks at correct picture when the image is named
- Imitates gestures
- Begins to use objects correctly (drinking from cup, brushing hair, dialing phone, listening to receiver)

Brain Development

As you've read in this chapter and the ones that preceded it, the early months of your child's life are crucial to her brain development. The environment to which you expose her and the experiences that she has at this time in life will have a powerful influence on the way her brain grows.

You have opportunities every day to nurture your child's brain. You can provide her with intellectual stimulation just by talking with her and by encouraging her to say words that she's learning. You can give her a comfortable and safe environment in which to explore the world around her. You can provide her with simple toys that challenge her brain to develop. You can play games with her that encourage her to stretch her memory.

In the box below, you'll find some suggestions that can be used day by day as your baby progresses from ages eight to twelve months. They really can make a difference in your child's life, and not only now—they'll build a foundation for brain growth for years to come.

Stimulating Infant Brain Growth: Age Eight Months Through Twelve Months

- Talk to your baby during dressing, bathing, feeding, playing, walking, and driving, using adult talk; check with your pediatrician if your baby does not seem to respond to sound or if syllables and words are not developing.

- Be attentive to your baby's rhythms and moods. Respond to her when she is upset as well as when she is happy.

- Your baby will be very tuned in to you and to others she encounters. Her ability to respond to your emotions is an important part of this developmental period. By eight to nine months of age, she can literally read your face for emotions, which underscores the need for you to temper strong emotions.

- Encourage your baby to play with blocks and soft toys, which helps her develop hand-to-eye coordination, fine motor skills, and a sense of competence.

- Provide a stimulating, safe environment where your baby can begin to explore and roam.

- Give consistent warm, physical contact—hugging, skin-to-skin, body-to-body contact—to establish your child's sense of security and well-being.

- Read to your baby every day.

- If you speak a foreign language, use it at home.

■ Try to be sure your baby is not exposed to events that could upset her or overwhelm her, or anything with content intended for older children or adults.

■ Play games like peekaboo and pattycake to stimulate your baby's memory skills.

■ Introduce your child to other children and parents.

■ Provide age- and developmentally appropriate toys that are safe and inexpensive. Toys do not need to be costly—ordinary household objects will do just fine. Remember, it's much more important to give your child more attention than more toys.

■ Teach your baby to wave "bye-bye" and to shake her head "yes" and "no."

■ Make sure other people who provide care and supervision for your baby understand the importance of forming a loving and comforting relationship with her.

■ Respect your baby's periodic discomfort around people who may not be her primary caregivers.

■ Spend time on the floor playing with your child every day.

■ Choose quality child care that is affectionate, responsive, educational, and safe. Visit your child care provider frequently and share your ideas about positive caregiving.

Emotional Development

During these months, your child sometimes may seem like two separate babies. First there's the one who's open, affectionate, and outgoing with you. But then there's another who's anxious, clinging, and easily frightened around unfamiliar people or objects. Some people may tell you that your child is fearful or shy because you're "spoiling" her, but don't believe it. Her widely diverse behavior patterns aren't caused by you or your parenting style; they occur because she's now, for the first time, able to tell the difference between familiar and unfamiliar situations. If anything, the predictable anxieties of this period are evidence of her healthy relationship with you.

Anxiety around strangers is usually one of the first emotional milestones your baby will reach. You may think something is wrong when this child of

The predictable anxieties of this period are evidence of your child's healthy relationship with you.

Social/Emotional Milestones for Your Eight- to Twelve-Month-Old

- Shy or anxious with strangers

- Cries when mother or father leaves

- Enjoys imitating people in play

- Shows specific preferences for certain people and toys

- Tests parental responses to his actions during feedings (What do you do when he refuses a food?)

- Tests parental responses to his behavior (What do you do if he cries after you leave the room?)

- May be fearful in some situations

- Prefers mother and/or regular caregiver over all others

- Repeats sounds or gestures for attention

- Finger-feeds himself

- Extends arm or leg to help when being dressed

yours who, at the age of three months, interacted calmly with people she didn't know is now beginning to tense up when strangers come too close. This is normal for this age, and you need not worry. Even relatives and frequent babysitters with whom your baby was once comfortable may prompt her to hide or cry now, especially if they approach her hastily.

At about the same time, she'll become much more "clutchy" about leaving you. This is the start of separation anxiety. Just as she's starting to realize that each object is unique and permanent, she'll also discover that there's only one of you. When you're out of her sight, she'll know you're somewhere, but not with her, and this will cause her great distress. She'll have so little sense of time that she won't know when—or even whether—you'll be coming back. Once she gets a little older, her memory of past experiences with you will comfort her when you're gone, and she'll be able to anticipate a reunion. But for now she's only aware of the present, so every time you leave her sight—even to go to the next room—she'll fuss and cry. When you leave her with someone else, she may scream as though her heart will break. At bedtime, she'll refuse to leave you to go to sleep, and then she may wake up searching for you in the middle of the night.

How long should you expect this separation anxiety to last? It usually peaks between ten and eighteen months and then fades during the last half of the second year. In some ways, this phase of your child's emotional development will be especially tender for both of you, while in others, it will be painful. After all, her desire to be with you is a sign of her attachment to her first and greatest love—namely you. The intensity of her feeling as she hurtles into your arms is irresistible, especially when you realize that no one—including your child herself—will ever again think you are quite as perfect as she does at this age. On the other hand, you may feel suffocated by her constant clinging, while experiencing guilt whenever you leave her crying for you. Fortunately, this emotional roller coaster eventually will subside along with her separation anxiety. But in the meantime, try to downplay your leave-taking as much as possible. Here are some suggestions that may help.

1. Your baby is more susceptible to separation anxiety when she's tired, hungry, or sick. If you know you're going to go out, schedule your departure so that it occurs after she's napped and eaten. And try to stay with her as much as possible when she's sick.

2. Don't make a fuss over your leaving. Instead, have the person staying with her create a distraction (a new toy, a visit to the mirror, a bath). Then say goodbye and slip away quickly.

3. Remember that her tears will subside within minutes of your departure. Her outbursts are for your benefit, to persuade you to stay. With you out of sight, she'll soon turn her attention to the person staying with her.

Acquainting Your Baby with a Sitter

Is your baby about to have a new babysitter for a few hours? Whenever possible, let your child get to know this new person while you're there. Ideally, have the sitter spend time with him on several successive days before you leave them alone. If this isn't possible, allow yourself an extra hour or two for this get-acquainted period before you have to go out.

During this first meeting, the sitter and your baby should get to know each other very gradually, using the following steps.

1. Hold the baby on your lap while you and the sitter talk. Watch for clues that your child is at ease before you have the sitter make eye contact with him. Wait until the baby is looking at her or playing contentedly by himself.

2. Have the sitter talk to the baby while he stays on your lap. She should not reach toward the child or try to touch him yet.

3. Once the baby seems comfortable with the conversation, put him on the floor with a favorite toy, across from the sitter. Invite the sitter to slowly come closer and play with the toy. As the baby warms up to her, you can move back gradually.

4. See what happens when you leave the room. If your baby doesn't notice you're missing, the introduction has gone well.

You can use leisurely introduction with anyone who hasn't seen the child in the past few days, including relatives and friends. Adults often overwhelm babies of this age by coming close and making funny noises or, worse yet, trying to take them from their mothers. You have to intervene when this occurs. Explain to these well-meaning people that your baby needs time to warm up to strangers and that he's more likely to respond well if they go slowly.

4. Help her learn to cope with separation through short practice sessions at home. Separation will be easier on her when she initiates it, so when she crawls to another room (one that's babyproofed), don't follow her right away; wait for one or two minutes. When you have to go to another room for a few seconds, tell her where you're going and that you'll return. If she fusses, call to her instead of running back. Gradually she'll learn that nothing terrible happens when you're gone and, just as important, that you always come back when you say you will.

5. If you take your child to a sitter's home or a child care center, don't just drop her off and leave. Spend a few extra minutes playing with her in this new environment. When you do leave, reassure her that you'll be back later.

If your child has a strong, healthy attachment to you, her separation anxiety probably will occur earlier than in other babies, and she'll pass through it more quickly. Instead of resenting her possessiveness during these months, maintain as much warmth and good humor as you can. Through your actions, you're showing her how to express and return love. This is the emotional base she'll rely on in years to come.

From the beginning, you've considered your baby to be a unique person with specific character traits and preferences. She, however, has had only a dim notion of herself as a person separate from you. Now her sense of identity is coming into bloom. As she develops a growing sense of herself as an individual, she'll also become increasingly conscious of you as a separate person.

One of the clearest signs of her own self-awareness is the way your baby watches herself in the mirror at this age. Up to about eight months, she treated the mirror as just another fascinating object. Perhaps, she thought, the reflection was another baby, or maybe it was a magical surface of lights and shadows. But now her responses will change, indicating she understands that one of the images belongs to her. While watching the mirror, for example, she may touch a smudge on her own nose or pull on a stray lock of her hair. You can reinforce her sense of identity by playing mirror games. When you're looking in the mirror together, touch different body parts: "This is Jenny's nose. This is Mommy's nose." Or move in and out of the mirror, playing peekaboo with the reflections. Or make faces and verbally label the emotions you are conveying.

As the months pass and your child's self-concept becomes more secure, she'll have less trouble meeting strangers and separating from you. She'll also become more assertive. Before, you could count on her to be relatively compliant as long as she was comfortable. But now, more often than not, she'll want things her own particular way. For instance, don't be surprised if she turns up her nose at certain foods or objects when you place them in front of her. Also, as she becomes more mobile, you'll find yourself frequently saying "no," to

Toys Appropriate for Your Eight- to Twelve-Month-Old

- Stacking toys in different sizes, shapes, colors
- Cups, pails, and other unbreakable containers
- Unbreakable mirrors of various sizes
- Bath toys that float, squirt, or hold water
- Large building blocks
- "Busy boxes" that push, open, squeak, and move
- Squeeze toys
- Large dolls and puppets
- Cars, trucks, and other vehicle toys made of flexible plastic, with no sharp edges or removable parts
- Balls of all sizes (but not small enough to fit in the mouth)
- Cardboard books with large pictures
- Music boxes, musical toys, and child-safe CD and MP3 players
- Push-pull toys
- Toy telephones
- Paper tubes, empty boxes, old magazines, egg cartons, empty plastic water bottles (without a lid or small cap as that could be a potential choking hazard)

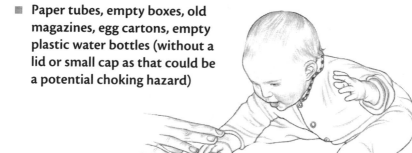

warn her away from things she shouldn't touch. But even after she understands the word, she may touch anyway. Just wait—this is only a forerunner of power struggles to come.

Developmental Health Watch

Each baby develops in his own manner, so it's impossible to tell exactly when your child will perfect a given skill. Although the developmental milestones listed in this book will give you a general idea of the changes you can expect as your child gets older, don't be alarmed if his development takes a slightly different course. Alert your pediatrician if your baby displays any of the following signs of *possible* developmental delay in the eight- to twelve-month age range.

- **Does not crawl**
- **Drags one side of body while crawling (for over one month)**
- **Cannot stand when supported**
- **Does not search for objects that are hidden while he watches**
- **Says no single words ("mama" or "dada")**
- **Does not learn to use gestures, such as waving or shaking head**
- **Does not point to objects or pictures**

Your baby also may become afraid of objects and situations that she used to take in stride. At this age, fears of the dark, thunder, and loud appliances such as vacuum cleaners are common. Later you'll be able to subdue these fears by talking about them, but for now, the only solution is to eliminate the source of the fears as much as possible: Put a night-light in her room, or vacuum when she's not around. And when you can't shield her from something that frightens her, try to anticipate her reaction and be close by so she can turn to you. Comfort her, but stay calm so she understands that you are not afraid. If you reassure her every time she hears a clap of thunder or the roar of a jet overhead, her fear gradually will subside until all she has to do is look at you to feel safe.

Basic Care

Feeding

At this age, your baby needs between 750 and 900 calories each day, about 400 to 500 of which should come from breast milk or formula (approximately 24 oz. [720 ml] a day). But don't be surprised if her appetite is less robust now than it

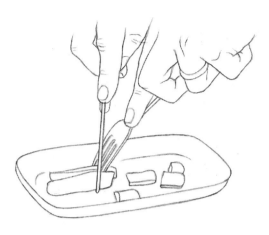

was during the first eight months. This is because her rate of growth is slowing, and she also has so many new and interesting activities to distract her.

At about eight months, you may want to introduce "junior" foods. These are slightly coarser than strained foods and are packaged in larger jars—usually 6 to 8 ounces (180–240 ml). They require more chewing than baby foods. You also can expand your baby's diet to include soft foods such as yogurt, oatmeal, forked mashed banana, potatoes, or even thicker pureed or lumpy pureed vegetables. Eggs (including scrambled) are an excellent source of protein, as are cottage cheese, Greek yogurt, and avocado. As always, introduce one food at a time, then wait three to five days before trying something else to be sure your child doesn't develop an allergic reaction.

At about eight to nine months, as your baby's ability to use her hands improves, give her a spoon of her own and let her play with it at mealtimes. Once she's figured out how to hold it, dip it in her food and let her try to feed herself. But don't expect much in the beginning, when more food is bound to go on the floor and high chair than into her mouth. A plastic cloth under her chair will help minimize some of the cleanup.

Be patient, and resist the temptation to grab the spoon away from her. She needs not only the practice but also the knowledge that you have confidence in her ability to feed herself. For a while you may want to alternate bites from her spoon with bites from a spoon that you hold. Once she consistently gets her own spoon to her mouth (which might not be until after her first birthday), you may keep filling her spoon for her to decrease the mess and waste, but leave the actual feeding to her.

In the early weeks of self-feeding, things may go more smoothly when she's really hungry and is more interested in eating than playing. Although your baby now eats three meals, just like the rest of the family, you may not want to impose her somewhat disorderly eating behavior on everyone else's dinnertime. Many

Transitional Objects

Almost everyone knows about the Charles Schulz character Linus and his blanket. He drags it around wherever he goes, nibbling on its corner or curling up with it when the going gets tough. Security objects such as blankets are part of the emotional support system every child needs in his early years.

Your child may not choose a blanket, of course. He may prefer a soft toy or even the satin trim on Mom's bathrobe. Chances are, he'll make his choice between months eight and twelve, and he'll keep it with him for years to come. When he's tired, it will help him get to sleep. When he's separated from you, it will reassure him. When he's frightened or upset, it will comfort him. When he's in a strange place, it will help him feel at home.

These special comforts are called transitional objects, because they help children make the emotional transition from dependence to independence. They work, in part, because they feel good: They're soft, cuddly, and nice to touch. They're also effective because of their familiarity. This so-called lovey has your child's scent on it, and it reminds him of the comfort and security of his own room. It makes him feel that everything is going to be OK.

Despite myths to the contrary, transitional objects are not a sign of weakness or insecurity, and there's no reason to keep your child from using one. In fact, a transitional object can be so helpful that you may want to help him choose one and build it into his nighttime ritual.

You also can make things easier for yourself by having two identical security objects. Doing this will allow you to wash one while the other is being used, thus sparing your baby (and yourself) a potential emotional crisis and a very bedraggled lovey. If your baby chooses a large blanket for his security object, you can easily turn it into two by cutting it in half. He has little sense of size and won't notice the change. If he's chosen a toy instead, try to find a duplicate as soon as possible. If you don't start rotating them early, your child may refuse the second one because it feels too new and foreign.

Parents often worry that transitional objects promote thumb sucking, and in fact they sometimes (but not always) do. But it's important to remember that thumb or finger sucking is a normal, natural way for a young child to comfort himself. He'll gradually give up both the transitional object and the sucking as he matures and finds other ways to cope with stress.

families compromise by feeding the baby most of her meal in advance and then letting her occupy herself with healthy finger foods while the others eat their meal.

Finger foods for babies include small pieces of steamed veggies, or soft fruit such as banana, well-cooked whole-grain pasta, small pieces of whole-wheat bread, chicken, scrambled eggs, or whole-grain cereals. Try to offer a selection of flavors, shapes, colors, and textures, but always watch her for choking in case she bites off a piece too big to swallow. (See *Choking*, page 691.) Also, because she's likely to swallow without chewing, never offer a young child chunks of peanut butter, large pieces of raw vegetables, whole nuts, whole grapes, popcorn, uncooked peas, celery, gum, hard

In the early weeks of self-feeding, things may go more smoothly when she's really hungry and is more interested in eating than playing.

Sample One-Day Menu for Your Eight- to Twelve-Month-Old

1 cup = 8 ounces (240 ml)
4 ounces = 120 ml
6 ounces = 180 ml

BREAKFAST
¼–½ cup cereal, or mashed or scrambled egg
¼–½ cup fruit, diced (if your child is self-feeding)
4–6 ounces breast milk or formula

SNACK
4–6 ounces breast milk, formula, or water
¼ cup diced cheese or cooked vegetables

LUNCH
¼–½ cup yogurt or cottage cheese or meat
¼–½ cup yellow or orange vegetables
4–6 ounces breast milk

SNACK
1 whole-grain cracker or teething biscuit
¼ cup yogurt or diced (if child is self-feeding) fruit
water

DINNER
¼ cup diced poultry, meat, or tofu
¼–½ cup green vegetables
¼ cup whole-grain pasta, rice, or potato
¼ cup diced or mashed fruit
4–6 ounces breast milk/formula

BEFORE BEDTIME
6–8 ounces breast milk, formula, or water (If breast milk, follow with water or
    brush teeth afterward.)

candies, or other hard round foods, and always observe your child eating. Choking can happen with hot dogs, grapes, or chunks of cheese or meat sticks (baby-food "hot dogs"), so these always should be cut lengthwise and then into smaller pieces before being fed to a child of this age.

Weaning from Breast to Bottle

Mothers wean their babies for a variety of reasons. The weaning process begins when the baby first receives anything in the diet besides breast milk.

In any event, you should continue to breastfeed until your baby is at least one year old. After one year of age, whole or 2 percent (reduced fat) cow's milk can be given. Many breastfed babies never use a bottle, but wean directly to a sippy or straw cup around this age. If you plan to introduce bottle-feedings of formula or expressed milk, it may be a bit more challenging if your baby has never been given a bottle before. She may object to it the first few times, especially if her mother tries to give it to her. By this age, she associates her mother with nursing, so it's understandable if she's confused and annoyed when there's a sudden change in the routine. Things may go more smoothly if her father or another family member feeds her—and Mom stays out of the room. After she's gotten used to the idea, then Mom can take over, but the baby should get lots of cuddling, stroking, and encouragement to make up for the lost skin-to-skin contact. Again, at this age you can also skip the bottle and wean straight to a sippy or straw cup of breast milk and later cow's milk.

Once your baby has learned to take an occasional bottle or cup, it should be relatively easy to wean her from the breast if you desire to do so. The time needed to wean her, however, will vary, depending on the emotional and physical needs of both child and mother. If your baby adapts well to change and you're ready for the transition, you can make a total switch in one or two weeks. For the first two days, substitute one bottle or cup of formula for one breastfeeding per day. (Don't express milk during this time.) On the third day, use a bottle or cup for two feedings. By the fifth day, you can jump to three or four bottle- or cup-feedings.

Once you've stopped breastfeeding entirely, breast milk production will cease very quickly. In the meantime, if your breasts should become engorged, you may need to express milk for the first two or three days to relieve the discomfort. Gradual weaning by eliminating one feeding at a time will help to minimize engorgement. Within a week, the discomfort should subside.

Many women prefer to wean more slowly, even when their babies cooperate fully. Breastfeeding provides a closeness between mother and child that's hard to duplicate any other way, and, understandably, you may be reluctant to give up such intimacy. In this case, you can continue to offer a combination of the breast milk and/or formula for up to one year of age, and breast milk and whole or 2 percent (reduced-fat) milk in a cup beyond one year of age. Some babies lose interest in breastfeeding between nine and twelve months, or when they learn to drink from a cup. It's important for you to remember that this is not a personal rejection, but a sign of your child's growing independence. Other times, older infants go through a period of time when they refuse the breast, the so-called nursing strike. Then without any warning or reason, they resume breastfeeding as though nothing changed. Breastfeeding can continue as part of the routine feeding beyond the first year of life.

Weaning to a Cup

A straw or sippy cup can be introduced anytime after six months of age. Babies who are breastfed may transition to a cup easier than to a bottle. To get started, give your baby a trainer cup that has two handles and a snap-on lid with a spout, or a straw cup. Either option will minimize spillage

Six months may pass before your baby is willing to take all his liquid from a cup.

as he experiments with different ways to hold (and most likely to throw) the cup.

In the beginning, fill the cup with a little water and offer it to him at just one meal a day. Show him how to maneuver it to his mouth and tip it so he can drink. Don't become dismayed, however, if he treats the cup as a plaything for several weeks; most babies do. Just be patient until he's finally able to get most of the liquid down his throat or suck out of the straw without the liquid dribbling down his chin or the cup flying around the room. Once he gets the hang of the cup, put breast milk or formula in the cup to get him used to drinking milk from something other than a bottle.

There are advantages to drinking from a cup: It will improve your child's hand-to-mouth coordination, and it will begin to prepare him for the weaning process, which frequently occurs around this age. Remember, the American Academy of Pediatrics believes that breastfeeding is the best source of nutrition for babies through at least their first birthday. But as you gradually transition him to receiving other types of liquids, your baby's readiness for drinking from a cup will be signaled by his:

1. Looking around while nursing or taking the bottle

2. Mouthing the nipple without sucking

3. Trying to slide off your lap before the feeding is finished

Even under the best of circumstances, weaning may not take place overnight. Six months may pass before your baby is willing to take all his liquid from a cup. Even so, you can start the process and proceed gradually, letting his interest and willingness guide you. You'll probably find it easiest at first to substitute a cup for the bottle or breast at the midday feeding. Once he's adjusted to this change, try doing the same in the morning. The bedtime feeding probably will be the last one abandoned, and for good reason: Your baby has become accustomed to this source of nighttime comfort and calming, and it will take him some time to give it up. If he's sleeping through the night and not waking up hungry, he doesn't physically need the extra nourishment from bedtime breast- or bottle-feeding. In this case, you might break the habit in stages, first by substituting a bedtime bottle with water instead of milk and then by switching to a drink of water from a cup.

During this process, you may be tempted to put milk in his bottle to help him go to sleep, but don't do it. If he falls asleep while feeding, the milk will pool around his teeth, and this can cause his incoming teeth to decay—a condition known as baby bottle tooth decay or early childhood caries. To make matters worse, drinking while lying flat on his back can contribute to middle ear infections, since the liquid may flow through the eustachian tube into the middle ear.

There's still one more disadvantage to prolonged bottle-feeding: The bottle can become a security object, particularly if your baby keeps it beyond about age one. To avoid this, don't let him carry or drink from a bottle while playing. Restrict the use of a bottle to feedings when he's sitting down or being held. At all other times, give him a cup. If you never allow him to take the bottle with him, he won't realize that bringing it along is even an option. Don't give in once this decision has been made; be consistent or he may get confused and demand a bottle again long after he has "officially" been weaned.

Sleeping

At eight months, your baby probably still takes two regular naps, one midmorning and the other mid-afternoon. She's also likely to sleep as much as ten to twelve hours at night without needing a middle-of-the-night feeding. But be aware of some possible problems ahead: As her separation anxieties intensify in the next few months, she may start to resist going to bed, and she may wake up more often looking for you.

During this difficult period, you may need to experiment with several strategies to find those that help your baby sleep. For example, some children go to sleep more easily with the door open (so they can hear you); others develop consoling habits, such as sucking their thumbs or rocking. As previously mentioned, your child also might adopt a special blanket or stuffed animal as a transitional object, which comforts her when you're not nearby. Anything that's safe, soft and huggable, and can be stroked or sucked will serve this purpose. You can encourage your child to use a transitional object by providing her with a lightweight blanket or soft toy.

Here are some additional suggestions to help this stage pass more quickly.

First of all, don't do anything that will reward your baby for calling you in the middle of the night. Go to her side to make sure she's all right, and tell her that you're nearby if she really needs you; but don't turn on the light, rock her, or walk with her. You might offer her a drink of water, but don't feed her, and certainly don't take her to your bed. If she's suffering from separation anxiety, taking her to your bed will only make it harder for her to return to her own crib.

When you do check on her, try to make her as comfortable as possible. Also make sure she isn't sick. Some problems, such as ear infections or the croup, can come on suddenly in the night. Once you're sure there's no sign of illness, then check her diaper, changing her only if she's had a bowel movement or if her diaper is uncomfortably wet. Do the change as quickly as possible in dim light and then settle her back in her crib—and on her back. Before leaving the room, whisper a few comforting words about how it's nighttime and time to sleep. If she continues to cry, wait a few minutes, then go back in and comfort her for a short time. This period can be extremely difficult for parents. After all, it's emotionally and physically exhausting to listen to your child cry, and you'll probably respond with a combination of emotions. But remember, her behavior is not deliberate. Instead, she's reacting to anxieties and stresses that are natural at her age. If you stay calm and follow a consistent pattern from one night to the next, she'll soon be putting herself to sleep. Keep this objective in sight as you struggle through the "training" nights. Doing so ultimately will make life much easier for both of you. See Chapter 35 for more information on sleep.

Behavior

Discipline

Your baby's desire to explore is almost impossible to satisfy. As a result, he'll want to touch, taste, and manipulate everything he can get into his hands. In the process, he's bound to find his way into places and situations that are off-limits. Although his curiosity is vital to his overall development and shouldn't be discouraged unnecessarily, he can't be allowed to jeopardize his own safety or to damage valuable objects. Whether he's investigating the burners on your stove or pulling up plants in your flower bed, you need to help him stop these activities.

Keep in mind that the way you handle these early incidents will lay the foundation for future discipline. Learning not to do something that he very much wants to do is a major first step toward self-control. The better he learns this lesson now, the less you'll have to intervene in years to come.

What's your best strategy? As we suggested earlier, distraction usually can deal effectively with undesirable behavior. Your baby's memory is still short, and thus you can shift his focus with minimal resistance. If he's headed for something he shouldn't get into, you don't necessarily have to say "no." Overusing that word will blunt its effect in the long run. Instead, pick him up and direct him toward something he can play with. Look for a compromise that will keep him interested and active without squelching his natural curiosity.

You should reserve your serious discipline for those situations where your child's activities can expose him to real danger—for example, playing with electric cords. This is the time to say "no" firmly and remove him from the situation. But don't expect him to learn from just one or two incidents. Because of his short memory, you'll have to repeat the scene over and over before he finally recognizes and responds to your directions. Never depend on an infant of this age to keep himself from danger, no matter how often he's been corrected. Find a spot where he can play safely—a no "No!" zone where everything is as safe as can be.

To improve the effectiveness of your discipline, consistency is absolutely critical. Make sure that everyone responsible for caring for your baby understands what the child is and isn't allowed to do. Keep the rules to a minimum, preferably limited to situations that are potentially dangerous to the child. Then make sure he hears "no" every time he strays into forbidden territory.

Immediacy is another important component of good discipline. React as soon as you see your baby heading into trouble, not five minutes later. If you delay your reprimand, he won't understand the reason you're angry and the lesson will be lost. Likewise, don't be too quick to comfort him after he's been scolded. Yes, he may cry, sometimes as much in surprise as distress; but wait a minute or two before you reassure him. Otherwise, he won't know whether he really did something wrong.

In the next chapter, we'll describe in some detail the importance of refraining from spanking or striking your child in any way when disciplining him. No matter what your child's age, or what his behavior has been, physical punishment is always an inappropriate way for you to respond. Spanking only teaches a child to act aggressively when he's upset. Yes, it may relieve your own frustration temporarily, and for the moment you actually might believe that it will do some good. But this is *not* an effective way of disciplining your child, and it certainly doesn't teach him any alternative way to act. It also undermines effective communication between the two of you, as well as weakening his own sense of security.

What's the alternative? The American Academy of Pediatrics recommends using "time-outs" instead of spankings—putting a child who has misbehaved in a quiet place for a few minutes, away from other people, TV, electronics, or books. When the time-out is over, explain to him exactly why his behavior was unacceptable. (For more information about spanking and more appropriate ways to discipline, see page 248.)

As you refine your own disciplinary skills, don't overlook the importance of responding in a positive way to your baby's *good* behavior. This kind of reaction is equally important in helping him learn self-control. If he hesitates before reaching for the stove, notice his restraint and tell him how pleased you are. And give him a hug when he does something nice for another person. As he grows older, his good behavior will depend, in large part, on his desire to please you. If you make him aware now of how much you appreciate the good things he does, he'll be less likely to misbehave just to get your attention.

Some parents worry about spoiling a child this age by giving him too much attention, but you needn't be concerned about that. At eight to twelve months, your baby still has a limited ability to be manipulative. You should assume that when he cries, it's not for effect but because he has real needs that aren't being met.

These needs gradually will become more complex, and as they do, you'll notice more variation in your baby's cries—and in the way you react to them. For example, you'll come running when you hear the shattering wail that means something is seriously wrong. By contrast, you may finish what you're doing before you answer the shrill come-here-I-want-you cry. You'll also probably soon recognize a whiny, muffled cry that means something like "I could fall asleep now if everyone would leave me alone." By responding appropriately to the hidden message behind your baby's cries, you'll let him know that his needs are important, but you'll respond only to deserving calls for attention.

Incidentally, there probably will be times when you won't be able to figure out exactly why your baby is crying. In these cases, he himself may not even know what's bothering him. The best response is some comfort from you, combined with consoling techniques that he chooses for himself. For instance, try holding him while he cuddles his favorite stuffed animal or special blanket, or take time to play a game or read a story with him. Both of you will feel better when he's cheered up. Remember that his need for attention and affection is just as real as his need for food and clean diapers.

Siblings

As your baby becomes more mobile, she'll be better able to play with her siblings, and those brothers and sisters usually will be glad to cooperate. Older children, particularly six- to ten-year-olds, often love to build towers for an eight-month-old to destroy. Or they'll lend a finger to an eleven-month-old just learning to walk. A baby this age can be a wonderful playmate to her siblings.

However, while the baby's mobility can turn her into a more active participant in games with her brothers and sisters, it also will make her more likely to invade their private territory. This may violate their budding sense of ownership and privacy, and it can present a serious safety hazard for the baby, since the toys of older children often contain small, easily swallowed pieces. You can ensure that everyone is protected by giving older siblings an enclosed place where they can keep and play with their belongings without fear of a "baby invasion."

A baby this age can be a wonderful playmate to his siblings.

Also, now that the baby can reach and grab just about everything in sight, sharing is another issue that must be dealt with. Children under three just aren't capable of sharing without lots of adult prodding and, in most cases, direct intervention. As much as possible, try to sidestep the issue by encouraging both children to play with their own toys, even if they're doing so side by side. When they do play together, suggest looking at books or listening to music, rolling a ball back and forth, or playing hide-and-seek games—in other words, activities requiring limited cooperation.

Grandparents

This childhood age (eight to twelve months) is a wonderful time to enjoy your grandchild. She is now much more physically active and has more language expressions and emotional enthusiasm. However, babies of this age also may experience stranger anxiety, and could be reluctant to go to Grandma and Grandpa with much eagerness. Don't take this personally; it's part of normal development. Simply hang in there, and continue to provide all of the love and attention that you always have, but don't feel you must overdo it in the midst of these pulling-back episodes by the baby. Be patient, and the apparent standoff-ishness will resolve over time.

In your activities with your grandchild, you can take advantage of her developmental progress in the following areas.

CRAWLING. Get down on the floor with your grandchild as much as you physically can. This "floor time" is both fun and reassuring for the baby. She'll show delight if you use yourself as her crawling target or object of exploration. Remember, though, to check the floor carefully for possible hazards, since babies will pick up every object within reach and put it in their mouths.

FINE MOTOR SKILLS. Develop your own set of fine motor "games" with your grandchild—for example, opening and closing items, dumping out and putting back games and toys, and operating latches. Expect plenty of repetition since babies seem tireless doing the same activity over and over.

LANGUAGE. Read books and listen to music with your grandchild. All the while, keep the language interactive. If you speak a language that's different from the one in which your grandchild is becoming proficient, don't be afraid to speak it to her. (Be sure her parents agree.) For more information on bilingual babies, see page 268.

BASIC CARE. When it comes to feeding and sleeping, consistency of routines is important in this age group. Keep "junior foods" in your home. You also can establish "Grandma's Special Menus" that your grandchild can come to expect. When the baby is staying at your home, nap times and nighttime sleep schedules should be maintained as close as possible to those at her own home. Changes of routine sometimes can create confusion for babies.

SAFETY. Follow the safety check items in your own home that are described at the end of this chapter to ensure your grandchild's well-being. Keep gates on the top and the bottom of stairways. Place soft, protective coverings around sharp or round edges. Don't use walkers. Also, since babies of this age can have a strong nature and are wiggly, changing diapers should be a two-person operation if possible; change the diapers on carpeted floors or sofas to minimize the risk that your grandchild will twist off the changing table. While you're changing the baby, try distracting her with something she can manipulate.

Immunization Update

At one year of age (or in the months immediately after your baby's first birthday), she should receive the measles, mumps, rubella (MMR) vaccine. This vaccine will protect your baby from three serious diseases that can cause fever, rash, and other symptoms, and potentially lead to serious complications (pneumonia in children with measles, and hearing impairment in children with mumps). The current recommendation is to have your child receive the first MMR vaccine between twelve and fifteen months of age.

The first dose of varicella vaccine, which protects your child against chickenpox, should be given between twelve and fifteen months of age if she is susceptible to the disease—that is, if she has not already had the chickenpox. The newer, combined vaccines have MMR and V in them and are given as one shot; however, because of the increased risk of febrile seizure when given at one year of age, many pediatricians use the combo at four years old and not at one year of age.

The third hepatitis B vaccine will also be given between six and eighteen months of age, and the first hepatitis A vaccine will be given on or after one year of age.

The fourth pneumococcal vaccine, which protects your child against pneumonia, meningitis, blood infection, and some ear infections, is also given at twelve to eighteen months of age.

Safety Check

Car Safety Seats

- Buckle the baby into an approved, properly installed car safety seat before you start the car. The American Academy of Pediatrics recommends that children ride rear-facing until age two, or until they reach the highest weight or height allowed by their car safety seat's manufacturer. It's important that such properly installed seats are in ALL cars in which your baby rides including child care providers, grandparents, and all the cars you may own. There are other elements of car safety seats that you need to be aware of, so for further information, see page 491 in Chapter 15.

Falls

- Use gates at the top and bottom of stairways, and in doorways to rooms with furniture or other objects that the baby might climb on or that have sharp or hard edges against which he might fall.

- Do not allow an infant to climb on a narrow-based ladder-back chair, since the child will try to climb the ladder and the chair will tip over, resulting in head injury and possible leg or arm fractures.

- Do not use a baby walker. A stationary activity center is a much safer choice.

Burns

■ Never smoke or carry hot liquids or foods near your baby or while you're holding him. When you must handle hot liquids or foods, put your baby in a safe place such as a crib, play yard, or high chair.

■ Never leave containers of hot liquids or foods near the edges of tables or counters or on low surfaces, such as coffee tables.

■ Do not allow your baby to crawl around hot stoves, floor heaters, or furnace vents.

Drowning

■ Never leave your baby alone in a bath or around containers of water, such as buckets, wading pools, swimming pools, sinks, or open toilets. Remove all water from containers immediately after use. If you have a swimming pool, install a four-sided fence of at least 4 feet in height that completely separates the house from the pool.

Poisoning and Choking

■ Never leave small objects in your baby's crawling area.

■ Do not give your baby hard pieces of food, or any soft foods that could become lodged in his airway, such as hot dogs and grapes.

■ Store all medicines and household cleaning products high and out of his reach.

■ Use safety latches on drawers and cupboards that contain objects that might be dangerous to him. It is best to store these items in high, out-of-reach, locked cabinets if possible.

~ 10 ~

Your One-Year-Old

YOUR BABY HAS turned one and becomes a toddler, crawling vigorously, starting or trying to walk, even talking a little. As she becomes more and more independent, the days of her unquestioning adoration and dependency on you are becoming numbered.

This realization probably makes you feel both sad and excited—not to mention a little nervous as you think about the coming clashes between her will and yours. In fact, you may already be getting some glimpses of these struggles. For instance, try to take something away from her and she may scream in protest. Or pull her away from a dangerous swinging door and she may quickly return to it, ignoring your warnings. Or offer her one of her favorite meals of cereal and bananas and she may reject it unexpectedly. These are her early experiments with control—testing your limits and discovering her own.

Exploring the boundaries established by your rules and her own physical and developmental limits will occupy much of her time for the next few years. Fortunately, this testing will begin slowly, giving both of you time to adjust to her emerging independence. As a toddler just learning to walk, she'll be most interested in finding out what the world looks like from an upright position. This curiosity, however, is bound to lead her into some forbidden situations. Remember, she's not consciously trying to be mischievous. She still very much counts on you to show her what's OK and what's not, and she'll look to you frequently for reassurance and security.

But as she becomes more confident on her feet, she'll also start showing more signs of assertiveness. By eighteen months, she'll probably have chosen "no" as her favorite word, and as she nears age two, she may throw a tantrum when you ask her to come with you against her will.

Your toddler also may be showing more signs of possessiveness with belongings and people close to her. Upon seeing you pick up another baby, she may react with an outpouring of tears. If another child grabs an attractive toy, she may engage in a strenuous tug-of-war for possession. In a few months, as her vocabulary grows, "mine" will become another of her favorite words.

For now, her vocabulary is still limited, although expanding rapidly. She understands much of what you say to her, provided you speak in clear, simple words, and you probably can decipher some of what she says to you. Hard as it may be to believe, in a year you'll be having running conversations.

Growth and Development
Physical Appearance and Growth

By the end of her first year, your baby's growth rate will begin to slow. From now until her next growth spurt (which occurs during early adolescence), her height and weight should increase steadily, but not as rapidly as during those first months of life. As an infant, she may have gained 4 pounds (1.8 kg) in four months or less, but during the entire second year, 3 to 5 pounds (1.4–2.3 kg) probably will be her total weight gain. Continue to plot her measurements every few months on the growth charts on pages 878–885 in the Appendix to make sure she's generally following the normal growth curve. As you'll see, there's now a much broader range of what's "normal" than there was at earlier ages.

At fifteen months, the average girl weighs about 23 pounds (10.5 kg) and is almost 30.5 inches (77 cm) tall; the average boy weighs about 24.5 pounds (11 kg) and is 31 inches (78 cm) tall. Over the next three months, they'll each gain approximately 1½ pounds (0.7 kg) and grow about an inch (2.5 cm). By two, she'll be about 34 inches (about 86 cm) tall and weigh 27 pounds (12.2 kg); he'll reach 34½ inches (87.5 cm) and almost 28 pounds (12.6 kg).

Your baby's head growth also will slow dramatically during the second year. Although she'll probably gain only about 1 inch (2.5 cm) in head circumference this entire year, by age two she'll have attained about 90 percent of her adult head size.

Your toddler's looks, however, probably will change more than her size. At twelve months, she still looked like a baby, even though she may have been walking and saying a few words. Her head and abdomen were still the largest parts of her body, her belly stuck out when she was upright, and her buttocks, by comparison, seemed small—at least when her diaper was off. Her arms and legs were still relatively short and soft, rather than muscular, and her face had softly rounded contours.

All this will change as she becomes more active, developing her muscles and trimming away some of her baby fat. Her arms and legs will lengthen gradually, and her feet will start to point forward as she walks, instead of out to the sides. Her face will become more angular and her jawline better defined. By her second birthday, it will be hard to remember how she looked as an infant.

Movement

If your baby hasn't started walking before his first birthday, he should within the next six months. In fact, perfecting this skill will be the major physical accomplishment of his second year. Even if he's already begun walking, it may take another full month or two before he can stand up and start moving smoothly without support. However, don't expect him to get up the way you would. Instead, his technique may be to spread his hands on the floor, straighten his arms, and lift his bottom in the air as he pulls his legs under him. Finally, while straightening his legs, he'll unbend at the waist and be off.

In the beginning, he really is toddling, which is quite different from mature walking. Instead of striding, he'll plant his legs wide apart, toes pointing outward, and lurch from side to side as he moves forward. As slow and painstaking as the process may seem in the beginning, he'll quickly pick up speed. In fact, don't be surprised if very soon you're running to keep up with him.

An inevitable part of this toddling, of course, is falling. In particular, walking on uneven surfaces will remain a challenge for some time. At first he'll trip on even small irregularities, such as a wrinkle in the carpet surface or an incline into another room. It will be months before he can walk up and down stairs, or turn corners without falling.

Also, at the beginning, don't expect him to use his hands during walking. While he'll use his arms for balance (bent and held at shoulder level in the "high guard" position), using his hands to carry, play with, or pick up a toy will be out of the question for a time. After he's been walking for two to three months, however, he'll have the entire process under control: Not only will he be stooping to pick up and carry a toy across the room, but he'll be able to push or pull a toy wagon, step sideways or backward, and even throw a ball while walking.

About six months after he takes his first steps, your baby's walking style will become much more mature. He'll keep his feet close together as he moves, making his gait much smoother. With your help he may even walk up and down stairs. However, when he tries this on his own, he'll crawl up on his hands and knees and back down one stair at a time on his stomach. Soon he'll take his first short, stiff runs straight ahead, though he probably won't run well until his third year. By his second birthday, your child will be moving with great efficiency. To think—just a year ago he could barely walk!

Movement Milestones Before Two Years of Age

- Walks alone
- Pulls toys behind her while walking
- Carries large toy or several toys while walking
- Begins to run
- Stands on tiptoe
- Kicks a ball
- Climbs up and down from furniture unassisted
- Walks up and down stairs holding on to support

Hand and Finger Skills

Given all the large motor skills your one-year-old is mastering, it's easy to overlook the more subtle changes in her ability to use her hands, both alone and in coordination with her eyes. These developments will allow her much more control and precision as she examines objects and tries new movements. They also will greatly expand her ability to explore and learn about the world around her.

At twelve months, it's still a challenge for her to pick up very small objects between her thumb and forefinger, but by the middle of her second year, this task will be simple. Watch how she'll manipulate small objects at will, exploring all the ways they can be combined and changed. Some of her favorite games might include:

- Building towers of up to four blocks, then knocking them down

- Covering and uncovering boxes or other containers

- Picking up balls or other objects in motion

- Turning knobs and pages

- Putting round pegs into holes

- Scribbling and painting

These activities not only will help her develop hand skills but also will teach her spatial concepts, such as "in," "on," "under," and "around." As she nears two years and her physical coordination improves, she'll be able to try more complex games, such as:

- Folding paper (if you show her how)

- Putting large square pegs into matching holes (which is more difficult than it is with round pegs, because it involves matching angles)

- Stacking up to five or six blocks

- Taking toys apart and putting them back together

- Making shapes from clay

Milestones in Hand and Finger Skills Before Two Years of Age

- **Scribbles spontaneously**
- **Turns over container to pour out contents**
- **Builds tower of four blocks or more**
- **Might use one hand more frequently than the other**

By her second birthday, your toddler may demonstrate a clear tendency toward right- or left-handedness. However, many children don't show this preference for several years. Other children are ambidextrous, being able to use both hands equally well. They may never establish a clear preference. There's no reason to pressure your toddler to use one hand over the other or to rush the natural process that leads her to this preference.

Language Development

Early in the second year, your toddler will suddenly seem to understand everything you say. You'll announce lunchtime and he'll be waiting by his high chair. You'll tell him you've lost your shoe and he'll find it. At first, his rapid response may seem a little unusual. Did he really understand, or is this just a dream? Rest assured, it's not your imagination. He's developing his language and comprehension skills right on schedule.

This giant developmental leap probably will alter the way you now talk to him and converse with others when he's around. For example, you may edit conversations held within his earshot, perhaps spelling out words you'd rather he didn't understand (as in, "Should we stop for I-C-E C-R-E-A-M?"). At the same time, you'll probably feel more enthusiastic about talking to him, because he's so responsive.

You may find yourself using less baby talk, no longer needing high-pitched

Language Milestones Before Two Years of Age

- **Points to object or picture when it's named for him ("Where's the . . . ?")**

- **Uses the names of familiar people, objects, and body parts ("What's that?" "Who's that?")**

- **Says several single words (by fifteen to eighteen months)**

- **Uses simple phrases (by eighteen to twenty-four months)**

- **Uses two- to four-word sentences**

- **Follows simple instructions**

- **Repeats words overheard in conversation**

singsong monologues to get his attention. Instead, try speaking slowly and clearly, using simple words and short sentences. Teach him the correct names of objects and body parts, and stop using cute substitutes such as "piggies" when you really mean "toes." By providing a good language model, you'll help him learn to talk with a minimum of confusion.

Most toddlers master at least fifty spoken words by the end of the second year and can put two words together to form a short sentence, although there are differences among children. Even among those with normal hearing and intelligence, some don't talk much during the second year. Boys generally develop language skills more slowly than girls. Whenever your child begins to speak, his first few words probably will include the names of familiar people, his favorite possessions, and parts of his body. You may be the only person who understands these early words, since he'll omit or change certain sounds. For example, he might get the first consonant (*b, d, t*) and vowel (*a, e, i, o, u*) sounds right, but drop the end of the word. Or he may substitute sounds he can pronounce, such as *d* or *b,* for more difficult ones.

You'll learn to understand what he's saying over time and with the help of his gestures. By all means, don't ridicule his language mistakes. Give him as much time as he needs to finish what he wants to say without hurrying, and then answer with a correct pronunciation of the word ("That's right, it's a ball!"). If you're patient and responsive, his pronunciation will improve gradually.

By midyear, he'll use a few active verbs, such as "go" and "jump," and words of direction, such as "up," "down," "in," and "out." By his second birthday, he'll have mastered the words "me" and "you" and use them all the time.

At first, he'll make his own version of a whole sentence by combining a single word with a gesture or grunt. He might point and say "ball"—his way of telling you he wants you to roll him the ball. Or he might shape a question by saying "Out?" or "Up?"—raising his voice at the end. Soon he'll begin to combine verbs or prepositions with nouns, to make statements like "Ball up" or "Drink milk," and questions like "What's that?" By the end of the year, or soon thereafter, he'll begin to use two-word sentences.

Cognitive Development

As you watch your toddler at play, have you noticed how hard she concentrates on everything she does? Each game or task is a learning proposition, and she'll gather all sorts of information about the way things work. She'll also now be able to draw on facts she's already learned in order to make decisions and find solutions to play-related challenges. However, she'll be interested in solving only those problems that are appropriate for her developmental and learning level, so hand her a toy that fascinated her at eleven months and she may walk away bored. Or suggest a game that's too advanced and she'll object. She'll be especially attracted to mechanical devices, such as wind-up toys, switches, buttons, and knobs. It may be difficult for you to judge exactly what she can and can't handle at this age, but it's not hard for her to decide. Provide her with a range of activities, and she'll select the ones that are challenging but not completely beyond her abilities.

Imitation is a big part of her learning process at this age. Instead of simply manipulating household objects, as she did during her first year, she'll actually use a brush on her hair, babble into the phone, turn the steering wheel of her toy car, and push it back and forth. At first, she'll be the only one involved in these activities, but gradually she'll include other players. She might brush her doll's hair, "read" to you from her book, offer a playmate a pretend drink, or hold her toy phone to your ear. Because imitation is such an important part of her behavior and learning, now, perhaps more than ever, you need to be aware of the behaviors that you are modeling for her. Remember, things that you say or do might be replayed (either to your great pleasure or dismay!) over and over again as she plays and learns. Older siblings are crucial here. This copying be-

Cognitive Milestones Before Two Years of Age

- **Finds objects even when hidden under two or three covers**
- **Begins to sort by shapes and colors**
- **Begins make-believe play**

havior happens between toddlers and their older siblings. It is an ideal time to take advantage of these natural developmental cues.

Well before her second birthday, your toddler will excel at hiding games, remembering where hidden objects are long after they leave her sight. If you pocket her ball or cracker while she's playing, you may forget all about it, but she won't!

As she masters hide-and-seek, she'll also become more understanding about separations from you. Just as she knows that a hidden object is somewhere, even when she can't see it, she'll now recognize that you always come back, even when you're away from her a whole day. If you actually show her where you go when you leave her—to work or to the grocery store, for example— she'll form a mental image of you there. This may make the separation even easier for her.

At this age, your toddler is very much the director; she lets you know what role she wants you to play in her activities. Sometimes she'll bring you a toy so you can help her make it work; other times she'll pull it away from you to try it by herself. Often, when she knows she's done something special, she'll pause and wait for your applause. By responding to these cues, you'll provide the support and encouragement she needs to keep learning.

You also must supply the judgment that she still lacks. Yes, she now understands how certain things behave, but—because she can't see how one thing affects another—she doesn't yet grasp the full notion of consequences. So even though she may understand that her toy wagon will roll downhill, she can't predict what will happen when it lands in the middle of the busy street below. Although she knows that a door swings open and shut, she doesn't know that she has to keep her hand from getting caught in it. And even if she's found out the hard way once, don't assume she's learned her lesson. Chances are she doesn't associate her pain with the chain of events that led up to it, and she almost certainly won't remember this sequence the next time. Until she develops her own common sense, she'll need your vigilance to keep her safe.

Social Development

Your toddler will develop a very specific image of his social world, friends, and acquaintances. He is at its center, and while you may be close at hand, he is most concerned about where things are in relation to himself. He knows that other people exist, and they vaguely interest him, but he has no idea how they think or what they feel. As far as he's concerned, everyone thinks as he does.

As you can imagine, his view of the world (technically, some experts call it egocentric or self-centered) often makes it difficult for him to play with other children in a truly social sense. He'll play alongside and compete for toys, but he doesn't play cooperative games easily. He'll enjoy watching and being around other children, especially if they're slightly older. He may imitate them or treat

them the way he does dolls, for example, trying to brush their hair, but he's usually surprised and resists when they try to do the same thing to him. He may offer them toys or things to eat but may get upset if they respond by taking what he's offered them.

Sharing is a meaningless term to a child this age. Every toddler believes that he alone deserves the spotlight. Unfortunately, most

Social Milestones Before Two Years of Age

- **Imitates behavior of others, especially adults and older children**
- **Increasingly aware of herself as separate from others**
- **Increasingly enthusiastic about company of other children**

are also as assertive as they are self-centered, and competition for toys and attention frequently erupts into hitting and tears. How can you minimize the combat when your child's "friends" are over? Try providing plenty of toys for everyone and be prepared to referee.

As we've suggested earlier, your child also may start to show possessiveness over toys that he knows belong to him. If another child even touches the plaything, he may rush over and snatch it away. Try reassuring him that the other child is "only looking at it" and that "it's OK for him to have a turn with it."

Gender Identification

If you were to take a group of one-year-olds, dress them alike, and let them loose on a playground, could you tell the boys from the girls? Probably not, because except for minor variations in size, there are very few differences between the sexes at this age. Boys and girls develop skills at about the same rate (although girls tend to talk earlier than boys), and they enjoy the same activities. Some studies have found boys to be more active than girls, but the differences in these first years are negligible.

Although parents generally treat boys and girls this age very similarly, they often encourage different toys and games for each sex. But aside from tradition, there's no basis for pushing girls toward dolls and boys toward trucks. Left to their own devices, both sexes are equally attracted to all toys, and they should be allowed to play with a variety of toys that they might be interested in.

Incidentally, young children learn to identify themselves as boys or girls by associating with other members of their own sex. But this process takes years. Dressing your girl exclusively in frills or taking your boy to baseball games won't make much of a difference at this age. What does matter is the love and respect you give your child as a person, regardless of sex. This will lay the foundation for high self-esteem.

But also acknowledge that "Yes, it's your toy, and he's not going to take it away from you." It may help to select a couple of particularly prized items and make them off-limits to everyone else. Sometimes this helps toddlers feel they have some control over their world and makes them less possessive about other belongings.

Because children this age have so little awareness of the feelings of others, they can be very physical in their responses to the children around them. Even when just exploring or showing affection, they may poke each other's eyes or pat a little too hard. (The same is true of their treatment of animals.) When they're upset, they can hit or slap without realizing they are hurting the other child. For this reason, be alert whenever your toddler is among playmates, and pull him back as soon as this physical aggressiveness occurs. Tell him, "Don't hit," and redirect all the children to friendlier play.

Masturbation

As your toddler explores the many parts of his body, he'll naturally discover his genitals. Since touching them will produce pleasant sensations, he'll do it often when his diaper is off. Although this may be accompanied by penile erections in boys, it's neither a sexual nor an emotional experience for toddlers. It just feels good. There's no reason to discourage it, worry, or call any attention to it. If you show a strong negative reaction when he touches his genitals, you're suggesting to him that there is something wrong or bad about these body parts. He may even interpret this to mean there's something wrong or bad about him. Wait until he's older to teach him about privacy and modesty. For now, accept his behavior as normal curiosity.

Fortunately, your toddler will show his self-awareness in less aggressive ways, as well. By eighteen months, he'll be able to say his own name. At about the same time, he'll identify his reflection in the mirror and start showing a greater interest in caring for himself. As he approaches age two, he may be able to brush his teeth and wash his hands if shown how to do it. He'll also help dress and, especially, undress himself. Many times a day you may find him busily removing his shoes and socks even in the middle of a store or the park.

Because your toddler is a great imitator, he will be learning important social skills from the way you handle conflicts between the two of you. Model for him the way words and listening can, at least on occasion, be used to resolve conflicts ("I know you want to get down and walk, but you must hold my hand

The Shy Child

Some children are naturally fearful about new people and situations. They hold back, watching and waiting before joining a group activity. If pushed to try something different, they resist, and when faced with someone new, they cling. For a parent trying to encourage boldness and independence, this behavior can be very frustrating. But challenging or ridiculing it will only make a shy child more insecure.

The best solution is to allow your child to move at her own individual pace. Give her the time she needs to adapt to new situations and let her hold your hand when she needs some extra assurance. If you take her behavior in stride, outsiders will be less likely to ridicule her, and she'll develop self-confidence much more quickly. If she continues this kind of behavior, discuss it with your pediatrician. She will be able to give you some individual advice and can, if necessary, refer you to a pediatric psychologist or child psychiatrist.

so I know you're safe"). As an imitator, he also will eagerly participate in anything you're doing around the house. Whether you're reading the paper, sweeping the floors, mowing the lawn, or making dinner, he'll want to "help." Even though it may take longer with him doing so, try to turn it into a game. If you're doing something he can't help with because it's dangerous or you're in a hurry, look for another "chore" he *can* do. By all means, don't discourage these wonderful impulses to be helpful. Helping, like sharing, is a vital social skill, and the sooner he develops it, the more pleasant life will be for everyone.

Emotional Development

Your one-year-old child will swing back and forth constantly between fierce independence and clinging to you. Now that she can walk and do things for herself physically, she has the power to move away from you and test her new skills. But at the same time, she's not yet entirely comfortable with the idea that she's an individual, separate from you and everyone else in the world. Especially when she's tired, sick, or scared, she'll want you there to comfort her and fend off loneliness.

It's impossible to predict when she'll turn her back on you and when she'll come running for shelter. She may seem to change from one moment to the next, or she may seem mature and independent for several whole days before suddenly regressing. You may feel mixed reactions to this, as well: While there are moments when it feels wonderful to have your baby back, there are bound to be other times when her fussing and whining is the last thing you need. Some people call this period the first adolescence. It reflects some of your child's mixed feelings about growing up and leaving you, and it's absolutely normal. Remember that the best way to help her regain her composure is to give her attention and reassurance when she needs it. Snapping at her to "act like a big girl" will only make her feel and act more insecure and needy.

The Aggressive Child

Some children are naturally aggressive in ways that begin to show during the second year. They want to take charge and control everything that goes on around them. When they don't get what they want, they may turn their energy toward violent behavior, such as kicking, biting, or hitting.

Does your toddler fit this description? If so, you'll need to watch him closely and set firm, consistent limits. Give him plenty of positive outlets for his energy through physical play and exercise. But when he's with other children, supervise him carefully to prevent serious trouble, and be sure to praise him when he gets through a play session without a problem.

In some families, a toddler's aggressive outbursts are considered an omen of future delinquency. Believing they have to come down hard on this behavior as soon as it appears, the parents spank or hit the child as punishment. However, children of this age copy their parents. Thus, a child treated this way can begin to believe that this is the correct way to handle people when you don't like their behavior, so—quite the opposite of what the parent intended—this reaction may just reinforce his aggressiveness toward others. The best way to teach your child how to hold his aggressive impulses in check is to instruct him in advance of what behavior is expected, praise him for playing well with others, and be firm and consistent when he misbehaves. Also, give him a good example to imitate with your own behavior and that of his siblings. (See also *Anger, Aggression, and Biting*, page 575.) Sometimes, more than words are needed to correct a toddler's misbehavior. Consider using a time-out.

Brief separations from you may help your toddler become more independent. She'll still suffer some separation anxiety and perhaps put up a fuss when you leave her—even if it's just for a few minutes. But the protest will be brief. Chances are, you may be more upset by these separations than she is, but try not to let her know that. If she believes her fussing has a chance of getting you to stay, she'll continue to fuss with similar occasions in the future. As tempting as it might be to quietly "sneak" away, she might actually become more clingy because she then never knows when you're going to disappear next. Instead, leave her with a kiss and a promise to return. And when you do come back, greet her enthusiastically and devote your full attention to her for a while before moving on to other chores or business. When your child understands that you always return and continue to love her, she'll feel more secure.

Basic Care

Feeding and Nutrition

You'll probably notice a sharp drop in your toddler's appetite after his first birthday. Suddenly he's picky about what he eats, turns his head away after just a few bites, or resists coming to the table at mealtimes. It may seem as if he should be eating more now that he's so active, but there's a good reason for the

Stimulating Child Brain Growth: One-Year-Old

- Your child learns through social interactions and play. Learning happens in the course of safe, stable, and nourishing relationships. If a child is fearful all the time, very little new learning will occur.

- Choose toys that encourage creativity. By selecting simple toys, you'll encourage your child to develop his own imagination.

- Encourage playing with blocks and soft toys, which helps your child develop hand-to-eye coordination, fine motor skills, and a sense of competence.

- Give consistent, warm, physical contact—hugging, skin-to-skin, body-to-body contact—to establish your toddler's sense of security and well-being. Avoid using food as a reward, but rather verbally praise and hug your child for good behavior.

- Be attentive to your child's rhythms and moods. Respond to her when she is upset as well as when she is happy. Be encouraging and supportive, with firm discipline as appropriate, but without yelling or hitting; provide consistent guidelines.

- Talk or sing to your child during dressing, bathing, feeding, playing, walking, and driving, using adult talk. Speak slowly and give your child time to respond. Try not to reply with "uh-huh," because your child will recognize when you're not listening; instead, expand on your child's phrases.

- Be consistent and predictable; establish routines for mealtimes, naps, and bedtime.

- Develop word associations by naming everyday objects and activities.

- Read to your child every day. Choose books that encourage touching and pointing to objects, and read rhymes, jingles, and nursery stories.

- If you speak a foreign language, use it at home.

- Play fun, calm, and melodic music for your child.

- Listen to and answer your child's questions. Also ask questions to stimulate decision-making processes.

- Begin to explain safety in simple terms; for example, feeling the heat from the stove teaches the meaning and danger of hot objects.

- Make sure other people who provide care and supervision for your child understand the importance of forming a loving and comforting relationship with her.

- Encourage your child to look at books and to draw.

- Help your child use words to describe emotions and to express feelings such as happiness, joy, anger, and fear ("glad," "mad," and "sad").

- Spend time on the floor playing with your child every day.

- Choose quality child care that is affectionate, responsive, educational, and safe. Visit your child care provider frequently and share your ideas about positive caregiving.

- If at all possible, avoid "adverse childhood experiences" (see pages xxxiv–xxxvii in the Introduction) and other causes of chronic stress that adversely affect brain development.

change. His growth rate has slowed, and he really doesn't require as much food now.

Your toddler needs about 1,000 calories a day to meet his needs for growth, energy, and good nutrition. If you've ever been on a 1,000-calorie diet, you know it's not a lot of food. But your child will do just fine with it, divided among three small meals and two snacks a day. Don't count on his always eating it that way, however, because the eating habits of toddlers are erratic and unpredictable from one day to the next. He may eat everything in sight at breakfast but almost nothing else for the rest of the day. Or he may eat only his favorite food for three days in a row, and then reject it entirely. Or he may eat 1,000 calories one day, but then eat noticeably more or less on the subsequent day or two. Your child's needs will vary, depending on his activity level, his growth rate, and his metabolism.

Mealtime should not turn into sparring matches to get your child to eat a balanced diet. He's not rejecting you when he turns down the food you prepared, so don't take it personally. Besides, the harder you push him to eat, the less likely he is to comply. Instead, offer him a selection of nutritious foods at each sitting, and let him choose what he wants. Vary the tastes and consistencies as much as you can.

If he rejects everything, you might try saving the plate for later when he's hungry. However, don't allow him to fill up on cookies or sweets after refusing his meal, since that will just fuel his interest in empty-calorie foods (those that are high in calories but relatively low in important nutrients, such as vitamins and minerals) and diminish his appetite for nutritious ones. Hard as it may be to believe, your child's diet will balance out over several days if you make a range of wholesome foods available and don't pressure him to eat a particular one at any given time. Your job as a parent is to offer nutritious, appropriate foods at appropriate times and your toddler needs to decide how much of these he will eat. When parents try to control how much a toddler eats by forcing him to clean his plate, the child may not learn to self-regulate. This can lead to continued eating and ignored signs of being full and resultant obesity. It can also lead to toddlers refusing to eat more foods and resulting in poor weight gain.

Your toddler needs foods from the same four basic nutrition groups that you do:

1. Meat, fish, poultry, eggs

2. Dairy products

3. Fruits and vegetables

4. Whole-grain cereal, bread, and pasta, potatoes and rice

Developmental Health Watch

Because each child develops at his own particular pace, it's impossible to tell exactly when yours will perfect a given skill. The developmental milestones listed in this book will give you a general idea of the changes you can expect as your child gets older, but don't be alarmed if he takes a slightly different course. Alert your pediatrician, however, if he displays any of the following signs of possible developmental delay for this age range.

- Cannot walk by eighteen months
- Fails to develop a mature heel-toe walking pattern after several months of walking, or walks exclusively on his toes
- Does not speak at least fifteen words by eighteen months
- Does not use two-word sentences by age two
- Does not seem to know the function of common household objects (brush, telephone, bell, fork, spoon) by fifteen months
- Does not imitate actions or words by the end of this period
- Does not follow simple instructions by age two
- Cannot push a wheeled toy by age two

When planning your child's menu, remember that cholesterol and other fats are very important for his normal growth and development, so they should not be restricted during this period. Babies and young toddlers should get about half of their calories from fat. You can gradually decrease the fat consumption once your child has reached the age of two (lowering it to about one-third of daily calories by ages four to five). While you should not lose sight of the fact that childhood obesity is a growing problem, youngsters in the second year of life need dietary fat. If you keep your child's caloric intake at about 1,000 calories a day, you shouldn't have to worry about overfeeding him and putting him at risk of gaining too much weight.

Adult eating preferences are developed now.

Emotional Milestones Before Two Years of Age

- **Demonstrates increasing independence**

- **Begins to show defiant behavior—particularly with adults with whom they feel comfortable**

- **Increasing episodes of separation anxiety toward midyear, then they fade**

By his first birthday, your child should be able to handle most of the foods you serve the rest of the family—but with a few precautions. First, be sure the food is cool enough so that it won't burn his mouth. Test the temperature yourself, because he'll dig in without considering the heat. Also, don't give him foods that are heavily spiced, salted, buttered, or sweetened. These additions prevent your child from experiencing the natural taste of foods, and they may be harmful to his long-term good health. Young children seem to be more sensitive than adults to these flavorings and may reject heavily spiced foods.

Your little one can still choke on chunks of food that are large enough to plug his airway. Keep in mind that children don't learn to chew with a grinding motion until they're about four years old. Make sure anything you give your toddler is mashed or cut into small, easily chewable pieces. Never offer him whole nuts, whole grapes (cut in half or quarters), cherry tomatoes (unless they're cut in quarters), carrots, popcorn, seeds (e.g., processed pumpkin or sunflower seeds), whole or large sections of hot dogs, meat sticks, or hard candies (including jelly beans or gummy bears), or chunks of peanut butter (it's fine to thinly spread peanut butter on a cracker or bread). Hot dogs and carrots in particular should be quartered lengthwise and then sliced into small pieces. Also make sure your toddler eats only while seated and supervised by an adult. Although he may want to do everything at once, "eating on the run" or while talking increases his risk of choking. Teach him as early as possible to finish a mouthful prior to speaking.

By his first birthday or soon thereafter, your toddler should drink his liquids from a cup. He'll need less milk now, since he'll get most of his calories from solid foods.

DIETARY SUPPLEMENTS. If you provide your child with selections from each of the four basic food groups and let her experiment with a wide variety of tastes, colors, and textures, she should be eating a balanced diet with plenty of vitamins. Some vitamins, such as the fat-soluble vitamins (A and D), may even

Toys Appropriate Before Two Years of Age

- **Board books with large pictures, simple stories**
- **Books and magazines with photographs of babies**
- **Blocks**
- **Nesting toys**
- **Simple shape sorters and pegboards**
- **Beginner's jigsaw puzzles**
- **Toys that encourage make-believe play (child lawn mower, kitchen sets, brooms)**
- **Digging toys (bucket, shovel, rake)**
- **Dolls of all sizes**
- **Cars, trucks, trains**
- **Unbreakable containers of all shapes and sizes**
- **Bath toys (boats, containers, floating squeak toys)**

pose risks; they're stored in the tissues when consumed in excess, and at very high levels could make your child sick. High doses of minerals such as zinc and iron taken over an extended time can have negative effects, as well.

For some children, however, supplementation may be important. Your child may need some vitamin and/or mineral supplementation if your family's dietary practices limit the food groups available to her. For example, if your household is strictly vegetarian, with no eggs or dairy products (which is not a diet recommended for children), she may need supplements of vitamins B_{12} and D as well as riboflavin and calcium. Rickets, for example, is a disease in which the bones soften, and it is associated with inadequate vitamin D intake and decreased exposure to sunlight. Consult your pediatrician about which supplements are needed and the amounts. (See information on vitamin D supplements on page 125.)

- Balls of all shapes and sizes
- Push and pull toys
- Outdoor toys (slides, swings, sandbox)
- Beginner's tricycle
- Connecting toys (links, large stringing beads, S-shapes)
- Stuffed animals
- Child keyboard and other musical instruments
- Large crayons
- Toy telephone
- Unbreakable mirrors of all sizes
- Dress-up clothes
- Wooden spoons, old magazines, baskets, cardboard boxes and tubes, other similar safe, unbreakable items she "finds" around the house (e.g., pots and pans)

Iron deficiency does occur among some young children and can lead to anemia (a condition that limits the ability of the blood to carry oxygen). In some cases the problem is dietary. Toddlers need to receive at least 15 milligrams of iron a day in their food, but many fail to do so. (See table of sources of iron, page 319.) Drinking large quantities of milk may lead to iron deficiency anemia, as the child will be less interested in other foods, some of which are potential sources of iron.

If your child is drinking 24 to 32 ounces (720–960 ml) of milk or less each day, there's little cause for concern. If she drinks much more than that and you can't get her to eat more iron-rich foods, consult your pediatrician about adding an iron supplement to her diet. In the meantime, continue to give her vitamin D drops (600 IU per day after age one) if taking less than 32 ounces of milk per day, and keep offering her a wide variety of iron-rich foods so that,

Discontinuing the Bottle

Infants who sleep with a bottle containing milk, juice, soda, or other sweetened liquids are at a high risk of developing tooth decay. It is recommended that the bottle be given up entirely at around age one and almost certainly by eighteen months. The sooner you start removing the bottle, the easier this task is, and if breastfeeding, bottles may be avoided altogether. Cup feeding may also be introduced as early as six months and by one year should be mastered. As long as your baby is drinking from a cup, he doesn't need to take liquids from a bottle. If you must give him a bottle, limit the contents to plain water. Unfortunately, weaning your baby from the bottle may not be as easy as it sounds. To help things along, eliminate the midday bottle first, then the evening and morning ones; save the bedtime bottle for last, but remember to limit the contents to plain water. If your baby will not take a bottle with plain water initially, slowly over a short period of time dilute the formula or other contents with water so that after a week or two the bottle contains *only* water.

It's easy to get into the habit of using a bottle to comfort a child or help him sleep. But at this age, he no longer needs anything to eat or drink during the night. If you are still feeding him at that time, you should stop. Even if he demands a bottle and drinks thirstily, nighttime feedings are a comfort rather than a nutritional necessity. The bottle soon turns into a crutch and prevents his learning to fall back to sleep on his own. If he cries for only a short time, try letting him cry back to sleep. After a few nights he'll probably forget all about the bottle. If this doesn't happen, consult your pediatrician and read the other sections on sleep in this book. (See, for example, pages 216 and 245.)

Incidentally, giving your toddler a drink or other healthy snack *before bedtime* is acceptable—provided you brush his teeth afterward. In fact, it may help him fall asleep. A short breastfeeding, a drink of cow's milk or other liquid, or even some fruit or another nutritious food will do. If the snack is a bottle, gradually phase it out by substituting a cup.

Whatever the snack, have your child finish it and then clean his teeth, using a soft cloth, gauze, or toothbrush. This can even be done while the child is sleeping on your lap. Not removing the food or liquid from your baby's teeth after he eats will allow it to remain on the teeth all night and can result in tooth decay. If he needs some comfort to get to sleep, let him use a cuddly toy, blanket, or his thumb—but never a bottle containing anything else but plain water.

Cutting Down on Sweets

Almost everyone naturally enjoys sweets, and your toddler is no different. Like other human beings, she was born with a taste for sugar, and she's already quite sensitive to different concentrations of sweetness. Offer her a yam and a baked potato, and she'll take the yam every time. Give her a choice between the yam and a cookie, and the cookie will win. Rest assured, it's not your fault if she makes a beeline for the candy and ice cream when you'd rather she take a piece of cheese. But it is your responsibility to limit her access to sweets and to provide a diet made up primarily of more nutritious foods that promote growth, not tooth decay.

eventually, supplementation won't be necessary. For more information on vitamin D, see page 125 in Chapter 4.

Fortunately, when sweets are out of your toddler's sight, they won't be on her mind, so either don't bring them into the house or keep them hidden. Also avoid adding sugar to her food, and don't make dessert an everyday event. As for snacks, instead of giving her sweet or fatty ones, let her have small portions of healthy food items such as fruit, whole-grain bread and crackers, and cheese. In other words, start encouraging good eating habits that can last a lifetime.

SELF-FEEDING. At twelve months, your baby was just getting used to drinking from a cup and feeding himself with a spoon and his fingers. By fifteen months, he'll be much more in control, getting food into his mouth with relative ease when he wants to and flinging it about the room when that seems like more fun. He'll be able to fill his spoon and get it to his mouth consistently, although occasionally it will tip the wrong way and spill at the last second. Unbreakable dishes, cups, and glasses are essential, since they, too, may go flying when he's bored with their contents. Such behavior should be discouraged by a firm reprimand and replacement of the utensils in the proper location. If these behaviors persist, consider taking him out of the high chair and waiting until the next meal.

By eighteen months, your toddler can use a spoon, fork, and unbreakable glass or cup when he wants to, but he may not

Make sure your toddler eats only while seated and supervised by an adult.

Sample One-Day Menu for a One-Year-Old

This menu is planned for a one-year-old child who weighs approximately 21 pounds (9.5 kg).

1 teaspoon = $\frac{1}{3}$ tablespoon = 5 ml
1 tablespoon = ½ ounce = 15 ml
1 cup = 8 ounces = 240 ml
1 ounce = 30 ml

BREAKFAST

½ cup iron-fortified breakfast cereal or
    1 cooked egg
¼–½ cup whole or 2 percent milk (with
    cereal or without)
Fruit can be added to cereal or on its own
½ banana, sliced
2–3 large sliced strawberries

SNACK

1 slice toast or whole-wheat muffin with 1–2 tablespoons cream cheese or
    peanut butter, or yogurt with cut-up fruit
½ cup whole or 2 percent milk

LUNCH

½ sandwich sliced turkey or chicken, tuna,
    egg salad, or peanut butter
½ cup cooked green vegetables
½ cup whole or 2 percent milk

SNACK

1–2 ounces cubed or string cheese, or 2–3 tablespoons fruit or berries
1 cup whole or 2 percent milk

DINNER

2–3 ounces cooked meat, ground or diced
½ cup cooked yellow or orange vegetables
½ cup whole-grain pasta, rice, or potato
½ cup whole or 2 percent milk

always want to. There will be times when he'd rather finger paint with his pudding or turn his plate into a soaring airplane. Some children get over this chaotic eating behavior by their second birthday, at which time they actually may become upset when they spill or get even a little smudge of food on their hands. Others, however, will remain very messy eaters well into their third year.

SOURCES OF IRON

Excellent

Red meats	Blackstrap molasses
Fortified bran cereal	

Good

Hamburger	Shrimp	Potato, baked in skin	Dried apricots
Lean beef	Frankfurter	Navy beans	Raisins
Chicken	Egg, egg yolks	Kidney beans	Prunes, prune juice
Tuna	Spinach, mustard greens	Soybeans	Strawberries
Ham	Asparagus	Split peas	Tomato juice

Adequate

Enriched rice	Avocado	Broccoli	Green peas
Enriched pasta, noodles	Cranberry juice	Tomato	Bacon
Enriched bread	Orange	Carrots	Peanut butter
Banana	Apple	Green beans	

WHERE WE STAND

CHILDHOOD OVERWEIGHT AND OBESITY is now a national health emergency. Obesity leads to shorter life spans, lower quality of life, and many chronic medical problems, many of which now even begin during childhood. We now fear that the current generation of children might live shorter lives than their parents due to the long-term effects of obesity. However, there is a lot that can be done to address and prevent obesity, and the earlier we're able to start the better. Small adjustments (regarding our approach to food, feeding, physical activity, etc.) in a young child could prevent many future health challenges. That is not to say that it will be easy, as currently the healthy choice is not always the easiest one, but it is well worth it! It was previously common to think that kids might outgrow or grow into their weight, but now more often than not, this is not happening. In fact, over the past two decades obesity rates have *doubled* in children and *tripled* among adolescents in the United States. Obesity affects all of our body systems and can lead to potentially serious health problems, including diabetes, high blood pressure, sleep apnea, liver failure, and more. It also can cause psychological stresses associated with children feeling different from their peers, leading to depression, anxiety, and low self-esteem.

The American Academy of Pediatrics believes that making small changes early on can prevent a lifetime of complications regarding childhood obesity, and that both parents and pediatricians can take steps to help children maintain and achieve a healthy weight. Your pediatrician should monitor your child's weight and rate of weight gain from infancy onward. Body mass index (BMI) and BMI percentile are indicators of how your pediatrician can ensure that your child is at a healthy weight for his or her age, sex, and height. A BMI at or above the 85th percentile falls into the overweight category; a BMI at or above the 95th percentile defines the obese category. (See *Growth Charts*, in Appendix.) These categories are basically risk categories for current and future medical problems and the higher the BMI (above the 85th percentile), the greater the risk. The AAP recently endorsed the World Health Organization's infant growth charts. This means that BMI can now be monitored as soon as your child is born. We definitely would not want an infant to lose weight! But, these growth charts can provide more confidence that your infant or toddler is growing well, and so may not need extra formula or supplementation. This can be particularly helpful reassurance if you are concerned that your child is fussy due to not eating enough.

Some children are more prone to gain extra weight because of family history (which can include things like genetics, having a slower metabolism, and family customs regarding the type and amount of food that is eaten), but in almost all cases, making healthy food changes and increasing physical activity can help improve your child's weight. Encourage your child to lead an active lifestyle at home, in child care settings, and in school to start them on the path to lifelong health. Talk to your pediatrician about ways to develop healthy eating habits that can begin in infancy, such as minimizing or eliminating juice and offering a variety of healthy foods, especially vegetables and fruits, and continuing these habits throughout childhood. Early on, encourage your child to eat a variety of healthy foods and allow them to decide when they are full. Don't forget that taste preferences can change over time and it can take your child ten times of trying a new food before he enjoys it. Choose nutritious snacks for him, including vegetables, fruits, low-fat dairy foods, and whole grains. Have him sit at the table and think about turning off the TV. Studies show that children who watch too much TV are more likely to be overweight because:

1. TV and screen time take away from time they could be running, jumping, and interacting with other people.

2. Kids tend to eat more when watching TV.

3. They're often exposed to commercials, leading to cravings for unhealthy foods.

These are among the reasons why the Academy recommends no television for children under two years of age and no more than two hours a day for older children. Also, try to keep mealtimes media/screen-free. With the TV off, meals can be a great time to have family conversations. (See *Media* chapter, page 813.) Keeping communication channels open with your children throughout their school years can be very protective. Family walks and physical activity are also a great opportunity to talk with your kids. As a parent, you have an enormous impact not only on your youngster's lifelong food choices, but also on other factors that can contribute to or prevent obesity. Consider leading by example—if you lead a healthy lifestyle, then your child is far more likely to lead one, too.

Getting Ready for Toilet Training

As your child approaches age two, you'll begin to think about toilet training. Perhaps you may be considering a child care or preschool program that requires her to be trained. Before you launch your campaign, however, be forewarned that toilet training generally becomes easier and is accomplished more quickly when your child is older. Yes, early training is possible—but not necessarily preferred. It may even place unnecessary pressure on your young toddler. She may not have the necessary bowel or bladder control or the motor skills needed to remove her clothes quickly and reliably before using the toilet.

Many children are ready to be toilet trained after their second birthday (boys often slightly later than girls), but your toddler might be ready earlier.

If your toddler appears ready, turn to page 356 for details. Even if she's not

quite ready, you still can familiarize her with the process by keeping her potty chair handy and explaining, in very simple terms, how it works. You might also consider choosing words that you'll use at home such as "pee-pee" and "poop" to familiarize her with what's taking place. Soon she'll be able to tell you after she has gone. While it is not a sign that she's completely ready to be toilet trained, it is a first step toward getting ready. As she gets older, you might also consider showing her where stool from her diapers goes, and allowing her to flush the toilet. The more familiar she is with the process, the less scary and confusing it will seem when you begin training her.

Sleeping

Sometimes it's tempting just to give up and let your child fall asleep in his tracks when he's overcome by exhaustion. But doing so will only make it more challenging to get on a routine sleep schedule, and this is very important for both daytime and nighttime sleeping. Instead, watch the clock to see when he shows signs of sleepiness, and then make that his regular bedtime. Establish a bedtime ritual and discuss it with your toddler. Whether you include a bath, story, or song, the routine should end with him quiet, but awake, in his crib, ready for your good-night kiss before you leave the room. If he cries continuously, use the methods described in Chapters 9 and 35 to teach him to fall asleep on his own.

Unfortunately, resistance at bedtime isn't the only sleep struggle you may have with your child. Remember the first time he slept through the night as a baby and you thought sleep problems were over? As the parent of a toddler, you now know the truth: He may go for a few days, weeks, or even months sleeping through the night, then begin waking up almost as frequently as a newborn.

A change in routine is a common cause of nighttime awakening. Changing rooms or beds, losing a favorite cuddly toy or blanket, taking a trip away from home, or illness may all disrupt his sleep. These are all valid reasons for him to wake up—but not for you to pick him up or take him to your room. He needs to put himself back to sleep, even if it means crying a bit first. The strategies outlined in Chapter 35 still apply.

But what if your toddler is used to getting lots of nighttime attention? In this case, you'll need to retrain him gradually. Let's say you've been giving him milk when he wakes up. It's time to change first to water and soon after stop it entirely. If you've been picking him up, restrict yourself to calming him with only your voice from a distance. Above all, don't get angry with him if he continues to protest. Show him kindness, even as you remain firm. It's not easy, but in the long run it will improve your sleep as well as his. See Chapter 35 for more information on sleep.

Behavior

Discipline

Having a toddler is a humbling experience and presents new challenges, adventures, and opportunities for fulfillment. Before your child was born, or even when she was a baby, it was easy for you to watch someone else's toddler throwing a temper tantrum and say, "My child will never do that." Now you realize there are times when any child acts up unexpectedly. You can guide your child and teach her what's right, and that will work most of the time. But you can't force her to act exactly as you want. So face the facts: There are bound to be times when the unruly child everyone is staring at is yours!

At this age, your toddler has a limited idea of what "good" and "bad" mean, and she does not fully understand the concept of rules or warnings. You may say, "If you pull the cat's tail, she'll bite you," but it may make no sense to her at all. Even "Be nice to kitty" may not be clear to her. So whether she's running into the street or turning her face away from Grandma's kiss, she's not deliberately behaving badly, nor do her actions mean that you've failed as a parent. She's simply acting on the impulses of the moment. It will take years of firm but gentle guidance before she fully understands what you expect from her and has the self-control to meet those expectations.

Many people think of discipline as punishment. In fact, discipline means to teach or instruct, and while punishment may be part of it, a much more important aspect of discipline is love. Affection and caring form the core of your relationship with your child, and they play a powerful role in shaping her behavior. Your love and respect will teach her to care about others as well as herself. Your own daily example of honesty, dedication, and trust will teach her to become honest, hardworking, and trustworthy herself. Also, the control you show in helping her to learn right from wrong will serve as a model for the self-discipline she develops later on. In short, if you want her to behave well, you need to act that way toward her.

If you were keeping a running tally, you'd want displays of affection to greatly outnumber punishments and criticisms. Even a quick hug or kiss, or a bit of good-natured roughhousing, will reassure your child that you love her. And on a day when your toddler is getting into everything and you find yourself being especially snappy with her, make sure you go out of your way when she does behave well to give her a hug and tell her she's doing a good job. "Catch" her being good as often as you can. Especially during this second year, pleasing you is very important to your toddler, so praise and attention are powerful rewards that can motivate her to obey the reasonable rules you set for her.

It's important to have realistic expectations for your child's behavior. They should reflect her own temperament and personality, not your fantasies. She may be much more active and inquisitive than you would like her to be, but insisting that she spend long stretches in the playpen or confined in her high chair will only make her more resistant and frustrated.

Even if your toddler is a "model" child, she still has to learn what you expect. Telling her once won't get the message across. She'll have to learn by trial and error (often, several errors) before she understands the rule.

If you're a single parent, you may encounter unique challenges related to that living situation, trying to manage a child's behavior issues on your own. But there are ways to minimize the stress you may feel at times, from utilizing available resources to help care for your child to keeping your own sense of humor as much as possible. (Also see *Single-Parent Families* on page 754 in Chapter 26.) One other important reminder: If you load too much on your child at this early age, you'll be frustrated, and she'll be hurt and bewildered. Make things easier for both of you by establishing some priorities and then building your list of rules gradually. Give precedence to limits that keep her safe. As your youngster learns to walk (between nine and sixteen months of age), safety should be the most important discipline issue, giving her the freedom to explore in safe ways, while making sure that childproof locks are on cabinets that contain heavy dishes or pots. Also be certain that she understands that there are prohibitions against hitting, biting, and kicking. Once she masters these rules, you can turn your attention to nuisance behavior, such as screaming in public, throwing food, writing on the wall, and removing her clothing at unexpected moments. Plan to save the finer points of polite social behavior for the next few years. It's too much to ask an eighteen-month-old to be nice when Grandma's kissing her at a time she'd rather be outside playing.

At this age, since your toddler can't understand everything that you say, it's also only fair to eliminate as many temptations as possible. She needs freedom to explore. Cluttering your home with "no-no's" will deprive her of this freedom and create more restrictions than she can possibly absorb. It also will frustrate her. While you can't get rid of the oven, you can lock away the china and place your houseplants out of reach. Redirection is also an important technique at this age. Instead of constantly saying "no" when she wants to play with the electrical outlet, and then dealing with the inevitable screaming fit that ensues, cut her off at the pass with a book or engage her in some play with blocks. Anticipating her every move can be exhausting, but it is a small price to pay to keep her both safe and content.

To prevent further unwanted behavior, pay extra attention to your toddler when she's tired, hungry, sick, or is in an unfamiliar setting—in other words, when she's most likely to be stressed. Also try to keep your own daily routine as flexible as possible so she doesn't feel extra pressure. If the two of you are at the grocery store during her nap time, don't be surprised if she acts up.

Despite all your attempts at prevention, sometimes your toddler will violate one or more of your top ten rules. When that happens, alert her with your facial expression and the displeased sound of your voice. Then move her to a different place. Sometimes this will be enough, but just as often, other measures still may be required. It's best to decide on these responses now, while you are calm and your toddler is young. Otherwise, in the heat of the moment, or when she becomes naturally more mischievous in the next few years, you may be more prone to lose your temper and do something you'll regret.

Here's an important pact to make with yourself. *Never* resort to punishments that physically or emotionally hurt your child. While you need to let her know that she's done something wrong, this doesn't mean you have to inflict pain. Spanking, slapping, beating, shaking, and screaming at children of any age do far more harm than good. Here are some of the main reasons why this is true.

1. Even if it stops the child from misbehaving at the moment, it also teaches her that it's OK to hit and yell when she's upset or angry. Think of the mother busily whacking her child as she yells at her: "I told you not to hit!" It's absurd, isn't it? But it's also tragically common, and has an equally tragic result: Children who are hit often become hitters themselves, having learned that violence is an acceptable way to express anger and to resolve conflicts. Remember, toddlers will imitate everything that you do.

2. Physical punishment can harm your child. If a little spank doesn't work, many parents will slap even harder as they become angrier and more frustrated.

3. Physical punishment makes the child angry at and resentful of the parent. So instead of developing self-discipline, the youngster is much more likely to try to get back at the parent by continuing to misbehave, but without getting caught.

4. Physical punishment gives a child a very extreme form of attention. Although it's unpleasant, even painful, it tells the child that she's gotten through to her parent. If the mother or father is usually too busy or preoccupied to pay much attention to her, the child may decide that the bad behavior and the punishment that follows it is worth it to get parental attention.

Physical punishment is harmful emotionally to both parent and child. It is the least effective way to discipline. So if spanking and yelling are wrong, what approach should you take? As difficult as it may be, the best way to deal with your misbehaving toddler is to isolate her briefly. No attention. No toys. No fun. This strategy, known as time-out, works like this:

1. You've told your toddler not to open the oven door, but she persists.

2. Without raising your voice, again say firmly, "No. Don't open the oven door," and pick her up with her back toward you.

3. Begin this "time-out training" in your lap with your child facing away from you. Hold her until she is quiet and still.

The keys to this form of discipline—or to any other, for that matter—are consistency and calmness. As hard as it may be, try to respond immediately every time your child breaks an important rule, but don't let your irritation get the better of you. If you're like most parents, you won't succeed 100 percent of the time, but an occasional slip-up won't make much difference. Just try to be as consistent as you can.

When you do feel yourself losing your temper, take a few deep breaths, count to ten, and, if possible, get someone else to watch your child while you leave the room. Remind yourself that you are older and should be wiser than your toddler. You know that at her age she's not deliberately trying to annoy or embarrass you, so keep your own ego out of it. In the end, the more self-discipline you exercise, the more effective you'll be at disciplining your child. Remember, they're watching and imitating you!

Coping with Temper Tantrums

While you're busily planning the rules and regulations by which your toddler must live, he's attempting to master his own destiny, and it's inevitable that you'll clash from time to time. Your first sign of this collision course will come when your one-year-old shakes his head and emphatically says "No!" after you've asked him to do something. By year's end, his protests may have escalated to screaming fits or full-blown tantrums in which he throws himself onto his back on the floor, clenches his teeth, kicks and screams, pounds his fists on the floor, and perhaps even holds his breath. As difficult as these performances may be for you to tolerate, they are a normal (even healthy) way for your toddler to deal with conflict at this age.

Look at the situation from his point of view. Like all young toddlers, he believes that the world revolves around him. He's trying hard to be indepen-

Preventing Temper Tantrums

(See also *Temper Tantrums*, page 587.)

When it comes to discipline, you have several distinct advantages over your child. First of all, because you know that there inevitably will be conflicts between you and your child (you can probably even predict which issues are likely to spark them), you can plan your strategy in advance to prevent friction as much as possible.

Use the following guidelines to help you minimize your child's temper tantrums, both in number and in intensity. Make sure everyone who takes care of her understands and follows these policies consistently.

1. When you ask your toddler to do something, use a friendly tone of voice and phrase your request like an invitation instead of a command. It also helps to say "please" and "thank you."

2. Don't overreact when she says "no." For quite some time, she may automatically say "no" to *any* request or instruction. She'll even say "no" to ice cream and cake at this stage! What she really means is something like "I'd like to be in control here, so I'll say 'no' until I think it through or until I see if you're serious." Instead of jumping on her, answer her hidden challenge by repeating your request calmly and clearly. Don't punish her for saying "no."

3. Choose your battles carefully. She won't throw a temper tantrum unless you push her first, so don't push unless there's something worth fighting for. For example, keeping her safely buckled into her car seat while the automobile is moving is a priority item. Making sure she eats her peas before her applesauce is not. So while she's saying "no" to everything all day long, you should be saying "no" only the few times a day when it's absolutely necessary.

4. Don't offer choices where none exists, and don't make deals. Issues like bathing, bedtime, and staying out of the street are nonnegotiable. She doesn't deserve an extra cookie or trip to the park for cooperating with these rules. Bribery will only teach her to break the rule whenever you forget to give her the agreed-on reward.

5. Do offer limited choices whenever possible. Let her decide which pajamas to wear, which story to read, which toys to play with. If you encour-

age her independence in these areas, she'll be much more likely to comply when it counts.

6. Anticipate situations that are likely to trigger a tantrum, and avoid them whenever possible. If she always makes a scene in the grocery store, arrange to leave her with a sitter the next few times you go shopping. If one of her playmates always seems to get her keyed up and irritable, separate the children for a few days or weeks and see if the dynamics improve when they're older.

7. Reward her good behavior with plenty of praise and attention. Even if you just sit with her while she looks at her books, your companionship shows her you approve of this quiet activity.

8. Keep your sense of humor. While it's not a good idea to laugh at your toddler as she kicks and screams (that just plays to her performance), it can be very therapeutic to laugh and talk about it with friends or older family members when she's out of earshot.

dent, and most of the time you're encouraging him to be strong and assertive. Yet every now and then, when he's trying to do something he very much wants to do, you pull him away or ask him to do something else. He can't understand why you're getting in his way, nor can he verbally tell you how upset he is. The only way he can express his frustration is by acting it out.

Outbursts, then, are all but inevitable, and your child's general temperament will set the tone for most of them. If he's very adaptable, easygoing, generally positive, and easily distracted, he may never kick and scream. Instead, he might pout, say "no," or simply head in an opposite direction when you try to guide him. The negativism is there, but it's low-key. On the other hand, if your child has been very active, intense, and persistent from infancy, he'll probably channel the same intensity into his tantrums. You'll need to remind yourself over and over that this is neither good nor bad, and it has nothing to do with your skill as a parent. Your child is not consciously trying to thwart you, but is simply going through a normal stage of development that soon (but perhaps not soon enough to suit you) will pass.

Here are some important points to keep in mind about living with temper tantrums.

■ **You may have** an easier time coping with your toddler's outbursts if you think of them as performances. This will help remind you of what you

WHERE WE STAND

THE AMERICAN ACADEMY OF PEDIATRICS strongly opposes striking a child for any reason. Spanking is never recommended; infants may be physically harmed by a parent who strikes the child. If a spanking is spontaneous, parents should later explain calmly why they did it, the specific behavior that provoked it, and how angry they felt. They also might apologize to their child for their loss of control. This usually helps the youngster to understand and accept the spanking, and it models for the child how to remediate a wrong.

Whenever a parent strikes a child, it may undermine the relationship of trust that the child needs to thrive. However, infants often frustrate their parents. Here are a few alternatives: First, put your baby in the crib or another safe place while you get control of yourself. Call a friend, relative, or partner to get some support or advice. If these don't help, reach out to your child's pediatrician for advice.

have to do to stop them: namely, eliminate the audience. Since you are the only audience that matters to your child, leave the room. If he follows, call time-out and put him in his playpen. Also, if he kicks or bites at any time during the tantrum, call time-out immediately. While it's normal for him to try out this kind of super aggressive behavior, you shouldn't let him get away with it.

- **When a tantrum** takes place away from home, it's much more difficult to remain calm. Especially when you're out in public, you can't just leave him and go to another room. And because you're trapped and embarrassed, you're much more likely to spank or snap at him. But that's not going to work any better here than it does at home, and it has the added disadvantage of making you look even worse than your child. Rather than lashing out or letting him have his way—either of which will only encourage his tantrums—calmly carry him to a restroom or out to the car, so he can finish his performance away from onlookers. Also, sometimes in public a big, immobilizing hug and calming voice will soothe and quiet such a child.

- **When the tantrum** or the time-out is over, don't dwell on it. Instead, if a request from you had triggered his outburst initially, calmly repeat it. Remain composed and determined, and he'll soon realize that acting out is a waste of his time as well as yours.

■ **He may hold** his breath during a severe temper tantrum. Sometimes this might last long enough to cause him to faint for a very short period of time. This can be very frightening when it occurs, but he will awaken in thirty to sixty seconds. Just keep him safe and protected during this brief episode and try not to overreact yourself, since this tends to reinforce tantrum breath-holding behavior. If not reinforced, this type of activity usually will disappear after a short period of time.

Family Relationships

Because your toddler is so self-centered, her older brothers and sisters might find her very taxing. Not only does she still consume the bulk of your time and attention, but with increasing frequency she will deliberately invade her siblings' territory and possessions. When they throw her out, she may respond with a tantrum. Even if the older siblings were tolerant and affectionate toward her as an infant, they are bound to display some antagonistic feelings toward her now—at least occasionally.

It will help keep the peace if you enforce off-limits rules to protect the older children's privacy, and you set aside time to spend just with them. No matter how old they are, all your children want your affection and attention. Whether they're preparing for the preschool picnic, planning a second-grade science project, trying out for the junior high soccer team, or fretting over a date for the junior prom, they need you as much as your toddler does.

If your toddler is the older sibling, the rivalry may be much more intense. (See *Sibling Rivalry*, page 751.) The normal feelings of jealousy are heightened by her self-centeredness, and she doesn't have the reasoning abilities to cope with them. Often her feelings of jealousy are not manifest as outright anger toward an infant, but as anger and belligerence toward you for not providing her with as much attention as she believes she deserves. And if she isn't getting enough attention for doing the "right" things (playing quietly by herself), she'll have no qualms about pushing your buttons (by jumping off the couch or biting or making a run for the electrical outlet!). Remember, there is no such thing as "negative" attention to a toddler—all attention is good. At times they'd rather have you angry with them than feel like they are being ignored (which, by the way, is the reason that time-out can be so effective). The way out of this vicious cycle (of acting out for attention followed by negative attention for acting out) is to catch her being good and to pick your battles. If you go out of your way to praise her for good behavior ("catching her being good"), she'll pick up a book the next time she's looking for attention, instead of jumping off the couch. By limiting your battles to egregious errors (biting or hitting) and issues of safety (playing with the electrical outlet), you'll limit the amount of negative attention that you are giving. If you're sure that she's doing something just to get your attention (like jumping off the couch), if you ignore that behavior, she'll probably stop that and try something else (remember, she's looking for attention). Despite her drive for independence, there are many times each day when she'll want to have the attention that you're giving the baby, and she isn't about to wait her turn.

It's important to begin preparing your toddler before the new baby arrives. She'll recognize the changes quite early in pregnancy, so don't try to hide anything from her. When she asks, tell her that a new baby is coming, but don't stress that it will be a brother or sister. Otherwise she'll expect a playmate instead of an infant. Also, try not to overemphasize the arrival of the new brother or sister far in advance of your delivery; your toddler is concerned only with events that happen in the immediate future.

As tempting as it may be to have her toilet trained before the new baby arrives—so you don't have two in diapers at the same time—it's not worth it if you have to pressure her to make it happen. (See Chapter 1, page 36.) Such efforts probably will backfire, and the added stress may make her resent the new baby. If major changes must be made, such as moving her to a new room, make them well in advance of the baby's due date. The less pressure you place on your toddler at the time of the new baby's arrival, the better everyone will fare.

After the new baby comes home, include your toddler as much as possible in your activities with the infant. Although she definitely can't be trusted alone with the infant, invite her to "help" as you feed, bathe, change, and dress her new sibling. Take advantage of the baby's naps to spend time alone with your toddler, and stress her importance to you and to the baby.

It's also essential to recognize that you can't satisfy the needs of both of them all the time, especially not by yourself. When you're feeling especially overwhelmed, "divide and conquer" by handing one child to your spouse, relative, or a close friend while you attend to the other. If possible, arrange for your toddler to go on special outings during this time, even if just to a park or the zoo. If the children get these occasional breaks from each other, everyone will feel less competitive—and a little more comfortable.

Immunization Update

Between twelve and fifteen months, your toddler will need booster doses of the Hib and pneumococcal conjugate vaccines. These vaccines help prevent meningitis, pneumonia, and joint infection caused by *Haemophilus influenzae* type b and several strains of *Streptococcus pneumoniae* bacteria. Your toddler also should receive her first measles, mumps, rubella (MMR) vaccine, chickenpox vaccine, and hepatitis A vaccine during these months. At twelve to eighteen months, your toddler also will require:

■ The fourth dose of the DTaP vaccine (which can be administered as early as twelve months, but is recommended at fifteen to eighteen months of age)

■ The third dose of the polio vaccine (if not already given)

■ The fourth dose of *pneumococcus*

■ The fourth dose of Hib

■ The second dose of hepatitis A vaccine, given at least six months after the first dose

Safety Check

Sleeping Safety

■ Keep the crib mattress at the lowest setting.

■ Keep the crib free of any objects that your toddler could stack and climb on to get out.

■ If your toddler can climb out of his crib, move him to a low bed.

■ Keep the crib away from all windows, drapery, and electrical and other cords.

■ Be sure all crib gyms, mobiles, and other hanging toys have been removed from the crib.

Toy Safety

■ Do not give your toddler any toy that has to be plugged into an electrical outlet.

A Message for Grandparents

You have an ongoing role to play in your grandchild's nurturing and development. Though you must carefully "re-childproof" your house as a grandparent (see Chapter 15), there are many wonderful things your grandchildren can do with grandparents. During this time of his young life, here are some activities in which you can participate and some things to keep in mind as you do:

MOTOR SKILLS

Help your grandchild practice skills that tie in with your own likes and preferences. For example:

- **Involve him in physical activities (such as sweeping, preparing food, or arranging items) around the house in which you can lend a helping hand to ensure his success and safety.**

- **Devise and initiate outdoor games and exercises that you and he can enjoy together.**

COGNITIVE MILESTONES

To help your grandchild develop cognitively:

- **Read special books to him.**

- **Play music and sing songs with him.**

- **Assist him as he begins to learn his numbers.**

- **Play hiding games like hide-and-seek and peekaboo.**

- **Mix fantasy play with real play.**

SOCIAL DEVELOPMENT

- **Encourage your grandchild to interact with his peers, but keep in mind that egocentric behavior is normal for this age.**

- **Don't overreact to selfishness or disregarding the feelings of others. Just reinforce that he should be sensitive to the feelings of other children.**

- Keep in mind that this period of self-centeredness will taper off by the age of three.

- Nurture his self-esteem at every opportunity, but not at the expense of others.

EMOTIONAL DEVELOPMENT

- Repeatedly tell your grandchild how special he is to you. Tell him how important your time together is to you.

- Don't overreact to the mood swings he goes through—clinging one moment, independent the next, and defiant after that.

- Don't reinforce his aggressiveness if it becomes abusive. Set limits, but do not physically restrain or punish him. Read the section on brain growth of children this age (page 309). Follow your own inclinations about the activities or areas that can promote his development.

- Do not give her a motorized riding toy.

- Do not give her a toy with any small parts or sharp edges. Stick with toys that are intended for toddlers, not for older children.

Water Safety

- Never leave your toddler, *even for a few seconds,* in or near any body of water without supervision. This includes a bathtub, toilet, wading pool, swimming pool, fishpond, whirlpool, hot tub, lake, or ocean.

Auto Safety

- The safest place for all children to ride is in their car safety seat in the backseat.

- Never let your toddler climb out of his car safety seat while the car is moving.

■ Never leave him alone in the car, even if it is locked and in your driveway.
(Also see the section on car safety seats, pages 491–499, of Chapter 15.)

Home Safety

■ Protect any open windows with window guards or barriers that your
toddler cannot possibly push out or open. Screens do not prevent falls
out of windows.

■ Make sure all electrical outlets have a safety covering on them. If possible, block electrical outlets with furniture or use outlet covers that are
not a choking hazard. Also make sure that all cabinets that contain
cleaning fluids or other dangerous items have safety locks on them.

■ Install ground-fault circuit interrupters (GFCIs) where appropriate—
usually in the kitchen and bathrooms—to prevent electrocution.

■ Keep electrical cords out of reach.

■ Guns should not be in the home of any child. The best way to protect
children from firearm-related injuries is to remove guns from homes and
communities. If you do have a gun, it is essential to store it unloaded in
a locked case, with the ammunition locked in a separate location.

■ Keep all medications and purses out of reach.

Outdoor Safety

■ Install door locks, barriers, and alarms to prevent your child from ac-
cessing pools, driveways, and streets without your knowledge. It is especially critical that pools be made entirely inaccessible by a four-sided
fence that completely separates the pool from the house and the rest of
the yard.

■ Hold on to your toddler whenever you're near streets, parking lots, and
driveways, even in quiet neighborhoods.

■ Set up fences or other barriers to make sure she stays within her outside
play area and away from the street, pools, and other hazards.

- Make sure there are sand, wood chips, or other soft surfaces under outdoor play equipment.

- Pay special attention anytime you or someone else is backing out of the garage or down the driveway. Make sure you know where your child is and that he cannot run into the path of the vehicle.

- Keep your vehicle locked when not in use so your child cannot get in. Even without starting the engine, he could set the car in gear, allowing it to roll, or could suffer heatstroke.

~ 11 ~

Your Two-Year-Old

YOUR CHILD IS now advancing from infancy toward and into the pre-school years. During this time, his physical growth and motor development will slow, but you can expect to see some tremendous intellectual, social, and emotional changes. His vocabulary will grow, he'll try to increase his independence from the other members of his family, and—upon discovering that society has certain rules that he is expected to observe—he'll begin to develop some real self-control.

These changes will present an emotional challenge for both you and your child. After all, these are the "terrible twos," when his every other word seems to be "no." This period will seem like a constant tug-of-war between his continuing reliance on you and his need to assert his independence. He may flip-flop between these extremes, clinging to you when you try to leave him and running in the opposite direction when you want him to obey you. You may find yourself longing for the cuddly infant he used to be while at the same time pushing him to behave like a "big kid." It's no wonder you occasionally lose patience with each other.

But on the other hand, this is also a time of joy and new independence for your two-year-old. His language grows, and his ability to really be "a real person" blossoms. He plays more games, entertains himself often for a longer period of time than earlier, and his imagination expands by telling stories and engaging with those around him.

By acknowledging and accepting these changes, all the positives and negatives, you'll make it easier for both of you through the next few hectic years. Largely through your responses to him—the encouragement and respect you show him, your appreciation for his accomplishments, the warmth and security you offer him—he'll learn to feel comfortable, capable, and special.

These feelings will help in later years as he goes to school and meets new people. Most important, they'll make him proud of himself as a person.

Growth and Development
Physical Appearance and Growth

Although your preschooler's growth rate will slow between his second and third birthdays, nevertheless he will continue his remarkable physical transformation from baby to child. The most dramatic change will occur in his bodily proportions. As an infant, he had a relatively large head and short legs and arms; now his head growth will slow, from ¾ inch (2 cm) in his second year alone to ¾ to 1¼ inches (2–3 cm) over the next ten years. At the same time, his height will increase, primarily because his legs and, to some degree, the rest of his body will be growing quickly. With these changes in the rates of growth, his body and legs will look much more in proportion.

The baby fat that seemed to make your infant so cuddly in the first months of life gradually will disappear during these preschool years. The percentage of fat, which reached a peak at age one, will steadily decrease to approximately half that by his fifth birthday. Notice how his arms and thighs become more slender and his face less round. Even the pads of fat under the arches, which have until now given the appearance of flat feet, will disappear.

His posture will change, as well, during this time. His pudgy, babyish look as a preschooler has been partly due to his posture, particularly his protruding abdomen and inwardly curving lower back. But as his muscle tone improves and his posture becomes more erect, he'll develop a longer, leaner, stronger appearance.

Although it will happen more slowly now, your child will continue to grow steadily. Preschoolers grow an average of 2½ inches (6 cm) annually and gain about 4 pounds (2 kg) each year. Plot your child's height and weight on the growth charts in the Appendix to compare his rate of growth to the average for this age. If you should notice a pronounced lapse in growth, discuss it with your pediatrician. She probably will tell you there is no need to become overly concerned, as some healthy children just may not grow as quickly during their second and third years as their playmates seem to do.

Less commonly, this pause in growth during the preschool years may signal something else—perhaps a chronic health problem, such as kidney or liver disease, or a recurrent infection. In rare cases, slow growth may be due to a disorder of one of the hormone glands or to gastrointestinal complications of some chronic illnesses. Your pediatrician will take all of these things into consideration when she examines your child.

At the age of two, don't be surprised if your child is eating less than you think he should. Children need fewer calories at this time because they're growing more slowly. But even though he's eating less, he still can remain well-nourished as long as you make a variety of healthy foods available to him. Encourage healthy snacks and begin establishing sound and healthful eating habits. At the same time, if he seems overly preoccupied with food and appears to be accumulating excess weight, talk to your pediatrician about ways to help manage his weight. Early eating behaviors can influence the risk of obesity throughout life, so managing your child's weight in childhood is as important as it is at any stage of life.

Movement

At this age, your child will seem to be continually on the go—running, kicking, climbing, jumping. His attention span, which was never particularly long, may now seem even shorter. Try starting a game with him, and he'll immediately change to a different one. Head in one direction, and he'll quickly detour to another. This yearlong energy spurt between ages two and three certainly will keep you on the go. But take heart—his activity level will strengthen his body and develop his coordination.

In the months ahead, your child's running will become smoother and more coordinated. He'll also learn to kick and direct the motion of a ball, walk up and down steps by himself while holding on, and seat himself confidently in a child-size chair. With a little help, he'll even be able to stand on one leg.

Watch your two-year-old walk, and you'll see how he has cast aside the stiff, spread-legged gait of a young preschooler, replacing it with a more adult, heel-to-toe motion. In the process, he has become much more adept at maneuvering his body, capable of walking backward and turning corners that are not

Movement Milestones for Your Two-Year-Old

- **Climbs well**

- **Walks up and down stairs, alternating feet**

- **Kicks ball (wearing closed-toed shoes, which are safer than flip-flops)**

- **Runs easily**

- **Pedals tricycle (be sure he wears a safety helmet on the tricycle)**

- **Bends over easily without falling**

too sharp. He also can do other things as he moves, such as using his hands, talking, and looking around.

Don't worry about finding activities that will help your child develop his motor skills. He'll probably be able to do that himself. When you are able to join in the fun, bear in mind that children this age love piggyback rides, rolling on mats, going down small slides, and climbing (with help) on the floor-level balance beam. The more running and climbing your games involve, the better.

If you can, set aside specific times during the day when he can go outside to run, play, and explore. This will help minimize wear and tear on the inside of the house as well as on your nerves. It's also safer for him to run around in the open than to bump into walls and furniture inside. While outdoors, let him use the yard, playground, or park—whichever is most available and safe for him. But be aware that since his self-control and judgment lag considerably behind his motor skills, you must remain vigilant and keep safety and injury prevention high on your priority list at all times.

Hand and Finger Skills

At age two, your child will be able to manipulate small objects with ease. He'll turn the pages of a book, build a tower six blocks high, pull off his shoes, and unzip a large zipper. He'll also coordinate the movements of his wrist, fingers, and palm so well that he can turn a doorknob, unscrew a jar lid, use a cup with one hand, and unwrap paper from a candy.

Milestones in Hand and Finger Skills for Your Two-Year-Old

- Makes vertical, horizontal, and circular strokes with pencil or crayon
- Turns book pages one at a time
- Builds a tower of six blocks
- Holds a pencil in writing position
- Screws and unscrews jar lids, nuts and bolts
- Turns rotating handles

One of his major accomplishments this year will be learning to "draw." Hand him a crayon and watch what happens: He'll place his thumb on one side of it and his fingers on the other, then awkwardly try to extend his index or middle finger toward the point. Clumsy as this grip may seem, it will give him enough control to create his first artistic masterpieces, using sweeping vertical and circular strokes.

Fortunately, your child's quiet play at this age will be much more focused than it was at eighteen months, when he was into everything. His attention span is longer, and now that he can turn pages, he'll be an active participant as you look at books or magazines together. He'll also be interested in activities such as drawing, building, or manipulating objects, so blocks and interlocking construction sets may keep him entertained for long periods. And if you let him loose with a box of nontoxic crayons or set of finger paints, his creative impulses will flourish.

Language Development

Your two-year-old not only understands most of what you say to him, but also speaks with a rapidly growing vocabulary of fifty or more words. Over the course of this year, he'll graduate from two- or three-word sentences ("Drink juice," "Mommy want cookie") to those with four, five, or even six words ("Where's the ball, Daddy?" "Dolly sit in my lap"). He's also beginning to use pronouns (I, you, me, we, they) and understands the concept of "mine" ("I want my cup," "I see my mommy"). Pay attention to how he also is using language to describe ideas and information and to express his physical or emotional needs and desires.

It's human nature to measure your preschooler's verbal abilities against those of other children his age, but you should try to avoid this. At this time, there's more variation in language development than in any other area. While some preschoolers develop language skills at a steady rate, others seem to master words in an uneven manner. And some children are naturally more talkative than others. This doesn't mean that the more verbal children are necessarily smarter or more advanced than the quieter ones, nor does it even mean that they have richer vocabularies. In fact, the quiet child may know just as many words but be choosier about speaking them. As a general rule, boys start talking later than girls, but this variation—like most others mentioned above—tends to even out as children reach school age.

Without any formal instruction, just by listening and practicing, your child will master many of the basic rules of grammar by the time he enters school. You can help enrich his vocabulary and language skills by making reading a part of your everyday routine. At this age, he can follow a story line and will understand and remember many ideas and pieces of information presented in

Language Milestones for Your Two-Year-Old

- **Follows a two- or three-part command, such as "Go to your room and bring back the teddy bear and the dog"**

- **Recognizes and identifies almost all common objects and pictures**

- **Understands most sentences**

- **Understands physical relationships ("on," "in," "under")**

- **Uses four- and five-word sentences**

- **Can say name, age, and sex**

- **Uses pronouns (I, you, me, we, they) and some plurals (cars, dogs, cats)**

- **Strangers can understand most of his words**

books. Even so, because he may have a hard time sitting still for too long, the books you read to him should be short. To keep his attention, choose activity-oriented books that encourage him to touch, point, and name objects or to repeat certain phrases. Toward the end of this year, as his language skills become more advanced, he'll also have fun with poems, puns, or jokes that play with language by repeating funny sounds or using nonsense phrases.

For some children, however, this language-development process does not run smoothly. In fact, about one in every ten to fifteen children has trouble with language comprehension and/or speech. For some children, the problem is caused by hearing difficulty, low intelligence, lack of verbal stimulation at home, or a family history of speech delays. In most cases, though, the cause is unknown. If your pediatrician suspects your child has difficulty with language, he'll conduct a thorough physical exam and hearing test and, if necessary, refer you to a speech/language or early childhood specialist for further evaluation. Early detection and identification of language delay or hearing impairment is critically important, so treatment can begin before the problem interferes with learning in other areas. Unless you and your pediatrician identify the difficulty and do something about it, your child may have continuous trouble with classroom learning.

Cognitive Development

Think back to your child's infancy and early preschooler months. That was a time when he learned about the world by touching, looking, manipulating, and

Cognitive Milestones for Your Two-Year-Old

- Makes mechanical toys work
- Matches an object in her hand or room to a picture in a book
- Plays make-believe with dolls, animals, and people
- Sorts objects by shape and color
- Completes puzzles with three or four pieces
- Understands concept of "two"

listening. Now, as a two-year-old, the learning process has become more thoughtful. His grasp of language is increasing, and he's beginning to form mental images for things, actions, and concepts. He also can solve some problems in his head, performing mental trial-and-error instead of having to manipulate objects physically. And as his memory and intellectual abilities develop, he'll begin to understand simple time concepts, such as "You can play *after* you finish eating."

Your child also is starting to understand the relationship between objects. For instance, he'll be able to match similar shapes when you give him shape-sorting toys and simple jigsaw puzzles. He'll also begin to recognize the purpose of numbers in counting objects—especially the number two. And as his understanding of cause and effect develops, he'll become much more interested in winding up toys and turning lights and appliances on and off.

You'll also notice your preschooler's play growing more complex. Most noticeably, he'll start stringing together different activities to create a logical sequence. Instead of drifting randomly from one toy to another, he may first put a doll to bed and then cover it up. Or he may pretend to feed several dolls, one after the other. Over the next few years, he'll put together longer and more elaborate sequences of make-believe, acting out much of his own daily routine, from getting up in the morning to taking a bath and going to bed at night.

If we were to single out the major intellectual limitation at this age, it would be your child's feeling that everything that happens in his world is the result of something he has done. With a belief like this, it becomes very difficult for him to understand correctly such concepts as death, divorce, or illness, without feeling that he played some role in it. So if parents separate or a family member gets sick, children often feel responsible. (See discussion in Chapter 26, *Family Issues.*)

Reasoning with your two-year-old is often difficult. After all, he views everything in extremely simple terms. He still often confuses fantasy with reality unless he's actively playing make-believe. Therefore, during this stage, be sure to choose your own words carefully: Comments that you think are funny or playful—such as "If you eat more cereal, you'll explode"—actually may panic him, since he won't know you're joking.

Social Development

By nature, children this age can be more concerned about their own needs and even act selfishly. Often they refuse to share anything that interests them, and they do not easily interact with other children, even when playing side by side, unless it's to let a playmate know that they would like a toy or object for themselves. There may be times when your child's behavior may make you upset, but if you take a close look, you'll notice that all the other preschoolers in the play group probably are acting the same way.

At age two, children view the world almost exclusively through their own needs and desires. Because they can't yet understand how others might feel in the same situation, they assume that everyone thinks and feels exactly as they do. And on those occasions when they realize they're out of line, they may not be able to control themselves. For these reasons, it's useless to try to shape your child's behavior using statements such as "How would you like it if she did that to you?" Save these comments until your child is older; then she'll be able to really understand how other people think and feel and be capable of responding to such reasoning.

Social Milestones for Your Two-Year-Old

- **Imitates adults and playmates**
- **Spontaneously shows affection for familiar playmates**
- **Can take turns in games**
- **Understands concepts of "mine" and "his/hers"**

Because your two-year-old's behavior seems only self-directed, you also may find yourself worrying that he's spoiled or out of control. In all likelihood, your fears are unfounded, and he'll pass through this phase in time. Highly active, aggressive children who push and shove usually are just as "normal" as quiet, shy ones who never seem to act out their thoughts and feelings.

Ironically, despite your child's being most interested in himself, much of his playtime will be spent imitating other people's mannerisms and activities. Imitation and "pretend" are favorite games at this age. So as your two-year-old puts his teddy to bed or feeds his doll, you may hear him use exactly the same words and tone of voice you use when telling him to go to sleep or eat his vegetables. No matter how he resists your instructions at other times, when he moves over into the parent role, he imitates you exactly. These play activities help him learn what it's like to be in someone else's shoes, and they serve as valuable rehearsals for future social encounters. They'll also help you appreciate the importance of being a good role model, by demonstrating that children often do as we do, not as we say.

The best way for your two-year-old to learn how to behave around other people is to be given plenty of trial runs. Don't let her relatively antisocial be-

Holding the Line on Tantrums

Frustration, anger, and an occasional tantrum are inevitable for all two-year-olds. As a parent, you should allow your preschooler to express his emotions but, at the same time, try to help him channel his anger away from violent or overly aggressive behavior. Here are some suggestions.

1. When you see your child starting to get worked up, try to turn his energy and attention to a new activity that is more acceptable.

2. If you can't distract your preschooler, ignore him. Every time you react to one of his outbursts in any way, you're rewarding his negative behavior with extra attention. Even scolding, punishing, or trying to reason with him may encourage him to act up more.

3. If you're in a public place where his behavior is embarrassing you, simply remove him without discussion or fuss. Wait until he's calmed down before you return or continue with your activities.

4. Do not use physical punishment to discipline your child. If you do, he may assume that aggression is an acceptable way to respond when he doesn't get his way.

5. If the tantrum involves hitting, biting, or some other potentially harmful behavior, you can't ignore it. But overreacting won't help your child. Instead, tell him immediately and clearly that he is not to behave this way, and move him off by himself for a few minutes. He can't understand complicated explanations, so don't try to reason with him. Just make sure he understands what he was doing wrong and give your consequence then and there. If you wait an hour, he won't connect the punishment with the "crime." (See *Temper Tantrums*, page 587.)

6. Limit and monitor his television viewing. (See *Media*, page 813.) Preschool children may behave more aggressively if they watch violent programs on TV.

Hyperactivity

By adult standards, many two-year-olds seem "hyperactive." But it's perfectly normal for a child this age to prefer running, jumping, and climbing to walking slowly or sitting still. He also may speak so fast that it's hard to understand him, and you may worry about his short attention span, but be patient. This excess energy usually subsides by the time he reaches school age.

While the energy level is high, it makes more sense for parents to adjust than to try to force the child to slow down. If your preschooler is a "mover," adjust your expectations accordingly. Don't expect him to stay seated through a long community meeting or restaurant meal. If you take him shopping, be prepared to move at his pace, not yours. In general, avoid putting him in confining situations where you know you'll both be frustrated, and give him plenty of opportunities to release his excess energy through games involving running, jumping, climbing, and throwing or kicking a ball.

Without strong guidance, a very active child's energy easily can turn toward aggressive or destructive behavior. To avoid this, you need to establish clear and logical rules and enforce them consistently. You also can encourage more low-key behavior by praising him whenever he plays quietly or looks at a book for more than a couple of minutes at a time. It helps, too, to keep his routine of bedtime, mealtimes, baths, and naps as regular as possible so that he has a sense of structure to his day.

Some preschool children have problems with hyperactivity and short attention spans that are very severe or persist beyond the preschool years. Only if these problems significantly interfere with preschool activities, preschool performance, or social behaviors do they warrant special treatment. (See *Hyperactivity and the Distractible Child*, page 583.) If you suspect that your child may be having difficulties in these areas, ask your pediatrician to evaluate him.

havior discourage you from getting play groups together. At first it may be wise to limit the groups to two or three children. And although you'll need to monitor their activities closely to be sure that no one gets hurt or overly upset, you should let the children guide themselves as much as possible. They need to learn how to play with one another, not with one another's parents.

High-quality early education offers daily structured opportunities to interact with other children in a safe environment. As he approaches three, your child may begin to develop real friendships. Inviting these new friends to play provides a great opportunity for him to develop his social skills.

Autism Spectrum Disorder

Awareness of Autism Spectrum Disorder (ASD) has increased in recent years, at a time when there has been a notable increase in the number of diagnosed cases of young children with the condition. When a child has ASD, he will likely have difficulties with communication and social skills.

Pediatricians recognize that the sooner ASD is identified, the sooner an intervention program directed at the child's symptoms of autism can start. For that reason, you need to be aware of the early warning signs of ASD, and talk to your pediatrician if you suspect that any of them are present. These symptoms may include:

- **Difficulty making or keeping eye contact**
- **A lack of, delay in, or loss of language**
- **A lack of response to a parent's smile or other facial expressions**
- **Repetitive body movements (such as hand-flapping or rocking)**
- **A lack of pretend play, or using toys in unusual, repetitive ways**
- **Difficulty in showing concern (empathy) for others**

The American Academy of Pediatrics recommends screening for ASD when children are between eighteen and twenty-four months of age, and at any age when you or your pediatrician are concerned that problems with development may be present. Remember, children develop at their own pace, but there are general developmental milestones to which you and your doctor should be attentive during the two- to three-year age range when children are speaking more and developing play skills with other children.

For more information about ASD, see pages 636–642.

Emotional Development

It's so difficult to follow the ups and downs of a two-year-old. One moment he's beaming and friendly; the next he's sullen and weepy—and often for no apparent reason. These mood swings, however, are just part of growing up. They are signs of the emotional changes taking place as your child struggles to take control of actions, impulses, feelings, and his body.

At this age, your child wants to explore the world and seek adventure. As a

Developmental Health Watch

The developmental milestones listed in this book give you a general idea of the changes you can expect as your child gets older, but don't be alarmed if his development takes a slightly different course. Do consult your pediatrician, however, if your child displays any of the following signs of possible developmental delay for this age range.

- ■ **Frequent falling and difficulty with stairs**
- ■ **Persistent drooling or very unclear speech**
- ■ **Inability to build a tower of more than four blocks**
- ■ **Difficulty manipulating small objects**
- ■ **Inability to communicate in short phrases**
- ■ **No involvement in "pretend" play**
- ■ **Failure to understand simple instructions**
- ■ **Little interest in other children**
- ■ **Extreme difficulty separating from mother**
- ■ **Poor eye contact**
- ■ **Limited interest in toys**

result, he'll spend most of his time testing limits—his own, yours, and his environment's. Unfortunately, he still lacks many of the skills required for the safe accomplishment of everything he needs to do, and he often will need you to protect him.

When he oversteps a limit and is pulled back, he often reacts with anger and frustration, possibly with a temper tantrum or sullen rage. He may even strike back by hitting, biting, or kicking. At this age, he just doesn't have much control over his emotional impulses, so his anger and frustration tend to erupt suddenly in the form of crying, hitting, or screaming. It's his only way of dealing with the difficult realities of life. He may even act out in ways that unintentionally harm himself or others. It's all part of being two.

Have sitters or relatives ever told you that your child never behaves badly when they're caring for him? It's not uncommon for preschoolers to be angels when you're not around, because they don't trust these other people enough to test their limits. But with you, your preschooler will be willing to try things

Emotional Milestones for Your Two-Year-Old

- **Expresses affection openly**
- **Expresses a wide range of emotions**
- **Objects to major changes in routine**

that may be dangerous or difficult, because he knows you'll rescue him if he gets into trouble.

Whatever protest pattern he has developed around the end of his first year probably will persist for some time. For instance, when you're about to leave him with a sitter, he may become angry and throw a tantrum in anticipation of the separation. Or he may whimper, or whine and cling to you. Or he simply could become subdued and silent. Whatever his behavior, try not to overreact by scolding or punishing him. The best tactic is to reassure him before you leave that you will be back and, when you return, to praise him for being so patient while you were gone. Take solace in the fact that separations should be much easier by the time he's three years old.

The more confident and secure your two-year-old feels, the more independent and well behaved he's likely to be. You can help him develop these positive feelings by encouraging him to behave more maturely. To do this, consistently set reasonable limits that allow him to explore and exercise his curiosity, but that draw the line at dangerous or antisocial behavior. With these guidelines, he'll begin to sense what's acceptable and what's not. To repeat, the key is consistency. Praise him every time he plays well with another child, or whenever he feeds, dresses, or undresses himself without your help, or when you help him to start with the activity and he completes it by himself. As you do, he'll start to feel good about these accomplishments and himself. With his self-esteem on the rise, he'll also develop an image of himself as someone who behaves a certain way—the way that you have encouraged—and negative behavior will fade.

Since two-year-olds normally express a broad range of emotions, be prepared for everything from delight to rage. However, you should consult your pediatrician if your child seems very passive or withdrawn, perpetually sad, or highly demanding and unsatisfied most of the time. These could be signs of depression, caused by either some kind of hidden stress or biological problems. If your doctor suspects depression, she'll probably refer your child to a mental health professional for a consultation.

Basic Care

Feeding and Nutrition

By age two, your child should be eating three healthy meals a day, plus one or two snacks. He can eat the same food as the rest of the family. With his improved language and social skills, he'll become an active participant at mealtimes if given the chance to eat with everyone else. Do not fixate on amounts and do not make mealtimes a battle. Do, however, pay attention to adopting healthy eating habits and making healthy food choices as a family. Sitting as a family at mealtime is the beginning of a good habit, too!

Fortunately, your child's feeding skills have become relatively "civilized" by now. At age two, he can use a spoon, drink from a cup with just one hand, and feed himself a wide variety of finger foods. But while he can eat properly, he's still learning to chew and swallow efficiently, and may gulp his food when he's in a hurry to get on with playing. For that reason, the risk of choking is high, so avoid the following foods, which could be swallowed whole and block the windpipe.

Hot dogs (unless sliced
  lengthwise, then across)
Whole nuts (especially peanuts)
Round, hard candies or gum
Whole grapes

Spoonfuls of peanut butter
Whole raw carrots
Raw cherries with pits
Raw celery
Marshmallows

Ideally, make sure your child eats from each of the basic four food groups each day:

1. Meat, fish, poultry, eggs

2. Milk, cheese, and other dairy products

3. Fruits and vegetables

4. Whole-grain cereals, potatoes, rice, flour products

Don't be alarmed, however, if he doesn't always meet this ideal. Many preschoolers resist eating certain foods, or for long periods insist on eating only one or two favorite foods. The more you struggle with your child over his eating preferences, the more determined he'll be to defy you. As we suggested earlier, if you offer him a variety of foods and leave the choices to him, he'll eventually consume a balanced diet on his own. He may be more interested in healthful foods if he can feed them to himself. So, whenever possible, offer him finger foods (e.g., fresh fruits or raw or cooked vegetables other than carrots and celery) instead of soft ones that require a fork or spoon to eat.

DIETARY SUPPLEMENTS. Vitamin supplements (except vitamin D or iron) are rarely necessary for preschoolers who eat a varied diet. However, supplemental iron may be needed if your child eats very little meat, iron-fortified cereal, or vegetables rich in iron. Large quantities of milk (more than 32 oz. [960 ml] per day) also may interfere with the proper absorption of iron, thus increasing the risk of iron deficiency. Your child should drink 16 ounces (480 ml) of low-fat or nonfat milk each day. This will provide most of the calcium he needs for bone growth and still not interfere with his appetite for other foods, particularly those that provide iron.

Sample One-Day Menu for a Two-Year-Old

This menu is planned for a two-year-old child who weighs approximately 27 pounds (12.5 kg).

1 teaspoon = ½ tablespoon = 5 ml
1 tablespoon = ½ ounce = 15 ml
1 ounce = 30 ml
1 cup = 8 ounces = 240 ml

BREAKFAST
½ cup nonfat or low-fat milk
½ cup iron-fortified cereal or ½ slice
    whole-wheat toast
⅓ cup fruit (for example, banana, canta-
    loupe, or strawberries)
1 egg

SNACK
4 crackers with cheese or hummus
    or ½ cup cut-up fruit or berries
½ cup water

LUNCH

½ cup low-fat or nonfat milk

½ sandwich—1 slice whole-wheat bread, 1 ounce
    meat, slice of cheese, veggie (avocado, lettuce,
    or tomato)

2–3 carrot sticks (cut up or cooked) or 2 table-
    spoons other yellow or green vegetable

½ cup berries or 1 small (½ oz.) low-fat oatmeal cookie

SNACK

½ cup nonfat or low-fat milk

½ apple (sliced), 3 prunes, $^1/_3$ cup grapes (cut up),
    or ½ orange

DINNER

½ cup nonfat or low-fat milk

2 ounces meat

$^1/_3$ cup whole-grain pasta, rice, or potato

2 tablespoons vegetable

A vitamin D supplement of 400 IU per day is important for children who are not regularly exposed to sunlight, are consuming less than 32 ounces per day of vitamin D–fortified milk, or do not take a daily multivitamin supplement containing at least 400 IU of vitamin D. This amount of vitamin D can prevent rickets.

Teething and Dental Hygiene

By age two and a half, your child should have all twenty of his primary (or baby) teeth, including the second molars, which usually erupt between twenty and thirty months. His secondary (or permanent) teeth probably won't start coming in until he's six or seven, although it's quite normal for them to arrive a little earlier or later than this. During this process of "teething," your child may experience some signs and symptoms including stomach upset, irritability, mild fever, etc. Although teething does not cause the above, it is recommended that you consult with your child's pediatrician if the condition persists. Some children while teething may experience irritation in their gums and respond by chewing on objects. Therefore it may be helpful that teething rings and other objects handled by the child be wiped down and kept clean, thereby reducing any infections. As you might guess, the number-one dental problem among preschoolers is tooth decay. Approximately one out of ten two-year-olds already have one or more cavities; by age three, 28 percent of children do; by age five, nearly 50 percent of children do. Many parents assume that cavities in baby teeth don't matter, because they'll be lost anyway. But that's not true. Dental decay in baby teeth can negatively affect permanent teeth and lead to future dental problems.

The best way to protect your child's teeth is to teach him good dental habits. With the proper coaching he'll quickly adopt good oral hygiene as a part of his daily routine. However, while he may be an enthusiastic participant, he won't yet have the control or concentration to brush his teeth all by himself. You'll need to supervise and help him so that the brush removes all the plaque— the soft, sticky, bacteria-containing deposits that accumulate on the teeth, causing tooth decay. Also, keep an eye out for areas of brown or white spots, which might be signs of early decay.

By this age you should be helping your child brush his teeth two times a day with a child-size toothbrush that has soft bristles. There are brushes designed to address the different needs of children at all ages, ensuring that you can select a toothbrush that is appropriate for your child. At this age you can start using a pea-size amount of fluoride toothpaste, which helps prevent cavities. If your child doesn't like the taste of the toothpaste, try another flavor or use plain water. Also try to teach your child not to swallow it, although at this age they are often still too young to learn to rinse and spit. Swallowing too much fluoride toothpaste can make white or brown spots on your child's adult teeth.

You'll hear all kinds of advice on whether the best brushing motion is up and down, back and forth, or around in circles. The truth is that the direction really doesn't matter. What's important is to clean each tooth thoroughly, top and bottom, inside and out. This is where you'll encounter resistance from your child, who probably will concentrate on only the front teeth that he can see. It may help to turn it into a game of "find the hidden teeth." Incidentally, a child cannot brush his teeth without help until he's older—about six to eight years old. So be sure to supervise or do the actual brushing if necessary.

Besides regular tooth brushing, your child's diet will play a key role in his dental health. And, of course, sugar is the big villain. The longer and more frequently his teeth are exposed to sugar, the greater the risk of cavities. "Sticky sugar" foods such as sticky caramel, toffee, gum, and dried fruit—particularly when it stays in his mouth and bathes his teeth in sugar for hours—could do serious damage. Make sure to always brush your child's teeth after a sugary food item. In addition, do not allow your child to have any sugar-containing liquid in a sippy cup for a prolonged period. During regular well-child visits, the pediatrician will check your child's teeth and gums to ensure their health. If she notices problems, she may refer your child to a pediatric dentist (pedodontist) or a general dentist with an interest in treating the dental needs of children. Both the American Academy of Pediatrics and the American Academy of Pediatric Dentistry recommend that all children see a pediatric dentist and establish a "dental home" by age one, so hopefully your child will be seeing a pediatric dentist by now.

As part of her dental checkup the dentist will make sure all teeth are developing normally and that there are no dental problems and give you further advice on proper hygiene. She also may apply a topical fluoride solution to provide extra protection against cavities. If you live in an area where the water is not fluoridated, she may prescribe fluoride drops or chewable tablets for your preschooler. For more guidance on fluoride supplements, talk to your pediatrician, and see page 127.

Toilet Training

By the time your child is two years old, you probably can hardly wait for him to be toilet trained. The pressure to reach that goal may be particularly intense if you want him to enter a preschool or child care program that requires the children to be trained. Be forewarned, though, that pushing him too early, before he is ready, actually may prolong the process.

In general, you won't cause any damage if you've started the training prior to eighteen months of age—as long as you keep your expectations for your child's success realistic and don't punish him if he has difficulty following instructions or has accidents. However, most experts think that toilet training is most effective if it is delayed until the child himself can control much of the process. Studies indicate that many children who begin training before eighteen months are not completely trained until after age four. By contrast, most of those who start around age two are completely trained before their third birthday. The average age of complete training is a little over two and a half years.

In order for a preschooler to be successfully potty trained, he needs to be able to sense the urge to go, be able to understand what the feeling means, and then be able to verbalize that he needs your help to make it to the toilet and actually go. Waiting until your child is truly ready will make the experience much faster and more pleasant for everyone involved.

In addition, chances are, toilet training won't be very successful until your child is past the extreme negativism and resistance that often occurs in early toddlerhood. He must want to take this major step. He'll be ready when he seems eager to please and imitate you, but also wants to become more independent. Since he needs to be independent, it is important to avoid power struggles, which will always delay training. Most children reach this stage sometime between eighteen and twenty-four months, but it's also normal for it to occur a little later. Often when your child is ready to be toilet trained, he will give you some verbal cues such as "need a clean diaper," or "need to go pee-pee" even though his diaper is already dirty or wet. This awareness indicates that your child is ready to be toilet trained.

Once your child is ready to begin this process, things should proceed smoothly as long as you maintain a relaxed, unpressured attitude. Praise him for his successes, and do not even mention his mistakes along the way. Punishing him or making him feel bad when he has an "accident" will only add an unnecessary element of stress, which is bound to hinder his progress. So keep things positive, and never criticize him if things don't always go right.

How should you introduce your child to the concept of using the toilet? The best way is to let him watch other family members of his sex if possible. Also talk to him frequently about the process.

For the first few weeks, let him sit on the potty fully clothed while you tell him about the toilet, what it's for, and when to use it.

The first goal is bowel training. Urination usually occurs with the bowel movement, so at first it is difficult for the child to separate the two acts. Once bowel training is established, however, most children (especially girls) quickly will relate the two. Boys usually learn to empty their bladders in the sitting position but gradually transfer to the standing one, particularly after watching older boys or their father do it that way.

The first step in training is to obtain a potty chair and place it in your child's room or in the nearest or most convenient bathroom. Then do the following:

1. For the first few weeks, let him sit on the potty fully clothed while you tell him about the toilet, what it's for, and when to use it.

2. Once he sits on it willingly, let him try it with his diaper off. Show him how to keep his feet planted solidly on the floor, since this will be important when he's having a bowel movement. Make the potty part of his routine, gradually increasing sitting on it from once to several times each day.

3. When he's comfortable with this pattern, try changing his diaper while he's seated, and actually drop the contents of the dirty diaper into the pot under him to let him know that this is the chair's real purpose.

4. Once your child grasps how this process works, he'll probably be more interested in using the potty properly. To encourage this, let him play near the chair without a diaper and remind him to use the potty when he needs to. He's bound to forget or miss at first, but don't show your disappointment. Instead, wait until he succeeds and reward him with excitement and praise.

5. After he is using the potty chair regularly, gradually switch over from diapers to training pants during the day. At this point, most boys quickly learn to urinate into an adult toilet by imitating their fathers or older boys. Both girls and boys may be able to use adult toilets outfitted with training seats.

Like most children, your own preschooler probably will take a little longer to complete nap and nighttime toilet training. Even so, encourage these steps along with daytime training, and stress them even more after he's routinely using the potty. The best approach is to encourage your child to use the potty immediately before going to bed and as soon as he wakes up. Be aware that some children will not achieve nighttime dryness until five or six years of age. You can use regular or disposable training pants at night, rather than the usual diapers that were used during the days previously, so your child can differenti-

At bedtime, put your child in a good frame of mind for sleep by playing quietly or reading a pleasant story.

ate. Yes, there will be a few accidents, but a plastic sheet under the cloth one will minimize the cleanup. Reassure your preschooler that all children have these accidents, and praise him whenever he makes it through the nap or night without wetting. Also tell him that if he wakes up in the middle of the night and needs to use the toilet, he can either go by himself or call for you to help him.

Your goal is to make this entire process as positive, natural, and nonthreatening as possible so he's not afraid to make the effort on his own. If nap-time or nighttime wetting is still a consistent problem one year after daytime training is complete, discuss the situation with your pediatrician.

Sleeping

When your child is two years old, he may sleep from nine to thirteen hours a day. Most children of this age still need to nap, and a two-hour daytime nap is common.

At bedtime, your child is likely quite familiar with his going-to-sleep ritual. He now knows that at a certain time each day he changes into his nightclothes, brushes his teeth, listens to a story, and takes his favorite blanket, toy, or stuffed animal to bed. If you change this routine, he may complain or even have trouble going to sleep.

However, even with a completely predictable bedtime routine, some children resist going to sleep. If they're still in a crib, they may cry when left alone or even climb out to look for Mom and Dad. If they've graduated to a bed, they

Transitioning to a Bed

Begin using a bed instead of the crib by the time your child is 35 inches tall. Transitioning to a regular or "big kid" bed can be difficult for two reasons. First, he is used to having the sides of his crib keep him on his mattress. Initially transitioning to a small mattress (like the one from his crib or a twin mattress) on the floor makes sense because he's probably going to roll out of his new bed anyway; better that it's already on the floor. Over time the crib mattress can be replaced with a larger mattress (even placed on the floor), and then later raised up onto a frame if you desire. The bed can be a child bed, or if she feels comfortable in a larger bed, then it's fine to move to a regular-size bed. The second difficulty with transitioning to a big bed involves getting him to stay on the bed. Consider using a guardrail to help keep him safe and secure while in bed. At the very least, his room needs to be childproofed; a gate might be needed at the door to keep him from wandering around the house at night. See Chapter 15 for more information on safety.

may get up again and again, insisting that they're not tired (even when they're clearly exhausted) or asking to join in whatever else is going on in the household.

To give a child like this a feeling of control, let him make as many of the choices as possible at bedtime—for example, which pajamas to wear and what story he wants to hear. Also, leave a night-light on and let him sleep with his security objects (see *Transitional Objects,* page 282) to help take the edge off his separation anxiety. If he still cries after you leave, give him several minutes or so (ten minutes, for example) to stop on his own before you go in to settle him down again; then leave for another several minutes, and repeat the process. Don't scold him, but also don't reinforce his behavior by feeding or staying with him.

When a nightmare awakens your child, the best response is to hold and comfort him. Let him tell you about the dream if he can, and stay with him until he's calm enough to fall asleep. Your child will have nightmares more frequently when he's anxious or under stress. If he has bad dreams often, see if you can determine what's worrying him in order to ease his anxiety. For example, if he's having nightmares during the period when he's being toilet trained, relax the pressure to use the potty. Also try talking with him (to the extent he can) about issues that might be bothering him. Some of his anxieties may involve his separation from you, time spent in child care, or changes at home. Talking sometimes can help prevent these stressful feelings from building up. If

Some Golden Rules of Preschooler Discipline

Whether you're a strict disciplinarian or use a more easygoing approach, the following guidelines should help you shape a strategy of discipline that ultimately will benefit both you and your child. Remember, your two-year-old is busy learning the rules—she doesn't want to be bad!

1. Always encourage and reward good behavior and punish the bad. Whenever you have a choice, take the positive route. For example, let's say your two-year-old is moving toward the stove; you should try to distract him with a safe activity instead of waiting for him to get into trouble. And when you notice that he has independently chosen to do something acceptable instead of misbehaving, congratulate him on making the right decision. By showing that you're proud of him, you'll make him feel good about himself and encourage him to behave the same way in the future.

2. Map out rules that help your child learn to control his impulsiveness and behave well socially without impairing his drive for independence. If your rules are overly restrictive, he may be afraid to explore on his own or try out new skills.

3. Always keep your child's developmental level in mind when you set limits, and don't expect more than he's capable of achieving. For example, a two- (as well as a three-) year-old can't control the impulse to touch things that attract him, so it's unrealistic for you to expect him not to touch displays at the grocery or toy store.

4. Set the punishment to your child's developmental level. For example, if you decide to send your preschooler to his room for misbehaving, don't keep him there for more than about five minutes; any longer, and he'll forget why he's there. If you prefer to reason with him, keep the discussion simple and practical. Never use hypothetical statements such as "How would you like it if I did that to you?" No preschooler can understand this kind of reasoning.

5. Don't change the rules or the punishments at random. That will only confuse your child. As he grows older, you naturally will expect more mature behavior, but when you change the rules at that time, tell him why. For example, you may tolerate his pulling on your clothes to get your attention when he's two, but by the time he's four, you may want him to find

more grown-up ways of approaching you. Once you make the decision to change a rule, explain it to him before you start to enforce it.

6. Make sure that all the adults in the house and other caregivers agree to and understand the limits and punishments used to discipline your child. If one parent says something is OK and the other forbids it, the child is bound to be confused. Eventually he'll figure out that he can get his way by playing one adult against the other, which will make your lives miserable now and in the future. You can prevent this game-playing by presenting a united front.

7. Remember that you are a key role model for your child. The more even-handed and controlled your behavior, the more likely your child will be to pattern himself after you. If, on the other hand, you hit or spank him every time he breaks a rule, you're teaching him that it's OK to solve problems through violence.

your child is watching television, carefully select programs as a precaution against nightmares. Even programs you consider innocent may contain images that are frightening to him. (See *Media*, page 813.)

Time-out

Although you can't ignore dangerous or destructive behavior, you can call a time-out. The foundation for its use can begin relatively early—eighteen to twenty-four months—by teaching your child that time-out means being quiet and still. Then you can build longer quiet-and-still time as your child gets older.

Since it's a skill that needs to be learned, this technique is most successful with three-year-olds (as well as four-year-olds), who generally know when they've done something seriously wrong and understand that this is why they're being disciplined. It should be used only in special circumstances—so pick your battles—and is coupled with a firm **NO**.

Here's how time-out works:

1. Have your child sit in a chair or go to a boring place where there are no distractions. By doing this you're separating him from his misbehavior and giving him time to cool off.

2. Briefly explain what you're doing and why. Tell him that you love him but that the behavior was unacceptable. No long lecture. Initially when children are young, time-out is over as soon as they are calm.

3. End time-out once they are quiet and still. This reinforces that time-out means quiet and still.

4. Once they have learned to calm themselves, a good rule of thumb is one minute of time-out for each year in the child's age.

5. When the time-out is over, there needs to be a "time-in," giving him plenty of positive attention when doing the right thing. Let him know what you expect for next time. For example, "Next time you're mad at your cousin, use your words."

At bedtime, put your preschooler in a good frame of mind for sleep by playing quietly with him or by reading him a pleasant story. Soothing music also may help calm him as he falls asleep, and a night-light will help reassure him if he wakes up. See Chapter 35 for more information on sleep.

Extinction

Extinction is a disciplinary technique that is most effective with two- as well as three-year-olds, although it can be useful into the school years. The idea is to ignore the child systematically whenever he breaks a certain rule. As you might guess, this method should be used for misbehavior that's annoying or undesirable but not dangerous or destructive; the latter needs the more direct, immediate approach already discussed.

Here's how "extinction" works.

1. Define exactly what your child is doing wrong. Does he scream for attention in public? Does he cling to you when you're trying to do something else? Be very specific about the behavior and the circumstances in which it occurs.

2. Keep track of how often your child does this, and what you do in response. Do you try to pacify him? Do you stop what you're doing to pay

attention to him? If so, you're unwittingly encouraging him to keep misbehaving over and over.

3. Keep recording the frequency of his misbehavior as you begin to ignore it. Remember, the key is consistency. Even if every person in the grocery store is glaring at you, do not show your child that you hear him screaming. Just keep doing what you're doing. At first, he'll probably act out more intensely and more frequently to test your will, but eventually he'll realize that you mean business. Be strong and—most important—ignore the misbehavior. If you give in to the outburst, you may reinforce the behavior you're trying to eliminate.

4. When your child acts properly in a situation where he usually misbehaves, be sure to compliment him. If, instead of screaming when you refuse to buy him a candy bar, he talks to you in a normal voice, praise him for acting so grown-up.

5. If you manage to extinguish the misbehavior for a while and then it reappears, start the process over again. It probably won't take as long the second time.

Discipline

What is the greatest challenge facing you as a parent during this and the next few years? Without a doubt, it's discipline. As you'll see, your child will develop the ability to control his impulses very gradually. At age two (and often continuing through age three), he'll still be very physical, using temper tantrums, pushing, shoving, and quarreling to get his own way. Most of these reactions are very impulsive; although he doesn't plan to behave this way, he cannot control himself yet. Whether he consciously understands it or not, the whole point of his misbehavior is to find not only his limits but yours, as well.

How you choose to establish and enforce these limits is a very personal issue. Some parents are quite strict, punishing their children whenever they violate a household rule; others are more lenient, preferring reason to punishment. Whatever approach you choose, if it's going to work, it must suit your child's temperament, and you also must feel comfortable enough with it to use it consistently. You'll find other helpful suggestions in *Some Golden Rules of Preschooler Discipline* on pages 361–362.

Family Relationships

A New Baby

During this year, if you decide to have another baby, you can expect your preschooler to greet this news with considerable jealousy. After all, at this age he doesn't yet understand the concept of sharing time, possessions, or your affection. Nor is he eager to have someone else become the center of the family's attention.

The best way to minimize his jealousy is to start preparing him several months before the new baby is born. If he understands, you can let him help shop

Stimulating Child Brain Growth: Your Two-Year-Old

The age of two is an important time in your child's life and in the development of his brain. As we described earlier, your child's physical growth may slow during this time, but his brain and his intellectual growth are moving full speed ahead. Just as you've made an effort to stimulate his brain growth from birth, you should continue doing so during this crucial year. Here are some suggestions:

- **Encourage creative play, building, and drawing. Provide the time and tools for playful learning.**

- **Be attentive to your child's rhythms and moods. Respond to him when he is upset as well as when he is happy. Be encouraging and supportive, with firm discipline as appropriate, but without yelling, hitting, or shaking. Provide consistent guidelines and rules.**

- **Give consistent warm, physical contact—hugging, skin-to-skin, body-to-body contact—to establish your child's sense of security and well-being.**

- **Talk to or sing to your child during dressing, bathing, feeding, playing, walking, and driving, using adult talk. Speak slowly and give your child time to respond. Try not to reply with "uh-huh" because your child will recognize when you're not listening; instead, expand on your child's phrases.**

- Read to your child every day. Choose books that encourage touching and pointing to objects, and read rhymes, jingles, and nursery stories.

- If you speak a foreign language, use it at home.

- Introduce your child to musical instruments (toy pianos, drums, etc.). Musical skills can influence math and problem-solving skills.

- Play calm and melodic music for your child.

- Listen to and answer your child's questions.

- Spend one-on-one personal time with your child each day.

- Offer your child simple choices in appropriate situations throughout the day (Peanut butter or cheese? Red T-shirt or yellow?).

- Help your child use words to describe emotions and to express feelings such as happiness, joy, anger, and fear.

- Limit your child's television viewing and video time; avoid violent cartoons. Monitor what your child does watch and discuss programs with your child. Don't use the TV as a babysitter.

- Promote out-of-home social experiences such as preschool programs and play groups in which your child can play and interact with other children.

- Acknowledge desirable behavior frequently (e.g., "I like it when the two of you play together").

- Make sure other people who provide care and supervision for your child understand the importance of forming a loving and comforting relationship with him.

- Spend time on the floor playing with your child every day.

- Choose quality child care (may want to consider National Association for the Education of Young Children [NAEYC] certified) that is affectionate, responsive, educational, and safe; visit your child care provider frequently and share your ideas about positive caregiving.

for baby items that you may need or help get the house or room ready. If your hospital offers a sibling preparation class, take him there during the last month of pregnancy so he can see where the baby will be born and where he can visit you. Discuss what it will be like having a new member of the family, how fun and important it is to be a big sibling, and how he can help his little brother or sister. (See *Preparing Your Other Children for the Baby's Arrival,* page 34.)

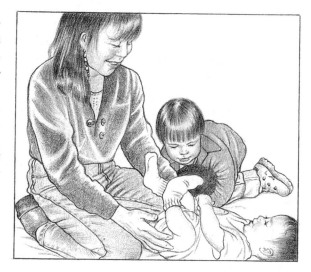

Once the baby is home, encourage your preschooler to help and play with the newborn (after washing his hands, of course), but don't force him. If he shows an interest, give him some tasks that will make him feel like a big brother, such as bringing you a diaper or blanket for the baby and picking out the baby's clothes or bath toys. And when you're playing with the baby, invite him to join you and show him how to hold and move the baby. Make sure he understands, however, that he's not to do these things unless you or another adult is present. Remember to reserve special time alone to spend with older siblings.

Hero Worship

Does your preschooler have older siblings? If so, you'll probably start seeing signs of hero worship around age two. In the young child's eyes, older brothers or sisters can do no wrong. They are perfect role models—people who are strong and independent, but still play like kids.

In your young child's eyes, his older brother or sister can do no wrong.

This kind of relationship has both benefits and drawbacks. Your preschooler probably will follow his older sibling around like a lapdog. This will give you some freedom, and it's usually fun for both children for a while. But before long, your older child will want his freedom back, which is bound to cause some disappointment—and perhaps tears or misbehavior—from your little one. Nevertheless, it's up to you to make sure that he doesn't overstay his welcome with big brother or sister. If you don't step in, their relationship will become strained.

If the older child is eight or more, he probably already has a fairly independent life, with friends and activities outside the home. Given the chance, your preschooler will tag along with him everywhere he goes. You shouldn't allow this unless the older child desires it or you, too, are going along and can keep the little one from becoming a pest. If the older child is of babysitting age, compensating him for taking care of your preschooler when you're out will help prevent resentment.

A Message for Grandparents

The third year of a child's life, encompassing the so-called terrible twos, is often a challenging one for parents and therefore for grandparents, as well. A child at this age is showing increased physical activity, greater mood swings, frequent tantrums or demanding behavior, and testing the limits of all adults.

As a grandparent, you may have forgotten what two-year-olds are like; after all, it's been many years since you raised your own children through this age. Here are some guidelines to keep in mind when you spend time with your two-year-old grandchild (although some of these steps are more easily said than done).

- Make an effort to "keep your cool." Don't overreact to outbursts. Try to take them in stride, and realize that much of this behavior is designed to get you to react. Maintain a flexible but firm and loving response.

- Be consistent in your approach to discipline, and make sure it's consistent with the disciplinary style of the child's parents. *Never use physical punishment.*

- Reinforce good behaviors with praise and compliments. Become a role model of the way you would like your grandchild to act.

- Try to encourage self-control.

- **Always be affectionate.**

- **Recognize that children of this age are very egocentric (i.e., they are thinking mostly of "me," not of the others in their lives), so don't take their lack of interest in you personally. This is normal for a two-year-old, and it won't last forever.**

Toilet training will be one of your grandchild's most important accomplishments at this age. Talk to his parents about the stage of training he's in, and how you can reinforce what he has already achieved, particularly when you're caring for him—babysitting on a Saturday afternoon or caring for him for the weekend. If he spends time in your home, purchase some extra training pants and have a potty chair identical to the one he is accustomed to at home.

Safety in your home remains important, so make sure your home is "child-proofed." See Chapter 15 for the specifics. Be especially careful of medications. Never leave them sitting out for his curious eyes or fingers; put them out of reach in a safe place that you will remember. Try to leave the medication there even after they leave, so that your home stays safe, even if they should stop by for a quick, unexpected visit. This is even more important if you cannot "unlock" the child-resistant caps and have chosen to put your pills in other types of containers. When medications are not in childproof containers, they can be easily opened by curious two-year-olds, so be especially vigilant with those.

Finally, always remember to place your grandchild in a car safety seat in the backseat for every trip in the automobile.

Pressures and rivalries are inevitable between siblings, but if there's a healthy balance between comradeship and independence, the bond between your children should grow and contribute to the self-esteem of both of them. Through her older sibling, your preschooler will get a sense of family values as well as a preview of what it's like to be a "big kid." The older child, meanwhile, will discover what it means to be a hero in his own home.

Being a role model for a younger brother or sister is a big responsibility, of course, and if you point this out to your older child, it may prompt an improvement in behavior. If you feel he's a bad influence on his younger sibling, however, and he doesn't improve, you have no choice but to separate the two whenever he's misbehaving. Otherwise, your preschooler will mimic him and soon pick up bad habits. Don't embarrass the older child by punishing him in front of the preschooler, but make sure the younger one understands the difference between "good" and "bad" behavior.

Visit to the Pediatrician

Beginning at twenty-four months of age, your child should see the pediatrician for a routine examination twice a year. In addition to the screening tests performed during his earlier examinations, he may undergo the following laboratory tests.

- A *blood test* to check for lead poisoning, as well as for cholesterol and hemoglobin (oxygen carrying protein, or iron, in red blood cells).

- A *urinalysis* to check for infection and kidney and metabolic diseases, but warranted only in symptomatic children. If the results of the first urinalysis are normal, it may not be repeated at future visits unless there are symptoms of a urinary-tract infection or related problems.

- A *skin test for tuberculosis* may be given, depending on the risk of possible exposure.

Immunization Update

By age two, your child should have received most of his childhood immunizations. These include:

- the hepatitis B series

- the Hib vaccine series against *Haemophilus influenzae* type b

- the vaccine series against pneumococcus

- the first three doses of the polio vaccine

- the first four doses of DTaP (diphtheria, tetanus, and pertussis [aka whooping cough])

- the first dose of the MMR vaccine (measles, mumps, rubella)

- two doses of the hepatitis A vaccine

- two or three doses of the rotavirus vaccine (depending on vaccine type given for doses one and two)

- the chickenpox (varicella) vaccine

Once a year, beginning at six months of age, your child also should receive the influenza vaccine. Also remember to have your child get booster shots for DTaP, polio, MMR, and varicella at elementary school entry or four to six years of age.

Safety Check

Your preschooler is now able to run, jump, and learn to ride a tricycle. His natural curiosity will drive him to explore many new things, including some dangerous places. Unfortunately, his self-control and ability to rescue himself are not yet fully developed, so he still needs careful supervision. (See Chapter 15 for additional information on safety.)

Falls

- Lock doors to any dangerous areas and hide the keys.

- Install stairway gates and window guards.

Burns

- Keep him away from kitchen appliances, irons, and wall or floor heaters (check for safety features on modern-day heaters and those in old houses).

- Block outlets with furniture or use outlet covers that are not a choking hazard.

- Keep electrical cords out of reach.

- Install and maintain working smoke detectors.

Poisoning

- Keep all medicines in child-resistant containers, locked up high, and out of sight and reach. Make sure you engage the child-resistant closure every time.

■ Store household cleaning products and medicines in their original containers in a locked cabinet.

■ Post the Poison Help phone number (1-800-222-1222) next to every telephone and in your cell phone contacts list. This number can be used everywhere in the United States.

Car Safety

■ Supervise your child closely whenever he's playing outside. Do not allow your child to play near the garage or driveway where cars may be coming or going. Many children are killed when someone, often a family member, unintentionally runs them over with a car. Most vehicles have large blind spots where a child cannot be seen as a car is backing up or moving. Keep cars locked when not in use so your child cannot get in without permission.

■ Use approved and properly installed car safety seats for every ride. Once they outgrow the height or weight limit for rear-facing in their convertible seats, children should ride forward-facing in a car seat equipped with a five-point harness as long as possible, or until they reach the highest weight or height allowed by the seat's manufacturer. Remember, never put your child in the front seat, even if it is for a short ride. Air bags are not little child–friendly, and should you be involved in a crash that sets off the air bag, your small child could get seriously injured. Always put them in their car safety seat in the rear seat, ideally the middle one. However, any spot in the rear seat is safe if the car safety seat can be installed there tightly. Never let him unbuckle or climb out of his car safety seat while the car is in motion.

■ Never leave your child alone in the car, even when it is locked and in your driveway.

~ 12 ~

Your Three-Year-Old

WITH YOUR CHILD'S third birthday, the "terrible twos" may be officially over and the "magic years" will begin. This is approximately a two-year period (ages three and four) when your child's world will be dominated by fantasy and vivid imagination. No longer a toddler, she is becoming more independent and, at the same time, more responsive to other children. This is a perfect age to introduce her to school or an organized play group, where she can stretch her skills while learning to socialize.

During this time, your child will mature in many areas, including toilet training and learning how to take proper care of her body. Since she can control and direct her movements now, she'll be able to play more organized games and sports. She also has mastered the basic rules of language and has built an impressive vocabulary that will increase daily as she experiments with words. Language will play an important role in her behavior, too, as she learns to express her desires and feelings verbally instead of through physical actions such as grabbing, hitting, or crying. Helping her put all her new skills together so she feels confident and capable is one of the most important ways you can guide her self-discipline during this period.

Your relationship with your child will change dramatically during this time. Emotionally, she is now able to view you as a separate person, with feelings and needs she's beginning to understand. When you're sad, she may render some sympathy or offer to solve your problems. If you become angry at another person, she may announce that she, too, "hates" that individual. She wants very much to please you at this age, and knows that she must do certain things and behave in certain ways to do so. At the same time, though, she wants to please herself, so she'll often try to bargain with you: "If I do this for you, will you do that for me?" At times when you simply want her to behave as you desire, this attempt at bargaining may be irritating, but it's a healthy sign of independence, and it shows that she has a clear sense of justice.

Growth and Development

Physical Appearance and Growth

Your child's body should continue to lose baby fat and gain muscle during this time, giving her a stronger and more mature appearance. Her arms and legs will become more slender and her upper body more narrow and tapered. In some children, gains in height occur so much more quickly than gains in weight and muscle that they may begin to look quite skinny and fragile. But this doesn't mean they are unhealthy or that anything is wrong; such children fill out gradually as their muscles develop.

In general, a preschooler's growth gradually will begin to slow this year and in the subsequent ones—from about a 5-pound (2.3-kg) gain and about a 3½-inch (8.9 cm) increase in height during the third year, and then decreasing to about 4½ pounds or 2 kg, and 2½ inches or 6.4 cm during the fifth. However, after age two, children of the same age can vary noticeably in size and weight, so try not to spend too much time comparing your child's measurements with those of her playmates. As long as she's maintaining her own individual rate of growth, there's no reason to worry.

Measure your child twice a year and record her measurements on her growth charts in the Appendix on pages 878–883. If her weight seems to be rising faster than her height, she may become overweight, or if her height does not increase at all in six months, she may have a growth problem. In either case, discuss this with your pediatrician.

Your child's face also will mature during these years. The length of her skull will increase slightly, and the lower jaw will become more pronounced. At the same time, the upper jaw will widen to make room for her permanent teeth. As a result, her face actually will become larger and her features more distinct.

Movement

At age three, your preschooler no longer has to concentrate on the mechanics of standing, running, jumping, or walking. Her movements are now quite agile, whether she's going forward, backward, or up and down stairs. While walking she stands erect, shoulders pulled back and belly held in by firm abdominal muscles. She uses a regular heel-toe motion, taking steps of the same length, width, and speed. She also can ride a tricycle with great ease.

However, not everything comes easily yet. Your child still may need to make a conscious effort while standing on tiptoes or on one foot, while getting up from a squatting position, or while catching a ball. But if she keeps her arms extended and stiffly forward, she can catch a large ball as well as throw a smaller one overhand quite smoothly.

Your three-year-old still may be as active as she was at two, but she'll probably be more interested in structured games at this age. Instead of running aimlessly or flitting from one activity to another, she'll probably ride her tricycle or play in the sandbox for long periods at a time. She also may enjoy active games such as tag, catch, or playing ball with other children.

Your preschooler may seem to be in constant motion much of the time. This is because she uses her body to convey thoughts and emotions that she still can't describe through language. Moving her body also helps her better understand many words and concepts that are new to her. For example, if you start talking about an airplane, she may spread her wings and "fly" around the room. While at times this level of activity may be annoying and distracting for you, it's a necessary part of her learning process and her fun.

Because your child's self-control, judgment, and coordination are still developing, adult supervision remains essential to prevent injuries. However, it's a mistake to fuss too much over her. A few bumps and bruises are inevitable and even necessary to help her discover her limits in physical activity. As a general rule, usually you can leave her alone when she's playing by herself in her room. She'll play at her own pace, attempting only those tasks that are within her abilities. Your concern and attention should be reserved for situations when

Movement Milestones for Your Three-Year-Old

- Hops and stands on one foot for up to five seconds
- Goes upstairs and downstairs without support
- Kicks ball forward
- Throws ball overhand
- Catches bounced ball most of the time
- Moves forward and backward with agility

she's around other children, hazardous equipment or machinery, and especially traffic. Other children may tease or tempt her to do things that are dangerous, while machines, equipment, and traffic defy her ability to predict their actions or speed. And she still cannot anticipate the consequences of actions such as chasing a ball into traffic or sticking her hand into the spokes of her tricycle, so you'll have to protect her in these situations.

Hand and Finger Skills

At age three, your child is developing both the muscular control and the concentration she needs to master many precision finger and hand movements. You'll notice that now she can move each of her fingers independently or together, which means that instead of grasping her crayon in her fist she can hold it like an adult, with thumb on one side and fingers on the other. Now she will be able to trace a square, copy a circle, or scribble freely.

Because her spatial awareness has developed quite a bit, she's more sensitive to the relationships among objects, so she'll position her toys with great care during play and control the way she holds utensils and tools to perform specific tasks. This increased sensitivity and control will allow her to build a tower of nine or more cubes, pour water from a pitcher into a cup (using two hands), unbutton clothes, possibly put large buttons into buttonholes, and use a fork and feed herself independently, spilling between the plate and her mouth only occasionally.

She's also extremely interested in discovering what she can do with tools such as scissors and paper and with materials such as clay, paint, and crayons. She now has the skill to manipulate these objects and is beginning to experiment with using them to make other things. At first she'll play randomly with craft materials, perhaps identifying the end product only after it's completed.

Looking at her scribbles, for example, she might decide they look like a dog. But soon this will change, and she'll decide what she wants to make before starting to work on it. This change in approach will motivate her to develop even more precision in moving and using her hands.

Quiet-time activities that can help improve your child's hand abilities include:

- Building with blocks

- Solving simple jigsaw puzzles (four or five large pieces)

- Playing with pegboards

- Stringing large wooden beads

- Coloring with crayons or chalk

- Building sand castles

- Pouring water into containers of various sizes

- Dressing and undressing dolls in clothing with large zippers, snaps, and laces

Milestones in Hand and Finger Skills for Your Three-Year-Old

- Copies square shapes
- Draws a person with two to four body parts
- Uses scissors
- Draws circles and squares
- Begins to copy some capital letters

You can encourage your child to use her hands by teaching her to use certain adult tools. She'll be thrilled to progress to a real screwdriver, a lightweight hammer, an eggbeater, or gardening tools. You'll need to supervise closely, of course, but if you let her help as you work, you may be surprised by how much of the job she can do herself.

Language Development

At age three, your child should have an active vocabulary of three hundred or more words. She'll be able to talk in sentences of three to four words and imitate most adult speech sounds. At times she'll seem to be chattering constantly— a phenomenon that sometimes may disturb you but that is essential to her learning of new words and gaining experience in using and thinking with them. Language allows her to express her thoughts, and the more advanced she is in speaking and understanding words, the more tools she'll have for thinking, creating, and telling you about it.

You should be able to see how your child uses language to help her understand and participate in the things going on around her. For instance, she can name most familiar objects, and she'll freely ask, "What's this?" when she can't call something by name. You can help her expand her vocabulary by providing additional words that she might not even request. For example, if she points to a car and says, "Big car," you might answer, "Yes, that's a big gray car. Look how shiny the surface is." Or if she's helping you pick flowers, describe each one she collects: "That's a beautiful white-and-yellow daisy, and that's a pink geranium."

You also can help her use words to describe things and ideas she can't see.

Stuttering

Many parents experience anxiety over their child's stuttering, even though such concern is usually unnecessary. After all, it's quite common for children to repeat syllables, sounds, or words occasionally, or to hesitate between words at around age two or three. Most of them never realize they're talking incorrectly, and they grow out of it without any special help. Only when this pattern persists over a long period of time (greater than two to three months) and interferes with communication is it considered actual stuttering.

About one in twenty preschool children stutter at some point, most often between the ages of two and six, when language is being developed, with a threefold greater incidence in boys than in girls. The cause is unknown. Some children may have trouble learning the normal timing and rhythm of speech, but most have no medical or developmental problems. Stuttering may increase when a child is anxious, tired, ill, or when she gets excited and tries to talk too rapidly. Some children stutter when learning too many new words at once. At other times, the child's thoughts are running ahead of her speech and she loses track of what she is saying in midsentence. Repeating a sound or word allows her to catch up. In some children who stutter, the pitch of their voices may rise as they repeat syllables or sounds; or they may open their mouths to speak but nothing comes out for a few moments.

The more frustrated a child becomes about her stuttering, the more trouble she will have with it. Thus the best approach for parents is simply to ignore the stuttering. Listen when she speaks, but don't correct her. Don't interrupt her or finish sentences for her, and make it clear through your body language that you're interested in listening to her. At the same time, you can set a good example by talking calmly and correctly, and using simple language when addressing her. It also may help if you slow the entire pace of your household, including the speed at which you (and other family members) speak; your own slower rate of speech will be more helpful than telling your child that she needs to talk more slowly.

You also should set aside some relaxed time each day to play and talk quietly with your child, giving her all of your attention free of distractions, and letting her decide the activities that you'll do together. You can build her self-esteem and confidence by praising her for all the activities she's doing correctly, while not drawing attention to her speech difficulties. Don't show any signs that you're annoyed, frustrated, or embarrassed by her stuttering (avoid statements like "Talk slower!" "Say it again more clearly this time!" or "Relax!"), and demonstrate that you are accepting of her. Reinforce the things that she does well. In an environment of acceptance, the anxiety associated with stuttering will be reduced, which will help her conquer the problem. With your support, usually she can overcome her true stuttering difficulty before entering school.

When a child's stuttering is severe, speech therapy may be necessary to help avoid a long-term problem. If your child frequently repeats sounds or parts of words, is very self-conscious, and shows obvious signs of tension (e.g., facial twitches or grimaces), let your pediatrician know. Also inform her of any family history of serious stuttering. She'll probably refer you to a speech and language specialist.

Language Milestones for Your Three-Year-Old

- **Understands the concepts of "same" and "different"**
- **Has mastered some basic rules of grammar**
- **Speaks in sentences of five to six words**
- **Speaks clearly enough for strangers to understand**
- **Tells stories**

When she's describing the "monster" in her dream, for example, ask her if the monster is angry or friendly. Ask her about the monster's color, where she lives, and whether she has friends. Not only will this help your child use words to express her thoughts, but it also may help her overcome her fear of such strange and frightening images.

Your three-year-old is still learning to use pronouns such as "I," "me," "mine," and "you." As simple as these words seem, they're difficult ideas to grasp because they indicate where her body, possessions, or authority ends and someone else's begins. And to complicate matters, the terms change depending on who's talking. Often she may use her name instead of saying "I" or "me." Or when talking to you, she may say "Mommy" instead of "you." If you try to correct her (e.g., by suggesting, "Say 'I would like a cookie' "), you'll only confuse her more, because she'll think you're talking about yourself. Instead, use these pronouns correctly in your own speech. So, for instance, say "I would like you to come" instead of "Mommy would like you to come." Not only will this help her learn the correct use of these words, but it also will help her establish a sense of you as an individual apart from your role as Mommy.

At this age, your child's speech should be clear enough that even strangers can understand most of what she says. Even so, she still may mispronounce as many as half the speech sounds she uses. For example, she may use *w* for *r* ("wabbit," "wice," "wose"), *d* for *th* ("dis," "dat," "den"), or *t* for any sounds she has trouble with ("tee" for "three," "tik" for "six"). The sounds *b, p, m, w,* and *h* will only begin to emerge midway through this year, and it may take months after that for her to perfect her use of them.

If your child's language abilities are delayed or poorly developed, and she also has shown behaviors such as social withdrawal, limited interests, or repetitive movements, she should be evaluated by a specialist skilled in diagnosing autism or autistic spectrum disorder (ASD). The earlier ASD is detected and treated, the greater the likelihood that your child will function up to her full

If the question is "Why can't the dog talk to me?" you can invite your child to look into the question further by finding a book about dogs.

potential. (For more information about ASD, see descriptions of this disorder and its management on pages 349 and 636.)

Cognitive Development

Your three-year-old will spend most of her waking hours questioning everything that happens around her. She loves to ask "Why do I have to . . . ?" and she'll pay close attention to your answers as long as they're simple and to the point. Don't feel that you have to explain your rules fully; she can't yet understand such reasoning and isn't interested in it anyway. If you try to have this kind of "serious" conversation, you'll see her stare into space or turn her attention to more entertaining matters, such as a toy across the room or a truck passing outside the window. Instead, telling her to do something "because it's good for you" or "so you don't get hurt" will make more sense to her than a detailed explanation.

Your child's more abstract "why" questions may be more difficult, partly because there may be hundreds of them each day and also because some of them have no answers—or none that you know. If the question is "Why does the sun shine?" or "Why can't the dog talk to me?" you can answer that you don't know, or invite her to look into the question further by finding a book about the sun or about dogs. Be sure to take these questions seriously. As you do, you help broaden your child's knowledge, feed her curiosity, and teach her to think more clearly.

When your three-year-old is faced with specific learning challenges, you'll find her reasoning still rather one-sided. She can't yet see an issue from two angles, nor can she solve problems that require her to look at more than one

Cognitive Milestones for Your Three-Year-Old

- **Correctly names some colors**
- **Understands the concept of counting and may know a few numbers**
- **Approaches problems from a single point of view**
- **Begins to have a clearer sense of time**
- **Follows three-part commands**
- **Recalls parts of a story**
- **Understands the concept of same/ different**
- **Engages in fantasy play**

factor at the same time. For example, if you take two equal cups of water and pour one into a short, fat container and the other into a tall, skinny one, she'll probably say the tall container holds more water than the short. Even if she sees the two equal cups to start with and watches you pour, she'll come up with the same answer. By her logic, the taller container is "bigger" and therefore must hold more. At around age seven, children finally understand that they have to look at multiple aspects of a problem before arriving at an answer.

At about three years of age, your child's sense of time will become much clearer. Now she'll know her own daily routine and will try hard to figure out the routines of others. For example, she may eagerly watch for the mail carrier who arrives nearly every day, but be perplexed that trash is picked up only one day out of seven. She'll understand that certain special events, such as holidays and birthdays, occur every once in a while, but even if she can tell you how old she is, she'll have no real sense of the length of a year.

But if you have any questions or concerns about your three-year-old's development, you should discuss them with your pediatrician. If he agrees that there is reason for concern, he will refer your child for further testing.

Social Development

At age three, your child will be much less selfish than she was at two. She'll also be less dependent on you, a sign that her own sense of identity is stronger and more secure. Now she'll actually play with other children, interacting instead of just playing side by side. In the process, she'll recognize that not everyone thinks exactly as she does and that each of her playmates has many unique qualities, some attractive and some not. You'll also find her drifting toward certain children and starting to develop friendships with them. As she creates these friendships, she'll discover that she, too, has special qualities that make her likable—a revelation that will give a vital boost to her self-esteem.

There's some more good news about your child's development at this age: As she becomes more aware of and sensitive to the feelings and actions of others, she'll gradually stop competing and will learn to cooperate when playing with her friends. She'll be capable of taking turns and sharing toys in small groups, even if she doesn't always do it. Instead of grabbing, whining, or screaming for something, she'll actually ask politely much of the time. As a result, you can look forward to less aggressive behavior and calmer play sessions. Often three-year-olds are able to work out their own solutions to disputes by taking turns or trading toys.

However, particularly in the beginning, you'll need to encourage this type of cooperation. For instance, you might suggest that she "use her words" to deal with problems instead of violent actions. Also, remind her that when two children are sharing a toy, each gets an equal turn. Suggest ways to reach a simple solution when she and another child want the same toy, perhaps drawing for the first turn or finding another toy or activity. This doesn't work all the time, but it's worth a try. Also, help her with the appropriate words to describe her feelings and desires so that she doesn't feel frustrated. Above all, show her by your own example how to cope peacefully with conflicts. If you have an explosive temper, try to tone down your reactions in her presence. Otherwise, she'll mimic your behavior whenever she's under stress.

No matter what you do, however, there probably will be times when your child's anger or frustration becomes physical. When that happens, restrain her from hurting others, and if she doesn't calm down quickly, move her away from the other children. Talk to her about her feelings and try to determine why she's so upset. Let her know that you understand and accept her feelings, but make it clear that physically attacking another child is not a good way to express these emotions.

Help her see the situation from the other child's point of view by reminding her of a time when someone hit or screamed at her, and then suggest more peaceful ways to resolve her conflicts. Finally, once she understands what she's done wrong—but not before—ask her to apologize to the other child. However, simply saying "I'm sorry" may not help your child correct her behavior; she also needs to know why she's apologizing. She may not understand right away, but give it time; by age four these explanations will begin to mean something to her.

Actually, the normal interests of three-year-olds will help keep fights to a minimum. They spend much of their playtime in fantasy activity, which tends to be more cooperative than play that's focused on toys or games. As you've probably already seen, your preschooler and her playmates enjoy assigning different roles to one another and then launching into an elaborate game of make-believe using imaginary or household objects. This type of play helps them develop important social skills, such as taking turns, paying attention, communicating (through actions and expressions as well as words), and responding to one another's actions. And there's still another benefit: Because pretend play allows children to slip into any role they wish—including superheroes or the Fairy Godmother—it also helps them explore more complex social ideas.

By watching the role-playing that goes on during your child's make-believe games, you'll also see that she's beginning to identify with her own sex. While playing house, boys naturally will adopt the father's role and girls the mother's, reflecting whatever differences they've noticed in their own families and in the world around them. At this age, your son also may be fascinated by his father, older brothers, or other boys in the neighborhood, while your daughter will be drawn to her mother, older sisters, and other girls.

Research shows that a few of the developmental and behavioral differences that typically distinguish boys from girls are biologically determined. For instance, the average preschool boy tends to be more aggressive, while girls generally are more verbal. However, most gender-related characteristics at this age are more likely to be shaped by cultural and family influences. Even if both parents work and share family responsibilities equally, your child still will find conventional male and female role models in television, magazines, books, billboards, and the families of friends and neighbors. Your daughter, for example, may be encouraged to play with dolls by advertisements, gifts from well-meaning relatives, and the approving comments of adults and other children. Boys, meanwhile, are generally guided away from dolls (although most enjoy them during the toddler years) in favor of more rough-and-tumble games and sports. Often, the girl who likes to roughhouse is called a tomboy, but the boy who plays that way is called tough or assertive. Not surprisingly, children sense the approval and disapproval in these labels and adjust their behavior accordingly. Thus, by the time they enter kindergarten, children's gender identities are well established.

Children this age often will take this identification process to an extreme. Girls may insist on wearing dresses, nail polish, and makeup to school or to the playground. Boys may swagger, be overly assertive, and carry their favorite

Social Milestones for Your Three-Year-Old

- Interested in new experiences
- Cooperates with other children
- Plays "Mom" or "Dad"
- Increasingly inventive in fantasy play
- Dresses and undresses self
- Negotiates solutions to conflicts
- More independent

ball, bat, or truck wherever they go. This behavior reinforces their sense of being male or female.

As your child develops her own identity during these early years, she's bound to experiment with attitudes and behaviors of both sexes. There's rarely any reason to discourage such impulses, except when the child is resisting or rejecting strongly established cultural standards. For instance, if your son wants to wear dresses every day or your daughter only wants to wear sport shorts like her big brother, allow the phase to pass unless it is inappropriate for a specific event. If the child persists, however, discuss the issue with your pediatrician.

Your child also may imitate certain types of behavior that adults consider sexual, such as flirting. If she's very dramatic and expressive, you may be concerned by these "suggestive" looks and movements, but often the suggestions are just an adult way of looking at the situation, while the child is just playing and is not aware of her actions. At this age, she has no mature sexual intentions, and her mannerisms are merely playful mimicry, so don't worry. If, however, her imitation of sexual behavior is very explicit or otherwise indicates that she may have been personally exposed to sexual acts, you should discuss this with your pediatrician, as it could be a sign of sexual abuse or the influence of inappropriate media or video games.

For more information about how the media could affect your child, see Chapter 32.

Emotional Development

Your three-year-old's vivid fantasy life will help her explore and come to terms with a wide range of emotions, from love and dependency to anger, protest, and fear. She'll not only take on various identities herself, but also she'll often assign living qualities and emotions to inanimate objects, such as a tree, a clock, a truck, or the moon. Ask her why the moon comes out at night, for example, and she might reply, "To say hello to me."

From time to time, expect your preschooler to introduce you to one of her imaginary friends. Some children have a single make-believe companion for as long as six months; some change pretend playmates every day, while still others never have one at all or prefer imaginary animals instead. Don't be concerned that these phantom friends may signal loneliness or emotional upset; they're actually a very creative way for your child to sample different activities, lines of conversation, behavior, and emotions.

You'll also notice that, throughout the day, your preschooler will move back and forth freely between fantasy and reality. At times she may become so involved in her make-believe world that she can't tell where it ends and reality begins. Her play experience may even spill over into real life. One night she'll come to the dinner table convinced she's Cinderella; another day she may come to you sobbing after hearing a ghost story that she believes is true.

While it's important to reassure your child when she's frightened or upset by an imaginary incident, be careful not to belittle or make fun of her. This stage in emotional development is normal and necessary and should not be discouraged. Above all, never joke with her about "locking her up if she doesn't eat her dinner" or "leaving her behind if she doesn't hurry up." She's liable to believe you and feel terrified the rest of the day—or longer.

From time to time, try to join your child in her fantasy play. By doing so, you can help her find new ways to express her emotions and even work through some problems. For example, you might suggest "sending her doll to school" to

Developmental Health Watch

Because each child develops in her own particular manner, it's impossible to tell exactly when or how she'll perfect a given skill. The developmental milestones listed in this book will give you a general idea of the changes you can expect as your child gets older, but don't be alarmed if her development takes a slightly different course. Alert your pediatrician, however, if your child displays any of the following signs of possible developmental delay for this age range.

- **Cannot throw a ball overhand**
- **Cannot jump in place**
- **Cannot ride a tricycle**
- **Cannot grasp a crayon between thumb and fingers**
- **Has difficulty scribbling**
- **Cannot stack four blocks**
- **Still clings or cries whenever her parents leave her**
- **Shows no interest in interactive games**
- **Ignores other children**
- **Doesn't respond to people outside the family**
- **Doesn't engage in fantasy play**
- **Resists dressing, sleeping, using the toilet**
- **Lashes out without any self-control when angry or upset**
- **Cannot copy a circle**
- **Doesn't use sentences of more than three words**
- **Doesn't use "me" and "you" appropriately**

see how she feels about going to preschool. Don't insist on participating in these fantasies, however. Part of the joy of fantasy for her is being able to control these imaginary dramas, so if you plant an idea for make-believe, stand back and let her make of it what she will. If she then asks you to play a part, keep your performance low-key. Let the world of pretend be the one place where *she* runs the show.

Emotional Milestones for Your Three-Year-Old

- Imagines that many unfamiliar images may be "monsters"
- Views self as a whole person involving body, mind, and feelings
- Often cannot distinguish between fantasy and reality

Back in real life, let your preschooler know that you're proud of her new independence and creativity. Talk with her, listen to what she says, and show her that her opinions matter. Give her choices whenever possible—in the foods she eats, the clothes she wears, the games you play together. Doing this will give her a sense of importance and help her learn to make decisions. Keep her options simple, however. When you go to a restaurant, for example, narrow her choices down to two or three items. Otherwise she may be overwhelmed and unable to decide. (A trip to an ice-cream store or frozen yogurt shop that sells several flavors can be agonizing if you don't limit her choices.)

What's the best approach? Despite what we've already said, one of the best ways to nurture her independence is to maintain fairly firm control over all parts of her life, while at the same time giving her some freedom. Let her know that you're still in charge and that you don't expect her to make the big decisions. When her friend is daring her to climb a tree, and she's afraid, it will be comforting to have you say no, so that she doesn't have to admit her fears. As she conquers many of her early anxieties and becomes more responsible in making her own decisions, you'll naturally give her more control. In the meantime, it's important that she feels safe and secure.

Basic Care

Feeding and Nutrition

As a preschooler, your child should have a healthy attitude toward eating. Ideally, by this age she no longer uses eating—or not eating—to demonstrate defiance, nor does she confuse food with love or affection. Generally (although almost certainly not always), she'll now view eating as a natural response to hunger and meals as a pleasant social experience.

Despite your preschooler's general enthusiasm for eating, she still may have very specific preferences in food, some of which may vary from day to day.

Your child may gobble down a particular food one day, and then push away the plate with the same food the next day. She may ask for a certain food for several days in a row, and then insist that she doesn't like it anymore. As irritating as it may be to have her turn up her nose at a dish she devoured the day before, it's normal behavior for a preschooler, and best not to make an issue of it. Let her eat the other foods on her plate or select something else to eat. As long as she chooses foods that aren't overly sugary, fatty, or salty, don't object. However, encourage her to try healthy new foods by offering her very small amounts to taste, not by insisting that she eat a full portion of an unfamiliar food.

As a parent, your job is to make sure that your preschooler has nutritious food choices at every meal. If she has healthy options on the dining room table, let her make the decision of what (and how much) to eat. If she's a picky eater—resisting eating vegetables, for example—don't get discouraged or frustrated. Keep giving them to her even if she repeatedly turns up her nose at the sight of them. Before long, she may change her mind, developing a taste for foods that she once ignored. This is the period of time that healthy snacking and healthy habits get reinforced and/or established.

Remember, meals don't need to be elaborate to be nutritious. If you have only a few minutes to prepare a meal, try a turkey sandwich, a serving of green beans, an apple, and a glass of nonfat or low-fat milk. A simple lunch like this takes less time to prepare than driving through a fast-food restaurant, and it is much healthier.

Television advertising, incidentally, can be a serious obstacle to your preschooler's good nutrition. Some studies show that children who watch over twenty-two hours of TV per week (over three hours of screen time a day) have a greater tendency to become obese. Children this age are extremely receptive to ads for sugary cereals and sweets, especially after they've visited other homes where these foods are served. Obesity is a growing problem among children in America. For this reason, you need to be aware of your child's eating habits, at home and away, and monitor them to make sure she's eating as healthy as possible.

Beyond Toilet Training

By about age three, many children are already fully toilet trained, although as a toddler your child may have used a potty chair rather than a toilet. But now, in preparation for preschool, she must get used to using toilets both at home and away.

If the small potty chair isn't in the bath-

As preschoolers, little boys begin to copy their fathers, friends, or older brothers, and stand up while urinating.

room, move it next to the regular toilet. If your child isn't already used to "going to the bathroom," this will help establish that routine. When she has fully adjusted to the potty seat, get a child-size toilet seat for the toilet, and provide a sturdy box or stool so she can climb up and down by herself. This also will give her a surface on which to plant her feet while using the toilet. Once she has completely and voluntarily made the transition from potty to toilet, remove the potty.

Little boys generally sit down to urinate during early toilet training, but as preschoolers, they'll begin to copy their fathers, friends, or older brothers, and stand up while urinating. As your son learns to do this, make sure he also lifts the toilet seat beforehand. You'd better be prepared to do some extra cleaning around the toilet bowl for a while, since he probably won't have perfect aim for some time. (Note: Make sure the toilet seat stays in the raised position when put there; falling seats have caused injuries.)

Away from home, teach your child to recognize restroom signs, and encourage her to use public bathrooms whenever necessary. You'll need to accompany and assist her in the beginning (although by the time she reaches her fifth year she should become comfortable enough to manage by herself). Whenever possible, however, an adult or older child should accompany her or at least wait outside the door.

She'll also need to learn that, at times, she'll have to use facilities when they're available, even before she feels a strong need. Doing this will make outings and especially car trips much more pleasant. Sometimes, however, a bathroom will not be available when it's really needed, so you may have to bring along a portable potty chair.

During the entire process just described, you'll need to help your child in the bathroom at first—whether at home or away. Plan not only on wiping, but also on helping her dress and undress. Before she goes to school, however, it's helpful to teach her to manage entirely on her own, especially if she is in a school that expects all children to be fully toilet trained to begin. A boy must learn to pull down his pants (if elastic-waist) or use the fly front. To make this procedure as simple as possible, dress your child in clothes that can be undone easily without help. Although overalls, for example, may be practical in other ways, they're very difficult for a child to get into and out of without help. For children of both sexes, elastic-waist pants or shorts are generally the most practical clothing at this age. A dress with elastic waist underpants will work equally well for girls.

If your child is starting preschool, other situations could arise. A common one occurs when a child tries to hold her urine flow because of the excitement of playing with other children, and ends up having an accident. Experiences like these are part of growing up. Never punish a child in circumstances like this, and know that she'll outgrow it.

Bed-Wetting

All young children occasionally wet their beds while going through nighttime toilet training. Also, even after your preschooler is able to stay dry at night for a number of days or weeks, she may start wetting at night again, perhaps in response to stress or changes occurring around her. When this happens, don't make an issue of it. Simply put her back in training pants at night for a while, but not as a punishment, only as a means to keep the sheets dry. As the stress decreases, she should stop wetting. If it persists, however, check with your pediatrician.

Most children with an ongoing bed-wetting pattern have never been consistently dry at night. Some may have unusually small bladders, and at age three (and even by age four or five in some children), they can't last a whole night without urinating. In other cases, the processes required for successful bladder control can take longer to develop, and the children may not be able to recognize when their bladder is full, awakening them to use the toilet.

If your preschooler persistently wets her bed, the problem probably will disappear gradually as she matures. Medication is not advisable during the preschool years, nor should she be punished or ridiculed. She is not wetting the bed on purpose; usually it simply indicates that she is a deep sleeper. Limiting her fluid intake and waking her up to use the bathroom probably won't help the situation much either, but reassuring her that these mishaps are "no big deal" may help her feel less ashamed. Also, make sure she understands that the bed-wetting is not her fault and that it probably will stop as she gets older. If there's a family history of bed-wetting, let her know that, too, in order to further take the burden off her shoulders. Should the bed-wetting continue after age five, your pediatrician may recommend one of several treatment programs. (See *Wetting Problems or Enuresis,* page 780.)

If a child who has been completely toilet trained for six months or longer suddenly begins wetting her bed again, there may be an underlying physical or emotional cause. As mentioned, perhaps stress in your child's life is contributing to this situation, or maybe she's reacting to a new baby in the family, a move to a new neighborhood, or a divorce. If she has frequent accidents during the day as well as at night, "dribbles" urine constantly, or complains of burning or pain while urinating, she may have a urinary tract infection or other medical problem. In any of these cases, see your pediatrician as soon as possible.

Sleeping

For many parents, their child's bedtime is the most challenging part of the day. This is more likely to be difficult if she has older brothers or sisters who stay up later. The younger one is bound to feel left out and afraid of "missing something" if the rest of the family is up after she's asleep. These feelings are understandable, and there's no harm in granting her some flexibility in her bedtime. But remember that most children at this age need at least ten to twelve hours of sleep each night. And what about napping in this age group? By the time children reach age three, most (about 90 percent) still nap each day. The typical nap in three-year-olds lasts from one to two hours, depending on the child.

The best way to prepare your preschooler for sleep is by establishing a bedtime routine. For example, read her a story. Once the story is over and you've said your good-nights, don't let her stall further, and don't let her talk you into staying with her until she falls asleep. She needs to get used to doing this on her own. Also, don't let her roughhouse or get involved in a lengthy play project right before bedtime. The calmer and more comforting the activity that precedes going to bed, the better and the more easily she'll go to sleep.

Although most preschoolers sleep through the night, some rouse several times to check their surroundings before falling back to sleep. There may be nights, however, when your child's very active dreams awaken her. These vivid dreams often represent the way she viewed some of the events of the day. They may reflect some impulse, aggressive feeling, or inner fear that comes to the surface only by way of these frightening images or dreams.

By the time she's a little older (about age five or even a bit older), she'll be better able to understand that these images are only dreams. But as a preschooler, she still may need to be reassured that they're not real. When she wakes up in the middle of the night, afraid and crying, try holding her, talking about the dream, and staying with her until she's calm. For your own peace of mind, don't forget that these are only nightmares and not a serious problem.

To further help your child overcome her nighttime fears, you might read her stories about dreams and sleep. As you talk about these stories together, she'll better understand that everyone has dreams and that she needn't be frightened of them. But always make sure that the books themselves aren't frightening to her. (For more information about nightmares and night terrors, see pages 421–423.)

Now, what about those instances in which you're sure your child is having neither a nightmare nor a night terror but is nevertheless waking up and calling for you? Simply reassure her that everything is all right, put her back to sleep, and then leave her. Don't reward her for waking up by giving her food or by taking her to your room. See Chapter 35 for more information on sleep.

Discipline

As a parent, one of your challenges is to teach your child which behaviors are acceptable, and which are not. This kind of learning is a process that won't happen overnight, but you've been doing it since your child was very young. All along, you should have been—and should continue to be—consistent about your expectations regarding her behavior. You need to set rules clearly, and stick to them.

At this age, your child's misconduct tends to be more conscious than it once was. As a toddler, she acted out of curiosity, trying to find and test her limits; now that she's a preschooler, her misbehavior may be less innocent. A three-year-old whose mother is pregnant or whose parents are separated, for example, may react by doing something that she well knows is forbidden. She may not understand the emotions that are driving her to break the rules, but she certainly realizes that she is breaking them.

To discourage such behavior, help your child learn to express her emotions through words instead of violent or obnoxious actions. The mother whose daughter hits her might say, "Stop it! You are very angry. Please tell me why." If she refuses to stop, a time-out may be necessary (see page 362 for a discussion on time-outs).

Sometimes your child won't be able to explain her anger, and it will be up to you to help her. This can be a real test of skill and patience, but is well worth it. Usually the problem will be fairly obvious if you examine the situation from her viewpoint. The pregnant mother just described, for example, can suggest, "You're very angry, but Mommy will help you feel better." This approach is most successful if you encourage your child to talk about her problems and feelings on an ongoing basis.

When setting limits, you'll need to be patient. Describe the undesirable behavior that your child has shown, and then tell her that she needs to stop doing it. Keep things simple: "Don't hit your brother. That's not nice."

Children test rules, particularly when those rules are new. But if you stay consistent, and repeat the new rule at appropriate times for a few days, she'll get the message and accept it.

(For more information about discipline, see pages 323 and 364, as well as the description of "extinction" on page 363.)

Preparing for School

Kindergarten usually is considered the "official" start of school. But many children get a taste of school much earlier, through preschool or group child care programs that may accept children as young as two or three. These programs generally are not designed to begin your child's academic or book-learning education, but they will help her get used to the idea of leaving home for a period of time each day and introduce her to the idea of learning in a group.

A good preschool is designed to get your child ready for when she reaches kindergarten entry age, and if its day-to-day programs are aligned with your child's developmental level and are emotionally supportive, your child will make a smoother transition to kindergarten when the time comes. She'll also be more likely to enjoy greater school success in the years ahead. Preschool will give her a chance to improve her social skills by meeting and playing with other children and adults, as well as introducing her to more formal rules than you may have established at home. A preschool program may be especially beneficial if your child doesn't have many opportunities to meet other children or adults, or if she has unusual talents or developmental problems that might benefit from special attention.

Aside from these advantages for your child, a preschool or child care program may help you meet some of your own needs. Perhaps you're going back to work now, or have a new baby at home. Maybe you just want a few hours to yourself each day. At this stage of your child's development, the separation can be good for both of you.

If you've never regularly spent much time apart from your child, you may feel sad or guilty about this new separation. You also may feel a little jealous if she becomes attached to her preschool teacher, especially if—in a moment of anger—she insists she likes her teacher better than you. But face it: You know very well that her teacher can't replace you, any more than preschool can replace your child's home life. These new relationships help her learn that there's a world of caring people in addition to her family. This is an important lesson for her to learn as she gets ready for the much larger world of primary school.

When you're hit by pangs of sadness, guilt, or jealousy, remind yourself that these structured separations will help your child become more independent, experienced, and mature, and also give you valuable time to pursue your own interests and needs. In the end, this time apart actually will strengthen the bond between the two of you.

Ideally, every preschool program should offer children a safe and stimulating environment supervised by attentive, supportive adults. At the same time, the community at large should be sensitive to and supportive of the need for high-quality, early childhood education. But unfortunately, not all preschool programs meet even the most basic requirements for an excellent environment for young children.

How can you distinguish the good from the bad? Here are some things to look for:

1. The school should have stated goals with which you agree. A good preschool tries to help children gain self-confidence, become more independent, and develop interpersonal skills. Be wary of programs that claim to teach academic skills or "speed up" children's intellectual development. From a developmental standpoint, most preschoolers are not yet ready to begin formal education, and pushing them may only take away the fun of learning and decrease their drive to learn. If you suspect that your child is ready to take on more educational challenges, ask your pediatrician to evaluate her or refer her to a child development specialist. If testing supports your suspicions, look for a program that will nurture her natural curiosity and talents without pressuring her to perform.

2. For a child with special needs—such as language or hearing impairment, behavioral or developmental problems—contact the director of special educa-

A preschool program may be especially beneficial if your child doesn't have many opportunities to meet other youngsters or adults.

tion in your local school system for a referral to appropriate programs in your area. Many neighborhood programs are not equipped to provide special therapy or counseling, and may make your child feel "behind" or out of place among the other children.

3. Look for programs with a relatively small class size. One- to three-year-olds do best in classes of eight to ten children, with close adult supervision. By the time your child is four, she will need slightly less direct supervision and thus may enjoy a group of up to sixteen. Here are the American Academy of Pediatrics' standards for the ratio of child to staff:

AGE	MAXIMUM CHILD:STAFF RATIO	MAXIMUM GROUP SIZE
13–30 months	4:1	8
31–35 months	5:1	10
3-year-olds	7:1	14
4-year-olds	8:1	16

4. Teachers and aides should be trained in early childhood development or education. Be suspicious of schools with an extremely high turnover rate among the staff. This may reflect poorly on the school's appeal to good teachers, and it also makes it difficult to find people who know anything about the teachers who are currently there.

5. Make sure you agree with the disciplinary methods used. Limit-setting should be firm and consistent without discouraging each child's need to explore. Rules should reflect the developmental level of the children in the program, and teachers should be supportive and helpful without stifling creativity and independent learning.

6. You should be welcome to observe your child at any time. While it may disrupt the daily routine to have parents coming and going, this openness reassures you that the program is consistent and the school has nothing to hide.

7. The school and grounds should be thoroughly childproofed. (See Chapter 15 on keeping your child safe.) Make sure there's an adult present at all times who knows basic first aid, including cardiopulmonary resuscitation (CPR—emergency breathing and heart stimulation techniques to revive a person who has stopped breathing or whose heart has stopped beating) and how to care for a child who's choking.

8. There should be a clear policy about illness among the children. In general, children with a fever should be excluded whenever the fever is accompanied by behavioral changes or by symptoms of illness that may need a doctor's attention. At the same time, keep in mind that the presence of a fever alone should not keep a child from participating in child care, since the fever itself isn't particularly relevant to whether the disease will spread to other children.

9. Hygiene is very important to minimize the spread of infectious illness among the children. Make sure there are child-height sinks and that children are encouraged to wash their hands when appropriate, especially after using the toilet and before eating. If the school accepts children who are not yet toilet trained, a diaper-changing area isolated from child activity and eating areas is absolutely necessary to control the spread of infectious disease.

10. Be certain you agree with the program's overall philosophy. Find out ahead of time how the school's philosophy affects the curriculum, and decide whether this is right for your family. Many preschools are connected with churches, synagogues, or other religious organizations. Children do not generally have to be members of the congregation in order to attend the program, but they may be exposed to certain rituals of faith.

For more information about child care and preschool programs, see Chapter 14.

Traveling with Your Preschooler

As your child gets older and more active, traveling will become more challenging. Your three-year-old will be restless when confined to a seat and, with her increasing willfulness, may protest loudly when you insist that she stay put. For safety's sake you will need to be firm, but if you provide enough distractions she actually may forget her restlessness. The specific tricks of traveling will vary somewhat with your mode of transportation.

TRAVELING BY CAR. Even on the shortest trips, your child must stay in her car safety seat. (See *Car Safety Seats,* page 491, for guidelines on selection and installation of car seats.) Most automobile crashes occur within five miles of home and at speeds under twenty-five miles per hour, so there can be no exceptions to the rule. If your child protests, refuse to start the car until she's buckled in. If you are driving and she escapes from her seat, pull over until she is secured again.

TRAVELING BY PLANE. When flying with a young child, choose a direct flight whenever possible to keep travel time to a minimum, and consider flying during your child's nap time or on a "redeye" (overnight) flight. Always let the airlines know in advance that you'll be traveling with one or more children. Special seating arrangements may be possible. Don't forget to pack healthy food and snacks because even if the airline does serve meals, they may not appeal to your toddler. Do not request seating in an emergency exit row since you will be moved, as your child is not capable of performing necessary emergency procedures.

Recently airport security procedures have become more rigorous. Be sure to allow your family additional time to move through the security checkpoints. The Federal Aviation Administration (FAA) recommends that when you're traveling with small children, give yourself even more time than usual to negotiate security. Remember, all child-related equipment—including strollers, car safety seats, infant carriers, and toys—must be visually inspected, as well as pass through an X-ray machine. You'll probably be asked to fold child-related equipment when you reach the X-ray belt so it all can pass through the inspection process more rapidly.

For your child's safety, dress her in bright colors when you travel so you can spot her more easily in a crowd. Tuck a card into her pocket on which you've written her name (and yours), your phone number (including cell phone), your address, and your travel itinerary. Have an up-to-date photograph of your child in your possession. (If possible, have a cell phone or smartphone picture taken of her on the day of your flight, with your child wearing the clothes that she has on the day that you're traveling.) It's also a good idea to carry a change of clothes with you in case your child needs to be changed on board.

While it makes sense to ask for preboarding when you're traveling with a baby, keep in mind that preboarding with a toddler or preschooler may not be wise if you think your child will become restless the longer she's on the plane.

One advantage of air travel is that you and your child can take brief walks when the "Fasten Seat Belt" sign is off. This is the best antidote to restlessness, especially if you should meet another preschooler in the aisles.

To amuse your child in her seat, take along an assortment of books and toys similar to those you would pack for a car trip.

Visit to the Pediatrician

Your preschooler should be examined by the pediatrician once a year. Now that she is better able to follow instructions and communicate, some screening procedures are possible that previously weren't. In particular, her maturity will allow more accurate testing of her hearing and vision. Your pediatrician will check your child's teeth and gums during routine visits, although your child should keep seeing a children's dentist for routine dental examinations (by age three, 28 percent of children have at least one cavity, and by age five, nearly 50 percent do, so good dental care is important).

Especially for Grandparents

A three-year-old child is becoming more of a real person. As that happens, your grandparent-grandchild relationship will become more meaningful and unique and will present many opportunities for additional growth for both of you.

The years from ages three through five are often known as "the magic years" for children. They are becoming more sociable, they engage in more make-believe and fantasy play, and they may have an "imaginary friend" for a while. As a grandparent, your role is to be part of her activities, play along, enjoy her creative mind at work, and develop favorite play scenarios with her that you can return to whenever you're with her. Make time for adventures at or near your house that will allow you to interact with her. For example:

- **Take her to the zoo or the aquarium, which your grandchild will find very enjoyable at this age.**

- **Visit and "lose yourselves" at the museum.**

- **Go with her to a safe playground with equipment that will allow her to exercise many of her muscle groups, while you hold, hug, and catch her.**

- **Attend young people's concerts and plays, which are short (about one hour long) and a good way to introduce her to music and the theater.**

- **Become a volunteer, reading to your grandchild's class at preschool.**

Be sure to follow all of the travel rules and advice that appear in this chapter.

Immunization Update

During your child's preschool years, you and your pediatrician should work together to ensure that your child is up-to-date on her immunizations. Refer to the chart on page 876 for an overview of the vaccines that she should have received in the first three years of life. Your doctor may recommend giving any missed vaccinations, according to a "catch-up" schedule approved by the American Academy of Pediatrics and other medical organizations.

Safety Check

Falls

Be sure to guard against falls from the following:

- Play equipment: Watch your child on slides and monkey bars. Do not allow your child to use playground equipment that does not have an energy-absorbent surface, such as wood chips, shredded rubber, sand, or rubber mats, under it.

- Tricycles: Avoid unstable tricycles, and use the kind that allows the child to be low to the ground. Use a bicycle helmet that fits your child properly and bears a label indicating that it is certified by the Consumer Product Safety Commission. Do not allow your child to ride in the street.

- Stairs: Continue to use gates at the top and bottom of staircases.

- Windows: Continue to use window guards at or above the second floor.

Burns

- Keep matches, cigarette lighters, and hot objects out of your child's reach. Install and maintain working smoke detectors in your home.

Car Safety

- If your child reaches the top weight and height for her car safety seat (see the manufacturer's recommendation), she may need a car safety seat that can be used to a higher weight and height. The majority of convertible, three-in-one, and combination car safety seats have forward-facing weight limits of 65 pounds or more, which should accommodate nearly all children this age. A five-point harness is much safer than a booster seat as long as your child fits within the weight and height limits.

- Your young child is not safe around cars. Keep her away from places where there are cars. Driveways and quiet streets can be dangerous, with injuries sometimes occurring when cars back into a child playing on the sidewalk or the driveway, who cannot be seen by the driver.

Keep cars locked when not in use so your child cannot get in without permission.

■ Do not allow children to ride tricycles in the street or near traffic; do not allow them to ride down driveways into the street.

Drowning

■ Never leave your preschooler unattended near water, even if she has taken swimming lessons and has some swimming skills. (See Chapter 15, pages 509–510 for guidelines on when to give your child swimming lessons.)

■ Swimming lessons do not provide "drown-proofing" for a child of any age. Continue practicing touch supervision (an adult is within arm's reach at all times) anytime your child is in or near water.

■ If you have a pool at home, make sure it is surrounded by a four-sided fence with a gate that is self-closing and self-latching.

~ 13 ~

Your Four- and Five-Year-Old

TIME PASSES QUICKLY, and before you know it, your child has turned four and then five years old. You may find that your somewhat calm child of three has now become a dynamo of energy, drive, bossiness, belligerence, and generally out-of-bounds behavior. You may be reminded of the earlier trials and tribulations you went through when he was two, but by age four, he is now taking different directions. Although he may seem to be chasing off in all directions at the same time, he is learning from all these experiences. Eventually this will let up (just when you thought you couldn't take it for another day), and gradually a more confident, calm child will emerge around his fifth birthday.

Meanwhile, this is a difficult age to handle. Each day there are new challenges to deal with. The emotional highs and lows will have him appearing secure and bragging one minute and insecure and whining the next. In addition, four-year-olds become set in some of their routines, not wanting to change for fear they will not know what to do. This fixation reveals some of the insecurity they are feeling during these months.

Their out-of-bounds behavior also is seen in the language they use. They enjoy using inappropriate words, and they love to watch your expression when they say them. They use these words more to get a response out of you than for any other reason, so don't overreact to them.

This energy machine of yours still has little sense of property. To him, all things are his. Four-year-olds are not thieves or liars, though. They simply believe that possession means ownership.

Also obvious during this time is the tremendous spurt of imaginative ideas that spring from children's minds and mouths. The "monsters" they talked with at school or the "dragon" who helped them across the street represent the normal tall tales told by four- to five-year-olds. They reflect the fact that children of this age are trying to distinguish fact from fantasy, and their fantasies sometimes get a bit out of control. All of this behavior and thinking will help your child build a secure foundation as he emerges into the world of kindergarten.

In fact, around his fifth birthday, your "baby" will be ready to tackle "real" school—the major occupation of childhood. This enormous step demonstrates that he's able to behave within the limits expected by school and society and has the skills to take on increasingly complex learning challenges. It also means that he's able to separate comfortably from you and move out on his own. Not only can he now share and show concern for others, but also he has learned to value friends—both children and adults—outside his own family.

Development

Movement

Your preschooler now has the coordination and balance of an adult. Watch him walk and run with long, swinging, confident strides, go up and down stairs without holding the handrail, stand on his tiptoes, whirl himself in a circle, and pump himself on a swing. He also has the muscular strength to perform challenging activities such as turning somersaults and doing a standing broad jump. It will be a toss-up as to who is excited more by his progress—you or him.

In your child's eagerness to prove just how capable and independent he is, he'll often run ahead of you when out on a walk. His motor skills are still way ahead of his judgment, however, so you'll need to remind him frequently to wait and hold your hand when crossing the street. The need for vigilance is just as important when he is anywhere near water. Even if he can swim, he probably

Movement Milestones for Your Four- and Five-Year-Old

- Stands on one foot for ten seconds or longer
- Hops, somersaults
- Swings, climbs
- May be able to skip

can't swim well or consistently. And should he accidentally go under, he may become frightened and forget how to keep himself afloat. So never leave him alone in a pool or in the water at the beach, even for a moment.

Hand and Finger Skills

Your four-year-old's coordination and ability to use his hands are almost fully developed. As a result, he's becoming able to take care of himself. He now can brush his teeth and get dressed with little assistance, and he may even be able to lace up his shoes.

Notice how he uses his hands with far more care and attention when he draws. He'll decide in advance what he wants to create and then go ahead with it. His figures may or may not have a body, and the legs may be sticking out of the head. But now they'll have eyes, a nose, and a mouth, and, most important to your child, they are people.

Because of this growing control over his hands, arts and crafts in general are becoming more exciting for him now. His favorite activities may include:

Milestones in Hand and Finger Skills for Your Four- and Five-Year-Old

- **Copies triangle and other geometric patterns**
- **Draws person with body**
- **Prints some letters**
- **Dresses and undresses without assistance**
- **Uses fork, spoon, and (sometimes) a table knife**
- **Usually cares for own toilet needs**

- Writing and drawing, holding the paper with one hand and the pencil or crayon with the other

- Tracing and copying geometric patterns, such as a star or diamond

- Card and board games

- Painting with a brush and finger painting

- Clay modeling

- Cutting and pasting (using safe, nonpointed child's scissors)

- Building complex structures with many blocks

These kinds of activities will not only permit him to use and improve many of his emerging skills, but he'll also discover the fun of creating. In addition, because of the success he'll feel with these activities, his self-esteem will grow. You may even notice certain "talents" emerging through his work, but at this age it's not advisable to push him in one direction over another. Just be sure to provide a broad range of opportunities so he can exercise all his abilities. He'll take the direction he enjoys most.

Language Development

At about age four your child's language skills will blossom. He'll now be able to pronounce most of the sounds in the English language, with the following

Language Milestones for Your Four- and Five-Year-Old

- **Recalls part of a story**
- **Speaks sentences of more than five words**
- **Uses future tense**
- **Tells longer stories**
- **Says name and address**

exceptions: *f, v, s,* and *z* probably will remain difficult for him until midway through age five, and he may not fully master *sh, l, th,* and *r* until age six or later.

Your preschooler's vocabulary will have expanded to around fifteen hundred words by now, and it will grow by another one thousand or so over the course of this year. He now can tell elaborate stories using relatively complex sentences of up to eight words. And he will tell you not only about things that happen to him and things he wants, but also about his dreams and fantasies.

Don't be surprised, however, if some of the words he uses are not ones you want to hear. After all, by now he's learned how powerful words can be, and he'll enthusiastically explore this power, for better and for worse. Thus, if your four-year-old is like most others, he'll be very bossy at times, perhaps commanding you and your spouse to "stop talking" or his playmates to "come here now." To help counteract this, teach your child how to use "please" and "thank you." But also review the way you and other adults in the family address him and each other. Chances are, he's repeating many of the commands he most often hears.

Your child also will probably pick up many swear words at this age. From his point of view, these are the most powerful words of all. He hears adults say them when they are most angry or emotional, and whenever he uses them himself, he gets quite a reaction. What's the best way to stop this behavior? Be a good role model and make a conscious effort not to use these words, even when you are stressed. In addition, try to minimize your child's use of these words without drawing too much attention to them. He probably has no idea what these words really mean; he just enjoys their energy.

When your child's upset, you may find he'll use words as insults. This is certainly preferable to physical violence, although it can be quite disturbing to you. Remember, though, that when your child uses these words, he's disturbed, too. If he says "I hate you!" what he really means is "I am very angry, and I want you to help me sort out my feelings." By getting angry and shouting back at him, you'll only make him feel more hurt and confused. Instead, remain

Learning to Read

Is your child interested in learning the names of letters? Does he look through books and magazines on his own? Does he like to "write" with a pencil or pen? Does he listen attentively during story time? If the answer is yes, he may be ready to learn some of the basics of reading. If not, he's like most preschoolers, and will take another year or two to develop the language skills, visual perception, and memory he needs to begin formal reading.

Although a few four-year-olds sincerely want to learn to read and will begin to recognize certain familiar words, there's no need to push your child to do so. Even if you succeed in giving him this head start, he may not maintain it once school begins. Some early readers lose their advantage over other children during the second or third grade, when the other students acquire the same basic skills.

The most crucial fact that determines whether a student will do well or poorly in school is a child's own enthusiasm, not how aggressively he was pushed early on. Parents should make learning to read fun, without forcing it on their child. Encouraging your child's enthusiasm in learning is more important than the age a child actually learns to read.

What's the most successful approach to early learning? Let your child set his own pace and have fun at whatever he's doing. Don't drill him on letters, numbers, colors, shapes, or words. Instead, encourage his curiosity and tendencies to explore on his own. Read him books that he enjoys, but don't push him to learn the words. Provide him with educational experiences, but make sure they're also entertaining.

When your child is ready to learn letters and reading, there are plenty of valuable tools to help him—books, puzzles, games, songs, educational television programs, and even some of the latest age-appropriate video/computer games and DVDs. But don't expect them to do the job alone. You need to be involved, too. If he's watching an educational TV show, for example, sit with him and talk about the concepts and information being presented. If he's playing with a computer program, do it with him so you can make sure it's appropriate for his abilities. If the game is too frustrating for him, it may diminish some of his enthusiasm and defeat the whole purpose. Active learning in a warm, supportive environment is the key to success.

calm and tell him you know he doesn't really hate you. Then let him know that it's OK to feel angry, and talk about the events leading up to his outburst. Try giving him the words that will allow him to tell you how he feels.

If the insults he chooses are mild ones, the best response may be a joke. For example, let's presume he calls you a "wicked witch"; you might laugh and respond: "And I'm just boiling up a pot of bats' wings and frogs' eyes. Care to join me for supper?" This kind of humor is an excellent way to take the edge off his anger as well as your own.

Of course, sometimes your preschooler doesn't have to say anything offensive to try your patience—his constant chatter can do it just as quickly. One solution at these moments is to redirect his verbal energy. For instance, instead of allowing him to chant mindless sound rhymes, teach him some limericks or songs, or take time out to read some poems. This will help him learn to pay more attention to the words he speaks and will boost his appreciation for the written language, as well.

Cognitive Development

By age four, your child is beginning to explore many basic concepts that will be taught in greater detail in school. For example, he now understands that the day is divided into morning, afternoon, and night, and that there are different seasons. By the time he's five and entering kindergarten, he may know some days of the week and that each day is measured in hours and minutes. He also may comprehend the essential ideas of counting, the alphabet, size relationships (big versus small), and the names of geometric shapes.

There are many good children's books that illustrate these concepts, but don't feel compelled to rush things. There's no advantage to him learning them this early, and if he feels pressured to perform now, he actually may resist learning when he gets to school.

The best approach is to offer your child a wide range of learning opportunities. For instance, this is the perfect age to introduce him to zoos and museums, if you haven't done so already. Many museums have special sections designed for children, where he can actively experience the learning process.

At the same time, you should respect his special interests and talents. If your child seems very artistic, take him to art museums and galleries, or let him try a preschool art class. Also, if you know an artist, take him for a visit so he can see what a studio is like. If he's most interested in machines and dinosaurs, take him to the natural history museum, help him learn to build models, and provide him with construction kits that allow him to create his own machines. Whatever his interests, you can use books to help answer his questions and open his horizons even further. At this age, then, your child should be discov-

Cognitive Milestones for Your Four- and Five-Year-Old

- **Can count ten or more objects**
- **Correctly names at least four colors**
- **Better understands the concept of time**
- **Knows about things used every day in the home (money, food, appliances)**

ering the joy of learning so that he will be self-motivated when his formal education begins.

You'll also find that, in addition to exploring practical ideas, your four-year-old probably will ask many "universal" questions about subjects such as the origin of the world, death and dying, and the composition of the sun and the sky. Now, for example, is when you'll hear the classic question "Why is the sky blue?" Like so many other parents, you may have trouble answering these questions, particularly in simple language your child will understand. As you grapple with these issues, don't make up answers; rely instead on children's books that deal with them. Your local library or bookstore should be able to recommend age-appropriate books to help you.

Social Development

By age four, your child should have an active social life filled with friends, and he may even have a "best friend" (usually, but not always, of his own sex). Ideally, he'll have friends in the neighborhood or in his preschool whom he sees routinely.

But what if your child is not enrolled in preschool and doesn't live near other families? And what if the neighborhood children are too old or too young for him? In these cases, you'll want to arrange play sessions with other preschoolers. Parks, playgrounds, and preschool activity programs all provide excellent opportunities to meet other children.

Once your preschooler has found playmates he seems to enjoy, you need to take some initiative to encourage their relationships. Encourage him to invite these friends to your home. It's important for him to "show off" his home, family, and possessions to other children. This will help him establish a sense of self-pride. Incidentally, to generate this pride, his home needn't be luxurious or filled with expensive toys; it needs only to be warm and welcoming.

Social Milestones for Your Four- and Five-Year-Old

- **Wants to please friends**
- **Wants to be like his friends**
- **More likely to agree to rules**
- **Likes to sing, dance, and act**
- **Shows more independence and may e visit a next-door neighbor by himself**

It's also important to recognize that at this age his friends are not just playmates. They also actively influence his thinking and behavior. He'll desperately want to be just like them, even during those times when their actions violate rules and standards you've taught him from birth. He now realizes that there are other values and opinions besides yours, and he may test this new discovery by demanding things that you've never allowed him—certain toys, foods, clothing, or permission to watch certain TV programs.

Don't despair if your child's relationship with you changes dramatically in light of these new friendships. For instance, he may be rude to you for the first time in his life. When you tell him to do something that he objects to, he may occasionally tell you to "shut up" or even swear at you. Hard as it may be to accept, this sassiness actually is a positive sign that he's learning to challenge authority and test the limits of his independence. Once again, the best way to deal with it is to express disapproval, and you might want to discuss with him what he really means or feels. The more emotionally you react, the more you'll encourage him to continue behaving badly. But if the subdued approach doesn't work, and he persists in talking back to you, a time-out is the most effective form of punishment (see page 362).

Bear in mind that even though your child is exploring the concepts of good and bad at this age, he still has an extremely simplified sense of morality. Thus, when he obeys rules rigidly, it's not necessarily because he understands or agrees with them, but more likely because he wants to avoid punishment. In his mind, consequences count but not intentions. When he breaks something of value, for instance, he probably assumes he's bad, whether he did it on purpose or not. But he needs to be taught the difference between accidents and misbehaving.

To help him learn this difference, you need to separate him—as a person—from his behavior. When he does or says something that calls for punishment, make sure he understands that he's being punished for a particular act that he's done, not because he's "bad." Instead of telling him that he is bad, describe specifically what he did wrong, clearly separating the person from the behavior. For example, if he is picking on a younger sibling, explain that it's wrong to make someone else feel bad, rather than just saying "You're bad." When he accidentally does something wrong, comfort him and tell him you understand it was unintentional. Try not to get upset yourself, or he'll think you're angry at him rather than about what he did.

It's also important to give your preschooler tasks that you know he can perform and then praise him when he does them well. He's quite ready for simple responsibilities, such as helping to set the table or cleaning his room. When you go on family outings, explain that you expect him to behave well, and congratulate him when he does so. Along with the responsibilities, give him ample opportunities to play with other children, and tell him how proud you are when he shares or is helpful to another child.

Finally, it's important to recognize that the relationship with older siblings can be particularly challenging, especially if the sibling is three to four years older. Often your four-year-old is eager to do everything his older sibling is doing; and just as often, your older child resents the intrusion. He may be resentful of the intrusion on his space, his friends, his more daring and busy pace, and especially his room and things. You often become the mediator of these squabbles. It's important to seek middle ground. Allow your older child his own time, independence, and private activities and space; but also foster times of cooperative play when and where appropriate. Family vacations are great opportunities to enhance the positives of their relationship and at the same time give each their own activity and special time.

Emotional Development

Just as it was when he was three, your four-year-old's fantasy life will remain very active. However, he's now learning to distinguish between reality and make-believe, and he'll be able to move back and forth between the two without confusing them as much.

Developmental Health Watch

Because each child develops in his own particular manner, it's impossible to predict exactly when or how your own preschooler will perfect a given skill. The developmental milestones listed in this book will give you a general idea of the changes you can expect as your child gets older, but don't be alarmed if his development takes a slightly different course. Alert your pediatrician, however, if your child displays any of the following signs of possible developmental delay for this age range.

- Exhibits extremely fearful or timid behavior
- Exhibits extremely aggressive behavior
- Is unable to separate from parents without major protest
- Is easily distracted and unable to concentrate on any single activity for more than five minutes
- Shows little interest in playing with other children
- Refuses to respond to people in general, or responds only superficially
- Rarely uses fantasy or imitation in play
- Seems unhappy or sad much of the time
- Doesn't engage in a variety of activities
- Avoids or seems aloof with other children and adults
- Doesn't express a wide range of emotions
- Has trouble eating, sleeping, or using the toilet
- Can't differentiate between fantasy and reality
- Seems unusually passive
- Cannot understand two-part commands using prepositions ("Put the cup on the table"; "Get the ball under the couch")

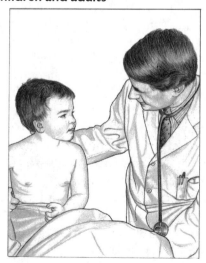

- ■ Can't correctly give his first and last name
- ■ Doesn't use plurals or past tense properly when speaking
- ■ Doesn't talk about his daily activities and experiences
- ■ Cannot build a tower of six to eight blocks
- ■ Seems uncomfortable holding a crayon
- ■ Has trouble taking off his clothing
- ■ Cannot brush his teeth efficiently
- ■ Cannot wash and dry his hands

As games of pretend become more advanced, don't be surprised if children experiment with make-believe games involving some form of violence. War games, dragon-slaying, and even games like tag all fall into this category. Some parents forbid their children to play with store-bought toy guns, only to find them cutting, pasting, and creating cardboard guns or simply pointing a finger and shouting "bang, bang." Parents shouldn't panic over these activities. This is no evidence that these children are "violent." A child has no idea what it is to kill or die. For him, toy guns are an innocent and entertaining way to be competitive and boost his self-esteem.

If you want a gauge of your child's developing self-confidence, listen to the way he talks to adults. Instead of hanging back, as he may have done at two or three, he now probably is friendly, talkative, and curious. He also is likely to be especially sensitive to the feelings of others—adults and children alike—and to enjoy making people happy. When he sees they're hurt or sad, he'll show sympathy and concern. This probably will come out as a desire to hug or "kiss the hurt," because this is what he most wants when he's in pain or unhappy.

At about the age of four and five, your preschooler also may begin to show an avid interest in basic sexuality, both his own and that of the opposite sex. He may ask where babies come from and about the organs involved in reproduction and elimination. He may want to know how boys' and girls' bodies are different. When confronted with these kinds of questions, answer in simple but correct terminology. A four-year-old, for example, doesn't need to know the details about intercourse, but he should feel free to ask questions, knowing he'll receive direct and accurate answers.

Along with this increased interest in sexuality, he'll probably also play with his own genitals and may even demonstrate an interest in the genitals of other

Emotional Milestones for Your Four- and Five-Year-Old

- **Aware of sexuality**

- **Able to distinguish fantasy from reality**

- **Sometimes demanding, sometimes eagerly cooperative**

children. These are not adult sexual activities but signs of normal curiosity and don't warrant scolding or punishment.

At what point should parents set limits on such exploration? This really is a family matter. It's probably best not to overreact to it at this age, since it's normal if done in moderation. However, children need to learn what's socially appropriate and what's not. So, for example, you may decide to tell your child:

- Interest in genital organs is healthy and natural.

- Nudity and sexual play in public are not acceptable.

- No other person, including even close friends and relatives, may touch his "private parts." The exceptions to this rule are doctors and nurses during physical examinations and his own parents when they are trying to find the cause of any pain or discomfort he's feeling in the genital area.

At about this same time, your child also may become fascinated with the parent of the opposite sex. A four-year-old girl can be expected to compete with her mother for her father's attention, just as a boy may be vying for his mother's attention. This so-called Oedipal behavior is a normal part of personality development at this age and will disappear in time by itself if the parents take it in stride. There's no need to feel either threatened or jealous because of it.

Basic Care

Healthy Lifestyle

As your child moves through the preschool years, this is a time to pay particular attention to adopting a healthy lifestyle for the entire family, and to encourage your child to stick with healthy habits. The lifestyle he becomes accustomed to at ages four and five is likely to influence the health-related choices he makes for the rest of his life. That means being conscientious about the food he eats and the amount of exercise he gets.

Pediatricians are more aware than ever that a growing number of children are overweight. Your doctor has been keeping track of your child's height and weight since infancy, and he'll be able to calculate whether your child weighs more than he should. Fortunately, there are steps you can take now to reduce your child's likelihood of becoming obese, and keep him on track for a healthy life.

Give some thought to the physical activity in your child's life. Even though he continues to be a bundle of endless energy, a lot of that energy often goes to waste. Many preschoolers spend several hours a day in front of the TV or computer screen, rather than playing outdoors. In fact, today's children are only one-fourth as active in their day-to-day lives as their grandparents were.

Whether or not your four- or five-year-old is overweight, you need to make sure that physical activity becomes and remains a priority in his life. These preschool years are a time when he should be developing his motor skills, im-

Sample One-Day Menu for a Preschooler

This menu is planned for a four-year-old child who weighs approximately 36 pounds (16.5 kg).

1 teaspoon = $\frac{1}{3}$ tablespoon = 5 milliliters
1 tablespoon = ½ ounce = 15 milliliters
1 ounce = 30 milliliters
1 cup = 8 ounces = 240 milliliters

BREAKFAST
½ cup nonfat or low-fat milk
½ cup whole-grain cereal
4–6 ounce or ½ cup cantaloupe,
    strawberries, or banana

SNACK
½ cup nonfat or low-fat milk
½ cup fruit such as melon, banana, or
    berries
½ cup yogurt

LUNCH

½ cup nonfat or low-fat milk
1 sandwich—2 slices whole-wheat bread with 1–2
    ounces of meat and cheese, veggie, and dressing
    (if needed), or peanut or almond butter (and jelly
    if needed)
¼ cup yellow or green vegetable

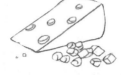

SNACK

1 teaspoon peanut or almond butter with 1 slice
    whole-wheat bread or 5 whole-grain crackers or
    string cheese or cut-up fruit

DINNER

½ cup nonfat or low-fat milk
2 ounces lean meat, fish, or chicken
½ cup whole-grain pasta, rice, or
    potato
¼ cup vegetable

If your family would like to include margarine, butter, or salad dressing as a "side" option to any meal, choose low-fat or healthier versions, if possible, and give only 1 or 2 teaspoons to your child.

proving his coordination, and playing games and sports with greater skill. You should make sure that he has access to age-appropriate play equipment, such as balls and plastic bats that will make exercise fun and something he looks forward to doing. Of course, these play periods must be supervised; you need to keep him away from dangerous situations like running into the street to chase a ball.

Make an effort to turn family time into a physically active time. On a Sunday afternoon, rather than going to the movies, take the entire family on a hike in the hills near your home. Or fly a kite in the park, play tag, or throw a ball back and forth.

As for TV watching, the American Academy of Pediatrics recommends limiting your child's time in front of the TV to no more than one to two hours a day, and that includes time spent playing computer and video games for entertainment. That will add up to less time on the couch and more time devoted to play where he can be physically active. Remember to limit your child's viewing to educational and nonviolent programming. And whenever possible, watch TV with your child and talk about what you see. (See *Media*, page 813.)

Feeding and Nutrition

Good nutrition is an important part of your child's healthy lifestyle. Fast-food restaurants may be tempting for their cost and convenience, but there are now many acceptable alternatives to the higher calorie, less nutritious items on the menu. During the preschool years, your child should be eating the same foods as the rest of the family, with an emphasis on those with nutritional value. This includes fresh vegetables and fruits, nonfat or low-fat dairy products (milk, yogurt, cheeses), lean meats (chicken, turkey, fish, lean hamburger), and whole-grain cereals and bread. At the same time, limit or eliminate the junk food in your child's diet, and get rid of sugared beverages as well. Since dairy is an important part of your child's diet, if flavored milk is the only way your child

How Much Is Enough?

Many parents worry whether their children are getting "enough" to eat. Here are some guidelines to help you make sure your child gets enough, but not too much.

1. Your child does not need the same serving size as an adult. Offer him small portions, with seconds only if he asks for them. A typical portion size should be about half of an adult size. For many foods, that's about the size of the palm of his hand. Here are some acceptable "child-size" portions.

   1 teaspoon = 5 ml
   1 ounce = 30 ml
   4–6 ounces milk or juice
   ½ cup cottage cheese or yogurt
   2 ounces hamburger
   1 slice toast
   4 tablespoons vegetables

   1 tablespoon = 15 ml
   1 cup = 8 ounces = 240 ml
   ½ cup cereal
   2 ounces chicken
   1 teaspoon margarine, butter, or dressing

2. In general, limit snacks to two a day. Choose healthy items instead of offering him unhealthy foods such as soft drinks, candy, pastries, or

salty and greasy items. As long as they are healthy, you can give him two snacks per day. More than two snacks a day may spoil his appetite for his main meals. Unhealthy snacks will expose his teeth to a higher risk of cavities over an extended period of time. To minimize the risk of cavities and excess calories, rely on nutritious snack foods like those listed below. Keep in mind that it often takes about a dozen times for a child to develop a taste for an unfamiliar food item:

fruit

carrot, celery, or cucumber sticks
   (can dip into low-fat ranch
   dressing or hummus)

yogurt

whole-grain toast/crackers
   (with healthy nut butter)

low-fat bran muffins

string cheese

On special occasions, your child can have dessert items or a sweet treat, but select low-fat oatmeal cookies or other low-fat choices whenever possible.

3. Don't use food as a reward for good behavior.

4. Make sure your child actually is hungry or thirsty when he asks for food or drink. If what he really wants is attention, talk or play with him, but don't use food as a pacifier.

5. Don't allow him to eat while playing, listening to stories, or watching television. Allowing him to do so will lead to "unconscious" eating well past the point when he's full.

6. Learn the calorie counts for the foods he eats most often and monitor how many calories he consumes on an average day. The total daily calories for a child age four to five should be 900 to 1,500, or about 40 calories per pound of body weight.

7. Don't worry if your child's food intake is inconsistent. One day he may seem to eat anything he can get his hands on, and the next he'll grimace at the sight of everything. When he refuses to eat, he may not be hungry because he's been less active than the day before. Also consider the possibility that he's using food as a means of exercising control. Especially during the period when he's being negative about nearly everything, he's bound to resist your efforts to feed him. When that happens, don't force him to eat. Rest assured that he will not starve himself, and he'll seldom, if ever, lose weight. If, however, a markedly decreased appetite

persists for more than one week, or there are other signs of illness, such as fever, nausea, diarrhea, or weight loss, consult your pediatrician.

8. Your child needs to drink approximately two cups (16 oz., or 480 ml) of nonfat or low-fat milk a day to meet his calcium requirement. Milk is an important food, mainly because of its calcium and vitamin D content. Too much milk, however, may reduce his appetite for other important foods.

will drink milk, be assured that research demonstrates that consuming either flavored or plain milk does not adversely affect body mass index measurements in children. Further, flavored milks can help your child meet his recommended daily dairy servings. The AAP 2006 report on optimizing bone health recommends consuming low-fat or fat-free flavored milks, cheeses, and yogurts containing modest amounts of added sugars to meet calcium recommendations in children. Desserts like ice cream and cake are fine once in a while, but certainly shouldn't be an everyday indulgence. Particularly if your child is overweight, pay attention to portion sizes, and for four- and five-year-olds, servings should be less than the adult-size portions that you and your spouse are eating.

While three-year-olds are frequently picky eaters, that behavior may continue in four-year-olds, as well, although the older child may be more vocal about his preferences. He may become more insistent about refusing to eat certain foods. His nutritional needs are the same as when he was a year younger, but he may have unpredictable emotional responses to the foods put in front of him. He may talk back and even swear if he doesn't like the food being served,

Hand-washing is an important part of a healthy lifestyle, too.

but if you put well-balanced meals on his plate, he'll have enough wholesome choices to keep him healthy.

At this age, your child should be good company at meals and be ready to learn basic table manners. By age four, he'll no longer grip his fork or spoon in his fist, because now he's able to hold them like an adult. With instruction, he also can learn the proper use of a table knife. You can teach him other table manners as well, such as not talking with his mouth full, using his napkin instead of his sleeve to wipe his mouth, and not reaching across another person's plate. While it's necessary to explain these rules, it's much more important to model them; he'll behave as he sees the rest of the family behaving. He'll also develop better table manners if you have a family custom of eating together. So make at least one meal a day a special and pleasant family time, and have your child set the table or help in some other way in the meal preparation.

Try to monitor your child's television viewing and exposure to advertisements. Television advertising, even if watched with the best explanations of commercial messages, does present a serious obstacle to your preschooler's good nutrition. Some research shows that screen time has been associated with obesity. Four- and five-year-olds are extremely receptive to ads for sugary cereals and sweets, especially after they've visited other homes where these foods are served. But to repeat, obesity is a growing problem among children in America. For this reason, you need to be aware of your child's eating habits, at home and away, and monitor them to make sure he's eating as healthy as possible.

To combat unhealthy influences, keep your own home as healthy as possible. Stock up on nutrient-rich, low-sodium, low-sugar, and low-fat products. Eventually he'll become accustomed to healthy, nutrient-rich foods, which may make him less susceptible to the temptation of the more sugary, salty, or greasy ones.

Sleeping

If your child is having difficulty with nighttime sleep, it often helps to establish sleep routines before bedtime. A four-year-old may respond positively to having a schedule that includes a bath, brushing his teeth, and a bedtime story, and then a time when the lights will be turned off. You might also try getting your child to sleep earlier rather than later; you may find that the nighttime struggles over sleep subside when your child is less tired and cranky. Your child's need for naps may gradually subside during this period.

Another nighttime issue in this age group is night terrors. Occasionally your preschooler will be in bed, appearing to be awake and upset, perhaps screaming and thrashing, eyes wide open and terrified, but he won't respond to you. In this case, he's neither awake nor having a nightmare. Rather, you're witnessing something called a night terror (or sleep terror)—a mysterious and, to parents, distressing form of sleep behavior common during the preschool and early school years. Typically, the child falls asleep without difficulty, but wakes up a few hours later, wide-eyed and terrified. He may point to imaginary objects, kick, scream, call out ("No, no!" "I can't!"), and generally be inconsolable. Parents

find these experiences particularly disturbing because the child looks and acts so differently from his usual self. (These events are much more unsettling for parents than for the child having them.) The only thing you really can do in this situation is hold the child to protect him from hurting himself. Reassure him: "You're fine. Mommy and Daddy are here." Keep the lights dim and speak softly. After ten to thirty minutes of this, he'll settle down and go back to sleep. The next morning, he'll remember nothing about the occurrence.

Some children may have just one episode of night terrors, while others experience them several times. It's not typical, however, for them to recur frequently or for a prolonged period. In cases of very frequent night terrors, sleep medications prescribed by your pediatrician may be helpful, but the best strategy seems to be to wait them out. Since some children have night terrors when they're overtired, try putting your child to bed about thirty minutes earlier than usual and see if the episodes diminish in frequency. In any case, they'll disappear naturally as the child grows older. For more information on night terrors, see the text box on page 423.

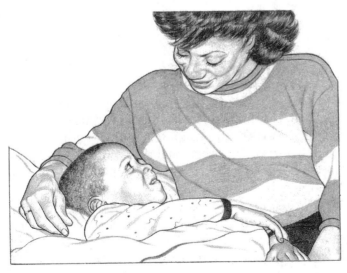

Unless a preschooler is very tired, he may resist going to sleep.

How to Tell a Nightmare from a Night Terror

Sometimes it's difficult to tell the difference between a nightmare and a night terror. This chart should help.

	Nightmare	Night Terror
Appearance and behavior	Frightening dream; child may awaken afraid and crying.	Screaming, crying, thrashing during sleep; may appear partially aroused, anxious, and agitated.
At what age does it start?	Frequently first occurs in toddlers and older.	May begin at age four or five (or at times later).
Timing of episodes	Often in the second part of the night during intense dreaming.	Mostly during nondreaming sleep; episodes start within two hours of going to sleep and last five to fifteen minutes; occur most often when child has a fever or sleep schedules are disrupted.
Return to sleep	May have trouble going back to sleep due to anxiety.	Goes back to sleep quickly.
Memory of experience	May remember the dream and talk about it.	No memory of the episode.
Underlying issues	Not associated with emotional problems, but may reflect inner fears surfacing in dreams.	Not associated with emotional problems.
Management	Awaken and comfort your child; talk to him to ease any stress that may be bothering him; avoid watching TV before bedtime.	Treatment with medications not effective; try putting child to bed a little earlier to avoid overtiredness.
Long-term	Talk to pediatrician if child complains of nightly nightmares.	Most children outgrow having night terrors.

Adapted from *Healthy Sleep Habits, Healthy Child*, by Marc Weissbluth, MD, FAAP.

Discipline

By age four, your preschooler may be getting some control over his unpredictable emotional responses, but he still won't be able to manage his feelings of defiance. Thus, at this age, he may openly disobey family rules, and, as mentioned earlier, even talk back or swear at you. Often he'll behave badly just to annoy you and to see your response. As irritating and embarrassing as this behavior may be, it's rarely a sign of emotional illness and usually disappears by school age if you take a relaxed approach to it.

This doesn't mean letting your child control or intimidate you. Believe it or not, even he doesn't want that. On the contrary, he expects you to restrain him when he gets too far out of line, just as he assumes you'll protect him when he does something dangerous.

One discipline technique is enforcing time-outs. After the time-out, review

Lying

Lying at this age is very common. Preschoolers lie for a variety of reasons. Sometimes it's because they're afraid of punishment, or it may be because they've gotten carried away with their fantasies, or perhaps they're imitating behavior they see among adults. Before you punish your child for not telling the truth, make sure you understand his motives.

When he's lying to avoid punishment, he may have broken one of the household rules. For instance, he may have damaged something he shouldn't have been handling. Or maybe he was too rough and he hurt one of his playmates. In any case, he's concluded that what he did is more serious an offense than lying. If you want him to confess, you must help him understand that lying is the greater misdeed. Save your anger and punishment for times when he conceals the truth, and instead of accusing him when you suspect he's done something wrong, say something like "This is broken. I wonder how it happened?" If he confesses, remain calm and even-tempered, and make the punishment less severe than if he persisted in the lie. This way he may be less afraid to divulge the truth next time.

Telling tall tales is entirely different from lying. This usually is just an expression of your child's imagination at work, and does no harm to anyone. It becomes a problem only if you—or your child—can no longer distinguish truth from fantasy. Although a tall tale doesn't require punishment, it does call for a lesson. Tell him the story of "The Boy Who Cried Wolf" and explain how it could be dangerous for him to keep making up falsehoods. (For example, what if he were hurt or ill, and you didn't know whether to believe him or not?) Make it clear that it's in his own best interests to tell the truth.

When your child's lying is just a copy of your behavior, you can best stop it by eliminating the model. When your child hears you telling "white lies," he may not understand that you're doing it to be tactful or in an effort to avoid hurting another person's feelings. All he knows is that you're not telling the truth—so he feels free to lie, as well. You can try teaching him the difference between outright lies and white lies, but he probably won't understand most of it. You're more likely to succeed by changing your behavior.

with your child why he received one. Another technique is the loss of privileges. However, do not use empty threats and never resort to physical abuse. So you must teach him what is acceptable behavior and what isn't. The only way he'll learn to set his own limits later is by having you set reasonable limits for him now. If you are firm and consistent, he will become more secure. It's also important to create opportunities for autonomy. For instance, if you're running an errand, ask your child if he wants to wear a sweater or jacket and ask him to help pick it out or find it. At the grocery store, ask him to help point out a product in the aisle that you are looking for.

In deciding what limits to set, keep in mind that many of the strategies you used when he was younger also are suitable now. It's still important to reward good behavior more often than punishing bad and to avoid physical punishments. And it's still essential to deal with misbehavior promptly and fairly, not waiting so long that your child forgets why he's being disciplined. Now more than ever, you also need to model appropriate behavior for him, by controlling your emotions (try not to overreact), carefully selecting the words you use (label the behavior and not the child), and using words (but not violence) to discuss emotions and settle disputes. Be sure to share your discipline strategies with your child's caregivers so your child receives consistent messages and appropriate forms of discipline.

For more information on discipline in preschoolers, see the section entitled *Discipline* on page 394, which is also largely applicable to four- and five-year-olds.

Preparing for Kindergarten

Kindergarten is a major turning point for your child. Even if he has attended preschool, he'll be expected to be much more grown-up as he enters elementary school, and he'll be given more responsibilities and more independence. "Regular" school is also a much larger and more confusing social setting than any he's known before. Even though his class may be no larger than the one in preschool, he may spend part of each day mixing with children from older classes. So he must be prepared emotionally not only for the tasks of kindergarten but also for the challenge of being one of the youngest in a big school.

As your child nears school age, you can start the preparations by talking to him about going to kindergarten. Explain how his routine will change when he starts school, and get him involved in choosing his back-to-school clothes. It also will help to drive or walk him by the school occasionally and even go in and show him the classroom so he'll see firsthand what to expect. Many schools open their classrooms before school begins so you can take your child in and introduce him to his teacher. All this preparation will help build his enthusiasm and lessen his anxiety about taking his next big step away from home.

Prior to beginning school, your child also should have a thorough physical examination. (Many states require it.) Your doctor will evaluate your child's vision, hearing, and overall physical development, make sure he has had the necessary immunizations, and give him any booster immunizations he needs. (See Chapter 31, *Immunizations*, and the immunization schedule in the Appendix.) Depending on state law and the likelihood of exposure, he also may administer a test for tuberculosis and may do routine labs in the office or send you to a laboratory for other tests.

In most school systems, children are accepted for kindergarten based on their age, often with a very rigid cutoff date as a guideline. While this approach

Kindergarten is a major turning point for your child.

works well for most children, it's not perfect. Developmental rates vary so widely that one child may be prepared for school at age four while another is not mature enough until age six.

If you are in doubt about your child's readiness, and your child is attending preschool, his teacher may be able to help you. He's seen him in action with other children and should be able to tell you if he's ready for a more structured classroom experience. Developmental testing of your child also may help determine whether he has the necessary skills to do well in kindergarten. Your pediatrician can help you make arrangements for such testing. These tests also can be helpful if you feel your child is advanced for his age, and you wish him to start school earlier than normal.

Many public school systems conduct preschool screening tests for all kindergarten-age children to assess their readiness for school and, in some instances, to allow children to start school at a slightly older age. This testing of developmental skills generally is held at the school during the spring or summer before the child is scheduled to enter kindergarten. At the same time,

school nursing personnel may collect information about the child's health, making sure he's been fully immunized, and perhaps examining his hearing and vision as well.

Unless there's evidence that your child will do very poorly, the best test may be a trial run when school opens. If there is a serious question about his progress during the school year, a decision will have to be made concerning his promotion. This decision will be based largely on his ability to learn, follow directions and routines, and relate to the other children as well as the teacher.

Talking about Bullying

Whether at preschool or on the playground, bullying can be a fact of life for many preschoolers. Bullying occurs when one child picks on another one, and it can happen at preschool or in the neighborhood (on playgrounds or in parks). The child being targeted is often smaller or weaker, shy, and feels helpless when confronted by bullying that can be physical (punching, pushing, kicking, choking), verbal (teasing, taunting, threatening, hate speech), or social (excluding from activities).

When children are bullied, they are often afraid to go to preschool. They may have difficulty paying attention at school, and they may complain of having headaches or stomach pains.

Make sure your child understands that bullying is not his fault. Talk to him about ways he can stay safe when he's being subjected to this aggressive behavior. Here are some strategies that are often effective for your child to use:

- **Look the bully directly in the eye.**

- **Stand tall and stay calm.**

- **Walk away.**

- **Say (in a firm voice) things such as, "I don't like what you're doing" or "Please don't talk to me like that."**

Have your child practice these approaches at home so they will happen more naturally when he needs to use them. Also, let him know that when bullying takes place, he can ask an adult for help. At the same time, you need to let preschool teachers and playground monitors know that bullying is going on, and ask them to help stop it if they see it occurring. When you are not around, an adult should be nearby who can keep watch and protect your child's safety.

Now, what if your child is the one who is doing the bullying? What if he is bullying other children in his preschool or in the neighborhood?

Take steps to put a stop to this behavior as soon as possible. Bullying needs to be taken seriously, and this is the time to change that undesirable behavior, before things get worse. Here are some guidelines:

- **Set consistent limits on your child's aggressive behavior. Make sure your child understands that bullying is never acceptable.**

- **Be a positive role model. Show your child that he can get what he needs without threatening or teasing other children.**

- When you need to discipline your child for his behavior, use nonphysical approaches—perhaps the loss of privileges. Make sure your child understands why this behavior is unacceptable.

- If you're having trouble putting a stop to your child's bullying, seek help from a teacher, a counselor, or a pediatrician.

Visit to the Pediatrician

You should continue to have your preschooler checked by your pediatrician once a year. He will confirm that your child is up-to-date on his immunizations. Booster doses of vaccines against polio, diphtheria, tetanus, pertussis, measles, mumps, rubella, and chickenpox are given at ages four to six years. Many states require these before kindergarten. (For a schedule of recommended immunizations, see the Appendix.)

HEARING. Around age four, your child can talk well enough to describe different sounds. Your pediatrician may suggest a thorough hearing check for your child, using tones at different frequencies. This test should be repeated every year or two, or more often if hearing problems are found.

VISION. At ages four and five, your child is able to understand directions and cooperate well enough to have a formal vision test. At this age, his visual acuity should be 20/30 or better. More important than the absolute vision in each eye is any difference in visual acuity between his two eyes. If you suspect a problem, he'll need to be seen by a pediatric ophthalmologist.

Safety Check

Throughout this book, there are recommendations for keeping your child safe at and away from home. In particular, Chapter 15 is devoted to safety in a number of areas, including safety on playgrounds, on bicycles and tricycles, and in your own backyard.

Here are some guidelines applicable specifically to four- and five-year-old children:

- As your child learns to ride a bicycle, he should *always* wear a helmet. When you purchase a bike, buy a helmet at the same time. Set a good example by wearing your own helmet every time you ride a bicycle.

- Never let your child ride a bike in the street. He is too young to ride safely in the street.

- If your child darts out into the street, he'll be in danger of being struck by a car. Accompany your child to play at the park or playground. Instruct him on the importance of stopping at the curb, and never crossing the street without an adult. Keep in mind, though, that your child may not remember this safety rule and must be supervised closely when near a street.

- While your child can learn to swim at this age, *never* let him swim alone, even if he seems capable of swimming. Your child should never play around a body of water (a lake, stream, pool, or ocean) unless an adult is nearby and watching at all times.

- Whenever you're on a boat with your child, make sure he wears a life jacket. Teach him that he should never dive into the water unless an adult has checked on the depth of the water.

- Teach your child never to play with matches or lighters, and make sure that these items are never left around the house where he can have access to them.

For additional information about safety, see Chapter 15, page 471.

Traveling with Your Child

Car crashes are the greatest danger to your child's life and well-being. A collision or a sudden stop, even when your car is traveling slowly, can cause devastating injuries. For that reason, your child should still be in a car safety seat with a five-point harness. The backseat is still the safest place for your child to ride.

Particularly when you're making a lengthy car trip with your four- or five-year-old, your child is less likely to resist the confinement of a car safety seat if you make the trips fun. Here are some suggestions to help pass the time.

- Talk about the passing sights. Ask your child what he sees out his window. Point out interesting sights. When he begins to learn colors, letters, and numbers, ask him to identify them in signs and billboards. Remember to keep your eyes on the road, however.

- Keep a variety of picture books and small, lightweight toys in the car within reach of his car safety seat.

- Keep children's songs or stories in the car. Encourage your child to sing along with his favorite tunes.

- For longer trips, take along a small box filled with age-appropriate activity materials, such as coloring or activity books, crayons, paper, stickers, or paper dolls. (Do not allow scissors in the car; they could be hazardous in the event of a sudden stop.) Also take along favorite CDs and DVDs, with sing-alongs, word rhymes, or other entertaining and familiar activities.

- Stop at least every two hours to break up the trip. This will allow your child a chance to stretch, perhaps eat a snack, and use the toilet.

- If your child is prone to motion sickness, it may help to give him an appropriate dose of nondrowsy motion-sickness medication one half hour before getting in the car. (See *Motion Sickness,* page 788.)

The trip will be more pleasant and comfortable for everyone if you follow several additional rules consistently, wherever you are.

- Never leave a child alone in the car, even for a minute.

- Don't allow yelling, hitting, biting, or loud noisemaking.

- Don't allow children to touch door handles. It may be helpful to use the child safety lock, if your car has one.

- Remind children to be considerate of other people in the car.

Especially for Grandparents

As you spend time with your grandchild, you'll probably notice a little change in his personality as he moves from a four-year-old to the more independent five-year-old. He may test your authority, show aggressiveness, be bossy, and at times even use "imitated" foul language. But fear not. Keep calm, knowing that this stage is only a stepping-stone to gaining greater mastery over his surroundings. Discipline him firmly but not harshly, and don't overreact to language you may find surprising and perhaps even offensive.

During this period in your grandchild's young life, he also will be developing larger social networks and some "best friends." You can expand this network even further if you can locate some other children nearby when he visits you, particularly if he's staying for a couple of days (or more). Set up some playdates with these other children of your neighbors or friends as well as with nearby cousins.

What if you live many miles from your grandchild, and frequent visits are not possible? There are many long-distance strategies for grandparents, taking advantage of the fact that children of this age are now quite verbal. Here are some suggestions.

- **The telephone is an obvious option. Establish a regular time when your grandchild can count on you to call. During these phone calls, talk about his activities. Ask questions about what he's doing and who his friends are. Preschool activities and "events" are often first on his mind. Keep notes so you can refer to his friends or special places by name in later conversations.**

- **If you don't get to see your grandchild very often, and both you and your children have a computer or smartphone with Internet access, you can use video conferencing to communicate. Simply viewing each other is worth a thousand words. Remember, though, that four-year-olds may not understand that you are not in the room or closer. An adult will likely have to explain how they can see Grandma, even though she is actually far away.**

- **Children _love_ to get regular mail or e-mail (using a parent's account). Sending cards and playful mementos of trips you have been on can keep the connection real.**

- **Exchanging family pictures and movies can mean a lot.**

■ Call to sing "Happy Birthday" and send a card to arrive on special occasions and holidays when you can't be there. It is important to make some contact for special celebrations.

■ Despite the distance, visits should become a priority. As important as the above suggestions are, nothing replaces actually being there with your grandchild. Even if it's only for a weekend, repeated contact and familiarity are keys to a meaningful relationship for both grandchild and grandparent.

~ 14 ~

Early Education and Child Care

WHO WILL CARE for your child during the hours when you are away? Sooner or later you're bound to face this question. Whether you need someone to care for your child a few hours a week or nine hours a day, you'll want to feel confident about the person who does it. But finding the right caregiver or team of caregivers to care for your child can be a big challenge. Your top priority should be to ensure the well-being of your child, and that should be the overriding consideration when selecting child care. This chapter provides suggestions to make your search easier. It also contains guidelines for preventing, recognizing, and resolving problems once you have made your choice.

The most important aspect of finding good child care is judging the quality of the child care program and the character and abilities of the caregiver involved with your child. Nearly six of every ten families use in-home or out-of-home care. Parents also may choose to share care between themselves or have relatives and nonrelatives provide that service. Some children participate in more than one type of child care arrangement at different times of the day or week. If your child's caregiver is not a member of your family, chances are you'll meet this person only a few times before entrusting your child to her. (Many, though not all, caregivers are women.) Even so, you'll want to feel as confident about your choice as if she were a member of your family. While it's impossible to be absolutely sure about anyone under these circumstances, you can tell a great deal about caregivers by observing them at work for a day or two and carefully checking references. Entrust your child to someone only after you have taken time to watch her with your child and other children, and you feel confident in her abilities and dedication.

In addition to this chapter's guidance on seeking, evaluating, and selecting child care, you'll find a checklist titled *Is This the Right Place for My Child?* on page 886 of the Appendix. It will help you choose high-quality, nurturing care.

What to Look for in a Care Provider: Guidelines for the Toddler and Preschool Child

(For infants, see Chapter 6, page 183.)

Children thrive when they're cared for in a safe, healthy environment by supportive adults who are warmly affectionate and who help children learn, interact, and work out solutions while protecting them from making choices that could lead to harm. The following list describes several things you should look for when you are observing someone who might take care of your child. More specific suggestions appear throughout this chapter, but remember that they are general guidelines. They apply to all out-of-home and in-home care, including babysitters, nannies, and teachers during preschool and the early primary school years. Also, keep these same criteria in mind as you play with your own child or supervise small groups of children.

A good caregiver will:

- Listen carefully to children and observe their behavior.

- Set reasonable limits for children and maintain those limits consistently.

- Tell children why certain things are not allowed, and offer acceptable alternatives.

Never entrust your child to anyone until you've taken time to watch her with your child and other children.

- Deal with difficult situations as they arise and before they get out of control.

- Anticipate trouble and intervene early to prevent it.

- Live up to promises made to the children.

- Join children at play without disrupting their activity.

- Ease transitions that can be stressful to children.

- Encourage children to think of their own ideas before offering suggestions.

- Reward children's efforts and relieve their "hurts" with an affectionate physical gesture, such as a hug or a pat.

- Talk naturally and conversationally with the children about what they are doing.

- Help children encourage each other by asking them to share their accomplishments.

- Encourage children to complete projects, even if they take longer than the time originally scheduled.

- Limit adult conversations in the children's presence.

- Show respect for the children's ideas and decisions.

- Avoid offering children choices when there is no choice.

- Allow children to make mistakes and learn from them (as long as there is no danger involved in doing so).

Choices in Care

In addition to the general suggestions just mentioned, you will want to identify your specific needs and desires. Before you meet and interview potential care-givers, the list of questions you need to answer should include:

- **Where do I** want my child to be during the day: At home? In someone else's home? In a child care center? If out-of-home care, how far away? What other family members or friends will my child be near?

- **What days and** hours do I need or want care each week?

- **How will I** handle my child's transportation to and from the program? If the caregiver needs transportation during the day or evening, how will it be handled?

- **What backup arrangements** can I make? How will I handle days when my child is sick or when my child's caregiver is unavailable because of illness or personal business? What are the arrangements for holidays, summertime, and vacations?

- **What can I** realistically afford?

- **What size program** do I want for my child? How much group interaction do I want for my child?

- **How much structure** and stimulation do I want for my child?

- **What qualifications do** I want the caregiver(s) to have?

- **How do I** want my child disciplined?

■ **What other basic** conditions would make me feel comfortable about leaving my child with someone else?

While a majority of young children in the United States are in some form of child care, nearly a quarter of this care is provided by relatives, mostly grandmothers. Not only are many grandparents caring for children for part of the day, but more and more of them are involved in taking children to and from other child care arrangements.

If you have family members or friends whom you would like to care for your child and who live nearby, ask yourself if you would be comfortable with their care and whether they would be willing to provide part-time care (perhaps for a few hours a day or for two to three days a week), either on a regular basis or as a backup if other arrangements fail. Consider also, when possible, that offering payment for these services makes the arrangement fairer and creates an additional incentive for the person you depend on for child care to help you.

Other options include bringing someone into your own home or taking your child to another person's home or a child care center. Your financial resources, the age and needs of your child, and your own preferences about child rearing will help you decide which choice is best.

Remember that your child will grow and develop quickly and the choice that is correct today may not be the best choice in the future. Keep reevaluating your child's needs and how good a fit your current child care arrangement is over time.

Here are some suggestions to keep in mind when deciding among in-home care, family child care, or a child care center:

In-Home Care/Nanny

If you are returning to work while your child is still an infant, one choice for child care (often a more expensive one) may be to have someone come into your home on a live-in or live-out basis. Since this person will not be required to be licensed, there are some important considerations that should be part of your evaluation and the hiring process.

■ Check references.

■ Perform a background check, if possible.

■ Ask for documented work experience (preferably as far back as five years).

- Ask for their approach to discipline, scheduling, feeding, comforting, and providing appropriate activities. Determine if their approach matches your style of child rearing and is right for your child. Make sure this individual shares your philosophy about how to react to excessive crying by your child, how to respond when he has an accident, or what to do when he doesn't sleep. (Sharing this kind of information is applicable no matter what type of setting your child is cared for in.)

HOW DO I FIND AN IN-HOME CAREGIVER?

- Ask friends for recommendations.

- Scan or place ads in the paper (especially local publications for parents).

- Go through a service.

AFTER CHOOSING AN IN-HOME CAREGIVER

- Arrange a trial period of at least a week when you can be home to watch the caregiver work under your supervision.

- In the days and weeks ahead, carefully monitor the performance of the person you hire.

ADVANTAGES OF IN-HOME CARE

1. Your child will stay in familiar surroundings and receive individualized care and attention.

2. He will not be exposed to the illnesses and negative behaviors of other children.

3. When your child is sick, you won't have to stay home from work or make different arrangements to take care of him.

4. Your caregiver may do some light housework and prepare family meals. If this is one of your expectations, make this clear from the start.

5. You will not need to worry about transportation for your child unless you want the caregiver to take him on outings.

DISADVANTAGES OF IN-HOME CARE

1. You may have difficulty finding someone who is willing to accept the wages, benefits, and confinement of working in your home, or you may find the costs of qualified in-home care prohibitive.

2. Since you will be considered an employer, you must meet minimum-wage, Social Security, and tax-reporting requirements. You also should provide health insurance for your employee, if she is not otherwise covered.

3. The presence of a caregiver may infringe on your family's privacy, especially if she lives in your home.

4. Because your caregiver will be alone with your child most of the time, you have no way of knowing exactly how she will perform her job.

5. Your caregiver may not always have backup help available for times when she isn't feeling well, has a family crisis, or wants to take a vacation. You will be responsible for securing a replacement.

6. Your caregiver will likely have less initial or ongoing training in child development and health and safety issues such as CPR, first aid, and medication administration. CPR and first aid are skills that she *has* to learn. Consider signing her up for a class in these life-saving skills, and offer to pay for it.

A Message for Grandparents

As a grandparent, you may become the person providing part-time care for your grandchild at times, perhaps on a scheduled day or two during the week or for a few hours here and there. Therefore, many of the guidelines in this chapter would apply to your caregiving. The recommendations about the best environment for the child, safety issues, special needs, and the size of the group (if you care for more than one child) should be considered.

As a grandparent, your role is unique and important. You are not just "another babysitter." You have a fundamental connection, providing the continuity between generations that your grandchild will come to understand and respect. Take advantage of this irreplaceable role. Your involvement with your grandchild, introducing him to your own world, is especially valuable. Treasure it. Make the most of those special days when you are the babysitter, and offer to do it regularly if you're able. Share stories with your grandchild (and read to him regularly).

At times, you may not be the actual caregiver for your grandchild, but rather you'll take him to and from a child care center or babysitter. You can make sure he is transported safely in an appropriate car safety seat, and provide another set of eyes to evaluate the quality of the center or sitter, which will help your grandchild's parents feel secure in their own choice of a child care setting.

As you know, times have changed, although caring love is still the universal and timeless ingredient in helping children to thrive. Educate yourself on the new medical discoveries since you raised your own children by asking your grandchild's parents to share information. The medical profession has learned a lot about having infants sleep safely on their backs and on safer over-the-counter medications for illnesses, as well as many other things. It keeps us young to learn new things.

By the way, if you've accepted the responsibility of picking up or dropping off your grandchild at regular times, introduce yourself to the responsible person at that site and provide them with your telephone number as a contact person. And remember, when driving with your grandchild, be sure he is properly buckled in a car safety seat at all times. At your home, make sure that you secure any of your personal medications by storing them up and away from sight or reach so that your grandchild can't get hold of them.

Family Child Care

Many people provide informal care in their homes for small groups of children, often looking after their own children or grandchildren at the same time. Some offer evening care, sick care, or care for children with special needs. Family child care is generally less expensive and more flexible than that offered by child care centers. A small family child care home typically has fewer than six children and one caregiver. Large family child care homes may have up to twelve children and one caregiver and an assistant.

Family child care may be licensed, registered, or unregulated. It is always best to seek out a setting that is licensed. (Licensing regulations vary from state to state and they can be found at places like the National Resource Center for Safe and Healthy Child Care, www.nrckids.org.)

IN CHOOSING A FAMILY CHILD CARE HOME

- Observe the caregiver's work.

- Look for signs of good quality care, such as hygienic diaper changing and safety measures.

In family child care, your child can be involved in many of the same household activities he'd find at your own home.

- Ask for references.

- Check certification and licensing compliance.

- Look over the home to ensure its safety.

- Find out how many children the provider has enrolled and during what hours.

- Inquire about substitute arrangements in case the caregiver is sick or cannot provide care.

- Request information on the caregiver's plans for emergency situations.

- Ask the provider what training he or she has.

- Ask if the provider's program is accredited by the National Association for Family Child Care.

HOW DO I FIND A FAMILY CHILD CARE PROVIDER?

- Ask friends for recommendations.

- Scan or place ads in the paper (especially local publications for parents).

- Contact a local resource and referral agency: www.naccrra.org or Child Care Aware at 1-800-424-2246.

AFTER CHOOSING A FAMILY CHILD CARE PROVIDER

- Monitor your child's adjustment and carefully observe interactions between the caregiver and your child.

- Keep the lines of communication open to address any issues that arise.

ADVANTAGES OF FAMILY CHILD CARE

1. In good family child care settings, there is a favorable child-to-adult ratio. In general, the total number of children to adults should be no more than about three children for one adult if some of the children are under the age of twenty-four months. (See page 397 for additional information on optimal child-staff ratios.)

2. Your child will have the comforts of being in a home and can be involved in many of the same household activities he'd find at home.

3. Your child will have social stimulation that comes from having playmates (when other children are present).

4. Family child care has the potential to be relatively flexible, so special arrangements can often be made to meet your child's individual interests and needs.

5. Your child may have more individualized attention and quiet time.

6. Your child may be exposed to fewer infectious diseases or less negative behavior from other children.

DISADVANTAGES OF FAMILY CHILD CARE

1. You cannot observe what happens to your child in your absence. While many providers carefully organize activities that are appropriate for children, others use the TV set as a babysitter—even letting children watch shows that are inappropriate for them.

2. Many family child care providers work without supervision or advice from other adults.

3. The caregiver might share the care of your child with relatives, boyfriends, or other people who might not give high-quality care.

Child Care Centers

Child care centers also may be called day care, child development centers, nursery schools, preschools, and other similar names. These facilities typically provide care for children in a nonresidential building with classrooms of children in different age groups. Most centers are licensed, caring for children from birth to six years old. Of the approximately 12 million children in child care in the US, about 9 million of them are in licensed facilities, and thus about 25 percent of children are cared for in unlicensed/unregulated facilities and settings. Centers demonstrate a higher commitment to quality by participating in the accreditation process.

There are several types of child care centers, most notably the following:

- *Chain centers* offer a wide variety of programs and very appealing activities for children. Because they are chains and run under central management, some do not offer any variation and room for individual creativity in their operations.

- *Independent for-profit centers* depend on enrollment fees to pay their overhead, and they typically earn a narrow profit for their owners. Because many of these programs are built around one or two dedicated people, they can be excellent—as long as those individuals remain actively involved in the daily operations.

- *Nonprofit centers* are sometimes linked to religious institutions, community centers, universities, or social service agencies, or they may be independently incorporated facilities. Some may have access to additional public funding, permitting discounted fees for lower-income families. Any income earned above expenses is put back into the program, directly benefiting the children.

- *Head Start* is a national child development program for children from birth to age five that provides services to promote academic, social, and emotional development, as well as providing social, health, and nutrition services for income-eligible families.

- *State-funded pre-kindergarten programs* are for four-year-olds, and are fully or partially funded by state education agencies. They are operated in schools or under the direction of state and local education agencies.

HOW DO I FIND A CHILD CARE CENTER?

- **Child care centers** are often listed on the Internet or in the phone book.

- **Ask your pediatrician** or other parents with children in child care to recommend a center.

- **Contact your community's** health or welfare agency, or a local or national resource and referral organization, such as Child Care Aware at www.childcareaware.org or 1-800-424-2246.

ADVANTAGES OF CHILD CARE CENTERS

1. More information is generally available about them since the majority of centers are regulated by licensing agencies.

2. Many centers have structured programs designed to meet children's developmental needs.

3. Most centers have several caregivers, so you are not dependent on the availability of just one person.

4. Workers in these centers have higher educational requirements and tend to be better supervised than caregivers in other settings.

5. Some centers may allow you to arrange shorter hours or fewer days of care if you work only part-time.

6. Many centers encourage parental involvement so you can help make the center better while your child is enrolled.

DISADVANTAGES OF CHILD CARE CENTERS

1. Regulations for child care centers vary widely based on the type of center.

2. Good programs may have waiting lists for admission because they are in such demand.

3. Due to the number of children cared for in this type of program, your child may receive less personalized attention than in a smaller program.

Making a Final Selection

When considering a particular child care setting, you need to know all of the rules and practices that would affect your child. If the program is formal enough to have a printed handbook, this may answer many of your questions. Otherwise, ask the program director about the following (some of which apply to in-home or family child care as well). Also see *Is This the Right Place for My Child?* in the Appendix to help you choose high-quality, nurturing care.

1. What are the hiring requirements for staff members? (Regulations vary from state to state.) In many good programs, caregivers must have at least two years of college, pass minimum health requirements, and receive basic immunizations. Ideally, they will have some background in early child development and perhaps have children themselves. Directors generally must have a college degree or many years of experience qualifying them as experts in both child development and administration. Staff members should also have training in CPR and first aid.

2. How many staff members are available per child? Although some children need highly personalized attention and others do well with less direct supervision, the general rule to follow is: The younger the child, the more adults there should be in each group. Each child should be assigned to one caregiver as the primary person responsible for that child's care, and that caregiver should provide most of the child's one-on-one care (e.g., feeding, diapering, putting the child to sleep).

The younger the child, the more adults there should be in each group.

3. How many children are in each group? Generally, smaller groups offer children a better chance to interact with and learn from one another. While fewer children per adult is usually better, there is a desirable maximum ratio and group size for each age category. The designated ratios vary from state to state, though, and some good facilities do not reach the ideal child-staff ratios. (Again, the chart *Is This the Right Place for My Child?* on page 886 of the Appendix provides these details.)

4. Is there a problem with frequent staff changes? If so, this may suggest that there are problems with the facility's operations. Ideally, most caregivers should have been with the program for several years, since consistency is desirable. Unfortunately, staff turnover in this profession is an issue for a variety of reasons, including low wages.

5. Are caregivers prohibited from smoking, even outside? This is important for your child's health.

6. Are caregivers required to have updated immunizations, including flu vaccines?

7. What are the goals of the program? Some are very organized and try to teach children new skills, or attempt to change or mold their behavior and beliefs. Others are very relaxed, with an emphasis on helping children develop at their own pace. Still others fall somewhere in between. Decide what you want for your child, and make sure the program you choose meets your desires. Avoid those that offer no personalized attention or support for your child.

8. What are the admission procedures? Quality child care programs require relevant background information on each child. Be prepared for very specific questions about your child's individual needs, developmental level, and health status. You also may be asked about your own child-rearing desires and any other children in your family.

9. Does the child care provider have a valid license and recent health certificate, and does the provider enforce health and immunization requirements for children in the program? Standard immunizations and regular checkups should be required for all children and staff members.

10. How are illnesses handled? Parents should be notified if a staff member or child contracts a significant communicable disease (not just a cold, but significant illnesses such as chickenpox or hepatitis). The program also should have a clear policy regarding sick children. You should know when to keep your child home and how the center will respond if he becomes ill during the day.

11. What are the costs? How much will you have to pay to start, and how often will you make installment payments? What do the payments cover specifically?

Will you need to pay when your child is absent for illness or vacations with the family?

12. What happens on a typical day? Ideally, there should be a mix of physical activity and quiet times. Some activities should be group-oriented and others individualized. Times for meals and snacks should be set aside. While a certain amount of structure is desirable, there also should be room for free play and special events.

13. How much parental involvement is expected? Some programs rely heavily on parent participation, while others request very little. At the least, quality programs should welcome your opinions and allow you to visit your child during the day. If the school maintains a closed-door policy for part or all of the day—typically for educational reasons—be sure that you are comfortable with this practice.

14. What are the general procedures? A well-organized program should have clearly defined rules and regulations regarding:

- Hours of operation

- Transportation of children

- Field trips

- Meals and snacks, whether they are provided by parents or are prepared on-site

- Administration of medication and first aid

- Emergency evacuations

- Notification of child's absence

- Weather cancellations

- Withdrawal of children from the program

- Supplies or equipment that parents must provide

- Sleep arrangements, especially for infants

- Special celebrations

- How parents may contact the staff during the day and at night

- Exclusion of children while they are sick with certain illnesses

- Security to ensure that everyone who enters the facility, including outdoor play areas, is screened by child care personnel, that strangers cannot enter the building, and that familiar adults who are acting oddly cannot get into any child care area, indoors or out

Once you've received this kind of basic information, you should take a tour of the building and grounds during operating hours to see how the caregivers interact with the children. Your first impressions are especially important, since they'll influence all your future dealings with the program. If you sense warmth and a loving approach to the children, you'll probably feel comfortable placing your own child there. If you see a worker spank or restrain one of the youngsters too forcefully, you should reconsider sending your own child, even if that's the only sign of abusive behavior you've noticed.

Try to observe the daily routine, paying attention to how the day is organized and what activities are planned for the children. Watch how food is prepared, and find out how often the children are fed. Check how frequently the children are taken to the toilet and/or diapered. While touring the child care home or center, also check to see if the following basic health and safety standards are being met:

- The premises are clean and reasonably neat (without discouraging play by the children).

- There is plenty of play equipment, and it is in good repair.

- The equipment is appropriate for the developmental skills of the children in the program.

- Children are closely supervised when climbing on playthings, roughhousing, or playing with blocks (which are sometimes thrown) and other potentially dangerous toys.

- Food is stored in an appropriate manner and if the child care site is preparing the food, that it is nutritious.

- Areas where food is handled are clearly separate from toilets and diaper-changing areas.

Napping in Child Care Settings

Sudden infant death syndrome (SIDS) has gotten plenty of attention in recent years, and many parents now know the importance of placing a baby to sleep on his back to minimize the risk of SIDS. Obviously, this same precaution should be followed in child care settings, where 20 percent of all SIDS cases occur—a disproportionately high amount. Although the American Academy of Pediatrics stresses the importance of using the back-sleeping position to lower the incidence of SIDS during child care, not all states in the United States have licensing regulations mandating that child care facilities place infants on their backs to sleep.

If your baby is going to be napping at his child care site, you must discuss this issue with the caregivers before making a final selection about a facility. Make sure that the child care setting you choose routinely follows this simple procedure. (For more information about SIDS, see page 195.)

One other important napping recommendation: For older children, make sure that bedding is clean and hypoallergenic.

Additional information about crib safety is available on pages 31–33.

■ Diaper-changing areas are cleaned and sanitized before and after being used for each child.

Hand-washing sinks are available where they are needed and are used not only by the children, but also by the staff members during the following:

While touring the child care home or center, also check to see if basic health and safety standards are being met.

- Upon arrival for the day

- When moving from one child care group to another

- Before and after eating or touching food or food preparation surfaces

- Before and after giving medication

- Before and after playing in water that is used by more than one person

- After diapering

- After using the toilet or helping children use the toilet

- After handling any body fluid, such as nasal discharge, blood, vomit, drool, or sores

- After playing in sandboxes

- After handling garbage

- Potty (or training) chairs are avoided in order to decrease the risk of spreading germs that cause diarrhea.

- Children are supervised by sight and sound at all times, even when napping.

Once you're satisfied that a particular program will provide your child with a safe, loving, healthy environment, let him test it out while you're present. Watch how the caregivers and your child interact, and make sure that all of you are comfortable with the situation.

Building a Relationship with Your Child's Care Providers

For your child's sake, you need to develop a good relationship with the person or people who care for him in your absence. The better you get along with his caregiver, the more comfortable your child will feel as he interacts with both of you. The better you communicate with the caregiver about your child, the more continuity there will be in his care throughout the day.

One way to build this relationship is by talking with the caregiver—even briefly—each time you leave or return for your child. If something exciting or upsetting happened during the early morning, it might affect your child's behavior during the rest of the day, so the caregiver should know about it. Share family stresses, both good and bad, like expecting the birth of a new sibling or a family illness.

When you arrive to take him home, you should be told about any important events that occurred in your absence, from a change in bowel movements or eating patterns to a new way of playing or his first steps. Also, if he's showing symptoms of a developing illness, you and the caregiver should discuss the situation and agree on what to do if symptoms get worse.

A rivalry may develop between you and the caregiver for your child's affection and control of his behavior. For example, you may hear "Funny, he never does that for me" when he misbehaves. Don't take this seriously—children usually save their worst behavior for the people they trust most.

If you treat caregivers as partners, they will feel that you respect them and probably will be more enthusiastic about looking after your child. Here are some ways to build this sense of partnership on a daily basis.

- **Show the caregiver** something that your child has made at home, or talk about things he's done that are particularly funny or interesting. Explain that sharing this kind of information is important to you, and encourage two-way communication.

- **Extend basic courtesy** to your child's caregivers.

- **Provide materials and** suggestions for special projects the caregivers can do with your child and/or the group, or ask if there are ways you can help with already planned activities.

- **Help out before** you leave your child by spending a few minutes getting him settled. If he's in a child care center, help him put away his things and join an activity. If he is being cared for at home, get him involved in an activity before you depart. Make sure your child always knows you are leaving. Say good-bye before you disappear, but leave without prolonging your departure. Don't just "slip away."

- **Help plan and** carry out special activities with the caregiver.

Periodically, you and the caregiver also should have longer discussions to review your child's progress, discuss any problems, and plan for future changes in your child's care. Schedule these extended conversations at a time when you won't be rushing to get somewhere, your child's caregiver isn't busy tending to other children, or the two of you aren't at a place where there will be distrac-

Tips for Transitioning

Getting the day started can be a challenge. So here are some suggestions to make your separation at the child care setting a little easier for both of you.

Your Child's Developmental Stage	Your Response

0 to 7 months

In early infancy your baby primarily needs love, comforting, and good basic care to satisfy his physical needs.

Although this period may be a difficult time of separation for you, young infants generally will transition to a consistent child care worker in almost any setting. Be patient during this initial settling-in period.

7 to 12 months

Stranger anxiety normally occurs at this time. Suddenly your baby may be reluctant to stay with anyone outside his family. The unfamiliar setting of a child care center also may upset him.

If possible, do not start child care during this period, or just ease into it. If your child is already in a program, take a little extra time each day before you say good-bye. Create a short good-bye ritual, perhaps letting him hold a favorite stuffed animal. Say good-bye and then quietly leave. Above all, be consistent from day to day.

12 to 24 months

This is when separation anxiety peaks and your child has the most difficulty with your leaving. He may not believe that you will return, and may weep and cling to you as you try to leave.

Be understanding but firm and persistent. Reassure him that you will return when you're done with work or have finished your errands. Once you have left, do not reappear unless you are prepared to stay or take your child home.

tions. If possible, arrange for someone else to care for your child while you are talking. Allow enough time to discuss all the facts and opinions that both of you have on your minds, and agree on specific objectives and plans.

Most parents find that this discussion goes more smoothly if they've made a list of important topics beforehand. You also should start the conversation on a positive note by talking about some of the things the caregiver is doing that please you. Then move on to any concerns. After presenting your own thoughts, ask for her opinions and listen carefully. Remember, there is little that's strictly right or wrong when it comes to child rearing, and most situations have several "right" approaches. Be open-minded and flexible in your discussion. Close the conversation with a specific plan of action and follow-up communication. Both of you will be more comfortable if something concrete comes out of the meeting, even if it's only a decision to stay on the same course for another month or two.

Resolving Conflicts

Let's assume that you've chosen a child care setting carefully. So what can you now expect?

Most parents are pleased with the child care they've chosen. Nevertheless, whenever two or more people share responsibility for a child, conflicts sometimes arise. In many cases, you can resolve a disagreement about child care simply by talking through the problem. You may find that the conflict is nothing more than a misunderstanding or a misreading of the situation. Other times, especially when several people are involved in the care of your child, you may need a more organized approach to resolving problems. The following step-by-step strategy can help.

The better you get along with her caregiver, the more comfortable your child will feel as she interacts with both of you.

1. Define the problem clearly. Make sure you understand who is involved, but avoid blaming anyone. For example, what if your child has been bitten by, or is biting, other children in his child care program? Find out which caregivers were on hand at the time. Ask what they observed and focus your attention on what realistic measures can be taken to prevent or decrease the likelihood of further incidents. Maybe you can suggest an alternate way in which the caregivers can respond if the incident recurs.

2. Listen to everyone's ideas in order to find other possible solutions.

3. Agree on a specific plan of action with clearly defined time limits and assignments to each of the caregivers—including you.

4. Consider everything that could go wrong with the plan you've devised, and decide how these problems might be avoided or handled if they occur.

5. Put the plan into action.

6. Meet again at a specified time to decide whether the plan is working. If it's not, go through the process again to decide what changes need to be made.

What to Do When Your Child Is Sick

If your child is like most others, he'll get his share of illnesses, whether he's in a child care program or not. In most cases these illnesses will be colds or other respiratory infections, which tend to occur more often between early fall and late spring. At times he may get one infection right after another and be sick for weeks. If both parents have full-time jobs, this can be a big problem and cause a great deal of stress since often one of the parents will need to stay home with the ill child.

Even children who seem to be only mildly ill may be sent home from child care programs, and, if based on good policies, for good reason. A sick child may be contagious and risks giving his illness to another child. Also, a sick child may need more individual care and attention than a child care provider or program can reasonably be expected to provide without interfering with the care of others.

States often have regulations that actually require child care programs to send sick children home. This makes sense, particularly when a child has a fever and is acting sick, is sneezing or coughing, is vomiting, or has diarrhea, since it is under those circumstances that contagious diseases are spread to others. The ultimate goal is both to provide your child with the care he needs and to limit the spread of contagious illnesses in the child care setting.

Ideally, you'll be able to stay home when your child is sick. However, there may be times when this option is particularly difficult or simply not possible. Be sure to talk to your employer ahead of time to see what arrangements you can make in the event that your child is ill. You might suggest telecommuting and taking your work home with you, or try to identify in advance coworkers who can substitute for you when this situation arises. Spouses, other family members, and trusted friends may be able to help in caring for your child.

If your job and your spouse's employer require full-time attendance, you'll have to make other arrangements for a sick child. These are days when you might arrange alternate care for him, preferably where both the caregiver and the setting are familiar. If you rely on a relative or hire a sitter to stay with him, make sure the caregiver understands the nature of the illness and how it should be treated.

If your child requires any medication, confirm your child care provider's policies regarding giving medication to children, and always obtain written instructions from your pediatrician to give to your caregiver. Don't expect your caregiver to follow your instructions without a pediatrician's authorization. Also, both prescription and over-the-counter medications should have a pharmacy or drugstore label on them with the child's name, the medication dosage, and the expiration date. Giving medication to children is a significant responsibility, and can be quite a challenge for caregivers. It should be requested only when it is necessary.

Your child's caregiver will need to know why the medication is being given, how it should be stored and administered (in what doses, at what intervals, and for how long), and what side effects to look for and what to do if they occur. Again, this should all be put in writing. Explain that medicine should not be disguised as food or described as candy; instead, your child should be told what the medicine is and why he needs to take it. Ask the caregiver to record the time each dose is given.

If your child is in a child care center, you should be prepared to sign a consent form, authorizing the staff to administer the medication. Also, you should expect your child's medications to be sent home each evening (since regulations typically do not allow them to be kept in the child care facility overnight).

A few communities have services that specialize in care for mildly ill children. These include the following:

HOME-BASED PROGRAMS

- Family child care homes that are equipped to care for both sick and well children. If a child becomes ill in such a program, he can continue attending in a segregated area, if necessary. Not all infections are contagious.

- Family child care homes that care only for sick children. Some of these are associated with well-child care centers.

- Agencies or child care centers that provide caregivers who can work in your home.

- Regular child care centers that have trained staff members to care for sick children in the usual child care setting, but apart from the main group of well children.

- Centers that offer a separate "get-well room" for sick children, staffed by a caregiver.

- Sick-child care centers that are set up specifically to care for ill children.

In sick-child programs, caregivers adjust the activity level of the youngsters to the child's ability to participate, and the children receive a lot of cuddling and personal attention. These programs should pay extra attention to hygiene for both caregivers and children. The premises and equipment, especially toys, should be cleaned thoroughly and often. Disposable toys may be necessary in some situations, depending on the nature of the illnesses involved. A pediatrician and public health consultant should be on call for every sick-child care facility.

Controlling Infectious Diseases

Whenever children gather in groups, their risk of getting sick increases. Infants and toddlers are particularly affected, since they can be expected to place their toys and their hands in their mouths, making it even easier to spread infectious diseases.

While it's impossible for adults to keep toys and other objects in the child care center in perfect sanitary condition, many precautions and practices can help control the spread of infection. Child care programs should be extremely careful about maintaining good hygiene. Children and teachers should have easy access to sinks. They should be reminded, and children should be assisted if necessary, to wash their hands after going to the bathroom. Staff members also should wash at all the times listed earlier in this chapter, and especially after changing diapers. Both the caregiver's and the child's hands should at least be wiped during diaper changing after removing the soiled diaper, and then both should wash their hands at the end of the diaper change routine. Hand-washing after blowing or wiping noses and before handling food or food surfaces can also significantly reduce the spread of infection.

If a center cares for infants, toddlers, and toilet-trained children, each of these groups should have a separate area, each with its own accessible sink for hand-washing. The facility and all equipment should be cleaned at least daily. Changing tables and toilets should be washed and disinfected.

As a parent, you can help control the spread of disease in your child's center by keeping him at home when he has an illness that's contagious or requires extra attention. Also notify his caregiver as soon as anyone in your family is diagnosed as having a particular illness, and request that all parents be alerted when any child in the program has a serious or highly contagious infectious illness.

Immunizations can greatly reduce outbreaks of serious infectious diseases. Centers should require children to be immunized (at appropriate ages) against hepatitis B, rotavirus, diphtheria, tetanus, pertussis, polio, influenza (flu), *Haemophilus influenzae* type b, pneumococcus, measles, mumps, rubella, hepatitis A, and chickenpox (also, the meningococcal vaccine is available for certain high-risk children). The immunity of your child's caregivers should be checked as well, and if there is any doubt, they should receive appropriate immunizations.

Remember, teach your child proper hygiene and hand-washing habits so that he's less likely to spread illnesses himself. Finally, educate yourself about the illnesses that are most common in child care settings, so you know what to expect and how to respond if they occur in your child's program. These include the following.

Colds and Flu

Children in child care typically have an average of seven to nine colds each year, and are more likely to get these infections than infants cared for at home. Fortunately, the chances of contracting some of the most severe illnesses or complications associated with the common cold can be decreased by immunizing children with the vaccines mentioned earlier. In child care centers, toys, tables, doorknobs, and other surfaces that are touched by hands should be sanitized frequently.

Colds are spread by direct or close contact with the mouth or nose secretions of an infected individual, or by touching contaminated objects. In child care settings, children can be taught to wash their hands frequently, and when that's not possible, to "give their sneezes the cold shoulder" by sneezing into their upper arm rather than their hands. They also should be taught proper disposal of tissues and not to share cups or eating utensils. (For more information about colds and flu, see pages 659–662 and pages 602–605, respectively.)

Cytomegalovirus (CMV) and Parvovirus Infection

Cytomegalovirus and parvovirus usually do not cause any (or cause only mild) illness in children and adults. However, these viruses can be dangerous to a pregnant woman who is not immune to them, because an infection sometimes can cause a serious infection in her unborn child. The infection can be transmitted through direct contact with body fluids (tears, urine, saliva). Fortunately, most adult women are already immune to these diseases, but if you are pregnant, have a child in child care, or work in a child care home or center yourself, you have an increased risk of exposure to CMV and parvovirus, and you should discuss this concern with your obstetrician.

Diarrheal Diseases

The average child has one or two episodes of diarrhea a year. These illnesses can spread easily in child care homes and centers. If your child has diarrhea, do not take him to child care unless all of his stool can be controlled by using the toilet. Children with loose stools who wear diapers or who cannot make sure that all of their stool ends up in the toilet should not be in child care unless your pediatrician has determined that the cause is not infectious. If he has a mild form of the illness, then several days away from the center should minimize the chances that he'll transmit it to other children. But if a more serious cause is suspected, further tests to identify the responsible agent (bacteria, virus, or parasite) may need to be done before the child returns. (See *Diarrhea*, page 530.)

Eye and Skin Infections

Conjunctivitis (pinkeye), impetigo, lice, ringworm, scabies, and cold sores are common problems in young children (lice and ringworm are described below). These afflictions of the skin and mucous membranes can be spread by touching a person on the affected area. The child care staff should notify you if this kind of problem occurs in any child in the program, so you can watch for symptoms in your own child. If these symptoms do appear, contact your pediatrician for early diagnosis and possible treatment. (See *Eye Infections*, page 728; *Impetigo*, page 841; *Ringworm*, page 846; *Scabies*, page 849; *Herpes Simplex* [cold sores], page 670.)

Head Lice

Head lice are small, tan-colored insects (less than one-eighth-inch long) that live on blood that they draw from the scalp. Although families and caregivers often become very upset about lice, they do not carry disease, but they can cause symptoms like itching on the scalp or neck.

Lice are spread by direct contact with infested hair. By using medications that kill lice and nits, the infestation in the hair can be controlled. After a child has received treatment, he can participate in child care where he will come in contact with other children. (Also see *Head Lice,* page 839.)

Hepatitis A Virus

Because of the success of the hepatitis A vaccine, this infection in child care settings is less common than it once was.

If a child in a care program gets hepatitis A, a viral infection of the liver, it can spread easily to other children and caregivers. In infants and preschool children, most infections are asymptomatic or cause mild, nonspecific symptoms. Older infected children may have only mild fever, nausea, vomiting, diarrhea, or jaundice (a yellowish skin color). However, adults who get this illness usually experience these symptoms to a much greater degree.

Hepatitis can be controlled through gamma globulin injections, but several staff members and parents may be infected before anyone realizes there's a problem. (See *Hepatitis,* page 542.)

Hepatitis B Virus

Infants receive the hepatitis B vaccine shortly after birth to protect them from catching this virus. The virus can be acquired during birth from an infected mother or after birth by exposure to infected blood such as during a needle stick. This type of exposure to blood rarely occurs in a child care setting; thus, there is no need to exclude a child with hepatitis B infection from group child care. (Also see descriptions of hepatitis B and the vaccine on pages 542–545.)

Human Immunodeficiency Virus (HIV)/AIDS

HIV (the AIDS virus) can produce a serious chronic infection, and children acquire HIV from their infected mothers before or during birth. HIV also can be transmitted from one child to another by passage of blood from an infected child into the body of someone not infected. There is no need to restrict placing an HIV-infected child in child care in the belief that this would protect others, since the risk of HIV transmission in this setting is extremely low when standard appropriate blood and body fluid precautions are used.

If an injury involving blood occurs, the caregiver should put on gloves and wash the wound, administer first aid, and apply a bandage. All blood-contaminated surfaces or clothing should be washed and disinfected. Diluted bleach kills HIV.

Also, since human milk can transmit HIV and other viruses, be sure that the child care facility has procedures to prevent feeding milk of one mother to another mother's child. If such an incident occurs, the situation should be handled following the national standards described in *Caring for Our Children* (published by the National Resource Center for Health and Safety in Child Care and Early Education: http://nrc.uchsc.edu). (Also see descriptions of HIV on pages 630–634.)

Ringworm

Ringworm is a mildly contagious fungal infection, causing red, circular patches with raised edges. On the scalp, ringworm can lead to patchy areas of dandruff-like scaling. Ringworm is spread by direct person-to-person contact by sharing combs, brushes, towels, clothing, or bedding. To control the infection, children should be treated early with medication. Once treatment is started, children can return to child care settings. (See also *Ringworm,* page 846.)

Preventing Injuries and Promoting Car Safety

Many injuries that occur at home or in child care settings are predictable and preventable. These issues are described earlier in this chapter on pages 447–452 in sections on assessing and selecting child care for your child. Safety for children (and adults) in and around cars is a special concern. The center should have well-marked pickup and drop-off points where children and adults are protected from street traffic, with signs such as CHILDREN AT PLAY placed in the pickup/drop-off areas as well as along nearby streets. The center should never allow a child to be in these areas, or in any area where cars come and go, unless he is being picked up or dropped off and is accompanied by an adult. Children also should never be permitted behind vehicles that could move and back over them. Also keep in mind that adults may need assistance when dealing with more than one child in the car. Cars should also not be left running, and should always be driven slowly.

If your child shares a ride to and from child care, be sure the other drivers have good driving records, and are using appropriate car safety seats for all children in their vehicles. The driver must check the vehicle to be sure that everyone is properly buckled in a car safety seat before pulling away and that everyone has left the vehicle before locking up at the parking spot. School buses and vans also need to follow measures that ensure the safety of children while they are being transported (see page 465).

Car-Pool Safety

If you drive children in a car pool, you must be as responsible for every child in the car as you are for your own. This means making sure that everyone is properly restrained in car safety seats appropriate for his size, not overloading the car, disciplining children who disobey safety rules, and checking that your insurance covers everyone on board. In addition, make sure that you and other drivers observe the following precautions, many of which will apply even when you, your spouse, or other family member (e.g., grandparent) are driving only your own child to his care setting.

- Pick up and drop off children only at the curb or in a driveway where the children are protected from other cars. They should be dropped off on the same side of the street as the school to avoid having them cross the street in traffic areas. There are too many vehicle-pedestrian collisions involving children crossing the street where there is no specific crosswalk or crossing guard.

- If possible, have each child's own parents or another responsible adult buckle him into the car and take him out when he returns home.

- Turn all children over to the direct supervision of a parent or child care staff member.

- Close and lock all car doors, but only after checking that fingers and feet are inside.

- Open passenger windows only a few inches, and lock all power window and door controls from the driver's seat if possible.

- Remind children about safety rules and proper behavior before starting out.

- Plan your routes to minimize travel time and avoid hazardous conditions.

- Pull over if any child in the group gets out of control or misbehaves. If any child consistently presents a problem, discuss the difficulty with his parents and exclude him from the car pool until his conduct improves.

- Have available emergency contact information for each child who rides in the car.

- Ideally, equip each vehicle with a fire extinguisher and first-aid kit.

- Be sure that no child is ever left in the car without a supervising adult.

If your child care program includes swimming, make sure appropriate safety precautions are followed. Any pool, lake, creek, or pond used by children should first be checked by public health authorities. If the pool is at or near the child care center itself, it should be entirely surrounded by at least a four-foot-high, four-sided childproof fence with a self-closing locked gate that completely separates the center from the pool. For hygienic and safety reasons, portable wading pools should be avoided.

Care for Children with Special Needs

If your child has a developmental disability or a chronic illness, don't let that keep him out of preschool or child care. In fact, quality child care may be good for him. He is likely to benefit from the social contact, physical exercise, and variety of experiences of a group program. Although the most common special health needs include asthma and allergies, there are a variety of developmental and behavioral issues that also fall into this category.

The time your child spends in a child care program will be good for you, too. Tending a child with special needs often places great demands on time, energy, and emotions. The challenge is to find a program that encourages normal childhood activities and at the same time meets his special needs; however, these are more widely available than in the past.

WHERE WE STAND

TO ENSURE THE SAFETY of children while they are being transported to school, the American Academy of Pediatrics strongly recommends that all children travel in age-appropriate and properly secured child restraint systems in all motor vehicles.

The AAP has had a long-standing position that new school buses should have safety restraints. Parents should work with school districts to encourage that every new bus be equipped with lap/shoulder seat belt restraints that also can accommodate car safety seats, booster seats, and harness systems. School districts should provide height- and weight-appropriate car safety seats and restraint systems for all children of preschool age; these systems include booster seats with a three-point belt.

When districts have policies on seat belt use, children tend to be better behaved and they are less likely to distract the driver.

School Transportation Safety

Whether you and your child rely on a bus or on alternative vehicles (such as vans) to take him to school, preschool, or child care, specific safety measures must be taken to protect him on that daily commute. The box on page 464, *Where We Stand*, describes the American Academy of Pediatrics' strong recommendation of the use of lap/shoulder seat belts on school buses. Also, make sure your child understands that on the school bus, he should:

- **Stay seated on the bus, never moving around once he's found and taken a seat.**

- **Always remain within view of the bus driver.**

- **Follow the instructions of the driver.**

- **Talk softly with classmates so the driver can concentrate.**

- **Never stick his hands, books, or other objects out the window.**

Safety is also important not only while your child is on the bus, but also *before* he boards and *after* he is dropped off at school or home. For example, he should:

- **Walk to the bus stop with you or another responsible adult.**

- **Arrive at the bus stop five minutes before the bus arrives so he won't need to rush.**

- **Wait for the bus to stop before approaching it to board.**

- **Tell the driver if he has dropped something near the bus; he shouldn't try to pick it up himself until he tells the driver that the item is there.**

- **Take his time while boarding and leaving the bus.**

- **Look both ways for traffic before crossing the street—looking to the left, then the right, and then the left again.**

(For other guidelines on car safety, see page 372.)

Federal law (the Individuals with Disabilities Education Act [IDEA], formerly known as the Amendments to the Education for All Handicapped Children Act) requires all states to develop special education programs for preschool (three- to five-year-old) children with developmental disabilities. This act also gives states the option to develop special education programs for infants and toddlers with developmental disabilities or delays. Parents should check with their pediatrician or their state education or health department regarding the availability of these early intervention programs.

Safety Walk Checklist

Next time you walk through your child's child care home or center, use the following checklist to make sure the facility is safe, clean, and in good repair. If there is a problem with any item on the list, bring it to the attention of the director or caregiver and follow up later to be sure it was corrected.

Indoors in All Programs

- Floors are smooth, clean, and have a nonskid surface.
- Medicines, cleaning agents, and tools are locked up and out of children's sight and reach.
- First-aid kit is fully supplied and out of children's reach.
- Windowsills, walls, and ceilings are clean and in good repair, with no peeling paint or damaged plaster. (Windowsills are the highest risk areas for lead poisoning.)
- Children are never left unattended.
- Electrical outlets are covered with childproof caps that are not a choking hazard.
- Electric lights are in good repair, with no frayed or dangling cords.
- Be especially careful about batteries being left around, particularly button batteries, which can be very damaging to the GI tract if swallowed.
- Heating pipes and radiators are out of reach or covered so children cannot touch them.
- Ask if the hot water is set at or below 120 degrees Fahrenheit (48.9 degrees Celsius) to lessen the risk of a scald burn.
- There are no poisonous plants or disease-bearing animals (e.g., turtles or iguanas).

■ Trash containers are covered.

■ Exits are clearly marked and easy to reach.

■ No smoking is allowed in the child care facility.

■ Windows at or above the second story have guards on them to prevent falls; and all window blind or drapery cords are secured out of children's reach. If possible, it is best to use cordless window products.

■ Leaks are fixed promptly and any mold is properly treated.

Outdoors in All Programs

■ Grounds are free of litter, sharp objects, and animal droppings.

■ Play equipment is smooth, well anchored, and free of rust, splinters, and sharp corners. All screws and bolts are capped or concealed.

■ Outdoor playground equipment is mounted over impact-absorbent surfaces for a distance of at least 6 feet (1.8 m) on all sides of the equipment. Playground surfaces should be made of at least 12 inches (30 cm) of wood chips, mulch, sand, pea gravel, or other impact-absorbing material under and around areas where falls are more likely to occur (under monkey bars, slides).

■ Swing seats are lightweight and flexible, and there are no open or S-shaped hooks.

■ Slides have wide, flat, stable steps with good treads, rounded rims along the sides to prevent falls, and a flat area at the end of the slide to help children slow down.

■ Metal slides are shaded from the sun.

■ Sandboxes are covered when not in use.

■ Childproof barriers keep children out of hazardous areas.

Infant and Toddler Programs

■ Toys do not contain lead or have any signs of chipping paint, rust, or small pieces that could break off. (The weight or softness of the material may provide clues that the toys are made of lead.)

- High chairs have wide bases and safety straps.

- Toddlers are not allowed to walk around with bottles or to take bottles to bed.

- Infant walkers are not used.

- Cribs, portable play yards, and beds meet safety standards.

- No recalled products or old products with broken or missing parts are used. Recalled products can be determined by checking the website of the Consumer Product Safety Commission: www.cpsc .gov. Caregivers can subscribe to e-mail alerts from the CPSC that will alert them when any toy or other children's product is recalled.

Start your search with your pediatrician by asking about the best type of group programs for your child to participate in. Also ask her for referrals to suitable centers. Your pediatrician can help you draft an individualized "care plan" to address your child's special health care needs and help your child care providers understand what your child will need. Although only one appropriate site may be available in some smaller communities, you will have several to choose from in many communities. The one you select should meet the same basic requirements outlined earlier in this chapter for other child care programs, plus the following.

1. The program should include children with and without chronic illnesses and special needs, to the extent possible. Having relationships with typically

If your child has a developmental disability or chronic illness, don't let that keep him out of child care.

developing playmates helps a child with a disability feel more relaxed and confident socially, and helps build his self-esteem. The arrangement also benefits the typically developing child and those with no special health needs by teaching them to look past the surface differences and helping them develop sensitivity and respect for all people.

2. The staff should be trained to provide the specific care your child requires. Some of the training needs can be specified in your child's care plan.

3. The program should have at least one physician consultant who is active in the development of policies and procedures affecting the type of special needs present among the children in the group. Your own pediatrician should also play an active role. Give permission for your child care providers to discuss questions and issues with your pediatrician.

4. All children should be encouraged to be as independent as their abilities allow, within the bounds of safety. They should be restricted only in activities that might be dangerous for them or that have been prohibited by doctor's orders.

5. The program should be flexible enough to adapt to slight variations in the children's abilities. For example, this may include altering some equipment or facilities for physically challenged or visually or hearing-impaired children.

6. The program should offer special equipment and activities to meet the special needs of children, such as breathing treatments for children with asthma. The equipment should be in good repair, and the staff should be trained to operate it correctly.

7. The staff should be familiar with each child's medical and developmental status. The staff should be able to recognize symptoms and determine when the child needs medical attention.

8. If the program includes off-site field trips or activities, the staff should be trained in safe transportation of children with special needs.

9. The staff should know how to reach each child's physician in an emergency and should be qualified to administer any necessary emergency medications. Emergency planning should be specified in the child's care plan.

These are very general recommendations. Because special needs vary so widely, it's impossible to tell you more precisely how to determine the best program for your own child. If you're having trouble deciding among the programs your pediatrician has suggested, go back and discuss your concerns with her. She will work with you to make the right choice.

Whatever your child's special needs, how he will be cared for in your absence is an important decision. The information you have just read should help. However, remember that you know your child better than anyone, so rely most heavily on your needs and impressions when choosing or changing a child care arrangement.

~ 15 ~

Keeping Your Child Safe

EVERYDAY LIFE IS full of well-disguised dangers for children: sharp objects, shaky furniture, reachable hot water faucets, pots on burning stoves, hot tubs, swimming pools, and busy streets. By adulthood we've learned to navigate this minefield so well that we no longer think of things like scissors and stoves as hazards. To protect your child from the dangers she'll encounter in and out of your home, you have to see the world as she does, and you must recognize that she cannot yet distinguish hot from cold or sharp from dull.

Keeping your child physically safe is your most basic responsibility—and a never-ending one. Unintentional injuries are the number-one cause of death and disability in children over the age of one. Each year, children experience over 6 million emergency department visits because of unintentional injury and over four thousand under the age of fifteen die. As might be expected, car crashes account for a large number of the injuries and deaths.

Many children are injured and killed by equipment designed specifically for their use. In one recent twelve-month period, high chair–related injuries sent almost 10,000 children to the hospital. In 2001, toys caused more than 200,000 injuries serious enough to require treatment in hospital emergency rooms in children under the age of fifteen. Even cribs account for about 32 deaths annually.

These are worrisome numbers, but we can prevent many injuries. In the past, injuries were called "accidents" because they seemed unpredictable and unavoidable. Today we know that injuries are not random. By understanding how a child grows and develops, and the risk of injury at each developmental stage, parents can take precautions that will prevent most, if not all, of these injuries.

Why Children Get Injured

Every childhood injury involves three elements: factors related to the child, the object that causes the injury, and the environment in which it occurs. To keep your child safe, you must be aware of all three.

Let's start with your child. His age makes a tremendous difference in the kind of protection he needs. The three-month-old who sits cooing in an infant seat requires quite different supervision from that needed by the ten-month-old who's started walking or the toddler who has learned to climb. So at each stage of your child's life, you must think again about the hazards that are present and what you can do to eliminate them. Repeatedly, as your child grows, you must ask: How far can he move and how quickly? How high can he reach? What objects attract his attention? What can he do today that he couldn't do yesterday? What will he do tomorrow that he can't do today?

During the first six months of life, you can secure your child's safety by never leaving him alone, even for a moment, in a dangerous situation such as on a bed or changing table where he might wiggle or roll off. As he grows, he'll create dangers of his own—perhaps by first rolling or crawling off the bed, then by creeping into places he shouldn't be, and finally by actively seeking out things to touch and taste that may be dangerous.

As your child begins to move about, you certainly will tell him "no" whenever he approaches something potentially hazardous, but he will not really understand the significance of your message. Many parents find the ages between six months and eighteen months extremely frustrating, because the child doesn't seem to learn from these reprimands. Even if you tell him twenty times a day to stay away from the toilet, he's still in the bathroom every time you turn your back. At this age your child is not being willfully disobedient; his memory just isn't developed enough for him to recall your warning the next time he's attracted by the forbidden object or activity. What looks like naughtiness is actually the testing and retesting of reality—the normal way of learning for a child of this age.

The second year is also risky for children because their physical abilities exceed their capacities to understand the consequences of their actions. Although your child's judgment will improve, his sense of danger won't be intense enough and his self-control won't be developed enough to make him stop once he's spotted something interesting. At this point, even the things he can't see will interest him, so his curiosity may take him to the bottom shelf of the refrigerator, into the medicine cabinet, and under the sink—to touch things and perhaps to taste.

Young children are extraordinary mimics, so they may try to take medicine just as they've seen Mom doing, or they may play with a razor just like Dad. Unfortunately, their notions of cause and effect aren't as advanced as their motor skills. Yes, your child may realize that tugging on the cord pulled the iron down on his head after it falls, but his ability to anticipate many similar consequences is still months away.

Gradually, between the ages of two and four, your child will develop a more mature sense of himself as a person who makes things happen—he flips a switch, for instance, and the light goes on. Although this thinking eventually will help children avoid dangerous situations, at this age they are so self-involved that they are likely to see only their own part in the action. A child whose ball rolls into the street will think only about retrieving the ball, not about the danger of being hit by a car.

The risks of this kind of thinking are obvious. And the risks are compounded by something the experts call magical thinking, which means that at this age a child behaves as if his wishes and expectations actually control what happens. A four-year-old, for example, may light a match because he wants to create the beautiful bonfire he saw on television last night. It probably won't occur to him that the fire could get out of control; but even if it did, he might discount the idea because it isn't his idea of what *should* happen.

This type of self-centered, magical thinking is entirely normal at this age. But because of it, you must be twice as careful about your child's safety until he outgrows this stage. You can't expect your two- to four-year-old to understand fully that his actions can have harmful consequences for himself or for others. He may, for example, throw sand at a playmate partly because it amuses him and partly because he wants it to be fun. Either way, he will find it difficult to understand that his friend is not enjoying the game.

For all these reasons, you must establish and consistently enforce rules related to safety during the early preschool years. Explain the reasons behind the rules: "You can't throw stones, because you'll hurt your friend"; "Never run into the street, because you could be hit by a car." But don't expect these reasons to persuade your child—or for him to consistently remember the rules. Repeat the rule itself every time your child is on the verge of breaking it until he understands that unsafe actions are always unacceptable. For most children, it takes dozens of repetitions before even the most fundamental safety rules are remembered. So be patient. In addition, even if he seems to understand, he is too young for you to assume he will always follow the rules. Make sure you still watch him very closely.

Your child's temperament also may determine his vulnerability. Studies suggest that children who are extremely active and unusually curious have more than their share of injuries. At certain stages of development, your child is likely to be stubborn, easily frustrated, aggressive, or unable to concentrate— all characteristics associated with injuries. So when you notice that your child is having a bad day or is going through a difficult phase, be especially alert: That's when he's most likely to test safety rules, even those he ordinarily follows.

Since you can't change your child's age, and you have little influence over his basic temperament, most of your efforts to prevent injury should focus on objects and surroundings. By designing an environment in which the obvious hazards have been removed, you can allow your young child the freedom he needs to explore.

Some parents feel they don't need to childproof their homes because they intend to supervise their children closely. And in fact, with constant vigilance, most injuries *can* be avoided. But even the most conscientious parents can't watch a child every moment. Most injuries occur not when parents are alert and at their best, but when they are under stress. The following situations are often associated with injuries:

- Hunger and fatigue (e.g., the hour or so before dinner)

- Mother's pregnancy

- Illness or death in the family

- Changes in the child's regular caregiver

- Tension between parents

- Sudden changes in the environment, such as moving to a new home or going on vacation

All families experience at least some of these stresses some of the time. Childproofing eliminates or reduces the opportunities for injury so that even when you are momentarily distracted—for example, by the ring of the telephone or doorbell—your child is less likely to encounter situations and objects that can cause him harm.

The pages that follow include advice about how to minimize dangers in and out of the home. The intention is to alert you to hazards—particularly those that, on the surface, might seem harmless—so you can take the sensible precautions that will keep your child safe and allow him the freedom he needs to grow up happy and healthy.

Safety Inside Your Home

Room to Room

Your lifestyle and the layout of your home will determine which rooms should be childproofed. Examine every room in which your child spends any time. (For most families, that means the entire house.) It's tempting to exclude a formal dining or living room that remains behind closed doors when not in use; but remember, the rooms that are forbidden to your child are the ones she'll want most to explore as soon as she's old enough. Any areas not childproofed will require extra vigilance on your part, even if their entrances are normally locked or blocked.

At the very least, your child's room should be a place where everything is as safe as it can be.

Nursery

CRIBS. Your baby usually will be unattended when in his crib, so this should be a totally safe environment. Falls are the most common injury associated with cribs, even though they are the easiest to prevent. Children are most likely to fall out of the crib when the mattress is raised too high for their height, or not lowered properly as they grow.

If you use a newer crib (one manufactured since June 2011), it is guided by safety standards that ban the manufacture or sale of drop-side rail cribs. There is a good chance that an older crib no longer meets all the current safety standards, especially if it has a drop side. If possible, it is best to use a newer crib that meets the current standards.

No matter what the age of your crib, inspect it carefully for the following features.

- Slats should be no more than 2⅜ inches (6 cm) apart so a child's head cannot become trapped between them. Widely spaced slats can allow an infant's legs and body to fall through but will trap the infant's head, which can result in death.

- There should be no decorative cut-outs in the headboard or footboard, as your child's head or limbs could become trapped in them.

- If the crib has corner posts, they should be flush with the end panels, or they should be very, very tall (such as posts on a canopy bed). Clothing and ribbons can catch on tall corner posts and strangle an infant.

- All screws, bolts, nuts, plastic parts, and other hardware should be present and original equipment. Never substitute original parts with something from a hardware store; replacement parts must be obtained from the manufacturer. They must be tightly in place to prevent the crib from coming apart; a child's activity can cause the crib to collapse, trapping and suffocating her.

- Before each assembly and weekly thereafter, inspect the crib for damage to hardware, loose joints, missing parts, or sharp edges. Do not use a crib if any parts are missing or broken.

You can prevent other crib hazards by observing the following guidelines.

1. The mattress should be the same size as the crib so there are no gaps to trap arms, body, or legs. If you can insert more than two fingers between the mattress and the sides or ends of the crib, the crib and mattress combination should not be used.

2. If you purchase a new mattress, remove and destroy all plastic wrapping material that comes with it, because it can suffocate a child.

3. Before your baby can sit, lower the mattress of the crib to the level where he cannot fall out either by leaning against the side or by pulling himself over it. Set the mattress at its lowest position before your child learns to stand. The most common falls occur when a baby tries to climb out, so move your child to another bed when he is 35 inches (89 cm) tall, or when the height of the side rail is less than three-quarters of his height (approximately nipple level).

4. In an older crib with a drop side or drop gate, the lowered crib side should be at least 9 inches (23 cm) above the mattress support in its lowest position to prevent the infant from falling out. Raised crib sides should be at least 26 inches (66.04 cm) above the mattress support in its lowest position. Be sure the locking latch that holds the side up is sturdy and can't be released by your child. Always leave the side up when your child is in the crib. If possible, consider replacing your older crib with a new one that meets current safety standards.

5. Periodically check the crib to be sure there are no rough edges or sharp points on the metal parts, and no splinters or cracks in the wood. If you notice tooth marks on the railing, cover the wood with a plastic strip (available at most children's furniture stores).

6. Do not use bumper pads in cribs. There is no evidence that they prevent injuries, and there is a possible risk of suffocation, strangulation, or entrapment. Infant deaths in cribs have been associated with bumper pads. In addition, toddlers can use a bumper guard to help them climb and fall out.

7. Pillows, quilts, comforters, sheepskins, stuffed animals, and other soft products should not be placed in a crib. Babies have suffocated on such items in the crib.

8. If you hang a mobile over your child's crib, be sure it is securely attached to the side rails. Hang it high enough so your baby cannot reach it to pull it down, and remove it when he is able to get up on his hands and knees, or when he reaches five months, whichever comes first.

9. Crib gyms are not recommended, as infants and toddlers may injure themselves falling forward onto the gym or pulling the gym down on top of their body.

10. To prevent the most serious of falls and to keep children from getting caught in cords from hanging window blinds or draperies and strangling, don't place a crib—or any other child's bed—near a window. The Consumer Product Safety Commission recommends using cordless window coverings if possible.

CHANGING TABLES. Although a changing table makes it easier to dress and diaper your baby, falls from such a high surface can be serious. Don't trust your vigilance alone to prevent falls; you should also consider the following recommendations.

1. Choose a sturdy, stable changing table with a 2-inch (5-cm) guardrail around all four sides.

2. The top of the changing table pad should be concave, so that the middle is slightly lower than the sides.

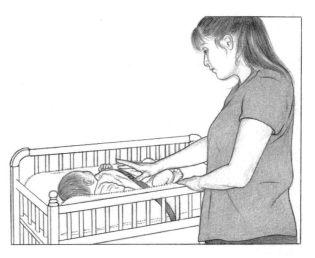

3. Buckle the safety strap, but don't depend on it alone to keep your child secure. Always keep a hand on your baby. Never leave a child unattended on a dressing table, even for a moment, even if he is strapped.

4. Keep diapering supplies within your reach—but out of your child's reach—so you don't have to leave your baby's side to get them. Never let him play with a powder container. If he opens and shakes it, he's likely to inhale particles of powder, which can injure his lungs.

5. If you use disposable diapers, store them out of your child's reach and cover them with clothing when he wears them. Children can suffocate if they tear off pieces of the plastic liner and swallow them.

BUNK BEDS. Although some children love them, bunk beds pose several serious dangers: The child on the top bunk can fall out, and the child on the lower bunk can be injured if the top bunk collapses. The bunk beds might be improperly constructed or assembled, causing dangerous structural flaws. Or a mattress that doesn't properly fit could entrap your child. If, despite these warnings, you choose to use bunk beds, take the following precautions.

1. Don't allow a child under six to sleep in the upper bunk. She won't have the coordination she needs to climb safely or to stop herself from falling out.

2. Place the beds in a corner of the room so there are walls on two sides. This provides extra support and blocks two of the possible four sites for falling out.

3. Don't place beds beside a window. This will help prevent children from falling out the window or being strangled by cords from hanging window blinds or draperies. The CPSC recommends using cordless window coverings if possible.

4. Be sure the top mattress fits snugly and cannot possibly slip over the edge of the frame. If there's a gap, your child might get trapped and suffocate.

5. Attach a ladder to the top bunk bed. Use a night-light so your child can see the ladder.

6. Install a guardrail on the top bunk. The gap between the side rail and guardrail should be no more than 3½ inches (8¾ cm). Be sure your child can't roll under the guardrail when the mattress on the top bunk is compressed by the weight of her body. If her head gets stuck under the guardrail, she may suffocate or be strangled. You may need a thicker mattress to prevent this.

7. Check the supports under the upper mattress. Wires or slats should run directly under the mattress and be fastened in place at both ends. A mattress that is supported only by the frame of the bed or unsecured slats could come crashing down.

8. If you separate bunks into two individual beds, make sure to remove all dowels or connectors.

9. To prevent falls and collapse of the bed, don't allow children to jump or roughhouse on either bunk.

10. Choose bunk beds with a label stating that they comply with ASTM Standard F1427-07 to help ensure that they are designed and constructed to be as safe as possible.

Kitchen

The kitchen is such a dangerous room for young children that some experts recommend they be excluded from it. That's a difficult rule to enforce, because parents spend so much time there and most young children want to be where the action is. While he's with you in the kitchen, sit him in a high chair or playpen so he can watch you and others in the room. He should be securely strapped in (if in a high chair) and within your vision. Keep a toy box or drawer with safe play items in the kitchen to amuse him. You can eliminate the most serious dangers by taking the following precautions.

1. Store strong cleaners, lye, furniture polish, dishwasher soap, and other dangerous products in a high cabinet, locked and out of sight. If you must store some items under the sink, buy a child safety lock that refastens automatically every time you close the cupboard. (Most hardware, baby supply, and department stores have them.) Never transfer dangerous substances into containers that look as if they might hold food, as this may tempt a child to taste them.

2. In the kitchen, keep knives, forks, scissors, and other sharp instruments separate from "safe" kitchen utensils, and in a latched drawer. Store sharp cutting appliances such as food processors out of reach and/or in a locked cupboard.

3. Unplug appliances when they are not in use so your child cannot turn them on. Don't allow electrical cords to dangle where your child can reach and tug on them, possibly pulling a heavy appliance down on himself.

4. Always turn pot handles toward the back of the stove so your child can't reach up and grab them. Whenever you have to walk with hot liquid—a cup of coffee, a pot of soup—be sure you know where your child is so you don't trip over him. Do not try to carry your child at the same time!

5. When shopping for an oven, choose one that is well insulated to protect your child from the heat if he touches the oven door. Also, never leave the oven door open.

6. If you have a gas stove, turn the dials firmly to the off position, and if they're easy to remove, do so when you aren't cooking so that your child can't turn the stove on. If they cannot be removed easily, use child-resistant knob covers and block the access to the stove as much as possible.

7. Keep matches out of reach and out of sight.

8. Don't warm baby bottles in a microwave oven. The liquid heats unevenly, so there may be pockets of milk hot enough to scald your baby's mouth when he drinks. Also, some overheated baby bottles have exploded when they were removed from the microwave.

9. Keep a fire extinguisher in your kitchen. (If your home has more than one story, mount an extinguisher in a place you will remember on each floor.)

10. Do not use small refrigerator magnets that your baby could choke on or swallow.

11. In addition to appliances and other items in the kitchen, make sure utensils and detergent or other cleaning products in the kitchen or laundry room are out of reach of young children, since they can look tempting to them. Such products can be extremely dangerous if swallowed or inhaled.

Bathroom

The simplest way to avoid bathroom injuries is to make this room inaccessible unless your child is accompanied by an adult. This may mean installing a latch on the door at adult height or a door top lock so the child can't get into the bathroom when you aren't around. Also, be sure any lock on the door can be unlocked from the outside, just in case your child locks himself in.

The following suggestions will prevent injuries when your child is using the bathroom.

1. Children can drown in only a few inches of water, so *never leave a young child alone in the bath, even for a moment.* Practice touch supervision by staying within arm's reach of your child anytime he is in or near water, such as a bathtub or swimming pool. If you can't ignore the doorbell or the phone, wrap your child in a towel and take him along when you go to answer it. Bath seats and rings are strongly *not* recommended and will not prevent drowning if the infant is left unattended. Never leave water in the bathtub when it is not in use.

2. Install no-slip strips on the bottom of the bathtub. Put a cushioned cover over the water faucet so your child won't be hurt if he bumps his head against it.

3. Get in the habit of closing the lid of the toilet, and use a toilet lid lock. A curious toddler who tries to play in the water can lose his balance, fall in, and drown. A toddler's head is disproportionately heavy, and he may not be able to lift it out of the water.

4. To prevent scalding, the hottest temperature at the faucet should be no more than 120 degrees Fahrenheit (48.9 degrees Celsius). In many cases you can adjust your water heater. When your child is old enough to turn the faucets, teach him to start the cold water before the hot.

5. Keep all medicines in containers with safety caps. Remember, however, that these caps are child-*resistant,* not childproof, so store all medicines and cosmetics high and out of sight and reach in a locked cabinet. Don't keep toothpaste, soaps, shampoos, and other frequently used items in the same cabinet. Instead, store them in a hard-to-reach cabinet equipped with a safety latch or locks.

6. If you use electrical appliances in the bathroom, particularly hair dryers and razors, be sure to unplug them and store them in a cabinet with a safety lock when they aren't in use. All bathroom wall sockets should have a special circuit to automatically shut off to lessen the likelihood of electrical injury if an appliance falls into the sink or bathwater. It is even better to use them in another room where there is no water. Ask an electrician to check your bathroom electrical outlets and to install GFCI safety outlets if needed.

Garage and Basement

Garages and basements tend to be places where potentially lethal tools and chemicals are stored. Keep garage doors locked, with self-closing doors, and make the room strictly off-limits to children. To minimize the risk when children do gain access to the garage and basement:

1. Keep paints, varnishes, thinners, pesticides, and fertilizers in a locked cabinet or locker. Be sure these substances are always kept in their original, labeled containers.

2. Store tools in a safe area out of reach and locked. This includes sharp items like saw blades. Be sure power tools are unplugged and locked in a cabinet when you finish using them.

3. Do not allow your child to play near the garage or driveway where cars may be coming and going. Many children are killed when someone, often a family member, unintentionally backs over them with a car. Most vehicles have large blind spots where a child cannot be seen even if the driver is watching the mirrors carefully.

4. If you have an automatic garage door opener, be sure your child is nowhere near the door before you open or close it. Keep the opener out of reach and out of sight. Make sure the automatic reversing mechanism is properly adjusted.

5. If, for some reason, you must store an unused refrigerator or freezer, remove the door so that a child cannot become trapped if he crawls inside.

All Rooms

Certain safety rules and preventive actions apply to every room. The following safeguards against commonplace household dangers will protect not only your small child, but your entire family.

1. Install smoke detectors throughout your home, at least one on every level and outside bedrooms. Check them monthly to be sure they are working. It is best to use smoke detectors with long-life batteries, but if these are not available, change the batteries annually on a date you will remember. Develop a fire escape plan and practice it so you'll be prepared if an emergency does occur.

2. Put safety plugs or covers that are not a choking hazard in all unused electrical outlets so your child can't stick her finger or a toy into the holes. If your child won't stay away from outlets, block access to them with furniture. Keep electrical cords out of reach and sight.

3. To prevent slipping, carpet your stairs where possible. Be sure the carpet is firmly tacked down at the edges. When your child is just learning to crawl and walk, install safety gates at both the top and bottom of stairs. Avoid accordion-style gates, which can trap an arm or a neck.

4. Certain houseplants may be harmful. The Poison Help Line (1-800-222-1222) or www.poisonhelp.hrsa.gov will have a list or description of plants to avoid. You may want to forgo house plants for a while or, at the very least, keep all house plants out of reach.

5.   Check your floors constantly for small objects that a child might swallow, such as coins, buttons, beads, pins, and screws. This is particularly important if someone in the household has a hobby that involves small items, or if there are older children who have small items.

6.   If you have hardwood floors, don't let your child run around in stocking feet. Socks make slippery floors even more dangerous.

7.   The Consumer Product Safety Commission recommends using cordless window coverings in all homes with children. If your window products are not cordless, attach cords for window blinds and drapes to floor mounts that hold them taut, or wrap these cords around wall brackets to keep them out of reach. Use safety stop devices on the cords. Cords with loops should be cut and equipped with safety tassels. Children can strangle on them if they are left loose.

8.   Pay attention to the doors between rooms. Glass doors are particularly dangerous, because a child may run into them, so fasten them open if you can. Swinging doors can knock a small child down, and folding doors can pinch little fingers, so if you have either, consider removing them until your child is old enough to understand how they work.

9.   Check your home for furniture pieces with hard edges and sharp corners that could injure your child if she falls against them. (Coffee tables are a particular hazard.) If possible, move this furniture out of traffic areas, particularly when your child is learning to walk. You also can buy cushioned corner- and edge-protectors that stick onto the furniture.

10. Test the stability of large pieces of furniture, such as floor lamps, bookshelves, and television stands. Put floor lamps behind other furniture and anchor bookcases and TV stands to the wall. Deaths and injuries can occur when children climb onto, fall against, or pull themselves up on large pieces of furniture. Secure televisions to the wall or to a low, stable stand that is designed to hold them; children have died when they were crushed by a falling television.

11. Keep computers out of reach so that your child cannot pull them over on herself. Cords should be out of sight and reach.

12. Open windows from the top if possible. If you must open them from the bottom, install operable window guards that only an adult or older child can open from the inside. A screen is not strong enough to prevent a fall. Never put chairs, sofas, low tables, or anything else a child might climb on in front of a window. Doing so gives her access to the window and creates an opportunity for a serious fall.

13. Never leave plastic bags lying around the house, and don't store children's clothes or toys in them. Dry-cleaning bags are particularly dangerous. Knot them before you throw them away so that it's impossible for your child to crawl into them or pull them over her head. Even a small piece torn off can become a potential choking hazard.

14. Think about the potential hazard of anything you put into the trash. Any trash container into which dangerous items will go—for example, spoiled food, discarded razor blades, or batteries—should have a child-resistant cover or be kept away and out of a child's reach.

15. To prevent burns, check your heat sources. Fireplaces, woodstoves, and kerosene heaters should be screened so that your child can't get near them. Check electric baseboard heaters, radiators, and even vents from hot-air furnaces to see how hot they get when the heat is on. They, too, may need to be screened.

16. A firearm should not be kept in the home or environment of a child. If you must keep a firearm in the house, keep it unloaded and locked up. Lock ammunition in a separate location. If your child plays in other homes, ask if guns are present there, and if so, how they are stored. (Also see *Where We Stand* below.)

17. Alcohol can be very toxic to a young child. Keep all alcoholic beverages in a locked cabinet and remember to empty any unfinished drinks immediately.

WHERE WE STAND

THE MOST EFFECTIVE WAY to prevent firearm-related injury to children is to keep guns out of homes and communities. The American Academy of Pediatrics strongly supports gun-control legislation. We believe that assault weapons and high-capacity ammunition magazines should be banned.

We recommend further that handguns and handgun ammunition be regulated, that restrictions be placed on handgun ownership, and that the number of privately owned handguns be reduced. Firearms should be removed from the environments where children live and play, but if they are not, they *must* be stored locked and unloaded. Safe storage practices can reduce the risk of death or injury, but loaded firearms and unloaded firearms and ammunition represent a serious danger to children.

Baby Equipment

During the past thirty years, the Consumer Product Safety Commission has taken an active role in setting standards to assure the safety of equipment manufactured for children and infants. Because many of these rules went into effect in the early 1970s, you must pay special attention to the safety of furniture made before then. The following guidelines will help you select the safest possible baby equipment, whether used or new, and utilize it properly.

High Chairs

Falls are the most serious danger associated with high chairs. To minimize the risk of your child falling:

1. Select a chair with a wide base, so it can't be tipped over if someone bumps against it.

2. If the chair folds, be sure the locking device is secure each time you set it up.

3. Strap your child in with the shoulder, waist, and crotch safety straps whenever he sits in the chair. Never allow him to stand in the high chair.

4. Don't place the high chair near a counter or table or within reach of a hot or dangerous object. Your child may be able to push hard enough against these surfaces to tip the chair over.

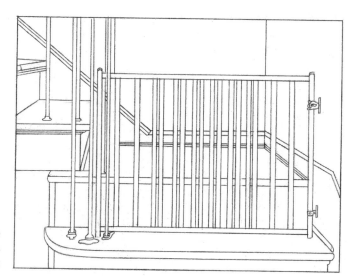

Safe, horizontal-type gate with slats 2⅜ inches (6 cm) apart

5. Never leave a young child unattended in a high chair, and don't allow older children to climb or play on it, as this could cause it to tip over.

6. A high chair that hooks onto a table is *not* a substitute for a more solid one. But if you plan to use such a model when you eat out or when you travel, look for one that locks onto the table. Be sure the table is heavy enough to support your child's weight without tipping. Also, check to see whether his feet can touch a table support. If he can push against it, he may be able to dislodge the seat from the table.

7. Check that all caps or plugs on chair tubing are firmly attached and cannot be pulled off; these could be choking hazards.

Infant Seats

Infant seats are not car safety seats, so not all the same regulations apply, and infant seats should be labeled to meet the safety standard. Use care in selecting an infant seat. Check the weight guidelines provided by the manufacturer, and don't use the seat after your baby has outgrown it. Here are some other safety guidelines to follow.

1. Never leave a baby unattended in an infant seat.

2. Never use an infant seat as a substitute for a car safety seat. Infant seats are designed only for propping a baby up, so that she can see, play, or be fed more easily.

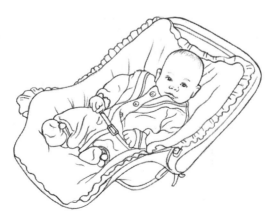

3. Always use the safety strap and harness when your baby is in the seat.

4. Choose a seat with an outside frame that allows the infant to sit deeply inside. Be sure the base is wide, so it is difficult to tip over.

5. Look at the bottom of the infant seat to see whether it's covered with a nonskid material. If it isn't, cut thin pieces of rubber, and glue them to the base so that the seat is less likely to slip when it's on a smooth surface.

6. Parents should remove the infant from the seat when moving the location of the seat to avoid falling or other injuries to the baby.

7. The most serious injuries associated with infant seats occur when a baby falls from a high surface, such as tables, couches, and chairs. Even small infants can jiggle a seat or carrier off a surface and fall, suffering head trauma and other injuries. Therefore, do not put the seat above floor level. To keep an active, squirming baby from tipping the seat over, place it on a carpeted area near you and away from sharp-edged furniture. Infant seats also may tip over when placed on soft surfaces, such as beds or upholstered furniture; these are not safe places for infant seats.

8. Never place a baby in an infant seat or a car safety seat on the roof or back of a car, even for a moment.

Playpens

Most parents depend on playpens (sometimes called play yards) as a safe place to put a baby when Mom or Dad isn't available to watch him every moment. Yet playpens, too, can be dangerous under certain circumstances. To prevent mishaps:

1. Choose a playpen or play yard with a label stating that it meets ASTM F406, a safety standard that will help ensure it is designed and built to prevent injuries. This standard is mandatory for all new play yards.

2. Never leave the side of a mesh playpen lowered. An infant who rolls into the pocket created by the slack mesh can become trapped and suffocate.

3. Do not tie toys to the sides or across the top of a playpen as a baby or toddler can become entangled in them.

4. If your playpen has a raised changing table, always remove the changing table when your child is in the playpen so he cannot become entrapped or strangled in the space between the changing table and the side rail of the playpen.

5. When your child can pull himself to a standing position, remove any boxes or large toys in the playpen that he could use to help him climb out.

6. Children who are teething often bite off chunks of the vinyl or plastic that cover the top rails, so you should check them periodically for tears and holes. If the tears are small, repair them with heavy-duty cloth tape; if they are more extensive, you may need to replace the rails.

7. Be sure that a playpen's mesh is free of tears, holes, or loose threads and that the openings are less than ¼ inch (0.6 cm) across, so that your child cannot get caught in it. The mesh should be securely attached to the top rail and floor plate. If staples are used, they should not be missing, loose, or exposed. Slats on wooden playpens should be no more than 2⅜ inches (6 cm) apart, so your child's head cannot become trapped between them.

8. Circular enclosures made from accordion-style fences are extremely dangerous, because children can get their heads caught in the diamond-shaped openings and the V-shaped border at the top of the gate. Never use such an enclosure, either indoors or out.

Walkers

The American Academy of Pediatrics does not recommend the use of infant walkers. Children can fall down stairs, and head injuries are common. Walkers do not help a child learn to walk, and they can delay normal motor development. A stationary walker or activity center is a better choice. These do not have wheels, but seats that rotate and bounce. You may also want to consider a sturdy wagon or a "kiddie push car." Be sure the toy has a bar she can push and that it's weighted so it won't tip over when she pulls herself up on it.

Pacifiers

Pacifiers will not harm your baby. In fact, there is some evidence that pacifiers may help reduce the risk of sudden infant death syndrome (SIDS), when putting your infant to sleep. However, for maximum safety use the following tips when giving your baby a pacifier:

1. Do not use the top and nipple from a baby bottle as a pacifier, even if you tape them together. If the baby sucks hard, the nipple may pop out of the ring and choke her.

2. Purchase pacifiers that cannot possibly come apart. If you are in doubt, ask your pediatrician for a recommendation.

3. The shield between the nipple and the ring should be at least 1½ inches (3.8 cm) across, so the infant cannot take the entire pacifier into her mouth. Also, the shield should be made of firm plastic with ventilation holes.

4. Never tie a pacifier to your child's crib or around your child's neck or hand. This is very dangerous and could cause serious injury or even death.

5. Pacifiers deteriorate over time. Inspect them periodically to see whether the rubber is discolored or torn. If so, replace them.

6. Follow the recommended age range on the pacifier, as older children can sometimes fit an entire newborn pacifier in their mouth and choke.

Toy Boxes and Toy Chests

A toy box can be dangerous for two reasons: A child could become trapped inside, or a hinged lid could fall on your child's head or body while he's searching for a toy. If possible, store toys on open shelves so that your child can get them easily. If you must use a toy box:

1. Look for one with no top, or choose one that has a lightweight removable lid or sliding doors or panels. Little fingers can easily become caught and injured under lids and between sliding doors and panels.

2. If you use a toy box with a hinged lid, be sure it has lid support that holds the lid open at any angle to which the lid is opened. If your toy box didn't come with such a support, install one yourself—or remove the lid.

3. Look for a toy box with rounded or padded edges and corners, or add the padding yourself, so your child won't be injured if he falls against it.

4. Children occasionally get trapped inside toy boxes, so be sure your box has ventilation holes or a gap between the lid and the box. Don't block the holes by pushing the box tight against a wall. Be sure the lid doesn't latch.

Toys

Most toy manufacturers are conscientious in trying to produce safe toys, but they cannot always anticipate the way a child might use—or abuse—their products. In 2011, there were an estimated 252,000 toy-related injuries treated in US hospital emergency rooms. Of these, 36 percent (91,600) involved children under the age of five years. If your child is injured by an unsafe product or if you would like to report a product-related injury, visit www.saferproducts.gov. The Consumer Product Safety Commission keeps a record of complaints and initiates recalls of dangerous toys, so your phone call may protect not only your child but others.

When selecting or using toys, always observe the following safety guidelines.

1. Match all toys to your child's age and abilities. Follow the manufacturers' guidelines on the packaging.

2. Rattles—probably your child's first toys—should be at least 1⅝ inches (4 cm) across. An infant's mouth and throat are very flexible, so one that's smaller than that could cause choking. Also, rattles should have no detachable parts.

3. All toys should be constructed of sturdy materials that won't break or shatter even when a child throws or bangs them.

4. Check squeeze toys to be sure the squeaker can't become detached from the toy.

5. Before giving your child a stuffed animal or a doll, be certain the eyes and other parts are firmly attached, and check them periodically. Remove all ribbons. Don't allow your child to suck on a pacifier or any other accessory that comes packaged with a doll and is small enough to be swallowed.

6. Swallowing and/or inhaling small parts of toys are serious dangers to young children. Inspect toys carefully for small parts that could fit in your child's mouth and throat. Look for toys labeled for children three and under, because they must meet federal guidelines requiring that they have no small parts likely to be swallowed or inhaled.

7. Toys with small magnets are especially dangerous for young children. If more than one magnet is swallowed, the magnets can attract each other in the child's body and cause intestinal blockages, perforations, and even death. Keep toys with small magnets away from children.

8. Toys with small parts that are purchased for older children should be stored out of the reach of younger ones. Impress on your older child the importance of picking up all the pieces from such toys when she's finished playing with them. You should check that there are no items dangerous for your baby left out. Consider restricting the use of these toys to a small area or places that are inaccessible to the baby.

9. Don't let a child play with balloons; she may inhale a balloon if she tries to blow it up. If a balloon pops, be sure to pick up and discard all the broken pieces. Mylar balloons are a safer choice than latex balloons.

10. To prevent both burns and electrical shocks, don't give young children (under age ten) a toy that must be plugged into an electrical outlet. Instead, buy toys that are battery-operated. Be sure that the battery cover is securely fastened in an enclosure that requires a screwdriver or other tool to open to prevent a loose battery from becoming a choking hazard.

11. Carefully inspect toys with mechanical parts for springs, gears, or hinges that could trap a child's fingers, hair, or clothing.

How to Report Unsafe Products

If you become aware of an unsafe product used by children—or if your own child suffers an injury related to a particular product—report it to the Consumer Product Safety Commission (CPSC) at www.saferproducts.gov. Your report is important for helping the CPSC identify hazardous products that may require further investigation or a potential recall.

12. To prevent cuts, check toys before you purchase them to be sure they don't have sharp edges or pointed pieces. Avoid toys with parts made of glass or rigid plastic that could crack or shatter.

13. Don't allow your child to play with very noisy toys, including squeeze toys with unexpectedly loud squeakers. Noise levels at or above 100 decibels can damage hearing.

14. Projectile toys such as dart guns or slingshots are not suitable for children, because they can so easily cause eye injuries. Never give your child a toy that actually fires anything except water.

Safety Outside the Home

Even if you create the perfect environment for your child inside your home, she'll be spending a lot of time outside, where surroundings are somewhat less controllable. Obviously, your personal supervision will remain the most valuable protection. However, even a well-supervised child will be exposed to many hazards. The information that follows will show you how to eliminate many of these hazards and reduce the risk that your child will be injured.

Car Safety Seats

Each year more children between the ages of one and nineteen are killed in car crashes than in any other way. Many of these deaths can be prevented if the children are properly restrained. Contrary to what some people believe, a parent's lap is actually the most dangerous place for a child to ride. In case of a car crash, sudden stop, or swerve, you wouldn't be able to hold on to your child, and your body would crush hers as you were thrown against the dashboard

Rear-facing-only car safety seat

and windshield. Not even the strongest adult can keep hold of a child while experiencing the massive forces of a crash. The single most important thing you can do to keep your child safe in the car is to buy, install, and use an approved car safety seat, appropriate for the age and size of your child, every time she rides in the car.

Car safety seats are required by law in all fifty states, the District of Columbia, and US territories. Unfortunately, studies consistently show that many parents do not use them properly. The most common mistakes include facing car safety seats in the wrong direction (that is, placing it facing forward too soon), not keeping your child in a car safety seat for a long enough time, placing rear-facing seats in front of an air bag, failing to strap or fasten the child into the car safety seat, failing to securely fasten the child's car safety seat to the vehicle seat, not using a booster seat for older children, and letting children ride in the front seat. Also, some parents don't use the car safety seat on short trips. They are not aware that most fatal crashes occur within 5 miles (8 km) of home and at speeds of less than 25 miles (40 km) per hour. For all these reasons, children continue to be at risk. It's not enough to have a car safety seat—you must use it correctly, every time, in the backseat.

Choosing a Car Safety Seat

Here are some guidelines you can use to help you select a car safety seat.

1. The American Academy of Pediatrics annually publishes a list of car safety seats that are available, "Car Safety Seats: A Guide for Families," which can be found online at www.healthychildren.org/carseatlist.

2. No one seat is "safest" or "best." The "best" car safety seat is one that fits your child's size and weight, and can be installed correctly in your car and used correctly on every trip.

3. Price does not always make a difference. Higher prices can mean added features that may or may not make the seat easier to use.

4. When you find a seat you like, try it out. Put your child in the seat and adjust the harnesses and buckles. Make sure it fits in your car and that the harnesses are easy to adjust when the seat is in your car.

5. Before you bring your baby home from the hospital, she should be observed in her car safety seat by hospital staff to make sure the semireclined position does not cause low heart rate, low oxygen, or other breathing problems. If the pediatrician advises that your baby needs to lie flat during travel, use a crash-tested car bed. If possible, an adult should ride in the backseat next to your baby to watch her closely.

Belt-positioning booster seat

6. Children with special health problems may need other restraint systems. Discuss this with your pediatrician. More information about safe transportation of children with special health needs is available from the Automotive Safety Program by phone at 1-317-274-2977 or 1-800-543-6227 or on their website at http://www.preventinjury.org/Special-Needs-Transportation.

Forward-facing car safety seat

7. Do not use a car safety seat that is too old. Look on the label for the date it was made. Many manufacturers recommend that seats be used for only six years. Check the instruction manual to find the expiration date; this may also be found on a label on the seat or stamped into the plastic shell. Over time, and with exposure to heat and cold, the car safety seat parts can become weakened, so it is important not to use a car safety seat past the manufacturer's expiration date.

8. If a car safety seat was in a moderate or severe crash, it may have been weakened and should not be used, even if it looks fine. Seats that were in a minor crash may still be safe to use. A crash is considered minor if the vehicle can be driven away from the crash, the door closest to the car safety seat was not damaged, no one in the vehicle was injured, the air bags did not go off, and you can't see any damage to the car safety seat. Some manufacturers still recommend replacing a seat after even a minor crash, so call the car safety seat manufacturer if you have questions about the safety of your seat. Do not use a seat if you do not know its full history.

9. It is best to use a new car safety seat. If you choose a used car safety seat, make sure you are absolutely sure that it has never been in any crash, all of the labels and instructions are present, and it has not been recalled.

10. Do not use a car safety seat that does not have a label with the date of manufacture and seat name or model number. Without these, you cannot check on recalls.

11. Do not use a car safety seat if it does not come with instructions. You need them to know how to use the car safety seat. Do not rely on the former owner's directions. Get a copy of the instruction manual from the manufacturer before you use the seat.

12. Do not use a car safety seat that has any cracks in the frame of the seat or is missing parts.

13. Register your car safety seat with the manufacturer so that you can be notified promptly in the event of a recall. If you do not have the registration card that came with the seat, you can register the seat on the manufacturer's website or by calling its customer service department.

14. You can find out if your car safety seat has been recalled by calling the manufacturer or the Department of Transportation's Vehicle Safety Hotline at 1-888-DASH-2-DOT (1-888-327-4236), from 8 a.m. to 10 p.m. ET, Monday through Friday. This information is also available on the National Highway Traffic Safety Administration website: www.nhtsa.gov/Safety/CPS. If the seat has been recalled, be sure to follow instructions to fix it or get the necessary parts.

Types of Car Safety Seats

Infants/Toddlers

All infants and toddlers should ride in a rear-facing car safety seat until they are two years old, or until they reach the highest weight or height allowed by the manufacturer of the car safety seat. This is the safest way to ride, so it is best for your child to ride rear-facing as long as he has not reached the weight or height limit set by the manufacturer. For many children, this may be well past the second birthday.

Toddlers/Preschoolers

All children two years or older, or those younger than two years who have outgrown the rear-facing weight or height limit for their car seat, should use a forward-facing car safety seat with a five-point harness for as long as possible, up to the highest weight or height allowed by their car safety seat's manufacturer.

School-Age Children

All children whose weight or height is above the forward-facing limit for their car safety seat should use a belt-positioning booster seat until the vehicle seat belt fits properly, typically when they have reached about 4 feet 9 inches in height and are between eight and twelve years old.

Older Children

When children are old enough and large enough to use the vehicle seat belt alone, they should always use lap and shoulder seat belts for optimal protection. All children younger than thirteen years should be restrained in the rear seats of vehicles for optimal protection.

Travel Vests

A travel vest may be an option while you are traveling, if your car or taxicab has only lap belts. Travel vests are designed for children between 20 and 168 pounds and can be an alternative to traditional forward-facing seats. They are useful in a vehicle that has lap-only seat belts in the rear or for children whose weight exceeds that allowed by traditional car safety seats. These vests may require use of a top tether.

Installing a Car Safety Seat

1. Read your vehicle owner's manual for important information on how to install the car safety seat correctly in your vehicle.

2. The safest place for all children to ride is in the backseat. Avoid driving more children than can be buckled safely in the backseat.

3. Never place a child in a rear-facing car safety seat in the front seat of a vehicle that has a passenger air bag. All new cars have air bags. When used with seat belts, air bags work very well to protect older children and adults. However, air bags are very dangerous when used with rear-facing car safety seats. If your car has a passenger air bag, children in rear-facing seats *must* ride in the backseat. Even in a low-speed crash, the air bag can inflate, strike the car safety seat, and cause serious brain injury and death. Toddlers who ride in forward-facing car safety seats also are at risk from air bag injuries. Remember, *all* children younger than thirteen years are safest in the backseat.

4. Car safety seats can be installed using either the vehicle seat belts or LATCH (*L*ower *A*nchors and *T*ethers for *Ch*ildren). LATCH is a system of lower anchors located in the seat bight (where the vehicle cushions meet) and tether anchors located on the shelf behind the seat (in most sedans) or on the floor, ceiling, or back of the seat (in most minivans, SUVs, and hatchbacks). The systems are equally safe, but in some cases it may be easier to install a seat tightly using LATCH.

5. Place the seat facing the correct direction for the size and age of your child. Route the seat belt or LATCH strap through the correct path on the car safety seat (check your instructions to make sure), and pull it tight. Before each trip, check to make sure the car safety seat is installed tightly enough by pulling on the car safety seat where the seat belt or LATCH strap passes through. It should not move more than an inch side to side or toward the front of the car.

6. If your infant's head flops forward, the seat may not be reclined enough. Tilt the seat back until it is reclined to the correct angle according to manufacturer's instructions. Your seat may have a recline indicator to help determine whether the angle is correct and a built-in adjuster for this purpose. If not, you may wedge firm padding, such as a rolled towel, under the front base of the seat.

7. If the seat belt buckle lies just at the point where the belt bends around the car safety seat, it may be impossible to make the belt tight enough. If you cannot get the belt tight, try another position in the car or consider using LATCH if it is available.

8. Many lap/shoulder belts allow passengers to move freely even when they are buckled. Read your car owner's manual to see if your seat belts can be locked into position or if you will need to use a locking clip. Locking clips come with all new car safety seats. (Some have built-in lock-offs in place of locking clips.) In many cases, the seat belt can be locked into place by pulling the shoulder belt all the way out, then feeding it back into the retractor. Read your instructions for information on how to use the locking clip or lock-off, if needed.

9. Some lap belts need a special, heavy-duty locking clip, available from the vehicle manufacturer. Check your car owner's manual for more information.

10. Before using LATCH, check the car safety seat and vehicle instructions for information including the weight limits for the lower anchors and attachments and which seating positions can be used for LATCH installation. Check the vehicle instruction manual to be sure you do not attach the tether to a cargo tie-down or other attachment point that is not a tether anchor.

11. Tethers should always be used with forward-facing car safety seats. Most anchors are located on the rear window ledge, the back of the vehicle seat, or the floor or ceiling of the vehicle. Tethers give extra protection by keeping the car safety seat from being thrown forward in a crash. All new cars, minivans, and light trucks are required to have upper tether anchors for securing the tops of car safety seats. If your vehicle was manufactured before September 2000, it may be possible to have a tether anchor installed by a dealer, often at no cost.

12. For specific information about installing your car safety seat, consult a certified Child Passenger Safety (CPS) Technician. A list of certified CPS Technicians is available by state or ZIP code at www.seatcheck.org or http://cert .safekids.org. A list of inspection stations staffed by certified CPS Technicians is also available on the Internet at www.nhtsa.dot.gov/. The information also can be accessed by telephone on the Department of Transportation's Vehicle Safety Hotline at 1-888-DASH-2-DOT (1-888-327-4236), from 8 a.m. to 10 p.m. ET, Monday through Friday.

Using the Car Safety Seat

1. A car safety seat can protect your child only if she is buckled securely in it *every* time she rides in the car—no exceptions, beginning with your baby's first ride home from the hospital. Help your child form a lifelong habit of buckling up by *always* using your own seat belt. If you have two cars, buy two seats or transfer the seat to the car in which your child will be traveling. Remember to never place a rear-facing car safety seat in the front seat if there is an air bag. The safest place for all children to ride is in the back.

2. Read and follow the car safety seat manufacturer's instructions, and always keep them with the car safety seat. If you lose the instructions, call or write the manufacturer and ask for a new set. In many cases, you can download the instructions from the manufacturer's website.

3. Most children go through a stage when they protest whenever you put them in the car safety seat. Explain firmly that you cannot drive until everyone is buckled up. Then back up your words with action.

4. Be sure to use the correct harness slots for the child. When riding rear-facing, the harness straps should be at or below the level of the child's shoulders. When riding forward-facing, they should be at or above the shoulders. Some seats do not have slots, but instead move the harness straps up and down by some other mechanism. Read the instructions to see how and where to adjust the harness strap height.

5. Be sure the harness straps are snug against your child's body. Dress your baby in clothes that allow the straps to go between her legs. Keep the straps snug to make sure they will hold your child securely; if you can pinch a fold of webbing between your fingers, it is too loose. Be certain the straps lie flat and are not twisted.

6.   If needed to keep your newborn from slouching, pad the sides of the seat and behind the crotch strap with rolled-up diapers or receiving blankets. Do not use add-on products that go behind the baby or between the baby and the harness straps; these can cause the straps not to restrain the baby properly in a crash. Never use any add-on products unless they came with your car safety seat or are specifically allowed by the manufacturer's instructions.

7.   In cold weather, dress your baby in thinner layers rather than thickly padded clothes, and tuck blankets around your baby *after* adjusting the harness straps snugly. Do not use bunting products that have a layer that goes underneath your baby.

8.   In hot weather, drape a towel over the seat when you leave the car in the sun. Before putting your child in the seat, touch the fabrics and the metal buckle with your hand to be sure they aren't hot.

9.   No matter how short your errand is, **never leave an infant or child alone in a car.** She can get overheated or too cold very quickly, even if the temperature outside seems mild, or she may become frightened and panicky when she realizes she's alone. Children who have been left alone in a car in hot weather have died from hyperthermia (overheating). Any child alone in a car is a target for abduction, or an older child may be tempted to play with things such as a cigarette lighter, power windows, or the gear shift, which could cause her serious injury or death. Any parent, no matter how loving and attentive, is capable of forgetting his or her child in the car. Take steps to prevent this by incorporating visual reminders or check-ins into your routine:

- Put something you will need at your destination, like your purse or briefcase, in the backseat where you have to open the back door to retrieve it.

- Put a large stuffed toy in the car safety seat when your child is not in the car, and put the toy in the front seat where you will see it when your child rides in the seat.

- Ask your child care provider to call you if your child does not arrive when expected.

- Be especially vigilant when there is a change in the usual routine; the risk of forgetting a child is higher during such a disruption.

■ Lock your car and set the parking brake when not in use so that children cannot get inside. Hyperthermia deaths have occurred when children got into a car to play.

10. Always use your own seat belt. In addition to setting a good example, you'll reduce your own risk of injury or death in a crash by 60 percent.

11. Children will outgrow their booster seats when they are older, often eight to twelve years of age. They can use the seat belt alone when it fits properly over strong bones, meaning that the lap belt fits low and snug across the thighs, the shoulder belt lies across the middle of the chest, and they can sit all the way back on the vehicle seat with knees bent over the edge without slouching and can stay in that position for the whole ride.

Air Bag Safety

An air bag can save your life. However, air bags and young children do not mix. The following information will help keep you and your children safe. (This information is worth repeating.)

■ The safest place for all infants and children under thirteen years of age to ride is in the backseat.

■ Never put a rear-facing car safety seat in the front seat of a car with an air bag. Your child can suffer a serious injury or death from the impact of the air bag against the back of the car safety seat.

■ Infants and toddlers should ride in a rear-facing car safety seat until they are at least two years of age or until they reach the height or weight limit set by the manufacturer. Rear-facing is the safest way to ride, so it is best to ride that way as long as possible.

■ All children should be properly secured in car safety seats or booster seats that are correct for their age and size.

■ Air bags enhance the safety of your car. Keep in mind, however, that young children—as well as children of any age—should ride in the backseat.

■ Side air bags improve safety for adults in side impact crashes. When children ride next to side air bags, it is essential that they be restrained in the

Keeping Your Child Happy and Safe on the Road

As hard as you may try to enforce car safety seat and seat belt use, your child may resist these constraints as he gets older. Here are some tips to keep him occupied and content—and also safe—while the car is in motion.

BIRTH TO NINE MONTHS

- Ensure your newborn's comfort by padding the sides of his car safety seat with receiving blankets if necessary to prevent slouching.

- If needed, place a small rolled-up cloth diaper or receiving blanket between the crotch strap and your baby to prevent his lower body from sliding too far forward.

- If your infant's head flops forward, double-check to see if the seat has been reclined enough. Follow the manufacturer's instructions on how to achieve the proper recline angle.

NINE MONTHS TO TWENTY-FOUR MONTHS

- Children this age love to climb, and may want desperately to get out of the car safety seat. If this describes your child, remind yourself that this is only a phase. As mentioned earlier, in a calm but stern voice, insist that he stay in his seat whenever the car is on the road. Let him know that the car cannot move unless everyone is buckled up, and then follow through if he tries to escape his seat. Keep the harness straps snug and the harness clip at chest level to make it more difficult for him to escape.

- Entertain your toddler by talking or singing with him as you drive. However, never do this to the point that it distracts you from paying attention to your driving.

TWENTY-FOUR MONTHS TO THIRTY-SIX MONTHS

- Make driving a learning experience by talking about the things your child sees out the window, as long as this doesn't distract you from driving.

- Encourage your child to buckle his toy animals or dolls into a seat belt and talk about how safe the toy is now that it's buckled up.

PRESCHOOLERS

■ Talk about safety as "grown-up" behavior, and praise your child whenever he voluntarily buckles up.

■ Encourage your child to accept the car safety seat or booster seat by suggesting make-believe roles, such as astronaut, pilot, or race-car driver.

■ Explain why the car safety seat is important: "If we have to stop suddenly, the straps keep you from bumping your head."

■ Show him books and pictures with safety messages.

■ Always wear your seat belt, and make sure everyone else in the car buckles up, too.

---

proper position. Read your car safety seat manual for guidance on placing the seat next to a side air bag, and refer to your vehicle owner's manual for recommendations that apply to your vehicle.

■ Seat belts must be worn correctly at all times by all passengers to provide the best protection.

Kids Around Cars

From a young age, teach children not to walk or play in the street or the driveway. Young children are not safe around streets and should not be playing near them. While they have the skills to get to roads and streets, they do not have the ability to recognize that streets and cars are dangerous. Children move quickly and impulsively. They are curious. Yet they have difficulty seeing cars in their peripheral vision, localizing sounds, and understanding traffic and the meaning of signs and signals. They cannot judge speed and vehicle distance. Couple this with drivers who may be multitasking and not looking out for young children who may run into the street, and a disaster could be in the making.

If children are near streets, "hands-on" supervision is necessary so you can quickly intervene if your child darts into the street to get a ball or run after an older child or adult.

To avoid injuries from vehicle backovers, driveways, alleyways, and any adjacent unfenced front yards should not be used as play areas. Parents should be reminded of the large blind spot behind the car (especially in bigger, elevated

WHERE WE STAND

ALL FIFTY STATES require that children ride in car safety seats. The American Academy of Pediatrics urges that all newborns discharged from hospitals be brought home in infant car safety seats. The AAP has established car safety seat guidelines for low-birth-weight infants, which include riding in a rear-facing seat and supporting the infant with ample padding around the sides, outside the harness system. A convertible car safety seat is recommended as a child gets older.

Infants and young children always should ride in car safety seats—preferably in the backseat—because it is safest. Never use a rear-facing car safety seat in the front seat of a vehicle equipped with a passenger-side air bag. An infant or child should never ride in an adult's arms. Children age twelve and younger should ride in the rear seat.

Older children should use booster seats until the vehicle safety belt fits well. This means that the child can sit all the way back on the vehicle seat with knees bent at the edge, the shoulder belt crosses the middle of the chest, the lap belt lies low and snug across the thighs, and the child can sit this way for the entire ride.

vehicles) and the need to walk completely around the car before getting in and starting the engine. Adults should make a point of knowing where the children are before putting a vehicle in reverse.

Baby Carriers—Backpacks, Front Packs, and Slings

Back and front carriers for infants are very popular. For your baby's—and your own—comfort and safety, follow these guidelines when purchasing and using baby carriers.

1. Infants born prematurely or with respiratory problems should not be placed in backpacks or other upright positioning devices as it may make it harder for them to breathe.

2. Some sling carriers may curl your baby's body into a C shape, which greatly increases the risk of breathing problems. If you use a sling, be sure your baby's neck is straight and his chin is not pressed into his chest.

3. In any type of carrier, check frequently to ensure that your baby's mouth and nose are not blocked by fabric or your body and that air flow is not restricted. The CPSC warns about the suffocation hazard to infants, particularly those who are younger than four months, who are carried in infant sling carriers. When infant slings are used for carrying, it is important to ensure that the infant's head is up and above the fabric, the face is visible, and the nose and mouth are clear of obstructions.

4. Take your baby with you when you shop for the carrier so that you can match it to his size. Make sure the carrier supports his back and that the leg holes are small enough so he can't possibly slip through. Look for sturdy material.

5. If you buy a backpack, be sure the aluminum frame is padded, so that your baby won't be hurt if he bumps against it.

6. Check the pack periodically for rips and tears in the seams and fasteners.

7. When using a baby carrier, be sure to bend at the knees, not the waist, if you need to pick something up. Otherwise, the baby may tip out of the carrier and you may hurt your back.

8. Babies over five months old may become restless in the carrier, so continue to use the restraining straps. Some children will brace their feet against the frame or against your body, changing their weight distribution. You should be certain that your child is seated properly before you walk.

Strollers

Look for safety features and take the following precautions.

1. If you string toys across your stroller, fasten them securely so they can't fall on top of the baby. Remove such toys as soon as the baby can sit or get on all fours.

2. Strollers should have brakes that are easy to operate. Use the brake whenever you are stopped, and be sure your child can't reach the release lever. A brake that locks two wheels provides an extra measure of safety.

3. Select a stroller with a wide base, so it won't tip over.

4. Children's fingers can become caught in the hinges that fold the stroller, so keep your child at a safe distance when you open and close it. Make sure the stroller is securely locked open before putting your child in it. Check that your baby's fingers cannot reach the stroller wheels.

5. Don't hang bags or other items from the handles of your stroller—they can make it tip backward. If the stroller has a basket for carrying things, be sure it is placed low and near the rear wheels.

6. The stroller should have a five-point harness (one with straps over both shoulders, at both hips, and between the legs), and it should be used whenever your child goes for a ride. For infants, use rolled-up baby blankets on either side of the seat if necessary to prevent slouching.

7. Never leave your child unattended.

8. If you purchase a side-by-side twin stroller, be sure the footrest extends all the way across both sitting areas. A child's foot can become trapped between separate footrests.

9. There are also strollers that allow an older child to sit or stand in the rear. Be mindful of weight guidelines and especially careful that the child in the back doesn't become overly active and tip the stroller.

Shopping Cart Safety

More than 20,000 children are treated in emergency rooms for shopping cart–related injuries each year. The most frequent kinds of injuries are contusions, abrasions, and lacerations, and most injuries are to the head or neck. Shopping cart–related injuries can be serious enough to require hospitalization, often because of head injuries and serious fractures. Some deaths have even occurred.

Shopping carts are often unstable; it may take as little as 16 pounds (7.26 kg) of force on the handle to tip a cart. The design of shopping carts makes it easier for them to tip over when a child is in the cart or in the seat designed to fit on the cart. Until shopping carts are redesigned to be more stable, you need to know that seats attached to the top of shopping carts or built into them won't prevent a child from falling out if she isn't properly restrained; these seats also won't prevent the cart from tipping over even if the child is restrained.

If possible, you should seek an alternative to placing your child in a shopping cart. If you must do so, make sure she is restrained at all times. Never allow her to stand up in the cart, be transported in the basket, or ride on the outside of the cart. Do not snap an infant car safety seat onto the built-in cart seat, as this can make the cart even more unstable. If one is available, use a shopping cart designed to carry children in a seat that is lower to the ground. Consider using a stroller or baby carrier instead. Never leave a child alone in a shopping cart, even for a moment.

Bicycles and Tricycles

If you like to ride a bicycle, you'll probably consider getting a child carrier that attaches to the back of the bike. You should be aware that even with the best carrier and safety helmet, your child is at risk for serious injury. This can occur when you lose control on an uneven road surface, or if you should happen to strike or be struck by another vehicle. It is wiser to wait to enjoy bicycling together until your child is old enough to ride with you on her own two-wheeler. (See below for further information about child carriers.)

As your child outgrows babyhood, she will want a tricycle of her own, and when she gets one, she'll be exposing herself to a number of hazards. For example, a child on a tricycle is so low to the ground that she can't be seen by a motorist who is backing up. Nevertheless, riding trikes and bikes is almost an essential part of growing up. Here are some safety suggestions that will help you reduce the risk to your child.

1. Don't buy a tricycle until your child is physically able to handle it. Most children are ready around age three.

2. Buy a tricycle that is built low to the ground and has big wheels. This type is safer because it is less likely to tip over.

3. Obtain a properly fitting bicycle helmet, and teach your child to use it every time she rides.

4. Tricycles should be used only in protected places. Don't allow your child to ride near automobiles, driveways, or swimming pools.

5. In general, children don't have the balance and muscle coordination to ride a two-wheel bicycle until around age six. Most children can safely begin to ride a two-wheeler with training wheels after age five, but not before. Again, to protect your child from injury, make sure she is wearing an approved bicycle helmet (certified on the label that it meets the Consumer Product Safety Commission standards).

6. If you're considering having your child ride as a passenger in a rear-mounted seat on an adult's bike, keep in mind that not only will she make the bike unstable, but she also will increase the braking time and raise the risk of serious injury to both you and your youngster. If you must carry your child on a bike, never put her in a seat on the back of your bicycle until she's at least one year old. A much better choice is for your child to ride in a bicycle-towed child trailer, although trailers should not be used in the roadway as they are low and may not be seen by motorists. Children who are old enough (twelve months to four years) to sit well unsupported and whose necks are strong enough to support a lightweight helmet may be carried in a rear-mounted seat, although it is not the preferred choice. *Never* carry infants in backpacks or front packs on a bike.

7. A rear-mounted seat must:

a. be securely attached over the rear wheel;

b. have spoke guards to prevent feet and hands from being caught in the wheels; and

c. have a high back and a sturdy shoulder harness and lap belt that will support a sleeping child.

8. A young passenger should always wear a lightweight infant bike helmet certified for young children to prevent or minimize head injury.

9. The child must be strapped into the bike seat with a sturdy harness.

10. Never ride with a child on the front handlebars or place a seat there.

Playgrounds

Whether it's a swing set in the backyard or the more elaborate apparatus in the park, there are many positive things to say about playground equipment. The use of this equipment encourages children to test and expand their physical abilities. However, there are some inevitable dangers. The risks can be minimized when equipment is well designed and children are taught basic playground manners. Here are some guidelines you can use in selecting playground equipment and sites for your child.

1. Children under five should play on equipment separate from older children.

2. Make sure there is sand, wood chips, or rubberized matting under swings, seesaws, and jungle gyms, and that these surfaces are of proper depth and well maintained. On concrete or asphalt, a fall directly on the head can be serious—even from a height of just a few inches.

3. Wooden structures should be made from all-weather wood, which is less likely to splinter. Examine the surfaces periodically to be sure they are smooth. Metal structures, for example, can get extremely hot in warmer months.

4. Conduct a periodic inspection of equipment, looking especially for loose joints, open chains that could come loose, and rusted cotter pins. Be sure there are no open S hooks or protruding pieces that could hook a child's clothing. On

metal equipment, check for rusted or exposed bolts as well as sharp edges and points. At home, cover them with protective rubber. In a public playground, report the hazard to the appropriate authorities.

5. Be sure swings are made of soft and flexible material. Insist that your child sit in the middle of the seat, holding on with both hands. Don't allow two children to share the same swing. Teach your child never to walk in front of or behind a swing while another child is on it. Avoid equipment in which the swings hang from overhead climbing bars.

6. Your child should wear closed-toe shoes at all times, as surfaces can become hot enough to cause serious burns to bare feet.

7. Be sure children on slides use the ladder instead of climbing up the sliding surface. Don't permit pushing and shoving on the ladder, and have children go up one at a time. Teach your child to leave the bottom of the slide as soon as he reaches it. If a slide has been sitting in the sun for a long time, check the sliding surface to see if it's too hot before letting him use it.

8. Don't allow children under four to use climbing equipment that is taller than they are (e.g., jungle gyms) without close supervision.

9. Between the ages of three and five, your child should use a seesaw only with other children of comparable age and weight. Children under three don't have the arm and leg coordination to use the equipment.

10. Although trampolines often are considered a source of fun for children, about 100,000 people per year are injured on them, including on backyard models. Childhood injuries have included broken bones, head injuries, neck and spinal cord injuries, sprains, and bruises. Parental supervision and protective netting aren't adequate to prevent these injuries. In a 2012 report, the American Academy of Pediatrics reported that there were 97,908 trampoline-related inju-

ries in 2009, resulting in 3,164 hospitalizations. Younger children (five years and younger) had a greater risk of injury, compared with older children. The American Academy of Pediatrics strongly discourages the use of trampolines for recreational use, whether at home, at a friend's house, at the playground, or in a routine gym class. Older children should use trampolines only in training programs for competitive sports such as gymnastics or diving, and only when supervised by a professional trained in trampoline safety.

If, despite these warnings, you choose to have a home trampoline, take the following precautions:

- Place the trampoline on a level surface free from surrounding hazards.

- Inspect the protective padding and the net enclosure often, and replace any damaged parts. (About 20 percent of trampoline injuries are related to direct contact with the springs and frame.)

- Allow only one person on the trampoline at a time. (Most trampoline injuries occur when there are multiple jumpers, particularly younger ones.)

- Do not permit users to do somersaults or flips.

- An adult should supervise any child while she's on the trampoline, and enforce the rules.

- Check your homeowners insurance policy to make certain that you are covered for trampoline-related claims. If not, a rider to the policy may be needed.

Your Backyard

Your backyard can be a safe play area for your child if you eliminate potential hazards. Here are some suggestions for keeping your yard safe.

1. If you don't have a fenced yard, teach your child the boundaries within which she should play. Again, she may not always follow your guidelines, so make sure to watch her very closely. Always have a responsible person supervise outdoor play as young children may wander off or get injured. (See a description of trampoline safety prior to this section on pages 507–508.)

2. Check your yard for dangerous plants. Among preschoolers, plants are a leading cause of poisoning. If you are unsure about any of the plants in your yard, call your local Poison Help Line (1-800-222-1222) and request a list of poisonous plants common to your area. If you have any poisonous plants, either replace them or securely fence and lock that area of the yard away from your child.

3. Teach your child never to pick and eat anything from a plant, no matter how good it looks, without your permission. This is particularly important if you let her help out in a vegetable garden where there's produce that could be eaten.

4. If you use pesticides or herbicides on your lawn or garden, read and follow the instructions carefully. Don't allow children to play on a treated lawn for at least forty-eight hours.

5. Don't use a power mower to cut the lawn when young children are around. The mower may throw sticks or stones with enough force to injure them. Never have your child on a riding mower even when you are driving. It is safest to keep young children indoors while the lawn is being mowed.

6. When you cook food outdoors, screen the grill so that your child cannot touch it, and explain that it is hot like the stove in the kitchen. Store propane grills so your child cannot reach the knobs. Be sure charcoal is cold before you dump it.

7. Never allow your child to play unattended near traffic or in the street, and do not allow her to cross the street by herself, even if it is just to go to a waiting school bus.

Water Safety

Water is one of the most ominous hazards your child will encounter. Young children can drown in only a few inches of water, even if they've had swimming instruction. Parents should know that swimming instruction and swimming skills do not provide "drown-proofing" for children of any age. However, swimming classes for young children are widely available, and the American Academy of Pediatrics now believes that children ages one to four (and older) may be less likely to drown if they have had formal swimming instruction. Even so, because the studies are small, and because they don't define what type of lessons work best, the American Academy of Pediatrics is not recommending *mandatory* swim lessons for all children ages one to four at this time. Instead, a parent's decision on whether to enroll individual children in swim lessons should be based on the child's frequency of exposure to water, his emotional development and physical abilities, and certain health concerns related to pool water infections and pool chemicals. Based on that information, you may want to consider swimming lessons for the following reasons:

1. You may be lulled into being less cautious because you think your child can swim, and children themselves may unwittingly be encouraged to enter the water without supervision.

WHERE WE STAND

THE AMERICAN ACADEMY OF PEDIATRICS feels strongly that parents should never—even for a moment—leave children alone near open bodies of water, such as lakes or swimming pools, nor near water in homes (bathtubs, spas). For backyard pools, rigid, motorized pool covers are not a substitute for four-sided fencing, since pool covers are not likely to be used appropriately and consistently. Parents should learn CPR and keep a telephone and emergency equipment (e.g., life preservers) at poolside.

2. Young children who are repeatedly immersed in water may swallow so much of it that they develop water intoxication. This can result in convulsions, shock, and even death.

3. Children at ages four and older can learn swimming skills more quickly than at a younger age, particularly as their motor development reaches the five-year-old level.

4. Safety training does not result in a significant increase in poolside safety skills of young children.

Children under the age of one may participate in swimming programs with a parent as a fun, recreational activity, but because there is no evidence that programs intended to prevent drowning in infants less than one year old are effective or safe, they should *not* be given this type of swim lessons.

When selecting a swimming program, be sure the class you choose adheres to guidelines established by the national YMCA. And remember that even a child who knows how to swim needs to be watched constantly. Whenever your child is near water (e.g., swimming pools, ponds, beach, etc.), follow these safety rules.

1. Be aware of small bodies of water your child might encounter, such as fishponds, ditches, fountains, rain barrels, watering cans—even the bucket you use when you wash the car. Empty containers of water when you're done using them. Children are drawn to places and things like these and need constant supervision to be sure they don't fall in.

2. Children who are swimming—even in a shallow toddler's pool—always should be watched by an adult, preferably one who knows CPR. (See *Cardiopulmonary Resuscitation and Mouth-to-Mouth Resuscitation*, page 691.) The adult should be within arm's length, providing "touch supervision" whenever young children are in or around water. Empty and put away inflatable pools after each play session.

3. Enforce safety rules: No running near the pool and no pushing others underwater.

4. Don't allow your child to use inflatable toys or mattresses to keep him afloat. These toys may deflate suddenly, or your child may slip off them into water that is too deep for him.

5. Be sure the deep and shallow ends of any pool your child swims in are clearly marked. Never allow your child to dive into the shallow end.

6. If you have a swimming pool at home, it should be completely surrounded with at least a 4-foot (1.2 m)-high fence that has a self-latching and self-locking gate that opens away from the pool. Check the gate frequently to be sure it is in good working order. Keep the gate closed and locked at all times. Be sure your child cannot manipulate the lock or climb the fence. No opening under the fence or between uprights should be more than 4 inches (10 cm) wide. Keep toys out of the pool area when not in use so that children are not tempted to try to get through the fence.

7. If your pool has a cover, remove it completely before swimming. Also, never allow your child to walk on the pool cover; water may have accumulated on it, making it as dangerous as the pool itself. Your child also could fall through and become trapped underneath. Do not use a pool cover in place of a four-sided fence because it is not likely to be used appropriately and consistently.

8. Keep a safety ring with a rope beside the pool at all times. If possible, have a phone in the pool area with emergency numbers clearly marked.

9. Spas and hot tubs are dangerous for young children, who can easily drown or become overheated in them. Don't allow young children to use these facilities.

10. Your child should always wear a life jacket when he swims or rides in a boat. A life jacket fits properly if you can't lift it off over your child's head after he's been fastened into it. For the child under age five, particularly the nonswimmer, it also should have a flotation collar to keep the head upright and the face out of the water.

11. Adults should not drink alcohol when they are swimming. It presents a danger for them as well as for any children they might be supervising. Adult supervisors should know CPR and how to swim.

12. Be sure to eliminate distractions while children are in the water. Talking on the phone, working on the computer, and other tasks need to wait until children are out of and away from the water.

Safety Around Animals

Children are more likely than adults to be bitten by domesticated animals, including your own family pet. This is particularly true when a new baby is brought into the home. At such times, the pet's response should be observed carefully, and it should not be left alone with the infant. After a two- or three-week get-acquainted period, the animal may become used to the baby. However, it is always wise to be cautious when the animal is around, regardless of how much your pet seems to enjoy the relationship.

If you are getting a pet as a companion for your child, wait until she is mature enough to handle and care for the animal—usually around age five or six. Younger children have difficulty distinguishing an animal from a toy, so they may inadvertently provoke a bite through teasing or mistreatment. Remember that you have ultimate responsibility for your child's safety around any animal, so take the following precautions.

1. Look for a pet with a gentle disposition. An older animal is often a good choice for a child, because a puppy or kitten may bite out of sheer friskiness. Avoid older pets raised in a home without children, however.

2. Treat your pet humanely so it will enjoy human company. Don't, for example, tie a dog on a short rope or chain, since extreme confinement may make it anxious and aggressive.

3. Never leave a young child alone with an animal. Many bites occur during periods of playful roughhousing, because the child doesn't realize when the animal gets overexcited.

4. Teach your child not to put her face close to an animal.

5. Don't allow your child to tease your pet by pulling its tail or taking away a toy or a bone. Make sure she doesn't disturb the animal when it's sleeping or eating.

6. Have all pets—both dogs and cats—immunized against rabies.

7. Obey local ordinances about licensing and leashing your pet. Be sure your pet is under your control at all times.

8. Find out which neighbors have dogs, so your child can meet the pets with which she's likely to have contact. Teach your child how to greet a dog: After asking the owner for permission, the child should stand still while the dog sniffs her; then she can slowly extend her hand to pet the animal.

9. Warn your child to stay away from yards in which dogs seem high-strung or unfriendly. Teach older children the signs of an unsafe dog: rigid body, stiff tail at "half mast," hysterical barking, crouched position, staring expression.

10. Instruct your child to stand still if she is approached or chased by a strange dog. Tell her not to run, ride her bicycle, kick, or make threatening gestures. Your child should face the dog and back away slowly until she's out of reach.

11. Wild animals can carry very serious diseases that may be transmitted to humans. You (and your family pets) need to avoid contact with rodents and other wild animals (raccoons, skunks, foxes) that can carry diseases ranging from hantavirus to plague, from toxoplasmosis to rabies. To avoid bites by wild creatures, notify the health department or Animal Control whenever you see an animal that seems sick or injured, or one that is acting strangely. Don't try to catch the animal or pick it up. Teach your child to avoid all undomesticated animals. Fortunately, most wild animals come out only at night and tend to shy away from humans. A wild animal that is found in your yard or neighborhood during the daylight hours might have an infectious disease like rabies, and you should contact the local authorities.

In the Community and Neighborhood

Many parents worry about keeping their child safe in and around the neighborhood. Fortunately, child abductions are rare, although they understandably get plenty of media attention when they occur. Most abductions occur when children are taken by noncustodial parents, although a smaller number of stranger abductions do take place each year.

Here are some suggestions to help keep your child safe.

- When you're shopping with your child, keep an eye on him at all times, as he can move quickly in and out of your line of vision in an instant.

- When choosing a preschool, ask about safety issues. Make sure a policy is in place where your child can be picked up only by his parent or someone else you designate.

- Although your child should be supervised by a trusted adult at all times, it is still important to teach him to never get into a car or go along with someone unfamiliar to him. If a stranger tells him something like "There's a lost puppy in my car; come into the car for a minute and see if you know him," he should emphatically say "no." In fact, tell him to run away as fast as possible from dangers like this and to yell very loudly and find a trusted adult in any situation in which he feels threatened.

- When hiring babysitters, always check references and/or ask for recommendations from friends and family members.

- For more information, contact the National Center for Missing & Exploited Children (1-800-843-5678; www.missingkids.com).

When planning ways to keep your child safe, remember that she is constantly changing. Strategies that protect her from danger when she's one year old may no longer be adequate as she becomes stronger, more curious, and more confident in later months and years. Review your family's home and habits often to make sure your safeguards remain appropriate for your child's age.

A Message for Grandparents

As a grandparent, your grandchild's well-being and safety are extremely important to you. Particularly when she is under your care—at your home, in her own home, in the car, or elsewhere—make sure that you've taken every step possible to ensure that she is safe and secure.

Take the time to read this chapter from beginning to end. It will provide you with guidelines to protect your grandchild in the situations that she's most likely to encounter. Before you have your grandchild visit or stay at your home, make certain that you've reviewed and adopted the recommendations you'll find here.

In this special section, you'll find the most important safety points for grandparents to keep in mind.

SAFETY INSIDE THE HOME

There are plenty of safety measures you should implement in your home to protect your grandchild. To keep some of these guidelines in the forefront of your mind, use the acronym SPEGOS to help remind you of the following:

- **S**moke detectors should be placed in the proper locations throughout the house.

- **P**ets and pet food should be stored out of a child's reach.

- **E**scape plans should be thought about in advance, and fire extinguishers should be readily available.

- **G**ates should be positioned at the top and bottom of stairs.

- Outlet covers that are not a choking hazard should be placed over sockets to prevent your grandchild from putting herself at risk of an electrical shock. Use furniture or other objects to block access to electrical outlets, wherever possible.

- Soft covers or bumpers should be positioned around sharp or solid furniture.

In addition to these general rules, be sure to keep important phone numbers by the telephone and programmed into your mobile cellular device. In an emergency, you'll want to call not only 911 when appropriate, but also certain specific family members. Another safety consideration: Your special chairs or walking aids could be unstable and present a risk; if possible, move them into the closet or a room that your grandchild won't be able to enter when he visits.

Read on to review safety measures for specific areas of your home.

NURSERY/SLEEPING AREA

- **If you saved your own child's crib, stored in your attic or garage, perhaps awaiting the arrival of a grandchild someday, you should replace it with a new one. Guidelines for children's furniture and equipment have changed dramatically, and a crib that is more than a few years old will not meet today's safety standards. This is likely also true for other saved and aging furniture that could pose risks to children, such as an old playpen.**

- **Buy a changing table (see page 477), use your own bed, or even a towel on the floor to change the baby's diapers. As she gets a little older, and she becomes more likely to squirm, you may need a second person to help in changing her diaper.**

- **Don't allow your grandchild to sleep in your bed.**

- **Keep the diaper pail emptied.**

KITCHEN

- **Put "kiddie locks" on the cabinets; to be extra safe, move unsafe cleansers and chemicals so they're completely out of reach.**

- **Remove any dangling cords, such as those from the coffeepot or toaster.**

■ Take extra precautions before giving your grandchild food prepared in microwave ovens. Microwaves can heat liquids and solids unevenly, and they may be mildly warm on the outside but *very hot* on the inside.

BATHROOMS

■ Store pills, inhalers, and other prescription or nonprescription medications, as well as medical equipment, locked and out of the reach of your grandchild. Be especially vigilant that all medications of any kind are kept up and away from a child's reach and sight.

■ Put nonslip material in the bathtub to avoid dangerous falls.

■ If there are handles and bars in the bathtub for your own use, cover them with soft material if you're going to be bathing the baby there.

■ Never leave a child unattended in a tub or sink filled with water.

BABY EQUIPMENT

■ Never leave your grandchild alone in a high chair or in an infant seat located in high places, such as a table or countertop.

■ Do not use baby walkers.

TOYS

■ Buy new toys for your grandchild that have a variety of sounds, sights, and colors. Simple toys can be just as good as more complex ones. Remember, no matter how fancy the toys may be, your own interaction and play with your grandchild are much more important.

■ Toys, CDs, and books should be age-appropriate and challenge children at their own developmental level.

■ Avoid toys with small parts that the baby could put into her mouth and swallow. Follow the recommendations on the package to find toys suitable for your grandchild's age.

■ Because toy boxes can be dangerous, keep them out of your home, or look for one without a top or lid.

GARAGE/BASEMENT

■ Make sure that the automatic reversing mechanism on the garage door is operating.

■ Keep all garden chemicals and pesticides as well as tools in a locked cabinet and out of reach.

SAFETY OUTSIDE THE HOME

Buy a car safety seat that you can keep inside your own car. Make sure you install it properly (or have a trained professional install it for you) and that you can strap your grandchild into it easily. Experiment with the buckles and clasps before you buy the car seat since their ease of use varies. Make sure you know that your grandchild is out of harm's way before backing your car out of the garage or down the driveway.

■ Purchase a stroller to use when taking the baby for a walk in your neighborhood.

■ On shopping trips, whenever possible choose stores that offer child-friendly shopping carts with seats that are low to the ground. Don't place your own car seat into a shopping cart, and avoid putting your grandchild in the seat at the top of the cart if possible.

■ If you have a tricycle or bicycle at your home for your grandchild, make sure you also have a helmet for her. Let her choose a helmet in a special design or color.

■ Although playgrounds can be fun, they also can be dangerous. Select one that has been designed to keep children as safe as possible; those at schools or at community-sponsored parks are often good choices.

■ Inspect your own backyard for anything hazardous or poisonous.

■ If you have a backyard swimming pool, or if you take your grandchild to another home or a park where there is a pool, *carefully read the water safety guidelines in this chapter (see pages 509–511). There should be at least a 4-foot-high fence with a locking gate surrounding the pool.* Make sure that neighbors' pools are enclosed by fences, as well. Practice touch supervision anytime your grandchild is in or near water. You should also know CPR and how to swim.

~ PART 2 ~

THE INFORMATION AND POLICIES in this section, such as first-aid procedures for the choking child and cardiopulmonary resuscitation (CPR), are constantly changing. Ask your pediatrician or other qualified health professional for the latest information on these procedures.

It is rare for children to become seriously ill with no warning. Based on your child's symptoms, you should usually contact your child's pediatrician for advice. Timely treatment of symptoms can prevent an illness from getting worse or turning into an emergency.

~ 16 ~

Abdominal/Gastrointestinal Tract

Abdominal Pain

CHILDREN OF ALL ages experience abdominal pain occasionally, but the causes of such pain in infants tend to be quite different from what they are in older children. So, too, is the way children of different age groups react to the pain. An older child may rub her abdomen and tell you she's having a "belly-ache" or "tummyache," while a very young infant will show her distress by crying and pulling up her legs or by passing gas (which is usually swallowed air). Vomiting or excessive burping also may accompany crying in babies.

Fortunately, most stomach-aches disappear on their own, and are not serious. However, if your child's complaints continue or worsen over a period of three to five hours, or if she has a fever, severe sore throat, or extreme change in appetite or energy level, you should notify your pediatrician immediately. These symptoms may indicate a more serious disorder.

In this section, you'll find descriptions of problems that lead to abdominal pain in children, from colic to intestinal infections. Also, because some causes of abdominal pain occur predominantly in older children rather than infants, a separate portion is devoted to those particular disorders (like constipation). You'll be referred to other sections of this chapter and other chapters in the book, as well, for more detailed descriptions of some of these disorders.

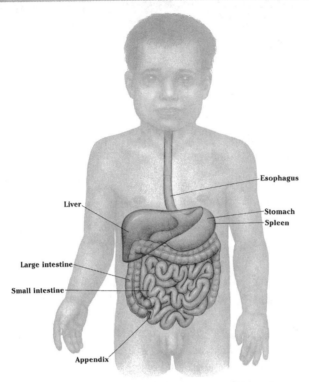

Liver

Large intestine

Small intestine

Appendix

Esophagus

Stomach
Spleen

Abdomen/Gastrointestinal Tract

Abdominal Pain in Infants

Colic usually occurs in infants between the ages of ten days and three months of age. While no one knows exactly what causes it, colic seems to result from rapid and severe contractions of the intestine that probably are responsible for the baby's pain. The discomfort often is more severe in the late afternoon and early evening, and may be accompanied by inconsolable crying, pulling up of the legs, frequent passage of gas, and general irritability. You can try a variety of approaches to colic, which might include rocking your baby, walking with her in a baby carrier, swaddling her in a blanket, or giving her a pacifier. (For more information about colic, see page 166 in Chapter 6, *The First Month*).

Intussusception is a rare condition that may cause abdominal pain in young infants. Intussusception is the most common abdominal emergency in children under age two. This problem occurs when one part of the intestine slides inside another portion of the intestine and becomes trapped, creating a blockage that causes severe pain. The child will intermittently and abruptly cry and pull her legs toward her stomach. This will be followed by periods without stomach pain and often without any distress. These children also may vomit and have dark, mucousy, bloody stools that often look like blackberry jelly. The pain is frequently severe, with periods of screaming followed by periods of quiet or even periods of lethargy.

It is important to recognize this cause of abdominal pain and to talk to your pediatrician immediately. She will want to see your child and perhaps order an X-ray called an air or barium enema. Sometimes doing this test not only enables the diagnosis but also unblocks the intestine. If the enema does not unblock the intestine, an emergency operation may be necessary to correct the problem.

Viral or bacterial infections of the intestine (gastroenteritis) are usually associated with diarrhea and/or vomiting. On-and-off abdominal pain is often also present. Most cases are viral, require no treatment, and will resolve on their own over a week or so; the pain itself generally lasts one or two days and then disappears. One exception is an infection caused by the *Giardia lamblia* parasite. This infestation may produce periodic recurrent pain not localized to any one part of the abdomen. The pain may persist for weeks or months and can lead to a marked loss of appetite and weight. Treatment with appropriate medication can cure this infestation and the abdominal pain that accompanies it. (For more information, see *Diarrhea,* page 530, and *Vomiting,* page 549.)

Abdominal Pain in Older Children

Constipation often is blamed for abdominal pain, and while it's rarely a problem in younger infants, it's a common cause of pain in older children, especially when pain is in the lower part of the abdomen. When a child's diet lacks plenty of fluids, fresh fruits and vegetables, and fiber rich in whole grains, bowel problems are more likely to occur. (For more information, talk to your pediatrician, and see *Constipation* on page 528.)

Urinary tract infections (UTI) are much more common in one- to five-year-old girls than in younger children. UTIs produce discomfort in the abdomen and the bladder area, as well as some pain and burning when urinating. These children also may urinate more frequently and possibly wet the bed. However, the infection usually does not produce a fever. If your child complains of these symptoms, take her to the pediatrician, who will examine her and check her urine. If an infection is present, an antibiotic will be prescribed, which will eliminate both the infection and the abdominal pain. (See *Urinary Tract Infections,* page 778.)

Strep throat is a throat infection caused by bacteria called *streptococci.* It occurs frequently in children over two years of age. The symptoms and signs include a sore throat, fever, and abdominal pain. There may be some vomiting and headache as well. Your pediatrician will want to examine your child and swab her throat to check for strep bacteria. If the results are positive for strep, your child will need to be treated with an antibiotic. (See *Sore Throat*, page 673.)

Appendicitis is very rare in children under age three and uncommon under the age of five. When it does occur, the first sign is often a complaint of constant stomachache in the center of the abdomen, and later the pain moves down and over to the right side. (See *Appendicitis*, page 525, for more detailed information.)

Lead poisoning most often occurs in toddlers living in an older house (built before the 1960s) where lead-based paint has been used. Children in this age group may eat small chips of paint off the walls and woodwork. The lead is then stored in their bodies and can create many serious health problems. Parents also should be aware of toys or other products with unacceptable lead content. (Recalls are posted on the US Consumer Product Safety Commission website at www.cpsc.gov.) Symptoms of lead poisoning include not only abdominal pain, but also constipation, irritability (the child is fussy, crying, difficult to satisfy), lethargy (she is sleepy, doesn't want to play, has a poor appetite), and convulsions. If your child is exposed to lead paint, has eaten paint chips or been exposed to toys with cracking, peeling, or chipping paint, and has any of the above symptoms, call your pediatrician. She can order a blood test for lead and advise you as to what else needs to be done. For all children, it is a good idea to be tested for lead. (See *Lead Poisoning*, page 716.)

Milk allergy is a reaction to the protein in milk, usually in younger infants, and can produce cramping abdominal pain, often accompanied by vomiting, diarrhea, and skin rash. (See *Milk Allergy*, page 566.)

Emotional upset in school-age children sometimes causes recurrent abdominal pain that has no other obvious cause. Although this pain rarely occurs before age five, it can happen to a younger child who is under unusual stress. The first clue is pain that tends to come and go over a period of more than a week, often associated with activity that is stressful or unpleasant. In addition, there are no other associated findings or complaints (fever, vomiting, diarrhea, coughing, lethargy or weakness, urinary tract symptoms, sore throat, or flulike symptoms). There also may be a family history of this type of illness. Finally, your child probably will act either quieter or noisier than usual and have trouble expressing her thoughts or feelings. If this type of behavior occurs with your child, find out if there's something troubling her at home or school or with siblings, relatives, or friends. Has she recently lost a close friend or a pet? Has there been a death of a family member, or the divorce or separation of her parents?

Your pediatrician can suggest ways

to help your child talk about her troubles. For example, he may advise you to use toys or games to help the child act out her problems. If you need additional assistance, the pediatrician may refer you to a child therapist, psychologist, or psychiatrist.

Appendicitis

The appendix is a narrow, finger-shaped, hollow structure attached to the large intestine. While it serves no known purpose in humans, it can cause serious problems when it becomes inflamed. Because of its location, this can happen quite easily; for instance, a piece of food or stool can get trapped inside, causing the appendix to swell and become infected and painfully inflamed. This inflammation—called appendicitis—is most common in children over the age of six, but can occur in younger children. Once infected, the appendix must be removed. Otherwise it may burst, allowing the infection to spread within the abdomen. Since this problem is potentially life-threatening, it's important to know the symptoms of

appendicitis so you can tell your pediatrician at the first sign of trouble. In order of appearance, the symptoms are:

1. Abdominal pain: This usually is the first complaint the child will have. Almost always, the pain is felt first around the belly button (periumbilical), and then may intensify in the lower right side. Sometimes, if the appendix is not located in the usual position, the discomfort may occur elsewhere in the abdomen or in the back, or there may be urinary symptoms, such as increased frequency or burning. Even when the appendix lies in its normal position and the pain is in the right lower abdomen, it may irritate one of the muscles that leads toward the leg, causing the child to limp or walk bent over.

2. Vomiting: After several hours of pain, vomiting may occur. It is important to remember that a stomachache usually comes before the vomiting with appendicitis, not after vomiting. Abdominal pain that follows vomiting is very commonly seen in viral illnesses such as the flu.

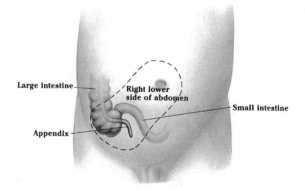

Large intestine

Right lower side of abdomen

Small intestine

Appendix

3. Loss of appetite: The absence of hunger occurs shortly after the onset of the pain.

4. Fever: Unless the appendix ruptures (breaks open), the fever is usually less than 102.2 degrees Fahrenheit (or 39 degrees Celsius).

Unfortunately, the symptoms associated with appendicitis sometimes may be hidden by a viral or bacterial infection that preceded it. Diarrhea, nausea, vomiting, and fever may appear before the typical pain of appendicitis, making the diagnosis much more difficult.

Also, your child's discomfort may suddenly vanish, thus persuading you that all is well. Unfortunately, this disappearance of pain also could mean that the appendix has just broken open or ruptured. Although the pain may leave for several hours, this is exactly when appendicitis becomes dangerous. The infection will spread to the rest of the abdomen, causing your child to become much more ill, develop a higher fever, and require hospitalization for surgery and intravenous antibiotics. Recovery may take much longer, and there may be more complications than with appendicitis diagnosed and treated earlier.

Treatment

Detecting the signs of appendicitis is not always easy, particularly with children under the age of three, who cannot tell you where it hurts or that the pain is moving to the right side. This is why it's better to act sooner rather than later if you have any suspicion that your child's pain or discomfort seems "different," more severe than usual, or out of the ordinary. While most children with abdominal pain don't have appendicitis, only a physician should diagnose this serious problem. If the abdominal pain persists for more than an hour or two, and if your child also has nausea, vomiting, loss of appetite, and fever, notify your pediatrician immediately. If the doctor is not certain that the problem is appendicitis, she may decide to observe your child closely for several hours, either in or out of the hospital. During this time, she will perform additional tests or examinations to see if more conclusive signs develop. If there is a strong probability of appendicitis, surgery usually will be done as soon as possible since surgically removing the appendix is usually the treatment of choice.

Celiac Disease

Celiac disease is a problem that causes malabsorption—that is, a failure of the bowels to absorb nutrients. It's caused by an immune reaction to gluten (the protein found in wheat, rye, barley, and oat products, which can be contaminated with gluten) that takes place in the intestine and stimulates the body's immune system to attack and damage the lining of the intestine, preventing nutrients from being absorbed into the system. As a result, food simply passes through the intestines, only partially digested. The result may be crampy abdominal pain, foul-smelling stools, diarrhea, weight loss, irritability, and a continuous feeling of being sick. In many cases, however, there may be constipation or no symptoms at all with celiac disease.

Treatment

Once your pediatrician suspects celiac disease, he'll order certain blood tests that can be used to screen for celiac disease. These tests measure the blood levels of antibodies to tissue transglutaminase, an enzyme normally present in the intestine and targeted in celiac disease. However, to make a definitive diagnosis, your pediatrician will refer your child to a pediatric gastroenterologist. This specialist will do a small-bowel biopsy, which entails the removal of a very tiny piece of the intestine for laboratory examination. This procedure usually is done by passing a small scope through the mouth and into the small intestine, where the biopsy is obtained.

If the intestinal lining turns out to be damaged, your child will be placed on a gluten-free diet. This means staying away from wheat, rye, barley, and the contaminated oat products. Your pediatrician or gastroenterologist will give you a complete list of foods to avoid, but you also need to carefully check the labels of any foods you purchase, since wheat flour is a hidden ingredient in many items. Because rice and rice products do not contain gluten, they'll probably become a major part of your child's diet. The number of gluten-free products in the grocery stores continues to increase, and some restaurants have gluten-free menus. Consultation with a dietitian is recommended, as the diet is very strict and must be followed exactly.

Some parents ask if they can just try a gluten-free diet without doing diagnostic testing. This is not recommended for several reasons. First, as stated before, the gluten-free diet in celiac disease is very strict. Few families can adhere rigidly enough to the diet without confidence that the diagnosis is correct. Second, it may take months for symptoms to completely resolve in a patient with celiac disease on a gluten-free diet. Finally, the gluten-free diet will cause both the serum and tissue markers of celiac disease to disappear, making it impossible to diagnose the disease accurately without putting your child back on a gluten-containing diet for several months.

Incidentally, your child may not be able to tolerate milk sugar for as long as several months after the initial diagnosis is made. In this case, you may be advised to eliminate milk temporarily, as well as gluten products, from her diet. During this time she might be given milk treated with enzymes, so that it will be predigested before reaching the intestine. Extra vitamins and minerals also might be necessary.

If your child does have celiac disease, she must remain on a gluten-free diet for her entire life, completely avoiding wheat, rye, barley, and contaminated oat products.

(See also: *Diarrhea,* page 530; *Malabsorption,* page 547; *Milk Allergy,* page 566; *Anemia,* page 621.)

Constipation

Bowel patterns vary in children just as they do in adults. Because of this, it is sometimes difficult to tell if your child is truly constipated. One child may go two or three days without a bowel movement and still not be constipated, while another might have relatively frequent bowel movements but have difficulty passing the stool. Or a child's constipation may go unnoticed if he passes a small stool each day, while a buildup of stool develops in his colon. In general, it is best to watch for the following signals if you suspect constipation:

■ In a newborn, firm stools less than once a day, though this can be normal in some exclusively breastfed infants

■ In an older child, stools that are hard and compact, with three or four days between bowel movements

■ At any age, stools that are large, hard and dry, and associated with painful bowel movements

■ Episodes of abdominal pain relieved after having a large bowel movement

■ Blood in or on the outside of the stools

■ Soiling between bowel movements

Constipation generally occurs when the muscles at the end of the large intestine tighten, preventing the stool from passing normally. The longer the stool remains there, the firmer and drier it becomes, making it even more difficult to pass without discomfort. Then, because the bowel movement is painful, your child may actively try to hold it in, making the problem still worse.

The tendency toward constipation seems to run in families. It may start in infancy and remain as a lifetime pattern, becoming worse if the child does not establish regular bowel habits or withholds stool. Stool retention occurs most commonly between the ages of two and five, at a time when the child is coming to terms with independence, control, and toilet training. Older children may resist having bowel movements away from home because they don't want to use an unfamiliar toilet. This, too, can cause constipation or make it worse.

If your child does withhold, he may produce such large stools that his rectum stretches. Then he may no longer feel the urge to defecate until the stool is too big to be passed without the help of an enema, laxative, or other treatment. In some of these cases, soiling occurs when liquid waste leaks around the solid stool. This looks like diarrhea or soiling on the child's underpants or diaper. In these severe cases, the rectum must be emptied under a physician's supervision, and the child must be retrained to establish normal bowel patterns. Consulting a pediatric gastroenterologist may be necessary.

Treatment

Mild or occasional episodes of constipation may be helped by the following suggestions.

Constipation due to breast milk is unusual, but if your breastfed infant is constipated, it is probably due to a reason other than diet. Consult your doctor before substituting formula for breast milk. (Keep in mind that the American Academy of Pediatrics recommends breastfeeding and avoiding cow's milk for the first twelve months of life.)

For infants, ask your pediatrician about giving small amounts of water or prune juice. In addition, for infants older than six months, fruits (especially prunes and pears) can often help resolve constipation.

For a toddler or older child who is eating solid foods and has problems with constipation, you may need to add high-fiber foods to his daily diet. These include prunes, apricots, plums, raisins, high-fiber vegetables (peas, beans, broccoli), and whole-grain cereals and bread products. At the same time, cut back on junk food, and cereals or breads that are not high in fiber. Increasing the daily water intake also may help.

In more severe cases, your pediatrician—alone or in consultation with a pediatric gastroenterologist—may prescribe a mild stool softener or enema. Follow such prescriptions exactly. Although some newer softeners are over the counter and simpler to use than these products used to be, never give your child a stool-loosening medication without first consulting with your doctor.

Prevention

Parents should become familiar with their children's normal bowel patterns and the typical size and consistency of their stools. Doing this is helpful in determining when constipation occurs and how severe the problem is. If the child does not have regular bowel movements each day or two, or is uncomfortable when they are passed, he may need help in developing proper bowel habits. This may be done by providing a proper diet and establishing a regular bowel routine.

In a child who is not yet toilet trained, the best way to guard against constipation is to provide a high-fiber diet. Increase the fiber as he gets older. A child should eat at a minimum his age plus five in fiber grams. For example, a three-year-old should eat at least 8 grams of fiber per day. To help reach that target, buy grains (cereals, crackers, breads, tortillas, pastas) that have at least 3 grams of fiber per serving. Make sure your child is getting five servings of fruits and vegetables each day. Read product labels about fiber content before choosing which items to serve your family.

Once the child is mature enough to be toilet trained, urge him to sit on the toilet every day, preferably after a meal. A book, puzzle, or toy can occupy him during this time so that he feels relaxed. Encourage him to stay on the toilet until he has a bowel movement, or for about fifteen minutes. Praise him if he is successful; if he is not, encourage him with positive statements. Eventually he should be able to use the toilet himself without parental guidance.

If the combination of a high-fiber diet, increases in fluids in the diet, and a daily toilet routine does not result in regular bowel movements, the child may consciously be withholding stool. In this case, you should consult your pediatrician, who may suggest an individualized approach to resolve the problem (every child's condition is unique). Your doctor can supervise stool softeners, laxatives, or suppositories, should they be necessary. Occasionally stool withholding becomes so severe that both the child and the family become upset by the symptoms. Much of each day's interactions focus on bowel movements. Programs have been devised to deal effectively with this problem.

Usually the withholding begins around the time of toilet training. The child is reluctant to move his bowels on the potty or toilet and withholds. The next bowel movement is painful. The child associates pain with bowel movements and now withholds stool because of this. The situation can progress to an all-consuming fear. When such severe symptoms develop, the rectum must be cleansed with enemas or rectal suppositories. Following this, a stool softener is given in amounts large enough to prevent the child from voluntarily withholding stool. Because the bowel movements are now no longer painful, the child will start to go on the potty without fear. This treatment may go on for several months while the laxative is slowly withdrawn. A diet high in fiber and regular toileting are also part of the routine.

Diarrhea

Normally your child's bowel movements will vary in number and consistency, depending on her age and diet. Breastfed newborns may have up to twelve small bowel movements a day, but by the second or third month, they may have some days without any. Most babies under one year of age produce less than 5 ounces (150 ml) of stool per day, while older children can produce up to 7 ounces (210 ml). By age two, most children will have only one or two large bowel movements a day, but your child can have several smaller ones and still be normal, especially if his diet includes juices or fiber-containing foods, such as prunes or bran.

An occasional loose stool is not cause for alarm. If, however, your child's bowel pattern suddenly changes to loose, watery stools that occur more frequently than usual, he has diarrhea.

Diarrhea occurs when the inner lining of the intestine is injured. The stools become loose because the intestine does not properly digest or absorb the nutrients from the foods that your child eats and drinks. Also, the injured lining tends to leak fluid. Minerals and salt are lost along with the fluid. This loss can be made even

Causes of Diarrhea

In young children, the intestinal damage that produces diarrhea is caused most often by viruses such as norovirus and rotavirus. Such viruses are easily transmitted from person to person. Diarrhea caused by bacteria and parasitic infections have decreased in frequency as a result of improvements in public health such as clean drinking water and proper disposal of sewage. Other causes of diarrhea are:

- Food poisoning (from things such as mushrooms, shellfish, or contaminated food)

- Side effects from oral medication (most commonly antibiotics)

- Food or milk allergy

- Infections outside the gastrointestinal tract, including the urinary tract, the respiratory tract, and even the middle ear (if your child is taking an antibiotic for such an infection, the diarrhea may become more severe.)

- Drinking fruit juice

worse if your child is fed food or beverages that contain large amounts of sugar such as found in fruit juice and sweetened beverages, since unabsorbed sugar draws even more water into the intestine, increasing the diarrhea.

When the body loses too much water and salt, dehydration results. This can be prevented by replenishing losses due to the diarrhea with adequate amounts of fluid and salt, as described under *Treatment* (page 532).

The medical term for intestinal inflammation is *enteritis*. When the problem is accompanied by or preceded by vomiting, as it often is, there is usually some stomach and small-intestinal inflammation, as well, and the condition is called *gastroenteritis*.

The causes of diarrhea are described in the box (*Causes of Diarrhea* above), and include viral or bacterial infections of the intestine. Children with viral diarrheal illnesses often have symptoms such as vomiting, fever, and irritability. (See *Vomiting,* page 549; Chapter 27, *Fever*.) Their stools tend to be greenish yellow in color and have a significant amount of water with them. (If they occur as often as once an hour, they usually won't have any solid stool at all.) If the stools appear red or blackish, they might contain blood; this bleeding may arise from the injured lining of the intestine or, more likely, simply may be due to irritation of the rectum by frequent, loose bowel movements. In any event, if you notice this or any other unusual stool color, you should notify your pediatrician.

A rotavirus vaccine is now given routinely to infants starting at two months of age. This is a liquid that is swallowed, not a shot. It is very good at preventing diarrhea and vomiting caused by rotavirus. Almost all babies who get rotavirus vaccine will be protected from severe rotavirus diarrhea. The vaccine will not prevent diarrhea or vomiting caused by other germs. Infants are given this rotavirus vaccine in an oral, three-dose regimen at two, four, and six months of age. There is an alternative to this RV5 immunization, called RV1, and it should be given orally in a two-dose regimen at two and four months of age. Either formulation is fine.

Treatment

There are no effective medications for treating viral intestinal infections, which cause most cases of diarrhea in infants. Prescription medications should be used only to treat certain types of bacterial or parasitic intestinal infections, which are much less common. When the latter conditions are suspected, your pediatrician will ask for stool specimens to be tested in the laboratory; other tests also may be done.

Some studies indicate that probiotics may be beneficial for certain causes of infectious diarrhea. In one study in otherwise healthy children, administering probiotics early in the course of diarrhea from viral gastroenteritis decreased its duration by one day. These dietary supplements are believed to help with the digestive process, as well as allergies and vaginal infections. (See *Probiotics and Prebiotics,* page 536.)

Over-the-counter antidiarrheal medications are not recommended for children under age two and should be used with caution in older children. They often worsen the intestinal injury and cause the fluid and salt to remain within the intestine, instead of being absorbed. With these medications, your child can become dehydrated without your being aware of it, because the diarrhea appears to stop. Always consult your pediatrician before giving your child any medication for diarrhea.

MILD DIARRHEA

If your child has a small amount of diarrhea but is not dehydrated (see the box on page 540 for signs of dehydration), does not have a high fever, and is active and hungry, you may not need to change her diet.

If your child has mild diarrhea and is vomiting, substitute a commercially available electrolyte solution for her normal diet. Your pediatrician will recommend these solutions to be given in small amounts, frequently to maintain normal body water and salt levels until the vomiting has stopped. In most cases, they're needed for only one to two days. Once the vomiting has subsided, gradually restart the normal diet.

Never give boiled milk (skimmed or otherwise) to any child with diarrhea. Boiling the milk allows the water to evaporate, leaving the remaining part dangerously high in salt and mineral content. In fact, you should never give boiled milk even to a well child.

SIGNIFICANT DIARRHEA

If your child has a watery bowel movement every one to two hours, or more frequently, and/or has signs of dehydration (see the box on page 540), consult his pediatrician. She may advise you to withhold all solid foods for at least twenty-four hours and to avoid liquids that are high in sugar (Jell-O, soft drinks, full-strength fruit juices, or artificially sweetened beverages), high in salt (packaged broth), or very low in salt (water and tea). She probably will have you give him only commercially prepared electrolyte solutions, which contain the ideal balance of salt and minerals. (See the table *Estimated Oral Fluid and Electrolyte Requirements by Body Weight* on page 535.) Breastfed babies usually are treated in a similar fashion except in very mild cases, when breastfeeding may be continued.

Remember, if your child has diarrhea, keeping him hydrated is very important. If he shows any signs of dehydration (such as decreased wet diapers, no tears, sunken eyes or fontanelle), call your pediatrician right away and withhold all foods and milk beverages until she gives you further instructions. Also contact your doctor if your child looks sick, and the symptoms aren't improving with time. *Take your child to the pediatrician or nearest emergency department immediately if you think he is moderately to severely dehydrated.* In the meantime, give your child a commercially prepared electrolyte solution.

For severe dehydration, hospitalization is sometimes necessary so that your child can be rehydrated intravenously. In milder cases, all that may be necessary is to give your child an electrolyte replacement solution according to your pediatrician's directions. The table on page 535 indicates the approximate amount of this solution to be used.

Exclusively breastfed babies are less likely to develop severe diarrhea. If a breastfed infant does develop diarrhea, generally you can continue breastfeeding, giving additional electrolyte solution only if your doctor feels this is necessary. Many breastfed babies can continue to stay hydrated with frequent breastfeeding alone.

Once your child has been on an electrolyte solution for twelve to twenty-four hours and the diarrhea is decreasing, you gradually may expand the diet to include foods such as applesauce, pears, bananas, and flavored gelatin, with a goal of returning to his usual diet over the next few days as he tolerates. In children over age one, milk can be withheld for one to two days until the diarrhea begins improving, or try lactose-free milk instead. In infants on formula, you can mix the formula with twice as much water as usual to make half-strength formula for a few feeds until the diarrhea seems to be improving and then you can mix it as usual. (Add an equal volume of water to your child's usual full-strength formula.) As the vomiting and diarrhea improve, an older child may be able to eat small quantities of bland foods such as rice, toast, potatoes, and cereal, and should be moved to an age-appropriate diet as soon as possible. You can continue to give the electrolyte replacement solution if your child likes it or they are not taking usual amounts of their regular fluids.

It is usually unnecessary to withhold food for longer than twenty-four hours, as your child will need some normal nutrition to start to regain lost strength. After you have started giving him food again, his stools may remain loose, but that does not necessarily mean that things are not going well. Look for increased activity, better appetite, more frequent urination, and the disappearance of any of the signs of dehydration. When you see these, you will know your child is getting better.

Diarrhea that lasts longer than two weeks (chronic diarrhea) may signify a more serious type of intestinal problem. When diarrhea persists this long, your pediatrician will want to do further tests to determine the cause and to make sure your child is not becoming malnourished. If malnutrition is becoming a problem, the pediatrician may recommend a special diet or special type of formula.

If your child drinks too much fluid, especially too much juice or sweetened beverages as mentioned earlier, a condition commonly referred to as toddler's diarrhea could develop. This causes ongoing loose stools but shouldn't affect appetite or growth or cause dehydration. Although toddler's diarrhea is not a dangerous condition, the pediatrician may suggest that you limit the amounts of juice and sweetened fluids your child drinks (limiting fruit juice is always a good idea). You can give plain water to children whose thirst does not seem to be satisfied by their normal dietary and milk intake.

When diarrhea occurs in combination with other symptoms, it could mean that there is a more serious medical problem. Notify your pediatrician immediately if the diarrhea is accompanied by any of the following:

■ Fever that lasts longer than twenty-four to forty-eight hours

■ Bloody stools

■ Vomiting that lasts more than twelve to twenty-four hours

■ Vomited material that is green-colored, blood-tinged, or like coffee grounds in appearance

■ A distended (swollen-appearing) abdomen

■ Refusal to eat or drink

■ Severe abdominal pain

■ Rash or jaundice (yellow color of skin and eyes)

If your child has another medical condition or is taking medication routinely, it is best to tell your pediatrician about any diarrheal illness that lasts more than twenty-four hours without improvement, or anything else that really worries you.

Estimated Oral Fluid and Electrolyte Requirements by Body Weight
1 Pound = 0.45 Kilograms
1 Ounce = 30 Milliliters

Body Weight (in pounds)	Minimum Daily Fluid Requirements (in ounces)*	Electrolyte Solution* Requirements for Mild Diarrhea (in ounces for 24 hours)
6–7	10	16
11	15	23
22	25	40
26	28	44
33	32	51
40	38	61

*NOTE: This is the smallest amount of fluid that a normal child requires. Most children drink more than this.

Prevention

The following guidelines will help lessen the chances that your child will get diarrhea.

1. Most forms of infectious diarrhea are transmitted from direct hand-to-mouth contact following exposure to contaminated fecal (stool) material. This happens most often in children who are not toilet trained. Promote personal hygiene (e.g., hand-washing after using the toilet or changing diapers and before handling food) and other sanitary measures in your household and in your child's child care center or preschool.

2. Do not give your child raw (unpasteurized) milk or foods that may be contaminated. (See *Food Poisoning,* page 537.)

3. Avoid unnecessary medications, especially antibiotics.

4. If possible, breastfeed your child through early infancy.

5. Limit the amount of juice and sweetened beverages.

6. Make sure your child has received the rotavirus vaccine, as it protects against the most common cause of diarrhea and vomiting in infants and young children.

Probiotics and Prebiotics

Probiotics (meaning "for life") are types of "good" bacteria. These living organisms inhabit the intestines, and may have beneficial health effects, although the evidence is not yet conclusive. Some studies have shown that foods or infant formula containing probiotics can prevent or even treat diarrhea in children, whether this condition is chronic or acute, or is associated with the use of antibiotics. To date, the strongest evidence suggests that probiotics may help avoid or improve viral gastroenteritis (see page 532); they also may strengthen a child's disease-fighting immune system and thus help fight off a number of infections that could lead to diarrhea. In one study of 326 children ages three to five years in a child care center over a six-month period, single and combination probiotics (twice a day for six months) lowered the incidence of fever by 53 percent and 72.7 percent in two groups receiving probiotics, compared to a control or placebo group; the presence of coughing was lowered by 41.4 percent and 62.1 percent in the two treatment groups, and the incidence of runny nose decreased 28.2 percent and 58.5 percent. Ongoing research will provide more guidance on the role of probiotics in children, but if your child has diarrhea, you may wish to talk to your doctor about the use of these organisms. Benefits from probiotics appear to occur only as long as probiotics are being taken.

Probiotics are available in many forms. Many infant formulas are now supplemented with probiotics. Some dairy products such as yogurt and kefir contain them, too. So do miso, tempeh, and soy beverages. Probiotic supplements (powders, capsules) are sold in health food stores; pediatricians are still debating the most appropriate use of these commercial probiotics—for example, what are the best dosages, how frequently should they be taken, and should they be used at all for preventing or managing certain health conditions? To date, there is not enough evidence to give probiotics to seriously ill children, nor is there persuasive data to recommend their routine use in infant formulas.

Foods containing probiotics appear to be safe for most children, although they can cause mild bloating or gas in some cases. If products like probiotic supplements have been exposed to heat or moisture, the living "good" bacteria may be killed, and thus the products will become useless. For now, if you're interested in trying probiotics, talk to your pediatrician first. (For more information about probiotics, see page 119.)

Some doctors recommend that rather than giving your child *probiot-*

ics, you should consider using *prebiotics* instead. While probiotics are living bacteria, prebiotics are nondigestible food components (such as complex sugars and fiber). They promote the growth of beneficial bacteria that are already present in the intestines, thus increasing the number of these good bacteria while also suppressing the growth of unhealthy strains. They also may decrease the levels of inflammation in the intestines and stimulate the absorption of calcium.

Breast milk is a good source of prebiotics. So are foods like bran, legumes, and barley, as well as certain vegetables (asparagus, spinach, onion) and fruits (berries, bananas).

(See also *Abdominal Pain*, page 521; *Celiac Disease*, page 526; *Malabsorption*, page 547; *Milk Allergy*, page 566; *Rotavirus*, page 812; and *Vomiting*, page 549.)

Food Poisoning and Food Contamination

Food poisoning occurs after eating food contaminated by bacteria. The symptoms of food poisoning are basically the same as those of stomach flu: abdominal cramps, nausea, vomiting, diarrhea, and fever. But if your child and other people who have eaten the same food all have the same symptoms, the problem is more likely to be food poisoning than stomach flu. The bacteria that cause food poisoning cannot be seen, smelled, or tasted, so your child won't know when she is eating them. These organisms include:

STAPHYLOCOCCUS AUREUS (STAPH)
Staph contamination is the leading cause of food poisoning. These bacteria ordinarily cause skin infections, such as pimples or boils, and are transferred when foods are handled by an infected person. When food is left at a specific temperature (100 degrees Fahrenheit [37.8 Celsius])—generally one that is lower than the temperature needed to keep food hot—the staph bacteria multiply and produce a poison (toxin) that ordinary cooking will not destroy. The symptoms begin one to six hours after eating the contaminated food, and the discomfort usually lasts about one day.

SALMONELLA
Salmonella bacteria (there are many types) are another major cause of food poisoning in the United States. The most commonly contaminated foods are raw meat (including chicken), raw or undercooked eggs, unpasteurized milk, and vegetables. Fortunately, salmonella are killed when the food is cooked thoroughly. For vegetables, make sure they are washed thoroughly. Symptoms caused by salmonella poisoning start sixteen to forty-eight hours after eating, and may last two to seven days. Although a salmonella in-

fection is usually self-limiting, it can be severe; so if your child appears sick and has a high fever, call your doctor.

E. COLI

Escherichia coli (or *E. coli*) is a group of bacteria that normally live in the intestines of children and adults. A few strains of these bacteria can cause food-related illnesses. Undercooked ground beef is a common source of *E. coli*, although raw produce and contaminated water have caused some outbreaks.

Symptoms of an infection typically include diarrhea (which can range from mild to severe) to abdominal pain, and in some cases nausea and vomiting. Some *E. coli* outbreaks have been quite severe and have even caused deaths in rare instances. The optimal treatment for an *E. coli*–related illness is rest and fluids (to counteract dehydration). But if symptoms are more severe, you should have a discussion with your pediatrician.

CLOSTRIDIUM PERFRINGENS

Clostridium perfringens (*C. perfringens*) is a bacterium frequently found in soil, sewage, and the intestines of humans and animals. It usually is transferred by the food handler to the food itself, where it multiplies and produces its toxin. *C. perfringens* often is found in school cafeterias because it thrives in food that is served in quantity and left out for long periods at room temperature or on a steam table. The foods most often involved are cooked beef, poultry, gravy, fish,

casseroles, stews, and bean burritos. The symptoms of this type of poisoning start eight to twenty-four hours after eating, and can last from one to several days.

SHIGELLOSIS

Shigella infections, or shigellosis, are intestinal infections caused by one of many types of shigella bacteria. These bacteria can be transmitted through contaminated food and drinking water, as well as via poor hygiene (in child care centers, for example). The organisms invade the lining of the intestine, and can lead to symptoms such as diarrhea, fever, and cramps.

Shigellosis and its symptoms usually subside after about five to seven days. In the meantime, your child should consume extra fluids and (if your pediatrician recommends it) a rehydrating solution. In severe cases, your doctor may prescribe antibiotics, which can shorten the duration and intensity of the infection.

CAMPYLOBACTER

One form of infectious food poisoning is caused by the bacteria *Campylobacter*, which a child may ingest when he eats raw or undercooked chicken, or drinks unpasteurized milk or contaminated water. This infection typically leads to symptoms such as watery (and sometimes bloody) diarrhea, cramps, and fever, about two to five days after the germs are consumed in food.

To diagnose a *Campylobacter* infection, your doctor will have a culture of a stool specimen analyzed in the laboratory. Fortunately, most cases of this infection run their course without any formal treatment, other than making sure that your child drinks plenty of fluids in order to replace the fluids lost from diarrhea. When symptoms are severe, however, your pediatrician may prescribe antibiotics. In most cases, your child will be back to normal in about two to five days.

BOTULISM

This is the deadly food poisoning caused by *Clostridium botulinum*. Although these bacteria normally can be found in soil and water, illness from them is extremely rare because they need very special conditions in order to multiply and produce poison. *Clostridium botulinum* grows best without oxygen and in certain chemical conditions, which explains why improperly canned food is most often contaminated and the low-acid vegetables, such as green beans, corn, beets, and peas, are most often involved. Honey also can be contaminated and frequently causes severe illness, particularly in children under one year of age. This is the reason why **honey should never be given to an infant under the age of one year.**

Botulism attacks the nervous system and causes double vision, droopy eyelids, decreased muscle tone, and difficulty in swallowing and breathing. It also can cause vomiting, diarrhea, and abdominal pain. The symptoms develop in eighteen to thirty-six hours and can last weeks to months. Without treatment, botulism can cause death. Even with treatment, it can cause nerve damage.

CRYPTOSPORIDIOSIS

In very uncommon situations, watery diarrhea, low-grade fever, and abdominal pain may be caused by an infection known as cryptosporidium. This infection is of special concern in children who do not have a normal immune system.

Other sources of food poisoning include poisonous mushrooms, contaminated fish products, and foods with special seasonings. Young children do not care for most of these foods and so will eat very little of them. However, it still is very important to be aware of the risk. If your child has unusual gastrointestinal symptoms, and there is any chance she might have eaten contaminated or poisonous foods, call your pediatrician.

Treatment

In most cases of food-borne illnesses, all that's necessary is to limit your child's eating and drinking for a while. The problem will then usually resolve itself. Infants can tolerate three to four hours without food or liquids; older children, six to eight. If your child is still vomiting or her diarrhea has not decreased significantly during this time, call your pediatrician.

Also notify the doctor if your child:

Signs and Symptoms of Dehydration (Loss of Significant Amounts of Body Water)

The most important part of treating diarrhea is to prevent your child from becoming dehydrated. Be alert for the following warning signs of dehydration, and notify the pediatrician immediately if any of them develop.

MILD TO MODERATE DEHYDRATION:

- Plays less than usual

- Urinates less frequently (for infants, fewer than six wet diapers per day)

- Parched, dry mouth

- Fewer tears when crying

- Sunken soft spot of the head in an infant or toddler

- Stools will be loose if dehydration is caused by diarrhea; if dehydration is due to other fluid loss (vomiting, lack of fluid intake), there will be decreased bowel movements

SEVERE DEHYDRATION (IN ADDITION TO THE SYMPTOMS AND SIGNALS ALREADY LISTED):

- Very fussy

- Excessively sleepy

- Sunken eyes

- Cool, discolored hands and feet

- Wrinkled skin

- Urinates only one to two times per day

- Shows signs of dehydration (See table *Signs and Symptoms of Dehydration* above.)

- Has bloody diarrhea

- Has continuous diarrhea with a large volume of water in the stool, or diarrhea alternating with constipation

- May have been poisoned by mushrooms

- Suddenly becomes weak, numb, confused, or restless, and feels tingling, acts drunkenly, or has hallucinations or difficulty breathing

Tell the doctor the symptoms your child is having, what foods she has eaten recently, and where they were obtained. The treatment your pediatrician gives will depend on your child's condition and the type of food poisoning. If she is dehydrated, fluid replacement will be prescribed. Sometimes antibiotics are helpful, but only if the bacteria are known. Antihistamines help if the illness is due to an allergic reaction to a food, toxin, or seasoning. If your child has botulism, she will require hospitalization and intensive care.

Prevention

Most food-borne illness is preventable if you observe the following guidelines.

CLEANLINESS

■ **Be especially careful** when preparing raw meats and poultry. After you have rinsed the meat thoroughly, wash your hands and all surfaces that have come in contact with the raw meat and poultry, with hot, sudsy water before continuing your preparation.

■ **Always wash your** hands before preparing meals and after going to the bathroom or changing your child's diaper.

■ **If you have** open cuts or sores on your hands, wear gloves while preparing food.

■ **Do not prepare** food when you are sick, particularly if you have nausea, vomiting, abdominal cramps, or diarrhea.

FOOD SELECTION

■ **Carefully examine any** canned food (especially home-canned goods) for signs of bacterial contamination.

Look for milky liquid surrounding vegetables (it should be clear), cracked jars, loose lids, and swollen cans or lids. *Don't use canned or jarred goods showing any of these signs. Do not even taste them. Throw them away so that nobody else will eat them.* (Wrap them first in plastic and then in a heavy paper bag.)

■ **Buy all meats** and seafood from reputable suppliers.

■ **Do not use** raw (unpasteurized) milk or cheese made from raw milk.

■ **Do not eat** raw meat.

■ **Do not give** honey to a baby under one year of age.

■ **If your child** turns away from a particular food or drink, try it yourself; you may find that it is spoiled and that it shouldn't be eaten.

■ **Call Poison Control** 1-800-222-1222 for guidance if your child becomes ill after eating.

FOOD PREPARATION AND SERVING

■ **Do not let** prepared foods (particularly starchy ones), cooked and cured meats, cheese, or anything with mayonnaise stay at room temperature for more than two hours.

■ **Do not interrupt** the cooking of meat or poultry to finish the cooking later.

- **Do not prepare** food one day for the next unless it will be frozen or refrigerated right away. (Always put hot food right into the refrigerator. Do not wait for it to cool first.)

- **Make sure all** foods are cooked thoroughly. Use a meat thermometer for large items like roasts or turkeys, and cut into other pieces of meat to check if they are done.

- **When reheating meals,** cover them and reheat them thoroughly.

- **You also may** want to contact the US Department of Agriculture, Washington, DC 20250, www.usda.gov. The department has a number of helpful pamphlets and newsletters, including topics such as cooking on a grill and preparing holiday turkeys.

Hepatitis

Hepatitis is an inflammation of the liver that, in children, is almost always caused by one of several viruses. In some children it may cause no symptoms, while in others it can provoke fever, jaundice (yellow skin), loss of appetite, nausea, and vomiting. There are at least six forms of hepatitis, each categorized according to the type of virus that causes it. The most common forms include:

1. Hepatitis A, also called infectious hepatitis or epidemic jaundice. Routine vaccination is recommended for all children at one year of age with a booster dose six to twelve months later.

2. Hepatitis B, also known as serum hepatitis or transfusion jaundice. Routine vaccination is now recommended for all infants at birth, with two booster doses given.

3. Hepatitis C, which is an important cause of chronic hepatitis. Currently there is no vaccine.

About one-half of all cases of hepatitis are caused by hepatitis B; of the remainder, slightly less than one-half are caused by hepatitis A, and nearly all of the rest are hepatitis C. Fortunately, with the routine vaccination now of nearly all children against hepatitis A and B (see above), the cases of hepatitis are decreasing.

Children, especially those in low socioeconomic groups, have the highest incidence of hepatitis A infection. However, because they often have no symptoms, their illnesses may go unrecognized.

Hepatitis A can be transmitted directly from person to person or through contaminated food or water. Commonly, human feces contain the virus, so in a child care or household setting, the infection can be spread when hands are not washed after having a bowel movement or after changing the diaper of an infected infant. Anyone who drinks water contaminated with infected human feces or who eats raw shellfish taken from polluted areas also may become infected. A child infected with hepatitis A virus may develop no symptoms or will become ill two to six weeks after the virus is transmitted. The illness usually disappears within one month after it begins.

Although hepatitis A is rarely transmitted via contaminated blood or semen, hepatitis B is usually spread through these body fluids. The incidence of hepatitis B infection is now greatest among adolescents, young adults, and in the newborns of women who are infected with the virus. When a pregnant woman has acute or chronic hepatitis B, she may transmit the infection to her newborn at the time of delivery. Therefore, all pregnant women should be tested for hepatitis B infection. Among adults and adolescents, the virus can be transmitted during sexual activity, and young children sometimes contract the infection through nonsexual, person-to-person contact.

In the past, hepatitis C was acquired from contaminated blood transfusions. With screening of all donors using new, sensitive tests, however, blood contaminated with the hepatitis C virus is now detectable and discarded. Hepatitis C also can be acquired by intravenous (IV) drug abusers who use contaminated needles. However, the use of sterile disposable needles and the screening of all blood and blood products has essentially eliminated the risk of transmission of hepatitis B and C in hospitals and doctors' offices. Infection with the hepatitis C virus commonly produces no symptoms, or only mild symptoms of fatigue and jaundice. In many cases, however, this form of hepatitis becomes chronic and can result in severe liver disease, liver failure, cancer of the liver, and even death later on in life.

Signs and Symptoms

A child could have hepatitis without anyone being aware of it, since many affected children have few, if any, symptoms. In some children the only signs of disease may be malaise and fatigue for several days. In others there will be a fever followed by jaundice (the sclera, or whites of the eyes, and the skin develop noticeable yellowish color). This jaundice is due to an abnormal increase in bilirubin (a yellow pigment) in the blood, caused by liver inflammation.

With hepatitis B, fever is less likely to occur, although the child may suffer loss of appetite, nausea, vomiting, abdominal pain, and malaise, in addition to jaundice. In children, hepatitis C doesn't always have symptoms.

If you suspect that your child has jaundice, notify your pediatrician. She will order blood tests to determine if hepatitis is causing the problem, or if it is due to another condition. You should contact your doctor anytime vomiting and/or abdominal pain persist beyond a few hours, or if appetite loss, nausea, or malaise continue for more than a few days or if your child becomes jaundiced. These may be indicators of hepatitis.

Treatment

In most settings, there is no specific treatment for hepatitis. As with most viral infections, the body's own defense mechanisms usually will overcome the infecting agent. Although you do not need to rigidly restrict the diet or activity of your child, you may need to make adjustments depending on his appetite and energy levels. Your doctor may recommend your child avoid aspirin and ibuprofen (and other nonsteroidal anti-inflammatory drugs) but acetaminophen can be used in children with chronic liver disease as long as there is not aggressive hepatitis present. Also, children on certain medications for long-term illnesses should have their dosages carefully reviewed by the pediatrician, again to avoid the toxicity that might result because the liver is unable to handle the usual medication load.

Medications are available to treat hepatitis B and hepatitis C under certain conditions. If your child's hepatitis becomes a chronic condition, your pediatrician will refer you to a pediatric gastroenterologist to help decide on appropriate follow-up care and to consider whether medications should be used.

Most children with hepatitis do not need to be hospitalized. However, if loss of appetite or vomiting is interfering with your child's fluid intake and posing a risk of dehydration, your pediatrician may recommend that he be hospitalized. You should contact your doctor immediately if your child appears very lethargic, unresponsive, or delirious, as these may indicate that his illness is worsening and hospitalization is indicated.

There is no chronic infection following hepatitis A; in comparison, about ten of every hundred children under five years of age infected with hepatitis B become chronic carriers of the virus. A high percentage of infants who are born to mothers with acute or chronic hepatitis B become chronically infected if they are not properly immunized after birth with the vaccine developed for protection against the hepatitis B virus. Children with chronic hepatitis B will need lifelong monitoring to reduce the lifetime risk of liver damage, cirrhosis, and liver cancer.

Prevention

All newborns should be immunized with the hepatitis B vaccine at birth. After birth, a second dose should be given at age one to two months. A hepatitis A vaccine is recommended for all children between their first and second birthdays (twelve to twenty-three months of age), as well as older children and adolescents who have not yet been vaccinated. In addition, certain international travelers, adults employed in certain high-risk occupations, and people with chronic liver disease, among other conditions, should ask their physician about receiving the hepatitis A vaccine. (See immunization schedules on pages 876–877.)

Hand-washing before eating and after using the toilet is the most important preventive measure against hepatitis. Children should be taught as young as possible to wash their hands at these times. If your child is in child care, check to be sure that members of the staff wash their hands after handling diapers and before feeding the children.

Hepatitis is not transmitted simply by being in the same school or room with an infected person, or by talking to him, shaking his hand, or playing a board game with him. Hepatitis A infection can occur if there has been a direct exposure to food or water contaminated with feces from a person infected with hepatitis A. It might be transmitted during kissing, the mouthing of toys, or sharing food or utensils. For hepatitis B, there must be direct contact with the blood or bodily fluids of an infected person.

If you find out that your child has been exposed to a person with hepatitis, immediately contact your pediatrician, who will determine if the exposure has placed your child at risk. If there's a chance of infection, the doctor may administer an injection of gamma globulin or a hepatitis vaccine, depending on which hepatitis virus was involved.

Prior to foreign travel with your child, consult your physician to determine the risk of exposure to hepatitis in the countries you plan to visit. In certain situations, gamma globulin and/or a hepatitis A vaccine may be indicated.

Inguinal Hernia

If you notice a small lump or bulge in your child's groin area or an enlargement of the scrotum, you may have discovered an inguinal hernia. This condition, which is present in up to five of every hundred children (most commonly in boys), occurs when an opening in the lower abdominal wall allows the child's intestine to squeeze through. This inguinal hernia is frequently confused with a more benign condition, a communicating hydrocele (see page 546).

The testicles of the developing male fetus grow inside his abdominal cavity, moving down through a tube (the inguinal canal) into the scrotum as birth nears. When this movement takes place, the lining of the abdominal wall (peritoneum) is pulled along with the testes to form a sac connecting the testicle with the abdominal cavity. This protrusion occurs in girls as well. A hernia in a child is due to a failure of this normal protrusion from the abdominal cavity to close properly before birth, leaving a space for a small portion of the bowel to later push through into the groin or scrotum.

Most hernias do not cause any discomfort, and you or the pediatrician will discover them only by seeing the bulge. Although this kind of hernia must be treated, it is not an emergency condition. You should, however, notify your doctor, who may instruct you to have the child lie down and elevate his legs. Sometimes this will cause the bulge to disappear. However, your doctor will still want to examine the area as soon as possible.

Rarely, a piece of the intestine gets trapped in the hernia, causing swelling and pain. (If you touch the area, it will be tender.) Your child may have nausea and vomiting as well. This condition is called an incarcerated (trapped) hernia and *does* require immediate medical attention. Call your pediatrician immediately if you suspect an incarcerated hernia.

Treatment

Even if the hernia is not incarcerated, it still should be surgically repaired. The surgeon also may check the other side of the abdomen to see if it, too, needs to be corrected, since it is very common for the same defect to be present there.

If the hernia is causing pain, it may indicate that a piece of intestine has become trapped or incarcerated. In that case, consult with your pediatrician immediately. He may try to move the trapped piece of intestine out of the sac. Even if this can be done, the hernia still needs to be surgically repaired soon thereafter. If the intestine remains trapped despite your doctor's efforts, emergency surgery must be performed to prevent permanent damage to the intestine.

Communicating Hydrocele

If the opening between the abdominal cavity and the scrotum has not closed properly and completely, abdominal fluid will pass into the sac around the testis, causing a mass called a communicating hydrocele. Many newborn boys have this problem; however, it usually disappears within one year without any treatment. Although most common in newborns, hydroceles also can develop later in childhood, most often with a hernia (see preceding section).

If your son has a hydrocele, he probably will not complain, but you or he will notice that one side of his scrotum is swollen. In an infant or young boy, this swelling decreases at night or when he is resting or lying down. When he gets more active or is crying, it increases, then subsides when he quiets again. Your pediatrician may make the final diagnosis by shining a bright light through the scrotum, to show the fluid surrounding the testicle. Your doctor also may

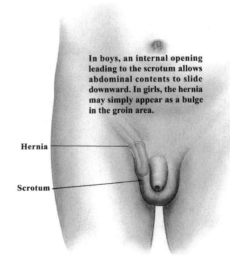

In boys, an internal opening leading to the scrotum allows abdominal contents to slide downward. In girls, the hernia may simply appear as a bulge in the groin area.

Hernia

Scrotum

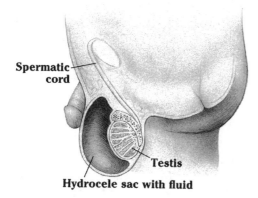

Spermatic cord

Testis

Hydrocele sac with fluid

request an ultrasound examination of the scrotum if it is very swollen or hard.

If your baby is born with a hydrocele, your pediatrician will examine it at each regular checkup until around one year of age. During this time your child should not feel any discomfort in the scrotum or the surrounding area. But if it seems to be tender in this area or he has unexplained discomfort, nausea, or vomiting, call the doctor at once. These are signs that a piece of intestine may have entered the scrotal area along with abdominal fluid. (See *Inguinal Hernia,* page 545.) If this occurs and the intestine gets trapped in the scrotum, your child may require immediate surgery to release the trapped intestine and close the opening between the abdominal wall and the scrotum.

If the hydrocele persists beyond one year without causing pain, a similar surgical procedure may be recommended. In this operation, the excess fluid is removed and the opening into the abdominal cavity closed.

Malabsorption

Sometimes children who eat a balanced diet suffer from malnutrition. The reason for this may be malabsorption, the body's inability to absorb nutrients from the digestive system into the bloodstream.

Normally the digestive process converts nutrients from the diet into small units that pass through the wall of the intestine and into the bloodstream, where they are carried to other cells in the body. If the intestinal wall is damaged by a virus, bacterial infection, or parasites, its surface may change so that digested substances cannot pass through. When this happens, the nutrients will be eliminated through the stool.

Malabsorption commonly occurs in a normal child for a day or two during severe cases of stomach or intestinal flu. It rarely lasts much longer since the surface of the intestine heals quickly without significant damage. In these cases, malabsorption is no cause for concern. However, chronic malabsorption may develop, and if two or more of the following signs or symptoms persist, notify your pediatrician.

Signs and Symptoms

Possible signs and symptoms of chronic malabsorption include the following:

■ Persistent abdominal pain and vomiting

- Frequent, loose, bulky, foul-smelling stools

- Increased susceptibility to infection

- Weight loss with the loss of fat and muscle

- Increase in bruises

- Bone fractures

- Dry, scaly skin rashes

- Personality changes

- Slowing of growth and weight gain (may not be noticeable for several months)

Treatment

When a child suffers from malnutrition, malabsorption is just one of the possible causes. She might be undernourished because she's not getting enough of the right types of food, or she has digestive problems that prevent her body from digesting them. She also might have a combination of these problems. Before prescribing a treatment, the pediatrician must determine the cause. This can be done in one or more of the following ways.

- **You may be** asked to list the amount and type of food your child eats.

- **The pediatrician may** test the child's ability to digest and absorb specific nutrients. For example, the doctor might have her drink a solution of milk sugar (lactose) and then measure the level of hydrogen in her breath afterward. This is known as a lactose hydrogen breath test.

- **The pediatrician may** collect and analyze stool samples. In healthy people, only a small amount of the fat consumed each day is lost through the stool. If too much is found in the stool, it is an indication of malabsorption.

- **Collection of sweat** from the skin, called a sweat test, may be performed to see if cystic fibrosis (see page 626) is present. In this disease, the body produces insufficient amounts of certain enzymes.

- **In some cases** the pediatrician might request that a pediatric gastroenterologist obtain a biopsy from the wall of the small intestine, and have it examined under the microscope for signs of infection, inflammation, or other injury.

Ordinarily, these tests are performed before any treatment is begun, although a seriously sick child might be hospitalized in order to receive special feedings while her problem is being evaluated.

Once the physician is sure the problem is malabsorption, she will try to identify a specific reason for its presence. When the reason is infection, the treatment usually will include antibiotics. If malabsorption occurs because the intestine is too active, certain medications may be used to counteract this, so that there's time for the nutrients to be absorbed.

Sometimes there's no clear cause for the problem. In this case, the diet may be changed to include foods or special nutritional formulas that are more easily tolerated and absorbed.

Reye Syndrome

Reye syndrome (often referred to as Reye's syndrome) is a rare but very serious illness that usually occurs in children younger than fifteen years of age. It can affect all organs of the body, but most often injures the brain and the liver. It is strongly associated with the use of aspirin or aspirin-containing medication.

Since the medical community issued a public warning against the use of aspirin during viral illnesses, the number of cases of Reye syndrome has decreased greatly.

Vomiting

Because many common childhood illnesses can cause vomiting, you should expect your child to have this problem several times during these early years. Usually it ends quickly without treatment, but this doesn't make it any easier for you to watch. That feeling of helplessness combined with the fear that something serious might be wrong and the desire to do something to make it better may make you feel tense and anxious. To help put your

mind at ease, learn as much as you can about the causes of vomiting and what you can do to treat your child when it occurs.

First of all, there's a difference between real vomiting and just spitting up. Vomiting is the forceful throwing up of stomach contents through the mouth. Spitting up (most commonly seen in infants under one year of age) is the easy flow of stomach contents out of the mouth, frequently with a burp.

Vomiting occurs when the abdominal muscles and diaphragm contract vigorously while the stomach is relaxed. This reflex action is triggered by the "vomiting center" in the brain after it has been stimulated by:

- Nerves from the stomach and intestine when the gastrointestinal tract is either irritated or swollen by an infection or blockage

- Chemicals in the blood (e.g., drugs)

- Psychological stimuli from disturbing sights or smells

- Stimuli from the middle ear (as in vomiting caused by motion sickness)

The common causes of spitting up or vomiting vary according to age. During the first few months, for instance, most infants will spit up small amounts of formula or breast milk, usually within the first hour after being fed. This "cheesing," as it is often called, is simply the occasional movement of food from the stomach, through the tube (esophagus) leading to it, and out of the mouth. It will occur less often if a child is burped frequently and if active play is limited right after meals. This spitting up tends to decrease as the baby becomes older, but may persist in a mild form until ten to twelve months of age. Spitting up is not serious and doesn't interfere with normal weight gain. (See *Spitting Up,* page 128.)

Occasional vomiting may occur during the first month. If it appears repeatedly or is unusually forceful, call your pediatrician. It may be just a mild feeding difficulty, but it also could be a sign of something more serious.

Around two weeks to four months of age, persistent forceful vomiting may be caused by a thickening of the muscle at the stomach exit. Known as hypertrophic pyloric stenosis, this thickening prevents food from passing into the intestines. It requires *immediate* medical attention. Surgery usually is required to open the narrowed area. The important sign of this condition is forceful vomiting occurring approximately fifteen to thirty minutes or less after every feeding. Anytime you notice this, call your pediatrician as soon as possible.

GERD. Occasionally the spitting up in the first few weeks to months of life gets worse instead of better—that is, even though it's not forceful, it occurs all the time. This happens when the muscles at the lower end of the esophagus become overly relaxed and allow the stomach contents to back up. This condition is known as gastroesophageal reflux disease, or GERD. This condition usually can be controlled by doing the following:

1. Avoid overfeeding or give smaller feeds more frequently.

2. Burp the baby frequently.

3. Leave the infant in a safe, quiet, upright position for at least thirty minutes following feeding.

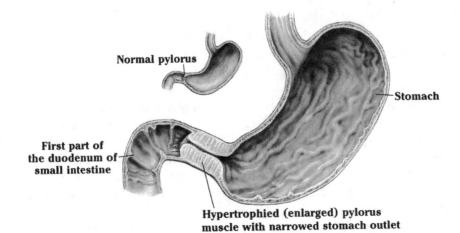

Normal pylorus

Stomach

First part of the duodenum of small intestine

Hypertrophied (enlarged) pylorus muscle with narrowed stomach outlet

4. Thicken the milk with small amounts of baby cereal as directed by your pediatrician.

If these steps are not successful, your pediatrician may refer you to a pediatric gastrointestinal (GI) specialist.

Infectious Causes. After the first few months of life, the most common cause of vomiting is a stomach or intestinal infection. Viruses are by far the most frequent infecting agents, but occasionally bacteria and even parasites may be the cause. The infection also may produce fever, diarrhea, and sometimes nausea and abdominal pain. The infection is usually contagious; if your child has it, chances are good that some of her playmates also will be affected.

Viruses are a leading cause of vomiting in infants and young children, with symptoms often progressing to diarrhea and fever. Some viruses are very contagious, but are becoming less common than in the past, due to the availability of a vaccine that can prevent the disease. The rotavirus is one of the viral causes of gastroenteritis, but other types of viruses—such as noroviruses and adenoviruses—can cause it as well. (For more information about gastroenteritis, see page 523.)

Occasionally infections outside the gastrointestinal tract will cause vomiting. These include infections of the respiratory system (also see discussions of middle ear infections, page 662; pneumonia, page 605), infections of the urinary tract (see page 778), meningitis (see page 785), and appendicitis (see page 525). Some of these conditions require immediate medical treatment, so be alert for the following trouble signs, whatever your child's age, and call your pediatrician if they occur.

■ Blood or bile (a green-colored material) in the vomit

■ Severe abdominal pain

■ Strenuous, repeated vomiting

■ Swollen or enlarged abdomen

■ Lethargy or severe irritability

■ Convulsions

■ Jaundice

■ Signs or symptoms of dehydration (see below under *Treatment,* as well as *Signs and Symptoms of Dehydration,* on page 540.)

■ Inability to drink adequate amounts of fluid

■ Vomiting continuing beyond twenty-four hours

Treatment

In most cases, vomiting will stop without specific medical treatment. The majority of cases are caused by a virus and will get better on their own.

You should never use over-the-counter or prescription remedies unless they've been specifically prescribed by your pediatrician for your child and for this particular illness.

When your infant or young child is vomiting, keep her lying on her stomach or side as much as possible. Doing this will minimize the chances of her inhaling vomit into her upper airway and lungs.

When there is continued vomiting, you need to make certain that dehydration doesn't occur. *Dehydration* is a term used when the body loses so much water that it can no longer function efficiently (see *Signs and Symptoms of Dehydration,* page 540). If allowed to reach a severe degree, it can be serious and life-threatening. To prevent this from happening, make sure your child consumes enough extra fluids to restore what has been lost through throwing up. If she vomits these fluids, notify your pediatrician.

For the first twenty-four hours or so of any illness that causes vomiting, keep your child off solid foods, and encourage her to suck or drink small amounts of fluids such as electrolyte solution (ask your pediatrician which one), instead of eating. Liquids not only help to prevent dehydration, but also are less likely than solid foods to stimulate further vomiting.

Be sure to follow your pediatrician's guidelines for giving your child fluids. Your doctor will adhere to requirements like those described in the box on page 535 (*Estimated Oral Fluid and Electrolyte Requirements by Body Weight*).

In most cases, your child will just need to stay at home and receive a liquid diet for twelve to twenty-four hours. Your pediatrician usually won't prescribe a drug to treat the vomiting, but some doctors will prescribe antinausea medications to children.

If your child also has diarrhea (see page 530), ask your pediatrician for instructions on giving liquids and restoring solids to her diet.

If she can't retain any clear liquids or if the symptoms become more severe, notify your pediatrician. He will examine your child and may order blood and urine tests or imaging tests such as X-rays to make a diagnosis. Occasionally hospital care may be necessary.

Until your child feels better, remember to keep her hydrated, and call your pediatrician right away if she shows signs of dehydration. If your child looks sick, the symptoms aren't improving with time, or your pediatrician suspects a bacterial infection, he may perform a culture of the stool, and treat appropriately.

~ 17 ~

Allergies

Asthma

ASTHMA IS A chronic disease of the breathing tubes that carry air to the lungs. In the last twenty years, there has been a major increase in the number of people with asthma, especially young children and those living in urban areas. In fact, asthma is now one of the most common chronic diseases of childhood, affecting about 5 million children. We don't know what caused this increase, but the main reasons seem to be air pollution, exposure to allergens, obesity, and respiratory illnesses.

Asthma symptoms can be different for each person, but wheezing is a hallmark sign. Wheezing is the high-pitched sound that occurs when the airways in the lungs are narrowed, typically due to inflammation. In asthma, wheezing occurs most often at night or in the early morning. Still, not everyone who wheezes has asthma. Although no specific test can determine asthma, the diagnosis is often made after a child has had three or more wheezing attacks. In between attacks children do well, but since they often get colds, the attacks can be as frequent as every month, particularly in toddlers or children less than three years of age. If a child has no other allergies—meaning that she does not have eczema or food allergy—and neither parent has asthma, wheezing will likely decrease between three and six years of age. If these children begin wheezing in the first years of life and continue to have repeated wheezing attacks, particularly beyond five and six years of age, they are diagnosed with asthma.

Every child is unique, and thus it is important to discuss your child's health with your primary physician or specialist. Asthma is such a variable disease that some infants and children may wheeze without much distress while others have such severe wheezing and breathing difficulty that it may create an emergency situation. In general, most exacerbations are manageable at home if symptoms are recognized early and treatment initiated as directed by your doctor.

If there is a history of asthma or allergy, a child who frequently wheezes is likely to continue wheezing for a number of years. However, asthma can also occur in children who are not allergic. It is not possible to cure asthma, but it *is* possible to control asthma symptoms. Proper treatment reduces wheezing and prevents future attacks. Children may wheeze from exercise, stress, and exposure to irritants—or

triggers—such as pollution, household cleaners (especially bleach), perfumes, and cold air. Cigarette smoke also is a major risk factor.

Many things can trigger an asthma attack, but in children under five, it's most common after a viral respiratory infection, including the common cold, for both allergic and nonallergic asthma.

Other common asthma triggers include:

- Dust mites, cockroaches, animal dander, pollens, and molds

- Cold air

- Certain medications (NSAIDs, ASA, etc.)

- Foods for those with food allergy (allergic reaction can include asthma symptoms)

Some less common triggers are:

- Stress and emotional upset

- Sinus infections

- Previous injury to the airways (e.g., in children who have had an endotracheal tube inserted or who have inhaled cigarette smoke)

- Gastroesophageal reflux

Signs and Symptoms

When your child has an asthma flare-up (or "attack"), the major symp-

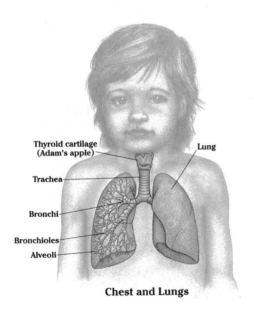

Thyroid cartilage (Adam's apple)

Lung

Trachea

Bronchi

Bronchioles

Alveoli

Chest and Lungs

tom will be a cough or wheeze that gets worse at night, with physical activity, or after contact with an irritant (e.g., cigarette smoke) or an allergen (e.g., animal dander, mold, dust mites, or cockroaches). As the attack progresses, the wheezing actually may decrease, as less air is able to move in and out. She also may experience shortness of breath, breathe fast, and have "retractions" when the chest and neck pull in while she works harder to take in air.

Many children with asthma have chronic symptoms, such as daily (or nightly) cough, cough whenever they exercise, or cough with exposures to pets, dust, and pollens. Asthma is considered "persistent" if there is a need for "rescue" medication (see *Treatment* section at right) more than twice a week or if there are more than two awakenings at night for asthma symptoms per month.

In some children, the physician may hear wheezing (especially when the child blows out hard) even without more obvious signs. Abnormalities may be detected by pulmonary function testing (PFT) in children old enough to cooperate with this breathing test (see page 556).

When to Call the Pediatrician

Children with well-controlled asthma can do the same activities as other children, including play outdoors and exercise. Watch your child closely when she's outside or exercising, and if symptoms develop or worsen, talk to your pediatrician.

For a child with asthma, you should know the situations that require *immediate* medical attention. As a rule, call your pediatrician immediately or consider going to the emergency room if:

- Your child has *severe* trouble breathing and seems to be getting worse, especially if she is breathing rapidly and there is pulling in of the chest wall when she inhales and forceful grunting when she exhales.

- Your child's mouth or fingertips appear blue.

- Your child acts agitated, unusually sleepy, or confused.

- There is any chest pain with breathing.

You also should call your pediatrician without delay if:

- Your child has a fever and persistent coughing or wheezing that is not responding to treatment.

- Your child is vomiting repeatedly and cannot take oral medication or drink fluids.

- Your child has difficulty speaking or sleeping because of wheezing, coughing, or troubled breathing.

Treatment

Asthma always should be treated under your pediatrician's supervision. The goals of treatment are to:

1. Decrease the frequency and severity of exacerbations, and reduce or prevent the chronic symptoms of coughing and difficulty breathing.

2. Develop a "plan of response" for asthma symptoms to minimize emergency medical treatment.

3. Allow your child to grow and develop normally and take part in normal childhood activities as fully as possible.

4. Control your child's symptoms with the smallest amount of medication possible to decrease the risk of drug side effects.

5. Ensure regular school attendance.

6. Minimize trips to the emergency room and the need for "rescue" treatments.

With these goals in mind, your pediatrician will prescribe medication and may refer you to a specialist who can evaluate your child's asthma. Your doctor also will help you plan your child's specific home treatment program. **This will include learning how to use the medicines and treatments that are prescribed and developing a plan to avoid the irritants and allergens that may be causing your child to cough or wheeze.** It may be helpful to have a written asthma management plan that you can read over now and then, which should describe your child's medications, when and how she should take them, and any other instructions that your pediatrician has given for caring for your child's condition.

If your child's asthma seems to be triggered by severe allergies, your pediatrician may refer you to a pediatric allergist or pulmonologist (lung specialist). Evaluating your child's lung function may include using a device called a spirometer, which measures the amount of air that your child is able to blow out of her lungs. Spirometry is usually not technically successful under three to five years of age.

The medication prescribed for your child will depend on the nature of the asthma. There are two main types of asthma drugs. One type opens up the breathing tubes and relaxes the muscles causing obstruction. These quick-relief or "rescue" medicines are called bronchodilators. The second type is controller or maintenance medications, which are used to treat the airway inflammation (swelling and mucus production).

■ **Quick-relief or rescue medications are intended for short-term use.** If your child has an asthma attack, with coughing and/or wheezing, a rescue medication should be given. Medicines such as albuterol are a common choice. By opening up her narrowed airways, these rescue medicines can relieve the tightness in her chest and ease her wheezing and feelings of breathlessness. They are prescribed on an as-needed basis. Should an attack become severe, your doctor may prescribe an additional medication—such as an oral corticosteroid. It is important to note that if there is no improvement or change after giving the rescue medicine, the child may need further evaluation. Usually breathing will improve for a few hours before the wheezing comes back. Some children continue to wheeze mildly despite treatment, but as long as your child is feeding and not in distress this may be OK.

The rescue medication can be given by HFA-propelled inhaler (HFA = hydrofluoroalkanes)—also known as a puffer—or by nebulizer (see next section).

- **Controller medications are intended to be used every day.** They are designed to control your child's asthma and lower the number of days and nights that he has asthma symptoms. In general, controller medicines are appropriate for children who have symptoms two or more times a week, who awaken with symptoms more than twice a month, who require more than two oral steroid courses within a year, or who have been hospitalized due to asthma symptoms. These drugs can reduce underlying inflammation gradually and over time but are not used to relieve symptoms immediately.

The most effective controller medication is an inhaled corticosteroid. There are several different types but they all work by preventing inflammation in the airway, which has the potential to reduce the number and severity of asthma episodes. In infants and young children, inhaled corticosteroids may be administered via nebulizer with facemask or via inhaler. An inhaler requires using a plastic tube called a spacer or volume holding chamber, which is required to allow the particles space to spread out and reach the small areas of the lungs. Without the spacer, most of the medication will travel to the back of the throat and be swallowed instead of inhaled. In infants and small children this is usually done with a mask (small or medium), which needs to be placed on the face with a good seal while the

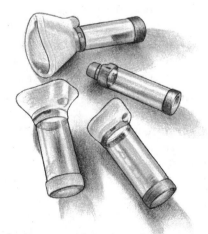

Spacers come in various shapes and sizes.

child takes several breaths. Spacers also come with a mouthpiece for older children, which requires the child to slowly inhale and hold her breath for ten seconds. Usually two puffs are given about a minute apart, with the child taking six breaths for each puff, which can be repeated every four to six hours or as directed by your doctor. After taking an inhaled steroid, it is important for your child to rinse and spit or brush her teeth.

Another way to deliver the medication is by nebulizer. The compressor (also known as breathing machine) connects by tubing to a device that is like a small cup into which the medication is placed. The compressor converts the liquid into a mist that is then breathed in. In small children a mask is used (see illustration on page 557) and needs to be on the face with a good seal. If there is not a good seal most of the medication escapes into the air and never reaches the lungs.

It is ideal to give the medication when your child is not crying, as it decreases the amount of medicine that can reach the lungs. This may not always be possible, but over time most children learn to accept the medication.

Although both techniques are equally effective, your child may be more cooperative with one over another. It may appear that the rescue medication (e.g., albuterol) is more effective through a nebulizer, but nebulized doses of albuterol are typically greater than two puffs delivered through an inhaler.

Because asthma can be a complicated disease and may differ from one person to another, your doctor will individualize your child's treatment. If your child's symptoms occur on an intermittent basis, your pediatrician might prescribe only a bronchodilator for episodic coughing or wheezing. If the asthma is chronic or recurrent, she usually will prescribe controller medications for regular daily use. These medicines typically take up to two weeks to provide their full effect.

Anti-inflammatory medications—most commonly inhaled corticosteroids—are recommended for all asthmatic children who have persistent symptoms. They are very effective and safe but must be used regularly to be effective. Often they fail because they are not taken consistently. Because they do not have an immediate effect, it is often tempting to stop using them. Doing so, however, will leave your child's airway unprotected, and she may experience an asthma attack.

A relatively newer class of controller medicine called leukotriene receptor antagonists block the activity of chemicals (leukotrienes) that are associated with airway inflammation; they are available only in oral preparations, such as in pill form as well as in a granule powder and chewable tablet. Although it is not as effective in preventing asthma attacks as inhaled corticosteroids, it may be an option for mild persistent symptoms or in addition to inhaled corticosteroids. Again, in order to prevent attacks it needs to be given every day.

Another way for a child to receive certain medication is through a dry powder inhaler. These release the medicine without a propellant. Your child must rely on the force of her own inhalation to take in the medicine and get it into her lungs. As a result, these are generally not prescribed until a child is school-age (at least five to six years of age).

Be sure to give medications according to your doctor's directions. *Do not stop medicines too soon*, give them less often than recommended, or switch to other drugs or treatments without first discussing the change with the doctor. In some children, several medicines may be prescribed at the same time to get the asthma controlled, and then the number of medications reduced once asthma symptoms are under control. If you do not understand why a particular treatment has been recommended, or how it should be given, ask for an explanation.

In some cases, children do not experience any improvement in their symptoms when they're using asthma medications. When that happens, more asthma medication may be needed, they might not have asthma after all, or other medical conditions may be interfering with their treatment. Your pediatrician will examine your child and check for problems that could be making her asthma worse, such as allergic rhinitis, sinus infections, and heartburn (gastroesophageal reflux).

Prevention

One of the most common allergic triggers for asthma, particularly in young children, is dust mites. While you cannot eliminate dust and other irritants, there are some things that can be done to reduce exposure and lower your child's chances of having asthma symptoms. For example, in your home you can:

- Cover your child's bed mattress and pillow with special dust mite–proof covers.

- Use pillows or comforters that can be machine-washed.

- Wash sheets, blankets, pillows, throw rugs, and stuffed animals every week in hot water to kill dust mites.

- Limit stuffed animals in your child's room (or reduce the time your child spends playing with stuffed animals).

- Consider removing pets from your home if the child is allergic.

- Keep your child out of rooms while you're vacuuming carpets and dusting furniture.

- Consider investing in a special air filter (called a high-efficiency particulate air filter, or HEPA) to keep your child's room clean.

- Maintain the humidity in your house below 50 percent when possible; dust mites and mold grow best in damp areas.

- Avoid perfumes, scented cleaning products, and other items with scents that could become irritants.

- Reduce mold in your house by repairing leaky plumbing.

- Keep your child away from cigarette, cigar, or pipe smoke, as well as smoke from a fireplace.

- Don't allow anyone to smoke in your home or car.

Eczema

Although many patients and practitioners use the terms *eczema* and *atopic dermatitis* interchangeably, *eczema* is really a general term used to describe a group of different skin conditions. Acute eczema may appear as reddened skin that is dry and peeling or may start oozing, occasionally resulting in small, fluid-filled bumps. When eczema becomes chronic (persists for a long time), the skin tends to thicken, experience hyperpigmentation, appear dry, and become scaly with coarse lines.

Atopic dermatitis and contact dermatitis are two of the most common types of eczematous dermatitis in children.

ATOPIC DERMATITIS

Atopic dermatitis often occurs in infants and children in families with a history of atopic dermatitis, food allergies, asthma, hay fever, and environmental allergies. Although the cause of atopic dermatitis is unknown, genetics clearly plays a role, but the relationship to allergies is unclear. Additionally, atopic dermatitis is the first condition to develop in most children who develop the other conditions listed above.

Eczema usually develops in three different phases. The first occurs between several weeks and six months of age, with itching, redness, and the appearance of small bumps on the cheeks, forehead, or scalp. This rash then often improves on the face and scalp and often spreads to the arms or trunk. Although atopic dermatitis can be confused with other types of dermatitis, severe itching is an essential clue that atopic dermatitis is the problem. In many cases the rash disappears or improves by two or three years of age.

In school-age children, atopic dermatitis is typically found on the elbows and knees. Scaly patches may be discrete and round or poorly defined. Severe and short flare-ups may have redness, crusts, blisters, and open areas, while chronic changes typically look like scaly, hyperpigmented, and thick skin.

The second phase of this skin problem occurs most often between the ages of four and ten years, and is characterized by circular, slightly raised, itchy, and scaly eruptions on the face or trunk. These are less oozy and more scaly than the first phase of eczema, and the skin tends to appear somewhat thickened. The most frequent locations for this rash are in the bends of the elbows, behind the knees, and on the backs of the wrists and ankles. All types are very itchy, and the skin generally tends to be very dry.

The third phase, characterized by areas of itching skin and a dry, scaly appearance, begins at about age twelve and occasionally continues on into early adulthood.

CONTACT DERMATITIS

Contact dermatitis can occur when the skin comes in contact with an irritating substance or allergen. One form of this problem results from repeated contact with irritating substances such as citrus juices or other acidic foods, bubble baths, strong soaps, certain foods and medicines, and woolen or rough-weave fabrics. In addition, one of the most common irritants is the child's own saliva, causing a lip licker's contact dermatitis. Contact dermatitis can be quite itchy, but the pattern often gives a clue to the diagnosis and helps to distinguish it from atopic dermatitis and other forms of eczematous dermatitis.

Another form of contact dermatitis develops after skin contact with substances to which the child is allergic. The most common of these are:

■ Nickel jewelry or snaps on jeans or pants

■ Certain flavorings or additives to toothpastes and mouthwashes (These cause a rash around or in the mouth.)

■ Glues, dyes, or leather used in the manufacture of shoes (They produce a reaction on the tops of the toes and feet.)

■ Dyes used in clothing (These cause rashes in areas where the clothing rubs or where there is increased perspiration.)

■ Plants, especially poison ivy, poison oak, and poison sumac. This rash usually appears within several hours after contact (one to three days with poison ivy); as well as being itchy, it may cause small blisters (see page 845)

■ Medications such as neomycin ointment

Treatment

If your child has a rash that looks like eczema, your pediatrician will need to examine it to make the correct diagnosis and prescribe the proper treatment. In some cases they may arrange for a pediatric dermatologist to examine it.

Although there is no cure for eczema, it generally can be well controlled and often will go away after several months or years. The most effective treatment is to prevent the skin from becoming dry and itchy and to avoid triggers that cause the condition to flare. To do this:

■ **Use skin moisturizers** (e.g., creams or ointments) regularly and frequently to decrease the dryness and itchiness.

■ **Give your child** daily soaking baths in lukewarm water. After a bath, rinse twice to remove any residual soap (which might be an irritant). Then apply the cream or ointment within three minutes of getting out of the bath to lock in the moisture.

- **Avoid harsh or** irritating clothing (wool or synthetic material).

- **If there is** exceptional itching, use cool compresses on the area, followed by the application of prescribed medications.

There are many types of medicated prescription creams and ointments available, so ask your pediatrician to suggest one that she prefers to control inflammation and itching. These preparations often contain a form of steroid, which is the first line of treatment. These creams or ointments should be used under the direction of your child's doctor. It's important to continue to apply the medications for as long as your pediatrician recommends their use. Stopping too soon will cause the condition to recur.

In addition to the skin preparations, your child also may take an antihistamine by mouth to relieve the itching and antibiotics (sometimes by mouth and sometimes as a cream) if the skin becomes infected. If your child develops frequent infections, talk to your pediatrician about bleach baths.

Treating allergic contact dermatitis is similar. Although a little detective work will often help identify the trigger, your pediatric dermatologist or allergist may conduct a series of patch tests. These tests are done by placing small patches of common irritants (or allergens) against your child's skin for forty-eight hours. If the skin reacts with redness and itching, that substance should be avoided.

Alert your pediatrician if any of the following occurs:

- Your child's rash is severe and is not responding to home treatment.

- There is any evidence of fever or infection (i.e., blisters, extensive redness, yellow crusts, pain, or oozing of fluid).

Food Allergy

While many foods can cause allergic reactions, true food allergies are less common than you might think. Food allergies are most likely to happen in infants and children, as well as in children with other allergies or whose family members have allergies. When food allergies do occur, they may be in response to any food, although particular items are more likely to cause reactions (see the list below). While in many cases food allergies may reveal themselves with mild symptoms, they can be potentially life-threatening.

While any food can trigger a food allergy, several cause the vast majority of cases in children. Cow's milk is among them (see *Milk Allergy*, page 566). Other common foods associated with allergies include:

- Eggs

- Peanuts and tree nuts (such as cashews, walnuts, etc.)

- Soy

- Wheat

- Fish (such as tuna, salmon, and cod) and crustacean shellfish (such as shrimp, crab, and lobster)

If your child has a food allergy, her immune system responds in an exaggerated way to otherwise harmless proteins in foods. When this food is consumed, her immune system manufactures antibodies that attempt to fight off the "offending" food. In the process, substances called "histamines" and other chemicals are released that cause allergic symptoms.

However, you may be able to reduce your child's likelihood of ever developing food allergies by exclusively breastfeeding her for a minimum of four months, but preferably for six months or more.

Another condition, called *food intolerance* or *food sensitivity,* occurs more often than true food allergies. Although the terms are often confused and sometimes used interchangeably,

food intolerance does not involve the immune system. For example, a child with lactose intolerance (a condition of food sensitivity) is deficient in an enzyme required to digest milk sugar, leading to stomachaches, bloating, and diarrhea. Other examples of intolerance include:

- Rashes. Sometimes the acids in foods, such as in orange juice or tomato products, can cause reactions like a rash around the mouth that is mistaken for food allergies.

- Diarrhea or vomiting. Food poisoning that is usually caused by bacteria in spoiled or undercooked food can trigger these responses. Also, when small children consume too much sugar in fruit juices, they may develop diarrhea.

Symptoms

A true food allergy happens when the body reacts against proteins found in foods. The reaction usually happens

How Allergies Develop

When an allergy-prone child is exposed to an allergen, his immune system produces an antibody (called IgE) in a process called allergic sensitization. Then the IgE sticks to mast cells in the skin and the linings of the airways and gut. The next time he comes in contact with allergens, these cells release chemicals (e.g., histamine and leukotrienes) that cause allergic symptoms.

shortly after a food is eaten. Food allergy reactions can vary from mild to severe and include:

- Skin problems (itchy skin rashes, hives, swelling)

- Stomach problems (nausea, vomiting, diarrhea)

- Breathing problems (sneezing, wheezing, throat tightness)

- Circulation problems (pale skin, light-headedness, loss of consciousness)

The intensity of the allergic reaction can range from mild to severe. If your child is highly allergic, even trace amounts of the food may trigger a potentially dangerous allergic response called anaphylaxis. But when they occur, they can develop without warning, progress rapidly, and must be treated immediately with a prescribed emergency injectable medication (called epinephrine, that is packaged in penlike form), which should be on hand at all times. They may trigger symptoms such as:

- Swelling of the throat and tongue

- Difficulty breathing

- Wheezing

- A sudden drop in blood pressure—which would make your child look pale, feel lethargic, or lose consciousness

- Turning blue

- Loss of consciousness

(See the box, *Anaphylactic Reactions: What You Should Do*, on page 571.)

Diagnosis and Management

Because some food allergies can be serious, talk to your pediatrician if you suspect that your child has one. To help make the diagnosis, your pediatrician will review your concerns and may perform some tests or refer you to an allergist, who may recommend additional testing. Sometimes the presence of a food allergy is obvious, like when a child gets hives and lip swelling after eating a walnut. But tests, including a skin prick test and blood tests, can confirm your doctor's suspicions:

- **With the** skin prick test (or scratch test), the doctor will place a drop of a liquid extract of the suspicious food on your child's back or forearm. Then he'll make a tiny scratch on the skin, allowing a bit of the substance to enter the outer layer of skin, which can result in swelling and itching at the site within fifteen minutes.

- **A blood test** can measure allergic antibodies to foods as well; these antibodies are called immunoglobulin E, or IgE. A sample of your child's blood will be drawn and sent to the laboratory, where it will be mixed with a number of food extracts to see if antibodies to that food can be detected. Results are usually available in one to two weeks.

However, these tests are not perfect. A positive skin or blood test alone is not sufficient to diagnose food allergy. Your doctor should discuss with you the specifics of your child's diet, including any of your concerns about reactions to particular foods, to know what tests to consider and how to interpret the results.

If it is unclear whether lingering symptoms are due to a food, the allergist may recommend placing your child on an "elimination diet." You'll be asked to remove for a period of time those foods that are suspected of causing your child's symptoms, and then you'll monitor whether symptoms subside or resolve when those foods are no longer being eaten. Several weeks later, the foods can be returned to your child's meals, one at a time, and you can determine whether symptoms have come back when a particular food is consumed again. This elimination diet should be done only under the guidance of an allergist or your pediatrician to ensure that your child is still receiving proper nutrition. In addition, sometimes returning a specific food to the diet requires a doctor-supervised feeding test.

The main way to treat food allergies is to avoid foods that cause them. For example, if an allergy to eggs has been detected, your pediatrician or allergist may recommend retesting your child periodically to see if she is still allergic. For foods like milk, soy, wheat, and egg, many children develop a tolerance naturally over time and outgrow their food allergy. Even though egg allergies are caused by a protein found in egg whites, the yolks can become contaminated with egg whites, and thus it is safer to avoid this food entirely, including products that contain eggs. Some children may be able to tolerate baked goods containing a smaller amount of egg that has been exposed to high heat. But if your child is not already eating baked egg products, then don't introduce them before discussing this first with an allergist.

Even once you're successful in keeping allergenic foods out of your refrigerator and off your dining room table, it may be more difficult to keep your child away from those items when she is out of your care. As your child gets older you'll have to educate her, as well as her friends, grandparents, teachers, child care workers, and caretakers, about the importance of avoiding specific foods that could trigger allergy symptoms. Every time you shop, read food labels and look for major allergens to which your child is allergic. Also, when your family is eating in restaurants, ask questions about the ingredients of menu items. While the waiter may be helpful, confirm the information by speaking with the chef.

As you make adjustments in your child's diet, talk to your pediatrician regularly about compensating for the missing foods and keeping her diet balanced. For example, if your child is allergic to milk, you will need to include other calcium-rich foods (like green leafy vegetables and calcium-fortified drinks) in her diet.

Keep in mind that there is no cure for food allergies. Fortunately, children often outgrow allergies over time with the maturing of their immune systems. But only reintroduce foods under your doctor's guidance. Certain food allergies—like those to peanuts and fish—are less likely to be "outgrown." Only 20 percent of children with peanut allergy outgrow or develop a natural tolerance. At some point, your pediatrician may decide to repeat allergy testing to confirm whether particular food allergies have run their course.

Milk Allergy

A true milk protein allergy usually appears in the first year of life, when an infant's digestive system is still quite immature.

Symptoms

Milk allergy symptoms may appear anywhere from a few minutes to a few hours after the child consumes a milk product, but the most severe symptoms usually occur within half an hour. The most common symptoms are:

■ Rashes

■ Vomiting and/or diarrhea (see pages 549 and 530)

Less common symptoms include blood in the stool.

In babies, if the milk allergy affects their respiratory system, they also may have cough, wheezing, or difficulty breathing. The allergy also can cause eczema, hives, swelling, or itching. (See *Cough,* page 598; *Eczema,* page 560; *Hives,* page 570.)

If you suspect your baby has an allergy to milk, tell your pediatrician, and be sure to mention whether there's a family history of allergy. Take your child to the doctor's office or emergency room *immediately* if he

■ Has difficulty breathing

■ Turns blue

■ Is extremely pale or weak

■ Has generalized hives

■ Develops swelling in the head and neck region

■ Has bloody diarrhea

Treatment

Breastfed babies. If your breastfed infant develops a milk allergy, your pediatrician may recommend that you follow a milk-free diet yourself. (You should take an extra calcium supplement in addition to the prenatal vitamin that you are already taking.) Discuss with your pediatrician or allergist about how and when to reintroduce milk into your child's diet. A medically supervised feeding test may be indicated.

Formula-fed babies. Infants with milk allergy should be given an alternative according to your pediatrician's guidelines. A small percentage of infants with a cow's milk allergy also have a soy protein allergy, so your doctor may recommend a brand of hypoallergenic formula made with extensive hydrolysate protein, which is processed in a way to avoid allergic reactions. (Also see *Choosing a Formula,* pages 116–118.)

Children over one year old. A young child who has a milk allergy will need to avoid cheese, yogurt, ice cream, and any food that contains milk. She will need a milk substitute like soy milk; if she's also sensitive to soy protein (some children are allergic to both soy and milk), your doctor can still suggest another "milk" substitute. Goat's milk and sheep's milk may not be acceptable alternatives, as they typically are not pasteurized. Consuming raw, unpasteurized milk can pose serious health risks. Other beverages based on rice, hemp, coconut, or almond do not have sufficient fat or protein to be the primary drink for a young child.

The main "treatment" is to eliminate milk and milk products from your child's diet. Be sure to tell all of your child's caregivers (including babysitters and those in child care settings) of your child's milk allergy so he does not receive milk by mistake.

Prevention

If possible, breastfeeding is recommended for the first four to six months of age. Research has shown that breastfeeding for at least four months (some recommend exclusive breastfeeding to six months or longer) can prevent or delay the development of allergies to cow's milk.

If you cannot breastfeed, ask your pediatrician to guide you in selecting an appropriate formula (as discussed above). For families with a strong family history of allergies, your doctor may recommend going straight to a hypoallergenic formula.

Hay Fever/Nasal Allergy

If your child's nose starts to run and his eyes become itchy, red, and swollen, but there are no other symptoms of a cold or an infection, he may be having hay fever (or allergic rhinitis). This is a reaction to allergens in the environment. The most common allergens that trigger hay fever are pollen, dust mites, mold, and animal dander.

Like other allergies, this condition tends to run in families. The symptoms may not appear immediately, however. Seasonal respiratory allergies (e.g., to pollen) are quite uncommon in children under age two.

It is sometimes difficult to tell the difference between a common cold and nasal allergy, because many of the symptoms are the same. Here are some of the signs of a possible nasal allergy.

- Sneezing, sniffling, stuffiness; itchy and runny nose (usually clear discharge)

- Tearing; itchy, red, or swollen eyes

- Coughing

- A horizontal crease across the bridge of nose from frequent wiping (nasal salute)

- Nosebleeds (see *Nosebleeds,* page 671)

- Dark rings (or allergic shiners) under the eyes

- Mouth breathing because of nasal congestion

- Fatigue (mostly from not sleeping well at night)

- Frequent throat clearing or clucking (rubbing tongue against roof of mouth)

If your child has nasal allergies, potential complications include frequent sinus and ear infections (see *Middle Ear Infections,* page 662, and *Sinusitis,* page 668), or if the allergy causes eye irritation, she may be more susceptible to eye infections (see page 728). Since chronic allergies also can interfere with sleep, your child often may be tired and cranky. These may also affect school performance.

Treatment

Call your pediatrician if your child's hay fever starts to interfere with sleeping or with school, social, or other activities. To prevent or treat allergy symptoms, the doctor can suggest a number of alternatives, including prescription and nonprescription antihistamines, nose sprays of various types, and other medications. In many cases, she will recommend an oral antihistamine; most are now available over the counter. The most common side effects of older antihistamines (diphenhydramine) are drowsiness, dry mouth, and, occasionally, change in behavior. Sometimes an antihistamine will have a stimulating effect, causing unusual activity and/or nervousness in the child. There are relatively newer antihistamines available that do not cause either hyperactivity or drowsiness. Nonsedating antihistamines include loratadine and fexofenadine. Low-sedating antihistamines include cetirizine. These may initially cause mild drowsiness, but it should occur less often with regular use. For more severe or persistent allergy symptoms, your physician may recommend a prescription steroid nasal spray that, when used on a daily basis, will help prevent nasal allergy symptoms.

You may be tempted to use decongestant nose drops or sprays that you can buy over the counter, but do not use these for more than three days, and never use them in children less than two years of age. Stopping after prolonged use may worsen nasal congestion. This increased congestion can be even more uncomfortable and difficult to treat than the original allergy. If your child's eyes are swollen, itchy, and red, your pediatrician may also recommend prescription or over-the-counter allergy eye drops.

Common Household Allergens

Source	What to Do
Pets (dogs, cats, guinea pigs, and hamsters) There's no such thing as a nonallergenic dog or cat, although some people are less sensitive to certain breeds. For dogs and cats, it's the *dander* (or skin sheddings) that triggers allergies, while for rodents, it is their urine that causes allergic symptoms.	If your child is allergic to an animal, don't allow that animal in the house and certainly not in the child's bedroom. The key to controlling mold is to limit humidity. Avoid using vaporizers, humidifiers, and swamp coolers. A dehumidifier in a damp basement can be helpful. Throughout the house, replace any carpet that's been saturated by a big water spill, or dry it completely. You can destroy mold with several types of disinfectants, but be careful to store them in a safe place, away from curious toddlers.
Mold Mold grows outdoors in cool, damp, dark places, such as in soil, grass, and dead leaves. Indoors, it's found in cluttered storage areas, recently flooded areas, basement areas, plumbing spaces, areas with poor ventilation such as closets and attics, as well as pillows and blankets that haven't been aired out in a long time.	
House Dust Mites Many people are allergic to house dust mites, which are found in bedding (pillows, blankets, sheets, and mattresses), upholstery, furniture, and carpet. These mites, which are too small to be seen by the naked eye, thrive in humid environments (humidity greater than 50 percent).	The most important measures for reducing exposure to house dust mites should be focused on the bedroom. Put mite-proof covers on mattresses and pillows, and wash sheets and blankets in hot water every week to remove allergens and kill the mites. It's also helpful to keep the humidity in the home at less than 50 percent to prevent the growth of mites. Using vacuum cleaners with HEPA filters may help limit the amount of airborne allergens during cleaning. If you're remodeling the bedroom, consider removing carpets from the room.

If possible, the best thing you can do for your allergic child is to remove the sources of allergens from your home. Refer to the box above for more information on common household allergens.

Hives

If your child has an itchy rash that consists of raised red bumpy areas or welts, perhaps with pale centers and no flaking skin over the lesions, he probably has hives. This rash may look like mosquito bites and can occur all over the body or just in one region, such as the face. The location may change with the hives disappearing in one area of the body and appearing in another, often in a matter of hours. When the rash remains in the same place for more than twenty-four hours, other diagnoses should be considered.

Among the most common causes of hives are:

- Response to an infection, most commonly a virus

- Foods (most commonly peanuts, tree nuts, egg whites, milk, shellfish, and sesame)

- Medications, either over-the-counter or prescription

- Bites or stings from bees or other insects

In at least half of the cases, it is not possible to identify the cause. If they last a few days or up to a few weeks and then go away, you may not need further evaluation. Foods, medications, and venom stings are generally not responsible for chronic hives (those lasting more than six weeks).

Treatment

An oral antihistamine should relieve or at least help reduce the itching of hives. It can be obtained without a prescription. You may need to use this type of medication for several days. Some of these medicines may need to be given to your child as often as every four to six hours while others can be given once or twice a day. Applying cool compresses to the area of itching and swelling also may help.

If your child is wheezing or having trouble swallowing, seek emergency treatment. The doctor usually will prescribe self-injectable epinephrine to stop the allergic response. Self-injectable epinephrine should be available at all times for such patients, including at home, in child care, or at school, in case of such reactions in the future. (For more information about these emergency kits, see the box *Anaphylactic Reactions: What You Should Do* on page 571.)

Prevention

In order to prevent subsequent outbreaks of hives, your doctor will try to determine what is causing the allergic reaction. If the rash is confined to a small area of skin, it probably was caused by something your child touched. (Plants and soaps are frequent culprits.) But if it spreads all over her body, something she ingested (a food or medication) or possibly an infection is most likely to blame.

Often the timing of when hives appear provides a clue to the cause.

Anaphylactic Reactions: What You Should Do

An anaphylactic reaction is always an emergency. It is potentially fatal and requires immediate medical attention. If symptoms such as swelling of the face or throat and wheezing occur, administer self-injectable epinephrine and then call 911 or go to the emergency room immediately.

When used properly and promptly, self-injectable epinephrine can reverse most serious reactions and allow for time to get to an emergency room for further treatment. In most cases, they reduce symptoms rapidly, but if they don't, another injection should be given.

To use an auto-injector, you'll press the device against your youngster's thigh and hold it there for a few seconds. Make sure to ask your doctor or nurse to give you precise instructions and demonstrate its use with a trainer. At the same time, your child

care center or preschool should have written instructions on how to recognize and react to a severe allergic reaction that may be life-threatening, and epinephrine should be available to them, along with a step-by-step guide and demonstration on how to administer it. Keep in mind that unused medication in these auto-injectors should be replaced at regular intervals, so check the expiration date and replace it as recommended by your doctor.

If your child has an anaphylactic reaction, see your pediatrician afterward, and find out exactly why the reaction happened and how to avoid another one. Your child should also wear a medical identification bracelet if she has had an anaphylactic episode in the past. This bracelet should give information about the allergies that your child has.

For example, does it usually happen after meals? Or after a specific medication? How quickly does it resolve? Does it take hours (food reaction) or last days to weeks (infection)? Consult your doctor for evaluation and management.

Insect Bites and Stings

Your child's reaction to a bite or sting will depend on her sensitivity to the particular insect's venom. While most children have only mild reactions, those who are allergic to certain insect venoms can have severe symptoms that require emergency treatment.

In general, bites are usually not a serious problem, but in some cases, stings may be. While it is true that most stings (from yellow jackets, wasps, and fire ants, for example) may cause pain and localized swelling, severe anaphylactic reactions are possible. Delayed allergic reactions to cat fleas, dog fleas, bedbugs, and mosquito bites are common and although uncomfortable, they are not life-threatening. Unfortunately, some children will develop chronic itchy bumps, which are quite persistent and difficult to treat, known as popular urticaria.

Treatment

Although insect bites can be irritating, they usually begin to disappear by the next day and do not require a doctor's treatment. To relieve the itchiness that accompanies bites by mosquitoes, flies, fleas, and bedbugs, apply a cool compress and calamine lotion or a low-potency topical steroid on the affected areas. Use oral antihistamines to control itch. If your child is stung by a wasp or bee, soak a cloth in cold water and press it over the area of the sting to reduce pain and swelling. Nonsteroidal anti-inflammatory drugs (ibuprofen) may also be helpful. Call your pediatrician if symptoms persist or become difficult to control. Your child may be prescribed an oral steroid if the swelling is significant.

If your child disturbs a beehive, get him away from it as quickly as possible. The base of a honeybee's stinger emits an alarm pheromone (hormone) that makes other bees more likely to sting as well.

It is very important to remove a bee stinger quickly and completely from the skin. The quick removal of a bee stinger will prevent a large amount of venom from being pumped into the skin. If the stinger is visible, remove it by gently scraping it off horizontally with a credit card or your fingernail. Avoid squeezing the stinger with a pair of tweezers; doing this may release more venom into the skin. The skin may be more swollen on the second or third day after a bee sting or mosquito bite.

Keep your child's fingernails short and clean to minimize the risk of infection from scratching. If infection does occur, the bite will become redder, larger, and more swollen. In some cases you may notice red streaks or yellowish fluid near the bite or your child may get a fever. Have your pediatrician examine any infected bite right away because it may need to be treated with antibiotics.

Call for medical help immediately if your child has any of these other symptoms after being bitten or stung:

- Sudden difficulty in breathing

- Weakness, collapse, or unconsciousness

- Hives or itching all over the body

- Extreme swelling near the eyes, lips, or penis that makes it difficult for the child to see, eat, or urinate

Prevention

Some children with no other known allergies may have severe reactions to insect stings. If your child has difficulty breathing, weakness, hives, or extreme facial swelling, collapses, or is unconscious, your doctor may recommend a

Insect Bites and Stings

Insect/Environment	Characteristics of Bite or Sting	Special Notes
Mosquitoes		
Water (pools, lakes, birdbaths)	Stinging sensation followed by small, red, itchy mound with tiny puncture mark at center	Mosquitoes are attracted by bright colors and sweat.
Flies		
Food, garbage, animal waste	Painful, itchy bumps; may turn into small blisters	Bites often disappear in a day but may last longer.
Fleas		
Cracks in floor, rugs, pet fur	Multiple small bumps clustered together on exposed areas, particularly arms, legs, face	Fleas are most likely to be a problem in homes with pets.
Bedbugs		
Cracks of walls, floors, crevices of furniture, bedding	Itchy red bumps occasionally topped by a blister; usually 2–3 in a row (same as fleas but may affect covered areas)	Bedbugs are most likely to bite at night and are less active in cold weather.
Fire ants		
Mounds in pastures, meadows, lawns, and parks in southern states	Painful, itchy bumps; may turn into small blisters	Fire ants usually attack intruders.
Bees and wasps		
Flowers, shrubs, picnic areas, beaches	Immediate pain and rapid swelling	A few children have severe reactions, such as difficulty breathing and hives/swelling all over the body.
Ticks		
Wooded areas	May not be noticeable; hidden on hair or on skin	Don't remove ticks with matches, lighted cigarettes, or nail polish remover; grasp the tick firmly with tweezers near the head; gently pull the tick straight out.

series of shots (venom immunotherapy injections) to decrease your child's risk of reaction to future insect stings (e.g., yellow jacket, wasp, hornet, fire ant). In addition, she will prescribe self-injectable epinephrine for you to keep on hand for use if your child is stung (see the box *Anaphylactic Reactions: What You Should Do* on page 571).

It is impossible to prevent all insect bites, but you can minimize the number your child receives by following these guidelines.

- Avoid areas where insects nest or congregate, such as garbage cans, stagnant pools of water, uncovered foods and sweets, and orchards and gardens where flowers are in bloom.

- When you know your child will be exposed to insects, dress her in long pants and a lightweight long-sleeved shirt as well as closed-toe shoes.

- Avoid dressing your child in clothing with bright colors or flowery prints, because they seem to attract insects.

- Don't use scented soaps, perfumes, or hair sprays on your child, because they also are inviting to insects.

Insect repellents are generally available without a prescription, but they should be used sparingly on infants and young children. In fact, the most common insecticides include DEET (N,N-diethyl m-toluamide), which is a chemical not recommended for use in children under two months of age. The AAP recommends that when used on children, repellents should contain *no more than 30 percent DEET.* In children who consistently get itchy bumps, topical treatment and oral antihistamines are of little help. For these children, wearing protective clothing, defleaing household pets, and applying insect repellent is the most effective way to manage the situation.

The concentrations of DEET vary significantly from product to product—ranging from less than 10 percent to over 30 percent—so read the label of any product you purchase. DEET's effectiveness peaks at a concentration of 30 percent, which is also *the maximum concentration currently recommended for children.*

An alternative to DEET is a product called picaridin (KBR 3023). While it has had wider use in Europe, picaridin has more recently become available in the US.

These repellents are effective in preventing bites by mosquitoes, ticks, fleas, chiggers, and biting flies, but have virtually no effect on stinging insects such as bees, hornets, and wasps.

The table on page 573 summarizes information about common stinging or biting insects.

~ 18 ~

Behavior

THERE ARE MANY times when your child's behavior warms and embraces your heart. But there are other times when it probably drives you a little crazy. From temper tantrums to dancing around your living room, she's expressing her feelings and needs, although not always in ways that you'd prefer.

Your child's behavior is partly innate; in a real sense, she was born to act this way. But there are a lot of other influences on her behavior in addition to her genetic makeup.

For example, your own parenting style will affect your child's behavior. So will the role models that she encounters and may imitate. So will the media—from television to movies to the Internet. Family circumstances are important, too, as are the stresses and transitions she'll encounter, including starting a new preschool or dealing with sickness.

Thus, your child's behavior doesn't happen in isolation. But no matter what the underlying cause or message that she's trying to communicate, her behavior will get your attention every day. As it does, there will be issues you'll have to deal with, both positive and negative, from computers to thumb sucking. These are the kinds of topics described in this chapter.

We all have feelings of anger and aggression, including your child. These impulses are normal and healthy, and part of your child's expected behavior. As a toddler or preschooler, your child may lack the self-control to express his anger peacefully. Instead, he may naturally lash out, perhaps hitting or biting in frustration. It's a behavior you should anticipate as he moves through this period of his life.

In a toddler (ages fifteen to thirty months), his expressive language skills (the speech and language your child produces), and his ability to articulate emotions such as happiness, anger, and sadness in particular, are not well developed. From the child's perspective, these are the terrific twos because they are so excited about all of the new things they are able to do developmentally. It's as if they are saying, "Look at what I can do!" As a result, all toddlers get frustrated at anyone or anything limiting their ability to do what they wish to do, even if they are not capable of it. This lack of independence leads to immediate and intense frustration and loss of control. When this happens, he needs you to take control for him and to help him develop judgment, self-discipline, and other tools to express his feelings in more acceptable and age-appropriate ways.

This is very hard for parents, since before the "terrific twos," your child was a cuddly, warm, interactive, and loving infant. Some parents will even think to themselves, "He is like a monster and just out to get me!" Do not take this behavior personally. Your toddler is simply overwhelmed. During this time, your overarching goal is to teach him how to regain control and to set limits on behaviors so he won't cause harm to himself, to others, or to property—but not to punish him.

While many parents think that discipline and punishment are the same thing, they are not. Discipline is a way of teaching and a way of enhancing a good parent-child relationship. When you discipline, you should provide your child with praise along with instruction in a firm tone, with the intent of improving his behavior. By contrast, punishment is a negative, in which you're dispensing an unpleasant consequence when your child does or doesn't do something. Punishment is a part of discipline, but only a small part. Until age three and sometimes later, children simply don't understand the concept of punishment. Setting limits is a much better approach than punishment; most children will respond to clear, calm, and decisive limit-setting.

Keep in mind that while occasional outbursts are normal, especially during temper tantrums (see page 587), it is not typical for a child to have frequent rages in which he attacks others or himself. Most children usually get angry at others only when they are provoked. Unless they are very tired or overstressed, they usually can be distracted or consoled, and will quickly forget their anger. They may cry, argue, or yell, but they resort to violence only when they are extremely frustrated.

Some children are supersensitive, easily offended, and quickly angered. Many of these children have been tense and unusually active since birth.

They are often more difficult to soothe and settle as infants. Beginning in the preschool years, they show signs of becoming aggressive toward other children, adults, and even animals. They often lash out suddenly and for no apparent reason, and may seem to be touchy or irritable most of the time. Even if they hurt someone in their anger, they may or may not feel sorry and may not feel responsible for the incident. Instead, they blame the other child for "making me angry," as if this excuses their actions.

Your child might go through a brief period of this kind of behavior if he's particularly worried, tired, or overstressed, but if it continues for more than a few weeks, and is especially aggressive, consult your pediatrician. If it becomes a routine daily pattern for more than three to six months, it should be viewed as a serious problem and may meet criteria for a conduct disorder.

This extreme form of aggressive behavior can lead to serious social and emotional problems if allowed to continue. Your child may eventually lose all his friends, which will make him even more tense and irritable, and seriously damage his self-esteem. There is always the danger that he will injure himself or others, and the problems will multiply when he reaches school age. Then his aggressive behavior may cause him to be suspended or expelled from school. Such a lack of self-esteem may later cause him to become self-destructive, abuse drugs or alcohol, become accident-prone, or even attempt suicide.

No one knows exactly what causes this kind of "conduct disorder" in a child (these children with conduct disorders lose their temper easily, annoy others intentionally, and are defiant or hostile toward parents and other authority figures). The problem may lie in the child's biological makeup, the relationships within the family, or a combination of the two. In many cases, other members of the child's family behave aggressively, and the atmosphere within the family is tense and stressful. In some cases, however, there is no clear explanation for the child's behavior.

What You Can Do

The best way to prevent aggressive behavior is to give your child a stable, secure home life with firm, loving discipline and full-time supervision during the toddler and preschool years. Everyone who cares for your child should be a good role model and agree on the rules he's expected to observe as well as the response to use if he disobeys. Whenever he breaks an important rule, he should be reprimanded *immediately* so that he understands exactly what he's done wrong.

Children don't know the rules of the house until they're taught them, so that is one of your important parenting responsibilities. Toddlers are normally interested in touching and exploring, so if there are valuables you don't want them to handle, hide or remove them. Consider setting up a separate portion of your home where he can play with books and toys.

For discipline to be most effective, it should take place on an ongoing basis, not just when your child misbehaves. In fact, it begins with parents smiling at their smiling baby, and it continues with praise and genuine affection for all positive and appropriate behaviors. Over time, if your child feels encouraged and respected, rather than demeaned and embarrassed, he is more likely to listen, learn, and change when necessary. It is always more effective to positively reinforce desired behaviors and to teach children alternative behaviors rather than just say, "Stop it or else." Tell them that the next time they are angry, they should use their words instead.

While teaching him other ways to respond, there's also nothing wrong with distracting him at times, or trying another approach. As long as you're not "bribing" him to behave differently by offering him sweet snacks, for example, there's nothing wrong with intentionally changing his focus.

Remember, your child has little natural self-control. He needs you to teach him not to kick, hit, or bite when he is angry, but instead to express his feelings through words. It's important for him to learn the difference between real and imagined insults and between appropriately standing up for his rights and attacking out of anger. The best way to teach these lessons is to supervise your child carefully when he's involved in disputes with his playmates. As long as a disagreement is minor, you can keep your distance and let the children solve it on their own. However, you must intervene when children get into a physical fight that continues even after they're told to stop, or when one child seems to be in an uncontrollable rage and is assaulting or biting the other. Pull the children apart and keep them separate until they have calmed down. If the fight is extremely violent, you may have to end the play session. Make it clear that it doesn't matter who "started it." There is no excuse for trying to hurt each other.

To avoid or minimize "high-risk" situations, teach your child ways to deal with his anger without resorting to aggressive behavior. Teach him to say "no" in a firm tone of voice, to turn his back, or to find compromises instead of fighting with his body. Through example, teach him that settling differences with words is more effective—and more civilized—than with physical violence. Praise him for his appropriate behavior and help explain to him how "grown-up" he is acting whenever he uses these tactics instead of hitting, kicking, or biting. And always reinforce and praise his behavior when he is demonstrating kindness and gentleness.

There's also nothing wrong with using a time-out when his behavior is inappropriate, and it can be used in children as young as one year old. These time-outs should be a last resort, however. Have him sit in a chair or go to a "boring" place where there are no distractions; in essence, you're separating him from his misbehavior, and giving him time to cool off. Briefly explain to your child what you're doing and why—but no long lectures.

Initially, when children are young, time-out is over as soon as they have calmed down and are quiet and still. Ending time-out once they are quiet and still reinforces this behavior, so your child learns that time-out means quiet and still. Once they have learned to calm themselves (to be quiet and still), a good rule of thumb is one minute of a time-out for each year in your child's age—thus, a three-year-old should have a three-minute time-out. When the time-out is over, there needs to be a time-in, while giving him plenty of positive attention when doing the right thing.

Always watch your own behavior around your child. One of the best ways to teach him appropriate behavior is to control your own temper. If you express your anger in quiet, peaceful ways, he probably will follow your example. If you must discipline him, do not feel guilty about it and certainly don't apologize. If he senses your mixed feelings, he may convince himself that he was in the right all along and you are the "bad" one. Although disciplining your child is never pleasant, it is a necessary part of parenthood, and there is no reason to feel guilty about it. Your child needs to understand when he is in the wrong so that he will take responsibility for his actions and be willing to accept the consequences.

When to Call the Pediatrician

If your child seems to be unusually aggressive for longer than a few weeks, and you cannot cope with his behavior on your own, consult your pediatrician. Other warning signs include:

- Physical injury to himself or others (teeth marks, bruises, head injuries)

- Attacks on you or other adults

- Being sent home or barred from play by neighbors or school

- Your own fear for the safety of those around him

The most important warning sign is the frequency of outbursts. Sometimes children with conduct disorders will go for several days or a week or two without incident, and may even act quite charming during this time, but few can go an entire month without getting into trouble at least once.

Your pediatrician can suggest ways to discipline your child and will help you determine if he has a true conduct disorder. If this is the problem, you probably will not be able to resolve it on your own, and your pediatrician will advise appropriate mental health intervention.

The pediatrician or other mental health specialist will interview both you and your child and may observe your child in different situations (home, preschool, with adults and other children). A behavior-management program will be outlined. Not all methods work on all children, so there will be a certain amount of trial and reassessment.

Once several effective ways are found to reward good behavior and discourage bad, they can be used in establishing an approach that works both at home and away. The progress may be slow, but such programs usually are successful if started when the disorder is just beginning to develop.

Coping with Disasters and Terrorism

Disastrous events—earthquakes, hurricanes, tornadoes, floods, and fires—can be frightening and traumatic for both children and adults. Events like these have always demanded that parents be available to talk with and reassure their children and be particularly sensitive to their children's needs. The AAP has compiled information for parents on talking with children about tragedies and other events at Healthy Children.org and AAP.org. Parents are understandably concerned about the effects of terrorism on their children, including the effects of the media's coverage of those events. In general, it is best to share basic information with children, not graphic details, or unnecessary details about tragic circumstances. Children and adults alike want to be able to understand enough so they know what's going on. Graphic information and images should be avoided.

Keep young children away from repetitive graphic images and sounds that may appear on television, radio, social media, computers, etc.

With older children, if you do want them to watch the news, record it ahead of time. That allows you to preview it and evaluate its contents before you sit down with them to watch it. Then, as you watch it with them, you can stop, pause, and have a discussion when you need to.

Children will generally follow good advice, but you have to give them some latitude to make decisions about what they're ready for. You can block them from seeing the newspaper that comes to the door, for example, but not the one on the newsstand. Today, most older children will have access to the news and graphic images through social media and other applications right from their cell phone. You need to be aware of what's out there and take steps in advance to talk to children about what they might hear or see.

What to Expect

Even if terrorism, natural disasters, or other traumatic events occur hundreds or thousands of miles from you and your child, television, online, and print news coverage can make the aftermath traumatizing. If the disaster actually has occurred in your own community, it can be especially frightening for your child.

In the aftermath of a crisis, children may react in different ways. Some may experience a type of post-traumatic stress reaction, with symptoms that may vary from child to child, depending in part on his age. A child up to age five:

- May have difficulty sleeping

- May exhibit a decreased appetite

- May cry and become cranky

- May show defiance, have tantrums, and exhibit hostility toward siblings

- May cling to you, "shadowing" you as you move from one room of the house to another, and show anxiety on leaving your side

- May have nightmares and refuse to sleep in his own bed

- May have bed-wetting episodes, even if he has previously been toilet trained

- May develop physical symptoms, such as stomachaches and headaches

- Might refuse to go to the preschool that he had attended enthusiastically for months or years

What You Can Do

Remember that children tend to personalize events. They may think that a terrorist attack or disaster is going to strike them or their family members. One of your primary goals as a parent is to talk with your child and make him feel secure and safe. Your words and actions can be very powerful in comforting him; talking with him about the events won't increase his fear and anxiety. As you interact with him, speak to him at a level he can understand. Here are some guidelines to keep in mind.

- **Listen to what** your child says to you. Help him use age-appropriate words to describe his feelings—perhaps "sad," "mad," or "scared." Don't make assumptions, and don't downplay what he's saying. Accept what he's feeling.

- **If your child** has difficulty expressing himself, encourage him to get his feelings out in other ways—perhaps by drawing pictures or playing with toys.

- **At his age,** your child may not need a lot of information about the events that have happened. Don't be surprised if he asks the same questions over and over. While you should be honest about what you tell him, don't overload him with information.

- **If a terrorist** attack has happened, explain that there are "bad" people in the world, and bad people do bad things. But make sure he understands that most people are not bad and that most people of all ethnic and religious groups are good. Use this event to teach tolerance to your child.

- **For an event** like a terrorist attack that occurred elsewhere in the country, let him know that the violence was isolated to particular areas, and not in your community.

■ **Although you always** should monitor what your child watches on television, this advice is *particularly* important when terrorism or other disasters are filling the screen. No matter what your child's age, he can be traumatized by what he sees on television, so restrict his viewing. When he does watch TV, make sure you are there with him, and talk about what you've seen.

■ **If you appear** particularly anxious over what has happened, he'll feel it and find coping more difficult. Try to stay as calm as possible in his presence, and maintain as many of the routines of the family's life as you can. If your child has been going to preschool, for example, the structure of continuing to do so can be comforting to him.

■ **Teach your child** the importance of helping out those who have been directly affected by the tragedy or disaster. Let him help you send a letter or care package or explain to him that you are sending money or supplies to help the victims.

■ **If your child** has been particularly traumatized by the events that have happened, talk with your pediatrician. She may suggest seeking the help of a mental health professional who specializes in treating children in tough emotional times.

■ **It is easier** for adults and children when there is a plan in place in advance of an emergency or disaster situation. Parents should develop a written disaster plan and discuss this plan with their children. Talking to children in advance of an emergency or disaster helps them to get better prepared and to develop strategies for coping with emergency situations. It is important to engage them in conversation and help them develop strategies to cope and adjust. For more information on helping children cope and adjust after a disaster, visit the Advocacy and Policy section on AAP.org.

If a Loved One Dies

The death of an important person in a child's life is among the most stressful events that a child can experience. When the death involves a parent or sibling, the potential for an adverse response by the child is compounded. When dealing with bereavement, here are some key things to consider.

■ **The child should** be told about a death honestly and in language that is developmentally appropriate.

■ **The family can** be reassured that their showing of feelings, such as shock, disbelief, guilt, sadness, and anger, is normal and helpful. A bereaved parent or other close family member who shares these feelings and memories (e.g., with pictures and stories) with a child reduces the child's sense of isolation.

- **Children need reassurance** that they will be cared for and loved by a consistent adult who attends sensitively to their needs. In addition, they must be assured that they did not cause the death, could not have prevented it, and cannot bring back the deceased. Parents should be encouraged to continue family routines and discipline.

- **The funeral services** can provide even a young child with an important way to grieve a loved one if such involvement is supportive, appropriately explained, and compatible with the family's values and approach. Children need to be prepared if they are to participate in the funeral process. The participation should be tailored according to the developmental level of the child. A trusted person should be with a child to explain what is happening and to offer support. Encouraging a child to commemorate loss through some form of participation, such as drawing pictures, planting a tree, or giving a favorite object, will promote inclusion in the process and provide a meaningful ritual.

- **Grief for a** child is a process that unfolds over time. The initial shock and denial of death may evolve into sadness and anger that can last for weeks to months and eventually end, in the best circumstances, with acceptance and readjustment.

Hyperactivity and the Distractible Child

Almost every child has days when she seems "inattentive and hyperactive," but true inattention and hyperactivity is a condition called attention deficit hyperactivity disorder (ADHD), which affects only about one to two in twenty children under age twelve. Children who have ADHD are inattentive, impulsive, move about a great deal, and have difficulty sitting still when it is required. They also can be easily distracted, often act on impulse, and have difficulty paying attention when listening to or watching events around them. They also may have trouble sleeping.

Particularly when your child is a toddler, you may worry that she shows signs of hyperactivity, but if you compare her with others her age, you probably will discover that her behavior is typical of her childhood peers. Around ages two and three, children naturally are very active and impulsive and have a short attention span. All children occasionally seem overactive or easily distractible—for example, when they're very tired, excited about doing something "special," or anxious about being in a strange place or among strangers. Truly hyperactive children, however, are noticeably more active, more easily distracted, and more excitable than their peers. Most important of all, these children never seem to be calm from one day to the next, and their behaviors continue into their school years.

Although most children with hyperactivity have normal intelligence, they frequently do not perform well in school settings, because they can't pay attention or follow instructions through to completion. They also are slower to develop control over their impulses and emotions and slower in developing the age-appropriate ability to concentrate and pay attention. They tend to be more talkative, emotional, demanding, disobedient, and noncompliant than others their age. Their behavior often remains immature throughout childhood and adolescence, and may lead to problems doing things that they need to do at home, in school, or among friends. Without support and treatment, children who are truly hyperactive have difficulty developing the self-esteem they need to lead healthy, productive lives.

Most of the children with inattention and hyperactivity have other family members with the same condition, which suggests that it may be mostly inherited. Sometimes the condition can be traced to illnesses affecting the brain or nervous system, such as meningitis, encephalitis, fetal alcohol syndrome, or severe prematurity. Most hyperactive children have never had such an illness, however, and most children who do suffer these ailments do not become hyperactive. Boys are two to four times more likely than girls to develop ADHD; no one knows precisely why these differences exist. Although there has also been much speculation that certain foods and food additives might be linked to ADHD, extensive research has not demonstrated that there is a substantial link. Children with these problems tend to elicit negative, punitive, and controlling responses from adults or parents who may not understand the true nature of hyperactivity. These children, when subjected to much criticism, only feel more negatively about themselves.

Whatever the source of hyperactivity, the way the problem is perceived, understood, and treated, and the way parents and teachers respond, can influence the outcome for the child. Parents who are emotionally healthy and who have knowledge of sound behavioral management principles help achieve the best results.

When to Call the Pediatrician

Observing your child alongside others her age over a period of days or weeks is the best way to determine if she is hyperactive. For this reason, those who care for her at preschool or child care may be your best source of information. They can tell you how she behaves in a group and whether she is acting in a typical manner compared to other children her age. Specific signs of ADHD include:

- Difficulty paying attention to activities that interest other children her age

- Difficulty following even simple instructions due to not paying attention

- Being impulsive, such as repeatedly running into the street without looking, interrupting other children's play, or racing through off-limit areas without considering consequences

- Unnecessarily hurried activity, such as running and jumping without periods of rest

- Sudden emotional outbursts, such as crying, angry yelling, hitting, or frustration, that seem inappropriate

- Persistent misbehavior because of not listening despite being told "no" many times

If you and others observe several of these warning signs on a continuing basis, consult your pediatrician. The doctor will go through the criteria for ADHD and examine your child to rule out any medical cause for the behavior, and then either conduct a further evaluation or refer you to a developmental behavioral pediatrician, psychologist, or child psychiatrist for a more formal evaluation. If this specialist determines that your preschooler has ADHD, the doctor or therapist probably will recommend some specific behavior strategies for managing her behavior and may suggest that you learn a system for fine-tuning your own behavior management skills, using so-called behavioral therapy or behavioral parent training (see also the section *How to Respond* at right).

Medications also may be recommended, depending on the effectiveness of behavioral measures with your child. Toddlers and preschoolers change so rapidly and so dramatically that what might seem like a behavioral problem at one point could disappear a few months later. Therefore it is important to determine if the behaviors have been persistent for more than six months.

Keep in mind that medications are used in more severe cases of attention deficit/hyperactivity disorder in younger children only after trying to control the behaviors with good parenting techniques. The American Academy of Pediatrics recommends that children with ADHD have a thorough patient history, family history, and physical exam before starting treatment with medications (specifically, with so-called stimulant drugs). In some cases, if the history or physical exam raises concerns, your doctor may advise that your child undergo an electrocardiogram (a test measuring the heart's activity) before she prescribes these medications.

As a parent of a child with ADHD, you may hear about "alternative" treatments, many of which are still unproven and some of which have been shown to be ineffective. Talk with your pediatrician before involving your child in any alternative therapies.

How to Respond

If your child shows signs of ADHD, it may mean that she cannot control her behavior on her own. In her hurry and

Effective Discipline

Child's Behavior*	Your Responses	
	Effective	*Constructive*
Temper tantrums	Give a time-out and walk away.	When child is calm, discuss the incident in an age-appropriate manner.
Overexcitement	Distract with another activity.	Talk about his behavior in an age-appropriate manner when he's calm.
Hitting or biting	Immediately remove him from situation or in anticipation of this behavior.	Discuss consequences of his actions (pain, damage, bad feelings) to him and others in an age-appropriate manner. Try a one-word time-out after a brief response.
Not paying attention	Establish eye contact to hold his attention.	Make sure your expectations are age-appropriate for your child's developmental level (ask him to listen to a story for three minutes instead of ten; don't insist he sit through a full church service).
Refuses to pick up toys	Don't let him play until he does his job.	Show him how to do the task and help him with it; praise him when he finishes.

*Note: In all these situations, try to determine what influences might cause or prolong the behavior: Is the child in need of attention, tired, worried, or fearful? What is your own mood or behavior? Remember, you always should praise your child for good or improved effort.

excitement, she may be accident-prone and may destroy property. To discipline a hyperactive child, you need to respond both effectively and constructively. If your actions are effective, your child's behavior will improve as a result. If they are constructive, they also will help develop her self-esteem and make her more personable. The box on page 586 (*Effective Discipline*) provides some examples of effective and constructive responses to common problems among hyperactive children.

It is important to respond immediately whenever your child misbehaves and to make sure that everyone caring for her responds to these incidents in the same way. Discipline means teaching self-control. If done effectively, you will rarely need to use punishment. Do not spank or slap your child since it does not encourage her to control herself and may contribute to a continued negative self-image and resentment toward you; at the same time, this approach tells her that it's OK to strike other people. Instead, acknowledge and point out those times when she displays appropriate behaviors ("catching her being good"), and learn to actively ignore inappropriate behaviors that are not dangerous; this approach is far more effective in the long run. Children with ADHD can be very challenging to manage and parents may find they need help or coaching in how to effectively manage their child's behaviors.

Temper Tantrums

As an adult, you have learned to control your strong emotions when it's not appropriate to fully express them—but your preschooler probably hasn't yet. His temper tantrums certainly are not fun for you or for him, but they are a normal part of life with most preschoolers. The first time your child screams and kicks because he can't have his way, you may feel angry, frustrated, humiliated, or frightened. You may wonder where you've gone wrong as a parent to produce such a miserable child. Rest assured, you are not responsible for this behavior, and tantrums are not ordinarily a sign of severe emotional or personality disorders. Almost all children have these episodes occasionally, especially around ages two and three. If handled successfully, they usually diminish in intensity and frequency by age four or five.

The section *Anger, Aggression, and Biting* (see page 575 in this chapter) explains the development of emotions in young children, and much of it applies to temper tantrums. In the developmental stage of separating from their parents, the word "no" is a perfectly understandable and a normal expression of children's emerging need for some independence. Tantrums are often an expression of frustration. Preschoolers are very eager to take control. They want to be more independent than their skills and safety allow, and they don't appreciate their limits. They want to make decisions, but they don't know how to compromise, and they don't deal well with disappointment or restraint. They also can't express their feelings well in words, so instead they act out their anger and frustration by crying or withdrawing, and sometimes by having temper tantrums. Although these emotional displays are unpleasant, they rarely are dangerous.

You often can tell when a temper tantrum is coming. For some time before it begins, the child may seem more sullen or irritable than usual, and neither gentle affection nor playing with her will change her moodiness. She may be tired, hungry, or lonely. Then she tries, or is expected, to do something beyond her capabilities, or asks for something she can't have. She begins to whimper or whine and becomes more demanding. Nothing will distract or comfort her, and finally she starts to cry. As the crying increases, she begins to flail her arms and kick her legs. She may fall to the ground or hold her breath—some children actually hold their breath until they turn blue or faint. As frightening as it is to watch these breath-holding spells, the child's normal breathing resumes as soon as she faints, and she will recover quickly and completely.

Don't be surprised if your child has tantrums only when you are around—most children act up only around their parents or other family members, seldom when with outsiders. She is also testing your rules and limits, whereas she wouldn't dare do this with someone she knows less well. When her challenge goes too far and you restrain her, she may respond with a tantrum. Don't take tantrums personally. Try to remain calm and understand the behavior. Ironically, her occasional outbursts are actually a sign that she trusts you.

This emotional explosion serves as a kind of energy release, which often exhausts the child so that she falls asleep soon afterward. When she awakens she usually is calm and her behavior is quiet and pleasant. If she is ill or there is a great deal of tension among the people around her, however, the frustration may start building all over again. Children who are anxious, ill, or temperamental, who get too little rest, or who live in very stressful households tend to have tantrums more frequently.

Prevention

You can't prevent every tantrum, but you may be able to decrease the number, duration, or intensity by making sure your child does not get overtired, overly anxious, or unnecessarily frustrated. Your child's temper may become very short if she doesn't have enough "quiet time," particularly when she is sick or anxious, or has been unusually active. Even if she doesn't sleep, lying down for fifteen or twenty minutes can help restore her energy and reduce the likelihood of tantrums from exhaustion. Children who do not nap may be particularly prone to tantrums and often need such a quiet period on a daily, scheduled basis. If your child resists, you might lie down with her or read her a story, but do not allow her to play or talk excessively.

Children whose parents fail to set appropriate limits, are overly strict, or forget to reinforce good behaviors tend to have more frequent and severe tantrums than children whose parents take a moderate approach. As a rule, it's best to set very few limits but to be firm about those that are set. Expect your child to tell you "no" many times each day. She needs to assert herself this way and it would not be normal if she never challenged you. You can allow her to have her way when the issue is minor—for example, if she wants to wander around slowly instead of walking quickly to the park, or if she refuses to get dressed before breakfast. But when she starts to run into the street, you must stop her and insist that she obey you, even if you have to hold her back physically. Be loving but firm, and respond the same way every time she violates the rule. She won't learn these important lessons immediately, so expect to repeat these interventions many times before her behavior changes. Also, make sure that every adult who cares for her observes the same rules and disciplines her in the same way.

One of the best strategies for preventing temper tantrums is to give your child appropriate choices. You might say, "Do you want me to read to you, or would you rather get dressed and go to the park?" Clearly each choice must be possible and reasonable—there may be days when the park is out of the question—and you will need to show some flexibility at times. Or what happens if you want to take your child outside in the winter so she can play in the snow—but she refuses to wear her snow clothes? In this instance, you might say, "Either you wear your snow clothes, or you have to carry them with you or I will carry them. Which choice do you want?" Once outside, she'll quickly realize that she is cold and she'll want to put on her snow clothes.

How to Respond

When your child has a temper tantrum, it's important that you try to remain calm yourself. If you have loud, angry outbursts, your child naturally will imitate your behavior. If you shout at her to calm down, you probably will make the situation worse. Maintaining a peaceful atmosphere will reduce the general stress level and make both you and your child feel better and more in control. In fact, sometimes gentle restraint, holding, or distracting comments such as "Did you see what the kitty is doing?" or "I think I heard the doorbell" will interrupt behavior such as breath holding before it reaches the point of fainting.

Sometimes, if you feel yourself losing control, humor will save the day. Turn a dispute over taking a bath into a race to the bathroom. Soften your command to "pick up your toys" by making a funny face. Unless your child is extremely irritable or overtired, she is more likely to be distracted into obedience if you temper discipline with a bit of fun or whimsy. Doing this might also make you feel better.

Some parents feel guilty every time they say "no" to their children. They try too hard to explain their rules, or apologize for them. Even at age two or three, children can detect uncertainty in a tone of voice, and they will try to take advantage of it. If the parent sometimes gives in, the child becomes even more outraged on those occasions when she doesn't get her way. There is no reason to be apologetic about enforcing your rules. It only makes it more difficult for your child to understand which of them are firm and which can be questioned. This does not mean that you should be unfriendly or abusive when you say no, but state your position clearly. As your child gets older, you can offer brief, simple reasons for your rules, but do not go into long, confusing explanations.

These important rules should be based on your child not hurting herself or destroying property. Also, everyone providing care for your child needs to agree to the same rules. It's wise to pick your battles as well. Toddlers can stay in a conflict situation for some time, which runs counter to the goal of limiting or avoiding the clash altogether. When you ask your child to do something against her will, follow through on the order with her. If you've asked her to put away her toys, offer to help her. If you've told her not to throw her ball against the window, show her where she *can* throw it. If you've reminded her not to touch the hot oven door, either remove her from the kitchen or stay there with her to make sure that she minds you.

(Never issue a safety order to a two- or three-year-old and then leave the room.)

Finally, use the cooling-off or time-out strategy described on page 362. Give your child some time alone to calm down and regain control. Put her in a separate place, removed from the activity in the house, and tell her clearly that her behavior was unacceptable (but that you still love her). The time-out plus your words will help her understand the reasons why.

When to Call the Pediatrician

Although occasional temper tantrums during the preschool years should be expected, they should become less frequent and less intense by the middle of the fourth year. Between tantrums, the child should behave like other kids her age and seem healthy. At no time should the behavior cause the child to harm herself or others or destroy property. When the outbursts are very severe, frequent, or prolonged, they may be an early sign of emotional disturbance.

Consult your pediatrician if your child shows any of the following warning signs.

■ Tantrums persist or intensify after age four.

■ Your child injures herself or others, or destroys property during tantrums.

■ Your child has frequent nightmares, extreme disobedience, reversal of toilet training, headaches or stomachaches, refusal to eat or go to bed, extreme anxiety, constant grumpiness, or clinging to you.

■ Your child holds her breath and faints during tantrums.

If your child holds her breath and faints, you probably should call the pediatrician. The doctor may want to examine her and possibly check for other causes of "fainting," such as seizures (see page 790). The pediatrician also can offer suggestions for disciplining your child and suggest parent education groups that might provide additional support and guidance. If your doctor feels the tantrums indicate a severe emotional disturbance, she will refer you to a child psychiatrist, psychologist, or mental health clinic.

Thumb and Finger Sucking

Do not be upset if your baby begins sucking his thumb or fingers. This habit is very common and has a soothing and calming effect. Some experts feel that one-half or more of all children engage in this activity at some time in their early life. It is largely the result of the normal rooting and sucking reflexes present in all infants at birth. There is evidence that some infants suck their thumbs and fingers even before delivery, and some, particularly finger suckers, will show that behavior immediately after being born.

By definition, a habit is a pattern of behavior that's repeated, and the child is not even aware that he's doing it. Of course, parents are very aware of it, and many of them worry. But habits like thumb sucking (as well as body rocking or head banging) often calm the child when he's feeling stress or fatigue. Because sucking is a normal reflex, thumb and finger sucking can be considered a normal habit.

All children have habits, and the only time thumb or finger sucking should cause you concern is if it continues too long or affects the shape of your child's mouth or the alignment of his teeth. Over half of thumb or finger suckers stop by age six or seven months. Sometimes young children, especially when they are feeling most vulnerable, even until age eight or so, still will suck their thumb occasionally. Don't even worry about it until your child is four to five years old. But because thumb sucking beyond the fifth birthday may cause changes in the roof of the mouth (palate) or in the way the teeth are lining up, you and your child's dentist might become concerned at that time. This also is a time when your child might begin to be affected by the negative comments of his playmates, siblings, and relatives. If these factors become worrisome, consult your pediatrician about treatment.

Treatment

Parents can help their children overcome habits like thumb sucking, but it takes time. Severe emotional or stress-related problems that might prolong this habit should be ruled out before any treatment program is begun. Also, your child should want to stop the habit and should be directly involved with the treatment chosen. Treatment usually is limited to children who persist in thumb sucking beyond their fifth birthday.

The techniques used usually begin with gentle reminders, particularly during the daytime hours. Friends or relatives might suggest that you use a pacifier, but there is no evidence that this is effective. It only substitutes one sucking habit for another.

If these measures are ineffective and your child is still uninterested in breaking the habit, some pediatricians may rarely recommend trying some type of "aversive" (unpleasant) treatment, but only as a last resort. This treatment is designed to serve as a reminder to your child when he begins to suck, and may include coating the finger or thumb with a bitter substance, or covering it with a bandage or "thumb guard" (an adjustable plastic cylinder that can be taped to the thumb).

Other pediatricians recommend motivating the child to "un-learn" the habit of thumb sucking by setting a series of attainable goals (e.g., no thumb sucking for an hour before bed, then after dinner, then all day) with praise or rewards for accomplishing those goals. Only once the child begins to catch themselves (become aware) will the behavior stop.

In those rare cases where there is severe tooth misalignment and the techniques described have all failed, some dentists will install a device in the mouth that prevents the fingers or thumb from putting pressure on the palate or teeth. Other options include using a sock, a bandage, or adhesive tape to serve as a reminder to your child to stop sucking. Whatever approach you use, it will work only if your child agrees that he wants to participate in stopping the thumb sucking.

It also is important to remember that your child may be one of the very few who for one reason or another cannot seem to stop thumb and finger sucking. Be assured that most of these children stop daytime sucking habits before they progress very far along in school due to peer pressure. Exerting excessive pressure on your child to stop this type of behavior probably would cause more harm than good, and even these children eventually stop the habit on their own.

Tics

Children who have tics experience involuntary movements or muscle spasms, most often of the face and neck. Their eyes may blink, their shoulders may shrug, their faces may grimace, or they may stretch their necks.

Some healthy newborns may show some jitteriness, most noticeable while the baby is crying; such tremors usually disappear after the second week of life. By contrast, true tics tend to develop later in childhood, sometimes as early as two to three years of age, but more often between ages seven and nine. These tics may start suddenly, and can be exaggerated in the aftermath of a physical or social stress. They can worsen when a child is anxious or tense, and become less frequent when he is able to relax.

The most serious tic disorder is called *Tourette's syndrome.* Children with this condition usually have a number of motor tics, starting in the face but before long affecting other parts of the body. These children also have vocal tics, such as uttering words or phrases (sometimes including obscene words), coughs, hiccups, sniffs, and snorts. The specific sounds and movements may change over time. Tourette's syndrome often is associated with other disorders, including hyperactivity, ADHD (attention deficit hyperactivity disorder), and obsessive thoughts and compulsive behaviors. It usually has its onset toward the middle of the first decade of life.

Management

You may find tics in your child annoying, and although you might be tempted to ask him to "stop doing that," they are beyond his control. In fact, when you call attention to them, they are more likely to persist or worsen.

If your pediatrician believes that there is a psychological component that is making your child's tics worse, these underlying emotional difficulties should be treated. Make an effort to reduce the stress, worries, or conflicts in your child's life, which may help relieve the severity of his tics. For Tourette's syndrome, your doctor may prescribe medications or refer you to a specialist to control the condition.

~ 19 ~

Chest and Lungs

Bronchiolitis

BRONCHIOLITIS IS AN infection of the small breathing tubes (bronchioles) of the lungs. It is one of the most common diseases of early childhood. (Note: The term *bronchiolitis* sometimes is confused with bronchitis, which is an infection of the larger, more central airways.)

Bronchiolitis is caused by a virus, most commonly respiratory syncytial virus (RSV). However, several other viruses can cause this condition, including human rhinovirus, metapneumovirus, parainfluenza, influenza, and adenovirus. The infection causes inflammation and swelling of the bronchioles, which in turn blocks the flow of air in and out of the lungs.

Most adults and older children who are infected by RSV get only an upper respiratory infection (a cold). In children under two years of age, however, an RSV infection is more likely to lead to bronchiolitis (inflammation of the bronchioles). It also may cause apnea, which means the baby stops breathing briefly for at least twenty seconds. This most often occurs in babies who were born prematurely. Bronchiolitis is associated with recurrent wheezing later in

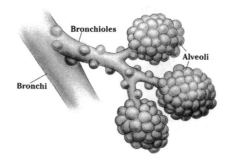

childhood; however, it is unclear whether bronchiolitis directly leads to the development of asthma.

In most parts of the US, RSV occurs from October or November through March. During the other months, bronchiolitis usually is caused by other viruses.

RSV is highly contagious and is spread by contact with an infected person. It can be found on surfaces for several hours and also spreads easily through families, child care centers, and hospital wards. Careful hand-washing with soap and water or alcohol-based hand sanitizers is the best way to prevent spreading the infection.

Signs and Symptoms

Almost all children get an RSV infection by the time they are three years old. The majority of them develop only an upper respiratory infection (a cold) with a runny nose, mild cough, and sometimes fever. Unfortunately, the RSV infection in a small number of infants will go into the lungs and cause bronchiolitis. After a day or two, the cough becomes more pronounced, and the child begins to breathe more rapidly and with more difficulty.

If your baby shows any of the following signs of breathing difficulty, or if his fever lasts more than three days (or if it is present at all in an infant under three months), call your pediatrician immediately.

■ He makes a high-pitched whistling sound, called a wheeze, each time he breathes in (inhales) or out (exhales).

■ Drawing in of the skin between and around the ribs and breastbone.

■ He is unable to drink fluids well because he is working so hard to breathe that he has difficulty sucking and swallowing.

■ He develops a bluish color around his lips or fingertips. This means the airways are so blocked that not enough oxygen is getting into his lungs and into the blood.

Also call the pediatrician if your child develops any of the following signs or symptoms of dehydration (not enough fluid in the body), which also can appear with bronchiolitis.

■ Dry mouth

■ Drinking less than his normal amount of fluids

■ Not making tears when he cries

■ Urinating less often than usual

If your child has any of the following conditions, notify your pediatrician:

■ As soon as you suspect that he has bronchiolitis

■ A persistent cough and runny nose

■ Any difficulty breathing

- Cystic fibrosis

- Congenital heart disease

- Bronchopulmonary dysplasia, seen in some infants who were born prematurely or were on a respirator (breathing machine) as newborns

- Low immunity

- Organ transplant

- Cancer for which he is receiving chemotherapy

Home Treatment

There are no medications to treat RSV infections at home. All you can do during the early phase of the illness is ease your child's cold symptoms. You can relieve some of the nasal stuffiness with a humidifier and salt water (saline) nose drops with or without nasal aspiration. Coughing is one way for the body to clear the lungs, and normally a cough does not need to be treated with medicine. If your child has a fever, you can give children's acetaminophen (Tylenol) as instructed on the box or children's ibuprofen (Motrin) if they are six months of age or older. Fever in children is a temperature at or over 100.4 degrees Fahrenheit (38 degrees Celsius) taken by a thermometer in the rectum (anus). (See *Fever,* page 763.)

Also, to avoid dehydration, make sure your child drinks lots of fluid during this time. (See *Diarrhea,* page 530.) He may prefer clear liquids rather than milk or formula. Because of his breathing difficulty, he also may feed more slowly or eat smaller amounts more frequently. He also may not eat solid foods very well due to decreased appetite. It's usually fine if he eats less solid food while sick as long as he is drinking enough fluids to avoid dehydration.

Professional Treatment

If your child is having mild to moderate breathing difficulty, your pediatrician may try using a medication that opens up the breathing tubes (bronchodilator). This is often given by a breathing machine (nebulizer) in the hopes of preventing hospitalization. These drugs seem to help with breathing in a small number of patients.

Bronchiolitis is the most common reason that infants are hospitalized, either because their breathing is very difficult, they cannot eat or drink normally, or they need to be treated with oxygen and bronchodilator or other medications. Very rarely, an infant will not respond to these treatments and might have to be placed on a breathing machine (respirator) to help his lungs and body get enough oxygen. This treatment usually is only a temporary measure that is stopped as soon as the child improves.

Prevention

The best way to protect your child from bronchiolitis is to keep him away from the viruses that cause it. Whenever possible, especially while he's an infant, avoid close contact with children or adults who are in the early (contagious) stages of respiratory infections. Even a mild cold in an older child or adult can cause breathing problems for an infant. If he is in a child care center where other children might have the virus, make sure that those who care for him wash their hands thoroughly and frequently. Infants should not be exposed to secondhand smoking, as this can increase the risk of infection.

There is a treatment that your pediatrician may prescribe that could reduce the risk of developing serious RSV disease requiring hospitalization. It is recommended only for a small number of high-risk babies such as those born very prematurely or with significant heart or lung disease. Palivizumab (known as Synagis) is a drug available to protect against severe RSV disease in children under the age of twenty-four months and is administered via injection on a monthly basis for three to five months prior to and during the RSV season. Ask your pediatrician which high-risk infants are most likely to benefit from this medication and whether your own child is a candidate.

Cough

Coughing is almost always an indication of an irritation in your child's air passages. When the nerve endings in the throat, windpipe, or lungs sense the irritation, a reflex causes air to be ejected forcefully through the passageways.

Coughs usually are associated with respiratory illnesses, such as colds/upper respiratory infection (see page 659), asthma (see page 553), bronchiolitis (see page 595), croup (see page 600), flu (see page 602), or pneumonia (see page 605). If your child's cough is accompanied by fever, he probably has such an infection.

When a child has a cold, the cough may sound wet (productive or congested), or dry and irritating. The cough may last longer than the accompanying runny nose. If he has a cough, a fever, and difficulty breathing (too fast, too slow, noisy, drawing in of the skin between and around the ribs and breastbone), he may have pneumonia. If he has these symptoms, see your doctor immediately.

To a large extent, the location of the problem determines the sound of the cough: An irritation in the larynx (voice box), such as croup, causes a cough that sounds like the bark of a dog or seal. Irritation of the larger airways, such as the trachea (windpipe) or bronchi, is a deeper, raspy cough.

Allergies and sinus infections can cause a chronic cough because mucus drips down the back of the throat, producing a dry, hard-to-stop cough, particularly at night upon lying down. A child who coughs only while asleep may have asthma (see page 553) or gastroesophageal reflux (a condition where the contents of the stomach rise up into the esophagus causing irritation and cough).

Here are some other cough-related issues that can affect children:

- **Anything more than** an occasional cough in an infant has to be taken seriously. The most common causes are colds and bronchiolitis, which usually get better in a few days. It is important to watch for signs of breathing difficulties and seek medical help if needed. These signs include not only rapid breathing, especially while asleep, but also drawing in of the skin between and around the ribs and breastbone (sternum).

- **Sometimes children cough** so hard that they throw up. Usually they vomit liquid and food from the stomach, but there also may be a lot of mucus, especially during a cold or an asthma attack.

- **Wheezing is a** high-pitched sound during breathing that occurs when there is an obstruction of the airway inside the chest. It is one of the symptoms of asthma, but also can occur if your child has bronchiolitis, pneumonia, or certain other disorders.

- **Children with asthma** often cough and wheeze together. This may happen when they are active or playing, or at night. Sometimes their cough can be heard, but the wheezing may be evident only to your doctor when she listens with a stethoscope. The cough and the wheeze usually get better after using asthma medications.

- **A cough is** commonly worse at night. When your child coughs at night, it may be caused by irritation in the throat or a sinus infection with post-nasal drip. Asthma is another major reason for a nighttime cough.

- **A sudden cough** can develop in children who are choking. It could mean that some food or liquid has "gone down the wrong way" and ended up in the lungs. The coughing helps clear the airways. However, if coughing continues for more than a few minutes, or if your child is having difficulty breathing, seek medical help right away. Don't put your fingers in your child's mouth to clear the throat because you may push the food or other cause of the obstruction down farther. (See *Choking*, page 691.)

When to Call the Pediatrician

An infant under two months of age who develops a cough should be seen by the doctor. For older infants and children, consult your physician immediately if the coughing:

- Makes it difficult for your child to breathe.

- Is painful, persistent, and accompanied by whooping, vomiting, or turning blue.

- Interferes with eating and sleeping.

- Appears suddenly and is associated with a fever.

- Begins after your child chokes on food or any other object. (See *Choking,* page 691.) In about 50 percent of cases, when a foreign body (food or toy) is inhaled into the bronchi and lungs the cough may develop a few hours or days later.

Your pediatrician will try to determine the cause of your child's cough; most commonly it's due to an upper respiratory virus. When the cough is from a medical problem other than a cold or the flu, such as a bacterial infection or asthma, it will be necessary to treat that condition before the cough will clear. Occasionally when the cause of a chronic cough (lasting longer than four weeks) is not apparent, further tests such as chest X-rays or tuberculosis skin tests may be necessary.

Treatment

Treating a cough depends on its cause. But whatever the cause, it is always a good idea to give extra fluids. Adding moisture to the air with a cool-mist humidifier or vaporizer also may make your child more comfortable, especially at night if they are mouth-breathers.

However, be sure to clean the device thoroughly each morning as recommended in the manufacturer's manual, so it doesn't become a breeding ground for harmful bacteria or fungi.

Nighttime coughs, particularly those associated with allergies or asthma, can be especially annoying, because they occur when everyone is trying to sleep. In some cases it may help to elevate the head of the older child's bed. If the night cough is due to asthma, use a bronchodilator or other asthma medication as directed by your pediatrician.

Although cough medicines can be purchased without a prescription, the American Academy of Pediatrics' position is that these cough medicines are not effective for children younger than six years old, and may even pose a health risk from serious side effects.

Croup

Croup is an inflammation of the voice box (larynx) and windpipe (trachea). It causes a barking cough and a high-pitched sound when breathing in. Although croup is sometimes associated with allergies, it usually is caused by a virus, most commonly the parainfluenza virus. The illness most often is "caught" from someone who is infected, sometimes from air droplets or from your child's own hand, which he uses to transfer the virus into his nose or mouth.

Croup tends to occur in the fall and winter when your child is between three months and three years old. Initially he may develop nasal stuffiness resembling a cold and fever. After a day or two, the sound of the cough will turn into something resembling a barking or seal-like cough. The cough tends to become worse at night.

The greatest danger with croup is that your child's airway will continue to swell, further narrowing his windpipe and making it difficult to breathe. As your child tires from the effort of breathing, he may stop eating and drinking. He also may become too fatigued to cough. Some children are particularly prone to getting a crouplike cough and seem to develop such a cough whenever they have a respiratory illness.

Treatment

If your child has mild croup symptoms, steam up the bathroom by turning on hot water in the shower, take her into the steamy bathroom, close the door, and sit in the bathroom with your child. Inhaling the warm, humidified air should ease her breathing within fifteen to twenty minutes. Or, weather permitting, you can take her outside to breathe in the cool, wet night air. While she is sleeping use a cold-water vaporizer or humidifier in your child's room.

Do *not* try to open your child's airway with your finger. Her breathing is being obstructed by swollen tissue beyond your reach, so you can't clear it away. She may throw up because of the coughing, but don't try to make her vomit. Pay close attention to your child's breathing. Take her to the nearest emergency room *immediately* if:

■ She seems to be struggling to get a breath.

■ She can't speak because of a lack of breath.

■ She gets excessively sleepy.

■ She turns blue when she coughs.

Your pediatrician may prescribe various medications, usually steroids, to help decrease the swelling in the upper airway and throat and make it easier for her to breathe. Steroids will also decrease the amount of time your child has symptoms of croup. Antibiotics are not helpful for croup because the infection is caused by a virus. Cough syrups do not help, either. In fact, as stated earlier, over-the-counter cough medicines may pose a health risk.

In the most serious cases, which are quite rare, your child will have a lot of difficulty breathing, and your pediatrician may admit her to the hospital until the swelling in the airway gets better.

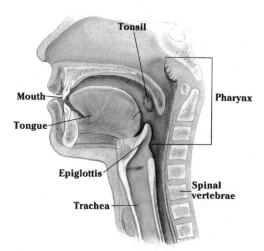

Tonsil

Mouth

Tongue

Pharynx

Epiglottis

Spinal vertebrae

Trachea

Flu/Influenza

Flu is the short term for influenza. It is an illness caused by a respiratory virus. The infection can spread rapidly through communities as the virus is passed from person to person. When someone with the flu coughs or sneezes, the influenza virus gets into the air, and people nearby, including children, can inhale it. The virus also can be spread when your child touches a hard surface, such as a door handle, and then places his hand or fingers in his nose/mouth or rubs his eye.

The flu season usually starts in the fall and ends in the spring. When there is an outbreak or epidemic, usually during the winter months, the illness tends to be most pronounced in preschool or school-age children. Adult caregivers are easily exposed and can contract the disease. The virus usually is transmitted in the first several days of the illness.

All flu viruses cause a respiratory illness that can last a week or more. Flu symptoms include:

■ A sudden fever (usually above 101 degrees Fahrenheit or 38.3 degrees Celsius)

■ Chills and body shakes

■ Headache, body aches, and being a lot more tired than usual

■ Sore throat

■ Dry, hacking cough

■ Stuffy, runny nose

Some children may throw up (vomit) and have loose stools (diarrhea).

After the first few days of these symptoms, a sore throat, stuffy nose, and continuing cough become most evident. The flu can last a week or even longer. A child with a common cold (see *Colds/Upper Respiratory Infection,* page 659) usually has a lower fever, a runny nose, and only a small amount of coughing. Children with the flu—or adults, for that matter—usually feel much sicker, more achy, and more miserable.

Healthy people, especially children, get over the flu in about a week or two, without any lingering problems. However, you might suspect a complication if your child says that his ear hurts or that he feels pressure in his face and head or if his cough and fever persist beyond two weeks. Talk with your child's doctor if your child has ear pain, a cough that won't go away, or a fever that won't go away.

Children who appear to have the greatest risk of complications from the flu are those with an underlying chronic medical condition, such as heart, lung, or kidney disease, an immune system problem, diabetes mellitus, some blood diseases, or malignancy. As these children may have more severe disease or complications, they should, when possible, be kept away from children with the flu or flulike symptoms. Their pediatrician may suggest additional precautions that should be taken. If your child has flulike symptoms along with any difficulty breathing, seek medical attention right away. There can be serious complications, even death, from the flu, but thanks to the flu vaccine (see information below) these are uncommon.

Treatment

For all children with the flu who don't feel well, lots of tender loving care is in order. Children can benefit from extra bed rest, extra fluids, and light, easy-to-digest meals. A cool mist humidifier or vaporizer in the room may add additional moisture to the air and make breathing through inflamed mucous membranes of the nose a little easier.

If your child is uncomfortable because of a fever, acetaminophen or ibuprofen in doses recommended by your pediatrician for his age and weight will help him feel better. (See Chapter 27, *Fever.*) Ibuprofen is approved for use in children six months of age and older; however, it should never be given to children who are dehydrated or who are vomiting continuously. *It is extremely important never to give aspirin to a child who has the flu or is suspected of having the flu. Aspirin during bouts of influenza is associated with an increased risk of developing Reye syndrome.* For more information about Reye syndrome, see page 549.

Prevention

Everyone should get the flu vaccine each year to update their protection. It is the best way to prevent getting the flu. Safe vaccines are made each year

and the best time to get the flu vaccine is the late summer/early fall or as soon as it is available in your community.

Vaccination is especially important for:

- All children, including infants born preterm, who are six months of age and older, especially those with conditions that increase the risk of complications from the flu

- Children of American Indian/Alaskan Native heritage

- All contacts and care providers of children with high-risk conditions and children younger than five years (especially infants younger than six months)

- All health care personnel

- All women who are pregnant, are considering pregnancy, have recently delivered, or are breastfeeding during the flu season

The flu virus spreads easily through the air with coughing and sneezing, and through touching things like doorknobs or toys and then touching your eyes, nose, or mouth. Here are some tips that will help protect your family from getting sick.

1. Everyone should wash their hands often. You can use soap and warm water for at least twenty seconds. That is about as long as singing the "Happy Birthday" song two times. And

an alcohol-based hand cleanser or sanitizer works well, too. Put enough on your hands to make them all wet, and then rub them together until dry.

2. Teach your child to cover his mouth and nose when coughing or sneezing. Show your child how to cough into the elbow or upper sleeve (not a hand) or use a tissue.

3. Throw all tissues used for runny noses and sneezes in the trash right away.

4. Wash dishes and utensils in hot, soapy water or the dishwasher.

5. Don't let children share pacifiers, cups, spoons, forks, washcloths, or towels without washing. *Never* share toothbrushes.

6. Teach your child to try not to touch her eyes, nose, or mouth.

7. Wash doorknobs, toilet handles, countertops, and even toys. Use a disinfectant wipe or a cloth with soap and hot water. (A *disinfectant* is a cleaner that kills germs.)

There are two types of the vaccine to protect against the flu—an inactivated (killed) vaccine, also called the "flu shot," which is given by injection; and a live, attenuated (weakened) influenza vaccine that is sprayed into the nostrils, often called "flu mist." The American Academy of Pediatrics recommends that an influenza vaccination be given annually to all healthy children starting at six months of age. If your child is receiving the flu vaccine for the first time, he will need two doses given at least one month apart. Flu vaccines are especially important for children at high risk for complications from the flu such as those with a chronic disease such as asthma, decreased immune system, renal disease, diabetes mellitus, or heart disease. All eligible children may receive the inactive vaccine, but only those two years and older who are healthy should receive the live nasal spray flu vaccine or "mist." Adults who live in the same household as someone who has a high risk for flu complications or who care for children under the age of five years should receive the flu vaccine yearly.

The flu vaccine has few side effects, the most common being redness, soreness or swelling at the injection site, and fever. Although flu vaccines are produced using eggs, as of 2012, influenza vaccines have been shown to have minimal egg protein so that virtually all children with presumed egg allergy may still safely receive the flu vaccine. For those having a history of severe egg allergy (anaphylaxis or respiratory and/or cardiovascular symptoms after egg ingestion), speak with your child's allergist about receiving the flu vaccine in their office.

Antiviral medications to treat an influenza infection are now available by prescription. Your pediatrician may be able to treat the flu with an antiviral medicine. Antiviral medications work best if started within the first one to two days of showing signs of the flu.

Call your pediatrician within twenty-four hours to ask about antiviral medications if your child is at high risk of influenza complications or if your child:

- Has any serious health problem like asthma, diabetes, sickle cell disease, or cerebral palsy.

- Is younger than two years, but especially if younger than six months, as young children are at an increased risk of influenza infection, hospitalization, and serious complications including death.

Pneumonia

The word *pneumonia* means "infection of the lung." While such infections were extremely dangerous in past generations, today most children recover from pneumonia if they receive proper medical attention.

Most cases of pneumonia follow a viral upper respiratory tract infection. Typically, the viruses that cause these infections (respiratory syncytial virus [RSV], metapneumovirus, influenza, parainfluenza, adenovirus) spread to the chest and produce pneumonia there. Pneumonia also can be caused by bacteria. Some of these are spread from person to person by coughing or by direct contact with the infected person's saliva or mucus. Also, if a viral infection has irritated the airway enough or weakened a child's immune system, bacteria may begin to grow in the lung, adding a second infection to the original one.

Children whose immune defenses or lungs are weakened by other illnesses, such as cystic fibrosis, asthma, or cancer (as well as by the chemotherapy used to treat cancer), are more likely to develop pneumonia. Children whose airways or lungs are abnormal in any other way also have a higher risk.

Because most forms of pneumonia are linked to viral or bacterial infections that spread from person to person, they're most common during the fall, winter, and early spring, when children spend more time indoors in close contact with others. The chance that a child will develop pneumonia is not affected by how warmly she is dressed or by air temperature.

Signs and Symptoms

Like many infections, pneumonia usually produces a fever, which in turn may cause sweating, chills, flushed skin, and general discomfort. The child also may lose her appetite and seem less energetic than normal. Babies and toddlers may seem pale and limp, and cry more than usual.

Because pneumonia can cause breathing difficulties, you may notice these other, more specific symptoms, too:

- Cough (see page 598)

- Fast, labored breathing

- Drawing in of the skin between and around the ribs and breastbone

- Flaring (widening) of the nostrils

- Pain in the chest, particularly with coughing or deep breathing

- Wheezing

- Bluish color to the lips or nails, caused by decreased oxygen in the bloodstream

Although the diagnosis of pneumonia usually can be made by a pediatrician on the basis of the signs, symptoms, and examination, a chest X-ray sometimes is necessary to make certain and to determine the extent of lung involvement.

Treatment

When pneumonia is caused by a virus, usually there is no specific treatment other than rest and the usual measures for fever control (see Chapter 27). Cough suppressants containing codeine or dextromethorphan should not be used, because coughing is helpful in clearing the excessive secretions caused by the infection. Viral pneumonia usually improves after a few days, although the cough may linger for several weeks. Ordinarily, no medication is necessary.

Because it is often difficult to tell whether the pneumonia is caused by a virus or by bacteria, your pediatrician may prescribe an antibiotic. All antibiotics should be taken for the full prescribed course and at the specific dosage recommended. You may be tempted to discontinue them early, but you should not do so. Your child will feel better after just a few days, but some bacteria may remain and the infection might return unless the entire course is completed.

Your child should be checked by the pediatrician as soon as you suspect pneumonia. Check back with the doctor if your child shows any of the following warning signs that the infection is worsening or spreading:

- Fever lasting more than a few days despite using antibiotics

- Breathing difficulties

- Evidence of an infection elsewhere in the body: red, swollen joints, bone pain, neck stiffness, vomiting, or other new symptoms or signs

Prevention

Your child can be vaccinated against pneumococcal infections, a bacterial cause of pneumonia. The American Academy of Pediatrics recommends that all children younger than two years old receive this immunization (called pneumococcal conjugate or PCV13). A series of doses needs to be given at two, four, six, and twelve to fifteen months of age, at the same time that children receive other childhood vaccines. One dose of PCV13 should also be given to all healthy children aged two through five years who are not completely vaccinated for their age and to children aged two through six years with certain underlying medical conditions. Check with your pediatrician about special catch-up circumstances and which children with high-risk conditions also should receive the PCV 13.

Another pneumococcal vaccine (pneumococcal polysaccharide or PPV23) also is recommended for older children (two through five years of age) who have a high risk of developing an invasive pneumococcal infection. These include children with sickle cell anemia, heart disease, lung disease, kidney failure, damaged or no spleen, organ transplant, and HIV (human immunodeficiency virus) infection. It's also recommended for children taking medications or who have diseases that weaken their immune system. Some children with certain underlying medical conditions may require a second dose of pneumococcal vaccine given at least eight weeks later.

(See also: *Asthma*, page 553, *Colds/Upper Respiratory Infection*, page 659; Chapter 27, *Fever*.)

Tuberculosis

Tuberculosis (TB) is an airborne infection that primarily affects the lungs. While TB is less common than it once was, some groups of children have a higher risk of developing tuberculosis, including:

- Children living in a household with an adult who has active tuberculosis or has a high risk of contracting TB

- Children infected with HIV or another condition that weakens the immune system

- Children born in a country that has a high prevalence of TB

- Children visiting a country where TB is endemic and who have extended contact with people who live there

- Children from communities that generally receive inadequate medical care

- Children living in a shelter or living with someone who has been in jail

Tuberculosis usually is spread when an infected adult coughs the bacteria into the air. These germs are inhaled by the child, who then becomes infected. Children younger than about ten years old with TB of the lungs rarely infect other people, because they tend to have very few bacteria in their mucus secretions and also have a relatively ineffective cough.

Fortunately, most children exposed to tuberculosis do not become ill. When the bacteria reach their lungs, the body's immune system attacks them and prevents further spread. These children have developed a symptom-free infection indicated only by a positive skin test. (See a description of this test below.) However, the symptom-free child still must be treated, as noted below, to prevent an active disease from ever occurring. Occasionally, in a small number of children without proper treatment, the infection does progress to disease, causing fever, fatigue, irritability, a persistent cough, weakness, heavy and fast breathing, night sweats, swollen glands, weight loss, and poor growth.

In a very small number of children (mostly those less than four years old), the tuberculosis infection can spread through the bloodstream, affecting virtually any organ in the body. This illness requires much more complicated treatment, and the earlier treatment is started, the better the outcome. These children have a much greater risk of developing tuberculosis meningitis, a dangerous form of the disease that affects the brain and central nervous system.

Children who are at risk for contracting TB should receive a tuberculin skin test, sometimes called a PPD (purified protein derivative of tuberculin). Your child may need a skin test if you answer yes to at least one of the following questions:

- Has a family member or contact had tuberculosis disease?

- Has a family member had a positive tuberculin skin test?

- Was your child born in a high-risk country (countries other than the US, Canada, Australia, New Zealand, or Western European countries)?

- Has your child traveled (had contact with resident populations) to a high-risk country for more than one week?

The test is performed in the pediatrician's office by injecting a purified, inactive piece of TB germ into the skin of the forearm. If there has been an infection, your child's skin will gradually swell and redden at the injection site. Your pediatrician must check the skin forty-eight to seventy-two hours after the injection, and measure the diameter of the reaction. This skin test will reveal a past infection by the bacteria, even if the child has had no symptoms and even if his body has fought the disease successfully.

If your child's skin test for TB turns positive, a chest X-ray will be ordered to determine if there is evidence of an active or past infection in the lungs. If the X-ray does indicate the possibility of an active infection, the pediatrician also will search for the TB bacteria in your child's cough secretions or in his stomach. This is done in order to determine the type of treatment needed.

Treatment

If your child's skin test turns positive, but he does not have symptoms or signs of active tuberculosis infection, he still is infected. In order to prevent the infection from becoming active, your pediatrician will prescribe a medication called isoniazid (INH). This medication must be taken by mouth once a day every day for a minimum of nine months. Antibiotics for shorter lengths of time may be possible.

For an *active* tuberculosis infection, your pediatrician will prescribe three or four medications. You will have to give these to your child every day for six to twelve months. Your child may have to be hospitalized initially for the treatment to be started, although most of it can be carried out at home.

Prevention

If your child has been infected with TB, regardless of whether he develops symptoms, it is *very* important to attempt to identify the person from whom he caught the disease. Usually this is done by looking for symptoms of TB in everyone who came in close contact with him, and having TB skin tests performed on all family members, child care providers, and housekeepers; the most common symptom in adults is a persistent cough, especially one that is associated with coughing up blood. Anyone who has a positive skin test should receive a physical examination, a chest X-ray, and treatment.

When an active infection is found in an adult, he will be isolated as much as possible—especially from young children—until treatment is under way. All family members who have been in contact with that person usually are also treated with INH, regardless of the results of their own skin tests. Anyone who becomes ill or develops an abnormality on a chest X-ray should be treated as an active case of tuberculosis.

Tuberculosis is much more common in underprivileged populations, which are more susceptible to disease due to crowded living conditions, poor nutrition, and the probability of inadequate medical care. AIDS patients, too, are at a greater risk of getting TB, because of their lowered resistance.

If untreated, tuberculosis can lie dormant for many years, only to surface during adolescence, pregnancy, or later adulthood. At that time, not only can the individual become quite ill, but he also can spread the infection to those around him. Thus, it's very important to have your child tested for TB if he comes in close contact with any adult who has the disease and to get prompt and adequate treatment for him if he tests positive.

Whooping Cough (Pertussis)

Pertussis, or whooping cough, is increasingly more common in young children than it used to be. Before the pertussis or whooping cough vaccine was developed, there were several hundred thousand cases of whooping cough each year in the United States.

Although that figure has decreased, there has actually been a rise in the number of cases in the US in recent years. In 2010, for example, there were 27,500 cases of pertussis reported. During 2012, forty-nine states and Washington, DC, reported increases in the disease compared with the same time period in 2011. As a result, giving the pertussis vaccine to children is even more important than ever.

This illness is caused by pertussis bacteria, which attack the lining of the breathing passages (bronchi and bronchioles), producing severe inflammation and narrowing of the airways. Severe coughing is a prominent symptom. If not recognized properly, the bacteria may spread to those in close contact with the infected person, through her respiratory secretions.

Infants under one year of age are at greatest risk of developing severe breathing problems and life-threatening illness from whooping cough. Because the child is short of breath, she inhales deeply and quickly between coughs. These breaths (particularly in older infants) frequently make a "whooping" sound—which is how this illness got its common name. The intense coughing scatters the pertussis bacteria into the air, spreading the disease to other susceptible persons.

Pertussis often acts like a common cold for a week or two. Then the cough gets worse (rather than better as usually happens with a cold), and the older child may start to have the characteristic "whoop." During this phase (which can last two weeks or more), the child often is short of breath and can look bluish around the mouth. She also may tear, drool, and vomit. Young infants with pertussis may have episodes where they appear to stop breathing or have vomiting after a long bout of cough. Infants with pertussis become exhausted and develop complications such as susceptibility to other infections, pneumonia, and seizures. Pertussis can be fatal in some infants, but the usual course is for recovery to begin after two to four more weeks. The cough may not disappear for months, and may return with subsequent respiratory infections.

When to Call the Pediatrician

Pertussis infection starts out acting like a cold. You should consider whooping cough if the following conditions are present.

- The child is a very young infant who has not been fully immunized and/or has been exposed to someone with a chronic cough or the disease.

- The child's cough becomes more severe and frequent, or her lips and fingertips become dark or blue.

- She becomes exhausted after coughing episodes, eats poorly, vomits after coughing, and/or looks "sick."

Treatment

The majority of infants with whooping cough who are less than six months old, and slightly less than one-half of older babies with the disease initially are treated in the hospital. This more intensive care can decrease the chances of complications. These complications can include pneumonia, which occurs in slightly less than one-fourth of children under one year old who have whooping cough. (If your child is older, she is more likely to be treated only at home.)

While in the hospital, your child may need to have the thick respiratory secretions suctioned. His breathing will be monitored, and he may need to have oxygen administered. For several days, your child will be isolated from other patients to keep the infection from spreading to them.

Whooping cough is treated with an antibiotic that is most effective when given in the first stage of the illness before coughing spells begin. Although antibiotics can stop the spread of the whooping cough infection, they cannot prevent or treat the cough itself. Because cough medicines do not relieve the coughing spells, your pediatrician probably will recommend other forms of home treatment to help manage the cough. Let your child rest in bed and use a cool-mist vaporizer to help soothe his irritated lungs and breathing passages. A vaporizer also will help loosen secretions in the respiratory tract. Ask your pediatrician for instructions on the best position for your child to help drain those secretions and improve breathing. Also ask your doctor whether antibiotics or vaccine boosters need to be given to others in your household to prevent them from developing the disease. Children who have been diagnosed with pertussis should be kept home from school or day care until finishing five days of antibiotics.

Prevention

The best way to protect your child against pertussis is with the DTaP vaccine (immunizations at two months, four months, and six months of age, and booster shots at twelve to eighteen months and at four or five years of age or prior to starting school). Parents or family members who will be in close contact with infants younger than one year old should also receive the DTaP booster to decrease the risk of passing the infection to the infant. In addition, all women who are pregnant should receive the DTaP vaccine during each pregnancy. This allows mothers to pass on protection against pertussis to their newborns.

~ 20 ~

Chronic Conditions and Diseases

Coping with Chronic (Long-Term) Health Problems

WE TEND TO think of childhood as a carefree and healthy time of life, but some children face chronic health problems during these early years. What distinguishes a *chronic* health problem from an *acute* health problem is that the acute problem is expected to resolve in a relatively short time frame and the child will return to normal. An acute health problem could mean an injury or a fracture that will heal, or an infection such as pneumonia, from which your child will recover completely. There are also a number of conditions that happen not infrequently to a young child that the

child will outgrow without any treatment or intervention. For example, a child with breath-holding spells will outgrow them by school age.

In contrast, a chronic health problem is expected to last at least twelve months and requires ongoing medical treatment to manage or control the disease. For example, a child with asthma may require inhalers every day to prevent the child from having an asthma attack. The parents of the child with asthma will need to learn about the condition, the treatment plan, and what to do if the child has an asthma attack, and bring the child to his primary care doctor, specialist, or both, several times throughout the year. The parents will need to become active participants in managing the condition and learn about the health care system and how to navigate it so the child gets the treatment he needs. Finally, the parents need to be able to help the child cope with the chronic condition emotionally and physically, and be able to help themselves and their family.

You can substitute "diabetes," "autism," "Down syndrome," or any other number of diagnoses and the above paragraph would read the same. The information that follows is aimed at helping parents and caregivers deal with the emotional and practical challenges of living with any child who has a long-term illness, special health care need, or disability. Some long-term health problems in children are relatively mild, and some children with chronic health conditions will not have any physical or psychological disability due to the success of ongoing medical treatment. Regardless, any type of lengthy illness, special health care need, or disability is stressful for both the child and his family. It is important to be able to manage all of these aspects and take care of yourself in the process. Learning about a child's chronic condition takes time and it can be very frustrating at times, and you will feel alone from time to time. Rest assured that you are not alone. Your reactions, grief, and frustration are normal, and your journey will be filled with many highs and lows; you will meet other parents on the same journey; and you will have many victories. Also remember that your child is still your child; your child is not, and should not be, defined by his condition.

The specific medical treatment of many chronic conditions is discussed elsewhere, under the names of those conditions. (See Index.)

Receiving the Diagnosis of a Chronic Condition

All parents, from the time they find out they are expecting a child, expect that the child will be healthy. You may have found out about your child's condition during pregnancy, in the newborn nursery, or afterward when you noticed that something was not quite right about your child's health. Regardless of when your child was diagnosed, being given a chronic diagnosis can cause a parent to feel sadness, fear, or grief at losing the expectation of a healthy child. This is a normal reaction and an adjustment that all parents of a child with a chronic condition endure.

That being said, receiving a chronic diagnosis can be devastating to a parent. It can mean that all of your hopes and expectations for your child have been replaced by fear of the unknown. What will happen to my child in two years? Five? Ten? Will the condition get better or worse? How am I going to manage all of these medications? Will I have to take time off from work? How much pain will my child have? You never forget the day that you were given the diagnosis for your child, but chances are you don't remember much else. There was probably a lot of information to absorb that day and it takes time to process it all.

Being a parent of a child with a chronic condition is a journey that you didn't ask for, but it is one that is OK, just different. It is a brand-new world, with a lot to learn in a relatively short period of time because your child's health depends on it. There will be highs and lows, flares and periods of quiet, denial and fear of the unknown. There will be days when you think you are the only parent with a special-needs child and you will wonder if anyone else knows how you feel. All of this can take a toll on your own well-being and health, which in turn affects how you can take care of your child. Recognizing these emotions will help you adjust to having a child with a chronic health condition and helping yourself and your child.

If your child is born with a serious medical problem or develops a chronic medical condition during her first years, you may face some of the following stressors and decisions.

■ **The realization that** your child is not perfectly healthy often leads to feelings of disappointment and guilt, and fear for their future. In trying to deal with these feelings, you may find yourself struggling with unexplained emotional swings ranging from hopefulness to guilt and depression.

■ **You will need** to select and work with a team of medical and community partners who can help your child and can partner with you in shared decision making.

■ **You may be** faced with learning about a new diagnosis and understanding your child's prognosis.

■ **You may face** decisions about treatment or surgery.

■ **You may have** to be responsible for giving your child certain medications, guide her in usage of special equipment, or help her perform special therapies.

■ **You will be** called on to provide the time, energy, money, and emotional commitment necessary for your child to receive the best possible treatment and coordinate care for your child.

■ **You will need** to learn how to access appropriate services and information to help your child.

■ **In adapting your** life to meet your child's needs without neglecting other family members, you will face many difficult choices, some of which may require compromise solutions.

Navigating the Health Care System

Parents of children with chronic conditions routinely describe navigating the health care system as their biggest challenge. Depending on your child's condition, you may be dealing with a few extra doctor visits per year, or you could be dealing with multiple specialists, pharmacies, therapists, insurance companies, and home health. All of this may lead to time away from work, your family, or other personal interests. Empowering yourself with information about your child's condition is a crucial aspect of navigating the health care system. You know your child's needs better than anyone else. Read about your child's condition, ask questions of your child's doctors and nurses, and talk with other parents. The information you learn, particularly the answers to questions that you don't know to ask in the early going, will help you engage with your child's doctors in making decisions. Health care and developmental outcomes are improved when the parents are engaged with the decision making and knowledgeable about the child's condition. Keep a notebook with your questions and make sure they are answered. If you see something at home that concerns you, call your doctor. Do not assume that you can wait until the next appointment. Doctors depend on and respect the information you provide them to make the right medical decision for your child.

You will need to make sure your child has a *medical home*. The American Academy of Pediatrics defines a medical home as care that is *accessible, continuous, comprehensive, family-centered, coordinated, compassionate, and culturally effective.* The medical home model of care means that the child and family work *in partnership* with the medical care team to meet all of the medical and nonmedical needs of a child. At a minimum, you need to ensure that your child has regularly scheduled visits with her doctors to actively manage your child's condition to keep your child healthy. A strong relationship with your child's primary care physician can help oversee all aspects of your child's care. It is also helpful to select one medical person as the overall coordinator of your child's medical care, taking a lead role in the medical home. This person may be someone in your pediatrician's office or another health professional who is most closely involved with your child's treatment. It should be someone who knows your family well, fosters shared decision making, values you as an equal team member, makes you feel comfortable, and is willing to spend time answering your questions, partnering with you, and working with other doctors and therapists involved in your child's care.

You know your child better than anyone else and thus you are the expert on your child. You should track and manage what goes on at home, ensure that you can carry out the medical care recommendations, and that your child gets good nutrition and all of her medications. You can make sure that your child's medical care needs are met *proactively*, that is, keeping your child healthy and making sure your child does not get sicker due to a complication of the chronic health problem. Many children with chronic health care problems have relatively long periods of being well-controlled, with occasional flares of disease activity. Your goal is to keep your child's condition under control and learn the signs and symptoms of a flare so you can ensure that your child's condition stays well-controlled.

Parent support groups will have meetings, either online or in person, and provide literature and emotional support. Learn about the options for treatment, including those that your doctor may not know about or is not familiar with. Regardless of whether those options are what you decide to take, information is about taking control of your child's treatment plan and having the knowledge to make the right decision for your child and your family.

Getting Help for Your Child

There are many ways that you can help your child with a chronic condition. You can start by making sure that you take your child to all of his doctor appointments. If you have to miss a doctor's appointment, you need to call the doctor and get it rescheduled—preferably *before* you miss the appointment. That way, your child's doctors can help you manage your child's condition before your child has a disease flare or gets sicker. If you find that you are unable to give your child his medications because of scheduling conflicts or your child is refusing, call your doctor. Your child's doctors may be able to arrange an alternative treatment plan. It is important that you let your child's doctors know what is going on at home and if something needs to be changed.

It is very important to provide your child with as much of a typical childhood experience as possible. No child wants to feel different from his friends, and to the extent that it is medically safe to do so, your child should be given the same opportunities as any other child to run and play. Your child should not be defined by his condition—your child is not an "asthmatic" or a "diabetic" but your child "who has asthma" or your child "who has diabetes." Nothing has changed about your child just because your child was given a diagnosis one day.

Good nutrition and growth are at the root of helping a child with a special health care need or chronic health problem. Some children with a chronic health problem have difficulty eating and swallowing. Others will lose their appetite from the medications they take. It is especially important for your child to be offered a good, healthy diet and, if necessary, you can work with your doctors or a nutritionist to make sure your child is not gaining too little weight—or too much. Some children with difficulty swallowing will cough or retch with feeds. If that is the case, you may also need to speak with a speech therapist who can focus on helping your child swallow properly.

Not all of your child's special needs will be medical, of course. He may require community supports such as special schooling, counseling, or other therapy. Many children with chronic conditions will attend day care or school. Some children may be in private day care; others may be in a center-based learning center specifically for children with disabilities. It is important that you speak with your child's teachers and caregivers about your child's medical needs. Specifically, you should let your child's teachers and caregivers know what your child's condition is, medications or therapies that are needed during the day, and warning signs that you need to be called about. School nurses are also excellent resources to help you and your child manage your child's condition.

Your family may need outside financial or governmental assistance. The person who coordinates your child's medical care also should provide some guidance in obtaining this extra help, but the best way to make sure you and your child get the services and support you need is to learn about the resources and regulations that apply to special services for children with chronic illnesses or disabilities. You also should find out what you can do if the services your family receives do not meet your child's needs.

Finally, focus on your child's emotional state and well-being. Help your child adapt to his chronic condition. You should offer your child every opportunity at a normal life to the extent that it is medically safe to do so. That means taking your child to the park to run and play, encouraging him to make friends, and attending school. As your child gets older, he will become increasingly aware of the medical treatments and the sense of being "different," regardless of whether your child has any actual physical disability or appearances.

Many children may not talk about their feelings, but will act out in different ways, including tantrums, having a short fuse, or being sad. Meeting other children with a chronic condition can help. It is also important to acknowledge your child's feelings and help your child's caregivers and teachers understand how your child is coping so they can help.

Balancing the Needs of Family and Child

For a while, the child with special needs may take all your attention, leaving little for other family members and outside relationships. Although this is normal, everyone in the family can be affected so try to find some way to restore a sense of balance and routine to your activities. Neither your sick child nor the rest of the family—nor your marital relationship—will benefit if the health problem becomes the central and overwhelming issue in your family's life. Eventually your child's medical care must become a part of your daily routine rather than its focus.

If your child must be hospitalized, returning her to normal family and community life is vital, not only for the family but also for her health and well-being. The longer she is treated like a "patient" instead of a growing child, the more problems she may have socially and emotionally later on. Although it's natural to want to protect a sick child, overprotection may make it more difficult for her to develop the self-discipline she needs as she matures. Also, if you have other children, you can't expect them to observe rules that you allow the child who is sick or disabled to ignore. Make sure these siblings receive adequate attention as well.

Your child needs your encouragement far more than your protection. Rather than concentrating on what she cannot do, try to focus instead on what she *can* do. Build on her strengths. If given a chance to participate in normal activities with children her age, she probably will do things that surprise everyone. Establishing this sense of normalcy is difficult if your child's condition is uncertain. You may find yourself withdrawing from your friends because you're so worried about your child, and you may hesitate to plan social activities if you're not sure she'll be well enough to attend. If you give in to these feelings all the time, resentment is bound to build up, so try not to let this happen. Even if there is a chance that your child's condition may worsen unexpectedly, take the risk and plan special outings, invite friends to your home, and get a babysitter from time to time so you can go out for an evening. Both you and your child will be better off in the long run if you take this approach.

The following suggestions may help you cope more effectively with your child's condition.

- **Whenever possible, both** parents/all caregivers should be included in discussions and decisions about your child's treatment, even if you and your spouse are separated or divorced. Too often, one parent may go alone to the medical appointment and then must explain what was said to the other parent. This may prevent one parent from getting some of his or her questions answered or learning enough about the choices.

- **Keep an open** line of communication with your pediatrician. Express your concerns and ask questions. Ask for a care plan to be developed with your input and regularly updated with relevant medical information and summaries.

- **Do not be** offended if your child's doctors ask personal questions about your family life. The more they know about your family, the better they can help you manage your child's care. For example, if your child has diabetes, she may need a special schedule of meals, so the pediatrician may want to suggest ways to work this diet into your family's normal meal plan. Or if your child needs a wheelchair, the doctor may ask about your home in order to suggest the best places for wheelchair ramps. If you have concerns about the doctor's suggestions, discuss them with him so you can reach an acceptable plan of action together.

- **Remember that although** you and your doctor want to be optimistic about your child's condition, you must be honest about it. If things are not going well, you should say so. Your child depends on you to speak up at these times and to work with the doctor to adjust the treatment or find a solution that will make the situation as good as possible.

- **Discuss your child's** condition frankly with her and the other members of your family. If you do not tell your child the truth, she may sense that you are lying; this can lead to feelings of isolation and rejection. Furthermore, she will imagine all the things that could be wrong—most of which may be worse than her real problem. So talk to her openly, and listen to her responses to make sure she understands. Answer her questions in clear, simple language.

- **Call on friends** and family members for support. You cannot expect to handle the strain created by your child's chronic condition all by yourself. Asking close friends to help you meet your own emotional needs will in turn help you to meet your child's.

- **If you have** other children, be sure to give them your attention and try to balance their needs and fears as well. There are resources available for siblings of children and youth with special health care needs.

- **Connecting with other** parents or caregivers that have children with the same or similar conditions as your child is incredibly helpful. Each state/commonwealth has a Family-to-Family Health Information Center that can help link you to other parents. In addition, certain diagnoses (cystic fibrosis, sickle cell disease, etc.) have specific family support networks that your health care providers or community partners can link you to.

- **Remember that your** child needs to be loved and valued as an individual. If you let the medical problems overshadow your feelings for her as a person, they may interfere with the bond of trust and affection between you. Be sure to reach out to your child's medical care team if you are feeling overwhelmed, lost, or don't know how to care for your child. Don't let yourself become so worried that you cannot relax and enjoy your child.

You are not alone. It is important to reach out to other parents who have a child with a chronic condition to see how they have coped with the journey. It is important for you to be proactive in learning about your child's condition as much as possible and what you can do to help. Read about your child's condition, talk with other families, and get to know your doctors well—they will be a tremendous resource to you and help you understand how to take care of your child's medical needs. If you are using web-based sources of information, be sure to check their validity and accuracy with your pediatrician. Family support groups are an important part of the journey. Knowing other families will help reassure you that you are not alone.

Anemia

Blood contains several different types of cells. The most numerous are the red blood cells, which absorb oxygen in the lungs and distribute it throughout the body. These cells contain hemoglobin, a red pigment that carries oxygen to the tissues and carries away carbon dioxide (the waste material). Anemia is a condition in which a decreased amount of hemoglobin is available in the red blood cells, making the blood less able to carry the amount of oxygen necessary for all the cells in the body to function and grow.

Anemia may occur for any of the following reasons:

1. The production of red blood cells is too slow.

2. Too many red blood cells are destroyed.

3. There is not enough hemoglobin within the red blood cells.

4. Blood cells are lost from the body.

Many cases of anemia are treatable. Young children most commonly become anemic when they fail to get enough iron in their diet. Iron is necessary for the production of hemoglobin. This iron deficiency causes a decrease in the amount of hemoglobin in the red blood cells. A young infant may get iron-deficiency anemia if he starts drinking cow's milk too early, particularly if he is not given an iron supplement or healthy food with iron. The deficiency occurs because cow's milk contains very little iron and the small amount is poorly absorbed through the intestines into the body. In addition, cow's milk given to an infant under twelve months of age can irritate the bowel and cause small amounts of blood loss. This results in a decrease in the number of red blood cells, which can cause anemia. Other nutritional deficiencies, such as a lack of folic acid, also can cause anemia, but such causes are rare.

Other causes of anemia, however, can be a result of a chronic condition that will need ongoing treatment and follow-up by your child's doctor. For example, anemia at any age can result from excessive blood loss from injury. In some cases, the blood loss may occur because the blood does not clot properly due to a condition such as hemophilia. Sometimes the red cells are prone to being easily destroyed. This condition, called hemolytic anemia, can result from disturbances on the surface of the red cells or other abnormalities in or outside the cells. Certain enzyme deficiencies can alter the function of red blood cells and increase the chances they will die or be destroyed early, causing anemia. A severe condition called sickle cell anemia involves an abnormal structure of hemoglobin, and is seen most often in children of African heritage. This disorder can be very severe and is associated with frequent "crises," often requiring repeated hospitalizations. (See page 623.)

Disorders called thalassemias are inherited blood conditions, and tend to occur most frequently in children of Asian, African, Middle Eastern, Greek, and Italian heritage. Children with these disorders have an abnormally low number of red blood cells, or not enough hemoglobin. They can develop anemia, sometimes severe cases.

Signs and Symptoms

Anemia frequently causes the skin to be mildly pale, usually most apparent as a decreased pinkness of the lips, the lining of the eyelids (conjunctiva), and the nail beds (pink part of the nails). Anemic children also may be irritable, mildly weak, or tire easily. Those with severe anemia may have shortness of breath, rapid heart rate, and swelling of the hands and feet. If the anemia continues, it may interfere with normal growth. A newborn with hemolytic anemia may become jaundiced (turn yellow), although many newborns are mildly jaundiced and don't become anemic.

If your child shows any of these symptoms or signs, or if you suspect he is not getting enough iron in his diet, consult your pediatrician. A simple blood count can diagnose anemia in most cases.

Some children are not anemic but still are deficient in iron. They may have a decreased appetite and be irritable, fussy, and inattentive, which may result in developmental delays or poor school performance. These problems will reverse when the children are given iron. Other signs of iron deficiency that may be unrelated to anemia include a tendency to eat unusual things, such as ice, dirt, clay, and cornstarch. This behavior, called pica, is not harmful unless the material eaten is toxic (e.g., lead). Usually the behavior improves after the iron deficiency is treated and as the child becomes older, although it may persist longer in children who are developmentally delayed.

Children with sickle cell anemia may have unexplained fever or swelling of the hands and feet as infants, and they are extremely susceptible to infection. If there is a history of sickle cell anemia or sickle cell trait in your family, make sure your child is tested for it at birth.

Although some cases of thalassemia have no symptoms, more moderate to severe cases can cause lethargy, jaundice, a poor appetite, slow growth, and an enlarged spleen.

Treatment

Since there are so many different types of anemia, it is very important to identify the cause before any treatment is begun. Do not attempt to treat your child with vitamins, iron, or other nutrients or over-the-counter medications unless it is at your physician's direction. This is important, because such treatment may mask the real reason for the problem and thus delay the diagnosis. The treatment for anemia may include medications, dietary supplements, or dietary restrictions.

If the anemia is due to a lack of iron, your child will be given an iron-containing medication that he will need to take under the direction of your child's pediatrician. This comes in a drop form for infants and a liquid or tablet form for older children. Because "iron overload" occurs when iron is given when it's not needed, your pediatrician will check your child's blood iron levels at regular intervals. Do not stop giving the medication until the physician tells you it is no longer needed.

Following are a few tips concerning iron medication.

- **It is best** not to give iron with milk because milk blocks iron absorption.

- **Vitamin C increases** iron absorption, so you might want to follow the dose of iron with a glass of orange juice.

- **Since liquid iron** tends to turn the teeth a grayish black color temporarily, have your child swallow it rapidly and then rinse his mouth with water. You also may want to brush your child's teeth after every dose of iron. Tooth-staining from iron is not permanent.

- **Iron medications cause** the stools to become a dark black color. Don't be worried by this change.

Safety precautions: Iron medications are extremely poisonous if taken in excessive amounts. (Iron is one of the most common causes of poisoning in children under five.) For that reason, *keep this and all medication out of reach of small children.*

Thalassemias are typically treated with transfusions of red blood cells and supplements of folic acid.

Sickle Cell Disease

Sickle cell disease (SCD) is a group of chronic genetic disorders affecting the red blood cells. In children with SCD, the red cells in the blood become sickle-shaped (appearing like an icicle under the microscope). This is important because it impacts how well the red blood cells transport oxygen around the body.

There are several types of sickle cell disease, including the best known, sickle cell anemia. Others include sickle–hemoglobin C disease and two types of sickle β-thalassemia. All of these disorders in the SCD complex have similar symptoms such as anemia (shortage of red blood cells), episodes of severe pain, and infections. (See *Signs and Symptoms,* on page 624.)

In the US, about 2,000 newborns each year have SCD (there are about 75,000 people who have SCD in the US). Although it is commonly thought of as affecting only people of African ancestry, it can occur in children of any race or ethnicity, including those whose ancestors come from South and Central America, India, Saudi Arabia, Italy, Greece, or Turkey.

In healthy children, red blood cells are normally round and flexible, and travel easily through blood vessels, transporting oxygen from the lungs to every part of the body. But children with SCD have abnormalities in hemoglobin (a component of every red blood cell), which can distort the shape of these red cells and contribute to the disease process. The irregularly shaped red cells become sticky, clumping together and interfering with the flow of nourishing blood to organs and limbs. These cells also can die prematurely, causing an ongoing deficiency of red blood cells.

Some children have "sickle cell trait," which is different from SCD. These children do not have the disease itself, but they carry the sickle cell gene responsible for causing it, and they can pass it along when they have children of their own. If a child inherits the sickle cell gene from one parent but not the other, pediatricians categorize the child as having sickle cell trait, but with no SCD symptoms.

Signs and Symptoms

In most cases, infants with SCD appear healthy at birth. However, after a child is a few months old, symptoms may emerge that can range from mild to severe.

Common signs and symptoms of SCD include:

- Inflammation and swelling of the hands and/or feet (called dactylitis or hand-foot syndrome); this is commonly the first symptom of SCD

- Anemia

- Pain

- Fatigue

- Shortness of breath

- Rapid heart rate

- Paleness

- Fever

- Jaundice (yellowing of the skin and eyes)

- Susceptibility to infections

- Delayed growth

A so-called sickle cell crisis may occur suddenly when an episode of pain develops, typically affecting the bones, joints, or abdomen. The intensity of pain can vary, and it can last from hours to many weeks. The trigger for these crises is unclear in many cases, although blocked blood flow plays a role, and in some cases, so can infections. Serious SCD complications can develop, including pneumonia, stroke, and organ damage (of the spleen, kidney, liver, or lung). When children with sickle cell trait are flying at high altitudes, "splenic infarction" (death of spleen tissue) can occur. Extreme exercise (such as by a student athlete with sickle cell trait) can cause problems as well. These children also have a greater risk of blood in the stool or urine and urinary tract infections.

Treatment

If your child has SCD, she should be diagnosed as early as possible so that appropriate treatment can be planned and started. Fortunately, most cases of SCD can be detected through a simple screening blood test that is universally given to infants in most states. SCD is the most common disorder identified by routine blood screening of newborns. Even if your state does not mandate such testing, you can request it from your pediatrician.

Children with SCD need long-term care, not only to relieve symptoms but also to promptly manage any future "sickle cell crisis." Commonly prescribed treatments include the following:

- Mild pain can be relieved with over-the-counter medications such as acetaminophen or nonsteroidal anti-inflammatory drugs (NSAIDs) such as ibuprofen. Heating pads also can be used for pain relief. In addition, good hydration is important.

- Antibiotics should be prescribed for all children with SCD, beginning by two months of age and given continuously until at least the age of five years. These medications are a preventive measure to reduce the risk of infections.

- Children with SCD should receive all childhood immunizations as recommended by the American Academy of Pediatrics (see page 876), including an annual influenza immunization.

Your child with SCD can benefit from various lifestyle measures. She should get plenty of rest and sleep. She should drink lots of water (particularly in warm weather) and avoid becoming overly hot or cold. Some doctors recommend folic acid supplements, which can help the body make more red blood cells.

If your child's pain becomes severe, or she develops other serious symptoms or complications, your pediatrician may recommend hospitalization. While hospitalized, your child could receive:

- Morphine or other drugs given intravenously (through a vein) for pain relief

- Intravenous antibiotics that can manage an infection if one develops

- Blood transfusions that can raise the number of red blood cells

- Supplemental oxygen given through a mask that can add oxygen to the blood

Because relatively mild symptoms (fever, pale skin, abdominal pain) can quickly progress to serious illness, parents should talk with their pediatrician in advance to make sure that the family has around-the-clock access to a medical facility experienced in treating SCD. If your child develops a fever, contact your pediatrician at once because of the risk of a major infection.

Eye involvement. Children with SCD can develop problems with their eyes and need to be examined by an ophthalmologist or pediatric ophthalmologist on a regular basis to make sure these complications do not occur. If they are found early, treatment is usually possible. Any type of eye injury in a child with SCD needs to be reported to your pediatrician immediately. What appears to be a minor injury to the eye might actually be serious, and possibly vision-threatening.

Cystic Fibrosis

Cystic fibrosis (CF) is the second most common inherited, life-shortening disease of childhood in the US (second only to sickle cell anemia). In the Caucasian population, 1 out of every 20 people is a carrier, and 1 out of every 2,500 Caucasian babies has CF. The disease is much less common in African Americans (1 in 15,100 live births) and Hispanics (1 in 13,500 live births), and even rarer among Asians. About 70,000 children and adults worldwide have been diagnosed with CF; a little less than half of them (30,000) are in the US.

Considerable progress has been made in treating cystic fibrosis and its symptoms, although there is still no cure. CF is a disease that changes the secretions of certain glands in the body. It is inherited from parents who carry the gene that causes this disease. For a child to get cystic fibrosis, both parents must be carriers of the gene that causes it. Although the sweat glands and the glandular cells of the lungs and pancreas are affected most often, the sinuses, liver, intestines, and reproductive organs also can be involved.

In 1989 researchers discovered the gene that causes CF. Couples planning to have children can undergo genetic testing and counseling to find out if they carry the CF gene. They can also receive prenatal testing to detect the gene in the fetus. If both parents are carriers, there are other options available, such as IVF (in vitro fertilization). Talk to your doctor about these alternatives.

Signs and Symptoms

The majority of CF cases are diagnosed within the first two years of life; in many states, newborn screenings now include mandatory testing for CF. More than half of CF cases are diagnosed because of repeated lung infections. These infections tend to recur because mucus in the airways is thicker than normal and more difficult to cough out, leading to a persistent cough and potentially pneumonia or bronchitis. Over time, these infections cause damage to the lungs, and are the major cause of death in CF. Most children with CF are also deficient in digestive enzymes, making it difficult for them to digest fats and proteins as well as they should. As a result, these children have large, bulky, foul-smelling stools, accompanied by poor weight gain.

To confirm the diagnosis, your pediatrician will order a sweat test to measure the amount of salt your child loses as he perspires. Children with cystic fibrosis have much more salt in their sweat than do children who do not have CF. Two or more of these tests may be required to ensure an accurate diagnosis, since the results are not always clearly positive or negative. If your child is diagnosed as having the disease, your pediatrician will help you get the additional specialized medical help that is necessary. At a medical center that specializes in treating children with CF you can find multidisciplinary experts to help your child and family.

Treatment

CF treatment is lifelong and typically requires many visits to a CF center where your child will be treated by a health care team specializing in CF care. Treating CF's lung infections is the most important aspect of your child's care. The goal is to help clear the thick secretions from your child's lungs, which may involve various techniques that help him cough out the sputum more easily. The lung infections themselves are treated with antibiotics. Your child will also be prescribed capsules containing digestive enzymes to be taken with every meal and every snack. The amount of enzymes is based on the level of fat in the diet and the weight of your child. Once the correct amount of enzymes is taken, your child's stool pattern will become more normal and he'll begin gaining more weight.

The majority of children with CF can expect to grow up and lead productive adult lives with good treatment. It is important to raise your child as you would if he did not have this disease. There is no reason to limit his educational or career goals. Your child needs both love and discipline, and should be encouraged to develop and test his limits. Balancing the physical and emotional demands created by this disease is hard on both the CF patient and his family, so it is very important that you get as much support as possible. Ask your pediatrician to put you in touch not only with the nearest CF center, but also with CF support groups. The Cystic Fibrosis Foundation also can be of help (www.cff.org; 1-800-344-4823). Connecting with other parents is essential to support you, your child, and your family.

Diabetes Mellitus

Diabetes mellitus occurs when specialized cells of the pancreas (a gland located behind the stomach) do not produce adequate amounts of the hormone insulin. Insulin enables the body to process the nutrients (proteins, fat, and carbohydrates) to make body tissues, promote growth, produce energy, and store energy. These nutrients are broken down into glucose, a type of sugar used by the cells of the body as a source of energy. Glucose is fuel for the body to use. Insulin transports glucose from the bloodstream into the cells maintaining blood sugar levels within a tight range. (Insulin transports glucose in people with or without diabetes.)

People with type 1 diabetes have a reduced supply of insulin or none at all. Eating causes blood glucose levels to rise (hyperglycemia). The nutrients in the food cannot be used by the cells but remain in the bloodstream. Without a source of energy, the cells think they are starving. In an attempt to nourish the starving cells, the liver makes sugar from the body stores of protein and fat, which also cannot be used without insulin. This leads to weight loss and weakness, because muscle and fat are being broken down and the body is not getting the energy it needs.

The body tries to eliminate the excess glucose circulating in the blood by excreting it in the urine and increasing the amount of urine in order to get rid of the large amount of sugar. This is why people who have diabetes urinate more frequently and can become very thirsty as they try to replace the fluid loss. Without insulin, the body tries to get energy from stored fat. The fat is broken down to certain kinds of acids known as ketones, which are also excreted in the urine.

Currently, there is no way to prevent type 1 diabetes. There is a genetic predisposition to developing type 1 diabetes, but only about 30 percent of children with type 1 diabetes have any close relatives with the disease. The destruction of the cells that make insulin results from a process in which the body's immune system views these cells as foreign invaders and mounts an immune response against them. This autoimmune process starts months to years before the first symptoms of diabetes show up. The trigger for this process may be viruses or other environmental factors, but none of this is known with certainty and hence there is no known way to prevent the autoimmune response.

In type 2 diabetes, the body does not make enough insulin and is not able to use the insulin properly. This is also known as insulin resistance. Type 2 diabetes was once considered a disease that only adults had to worry about (indeed, the condition was once called "adult onset diabetes"). Today, type 2 diabetes in children and adolescents is usually associated with obesity, and is increasing in children as the rates of obesity grow. Among children diagnosed with type 2 diabetes, eighty-five out of one hundred are obese. Children who are inactive, overeat, and have a family history of diabetes have the greatest risk of developing type 2 diabetes. Children in minority groups also have a higher incidence of type 2 diabetes. According to the American Diabetes Association, an estimated 2 million children have "pre-diabetes," which is a collection of risk factors that often leads to type 2 diabetes.

Diabetes can appear at any time, even in the first year of life. However, the diagnosis often is delayed in infants and toddlers until the child is very sick, because the symptoms may be attributed to other illnesses.

It is important to notify your pediatrician immediately if your child displays any of the following warning signs and symptoms of diabetes:

- Increased thirst

- Increased or frequent urination. A toilet-trained child may start bed-wetting, or a baby in diapers will need more frequent changes.

- Weight loss with either increased appetite and food intake or marked persistent loss of appetite (more common in the younger child)

- Dehydration (see page 540 for signs)

- Severe diaper rash that does not respond to the usual treatment

- Unexplained tiredness or fatigue

- Vomiting that is persistent, particularly if it is accompanied by weakness or drowsiness

- Blurred vision

- Slow-to-heal cuts and sores

If your child goes to the doctor with any suspicious symptoms, be sure that a urine or blood test is done to determine whether his glucose levels are too high. This simple test will provide a clue to diabetes and prevent your child from becoming more ill.

Treatment

When blood tests confirm diabetes, treatment begins immediately. Insulin injections are often given for type 1 diabetes. When the child does not require intravenous fluids to correct dehydration and vomiting, many specialists do not hospitalize patients with diabetes, but care for them in an outpatient setting with frequent office visits.

A health care team that specializes in diabetes will teach the entire family how to manage diabetes. Members of the health care team include a physician (usually with advanced training in the care of youth with diabetes), a nurse educator, and a dietitian who all work together to educate the family. You'll learn how to test blood glucose levels from a drop of blood from a finger stick and how to give insulin injections. You will learn about food, planning meals and snacks, and activity and exercise. Your team will help determine how many insulin injections your child may need to control his blood sugars and successfully manage his diabetes. Parents should learn as much as possible about the care and management of their child's diabetes.

Having children participate as much as possible in their diabetes management gives them some measure of control. Children under age three can choose which finger to stick for blood sugar tests. They can also choose which place to use for the insulin injection. Some children now get insulin through a pump, which offers flexibility and convenience for some children.

Child care and school personnel need to know about your child's diabetes, her insulin schedule, and her snack needs. School personnel also need to be able to recognize and treat hypoglycemia (low blood sugar). They also need to know how to test blood sugar levels and have guidelines for giving insulin and testing for urine ketones. They should always have the parent's emergency phone number on hand. To learn more about type 1 diabetes go to the Juvenile Diabetes Research Foundation (www.jdf.org; 1-800-533-2873) and the American Diabetes Association (www.diabetes .org; 1-800-342-2383).

HIV Infection and AIDS

HIV (human immunodeficiency virus) is a virus that can lead to AIDS (acquired immunodeficiency syndrome).

The rate of new HIV diagnoses increased about 30 percent from 2006 to 2009 among adolescents and young adults in the US, usually contracted via sexual activity. Heterosexual activity is the risk behavior responsible for the majority of HIV infections in women, while intravenous drug use has declined as a cause of HIV infection. Children, on the other hand, ac-

quire the infection primarily from their HIV-infected mothers, either in utero (as the virus passes across the placenta), during delivery (when the newborn is exposed to the mother's blood and body fluids), or by ingesting infected breast milk. An HIV infection will develop in 13 to 39 of 100 infants born to HIV-infected mothers who are untreated. Treating the mother and newborn with Zidovudine (or AZT) reduces the risk of HIV infection from mothers to babies to about 8 of 100, and more powerful combinations of drugs can reduce this figure to 2 of 100 or less.

Once a person is infected with HIV, the virus will be in his body for life. People with HIV infection may be free of symptoms for years. AIDS occurs only after the progressive weakening of the immune defense system by HIV, a process that may take many months or years. Without treatment, children usually develop signs of HIV infection by the age of two, but the average time to develop AIDS is about five years.

Infants with the HIV infection initially may appear well, but problems gradually develop. For example, their weight and height fail to increase appropriately within the first six months to one year. They have frequent episodes of diarrhea or minor skin infections. The lymph nodes (glands) anywhere in the body may enlarge, and there is a persistent fungus infection of the mouth (thrush). The liver and spleen may enlarge. Because neurological development may be affected, children may have a delay in walking and other motor skills, a delay in their ability to think and talk, and diminished head growth during infancy.

Eventually, if the HIV infection progresses as the body's immune system further deteriorates, AIDS-related infections and cancers may occur. The most common of these, *Pneumocystis jirovecii* pneumonia, is accompanied by fever and breathing difficulties. This common infection occurs predominantly in infants between three months and one year of age. It is possible to prevent this infection with antibiotics, and doctors recommend that all babies born to HIV-infected women be placed on preventive antibiotics as early as six weeks of age until tests show that the infant does not have an HIV infection.

Care of an HIV-Infected Child

Many children with HIV can now grow and lead productive and fulfilling lives with good medical care, and well over 90 percent of children with HIV reach adulthood. Your child with HIV is typically cared for by an infectious disease specialist as well as a primary care physician. Other specialists and therapists may work with you and your family. It is important to keep all of your appointments and take all medications that are prescribed. A number of approved anti-HIV or "antiretroviral" drugs are available for use in children. These medications suppress virus reproduction and improve the child's growth and neurologic development.

They also delay the progression of the disease. It is essential that your doctor know about the baby's HIV infection as early in life as possible and that you administer antiretroviral therapy as the doctor advises.

Children who are HIV positive need love and attention like all other children, and you should be aware of addressing the "stigma" that may come with having HIV infection. It is important that you advocate for your child and ensure that people understand HIV cannot be transmitted by just holding a child who is HIV positive. Common infections can cause serious complications in children with HIV infection. These children with HIV should attend child care and school when they are able. At the same time, they may be accidentally exposed to communicable illnesses like chickenpox, and the school or child care facility should inform parents of these exposures and report them to their child's doctor. Call the doctor immediately if your HIV-infected child develops a fever, breathing difficulties, diarrhea, swallowing problems, or skin irritation, or if he's been exposed to a communicable disease. In fact, any change in your child's health status should prompt you to seek medical attention, since the child with HIV may have few reserves to combat even minor illnesses.

Whenever seeking any medical attention for your child, be sure to inform the physician of the HIV infection so that she can assess and

WHERE WE STAND

THE AMERICAN ACADEMY OF PEDIATRICS supports legislation and public policy directed toward eliminating any form of discrimination based on whether a child is infected with HIV (the virus that causes AIDS).

- **AIDS in the schools:** All HIV-infected children should have the same right as those without the infection to attend school and child care. Infected children should receive access to special education and other related services (including home instruction) if their disease progresses and the need arises. The confidentiality of a child's HIV-infection status should be respected, with disclosure given only with the consent of the parent(s) or legal guardian(s).

- **AIDS legislation:** As the number of HIV-infected children, adolescents, and young women continues to grow, the Academy supports federal funding for AIDS research and health care services for HIV-infected individuals and their families.

- **AIDS testing:** The Academy recommends that information about HIV infection, prevention of mother-to-child HIV transmission, and HIV antibody testing be routinely provided as part of a comprehensive health care program for pregnant women. Documented, routine HIV antibody testing should be performed for all pregnant women in the United States after notifying them that testing will be performed, unless the patient declines HIV testing (called "opt-out" consent or "right of refusal"). The Academy also recommends HIV testing with parental or guardian consent for *newborns* whose mothers' HIV status (i.e., whether the virus is present in her blood) is not known.

care for the illness appropriately, as well as give correct immunizations.

If You're Pregnant

All pregnant women should be tested for HIV infection during every pregnancy. When a pregnant woman is infected with HIV, it is important that she be treated appropriately (with three combinations of anti-HIV drugs) to reduce the likelihood of transmission of the virus from mother to infant. Once the baby is born, women who are HIV-infected should not breastfeed their infant because of the risk of transmitting the virus via breastfeeding; safe alternative sources of infant nutrition are available, such as infant formulas.

WHERE WE STAND

WHEN CHILDREN HAVE a chronic, serious illness or disability, their parents often turn to "natural" therapies. Words that describe these therapies include *alternative, complementary,* and *folk remedy.* These treatments can be used in addition to the care their child is receiving from their pediatrician or other mainstream practitioner, even when they're happy with this traditional care. In some cases, they may have become frustrated with what mainstream medicine offered their child, and they've turned to natural therapies, which continue to increase in popularity.

If you've made the decision to seek natural therapies for your child's care, involve your pediatrician in the process. Your doctor may be able to help you better understand these therapies, whether they have scientific merit, whether claims about them are accurate or exaggerated, and whether they pose any risks to your child's well-being. Keep in mind that a "natural" treatment does not always mean a "safe" one. Your pediatrician can help you determine whether there is a risk of interactions with your child's other medications.

The American Academy of Pediatrics has encouraged pediatricians to evaluate the scientific merits of natural therapies, determine whether they might cause any direct or indirect harm, and advise parents on the full range of treatment options. If you decide to use a natural therapy, your pediatrician also may be able to assist in evaluating your child's response to that treatment.

In the Classroom

There is no risk of HIV transmission in routine classroom activities. The virus is not spread through casual contact. It cannot be transmitted through the air, by touching, or via toilet seats. School-age children with HIV infection can attend a regular school. You should not be required to disclose the HIV status of your child in order for him to attend school and participate in all school-related activities.

Although HIV transmission has not occurred in schools and child care centers, these settings are required to adopt routine precautionary procedures for handling blood, stool, and bodily secretions. The standard precaution is to wash exposed skin immediately with soap and water after any contact with blood or body fluids. Soiled surfaces should be cleaned with disinfectants such as bleach (a 1-to-10 dilution of bleach to water). Disposable towels or tissues should be used whenever possible. Gloves are recommended when contact with blood or blood-containing body fluids may occur, and therefore gloves should be available in schools and child care centers. It is important for staff members to wash their hands thoroughly after changing diapers, whether gloves are used or not.

Schools should ensure that children wash their hands before eating, and the staff should wash their hands before food preparation or feeding children. Though many parents worry about biting, HIV has not been transmitted in school settings. Also, it is critically important that schools incorporate HIV education into their curriculum. All children should learn about how HIV is and is not spread. They should learn how to avoid exposure to blood and body fluids that might contain HIV. They should also learn that HIV is not spread through casual contact.

~ 21 ~

Developmental Disabilities

IT'S NATURAL TO compare your child with others his age. When the neighbor's baby walks at ten months, for example, you may worry if yours isn't walking by twelve months, although many children do not walk until they are sixteen or seventeen months of age. And if your toddler is using words at an earlier age than his playmates, probably you'll be very proud. Usually, however, such differences are not significant in the long run. Each child has his own unique rate of development, so some learn certain skills faster than others. Sometimes, a slight developmental delay may simply be that a normal child needs a little more time, but any significant delay should be identified and, if needed, treated early to ensure that the child reaches his full developmental potential.

A true developmental disability, however, is likely to be a more permanent issue and to require more intensive treatment. Yet only when a baby or preschooler lags far behind, or fails to reach the developmental milestones outlined in Chapters 6 through 13 of this book, or loses a previously acquired skill, is there reason to suspect a mental or physical problem serious enough to be considered a developmental disability. Developmental disabilities that can be identified during childhood include intellectual disability, language and learning disorders, cerebral palsy, autism, and sensory impairments such as vision and hearing loss. (Some pediatricians include seizure disorders in this category, but a large percentage of children who have seizures develop typically.)

Within each developmental disability there is a range of severity that may impact daily functioning a lot or just a little bit. Also, some children have more than one disability, each requiring different care.

If your child does not seem to be developing at the same pace as other children the same age, he should have a complete medical and developmental evaluation, perhaps including a consultation with a developmental pediatrician, child neurologist, or pediatric rehabilitation medicine physician who is a specialist trained in the evaluation, diagnosis, and care planning for children with disabilities. Your pediatrician will refer you to the most appropriate professional for further assessment. Doing this will give your pediatrician the information she needs to determine whether a true disability exists, and, if so, how it should be managed. Your physician may recommend additional evaluation by a physical, speech and language, or occupational therapist. Early intervention services are typically recommended for many children under the age of three with developmental delays or medical conditions that place children at high risk for delay. Your pediatrician should be able to help you arrange these consultations. These evaluations may be available through early intervention for children under three years of age or by the school district if your child is over

three. You should contact your school district to find out if they can do these evaluations if you or your physician have concerns about developmental delays. You don't need a referral from a doctor for an evaluation by early intervention or the school system.

Today every child over the age of three years with a developmental disability is entitled by federal law to a free and appropriate public education. For children under three, such intervention may be provided in your home. Most states also offer special early intervention programs for infants and toddlers less than three years old with developmental delays or disabilities or who are at risk for these difficulties. Between the ages of three and five years, therapy or education for identified delays may take place in a preschool or at home.

The families of children with disabilities also need special support and education. Families often worry about how they can help their child once a developmental disability is identified. To understand how your child can realize his full potential, each member of your family should be educated about his developmental condition and counseled about how to help him develop new skills.

Autism Spectrum Disorder

Autism spectrum disorder (ASD) affects a child's behavior, social, and communication skills. ASD is lifelong and can significantly impair the way children interact with others. Symptoms and their severity vary, ranging from mild differences in social awareness to severe disabilities. Affected children commonly have unusual or delayed language. They may have habitual behaviors (such as eating very few foods) or repetitive behaviors (such as turning a light switch off and on, a singular interest in one topic, or physical behaviors like rocking from side to side), and they may have poor eye contact with others.

Autism affects children of all races, ethnicities, and socioeconomic groups. It occurs about four times more often in boys than in girls, and is diagnosed in nearly 1 of every 68 children in the US. Although autism was once thought of as relatively rare, the number of children with this condition has risen in recent years. This increase in cases may be due in part to a greater awareness of autism's signs and symptoms by parents, teachers, and pediatricians. Thus, more children are being diagnosed with the condition. At the same time, there are better screening tools that doctors can use to detect the condition, and that allow it to be diagnosed even in children with milder symptoms. The exact cause of autism is not known. Studies of families, including those with twins, have shown that genetics play an important role in autism, although there are other causes as well. In a family in which one child has been diagnosed with autism, there is a greater likelihood that a sibling will also have a form of the disorder, compared with the population at large. Even so, in most individual cases of autism, the exact cause remains unclear. In addition to the role of genetics, researchers are also studying factors in the environment that may interact with genes to increase a child's risk of developing symptoms of autism.

Some parents have been concerned about a possible link between autism and certain childhood immunizations. About one-quarter of children with autism will initially develop a few words then lose them between eighteen and twenty-four months. This is likely related to the underlying differences in brain development. Many studies have now examined the claim that vaccines given in this time frame cause autism, and there is no scientific evidence supporting an association between autism and vaccinations. If you have questions about vaccines for your child, talk to your pediatrician who can provide scientifically confirmed information about the safety of vaccines.

Reflecting scientific consensus, autism spectrum disorder (ASD) now is considered a single condition. It replaces four separate disorders (autistic disorder, Asperger disorder, childhood disintegrative disorder, and pervasive developmental disorder-not otherwise specified [PDD-NOS]).

Children with ASD have difficulties with speech and language, problems relating to others, and unusual, repetitive behaviors. The social symptoms are typically seen in the first year of life (although they may be subtle), language problems are more obvious in the second year, while repetitive behaviors may appear even later. Many children also have intellectual deficits, although the majority have typical scores on intellectual testing.

Children with ASD and typical intelligence used to be classified as having *Asperger syndrome (or disorder)*. But even though some children with ASD have better language skills, they have problems with social skills and have difficulty understanding how they should interact with others. They may be preoccupied with their "own world," be unaware of their impact on other people, talk about only one or two topics that they focus on repeatedly, and interpret language literally, having trouble with humor, teasing, and figures of speech. They may be described as having "quirky" interests and behavior. Their voice may have little variation in tone and they may exhibit only limited facial expressions or eye contact. Children with ASD and typical intelligence may not be diagnosed until preschool age or later. Many also have symptoms of ADHD.

Children with fewer overall symptoms than would lead to a diagnosis of ASD may still have challenging behaviors that impair function and merit intervention.

Signs and Symptoms

The following characteristics may be seen in children with ASD. Keep in mind that no two children with these disorders are alike, and signs and symptoms can differ from one child to another.

■ **Some children with** ASD never develop the ability to speak, or may have delayed or poorly developed language skills. They may use words without attaching the usual meanings to them or simply repeat what they hear others saying (known as echolalia). They may not be capable of starting or continuing a conversation, using language for social discussions, or following rules for conversations and storytelling (language pragmatics).

■ **Some children may** not be able to understand what people say to them, or interpret or respond appropriately to cues such as the facial expressions and the body language of others. They might not respond when their name is called, but may react when they hear other types of sounds (a dog's bark, the crinkle of a bag of potato chips).

■ **These children may** be socially withdrawn and have trouble relating to people and making eye contact. They may appear to be unaware of their surroundings.

■ **Their behavior and** body movements are sometimes repetitive. For instance, they may have repetitive motor movements like rocking, spinning, flapping their hands, or lining things up. They may be fascinated by spinning objects like fans or tops. They also may engage in activity that could be harmful to themselves, such as head banging or biting, or may be aggressive toward others and have tantrums.

- **They may become** upset and have tantrums or disruptive behavior when changes in everyday routines occur (e.g., mealtimes) or when they have to transition from one activity to another.

- **They may have** a limited (restricted) range of interests and activities. Their play may not be creative or imaginative in the usual sense of "play," and may include repetitive behavior.

- **They may play** with toys in ways in which they are not designed to be used. They may play with parts of a toy (only the wheels on a toy truck, for example) rather than the entire toy. They may line up toys repeatedly.

- **Instead of forming** attachments to a blanket or stuffed animal, they might prefer unusual objects (keys, a ballpoint pen, a flashlight), and may not want to give up holding them all the time.

- **They may be** very sensitive to smells, lights, sounds, touch, and textures; they may seem to have a high threshold to pain.

Diagnosis

The earlier treatment is started after diagnosis, the better the response. Therefore, if your child has shown delays in developing language, or has unusual behaviors, talk to your pediatrician. Other early signs should raise concerns and may lead to a diagnosis. Contact your doctor if your child is not doing the following activities by the stated age:

By Twelve Months

- Looks at an object when you point to it and say, "Look!"

- Uses simple gestures like waving "bye"

- Says "mama," "dada," and at least one other word

By Eighteen Months

- Points to show you interesting objects or events

- Uses at least ten words correctly

- Will do pretend play, e.g., feed a doll

By Twenty-Four Months

- Points to several body parts, objects, and pictures

- Imitates behavior of others, especially adults and older children

- Speaks two-word phrases and has a fifty-word vocabulary

By Thirty-Six Months

- Enjoys playing with and imitating other children

- Speaks three-word sentences and can use some pronouns

- Talks for doll or action figure in pretend play

By Forty-Eight Months
- Can name friends when asked

- Answers "wh" questions (what, when, who, where)

- Speaks clearly in five- to six-word sentences

Further signs and symptoms can be found at the Centers for Disease Control and Prevention website, www.cdc.gov/actearly.

If you observe signs like these in your child, or are concerned about other aspects of his language and social development, let your pediatrician know—and the earlier, the better. In fact, as soon as the diagnosis of autism is suspected, treatment should begin, even before a diagnosis is conclusively made. Children with other types of delays may have some of these symptoms as well. These other developmental diagnoses also benefit from intervention, so getting your child evaluated is important even if you are not concerned about autism.

Unfortunately, no laboratory test is available to diagnose autism, nor does a single set of symptoms always characterize it. But your pediatrician or a team of health care specialists with expertise in ASD will make the diagnosis based largely on the pres-

ence (or absence) of a collection of symptoms. As part of the diagnostic process, your child's play behavior will be observed, as will his interactions with his caregivers. Your pediatrician also will take a detailed history, conduct a physical examination, and perhaps order laboratory tests to rule out medical conditions that can cause symptoms that may mimic some of those associated with autism. Standardized screening tests and other diagnostic tools, including language evaluations, are available to add to the information that can assist in reaching a diagnosis. Children with these signs should always be evaluated to make sure they can hear normally.

To help make the diagnosis, you can contact a specialist in ASD, typically found in major medical centers. Ask your pediatrician for a referral, or call your state's public early childhood system to request a free evaluation to find out if your child qualifies for intervention services.

Treatment

There is no known cure for autism spectrum disorder. A child diagnosed with ASD will need specialized services aimed at the management of the specific findings associated with his ASD. Early treatment may improve the ability of a child with autism to function more effectively in life.

Some commonly used approaches include Applied Behavior Analysis (ABA), DIR (Floortime or Greenspan method), and TEACCH (*Treatment and Education of Autistic and*

WHERE WE STAND

THE AMERICAN ACADEMY OF PEDIATRICS (AAP) encourages doctors to be aware of the signs of ASD, and to be on the lookout for these signs during every well-child visit.

At the same time, the Academy urges parents to always let their pediatricians know of any concerns they may have about their child's behavior and development. The AAP recommends autism-specific screening when children are at eighteen and twenty-four months of age; the sooner an intervention program is started, the better. However, children should be evaluated at any age if a parent or professional has concern about the possibility of an ASD. If ASD is suspected or diagnosed, parents should seek a referral for early intervention and local specialists (like speech therapy or behavioral intervention to promote social skills). Early intervention programs are specific for children zero to three years of age. Above the age of three, a referral should be made to your school district. Parents should make an effort to become as familiar as possible with available treatments and programs in their community, and support their child in learning the skills needed to be successful in the least restrictive educational setting.

Communications-handicapped Children). The most effective techniques are intensive, and are designed to address behavioral issues, and help the child develop communication and social skills.

Children with ASD require an individualized educational program that addresses their language and social learning needs in the least restrictive environment. Sometimes, children will benefit from smaller learning environments that provide less distraction. Generally, younger children benefit from intensive educational and other therapies that may be up to twenty-five hours a week, twelve months a year. Like other children with developmental disabilities, families should evaluate educational options that promote development of social skills. At times, medications also are helpful to manage the behavioral difficulties with autism and related disorders as part of an overall behavioral plan.

Children with ASD can vary considerably in their ability for independence in adulthood, as well as in their behavior and language skills. It is impossible to predict in early childhood the adult abilities of a young child with ASD, so it is important to begin interventions for language, social, academic, and behavioral symptoms as early and intensely as possible. No two children with ASD have the same needs, and the approach that is appropriate for one child may be different from what is used for another. Be as involved as you possibly can in your child's treatments. Your pediatrician can help you find community agencies that provide services for your child, as well as family support networks, counseling, and advocacy groups. On the Internet, seek out reliable sources of information and education, such as the Centers for Disease Control and Prevention (www.cdc.gov) or the American Academy of Pediatrics (www.aap.org/autism). You may get conflicting advice about interventions besides those recommended at the time of your child's evaluation. It is important to confer with your pediatrician about therapies that you might be considering. Through support groups, you also can meet parents of other children with ASD and share experiences, concerns, and solutions.

As mentioned earlier, if one of your children is diagnosed with autism, there is an increased risk (of about 3 to 7 percent) that the same disorder will occur in your other children. Speak to your pediatrician about receiving counseling to discuss this increased risk.

Also see the section on autism in Chapter 11 (*Your Two-Year-Old*) on page 349.

Cerebral Palsy

Children with cerebral palsy have an abnormality or damage to the area of the brain that controls movement and muscle tone. Many of these youngsters have typical intelligence, even though they have difficulty with motor control and movement. The condition causes different types of motor difficulties, which can vary from quite mild and barely noticeable to very profound. Depending on the severity of the problem, a child with cerebral palsy may have clumsy movement patterns, or he may be unable to walk. Some children have weakness and poor motor control of one arm and one leg on the same side of the body (called hemiparesis), some have difficulties with both their legs (diplegia), and some have problems with control of both upper and lower extremities (quadriplegia). In some children the muscle tone generally is increased (called spasticity or hypertonia), while in others it is very low (called hypotonia). While many children with cerebral palsy have preserved understanding of language, they may have difficulty in coordinating the mouth movements needed to produce speech.

Cerebral palsy is caused by malformation or damage to the brain, usually before birth while the brain is being formed, but occasionally during delivery, or after birth. Premature birth is associated with an increased risk of cerebral palsy due to the fragility of the developing brain. A baby also can get cerebral palsy from very severe jaundice after birth, or later on in infancy from an injury or illness affecting the brain. Although it may be challenging, it is important to focus your energy on optimizing your child's development and remember that in many cases a cause cannot be identified.

A report by the American Academy of Pediatrics and the American College of Obstetricians and Gynecologists concluded that the majority of cases of cerebral palsy are not the result of events during labor and delivery, such as an insufficient supply of oxygen (hypoxia).

Signs and Symptoms

The signs and symptoms of cerebral palsy vary tremendously because there are many different types and degrees of motor problems. The main clue that your child might have cerebral palsy is a delay in achieving the motor milestones listed in Chapters 5 through 13 of this book. Here are some specific warning signs.

IN A BABY OVER TWO MONTHS

- **His head lags** when you pick him up while he's lying on his back.

- **He feels stiff.**

- **He feels floppy.**

- **When held cradled** in your arms, he seems to overextend his back and neck—constantly acts as if he is pushing away from you.

- **When you pick** him up, his legs get stiff and they cross or "scissor."

IN A BABY OVER TEN MONTHS

- **He crawls in** a lopsided manner, pushing off with one hand and leg while dragging the opposite hand and leg.

- **He scoots around** on his buttocks or hops on his knees, but does not crawl on all fours.

If you have any concerns about your child's development, talk to your pediatrician at your routine visit. Because children's rates of development vary widely, it is sometimes difficult to make a definite diagnosis of mild cerebral palsy in the first year or two of life. Often a consultation with a developmental pediatrician, pediatric neurologist, or pediatric rehabilitation medicine physician will assist in the diagnosis. Your pediatrician will refer you to the appropriate professional. Your child will also be referred to a physical and/or occupational therapist for additional assessment of their motor skills. A CT (computed tomography) or MRI (magnetic resonance imagery) of the head may be recommended to determine whether a brain abnormality exists. Even when a firm diagnosis is made during these early years, it often is difficult to predict how severe the motor problems will be in the future. However, usually by three to four years of age a child's motor symptoms become clear.

Treatment

If your pediatrician suspects that your child has cerebral palsy, you may be referred to an early intervention program. These programs are staffed by early childhood educators; physical, occupational, and speech and language therapists; nurses; social workers; and medical consultants. In such a program, your child will get therapies specifically targeting their needs and you'll learn how to become your child's own teacher and therapist. You will be taught by a physical and/or occupational therapist what exercises to do with your infant, what positions are most comfortable and beneficial to him, and how to help with specific problems such as feeding difficulties. Sometimes medications such as baclofen may be suggested to minimize the spasticity associated with cerebral palsy. Sometimes botulinum toxin type A, a muscle-relaxing drug, is injected to decrease muscle tightness in the legs or arms. Medication for spasticity is not typically recommended for young children. Older children may be treated with implantable baclofen pumps or have surgical procedures to decrease spasticity. You may receive information about adaptive equipment that can help your child participate in everyday activities and position him so he can use his hands better in play. Special equipment may include customized utensils to make eating easier, pencils that can be held more easily, wheelchairs, and walkers. Through support groups, you also can meet parents of other children with similar disabilities and share experiences, concerns, and solutions.

The most important thing you can do for your child is to help him develop skills, become resilient, and gain positive self-esteem. Encourage him to perform the tasks he is capable of and practice more challenging tasks so that he learns to do them with as little assistance as possible. The professionals at early intervention centers can help you evaluate your child's abilities and teach you how to reach appropriate goals.

You may be offered advice about other types of therapies than those offered by the conventional therapy team. Ask your pediatrician before trying nonstandard therapies. You can contact the United Cerebral Palsy Association at www.ucp.org, for information about resources and programs available in your area and to read additional information about cerebral palsy.

Associated Problems

INTELLECTUAL DISABILITY

It has been estimated that more than half of children with cerebral palsy have global developmental delays that include thinking and problem solving. Many children with cerebral palsy also are diagnosed with intellectual disabilities (what used to be called mental retardation), while others have average intellectual abilities or specific learning disabilities. (See also *Intellectual Disability*, page 656.)

SEIZURES

One out of every three people with cerebral palsy has or will develop seizures. They may not start until later in childhood. Fortunately, these seizures usually can be controlled with anticonvulsant medications. (See also page 790.)

VISION DIFFICULTIES

Because the injury to the brain often affects eye muscle coordination, more than three out of four children with cerebral palsy have strabismus, a problem with one eye turning in or out. If this problem is not corrected early, the vision in the affected eye will get worse and eventually will be lost permanently (amblyopia). Thus it is extremely important to have your child's eyes checked regularly by your pediatrician. (See also *Strabismus,* page 732.)

JOINT CONTRACTURES AND SCOLIOSIS

In children with spastic forms of cerebral palsy, it is often difficult to prevent "contracture," an extreme stiffening of the joints caused by the unequal pull of one muscle over the other. A physical therapist, developmental pediatrician, or pediatric rehabilitation medicine physician can teach you how to stretch the muscles to try to prevent the onset of contracture. Sometimes braces, casting, or medication may be used to improve joint mobility and stability. In some situations, orthopedic surgery is performed as part of contracture management.

Some children with asymmetry of their muscle tone may have differences in the size of the affected arm or leg or contractures of joints. An orthopedic surgeon might be consulted to prescribe orthotics (splints or braces) to prevent contractures from worsening. Sometimes children develop scoliosis or curvature of the spine that requires a special back brace. If physical therapy, orthotics, medical management of spasticity or tone, and positioning cannot prevent contractures, surgery may be needed to maximize motor abilities.

DENTAL PROBLEMS

Many children with cerebral palsy have a greater risk of developing oral diseases. This can mean more gingivitis (gum disease) and cavities. One reason may be that it is difficult for them to brush their teeth. However, they also have more enamel defects than other children, which may make their teeth more susceptible to decay. In addition, some medications such as seizure or asthma drugs may contribute to cavity formation. Because of the special skills needed to monitor their dental needs, families often seek out pediatric dentists for their children with cerebral palsy.

HEARING LOSS

Some children with cerebral palsy have a complete or partial hearing loss. One cause of cerebral palsy commonly associated with hearing loss is severe jaundice or anoxia (a deficiency of oxygen) at birth. If you find that your baby does not blink or startle at loud noises by one month, is not turning his head toward a sound by three to four months, or is not saying words by twelve months, discuss it with your pediatrician. The results of newborn hearing screening should be reviewed and follow-up hearing evaluation should be obtained along with formal speech and language testing. (See also *Hearing Loss,* page 652.)

PROBLEMS WITH SPATIAL AWARENESS

Over half the children with cerebral palsy affecting one side of the body have challenges sensing the position of their arm, leg, or hand on the affected side. (For example, when a child's hands are relaxed, he cannot tell whether his fingers are pointing up or down without looking at them.) If this problem exists, the child may limit use of the involved hand, even if the motor disability is minimal. He might act as if it is not there. Physical or occupational therapy can help him learn to use the affected parts of his body, despite this disability.

Congenital Abnormalities

Congenital abnormalities are caused by problems during the fetus's development before birth. About 3 of every 100 babies born in the United States have congenital abnormalities.

There are five categories of these abnormalities, grouped according to the cause.

CHROMOSOME ABNORMALITIES

Chromosomes carry the genetic material inherited from one generation to the next in the egg and sperm. Normally, twenty-three chromosomes come from the father and twenty-three from the mother, and all are found in the center of every cell in the body except the red blood cells. The genes carried on the chromosomes determine a child's characteristics.

When a child does not have the normal forty-six chromosomes, or when pieces of the chromosomes are missing or duplicated, there may be problems in the development and function of organs including the brain. Down syndrome is an example of a condition that can occur when a child is born with an extra chromosome.

SINGLE-GENE ABNORMALITIES

Sometimes the chromosomes are normal in number, but one or more of the genes on them are abnormal. Some of these genetic abnormalities are inherited from a parent who also has that abnormality. This is known as autosomal dominant inheritance.

Other genetic problems can be passed to the child only if both parents carry the same gene. (Cystic fibrosis, Tay-Sachs disease, and sickle cell anemia are all examples of disorders inherited in this fashion.) In these cases neither parent has the disorder, but each carries the gene for it. One in four of their children would inherit this gene from both parents and be affected. This is known as autosomal recessive inheritance.

A third type of genetic abnormality is called sex-linked, and generally is passed on to boys only. Girls may carry the gene that causes these disorders but not show the actual disease. (Examples of this problem include hemophilia, color blindness, and the common forms of muscular dystrophy.)

CONDITIONS DURING PREGNANCY THAT AFFECT DEVELOPMENT

Certain illnesses of the mother during pregnancy, particularly during the first nine weeks, can cause serious congenital abnormalities—German measles and diabetes, for example. Alcohol consumption and certain drugs if used during pregnancy significantly increase the risk of problems with brain development. There are medications that, if taken during pregnancy, also can cause harm to the fetus, as can certain chemicals that can pollute air, water, and food. Always check with your doctor before using any medication or nutritional supplement while you are pregnant.

COMBINATION OF GENETIC AND ENVIRONMENTAL PROBLEMS

Spina bifida and cleft lip and palate are types of congenital abnormalities that may occur when there is a genetic tendency for the condition combined with exposure to certain environmental influences within the womb during critical stages of the pregnancy. Women are prescribed prenatal vitamins to help prevent the fetus from having spina bifida.

UNKNOWN CAUSES

The vast majority of congenital abnormalities have no known cause. If you and your family have had one child with congenital abnormalities or developmental problems without a known cause, ask your pediatrician for a referral to a geneticist or genetic counselor. They can review with you your risk for having another child with similar problems.

When Your Child Has a Congenital Disorder

Despite advances in prenatal diagnostics like ultrasound, most families learn their baby has a congenital abnormality after she is born. With all of the new medical information and stress about medical decision making that families are faced with, it is often helpful to have one person who fields questions from family and friends. It is very important to ask the doctors caring for your baby to explain everything so you understand and to make certain that you have the support of friends and family. Siblings need to be informed about the condition of the baby in words that are appropriate to their developmental level. Once a diagnosis is made, many families find it very helpful to be put in contact with family support groups for that disorder.

Congenital Conditions

Congenital abnormalities are so diverse, and require such different types of treatment, that it would be impossible to discuss them all in this section. Instead, we will look only at the medical management of two conditions: Down syndrome and spina bifida.

DOWN SYNDROME

Approximately 1 out of every 800 babies is born with Down syndrome. Fortunately, through amniocentesis, Down syndrome can be detected prenatally. Down syndrome is caused by the presence of an extra chromosome—resulting in a characteristic appearance including up-slanted eyes with extra folds of skin at the inner corners, flattening of the bridge of the nose, a relatively large tongue, and a decrease in the muscle and ligament tone of the body.

Almost all children with Down syndrome have some degree of intellectual disability. The degree of intellectual disability varies as does the amount and intelligibility of spoken language. Children with Down syndrome are often quite social, but there are some who have ADHD, autism, or both. Educational approaches are used to promote independence in self-care skills and the skills necessary for employment in adulthood.

Prenatal diagnosis allows for the doctors to anticipate the need for early treatment for abnormalities of the heart, intestinal tract, and/or blood that babies with Down syndrome might have. Once suspected on prenatal ultrasound, Down syndrome can be confirmed by a blood test on the mother. Since most of the time newborns with Down syndrome have no medical problems that require immediate treatment, most can leave the hospital after the normal newborn stay.

If you have a newborn with Down syndrome, your pediatrician will recommend early intervention services for you and your baby. Early intervention programs will provide therapy for your baby to learn how to reach her milestones and will help you with strategies to maximize her skills.

There are many types of therapy that are not scientifically proven that you might read about. You should discuss any intervention that you are considering with your clinician to make certain it is safe and effective.

In addition to developmental delay, Down syndrome can result in physical problems as your child gets older. Her growth should be closely watched, since extremely slow growth in height and/or excessive weight gain may indicate a lack of thyroid hormone, a problem that affects many youngsters with Down syndrome. Even without thyroid problems, chances are that she'll be shorter and weigh less than average for her age as an infant. When they're older, children with Down syndrome may be overweight. One-half of children with Down syndrome also have heart problems diagnosed at birth that may require medication or surgery. Over one-half have vision and hearing defects.

Another problem, which affects 15 of every 100 children with Down syndrome, is an abnormality in the ligaments of the neck (neck instability) that can cause serious spinal injury if the neck is extended (bent backward) during exercise or anesthesia. For this reason, consult your pediatrician for advice regarding whether neck X-rays are needed before she's allowed to participate in vigorous athletic activities (especially tumbling and gymnastics) or before elective surgery so the anesthesia doctor knows how to manage your child's sedation. If X-rays show this abnormality, her physical activities should be limited to movements that cannot cause injury.

SPINA BIFIDA

Spina bifida occurs when the spinal bones fail to close properly during early fetal development. There are many different subtypes of spina bifida. The most common form, spina bifida occulta, occurs when the spinal bones don't close but there are no problems with the nerves that are protected by the spinal column. Most people with spina bifida occulta don't even know they have it. Another form is meningocele, in which there is a sac of fluid that is present but no spinal nerve tissue involved. Another type is myelomeningocele. This type includes the bones of the spine, the sac of fluid, and parts of the spinal nerves and spinal cord. Most of the time, when people say spina bifida, they are referring to myelomeningocele. Spina bifida is caused by an interaction between genes and the environment. A parent who has one child with spina bifida has a greater chance (1 out of 100) of having another. This increased frequency appears to be due to some combined effect of heredity and environment. Vitamins including folic acid are given to pregnant women to minimize the risk for spina bifida in the fetus. Ultrasound examination can identify spina bifida during pregnancy, and blood tests done on the mother can help to identify an increased risk of having a baby with spina bifida. Knowing that a baby will have spina bifida allows the family to plan for delivery at a medical center that has specialty surgery and neonatal care. At some highly specialized centers with experts in high-risk maternal fetal medicine and surgeons that specialize in fetal surgery, pregnant women may choose to be evaluated for fetal surgery. Fetal surgery for spina bifida is not a cure but can lessen the impacts of the condition.

A newborn with spina bifida has a sac protruding from the spine that contains spinal fluid and a portion of the spinal cord. These are the nerves that control the lower part of the body. On the first or second day of life, surgery must be performed to close the opening in the spine. Unfortunately, little can be done to repair the damaged nerves, but a lot can be done to help children be as functional as possible.

Most babies with spina bifida have several other medical complications. These include:

Hydrocephalus. Up to 9 out of 10 children with spina bifida eventually develop hydrocephalus, caused by an excessive increase in the fluid that normally cushions the brain from injury. The increase occurs because the path through which the fluid ordinarily flows is altered. This condition is serious and must be treated surgically.

The pediatrician should suspect hydrocephalus if the baby's head is growing more rapidly than expected. The condition is confirmed by a computerized X-ray of the head, called a CT (computed tomography) scan, magnetic resonance imagery (MRI), or ultrasound. If the condition exists, surgery will be required to relieve fluid buildup by placement of a shunt to remove the fluid.

Latex allergies. People with spina bifida are more likely to be allergic to latex. Allergic reactions can vary from mild to very severe. All children with spina bifida should take precautions to avoid latex. Those children with latex allergies should have an emergency care plan should an allergic event occur. You can reduce the chances that he will acquire the sensitivity by avoiding exposure to latex. But be aware that many infant products contain latex (bottle nipples, pacifiers, teething toys, changing pads, mattress covers, and some diapers), so products containing latex should be avoided.

Muscle weakness or paralysis. Because the congenital abnormality of the spinal cord impacts the development of nerves connecting the brain to the lower limbs, the muscles in the legs may be very weak or not function at all in children with spina bifida. Because they may not be able to move their feet, knees, or hips, they may be born with contractures of these joints. Surgery can be performed to correct some of these problems, and the muscle weakness can be treated with physical therapy and bracing. Depending on the level of the spinal lesion, children with spina bifida may be able to walk independently or with walkers. Many use wheelchairs, however.

Bowel and bladder problems. Often the nerves that control bowel and bladder function do not work properly with spina bifida. As a result, these children are more likely to develop urinary tract infections and can

have urine back up from the bladder and damage the kidneys. Your pediatrician will refer your child to a urologist, who will monitor your child's bladder function and determine if he needs to have urine drained through a catheter to protect his kidneys.

Bowel control may be a problem because of the lack of nerve control of the rectum. Careful dietary management (to keep the stools soft), and the occasional use of suppositories, bowel stimulants, or special enemas may be recommended to help with bowel management.

Infection. Parents of children who have spina bifida and hydrocephalus or urinary tract problems must be ever alert for signs of infection. Your pediatrician will prescribe antibiotics if your child gets an infection.

Educational and social problems. Seven out of 10 children with spina bifida have developmental and learning disabilities requiring some educational supports for learning needs. Issues of health and wellness, including weight control, physical activity, and social inclusion, are particularly important to the long-term physical, emotional, and social well-being of children with spina bifida.

Parents of a child with spina bifida need more than one physician to manage their child's medical care. In addition to the basic care your pediatrician delivers, this disorder requires a team approach that involves neurosurgeons, orthopedic surgeons, urologists, reha-

WHERE WE STAND

IN AN EFFORT to reduce the prevalence of spina bifida, the American Academy of Pediatrics endorses the recommendation of the US Public Health Service that all women capable of becoming pregnant consume 400 micrograms per day of folic acid (a B vitamin). Folic acid helps to prevent neural tube defects (NTDs), which include spina bifida. Although some foods are fortified with folic acid, it is not possible for women to meet the 400-microgram goal through a typical diet. Thus, an Academy policy statement recommends a daily multivitamin tablet that contains folic acid in the recommended dose. Studies show that if all women of childbearing age met these dietary requirements, 50 percent or more of NTDs could be prevented.

Women who are at high risk for an NTD-affected pregnancy (for example, because of a previous NTD-affected pregnancy, having diabetes mellitus, or taking antiseizure medications) are advised to discuss their risk with their doctor. This includes possible treatments with very high doses of folic acid (4,000 mcg per day), beginning one month before becoming pregnant and continuing throughout the first trimester. As the doctor will explain, however, women should not attempt to achieve this very high dose of folic acid by taking multivitamin supplements, but rather only under the care of a physician.

bilitation experts, physical therapists, psychologists, and social workers. Many medical centers run special spina bifida clinics, which offer the services of all these health professionals in one location. Having all members of the team together makes it easier for everyone to communicate and usually provides better access to information and assistance when parents need it.

Resources

Information and support for parents are available from various organizations.

March of Dimes
1-914-997-4488
www.marchofdimes.com

The National Down Syndrome Congress
1-800-232-NDSC (6372)
www.ndsccenter.org

The Spina Bifida Association of America
1-800-621-3141
www.spinabifidaassociation.org

United Cerebral Palsy Association
1-800-872-5827
www.ucp.org

Hearing Loss

Although hearing loss can occur at any age, hearing difficulties at birth or that develop during infancy and the toddler years can have serious consequences. This is because normal hearing is needed to understand spoken language and then, later, to produce clear speech. Consequently, if your child experiences hearing loss during infancy and early childhood, it demands immediate attention. Even a temporary but significant hearing loss during this time can make it very difficult for the child to learn proper oral language.

Most children experience mild hearing loss when fluid accumulates in the middle ear from congestion, colds, or ear infections. This hearing loss is usually only temporary; normal hearing commonly returns once the congestion or infection subsides and the Eustachian tube (which connects the middle ear to the throat) drains the remaining fluid into the back of the throat. In many children, perhaps 1 in 10, fluid stays in the middle ear following an ear infection (see page 662) because of problems with the Eustachian tube. These children don't hear as well as they should, and sometimes develop speech delays. Much less common is the permanent kind of hearing loss that always endangers normal speech and language development. Permanent hearing loss varies from mild or partial to complete or total deafness.

There are two main kinds of hearing loss:

Conductive hearing loss. When a child has a conductive hearing loss, there may be an abnormality in the structure of the outer ear canal or middle ear, there may be a large amount of cerumen (wax) lodged in the ear canal, or there may be fluid in the middle ear that interferes with the transfer of sound.

Sensorineural hearing loss. This type of hearing impairment is caused by an abnormality of the inner ear or the nerves that carry sound messages from the inner ear to the brain. The loss can be present at birth or occur any time thereafter. Even without a family history of deafness, the cause is frequently inherited (genetic). If the mother had rubella (German measles), cytomegalovirus (CMV), or another infectious illness that affects the inner ear during pregnancy, the fetus could have been infected and may lose hearing as a result. The problem also may be due to a malformation of the inner ear. Most often the cause of severe sensorineural hearing loss is inherited. Still, in most cases, no other family member on either side will have hearing loss because each parent is only a carrier for a hearing loss gene. This is called an "autosomal recessive pattern," rather than "dominant" where it would be expected that other family members would have hearing loss. Future brothers and sisters of the child have an increased risk of being hearing impaired, and the family should seek genetic counseling if the hearing loss is determined to be inherited.

Hearing loss must be diagnosed as soon as possible, so that your child isn't delayed in learning language—a process that begins the day she is born. The American Academy of Pediatrics recommends that before a newborn infant goes home from the hospital, she undergo a hearing screening. In fact, every state and territory in the US now has an Early Hearing Detection and Intervention (EHDI) program, which mandates that all newborns be screened for hearing loss before they are discharged from the hospital. At any time during your child's life, if you and/or your pediatrician suspect that she has a hearing loss, insist that a formal hearing evaluation be performed promptly. (See *Hearing Loss: What to Look For* on page 655.) Although some family doctors, pediatricians, and well-baby clinics can test for fluid in the middle ear—a common cause of hearing loss—they cannot measure hearing precisely. Your child should go to an audiologist, who can test your child's hearing at any age. If she has hearing loss, she must also be seen by an ear, nose, and throat doctor (ENT; an otolaryngologist).

If your child is under age six months, or uncooperative during her hearing examination, she may be given one of two available tests, which are similar to the tests performed during newborn hearing screenings. They are painless, and can take anywhere from five to sixty minutes. They are as follow:

■ **The auditory brainstem** response test (ABR) measures how the brain responds to sound during deep sleep. Clicks or tones are played into the baby's ears through soft earphones, and electrodes placed on the baby's head measure the brain's response. This allows the doctor to test your child's hearing without having to rely on her cooperation. ABRs are performed during a "natural sleep" in infants under three or four months old. Older babies and toddlers need to be sedated to undergo an ABR.

■ **The otoacoustic emissions** test measures sound waves produced by the ear. A tiny probe is placed just inside the baby's ear canal, which then measures the response when clicks or tones are played into the baby's ear. Babies and young children usually do not need to be napping or sedated for this, as it is a brief screening exam. This can be done at any age.

Behavioral audiometry, or "conditioned response audiometry," can be performed with a cooperative baby as young as six months old. A combination of visual and auditory stimuli are provided, and can determine frequency-specific (although not ear-specific) hearing levels in infants and toddlers.

Formal behavioral audiometry can determine hearing levels as well as eardrum function in each ear. This is performed using soft earphones that send sounds and words to the ear, and is typically well tolerated by children in the three-to-five-year age range, depending on the individual child's cooperation in the testing setting.

These tests may not be available in

your immediate area, but the consequences of undiagnosed hearing loss are so serious that your doctor may advise you to travel to where one of them can be done. Certainly, if these tests indicate that your baby may have a hearing problem, your doctor should recommend a more thorough hearing evaluation as soon as possible to confirm whether your child's hearing is impaired.

Treatment

Treating a hearing loss will depend on its cause. If it is a mild conductive hearing loss due to fluid in the middle ear, the doctor may simply recommend that your child be retested in a few months to see whether the fluid has cleared by itself. Medications such as antihistamines, decongestants, or antibiotics are ineffective in clearing up middle ear fluid.

If there is no improvement in hearing over a three-month period, and there is still fluid behind the eardrum, the doctor may recommend a referral to an ENT specialist. If the fluid persists and there is sufficient (even though temporary) conductive hearing impairment from the fluid, the specialist may recommend draining the fluid through ventilating tubes. These are surgically inserted through the eardrum. This is a minor operation and takes about fifteen minutes, but your child must receive a general anesthetic for it to be done properly, so she usually will spend part of the day in a hospital or an outpatient surgery center.

Even with the tubes in place, future infections can occur, but the tubes help reduce the amount of fluid and decrease your child's risk of repeated infection. If the cause for the hearing loss was purely the fluid, the tubes will improve the hearing.

If a conductive hearing loss is due to a malformation of the outer or middle ear, a hearing aid may restore hearing to normal or near-normal levels. However, a hearing aid will work only when it's being worn. You must make sure it is on and functioning at all times, particularly in a very young child. Reconstructive surgery may be considered when the child is older.

Early placement of hearing aids for infants even with severe to profound hearing loss is important to give them self-awareness of receptive language. Early exposure to either aural (spoken) or visual (sign) language has a very significant impact on language development.

Hearing aids can improve hearing levels in children with mild to moderate sensorineural hearing loss, such that most can develop normal speech and oral language. Should your child have severe or profound hearing impairment in both ears and receive little or no benefit from hearing aids, she could become a candidate for cochlear implants. Cochlear implants have been approved by the government for children since 1990. If your family is considering an implant for your child, results for developing useful speech and hearing are better with early (ideally by one year of age) rather than late (over three years old) implantation, when the hearing loss occurred at birth. Therefore it is extremely important to seek out early and efficient evaluation and treatment of this type of hearing loss. Most children with normal brain development and early implantation can develop good to excellent hearing and mainstream oral language with cochlear implants. Almost all children gain better awareness of sounds in their environment. The potential for children with profound hearing loss to maximally benefit from cochlear implants in terms of developing oral language and hearing skills is significantly optimized through enrollment in extensive therapies and re-

When to Call the Pediatrician
Hearing Loss: What to Look For

Here are the signs and symptoms that should make you suspect that your child has a hearing loss and alert you to call your pediatrician.

- Your child doesn't startle at loud noises by one month or turn to the source of a sound by three to four months of age.

- He doesn't notice you until he sees you.

- He concentrates on gargling and other vibrating noises that he can feel, rather than experimenting with a wide variety of vowel sounds and consonants. (See *Language Development* in Chapters 8 and 9.)

- His speech is delayed or hard to understand, or he doesn't say single words such as "dada" or "mama" by twelve to fifteen months of age.

- He does not say five to ten words by eighteen months of age.

- He does not put two to three words together at two years of age.

- His speech is not understandable 50 percent of the time by two and a half years of age.

- He doesn't always respond when called. (This is usually mistaken for inattention or resistance, but could be the result of a partial hearing loss.)

- He seems to hear some sounds but not others. (Some hearing loss affects only high-pitched sounds; some children have hearing loss in only one ear.)

- He seems not only to hear poorly but also has trouble holding his head steady, or is slow to sit or walk unsupported. (In some children with sensorineural hearing loss, the part of the inner ear that provides information about balance and movement of the head is also damaged.)

sources for hearing development including speech therapy, specialized teachers for the hearing impaired, and parent resources and counseling.

Parents of children with sensorineural hearing loss usually are most concerned about whether their child will learn to talk. The answer is that, although optimally timed cochlear implantation will greatly improve the chances of learning oral language, not all may learn to speak clearly. However, all children with a hearing impairment can be taught to communicate. Some children learn to lip-read well, while others never fully master the skill. However, oral speech is only one form of language. For children in whom hearing aids or cochlear implants cannot offer enough improvement in hearing to develop oral language, or for those families who have chosen not to pursue oral language, sign language is another mode of communication that can be learned. If your child is learning sign language, you and your immediate family also must learn it. This way you will be able to teach, discipline, praise, comfort, and laugh with her. You should encourage friends and relatives to learn signing, too. Written language also is very important because it is the key to educational and vocational success. Although some advocates in the deaf community prefer separate schools for deaf children, there is no reason for children with severe hearing impairment to be separated from other people because of their hearing loss. With proper early language intervention, education, and support, these children will grow to be fully integrated into their social structure and active participants in the world around them.

Intellectual Disability

The term *intellectual disability* (ID) is used when a child's intelligence and abilities to adjust to his surroundings are significantly below average and affect the way he learns and develops new skills. The more severe the disability, the more delayed a child's behavior will be for his age.

Intelligence in children over age two years generally is measured in terms of IQ (intelligence quotient). To determine IQ, the child is given a test to assess his problem-solving skills in language and nonlanguage areas. The tests are designed for the average score to be 100 and for most people to test within a range above and below 100.

In some cases, standard IQ tests are not accurate or reliable, because cultural differences or language problems or physical problems interfere with testing. In such cases, special tests that measure the child's ability to function and reason, despite these problems, should be used.

Signs and Symptoms

Generally, the more severe the degree of intellectual disability, the earlier you will notice the signs. It may be difficult to predict in young children who have delays in both language and problem-solving skills what their delays might be as they develop.

When a baby is late in developing basic motor skills (e.g., holding his head up by himself by three to four months or sitting unsupported by seven to eight months), there also may be some associated intellectual disability. However, this is by no means always the case. Nor does normal motor development guarantee normal intelligence. Some children with mild to moderate degrees of intellectual disability have normal physical development during the first few years of life. In such cases, the first sign of intellectual disability may be a delay in language development or in learning simple imitation skills, such as waving bye-bye or playing patty-cake.

In many cases of mild disability, except for delays in speech, the young child otherwise may reach developmental milestones at typical times. Later, when he begins preschool or school, he may have difficulty performing academic skills at his grade level. He might have trouble completing puzzles, recognizing colors, or counting when his classmates already have mastered these tasks. Remember, however, children do develop at very different rates, and problems in school certainly are not always a sign of intellectual disability. Developmental delays also can be caused by disorders such as hearing loss, vision problems, learning disabilities, or lack of experience due to environmental challenges.

When to Call the Pediatrician

If you are concerned about a delay in your child's development (see the sections on development in Chapters 6 through 13), call your pediatrician, who will review your child's overall development and determine whether it is appropriate for his age. If the pediatrician is concerned, she will probably refer you to a pediatric developmental specialist, a pediatric neurologist, or a multidisciplinary team of professionals for further assessment. With older children, formal psychological testing may be helpful.

Treatment

The main treatment for children with intellectual disability is educational. There is a range of intellectual disability with symptoms that can be mild, moderate, or severe in degree. Adults with mild intellectual disability may have the academic skills for competitive community employment. With increasing functional impairment, there is increasing likelihood of the need for adult supports for daily needs and employment support.

In the past, people with ID lived in large residential facilities. The goal is now for adults with ID to live with their families, in their communities, or in small supported living units with meaningful work options. For more information, visit The Arc website at www.thearc.org.

Prevention

While an increasing number of genetic causes for ID can be identified, early screening can only prevent symptoms due to metabolic disorders such as phenylketonuria (PKU) and hypothyroidism. If these conditions are detected soon after birth through standard screening tests performed in the hospital nursery, they can be treated. Another condition that can cause intellectual disability if not detected early in life is hydrocephalus (excess fluid causing increased pressure in the brain; see page 649). This condition usually is treated by draining the fluid to another part of the body to release the pressure and thereby prevent brain damage.

In many cases of intellectual disability, there is not an identifiable cause. Consult your pediatrician, local advocacy organizations such as The Arc of the United States at www.thearc.org, and other reputable professionals to find out what programs (e.g., the Special Olympics) are available in your community. Professional assistance can be extremely helpful. In the long run, however, you are your child's most important advocate.

With your child's teachers and therapist you can set realistic objectives for him, and encourage him to reach them. Assist him if necessary, but let him do as much as possible on his own. You and your child will feel most rewarded when he reaches a goal by himself.

~ 22 ~

Ears, Nose, and Throat

Colds/Upper Respiratory Infection

YOUR CHILD PROBABLY will have more colds, or upper respiratory infections, than any other illness. In the first two years of life alone, most children have eight to ten colds. And if your child is in child care, or if there are older school-age children in your house, she may have even more, since colds spread easily among children who are in close contact with one another. That's the bad news, but there is some good news, too: Most colds go away by themselves and do not lead to anything worse.

Colds are caused by viruses, which are extremely small infectious organisms (much smaller than bacteria). A sneeze or a cough may directly transfer a virus from one person to another. The virus also may be spread indirectly, in the following manner.

1. A child or adult infected with the virus will, in coughing, sneezing, or touching her nose, transfer some of the virus particles onto her hand.

2. She then touches the hand of a healthy person.

3. This healthy person touches her newly contaminated hand to her own nose, introducing the infectious agent to a place where it can multiply and grow—the nose or throat. Symptoms of a cold soon develop.

4. The cycle then repeats itself, with the virus being transferred from this newly infected child or adult to the next susceptible one, and so on.

Once the virus is present and multiplying, your child will develop the familiar symptoms and signs:

■ Runny nose (first, a clear discharge; later, a thicker, often colored one)

■ Sneezing

■ Mild fever (101–102 degrees Fahrenheit [38.3–38.9 degrees Celsius]), particularly in the evening

■ Decreased appetite

■ Sore throat and, perhaps, difficulty swallowing

■ Cough

■ On-and-off irritability

■ Slightly swollen glands in the neck

If your child has a typical cold without complications, the symptoms should disappear gradually after seven to ten days.

Treatment

An older child with a cold usually doesn't need to see a doctor unless the condition becomes more serious. If she is three months or younger, however, call the pediatrician at the first sign of illness. With a young baby, symptoms can be misleading, and colds can quickly develop into more serious ailments, such as bronchiolitis (see page 595), croup (see page 600), or pneumonia (see page 605). For a child older than three months, call the pediatrician if:

■ The nostrils are widening with each breath, there is drawing in of the skin between and around the ribs and breastbone, or your child is breathing rapidly or having any difficulty breathing.

■ The lips or nails turn blue.

■ Nasal mucus persists for longer than ten to fourteen days.

■ The cough just won't go away (it lasts more than one week).

■ She has pain in her ear (see *Middle Ear Infections*, page 662) or persistent fussiness or crying.

■ Her temperature is over 102 degrees Fahrenheit (38.9 degrees Celsius).

■ She is excessively sleepy or cranky.

Your pediatrician may want to see your child, or he may ask you to watch her closely and report back if she doesn't improve each day and is not completely recovered within one week from the start of her illness.

Unfortunately, there's no cure for the common cold. Antibiotics may be used to combat *bacterial* infections, but they have no effect on viruses (and may have adverse effects if used on viruses), so the best you can do is to make your child comfortable. Make sure she gets extra rest and drinks a lot of fluids. If she has a fever or is uncomfortable, give her single-ingredient acetaminophen or ibuprofen. Ibuprofen is approved for children six months of age and older; however, it should never be given to children who are dehydrated or who are vomiting repeatedly. (Be sure to follow the recommended dosage for your child's age and the time interval for repeated doses.)

It's important to note, though, that the American Academy of Pediatrics' position is that over-the-counter cough medicines are not effective for children younger than six years old. Several studies show that cold and cough products don't work in children younger than six years of age and can have potentially serious side effects. In addition, keep in mind that coughing clears mucus from the lower part of the respiratory tract, and ordinarily there's no reason to suppress it.

If your infant is having trouble breathing or drinking because of nasal congestion, clear her nose with saline (salt water) nose drops or spray, which are available without a prescription. This can then be followed by suction with a rubber suction bulb every few hours or before each feeding or before bed. For the nose drops, use a dropper that has been cleaned with soap and water and rinsed well with plain water. Place two drops in each nostril fifteen to twenty minutes before feeding, and then immediately suction with the bulb. *Never use nose drops that contain any medication, since excessive amounts can be absorbed. Only use normal saline nose drops.*

When using the suction bulb, remember to *squeeze the bulb part of the syringe first, gently stick the rubber tip into one nostril, and then slowly release the bulb.* This slight amount of suction will draw the clogged mucus out of the nose and should allow her to breathe and suck at the same time once again. You'll find that this technique works best when your baby is under six months of age. As she gets older, she'll fight the bulb, making it difficult to suction the mucus, but the saline drops will still be effective.

Placing a cool-mist humidifier or vaporizer in your child's room also will help keep nasal secretions more liquid and make her more comfortable. Set it close to her (but safely beyond her reach) so that she gets the full benefit of the additional moisture. Be sure to clean and dry the humidifier thoroughly each day as recommended in the manufacturer's manual to prevent bacterial or mold contamination. *Hot-water vaporizers are not recommended since they can cause serious scalds or burns.*

Prevention

If your baby is under three months old, the best prevention against colds is to keep her away from people who have them. This is especially true during the winter, when many of the viruses that cause colds are circulating in larger numbers. A virus that causes a mild illness in an older child or an adult can cause a more serious one in an infant.

If your child is in child care and has a cold, teach her to cough and sneeze away from others, and to use a tissue to cough into and wipe her nose. Doing this may prevent her from spreading the cold to others. Similarly, if your child would be in contact with children who have colds and it is convenient for you to keep her away from them, by all means do so. Also teach her to wash her hands regularly during the day; this will cut down on the spread of viruses.

Teach your child to sneeze or cough into the crook of her elbow or shoulder. Even using a tissue or a handkerchief is better than having your child cover her mouth with her hand when sneezing and coughing. If the virus lands on her hand, it can be transmitted to whatever she touches—a sibling, a friend, or a toy.

Middle Ear Infections

During your child's first few years of life, there's a good chance that he'll get a middle ear infection. At least 70 percent of the time, middle ear infections occur after colds that have weakened the body's ability to prevent bacteria from entering the middle ear. Doctors refer to this middle ear infection as acute otitis media.

Middle ear infections are one of the most prevalent treatable childhood illnesses, occurring most often in children between six months and three years of age. Two-thirds of all children have at least one ear infection by their second birthday. It's a particularly common problem among young children because they are more susceptible to colds and because of the length and shape of their tiny Eustachian tubes, which normally ventilate the middle ear.

Children under one year of age who spend time in child care programs tend to get more middle ear infections than those cared for at home, primarily because they are exposed to more viruses. Also, infants who self-feed from a bottle when lying on their backs are susceptible to ear infections since this may allow small amounts of formula to enter the Eustachian tube. Two things may explain the fact that, as your child enters school, his likelihood of getting a middle ear infection will decrease: The growth of his middle ear structures reduces the likelihood of fluid blockage, and the body's defenses against infection improve with age.

Other characteristics may place children at a higher risk of middle ear infections:

Gender. Although researchers are not sure why, boys have more middle ear infections than girls.

Heredity. Ear infections can run in families. Children are more likely to have repeated middle ear infections if a parent or a sibling also had numerous ear infections.

Secondhand smoke. Children who breathe in secondhand tobacco smoke

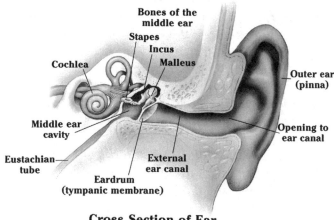

Bones of the
middle ear

Stapes

Incus

Malleus

Cochlea

Outer ear
(pinna)

Middle ear
cavity

Opening to
ear canal

Eustachian
tube

External
ear canal

Eardrum
(tympanic membrane)

Cross Section of Ear

have a markedly increased risk of ear infections as well as respiratory infections, bronchitis, pneumonia, and asthma.

There are certain things you can do to protect your infant from ear infections, such as breastfeeding, not smoking, making sure he is up-to-date on her vaccines, and practicing good hygiene and proper nutrition to prevent illness.

Signs and Symptoms

Middle ear infections are usually, but not always, painful. A child old enough to talk will tell you that his ear hurts; a younger child may pull at his ear and cry. Babies with ear infections may cry even more during feedings, because sucking and swallowing cause painful pressure changes in the middle ear. A baby with an ear infection may have trouble sleeping. Fever is another warning signal; ear infections sometimes (one out of three) are

accompanied by elevated temperatures ranging from 100.4 to 104 degrees Fahrenheit (38–40 degrees Celsius). In addition, children may appear off balance or clumsier because the fluid or infection in the middle ear may affect their sense of balance (vestibular system).

You might see blood-tinged yellow fluid or pus draining from the infected ear. This kind of discharge means that the eardrum has developed a small hole (called a perforation). This hole usually heals by itself without complications, but you will want to describe the discharge to your pediatrician.

You also may notice that your child may not hear well. This occurs because the fluid behind the eardrum interferes with sound transmission. But the hearing loss is usually temporary; normal hearing will be restored once the middle ear is free of fluid. Occasionally, when ear infections recur, fluid may remain behind the eardrum for many weeks and continue to interfere with hearing. If you feel your child's hearing is not as good as it was, including before his ear became infected, consult your pediatrician. If you remain concerned, request a consultation with an ear, nose, and throat doctor (ENT; otolaryngologist). After several months of watchful waiting, your pediatrician may recommend a hearing test or referral to a hearing specialist (audiologist) if your child has had middle ear fluid in both ears for more than three months, or in one ear for more than six months.

Middle ear infections are most common during the cold and flu season of winter and early spring. When your child complains of moderate or severe pain in his ear during the summer, especially when you touch or pull on the ear, he could be suffering from an infection of the *outer* ear canal, called swimmer's ear. Swimmer's ear is essentially an infection of the skin lining the inside of the outer ear canal. Although this may temporarily affect hearing, it poses no long-term hearing loss. Swimmer's ear can be extremely painful and should be treated. (See *Swimmer's Ear,* page 677.)

Treatment

Whenever you suspect an ear infection, call your pediatrician. In the meantime, follow these steps to make your child more comfortable.

■ **If he has** a high fever, cool him using the procedures described in Chapter 27.

■ **Give acetaminophen or** ibuprofen in the dose appropriate for his age. (Don't give aspirin to your child; it has been associated with Reye syndrome, a disease that affects the liver and brain. See page 549 for more information about Reye syndrome.)

■ **Your pediatrician might** suggest placing warm (not hot) compresses or a heating pad on your child's ear to help relieve pain. (This is not recommended for young babies.) Putting a pain-relieving drop into the ear canal may help reduce pain, but ask your pediatrician whether these should be used. The pediatrician will look into your child's ears with a lighted magnifying instrument called an otoscope to determine whether there is fluid in the middle ear space behind the eardrum. The doctor may attach a piece of rubber tubing to the otoscope and press on a rubber bulb to gently blow air into the ear to check for sensitivity and eardrum movement. Your doctor may also use a special instrument such as a tympanometer to determine whether there is fluid in the middle ear. He may also perform a test called acoustic reflectometry to detect fluid in the middle ear.

If there's a fever, the doctor will examine your child to determine whether there are any other problems. To treat middle ear infections, the doctor will recommend steps to ease pain and may prescribe an antibiotic.

Antibiotic Overuse

Antibiotics are an important treatment in managing bacterial infections such as severe ear infections and strep throat. But infections caused by viruses will not improve with antibiotics. That is why the common cold, certain types of mild ear infections, and the vast majority of sore throats do not require an antibiotic. When an antibiotic is prescribed, the goal is to make sure the antibiotic is specific for the type of bacteria causing the infection, and it is given for the right length of time.

If antibiotics are used when they are not needed—or if patients do not take a complete course of the drug—new strains of bacteria may develop. When that happens, antibiotics eventually may stop working and the infections they're designed to treat will no longer be curable by the use of these medications, because the bacteria have become "resistant" to them. In addition, antibiotics can produce side effects including allergic reactions or a potentially serious form of antibiotic-associated diarrhea.

Here are three important points to keep in mind if your child has an infection, to make sure your child gets the right kind of antibiotic and only when it's necessary.

- Ask your pediatrician if the infection causing your child's illness is caused by a bacterium. Antibiotics work only against bacterial illnesses, not those caused by viruses. So while they may be appropriate for treating ear infections, you should not ask your pediatrician for a prescription for antibiotics to treat your child's colds and flu (as well as many sore throats and coughs), which are viral infections.

- If an antibiotic is not necessary because your child has a viral infection, ask what other measures are recommended to help with your child's symptoms. For children with mild ear infections, your child's doctor may recommend medicine to treat ear pain.

- If your child's doctor prescribes an antibiotic for an ear infection or other bacterial infection, ask how to follow up if your child's condition worsens or has not improved in forty-eight to seventy-two hours. Make sure that your child takes the prescribed antibiotic exactly as your doctor instructs. That means taking all of the medicine that was prescribed, even if your child seems well before he has finished the entire course. And don't give your child antibiotics that have been prescribed for another family member or for another illness. If your child develops an itchy rash, hives, or watery diarrhea while taking antibiotics, notify your child's doctor.

Eardrops sometimes are used to relieve pain. For swimmer's ear or a middle ear infection with perforation, antibiotic ear drops may be prescribed as well. Unless your child's ear infections are associated with allergies, antihistamines and decongestants probably won't help.

An antibiotic is one of the treatment options for ear infections. If recommended, your doctor will specify the schedule for giving it to your child; it may include dosing once, twice, or three times a day. Follow the schedule precisely. As the infection begins to clear, some children experience a sense of fullness or popping in the ears; these are normal signs of recovery. There should be clear signs of improvement and disappearance of ear pain and fever within two days.

When your child starts feeling better, you may be tempted to discontinue the medication—but don't. Some of the bacteria that caused the infection still may be present. Stopping the treatment too soon may allow them to multiply again and permit the infection to return with full force. Your pediatrician may want to see your child after the medication is finished, to check if any fluid is still present behind the eardrum, which can occur even if the infection has been controlled. This condition (fluid in middle ear), known as otitis media with effusion, is extremely common: 5 out of every 10 children still have some fluid three weeks after an ear infection is treated. In 9 out of 10 cases, the fluid will disappear within three months without additional treatment.

Also, this fluid accumulation may be caused by something other than an ear infection, such as swollen adenoid tissue in the upper throat that interferes with drainage; for that reason, seeing a doctor is especially important to determine the cause of and best care for the problem.

Occasionally an ear infection won't respond to the first antibiotic prescribed. If your child continues to complain of significant ear pain and still has a high fever for more than two days after starting an antibiotic, call the pediatrician. To determine if the antibiotic is working, your doctor may refer you to an ENT specialist in order to take a sample of the fluid from the ear by inserting a needle through the eardrum. If the analysis of this sample reveals that the infection is caused by bacteria resistant to the antibiotic your child has been taking, your pediatrician will prescribe a different one. In very rare instances, an ear infection may linger even though other drugs are used. In these cases, a child may be hospitalized so that antibiotics can be given intravenously and the ear can be drained surgically.

Should a child with an ear infection be kept home? It won't be necessary if he's feeling well, as long as someone at child care or school can administer his medication properly. Talk with the staff nurse or your child's caregiver, and review the dosage and the times when it should be given. You also should check to be sure that storage facilities are available if the medication must be refrigerated. Medicine that doesn't require refrigeration should be kept in a locked cabinet separate from other items, and its container should be clearly identified with your child's name and the proper dosage.

If your child's eardrum has ruptured, he'll be able to engage in most activities, although he may not be permitted to swim until the ear is dry and healed. Ordinarily, there's no reason to prevent him from flying in an airplane, although he may have some discomfort from the pressure change.

Prevention

Occasional ear infections cannot be prevented. In some children, ear infections may be related to seasonal allergies, which also can cause congestion and block the natural drainage of fluid from the ear to the throat. If your child seems to get ear infections more frequently when his allergies flare up, mention this to your pediatrician, who may suggest additional testing or prescribe antihistamines.

If your baby is being bottle-fed, hold his head above the stomach level during feedings. Doing this keeps the Eustachian tubes from becoming blocked. You and others also should not smoke around your baby. Again, children exposed to secondhand tobacco smoke have more respiratory infections, bronchitis, pneumonia, poor lung function, and asthma than children who aren't exposed. In addition, careful hand-washing can also help protect your baby from illness and subsequent ear infections. Breastfeeding is also associated with fewer ear infections in children.

And what about children who recover from one ear infection only to get another shortly thereafter? If your child continues to have ear infections, and continues to have hearing loss, he probably will be referred to an ear, nose, and throat (ENT; otolaryngologist) specialist, who may recommend that tiny ventilation tubes (sometimes called tympanostomy tubes) be inserted in the eardrum under anesthesia. While the tubes are in place, they usually restore hearing to normal, and also prevent fluid and harmful bacteria from becoming trapped in the middle ear, where they can cause another infection.

Use of tubes has become standard care for the following specific indications: (1) persistent fluid in both middle ears for more than three months with hearing loss; (2) persistent fluid in one middle ear longer than six months; or (3) recurrent ear infections with significant symptoms occurring more than three times in six months or more than four to five times in twelve months. If the placement of

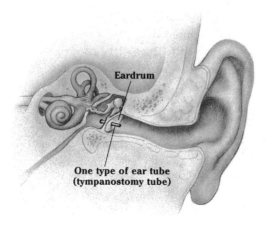

Eardrum

One type of ear tube (tympanostomy tube)

ventilation tubes is proposed for your child, discuss his specific problem with your child's specialist and pediatrician so you fully understand the advantages and disadvantages.

Keep in mind that although ear infections are bothersome and uncomfortable, they are usually minor and clear up without causing any lasting problems. Most children stop getting ear infections by the time they are four to six years old.

Sinusitis

Sinusitis is an inflammation of one or more of the sinuses (bony cavities) around the nose. It usually occurs as a complication of a cold or allergic inflammation in children over two years of age. These conditions cause swelling of the lining of the nose and sinuses. This swelling blocks the openings that normally allow the sinuses to drain into the back of the nose, so the sinuses fill with fluid. Although nose blowing and sniffing may be natural responses to this blockage,

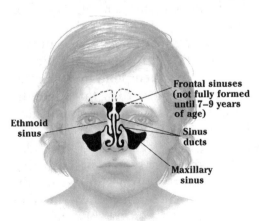

Frontal sinuses (not fully formed until 7–9 years of age)

Ethmoid sinus

Sinus ducts

Maxillary sinus

they can make the situation worse by pushing bacteria from the back of the nose into the sinuses. Since the sinuses can't drain properly, the bacteria will multiply there, causing an infection.

Several signs of sinusitis should alert you to call your pediatrician:

■ **Persistent cold or** upper respiratory infection symptoms, including cough and nasal discharge lasting for more than seven to ten days, without any improvement. The nasal discharge may be thick and yellow, or clear, or whitish, and the cough usually will continue during the day as well as at night. In some cases a child with sinusitis will have swelling around the eyes when he wakes up in the morning. Also, a preschooler with sinusitis sometimes may have persistent bad breath along with cold symptoms. (However, this also could mean that he has put something into his nose or has a sore throat, or that he isn't brushing his teeth.)

■ **Your child's cold** is severe and is accompanied by high fever and thick yellow nasal discharge. His eyes might be swollen in the early morning, and he might have a severe headache that he describes (if he's old enough) as behind or above the eyes.

In very rare cases, a sinus infection may spread to either the eye or the central nervous system (the brain). If this occurs, you'll see swelling around the eye not just in the morning but all through the day, and you should call your pediatrician immediately. If your child has a very severe headache, becomes sensitive to light, or is increasingly irritable, the infection may have spread into the central nervous system. This is serious and requires immediate medical attention.

Treatment

If your pediatrician thinks your child has sinusitis, she may prescribe an antibiotic, usually for a fourteen- to twenty-one-day period. Once your child is on the medication, his symptoms should start to go away very quickly. In most cases the nasal discharge will clear and the cough will improve over a week or two. *But even though he may seem better, he must continue to take the antibiotics for the prescribed length of time.*

If there's no improvement after two to four days, your pediatrician might want to conduct some further tests, after which a different medication may be prescribed or an additional one added for a longer period of time.

Epiglottitis

The epiglottis is a tonguelike flap of tissue at the back of the throat that may become infected, usually by bacteria called *Haemophilus influenzae* type B. Fortunately, this infection (epiglottitis) is now *un*common thanks to the Hib vaccine, which prevents infections due to *Haemophilus influenzae* type B.

Epiglotittis, which can be life-

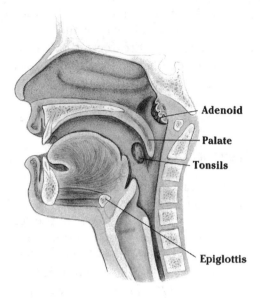

threatening when it occurs, begins with a sore throat and a fever that usually is greater than 101 degrees Fahrenheit (38.3 degrees Celsius) and quickly makes your child feel very sick. Her throat will become extremely sore. With each breath, she may make a harsh or raspy noise, called stridor. She may have such difficulty swallowing that she begins to drool.

If your child has an unusually sore throat and is drooling and/or breathing with difficulty, call your physician immediately or go to the emergency room. Because epiglottitis progresses so rapidly and has such serious consequences, do not attempt to treat it at home. After contacting your pediatrician, try to keep your child calm. Don't try to examine her throat or insist that she lie down. Also, avoid offering food or water, because that might cause vomiting, which often makes breathing even more difficult.

It's important to remember that epiglottitis progresses very rapidly and can become life-threatening if it goes untreated. If the doctor determines that your child has epiglottitis, she will be urgently admitted to the hospital for treatment including antibiotics.

Prevention

The Hib vaccine is available to combat the bacteria that cause epiglottitis. Your child should receive the full series of the Hib vaccine, according to your pediatrician's recommendations. (See *Recommended Immunization Schedule* on page 876.) However, even if she has had the vaccine, consult your doctor if you know there has been an exposure to another child who has the infection. Your physician might want to take added precautions.

Herpes Simplex

Oral herpes is a common viral disease of childhood. This condition produces sores ("cold sores"), blisters ("fever blisters"), and swelling of the inside of the mouth and lips. (When most people hear the word *herpes,* they associate it with genital herpes, the sexually transmitted disease; however, a different strain of this virus usually causes cold sores in children.) Oral herpes is highly contagious, and is spread by direct contact, frequently by kissing. Most infants are protected by their mothers' antibodies up to about age six months, but they become susceptible after that.

When the virus is transmitted to a child for the first time, she is said to have primary herpes. This may cause pain, swelling and reddening of the gums, and an increase in saliva, followed a day or two later by blisters inside the mouth. When the blisters break, they leave sore areas that take several days to heal. The child also may develop a fever and headache, act irritably, lose her appetite, and have swollen lymph glands for a week or so. Many children, however, have such mild symptoms that no one realizes they have the virus.

Once a child has had primary herpes, she becomes a carrier of the virus. This means that the virus, usually in an inactive state, remains within her system. However, during episodes of stress (including other infections), injury to the mouth, sunburn, allergies, and fatigue, the virus can become reactivated, producing what's called recurrent herpes. This condition is milder than the primary infection, and usually doesn't occur until later in childhood or adulthood. Cold sores and fever blisters are the symptoms of recurrent herpes.

Treatment

If your child complains of symptoms resembling those of herpes, consult your pediatrician. Primary herpes is not a serious illness, but it can make your child uncomfortable. The treatment, which should be aimed at reducing this discomfort, includes:

- **Bed rest and** sleep

- **Plenty of cold** fluids, including non-acidic drinks like apple or apricot juice

- **Acetaminophen, if there's** fever or excessive discomfort

- **Mouth rinse or** gargles prescribed by your pediatrician. These medications may contain a painkiller that will numb the areas affected by the mouth sores. Carefully follow the directions for these preparations.

- **A soft, bland,** but nutritious diet

- **Antiviral medication (such** as acyclovir or a similar type of drug) that may be prescribed by your pediatrician. This will stop the virus from multiplying, but will not prevent reactivation after the medication is stopped.

Occasionally a child infected with primary herpes refuses to drink fluids because of the associated mouth pain. In some cases, such a child must be hospitalized if she is showing signs of dehydration.

Never use any creams or ointments containing steroids (cortisone) if there is the slightest suspicion that the mouth sores are due to herpes. These preparations can make the viral infection spread.

Prevention

Direct contact is required to spread the herpes virus, so you should not let anyone with herpes blisters or sores kiss your child. People with a history of oral herpes often shed the virus in their saliva even when they have no sores. In general, to prevent spread of germs, discourage individuals from kissing your baby or child directly on the lips.

Also, try to discourage your child from sharing eating utensils with other children. (This is more easily said than done.) If your child has primary herpes, keep her home to prevent other children from getting this infection from her.

Nosebleeds

Your child is almost certain to have at least one nosebleed—and probably many—during these early years. Some preschoolers have several a week. This is neither abnormal nor dangerous, but it can be very frightening. If blood flows down from the back of the nose into the mouth and throat, your child may swallow a great deal of it, which in turn may cause vomiting.

There are many causes of nosebleeds, most of which aren't serious. Beginning with the most common, they include:

- **Colds and allergies:** A cold or allergy causes swelling and irritation inside the nose and may lead to spontaneous bleeding.

- **Trauma: A child** can get a nosebleed from picking his nose, or putting something into it, or just blowing it too hard. A nosebleed also can occur if he is hit in the nose by a ball or other object or if he falls and hits his nose.

- **Low humidity or** irritating fumes: If your house is very dry, or if you live in an arid climate, the lining of your child's nose may dry out, making it more likely to bleed. If he is frequently exposed to toxic fumes (fortunately, an unusual occurrence), they may cause nosebleeds, too.

- **Anatomical problems: Any** abnormal structure inside the nose can lead to crusting and bleeding.

- **Abnormal growths: Any** abnormal tissue growing in the nose may cause bleeding. Although most of these growths (usually polyps) are benign (not cancerous), they still should be treated promptly.

- **Abnormal blood clotting:** Anything that interferes with blood clotting can lead to nosebleeds. Medications, even common ones like aspirin, can alter the blood-clotting mechanism just enough to cause bleeding. Blood diseases, such as hemophilia, also can provoke nosebleeds.

- **Chronic illness: Any** child with a long-term illness, or who may require extra oxygen or other medication that can dry out or affect the lining of the nose, is likely to have nosebleeds.

Treatment of Nosebleeds

There are many misconceptions and folktales about how to treat nosebleeds. Here's a list of dos and don'ts.

DO . . .

1. Remain calm. A nosebleed can be frightening, but is rarely serious.

2. Keep your child in a sitting or standing position. Tilt his head slightly forward. Have him gently blow his nose if he is old enough.

3. Pinch the lower half of your child's nose (the soft part) between your thumb and finger and hold it firmly for a full ten minutes. If your child is old enough, he can do this himself. *Don't release the nose during this time to see if it is still bleeding* (no peeking!). Stopping the pressure may interfere with the forming of the clot and allow the bleeding to continue.

Release the pressure after ten minutes and wait, keeping your child quiet. If the bleeding hasn't stopped, repeat this step. If after ten more minutes of pressure the bleeding hasn't stopped, call your pediatrician or go to the nearest emergency department.

DON'T . . .

1. Panic. You'll scare your child.

2. Have him lie down or tilt back his head.

3. Stuff tissues, gauze, or any other material into your child's nose to stop the bleeding.

Also, call your pediatrician if:

- **You think your** child may have lost too much blood. (But keep in mind that the blood coming from the nose always looks like a lot.)

- **The bleeding is** coming only from your child's mouth, or he's coughing or vomiting blood or brown material that looks like coffee grounds.

- **Your child is** unusually pale or sweaty, or is not responsive. *Call your pediatrician immediately in this case, and arrange to take your child to the emergency department.*

- **He has a** lot of nosebleeds, along with a chronically stuffy nose. This may mean he has a small, easily broken blood vessel in the nose or on the surface of the lining of the nose, or a growth in the nasal passages.

If a blood vessel is causing the problem, the doctor may touch that point with a chemical substance (silver nitrate) to stop the bleeding.

Prevention

If your child gets a lot of nosebleeds, ask your pediatrician about using saltwater (saline) nose drops every day and/or putting a small amount of petroleum jelly in each nostril at night. Doing so may be particularly helpful if you live in a very dry climate, or when the furnace is on. In addition, a humidifier or vaporizer will help maintain your home's humidity at a level high enough to prevent nasal drying. Also tell your child not to pick his nose.

Sore Throat (Strep Throat, Tonsillitis)

The terms *sore throat, strep throat,* and *tonsillitis* often are used interchangeably, but they don't mean the same thing. Tonsillitis refers to tonsils that are inflamed. (See *Tonsils and Adenoid,* page 675.) Strep throat is an infection caused by a specific type of bacteria, *Streptococcus.* When your child has a strep throat, the tonsils are usually very inflamed, and the inflammation may affect the surrounding part of the throat as well. Other causes of sore throats are viruses and may cause inflammation only of the throat around the tonsils and not the tonsils themselves.

In infants, toddlers, and preschoolers, the most frequent cause of sore throats is a viral infection. No specific medicine is required when a virus is responsible, and the child should get better over a seven- to ten-day period. Often children who have sore throats due to viruses also have a cold at the same time. They may develop a mild fever, too, but they generally aren't very sick.

One particular virus (called Coxsackie), seen most often during the summer and fall, may cause the child to have a somewhat higher fever, more difficulty swallowing, and a sicker overall feeling. If your child has a Coxsackie infection, she also may have one or more blisters in her throat and on her hands and feet (often called hand, foot, and mouth disease). Infectious mononucleosis can produce a sore throat, often with marked tonsillitis; however, most young children who are infected with the mononucleosis virus have few or no symptoms.

Strep throat is caused by a bacterium called *Streptococcus pyogenes*. To some extent, the symptoms of strep throat depend on the child's age. Infants with strep infections may have only a low fever and a thickened or bloody nasal discharge. Toddlers (ages one to three) also may have a thickened or bloody nasal discharge with a fever. Such children are usually quite cranky, have no appetite, and often have swollen glands in the neck. Sometimes toddlers will complain of tummy pain and/or experience vomiting instead of a sore throat. Children over three years of age with strep are often more ill; they may have an extremely painful throat, fever over 102 degrees Fahrenheit (38.9 degrees Celsius), swollen glands in the neck, and pus on the tonsils. It's important to be able to distinguish a strep throat from a viral sore throat, because strep infections are treated with antibiotics.

Diagnosis and Treatment

If your child has a sore throat that persists (not one that goes away after her first drink in the morning), whether or not it is accompanied by fever, headache, stomachache, or extreme fatigue, you should call your pediatrician. That call should be made even more urgently if your child seems extremely ill, or if she has difficulty breathing or extreme trouble swallowing (causing her to drool). This may indicate a more serious infection (see *Epiglottitis,* page 669).

Most pediatric offices perform rapid strep tests that provide findings within minutes. If the rapid strep test is negative, your doctor may confirm the result with a culture. A negative test means that the infection is presumed to be due to a virus. In that case, antibiotics (which are antibacterial) will not help and need not be prescribed.

The doctor will examine your child and may perform a rapid strep test or a throat culture to determine the nature of the infection. To do this, he will touch the back of the throat and tonsils with a cotton-tipped applicator and then smear the tip onto a special culture dish that allows strep bacteria to grow if they are present. The culture dish usually is examined twenty-four hours later for the presence of the bacteria.

If the test shows that your child does have strep throat, your pediatrician will prescribe an antibiotic to be taken by mouth or by injection. If your child is given the oral medication, it's very important that she take it for the full course, as prescribed, even if the symptoms get better or go away.

If a child's strep throat is not treated with antibiotics, or if she doesn't complete the treatment, the infection may worsen or spread to other parts of her body, leading to conditions such as abscesses of the tonsils or kidney problems. Untreated strep infections also can lead to rheumatic fever, a disease that affects the heart. However, rheumatic fever is rare in the US and in children under five years old.

Prevention

Most types of throat infections are contagious, being passed primarily through the air on droplets of moisture or on the hands of infected children or adults. For that reason, it makes sense to keep your child away from people who have symptoms of this condition. However, most people are contagious before their first symptoms appear, so often there's really no practical way to prevent your child from contracting the disease.

In the past when a child had several incidents of sore throat, her tonsils might have been removed in an attempt to prevent further infections. But this operation, called a tonsillectomy, is recommended today only for the most severely affected children. Even in difficult cases, where there is repeated strep throat, antibiotic treatment is usually the best solution.

(See also *Swollen Glands,* page 680.)

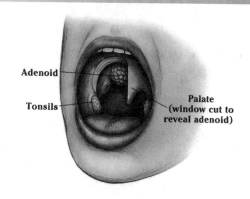

Adenoid

Tonsils

Palate
(window cut to
reveal adenoid)

Tonsils and Adenoid

If you look into your child's throat, you may see a pink, oval-shaped mass on each side. These are the tonsils. The tonsils are small in infants and increase in size over the early years of childhood. They produce antibodies during periods when the body is fighting infection.

Like the tonsils, the adenoid is part of your child's defense against infections. The adenoid is located in the very upper part of the throat, above the uvula and behind the nose. This area is called the nasopharynx. The adenoid can be seen only with special mirrors or instruments passed through the nose, or indirectly by X-ray.

A common illness associated with the tonsils is tonsillitis. This is an inflammation of the tonsils usually due to an infection. Sometimes, tonsils can be enlarged and not be infected. However, most of the time there is an infection that has caused them to be larger than normal. There are several signs of tonsillitis, including:

- Red and swollen tonsils

- White or yellow coating over the tonsils

- A "throaty" voice

- Sore throat

- Uncomfortable or painful swallowing

- Swollen lymph nodes ("glands") in the neck

- Fever

It is not always easy to tell when your child's adenoid is enlarged. Some children are born with a larger adenoid. Others may have temporary enlargement of their adenoid due to colds or other infections; this is especially common among young children. Also, chronic rhinitis (a persistent runny nose) is more frequently the cause of these symptoms, and can be treated with corticosteroid nasal sprays. But the constant swelling or enlargement of the adenoid can cause other health problems, such as ear and sinus infections. Some signs of adenoid enlargement are:

- Breathing through the mouth instead of the nose most of the time

- Nose sounds "blocked" when the child talks

- Noisy breathing during the day

- Snoring at night

Both the tonsils and the adenoid may be enlarged if your child has the above symptoms along with any of the following:

- Breathing stops for a short period of time at night during snoring or loud breathing; this condition, called sleep apnea, is uncommon, but not unheard of.

- Choking or gasping during sleep

- Difficulty swallowing, especially solid foods

- A constant "throaty voice," even when there is no tonsillitis

In severe cases, your child may have such difficulty breathing that it interferes with the normal exchange of oxygen and carbon dioxide in his lungs. This is important to recognize since it may interrupt your child's normal sleep pattern. If your child has severe breathing difficulties, seems drowsy during waking hours, and lacks energy despite what should have been adequate amounts of sleep, consult your pediatrician; when breathing problems are severe, call 911.

Treatment

If your child shows the signs and symptoms of enlarged tonsils or adenoid, and doesn't seem to be getting better over a period of weeks, mention it to your pediatrician.

SURGERY TO REMOVE TONSILS AND/ OR ADENOID (TONSILLECTOMY AND ADENOIDECTOMY)

Although these two operations (often combined and called T & A) were done almost routinely in the past and remain one of the most common major operations performed on children, not until recently has their long-term effectiveness been adequately tested. In light of current studies, today's physicians are much more conservative in recommending these procedures, even though some children still need to have their tonsils and/or adenoid taken out.

According to the guidelines of the American Academy of Pediatrics, your pediatrician may recommend surgery in the following circumstances:

- Tonsil or adenoid swelling makes normal breathing difficult (causing problems such as behavioral issues, bed-wetting, apneas, school performance problems, etc.).

- Tonsils are so swollen that your child has a problem swallowing.

- An enlarged adenoid makes breathing uncomfortable, severely alters speech, and possibly affects normal growth of the face. In this case, surgery to remove only the adenoid may be recommended.

- The child has an excessive number of severe sore throats each year.

If your child needs surgery, make sure he knows what will happen before, during, and after surgery. Don't keep the surgery a secret from your child. An operation can be scary, but it's better to be honest than to leave your child with fears and unanswered questions.

The hospital may have a special program to help you and your child get familiar with the hospital and the surgery. If the hospital allows, try to stay with your child during the entire hospital visit. Let your child know that you'll be nearby during the entire operation. Your pediatrician also can help you and your child understand the operation and make it less frightening.

Swimmer's Ear (External Otitis)

Swimmer's ear is an infection of the skin inside the ear canal (or outer ear) that occurs most often after swimming or other activities that allow water into the ears. Swimmer's ear develops because moisture in the ear canal encourages the growth of certain bacteria and, at the same time, causes the skin that lines the ear canal to soften (like the white, swollen area that forms under a wet bandage). The bacteria then invade the softened skin and multiply there, causing an often painful infection.

For reasons that are not clear, some children are more prone to it than others. Injury to the canal (cotton swab abuse), and conditions such as eczema (see page 560) and seborrheic dermati-

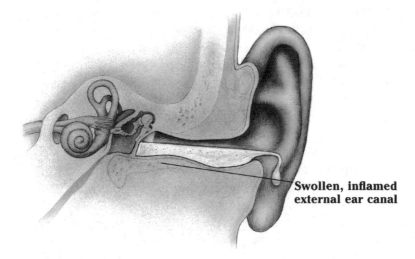

Swollen, inflamed external ear canal

tis (see page 836), can increase the likelihood of getting swimmer's ear.

With the mildest form of swimmer's ear, your child will complain only of itchiness or a plugged feeling in the ear, or—if he's too young to tell you what's bothering him—you might notice him sticking his finger in his ear or rubbing it with his hand. Within hours to days the opening of his ear canal may become swollen and slightly red, causing a dull pain. If you push on the opening or pull up on his ear, it may be painful.

In more severe cases of swimmer's ear, the pain will be constant and intense, and your child may cry and hold his hand over his ear. The slightest motion, even chewing, will hurt a lot. The ear canal opening may be swollen shut, with a few drops of pus or cheesy material oozing out, and there may be a low-grade fever (rarely more than one or two degrees above normal). In the most serious infections, the redness and swelling may spread beyond the ear canal to the entire outer ear.

Since swimmer's ear doesn't involve the middle ear or the hearing apparatus, any loss of hearing due to blockage of the canal is temporary.

Treatment

If your child has pain in his ear, or if you suspect swimmer's ear, call your pediatrician. Although the condition usually isn't serious, it still needs to be examined and treated by a doctor.

Until you see your pediatrician, you can help relieve your child's pain with acetaminophen, along with a heating pad (on a low setting) or a warm-water bottle placed around the ear. Keep him out of the water for several days, and see if the pain subsides. For severe pain in an older child, your pediatrician may prescribe a pain medication with codeine to be used temporarily while the infection is being treated.

Do *not* insert a cotton swab or anything else into the ear in an attempt to relieve itching or promote drainage; doing so will only cause further skin damage and provide additional sites for bacteria to grow. At the pediatrician's office, the doctor first will examine the affected ear and then, perhaps, carefully clean out pus and debris from the canal. In mild cases this may be the only treatment your child needs, although most doctors also prescribe eardrops for five to seven days. The eardrops combat infection and thereby decrease swelling, which helps to relieve the pain. In order to be effective, however, eardrops have to be used properly. Here's how to administer them:

1. Lay your child on his side with his affected ear up.

2. Put the drops in so that they run along the side of the ear canal, permitting air to escape as the medicine flows in. You can gently move the ear to help the drops along.

3. Keep your child lying on his side for two or three minutes to make sure that the drops reach the deepest part of the ear canal.

4. Use these drops as directed for the length of time prescribed. Rarely, oral antibiotics also are prescribed.

If the ear canal is too swollen for drops to enter, your pediatrician may insert a "wick"—a small piece of cotton or spongy material that soaks up the medicine and holds it in the canal. In this case, you'll need to resaturate the wick with the drops three or four times per day.

When your child is being treated for swimmer's ear, he should stay out of the water for about a week. However, he can take brief showers or baths daily and have his hair washed, as long as you dry the ear canal afterward with the corner of a towel or a blow-dryer (on a very low setting, held away from the ear). Once that's done, put in more eardrops.

Prevention

There's no need to try to prevent swimmer's ear unless your child has had this infection frequently or very recently. Under these circumstances, limit his stays in the water, usually to less than an hour. Then, when he comes out, remove the excess water from his ear with the corner of a towel, or have him shake his head.

As a preventive measure, many pediatricians recommend acetic acid eardrops. They are available in various preparations, some of which require a prescription. They usually are used in the morning, at the end of each swim, and at bedtime. A mixture of white vinegar and rubbing alcohol is a practical and effective home remedy. A few drops in each ear can be used after swimming. Earplugs or a bathing cap sometimes helps keep the ears dry and prevents this problem from occurring.

Resist the temptation to clean out your child's ear with cotton swabs, your finger, or any other object as doing so can cause trauma to the ear canal or eardrum.

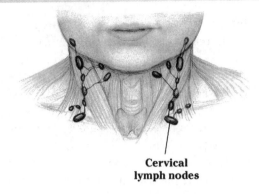

Cervical lymph nodes

Swollen Glands

Lymph glands (or lymph nodes) are an important part of the body's defense system against infection and illness. These glands normally contain groups of cells, called lymphocytes, which act as barriers to infection. The lymphocytes produce substances called antibodies that destroy or immobilize infecting cells or poisons. When lymph glands become enlarged or swollen, it usually means that the lymphocytes have increased in number due to an infection or other illness and that they are being called into action to produce extra antibodies. Rarely, swollen glands—particularly if long-lasting and without other signs of inflammation, such as redness or tenderness— may indicate a tumor.

If your child has swollen glands, you'll be able to feel them or actually see the swelling. They also may be tender to the touch. Sometimes, if you look near the gland, you can find the infection or injury that has caused it to swell. For example, a sore throat often will cause glands in the neck to swell, or an infection on the arm will produce swollen glands under the arm. Sometimes the illness may be a generalized one, such as those caused by a virus, in which case many glands might be slightly swollen. In general, because children have more viral infections than adults, lymph nodes, particularly in the neck, are more likely to be enlarged. Swollen glands at the base of the neck and just above the collarbone may be an infection or even a tumor within the chest, and should be examined by a physician as soon as possible.

Treatment

In the vast majority of cases, swollen glands are not serious. Young children almost always have a few small glands (less than 1 cm) in their neck that can be felt, but it is nothing to be concerned about. Lymph node swelling usually disappears after the illness that caused it is gone. The glands gradually return to normal over a period of weeks. You should call the pediatrician if your child shows any of the following:

- Lymph glands swollen and tender for more than five days

- Fever higher than 101 degrees Fahrenheit (38.3 degrees Celsius)

- Glands that appear to be swollen throughout the body

- Tiredness, lethargy, or loss of appetite

- Glands that enlarge rapidly, or the skin overlying them turning red or purple

As with any infection, if your child has a fever or is in pain, you can give her acetaminophen in the appropriate dosage for her weight and age until you can see the pediatrician. When you call, your doctor probably will ask you some questions to try to determine the cause of the swelling, so it will help if you do a little investigating beforehand. For instance, if the swollen glands are in the jaw or neck area, check if your child's teeth are tender or her gums are inflamed, and ask her if there is any soreness in her mouth or throat. Mention to your doctor any exposure your child has had to animals (especially cats) or wooded areas. Also check for any recent animal scratches, tick bites, or insect bites or stings that may have become infected.

The treatment for swollen glands will depend on the cause. If there's a specific bacterial infection in nearby skin or tissue, antibiotics will clear it, allowing the glands gradually to return to their normal size. If the gland itself has an infection, it may require not only antibiotics but also warm compresses to localize the infection or surgical drainage. If this is done, the material obtained from the wound will be cultured to determine the exact cause of the infection. Doing this will help the doctor choose the most appropriate antibiotic.

If your pediatrician cannot find the cause of the swelling, or if the swollen glands don't improve after antibiotic treatment, further tests will be needed. For example, infectious mononucleosis might be the problem if your child has a fever and a bad sore throat (but not strep), is very weak, and has swollen (but not red, hot, or tender) glands, although mononucleosis occurs more often in older children. Special tests can confirm this diagnosis. In cases where the cause of a swollen gland is unclear, the pediatrician also may want to do a tuberculosis skin test.

If the cause of prolonged swelling of lymph nodes cannot be found in any other way, it may be necessary to perform a biopsy (remove a piece of tissue from the gland) and examine it under a microscope. In rare cases this may reveal a tumor or fungus infection, which would require special treatment.

Prevention

The only swollen glands that are preventable are those that are caused by bacterial infections in the surrounding tissue. In cases of suspected infection, you can avoid involving the lymph nodes by properly cleaning all wounds (see *Cuts and Scrapes,* page 692) and receiving early antibiotic treatment.

~ 23 ~

Emergencies

THE INFORMATION and policies in this section, such as first-aid procedures for the choking child and cardiopulmonary resuscitation (CPR), are constantly changing. Ask your pediatrician or other qualified health professional for the latest information on these procedures.

It is rare for children to become seriously ill with no warning. Based on your child's symptoms, you should usually contact your child's pediatrician for advice. Timely treatment of symptoms can prevent an illness from getting worse or turning into an emergency.

At the same time, take steps *before* an emergency occurs to prepare for such an event if it should happen (see guidelines for emergency phone numbers on page 684). Also read the description of how to assemble a first-aid kit (page 695). For the CPR guidelines chart, please see page 889.

A true emergency is when you believe a severe injury or illness is threatening your child's life or may cause permanent harm. In these cases, a child needs emergency medical treatment immediately. Discuss with your child's pediatrician in advance what you should do in case of a true emergency.

Many true emergencies involve sudden injuries. These injuries are often caused by the following:

- Motor vehicle–related injuries (car crashes, pedestrian injuries), or other sudden impacts such as from bicycle-related injuries, falling TVs or furniture, or falls from heights such as a window.

Emergency Phone Numbers

Keep the following phone numbers and addresses handy by programming them into your cell phone and those of anyone who cares for your child. You can also post them on your refrigerator or near other phones and insert a copy in your wallet.

- Your cell phone number

- Your home phone and address

- A nearby relative's or trusted neighbor's or friend's phone

- Your child's pediatrician

- Emergency medical services (ambulance) (911 in most areas)

- Police (911 in most areas)

- Fire department (911 in most areas)

- Poison Help Line (1-800-222-1222)

- Hospital

- Dentist

It is important that everyone who cares for your child, including care providers or sitters, knows where to find emergency phone numbers. If you have 911 service in your area, make sure your older children and your sitter know to dial 911 in case of an emergency. Be certain that they know your home address and phone number, since an emergency operator will ask for or confirm this information. Always leave your cell phone number and the phone number and address where you can be located. You should also make sure your sitter knows any medications your child takes and any allergies he may have. Those caring for your child (including you and your spouse and family) also should take a CPR class.

Remember, for a medical emergency, always call 911 and/or your child's pediatrician. If your child is seriously ill or injured, it may be safer for your child to be transported by emergency medical services (an ambulance).

- Poisoning

- Burns or smoke inhalation

- Choking

- "Nonfatal drowning" (once referred to as "near drowning") in a swimming pool, bathtub, etc.

- Firearms or other weapons

- Electric shocks

Other true emergencies can result from either medical illnesses or injuries. Often you can tell that these emergencies are happening if you observe that your child has any of the following symptoms:

- Acting strangely or becoming more withdrawn and less alert

- Increasing difficulty with breathing

- Skin or lips that look blue or purple (or gray for darker-skinned children)

- A cut or burn that is large or deep

- Bleeding that does not stop

- Rhythmical jerking and loss of consciousness (a seizure)

- Unconsciousness

- Any change in level of consciousness, confusion, a bad headache, or vomiting several times *after a head injury*

- Very loose or knocked-out teeth, or other major mouth or facial injuries

- Increasing or severe persistent pain

- Decreasing responsiveness when you talk to your child

Call your child's pediatrician or the Poison Help Line (1-800-222-1222) at once if your child has swallowed a suspected poison or any medication you did not intend him to ingest, even if your child has no signs or symptoms. You should not make your child vomit by any means. Making your child vomit is not recom-mended as it can cause further injury to your child's body. Do not give him syrup of ipecac, make him gag, or give him salt water. If you have syrup of ipecac in your home, properly dispose of it and throw away the container.

Always call for help if you are concerned that your child's life may be in danger or your child is seriously hurt.

IN CASE OF A TRUE EMERGENCY

- Stay calm.

- If it is needed and you know how, start CPR (cardiopulmonary resus-citation). For information on CPR, see page 691.

- If you need immediate help, call 911. If you do not have 911 service in your area, call your local emer-gency ambulance service or county emergency medical service. Other-wise, call your child's pediatrician's office and state clearly that you have an emergency.

- If there is bleeding, apply continu-ous pressure to the site with a clean cloth.

- If your child is having a seizure, place her on a carpeted floor with her head turned to the side, and stay with her until help arrives.

After you arrive at the emergency room, make sure you tell the emer-gency staff the name of your child's pediatrician; he will work closely with the emergency department and can provide them with additional information about your child. Bring any medication your child is taking and her immunization record with you to the hospital. Also bring any suspected poisons or medications your child might have taken.

In the event of a crash, the driver or other adults in the car may be unconscious or otherwise unable to give first responders information about the child. Medical personnel may be delayed in providing needed care to your child if they cannot find you to give permission. To help ensure that your child can be identified and treated promptly, consider attaching a sticker to his seat with his name, date of birth, parents' names and phone numbers, and any other information you think might be important to emergency personnel (e.g., special health care needs or severe allergies). Place the sticker in a spot where first responders will be able to find it but where it is not easily visible from outside the car. Many police and fire departments, hospitals, and health departments keep a stock of preprinted stickers for this purpose, or you can make your own.

Bites

Animal Bites

You need to keep your child safe around animals, including family pets. Review the section *Safety Around Animals* on page 512.

Many parents assume that children are most likely to be bitten by strange or wild animals, but in fact most bites are inflicted by animals the child knows, including the family pet. Although the injury often is minor, biting does at times cause serious wounds, facial damage, and emotional problems.

As many as 1 percent of all visits to pediatric emergency centers during the summer months are for human or animal bite wounds. An estimated 4.7 million dog bites, 400,000 cat bites, 45,000 snake bites, and 250,000 human bites occur annually in the United States. About 6 of 10 of those bitten by dogs are children.

Treatment

If your child is bleeding from an animal bite, apply firm continuous pressure to the area for five minutes or until the bleeding stops. Then wash the wound gently with soap and water, and consult your pediatrician.

If the wound is very large, or if you cannot stop the bleeding, continue to apply pressure and call your pediatrician to find out where to take your child for treatment. If the wound is so large that the edges won't come together, it probably will need to be sutured (stitched). Although this will help reduce scarring, in an animal bite it increases the chance of infection, so your doctor may prescribe antibiotics.

Contact your pediatrician whenever your child receives an animal bite that breaks the skin, no matter how minor the injury appears. The doctor will need to check whether your child has been adequately immunized against tetanus (see *Immunization Schedule* on pages 876–877) or might require protection against rabies. Both of these diseases can be spread by animal bites.

Rabies is a viral infection that can be transmitted by an infected animal through bites or scratches. It causes a high fever, difficulty in swallowing, convulsions, and ultimately death. Fortunately, rabies in humans is rare today, with an average of two to three deaths each year in the US; the decline in recent years is due to the availability of animal control and vaccination programs, as well as effective human rabies vaccines and immunoglobulin treatments. Nevertheless, because the disease is so serious and the incidence has been increasing in animals, your pediatrician will carefully evaluate any bite for the risk of contracting this disease. Bites from wild animals—especially bats but also skunks, raccoons, coyotes, and foxes—are much more dangerous than those from tame, immunized (against rabies) dogs and cats. *If the animal has been killed, do not dispose of its body or brain.* The brain can be examined for rabies, so call your pediatrician immediately for advice on how to handle the situation.

If the risk of rabies is high as determined by your pediatrician, he immediately will give, or arrange to have given, injections of the rabies vaccine to prevent the disease. If the biting animal is a healthy dog or cat, he will recommend that it be observed for ten days, starting treatment for your child only if the animal shows signs of rabies. If the animal is a wild one, it usually is euthanized immediately so that its brain can be examined for signs of rabies infection.

As noted earlier, an animal bite, even when it doesn't cause rabies, can become infected. Notify your pediatrician immediately if you see any of the following signs of infection.

- Pus or drainage coming from the bite

- The area immediately around the bite becoming swollen and tender (It normally will be red for two or three days, but this in itself is not cause for alarm.)

- Red streaks that appear to spread out from the bite

- Swollen glands above the bite

(See also *Safety Around Animals,* page 512.)

Your pediatrician may recommend antibiotic therapy for a child who has:

- Moderate or severe bite wounds

- Puncture wounds, especially if the bone, tendon, or joint has been penetrated

- Facial bites

- Hand and foot bites

- Genital area bites

Children who have a weakened immune system or have no spleen often receive antibiotic treatment.

Your pediatrician may recommend a follow-up visit to inspect any wound for signs of infection within forty-eight hours.

Many children who have been bitten by dogs may also show signs of traumatic stress in the weeks and months after the incident. Long after the physical wound has healed, these children may continue to experience traumatic stress associated with the bite. They may feel fear, including anxiety about being bitten again, especially when they see or hear about another dog. They may withdraw, or cling to their parents. They may resist going outside to play, have trouble sleeping, have nightmares, and wet the bed.

To help the healing process, be attentive to what your child is saying and feeling. Give her extra attention, particularly when you sense that she needs it. Some children with traumatic stress may require treatment by a mental health professional.

Human Bites

Children often experience a human bite by a sibling or a playmate. If your child is bitten by another person, call your pediatrician immediately to de-scribe the severity of the injury. Doing this can be especially important if the biter's teeth pierced your child's skin or if the injury is large enough to require stitches.

Be sure to wash a serious bite carefully with cool water and soap before going to the pediatrician. Your pediatrician will check your child's tetanus and hepatitis B vaccine status and assess the risk for other infections. For a bite that barely breaks the skin, such as a cut or scrape, a good washing with soap and water, followed by bandaging and close follow-up, is all that is needed. (For more information on human biting, aggressive behavior, or biting in situations with AIDS, see Chapter 14, page 461; Chapter 20, page 630.)

Burns

Burns are divided into three categories, according to their severity. First-degree burns are the mildest and cause redness and perhaps slight swelling of the skin (like most sunburns). Second-degree burns cause blistering and considerable swelling. Third-degree burns may appear white or charred and cause serious injury, not just to the surface but also to the deeper skin layers.

There are many different causes of serious burns in children, including sunburn, hot water or other hot liquids, and those due to fire, electrical contact, or chemicals. All of these can cause permanent injury and scarring to the skin.

Treatment

Your *immediate* treatment of a burn should include the following.

1. As quickly as possible, soak the burn in cool water. Don't hesitate to run cool water over the burn long enough to cool the area and relieve the pain immediately after the injury. *Do not use ice on a burn. It may delay healing.* Also, do not rub a burn; it can increase blistering.

2. Cool any smoldering clothing immediately by soaking with water, then remove any clothing from the burned area unless it is stuck firmly to the skin. In that case, cut away as much clothing as possible.

3. If the injured area is not oozing, cover the burn with a sterile gauze pad or a clean, dry cloth.

4. If the burn is oozing, cover it lightly with sterile gauze if available and immediately seek medical attention. If sterile gauze is not available, cover burns with a clean sheet or towel.

5. Do not put butter, grease, or powder on a burn. All of these so-called home remedies actually can make the injury worse.

For anything more serious than a superficial burn, or if redness and pain continue for more than a few hours, consult a physician. *All* electrical burns and burns of the hands, mouth, or genitals should receive immediate medical attention. Chemicals that cause burns also may be absorbed through the skin and cause other symptoms. Call the Poison Help Line (1-800-222-1222) or your pediatrician after washing off all the chemicals. (For treatment of a chemical contact to a child's eye, see *Poison in the Eye,* page 707.)

If your physician thinks the burn is not too serious, he may show you how to clean and care for it at home using medicated ointments and dressings. Under the following circumstances, however, hospitalization may be necessary:

- If the burns are third degree

- If 10 percent or more of the body is burned

- If the burn involves the face, hands, feet, or genitals, or involves a moving joint

- If the child is very young or fussy, and therefore too difficult to treat at home

When treating a burn at home, watch for any increase in redness or swelling or the development of a bad odor or discharge. These can be signs of infection, which will require medical attention.

Prevention

Chapter 15, *Keeping Your Child Safe,* provides ways to safeguard your child against fire and scalding at home. For added protection, here are a few more suggestions.

- **Install smoke detectors** in hallways outside bedrooms, the kitchen, living room, and near the furnace, with at least one on every floor of the house. Test them every month to be sure they work. It is best to use alarms that have long-life batteries, but if these are not available, change batteries at least annually on a specific date that you'll remember (such as January 1 of each year). Consider investing in an alarm that allows you to record your own voice calling to your children by name; these new alarms may be more effective in rousing sleeping children than alarms with loud beeping tones.

- **Practice home fire** drills. Make sure every family member and others who care for your children in your home know how to leave any area of the home safely in case of a fire.

- **Have several working** fire extinguishers readily available and familiarize yourself with how to use them. Place fire extinguishers around the home where the risk of fire is greatest, such as in the kitchen, furnace room, and near the fireplace.

- **Teach your children** to crawl to the exits if there's smoke in the room. (They will avoid inhaling the smoke by staying below it.)

- **Purchase a safety** ladder if your home has a second story, and teach your children how to use it. If you live in a high-rise building, teach your children the locations of all exits and make sure they understand never to use the elevator in a fire. (It can become trapped between floors or open on a floor where the fire is burning.)

- **Agree on a** family meeting point outside the house or apartment so you can make certain everyone has gotten out of the burning area.

- **Teach your children** to stop, drop, and roll on the ground if their clothing catches fire.

- **Avoid smoking indoors.**

- **Do not leave** food cooking on the stove unattended.

- **Lock up flammable** liquids in the home. It is best to store them outside the home, out of children's reach, and away from heat or ignition sources.

- **Lower the temperature** of your water heater to below 120 degrees Fahrenheit (48.9 degrees Celsius) to prevent hot-water scalds and burns.

- **Don't plug appliances** or other electrical equipment into extension cords if they place too much "amperage" or load on the cord, thus creating a potentially unsafe situation.

- **Keep matches and** lighters away from children, locked and out of reach.

- **Avoid all fireworks,** even those meant for consumer use.

Cardiopulmonary Resuscitation (CPR) and Mouth-to-Mouth Resuscitation

CPR can save your child's life if his heart stops beating or he has stopped breathing for any reason such as drowning, poisoning, suffocation, smoke inhalation, or choking. Become familiar with the CPR instructions in the Appendix of this book. However, reading about CPR is not enough to teach you how to perform it. *The American Academy of Pediatrics strongly recommends that all parents and anyone who is responsible for the care of children should complete a course in basic CPR and treatment for choking.*

This training is especially vital if you own a swimming pool or live near water, such as a lake or community swimming pool or spa. Contact your local chapter of the American Heart Association or the American Red Cross to find out where and when certified courses are given in your community. Most of the classes teach basic first aid, CPR, and emergency prevention, along with what to do for a choking infant or child.

Choking

Choking occurs when a person inhales something other than air into the windpipe or when food or other objects block the windpipe. Among children, choking often is caused by liquid that "goes down the wrong way." The child will cough, wheeze, gasp, and gag until the windpipe is cleared, but this type of choking is usually not harmful.

Choking becomes life-threatening when a child swallows or inhales an object—often food—that blocks air flow to the lungs. This is an emergency that calls for immediate first aid. For specific and complete choking/CPR instructions, familiarize yourself with the chart in the Appendix on pages 883–885, and take a course on CPR for children.

A child who begins to breathe by herself two or three minutes after a choking incident probably will not suffer any long-term damage. The longer she is deprived of oxygen, however, the greater the risk of permanent injury.

Occasionally a choking episode is followed by persistent coughing, gagging, wheezing, excessive salivation, or difficulty in swallowing or breathing. If this occurs, it may mean that an object is still partially blocking the airway—possibly in the lower breathing tubes. In this case, the object can cause continued breathing difficulty, irritation, and possibly pneumonia. Notify your pediatrician if any symptoms persist, so that further tests, such as chest X-rays, can be done. If they show that your child has inhaled something, she probably will need to be admitted to the hospital for a procedure to remove the object.

Prevention

Choking is a significant danger for children, especially until age seven. Objects such as safety pins, small parts from toys, and coins cause choking, but food is responsible for most incidents. You must be particularly watchful when children around the age of one are sampling new foods. Here are some additional suggestions for preventing choking.

- **Don't give young** children hard, smooth foods (e.g., peanuts, raw vegetables) that must be chewed with a grinding motion. Children don't master that kind of chewing until age four, so they may attempt to swallow the food whole. Do not give whole peanuts or other nuts to young children. When they do start to eat peanuts (and you know they don't have an allergy to peanuts), make sure to watch your child very closely while chewing.

- **Don't give your** child round, firm foods (like hot dogs and carrot sticks) unless they are chopped completely. Cut or break food into bite-size pieces (no larger than ½ inch [1.27 cm]) and encourage your child to chew thoroughly.

- **Supervise mealtime for** your infant or young child. Don't let her eat while playing or running. Teach her to chew and swallow her food before talking or laughing.

- **Chewing gum is** dangerous as a choking hazard for young children.

Because young children put everything into their mouths, small non-food objects are also responsible for many choking incidents. Look for age guidelines in selecting toys, but use your own judgment concerning your child. Also be aware that certain objects have been associated with choking, including uninflated or broken balloons; baby powder; items from the trash (e.g., eggshells, pop-tops from beverage cans); safety pins; coins; marbles; small balls; pen or marker caps; magnets; and small, button-type batteries. Foods that pose particular risk include hot dogs; hard, gooey, or sticky candy or vitamins; grapes; and popcorn. If you're unsure whether an object or food item could be harmful, you can purchase a standard small-parts cylinder at juvenile products stores.

Cuts and Scrapes

Your child's natural curiosity and eagerness are likely to produce some scrapes and cuts along the way. His reaction may be far more severe than the actual damage. In most cases, good treatment will require little more than cleansing the injury, protecting it, and providing plenty of reassurance (and perhaps a kiss on the minor bump or bruise).

Scrapes

Most minor injuries in young children are scrapes, or abrasions, which means that the outer layers of skin literally have been scraped off. If the abrasion covers a large area, it may appear to be very bloody, although the actual amount of blood lost is small. The area should be rinsed first with cool water to flush away debris and then washed gently with warm water and soap. Avoid using iodine and other antiseptic solutions. They have little protective value, and can add to the pain and discomfort.

If left alone, most abrasions "scab" over quickly, and this was thought to be the best natural remedy. But scabs actually slow the healing process and can lead to more scarring. Treat large or oozing scrapes with an antibiotic ointment and then cover them with a sterile (germ-free) dressing. These can be obtained at your local pharmacy, either in the form of an adhesive bandage or a separate gauze pad that is held in place by roller gauze or adhesive tape. Antibiotic ointment also helps prevent the dressing from sticking to the healing wound surface. The purpose is to prevent the injury from becoming infected while healing occurs. It is best to keep the bandage in place, except for dressing changes, until the wound heals. Take care that dressings around such areas as fingers or toes are not so tight as to interfere with circulation.

Some dressings are made of materials such as Telfa, which are less likely to adhere to the raw surface of a wound. Examine the wound daily during the dressing change, or whenever it becomes dirty or wet. If a bandage sticks when you try to remove it, soak it off with warm water.

Most wounds require a dressing for only two or three days, but your child may be reluctant to stop applying bandages that quickly, because small children regard bandages as badges or medals. There is no harm in leaving the area loosely covered as long as the bandage is kept dry and clean and the wound is checked daily.

Call your pediatrician if you can't get a wound clean or notice drainage of pus, increasing tenderness or redness around the site, or fever. These are signs that the wound may be infected. If necessary, the doctor can use a local anesthetic to prevent severe pain while cleaning out dirt and debris that you are not able to remove. If the wound is infected, she may prescribe antibiotics in the form of an oral medicine or an ointment or cream.

Cuts, Lacerations, and Bleeding

A cut or laceration is a wound that breaks through the skin and into the tissues beneath. Because the injury is deeper than a scrape, there are more likely to be problems, such as bleeding, and there is the possibility of damage to nerves and tendons. The following simple guidelines will help you prevent serious bleeding and other problems such as scarring when your child gets a cut.

1. Apply pressure. Almost all active bleeding can be stopped by applying direct pressure with clean gauze or cloth over the site for five or ten minutes. The most common mistake is interrupting the pressure too early in order to peek at the wound. Doing this may result in more bleeding or in the buildup of a clot that can make it harder to control the problem with further pressure. If bleeding starts again after five minutes of continuous pressure, reapply pressure and call your doctor for help. Do not use a tourniquet or tie-off on an arm or leg unless you are trained in its use, since this can cause severe damage if left on too long.

2. Stay calm. The sight of blood can be frightening, but this is an important time to stay in control. You'll make better decisions if you are calm, and your child will be less likely to get upset by the situation. Remember, by using direct pressure you will be able to control bleeding from even the most severe lacerations until help can arrive. Relatively minor cuts to the head and face will bleed more than cuts to other parts of the body because of the greater number of small, superficial blood vessels.

3. Seek medical advice for serious cuts. No matter how much (or how little) bleeding occurs, call your doctor if the laceration is deep (through the skin) or more than ½ inch (1.27 cm) long. Deep cuts can severely damage underlying muscles, nerves, and tendons, even if on the surface the wound does not appear serious. Long lacerations and those on the face, chest, and back are more likely to leave disfiguring scars. In these situations, if the wound is properly closed, the scar probably will be much less apparent. In some circumstances a skin adhesive (a gluelike substance) may be used to close the wound. If in doubt about whether stitches, adhesives, or staples are needed, call your doctor right away for advice, as it's important for repair to occur within eight to twelve hours of the injury.

You should be able to treat short, minor cuts yourself, as long as the edges come together by themselves, or with the aid of a "butterfly" bandage, and if there is no numbness beyond the wound and no reduction in sensation or movement. (A butterfly bandage is a strip of adhesive with ends that flare. It's used to keep the edges of a cut together during the healing process.) However, have your doctor examine your child if there is any possibility that foreign matter, such as dirt or glass, is trapped in the cut. Any injury that you cannot manage should be seen by your pediatrician or emergency medical services as soon as possible to maximize healing. Your child may not like to let you examine a laceration thoroughly because of the pain involved. The pediatrician, however, can use a local anesthetic, if neces-

First-Aid Supplies for Your Home and Car

You should prepare a first-aid kit for your home as well as one for each of your cars. The kit should contain:

- Acetaminophen or a nonsteroidal anti-inflammatory medication (such as ibuprofen)
- Antibiotic ointment
- Prescription medications (a month's supply)
- Sterile adhesive bandages (in various sizes)
- Gauze pads

- Scissors
- Tweezers
- Soap or another cleansing agent
- Petroleum jelly or another lubricant
- Moistened towelettes
- Thermometer

sary, to ensure a thorough exam. He may also use topical skin adhesives.

4. Clean and dress the wound. If you feel comfortable handling the problem, wash the wound with plain water and examine it carefully to be sure it is clean. Apply an antibiotic ointment, then cover it with a sterile dressing. It's easy to underestimate the extent or severity of a cut, so even if you choose to treat it yourself, don't hesitate to call your pediatrician for advice. If any redness, swelling, or pus appears around the wound, or if bleeding recurs, consult your physician as soon as possible. Antiseptics such as iodine and alcohol are not necessary and increase your child's discomfort, so do not use them on cuts. If your child's immunizations are current, tetanus shots are not necessary after most abrasions and lacerations. However, if your child is not up-to-date on his tetanus booster or it is time for a booster dose, your pediatrician may recommend that one be given.

See the box *First-Aid Supplies for Your Home and Car* for information on assembling items needed to treat your family's wounds and injuries.

Prevention

It is almost impossible for a curious and active child to avoid some scrapes and minor cuts, but there are things you can do to decrease the number your child will have and to minimize their severity. Keep potentially dangerous objects like sharp knives, easily breakable glass objects, and scissors out of his reach. When he gets old enough to use knives and scissors himself, teach him how to handle them properly and insist that they be used safely. At regular intervals make a safety check of your house, garage, and yard. If you find objects that are potentially dangerous because your child is older and can get into them, store them securely out of his reach.

Also see Chapter 15, *Keeping Your Child Safe.*

Drowning

Drowning is a leading cause of death among children, including infants and toddlers. Most infant drownings occur in bathtubs and buckets. Toddlers between one and four years most commonly drown in swimming pools. However, many children in this age group drown in ponds, rivers, and lakes. Children older than five years old are more likely to drown in rivers and lakes, but this varies from one area of the country to another. It is important to know that children can drown in even 1 inch of water, such as a bathtub or toilet.

Drowning refers to death that occurs in this way. When a child is rescued before death, the episode is called a nonfatal drowning.

What You Should Do

Get your child out of the water immediately, then check to see if she is breathing on her own. If she is not, begin CPR immediately (see Appendix). If someone else is present, send him or her to call for emergency medical help, but don't spend precious moments looking for someone, and don't waste time trying to drain water from your child's lungs. Concentrate instead on giving her rescue breathing and CPR until she is breathing on her own. Vomiting of swallowed water is very likely during CPR. Only when the child's breathing has resumed should you stop and seek emergency help. Call 911. Once the paramedics arrive, they will administer oxygen and continue CPR if necessary.

Any child who has come close to drowning should be given a complete medical examination, even if she seems all right. If she stopped breathing, inhaled water, or lost consciousness, she should remain under medical observation for at least twenty-four hours to be sure there is no damage to her respiratory or nervous system.

A child's recovery from a nonfatal drowning depends on how long she was deprived of oxygen. If she was underwater only briefly, she is likely to recover completely. Longer periods without oxygen can cause damage to the lungs, heart, or brain. A child who doesn't respond quickly to CPR may have more serious problems, but it's important to keep trying, because sustained CPR has revived children who have appeared lifeless or who have been immersed in very cold water for lengthy periods.

Prevention

For newborn infants and children under five years of age, parents and caregivers should never—even for a moment—leave children alone or in the care of another child, while in or near bathtubs, pools, spas, or wading pools, or near irrigation ditches or other open bodies of water. With children of this age, use "touch supervision"; that means that a supervising adult should be within an arm's length of the child with full attention focused on the child at all times when she is in or near water. The supervising adult should not be engaged in distracting activities, such as talking on a telephone, socializing, or tending to household chores.

Home swimming pools should be surrounded by a fence that prevents a child from getting to the pool from the house. There is no substitute for at least a 4-foot-high, nonclimbable, four-sided fence with a self-closing, self-latching gate. Parents, caregivers, and pool owners should know CPR and how to swim and should keep a telephone and equipment approved by the US Coast Guard (life preservers, life jackets, shepherd's crook) at poolside.

Toddlers, youngsters with intellectual disabilities, and children with seizure disorders are particularly vulnerable to drowning, but all youngsters are in danger if unsupervised in or near water. Even a child who knows how to swim may drown a few feet from safety. Remember, children should be supervised at all times. Swimming lessons should *not* be considered as a way to "drown-proof" your child. (For more information on water safety, see page 509.)

Electric Shock

When the human body comes in direct contact with a source of electricity, the current passes through it, producing what's called an electric shock. Depending on the voltage of the current and the length of contact, this shock can cause anything from minor discomfort to serious injury to death.

Young children, particularly toddlers, experience electric shock most often when they bite into electrical cords or poke metal objects such as forks or knives into unprotected outlets or appliances. These injuries also can take place when electric toys, appliances, or tools are used incorrectly, or when electric current makes contact with water in which a child is sitting or standing. Lightning accounts for about 20 percent of the cases that occur. Christmas trees and their lights are a seasonal hazard.

What You Should Do

If your child comes in contact with electricity, *always* try to turn the power off first. In many cases you'll be able to pull the plug or turn off the switch. If this isn't possible, consider an attempt to remove the live wire— but *not with your bare hands,* which would bring you in contact with the current yourself. Instead, try to cut the wire with a wood-handled ax or well-insulated wire cutters, or move the wire off the child using a dry stick, a rolled-up magazine or newspaper, a rope, a coat, or another thick, dry object that won't conduct electricity.

If you can't remove the source of the current, try to pull the child away. Again, *do not touch the child with your bare hands* when he's attached to the source of the current, since his body will transmit the electricity to you. Instead, use a nonconducting material such as rubber (or those described above) to shield you while freeing him. (*Caution:* None of these methods can be guaranteed safe unless the power can be shut off.)

As soon as the current is turned off (or the child is removed from it), check the child's breathing, skin color, and ability to respond to you. If his breathing or heartbeat has stopped, or seems very rapid or irregular, immediately use cardiopulmonary resuscitation (CPR; see page 691) to restore it, and have someone call for emergency medical help. At the same time, avoid moving the child needlessly, since such a severe electrical shock may have caused a spinal fracture.

If the child is conscious and it seems the shock was minor, check him for burned skin, especially if his mouth was the point of contact with the current. Call 911. Electric shock can cause internal organ damage that may be difficult to detect without a medical examination. For that reason, *all* children who receive a significant electric shock should see a doctor.

In the pediatrician's office, any minor burns from the electricity will be cleansed and dressed. The doctor may order laboratory tests to check for signs of damage to internal organs. If the child has severe burns or any sign of brain or heart damage, he will need to be hospitalized.

Prevention

The best way to prevent electrical injuries is to use outlet covers that are not a choking hazard, make sure all wires are properly insulated, tuck wires away from your child's reach, and provide adult supervision whenever children are in an area with potential electrical hazards. Small appliances are a special hazard around bathtubs, sinks, or pools. (See also Chapter 15, *Keeping Your Child Safe.*)

Fingertip Injuries

Children's fingertips get smashed frequently, usually getting caught in closing doors. The child is either unable to recognize the potential danger, or she fails to remove her hand quickly enough before the door is shut. Fingers also sometimes get crushed when youngsters play with a hammer or other heavy object, or when they're around a car door.

Because fingertips are exquisitely sensitive, your child will let you know immediately that she's been injured. Usually the damaged area will be blue and swollen, and there may be a cut or bleeding around the cuticle. The skin, tissues below the skin, and the nail bed—as well as the underlying bone and growth plate—all may be affected. If bleeding occurs underneath the nail, it will turn black or dark blue, and the pressure from the bleeding may be painful.

Home Treatment

When the fingertip is bleeding, wash it with soap and water, and cover it with a soft, sterile dressing. An ice pack or a soaking in cold water may relieve the pain and minimize swelling.

If the swelling is mild and your child is comfortable, you can allow the finger to heal on its own. But be alert for any increase in pain, swelling, redness, or drainage from the injured area, or a fever beginning twenty-four to seventy-two hours after the injury. These may be signs of infection, and you should notify your pediatrician.

When there's excessive swelling, a deep cut, blood under the fingernail, or if the finger looks as if it may be broken, call your doctor immediately. Do not attempt to straighten a fractured finger on your own.

Professional Treatment

If your doctor suspects a fracture, he may order an X-ray. If the X-ray confirms a fracture—or if there's damage to the nail bed, where nail growth occurs—an orthopedic consultation may be necessary. A fractured finger can be straightened and set under local anesthesia. An injured nail bed also must be repaired surgically to minimize the possibility of a nail deformity developing as the finger grows. If there's considerable blood under the nail, the pediatrician may drain it by making a small hole in the nail, which should relieve the pain.

Although deep cuts may require stitches, often all that's necessary is sterile adhesive strips (thin adhesive strips similar to butterfly bandages). A fracture underneath a cut is considered an "open" fracture and is susceptible to infection in the bone. In this case, antibiotics will be prescribed. Depending on your child's age and immunization status, the doctor also may order a tetanus booster.

(See also *Fractures/Broken Bones*, below.)

Fractures/Broken Bones

Although the term *fracture* may sound serious, it is just another name for a broken bone. As you probably remember from your own childhood, fractures are very common. In fact, they are the fourth most common injury among children under age six. Falls cause most of the fractures in this age group, but the most serious bone breaks usually result from car crashes.

A broken bone in a child is different from one in an adult, because young bones are more flexible and have a thicker covering, which makes them better able to absorb shock. Children's fractures rarely require surgical repair. They usually just need to be kept free of movement, most often through the use of a molded cast.

Most youngsters' broken bones are either "greenstick" fractures, in which the bone bends like green wood and breaks only on one side, or "torus" fractures, in which the bone is buckled, twisted, and weakened but not completely broken. A "bend" fracture refers to a bone that is bent but not broken, and is also relatively common among youngsters. "Complete" fractures, in which the bone breaks all the way through, also occur in young children.

Because your child's bones are still growing, he is vulnerable to an additional type of fracture that does not occur in adults. This involves damage to the growth plates at the ends of the bones, which regulate future growth. If this part of the bone does not heal properly after the fracture, the bone may grow at an angle or more slowly than the other bones in the body. Unfortunately, the impact on the bone's growth may not be visible for a year or more after the injury, so these fractures must be followed carefully by the pediatrician for twelve to eighteen months to make sure no growth damage has occurred. Fractures that involve injury to the growth plate sometimes need surgery to minimize the risk of future growth problems.

Fractures around the elbow often cause the arm to heal abnormally, resulting in a crooked position. Many require surgery to minimize this risk. Children with fractures near the elbow may be referred to a sports medicine or orthopedic specialist.

Fractures also are classified as "nondisplaced," when the broken ends are still in proper position, or "displaced," when the ends are separated or out of alignment. In an "open" or "compound" fracture, the bone sticks through the skin. If the skin is intact, the fracture is "closed."

Signs and Symptoms

It's not always easy to tell when a bone is broken, especially if your child is too young to describe what he's feeling. Ordinarily with a fracture, you will see swelling and your child will clearly be in pain and unable—or unwilling—to move the injured limb. However, just because your child can move the bone doesn't necessarily rule out a fracture. Anytime you suspect a fracture, notify your pediatrician immediately.

Home Treatment

Until your child can be seen in the pediatrician's office, emergency room, or urgent care center, use an improvised sling or rolled-up newspaper or magazine as a splint to protect the injury from unnecessary movement.

Don't give the child anything by mouth to drink or to relieve pain without first consulting the doctor, but if yours is an older child, you can use a cold pack or a cold towel, placed on the injury site, to decrease pain. Extreme cold can cause injury to the delicate skin of babies and toddlers, so do not use ice with children this young.

If your child has broken his leg, do not try to move him yourself. Call 911 for an ambulance; let the paramedics supervise his transportation and make the child as comfortable as possible.

If part of the injury is open and bleeding, or if bone is protruding through the skin, place firm pressure on the wound (see *Cuts, Lacerations, and Bleeding,* page 693); then cover it with clean (preferably sterile) gauze. Do not try to put the bone back underneath the skin. After this injury has been treated, be alert to any fever, which may indicate that the wound has become infected.

Professional Treatment

After examining the break, the doctor will order X-rays to determine the extent of the damage. If the doctor suspects that the bone's growth plate is affected, or if the bones are out of line, an orthopedic consultation will be necessary.

Because children's bones heal rapidly and well, a plaster or fiberglass cast, or sometimes just an immobilizing splint, is all that is needed for most minor fractures. For a displaced fracture, an orthopedic surgeon may have to realign the bones. This may be done as a "closed reduction," in which the surgeon uses local or general anesthesia, manipulates the bones until they're straight, and then applies a cast. An "open reduction" is a surgical procedure done in an operating room, but this is rarely necessary for children. After the surgical reduction, a cast will be used until the bone has healed, which usually takes about half the time that adult bones require, or less, depending on the child's age. The nice thing about young bones is that they don't have to be in perfect alignment. As long as they are more or less in the right place, they will remodel as they grow. Your pediatrician may order periodic X-rays while the bone is healing, just to make sure they are aligning properly.

Usually casting brings rapid relief or at least a decrease in pain. If your child has an increase in pain, numbness, or pale or blue fingers or toes, call your doctor immediately. These are signs that the extremity has swollen and requires more room within the cast. If the cast is not adjusted, the swelling may press on nerves, muscles, and blood vessels, which can produce permanent damage. To relieve the pressure, the doctor may split the cast, open a window in it, or replace it with a larger one.

Also let the doctor know if the cast breaks or becomes very loose, or if the plaster gets wet and soggy. Without a proper, secure fit, the cast will not hold the broken bone in position to mend correctly. Newer casts may permit swimming and bathing, but be sure to follow the instructions for drying out your child's cast after it gets wet.

Bones that have been broken often will form a hard knot at the site of the break during the healing process known as a callus. Especially with a broken collarbone, this may look unsightly, but there is no treatment for this, and the knot will not be permanent. The bone will remodel and resume its normal shape in a few months.

Head Injury/Concussion

It's almost inevitable that your child will hit her head every now and then, especially when she's a toddler, falling off playground equipment or bunk beds, for example. These blows may upset you, but your anxiety is usually worse than the bump. Most head injuries are minor, causing no serious problems. Even so, it's important to know the difference between a head injury that warrants medical attention and one that needs only a comforting hug.

If your child suffers a brief, temporary loss of consciousness after a hard blow to the head, she is said to have had a concussion. By definition, a concussion is a hard strike to the head resulting in temporary confusion or a change in behavior, and sometimes with a loss of consciousness. Particularly if a child has significant memory loss, disorientation, altered speech, visual changes, or nausea and vomiting after a head injury, call 911 and contact your pediatrician. In fact, if your child experiences any type of concussion, your child should be examined by her doctor.

Treatment

If a child's head injury has been mild, she'll remain alert and awake after the incident, and her color will be normal. She may cry out due to momentary pain and fright, but the crying should last no more than ten minutes and then she'll go back to playing as usual.

Occasionally a minor head injury also will cause slight dizziness, nausea, and headache. Even so, if the injury seems minor and there's not a significant cut (one that's deep and/or actively bleeding) that might require immediate medical attention or possibly stitches (see *Cuts and Scrapes,* page 692), you may be able to treat your child at home. Just wash the cut with soap and water. If there's a bruise, apply a cold compress. This will help minimize the swelling if you do it in the first few hours after the injury. Even in these cases, however, it may be wise to call your pediatrician and explain the circumstances and your child's condition.

Even after only a minor head injury, you should observe your child for twenty-four to forty-eight hours to see if she develops any signs that the injury was more severe than it first appeared. Although it's very rare, children can develop a serious brain injury after a seemingly minor bump on the head that causes no immediate obvious problems. If your child develops any of the following symptoms, be sure to consult your pediatrician immediately or seek prompt attention from the nearest emergency room:

- **She seems excessively** sleepy or lethargic during her usual wakeful hours, or you cannot awaken her while she's asleep at night.

- **She has a** headache that won't go away (even with acetaminophen) or vomits. Headache and vomiting occur commonly after head trauma, but they are usually mild and last only a few hours. (Small children may not be able to let you know that they have a headache so they may cry or be inconsolable.)

- **She's persistently and/or** extremely irritable. With an infant who cannot tell you what she's feeling, this may indicate a severe headache.

- **Any significant change** in your child's mental abilities, coordination, sensation, or strength warrants immediate medical attention. Such worrisome changes would include weakness of arms or legs, clumsy walking, slurred speech, crossed eyes, or difficulty with vision.

- **She becomes unconscious** again after being awake for a while, or she has a seizure (convulsion) or starts to breathe irregularly.

If your child loses consciousness *at any time* after hitting her head, notify the pediatrician. If she doesn't awaken within a few minutes, she needs *immediate medical attention.* Call 911 for help while you follow these steps.

1. Move your child as little as possible. *If you suspect that she might have injured her neck, do not attempt to move her. Changing the position of her neck might make her injuries worse.* One exception: Move her only if she's in danger of being injured further where she is (e.g., on a ledge or in a fire), but try to avoid bending or twisting her neck.

2. Check to see if she's breathing. If she isn't, perform CPR (see page 691).

3. If she's bleeding severely from a scalp wound, apply direct pressure with a clean cloth over the wound.

4. After calling 911, wait for the ambulance's arrival rather than taking your child to the hospital yourself.

Loss of consciousness following a head injury may last only a few seconds or as long as several hours. If you find the child after the injury happened, and you are not sure if she lost consciousness, notify the pediatrician. (An older child who has had a concussion may say that she can't remember what happened just prior to and just after the injury.)

Most children who lose consciousness for more than a few minutes will be hospitalized overnight for observation. Hospitalization is essential for youngsters with severe brain injury and irregular breathing or convulsions. Fortunately, with modern pediatric intensive care, many children who have suffered serious head injury—and even those who have been unconscious for several weeks—eventually may recover completely.

Poisoning

About 2.2 million people swallow or have contact with a poisonous substance each year. More than half of these poison exposures occur in children under six years of age.

Most children who are poisoned are not permanently harmed, particularly if they receive immediate treatment. If you think your child has been poisoned, stay calm and act quickly.

You should suspect poisoning if you ever find your child with an open or empty container of a toxic substance, especially if she is acting strangely. Be alert for these other signs of possible poisoning:

- Unexplained stains on her clothing

- Burns on her lips or mouth

- Unusual drooling, or odd odors on her breath

- Unexplained nausea or vomiting

- Abdominal cramps without fever

- Difficulty in breathing

- Sudden behavior changes, such as unusual sleepiness, irritability, or jumpiness

- Convulsions or unconsciousness (only in very serious cases)

Treatment

Anytime your child has been exposed to a poison of any kind, you should notify your pediatrician. However, your regional Poison Center will provide the immediate information and guidance you need when you first discover that your child has been poisoned. These centers are staffed twenty-four hours a day with experts who can tell you what to do without delay. Call the national toll-free number for the Poison Help Line at 1-800-222-1222, which will provide immediate and free access around the clock to your regional Poison Center. *If there's an emergency and you cannot find the number, dial 911 or Directory Assistance and ask for the Poison Help Line. Keep the number in your cell phone.*

The immediate action you need to take will vary with the type of poisoning. The Poison Help Line can give you specific instructions if you know the particular substance your child has swallowed. However, carry out the following instructions before calling them.

(For more information about poisoning, see *Food Poisoning and Food Contamination* in Chapter 16, page 537.)

SWALLOWED POISON

First, get the poisonous substance away from your child. If she still has some in her mouth, make her spit it out, or remove it with your fingers. Keep this material along with any other evidence that might help determine what she swallowed.

Next, check for these signs:

- Severe throat pain

- Excessive drooling

- Breathing difficulty

- Convulsions

- Excessive drowsiness

Poison-Proofing Your Home

- Store drugs and medications in a medicine cabinet that is locked or out of reach. Do not keep toothpaste, soap, or shampoo in the same cabinet. If you carry a purse, keep potential poisons out of your purse, and keep your child away from other people's purses.

- Buy and keep medications in their own containers with child safety caps. (Remember, however, that these caps are child-resistant, not childproof, so keep them in a locked cabinet.) Safely dispose of leftover prescription medicines when the illness for which they were prescribed has passed. Many pharmacies and municipalities accept leftover medications and will dispose of them safely.

- Do not take medicine in front of small children; they may try to imitate you later. Never tell a child that a medicine is candy in order to get him to take it.

- Check the label every time you give medication, to be sure you are giving the right medicine in the correct dosage. Mistakes are most likely to occur in the middle of the night, so always turn on the light when handling any medication.

- Read labels on all household products before you buy them. Try to find the safest ones for the job, and buy only what you need to use immediately.

- Store hazardous products in locked cabinets that are out of your child's reach. Do not keep detergents and other cleaning products under the kitchen or bathroom sink unless they are in a cabinet with a safety latch that locks every time you close the cabinet. (Most hardware stores and department stores sell these safety latches.) In recent years, in part because of convenience, some parents use detergent packaged in single-load packets or "pods"—which may be tempting for children to put in their mouth, but can make them violently ill very quickly. Make sure they're kept out of sight and reach of children.

- Never put poisonous or toxic products in containers that were once used for food, especially empty drink bottles, cans, or cups.

- Always open the garage door before starting your car, and never run the car in a closed garage. Be sure that coal, wood, or kerosene stoves are properly maintained. If you smell gas, turn off the stove or gas burner, leave the house, and then call the gas company.

- Post the Poison Help Line number, 1-800-222-1222, near every telephone in your home and in your cell phone, along with other emergency numbers. Be sure that your child care provider and anyone else caring for your child knows when and how to use these numbers.

Keep in mind that these guidelines should apply to not only your home, but also any other settings where your child visits, including the homes of grandparents and babysitters.

If any of these are present, or if your child is unconscious or has stopped breathing, start emergency procedures and get medical help immediately by calling 911. Take the poison container and remnants of material with you to help the doctor determine what was swallowed. *Do not make your child vomit by any means*—even if the label on the container suggests it—as this may cause further damage.

If your child is not showing these serious symptoms, call the Poison Help Line number, 1-800-222-1222, which will direct your call to your regional poison center. The person answering the phone will need the following information in order to help you:

- **Your name and** phone number.

- **Your child's name,** age, and weight. Also be sure to mention any serious medical conditions she has or medications she is taking.

- **The name of** the substance your child swallowed. Read it off the container, and spell it if necessary. If ingredients are listed on the label, read them, too. If your child has swallowed a prescription medicine, and the drug is not named on the label, give the center the name of the pharmacy and its phone number, the date of the prescription, and its number. Try to describe the tablet or capsule, and mention any imprinted numbers on it. If your child swallowed another substance, such as a part of a plant, provide as full a description as possible to help identify it.

- **The time your** child swallowed this poison (or when you found her), and the amount you think she swallowed.

If the poison is extremely dangerous, or if your child is very young, you may be told to take her directly to the nearest emergency department for medical evaluation. Otherwise, you will be given instructions to follow at home.

Vomiting may be dangerous, so never make a child vomit. Strong acids (e.g., toilet bowl cleaner) or strong alkalis (e.g., lye, drain or oven cleaner, or dishwasher detergent) can burn the throat—and vomiting will only increase the damage. Syrup of ipecac is a drug that was used in the past to make children vomit after they had swallowed a poison; although this may seem to make sense, it is no longer considered a good poison treatment. You should not make your child vomit by any means. Making your child vomit is not recommended as it can cause further injury to your child's body. If you have syrup of ipecac in your home, properly dispose of it and throw away the container. Do not make a child vomit by any means, whether by giving him syrup of ipecac, making him gag, or giving him salt water. Instead, you may be advised to have the child drink milk or water.

POISON ON THE SKIN

If your child spills a dangerous chemical substance on her body, remove her clothes and rinse the skin with lukewarm—not hot—water. If the area shows signs of being burned, continue rinsing for at least fifteen minutes, no matter how much your child may protest. Then call the Poison Help Line for further advice. Do not apply ointments or grease.

POISON IN THE EYE

Flush your child's eye by holding her eyelid open and pouring a steady stream of lukewarm water into the inner corner. A young child is sure to object to this treatment, so get another adult to hold her while you rinse the eye. If that's not possible, wrap her tightly in a towel and clamp her under one arm so you have one hand free to hold the eyelid open and the other to pour in the water.

Continue flushing the eye for fifteen minutes. Then call the Poison Help Line, 1-800-222-1222, for further instructions. Do not use an eyecup, eyedrops, or ointment unless the Poison Center tells you to do so. If there is any question of continued pain or severe injury, seek emergency assistance immediately.

POISONOUS FUMES

In the home, poisonous fumes are most likely to be produced by an idling automobile in a closed garage; leaky gas vents; wood, coal, or kerosene stoves that are improperly vented or maintained; or space heaters, ovens, stoves, or water heaters that use gas. If your child is exposed to fumes or gases from these or other sources, get her into fresh air immediately. If she is breathing, call the Poison Help Line, 1-800-222-1222, for further instructions. If she has stopped breathing, start CPR (see page 691), and don't stop until she breathes on her own or someone else can take over. If you can, have someone call 911 for emergency medical help immediately; otherwise, try one minute of CPR and then call for emergency assistance.

Prevention

Young children, especially those between ages one and three, are commonly poisoned by things in the home such as drugs—even those sold over the counter—and medications, cleaning products, plants, cosmetics, pesticides, paints, solvents, antifreeze, windshield wiper fluid, gasoline, kerosene, and lamp oil. This happens because tasting and mouthing things is a natural way for children to explore their surroundings, and because they imitate adults without understanding what they are doing.

Most poisonings occur when parents are distracted. If you are ill or under a great deal of stress, you may not watch your child as closely as usual. The hectic routines at the end of the day cause so many lapses in parental attention. So keep all poisons, medications, and toxins high out of children's sight and reach. The best way to prevent poisonings is to store all toxic substances in a locked cabinet where your child cannot possibly get to them, even when you are not directly watching her. Also, supervise her even more closely whenever you're visiting a store or a friend or relative's home that has not been childproofed. (See also Chapter 15, *Keeping Your Child Safe*.)

~ 24 ~

Environmental Health

ALL CHILDREN ARE potentially exposed to environmental toxins in the world in which we live. But even though you can't protect your child from every environmental hazard that exists, whether indoors or out, you can lower his exposure by taking the steps described in this chapter.

Air Pollution and Secondhand Smoke

The outdoor air contains several substances that could be harmful to children. One of the most worrisome is ozone, which is a colorless gas that can cause harm when it is present near the ground. Ozone is formed when sunlight on certain chemicals (nitrogen oxide, reactive hydrocarbon) is released by automobiles and industry. Ozone concentrations are likely to be greatest in the summer on warm, sunny days, peaking in the mid- to late afternoon.

If you live near a major roadway, your child will be exposed to problematic diesel exhaust. Because children spend time playing outdoors, they are particularly susceptible to ozone's effects, with breathing difficulties most likely to occur in youngsters with asthma. Children also breathe more rapidly than adults and inhale more pollutants per pound of body weight.

Another common air pollutant is an indoors issue—secondhand (or environmental) cigarette smoke—which is exhaled smoke from burning tobacco, or smoke from the mouthpiece end or filter of a cigarette, cigar, or pipe. According to the Centers for Disease Control and Prevention, about 25 percent of children ages three to eleven years old live in a household with at least one smoker. If you or others in your home use cigarettes, pipes, or cigars, your child is being exposed to their smoke. This smoke contains thousands of chemicals, some of which have been shown to cause cancer and other illnesses, including respiratory infections, bronchitis, and pneumonia. Children exposed to cigarette smoke also have a greater likelihood of developing ear infections and asthma, and they may have a more difficult time getting over colds. They are more susceptible to headaches, sore throats, hoarseness, irritated eyes, dizziness, nausea, lack of energy, and fussiness. For these reasons, many parents have designated their homes as nonsmoking areas.

Thirdhand smoke exposure is a relatively new concept, and is usually defined as the smoke, residual nicotine, and other chemicals that tobacco smoke leaves behind on clothes, furniture, carpets, a person's hair, and her skin after a cigarette has already been extinguished.

If a parent smokes around her newborn, the baby has a greater risk of dying from sudden infant death syndrome (SIDS). In addition, nicotine and dangerous chemicals from cigarettes are in the breast milk of nursing mothers, who thus expose their babies.

When children are exposed to tobacco smoke, they might develop life-threatening illnesses later in life, including lung cancer and heart disease. They also may be more likely to have cataracts as adults.

One other important point: When you smoke in your home, you create a risk of fires and burns to your child and others. Children can suffer burns if they find and play with a lit cigarette or with matches or a lighter.

According to the 2006 Surgeon General's Report, there is no risk-free level of tobacco exposure. One study showed that when just one cigarette was smoked in a bedroom with a closed door, two hours were needed for particulates in the air to return to a threshold lower than harmful levels.

As your child grows, keep in mind that you are a role model. If your child sees you smoking, she may want to try it as well, and you could be laying the foundation for a lifetime of smoking.

Prevention

To protect your child from air pollution, limit his playtime outdoors when local agencies have issued health advisories or smog alerts—particularly if your child has a respiratory problem like asthma. Newspapers and TV news programs often provide information about the air quality in the community.

To reduce the air pollution from automobiles on smoggy days, keep your car in the garage and use public transportation or car pools instead. Do not use gasoline-powered lawn mowers on high-pollution days and limit their use at other times. Work with your local, state, and national governments to enforce and tighten air pollution laws and regulations.

To reduce your child's exposure to environmental tobacco smoke, here are some additional steps you can take:

- **If you or** other family members smoke, stop! If you've been unable to quit, talk to your doctor, who can refer you to low-cost stop-smoking programs available in your community. Or contact 1-800-QUITNOW (1-800-784-8669) or www.smoke free.gov to assist you in quitting smoking.

- **Don't allow anyone** to smoke in your home or your car, particularly when children are present. Don't place ashtrays around your house that may encourage people to light up. Your home and car should always remain smoke-free.

- **Store matches and** lighters out of reach of children.

- **When selecting a** babysitter or child care provider, make it clear that no one is permitted to smoke around your child.

- **When you're in** public places with your child, ask others not to smoke around you and your child. Choose restaurants that don't allow smoking.

Asbestos

Asbestos is a natural fiber that was widely used as a spray-on material for fireproofing, insulation, and sound-proofing in schools, homes, and public buildings from the 1940s through the 1970s. It does **not** pose health risks unless it deteriorates and becomes crumbly, when it can release microscopic asbestos fibers into the air. When asbestos fibers are inhaled, they can cause chronic health problems to the lungs, throat, and gastrointestinal tract, including a rare type of chest cancer (called meso-thelioma) that can occur as long as five decades after asbestos exposure.

Today, schools are mandated by law to either remove asbestos or otherwise ensure that children are not exposed to it. However, it is still in some older homes, especially as insulation around pipes, stoves, and furnaces, as well as in walls and ceilings.

Prevention

Follow these guidelines to keep your child safe from asbestos.

- **If you think** there may be asbestos in your home, have a professional inspector check for it. Local health departments and regional offices of the Environmental Protection Agency (EPA) can provide the names of individuals and labs certified to inspect homes for asbestos. To locate the regional EPA office nearest you, go to www.epa.gov/asbestos.

- **Do not let** your youngster play near any exposed or deteriorating materials that could contain asbestos.

- **If asbestos is** found in your home, it may be acceptable to leave it there if it is in good condition. But if it is deteriorating, or if it might be disturbed by any renovations you're planning, have a properly accredited and certified contractor remove the asbestos, which must be taken off in a safe manner. Again, ask the local health department or the EPA for information on finding a certified contractor in your community.

Carbon Monoxide

Carbon monoxide is a toxic gas that is a by-product of appliances, heaters, and automobiles that burn gasoline, natural gas, wood, oil, kerosene, and propane. It has no color, no taste, and no odor. It can become trapped inside your home if appliances are not working, if a furnace, stove, or fireplace has a clogged vent or chimney, or if a charcoal grill is used in an enclosed area. Carbon monoxide also might enter your home when an automobile is left running in an attached garage.

When your child breathes carbon monoxide, it harms the ability of his blood to transport oxygen. Although everyone is at risk for carbon monoxide poisoning, it is particularly dangerous for children because they breathe faster and inhale more carbon monoxide per pound of body weight. Symptoms may include headaches, nausea, shortness of breath, fatigue, confusion, and fainting. Persistent exposure to carbon monoxide can lead to personality changes, memory loss, severe lung injury, brain damage, and death.

Prevention

You can reduce your child's risk of carbon monoxide poisoning by:

- **Buying and installing** carbon monoxide detectors in your home, particularly near the bedrooms, or near a furnace or woodstove

- **Never leaving your** car running in an attached garage (even if the garage door is open)

- **Never using a** charcoal or propane grill, hibachi, or portable camping stove indoors or in an enclosed area

- **Scheduling an annual** inspection and servicing of oil and gas furnaces, woodstoves, gas ovens and ranges, gas water heaters, gas clothes dryers, and fireplaces

- **Never using your** nonelectric oven to heat your kitchen or your house

Contaminated Fish

Fish is a protein-rich food that is healthy for both children and adults. It contains a good type of fat (omega-3 fatty acids), as well as nutrients such as vitamin D. It also is low in saturated fat. At the same time, a lot of attention has focused on the contaminants that may be in fish and that could pose health risks.

One of the most widely discussed contaminants is mercury, which at high levels can be toxic. It gets into oceans, rivers, lakes, and ponds, and can end up in the fish we eat. Mercury in bodies of water like lakes and streams—some of it discharged from industrial plants—can be converted by bacteria into mercury compounds such as methylmercury. As a result, certain predatory fish (including shark and swordfish) can contain high quantities of mercury, which when consumed can have a serious negative effect on a young child's developing nervous system.

Other environmental pollutants have been found in fish and other foods, including polychlorinated biphenyls (PCBs) and dioxins. Although PCBs are chemicals that were manufactured primarily for use as fire retardants and in electrical transformers, they were banned in the US in the late 1970s. However, they have remained in the environment in water, soil, and air, and have been found in fish. PCBs have been associated with thyroid problems, lowered IQ, and memory impairment in young children.

Dioxin is another pollutant that has been detected in fish. It is the byproduct of certain chemicals by incineration and can interfere with the developing nervous system and other organs, particularly when the exposure is long-term. Fortunately, PCBs and dioxins have decreased significantly in recent years.

Prevention

You need to make an effort to reduce your child's exposure to toxic substances in food. Government agencies are recommending that young children reduce their intake of certain fish that may contain high levels of mercury. Specifically, young children should not consume king mackerel, swordfish, shark, and tilefish. At the same time, other types of fish and shellfish are lower in mercury, including canned light tuna, salmon, shrimp, cod, catfish, clams, flatfish, crab, scallops, and pollock, so these are much better choices for your child. Nevertheless, you should limit your child's intake of even these safer selections to less than 12 ounces per week.

For information about the safety of fish and shellfish caught in your area, contact state and local health departments. Also check fish advisories on the Environmental Protection Agency's website: http://www.epa .gov/waterscience/fish/. The health department in your state also can provide any advisories issued about the presence of other toxins in fish in your area.

Drinking Water

Children drink much more water for their size than adults. Most of this water comes from the tap, and the quality of this water is regulated by standards instituted by Congress, included in the Safe Drinking Water Act of 1974. Subsequent laws have set drinking water standards for chemicals that were known to be in some water supplies.

Today the drinking water in the US is among the safest in the world, although problems can occur from time to time. Violations in water safety standards are most likely to occur in small systems that serve less than a thousand people. Also, keep in

Plastics (Bisphenol A; BPA)

Breastfeeding is safe and the most important way to nourish your baby. Many food and liquid containers, including some baby bottles, are made of polycarbonate, or have a lining that contains the chemical bisphenol A (BPA). BPA is used to harden plastics, keep bacteria from contaminating foods, and prevent cans from rusting. Other man-made chemicals—phthalates—are used in soft, flexible plastics.

There are concerns over the possible harmful effects that BPA and phthalates may have on humans, particularly on infants and children. For example, animal studies have shown effects on the endocrine functions in animals, related to BPA and phthalate exposure. BPA acts as a weak estrogen in animals and perhaps in humans, too. Additional and ongoing studies will determine what level of exposure to these chemicals might cause similar effects in humans.

Risk Reduction

As research continues, concerned parents can take the following precautionary measures to reduce babies' exposure to BPA:

- Avoid clear plastic baby bottles or containers with the recycling number 7 and the letters "PC" imprinted on them. Many contain BPA, although newer bottles should be BPA-free.

- Consider using certified or identified BPA-free plastic bottles.

- Glass bottles can be an alternative, but be aware of the risk of injury to you or your baby if the bottle is dropped or broken.

- Because heat may cause the release of BPA from plastic, do not heat polycarbonate bottles in the microwave and do not wash polycarbonate bottles in the dishwasher.

- Breastfeeding is another way to reduce potential exposure to unwanted chemicals. The AAP recommends exclusive breastfeeding for a minimum of four months but preferably for six months.

Breastfeeding should be continued thereafter as long as it is mutually desired by mother and infant.

If you are considering switching from canned liquid to powdered formula, note that the mixing procedures may differ, so pay special attention when preparing formula from powder.

If your baby is on specialized formula to address a medical condition, you should not switch to another formula, as the known risks would outweigh any potential risks posed by BPA in particular.

Risks associated with giving infants inappropriate (homemade condensed milk) formulas or alternative (soy or goat) milk are far greater than the potential effects of BPA and phthalates.

mind that private wells are not federally regulated, and should be tested for nitrates and other environmental toxins if appropriate (see *Where We Stand* on page 716).

Contaminants that can cause illness in the drinking water include: germs, nitrates, man-made chemicals, heavy metals, radioactive particles, and by-products of the disinfecting process.

Although bottled water can be purchased in markets, many brands are just tap water that has been bottled for sale. Bottled water is generally much more expensive than tap water, and unless there are known contamination problems in your community's water supply, it is not necessary. In summary, be careful about using bottled water with children on a regular basis.

Prevention

To ensure that your child is consuming safe drinking water, you can check the water quality by contacting the county health department, the state environment agency, or the Environmental Protection Agency's Safe Drinking Water Hotline (1-800-426-4791). Local water companies are mandated to report what is in the water on an annual basis. Well water should be tested yearly.

Other guidelines include:

■ **Use cold water** for cooking and drinking. Contaminants can accumulate in hot water heaters.

■ **If you are** concerned about the quality of your plumbing, run the faucet for two minutes each morning prior to using the water for cooking or drinking. This will flush the pipes and lower the likelihood that contaminants will end up in the water you consume.

■ **Have well water** tested for nitrates before giving it to infants under one year of age.

WHERE WE STAND

IN THE US, about 15 million families get their drinking water from private, unregulated wells. Studies show that a significant number of these wells have concentrations of nitrates that exceed federal drinking-water standards. These nitrates are a natural component of plants and nitrate-containing fertilizers that can seep into well water, and don't pose any toxic risk to humans on their own. But in the body, they can be converted to nitrites, which are potentially hazardous. In infants, they can lead to a condition called methemoglobinemia, a dangerous and often fatal blood disorder that interferes with the circulation of oxygen in the blood.

Babies whose formula is prepared using well water may have a high risk of nitrate poisoning. The AAP recommends that if your family drinks well water, the well should be tested for nitrates. If the well water contains nitrates (above a level of 10 mg/L), it should not be used for infant formula or food preparation. Instead, you should prepare food or formula by using purchased water, public water supplies, or water from deeper wells with minimal nitrate levels.

How often should well water be tested? Tests should be done every three months for at least one year to determine the levels of nitrates. If these tests show safe levels, then a follow-up test once a year is recommended.

Breastfeeding is the safest way to nourish your infant, since high levels of nitrates are not passed through breast milk.

■ **Drinking water that** may be contaminated with germs should be boiled and then allowed to cool before drinking. Boil for no more than one minute. However, it is important to remember that boiling water only kills bacteria and other germs; it does **not** remove toxic chemicals. If you don't like the taste or smell of your tap water, filters made with activated carbon will remove the odd taste or smell. Such filters will also remove undesirable chemicals without removing fluoride that prevents tooth decay.

Lead Poisoning

Contrary to popular belief, lead poisoning is not caused by chewing on a pencil or being stabbed with its point. Lead poisoning is caused most often by touching and then mouthing dusty toys, bits of old paint, or dirt; by breathing lead in the air; or by drinking water from pipes lined or soldered with lead. There also may be lead in hobby materials such as stained glass, paints, solders, and fishing weights. It might be in mini-blinds manufactured outside the US prior to July 1997. If you buy new mini-blinds, look for those that have a label that says "new formulation" or "nonleaded formula." Lead also might be in food cooked or stored in some imported ceramic dishes. Do not serve acidic substances (e.g., orange juice) in these dishes, since the acids can leach lead from the dishes into the food. Although food cans with soldered seams could add lead to the food inside them, these cans generally have been replaced by seamless aluminum containers in the US.

Other sources of lead can include candy and alternative sources of medicine from countries like Mexico, as well as some spices, cosmetics, and ayurvedic treatments from India, the Middle East, and Southeast Asia.

Lead was an allowable ingredient in house paint before 1978 and so may be on the walls, doorjambs, and window frames on many older homes. As the paint ages, it chips, peels, and comes off in the form of dust. Toddlers may be tempted by such bite-size pieces and will taste or eat them out of curiosity. Even if they don't intentionally eat the material, the dust can get on their hands and into their food. Sometimes the lead-containing finish

has been covered with other layers of newer, safer paints. This can give you a false sense of reassurance, however, since the underlying paint still may chip or peel off with the newer layers and fall into the hands of toddlers.

Although there has been a decline in high lead levels in children's blood, somewhere between half a million and 1 million children in the US still have unacceptably high levels. Living in a city, being poor, and being African American or Hispanic are all risk factors that increase the chances of having an elevated blood-lead level. But even children living in rural areas or who are in well-to-do families still can be at risk.

In a child who continues consuming lead, it will accumulate in the body. Although it may not be noticeable for some time, ultimately it can affect many areas of the body, including the brain. Lead poisoning can cause learning disabilities and behavioral problems. Very high levels will likely cause the most severe problems, but the extent of damage for any individual child cannot be predicted. Lead also can cause stomach and intestinal problems, loss of appetite, anemia,

WHERE WE STAND

LEAD CAUSES SERIOUS damage to children's brains even at relatively low levels of exposure—the effects of which are largely irreversible. The American Academy of Pediatrics supports widespread lead screening of children, as well as funding programs to remove lead hazards from the environment.

headaches, constipation, hearing loss, and even short stature. Iron deficiency increases the risk for lead poisoning in children, which is why these two disorders are often found together in children. (See *Abdominal Pain,* page 521.)

Prevention

If your home was built after 1977, when federal regulations restricted the amount of lead in paint, the risk for having dangerous amounts of lead in the dust, paint, or soil of your residence is low. However, if your home is older, the likelihood of having dangerous amounts of lead there can be very high, especially for the oldest homes (those built before 1960). If you think your home may contain lead, clean up any paint dust or chips using water. During this cleanup, if you add a detergent to the water, it will help bind the lead into the water. Also, keeping surfaces (floors, window areas, porches, etc.) clean may lower your child's chance of being exposed to lead-containing dust. Older windows are of particular concern since paint on wood frames frequently is damaged and the action of opening and closing windows can produce lead-containing dust. Do not vacuum the chips or dust as the vacuum will spread the dust out through its exhaust hole, although a HEPA vacuum may be OK to use. It's also a good idea to have your child leave his shoes at the door and wash his hands often, particularly before he eats.

Another step is to identify surfaces in your home with lead-contaminated paint, or areas with dangerous amounts of lead in the dust or dirt. A home inspection is necessary to do this, and you can get help from your local or state health department to find a lead inspector in your area.

Diagnosis and Treatment

Children who have lead poisoning rarely show any physical symptoms. However, learning and behavior problems from lead may show up in the preschool child or may not show up until the child reaches school age. At that point they need to learn more complicated tasks like reading or arithmetic and may have trouble keeping up with class work. Some may even seem overly active, due to the effects of the lead. For this reason, the only sure way to know if your child has been exposed to excessive lead is to have him tested. In fact, a blood test for lead around ages one and two years old is recommended for children.

The most common screening test for lead poisoning uses a drop of blood from a finger prick. If the results of this test indicate that a child has been exposed to excessive lead, a second test will be done using a larger sample of blood obtained from a vein in the arm. This test is more accurate and can measure the precise amount of lead in the blood.

Children who have lead poisoning should immediately be removed from the home where they are being exposed to this toxic substance. In rare instances, they may require treatment

ORGANIC FOODS

Organic foods used to be available only in specialty markets. But their popularity has grown so much in recent years that you can now find them in most neighborhood supermarkets as well as health food stores. In cities and towns across the country, the organic fruits and vegetables that land in shopping carts most often are tomatoes, carrots, peaches, leafy vegetables, apples, bananas, potatoes, and squash.

Research has shown that parents with children under eighteen years of age are more likely to buy and serve organic produce than other people. The reason? In explaining their preference for organic foods, many mothers and fathers say that they're putting these organic products on their dining room table for reasons of personal health and food safety, as well as for environmental concerns. These parents often voice worries about the effects of agricultural chemicals like pesticides in the foods they give their children.

The US Department of Agriculture has established a certification program that requires farmers to meet government guidelines for growing and processing foods before the "organic" label can be attached to them. When foods like fruits, vegetables, and grains are organic, they are grown in soil fertilized with manure and compost, and without the use of pesticides, herbicides, dyes, or waxes; these standards prohibit the use of nonorganic ingredients for at least three years before crops are harvested. Organically produced meats must be raised free of growth hormones or antibiotics.

But does it really make a difference to buy organic? Are these foods actually safer and more nutritious—and are they worth the premium prices often charged for them?

Several studies have examined whether health risks can be reduced by limiting or eliminating exposure to pesticides. These pesticides are sprayed on crops to safeguard them from insects and molds, and their residue can be left on fruits and vegetables and then later consumed. But here are the facts: Any risk to children and adults when eating these foods is minimal. The traces of pesticides found on produce are usually much lower than the safety levels established by government agencies.

To complicate the issue of whether to buy organic, even organic foods may not be completely chemical-free. Although they haven't been treated with pesticides, small amounts of these chemicals can be carried by the wind or water, and end up on organic crops. Similar concerns surround other chemicals as well, such as nitrates; the levels of nitrates in organically grown plant foods vary from one producer to another, and are dependent on factors like the season in which they're grown, the geographic location, and the post-harvest processing.

No matter what you decide, don't let any concerns about chemicals keep you from feeding your children a healthy diet rich in fruits, vegetables, whole grains, and low-fat or fat-free dairy products, whether those are conventional or organic foods. In fact, there are greater risks in *not* making fruits and vegetables part of your child's meals, compared with any hazards posed by pesticides or herbicides.

Chemicals aside, what's the nutritional value of organic foods? Are these foods more nutritious for your child? Bear in mind that there is *no* convincing evidence that the nutritional content of organic foods differs in any significant way from conventional foods—in other words, there's no persuasive research showing that organic foods are more nutritious, safer, or even more tasty for your family.

If you have easy access to organic foods in local farmer's markets or stores, and their higher prices fit into your budget, there is certainly little downside to choosing organic items. However, keep in mind that organically grown produce may spoil more rapidly because it is not protected against damage from insects and bacteria.

with a drug that binds the lead in the blood and greatly increases the body's ability to eliminate it. When treatment is necessary, usually oral medicines are used on an outpatient basis. Much less frequently, the treatment may involve hospitalization and a series of injections.

Some children with lead poisoning require more than one course of treatment. Unfortunately, standard treatments for lead-poisoned children produce only a short-term or marginal lowering of the child's body lead levels and do not lower the child's chance of developing lead-related behavioral or learning problems. Children who have had lead poisoning will need to have their physical health, behavior, and academic performance monitored for many years and should receive special schooling and therapy to help them overcome learning and behavior problems.

The best treatment for lead poisoning is prevention. If you buy an older home, you may want to have it tested first. In the same way, children who spend time in older buildings for day care or other reasons may be at risk.

Pesticides/Herbicides

Pesticides and herbicides are used in a variety of settings, including homes,

Hand-washing is an important part of a healthy lifestyle.

schools, parks, lawns, gardens, and farms. While they may kill insects, rodents, and weeds, many are toxic to people when consumed in food and water.

More research is needed to determine the short- and long-term effects of pesticides and herbicides on humans. Although some studies have found connections between some childhood cancers and an exposure to pesticides, other studies have not reached the same conclusions. Many pesticides disrupt the nervous system of insects, and research has shown that they have the potential to damage the neurological system of children.

Prevention

Try to limit your child's unnecessary exposure to pesticides or herbicides. To reduce such exposure:

- Minimize using foods in which chemical pesticides or herbicides were used by farmers.

- Wash all fruits and vegetables with water before your child consumes them.

- For your own lawn and garden, use nonchemical pest control methods whenever possible. If you keep bottles of pesticides in your home or garage, make sure they're out of the reach of children to avoid any accidental poisoning.

- Children and adults who eat organic foods have lower levels of pesticide metabolites in their system.

- Avoid routinely spraying homes or schools to prevent insect infestations.

- Integrated pest management focuses on the use of baits, and blocking the sources of entry, as safer methods of entry.

Radon

Radon is a gas that is a product of the breakdown of uranium in soil and rock. It also may be in water, natural gas, and building materials.

High levels of radon are in homes in many regions of the United States. It makes its way into homes through cracks or openings in the foundation, walls, and floors, or occasionally in well water. It does not cause health problems immediately upon inhalation. Over time, however, it can increase the risk of lung cancer. In fact, next to cigarette smoking, radon is thought to be the most common cause of lung cancer in the United States.

Prevention

To reduce your child's risk of radon exposure:

- Ask your pediatrician or the local health department whether radon levels are high in your community.

- Have your home tested for radon, using an inexpensive radon detector. (Hardware stores sell these detectors.) A certified laboratory should analyze the results of this test.

- If the levels are too high in your home, call the Radon Hotline (operated by the National Safety Council in conjunction with the Environmental Protection Agency) at 1-800-767-7236; this is also a good resource for information on reducing the radon risk in your home.

~ 25 ~

Eyes

YOUR CHILD RELIES on the visual information he gathers to help him develop throughout infancy and childhood. If he has difficulty seeing properly, he may have problems in learning and relating to the world around him. For this reason it is important to detect eye deficiencies as early as possible. Many vision problems can be corrected if treated early but become much more difficult to care for later on.

Your infant should have his first eye examination at your first visit with your pediatrician to check for problems that may be present. Routine vision checks then should be part of every visit to the pediatrician's office. If your family has a history of serious eye diseases or abnormalities, your pediatrician may refer your baby to an ophthalmologist

(an eye specialist with a medical degree) for an early examination and follow-up visits if necessary.

If a child is born prematurely, he will be checked for a vision-threatening condition called retinopathy of prematurity (ROP), especially if he required oxygen over a prolonged period of time during his early days of life. The risk is greater in the premature infant with a birth weight of less than 1,500 grams (3.3 lb.). This condition may not be prevented even with ideal neonatal care, but in many cases, if detected early, it can be treated successfully. All neonatologists are aware of potential problems resulting from ROP and will let parents know about the necessity for evaluation by an ophthalmologist. Parents also should be told that all premature children are at

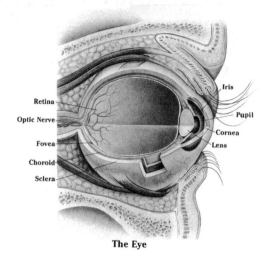

Retina
Optic Nerve
Fovea
Choroid
Sclera

Iris
Pupil
Cornea
Lens

The Eye

greater risk for developing astigmatism, nearsightedness, and strabismus (these medical eye conditions are described below), and that they therefore should be screened periodically throughout childhood.

How much does a newborn baby see? Until fairly recently, doctors thought that a newborn infant could see very little; however, newer information indicates that even during the early weeks of life, an infant can see light and shapes and can detect movement. Distance vision remains quite blurry, with the optimal-viewing length being 8 to 15 inches (20 to 38 cm), which is roughly the distance from his eyes to yours as you are nursing or feeding your baby.

Until your baby learns to use both eyes together, they may "wander," or move randomly. This random movement should be decreasing by two to three months of age. Around three months old, your baby probably will focus on faces and close objects and follow a moving object with his eyes.

By four months of age, he should be using his vision to detect various objects close to him, which he probably will reach for and grasp. By six months old he should be able to visually identify and distinguish between objects.

Between one and two years of age, your child's ability to see will develop rapidly, and by ages three to five, the child with normal vision will reach typical adult visual acuity levels.

By the time your child is ten, his visual system will be fully mature. At this point, many early onset eye and vision problems may no longer be reversed or corrected. This is why early detection and treatment of eye problems in children are so important and why your pediatrician will examine your baby's eyes at every routine physical examination.

Vision Screening Recommendations

Vision screening is a very important factor in identifying vision-threatening conditions. Regular eye checks during pediatric visits are done to determine if your baby's eyes are developing normally. The American Academy of Pediatrics recommends that children be screened in four stages:

1. In the newborn nursery: Pediatricians should examine all infants prior to their discharge from the nursery to check for infections (page 728) and ocular defects, cataracts (page 727), or congenital glaucoma. If a problem is suspected, a pediatric ophthalmologist should see the newborn. All children with multiple medical problems or with a history of prematurity should be examined by an ophthalmologist.

2. By the age of six months: Pediatricians should screen infants at the time of their well-baby visits to check for ocular alignment (eyes working together) and the presence of any eye disease. From six months to three years of age, photo screening may be electively performed for earlier detection of amblyopia or its risk factors.

3. At the age of three to five years: Vision screening by a pediatrician should be done annually during these ages. The visual acuity is checked and the eyes are examined for any other abnormality that may cause a problem with the child's educational development. Any abnormality requires referral to an ophthalmologist.

4. At the age of six years and older: Pediatricians should screen children annually until the age of six, and every other year thereafter. These tests measure visual acuity and evaluate other ocular functions.

By three to four years of age, most children can follow directions and describe what they see, so visual acuity testing is much more reliable. Your pediatrician may use eye charts with shapes rather than letters to estimate your preschool-age child's visual acuity. By this age, visual acuity should have reached the 20/40 level in each eye, and any child with less than 20/40 vision should be referred to an ophthalmologist to determine the cause of the visual deficiency. From ages six years and onward, normal visual acuity results in each eye of 20/30 or better are expected.

Your pediatrician may use a newer method for screening vision, especially in younger children, called photoscreening, in which a specially designed camera is used to help detect potential abnormalities with your child's vision. These devices are becoming an increasingly accepted method for screening youngsters, especially for those who are either too young or otherwise unable to have their vision reliably tested with a symbol or letter eye chart.

When to Call the Pediatrician

As noted above, vision screening is a very important factor in identifying vision-threatening conditions. These routine eye checks can detect hidden eye problems, but occasionally you may notice obvious signs that your child is having trouble seeing or that his eyes are not normal. Notify the pediatrician if your child shows any of the following warning signs.

- A white appearance of the pupil (a condition called leukocoria) in one or both eyes

- Persistent (lasting more than twenty-four hours) redness, swelling, crusting, or discharge in his eyes or eyelids

- Excessive tearing

- Sensitivity to light, especially a change in the child's light sensitivity

- Eyes that look crooked or crossed, or that don't move together

- Head consistently held in an abnormal or tilted position

- Frequent squinting

- Drooping of one or both eyelids

- Pupils of unequal size

- Continuous eye-rubbing

- Eyes that "bounce" or "dance"

- Inability to see objects unless he holds them close

- Eye injury (see page 728)

- Cloudy cornea

You also should take your child to the pediatrician if he complains of any of the following:

- Seeing double

- Frequent headaches

- Persistent eye pain or mild headaches after doing close-up eye work (reading, watching television)

- Blurred vision

- Itching, scratching, or burning eyes

- Difficulty with color vision

Depending on the symptoms your child displays, your pediatrician probably will check for vision difficulties and/or some of the other problems discussed in the remainder of this chapter.

Amblyopia

Amblyopia, or lazy eye, is a fairly common eye problem (affecting about 2 out of 100 children) that develops when a child has one eye that doesn't see well, and she uses the other eye almost exclusively. In general, this problem must be detected as early as possible in order to treat and restore normal vision in the affected eye. If this situation persists for too long (past seven to ten years of age), vision is often lost permanently in the unused eye.

Once an ophthalmologist diagnoses the problems in the unused eye, your child may need to wear a patch over the "good" eye for periods of time. This forces her to use and strengthen the eye that has become "lazy." Patching therapy will be continued for as long as necessary to bring the weaker eye up to its full potential and maintain it there. This could take weeks, months, or even a few years. As an alternative to the patch, the ophthalmologist might prescribe eye drops to blur the vision in the good eye, thereby stimulating your child to use the amblyopic eye better.

Cataracts

Although we usually think of cataracts as affecting elderly people, they also may be found in infants and young children, and are sometimes present at birth. A cataract is a clouding of the lens (the transparent tissue inside the eye that helps bring light rays into focus on the retina). While rare, congenital cataracts are nonetheless a leading cause of visual loss and blindness in children.

Cataracts in children need to be detected and treated early so their vision can develop more appropriately. A cataract usually shows up as a white discoloration in the center of the child's pupil. If a baby is born with a cataract that blocks most of the light entering the eye, the affected lens has to be removed surgically to permit the baby's vision to develop. Most pediatric ophthalmologists recommend that this procedure be performed during the first month of life. After the clouded lens is removed, the baby must be fitted with a contact lens or with an eyeglass correction. At the age of about two years, the placement of a lens within the eye is recommended. In addition, visual rehabilitation of the affected eye will almost always involve use of a patch until the child's eyes are fully mature (at about age ten years).

Occasionally a child will be born with a small pinpoint cataract that will not initially impede visual development. These tiny cataracts often do not require treatment; however, they need to be monitored carefully to ensure that they do not become large enough to interfere with normal vision development.

In many cases, the cause of cataracts in infants cannot be determined. Cataracts may be attributed to a tendency inherited from parents; they may result from trauma to the eye; or they may occur as a result of viral infections such as German measles and chickenpox or an infection from other microorganisms, such as those that cause toxoplasmosis. To protect the unborn child from cataracts and from other serious disorders, pregnant women should take care to avoid unnecessary exposure to infectious diseases. In addition, as a precaution against toxoplasmosis (a disease caused by parasites), pregnant women should avoid handling cat litter or eating raw meat, both of which may contain the organism that causes this disease.

Eye Infections

If the white of your child's eye and the inside of his lower lid become red, he probably has a condition called conjunctivitis. Also known as pinkeye, this inflammation, which can be painful and itchy, usually signals an infection, but may be due to other causes, such as an irritation to smoke or fumes, an allergic reaction, or (rarely) a more serious condition. It's often accompanied by tearing and discharge, which is the body's way of trying to heal or remedy the situation.

If your child has a red eye, he needs to see the pediatrician as soon as possible. Eye infections typically last seven to ten days. The doctor will make the diagnosis and prescribe necessary medication if it is indicated. *Never put previously opened medication or someone else's eye medication into your child's eye. It could cause serious damage.*

In a newborn baby, serious eye infections may result from exposure to bacteria or viruses during pregnancy or during passage through the birth canal—which is why all infants are treated with antibiotic eye ointment or drops in the delivery room. Such infections must be treated early to prevent serious complications. Eye infections that occur after the newborn period may be unsightly, because of the redness of the eye and the yellow discharge that usually accompanies them, and they may make your child uncomfortable, but they are rarely serious. If your pediatrician feels the problem is caused by bacteria, antibiotic eyedrops are the usual treatment. Viral causes of conjunctivitis do not respond to antibiotics, but antibiotic eye drops may still be used if a bacterial infection is suspected.

Eye infections are very contagious. Except to administer drops or ointment, you should avoid direct contact with your child's eyes or drainage from them until the medication has been used for several days and there is evidence of clearing of the redness. Carefully wash your hands before and after touching the area around the infected eye. If your child is in a child care or nursery school program, you should keep him home until the pinkeye is no longer contagious. Your pediatrician will tell you when you can safely send him back to child care or nursery school.

Eye Injuries

When dust or other small particles get in your child's eyes, the cleansing action of tears usually will wash them out. If that fails to occur, or if a serious accident affecting the eye takes place, call your pediatrician or take your child to the nearest emergency room after heeding the following emergency guidelines.

CHEMICALS IN THE EYE (see further discussion, Chapter 23)
Flush the eye extensively with water, making sure you get the water into the eye itself. Then take the child to the emergency room.

Preventing Eye Injuries

Nine out of ten eye injuries are preventable, and almost half occur around the home. To minimize the risk of such accidents in your family, follow these safety guidelines.

- Keep all chemicals out of reach and separate from medications. That includes detergents, ammonia, spray cans, Super Glue, and all other cleaning fluids.

- Choose your child's toys carefully. Watch out for sharp or pointed parts, especially if your child is too young to understand their danger.

- Keep your child away from darts and pellet and BB guns.

- Teach your preschooler how to handle scissors and pencils properly. If she's too young to learn, don't allow her to use them.

- Keep your child away from power lawn mowers and trimmers, which can hurl stones or other objects.

- Don't let your child near you when you're lighting fires or using tools. If you want her to watch you hammer nails, make her wear protective goggles. Safety glasses should also be worn for your safety and to set a good example for your child.

- If your child begins participating in youth sports, have her wear eye protectors appropriate for her sport. Baseball is the leading cause of sports-related eye injuries in children, with many such injuries resulting from being struck by a pitched ball. Eye protectors (made of polycarbonate) should be seriously considered for use as part of her batting helmet. Protective sports eye equipment (again using polycarbonate lenses) also should be worn during youth sports such as soccer or basketball, as well as other recreational sports such as skiing. Prescription sports goggles are also available and are a good way to protect the eye while providing vision help.

- Tell your youngster not to look directly into the sun, even with sunglasses. Doing so can cause severe and permanent eye damage. Never allow a child to look directly at an eclipse of the sun.

- Never allow your child near fireworks of any kind. The American Academy of Pediatrics encourages children and their families to enjoy fireworks at public fireworks displays rather than purchasing fireworks for home use. In fact, the Academy would support a ban on public sales of all fireworks.

LARGE PARTICLE IN THE EYE

If the particle won't come out with tears or by flushing with water, or if your child is still complaining of pain after an hour, call your pediatrician. The doctor will remove the object or, if necessary, refer you to an ophthalmologist. Sometimes such particles cause scratches on the cornea (corneal abrasions), which are quite painful but heal rapidly with proper treatment. Corneal injuries also can be caused by blows or other injuries to the eye.

CUT EYELID

Minor cuts usually heal quickly and easily, but a deep cut requires emergency medical attention and probably will need stitches. (See *Cuts and Scrapes,* page 692.) Cuts on the border of the eyelids by the eyelashes, or near the tear duct openings, can be a special concern. If the cut is located in these areas, call your pediatrician right away for advice on how to handle the situation.

BLACK EYE

To reduce swelling, apply a cold pack or towel to the area for ten to twenty minutes. Then consult the doctor to make sure there is no internal damage to the eye or the bones surrounding the eye.

Eyelid Problems

Droopy eyelid (ptosis) may appear as a weak or heavy upper lid; or, if it is very slight, it may be noticed only because the affected eye appears somewhat smaller than the other eye. Ptosis usually involves only one eyelid, but both may be affected. Your baby may be born with ptosis, or it may develop later. Ptosis may be partial, causing your baby's eyes to appear slightly asymmetrical; or it may be total, causing the affected lid to cover the eye completely. If the ptotic eyelid covers the entire pupillary opening of your child's eye, or if the weight of the lid causes the cornea to assume an irregular shape (astigmatism), it will threaten normal vision development and must be corrected as early as possible. If vision is not threatened, surgical intervention, if necessary, is usually delayed until the child is four or five years of age or older, when the eyelid and surrounding tissue are more fully developed and a better cosmetic result can be obtained.

Most **birthmarks** and growths involving the eyelids of the newborn or young child are benign; however, because they may increase in size during the first year of life, they sometimes cause parents to become concerned. Most of these birthmarks and growths are not serious and will not affect your child's vision. However, any irregularity should be brought to the attention of your child's pediatrician so that it can be evaluated and monitored.

Some children will develop lumps and bumps on their lids that can impair development of good eyesight. In particular, a blood vessel tumor called a capillary or strawberry hemangioma can start out as a small swelling, and rapidly enlarge. It may enlarge over the first year of life, and then start to spontaneously resolve over the next few years of life. If it becomes large enough, it can interfere with your baby's development of good vision in the affected eye and will need to be treated. Because of their potential to cause vision problems, any child who starts to show any rapidly enlarging lumps or bumps around either eye should be evaluated by your pediatrician and perhaps an ophthalmologist as well.

A child might also be born with a flat, purple-colored lesion on their face called a port wine stain, because of its resemblance to a dark red wine. If this birthmark involves the eye, especially the upper lid, the child may be at risk for development of glaucoma (a condition where pressure increases inside the eyeball) or amblyopia (weak vision). Any child born with this birthmark needs to be examined by an ophthalmologist shortly after birth.

Small dark moles, called **nevi**, on the eyelids or on the white part of the eye itself rarely cause any problems or need to be removed. Once they have been evaluated by your pediatrician, these marks should cause concern only if they change in size, shape, or color.

Small, firm, flesh-colored bulges underneath your child's eyebrows are usually **dermoid cysts**. These cysts are noncancerous tumors that usually are present from birth. Because they tend to increase in size during early childhood, their removal is preferred in most cases before they rupture under the skin and cause inflammation.

Two other eyelid problems—**chalazia** and **hordeola** or **sties**—are common, but not serious. A chalazion is a cyst resulting from a blockage of an oil gland. A sty, or hordeolum, is a bacterial infection of the cells surrounding the sweat glands or hair follicles on the *edge* of the lid. Call your pediatrician regarding treatment of these conditions. He probably will tell you to apply warm compresses directly to the eyelid for twenty or thirty minutes three or four times a day until the chalazion or sty clears. The doctor may want to examine your child before prescribing additional treatment, such as an antibiotic ointment or drops.

Once your child has had a sty or chalazion, she may be more likely to get them again. When they occur repeatedly, it's sometimes necessary to perform lid scrubs to reduce the bacterial colonization of the eyelids and open the glands and pores in the eyelids.

Impetigo is a very contagious bacterial infection that may occur on the eyelid. Your pediatrician will advise you on how to remove the crust from the lid and then prescribe an antibiotic eye ointment and oral antibiotics. (See *Impetigo*, page 841.)

Glaucoma

Glaucoma is a serious eye disorder caused by increased pressure within the eye. It may be due to either overproduction or inadequate drainage of the fluid within the eye. If this increased pressure persists too long, it can damage the optic nerve, resulting in permanent loss of vision.

Although a child can be born with glaucoma, this is quite rare. More often it develops later in life. The earlier it is detected and treated, the better the chance of preventing permanent loss of vision. Warning signs of glaucoma in infants include:

- Excessive tearing associated with extreme sensitivity to light (the child will turn her head into the mattress or blankets to avoid light).

- Hazy or overly prominent appearance of either eye.

- Increased irritability (typically due to persistent eye pain and redness).

Call your pediatrician promptly if you are concerned about any of these signs.

Usually glaucoma must be treated surgically to create an alternate route for fluid to leave the eye. Any child who has this disease must be watched very carefully throughout her life so that the pressure is kept under control and the optic nerve and cornea stay as healthy as possible.

Strabismus

Strabismus is a misalignment of the eyes caused by an imbalance in the muscles controlling the eye. This condition makes it impossible for the eyes to focus on the same point at the same time. Strabismus occurs in about 4 out of 100 children. It may be present at birth (infantile strabismus), or it may develop later in childhood (acquired strabismus). Strabismus can develop if your child has another visual impairment, sustains an eye injury, or develops cataracts. Always report the sudden onset of strabismus to your pediatrician immediately. Although very rare, it may indicate the development of a tumor or other serious nervous system problem. In all cases, it is important to diagnose and treat strabismus as early in your child's life as possible. If a turned eye is not treated early, the child may never develop the ability to use both eyes together (binocular vision); and if both eyes are not used together, it is common for one to become "lazy," or amblyopic (see page 726). Amblyopia often coexists with strabismus and must be treated separately with patching or the use of eyedrops in the opposite eye.

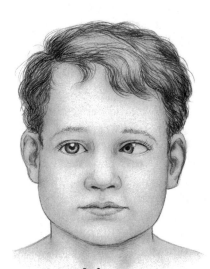

**Left eye
turning inward**

It is important to note that a newborn baby's eyes commonly and normally wander. However, within a few weeks, he learns to move his eyes together, and this strabismus should disappear within a few months. However, if this intermittent wandering continues, or if your baby's eyes don't turn in the same direction (if one turns in, out, up, or down), he needs to be evaluated by your pediatrician, and often a pediatric ophthalmologist as well.

If your child is born with strabismus and it does not resolve on its own in a few months, it's important for his eyes to be realigned as soon as possible so he can focus them together on a single object. Eye exercises alone cannot accomplish this, so the treatment usually involves eyeglasses or surgery.

If your child needs an operation, this surgery is frequently done between six and eighteen months of age. The operation is usually safe and effective, although it's not uncommon for a child to need more than one procedure. Even after surgery, your child still may need glasses.

Some children look as if they have strabismus because of the way their faces are structured, but in fact their eyes may be well-aligned. These children often have a flat nasal bridge and broad skin folds alongside the nose, termed *epicanthus,* which can distort the appearance of the eyes, making these youngsters appear cross-eyed when they really aren't. This condition is called pseudostrabismus (meaning false eye turning). The child's vision is not affected, and, in most cases, as the child grows and the nasal bridge be-comes more prominent, the child loses the appearance of crossed eyes.

Because of the importance of early diagnosis and treatment of a true misalignment (or true strabismus), if you have any suspicion that your baby's eyes may not be perfectly aligned and working together, you should bring it to the attention of your pediatrician, who can best determine whether your baby has an actual problem.

Tear (or Lacrimal) Production Problems

Tears play an important role in maintaining good eyesight by keeping the eyes wet and free of particles, dust, and other substances that might cause injury or interfere with normal vision. The so-called lacrimal system maintains the continuous production and circulation of tears, and depends on regular blinking to propel tears from the lacrimal gland across the surface of the eye, finally draining through the tear ducts and into the nose.

This lacrimal system develops gradually over the first three or four years of life. Thus, while a newborn will produce enough tears to coat the surface of the eyes, it may be several months after birth before he "cries real tears."

Blocked tear ducts, which are very common among newborns and young babies, can cause the appearance of excessive tearing in one or both eyes, because the tears run down the cheek instead of draining through the duct and into the nose. In newborns,

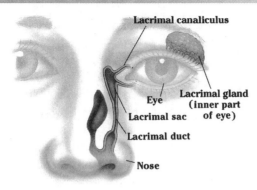

Lacrimal canaliculus

Eye

Lacrimal gland
(inner part
of eye)

Lacrimal sac

Lacrimal duct

Nose

blocked tear ducts usually occur when an internal membrane covering them fails to disappear around birth. Your pediatrician will demonstrate how to massage the tear duct. She'll also show you how to clean the eye with moist compresses to remove all secretions and crusting. Until the tear duct finally opens, the sticky mucus discharge may not go away. Since this is not typically a true infection or pinkeye, antibiotics are not always necessary or helpful.

Sometimes a persistent membrane (or even a small cyst) can cause a blocked tear duct that does not resolve on its own or with massaging. When this occurs and the methods described above are unsuccessful, the ophthalmologist may decide to probe open the blocked tear duct surgically. Rarely, this procedure must be repeated more than once.

Vision Difficulties Requiring Corrective Lenses

NEARSIGHTEDNESS

The inability to see distant objects clearly is the most common visual problem in young children. This inherited trait occasionally is found in newborns, especially premature infants, but it more often develops after six to nine years of age.

Contrary to popular belief, reading too much, reading in dim light, or poor nutrition cannot cause or affect nearsightedness. It's usually the result of an eyeball that is longer in shape, causing the image to be focused improperly. Less frequently, it is due to a change in the shape of the cornea or lens.

The treatment for nearsightedness is corrective lenses—either eyeglasses or contact lenses. Keep in mind that when your child grows, so do his eyes, so he may need new lenses as often as every six to twelve months. Nearsightedness usually changes rapidly for several years and then stabilizes during or after adolescence.

FARSIGHTEDNESS

This is a condition in which the eyeball is shorter than its focusing ability. Most infants are actually born farsighted, but as they grow, their eyeballs get longer and the farsightedness diminishes. Glasses or contact lenses rarely are needed unless the condition is excessive. If your child has eye discomfort or frequent mild headaches related to prolonged reading, she may be suffering from a severe degree of farsightedness and should be examined by your pediatrician or pediatric ophthalmologist. Excessive farsightedness also may lead to crossed eyes (see *Strabismus,* page 732) and *Amblyopia* (see page 726), both of which require treatment in addition to glasses.

ASTIGMATISM

Astigmatism is an uneven curvature of the surface of the cornea and/or lens. (Think of the eye as having the shape of a football.) If your child has an astigmatism, vision both near and far may be blurred. Astigmatism can be corrected with either glasses or contact lenses, and, like farsightedness, may cause amblyopia if one eye is affected more than the other.

~ 26 ~

Family Issues

Adoption

IF YOU ARE about to adopt or have just adopted a child, you are likely experiencing conflicting emotions. Along with excitement and delight, you also may feel some anxiety and apprehension. These are emotions common to all parents, regardless of whether a child joins their family by birth or by adoption. Choosing an understanding, supportive, and collaborative pediatrician will be helpful as you begin your new job as a parent. Even before a child joins your family, a pediatrician can discuss your feelings about impending parenthood. If you are adopting a child internationally or domestically, a pediatrician will also be able to address any medical issues that may arise.

Once your child is home with you, schedule a visit to a pediatrician as soon as possible. Similar to an initial newborn exam, this initial postadoptive visit can provide an opportunity to ask any questions you have about your child's physical and mental health and development. Schedule future exams as required by the child's age and medical needs. Many families find that they benefit from additional visits with their pediatrician during the first year or so to help address concerns that may arise as parents and child start to develop a relationship.

In addition to the typical challenges of parenting, adoptive parents also face several issues and questions that nonadoptive parents do not. They include the following:

HOW AND WHEN SHOULD I TELL MY CHILD SHE IS ADOPTED?

Your child should learn the truth about her birth family and her adoptive family as early as she is able to understand, which probably will be between ages two and four. It is important to adjust the information to her maturity level, so that she can make sense of it. For example: "Your birth parents loved you very much, but they knew they could not take care of you. So they looked for someone who also loved little children and was looking to have a bigger family." As she gets older and asks more specific questions, give her honest answers, but do not press information on her if she seems uncomfortable, fearful, or disinterested about it. Children should come to know about and understand adoption gradually, as they mature, just as they come to understand many other complicated ideas.

ARE THERE SPECIAL CONCERNS TO WATCH FOR?

Adopted children have the same problems that other children of the same age and background have. Children with a history of living in an orphanage or in foster care have often experienced significant adversity or trauma, and may benefit from specific parenting strategies to address those. They may also benefit from counseling at the time of placement, or at different times in their lives.

SHOULD I TELL OTHERS THAT MY CHILD IS ADOPTED?

If you are asked, answer the question honestly, with as much detail as seems appropriate for the situation. Recognize that the most important audience for your answer is your child. Many professionals believe that your child's "adoption story" is hers to own and share as she desires as she gets older. You may wish to share general information with friends and family, but hold sensitive details privately until your child is old enough to understand them and decide for herself how and with whom she would like them to be shared.

WHAT IF SHE WANTS TO FIND HER BIRTH PARENTS?

Many adoptions today include some degree of openness, or ongoing identified contact between birth parent, adoptee, and adoptive parents, and there is a lot of evidence that this arrangement is helpful to children in many ways. If your adoption is not open, though, it is still very natural for children to wonder about birth parents, and this in no way diminishes the love that your child has for you. Talking with your child about his birth parents helps him to know that you understand this, and that he can share those thoughts and feelings with you. Circumstances will vary, but let your child know that when he is old enough, you will help him to search for them if he wants to. Your adoption agency and adoption search specialists can help.

Your pediatrician may be able to help you with more detailed answers to these and other questions that arise in adoptive families.

WHERE WE STAND

INCREASING NUMBERS OF children have been adopted by gay or lesbian individuals or couples in recent years. In some states this has stimulated political debate and public policy change. A growing body of scientific literature reveals that children who grow up with one or two gay and/or lesbian parents will develop emotionally, cognitively, socially, and sexually as well as children whose parents are heterosexual. Parents' sexual orientation is much less important than having loving and nurturing parents.

The American Academy of Pediatrics recognizes the diversity of families. We believe that children who are born to, or adopted by, one member of a gay or lesbian couple deserve the security of two legally recognized parents. Therefore, we support statutory and legal means to enable children to be adopted by the second parent or coparent in families headed by gay and lesbian couples.

Child Abuse and Neglect

Child abuse is common. It is important to understand and reduce the risks of abuse for your child and familiarize yourself with the signs of abuse. Approximately 3 million cases of child abuse and neglect involving almost 5.5 million children are reported each year. The majority of cases reported to Child Protective Services involve neglect, followed by physical and sexual abuse. According to Prevent Child Abuse, "Neglect occurs when children's basic needs are not adequately met, resulting in actual or potential harm. Child neglect can harm children's physical and mental health as well as their social and cognitive development in many different ways." There is considerable overlap among children who are abused, with many suffering a combination of physical abuse, sexual abuse, and/or neglect.

Sexual abuse is any sexual activity that a child cannot comprehend or consent to. It includes acts such as fondling, oral-genital contact, and genital and anal intercourse, as well as exhibitionism, voyeurism, and exposure to pornography. Studies have suggested that up to one in four girls and one in eight boys will be sexually abused before they are eighteen years old. Physical abuse occurs when a child's body is injured as a result of hitting, kicking, shaking, burning, or other show of force. One study suggests that about 1 in 20 children has been physically abused in their lifetime. Teach your child that it is not OK for adults to touch his body if he does not consent or understand what is happening.

Most child abuse occurs within the family. Risk factors include parental depression or other mental health issues, a parental history of childhood abuse, and domestic violence. Child neglect and other forms of maltreatment are also more common in families living in poverty and among parents who are teenagers or who abuse drugs or alcohol. More children are abused by a caregiver or someone they know, than abused outside of the home by a stranger.

Child neglect can include physical neglect (failing to provide food, clothing, shelter, or other physical necessities), emotional neglect (failing to provide love, comfort, or affection), or medical neglect (failing to provide needed medical care). Psychological or emotional abuse results from all of the above, but also can be associated with verbal abuse, which can harm a child's self-worth or emotional well-being.

Signs and Symptoms

It is not always easy to recognize when a child has been abused. Children who have been maltreated are often afraid to tell anyone, because they think they will be blamed or that no one will believe them. Sometimes they remain quiet because the person who abused them is someone they love very much, or because of fear, or both. Parents also tend to overlook signs and symptoms of abuse, because they don't want to face the truth. This is a serious mistake. A child who has been abused needs special support and treatment as early as possible. The longer he continues to be abused or is left to deal with the situation on his own, the harder it is for children to be able to heal and develop optimally physically and mentally.

It is important to remember that there are important consequences for the parent as well when a child has gone through an adverse childhood experience (ACE). Parents should always be alert to any unexplainable changes in the child's body or behavior. While injuries are often specific for an incident of physical abuse, behavioral change tends to reflect the anxiety that results from a variety of acute and chronic stressful situations. There are no behaviors that relate to a particular type of child abuse or neglect. Here is a short list of physical signs and behavioral changes in children who may have experienced abuse or neglect:

Physical Signs

- Any injury (bruise, burn, fracture, abdominal or head injury) that cannot be explained

- Failure to gain weight (especially in infants) or sudden dramatic weight gain

- Genital pain or bleeding

- A sexually transmitted disease

BEHAVIORAL AND MENTAL HEALTH CHANGES THAT RAISE CONCERN ABOUT POSSIBLE ABUSE OR NEGLECT

- Fearful behavior (nightmares, depression, unusual fears)

- Abdominal pain, bed-wetting (especially if the child has already been toilet trained)

- Attempts to run away

- Extreme sexual behavior that seems inappropriate for the child's age

- Sudden change in self-confidence

- Headaches or stomachaches with no medical cause

- Abnormal fears, increased nightmares

- School failure

- Extremely passive or aggressive behavior

- Desperately affectionate behavior or social withdrawal

- Big appetite and stealing food

Long-Term Consequences

In most cases, children who are abused or neglected suffer greater mental health than physical health damage. Emotional and psychological abuse and neglect deny the child the tools needed to cope with stress, and to learn new skills to become resilient, strong, and successful. So a child who is maltreated or neglected may have a wide range of reactions and may even become depressed or develop suicidal, withdrawn, or violent behavior. As he gets older, he may use drugs or alcohol, try to run away, refuse discipline, or abuse others. As an adult, he may develop marital and sexual difficulties, depression, or suicidal behavior. Identifying a child victim is the first step. Recognizing the important influence of early trauma on future development is crucial to assisting the child.

Not all children who are abused have severe reactions (see previous discussion on the resilient child, page xxxiv). Usually the younger the child, the longer the abuse continues, and the closer the child's relationship with the abuser, the more serious the mental health effects will be. A close relationship with a very supportive adult can increase resiliency, reducing some of the impact.

Getting Help

If you suspect your child has been abused, get help immediately through your pediatrician or a local child protective agency. Physicians are *legally obligated* to report all suspected cases of abuse or neglect to state authorities. Your pediatrician also will detect and treat any medical injuries or conditions, recommend a therapist, and provide necessary information to investigators. The doctor also may testify in court if necessary to obtain legal protection for the child or criminal prosecution of the person suspected of perpetrating the abuse or neglect.

If he has been abused, your child will benefit from the services of a qualified mental health professional.

You and other members of the family may be advised to seek counseling so that you'll be able to provide the support and comfort your child needs. If someone in your family is responsible for the abuse, a mental health professional may be able to help that person successfully, as well.

If your child has been abused, you may be the only person who can help him. There is *no* good reason to delay reporting your suspicions of abuse. Denying the problem will only make the situation worse, allowing the abuse or neglect to continue unchecked and decreasing your child's chance for optimal physical and mental health and well-being.

In any case of abuse or neglect, the child's safety is of primary concern. He needs to be in a safe environment free of the potential for continuing abuse and neglect.

Preventing Abuse and Neglect

The major reasons for physical and psychological maltreatment of children within the family often are parental feelings of isolation, stress, and frustration. Parents need support and as much information as possible in order to raise their children responsibly. They need to be taught how to cope with their own feelings of frustration and anger without venting them on children. They also need the companionship of other adults who will listen and help during times of crisis. Support groups through local community organizations often are helpful first steps to diminish some of the isolation or frustration parents may be feeling. Parents who were themselves abused as children are in particular need of support. Confronting, addressing, and healing parental mental and emotional health take uncommon courage and insight, but this is often the best way to reduce the chances that the past abuse is not passed on to the next generation of their children.

Personal supervision of and involvement in your child's activities are the best ways to prevent physical and sexual abuse outside the home. Any school or child care program you select for your child should allow unrestricted and unannounced parental visits without prearrangement. Parents should be allowed to help in the classroom on a volunteer basis and be informed about the selection or changes of staff members. Parents should pay careful attention to their child's reports about and reactions to his experiences at child care and school. Always investigate if your child tells you he's been maltreated or if he undergoes a sudden unexplained change in behavior.

Although you don't want to frighten your child, you can teach him some basic rules of safety in a nonthreatening manner. Teach him to keep his distance from strangers, not to wander away from you in unfamiliar territory, to say "no" when someone asks him to do something against his will, and always to tell you if someone hurts him or makes him feel bad. Always remember that open, two-way communication with your child provides the best chance that you will know early when a problem occurs. Emphasize that he will not get in trouble if he tells you about abuse or other confusing events. Emphasize that you need to know this to be able to keep him safe and that he will be OK if he tells you. Instead of teaching him that he's surrounded by danger, teach him that he is strong, capable, and can count on you to keep him safe, as long as he can tell you about it.

Divorce

Every year over 1 million children in the US are involved in a divorce. Even those children who had lived with parental conflict and unhappiness for a long time may find the changes that follow divorce more difficult than anything they'd experienced before. At the very least, the child must adjust to living apart from one parent or, if in shared custody, to dividing her life between two homes. Because of financial changes, she also may have to move to a smaller home and a different neighborhood. A mother who stayed at home before now may have to go to work. Even if she doesn't, the stress and depression that accompany divorce may make some mothers less attentive to and loving with their children.

No one can predict specifically how divorce will affect your child. Her response will depend on her own sensitivity, the quality of her relationships with each parent, and the parents' ability to work together to meet her emotional needs during this time. It also will depend to some extent on her age and resiliency or vulnerability that her previous life experiences have given her.

In a very general way, you can anticipate how your child will react to divorce based on her age at the time it occurs:

Children under two often revert to more infantile behavior. They may become unusually clingy, dependent, or frustrated. They may refuse to go to sleep and may suddenly start waking up during the night. Under the age of three, they may show signs of sadness and fear of others. They also may have angry outbursts and tantrums, lose interest in eating, and have problems with toilet training.

Children between three and five also may act more like infants and they may feel that they are responsible for their parents' breakup. At this age, children do not fully understand that their parents' lives are separate from their own. They believe that they are the center of their family's universe and therefore blame themselves when significant events happen in their lives. Boys often become more aggressive and defiant toward their mothers. Girls may become insecure and distrustful of males. The less contact the child has with the noncustodial parent, or the more tense the postdivorce relationship, the more serious these reactions are likely to be. In the process, the child's self-worth may be impacted negatively.

Your child's response to the divorce probably will be most intense during and immediately following the physical separation. As she grows older, she may continue to think about the past and struggle to understand why her parents separated. For years she may have some sense of loss, which might become especially painful during holidays and on special occasions like birthdays and family reunions.

Most children of divorce wish desperately for their parents to get back together. However, it is much more difficult for them if the parents repeatedly attempt to reconcile and then part again than if the initial separation is final. When the parents act indecisively, the child is likely to become suspicious, confused, and insecure.

In some cases, a child's behavior and self-esteem actually improve after the parents' divorce. Sometimes this is because the parents are relieved of the tension and sadness of an unhappy marriage and now can give the child more affection and attention. Sometimes it is because the divorce ends an emotionally or physically abusive situation. Often, however, even children who have been abused by a parent still yearn for that abusive parent's love and for the family to be restored.

In summary, some children have serious and lasting psychological aftereffects from a divorce, but many others do well once the initial impact has been experienced and coped with, and the child and other family members have learned how to successfully adapt and support each other with their new life circumstances.

How Parents Can Help the Child

A child integrates and mirrors her parents' emotions. If her parents are angry, depressed, or violent during the separation process, a child is likely to absorb these disturbing feelings and may turn them against herself. If the parents argue about her, or if she hears her name during their disputes, she may believe even more strongly that she is to blame. Secrecy and silence probably won't make her feel much better, however, and actually may intensify the unhappiness and tension she feels around her. If you're divorcing, the best approach is to be honest about your feelings but make a special effort to be loving and reassuring with your child. She will have to accept that her parents no longer love each other—and you shouldn't try to pretend otherwise—but make sure she understands and feels that both parents love her just as much as ever and want to help her through this process.

When parents are sensitive to what their child is going through, the child has a greater likelihood of coping and rebounding from the uncertainty and anxiety that are often present due to the divorce. But each child is different. Children have their own way of reacting to the situations around them—some respond with resilience and a sense of optimism while others tend to think negatively and disastrously about the present and the future. One of your tasks is to help your child deal with the divorce realistically, and avoid any thoughts that these major life changes will negatively impact her life.

To help in the adjustment process, make it clear to your child that even though she may be spending time in two homes now, emphasize and reemphasize that she will continue to be loved just as much as always by both parents. She will continue to be safe. In fact, explain that you and your spouse will each have more special time to devote to her. Also, point out that you and your spouse expect to be happier because of the divorce, and the household will be a more pleasant place.

In the weeks, months, and years after a divorce, keep the dialogue with your child open and appropriate for her age level. Repeatedly encourage her to talk about her feelings. Respond to her questions with clear and simple answers, and don't hesitate to bring up issues that she may have never raised on her own but are common among children of divorce. (She may be thinking, "Is it my fault that Mommy and Daddy are going to be apart?" . . . "If I'm a good girl, will Mommy and Daddy get together again?" . . . "Will Mommy and Daddy still always love me?")

If your child is younger than two years, you can't get these messages across very well with words. You will have to convey them through your actions. When you are with your child, try to put your own issues and worries aside and concentrate on her needs. Keep the daily routine as consistent as possible, and do not expect her to make any other major changes (e.g.,

toilet training, moving from a crib to a bed, or, if avoidable, adjusting to a new care provider or home arrangement) during this transitional period. In the beginning, try to be understanding and patient if your child's behavior regresses, but if this regression continues even after the divorce is completed and your life has settled back into a regular routine, ask your pediatrician for advice.

If your child is older, she needs to feel that both of her parents care about her and that they are willing to put their differences aside when it comes to her welfare. This means that you both must maintain an active involvement in her life. In the past, most fathers gradually withdrew from their children following divorce. Today courts and psychologists are trying to correct this pattern, in part by making a distinction between physical and legal custody. In this way, one parent can be granted physical custody, so that the child can have a home base, while legal custody can be awarded jointly, so that both parents remain involved in decisions about the child's education, medical care, and other basic physical, mental, and social needs. The child can visit regularly with the parent who does not have physical custody.

It is also possible to have both joint physical custody and joint legal custody. This arrangement has the advantage of keeping both parents fully involved with the child. However, it also may have serious drawbacks. Especially if they are under ten, the children may feel split between two

Helping Your Child Move Forward

To ease your child through the divorce, here are some suggestions:

- Talk with your child on an ongoing basis, and make her feel safe despite her fears and worries.

- Be honest, but keep things simple ("Your daddy and I are having trouble getting along").

- Show patience with your child, who may ask questions like "Why is Daddy moving away?" "How often will I see Daddy?" "When is he moving back?" "Where am I going to live?"

- Make it clear that your child did not cause your marital problems.

- Do not blame your spouse or express any anger in front of your child.

- Reassure your child that despite the divorce, both you and your spouse love her and will not abandon her. Let her experience demonstrations of love from both parents.

- Keep your child on simple schedules and routines. Keep activities, meals, and bedtime at regular times to give her stability and comfort, and so that she knows what to expect each day.

homes, two sets of friends, and two routines. Many parents who have joint physical custody find it difficult to manage all the day-to-day decisions about scheduling, birthday parties, lessons, and schoolwork. Unless both parents are fully committed to making this arrangement work, it can lead to more conflict, confusion, and stress for the child. Any custody arrangement should give a high priority to the child's mental health, as well as her emotional and developmental needs.

Whatever your custody arrangement, both of you, as your child's parents, will continue to play key roles in her life. Try to support each other in these roles. As much as possible, avoid criticizing each other in front of your child. There's no place for your child to witness anger and hostility between you and your spouse; it can only confuse and upset her. Your child needs reassurance that it is still OK for her to love both of you. She needs you to help her feel that she's safe with either of you and that there is no need for secrets or guilt.

If you and her other parent cannot actively cooperate, at least be tolerant of each other's routines, rules, and plans, even if you have minor reservations. Under the circumstances, arguments over how much television your child watches or what foods she eats can cause her far more damage than will the TV or the snacks. If necessary, discuss your concerns when your child is not around. If a child hears you trying to undermine each other's authority, she may come to feel that she cannot trust either of you or that she can't talk about her feelings openly. An atmosphere of hostility may make it hard for her to feel secure and comfortable about her relationships with her parents and with others in her life.

As your child reaches age four or five, her life will broaden to include school and neighborhood activities, and she will develop much more complex feelings about her place in the world. You and your former spouse should discuss how she behaves and what she talks about when she is with each of you. Even though you are divorced, you still share responsibility for your child, and you need to work together to resolve any emotional or behavioral problems she may develop. Be especially alert for any signs of low self-esteem, unusual moodiness or depression, or excessive apologizing or self-criticism. These signs may indicate that she is blaming herself for the divorce. If this is the case, and you cannot convince her that she is blameless, talk to your pediatrician. She may advise you to consult a child psychiatrist or psychologist or other mental health professional.

If you feel very depressed or disturbed after your divorce and cannot seem to regain control of your life, you will not be able to give your child the nurturing and support she needs and that you wish to provide. For everyone's sake, it is very important for you to consult with a professional for yourself for psychological counseling as soon as you realize you are having difficulty.

Although there are always difficult moments in any divorce, you and your spouse can help your child adjust by making an effort to keep the divorce as nonconfrontational as possible. Consider using a "collaborative law" approach, where couples reach a settlement outside of the court system. Although each partner often hires his or her own lawyer, both sides have the same goal—namely, to reach an agreement that is acceptable to everyone, with the intent to cooperate and avoid rivalry—for their own sake and the sake of their children. A growing number of divorce lawyers now specialize in this collaborative law; your attorney is an advocate on your behalf, but is trained to minimize problems and reach a resolution that everyone finds acceptable.

If your divorce is full of tension and anger, you may worry that the battles will never end and that your child will not be able to experience good physical and mental health and well-being. Although it is true that some of the emotional effects of divorce may remain with your child permanently, she will have every chance to grow up healthy and happy if she receives the love, affection, and support she needs from her parents and other caregivers. With time, most children accept the changes that occur because of the divorce, and in many families, children become much closer to both parents.

(See also *Single-Parent Families*, page 754; *Stepfamilies*, page 756.)

Grief Reactions

Losing a parent is one of the most traumatic events that can happen to any child, and grief is the natural response. Your child may experience grief not only if a parent dies but also if one becomes chronically or seriously ill, or if there is a divorce. (Even if he remains in touch with both parents following divorce, he may mourn the loss of the family as he's known it.) Children also may grieve for siblings, grandparents, a beloved caregiver, or a pet.

WHEN A CHILD LOSES A PARENT

For a young child, losing a parent is an overwhelming crisis that is impossible for the child to understand. Children under five developmentally cannot grasp the permanence of death. Because of this, the first stage of grief is often a period of protest and hope that the lost parent will return. Many children will try to use fantasy to make this happen, imagining the missing parent in familiar situations or places.

Once the child begins to realize that his parent is truly gone forever, despair sets in. Infants, with their limited communication skills, generally express their distress by crying, feeding poorly, and being difficult to console. Toddlers will cry and be easily excitable and uncooperative, and may regress to infantile behavior. Older children may become withdrawn. A preschooler might have a faraway look on his face, or be less creative and less enthusiastic about play during this period. The more anguished or emotionally distant the other members of the family are, the more intense a young child's despair is likely to be.

Eventually he will emerge from this mood of despair and begin to shift his love and trust to others. This does not mean that he's forgotten the missing parent or that the hurt has gone away. Throughout his life there will be times when he will experience conscious and unconscious feelings of loss, especially on birthdays and holidays, during special occasions such as a graduation, and when he's ill. At these times the child may voice his sadness and ask about his missing parent.

If the deceased parent was the same sex as the child, these questions probably will come up frequently between ages four and seven, when he is struggling to understand his own gender identity. In the best of outcomes, these remembrances will be brief and positive and will not create serious distress. If they are prolonged or if they noticeably disturb the child, you should discuss them with the pediatrician.

WHEN A CHILD LOSES A SIBLING

Losing a sibling also is a devastating experience. Although it might not strike as deeply as the loss of a parent, it may be more complicated because many children, even those old enough to understand how their sibling died, may feel that in some way they are to blame. These feelings may be intensified if parents, deep in their own feelings, become withdrawn or angry and unwittingly shut themselves off from the child.

The surviving sibling often watches helplessly as his parents go through the same agony of grief that he would experience if he'd lost them. First he will see the shock and emotional numbness, then denial, then anger that such a thing could possibly happen. Through it all, he is likely to hear guilt in his parents' words and voices. He may interpret this guilt to mean that they were devoting time or attention to him that should have been given to his lost sibling.

His parents may feel driven to talk about their lost child, how the death occurred, and what they could have done to prevent it. The surviving child may try to comfort his parents even though that is not an appropriate role for him and it is more appropriate for him to work on learning to cope effectively with what has happened. The realization that the surviving child cannot make his parents happy, no matter what he does, may seriously damage his own feelings of security and self-esteem. If either parent unwittingly reacts by becoming restrained, short-tempered, and preoccupied with distractions outside the family, the surviving sibling may feel frightened and rejected by them.

In a household where one parent intensively feels the need to talk and the other avoids talking, the essential mutual support and understanding they each need is difficult to achieve. As a result, the marriage may suffer.

The surviving child feels this stress as keenly as his grief for the sibling he's lost, and may assume that he's responsible for his parents' disputes as well as for his sibling's death. The entire family will benefit from professional counseling after a child dies. Your pediatrician can recommend a qualified family therapist, psychologist, or child psychiatrist to help you all cope with your grief and help your family learn to cope, heal, and rebuild healthy and supportive relationships and interactions.

HELPING YOUR GRIEVING CHILD

When you are grieving for your spouse or your child, it is easy to overlook your surviving child's needs. The following suggestions can help you provide the love, comfort, and trust your child needs during and after the grieving process.

1. Maintain your child's familiar day-to-day routine as much as possible. Ask the people he loves and trusts—family members, familiar care providers, or preschool teachers—to be there for him when you are unavailable.

2. Offer frequent, calm explanations, keeping in mind your child's level of understanding and possible feelings of guilt. Keep the explanations as simple as possible, but be truthful. Do not construct fairy tales that will leave him more confused or hopeful that the death can be reversed. If your child is older than three, reassure him that nothing he did or thought caused the death and that no one is angry with him. To help ensure that he understands, it may help to ask him to repeat what you've said.

3. Get help from loved ones. It is difficult to give your grieving child all the attention and support he needs when you are grief-stricken yourself. Close friends and family members may be able to give you some relief, while at the same time providing a comforting sense of family and community when he may feel alone and lost. If you have lost a child, it is especially important for the family's sake that you and your spouse try to be mutually supportive during this time.

4. Be open to discussions about the loss over the ensuing weeks, months, and years. Even if your child appears to recover from grief faster than you do, his grieving process will go on below the surface for many years—possibly, in a quiet way, for a lifetime. He will need your continuing support and understanding as he tries to come to terms with his loss. As he grows older, he will ask more sophisticated questions about the circumstances and reasons for the death. As painful as it may be for you to recall these events, try to answer him honestly and directly. The more he understands what happened, the easier it will be for him to make his peace with it.

SHOULD YOUR PRESCHOOLER ATTEND THE FUNERAL?

Whether a young child attends a funeral for a loved one depends on the child's individual level of understanding, emotional maturity, and desire to participate in this ritual. If he seems very fearful and anxious, and cannot understand the purpose of the ceremony, then he probably should not attend. On the other hand, if he seems able to understand the situation to some degree and wishes to be there to say good-bye one last time, attending may be consoling and actually help him deal with his grief.

If you decide to have him at the funeral, prepare him for what will happen. Also, make arrangements ahead of time for a close family member or caregiver to take the child if he needs to leave, so you can remain at the funeral. Having this extra help also will free you to meet your own emotional needs during the ceremony.

If you decide not to have your child at the funeral, you might arrange a private, less formal visit later to the gravesite. Although this, too, will be stressful, it may make it easier for him to understand what has happened. If there is one, you might also consider having him attend a family gathering afterward, where he may find it comforting to be around family members.

When to Get Professional Help

You may want to consult your pediatrician for advice soon after the death has occurred. With the experience and knowledge to help you guide your child through the grieving process, the physician can help you decide how and what to tell your child, and can discuss how your child may be feeling and behaving in the months to come.

It is not possible to say how long your child will continue to grieve. Ordinarily, a grieving child will show signs of gradual recovery, within, at first, hours, then days, and eventually weeks when he acts pretty much as he did before the death. If he does not start to have these periods of normalcy within four to six weeks, or if you feel that his initial feelings and behaviors are too intense or are lasting too long, talk with your pediatrician.

Although it is normal for a child to miss a deceased parent or sibling at times, it is not normal for the preoccupation to overshadow the child's entire life for years to come. If your child seems to be thinking constantly about the death, so that his grief dominates every family occasion and interferes with his social and psychological development, he needs psychological counseling. Your pediatrician can refer you to a qualified mental health professional. If a dying relative is in a hospice facility or program, they often have grief counseling expertise that would be of help to parents and to children.

Your child also needs you to return gradually to normal functioning. After you have lost a child or your spouse, it may take many months before you are able to return to your usual daily routine and much longer before your strong sad feelings begin to subside. If a year has passed since the death and you still do not feel that you can resume your former activities, or if your grieving is replaced by ongoing depression, it's good to seek help from a mental health professional, not only for your benefit but for your child's as well.

Sibling Rivalry

If you have more than one child, you almost certainly will have to deal with some amount of sibling rivalry. Competition between youngsters in a family is natural. All children want parental affection and attention, and each child believes he rightly should receive all of yours. Your child does not want to share you with his brother or sister, and when he realizes he has no choice in the matter, he may become jealous, possibly even violent, toward his sibling.

Sibling rivalry between younger children tends to be most troublesome when the age difference is from one and a half to three years. This is because the preschool child is still very dependent on his parents and has not yet established many secure relationships with friends or other adults. However, even when the spread is as many as nine years or more, the older child still needs parental attention and affection. If he feels that he is being left out or rejected, he likely will blame the baby. In general, the older the child, the less jealousy he will feel toward his younger sibling. The jealousy is often most intense for preschoolers when the sibling is a newborn.

There may be days when you're convinced your children really do hate each other, but these emotional outbursts are only temporary. Despite their feelings of resentment, siblings usually have true affection for one another. You may have difficulty seeing this, however, since they may reserve their worst behavior for moments when you are around, and they are competing directly for your attention. When you are absent, they may be fine companions. As they get older and their need for your complete and undivided attention decreases, their feelings of affection probably will overcome their jealousy of each other. Intense sibling rivalry that lasts into adulthood is rare.

What to Expect

You may notice the first signs of sibling rivalry even before your younger child is born. As the older one watches you preparing the nursery or buying baby equipment, he may demand gifts for himself. He may want to wear diapers again or drink from a bottle "like the baby." If he senses that you're preoccupied with the baby, he may misbehave or act out in order to get your attention.

This unusual or regressive behavior may continue after the baby is home. Your older child may cry more frequently, become more clingy and demanding, or simply withdraw. He may imitate the baby by asking for his old baby blanket, sucking on a pacifier, or even demanding to nurse. School-age children often appear very interested and affectionate toward the baby, but may be aggressive or misbe-

have in other ways to get attention. Among all siblings, the demand for attention is usually greatest when the parents are actively and intimately involved with the baby—for example, during breastfeedings or bath time.

As your younger child gets older and becomes more mobile, quarrels will erupt over the older child's toys and other possessions. The toddler will go straight for what he wants, without caring who owns it, while your preschooler will guard his own territory jealously. When the toddler intrudes on this space, the older child usually reacts strongly.

Sometimes, particularly when the children are several years apart, the older one is accepting and protective of the younger sibling. However, as the younger one grows and begins to develop more mature skills and talents (e.g., in schoolwork, athletics, talking, singing, or acting), the older child may feel threatened or embarrassed by "being shown up." He may then become more aggressive or irritating, or start to compete with the younger sibling. The younger child, too, may experience jealousy about the privileges, talents, accomplishments, or advantages that his older sibling accumulates as he gets older. Often it is almost impossible to tell which child is contributing more to the rivalry.

How Should Parents React?

It is important not to overreact to jealousy between your children, especially if the older child is a preschooler. Feelings of resentment and frustration are understandable—no child wants to give up the spotlight of parental affection. It takes time for a child to discover that his parents don't love him any less because they have a second child.

If your older child starts imitating the baby, do not ridicule or punish him. You can indulge him briefly by allowing him to drink from a bottle or climb into the crib or playpen, but only once or twice at the most, and don't reward this behavior by giving him extra attention. Make it absolutely clear that he does not have to behave like a baby to gain your approval, love, or affection. Praise him when he acts "grown-up," and give him plenty of opportunities to be a "big brother" (or, in the case of a girl, a "big sister"). If you intentionally try to catch him being good, it should not take long for him to realize that he benefits more by acting maturely than by behaving like a baby.

If your older child is between three and five years old, try to minimize conflicts over space by guaranteeing some secure, protected area. Separating his private possessions from shared ones will help reduce quarreling.

It is natural for parents to compare their children, but do not do this in front of them. Each child is special, and should be treated as such. Comparisons inevitably make one child feel inferior to the other. A statement such as "Your sister is always so much neater than you," for example, will make a child resent both you and his sister, and actually may encourage him to be messy.

When your children get into an argument, usually the best strategy is to stay out of it. Left alone, they probably will settle it peacefully. If you get involved, you may be tempted to take sides, making one child feel triumphant and the other betrayed. Even if they bring their fight to you, try to be impartial and tell them to settle it peacefully on their own. Instead of blaming either one, explain that they're both responsible for creating the dispute and for ending it. Doing so encourages them to problem solve together, a social skill that will serve them well in the future.

Obviously, you must intervene if the situation becomes violent, especially if the older child might harm the younger one. In this case you must first protect the younger child. Make sure the older child understands that you will not tolerate any abusive behavior. If the age difference is large or if there is any reason to suspect that violence may erupt, supervise them closely when they are together. Preventing aggressive behavior is always better than punishment, which all too often increases rather than decreases the older child's feelings of rivalry.

It is important to spend time separately with each child. Finding the right balance of attention is not always easy, but if your older child's acting out is becoming extreme, it could be a signal that he needs more of your time.

If the older sibling remains extremely aggressive, or if you feel that you don't know how to handle the situation, consult your pediatrician, who can determine whether this is normal sibling rivalry or a problem that requires special attention. The pediatrician also can suggest ways to ease the tensions. If necessary, she will refer you to a qualified mental health professional.

(See also *Preparing Your Other Children for the Baby's Arrival*, page 34.)

Single-Parent Families

Single-parent families are becoming more common. Most children of divorce spend at least some years in single-parent households. Another increasingly large group of children live with single parents who were never married or involved in a long-term relationship. A smaller number of children have widowed parents.

From a parent's viewpoint, there are some benefits to being single. You can raise the child according to your own beliefs, principles, and rules, with no need for conflict or resolving differences. Single parents often develop closer bonds with their children. When the father is the single parent, he may become more nurturing and more active in his child's daily life than some fathers in two-parent households. Children in single-parent households may become more independent and mature because they have more responsibility within the family.

Single parenthood is not easy, for parents or children. If you can't arrange or afford child care, getting and holding a job may be difficult. (See Chapter 14, *Early Education and Child Care*.) Without another person to share the day-in, day-out job of raising the child and maintaining the household, you may find yourself so busy that you become socially isolated. When you are under stress, the child may sense and share this stress. You can easily become too tired and distracted to be as emotionally supportive or consistent about rules and discipline as you would like to be. This can lead to distress and behavior problems for the child. Some single parents worry that the lack of a same-sex parent may deprive their son or daughter of a potential role model.

Here are some suggestions that may help you meet your own emotional needs while providing your child with the guidance she needs.

- **Take advantage of** all available resources in finding help in caring for your child. Use the guide to child care in Chapter 14.

- **Maintain your sense** of humor as much as possible. Try to see the positive or funny side of everyday surprises and challenges.

- **For your family's** sake as well as your own, take care of yourself. See your doctor regularly, eat properly, and get enough rest, exercise, and sleep.

- **Set a regular** time when you can take a break without your child. Relax with friends. Go to a movie. Pursue hobbies. Join groups. Do things that interest you. Pursue a social life of your own.

Parenting in Military Families

Being a parent in the military can present unique challenges, particularly in times of deployment or military conflict, when the stresses of being away from a child can be difficult for the entire family. Young children may demonstrate a number of behaviors in response to being separated from a parent, such as clinginess to the other parent and/or a caregiver, regressive behaviors (e.g., bed-wetting after having being toilet trained), anxiety over new people or circumstances, and being quiet and pulling away from others.

If you're the parent remaining at home with your child, try to keep things as normal as possible, including maintaining usual daily routines. Answer questions as honestly as possible (keeping in mind his level of understanding), and reassure him that the deployed parent is fine and doing well. Try to maintain as much communication as possible with the absent parent, letting your child communicate by phone, letter, e-mail, or videoconferencing. If your child seems to be in particular distress, talk with your pediatrician, who might make a referral to a mental health professional. Also there is a website for all military spouses to access mental health services, regardless of location, at: www.MilitaryOneSource.com.

The AAP's Deployment and Military Medical Home Resources webpage has been designed to support military youth, families, and the other professionals caring for this population. Please spend some time on the site to learn more about what military pediatricians and other youth-serving professionals are doing to help military children and adolescents every day: http://www.aap.org/en-us/advocacy-and-policy/aap-health-initiatives/Pages/Deployment-and-Military.aspx.

■ **Do not feel** guilty because your child has only one parent. There are plenty of families in the same situation. You didn't "do it to her," and you don't need to penalize yourself or spoil her to make amends. Feeling and acting guilty won't help anyone.

■ **Do not look** for problems where none exist. Many children grow up very well in single-parent homes, while others have a great many problems in two-parent homes. Being a single parent does not necessarily mean you'll have more problems or have more trouble resolving them.

■ **Set firm but** reasonable limits for your children, and do not hesitate to enforce them. Children feel more secure and develop responsible behavior better when limits are clear and consistent. Expand these limits as the child demonstrates the ability to accept increased responsibility.

- **Find some time** each day with your child—playing, talking, reading, helping with homework, or watching television.

- **Praise your child** often, showing genuine affection and unconditional, positive support.

- **Create as large** a support network for yourself as possible. Keep active lists of relatives, friends, and community services that can help with child care. Establish friendships with other families who will let you know of community opportunities (soccer, cultural events, etc.) and are willing to exchange babysitting.

- **Talk to trusted** relatives, friends, and professionals such as your pediatrician about your child's behavior, development, and relationships within the family.

Stepfamilies

A single parent's remarriage can be a blessing for the parent and child alike—restoring the structure and security that were lost through divorce, separation, or death.

Benefits may include additional love and companionship for a parent as well as the children. Often a stepparent becomes as appropriate a role model of the same sex as the former spouse. In addition, there may be financial benefits of having another caregiver in the house.

But creating a stepfamily also requires many adjustments and can be very stressful. If the stepparent is introduced as a substitute for your child's absent parent, the child may feel torn by her loyalty to her biologic parent and may reject the stepparent immediately. There is often a great deal of jealousy between stepparents and stepchildren, as well as competition for the love and attention of the parent who has brought them together. If a child feels that her new stepparent is coming between her and her parent, she may reject the stepparent and act out in order to regain her parent's attention. The situation becomes even more complex and stressful when there are children on both sides who are suddenly expected to accept each other's parents and get along as siblings. With time, most blended families do manage to sort through these conflicts, but it requires a great amount of patience and commitment on the part of the adults, as well as the willingness to get professional help early to prevent significant problems from developing.

As difficult as the transition may seem at first, try to keep in mind that relationships between stepparents and stepchildren tend to develop gradually over a period of one to several years, rather than over weeks or months.

An important factor in the development of the step-relationship may be support from the other biological parent. The child may resent a rela-

Suggestions for Stepfamilies

Making a smooth transition from a single-parent family to a successful stepfamily requires special sensitivity and effort from the biological parent and stepparent. Here are some suggestions that may help.

- Inform your former spouse of your marriage plans, and try to work together to make the transition as easy as possible for your child. Make sure everyone understands that the marriage will not change your former spouse's role in your child's life.

- Give your child time to get to know the stepparent (and stepsiblings, if any) before you begin living together. Doing this will make the adjustment easier for everyone and will often eliminate much of your child's anxiety about the new arrangement.

- Watch for signs of conflict, and work together to correct them as early as possible.

- Parent and stepparent should decide together what will be expected of the child, where and how limits will be set, and what forms of discipline are acceptable.

- Parent and stepparent need to share the responsibilities of parenthood. This means that *both* will give affection and attention and that *both* will have authority in the household. Deciding together how the child should be disciplined, and supporting each other's decisions and actions, will make it easier for the stepparent to assume a role of authority without fear of disapproval or resentment.

- If a noncustodial parent visits the child, these visitations should be arranged and accepted so that they do not create disagreement within the stepfamily.

- Try to involve both biological parents and stepparent(s) in all major decisions affecting a child. If possible, arrange for all the adults to meet together to share insights and concerns; doing this will let the child know that the grown-ups are willing to overcome their differences for his benefit.

- Be sensitive to your child's wishes and concerns about his role within the stepfamily. Respect his level of maturity and understanding when, for example, you help him decide what to call the stepparent or introduce him to the stepparent's relatives.

tionship with a biological parent that prevents closeness to the stepparent and may feel guilty whenever she is emotionally drawn to the stepparent. Good communication among all three (or four) parents can minimize this guilt, as well as reduce the confusion that a child could feel when she tries to adjust to the values and expectations of several adults. For this reason, when a child is spending time in two households, occasional meetings with all of the parents, if possible, may be very helpful. Sharing perspectives on rules, values, and scheduling tells the child that all her parents can talk with one another, are mutually respectful, and have her health and well-being as a central priority.

In an atmosphere of mutual respect between biological and stepparents, the child is more likely to have the benefits of stepfamilies mentioned earlier. The child again has the opportunity of living in a household with two parents. The remarried parent often is happier and thus better able to meet the child's needs. As the child gets older, her relationship to the stepparent may give her additional support, skills, and perspectives. These benefits, together with the economic advantages of the stepfamily situation, may give the child a broader range of opportunities.

Multiples

Having twins (or other "multiples," such as triplets) means much more than simply having two or more ba-

bies at once, and the challenges go beyond having twice or three times the work or pleasure. Twins and other multiples quite frequently are born early and therefore tend to be smaller than the average newborn, so you may need to consult your pediatrician even more frequently than you would with a single baby. Feeding twins, whether by breast or bottle, also requires some special strategies, and the doctor can provide advice and support. There may be added financial pressures upon the family as well, spending a lot more on diapers, clothing, food, car safety seats, and dozens of other items—and perhaps needing a larger family car or even a larger home. (See Chapter 1.)

The twin birth rate in the US is just over 3 percent. But as your obstetrician and pediatrician may have explained to you, the number of multiple births has risen in recent years. It has increased 42 percent since 1990 and 70 percent since 1980. Some researchers have attributed much of this increase to the more frequent use of infertility treatments and procedures such as in vitro fertilization. In vitro fertilization may involve implanting more than one fertilized egg into the uterus, while using infertility drugs can stimulate the ovaries to release two or more eggs.

This section is written primarily with twins in mind, but most of the same information and guidelines apply to triplets and other multiple births. For more information on multiples, check out *Raising Twins: Parenting Multiples From Pregnancy*

Through the School Years by Shelly Vaziri Flais, MD, FAAP.

Raising Multiples

You should care for your healthy multiples just like any other infants. From the very beginning, it is important that you recognize that your babies are separate individuals. If they are identical, it is easy to treat them as a "package," providing them with the same clothing, toys, and quality of attention. But as similar as they may appear physically, emotionally, behaviorally, and developmentally, they are different, and in order to grow up happy and secure as individuals, they need you to support their differences. As one twin explained, "We're not twins. We're just brothers who have the same birthday!"

Identical twins come from the same egg, are always the same sex, and look very much alike. Fraternal twins come from two separate eggs, which are fertilized at the same time. They may or may not be the same sex. Whether identical or fraternal, all twins have their individual personalities, styles, and temperament. Both identical and fraternal twins may become either competitive or interdependent as they grow. Sometimes one twin acts as the leader and the other as the follower. Whatever the specific quality of their interaction, most twins develop very intense relationships early in life simply because they spend so much time with each other.

If you also have other children, your twin newborns may prompt more than the usual sibling rivalry. They will require a large amount of your time and energy, and will attract a great deal of extra attention from friends, relatives, and strangers on the street. You can help your other children accept, and perhaps even take advantage of, this unusual situation by offering them "double rewards" for helping with the new babies and encouraging even more involvement in the daily baby care chores. It also becomes even more essential that you spend some special time each day alone with the other children doing their favorite activities.

As your twins get older, particularly if they are identical, they may choose to play only with each other, making their other siblings feel left out. To discourage the twins from forming such exclusive bonds, urge them to play individually (not as a unit) with other children. Also, you or a babysitter might play with just one twin while the other plays with a sibling or friend.

You may find that your twins do not develop in the same pattern as do other children their age. Some twins seem to "split the work," with one concentrating on motor skills while the other perfects social or communication abilities. Because they spend so much time together, many twins communicate better with each other than with other family members or friends. They learn how to "read" each other's gestures and facial expressions, and occasionally they even have their own verbal language that no one else can

Transporting Your Newborn Multiples

In many cases, twins and other multiples are smaller and weigh less than the average newborn. When bringing your babies home from the hospital and for subsequent trips in the car, keep the same guidelines in mind for choosing and using car safety seats. That means choosing rear-facing car safety seats and relying on them until your babies have reached two years of age or have outgrown the rear-facing weight or height limit for their seats. Rear-facing-only seats have carrying handles, and may be sold with a base that can stay in your car. Convertible seats are larger than rear-facing-only seats and can be used both rear-facing and forward-facing, so some parents choose to use a convertible seat from birth.

But here's a very important point to keep in mind if your babies were born prematurely: rear-facing *convertible* car seats may be too large to fit your preemies appropriately. Before your newborns are discharged from the hospital, make sure they are tested to determine if they can ride safely while reclining in a car seat. If they have certain medical issues related to breathing or heart rate, they may not be able to ride in a semi-reclined position. In these instances, preemies should lie flat when they're riding in a car. In this case, your babies should ride in a crash-tested car bed. (In most cases, the car bed will be purchased through the hospital.) Always use the harnesses and buckle that are part of the car beds, and install the beds lengthwise in the backseat; position your babies so their heads are toward the center of the car.

understand. (This is particularly true of identical twins.) Because they can entertain each other, they may not be very motivated to learn about the world beyond them. This unique developmental pattern does not represent a problem, but it does make it very important to separate your twins occasionally and expose them individually to other playmates and learning situations.

Twins are not always happy about being apart, especially if they have established strong play habits and preferences for each other's company. For this reason, it is important to begin separating them occasionally as early as possible. If they resist strongly, try a gradual approach using very familiar children or adults to play with them individually but in the same room or play area. Being able to separate will become increasingly important as the twins approach school age. In preschool most twins can stay together in the same room, but many elementary schools prefer twins to be in separate classes.

As much as you appreciate the individual differences between your twins, you no doubt will have certain feelings for them as a unit. There is nothing wrong with this, since they do share many similarities and are themselves bound to develop a dual identity—as individuals and as twins. Helping them understand and accept the balance between these two identities is one of the most challenging tasks facing you as the parent of twins.

Your pediatrician can advise you on how to cope with the special parenting challenges with twins. He also can suggest helpful reading material or refer you to organizations that help parents with multiples. One organization to look for in your area may be Multiples of America.

At the same time, take care of yourself, getting as much rest as possible. Many parents find that raising twins and other multiples is much more physically demanding and emotionally stressful than having just one baby. So make an effort to catch up on your own sleep whenever you can. Take turns with your spouse on who's going to handle the "middle-of-the-night" feedings, and who will bathe and feed the babies. If your budget can afford it, get some extra help for routine tasks like bathing the newborns and grocery shopping—or ask friends and family members for help. An extra set of hands, especially when there are more than twins, even for just a few hours a week, can make an enormous difference, and can give you not only more time to enjoy your babies, but also more time for yourself.

~ 27 ~

Fever

YOUR CHILD'S NORMAL temperature will vary with his age, activity, and the time of day. Infants
tend to have higher temperatures
than older children, and everyone's temperature is highest between late afternoon and early
evening and lowest between midnight and early morning. Ordinarily, a rectal reading of 100.4
degrees Fahrenheit (38 degrees
Celsius) and higher indicates
fever. Other methods of temperature taking such as oral, tympanic, and temporal should still
generally use 100.4 degrees or
more as the cutoff for a true fever
while axillary (underarm) measurements may have a lower cutoff. A rectal reading is the gold
standard for infants.

By itself, fever is *not* an illness. Rather, it is a sign or symptom of sickness. In fact, usually it
is a positive sign that the body is
fighting infection. Fever stimulates certain defenses, such as the
white blood cells, which attack
and destroy invading bacteria
and viruses. The fever may actually be important in helping your
child fight his infection. However, fever is often associated
with discomfort. It increases his
need for fluids and makes his
heart rate and breathing rate
faster.

Fever may accompany any
infection. This includes respiratory illnesses such as croup or
pneumonia, ear infections, influenza (flu), colds, and sore throats.
Fever may occur with infections
of the bowel, blood, or urinary
tract, brain and spinal cord
(meningitis), and with most viral
illnesses.

In children between six months

and five years, fever can trigger seizures (called febrile convulsions), although they happen only rarely. These convulsions tend to run in families, and usually happen during the first few hours of a febrile illness. Children may look "peculiar" for a few moments, then stiffen, twitch, and roll their eyes. They will be unresponsive for a short time, and their skin may appear to be a little darker than usual during the episode. The entire convulsion usually lasts less than one minute, and may be over in a few seconds, but it can seem like a lifetime to a frightened parent. Although uncommon, convulsions can last for up to fifteen minutes or longer. It is reassuring to know that febrile convulsions almost always are harmless—they do not cause brain damage, nervous system problems, paralysis, intellectual disability, or death—although they should be reported promptly to your pediatrician. If your child is having trouble breathing or the convulsion (also referred to as a seizure) does not stop within fifteen minutes, call 911.

What Type of Thermometer Is Best?

The American Academy of Pediatrics no longer recommends mercury thermometers because these glass thermometers may break and, as their mercury vaporizes, it can be inhaled, resulting in toxic levels. Digital electronic thermometers are better choices.

- **Digital devices can** measure temperatures in your child's mouth or rectum. As with any device, some digital thermometers are more accurate than others. Follow the manufacturer's instructions carefully, and be sure the thermometer is calibrated as recommended by the manufacturer.

- **Ear thermometers are** another acceptable choice. Their accuracy depends on the ability of the beam emitted by the device to reach the eardrum. Thus, some of these devices may not be as reliable because of earwax or a small curved ear canal. For that reason, most pediatricians prefer that parents use digital electronic thermometers.

- **Temporal artery thermometers** are also available. They use an infrared scanner to determine the temperature of the temporal artery, which runs across the forehead just below the skin. They are most useful in children three months and older, although recent research shows that they are reliable in babies younger than three months as well. They also are simple to use, even while your child is asleep.

Children younger than one year at the time of their first simple febrile convulsion have approximately a 50 percent chance of having another such seizure, while children over one year of age when they have their first sei-

Best Ways to Take a Temperature

There are several ways to take your child's temperature. A digital thermometer (which shows the temperature in numbers in a small window) reads the body temperature when its sensor (located in the tip of the thermometer) touches the part of the body where it is used (in the mouth, under the arm, or in the rectum). An ear thermometer or a temporal artery thermometer can also be used. (See page 764 for more information about the digital and other types of thermometers.) Whatever approach you use, clean the thermometer as directed—usually with lukewarm soapy water or rubbing alcohol—before each use, and then rinse with cool water.

Here are some other guidelines to keep in mind:

■ To take the temperature in your child's bottom (rectally), turn on the digital thermometer and then put a small amount of lubricant, such as petroleum jelly, on the end of the thermometer that will be inserted into your baby. Place your child across your lap or on something firm, either faceup or facedown (if he's facedown, put one hand on his back; if he's faceup, bend your child's leg to his chest, resting your free hand on the back of his thighs). Then gently insert the small end of the thermometer in your child's bottom (or rectum), putting it in about ½ inch to 1 inch. Hold the thermometer in place for about one minute or until the device signals that it's done (by beeping or lighting up). Remove it and read the number.

■ Taking a rectal or oral temperature is more accurate than taking it under your child's arm. Also, in your household, use one digital thermometer labeled "oral," and another one labeled "rectal." Don't use the same thermometer in both places.

■ At ages four or five years old, you also can take your child's temperature by placing the thermometer in his mouth (orally). After turning on the thermometer, place the small end under your child's tongue, toward the back of his mouth. Ask him to close his mouth around the thermometer, and hold it in place. After about a minute, you should hear the thermometer "beep" or see it light up. Remove it and read the number.

■ Tympanic (ear) and temporal artery (side of forehead) thermometers are increasingly popular among parents and health care providers, and appear to be quite accurate when used correctly.

zure have about a 30 percent chance of having a second one. Nevertheless, febrile convulsions rarely happen more than once within a twenty-four-hour (one-day) period. Although many parents worry that a febrile convulsion will lead to epilepsy, keep in mind that epileptic seizures are not caused by a fever, and children with a history of fever-related convulsions have only a slightly higher likelihood of developing epilepsy by age seven.

A rare but serious problem that is easily confused with fever is *heat-related illness,* or *heatstroke.* This is not caused by infection or internal conditions, but by surrounding heat. It can occur when a child is in a very hot place—for example, a hot beach in midsummer or an overheated closed car on a summer day. Leaving children unattended in closed cars is the cause of several deaths a year; *never* leave an infant or child unattended in a closed car, even for a few minutes. Heatstroke also can occur if a baby is overdressed in hot, humid weather. Under these circumstances, the body temperature can rise to dangerous levels (above 105 degrees Fahrenheit [40.5 degrees Celsius]), which must be reduced quickly by removing some of the clothing, cool-water sponging, fanning, and removal to a cool place. After the child has been cooled, he should be taken immediately to a pediatrician or emergency room. Heatstroke is an emergency condition.

Whenever you think your child has a fever, take his temperature with a thermometer. (See *Best Ways to Take a Temperature* on page 765.) Feeling the skin (or using temperature-sensitive tape) is not accurate, especially when the child is experiencing a chill.

When to Call the Pediatrician

If your child is *two months or younger* and has a rectal temperature of 100.4 degrees Fahrenheit (38 degrees Celsius) or higher, call your pediatrician immediately. *This is an absolute necessity.* The doctor will need to examine the baby to rule out any serious infection or disease.

You also may need to notify the doctor if your child is between three and six months and has a fever of 101 degrees Fahrenheit (38.3 degrees Celsius) or greater, or is older than six months and has a temperature of 103 degrees Fahrenheit (39.4 degrees Celsius) or higher. Such a high temperature may indicate a significant infection or dehydration, which may require treatment. However, in most cases, your decision to call the pediatrician should depend on associated symptoms, such as a sore throat, an earache, a cough, unexplained rash, or repeated vomiting or diarrhea. Also, if your child is very fussy or sleeping more than usual, call your doctor. In fact, your child's activity level tends to be a more important indicator than the height of the fever. Again, fever in and of itself is not a sickness. It is a sign of sickness.

If your child is over one year of age, is eating and sleeping well, and has playful moments, there usually is no need to call the doctor immediately. If a high fever (as defined earlier)

Acetaminophen Dosage Chart

Dosages may be repeated every four hours, but should not be given more than five times in twenty-four hours. (*Note:* Milliliter is abbreviated as ml; 5 ml equals 1 teaspoon [tsp]. Use only a syringe or accurate measuring device, not household teaspoons, which can vary in size.) Be sure to read the label to make sure you are using the right product.

Age*	Weight**	Infant/Children's Oral Suspension 160 mg/5 ml	Chewable Tablets 80 mg tabs†
0–5 mos.	6–11 lbs. (2.7–5 kg)	—	—
6–11 mos.	12–17 lbs. (5.5–7.7 kg)	½ tsp	1 tab
1–2 yrs.	18–23 lbs. (8.2–10.5 kg)	¾ tsp	1½ tabs
2–3 yrs.	24–35 lbs. (10.9–15.9 kg)	1 tsp	2 tabs
4–5 yrs.	36–47 lbs. (16.3–21.4 kg)	1½ tsps	3 tabs

*Note: Age is provided as a convenience only. Dosing for fever should be based on current weight.
**Weight given is representative of the age range.
†Note: Make sure, when using chewable tablets, to refer to the 80 mg chewable dosage.

We do not recommend using aspirin to treat a simple fever in infants, children, or teens, unless recommended by your pediatrician.

persists for more than twenty-four hours, however, it is best to call even if there are no other complaints or findings.

If your child becomes delirious (acts frightened, "sees" objects that are not there, talks strangely) while he has a high fever, call your pediatrician, particularly if this has not occurred before. These unusual symptoms probably will disappear when the temperature returns to normal, but the doctor may want to examine your child and determine it is not caused by something more serious, such as an inflammation of the brain (encephalitis) or membranes covering the brain and spinal cord (meningitis).

Ibuprofen Dosage Chart

Dosages may be repeated every six to eight hours, but should not be given more than four times in twenty-four hours. (*Note:* Milliliter is abbreviated as ml; 5 ml equals 1 teaspoon [tsp]. Use only a syringe or accurate measuring device, not household teaspoons, which can vary in size.) Be sure to read the label to make sure you are using the right product.

Age*	Weight**	Infant Drops 50 mg/1.25 ml	Children's Suspension 100 mg/5 ml	Chewable Tablets 100 mg tabs
6–11 mos.	12–17 lbs. (5.5–7.7 kg)	1.25 ml	2.5 ml	½ tablet
1–2 yrs.	18–23 lbs. (8.2–10.5 kg)	1.875 ml	3.75 ml	½ tablet
2–3 yrs.	24–35 lbs. (10.9–15.9 kg)	2.5 ml	5 ml	1 tablet
4–5 yrs.	36–47 lbs. (16.3–21.4 kg)	—	7.5 ml	1½ tablets

*Note: Age is provided as a convenience only. Dosing for fever should be based on current weight.
**Weight given is representative of the age range.

We do not recommend using aspirin to treat a simple fever.

Home Treatment

Fevers generally do not need to be treated with medication unless your child is uncomfortable. Even higher temperatures are not in themselves dangerous or significant unless your child has a chronic disease. If your child has a history of a fever-related convulsion, treating the fever with medication has not been shown as a strategy to prevent this kind of seizure. It is more important to watch how your child is behaving. If he is eating and sleeping well and has periods of playfulness, he probably doesn't need any treatment. You should also talk with your pediatrician about when to treat your child's fever. A good time to do this is at well-child visits.

When your child has a fever and seems to be quite bothered or uncomfortable by it, you may treat it with the following approaches.

MEDICATION
Several medications can reduce body temperature by blocking the mecha-

nisms that cause a fever. These so-called antipyretic agents include acetaminophen, ibuprofen, and aspirin. All three of these over-the-counter drugs appear to be equally effective at reducing fever. *However, because aspirin may cause or be associated with Reye syndrome, the American Academy of Pediatrics does not recommend using aspirin to treat a fever in children.* Acetaminophen can be given without a doctor's advice once your child is older than three months, and ibuprofen can be given to children older than six months of age. However, if your child has a disease affecting his liver, ask your doctor if acetaminophen is safe to use. Similarly, if your child has kidney disease, asthma, an ulcer, or other chronic illness, ask your doctor first if ibuprofen is safe. If your child is dehydrated or vomiting, ibuprofen should be given only under the supervision of a doctor due to risk of kidney damage.

Ideally, the doses of acetaminophen and ibuprofen should be based on a child's weight, not his age. (See the dosage charts on pages 767 and 768.) However, the dosages listed on the labels of acetaminophen bottles (which are usually calculated by age) are generally safe and effective unless your child is unusually light or heavy for his age. Keep in mind that at too-high doses of acetaminophen, a toxic response in the liver can develop, although it happens only rarely. When a toxic reaction does occur, the symptoms may include nausea, vomiting, and abdominal discomfort.

As a general guideline, read and follow the instructions on the manufacturer's label when using *any* medication. Following the instructions is important to ensure that your child receives the proper dosages. Also, other over-the-counter medications, such as cold and cough preparations, may contain acetaminophen. The simultaneous use of more than one acetaminophen-containing product may be dangerous, so read all medication labels to ensure that your child is not receiving multiple doses of the same medicine. Also, as a general rule, do not give a child under two months old either acetaminophen or any other medication without the advice of your pediatrician.

Some parents have tried alternating between giving acetaminophen and ibuprofen when their child is running a fever. This approach, however, can theoretically cause medication errors—"Which medicine am I supposed to give him next?"—and could lead to potential side effects. So if your child is uncomfortable with a fever, choose which medicine to give, and then give it according to the dosing recommendations and only if your child still needs it. Either ibuprofen or acetaminophen is effective in reducing fever and making your child feel better. Always consult your doctor before changing the dose schedule, or using these medicines in combination.

Also keep in mind that over-the-counter cough and cold medicines should *not* be given to infants and children under six years of age because of potentially serious side effects. Studies also have shown that these cough and cold products are not effective in treating the symptoms of children under six years old, and may even pose health risks.

OTHER TREATMENT SUGGESTIONS FOR FEVER

- **Keep your child's** room and your home comfortably cool, and dress him lightly.

- **Encourage him to** drink extra fluid or other liquids (water, diluted fruit juices, commercially prepared oral electrolyte solutions, gelatin [Jell-O], Popsicles, etc.).

- **If the room** is warm or stuffy, place a fan nearby to keep cool air moving.

- **Your child does** not have to stay in his room or in bed when he has a fever. He can be up and about the house, but should not run around and overexert himself.

- **If the fever** is a symptom of a highly contagious disease (e.g., chickenpox or the flu), keep your child away from other children, elderly people, or people who may not be able to fight infection well, such as those with cancer.

Treating a Febrile Seizure

If your child has a febrile seizure, take the following steps immediately to prevent injury:

- Place him on the floor or bed away from any hard or sharp objects.

- Turn his head to the side so that any saliva or vomit can drain from his mouth.

- Do not put anything into his mouth; he will not swallow his tongue.

- Call your pediatrician.

- Call 911 if the seizure lasts longer than fifteen minutes.

~ 28 ~

Genital and Urinary Systems

Blood in the Urine (Hematuria)

IF YOUR CHILD'S urine has a red, orange, or brown color, it may contain blood. When the urine specifically contains red blood cells, doctors use the medical term *hematuria* to describe this condition. Many things, including a physical injury or inflammation or infection in the urinary tract, can cause it. Hematuria also is associated with some general medical problems, such as defects of blood clotting, exposure to toxic materials, hereditary conditions, or immune system abnormalities.

Sometimes there may be such small amounts of blood in the urine that you cannot see any color change, although it may be detected by a urine test performed by the pediatrician. In some cases the reddish color is not associated with hematuria at all, and may be due simply to something your child has eaten or swallowed. Beets, blackberries, red food coloring, phenolphthalein (a chemical sometimes used in laxatives), pyridium or phenazopyridine (medicine used to relieve bladder pain), and the medicine rifampin may cause the urine to turn red or orange if your child ingests them. Anytime you are not sure that one of these alternative explanations is responsible for the color change, call your pediatrician. Blood in the urine, when accompanied by protein (albumin), is usually due to inflammation of the filtering membranes of the kidney; the general term for this condition is *nephritis*. Your doctor may recommend further tests to distinguish among several different kinds of nephritis.

Treatment

Your pediatrician will ask you about any possible injury, foods, or health symptoms that might have caused the change in urine color. He will perform a physical exam, checking particularly for any increase in blood pressure, tenderness in the kidney area, or swelling (particularly of the hands or feet or around the eyes) that might indicate kidney problems. He also will conduct tests on a sample of urine and may order blood tests, imaging studies (such as an ultrasound scan or X-rays), or perform other examinations to check your child's kidneys, bladder, and immune system. If none of these reveals the cause of the hematuria, and it continues to occur, your pediatrician may refer you to a children's kidney specialist, who will perform additional tests. (Sometimes these tests include examining a tiny piece of kidney tissue under the microscope, a procedure known as a biopsy. This tissue may be obtained by surgery or by performing what's called a needle biopsy.)

Once your pediatrician knows more about what is causing the hematuria, a decision can be made whether treatment is necessary. Often no treatment is required, indicating that there is nothing to worry about. Occasionally medication is used to suppress the inflammation that is the hallmark sign of nephritis. Whatever the treat-

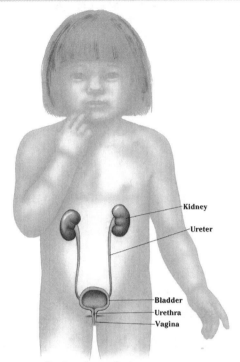

Genitourinary System

Kidney

Ureter

Bladder
Urethra
Vagina

ment, your child will need to return to the doctor regularly for repeat urine and blood tests and blood pressure checks. This is necessary to make sure that she isn't developing chronic kidney disease, which can lead to kidney failure.

Occasionally hematuria is caused by kidney stones, or, rarely, by an abnormality that will require surgery. If this is the case, your pediatrician will refer you to a pediatric urologist or nephrologist (kidney specialist) who can perform such procedures.

Proteinuria

A child's urine sometimes contains abnormally high amounts of protein. Although the body needs proteins to perform essential functions, such as guarding against infections and helping the blood to clot, a minimal amount of these proteins should leak into the urine. If high amounts of protein are detected in the urine, this may indicate that the kidneys are not working properly and are allowing proteins (which are large molecules) to leak out into the urine. This leakage of protein may be due to various abnormalities of the kidney's filtering membranes.

Diagnosis

Proteinuria often causes no symptoms. But when high levels of protein are in the urine, blood protein levels may drop and your child could develop swelling in the legs, ankles, abdomen, or eyelids. At the same time, the blood pressure may be elevated, another sign of likely kidney disease. If your pediatrician detects proteinuria, she can use a simple test in which a chemically treated paper strip is dipped into the urine, and will change colors if protein is present. She may recommend that you collect urine samples from your child just after awakening in the morning (if the proteinuria disappears, the condition is benign), and that the urine specimens be examined in the laboratory, or that your child have some blood tests. In some children, a small amount of protein may be found in the urine for a short time and later disappear without any consequences.

At times, your pediatrician may decide to have your child seen by a kidney specialist (nephrologist), who might recommend further testing that may include a kidney biopsy. During a kidney biopsy, a needle is used to remove a small amount of kidney tissue for examination in the laboratory. Your child will be sedated for this procedure and the area over the kidney will be made numb by injecting a local anesthetic.

Treatment

Medication can be given to treat some underlying kidney problems associated with proteinuria. Your pediatrician might recommend that your child consume less salt to curtail the swelling associated with proteinuria. Children who have had proteinuria, even if it appears to be one of the harmless varieties, probably will be monitored over time with regular urine tests.

Circumcision

Circumcision is a common procedure in many infant boys. It involves removing the foreskin covering the tip of the penis. There are benefits and risks to circumcision, and you should discuss them with your pediatrician and your spouse before your baby is born. Although it is not routinely recommended for all newborn boys, there may be medical, religious, and other reasons why you may decide that it is appropriate for your son. Circumcision is discussed in detail on pages 24–26 and 138–139.

Hypospadias

In boys, the opening through which urine passes (the meatus) is located at the tip of the penis. A condition known as hypospadias is a birth defect that leaves the opening on the underside of the penis. There also may be an abnormal bending of the penis called chordee, which may cause sexual problems in adulthood. The meatus (the opening where urine passes) may direct the urinary stream downward and cause the stream to spray. A concern of many parents is the abnormal appearance of the penis in severe hypospadias, which can be a source of embarrassment to boys as they grow older.

Treatment

After detecting hypospadias in your newborn, your pediatrician probably will advise against circumcision until after consultation with a pediatric urologist or surgeon. This is because circumcision makes future surgical repair more difficult.

Mild hypospadias may require no treatment, but moderate or severe forms require surgical repair. At this time, most children with hypospadias undergo outpatient surgery at around six months of age. In severe cases, more than one operation may be needed to repair the condition completely. After surgery your child's penis will appear nearly normal and he'll be able to urinate normally and—when he's older—have sexual relations.

Meatal Stenosis

Sometimes, particularly in circumcised boys, irritation of the tip of the penis causes scar tissue to form around the meatus, making it smaller. This narrowing, called meatal stenosis, may develop at any time during childhood, but is most commonly found between ages three and seven.

Boys with meatal stenosis have a narrowed and abnormally directed urinary stream. The stream is directed upward (toward the ceiling), making it difficult to urinate into the toilet without pushing the penis down between the legs. Your son may take longer to urinate, and have difficulty emptying his bladder completely.

Treatment

If you notice that your son's urinary stream is very small or narrow, or if he strains to urinate or dribbles or sprays urine, discuss it with your pediatrician. Meatal stenosis is not a serious condition, but it should be evaluated to see if it needs treatment. In some minor cases, a steroid cream can be applied to the penis to correct the problem. If an operation is needed, this surgery is very minor and usually requires only local anesthesia. Your child will have some minor discomfort after the procedure, but this should disappear after a very short period of time.

Labial Adhesions

Ordinarily the lips of skin (labia) surrounding the entrance to the vagina are separated. In rare cases, they grow together to block the opening, partially or completely. This condition, called labial adhesions (sticking together of labia), may occur in the early months of life or, less frequently, later on if there is constant irritation and inflammation in this area. In these latter cases, the problem is usually traceable to diaper irritation, contact with harsh detergents, or underwear made with synthetic fabric. Usually labial adhesions do not cause symptoms, but they can lead to difficulty with urination and increase a girl's susceptibility to urinary tract infections. If the vaginal opening is significantly blocked, urine and/or vaginal secretions will build up behind the obstruction.

Treatment

If the opening of your daughter's vagina appears to have closed or looks partially blocked, notify your pediatrician. He will examine your child and advise you whether any treatment is necessary. The majority of such adhesions resolve on their own as the child gets older and require no treatment.

At first, your doctor will attempt to spread the labia gently. If the connecting tissue is weak, this mild pressure may expose the opening.

But if the connecting tissue is too strong, the doctor may prescribe a cream that contains the female hormone estrogen for you to apply to the area as you very gently and gradually spread the labia apart over a period of time. Once the labia are separated, you will need to apply the cream for a short while (three to five days) until the skin on both sides heals completely.

Occasionally some adhesions return once the cream is discontinued. Repeat application of the cream may be tried or a different type of topical steroid ointment similar to hydrocor-

Normal labia

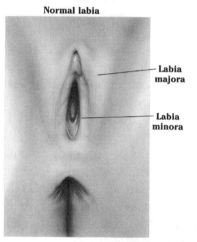

Labia
majora

Labia
minora

Labia with adhesions

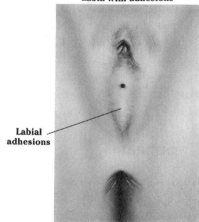

Labial
adhesions

tisone cream may be used. In rare cases, the adhesions will not improve with treatment and may become so severe that they block the flow of urine. In this situation, they may need to be separated in the office (after application of a topical anesthetic) or separated in the operating room with a short surgical procedure.

Undescended Testicles (Cryptorchidism)

During a woman's pregnancy, the baby boy's testes develop in his abdomen. As he nears birth, they descend through a tube (the inguinal canal) into the scrotum. In a small number of boys, especially those who are premature, one or both testicles fail to descend by the time of birth. In many of these boys, descent will occur during the first few months of life. In some, however, this does not happen.

Most boys will have a normal re-

traction of the testes under certain situations, such as while sitting in cold water (i.e., the testes "disappear" temporarily up into the inguinal canal). However, in general, when the boy is warm, testes should be low in the scrotum. The cause of most cases of undescended testicles is unknown.

If your child has undescended testicles, his scrotum may be small and appear underdeveloped. If only one testicle is undescended, the scrotum may look asymmetrical (full on one side, empty on the other). If the testicles sometimes are in the scrotum and at other times (e.g., when he is cold or excited) are absent, and located above the scrotum, they are said to be retractile. This condition usually self-corrects as a boy grows older.

Rarely the undescended testicle may be twisted, and in the process, its blood supply may be stopped, causing pain in the inguinal (groin) or scrotal area. If this situation is not corrected, the testicle can be damaged severely and permanently. If your son has an undescended testicle and complains of pain in the groin or scrotal area, call your pediatrician immediately.

Undescended testicles should be reevaluated at each regular checkup. If they do not descend into the scrotum by six months of age, treatment should be considered.

Treatment

Undescended testicles may be treated with hormone injections and/or surgery. Currently, hormonal treatment is used only in very limited cases of a

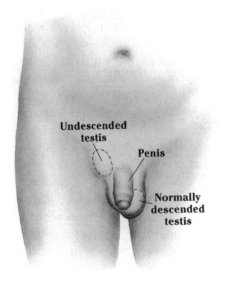

Undescended testis

Penis

Normally descended testis

very low undescended testis or some retractile testes. The vast majority of children with an undescended testis will require surgery. Many children with true undescended testes will also have an inguinal hernia (see page 545), and the hernia will be repaired at the same time that the undescended testis is surgically moved to the scrotum.

If your son's undescended testicle is allowed to remain in that position for more than two years, he may have a higher than average risk of being unable to father children (infertility). Undescended testes are also at higher risk of developing testicular tumors in adult life. The risk is small but is still present even after the testis is surgically brought into the scrotum. Therefore it is important that children with an undescended testis be taught the importance of testicular self-exam when they become adults.

Urethral Valves

Urine leaves the bladder through a tube called the urethra, which in boys passes through the penis. Rarely, small membranes form across the urethra in boys early in pregnancy, and they can block the flow of urine out of the bladder. These membranes are called posterior urethral valves and can have life-threatening consequences by causing blockage of normal urine flow, thus interfering with development of the kidneys. If there is abnormal kidney development, there can be abnormal development of the lungs.

The severity of posterior urethral

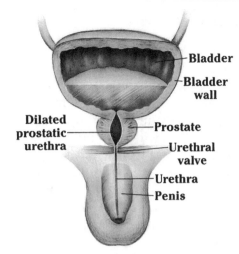

valves can vary widely. Most cases are diagnosed before birth with a screening ultrasound. This condition may be suspected in boys if there appears to be a decrease in the amount of amniotic fluid. Consulting a pediatric urology specialist is always advisable before the baby is born.

In boys who are not diagnosed before birth with posterior urethral valve, sometimes the newborn exam may reveal that the baby's bladder is distended and enlarged. Other warning signals include a continual dribbling of urine and a weak stream during urination. More commonly though, posterior urethral valve is diagnosed when the boy develops a urinary tract infection with fever and poor feeding. If you notice these symptoms, notify your pediatrician at once.

Posterior urethral valves require immediate medical attention to prevent serious urinary tract infections or damage to the kidneys. If the blockage is severe, the urine can back up through the ureters (the tubes between the bladder and the kidneys), creating pressure that can damage the kidneys.

Treatment

If your child has a posterior urethral valve, your pediatrician may pass a small tube (catheter) into the bladder to relieve the obstruction temporarily and allow the urine to flow out of the bladder. He will then take an ultrasound of the bladder and kidneys to confirm the diagnosis and see if any damage has occurred to the upper urinary tract. Your pediatrician will consult with a pediatric nephrologist or urologist, who may recommend surgery to remove the obstructing valves and prevent further infection or damage to the kidneys or urinary system.

Urinary Tract Infections

Urinary tract infections are common among young children, particularly girls. They generally are caused by bacteria that enter through the urethra. In infants, though, they may also rarely be caused by bacteria carried through the bloodstream to the kidneys from another part of the body. As the bacteria move through the urinary tract, they may cause an infection in different locations. *Urinary tract infection (UTI)* is a general term used for all the following specific infections.

- *Cystitis:* infection of the bladder

- *Pyelonephritis:* infection of the kidney

- *Urethritis:* infection of the urethra

The bladder is the area most commonly infected. Usually cystitis is caused by bacteria that get into the urinary tract through the urethra. The urethra is very short in girls, so bacteria can get into the bladder easily. Fortunately, these bacteria normally wash out when urinating.

Cystitis can cause lower abdominal pain, vomiting, tenderness, pain during urination, frequent urination, blood in the urine, recurrence of day- or nighttime wetting in a previously toilet-trained child, and a low-grade fever. Infection of the upper urinary tract (the kidneys) will cause more general abdominal pain and a higher fever, but is less likely to cause frequent and painful urination. In general, urinary tract infections in infants and young children (up to two years of age) may have few recognizable signs or symptoms other than a fever; they also have a greater potential for causing kidney damage than those occurring in older children.

Urinary tract infections must be treated with antibiotics as quickly as possible, so you should notify your pediatrician promptly if you suspect your child has developed one. This is especially the case for infants, in whom an unexplained high fever (that is, not explained by a respiratory infection or diarrhea) may be the only indicator of a urinary tract infection. If your infant has a fever with no other symptoms for more than three days, make sure to talk to your pediatrician, as an evaluation may be indicated.

Diagnosis/Treatment

When a urinary tract infection is suspected, particularly in a child with symptoms, your pediatrician will measure her blood pressure (since an increase in blood pressure can be a sign of a related kidney problem) and examine her for lower abdominal tenderness that might indicate a UTI. Your doctor will want to know what your child has been eating and drinking, because certain foods can irritate the urinary tract, causing symptoms similar to those of an infection.

Your pediatrician also will want a urine sample from your child for analysis. This must be collected either by using a catheter in infants and small children that are not toilet trained, or by the "clean catch" method in an older child that is toilet trained. In toilet-trained children, the urine can be collected by having the child void into a sterile container. First, you'll use soap and water or special wipes provided by your pediatrician to cleanse the urethral opening (with an uncircumcised boy, hold the foreskin back). Then allow your child to start to urinate, but wait just a moment before you start to collect the sample in the container provided by the doctor. In this way, any bacteria around the outside of the urethral opening will be washed away by the early urine voided and won't contaminate the specimen. In infants who are very sick or have a fever, the urine will be collected by catheterization in which a small tube is passed through the urethra into the bladder. In rare cases, a doctor may alternatively perform a suprapubic tap in which a small needle is inserted through the skin of the lower abdomen into the bladder. The urine that is collected will be examined for any sign of blood cells or bacteria, and special tests (cultures) will be done to identify the bacteria. An antibiotic will be started if an infection is suspected, although depending on what the final results of the culture show, the particular antibiotic may need to be changed.

In agreement with recently revised guidelines for the treatment of UTI in infants and children (up to age twenty-four months), your pediatrician may prescribe antibiotics for a total of seven to fourteen days. Prompt treatment is important in order to eliminate the infection and prevent its spread, and also to reduce the chances of kidney damage.

Make sure your child takes the full course of medication prescribed, even if the discomfort goes away after just a few days. Otherwise, the bacteria may grow again, causing further infection and more serious damage to the urinary tract. After the treatment is complete, your doctor may want to obtain and analyze another urine sample to make sure that the infection is completely gone and no bacteria remain, though this is no longer a requirement.

The American Academy of Pediatrics recommends that imaging tests (such as ultrasound, X-rays, or renal scans) may be done in children under age two after their first urinary tract infection. Some imaging studies may not be necessary following a urinary tract infection if prenatal ultrasound studies have adequately visualized the structure of the infant's urinary tract. Your pediatrician may conduct other tests to check the functioning of the kidneys. If any of these examinations indicate an anatomical abnormality of the bladder, ureters, or kidneys that should be corrected, your doctor will recommend that your child see a pediatric urologist or nephrologist.

The AAP does *not* currently recommend after a course of antibiotics that additional antibiotics be given as a preventive (prophylactic) measure to prevent a recurrence of the infection, since research shows that this does not prevent future UTIs.

Wetting Problems or Enuresis

After your child is toilet trained (usually between ages two and four), it is not uncommon for children to wet the bed at night. This may happen as often as two to three times per week early in this period, and gradually become less and less until it is completely gone at around age five in most children.

The exact cause of this incontinence (wetting) is not known. The best way to approach it is to consider it to be something natural and unimportant, and not to scold or punish your child.

Some children continue to wet at night past the age of five. When wetting occurs only during sleep, it is called nocturnal (nighttime) enuresis, or bed-wetting. It affects one out of every four children at age five, one in five at age seven years, and about one in twenty at age ten years. Boys make up two-thirds of this group, and often there is a family history of bed-wetting (usually in the father). Although the reasons for bed-wetting are not fully understood, it may be related to the time it takes different children to develop control over the nervous, muscular, and nighttime full bladder sensation that needs to be subconsciously suppressed. Bed-wetting generally is *not* associated with other physical or emotional problems. It is important to realize that a child has no conscious control of their bladder when they are sleeping. Thus, they should never be made to feel that the bed-wetting is something that they can consciously control and stop on their own.

A much smaller number of children over age five have daytime wetting problems, and an even smaller group is unable to hold their urine both day and night. When incontinence does occur during both the day and night, it may signal a more complicated problem with the bladder or the kidneys.

If your child wets at night, here are some possible causes:

- Slow development to awaken when the bladder is full

- Constipation, which can cause extra pressure on the bladder from the rectum

■ An early sign of diabetes mellitus (see page 627), a urinary tract infection (see page 778), or emotional distress caused by an upsetting event or unusual stress—but only if wetting began suddenly after an extended dry period

Signs of a Problem

When your child is starting toilet training, he is sure to have "accidents." Therefore, you shouldn't be concerned about wetting until at least six months to a year after the training is successful. Even then, it is still normal for him to have some accidents, but they should decrease in number, so that by six months after toilet training is achieved, he should have only occasional accidents during the day, with perhaps a few more at night. If your child continues to wet frequently, or if you notice any of the following signals, talk with your pediatrician.

■ Wet underpants, nightclothes, and bed linens, even when the child regularly uses the toilet

■ Unusual straining during urination, a very small or narrow stream of urine, or dribbling after urination

■ Cloudy or pink urine, or bloodstains on underpants or nightclothes

■ Redness or rash in the genital area

■ Hiding underwear to conceal wetting

■ Daytime as well as nighttime wetting

Treatment

Up to about the age of five years old, it is perfectly normal for your child to have occasional nighttime wetting or daytime accidents when she is laughing, engaged in physical activity, or just too busy playing; in these cases, you should not be concerned. Although annoying to you and perhaps embarrassing for your child, these episodes should stop on their own. There probably is no need for a medical investigation. However, your pediatrician will want to know the answers to the following questions.

■ Is there a family history of wetting?

■ How often does your child urinate, and at what times of the day?

■ When do the accidents occur?

■ Do accidents happen when your child is very active or upset, or when she's under unusual stress?

■ Does your child tend to have accidents after drinking a lot of fluids or eating a lot of salty foods?

■ Is there anything unusual about your child's urination or the way her urine looks?

If your pediatrician suspects a problem, he may check a urine sample for signs of a urinary tract infection (see page 778). If there is an infection, the doctor will treat it with antibiotics, and this may cure the wetting problems. Usually, however, an infection is not the cause.

If there are other indications that wetting is due to more than just slow development of being able to respond to a full bladder, and the wetting persists well beyond age five, your pediatrician may request additional tests, such as X-rays of the bladder (voiding cystourethrogram or VCUG) or an ultrasound examination of the kidneys. If an abnormality is found, the doctor may recommend that you consult a pediatric urologist.

If no physical cause can be found in a child who wets and is over five years of age, and the wetting is causing significant family disruption, your pediatrician may recommend a home treatment program. The program will vary, depending on whether your child wets during the day or the night.

HOME TREATMENT FOR DAYTIME WETTING AFTER TOILET TRAINING

1. **Prevent skin** irritation in the genital area by avoiding harsh detergents or underclothing, as well as bubble-making products in the bathwater. Also, choose mild soaps for bathing, and apply petroleum jelly to protect the affected areas from further irritation from the water and urine.

2. **Prevent constipation** or treat it if it occurs (see page 528).

3. **Try using** a timed voiding program, reminding your child to empty his bladder every few hours rather than waiting until he "has to go"—which by then may be too late.

HOME TREATMENT FOR NIGHTTIME BED-WETTING OVER THE AGE OF FIVE

The following plan usually is helpful, but you should discuss it with your pediatrician before beginning.

1. **Explain the** problem to your child, emphasizing that you understand and know it's not his fault.

2. **Discourage him** from drinking fluids during the two hours before bedtime.

3. **Treat constipation** if it is present.

If your child is still wetting after one to three months on this plan, your pediatrician may recommend using a bed-wetting alarm device. This alarm will awaken your child automatically as soon as he begins to wet, so he can get up and complete his urination in the toilet. Oftentimes, children will sleep through the alarm and not wake up when it goes off. When this occurs, parents will need to be able to hear the alarm so they can assist in waking the child up. When used consistently and according to your pediatrician's guidelines, this bladder-conditioning method is successful for more than half of the children who try it. However, it may take up to four months to work. The relapse rate for the sleep alarm is generally low. It is important to follow your pediatrician's directions carefully in order to give this device the best chance to work.

Another option may be oral medications. These work in about half to two-thirds of the children who use them and side effects are rare. However, relapse rates are high. Oral medications can also be used intermittently for camp, sleepovers, and other similar situations. It is important to limit drinking water before bedtime when on certain oral medications. This should be discussed with your doctor.

If None of the Treatments Work

A small number of children with bed-wetting simply do not respond to any treatment. However, almost all will outgrow the problem by adolescence. Only 1 in a 100 adults is troubled by persistent bed-wetting. Until your child does outgrow his wetting problem, he may need some emotional support from the family, and he also may benefit from speaking with his pediatrician about this condition, or receiving counseling with a child mental health professional.

Because bed-wetting is such a common problem, you may see advertisements for many mail-order treatment programs. You should be wary of them, however, as many false claims and promises are made. Your pediatrician is still your most reliable source for advice, and you should ask him for it before enrolling in or paying for any treatment program.

Read more about bed-wetting. A recommended book is *Waking Up Dry* by Howard J. Bennett, MD, FAAP.

Head, Neck, and Nervous System

Meningitis

MENINGITIS IS AN inflammation of the tissues that cover the brain and spinal cord. The inflammation sometimes affects the brain itself. With early diagnosis and proper treatment, a child with meningitis has a reasonable chance of a good recovery, though some forms of bacterial meningitis develop rapidly and have a high risk of complications.

Thanks to vaccines that protect against serious forms of bacterial meningitis, today most cases of meningitis are caused by viruses. The *viral* form usually is not very serious, except in infants less than three months of age and with certain viruses such as herpes simplex, which typi-cally causes another serious infection. Once meningitis is diagnosed as being caused by a virus, there is no need for antibiotics and recovery should be complete. *Bacterial* meningitis (several types of bacteria are involved) is a very serious disease. It occurs rarely in developed countries (because of the success of vaccines), but when it does occur, children under the age of two are at greatest risk.

The bacteria that cause meningitis often can be found in the mouths and throats of healthy children. But this does not necessarily mean that these children will get the disease. That doesn't happen unless the bacteria get into the bloodstream.

We still don't understand exactly why some children get meningitis and others don't, but we

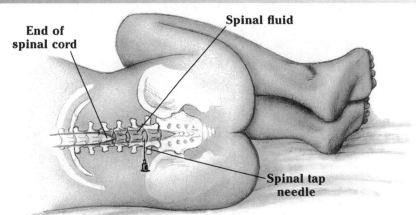

End of spinal cord

Spinal fluid

Spinal tap needle

A spinal tap is taken from the space below the spinal cord so that the needle will not touch the spinal cord.

do know that certain groups of children are more likely to get the illness. These include the following:

■ Babies, especially those under two months of age (Because their immune systems are not well developed, the bacteria can get into the bloodstream more easily.)

■ Children with recurrent sinus infections

■ Children with recent serious head injuries and skull fractures

■ Children who have just had brain surgery

With prompt diagnosis and treatment, 7 out of 10 children who get bacterial meningitis recover without any complications. However, bear in mind that meningitis is a potentially fatal disease, and in about 2 out of 10 cases, it can lead to serious nervous-system problems, deafness, seizures, paralysis of the arms or legs, or learn-

ing difficulties. Because meningitis progresses quickly, it must be detected early and treated aggressively. This is why it's so important for you to notify your pediatrician immediately if your child displays any of the following warning signs:

If your child is less than two months old: A fever, decreased appetite, listlessness, or increased crying or irritability warrants a call to your doctor. At this age, the signs of meningitis can be very subtle and difficult to detect. It's better to call early and be wrong than to call too late.

If your child is two months to two years old: This is the most common age for meningitis. Look for symptoms such as fever, vomiting, decreased appetite, excessive crankiness, or excessive sleepiness. (His cranky periods might be extreme and his sleepy periods might make it impossible to arouse him.) Seizures along with a fever may be the first signs of meningitis, although most brief, generalized (so-called tonic-clonic) convulsions turn out to be simple febrile seizures, not meningitis. (See *Seizures, Convulsions, and Epilepsy,* page 790.) A rash also may be a symptom of this condition.

If your child is two to five years old: In addition to the above symptoms, a child of this age with meningitis may complain of a headache, pain in his back, or a stiff neck. He also may object to looking at bright lights.

Treatment

If, after an examination, your pediatrician is concerned that your child may have meningitis, she will conduct a blood test to check for a bacterial infection and also will obtain some spinal fluid by performing a spinal tap, or lumbar puncture (LP). This simple procedure involves inserting a special needle into your child's lower back to draw out spinal fluid. This is usually a safe technique in which fluid is sampled from the bottom of the sac surrounding the spinal cord. Signs of infection in this fluid will confirm that your child has bacterial meningitis. In that case he'll need to be admitted to the hospital for intravenous antibiotics and fluids and for careful observation for complications. During the first days of treatment, your child may not be able to eat or drink, so intravenous fluids will provide the medicine and nutrition he needs. For certain types of meningitis, intravenous antibiotics may be necessary for seven to twenty-one days, depending on the age of the child and the bacteria identified.

Prevention

Some types of bacterial meningitis can be prevented with vaccines. Ask your pediatrician about the following.

HIB (*HAEMOPHILUS INFLUENZAE* type b) VACCINE

This vaccine will decrease the chance of children becoming infected with *Haemophilus influenzae* type b (Hib) bacteria, which was the leading cause of bacterial meningitis among young children before this immunization became available. The vaccine is given by injection to children at two months, four months, and six months, and then again between twelve and fifteen months of age. (Some combined vaccines may allow your doctor to omit the last injection.)

PNEUMOCOCCAL VACCINE

This vaccine is effective in preventing many serious infections caused by the pneumococcus bacteria, including meningitis as well as bacteremia (an infection of the bloodstream) and pneumonia. It is recommended starting at two months of age, with additional doses at four, six, and between twelve and fifteen months of age. Some children who have an increased susceptibility to serious infections (these high-risk children include those with abnormally functioning immune systems, sickle cell disease, certain kidney problems, and other chronic conditions) may receive an additional pneumococcal vaccine between ages two and five years.

MENINGOCOCCAL VACCINE

There are two kinds of meningococcal vaccines available in the US, but the preferred vaccine for children is called the meningococcal conjugate vaccine (MCV4). Although it can prevent four types of meningococcal disease, it is not routinely recommended for very young children, but rather for young adolescents (eleven to twelve years of age), or teenagers at the time they start high school (or at fifteen years old).

Motion Sickness

Motion sickness occurs when the brain receives conflicting signals from the motion-sensing parts of the body: the inner ears, the eyes, and nerves in the extremities. Under usual circumstances, all three areas respond to any motion. When the signals they receive and send are inconsistent—for example, if you watch rapid motion on a movie screen, your eyes sense the motion, but your inner ear and joints do not—the brain receives conflicting signals and activates a response that can make you sick. The same thing can happen when a child is sitting so low in the backseat of a car that she cannot see outside. Her inner ear senses the motion, but her eyes and joints do not.

Motion sickness usually starts with a vague feeling of stomach upset (queasiness), a cold sweat, fatigue, and loss of appetite. This usually progresses to vomiting. A young child may not be able to describe queasiness, but will demonstrate it by becoming pale and restless, yawning, and crying. Later she may lose interest in food (even her favorite ones), and even vomit. This response can be affected by previous car trips that made her sick, but it usually improves over time.

We do not know why motion sickness happens more often in some children than others. Since many of these children years later experience occasional headaches, there is a belief that motion sickness may be an early form of migraine. Motion sickness occurs most often on a first boat or plane ride, or when the motion is very intense, such as that caused by rough water or turbulent air. Stress and excitement also can start this problem or make it worse.

What You Can Do

If your child starts to develop motion sickness, the best approach is to stop the activity that is causing the problem. If it occurs in the car, stop as soon as safely possible and let her get out and walk around. If you are on a long car trip, you may have to make frequent short stops, but it will be worth it. If this condition develops on a swing or merry-go-round, stop the motion promptly and get your child off the equipment.

Since "car sickness" is the most common form of motion sickness in children, many preventive measures have been developed. In addition to frequent stops, try the following.

- If she has not eaten for three hours, give your child a *light* snack before the trip—which also helps on a boat or plane. This relieves hunger pangs, which seem to add to the symptoms.

- Try to focus her attention away from the queasy feeling. Listen to the radio, sing, or talk.

- Have her look at things outside the car, not at books or games.

If none of the above works, stop the car, remove her from her car seat, and have her lie on her back for a few minutes with her eyes closed. A cool cloth on the forehead also tends to lessen the symptoms.

If you are going on a trip and your child has had motion sickness in the past, you might want to give her medication ahead of time to prevent problems. Some of these medications are available without a prescription, but ask your pediatrician before using them. Although they can help, they often produce side effects, such as drowsiness (which means that when you get to your destination your child might be too tired to enjoy it), dry mouth and nose, or blurred vision.

If your child has symptoms of motion sickness at times when she is not involved with a movement activity—particularly if she also has a headache; has difficulty hearing, seeing, walking, or talking; or stares off into space—tell your pediatrician about it. These may be symptoms of problems other than motion sickness.

Mumps

Mumps is a viral infection that usually causes swelling of the salivary glands (the glands that produce the digestive juices in the mouth). Thanks to the MMR (measles, mumps, and rubella) vaccine given at twelve to fifteen months and a booster at age four to six years, most children in developed countries will never get this disease.

The American Academy of Pediatrics recommends that if your child has not been immunized with the MMR vaccine in early childhood as suggested, your child (eighteen years old and younger) should be given two doses of MMR, separated by four weeks.

While the administration of the MMR vaccine is very important, if a child has not been immunized, the parent should know how to identify mumps and distinguish it from similar ailments. The parotid gland, located in front of the ear at and above the angle of the jaw, is the one most often affected by mumps. However, other salivary glands in and around the face may be involved. Although not all children with mumps appear swollen (in milder cases), anyone who has the virus in his system will become immune to it.

The mumps virus is transmitted when an infected individual coughs droplets containing the virus into the air or onto his hands. A nearby child can inhale these particles, and the virus can pass through his respiratory

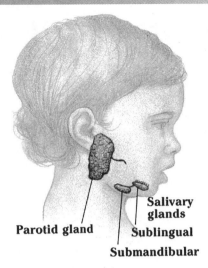

Parotid gland **Salivary glands** **Sublingual** **Submandibular**

system into his bloodstream, finally settling in his salivary glands. At this point, the virus usually causes swelling of the glands along the side of one or both cheeks.

Other symptoms of mumps may include swelling and pain in the joints and, in boys, swelling of the testes. In extremely rare cases, the virus can cause swelling of the brain in boys or girls, or swelling of the ovaries in girls.

It's important to note that salivary gland swelling can be caused by infections other than mumps. This explains why some parents are convinced that their children have had the disease more than once. If your child has been immunized or already has had mumps and his cheeks become swollen, consult your pediatrician to determine the cause.

Treatment

There is no specific treatment for mumps, aside from making the child as comfortable as possible with rest, lots of fluids, and acetaminophen for fever. Although a child with the disease may not be too eager to take fluids, you should keep a glass of water or noncitrus juice nearby, and encourage him to take frequent sips. Sometimes a warm compress over the swollen gland will give some short-term relief.

If your child's condition worsens, or if he develops complications such as painful testes, severe abdominal pain, or extreme listlessness, contact your pediatrician right away. Complications are extremely rare, but the doctor will want to examine your child to see if he needs more extensive medical treatment.

Seizures, Convulsions, and Epilepsy

Seizures are sudden temporary changes in consciousness, physical movement, sensation, or behavior caused by abnormal electrical impulses in the brain. Depending on what part(s) of the body are affected by the abnormal electrical impulses, a seizure may cause sudden stiffening of the body, rhythmic shaking, isolated body jerks, complete relaxation of the muscles (which can make a person appear to be paralyzed temporarily), or staring spells. Sometimes these seizures are referred to as "fits" or "spells." The terms *convulsion* and *seizure* are often used interchangeably.

A convulsion that involves the whole body (sometimes called a "generalized tonic-clonic" or "grand mal" seizure) is the most dramatic type of seizure, causing rapid, violent movements and loss of consciousness. Convulsions occur in about 5 out of every 100 people at some time during childhood. By contrast, "absence" seizures (previously called "petit mal" seizures) are momentary episodes with a vacant stare or a brief (one- or two-second) lapse of attention. These occur mainly in young children and may be so subtle that they aren't noticed until they begin affecting schoolwork.

Febrile convulsions (seizures caused by high fever in the absence of acute or chronic neurological disease) occur in 3 or 4 out of every 100 children between six months and five years of age, but most often around twelve to eighteen months old. Children younger than one year at the time of their first simple febrile seizure convulsion have approximately a 50 percent chance of having another, while children over one year of age when they have their first seizure have about a 30 percent chance of having a second one. Nevertheless, only a very small number of affected children will go on to develop epilepsy (chronic seizures without a fever). A febrile convulsion can cause reactions as mild as a rolling of the eyes or stiffening of the limbs, or as startling as a generalized convulsion with twitching and jerking movements that involve the whole body. Febrile convulsions usually last less than two or three minutes, and ordinarily the child's behavior shortly returns to normal.

The term *epilepsy* is used to describe seizures that occur repeatedly over time without an acute illness (like fever) or other trigger. Sometimes the cause of the recurring seizures is known (symptomatic epilepsy), and sometimes it is not (idiopathic epilepsy).

Some children experience sudden episodes that might masquerade as or imitate seizures, but are really not. Examples include breath holding, fainting (syncope), facial or body twitching (myoclonus), and unusual sleep disorders (night terrors, sleepwalking, and cataplexy). They may occur just once or may recur over a limited time period. Again, although these episodes may resemble epilepsy or true seizures, they are not, and they require quite different treatment.

Treatment

Most seizures will stop on their own and do not require immediate medical treatment. If your child is having a convulsion, protect her from injuring herself by laying her on her side with her hips higher than her head, so she will not choke if she vomits.

If the convulsion does not stop within two or three minutes or is unusually severe (difficulty breathing, choking, blueness of the skin, having several in a row), call 911 for emergency medical help. Do not leave your child unattended. After the seizure stops, call the pediatrician immediately and arrange to meet in the doctor's office or the nearest emergency department. Also call your doctor if your child is on an anticonvulsant medication, since this may mean that the dosage must be adjusted.

If your child has a fever, the pediatrician will check to see if there is an infection. If there is no fever and this was your child's first convulsion, the doctor will try to determine other possible causes by asking if there is a family history of seizures or if your child has had any recent head injury. He will examine your child and also may order blood tests or testing with an electroencephalogram (EEG), which measures the electrical activity of the brain. In some cases, your child may require pictures of the brain using computed tomography (CAT scan) or magnetic resonance imaging (MRI). Sometimes a spinal tap will be performed to obtain a specimen of spinal fluid that can be examined for some causes of convulsions such as meningitis, an infection of the lining of the brain (see page 785). If no explanation or cause can be found for the seizures, the doctor may consult a pediatric neurologist, a pediatrician who specializes in disorders of the nervous system.

If your child has had a febrile convulsion, some parents may try controlling the fever using acetaminophen and sponging. However, these approaches do *not* prevent future febrile seizures, but only make the child more comfortable. If a bacterial infection is present, your doctor will probably prescribe an antibiotic. If a serious infection such as meningitis is responsible for the seizure, your child will have to be hospitalized for further treatment. Also, when seizures are caused by abnormal amounts of sugar, sodium, or calcium in the blood, hospitalization may be required so that the cause can be found and the imbalances corrected.

If epilepsy is diagnosed, your child usually will be placed on an anticonvulsant medication. When the proper dosage is maintained, the seizures are often well-controlled. Your child may need to have her blood checked periodically after starting some medications to make certain there is an adequate amount of medication in her system. She also may need periodic EEGs. Medication usually is continued until there have been no seizures for a year or two.

As frightening as seizures can be, it's encouraging to know that the likelihood that your child will have another one drops greatly as she gets older. (Only 1 in 100 adults ever has a seizure.) Unfortunately, a great deal of misunderstanding and confusion about seizures still exists, so it is important that your child's friends and teachers become educated about her condition. If you need additional support or information, consult with your pediatrician or contact your local or state branch of the Epilepsy Foundation of America (www.epilepsy foundation.org; 1-800-332-1000).

Head Tilt (Torticollis)

Head tilt is a condition that causes a child to hold her head or neck in a twisted or otherwise abnormal position. She may lean her head toward one shoulder and, when lying on her stomach, always turn the same side of her face toward the mattress. This can cause her head to flatten on one side and her face to appear uneven or out of line. If not treated, head tilt may lead to permanent facial deformity or unevenness and to restricted head movement.

Most cases of head tilt are associated with a condition called torticollis (described below), although in rare instances a head tilt can be due to other causes such as hearing loss, misalignment of the eyes, reflux (a flowing back of stomach acid), a throat or lymph node infection, or, very uncommonly, a brain tumor.

CONGENITAL MUSCULAR TORTICOLLIS
By far the most common cause of head tilt among children under age five is congenital torticollis. This condition commonly occurs due to positioning while the baby is still in the womb and rarely may occur during birth (particularly breech and difficult first-time deliveries). Whatever the cause, this condition usually is detected in the first six to eight weeks of life, when the pediatrician notices a small lump on the side of the baby's neck in the area of the injured muscle. The affected muscle is the sternocleidomastoid muscle, which connects the breastbone, head, and neck. Later the muscle contracts and causes the head to tilt to one side and look toward the opposite side.

ACQUIRED TORTICOLLIS (DUE TO INJURY OR INFLAMMATION)
This is more likely to occur in older children, up to the age of nine or ten.

This type of torticollis usually results from an inflammation of the throat caused by an upper respiratory infection, a sore throat, an injury, or some unknown factor. The swelling, for reasons still not known, causes the tissue surrounding the upper spine to loosen, allowing the vertebral bones to move out of normal position. When this happens, the neck muscles go into spasm, causing the head to tilt to one side. Onset of this condition is typically sudden and very painful.

Treatment

Each type of head tilt requires different treatment. It is very important to seek such treatment early, so that the problem is corrected before it causes permanent deformity.

Your pediatrician will examine your child's neck and may order X-rays of the area in order to identify the cause of the problem. X-rays or ultrasound of the hip also may be ordered, as some children with congenital muscular torticollis also have an abnormality known as developmental dysplasia of the hip. If the doctor decides that the problem is congenital muscular torticollis, you will learn an exercise program to stretch the neck muscles. The doctor will show you how to gently move your child's head in the opposite direction from the tilt. You'll need to do this several times a day, very gradually extending the movement as the muscle stretches.

When your child sleeps, it is best to place her on her back, with her head positioned opposite to the direction of

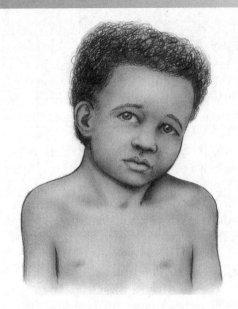

the tilt. In rare instances, your pediatrician may suggest adjustments to her sleep position. When she is awake, position her so those things she wants to look at (windows, mobiles, pictures, and activity) are on the side away from the injury. In that way, she'll stretch the shortened muscle while trying to see these objects. Your pediatrician may also recommend placing her on her stomach while awake and turning her face away from the affected side.

These simple strategies cure this type of head tilt in the vast majority of cases, preventing the need for later surgery. (Your pediatrician may refer your child to a physical therapist to help work on this condition.)

If the problem is not corrected by exercise or position change, your pediatrician will refer you to a pediatric neurologist or orthopedist. In some cases it may be necessary to lengthen the involved tendon surgically.

If your child's head tilt is caused by something other than congenital muscular torticollis, and the X-rays show no spinal abnormality, other treatment involving rest, a special collar, gentle stretching, massage, traction, application of heat to the area, medication, or, rarely, further imaging or surgery may be necessary. For treating torticollis due to injury or inflammation, your doctor may recommend applying heat, as well as using massage and stretching to ease head and neck pain. Your pediatrician can refer you to a specialist for a definitive diagnosis and treatment program.

~ 30 ~

Heart

Arrhythmias

YOUR CHILD'S HEART rate normally will vary to some degree. Fever, crying, exercise, or other vigorous activity makes any heart beat faster. The younger the child, the faster the normal heart rate. As your child gets older, the heart rate will slow down. A resting heart rate of 130 to 150 beats per minute is normal for a newborn infant, but it is too fast for a five-year-old child at rest. In a very athletic teenager, a resting heart rate of 50 to 60 beats per minute may be normal.

The heart's regular rhythm or beat is maintained by a small electrical circuit that runs through nerves in the walls of the heart. When the circuit is working properly, the heartbeat is quite regular; but when there's a problem in the circuit, an irregular heartbeat, or arrhythmia, can occur. Some children are born with abnormalities in this heart circuitry, but arrhythmias also can be caused by infections or chemical imbalances in the blood. Even in healthy children, there can be other variations in the rhythm of the heartbeat, including changes that occur just as a result of breathing. Such a fluctuation is called *sinus arrhythmia,* and requires no special evaluation or treatment because it is normal.

So-called premature heartbeats are another form of irregular rhythm that requires no treatment. If these occur in your child, she might say that her heart "skipped a beat" or did a "flip-flop." Usually these symp-

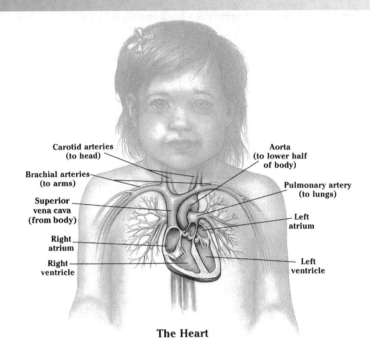

Carotid arteries
(to head)

Brachial arteries
(to arms)

Superior
vena cava
(from body)

Right
atrium

Right
ventricle

Aorta
(to lower half
of body)

Pulmonary artery
(to lungs)

Left
atrium

Left
ventricle

The Heart

toms do not indicate the presence of significant heart disease.

If your pediatrician says that your child has a true arrhythmia, it could mean that her heart beats faster than normal (tachycardia), very fast (flutter), fast and with no regularity (fibrillation), slower than normal (bradycardia), or that it has isolated early beats (premature beats). While true arrhythmias are not very common, when they do occur they can be serious. On rare occasions they can cause fainting or even heart failure. Fortunately, they can be treated successfully so it's important to detect arrhythmias as early as possible.

Signs and Symptoms

If your child has a true arrhythmia, your pediatrician may discover it during a routine visit. But should you notice any of the following warning signs between pediatric visits, notify your doctor immediately.

- Your infant suddenly becomes pale and listless; the body feels limp.

- Your child complains of "the heart beating fast," while at rest.

- She tells you she feels uncomfortable, weak, or dizzy.

- She blacks out or faints.

It's unlikely that your child will ever experience any of these symptoms, but if she does, your pediatrician will perform additional tests and perhaps consult with a pediatric cardiologist. In the process the doctors may do an electrocardiogram (ECG) to better distinguish a normal sinus arrhythmia from a true arrhythmia. An ECG is the recording of the electrical activity of the heart, and it will allow the doctor to observe any irregularities more closely.

Sometimes your child's unusual heartbeats may occur at unpredictable times, often not when the ECG is being taken. In that case the cardiologist may suggest that your child carry a small portable recorder called a Holter monitor that continuously records her heartbeat over a one- to two-day period. During this time you'll be asked to keep a log of your child's activities and symptoms. Comparing the ECG with your observations will help make a diagnosis. For example, if your child feels her heart "flutter" and becomes dizzy at 2:15 p.m. and the ECG shows her heart suddenly beating faster at the same time, the diagnosis of arrhythmia will probably be established.

Occasionally irregular heartbeats will occur only during exercise. If that's the case with your child, the cardiologist may have her ride a stationary bicycle or run on a treadmill while her heartbeat is being recorded. When your child is old enough to participate in sports, ask your pediatrician if any special tests or restrictions are necessary.

Heart Murmur

Technically, a heart murmur is simply a noise heard between the beats of the heart. When a doctor listens to the heart, she hears a sound something like *lub-dub, lub-dub, lub-dub*. Most often, the period between the *lub* and the *dub* and between the *dub* and the *lub* is silent. If there is any sound during this period, it is called a murmur. Heart murmurs are extremely common, and are usually normal (that is, the sounds are caused by a healthy heart pumping blood normally).

In preschool and school-age children, heart murmurs are almost always not a concern. Most children with a murmur require no special care, and the sound eventually disappears. These children have "normal" or so-called functional or innocent heart murmurs.

If your child has such a murmur, it probably will be discovered between the ages of one and five years during a routine examination. The doctor then will listen carefully to determine if this is a "normal" heart murmur or one that might indicate a problem. Usually, just by listening to its sound, the pediatrician will be able to tell if a murmur is innocent (normal blood flow through a normal heart). If necessary, she will consult a pediatric cardiologist to be certain, but additional tests are usually not needed.

On rare occasions, a pediatrician will hear a murmur that sounds abnormal enough to indicate that something might be wrong with the heart. If the doctor suspects this, your child will be referred to a pediatric cardiologist to enable a precise diagnosis to be made.

When do heart murmurs become a concern? When they occur very early at birth or during the first six months of life. These murmurs are *not* functional or innocent, and most likely they will require the attention of a pediatric cardiologist immediately. They may be due to abnormal connections between the pumping chambers (septal defects) or the major blood vessels coming from the heart (e.g., transposition of vessels). Your infant will be observed for changes in skin color (turning blue), as well as breathing or feeding difficulties. He also may undergo additional tests, such as a chest X-ray, electrocardiogram (ECG), and an ultrasound of the heart (echocardiogram). This echocardiogram creates a picture of the inside of the heart by using sound waves. The cardiologist and pediatrician together will make a decision as to next steps depending on the results of these tests. If all of these tests prove normal, then it is safe to conclude that the baby has an innocent murmur and he will not need to be seen again by a cardiologist.

When a specific condition called patent ductus arteriosus (PDA) occurs, it is often detected shortly after birth, most commonly in premature babies. In infants with a PDA, blood circulates abnormally between the two major arteries that come off the heart. In most cases, the only symptom of PDA is a heart murmur until the ductus closes on its own shortly after birth, which often happens in otherwise healthy, full-term newborns. Sometimes, especially in premature babies, it may not close on its own, or it may be large and permit too much blood to pass through the lungs, which can place extra strain on the heart, forcing it to work harder and causing a rise in pressure in the arteries of the lungs. If this is the case, a medication may be tried initially, but if not successful, surgery may be needed to close the PDA.

Treatment

Innocent heart murmurs are normal and therefore require no treatment. Children with these innocent heart murmurs do not need repeated evaluations or long-term follow-up care from cardiologists, nor do they require restrictions on sports or other physical activities.

Innocent heart murmurs generally disappear by mid-adolescence. Cardiologists don't know why they go away, any more than we know why they appear in the first place. In the meantime, don't be discouraged if the murmur is softer on one visit to the pediatrician and loud again on the next. This may simply mean that your child's heart is beating at a slightly different rate each time. Most likely, this normal murmur will go away eventually.

Patent ductus arteriosus is a self-correcting problem in some cases, or medications can be used to close a PDA. But if the ductus arteriosus remains open, it may need to be corrected surgically or with a catheter.

If other, more serious, heart conditions are diagnosed from birth or shortly thereafter, and the evaluation reveals more serious defects, the pediatric cardiologist and pediatrician will consult a pediatric cardiac surgeon at a regional Pediatric Cardiac Center where complete pediatric cardiac diagnostic and intervention capabilities exist.

Hypertension/High Blood Pressure

We usually think of high blood pressure, or hypertension, as a problem that affects adults. But, in fact, this condition can occur at any age, even in infancy. About 5 of every 100 children have higher than normal blood pressure, although fewer than 1 in 100 has medically significant hypertension.

The term *blood pressure* actually refers to two separate measurements: *Systolic* blood pressure is the highest pressure reached in the arteries as the heart pumps blood out for circulation through the body; *diastolic* blood pressure is the lower pressure that occurs in the arteries when the heart relaxes between beats. If either or both of these measurements are above the range found in healthy people of the same age and sex, it's called hypertension.

In many cases, hypertension seems to develop with age. As a result, your child may show no signs of high blood pressure as an infant, but may develop the condition as she grows. Children who are overweight are much more prone to have hypertension (as well as other health problems). Thus, good eating habits (without overeating and without emphasizing high-fat foods) and plenty of physical activity are important throughout the early years of childhood (and for the rest of her life).

In most instances of high blood pressure, other than those cases caused or made worse by obesity, no known cause can be identified. However, when hypertension becomes *severe* in children, it's usually a symptom of another serious problem, such as kidney disease or abnormalities of the heart or of the nervous or endocrine (gland) system.

Fortunately, high blood pressure alone rarely causes serious problems in children, and can be controlled through dietary changes, medication, or a combination of the two. However, if hypertension is allowed to continue or become worse over many years, the prolonged extra pressure can lead to heart failure or stroke in adulthood. Also, long-term hypertension causes changes in blood vessel walls that may result in damage to the kidneys, eyes, and other organs. For these reasons it's important for children with hypertension to have their blood pressure checked regularly by their pediatrician, and for you to follow the doctor's treatment advice carefully.

Treatment

In most routine physical examinations, your child's blood pressure will be measured. This is how hypertension is usually discovered. Most often this condition causes no noticeable discomfort, but any of the following may indicate high blood pressure:

High-Sodium (Salt) Foods

(more than 400 mg/serving)

Seasonings: Bouillon, salted meat tenderizers, salted spices (e.g., garlic salt, onion salt, seasoned salt), soy sauce, teriyaki sauce
Snack foods: Salted pretzels, crackers, chips, and popcorn
Commercially prepared foods: Most frozen dinners and commercially prepared entrees; dry and canned soups
Vegetables: Any vegetables prepared in brine (e.g., olives, pickles, sauerkraut); vegetable juices (e.g., tomato juice)
Cheeses: Processed cheese foods, some types of cheeses including American cheese, blue cheese, cottage cheese, and Parmesan cheese
Meat: Any smoked, cured, pickled, or processed products (e.g., corned beef, bacon, dried meat and fish, ham, luncheon meats, sausages, and frankfurters)

Low- and Moderate-Sodium (Salt) Foods

(less than 400 mg/serving)

Seasonings: Spices without added salt (e.g., garlic powder, onion powder); "plain" spices (oregano, thyme, dill, cinnamon, etc.); condiments (e.g., mayonnaise, mustard, hot pepper sauce, steak sauce, ketchup)
Vegetables: All fresh, frozen, and canned, particularly those canned with no added salt
Fruits and fruit juices: Fruit juices; all fresh, canned, frozen, and dried fruits
Grain products: Pasta, bread, rice, cooked cereals, most ready-to-eat cereals, pancakes, pastries, cakes, cookies
Dairy products: Milk, yogurt, custard, pudding, ice cream
Meat and other protein foods: Fresh meat, fish, and eggs; unsalted nuts; dried beans and peas

- Headache

- Dizziness

- Shortness of breath

- Visual disturbances

- Fatigue

If your child has high blood pressure, your pediatrician will order tests to see if there is an underlying medical problem. These tests include examining the urine and blood. Sometimes special X-rays are used to examine the blood supply to the kidneys. If no medical problem can be found, your child will be diagnosed with *essential hypertension*. (In medical terms, the word *essential* refers only to the fact that no cause could be found.)

What will the doctor tell you to do? If obesity is the cause, the first step may be to have your child lose weight. This will need to be very closely monitored by your pediatrician. Not only will weight loss lower blood pressure, it can provide many other health benefits as well.

The next step toward reducing your child's blood pressure is to limit the salt in her diet. (See box on page 800, *High-Sodium [Salt] Foods* and *Low- and Moderate-Sodium [Salt] Foods*.) Giving up the use of table salt and restricting salty foods can reverse mild hypertension and will help lower more serious blood pressure levels. You'll also have to be cautious when shopping for packaged foods; most canned and processed foods contain a great deal of salt, so check labels carefully to make sure the items have little or no salt added. Fast food and other types of restaurant foods are often high in salt, so minimize their intake. Your pediatrician also may suggest that your child get more exercise. Physical activity seems to help regulate blood pressure and thus can reduce mild hypertension.

Once your pediatrician knows your child has high blood pressure, he'll want to check it frequently to make sure the hypertension is not becoming more severe. Depending on how high the blood pressure is, he may refer your child to a child hyper-tension specialist, usually a pediatric nephrologist (kidney specialist) or pediatric cardiologist (heart specialist). If it does become worse, it may be treated with medication as well as diet and exercise. Many types of medications are available, which work through different parts of the body. When your child's blood pressure is brought under control with diet or medication it is important to continue the treatment according to your doctor's recommendations, including changes in diet, or the hypertension will return.

Prevention

It's very important to detect hypertension early. Uncontrolled long-standing hypertension can have damaging effects on several other organs in the body such as the heart, kidneys, and brain. It is now recommended that all children have their blood pressure checked beginning at age three, sooner for those at high risk. These include infants who were preterm, or of low birth weight, or who had a difficult or prolonged hospital stay. It also includes children who have congenital heart disease, who are receiving medications that might increase blood pressure, or who have any other condition that might lead to high blood pressure.

Because overweight children are more likely to develop hypertension (as well as other health problems), watch your child's caloric intake and make sure she gets plenty of exercise. Even relatively small decreases in weight or small increases in physical activity may prevent hypertension in overweight children.

Kawasaki Disease

Kawasaki disease is a systemic process where blood vessels throughout the body become inflamed. It is a potentially serious and perplexing disease, the cause of which is unknown. One sign of this disease includes fever, usually quite high, that lasts for at least five days and doesn't respond to antibiotics and does not have an alternative cause. Fever should be present to consider a diagnosis of Kawasaki disease in the ill child and in addition other signs must be present on examination. Most often, four of the six following signs appear in the first week of a typical case:

1. Rash over some or all of the body, often more severe in the diaper area, especially in infants under twelve months of age.

2. Redness and swelling of the palms and soles and/or in the later stage, peeling of the skin around the base of the nails.

3. Red, swollen, and cracked lips and/or a strawberry tongue (red and bumpy).

4. Red, inflamed eyes, involving the sclerae (white part).

5. A single swollen lymph gland, particularly on one side of the neck.

6. Irritability or listlessness. Children with Kawasaki disease are usually crankier or more lethargic than usual. They also may complain of abdominal pain, headache, and/or joint pain.

When Kawasaki disease associated inflammation of the blood vessels occurs, it often involves the arteries of the heart (the coronary arteries) and can be present in up to 25 percent of cases. Blood tests are used to demonstrate inflammation and a heart ultrasound (echocardiogram) will be used to evaluate the coronary arteries in the child with Kawasaki disease. The echocardiogram can identify inflammation, which can weaken the walls of the blood vessels, and in some cases this weakening may even balloon out, causing aneurysms (blood-filled swellings of the blood vessels). In most cases the inflammation in the blood vessels appears to resolve after several months to years, but in some cases, the coronary artery may become stenotic (narrow).

Kawasaki disease occurs most frequently in Japan and Korea and in individuals of Japanese and Korean ancestry, but it can be found among all racial groups and on every continent. The exact number of cases is not known, but it is probably between 5,000 and 10,000 per year in the US, typically occurring in infants between eighteen and twenty-four months of age and preschoolers. Kawasaki disease occurs rarely in infants between six weeks and six months of age, and in this age group, unremitting fever may be the only sign noted. The peak age of occurrence in the United States is between six months and five years.

Kawasaki disease is not contagious. It is extremely uncommon for two children in the same household to get the disease. Likewise, it does not spread among children in child care programs, where there is daily close contact. Although Kawasaki disease can occur in community outbreaks, particularly in the winter and early spring, no one knows the cause. Despite intense research, no bacterium, virus, or toxin has been identified as a cause of the disease. No specific test makes the diagnosis. The diagnosis is made by meeting the signs of illness mentioned previously and by excluding other possible diseases.

Treatment

Though the cause of Kawasaki disease is unknown, it can be treated but not prevented. If it is diagnosed early enough, intravenous gamma globulin (a mixture of human antibodies) can greatly reduce the risk of a child developing coronary aneurysms. If your child receives gamma globulin infusion, this may impact the routine immunization schedule related to so-called live virus vaccines (varicella and MMR vaccine), so parents should check with their pediatrician. However, all vaccines that are inactivated vaccines, including influenza vaccine, should be given on schedule.

In addition to gamma globulin, the child with Kawasaki disease will receive aspirin, initially in high doses during the first stage of Kawasaki disease and in low doses during the recovery stage, until your pediatrician tells you it is okay to stop. Aspirin can decrease the tendency of blood to clot in damaged blood vessels and it is used to prevent clots from developing in the coronary arteries. Although it's appropriate to use aspirin to treat Kawasaki disease, aspirin should not be used to treat children with minor illnesses (e.g., a cold or influenza) as it has been linked with a serious disease called Reye syndrome. If a child is treated with aspirin for Kawasaki disease and exposed to influenza or chickenpox, the aspirin should be stopped and parents should discuss a suitable temporary substitute medicine with their pediatrician.

~ 31 ~

Immunizations

IMMUNIZATIONS have helped children stay healthy for more than half a century. Routine vaccines have become one of the best weapons available to protect your child against major childhood diseases.

Immunizations, in fact, are one of the greatest public health success stories of our times. Many diseases that were once a routine part of growing up—some of them life-threatening—are now preventable and relatively rare, thanks to improvements in sanitation, better nutrition, less crowded living conditions, antibiotics—and, most important, vaccines. At one time, most people did not reach adulthood without someone in their family or circle of friends being touched by a very serious illness or death caused by an infectious disease. But now those same diseases are at record low levels in the US as well as many other countries in the world—and that's because immunization rates are at record highs. Routine immunization against sixteen infectious diseases is now recommended between birth and eighteen years of age. Vaccines work extremely well—most are more than 90 percent effective in preventing diseases—so they are important weapons in keeping children safe and healthy. When parents learn of the risks of these infections—for example, whooping cough causing seizures, brain disease, and even death—the argument in favor of childhood immunizations is persuasive. Although chickenpox, for example, is usually a mild disease, before the vaccine was available, more than 11,000 children were hospitalized each year when chickenpox sores became infected. Before the vaccine, about 100 people died of chickenpox complications each year. But now this disease can be prevented.

Important and Safe

Because many parents (and even some doctors) have never seen a child with diseases like whooping cough or diphtheria or measles, mothers and fathers sometimes ask their pediatrician whether their child really needs vaccines at all. But while many of the illnesses that once caused lifelong disabilities or even death are now uncommon, they haven't been wiped out completely. Yes, they are preventable, but the germs that cause many of them are still around, and are constantly being brought into the country by international travelers.

Just consider the case of the *Haemophilus influenzae* type b (Hib) vaccine. It protects children from serious childhood diseases like meningitis (an inflammation and swelling of the tissues that cover the brain and spinal cord) and throat infections that can block the airway (epiglottitis). Before this vaccine became available in the 1980s, there were about 20,000 cases of Hib disease in the United States every year. *H. influenzae* type b was the most common cause of bacterial meningitis in the United States and it was a major cause of intellectual disability and deafness. It caused about 12,000 cases of meningitis each year in children younger than five years of age—especially in babies six to twelve months old. Of those children infected, 1 in 20 died from this disease, and 1 in 4 developed permanent brain damage. Today, because Hib disease is prevented by immunization, there are fewer than 100 cases annually in the United States.

At the same time, vaccines are very safe—but they're not perfect. Like medications, they can cause occasional reactions, but usually these are mild (see *More About Immunizations* on page 807). Side effects like redness or discomfort at the site of the injection can happen in as many as 1 out of 4 children. They appear soon after the shot is given, and then usually go away within a day or two. Your child also may be fussy afterward. Although more severe reactions can occur, they are much less common. Some children with certain health conditions should not receive vaccines. Talk to your doctor if your child had a serious reaction to a previous vaccine, has certain allergies, or is sick on the day of the appointment. This type of information can help your doctor determine if your child should not get a vaccine. In recent years, some critics of immunizations have pointed to a preservative called thimerosal, which for decades had been added to some vaccines to prevent contamination of vaccines by bacteria. Thimerosal has a small amount of organic mercury in it, which worried some parents. They were concerned about a link between disorders such as autism and vaccines that contain thimerosal. Numerous

More About Immunizations

When you have your children immunized:

- You protect them from dangerous and potentially fatal diseases.

- You lower the severity of the disease if your children happen to get it.

- You cut down the chances that contagious diseases will spread.

- You safeguard other people in your community who are too young to receive the vaccine or cannot receive vaccinations due to medical issues.

Also of Note

- After receiving a vaccine, some children experience mild symptoms such as a low fever and fussiness, as well as tenderness, swelling, or redness where the shot was given. They also may sleep a little longer than usual in the day or two after receiving the shot.

- On very rare occasions, children may react to a vaccine with a more serious response, such as a high fever, a rash, or seizures. Call your pediatrician if your child develops a fever over 103 degrees Fahrenheit (39.4 degrees Celsius), a generalized rash (including hives), a large amount of swelling in the limb where the shot was given, or any other symptoms that worry you. These guidelines apply to all of the immunizations described in this chapter.

---

scientific studies now show there is no link between thimerosal in vaccines and autism. In addition, all vaccines manufactured for infants in the United States are thimerosal-free or contain only trace levels.

While some parents also worry that their child is receiving "too many vaccines" at one time, there is plenty of research showing that multiple childhood vaccines can be given at the same time safely. In fact, a vaccine cannot be licensed and recommended until the manufacturers show that it can be given safely with other recommended vaccines. And although children receive more vaccines than in years past, the ones they're receiving have been purified and improved so that children are actually receiving fewer antigens (substances that help a body build up an immunity) with each shot. These shots are effective and safe when they're given according to the guidelines recommended by the American Academy of Pediatrics.

The important point to remember is that getting these preventable diseases is much more dangerous than getting the vaccines. If you have questions or concerns about immunizations, talk with your pediatrician.

Easing the "Hurt"

Shots can hurt. When your child receives a vaccine, she can be uncomfortable and may cry for several minutes. But fortunately, any pain is very short-lived. At the moment the immunization is given, you may be able to soften the experience by distracting your child. Talk soothingly, and make eye contact with her. Afterward, comfort and play with her for a while.

If your child develops side effects, you may be able to ease any fever or irritability by giving her acetaminophen or ibuprofen. Be sure to discuss the use and proper dosage of these medicines with your pediatrician. If your child has pain at the site where the shot was given, your doctor might recommend applying cool compresses to lessen the discomfort. Certainly, if any reaction makes your child uncomfortable for more than four hours, notify your pediatrician, who will want to note it in your child's records and prescribe appropriate treatment.

Before immunizing your child, it's a good idea to talk with your doctor about what reactions could occur, if any. If unusual or severe reactions (like a high fever or changes in behavior) happened in the past, you and your pediatrician should discuss the pros and cons of whether another dose of the same vaccine is appropriate when the next one is scheduled.

As painful as it may be for you to watch your child experience the discomfort of a shot, don't lose sight of the fact that you're doing enormous good for her by making sure she is protected from the diseases that vaccines can prevent.

What Shots Does Your Child Need?

Your child should be vaccinated according to the schedule of immunizations recommended by the American Academy of Pediatrics. The entire schedule appears in the Appendix, and includes the immunizations described below for young children. Please refer to the chart often for information on the immunizations your child needs and when they should be given. Also, recommendations change as vaccines are improved and new ones are developed; so be sure to speak with your pediatrician or visit www.aap.org for the most current immunization schedule.

DIPHTHERIA, TETANUS, AND PERTUSSIS
The DTaP vaccine protects your child against diphtheria (D), tetanus (T), and pertussis (aP). The diphtheria portion of this vaccine guards against a throat infection that can trigger breathing difficulties, paralysis, or

WHERE WE STAND

THE AMERICAN ACADEMY OF PEDIATRICS believes that immunizations are the safest and most cost-effective way of preventing disease, disability, and death. We urge parents to make sure that their children are immunized against dangerous childhood diseases since it is always better to prevent a disease than to have to treat it or live with the consequences of having it.

heart failure. The tetanus portion protects against a disease that causes the tightening or "locking" of all of the muscles in the body, especially the jaw, and is potentially fatal. The vaccine for pertussis (also called whooping cough) prevents bacteria from causing severe and violent coughing spells in infants that can make breathing and eating difficult.

What about expected side effects? Redness and tenderness may occur with the diphtheria and tetanus portions of the vaccine. Sometimes the fourth or fifth dose is followed by swelling of the arm or leg in which the shot was given. Severe, but very rare, problems that have been reported after the DTaP vaccine include long-term seizures, coma, and permanent brain damage. Don't keep your child from getting this—or any—vaccine without first speaking with your pediatrician. He can address any concerns you may have. For the vast majority of children, the dangers of the diseases themselves far outweigh any risks of the shots; keep in mind, for example, that 2 out of 10 people who get tetanus die from it; and 1 out of 100 babies under two who get pertussis die. More than 1 out of 10 children who

get diphtheria die of complications. Immunizations are very important.

MEASLES, MUMPS, AND RUBELLA (MMR)

The measles portion of this vaccine protects against an infection that causes an extensive red or brownish blotchy rash, as well as flulike symptoms; measles can lead to severe complications such as pneumonia, seizures, and brain damage. The mumps vaccine gives your child protection against a virus that causes swollen salivary glands, a fever, and headaches, and can lead to deafness, meningitis, and painful swelling of the testicles or ovaries. The rubella (German measles) vaccine guards against an infection of the skin and lymph nodes, in which the child may have a pink rash and swollen, tender glands at the back of the neck.

There has been considerable media attention in recent years about a connection between the MMR vaccine and autism. In fact, extensive research shows that there is no connection. There has been confusion because autism is often diagnosed at about the age at which children receive the MMR vaccine. This has led to the erroneous conclusion that the vaccine somehow causes autism. But, in fact, studies now show that autism actually begins before a baby is born and vaccines play no role.

Use of the MMR vaccine was once discouraged for children who had an allergy to eggs. But because the MMR vaccine now contains only trace amounts of egg protein, the recommendation has been adjusted and now the vaccine can be safely administered to egg-allergic children without special precautions. Also, if your child is taking any medication that interferes with the immune system, or if her immune system is weakened for any reason, she generally should not receive this immunization. As for side effects, sometimes, around seven to twelve days after the MMR vaccine, a child may develop mild swelling of the glands in the cheeks or neck, and a fever or mild rash. If this mild vaccine side effect does occur, it is important to note that it is not dangerous or contagious and will resolve on its own. Such findings occur less often after the second dose. Severe problems such as seizures caused by fever occur in 1 out of 3,000 doses. Serious allergic reactions are very rare (about 1 out of 1,000,000 doses).

CHICKENPOX (VARICELLA)

The vaccine to protect against the varicella virus became available in 1995, and protects against not only chickenpox but also shingles in later life. Natural chickenpox infection can cause a fever and an itchy, blisterlike rash all over the body. There may be as many as 250 to 500 of these blisters. Some-times, the infection causes serious complications, including skin infections, brain swelling, and pneumonia.

Varicella vaccine is safe. Reactions to the vaccine are generally mild. About 20 percent will develop mild pain, redness, or swelling at the injection site. Very rarely, in less than 1 in 1,000 children, a febrile seizure may occur after the vaccine. If your child has a weakened immune system, or is taking steroids or other drugs that can affect the immune system, check with your doctor before she gets the chickenpox immunization.

Two doses of the vaccine provide more than 90 percent protection against infection. Currently if someone who has been vaccinated does get chickenpox, it is usually very mild. They will have few spots, are less likely to have a fever or serious complications, and will recover faster.

INFLUENZA

Influenza (or "the flu") is a respiratory illness caused by a virus. This infection leads to symptoms such as a high fever, muscle aches, sore throat, and cough, and it may take your child several days of rest to recover. There are two types of influenza vaccine to protect your child:

■ The inactivated (killed) vaccine or the "flu shot," given by injection

■ The live attenuated (weakened) vaccine, sprayed into the nostrils

Children six months of age and older—including all children, adolescents, young adults, and those caring for a child too young to receive a vaccine—should receive the annual seasonal influenza vaccine. Special efforts should be made to vaccinate those who have chronic medical conditions that increase their risk of severe influenza complications (such as asthma, diabetes, immunosuppression, or neurological disorders). The formulation of the influenza vaccine changes yearly, depending on the expected prevalence of the various influenza strains. This is one reason the influenza vaccine must be administered every year.

POLIO

The polio vaccine provides protection from the virus that causes polio. While some infections with the polio virus cause no symptoms, it can cause paralysis and death in other cases. Before the polio vaccine was available, millions of children throughout the world were left paralyzed from polio.

Today, all children need four doses of the polio vaccine before they start school, starting with shots at two months of age. The inactivated polio vaccine is given as shots, and there is no risk of the vaccine causing the disease. An oral form of the vaccine is no longer available in the US.

HIB (*HAEMOPHILUS INFLUENZAE TYPE B*)

The Hib vaccine protects your child from the bacterium that (before the vaccine became available) was the leading cause of meningitis. This serious disease occurs most often in chil-dren from ages six months to five years, leading to symptoms such as fever, seizures, vomiting, and a stiff neck. Meningitis also can cause hearing loss, brain damage, and death. These same bacteria can also lead to a rare but serious inflammation of the throat called epiglottitis.

The first Hib vaccine should be given at two months of age, with additional doses to follow. It is important to have your child immunized with this vaccine in order to lower her risk of getting Hib diseases during the early years of life when she is most vulnerable to these infections. There are no reasons to withhold this vaccine from your child unless she has had a rare life-threatening allergic reaction to a previous dose of the vaccine.

HEPATITIS B

The hepatitis B vaccine offers protection against a liver disease that can be spread by infected blood and body fluids. The infection is caused by the hepatitis B virus, and can lead to cirrhosis and liver cancer. The infection can be passed from an infected mother to her baby at the time of birth, or from one household member to another.

The first hepatitis B shot should be given shortly after birth, even before your baby is discharged from the hospital. A second dose should be given at one to two months of age, and a third dose when the child is six to eighteen months old. The hepatitis B vaccine is very safe. Severe problems are rare. Possible mild reactions include soreness where the shot was given, and in one out of fifteen people, a temperature of 99.9 degrees Fahrenheit (37.7 degrees Celsius) or higher.

HEPATITIS A

Like the hepatitis B vaccine, the hepatitis A immunization protects against a common liver disease, which your child can catch by eating food or drinking water contaminated with the hepatitis A virus. This common infection can sometimes be spread in child care settings when caregivers do not follow good hand-washing procedures.

The hepatitis A vaccine is very safe. Reactions to this vaccine are very uncommon and usually nothing more than soreness where the shot was given.

PNEUMOCOCCAL VACCINE

The pneumococcal conjugate vaccine protects your child from meningitis, as well as common forms of pneumonia, blood infections, and certain ear infections. A pneumococcal infection is one of the most common causes of vaccine-preventable deaths in children. Only mild reactions are associated with the vaccine. Some children become fussy or drowsy, lose their appetite, or develop a fever.

ROTAVIRUS

The rotavirus vaccine protects against a potentially serious stomach virus (often referred to as the "stomach flu"), which can cause vomiting, diarrhea, and related symptoms in children. The rotavirus is the most common cause of severe diarrhea in children under the age of two years. In the US, before the rotavirus vaccine was given, about 50,000 children less than five years of age were hospitalized each year because of rotavirus infection.

Some children may experience mild, temporary diarrhea or, rarely, vomiting within seven days of getting a dose of the rotavirus vaccine. There are no severe reactions associated with this vaccine. As with some other vaccines mentioned earlier, talk with your doctor before getting the rotavirus vaccine if your child's immune system might be weakened by conditions like HIV or steroid use.

MENINGOCOCCAL VACCINE

The meningococcal vaccine will protect your child against some of the most common types of germs that cause meningitis. This vaccine is recommended for children starting at eleven or twelve years of age. Children with an increased risk of infection should be immunized early in the first year of life. Check with your pediatrician about when the vaccine should be administered if your child has a weakened immune system.

HUMAN PAPILLOMAVIRUS VACCINE

Human papillomavirus causes cervical cancer in females as well as anogenital cancer and genital warts in males and females. This vaccine works only if it is administered *before* your child becomes infected with this virus, and more than 80 percent of people will become infected at some time in their life. The first three doses should be administered at eleven or twelve years of age to all males and females.

~ 32 ~

Media

TECHNOLOGY SUCH AS TV, mobile devices, and Internet-related games offer entertainment, culture, and education to our children. They are an important part of the average daily lifestyle. While it may offer many benefits, media use has also been associated with the risk of obesity, sleep issues, aggressive behaviors, and attention issues in preschool- and school-age children. When it comes to incorporating technology into your child's daily routine, she needs your experience, judgment, and supervision.

Early Years

Some doctors specialize in early brain development in children and the best ways to help them learn. The effect of various types of media stimulation and screen time activities is an area of ongoing study, but early results lead us to recommend that children under age two should be as "screen-free" as possible. Many digital media programs are marketed as "educational," even when evidence shows that very young children cannot learn from such a format.

Quality programs are educational at an age when children can understand the content and context of what they are seeing. Studies consistently find that children over two years old typically have this understanding. It's important for parents to remember that unstructured play time is more valuable for the developing brain than electronic media. Children learn to think creatively, problem solve, and de-

WHERE WE STAND

THE AAP RECOMMENDS that parents and caregivers minimize or eliminate altogether media exposure for children under the age of two. For older preschool-age children, media limits are very appropriate, and parents should have a strategy for managing electronic media when choosing to maximize its benefits. Remember that supervised independent play for infants and young children has been shown to have superior benefit to the use of screen media when you cannot sit down and actively engage in play with your child. For example, have your child play with nesting cups on the floor nearby while you prepare dinner. Also avoid placing a television set in your child's bedroom and recognize that your own media use can have a negative effect on children.

velop reasoning and motor skills at early ages through unstructured, unplugged play much better than with passive screen time. Free play also teaches them how to entertain themselves. While children may remember some things viewed on a program (especially when viewed repeatedly), children learn much more from a live person presenting the same material.

When parents are watching their own programs and using cellular devices or computers, it is important to remember that this *background media* may not be desirable for children. It can be distracting for parents and decreases parent-child interaction. Background media may also interfere with a young child's learning from play and activities. Young children with heavy media use are at risk for delays in language development once they start school, but more research is needed as to the reasons. Background media is distracting for both the parent and the child. When adult programs are on, the adult's attention is turned to the screen and there is significantly less casual "talk time" going on between parent and child. Research shows that "talk time" is valuable for children's emerging language development. And background media is also distracting for a child who may be sitting in the same room, playing with his toys. Research shows that even when a show is not intended for a child audience, a child will glance up at the screen three times every minute. It disrupts a child's concentration when he is "at work" (playing). Children are less focused and more likely to move on to a new toy more quickly when a screen is on.

Ages Two and Three

By the age of two, children can benefit from watching educational content such as programming with music, movement, or simple stories. Passive screen time is not a substitute for reading, playing, or problem solving, but through moderation it can play a

WHERE WE STAND

ALTHOUGH THE AMERICAN ACADEMY OF PEDIATRICS does not hold media solely responsible for violence in our society, we believe that violence in television, movies, or video games has a clear effect on the behavior of children and contributes to the frequency with which violence is used to resolve conflict. Entertainment media also distort reality on matters such as drugs, alcohol, tobacco, sexuality, and family relations.

We encourage parents to manage both the quantity and the quality of their family's screen time. Parents can create a healthy media diet and lead by example. Children's TV programming is supported by commercial advertisers whose primary motivation is to sell products. Many young children are not prepared to distinguish between programs and the commercials that interrupt them, nor do they fully understand that commercials are designed to sell them (and their parents) something.

Together, parents, broadcasters, and advertisers must be held responsible for the media that children consume. The American Academy of Pediatrics strongly supports legislative efforts to improve the quality of children's programming. We urge parents to limit and monitor the amount of screen time (including television, videos, computer, and video games) for their children, to monitor what their children are watching, and to watch media with them to help them learn from what they see.

role in developing specific skill sets. Carefully chosen programs can help introduce young children to letters, numbers, and certain life experiences. Children who are inadvertently exposed to adult content, however, may absorb some negative messages if present. A child watching a show with adult content may observe characters engaging in violence or using inappropriate language. These types of programs may also present sexuality, drugs, and alcohol to children who are too young to understand the reality of these issues. In addition, a great deal of screen time perpetuates myths and stereotypes of certain gender tasks and racial associations that will serve as poor influences on children. Children view social interactions on video programs as a glimpse of the "real world" when, in reality, they are often far from reality. This is why it is important for parents to preview or watch programs with their child to discuss what is happening on the screen and answer questions.

A mounting body of research shows that screen time is associated with obesity. Some experts believe it is due to excessive snacking while watching programs and that exposure to ads for junk food and fast food also increases children's desire for these foods. Snacking outside of normal meal times increases while watching TV or movies. In addition, most screen time is sedentary time for young children, where they are not running around and playing.

All children need active play, not only for the physical exercise but also for proper mental and social development. Most media use is passive. Sitting and watching TV all the time, for example, does not help your child acquire the most important skills and experiences she needs at this age, such as communication, creativity, fantasy, judgment, and experimentation. The more time your child spends in front of a screen, the less time there is to spend on the wide variety of activities that create a fun and memorable childhood. While there may be some educational benefits to screens, children need a healthy variety of daily activities. Independent play encourages creativity. Playing with other children fosters social skills and problem solving. And physical activity is critical for a healthy lifestyle. This is why children need a balance of activities in their day.

Ages Four and Five

In a fast-changing, increasingly technological world, it is important for children to become adept at using various forms of technology as they grow older. Carefully monitoring your child's usage will lead to a safe and fun experience.

If your child chooses to play games on a tablet, mobile device, or family computer, ensure that she plays games that are suited to her age. If the game requires using the Internet, check that it is housed on a safe, kid-friendly website. This will limit the possibility of her encountering inappropriate material inadvertently. Furthermore, the American Academy of Pediatrics recommends using your computer operating system's parental controls, which can block or filter Internet content. This is also consistent with cell phones and other mobile devices. Many Internet service providers have software for the same purpose, generally free of charge. Parents can choose to purchase a separate software program or app that can block and track inappropriate or unwanted websites, and lock parts of the device to prevent your child from viewing other areas. There are also apps that can control the *length* of time a child is on a screen.

TV shows and movies often come with a rating that indicates the type of content included in the program. These are usually located in the TV listings or TV guide. News programs do not have ratings, and certain information presented may not be suitable for children to hear. Be firm with your child about what is appropriate material for her to view.

Technology devices, whether it's TV or a tablet, can be a part of the bedtime routine for many children. Parents mistakenly believe that these can sometimes be a calming sleep aid, but some TV programs actually increase bedtime resistance, and can

Special-Needs Children and Computers

If your child has special needs, you can get equipment that makes it easier for her to use computers. For example, special screens, keyboards, joysticks, and computerized voice programs allow children with disabilities to enjoy using a computer.

For additional information, contact:

- ERIC—the Education Resources Information Center (1-800-538-3742; www.eric .ed.gov). This resource is an online digital library of education research and information.

- The Starlight Foundation (1-310-479-1212; www.starlight.org) is another excellent resource. It is an organization dedicated to developing projects that empower seriously ill children to face their day-to-day challenges.

In addition, your child should clearly understand that people online are not always who they say they are, and may not be the "friends" they claim to be.

cause anxiety about falling asleep. Research has shown that television viewing is associated with irregular sleep schedules in children who watch television around bedtime, and can shorten sleep duration by delaying the onset of sleep. In addition, research shows that the glow of screens will interfere with the release of melatonin, a body chemical that is needed to wind down to sleep. For these reasons it is important to keep screens out of your child's bedroom at night. Poor sleep habits have adverse effects on mood, behavior, and learning. Limit watching TV or engaging in digital or computer games that are stimulating to earlier in the day and have a "bedtime" or "electronic curfew" for screens about an hour before your child's bedtime.

Guidelines for Media Use

- Your child should use the computer only when you're sitting with her or are close by and can supervise online activities.

- Keep the family computer in a public area of the house and create clear rules for its use.

- Set and enforce a daily or weekly time limit or curfew for all media usage.

- Make sure that your child understands not to share personal information over the Internet. Websites aimed at children should not request detailed information without a parent's permission, but if they do, inform your child to talk with you first.

A Message to Parents

For children over age two, limit screen time to less than one or two hours a day. Teach your child that screen time means television, movies, and digital gaming, and that these are privileges that one can enjoy but that also come with responsibilities.

Be media-smart by:

■ Setting limits and offering guidance for your child's media time

■ Helping your child to plan which programming and movies to watch and when

■ Turning the screen off when the show is over or they have reached their maximum allowed usage time

■ Being mindful of times when you use media as a "babysitter"

■ Keeping TV, DVD players, video games, and computers out of your child's bedroom and in open family areas of your home

■ Watching TV with your child to help educate her about advertising and commercials

To increase her interest in other activities that don't involve forms of media, invite her to join you in reading, playing board or outdoor games, coloring, cooking, building, or visiting with friends. Praise her when she entertains herself without relying on television or the computer, and present a good model by restricting your own media time. You are your child's best role model. You have to show her that you value human interactions and that you also have limits on your screen time. And *do not* use television as a reward or withhold it as a punishment, as it will only make it seem more enticing. Set up the ground rules and be consistent. Maybe your house rules are "no videos or TV shows on school nights" or "up to two hours of recreational screen time after homework is done"—media is earned after the homework is done. No matter what your family's rules are, having and enforcing rules is the key.

Monitoring your children's "media diet" is important to establish at an early age. Media education can lead to a better understanding of the pros and cons of all types of media, and how best to introduce and use it in your home.

~ 33 ~

Musculoskeletal Problems

Arthritis

ARTHRITIS involves inflammation of the joints that produces swelling, stiffness, redness, heat, tenderness, and pain with motion. Although arthritis is typically thought of as a condition of the elderly, children can also develop arthritis. The four most common forms of childhood arthritis are as follows:

TRANSIENT SYNOVITIS (INFLAMMATION) OF A HIP
This is the most common form of arthritis in children. It typically develops suddenly between two and ten years of age, and then it resolves after a short period of time (days to weeks), with no serious lasting effects. The most common cause involves the im-

mune system's overreaction to a virus, so it is frequently seen after an upper respiratory infection. Treatments include rest and anti-inflammatory medications (such as ibuprofen), which may help symptoms go away faster.

BACTERIAL INFECTION OF A JOINT
When a joint becomes infected with bacteria, it becomes very painful, hot, swollen, and stiff. An affected child will often walk with a limp, refuse to bear weight, or have decreased movement in an arm. An affected child also will typically have a fever, and very young children may simply be irritable and refuse to walk or use an extremity. Notify your pediatrician immediately if these signs or symptoms appear, as rapid treatment can prevent joint

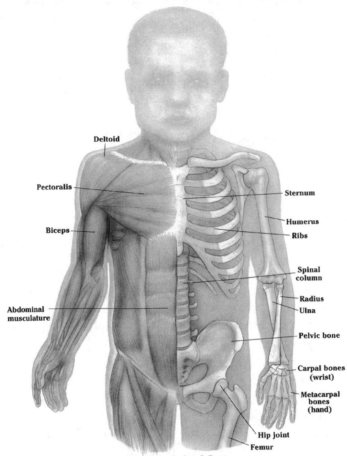

Deltoid
Pectoralis
Biceps
Abdominal
musculature

Sternum
Humerus
Ribs
Spinal
column
Radius
Ulna
Pelvic bone
Carpal bones
(wrist)
Metacarpal
bones
(hand)
Hip joint
Femur

Musculoskeletal System

damage. If infection involves the hip or other deep and inaccessible joints, it can be difficult to diagnose; and infection of the large weight-bearing joints is a very serious condition that needs to be properly diagnosed and treated by a specialist (usually an orthopedist). Treatment may include needle aspiration or surgical drainage of the infected joint, and intravenous (IV) antibiotics.

LYME DISEASE

An infection transmitted by the deer tick can cause a form of arthritis known as Lyme disease. It is called this because it was first diagnosed in a child in Old Lyme, Connecticut. This infection often starts with a red mark that is surrounded by a light ring or halo (having the appearance of a red and white target) at the site where your child was bitten by a deer tick. Later, a similar but smaller rash may appear on other areas of the body. Your child also may develop flulike symptoms such as headache, fever, swollen lymph nodes, fatigue, and muscle aches. Arthritis then typically develops weeks to months after the skin rash. If arthritis is severe, medications can be prescribed to control inflammation and pain until the condition gradually resolves on its own.

If a joint is involved, Lyme disease is often treated with antibiotics. However, the American Academy of Pediatrics does not recommend routinely taking antibiotics after a tick bite in an effort to *prevent* Lyme disease due to the fact that most tick bites do not transmit the germ that causes Lyme disease, possible side effects of antibiotics, cost, and the risk of promoting antibiotic-resistant bacteria. The Academy also does not recommend testing your child's blood for Lyme disease shortly after a tick bite, since it takes quite a while for antibodies to show up in the blood even with an infected tick bite. To prevent Lyme disease, your child should avoid tick-infested areas such as wooded regions, high grasses, or marshes. Children also can protect themselves from ticks by wearing long-sleeved shirts, tucking their pants into their socks, and using an insect repellent that has DEET as the active ingredient when outside. (See page 854 for more information on DEET.)

Almost all cases of Lyme disease can be readily treated with antibiotics, even if arthritis develops.

JUVENILE IDIOPATHIC ARTHRITIS (JIA)

Juvenile idiopathic arthritis (JIA) has previously been referred to as juvenile rheumatoid arthritis or juvenile chronic arthritis, and is the most common form of chronic joint inflammation in children. JIA is a puzzling disorder that is often difficult to diagnose and challenging for families to understand. Common symptoms in-

How to Remove a Tick

1. Gently cleanse the area with an alcohol-soaked sponge or cotton ball.

2. Using forceps, tweezers, or fingers (protected by a tissue or cloth), grasp the tick as near to the mouth parts and as close to the skin as possible.

3. Using gentle but steady tension, pull the entire tick up and out.

4. Be sure the tick is dead before disposing of it. Removal and disposal of ticks should be done with a protective barrier (tissue or cloth) so you do not get exposed to any bacteria or infectious agents that could be spread by a tick.

5. After the tick is out, cleanse the bitten area thoroughly with alcohol or other cleansing (soap) agent.

clude persistent joint stiffness and swelling, and pain with motion of affected joints. If your child has these symptoms, and/or an unusual pattern of walking, especially in the morning or after naps, call your pediatrician to have your child evaluated. Surprisingly, many children with JIA do not complain of much pain; stiffness and swelling are often the most prominent signs of arthritis.

JIA can occur at almost any age, but it is very uncommon before the first birthday. Particular types of JIA are common before the age of six or around the time of puberty. Although this condition can be disabling, with proper treatment most children have good outcomes, and in many children the condition will resolve on its own over time. The exact cause of JIA is unknown. Researchers believe that JIA may be triggered by an infection that causes an abnormal response of the immune system, which leads to autoimmune joint inflammation.

Signs, symptoms, and long-term consequences vary depending on the subtype of JIA. A form of JIA known as systemic JIA involves not only arthritis, but also inflammation throughout the body, with associated fever and rash, and possible effects on other organs. For example, a child with systemic JIA can develop pericarditis (inflammation of the sac that surrounds the heart), myocarditis (inflammation of the heart muscle), pleuritis (an inflammation of the inner lining of the chest), or pneumonitis (inflammation of the lungs). Other subtypes of JIA include oligoarthritis, polyarthritis–

rheumatoid factor negative, polyarthritis–rheumatoid factor positive, psoriatic arthritis, enthesitis-related arthritis, and undifferentiated arthritis. Oligoarticular JIA affects no more than four joints and is most common in preschool girls. The two forms of polyarticular JIA affect at least five joints, and the rheumatoid factor positive subtype is similar to adult rheumatoid arthritis. Psoriatic JIA occurs in children with the skin condition of psoriasis or children who have typical features of psoriatic JIA (swelling of entire digits, nail changes, first-degree relative with psoriasis). Enthesitis-related arthritis involves both arthritis as well as enthesitis (inflammation of sites where tendons and ligaments attach to bone). This subtype of JIA is often associated with a gene, HLA-B27, and is the only form of JIA that is more common in boys. Undifferentiated JIA does not fit neatly into one of the other categories, or it often has features of more than one JIA subtype. Importantly, some children with JIA can have associated inflammation in the front of the eye and this is most common in JIA patients who have a positive ANA test. This should be evaluated by an ophthalmologist early in the course of the disease.

JIA TREATMENT

Great strides have been recently made in the treatment of JIA. Treatment varies depending on the severity and location of arthritis, but it often includes both medications and exercise. It is important to follow the treatment plan that is recommended by your doctor to ensure the best outcome for the child.

The main goal of medical treatment of JIA is reduction of joint inflammation. Nonsteroidal anti-inflammatory drugs (NSAIDs) are often used initially to decrease pain and stiffness. Commonly used NSAIDs include ibuprofen, naproxen, and meloxicam. NSAIDs work quickly, but they can cause stomach upset and should always be taken with food. Call your doctor if a child taking NSAIDs complains of abdominal pain or loses appetite. Children with an inadequate response to NSAIDs may be treated with more effective medications, but these often also have more risk of side effects and higher cost. These medications include methotrexate, as well as relatively new biologics, such as etanercept, adalimumab, abatacept, and tocilizumab. These medications have more risks that require careful monitoring, but they can also make a huge difference in the lives of children with arthritis. Another treatment option that is commonly used when only one or a few joints have arthritis involves directly injecting a long-acting steroid into affected joints, which can rapidly restore function in even severely affected joints.

Exercise also plays an important role in slowing progression of JIA and preventing joints from getting too stiff. Although it may be uncomfortable at times, especially when a child's joints are already sore, it is important for families to help their child work through the discomfort for the long-term benefits. Involvement of physical and occupational therapies is often helpful to guide an exercise program, and for very stiff joints, these therapies can also provide a splinting program to prevent and/or reduce deformities of affected joints.

Living with JIA requires a great deal of adjustment and dedication, not only for affected children but also for their families. Working as a team with your health care providers can help decrease the risk of a child with JIA having long-term problems or disabilities.

Bowlegs and Knock-Knees

Toddlers' legs often have a bowed appearance. In fact, many children have bowing of the legs until they are about two years old. After this age, they often will look progressively knock-kneed until they are about six years of age; afterward this returns to normal. At times, children may not have straight lower legs until they are nine or ten years old.

Bowlegs and knock-knees usually are variations of normal and normally require no specific treatment. Typically, a child's legs will straighten naturally by the teen years, but treatment may become necessary if there is a severe deformity or the deformity occurs during the teen years. Bracing, corrective shoes, and exercise are rarely helpful except for severe deformities, and may hinder a child's physical development and cause unnecessary emotional stress. Rarely, bowlegs or knock-knees are the result of a disease. Arthritis, injury to the growth plate around the knee (see *Fractures/Broken Bones*, page 699), infection, tumor, Blount's disease (a growth disorder of the knee and shinbone), and rickets (caused by vitamin D deficiency) all can cause changes in the curvature of the legs.

Here are some signs that suggest a child's bowlegs or knock-knees may be caused by a serious problem:

■ The curvature is extreme.

■ Only one side is affected.

■ The bowlegs get worse after age two.

■ The knock-knees persist after age seven.

■ Your child also is unusually short for his age.

If your child fits any of these descriptions, talk to your pediatrician. In some cases, treatment, including referral to a pediatric orthopedist, may be needed.

Elbow Injuries

A pulled elbow (also known as nursemaid's elbow) is a common, painful injury generally among children under four years old but occasionally older. It occurs when the outer part of the elbow becomes dislocated or slips out of its joint. This happens because the child's elbow joint is loose enough to separate slightly when her arm is pulled to full length (while being lifted,

yanked, or swung by the hand or wrist, or if she falls on her outstretched arm). The nearby tissue slides into the space created by the stretching and becomes trapped after the joint returns to its normal position.

A nursemaid's elbow injury usually doesn't cause swelling, but the child will complain that the elbow hurts, or cry when her arm is moved. A child will typically hold her arm close to the side, with the elbow slightly bent and the palm turned toward the body. If someone tries to straighten the elbow or turn the palm upward, the child will resist because of the pain.

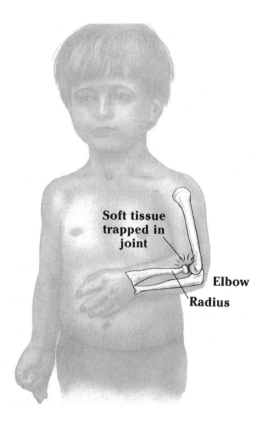

Soft tissue trapped in joint

Elbow

Radius

Treating Nursemaid's Elbow

This injury should be treated by a pediatrician or other trained health care provider. Since elbow pain can also be due to a fracture, your pediatrician may need to consider this before the elbow is "reduced" or put back into place.

Your doctor will check the injured area for swelling and tenderness and any limitation of motion. If an injury other than nursemaid's elbow is suspected, X-rays may be taken. If no fracture is noted, the doctor will move and twist and flex the arm gently to release the trapped tissue and allow the elbow to return to its normal position. Once he has moved the elbow back in place, the child will generally feel immediate relief and within a few minutes should be using her arm normally without any discomfort. Occasionally, the doctor may recommend a sling for comfort for two or three days, particularly if several hours have passed before the injury is treated successfully. If the injury occurred several days earlier, a hard splint or cast may be used to protect the joint for one to two weeks. Persisting pain after a "reduction" may mean that a fracture occurred that may not have been apparent at the time of initial X-rays.

Prevention

Nursemaid's elbow can be prevented by not pulling or lifting your child by the hands or wrists, or swinging her by the arms. Instead, lift your child by grasping her body under the arms.

Flat Feet/Fallen Arches

Babies are often born with flat feet, which may persist well into their childhood. This occurs because children's bones and joints are flexible, causing their feet to flatten when they stand. Young babies also have a fat pad on the inner border of their feet that hides the arch. You still can see the arch if you lift your baby up to stand on the tips of the toes, but it may disappear when he's standing normally. The foot may also turn out, increasing the weight on the inner side and making it appear even more flattened.

Normally, flat feet disappear by age six as the feet become less flexible and the arches develop with increased leg muscle strength. Only about 1 or 2 out of every 10 children will continue to have flat feet into adulthood. For children who do not develop an arch, treatment is not recommended unless the foot is stiff or painful, which may mean that there is a possible connection between some of the small foot bones called a tarsal coalition (fused or connected bones). This may mean an X-ray is indicated. Shoe inserts won't help your child develop an arch, and may cause more problems than the flat feet themselves.

However, certain forms of flat feet may need to be treated differently. For instance, a child may have tightness of the heel cord (Achilles tendon) that limits the motion of his foot. This tightness can result in a flat foot, but it usually can be treated with special stretching exercises to lengthen the

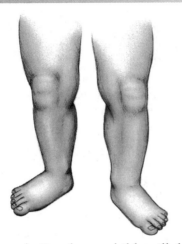

heel cord. Rarely, a child will have truly rigid flat feet due to a tarsal coalition (fused or connected bones), a condition that can cause problems. These children have difficulty moving the foot up and down or side to side at the ankle. The rigid foot can cause pain and, if left untreated, can lead to arthritis. This rigid type of flat foot is seldom seen in an infant or very young child. (More often, rigid flat feet develop during the teen years and should be evaluated by your child's pediatrician.)

Symptoms that should be checked by a pediatrician include foot pain, sores or pressure areas on the inner side of the foot, a stiff foot, limited side-to-side foot motion, or limited up-and-down ankle motion. For further treatment you should see a pediatric orthopedic surgeon or podiatrist experienced in childhood foot conditions.

Limp

Limping can be caused by something as simple as a pebble in your child's shoe, a blister on her foot, or a pulled muscle. But a limp also can be a sign of more serious trouble, such as a broken bone, arthritis, infection, or hip dysplasia. For that reason, it's important to have your pediatrician examine a child with a limp to make sure that no serious problems exist.

Some children limp when they first learn how to walk. Early limping can be caused by neurological damage (such as cerebral palsy; see page 642). But any limp around the time your child begins to walk needs to be investigated as soon as possible, since the longer it goes untreated, the more difficult it may be to correct. Once walking is well established, significant sudden limping usually indicates one of several conditions:

■ A "toddler" fracture

■ Hip injury or inflammation (synovitis)

■ Previously undiagnosed developmental dysplasia (abnormal development) of the hip (DDH)

■ Infection in the bone or joint

■ Kohler's disease (loss of blood supply to a bone in the foot)

■ Juvenile idiopathic arthritis

A "toddler" fracture is a spiral fracture of the tibia (one of the leg bones that extends from the knee to the ankle; see *Fractures/Broken Bones*, page 699). It can occur with minor accidents such as when children trip, jump, or fall, or when they go down a slide in an older child's or an adult's lap with their feet tucked under them. Sometimes children can explain how the injury occurred, but usually they have difficulty recalling exactly what happened. At times an older sibling or child care provider can solve the mystery.

Hip problems that cause a limp at this age usually are due to a viral joint infection causing transient synovitis and should be evaluated by your pediatrician. When a child has an infection in the bone or joint, she usually experiences a fever, swelling of the joint, and redness. If the infection is in the hip joint, she will hold her leg flexed or bent at the hip and be extremely irritable and unwilling to move the hip and leg in any direction, although swelling and redness may not be obvious in this deep joint.

Sometimes a child is born with a dislocated hip (DDH, developmental dysplasia of the hip) that may not be noticed until she starts to walk. As one limb is shorter, the hip is less stable and the buttock muscles are weaker than the other side, the child may walk with an obvious limp.

Perthes disease is another disorder that causes children to limp and that is most often *not* associated with any pain complaints. It is more often only a minor problem in children younger than six years old, but in older children, usually older than ten years of age, it can be a significantly disabling problem.

Limping is a major reason that parents of children with juvenile idiopathic arthritis seek medical care. In a typical case, a child will not complain of being in pain. But she limps nevertheless, with this limping at its worst after waking in the morning or from a nap, and becoming less noticeable with activity.

Treatment

With minor injuries, such as a blister, cut, or sprain, simple first-aid treatment can be performed at home. However, if your child has just started walking and is constantly limping, your pediatrician should evaluate her. It is all right to wait twenty-four hours if your older child develops a limp since sometimes the problem will disappear overnight. But if your child is still limping the next day, or is in extreme pain, see your pediatrician.

X-rays of the hip or the entire leg may be necessary to make the diagnosis. If there is an infection, antibiotics should be started and hospitalization may be required. Intravenous (IV) antibiotics may be given in high doses to allow them to get to the joint and bone. If a bone is broken or dislocated, the limb will be placed in a splint or cast and the child will be referred to an orthopedist for evaluation and further management. It is also advisable to see a pediatric orthopedist if a congenital dislocated hip (DDH) or Perthes disease is diagnosed.

Pigeon Toes (Intoeing)

Children who walk with their feet turned in are described as being "pigeon-toed" or having "intoeing." This is a very common condition that may involve one or both feet, and it occurs for a variety of reasons.

INTOEING DURING INFANCY
Infants are sometimes born with their feet turning in. If this turning occurs from the front part of their foot only, it is called metatarsus adductus (see figure below). It most commonly is due to being positioned in a crowded space inside the uterus before the baby is born.

You can suspect that metatarsus adductus may be present if:

■ The front portion of your infant's foot at rest turns inward.

■ The outer side of the child's foot is curved like a half-moon.

**Appearance of foot in
metatarsus adductus**

This condition is usually mild and will resolve before your infant's first birthday. Sometimes it is more severe, or accompanied by other foot deformities that result in a problem called clubfoot. This condition requires a consultation with a pediatric orthope-

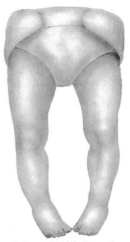

Internal tibial torsion

dist, and there is extremely effective nonoperative treatment with early casting or splinting.

INTOEING IN LATER CHILDHOOD
When a child is intoeing during her second year, this is most likely due to inward twisting of the shinbone (tibia). This condition is called internal tibial torsion (see figure above). When a child between ages three and ten has intoeing, it is probably due to an inward turning of the thighbone (femur), a condition called medial femoral torsion. Both of these conditions tend to run in families.

Treatment

Some experts feel no treatment is necessary for intoeing in an infant under six months of age. For severe metatarsus adductus in infancy, early casting may be useful.

Studies show that most infants who have metatarsus adductus in early infancy will outgrow it with no treatment necessary. If your baby's intoeing persists after six months, or if it is rigid and difficult to straighten out, your doctor may refer you to a pediatric orthopedist who may recommend a series of casts applied over a period of three to six weeks. The main goal is to correct the condition before your child starts walking.

Intoeing in early childhood often corrects itself over time, and usually requires no treatment. But if your child has trouble walking, discuss the condition with your pediatrician who may refer you to an orthopedist. A night brace (special shoes with connecting bars) was used in the past for this problem, but it hasn't proven to be an effective treatment. Because intoeing often corrects itself over time, it is very important to avoid nonprescribed "treatments" such as corrective shoes, twister cables, daytime bracing, exercises, shoe inserts, or back manipulations. These do not correct the problem and may be harmful because they interfere with normal play or walking. Furthermore, a child wearing these braces may face unnecessary emotional strain from her peers.

Nevertheless, if a child's intoeing remains by the age of nine or ten years old, surgery may be required to correct it.

Sprains

Sprains are injuries to the ligaments that connect bones to one another. A sprain occurs when a ligament is stretched excessively or torn. Sprains are less common in young children, because their ligaments are usually stronger than the growing bones and cartilage to which they are attached. Therefore, the growing part of the bone might separate or tear away before the ligament is injured.

In young children, the ankle is the most commonly sprained joint, followed by the knee and wrist. In a mild sprain (grade 1), the ligament simply is overstretched, while more severe sprains can involve partial tearing of the ligament (grade 2), or complete tearing (grade 3).

Call your child's pediatrician if your child has a joint injury and is unable to bear weight or has excessive swelling or pain. Often the doctor will want to examine your child. In some instances, special X-rays may be ordered to rule out a fracture (a break in the bone). If there is a fracture, your pediatrician may consult with or refer you to an orthopedist or sports medicine specialist. When a sprain is diagnosed, treatment usually involves compression using an elastic bandage or immobilization with a splint. A walking cast or removable device may be necessary if the ankle or foot injury has been severe.

Most grade 1 sprains will heal within two weeks without subsequent complications. Your child's physician should be called anytime a joint injury fails to heal or swelling recurs. Ignoring these signs could result in serious damage to the joint and long-term disability.

~ 34 ~

Skin

SKIN PROBLEMS IN children often get the attention—and sometimes raise the anxiety levels—of parents. After all, these skin conditions are immediately visible, and while the overwhelming majority are not serious, they can still become a source of worry. In this chapter, you'll find an alphabetical description of common skin problems. Other related skin conditions (specifically eczema, hives, and insect bites and stings) are discussed in Chapter 17, *Allergies*.

Birthmarks and Hemangiomas

Dark-Pigmented Birthmarks (Nevi or Moles)

Nevi, or moles, are either congenital (present at birth) or acquired. Composed of so-called nevus cells, these spots range in color from light tan to dark brown or black.

CONGENITAL NEVI

Small nevi appear at birth and are relatively common, occurring in about 1 out of every 100 newborns. They tend to grow with the child and usually don't cause any problems. Rarely, however, these moles may develop into a type of serious skin cancer (melanoma) at some later time. Therefore, while you don't have to worry about them right away, it's a good idea to watch them carefully and have them checked by your pediatrician at regular intervals or if there is any change in appearance (color, size, or shape). She may refer you to a pediatric dermatologist who will advise you on removal and any follow-up care.

A much more serious type of nevus is a large congenital one that is over 20 centimeters (7⅞ in) in diameter. It might be flat or raised, may have hair growing from it (although small, insignificant nevi sometimes also have hair), and can be so large that it covers an arm or a leg. Fortunately, these nevi are very rare (occurring in 1 out of every 20,000 births). However, they are more likely than the smaller ones to develop into a melanoma (maybe up to 5 percent), so early consultation with a pediatric dermatologist and regular mole checks are advisable.

ACQUIRED NEVI, OR MOLES

Most light-complected people develop ten to thirty pigmented nevi, or moles, throughout the course of their lives. They usually occur after the age of five, but sometimes develop earlier. These acquired moles are seldom a cause for worry. However, if your child develops one that's irregularly shaped (asymmetrical), has multiple colors within its structure, and is larger than a pencil eraser, ask your pediatrician to examine it.

One final note: Probably the most common acquired dark spots on the skin are freckles. They can appear as early as ages two to four years, are found more often on parts of the body exposed to the sun, and tend to run in families. They often become darker or larger during the summer and are less prominent in the winter. Although they represent no danger, they may be an indicator of excessive sun exposure. They are also an important reminder to keep kids out of the sun when possible and to use UV protective clothing, hats, sunglasses, and sunscreen to protect their skin.

Blood Vessel Birthmarks on the Skin

Your baby has a flat red patch on the back of the neck at birth and then at two to three weeks of age develops a new red raised bump on the forehead. They're unsightly, but are they harmful?

Although some of these blood vessel or vascular marks are usually innocent and do not cause trouble, it's important to recognize the difference between these marks and those that may be associated with medical complications. Your pediatrician will also evaluate such birthmarks at each visit.

CAPILLARY MALFORMATIONS (SALMON PATCHES AND PORT WINE BIRTHMARKS)

Capillary malformations are recognized as flat red patches in the newborn and include salmon patches (most common) and port wine birthmarks (less common). Salmon patches occur in more than 80 percent of infants and most commonly involve the back of the neck, the mid forehead, the upper eyelids, the sides of the nose, and the middle of the upper lip. Although they fade during the first few years of life and are not associated with any serious medical problems, they may still be noticeable when children are overheated or having a temper tantrum, especially in light-complected individuals.

Port wine birthmarks occur in other areas of the skin, tend to be darker at birth, do not fade, and usually gradually darken with increasing age. They may be associated with other birth defects including abnormalities of the underlying veins and arteries in the involved skin. When a port wine birthmark involves the skin around the eye, forehead, or scalp, it may be associated with abnormalities of the eye and brain known as Sturge-Weber syndrome. Affected children should be checked for glaucoma and other eye birth defects as well as abnormalities of the brain. This evaluation may be performed by your pediatrician in collaboration with a pediatric neurologist, ophthalmologist, and dermatologist or in a center of excellence specializing in Sturge-Weber syndrome.

Since port wine birthmarks usually intensify during childhood and adult life, treatment with pulsed dye laser, which involves multiple treatments spaced by six to twelve weeks, should be considered in infancy or early childhood. Special medical makeup can also be used to camouflage these marks.

HEMANGIOMAS OF INFANCY (HOI)

Hemangiomas of infancy (often referred to by parents as strawberry marks) occur in 10 percent of babies by two months of age with most appearing by two to three weeks of age. They often are not present at birth or only noted as subtle flat red spots that often are mistaken for bruises. They can involve any part of the body, but there is a predilection for the head and neck. Most children have a single HOI, but in rare cases some infants have hundreds. For reasons that are not well understood, two-thirds to three-fourths occur in girls and they are much more common in premature infants, especially in infants of low birth weight. HOI usually peak in size by three to four months of age, followed by slow but steady regression without treatment.

If your infant develops a hemangioma, have your pediatrician examine it so he can follow its course from the start. Quite often, the large reddish-purplish appearance of these innocent growths upsets parents to the point they want to have them removed immediately. However, since the vast majority will gradually reduce in size without treatment, it's generally best to leave them alone. Studies have shown that when this type of hemangioma is left untreated, few complications or cosmetic problems result.

At times, hemangiomas may need to be treated or removed—namely, when they occur close to vital structures, such as the eye, throat, or mouth; when they seem to be growing much faster than usual; or when they are likely to bleed profusely or become infected. Such conditions are uncommon, but require careful evaluation and management by your pediatrician and pediatric dermatologist. In some cases, hemangiomas on the face are treated in infancy because of the social stigma from having this facial mark and because of only minor scarring that occurs in this age group; this is a decision that can be made with your pediatrician and pediatric dermatologist, as well as with the plastic surgeon. Several treatment options are available including oral medications to help shrink the hemangioma and, rarely, surgical removal.

Very rarely, HOI are found in large numbers widely scattered over the skin surface. In some of these infants they also may be located on organs inside the body. If this is suspected, your pediatrician may need to conduct further tests. Especially large HOI in certain locations such as the head and neck, the chin in a beard distribution, and the lower spine may be associated with problems in underlying bony structures and soft tissues and may require additional evaluation by your pediatrician.

(See also *How Your Newborn Looks,* page 134.)

Chickenpox

Chickenpox was once one of the most common childhood illnesses. But thanks to the varicella vaccine, far fewer children now get this disease. Chickenpox is a highly contagious infection causing an itchy, blisterlike rash that can cover most of the body. Children often get a mild fever along with the rash.

After your child has been exposed to the virus that causes chickenpox, the rash usually begins fourteen to sixteen days later. Small blisters, which may have a red area around them, will begin to appear on the body and scalp, then spread to the face, arms, and legs. There may be as many as 250 to 500 of these blisters. Normally the blisters will crust over and then heal, but tiny sores and possibly small scars may develop if your child scratches them and they become infected. The skin around some of the blisters may become darker or lighter, but this change in coloring will disappear gradually after the rash is gone.

Treatment

From your own childhood, you may remember just how itchy chickenpox can be. You should discourage your child from scratching, because that can cause additional infection. Acetaminophen (in the appropriate dose for your child's age and weight) may decrease the discomfort from the rash or fever. Trimming her fingernails and bathing her daily with soap and water also can help prevent secondary bacterial infection. Oatmeal baths, available without prescription from your pharmacy, will ease the itch. Antihistamines can be used to decrease the itch. (Be sure to follow the dosing instructions carefully.) A prescription medicine (acyclovir or valacyclovir) also can modestly decrease the severity of the symptoms if started within twenty-four hours of the onset of the disease. This medicine, while not recommended for healthy children younger than twelve years of age, should be considered for those at risk for moderate to severe disease (e.g., children with weakened immune systems or those with certain skin disorders such as eczema).

Do not give your child aspirin or any medication that contains aspirin or salicylates when they have chickenpox. These products increase the risk of Reye syndrome (see page 549), a serious illness that involves the liver and brain. You also should avoid steroids and any medicines that interfere with the immune system. If you are not sure about what medications you can safely use at this time, ask your pediatrician for advice.

Incidentally, the doctor probably won't need to see your child unless she develops a complication such as a skin infection, trouble breathing, or if her temperature rises above 102 degrees Fahrenheit (38.9 degrees Celsius) or lasts longer than four days. Let the pediatrician know if areas of the rash become very red, warm, or tender; this may indicate a bacterial infection. Be sure to call your pediatrician *immediately* if your child develops any signs of Reye syndrome or encephalitis: vomiting, nervousness, confusion, convulsions, lack of responsiveness, increasing sleepiness, or poor balance.

If your child does have chickenpox, you should mention it to your pediatrician and other parents whose children may have been exposed. Your child may be contagious one to two days before the rash starts and for twenty-four hours after the last new blister appears (usually five to seven days). In some cases, the contagious period lasts until all the blisters are dry and crusted over. Only individuals who have never had chickenpox (or the chickenpox vaccine) are susceptible. After she's recovered from the chickenpox, your child usually will be immune to it for the rest of her life.

Prevention

A vaccine to protect against chickenpox is recommended for all healthy children, with the first dose given between twelve and fifteen months of age, plus a second (booster) dose given between four and six years of age. Until your child has received this vaccine, the only sure way to protect her is to avoid exposure to the chickenpox virus. Protection from exposure is important for newborn infants, especially premature babies, in whom the disease can be more severe (but rarely fatal).

Most infants whose mothers have had chickenpox are immune to the disease for the first few months of life since mothers pass short-lived protective antibodies to their infants. Susceptible children who have diseases affecting the immune system (e.g., cancer) or who are using certain drugs (e.g., prednisone) should avoid being exposed to chickenpox. If these children are exposed, they may be eligible for a special immunization that will provide immunity to the disease for a limited period. It's important to remember that since the varicella vaccine is a live virus vaccine, children who have a weakened immune system may not have a normal response to it and may not be able to receive the vaccine.

Cradle Cap and Seborrheic Dermatitis

Your beautiful one-month-old baby has developed scaliness and redness on his scalp. You're concerned and think maybe you shouldn't shampoo as usual. You may be concerned if you see some redness in the creases of his neck and armpits and behind his ears. What is it and what should you do?

When this rash occurs on the scalp alone, it's known as cradle cap. But although it may start as scaling and redness of the scalp, it also can be found later in the other areas just mentioned. It can extend to the face and diaper area, too, and when it does, pediatricians call it seborrheic dermatitis (because it occurs where there is the greatest number of oil-producing sebaceous glands). Seborrheic dermatitis is a noninfectious skin condition that's very common in infants, usually beginning in the first weeks of life and slowly disappearing over a period of weeks or months. Unlike eczema or contact dermatitis (see pages 560–562), it's rarely uncomfortable or itchy.

No one knows for sure the exact cause of this rash. Some doctors have speculated that it may be influenced by the mother's hormonal changes during pregnancy, which stimulate the infant's oil glands. This overproduction of oil may have some relationship to the scales and redness of the skin.

Treatment

If your baby's seborrheic dermatitis is confined to his scalp (and is, therefore, just cradle cap), you can treat it yourself. Don't be afraid to shampoo the hair; in fact, you should wash it (with a mild baby shampoo) more frequently than before. This, along with soft brushing, will help remove the scales. Stronger medicated shampoos (antiseborrhea shampoos containing sulfur, salicylic acid, selenium sulfide, ketoconazole, or coal tar) may loosen the scales more quickly, but since they also can be irritating, use them only after consulting your pediatrician.

Some parents have found using petroleum jelly or ointments beneficial. But baby oil is not very helpful or necessary. In fact, while many parents tend to use unperfumed baby oil or mineral oil and do nothing else, doing so allows scales to build up on the scalp, particularly over the soft spot on the back of the head, or fontanelle. Instead, your doctor also might prescribe a cortisone cream or lotion, such as 1 percent hydrocortisone cream. Once the condition has improved, you can prevent it from recurring, in most cases, by continuing with frequent hair washing with a mild baby shampoo. Fortunately, most babies' conditions clear up during the second half of the first year of life, so prolonged treatment is usually unnecessary.

Sometimes yeast infections occur on the affected skin, most likely in the crease areas rather than on the scalp. If this occurs, the area will become extremely reddened and quite itchy. In this case, your pediatrician might prescribe a medication such as an anti-yeast cream.

Rest assured that seborrheic dermatitis is not a serious condition, or an infection. Nor is it an allergy to something you're using, or due to poor hygiene. It will go away without any scars.

Fifth Disease (Erythema Infectiosum)

Rosy cheeks are often considered a sign of good health, but if your child suddenly develops bright-red patches on her cheeks that are also raised and warm, she may have a viral illness known as fifth disease. Like so many other childhood illnesses, this one is spread from person to person. The virus causing this disease is called a parvovirus. Once your child is exposed to the virus, it may take from four to fourteen days for symptoms to appear.

This is a mild disease, and most children feel well even when the rash appears. However, there can be mild coldlike symptoms: sore throat, headache, pinkeye, fatigue, a mild fever, or itching. In rare cases there may be aches in the knees or wrists. The disease process may be more severe in children with abnormal hemoglobin or red blood cells, such as sickle cell anemia, and in children with cancer.

The rash usually begins on the cheeks, causing them to look as if they've been slapped. During the next few days, the arms and then the trunk, thighs, and buttocks will develop a pink, slightly raised rash that has a lacelike pattern. Fever is usually absent or mild. After five to ten days the rash will fade, with the face clearing first, followed by the arms, and then the trunk and legs. Interestingly, the rash may reappear briefly weeks or months later, particularly if your child becomes hot from bathing, exercise, or sunlight, or spends time in the sun.

Treatment

For most children, fifth disease is not serious. The rash, however, may look similar to other rashes that may be more serious, as well as certain drug-related rashes; as a result, it's important to discuss the rash with your pediatrician and let him know about any medications your child may be taking. When you describe the symptoms over the phone, the doctor may suspect fifth disease, but he still may want to examine your child to be certain.

There is no specific medicine for fifth disease; treatment is geared to providing relief of the symptoms. For instance, if your child has a fever or aches and pains, you can treat her with acetaminophen. If she exhibits new symptoms, feels sicker, or develops a high fever, call your pediatrician.

A child with fifth disease is contagious when she is suffering from the coldlike symptoms that *precede* the rash. But by the time they demonstrate a rash they are no longer contagious. Nevertheless, as a rule, whenever your child has a rash or a fever, you should keep her away from other children until your doctor identifies the illness. As a precaution, wait until she no longer has a fever and is feeling normal before allowing her to play with other children. Also, it is important to keep your child away from pregnant women (particularly in their first trimester), since the virus that causes this disease may cause serious illness or even death in the fetus if the mother becomes infected.

Hair Loss (Alopecia)

Almost all newborns lose some or all of their hair. This is normal and to be expected. The baby hair falls out at three to five months of age and is gradually replaced by the mature hair. So hair loss occurring in the first six months of life in this pattern is not a cause for concern.

Very commonly, a baby loses her hair where she rubs her scalp against the mattress or as a result of a head-banging habit. As she starts to move more and sit up or outgrow this head-rubbing or -banging behavior, this type of hair loss will correct itself. Many babies also lose hair on the back of the scalp at age four months as their hair grows at varying times and rates.

In very rare cases, babies may be born with alopecia (hair loss), which can occur by itself or in association with certain abnormalities of the nails and the teeth. Later in childhood, hair loss may be due to medications, a scalp injury, or a medical or nutritional problem.

An older child may also lose her hair if it's braided too tightly or pulled too hard when combing or brushing. Some children (under age three or four) twirl their hair as a comforting habit and innocently break it off or pull it out. Other children (usually older ones) may pull their hair out on purpose but deny doing so, or they simply may be unaware that they are doing it; this often is a signal of emotional stress, which you should discuss with your pediatrician.

Alopecia areata, a condition common in children and teenagers, seems to be an "allergic" reaction to one's own hair. In this disorder, children lose hair in a circular area, causing a bald spot. In general, when it's limited to a few patches, the outlook for complete recovery is good. But when the condition persists or worsens, steroid creams and even steroid injections and other forms of therapy at the site of the hair loss often are used. Unfortunately, if the hair loss is extensive, it may be difficult to renew its growth.

Because alopecia and other types of hair loss can be a sign of other medical or nutritional problems, bring these conditions to your pediatrician's attention whenever they occur after the first six months of age. The doctor will look at your child's scalp, determine the cause, and prescribe treatment. Sometimes, a referral to a pediatric dermatologist is necessary.

Head Lice

Head lice commonly occur in young children who play together, share clothing, hats, or hairbrushes, or are generally in close contact. Although often misunderstood and embarrassing to parents, head lice are neither a painful nor a serious medical problem. Head lice do not transmit diseases or cause permanent problems. Many parents with children in school or child care have received a note informing them of a case of head lice in their child's classroom. This condition occurs in all socioeconomic groups, is most common in children ages three to twelve, and only rarely occurs in African American children.

Usually you first become aware of head lice by noticing that your child has an extremely itchy scalp. On close inspection, you may see little white dots in the hair or on the neck at the hairline. Sometimes, you may confuse this with dandruff or seborrhea. Dandruff generates larger flakes, however, while lice infestation results in more discrete dots that usually are stuck onto the shaft of the hair near the scalp. These are the eggs of the lice attached to the hair shaft. In addition you may find living lice in the hair as well. They avoid light and will move rapidly to get out of the light so living lice can be hard to see. Also, the itchiness of the scalp is usually far more uncomfortable with lice than with seborrhea or dandruff.

These symptoms may indicate the head louse, *Pediculus humanus capitis,* and its eggs or nits. Try not to overreact when you first realize this or when your child's school phones or sends home a note. It is a very common condition that should not reflect negatively on your family's personal hygiene. It is merely the result of having your child in contact with other children infected with head lice. Because children in the same family spend so much time together in such close proximity, it is not unusual for lice to be spread from one sibling to another.

Treatment

Once you recognize that your child has head lice, there are several treatments available. They come in a variety of forms such as cream rinse, shampoo, gel, and mousse. Most should be applied to dry hair because wet hair can dilute the chemicals in the treatment, and they should be kept on the hair for the full amount of time recommended on the product label. While the treatments are effective at killing live lice, they may not always kill all of the eggs, and thus a second treatment may be needed seven to ten days after the first one.

The most widely used products for treating head lice contain 1 percent permethrin. These are the treatments currently recommended by the American Academy of Pediatrics as the initial way to manage head lice. They have advantages over other treatments, such as low toxicity, and they do not cause allergic reactions in individuals with plant allergies. Apply the permethrin, available as a cream rinse, to the hair after shampooing with a nonconditioning shampoo and towel-drying. Then reapply it one week later.

Some available medications to kill lice are potentially dangerous insecticides. So use only according to package instructions and your pediatrician's recommendations. Some head lice treatments are available by prescription, but they are usually not the first choice for treating this condition; your pediatrician may recommend them if an over-the-counter product doesn't work.

Some parents also try home remedies for head lice, which often involve "washing" their child's hair with thick or oily substances like petroleum jelly, olive oil, tub margarine, or mayonnaise, and then leaving these products on the hair overnight. Proponents of these approaches believe that coating the hair will smother and kill the lice. However, there is no scientific proof that they work, even though they won't hurt your child if you decide to try them. On the other hand, certain home treatments must be avoided, particularly coating the hair with toxic or highly flammable substances such as gasoline or kerosene, or using products that are manufactured for use on animals.

After using one of the over-the-counter or prescription medications, you do not have to remove nits manually to prevent the spread of head lice, although doing so may be prudent for aesthetic reasons. Carefully combing the hair with a fine-tooth comb can remove the dead egg cases and any eggs (nits) that have survived treatment. This nit removal is tedious and often requires once-a-day combing until no more nits are seen; then continue with the combing every few days for a week or two.

To prevent reinfection, wash all bedclothes and clothing (hats are a big culprit) that have been in contact with the child for the forty-eight hours immediately preceding you noticing the head lice. Use the hot cycles to wash the clothes, or have them dry-cleaned if you prefer. Wash combs and brushes in a shampoo specific against lice, or soak in boiling water for five to ten minutes. In addition, if your child has lice, it's important to inform the child care center or school. However, the American Academy of Pediatrics believes that no healthy child should be excluded from or allowed to miss school because of head lice. The Academy also discourages "no nit" policies that require the absence of nits in order for a child to return to school. A child with an active head lice infestation likely has had this outbreak for a month or more by the time it is discovered. So because he poses little risk to others, he should remain in class while trying to avoid direct head contact with other children. Also, to prevent your child from contracting head lice, teach him not to share personal items such as hats, combs, and brushes. If your active, engaging three-year-old has head lice, someone else in the group probably does, too. Because head lice are very contagious, *other family members also may need to be examined and treated* and have their clothing and bedding laundered.

Impetigo

Impetigo is a contagious bacterial skin infection that often appears around the nose, mouth, and ears. More than 90 percent of impetigo cases are caused by staphylococcal bacteria, while the rest are caused by the streptococcal bacteria (which also are responsible for "strep" throat and scarlet fever).

If staphylococcal bacteria are to blame, the infection may cause blisters filled with clear or yellow fluid. These can break easily, leaving a raw, glistening area that soon forms a scab with a honey-colored crust. By contrast, infections with strep bacteria usually are not associated with blisters, but they do cause crusts over larger sores and ulcers.

Treatment

Impetigo needs to be treated with antibiotics, either topically or by mouth, and your pediatrician may order a culture in the lab to determine which bacteria are causing the rash. Make sure your child takes the medication for the full prescribed course, or the impetigo could return.

One other important point to keep in mind: Impetigo is contagious until the rash clears, or until at least two days of antibiotics have been given and there is evidence of improvement. Your child should avoid close contact with other children during this period, and you should avoid touching the rash. If you or other family members do come in contact with it, wash your hands and the exposed site thoroughly with soap and water. Also, keep the infected child's washcloths and towels separate from those of other family members.

Prevention

The bacteria that cause impetigo thrive in breaks in the skin. The best ways to prevent this rash are to keep your child's fingernails clipped and clean and to teach him not to scratch minor skin irritations. When he does have a scrape, cleanse it with soap and water, and apply an antibiotic cream or ointment. Be careful not to use washcloths or towels that have been used by someone else who has an active skin infection.

When certain types of streptococcal bacteria cause impetigo, a rare but serious complication called glomerulonephritis can develop. This disease injures the kidney and may cause high blood pressure and blood to pass in the urine. Therefore, if you notice any blood or dark brown color in your child's urine, let your pediatrician know so he can evaluate it and order further tests if needed.

Measles

Thanks to vaccinations, cases of measles were on the decline until recently. But in fact, they have been on the rise in the US. According to the national Centers for Disease Control and Prevention, there were 222 measles cases in 2011, which was the highest number of cases in fifteen years in the US. The majority of these measles cases were in people younger than twenty years old. Most cases that occur now are imported from other countries and occur in children who have never been vaccinated or are too young to receive the vaccine. If your child has never been immunized or had the measles, he can get them if he is exposed. The measles virus is passed through the air droplets transmitted by an infected person. Almost everyone who breathes the droplets and is not immune to the disease will become infected.

Signs and Symptoms

For the first eight to twelve days after being exposed to the measles virus, your child probably will have no symptoms; this is called the incubation period. Then he may develop an illness that seems like a common cold, with a cough, runny nose, and pinkeye (conjunctivitis; see page 728). The cough may be severe at times and will last for about a week, and your child probably will feel miserable.

During the first one to three days of the illness, the coldlike symptoms will become worse, and he'll develop a fever that may run as high as 103 to 105 degrees Fahrenheit (39.4–40.5 degrees Celsius). The fever will last until two to three days after the rash first appears.

After two to four days of illness, the rash will develop. It usually begins on the face and neck, and spreads down the trunk and out to the arms and legs. It starts as very fine red bumps, which may join together to form larger splotches. If you notice tiny white spots, like grains of sand, inside his mouth next to his molars, you'll know the rash will follow soon. The rash will last five to eight days. As it fades, the skin may peel a little.

Treatment

Although there is no treatment for the disease, it is important that the pediatrician examine your child to determine that measles is, in fact, the cause of the illness. If your illness is due to measles, a dose of vitamin A may be indicated. Treatment of children with measles with vitamin A has been found to lessen the chances of the associated complications and death due to the infection. Your pediatrician will advise you on the correct dose of vitamin A. Many other conditions can start in the same way, and measles has its own complications (see below) that the doctor will want to watch for. When you call, describe the fever and rash, so that the doctor knows that you suspect measles. When you visit the office, the pediatrician will want to separate your child from other patients, so that the virus is not transmitted to them.

Your child is contagious from several days before the rash breaks out until the fever and rash are gone. During this period he should be kept at home (except for the visit to the doctor) and away from anyone who is not immune to the illness.

At home, make sure your child drinks plenty of fluids and give acetaminophen in the proper dose if your child is uncomfortable due to the fever. The conjunctivitis that accompanies measles can make it painful for the child to be in bright light or sunshine, so you may want to darken his room to a comfortable level for the first few days.

Sometimes bacterial infections develop as a complication of the measles. These most often include pneumonia (see page 605), middle ear infection (see page 662), or encephalitis (inflammation of the brain). In these cases, your child must be seen by the pediatrician, who may prescribe antibiotic treatment or admit your child to the hospital.

Prevention

Almost all children who receive two doses of the MMR (measles, mumps, rubella) vaccine after their first birthday are protected against measles for life—the first dose should be administered between ages twelve and fifteen months, and the second one between ages four and six years old. Because up to 5 percent of children may not respond to the initial vaccination, the second (booster) dose is recommended for all children. (See Chapter 31, *Immunizations*.)

If your unimmunized child has been exposed to someone who has the measles, or if someone in your household has the virus, notify your pediatrician at once. The following steps can help keep your child from getting sick.

1. If he is under one year old or has a weakened immune system, he can be given immune globulin (gamma globulin) up to six days following exposure. This may temporarily protect him from becoming infected, but will not provide extended immunity.

2. An infant six through eleven months of age may receive the measles vaccine alone if he is exposed to the disease or if he is living in a community where exposure is highly likely or in an epidemic situation. If doses are given during these months, your child still may need additional doses to be fully immunized.

3. If your child is otherwise healthy and over one year old, he can be vaccinated. The vaccine may be effective if given within seventy-two hours of his exposure to an infected person, and *will* provide extended immunity. If your child has received one dose of the measles vaccine and at least one month has elapsed since that dose, he may be given a second dose after exposure.

MRSA Infections

Methicillin-resistant *Staphylococcus aureus* (MRSA) is the name of a staphylococcal bacterium that can cause infections not only on the surface of the skin, but also into the soft tissue where a boil or abscess can form. In recent years, MRSA has become a major public health problem because this bacterium has become resistant to antibiotics called beta-lactams, which include methicillin and other commonly prescribed antibiotics. This resistance has made treating these infections more difficult. While MRSA was once limited to hospitals and nursing homes, it has spread into the community in schools, households, and child care centers, among other places. It can be transmitted from person to person through skin-to-skin contact, particularly through cuts and abrasions.

If your child has a wound that appears to be infected—specifically, if it is red, swollen, hot, and draining pus—have it checked by your pediatrician. He may drain the infection and prescribe topical and/or oral antibiotics. The most serious MRSA infections may cause pneumonia and bloodstream infections. Even though MRSA infections are resistant to some antibiotics, they are treatable with other medications.

To prevent your child from getting MRSA at school or other public places, the following strategies can be helpful:

- **Follow good hygiene** practices. Your child should wash his hands frequently with soap and warm water, or use alcohol-based hand sanitizers.

- **Use a clean** dry bandage to cover any cuts, scrapes, or breaks in your child's skin. These bandages should be changed at least daily.

- **Don't let your** child share towels, washcloths, or other personal items (including clothing) with anyone else.

- **Frequently clean surfaces** that your child touches.

Pinworms

Fortunately, the most common type of worm infesting children, the pinworm, is essentially harmless. The pinworm is unpleasant to look at and may cause rectal itching and, in girls, vaginal discharge, but it is not responsible for more serious health concerns. Pinworms cause more social concern than medical problems.

Pinworms are spread easily from one child to another by the transfer of eggs. Often an infected child scratches her rectum, picking up an egg, and then transfers it to the sandbox or a toilet seat where another child unknowingly picks up the egg and later transfers it to his mouth. The eggs are swallowed, later hatch, and the pinworm makes its way to the anus to again deposit its eggs. Pinworms usually present with itching around your child's behind at night. Girls may also have vaginal itching. If you take a look at the skin around the anus first thing in the morning before the child has gotten up from bed, you may see the adult worms, which are whitish gray and threadlike, measuring about

¼ to ½ inch (0.63–1.27 cm) long. Your pediatrician might collect some of the worms and eggs by applying the sticky side of a strip of clear cellophane tape to the skin around the anus. The tape can be examined under a microscope to confirm the presence of the parasite.

Treatment

Pinworms can be treated easily with an oral medication, taken in a single dose and then repeated in one to two weeks. This medication causes the mature pinworms to be expelled through bowel movements. Some pediatricians may advise treating the other family members, as well, since one of them may be a carrier without having any symptoms. This medication is not recommended for use in children under two years of age. Also, when the infection is resolved, the child's underclothes, bedclothes, and sheets should be washed carefully to reduce the risk of reinfection.

Prevention

It is very difficult to prevent pinworms, but here are some hints that might be helpful.

- Encourage your child to wash her hands after using the bathroom.

- Encourage her sitter or child care provider to wash the toys frequently, particularly if pinworms have been detected in one or more of the children.

- Encourage your child to wash her hands after playing with a house cat or dog, since these pets can carry the eggs in their fur.

Poison Ivy, Poison Oak, and Poison Sumac

Poison ivy, poison oak, and poison sumac commonly cause skin rashes in children during the spring, summer, and fall seasons. An allergic reaction to the oil in these plants produces the rash. The rash occurs from several hours to three days after contact with the plant and begins in the form of blisters, accompanied by severe itching.

Contrary to popular belief, it is not the fluid in the blisters that causes the rash to spread. This spreading occurs when small amounts of oil remain under the child's fingernails, on her clothing, or on a pet's hair that then comes in contact with other parts of her body. The rash will not be spread to another person unless the oil that remains also comes in contact with that person's skin.

Poison ivy grows as a three-leafed green weed with a red stem at the center. It grows in vinelike form in all parts of the country except the Southwest. Poison sumac is a shrub, not a vine, and has seven to thirteen leaves arranged in pairs along a central stem. Not nearly as abundant as poison ivy, it grows primarily in the swampy areas of the Mississippi River region. Poison oak grows as a shrub, and it is seen primarily on the West Coast. All three plants produce similar skin reactions. These skin reactions are forms of contact dermatitis. (See *Eczema,* page 560.)

Treatment

Treating reactions to poison ivy—the most frequent of these forms of contact dermatitis—is a straightforward matter.

- **Prevention is the** best approach. Know what the plant looks like and teach your children to avoid it.

- **If there is** contact, wash all clothes and shoes in soap and water. Also, wash the area of the skin that was exposed with soap and water for at least ten minutes after the plant or the oil has been touched.

- **If the eruption** is mild, apply calamine lotion three or four times a day to cut down on the itching. Avoid those preparations containing anesthetics or antihistamines, as often they can cause allergic eruptions themselves.

- **Apply topical 1** percent hydrocortisone cream to decrease the inflammation.

- **If the rash** is severe, on the face, or on extensive parts of the body, the pediatrician may need to place your child on a high-potency topical steroid or oral steroids. These will need to be given for about ten to

fourteen days, often with the dose tapering in a specific schedule determined by your pediatrician. This treatment should be reserved for the most severe cases.

Call the pediatrician if you notice any of the following:

- Severe eruption not responsive to the previously described home methods

- Any evidence of infection, such as blisters, redness, or oozing

- Any new eruption or rash

- Severe poison ivy on the face

- Fever

Ringworm

If your child has a scaly round patch on the side of his scalp or elsewhere on his skin, and he seems to be losing hair in the same area of the scalp, the problem may be a contagious infection known as ringworm or tinea.

This disorder is caused not by worms but by a fungus. It's called ringworm because the infections tend to form round or oval spots that, as they grow, become smooth in the center but keep an active red scaly border.

Scalp ringworm often is spread from person to person, sometimes when sharing infected hats, combs, brushes, and barrettes. If ringworm appears elsewhere on your child's body, he may have the type spread by infected dogs or cats.

The first signs of infection on the body are red, scaly patches. They may not look like rings until they've grown to half an inch in diameter, and they generally stop growing at about 1 inch. Your child may have just one patch or several. These lesions may be mildly itchy and uncomfortable.

Scalp ringworm starts the same way the body variety does, but as the rings grow, your child may lose some hair in the infected area. Certain types of scalp ringworm produce less obvious rings and are easily confused with dandruff or cradle cap. Cradle cap, however, occurs only during infancy. If your child's scalp is continually scaly and he's over a year old, you should suspect ringworm and notify your pediatrician.

Treatment

A single ringworm patch on the body can be treated with an over-the-counter cream recommended by your pediatrician. The most frequently used ones are tolnaftate, miconazole, and clotrimazole. A small amount is applied two or three times a day for at least a week, during which time some clearing should begin. If there are any patches on the scalp or more than one on the body, or if the rash is getting worse while being treated, check with your pediatrician again. She will prescribe a stronger medication and, in the case of scalp ringworm or widespread body ringworm, will use an oral antifungal preparation. Your child will have to take medicine for several weeks depending on the medication to clear the infection.

You also may need to wash your child's scalp with a special shampoo when he has scalp ringworm. If there's any possibility that others in the family have caught the infection, they also should use this shampoo and be examined for possible signs of infection. Do not allow your child to share combs, brushes, hair clips, barrettes, or hats.

Prevention

You can help prevent ringworm by identifying and treating any pets with the problem. Look for scaling, itchy, hairless areas on your dogs and cats, and have them treated right away. Any family members, playmates, or schoolmates who show symptoms also should be treated.

Roseola Infantum

Your ten-month-old doesn't look or act very ill, but she suddenly develops a fever between 102 degrees Fahrenheit (38.9 degrees Celsius) and 105 degrees Fahrenheit (40.5 degrees Celsius). The fever lasts for three to seven days, during which time your child may have less appetite, mild diarrhea, a slight cough, and a runny nose, and seems mildly irritable and a little sleepier than usual. Her upper eyelids may appear slightly swollen or droopy. Finally, *after her temperature returns to nor-*

mal, she gets a slightly raised, spotty pink rash on her trunk, which spreads only to her upper arms and neck and fades after just twenty-four hours. What's the diagnosis? Most likely it's a disease called roseola—a contagious viral illness that's most common in children under age two. Its incubation period is thought to be nine to ten days. The key to this diagnosis is that the rash appears *after* the fever is gone. We now know that a specific virus causes this condition.

Treatment

Whenever your infant or young child has a fever of 102 degrees Fahrenheit (38.9 degrees Celsius) or higher for twenty-four hours, call your pediatrician, even if there are no other symptoms. If the doctor suspects the fever is caused by roseola, he may suggest ways to control the temperature and advise you to call again if your child becomes worse or the fever lasts for more than three or four days. For a child who has other symptoms or appears more seriously ill, the doctor may order a blood count, urinalysis, or other tests.

Since illnesses that cause fever can be contagious, it's wise to keep your child away from other children, at least until you've conferred with your pediatrician. Once her fever is gone for twenty-four hours, even if the rash has appeared, your child can return to child care or preschool, and resume normal contact with other children.

While your child has a fever, dress her in lightweight clothing. If she is very uncomfortable because of the fever, you can give her acetaminophen in the appropriate dose for her age and weight. (See Chapter 27, *Fever.*) Don't worry if her appetite is decreased, and encourage her to drink extra fluids.

Although this disease rarely is serious, be aware that early in the illness, when fever climbs very quickly, there's a chance of convulsions (see *Seizures, Convulsions, and Epilepsy,* page 790). There may be a seizure regardless of how well you treat the fever, so it's important to know how to manage convulsions even though they're usually quite mild and occur only briefly, if at all, with roseola.

Rubella (German Measles)

Although some of today's parents had rubella, or German measles, during their childhood, it is a rare illness now, thanks to an effective vaccine. Even when it was prevalent, however, rubella was usually a mild disease.

Rubella is characterized by a mild fever (100–102 degrees Fahrenheit [37.8–38.9 degrees Celsius]), swollen glands (typically on the back of the neck and base of the skull), and a rash. The rash, which varies from pinhead size to an irregular redness, is raised and usually begins on the face. Within two to three days it spreads to the neck, chest, and the rest of the body as it fades from the face.

Once exposed to rubella, a child usually will develop the disease in fourteen to twenty-one days. The contagious period for rubella begins several days before the rash appears and continues for five to seven days after it develops. Because the disease can be so mild, it goes unrecognized in about half the children who contract it.

Before the rubella vaccine was developed, this illness tended to occur in epidemics every six to nine years. Since the vaccine was introduced in 1968, there have been no significant epidemics in the United States. Even so, the disease still occurs. Each year unvaccinated and susceptible teenagers, often in college campus settings, develop the illness. Fortunately, except for causing fever, discomfort, and occasional pain in the joints, these small epidemics are of little consequence.

What You Can Do

If your pediatrician diagnoses rubella in your child, you may be able to make him more comfortable by giving him extra fluids, bed rest (if he's fatigued), and acetaminophen if he has a fever. Keep him away from other children or adults unless you are sure that they're immunized. As a general rule, children with rubella should not be in child care or any other group setting for seven days after the rash first appears. In particular, make a special effort not to expose pregnant women to a child with rubella.

If your child is diagnosed as having the congenital form of rubella, your pediatrician can advise you on the best way to manage his complex and difficult problems. Infants born with congenital rubella are often infectious for a year after birth and therefore should be kept out of any group child care setting, where they could expose other susceptible children or adults to the infection.

When to Call the Pediatrician

If your child has a fever and a rash and appears uncomfortable, discuss the problem with your pediatrician. If rubella is diagnosed, follow the guidelines suggested earlier for treatment and isolation.

Prevention

Being immunized is the best way to prevent German measles. The vaccine usually is administered as part of a three-in-one shot called MMR (measles, mumps, rubella), given when the child is twelve to fifteen months old. A booster dose needs to be given as well. (See Chapter 31, *Immunizations*.)

There are relatively few adverse reactions to the rubella vaccine. Occasionally children will get a rash and a slight fever. *A child can be immunized even if his mother is pregnant at the time.* However, a susceptible pregnant woman should not be immunized herself. She also should be extremely careful to avoid contact with any child or adult who may be infected with the virus. After delivery, she should be immunized immediately.

Scabies

Scabies is caused by a microscopic mite that burrows under the top layers of skin and deposits its eggs. The rash that results from scabies is actually a reaction to the mite's body, eggs, and excretions. Once the mite gets into the skin, it takes two to four weeks for the rash to appear.

In an older child, this rash appears as numerous itchy, fluid-filled bumps that may be located under the skin next to a reddish burrow track. In an infant, the bumps may be more scattered and isolated and often are found on the palms and soles. Because of scratch marks, crusting, or a secondary infection, this annoying rash often is difficult to identify except in infants who usually demonstrate distinct burrows.

According to legend, when Napoleon's troops had scabies, one could hear the sound of scratching at night from over a mile away. A bit of exaggeration perhaps, but it illustrates two key points to remember if you think your child has scabies: It's very itchy and contagious. Scabies is spread only by person-to-person contact, and this happens extremely easily. If one person in your family has the rash, the others may get it, too.

Scabies can be located almost anywhere on the body, including the area between the fingers. Older children and adults usually don't get the rash on their palms, soles, scalp, or face, but babies may.

Treatment

If you notice that your child (and possibly others in the family) is scratching constantly, suspect scabies and call the pediatrician, who will examine the rash. The doctor may gently scrape a skin sample from the affected area, and look under the microscope for evidence of the mite or its eggs. If scabies turns out to be the diagnosis, the doctor will prescribe one of several antiscabies medications. Most are lotions that are applied over the entire body—from the scalp to the soles of the feet—and are washed off after several hours. You may need to repeat the application one week later.

Most experts feel the whole family must be treated—even those members who don't have a rash. Others feel that although the entire family should be examined, only those with a rash should be treated with antiscabies medications. Any live-in help, overnight visitors, or frequent babysitters also should receive care.

To prevent infection caused by scratching, cut your child's fingernails. If the itching is very severe, your pediatrician may prescribe an antihistamine or other anti-itch medication. If your child shows signs of bacterial infection in the scratched scabies, notify the pediatrician. She may want to prescribe an antibiotic or another form of treatment.

Following treatment, the itching could continue for two to four weeks, because this is an allergic rash. If it persists past four weeks, call your doctor, because the scabies may have returned and need retreatment.

Incidentally, there is some controversy over the possible spread of scabies from clothing or linen. Evidence indicates that this occurs very rarely.

Thus, there's no need for extensive washing or decontamination of the child's room or the rest of the house, since the mite usually lives only in people's skin.

Scarlet Fever

When your child has a strep throat (see page 673), there's a chance that he'll get a rash. This is known as scarlet fever. The symptoms of scarlet fever begin with a sore throat, a fever of 101 to 104 degrees Fahrenheit (38.2–40 degrees Celsius), and headache. This is followed within twenty-four hours by a red rash covering the trunk, arms, and legs. The rash is slightly raised, which makes the skin feel like fine sandpaper. Your child's face may turn red, too, with a pale area around his mouth. This redness will disappear in three to five days, leaving peeling skin in the areas where the rash was most intense (neck, underarms, groin, fingers, and toes). He may also have a white-coated, then reddened, tongue, and mild abdominal pain.

Treatment

Call your pediatrician whenever your child complains of a sore throat, especially when a rash or fever also is present. The doctor will examine him and swab his throat to check for streptococcal bacteria. If the streptococcal bacteria are found, an antibiotic (usually penicillin or amoxicillin) will be given. If your child takes the antibiotic by mouth instead of as an injection, it's extremely important to complete the entire course because shorter treatment sometimes results in a return of the disease.

Most children with streptococcal throat infections respond very quickly to antibiotics. The fever, sore throat, and headache usually are gone within twenty-four hours. The rash, however, will remain for about three to five days.

If your child's condition does not seem to improve with treatment, notify your pediatrician. If other family members develop a fever or sore throat at this time—with or without a rash—they, too, should be examined and tested for strep throat.

If not treated, scarlet fever (like strep throat) can lead to ear and sinus infections, swollen neck glands, and pus around the tonsils. The most serious complication of untreated streptococcal throat is rheumatic fever, which results in joint pain and swelling and sometimes heart damage. Very rarely, the streptococcal bacteria in the throat can lead to glomerulonephritis, or inflammation of the kidneys, causing blood to appear in the urine and sometimes high blood pressure.

Sunburn

While those with darker skin coloring tend to be less sensitive to the sun, everyone is at risk for sunburn and its associated disorders. Children especially need to be protected from the sun's burning rays, since most sun damage occurs in childhood. Like other burns, sunburn will leave the skin red, warm, and painful. In severe cases it may cause blistering, fever, chills, headache, and a general feeling of illness.

Your child doesn't actually have to be burned, however, in order to be harmed by the sun. The effects of exposure build over the years, so that even moderate exposure during childhood can contribute to wrinkling, toughening, freckling, and even cancer of the skin in later life. Also, some medications can cause a skin reaction to sunlight, and some medical conditions may make people more sensitive to the sun.

Treatment

The signs of sunburn usually appear six to twelve hours after exposure, with the greatest discomfort during the first twenty-four hours. If your child's burn is just red, warm, and painful, you can treat it yourself. Apply cool compresses to the burned areas or bathe the child in cool water. You also can give acetaminophen to help relieve the pain. (Check the package for appropriate dosage for her age and weight.)

If the sunburn causes blisters, fever, chills, headache, or a general feeling of illness, call your pediatrician. Severe sunburn must be treated like any other serious burn, and if it's very extensive, hospitalization sometimes is required. In addition, the blisters can become infected, requiring treatment with antibiotics. Some-

times extensive or severe sunburn also can lead to dehydration (see *Diarrhea*, page 530, for signs of dehydration) and, in some cases, fainting (heatstroke). Such cases need to be examined by your pediatrician or the nearest emergency facility.

Prevention

Many parents incorrectly assume that the sun is dangerous only when it's shining brightly. In fact, it's not the visible light rays but rather the invisible ultraviolet rays that are harmful. Your child actually may be exposed to more ultraviolet rays on foggy or hazy days because she'll feel cooler and therefore stay outside for a longer time. Exposure is also greater at higher altitudes. Even a big hat or an umbrella is not absolute protection because ultraviolet rays reflect off sand, water, snow, and many other surfaces.

Try to keep your child out of the sun when the peak ultraviolet rays occur (between 10 a.m. and 4 p.m.). In addition, follow these guidelines.

- **Always use a** sunscreen to block the damaging ultraviolet rays. Choose a sunscreen made for children with a sun protection factor (SPF) of 30 or higher and with broad-spectrum coverage for UVA and UVB light. (Check the label.) Apply the protection half an hour before going out. Keep in mind that *no* sunscreens are truly waterproof, and thus they need to be reapplied every one and a half to two hours, particularly if your child spends a lot of time in the water. Consult the instructions on the bottle, and choose a product that is labeled "water resistant."

- **Dress your child** in lightweight cotton clothing with long sleeves and long pants. SPF clothing and hats are also a good idea to protect your child's skin when she's outdoors.

- **Use a beach** umbrella or similar object to keep her in the shade as much as possible.

- **Have her wear** a hat with a wide brim.

- **Babies under six** months of age should be kept out of direct sunlight. If adequate clothing and shade are not available, sunscreen may be used on small areas of the body, such as the face and the backs of the hands.

(See also *Burns,* page 688.)

Warts

Warts are caused by a virus—the human papillomavirus (HPV). These firm bumps (although they also can be flat) are yellow, tan, grayish, black, or brown. They usually appear on the hands, on the toes, around the knees, and on the face, but can occur anywhere on the body. When they're on the soles of the feet, doctors call them plantar warts. Although warts can be contagious, they appear infrequently in children under the age of two.

Treatment

Your pediatrician can give you advice on treating warts. Sometimes he will recommend an over-the-counter medication that contains salicylic acid or even treat them in the office using a liquid nitrogen–based solution or spray. If any of the following are present, he may refer you to a dermatologist:

- Multiple, recurring warts

- A wart on the face or genital area

- Large, deep, or painful plantar warts (warts on the soles of the feet)

- Warts that are particularly bothersome to your child

Some warts will just go away by themselves. Others can be removed using prescription or nonprescription preparations. However, surgical removal by scraping, cauterizing, or freezing is sometimes necessary with multiple warts, those that continue to recur, or deep plantar warts. Although surgery or laser treatment might help, there are no good, well-controlled studies showing that painful, destructive treatments are any better than no treatment at all. Fortunately, the natural history is for most children to develop immunity against warts within two to five years, resulting in clearing of warts even without treatment.

West Nile Virus

The West Nile virus has received plenty of attention in recent years. It is spread to humans through the bite of an infected mosquito. The first outbreak occurred in the United States in 1999. Although some children have become ill when infected with the virus, in most cases the symptoms are mild.

Mosquitoes become carriers of the virus by feeding on infected birds. Although other animals have been infected with the virus—including horses, bats, squirrels, and domestic animals—birds are the most common reservoir. Once the virus has been transmitted to a human through a bite, it can multiply in an individual's bloodstream and in some cases cause illness. However, even if your child is bitten, she'll probably have only mild symptoms or none at all. Among people who have been bitten and contracted the infection, about one in five develop mild flulike symptoms (e.g., a fever, headaches, and body aches) and at times a skin rash. These symptoms tend to last only a few days. In fewer than 1 out of 100 infections, a severe illness can occur (so-called West Nile encephalitis or meningitis), with symptoms such as a high fever, a stiff neck, tremors, muscle weakness, convulsions, paralysis, and loss of consciousness.

Prevention

Like all people, your own child's risk of West Nile virus comes mostly from mosquito bites. She cannot catch the disease from an infected playmate or from touching or kissing a person with the infection (or even by touching a bird infected with the virus).

There is no vaccine to protect your child from the West Nile virus. But you can reduce her likelihood of developing the disease by taking steps to reduce the chance that she will be bitten by a mosquito that could be carrying the virus. Here are some strategies to keep in mind. (Some of them are described in the *Insect Bites and Stings* section on page 571.)

- **Apply insect repellent** to your child, using just enough to protect her exposed skin.

- **The concentrations of** DEET vary significantly from product to product—ranging from less than 10 percent to over 30 percent—so be sure to read the label before you buy. The higher the concentration of DEET, the longer the action and the greater the effectiveness of the product. Effectiveness peaks at 30 percent, which is also the maximum concentration recommended for children. Check the label for this percentage because some products can have concentrations much higher than 30 percent. DEET's safety does not appear to be related to its level of concentration, however; a prudent approach is to select the lowest effective concentration for the amount of time your child spends outdoors.

- **Avoid products that** include DEET in a sunscreen because the sunscreen needs to be applied frequently, while the DEET should be used just once a day. More frequent applications of DEET may be associated with toxicity. Also be sure to wash the DEET off with soap and water at the end of the day. Even older children should not apply DEET-containing repellents more than once a day.

- **Do not use** DEET preparations on infants under two months of age. In older children, apply it sparingly around the ears, and don't use it on the mouth or the eyes. Don't put it over cuts.

- **An alternative to** DEET is called picaridin. It is a pleasant-smelling product without the oily residue of DEET. It is used in concentrations of 5 to 10 percent.

- **Whenever possible, dress** your child in long sleeves and long pants while she's outside. Use mosquito netting over a baby's infant carrier.

- **Keep your child** away from locations where mosquitoes are likely to congregate or lay their eggs, such as standing water (e.g., in birdbaths and pet water dishes).

- **Because mosquitoes are** more likely to bite humans at certain times of day—most commonly at dawn, dusk, and in the early evening—consider limiting the amount of time your child is outdoors during those hours.

- **Repair any holes** in your screens.

~ 35 ~

Your Child's Sleep

SLEEP IS AN essential, healthy part of your child's life. In the same way that good nutrition is important for the development of his body, sleep is crucial for the development of his brain. As your young child establishes and maintains a regular sleep schedule, he is more likely to sleep longer and less likely to awaken during the night, with all the health benefits of that kind of sound sleep. The sleeping brain is not a resting brain, but rather is functioning in a different manner. By providing your child's growing brain with sufficient sleep, your child will be better able to concentrate and his temperament will be more even.

Not surprisingly, many parents worry about the sleep habits and behaviors of their child. "Is he getting too little sleep? Or too much? How important are naps, and how many hours of napping are enough? Should I let him cry himself to sleep at night, or should I pick him up when he's in tears? Why does he seem to go to sleep later—or earlier—than other children of the same age?"

Even though many parents are anxious about their child's sleep patterns, the good news is that many of their concerns can easily be addressed. Many moms and dads may be unclear about the optimal sleep schedule for a child at different ages. Even when they ask questions and get some clarification from their pediatrician, they still may be left frustrated with general advice that may be applicable to children at large, but not necessarily to their own child. After all, children aren't alike, and there are normal variations from one child to another; some children may develop regular sleep rhythms in the first six to eight weeks of life, and they may sleep for many hours at a time; others, however, may have unpredictable sleep behaviors that stay that way for many months—or longer. It's reasonable to discuss with your pediatrician the specific questions you have and to review your own family's routines, problems, and challenges that may affect your child's sleep patterns.

In fact, although some parents

SCENARIO #1

The mother of a four-month-old baby complained to friends that while her infant had slept extremely well in the first week of his life, his sleep patterns seemed to have unraveled after that. More than anything, his sleep times were erratic and unpredictable. She conceded that she tried to keep her baby awake well into the evening so her husband could play with the infant upon returning home from work between 8:00 and 8:30 p.m. But before his arrival, her baby would often fuss and cry. Even though he seemed drowsy at times, she would try keeping him awake for a little while longer, awaiting her husband's arrival. But more often than not, the infant had become so overtired that he just couldn't be consoled.

Mother and father were conflicted over what to do: Dad seemed comfortable with the baby crying until he arrived home, while Mom worried they were being heartless. Sometimes, she would try putting him down for a brief nap in the very late afternoon, but he would still become cranky later that night, and tension escalated between husband and wife.

They decided to ask their pediatrician for advice. The doctor explained the importance of being respectful of the child's evolving sleep schedule. For a typical four- to eight-month-old, a healthy nightly bedtime is between 6 and 8 p.m. Keeping the child up longer to greet his father would leave him overtired and out of sync with his own biological rhythms.

Always be mindful of your own child's sleep needs. His biological clock is evolving, and when he feels the need to sleep, he should be allowed to do so. If his sleep-wake schedule is artificially disrupted, he will probably become moody and less attentive when he is awake. If he goes to bed earlier, he may get up a *little* earlier, but his total night sleep will be longer. This will allow more time for a working parent to spend with his or her child in the morning. If any adjustments in schedules need to be made, they should begin with Mom and Dad, who should find a way to be available to their child when he's awake and alert.

may ask their doctor questions like "How many hours should my child sleep at night?", there's no universal answer that applies to every child. In the first two years of life in particular, your child's unique genetics has a powerful influence on sleep; whether he takes long naps or short ones, his genetic makeup may be the reason. Or his distinctive temperament could be influencing his sleep behavior. Also, family circumstances can vary, affecting when, how long, and how well a child sleeps. A child whose parents are divorced may encounter markedly differing sleep environments when he's sleeping at the home of one parent during the week, and the other on weekends. If the parent works at night and sleeps during the day, this can also affect the baby's sleep schedule.

Getting Sleep in Sync

Despite parental concerns—or in some cases, perhaps because of them—moms and dads sometimes unknowingly disrupt the sleep of their children. For example, even though parents want to do what's healthy for their child, they don't always appreciate the effect that their own busy schedules and family decision making may have on their child's sleep.

Most commonly, parents may not recognize the importance of adopting a lifestyle that keeps their child in sync with his emerging biological system. Timing is everything (or at least it's pretty close). Because the timing of sleep is critical, it is important to understand that *when* your children

sleep is probably more important than *how long* they sleep. The quality of a child's sleep, which can restore alertness and maintain an even temperament, depends largely on when sleep occurs. That means encouraging him to sleep in rhythm with his own biological clock.

Pay attention to your child, and you'll find that, just like adults, he has "drowsy times" during the day. If he sleeps during these drowsy periods, the quality of that sleep will be greater than sleep that occurs out of phase with his biological cycles. But if you wait to put him down for sleep until well after he's shown signs of drowsiness, he's likely to be overtired by then, which may make it more difficult for him to fall asleep.

THE FIRST YEAR OF LIFE

As a parent, you need to nurture and support your child's need to sleep. As much as possible, encourage him to sleep during those times of the day when he's likely to benefit the most from it. However, adopting an optimal sleep schedule won't happen overnight. For infants, it takes a while for a baby's biological (circadian) rhythms to develop, with your ultimate goal of getting his sleep patterns to match his internal mechanisms. Give it time, and it will develop naturally. Your challenge as a parent is to be sensitive to those moments when his body is telling him (and you) that he's ready for sleep. Otherwise, you may be putting him down in his crib or bed way too early or way too late, and the ease with which he falls asleep—and the restorative capacity of that sleep—will be affected.

YOUR TODDLER OR SCHOOL-AGE CHILD

For clues on whether your older child is getting enough sleep—particularly quality sleep—observe him at the end of the day. Is he sweet, adaptable, friendly, cooperative, independent, and engaging? Or is he whiny, crabby, excitable, wired, and irritable? He may be running out of steam as the day draws to a close, all because of mild but chronic sleep deprivation. So pay attention to him, and you'll find that, just like with adults, he experiences a drowsy time during the day. If he's consistently melting down, you may need to make some adjustments in the times when you put him to sleep. He may need to go to bed earlier. The earlier bedtime will get rid of his unpleasant behavior near the end of the day.

Also keep the following caveat in mind: At times, when parents move their baby's bedtime earlier, they see no improvement in the baby's pre-sleep behavior. In cases like this, the earlier bedtime may still be too late, and needs to be adjusted further, so that it is even earlier.

Sleep Routines and Dealing with Crying

Some babies cry every night when they're placed in their crib for sleep; others almost never do. For many parents, it can be gut-wrenching when a child cries in his crib for long periods of time. As a baby cries, your heart may be breaking, and it can be anguishing to keep your distance while you wait for him to fall asleep. Or you might feel frustration or anger at his apparent unwillingness or inability to quiet down and sleep. Even just a few minutes of tears can seem like an eternity.

Often concerned about why their baby is crying, parents may wonder whether the infant is simply letting off steam, is feeling lonely, or whether he's really in distress. Many parents just give in, rushing to their infant's crib side, unable to bear the sound of the sobs.

Not surprisingly, some of the most common questions asked of pediatricians are "Should I let my baby cry himself to sleep, or should I pick him up and comfort him?", as well as the more fundamental question, "How much sleep should he really be getting?" To a large degree, the answers to these questions depend on the age of the child.

THE FIRST MONTH OF LIFE

During this period, your baby will spend most of his time asleep. When you place him in his crib for sleep, or when he awakens, try to avoid letting him cry. Instead, respond to those tears, and do whatever you can to soothe your baby, such as singing quietly, talking to him quietly, playing soft music, keeping the lights dim, and/or rocking him gently. Pick him up if necessary, placing him back in the crib again five to ten minutes later.

By minimizing his discomfort in whatever way works, you'll maximize his sleep time and its quality. (For additional information about soothing a crying baby, see below, as well as pages 863 and 865 later in this chapter.)

When is an infant of this age ready for sleep, whether or not he's in tears? In general, after he has been awake for one to two hours, he needs sleep. Sometimes he may need to fall asleep even before an hour goes by, and rarely he may stay awake for three hours. If he is a little fussy or has some low-level crying, wait to see if it escalates once you place him back in the crib, and if it does, then of course pick him up. But he just might drift off to sleep.

Generally, no matter what the circumstances, he will begin to show signs of being overtired and irritable if he doesn't get his nap when he needs it. So start soothing him to sleep. After he's been awake for an hour or two, he may need to be soothed. Place him in his crib when he's drowsy but still awake (this approach will be particularly helpful for daytime napping). If you wait too long, he's likely to become cranky, and have even more difficulty falling asleep.

Sharing the Bedtime Routine

During these early weeks of life, it is also important to get other adults, such as your spouse or partner, a grandmother, a sitter, or a nanny, involved in bedtime rituals. When you are the only one participating in getting him into bed, he will associate only you with putting him to sleep. The more people who are involved, the less likely that your baby will associate a certain scenario with falling asleep. This notion is sometimes called "many hands." If a baby associates only you with sleep—falling asleep while being held in your arms or while rocking—he will be able to fall asleep only when in those situations.

Parent Sleep Deprivation

In your baby's first weeks of life, another issue may surface: Mom or Dad may be sleep deprived. Various sleep schedules may leave your spouse anxious and overwhelmed, particularly if she feels that there are more responsibilities added to her life when she herself is feeling so sleep deprived and exhausted. You should support each other, and when necessary give the primary caretaker additional periods when she can take a break to catch a nap or adopt another approach to recharge her batteries.

IMPLEMENTING A SLEEP PLAN

It is important that both you and your spouse/partner agree to a sleep plan for your child. If only one parent is on board, the plan is unlikely to succeed. Decide together whether to adopt any new steps gradually or quickly. Many pediatricians advise small, simple steps first, making it a little easier for both parent and child to adjust. A slightly earlier bedtime, for example, may improve your child's mood and lead to less disappointment.

Whenever a change is made, wait and watch for a while to see how successful it is. Do not make your evaluation on a day-by-day (or night-by-night) basis. Try a new approach for at least several days before concluding that the change is worth continuing.

■ *At about six weeks of age (counting from the baby's due date).* Your baby's sleep-wake schedule will start to settle into more of a routine at this time. He will begin to sleep longer at night, and may exhibit signs of drowsiness (and perhaps some crying) earlier in the evening. For example, while he may have once been ready for sleep between 9 and 11 p.m., he may start to need sleep somewhat earlier—perhaps between 6 and 8 p.m. His longest sleep period will be in the late evening, lasting for three to five hours.

Variations exist, of course, so be sensitive to your own baby's needs and anticipate that he may require an earlier bedtime—no longer at 11 p.m. but rather at 8 p.m. So to minimize crying, put your child to sleep earlier, spend some time soothing him if needed (although if he fusses a little, it won't cause any harm), and let his own biological rhythm dictate whether it will turn into a thirty-minute nap or a four-hour snooze.

As you and your baby get in tune with his rhythms, he'll gradually learn to soothe himself to sleep when you put him down. As that

happens, there will be little or no crying. By about three months of age, most babies sleep six to eight hours during the night without waking their parents up. If he awakens too early, you might be able to encourage him to go back to sleep by soothing him, and keeping the lights off and the shades drawn. Avoid picking him up or feeding him, if possible.

■ *Four to twelve months of age.* With a four-month-old, and continuing into the weeks and months ahead, keep working at being sensitive to your baby's bodily rhythms, which will minimize episodes of crying. From four months through the rest of the first year of life, most infants need at least two naps—one at mid-morning and the other at midday; some children may nap a third time later in the afternoon. Try to get him on a schedule of napping at about 9 a.m., then at 1 p.m., and finally a late afternoon nap if he needs it. Most parents hate to awaken a young child from a nap because sleep is precious for him. Let him nap for as long as he wishes unless he has difficulty falling asleep at night; in that case, talk to your pediatrician about awakening him from his afternoon nap a little earlier than he might wake up on his own. If he takes late and lengthy naps, it might be because his bedtime is too late, and he is partially compensating for lost sleep at night by taking long naps. Skipping the third nap and having an earlier

SCENARIO #2

A mother and father brought their five-month-old daughter to the pediatrician, and explained that her napping (or lack of it) had become a serious problem that affected the entire family. They would put their child down for a daytime nap, but she would awaken about thirty-five to forty minutes later, ready to continue her day, at least for a while. They agreed that their baby needed lengthier naps, but were frustrated in their attempts to make them longer. They had tried leaving their baby in her crib for twenty more minutes after awakening, but she would cry nonstop and resisted returning to sleep.

Their pediatrician explained that in infants four to five months old, it can be challenging to initiate a regular nap schedule because their biological rhythms are continuing to change and mature, and thus nap times may not become well established for about another month or two. The doctor suggested that they could try extending the naps by responding promptly when the child first makes noises or calls out for attention.

When that happens, they can try gently patting their baby, giving her a massage, or offering breastfeeding for a short time. With this approach, many children will fall back asleep for another twenty to thirty minutes, providing a truly restorative nap that leads to greater alertness and attention spans later in the day.

As a child becomes older, however, these particular approaches can become more stimulating than soothing in some children, and thus become counterproductive. After discussing the matter further with the parents, the pediatrician felt there were a couple of factors at play. The child's bedroom might not be dark enough and the apartment might not be quiet enough to encourage sleep. But more important, the timing of the child's naps were likely not in sync with her natural rhythms. He recommended that they adjust the sleep environment to make it more conducive to napping, and to be patient until their child's biological rhythms made her body more agreeable to predictable daytime napping.

bedtime might be warranted. By about nine months of age, try to dispense with late afternoon naps so he'll be ready for bedtime for the night at an earlier time than if those late afternoon naps continued.

At this age, a child's nighttime sleep will be his longest sleep period of the day, and by about eight months old, it should last from ten to twelve hours without him awakening for a nighttime feeding. But if a child of this age seems overtired and he cries at the mere sight of his bed, his naps may be too short (less than thirty minutes long), his naps may not be occurring with his sleep rhythms, or perhaps you're putting him to bed too late at night. In the latter case, place him in bed much earlier, at least temporarily—perhaps at 5:30 or 6 p.m.—to respond to his excessive tiredness. If he cries, check on him and console him with a few comforting words. Change his diaper if needed, make sure he is comfortable, but keep the lights dim and don't arouse him more fully by picking him up and walking with him. Then leave the room quietly. As the days and weeks pass, gradually give him less attention at night, which will help him stop anticipating that you'll show up whenever he cries or calls out for you, and he'll be more likely to learn self-soothing such as sucking on his hand, rocking his head, or rubbing the sheet.

It's important to keep in mind that there are times when you may need to let your baby cry himself to sleep; it won't cause any harm and there's no need to worry about the possible messages behind those tears. Remember, you have all day to show your infant how much you love him and care for him. At night, he'll get the message that nighttime is for sleeping, and on those nights when you let him cry, you're helping him learn to soothe himself. He won't be thinking that you're abandoning him or that you don't love him anymore; he knows by your daytime behaviors that this isn't the case at all. In other words, there's no need to worry.

Daytime Nap Evolution

- *At about ages ten to twelve months,* the baby's morning nap will begin to taper off in the minority of children. Around twelve months of age, some babies may drop their morning nap. As that happens, you can start moving his nighttime bedtime somewhat earlier (perhaps by about twenty to thirty minutes); the afternoon nap can be started a little sooner, too. The time when you put your baby down for nighttime sleep may vary for a while, depending on factors such as how tired your child seems, and the quality of his daytime napping.

- *Thirteen to twenty-three months of age.* The amount of time that your child spends napping will begin to change during this time of life. By age fifteen months, about half (but certainly not yet all) children will be taking only one nap a day, typically in the afternoon. The morning nap may simply fade away on its own, although there could be some rough periods as this transition to a single daily nap takes place. Even so, for most children, the morning nap will gradually disappear. As that happens, if you put your child to bed earlier for the night, he'll actually be less likely to miss those

SCENARIO #3

Many parents recognize the importance of bedtime routines—but for some parents, these routines don't always work. One mother tried out many of those that she had heard about, including bathing her baby, massaging her after the bath, singing soft lullabies, and swaddling the baby, but none was effective. In fact, her baby often became *more* irritable as these approaches were used.

When this mother expressed her frustration to her pediatrician, he offered some pointers to make these bedtime routines more effective. He told her to begin using them early, *before* the child is already overtired and becoming crabby. He also urged her to be consistent, using the same bedtime routines day after day until the child begins to associate them with sleep. He stressed persistence, explaining that changes don't happen overnight, and that routines need to be relied on over time to have a positive effect.

The pediatrician had another suggestion. He asked the parents to place the infant in the crib for a nap about twenty to thirty minutes *before* they thought the nap should actually begin. As the baby relaxed in her crib, she almost always had a bowel movement within ten to twenty minutes, which prompted her to cry. But then once her diaper was changed, she was now in the correct biological time frame for her nap to begin. Her parents soothed her, and she fell asleep for a lengthy nap.

morning naps, and he's more likely to wake up rested.

- *By twenty-four months of age*, nearly all children have transitioned to just a single afternoon nap, although this napping remains biologically important for them to function well during the rest of the day.

- *Between two and three years old*, most children continue needing one daytime nap so they're not irritable and fussy by late afternoon. By about three years old, the average child will sleep about two hours during the daytime. However, some will sleep more and others less (as little as an hour in some cases). Try to make the timing of naps and nighttime sleep regular, although the need for some flexibility is inevitable. Some children will go through periods where they resist napping, even though their body is telling them (and you) that they need a nap; in those instances, try out an earlier or later bedtime at night, and see if that helps your child rest better during the day.

The best rule of thumb about the length of napping is that your child's naps should be long enough to be restorative. There is some evidence that longer naps tend to improve a child's attention span and his ability to learn. Conversely, if he's having very brief mini-naps that are just a few minutes in length, they simply won't sustain him through the day. A child's need for an afternoon nap about one to two hours in length tends to persist until he is about three years old, and then the length will shorten after that. Research shows that 90 percent of three-year-olds are still napping.

- *Three to five years of age.* Most children in this age range are ready for nighttime sleep between 7 and 9 p.m., or earlier if naps are brief or absent, and they'll sleep through the night until about 6:30 to 8 a.m. Naps tend to become less common in some children by age three or four.

  During this age, get in tune with your child's need for sleep, and set a regular bedtime. With less napping time and greater physical activity, the sleep needs at night actually increase in some children.

For more detailed information and specific guidance on sleep for particular age groups, see the sections on this topic in Part I of the book, including on pages 59–63, 216, 245, 287–288, 322–323, 359, 393, and 421.

Getting the Most Out of Sleep

So how do you prepare and soothe your child to sleep? Soothing techniques may vary based on the age of your child. Some gentle rubbing of his back can help at almost any age. For young infants, so can touching your own cheek to his in a rhythmic pattern that coincides with his own breathing. Patting him, kissing his forehead, or encouraging sucking behavior with a pacifier or finger, for example, may also be useful for young infants.

Bedtime routines can start as early as four to six months of age, and they'll help get your child ready for rest, particularly as he starts to associate them with sleep. Try reading him a story. Or give him a warm bath or a massage, sing him a lullaby, or play soothing music. Cut down on your playtime with him right before bedtime, close the curtains, dim the lights, and unplug the phones.

More important than your choice of a specific routine or ritual, you need to continue to stay in rhythm with your child's circadian clock. When it's time to sleep, keep your child away from situations where there is a lot of stimulation, which can lead to crankiness and make sleep difficult. Family activities with the baby before bedtime should be low-key, so as not to overstimulate him. Remember, timing is the key to healthy sleep. So while it's fine to sit quietly with your child for ten to twenty minutes and read him a story, what you choose to do is usually of less importance than the time you choose to do it.

With this in mind, many mothers and fathers try to change their own behaviors to encourage better sleep in their children. If possible, parents can share a parenting plan, similar to creating a sleep or bedtime routine. While one parent stays home with a child, the other parent is able to run errands or visit friends, and vice versa. This type of schedule can be implemented into their daily, weekly, or monthly routine in a way that works best with the family. Once your baby adopts a regular schedule in sync with his own internal clock, it can be liberating for Mom and Dad. You can take your child out for special events, and he won't fuss or cry. If your baby sticks to a routine for at least 80 percent of the time, the other 20 percent may not be a problem if you need to adjust his sleep schedule.

If your infant is in child care during the first year of life, ask his caregivers to keep him on a regular napping schedule as much as possible. It should be the same schedule that you follow at home to minimize disruptions. Sometimes, you may not even observe if he is overtired because he is so excited to see you when you pick him up at the child care facility, and you are so enthusiastic to see him. But pay attention to what he's experiencing. The staff's willingness to adapt to your own preferences for

SCENARIO #4

A father called the family's pediatrician with a problem that he and his wife were trying to solve. They understood the value of keeping their nine-month-old infant on a sleep schedule. At the same time, however, they had two older children with activities that didn't always fit in with the parents' commitment to be protective of their baby's need to nap.

Their pediatrician recommended that the parents work hard at finding a balance between the older children's social needs, and the baby's biologic requirement to nap during the day. Noting that they may not always find the perfect solution that meets the needs of everyone, the doctor added that compromises may be necessary. "Sometimes," he said, "you may have to tell an older child, 'You'll be a little late to your playdate because we're going to wait a few extra minutes until Owen finishes sleeping.' But other times, when the older child has a special event, you may decide to wake up the infant to make sure the older brother or sister gets to where he or she needs to go on time."

It's true that, in most cases, you should try to avoid awakening a sleeping baby. But a slightly shorter nap now and then won't cause harm, as long as it doesn't become a regular pattern.

napping may be an important factor when you're choosing a facility.

Of course, many (but not all) child care facilities are willing and able to make the timing of napping a priority. However, depending on where your child is being cared for, there may not be a dark, quiet room for napping, which can make sleeping difficult. Your child may be ready for a nap between 9 and 10 a.m. and then again between 1 and 3 p.m.—but the child care environment may not be conducive to napping at those times. There might be too much light, or lots of noise (including crying) from other children. As a result, he may not get the sleep he needs at the time when he most needs it. When that happens, he could be overtired when you pick him up at the end of your workday, and it may be particularly hard to keep him on a regular schedule. Your own time spent with the baby, bathing, feeding, and dressing him in the morning, can help make up for any time lost later in the day.

Even with cooperative child care staff, however, the situation can become mixed up on weekends. If your child has been in child care all week while you've been at your job, you'll probably be eager to spend as much time as possible with him on Saturday and Sunday. You may give in to his crying or demands to play because of your own guilt about being away so much, and good-quality naps may fall by the wayside. Then, after the weekend, the child care workers won't need a calendar to tell that it's Monday—they'll know just by how irritable your child is from a change in his weekday sleep routines.

Nevertheless, some disruptions in sleep schedules are inevitable. Holidays, vacations, or a family gathering can keep your child from napping or getting to bed on time. Because the temperament of children varies, some are much more adaptable to changes like these than others; while one child will adjust to changing circumstances very easily, others may not.

As much as possible, respect your child's nature, and try to maintain normal sleep routines. At the same time, if you know that a disruption of his sleep schedule is on the horizon, he will fare better and adapt more successfully, and have a cheerier disposition, if he is more rested ahead of time. So when you look ahead to a family party, for example, try to keep your child well rested in the preceding day or two so that this intrusion into his sleep schedule will unfold as smoothly as possible. The more rested your child is, the better his temperament and the more adaptable he will be to changes in his environment— and the better he will sleep.

How often can you disrupt your child's sleep schedule? Exceptions to sleep routines can occur once or twice a month—where you can forget or adjust naps and bedtimes—and you and your baby can enjoy holidays, birthdays, and other special events. Most well-rested children adapt to these occasional events, but do not overdo it with disruptions once or twice a week.

If your baby does get off schedule— perhaps because of a grandparent's visit, or when an unexpected illness occurs—think of the notion of a "reset" that lasts just one night. For this one night only of readjustment, put your child to bed very early, ignoring protest crying related to the sleep debt he has accumulated. A more gradual approach often fails due to the child's overtiredness and his battle to get extra attention. It can be frustrating for parents, but a single "reset" night should resolve the problem.

Dealing with Other Sleep Concerns

You and your spouse should work on other issues that could be disrupting your child's sleep. Do you have trouble setting limits with him? Is there marital discord between you and your partner that you're just too tired to address, but that is creating tension in the household? Do money worries or other problems create stress that makes it difficult for you to devote energy to establishing sleep routines? If you're not dealing effectively with problems like these, your child's sleep may pay the price.

Also, does your child have health issues that make sleeping difficult, such as colic, severe eczema, or sleep apnea? (Colic is a frequent cause of sleep-disrupting fussiness in very young babies; see page 166 for more information and guidance.) Or your child could have a short-term health problem like an ear infection that is causing pain and keeping him awake. Tend to his immediate needs, following your pediatrician's instructions on how to manage the problem and ease your child's discomfort.

Putting Sleep in Perspective

When it comes to your child's sleep, do the best you can, but don't feel bad if things don't always go smoothly. Make a concerted effort to get your child to bed on time for naps and at night. If your baby spends time at child care or with a nanny, and you're simply not present to put him to sleep at nap time, make sure that his caretakers understand and are trying to comply with your own preferences about your child's sleep schedule. But as a parent, you also need to set aside any anxiety and blame you might feel if you aren't doing everything perfectly. Inevitably, there will be days and nights when your child doesn't sleep well. Don't beat yourself up if your child goes to bed a little late for a night or two (or more). Just get back on track as soon as possible, and help him return to a normal sleeping routine. Dealing effectively with your child's sleeping problems is important, not only for your child but also because his sleep difficulties can interfere with your own need to rest. Meeting your own sleep needs (as well as those of your partner) is important to effectively care for your baby and the rest of your family. Chronically overtired parents also have a greater risk of becoming depressed.

Keep in mind that helping your

child sleep can be one of parenting's biggest challenges. But it can have an enormous payoff in terms of your child's health, now and in the future. Many adults are chronically poor sleepers because of patterns that often began during their own childhood and continued on. Sleeping poorly is a learned behavior, and when a child doesn't get quality sleep, he may not learn how to sleep well. In many cases, such sleep issues are likely to become part of his life for many years. The younger your child is when you begin to deal with his sleep problems, the more likely you are to resolve them. Remember that your pediatrician can be an ongoing source of support, advice, and reassurance. Additionally, many pediatric medical centers have individuals who specialize in helping children sleep better.

~ APPENDIX ~

Recommendations for Preventive Pediatric Health Care

Bright Futures/American Academy of Pediatrics

Each child and family is unique; therefore, these Recommendations for Preventive Pediatric Health Care are designed for the care of children who are receiving competent parenting, have no manifestations of any important health problems, and are growing and developing in satisfactory fashion. Additional visits may become necessary if circumstances suggest variations from normal.

Developmental, psychosocial, and chronic disease issues for children and adolescents may require frequent counseling and treatment visits separate from preventive care visits.

AGE[1]		INFANCY							EARLY CHILDHOOD						
	Prenatal[2]	Newborn[3]	3-5 d[4]	By 1 mo	2 mo	4 mo	6 mo	9 mo	12 mo	15 mo	18 mo	24 mo	30 mo	3 y	4 y
HISTORY Initial/Interval	●	●	●	●	●	●	●	●	●	●	●	●	●	●	●
MEASUREMENTS															
Length/Height and Weight		●	●	●	●	●	●	●	●	●	●	●	●	●	●
Head Circumference		●	●	●	●	●	●	●	●	●	●	●			
Weight for Length		●	●	●	●	●	●	●	●	●	●				
Body Mass Index[5]												●	●	●	●
Blood Pressure[6]		★	★	★	★	★	★	★	★	★	★	★	★	●	●
SENSORY SCREENING															
Vision		★	★	★	★	★	★	★	★	★	★	★	★	●[7]	●
Hearing		●[8]	★	★	★	★	★	★	★	★	★	★	★	★	●
DEVELOPMENTAL/BEHAVIORAL ASSESSMENT															
Developmental Screening[9]								●			●		●		
Autism Screening[10]											●	●			
Developmental Surveillance		●	●	●	●	●	●		●	●		●		●	●
Psychosocial/Behavioral Assessment		●	●	●	●	●	●	●	●	●	●	●	●	●	●
Alcohol and Drug Use Assessment[11]															
Depression Screening[12]															
PHYSICAL EXAMINATION[13]		●	●	●	●	●	●	●	●	●	●	●	●	●	●
PROCEDURES[14]															
Newborn Blood Screening[15]		←	●	→											
Critical Congenital Heart Defect Screening[16]		●													
Immunization[17]		●	●	●	●	●	●	●	●	●	●	●	●	●	●
Hematocrit or Hemoglobin[18]						★			●	★	★	★	★	★	★
Lead Screening[19]							★	★	● or ★[20]		★	● or ★[20]		★	★
Tuberculosis Testing[21]			★				★		★			★		★	★
Dyslipidemia Screening[22]												★			★
STI/HIV Screening[23]															
Cervical Dysplasia Screening[24]															
ORAL HEALTH[25]							★	★	● or ★		● or ★	● or ★	● or ★	●	
ANTICIPATORY GUIDANCE	●	●	●	●	●	●	●	●	●	●	●	●	●	●	●

KEY ● = to be performed   ★ = risk assessment to be performed with appropriate action to follow, if positive

← ● → = range during which a service may be provided

American Academy of Pediatrics
DEDICATED TO THE HEALTH OF ALL CHILDREN™

Bright Futures.
prevention and health promotion for infants,
children, adolescents, and their families™

These guidelines represent a consensus by the American Academy of Pediatrics (AAP) and Bright Futures. The AAP continues to emphasize the great importance of continuity of care in comprehensive health supervision and the need to avoid fragmentation of care.

Refer to the specific guidance by age as listed in *Bright Futures* guidelines (Hagan JF, Shaw JS, Duncan PM, eds. *Bright Futures Guidelines for Health Supervision of Infants, Children and Adolescents*. 3rd ed. Elk Grove Village, IL: American Academy of Pediatrics; 2008).

	MIDDLE CHILDHOOD						ADOLESCENCE										
5 y	6 y	7 y	8 y	9 y	10 y	11 y	12 y	13 y	14 y	15 y	16 y	17 y	18 y	19 y	20 y	21 y
●	●	●	●	●	●	●	●	●	●	●	●	●	●	●	●	●
●	●	●	●	●	●	●	●	●	●	●	●	●	●	●	●	●
●	●	●	●	●	●	●	●	●	●	●	●	●	●	●	●	●
●	●	●	●	●	●	●	●	●	●	●	●	●	●	●	●	●
●	●	★	●	★	●	★	●	★	★	●	★	★	●	★	★	★
●	●	★	●	★	●	★	★	★	★	★	★	★	★	★	★	★
●	●	●	●	●	●	●	●	●	●	●	●	●	●	●	●	●
●	●	●	●	●	●	●	●	●	●	●	●	●	●	●	●	●
						★	★	★	★	★	★	★	★	★	★	★
						●	●	●	●	●	●	●	●	●	●	●
●	●	●	●	●	●	●	●	●	●	●	●	●	●	●	●	●
●	●	●	●	●	●	●	●	●	●	●	●	●	●	●	●	●
★	★	★	★	★	★	★	★	★	★	★	★	★	★	★	★	★
★	★															
★	★	★	★	★	★	★	★	★	★	★	★	★	★	★	★	★
	★		★	←	●	→	★	★	★	★	★	★	←		●	→
						★	★	★	★	★	←		●	→	★	★
																●
	●															
●	●	●	●	●	●	●	●	●	●	●	●	●	●	●	●	●

The recommendations in this statement do not indicate an exclusive course of treatment or standard of medical care. Variations, taking into account individual circumstances, may be appropriate.

1. If a child comes under care for the first time at any point on the schedule, or if any items are not accomplished at the suggested age, the schedule should be brought up to date at the earliest possible time.
2. A prenatal visit is recommended for parents who are at high risk, for first-time parents, and for those who request a conference. The prenatal visit should include anticipatory guidance, pertinent medical history, and a discussion of benefits of breastfeeding and planned method of feeding, per the 2009 AAP statement "The Prenatal Visit" (http://pediatrics.aappublications.org/content/124/4/1227.full).
3. Every infant should have a newborn evaluation after birth, and breastfeeding should be encouraged (and instruction and support should be offered).
4. Every infant should have an evaluation within 3 to 5 days of birth and within 48 to 72 hours after discharge from the hospital to include evaluation for feeding and jaundice. Breastfeeding infants should receive formal breastfeeding evaluation, and their mothers should receive encouragement and instruction, as recommended in the 2012 AAP statement "Breastfeeding and the Use of Human Milk" (http://pediatrics.aappublications.org/content/129/3/e827.full). Newborn infants discharged less than 48 hours after delivery must be examined within 48 hours of discharge, per the 2010 AAP statement "Hospital Stay for Healthy Term Newborns" (http://pediatrics.aappublications.org/content/125/2/405.full).
5. Screen, per the 2007 AAP statement "Expert Committee Recommendations Regarding the Prevention, Assessment, and Treatment of Child and Adolescent Overweight and Obesity: Summary Report" (http://pediatrics.aappublications.org/content/120/Supplement_4/S164.full).
6. Blood pressure measurement in infants and children with specific risk conditions should be performed at visits before age 3 years.
7. If the patient is uncooperative, rescreen within 6 months, per the 2007 AAP statement "Eye Examination in Infants, Children, and Young Adults by Pediatricians" (http://pediatrics.aappublications.org/content/111/4/902.abstract).
8. All newborns should be screened, per the AAP statement "Year 2007 Position Statement: Principles and Guidelines for Early Hearing Detection and Intervention Programs" (http://pediatrics.aappublications.org/content/120/4/898.full).
9. See 2006 AAP statement "Identifying Infants and Young Children With Developmental Disorders in the Medical Home: An Algorithm for Developmental Surveillance and Screening" (http://pediatrics.aappublications.org/content/118/1/405.full).
10. Screening should occur per the 2007 AAP statement "Identification and Evaluation of Children with Autism Spectrum Disorders" (http://pediatrics.aappublications.org/content/120/5/1183.full).
11. A recommended screening tool is available at http://www.ceasar-boston.org/CRAFFT/index.php.
12. Recommended screening using the Patient Health Questionnaire (PHQ)-2 or other tools available in the GLAD-PC toolkit and at http://www.aap.org/en-us/advocacy-and-policy/aap-health-initiatives/Mental-Health/Documents/MH_ScreeningChart.pdf.
13. At each visit, age-appropriate physical examination is essential, with infant totally unclothed and older children undressed and suitably draped. See 2011 AAP statement "Use of Chaperones During the Physical Examination of the Pediatric Patient" (http://pediatrics.aappublications.org/content/127/5/991.full).
14. These may be modified, depending on entry point into schedule and individual need.
15. The Recommended Uniform Newborn Screening Panel (http://www.hrsa.gov/advisorycommittees/mchbadvisory/heritabledisorders/recommendedpanel/uniformscreeningpanel.pdf), as determined by The Secretary's Advisory Committee on Heritable Disorders in Newborns and Children, and state newborn screening laws/regulations (http://genes-r-us.uthscsa.edu/sites/genes-r-us/files/nbsdisorders.pdf), establish the criteria for and coverage of newborn screening procedures and programs. Follow-up must be provided, as appropriate, by the pediatrician.
16. Screening for critical congenital heart disease using pulse oximetry should be performed in newborns, after 24 hours of age, before discharge from the hospital, per the 2011 AAP statement "Endorsement of Health and Human Services Recommendation for Pulse Oximetry Screening for Critical Congenital Heart Disease" (http://pediatrics.aappublications.org/content/129/1/190.full).
17. Schedules, per the AAP Committee on Infectious Diseases, are available at: http://aapredbook.aappublications.org/site/resources/izschedules.xhtml. Every visit should be an opportunity to update and complete a child's immunizations.
18. See 2010 AAP statement "Diagnosis and Prevention of Iron Deficiency and Iron Deficiency Anemia in Infants and Young Children (0-3 Years of Age)" (http://pediatrics.aappublications.org/content/126/5/1040.full).
19. For children at risk of lead exposure, see the 2012 CDC Advisory Committee on Childhood Lead Poisoning Prevention statement "Low Level Lead Exposure Harms Children: A Renewed Call for Primary Prevention" (http://www.cdc.gov/nceh/lead/ACCLPP/Final_Document_030712.pdf).
20. Perform risk assessments or screenings as appropriate, based on universal screening requirements for patients with Medicaid or in high prevalence areas.
21. Tuberculosis testing per recommendations of the Committee on Infectious Diseases, published in the current edition of *AAP Red Book: Report of the Committee on Infectious Diseases*. Testing should be performed on recognition of high-risk factors.
22. See AAP-endorsed 2011 guidelines from the National Heart Blood and Lung Institute, "Integrated Guidelines for Cardiovascular Health and Risk Reduction in Children and Adolescents" (http://www.nhlbi.nih.gov/guidelines/cvd_ped/index.htm).
23. Adolescents should be screened for sexually transmitted infections (STIs) per recommendations in the current edition of the *AAP Red Book: Report of the Committee on Infectious Diseases*. Additionally, all adolescents should be screened for HIV according to the AAP statement (http://pediatrics.aappublications.org/content/128/5/1023.full) once between the ages of 16 and 18, making every effort to preserve confidentiality of the adolescent. Those at increased risk of HIV infection, including those who are sexually active, participate in injection drug use, or are being tested for other STIs, should be tested for HIV and reassessed annually.
24. See USPSTF recommendations (http://www.uspreventiveservicestaskforce.org/uspstf/uspscerv.htm). Indications for pelvic examinations prior to age 21 are noted in the 2010 AAP statement "Gynecologic Examination for Adolescents in the Pediatric Office Setting" (http://pediatrics.aappublications.org/content/126/3/583.full).
25. Refer to a dental home, if available. If not available, perform a risk assessment (http://www2.aap.org/oralhealth/docs/RiskAssessmentTool.pdf). If primary water source is deficient in fluoride, consider oral fluoride supplementation. For those at high risk, consider application of fluoride varnish for caries prevention. See 2008 AAP statement "Preventive Oral Health Intervention for Pediatricians" (http://pediatrics.aappublications.org/content/122/6/1387.full) and 2009 AAP statement "Oral Health Risk Assessment Timing and Establishment of the Dental Home" (http://pediatrics.aappublications.org/content/111/5/1113.full).

Summary of changes made to the
2014 Bright Futures/AAP Recommendations for Preventive Pediatric Health Care
(Periodicity Schedule)

Changes to Developmental/Behavioral Assessment

- **Alcohol and Drug Use Assessment**- Information regarding a recommended screening tool (CRAFFT) was added.

- **Depression**- Screening for depression at ages 11 through 21 has been added, along with suggested screening tools.

Changes to Procedures

- **Dyslipidemia screening**- An additional screening between 9 and 11 years of age has been added. The reference has been updated to the AAP-endorsed National Heart Blood and Lung Institute policy (http://www.nhlbi.nih.gov/guidelines/cvd_ped/index.htm)

- **Hematocrit or hemoglobin**- A risk assessment has been added at 15 and 30 months. The reference has been updated to the current AAP policy (http://pediatrics.aappublications.org/content/126/5/1040.full).

- **STI/HIV screening**- A screen for HIV has been added between 16 and 18 years. Information on screening adolescents for HIV has been added in the footnotes. STI screening now references recommendations made in the AAP Red Book. This category was previously titled "STI Screening."

- **Cervical dysplasia**- Adolescents should no longer be routinely screened for cervical dysplasia until age 21. Indications for pelvic exams prior to age 21 are noted in the 2010 AAP statement "Gynecologic Examination for Adolescents in the Pediatric Office Setting" (http://pediatrics.aappublications.org/content/126/3/583.full).

- **Critical Congenital Heart Disease**- Screening for critical congenital heart disease using pulse oximetry should be performed in newborns, after 24 hours of age, before discharge from the hospital, per the 2011 AAP statement, "Endorsement of Health and Human Services Recommendation for Pulse Oximetry Screening for Critical Congenital Heart Disease" (http://pediatrics.aappublications.org/content/129/1/190.full).

For several recommendations, the AAP Policy has been updated since 2007 but there have been no changes in the timing of recommendations on the Periodicity Schedule. These include:

- Footnote 2- The Prenatal Visit (2009):
http://pediatrics.aappublications.org/content/124/4/1227.full

- Footnote 4- Breastfeeding and the Use of Human Milk (2012):
http://pediatrics.aappublications.org/content/129/3/e827.full and Hospital Stay for Healthy Term Newborns (2010):
http://pediatrics.aappublications.org/content/125/2/405.full

- Footnote 8- Year 2007 Position Statement: Principles and Guidelines for Early Hearing Detection and Intervention Programs (2007):
http://pediatrics.aappublications.org/content/120/4/898.full

- Footnote 10- Identification and Evaluation of Children with Autism Spectrum Disorders (2007); http://pediatrics.aappublications.org/content/120/5/1183.full

- Footnote 17- Immunization Schedules (2014):
http://aapredbook.aappublications.org/site/resources/IZSchedule0-6yrs.pdf,
http://aapredbook.aappublications.org/site/resources/IZSchedule7-18yrs.pdf
and

- Footnote 19- CDC Advisory Committee on Childhood Lead Poisoning Prevention statement "Low Level Lead Exposure Harms Children: A Renewed Call for Primary Prevention" (2012):
http://www.cdc.gov/nceh/lead/ACCLPP/Final_Document_030712.pdf

- Footnote 22- AAP-endorsed guideline "Integrated Guidelines for Cardiovascular Health and Risk Reduction in Children and Adolescents" (2011):
http://www.nhlbi.nih.gov/guidelines/cvd_ped/index.htm

- Footnote 25- Preventive Oral Health Intervention for Pediatricians (2008):
http://pediatrics.aappublications.org/content/122/6/1387.full and Oral Health Risk Assessment Timing and Establishment of the Dental Home (2009):
http://pediatrics.aappublications.org/content/111/5/1113.full. Additional information from the policies regarding fluoride supplementation and fluoride varnish has been added to the footnote.

New references were added for several footnotes, also with no change to recommendations in the Periodicity Schedule:

- Footnote 5- Expert Committee Recommendations Regarding the Prevention, Assessment, and Treatment of Child and Adolescent Overweight and Obesity: Summary Report (2007):
http://pediatrics.aappublications.org/content/120/Supplement_4/S164.full

- Footnote 13- Use of Chaperones During the Physical Examination of the Pediatric Patient (2011):
http://pediatrics.aappublications.org/content/127/5/991.full

- Footnote 15- The Recommended Uniform Newborn Screening Panel
(http://www.hrsa.gov/advisorycommittees/mchbadvisory/heritabledisorders/reco mmendedpanel/uniformscreeningpanel.pdf), as determined by The Secretary's Advisory Committee on Heritable Disorders in Newborns and Children, and state newborn screening laws/regulations (http://genes-r-us.uthscsa.edu/sites/genes-r-us/files/nbsdisorders.pdf), establish the criteria for and coverage of newborn screening procedures and programs. Follow-up must be provided, as appropriate, by the pediatrician.

For consistency, the title of "Tuberculin Test" has been changed to "Tuberculosis Testing." The title of "Newborn Metabolic/Hemoglobin Screening" has been changed to "Newborn Blood Screening."

Figure 1. Recommended immunization schedule for persons aged 0 through 18 years – United States, 2014.

(FOR THOSE WHO FALL BEHIND OR START LATE, SEE THE CATCH-UP SCHEDULE [FIGURE 2]).

These recommendations must be read with the footnotes that follow. For those who fall behind or start late, provide catch-up vaccination at the earliest opportunity as indicated by the green bars in Figure 1. To determine minimum intervals between doses, see the catch-up schedule (Figure 2). School entry and adolescent vaccine age groups are in bold.

Vaccine	Birth	1 mo	2 mos	4 mos	6 mos	9 mos	12 mos	15 mos	18 mos	19–23 mos	2–3 yrs	4–6 yrs	7–10 yrs	11–12 yrs	13–15 yrs	16–18 yrs
Hepatitis B[1] (HepB)	1st dose	←——2nd dose——→			←—————————3rd dose—————————→											
Rotavirus[2] (RV) RV1 (2-dose series); RV5 (3-dose series)			1st dose	2nd dose	See footnote 2											
Diphtheria, tetanus, & acellular pertussis[3] (DTaP: <7 yrs)			1st dose	2nd dose	3rd dose		←————4th dose————→					5th dose				
Tetanus, diphtheria, & acellular pertussis[4] (Tdap: ≥7 yrs)														(Tdap)		
Haemophilus influenzae type b[5] (Hib)			1st dose	2nd dose	See footnote 5		3rd or 4th dose, See footnote 5									
Pneumococcal conjugate[6] (PCV13)			1st dose	2nd dose	3rd dose		←———4th dose———→									
Pneumococcal polysaccharide[6] (PPSV23)																
Inactivated poliovirus[7] (IPV) (<18 yrs)			1st dose	2nd dose	←—————————3rd dose—————————→							4th dose				
Influenza[8] (IIV; LAIV) 2 doses for some: See footnote 8					Annual vaccination (IIV only)								Annual vaccination (IIV or LAIV)			
Measles, mumps, rubella[9] (MMR)							←——1st dose——→					2nd dose				
Varicella[10] (VAR)							←——1st dose——→					2nd dose				
Hepatitis A[11] (HepA)							←—2-dose series, See footnote 11—→									
Human papillomavirus[12] (HPV2: females only; HPV4: males and females)							See footnote 13							(3-dose series)		
Meningococcal[13] (Hib-Men-CY ≥6 weeks; MenACWY-D ≥9 mos; MenACWY-CRM ≥2 mos)														1st dose		Booster

Legend:

- Range of recommended ages for all children
- Range of recommended ages for catch-up immunization
- Range of recommended ages for certain high-risk groups
- Range of recommended ages during which catch-up is encouraged and for certain high-risk groups
- Not routinely recommended

This schedule includes recommendations in effect as of January 1, 2014. Any dose not administered at the recommended age should be administered at a subsequent visit, when indicated and feasible. The use of a combination vaccine generally is preferred over separate injections of its equivalent component vaccines. Vaccination providers should consult the relevant Advisory Committee on Immunization Practices (ACIP) statement for detailed recommendations, available online at http://www.cdc.gov/vaccines/hcp/acip-recs/index.html. Clinically significant adverse events that follow vaccination should be reported to the Vaccine Adverse Event Reporting System (VAERS) online (http://www.vaers.hhs.gov/) or by telephone (800-822-7967). Suspected cases of vaccine-preventable diseases should be reported to the state or local health department. Additional information, including precautions and contraindications for vaccination, is available from CDC online (http://www.cdc.gov/vaccines/recs/vac-admin/contraindications.htm) or by telephone (800-CDC-INFO [800-232-4636]).

This schedule is approved by the Advisory Committee on Immunization Practices (http://www.cdc.gov/vaccines/acip/), the American Academy of Pediatrics (http://www.aap.org), the American Academy of Family Physicians (http://www.aafp.org), and the American College of Obstetricians and Gynecologists (http://www.acog.org).

NOTE: Visit www.healthychildren.org/immunizations for the most current information and footnotes.

FIGURE 2. Catch-up immunization schedule for persons aged 4 months through 18 years who start late or who are more than 1 month behind —United States, 2014.

The figure below provides catch-up schedules and minimum intervals between doses for children whose vaccinations have been delayed. A vaccine series does not need to be restarted, regardless of the time that has elapsed between doses. Use the section appropriate for the child's age. Always use this table in conjunction with Figure 1 and the footnotes that follow.

Vaccine	Minimum Age for Dose 1	Minimum Interval Between Doses			
		Dose 1 to dose 2	Dose 2 to dose 3	Dose 3 to dose 4	Dose 4 to dose 5
Persons aged 4 months through 6 years					
Hepatitis B[1]	Birth	4 weeks	8 weeks and at least 16 weeks after first dose; minimum age for the final dose is 24 weeks		
Rotavirus[2]	6 weeks	4 weeks	4 weeks[2]		
Diphtheria, tetanus, & acellular pertussis[3]	6 weeks	4 weeks	4 weeks	6 months	6 months[3]
Haemophilus influenzae type b[5]	6 weeks	4 weeks if first dose administered at younger than age 12 months / 8 weeks (as final dose) if first dose administered at age 12 through 14 months / No further doses needed if first dose administered at age 15 months or older	4 weeks[5] If current age is younger than 12 months and first dose administered at < 7 months old / 8 weeks (as final dose)[5] if current age is younger than 12 months and first dose administered between 7 through 11 months (regardless of Hib vaccine [PRP-T or PRP-OMP] used for first dose); OR if current age is 12 through 59 months and first dose administered at younger than age 12 months; OR first 2 doses were PRP-OMP and administered at younger than 12 months. / No further doses needed if previous dose administered at age 15 months or older	8 weeks (as final dose) This dose only necessary for children aged 12 through 59 months who received 3 (PRP-T) doses before age 12 months and started the primary series before age 7 months	
Pneumococcal[6]	6 weeks	4 weeks if first dose administered at younger than age 12 months / 8 weeks (as final dose for healthy children) if first dose administered at age 12 months or older / No further doses needed for healthy children if first dose administered at age 24 months or older	4 weeks if current age is younger than 12 months / 8 weeks (as final dose for healthy children) if current age is 12 months or older / No further doses needed for healthy children if previous dose administered at age 24 months or older	8 weeks (as final dose) This dose only necessary for children aged 12 through 59 months who received 3 doses before age 12 months or for children at high risk who received 3 doses at any age	
Inactivated poliovirus[7]	6 weeks	4 weeks[7]	4 weeks[7]	6 months[7] minimum age 4 years for final dose	
Meningococcal[13]	6 weeks	8 weeks[13]	See footnote 13	See footnote 13	
Measles, mumps, rubella[9]	12 months	4 weeks			
Varicella[10]	12 months	3 months			
Hepatitis A[11]	12 months	6 months			
Persons aged 7 through 18 years					
Tetanus, diphtheria; tetanus, diphtheria, & acellular pertussis[4]	7 years[4]	4 weeks	4 weeks if first dose of DTaP/DT administered at younger than age 12 months / 6 months if first dose of DTaP/DT administered at age 12 months or older and then no further doses needed for catch-up	6 months if first dose of DTaP/DT administered at younger than age 12 months	
Human papillomavirus[12]	9 years	Routine dosing intervals are recommended[12]			
Hepatitis A[11]	12 months	6 months			
Hepatitis B[1]	Birth	4 weeks	8 weeks (and at least 16 weeks after first dose)		
Inactivated poliovirus[7]	6 weeks	4 weeks	4 weeks[7]	6 months[7]	
Meningococcal[13]	6 weeks	8 weeks[13]			
Measles, mumps, rubella[9]	12 months	4 weeks			
Varicella[10]	12 months	3 months if person is younger than age 13 years / 4 weeks if person is aged 13 years or older			

NOTE: Visit www.healthychildren.org/immunizations for the most current information and footnotes.

Birth to 24 months: Boys
Length-for-age and Weight-for-age percentiles

NAME _____

RECORD # _____

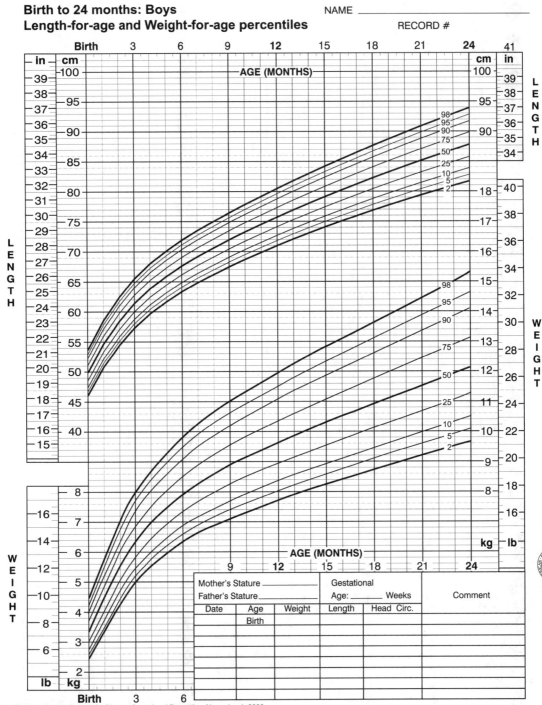

Published by the Centers for Disease Control and Prevention, November 1, 2009
SOURCE: WHO Child Growth Standards (http://www.who.int/childgrowth/en)
SAFER · HEALTHIER · PEOPLE™
Additional copies are available for purchase in quantities of 100. To order, contact:
American Academy of Pediatrics · 141 Northwest Point Blvd · Elk Grove Village, IL 60007-1098
Web site—http://www.aap.org. · Minimum order 100.   HE0510

American Academy
of Pediatrics
DEDICATED TO THE HEALTH OF ALL CHILDREN™

Birth to 24 months: Girls
Length-for-age and Weight-for-age percentiles

NAME _____

RECORD # _____

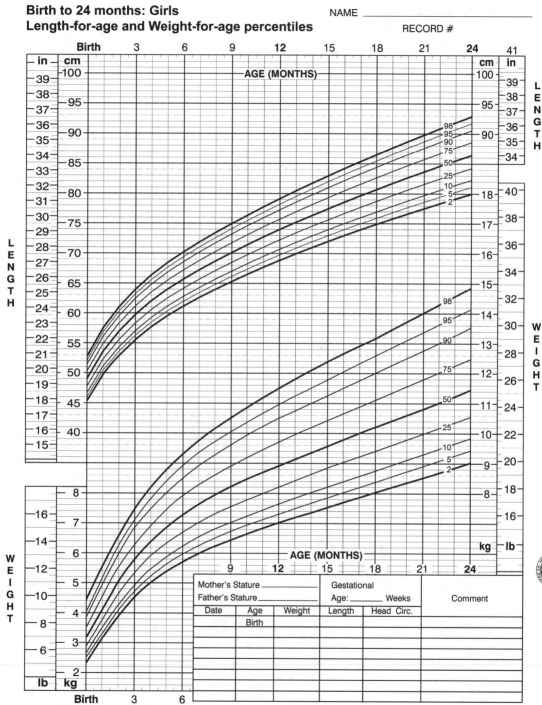

Published by the Centers for Disease Control and Prevention, November 1, 2009
SOURCE: WHO Child Growth Standards (http://www.who.int/childgrowth/en)

Reprinted by the American Academy of Pediatrics

The recommendations in this publication do not indicate an exclusive course of treatment or serve as a standard of medical care. Variations, taking into account individual circumstances, may be appropriate.
© 2011 American Academy of Pediatrics

9-284-Rep1013

Additional copies are available for purchase in quantities of 100.

To order, contact:
American Academy of Pediatrics
141 Northwest Point Blvd
Elk Grove Village, IL 60007-1098
Web site—http://www.aag.org. Minimum order 100.
HE0511

American Academy of Pediatrics

DEDICATED TO THE HEALTH OF ALL CHILDREN™

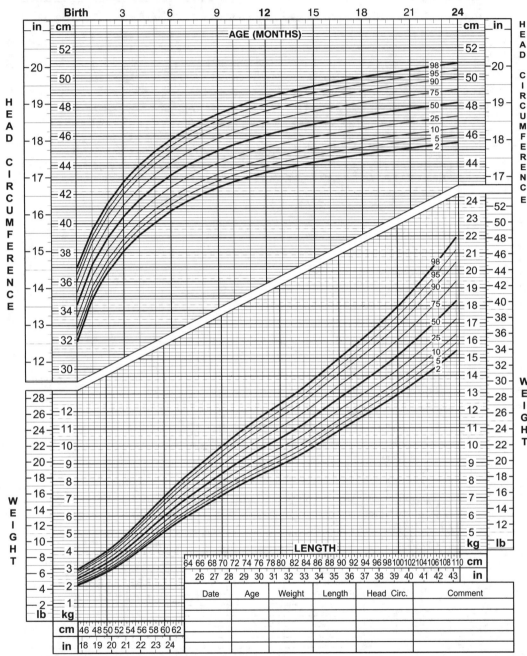

Birth to 24 months: Boys
Head circumference-for-age and
Weight-for-length percentiles

NAME _____

RECORD # _____

Published by the Centers for Disease Control and Prevention, November 1, 2009
SOURCE: WHO Child Growth Standards (http://www.who.int/childgrowth/en)

Additional copies are available for purchase in quantities of 100. To order, contact:
American Academy of Pediatrics • 141 Northwest Point Blvd • Elk Grove Village, IL 60007-1098
Web site—http://www.aap.org. • Minimum order 100.   HE0510

Reprinted by the American Academy of Pediatrics
The recommendations in this publication do not indicate an exclusive course of
treatment or serve as a standard of medical care. Variations, taking into account
individual circumstances, may be appropriate.
© 2011 American Academy of Pediatrics   9-283/REP1013

American Academy
of Pediatrics

Birth to 24 months: Girls
Head circumference-for-age and
Weight-for-length percentiles

NAME _____

RECORD # _____

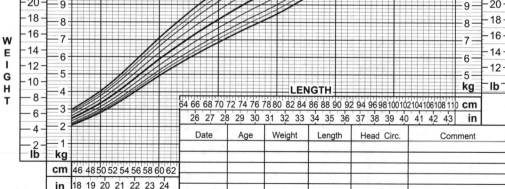

Published by the Centers for Disease Control and Prevention, November 1, 2009
SOURCE: WHO Child Growth Standards (http://www.who.int/childgrowth/en)

Reprinted by the American Academy of Pediatrics

The recommendations in this publication do not indicate an exclusive course of treatment or serve as a
standard of medical care. Variations, taking into account individual circumstances, may be appropriate.
© 2011 American Academy of Pediatrics   9-284-Rep1013

Additional copies are available for purchase in quantities of 100.

To order, contact:
American Academy of Pediatrics
141 Northwest Point Blvd
Elk Grove Village, IL 60007-1098
Web site—http://www.aag/org. Minimum order 100.
HE0511

American Academy
of Pediatrics

DEDICATED TO THE HEALTH OF ALL CHILDREN™

Boys, 2 to 20 years

STATURE FOR AGE AND WEIGHT FOR AGE PERCENTILES

Name _____

Record # _____

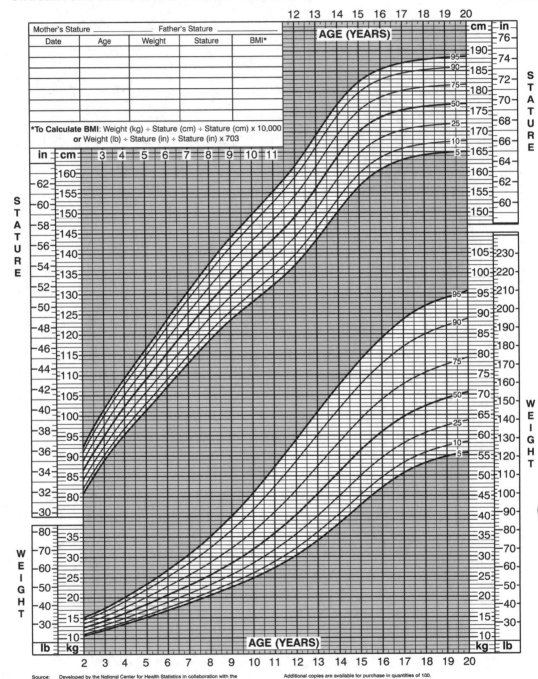

*To Calculate BMI: Weight (kg) ÷ Stature (cm) ÷ Stature (cm) x 10,000
or Weight (lb) ÷ Stature (in) ÷ Stature (in) x 703

Source: Developed by the National Center for Health Statistics in collaboration with the National Center for Chronic Disease Prevention and Health Promotion (2000). http://www.cdc.gov/growthcharts

Reprinted by the American Academy of Pediatrics

The recommendations in this publication do not indicate an exclusive course of treatment or serve as a standard of medical care. Variations, taking into account individual circumstances, may be appropriate.

©2000 American Academy of Pediatrics

Additional copies are available for purchase in quantities of 100.

To order, contact:
American Academy of Pediatrics
141 Northwest Point Blvd
Elk Grove Village, IL 60007-1098
Web site — http://www.aap.org
Minimum order 100.

American Academy of Pediatrics

DEDICATED TO THE HEALTH OF ALL CHILDREN™

Girls, 2 to 20 years

STATURE FOR AGE AND WEIGHT FOR AGE PERCENTILES

Name _____

Record # _____

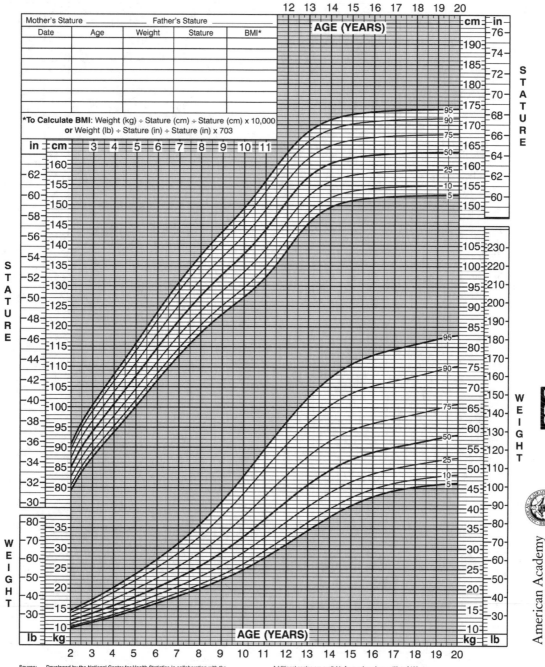

Mother's Stature _____ Father's Stature _____

Date	Age	Weight	Stature	BMI*

*To Calculate BMI: Weight (kg) ÷ Stature (cm) ÷ Stature (cm) x 10,000
or Weight (lb) ÷ Stature (in) ÷ Stature (in) x 703

American Academy of Pediatrics

DEDICATED TO THE HEALTH OF ALL CHILDREN™

Source: Developed by the National Center for Health Statistics in collaboration with the National Center for Chronic Disease Prevention and Health Promotion (2000).
http://www.cdc.gov/growthcharts

Reprinted by the American Academy of Pediatrics

The recommendations in this publication do not indicate an exclusive course of treatment or serve as a standard of medical care. Variations, taking into account individual circumstances, may be appropriate.

©2000 American Academy of Pediatrics

Additional copies are available for purchase in quantities of 100.

To order, contact
American Academy of Pediatrics
141 Northwest Point Blvd
Elk Grove Village, IL 60007-1098
Web site — http://www.aap.org
Minimum order 100.

Boys, 2 to 20 years

BODY MASS INDEX-FOR-AGE PERCENTILES

Name _____

Record # _____

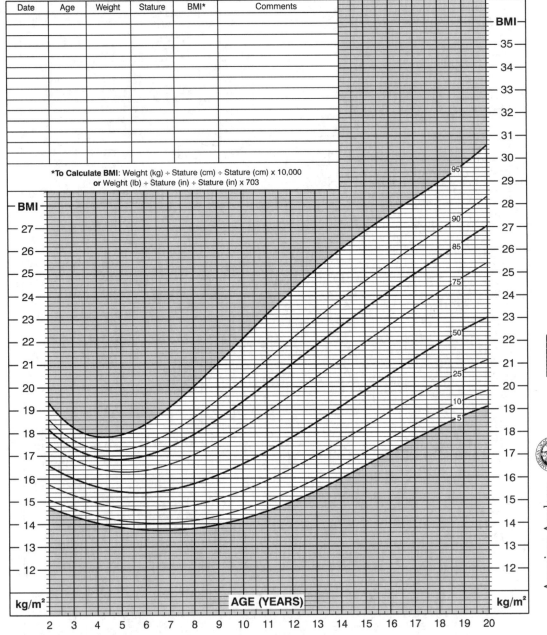

Date	Age	Weight	Stature	BMI*	Comments

*To Calculate BMI: Weight (kg) ÷ Stature (cm) ÷ Stature (cm) x 10,000
or Weight (lb) ÷ Stature (in) ÷ Stature (in) x 703

AGE (YEARS)

kg/m²

American Academy
of Pediatrics

DEDICATED TO THE HEALTH OF ALL CHILDREN™

Source: Developed by the National Center for Health Statistics in collaboration with the
National Center for Chronic Disease Prevention and Health Promotion (2000).
http://www.cdc.gov/growthcharts

Reprinted by the American Academy of Pediatrics

The recommendations in this publication do not indicate an exclusive course of treatment or serve as a
standard of medical care. Variations, taking into account individual circumstances, may be appropriate.

©2000 American Academy of Pediatrics, Revised—5/01

9-8/REP1013

Additional copies are available for purchase in quantities of 100.

To order, contact:
American Academy of Pediatrics
141 Northwest Point Blvd
Elk Grove Village, IL 60007-1098
Web site — http://www.aap.org
Minimum order 100.

HE0304

Girls, 2 to 20 years

Name _____

BODY MASS INDEX FOR AGE PERCENTILES

Record # _____

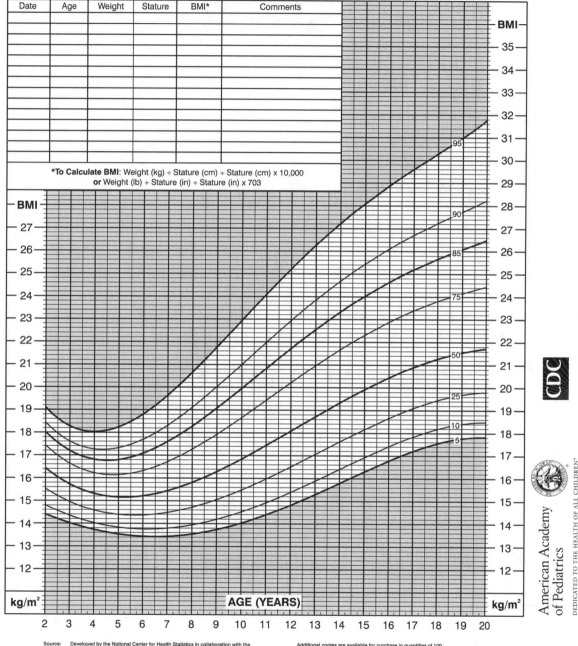

Date	Age	Weight	Stature	BMI*	Comments

*To Calculate BMI: Weight (kg) ÷ Stature (cm) ÷ Stature (cm) x 10,000
or Weight (lb) ÷ Stature (in) ÷ Stature (in) x 703

AGE (YEARS)

Source: Developed by the National Center for Health Statistics in collaboration with the
National Center for Chronic Disease Prevention and Health Promotion (2000).
http://www.cdc.gov/growthcharts

Reprinted by the American Academy of Pediatrics

The recommendations in this publication do not indicate an exclusive course of treatment or serve as a
standard of medical care. Variations, taking into account individual circumstances, may be appropriate.

©2000 American Academy of Pediatrics, Revised—5/01
9-10/REP0113

Additional copies are available for purchase in quantities of 100.
To order, contact
American Academy of Pediatrics
141 Northwest Point Blvd
Elk Grove Village, IL 60007-1098
Web site — http://www.aap.org
Minimum order 100.

HE0306

American Academy of Pediatrics

DEDICATED TO THE HEALTH OF ALL CHILDREN®

CDC

Is This The Right Place For My Child?

(Make a copy of this checklist to use with each program you visit.)

Place a check in the box if the program meets your expectations.

Notes:

Will my child be supervised?

Are children watched at all times, including when they are sleeping?[15]

Are adults warm and welcoming? Do they pay individual attention to each child?[40]

Are positive guidance techniques used?
Do adults avoid yelling, spanking, and other negative punishments?[16]

Are the caregiver/teacher-to-child ratios appropriate and do they follow the recommended guidelines:

➤ One caregiver per 3 or 4 infants
➤ One caregiver per 3 or 4 young toddlers
➤ One caregiver per 4 to 6 older toddlers
➤ One caregiver per 6 to 9 preschoolers[19]

Have the adults been trained to care for children?

If a center,

➤ Does the director have a degree and some experience in caring or children? [27/28/29]
➤ Do the teachers have a credential*** or Associate's degree and experience in caring for children?[27/28/29]

If a family child care home:

➤ Has the provider had specific training on children's development and experience caring for children?[30]

Is there always someone present who has current CPR and first aid training?[32]

Are the adults continuing to receive training on caring for children?[33]

Have the adults been trained on child abuse prevention and how to report suspected cases?[12/13]

Will my child be able to grow and learn?

For older children, are there specific areas for different kinds of play (books, blocks, puzzles, art, etc.)?[21]

For infants and toddlers, are there toys that "do something" when the child plays with them?[41]

Is the play space organized and are materials easy-to-use? Are some materials available at all times?[21]

Are there daily or weekly activity plans available? Have the adults planned experiences for the children to enjoy? Will the activities help children learn?[22]

Do the adults talk with the children during the day? Do they engage them in conversations? Ask questions, when appropriate?[43]

Do the adults read to children at least twice a day or encourage them to read, if they can read?[43]

Is this a safe and healthy place for my child?

Do adults and children wash their hands (before eating or handing food, or after using the bathroom, changing diapers, touching body fluids, eating, etc.)?[4]

Are diaper changing surfaces cleaned and disinfected after each use?[5]

Do all of the children enrolled have the required immunizations?[6]

Are medicines labeled and out of children's reach?[7]

Are adults trained to give medicines and keep records of medications?[7]

Place a check in the box if the program meets your expectations.

Are cleaning supplies and other poisonous materials locked up, out of children's reach?[8]

Is there a plan to follow if a child is injured, sick or lost?[9]

Are first aid kits readily available?[10]

Is there a plan for responding to disasters (fire, flood, etc.)?[11]

Has a satisfactory criminal history background check been conducted on each adult present?

➤ Was the check based on fingerprints?[14]

Have all the adults who are left alone with children had background and criminal screenings?[13]

Is the outdoor play area a safe place for children to play?[39]

➤ Is it checked each morning for hazards before children use it?[23]

➤ Is the equipment the right size and type for the age of the children who use it?[24]

➤ In center-based programs, is the playground area surrounded by a fence at least 4 feet tall?[25]

➤ Is the equipment placed on mulch, sand, or rubber matting?[23]

➤ Is the equipment in good condition?[39]

Is the number of children in each group limited?

➤ In family child care homes and centers, children are in groups of no more than**

- 6-8 infants
- 6-12 younger toddlers
- 8-12 older toddlers
- 12-20 preschoolers
- 20-24 school-agers[20]

Is the program well-managed?

Does the program have the highest level of licensing offered by the state?[42]

Are there written personnel policies and job descriptions?[17]

Are parents and staff asked to evaluate the program?[37]

Are staff evaluated each year; do providers do a self-assessment?[18]

Is there a written annual training plan for staff professional development?[33]

Is the program evaluated each year by someone outside the program?[38]

Is the program accredited by a national organization?[36]

Does the program work with parents?

Will I be welcome any time my child is in care?[1]

Is parents' feedback sought and used in making program improvements?[1]

Will I be given a copy of the program's policies?[2]

Are annual conferences held with parents?[3]

Notes:

_____

_____

_____

_____

_____

_____

_____

_____

_____

_____

_____

_____

_____

_____

_____

_____

_____

_____

_____

_____

_____

_____

_____

_____

_____

_____

_____

These questions are based on research about child care; you can read the research findings on the NACCRRA website under "Questions for Parents to Ask" at http://www.naccrra.org.

* These are the adult-to-child ratios and group sizes recommended by theNational Association for the Education of Young Children. Ratios are lowered when there are one or more children who may need additional help to fully participate in a program due to a disability, or other factors.

** Group sizes are considered the maximum number of children to be in a group, regardless of the number of adult staff.

*** Individuals working in child care can earn a Child Development Associate credential.

For help finding child care in your area, contact Child Care Aware®, a Program of NACCRRA toll-free at 1-800-424-2246 or visit online at www.childcareaware.org.

For information about other AAP publications visit: www.aap.org

Endorsed by:

American Academy of Pediatrics
DEDICATED TO THE HEALTH OF ALL CHILDREN™

✦Office of Child Care
♡

CHOKING/CPR

LEARN AND PRACTICE CPR (CARDIOPULMONARY RESUSCITATION).

IF ALONE WITH A CHILD WHO IS CHOKING...

1. SHOUT FOR HELP. 2. START RESCUE EFFORTS. 3. CALL 911 OR YOUR LOCAL EMERGENCY NUMBER.

START FIRST AID FOR CHOKING IF	DO *NOT* START FIRST AID FOR CHOKING IF
• The child cannot breathe at all (the chest is not moving up and down). • The child cannot cough or talk, or looks blue. • The child is found unconscious/unresponsive. (Go to CPR.)	• The child can breathe, cry, or talk. • The child can cough, sputter, or move air at all. The child's normal reflexes are working to clear the airway.

FOR INFANTS YOUNGER THAN 1 YEAR

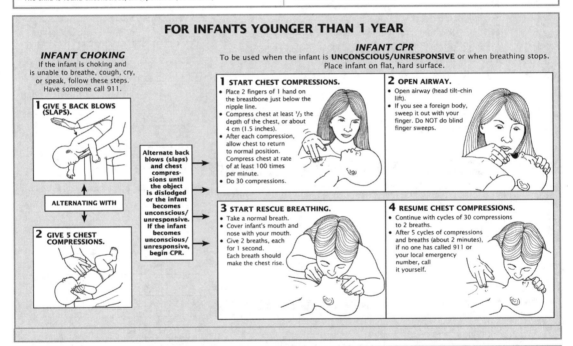

INFANT CHOKING
If the infant is choking and is unable to breathe, cough, cry, or speak, follow these steps. Have someone call 911.

1 GIVE 5 BACK BLOWS (SLAPS).

ALTERNATING WITH

2 GIVE 5 CHEST COMPRESSIONS.

Alternate back blows (slaps) and chest compressions until the object is dislodged or the infant becomes unconscious/unresponsive. If the infant becomes unconscious/unresponsive, begin CPR.

INFANT CPR
To be used when the infant is **UNCONSCIOUS/UNRESPONSIVE** or when breathing stops. Place infant on flat, hard surface.

1 START CHEST COMPRESSIONS.
• Place 2 fingers of 1 hand on the breastbone just below the nipple line.
• Compress chest at least 1/3 the depth of the chest, or about 4 cm (1.5 inches).
• After each compression, allow chest to return to normal position. Compress chest at rate of at least 100 times per minute.
• Do 30 compressions.

2 OPEN AIRWAY.
• Open airway (head tilt–chin lift).
• If you see a foreign body, sweep it out with your finger. Do NOT do blind finger sweeps.

3 START RESCUE BREATHING.
• Take a normal breath.
• Cover infant's mouth and nose with your mouth.
• Give 2 breaths, each for 1 second. Each breath should make the chest rise.

4 RESUME CHEST COMPRESSIONS.
• Continue with cycles of 30 compressions to 2 breaths.
• After 5 cycles of compressions and breaths (about 2 minutes), if no one has called 911 or your local emergency number, call it yourself.

If at any time an object is coughed up or the infant/child starts to breathe, stop rescue breaths and call 911 or your local emergency number.

Ask your pediatrician for information on choking/CPR instructions for children older than 8 years and for information on an approved first aid or CPR course in your community.

CHOKING/CPR

LEARN AND PRACTICE CPR (CARDIOPULMONARY RESUSCITATION).

IF ALONE WITH A CHILD WHO IS CHOKING...

1. SHOUT FOR HELP. 2. START RESCUE EFFORTS. 3. CALL 911 OR YOUR LOCAL EMERGENCY NUMBER.

START FIRST AID FOR CHOKING IF	DO *NOT* START FIRST AID FOR CHOKING IF
• The child cannot breathe at all (the chest is not moving up and down). • The child cannot cough or talk, or looks blue. • The child is found unconscious/unresponsive. (Go to CPR.)	• The child can breathe, cry, or talk. • The child can cough, sputter, or move air at all. The child's normal reflexes are working to clear the airway.

FOR CHILDREN 1 TO 8 YEARS OF AGE

CHILD CHOKING (HEIMLICH MANEUVER)

Have someone call 911. If the child is choking and is unable to breathe, cough, cry, or speak, follow these steps.

1. Perform Heimlich maneuver.
   • Place hand, made into a fist, and cover with other hand just above the navel. Place well below the bottom tip of the breastbone and rib cage.
   • Give each thrust with enough force to produce an artificial cough designed to relieve airway obstruction.
   • Perform Heimlich maneuver until the object is expelled or the child becomes unconscious/unresponsive.

2. If the child becomes UNCONSCIOUS/UNRESPONSIVE, begin CPR. ➡

CHILD CPR

To be used when the child is **UNCONSCIOUS/UNRESPONSIVE** or when breathing stops.
Place child on flat, hard surface.

1 START CHEST COMPRESSIONS.
• Place the heel of 1 or 2 hands over the lower half of the sternum.
• Compress chest at least $1/3$ the depth of the chest, or about 5 cm (2 inches).
• After each compression, allow chest to return to normal position. Compress chest at rate of at least 100 times per minute.
• Do 30 compressions.

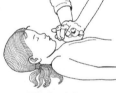

1-hand technique   2-hand technique

2 OPEN AIRWAY.
• Open airway (head tilt–chin lift).
• If you see a foreign body, sweep it out with your finger. Do NOT do blind finger sweeps.

3 START RESCUE BREATHING.
• Take a normal breath.
• Pinch the child's nose closed, and cover child's mouth with your mouth.
• Give 2 breaths, each for 1 second. Each breath should make the chest rise.

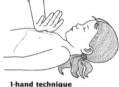

4 RESUME CHEST COMPRESSIONS.
• Continue with cycles of 30 compressions to 2 breaths until the object is expelled.
• After 5 cycles of compressions and breaths (about 2 minutes), if no one has called 911 or your local emergency number, call it yourself.

If at any time an object is coughed up or the infant/child starts to breathe, stop rescue breaths and call 911 or your local emergency number.

Ask your pediatrician for information on choking/CPR instructions for children older than 8 years and for information on an approved first aid or CPR course in your community.

~ INDEX ~

Page numbers of illustrations appear in italics.

Abdominal/gastrointestinal tract, 521–52, *522, 525*
abdominal distention in newborns, 137, 150, 534
appendicitis, 524, 525–26, *525*
bacterial infections, 523
botulism, 539
campylobacter, 538–39
celiac disease, 526–28
clostridium perfringens, 538
colic, 522
communicating hydrocele, 546–47, *547*
constipation, 193, 521, 523, 528–30, 782
cryptosporidiosis, 539
diarrhea, 530–35
e. coli, 538
food poisoning, 531, 537–42
gastroenteritis, 523, 531, 551
GERD, 550–51
hepatitis, 461, 542–44
hydrocele, 138, 545, 546, 547
inguinal hernia, 545–46, *546*
intestinal infection, 523
intussusception, 522–23
lead poisoning, 524
malabsorption, 547–49
milk allergy, 524
pain, 523–26, 534, 581
pinworms, 844–45
Reye syndrome, 549
salmonella bacteria, 537–38
shigellosis, 538
staphylococcus aureus, 537, 843
strep throat, 523–24
urinary tract infections, 523
viral infections, 523
vomiting, 549–52, *550*
Abusive head trauma, 168–169
ACEs (adverse childhood experiences), xxxiv, 310

Acetaminophen. *See also treatment for specific illnesses*
dosage chart, 767
first-aid, 695
Adenoids, 675–77, *675*
Adenoidectomy, 677
Adenovirus, 595
ADHD (attention deficit hyperactivity disorder), 583–86, 587, 638
Adoption, 737–39
Aggressive children, 306, 308, 428–29, 575–80, 639
Air pollution, 709–11
Alcohol
breastfeeding and, 96
during pregnancy, 5, 8–9, 141, 164
fetal alcohol syndrome (FAS), 5, 584
poisoning danger, 484
Allergic rhinitis, 559, 567–68, 676
Allergies, 553–74
anaphylactic reactions, 564, 570, 571, 604
animals, 559, 569
asthma, 553–60
bee sting, 571–74
breastfeeding and, 85, 114, 117, 566, 567
common household, 569
diarrhea and, 179, 564, 566
DTaP vaccine, 808–9
dust mites, 554, 559, 569
eczema or dermatitis, 560–62
eggs, 562, 810
fish, 563
food, 179, 527, 562–66
hay fever/nasal allergy, 567–68
hives, 570–71
how allergies develop, 563
latex, 649–50
milk or dairy products, 116–17, 524, 566–67

mold, 569
peanuts/tree nuts, 562, 565, 570
respiratory, 567–68
responses to, 254
scabies and, 849–51
solid food introduction, 242
soy protein, 118, 563
testing for, 564–65
Alopecia/alopecia areata, 838
Amblyopia, 726–27, 732, 734
American Academy of Pediatrics (AAP) positions
adenoid surgery, 677
adoption by same-sex couples, 739
alcohol during pregnancy, 8–9
antibiotics for tick bites, 821
aspirin for fever, 769
autism spectrum disorders, 641
baby checkups and immunizations, 20, 21–22
baby walkers, 264, 488
blood pressure testing, 779
breastfeeding, 84–85, 286
car and school bus safety seats, 462, 492
circumcision, 26
complementary or alternative medicine, 633
CPR training, 691
discipline methods, 289, 329
folic acid, 651
fluoride supplements, 127–28
flu vaccine, 603
fruit juice, 127
gun safety, 484
head lice, 839, 840
HIV/AIDS, 461–62, 632
homemade formulas, 115
imaging tests for UTIs, 779–80
immunizations, 809
insect repellents/DEET, 574

American Academy of
   Pediatrics (AAP) positions
   (*cont.*)
iron supplements, 126
lead poisoning, 717
media and technological
   devices, 417, 814, 815
newborn examinations, 22,
   155
newborn hospital discharge,
   144
newborn sleep position, 63,
   195, 196
obesity, 319–21
pediatrician board-
   certification, 18–19
physical punishment, 329
pneumococcal vaccine, 606
preschool child-to-staff
   ratio, 397
shaking a baby, 61, 168–69
SIDS, child care settings,
   451
sleeping of new babies near
   but not with parents, 33
smoking and pregnancy, 9
sunscreens, 125
thermometers, 764
tonsillectomy, 677
trampolines, 508
transportation safety, 464
urine testing, 779
vitamin supplements, 124,
   178
water safety, 509, 510
well water source safety, 716
American Academy of
   Pediatrics' *New Mother's
   Guide to Breastfeeding*
   (Meek, ed.), 108, 131
American Academy of
   Pediatrics (AAP) website,
   580
   Advocacy and Policy, 582
   autism, 642
American Diabetes Assn., 628,
   630
American Heart Assn., 691
American Red Cross, 691
Amniocentesis, 12, 13
Anaphylactic reactions, 570,
   571, 572, 604

Anemia, 621–23
lead poisoning and, 718
of prematurity, 55
SCD and, 624
thalassemia, 13, 622, 623
Anger, 575–80
parental, 212–14
Animals
allergies to, 569
asthma and, 559
bites, 686–88
cat scratches, 681
flea bites and, 573
rabies, 512, 513, 687
safety around, 512–13
stress and trauma, 688
toxoplasmosis, 7, 513
Antibiotic ointment or cream,
   561, 693, 695, 731, 841
Antibiotics, 253–54. *See also
   treatment of specific
   illness*
resistance to, 843–44
risk of overuse, 665
Antihistamines, use of, 562,
   568, 570, 572, 834
Antihypertensives, 801
Anti-inflammatory drugs, 556,
   558, 823
Antipyretic drugs, 767, 768
Antiviral medication, 7, 79,
   254, 604–5, 671
Apgar scores, 48–49
Apnea, 55, 195, 595, 676
Appendicitis, 524, 525–26,
   525
Appetite, 309, 311
Appetite loss, xxxi, 116, 224,
   254, 309, 311, 419, 420,
   521, 526, 534, 543, 622,
   629, 660, 670, 674, 680,
   717, 786, 788, 812, 823,
   847, 848
when to call the doctor,
   224
Arachidonic acid (ARA), 117
Arrhythmias, heart, 795–97
Arthritis, 819, 821–23
bacterial infection of the
   joint, 819–20
juvenile idiopathic arthritis
   (JIA) 821–23

Lyme disease and, 820–21
transient synovitis of hip,
   819
Asbestos, 711–12
Asperger syndrome, 637, 638
Aspirin
for fever, 603, 769
for Kawasaki disease, 803
nosebleeds and, 672
warning, 220, 224, 549,
   603, 803
Arc, The, 658
Asthma, 553–60, *554, 557*
air pollution and, 709
breastfeeding and, 26, 86
bronchiolitis and, 595
nebulizer (bronchodilator),
   557–58
common triggers, 554, 556,
   559
compressor or breathing
   machine, 558
controller meds, 557–59
coughing and, 598, 599
pneumonia and, 605
puffer or nebulizer, 557–58
pulmonary function testing
   (PFT), 555
quick-relief or rescue meds,
   556–57, 558
second-hand smoke, 709–11
spacer, 557–58, *557*
when to call the doctor, 555
Atopic dermatitis, 221–22,
   560–62
Autism/Autistic spectrum
   disorder (ASD), 349,
   636–42
diagnosis, 639–40
immunizations and, 637,
   809–10
signs and symptoms,
   239–40, 349, 381–82,
   638–39
treatment, 640–42
Automotive Safety for
   Children Program, 493

Baby acne, 158–59
Baby carriers, 502–3
Baby oil, 73

Baby powder, 73, 199, 478, 692
Baby sitters. *See* Child care
Bacterial infections, 254. *See also specific diseases*
Baldness, 158, 838
Balloons, dangers, 490, 692
Balls, 232, 279, 315
Bassinets, 29, 33, 63
Bathing
  infants, 69–72, *69, 70–71*
  safety check, 72, 198–99, 256
  washtub (for infant), 29–30
  water temperature, 252
Bedbug bites, 573
Bedding, 29, 62, 477, 559
Bed-wetting, 392–93, 581, 780–83
Bee stings, 571–74
  anaphylactic reactions, 570, 571, 572
Behavior, 575–93. *See also* Discipline; Temper tantrums
  anger, aggression, biting, 575–80, 586
  autism and, 638–39
  bullying, 428–29
  coping with disasters and terrorism, 580–82
  death of a loved one and, 582–83, 748–51
  hyperactivity and distractible child, 348, 583–85, 587
  lead poisoning and, 718
  media use and, 347, 421, 576–80
  thumb sucking, 282, 591–92
  tics, 592–93
Bicycle safety, 430, 505–6, 517. *See also* Tricycles
Bilingual babies, 268
Bilirubin, 55, 152–53
Birth, 38–41. *See also* Newborns
  birth plan, 15–16
  breech, 11, 155
  Cesarean, 7, 11, 40, 46–48
  episiotomy, 39, 45
  inducing labor, 39, 41

injuries during, 140, 150–51, 793
last-minute activities, 16–17
pain and medication, 39–40
preparing for delivery, 14–17
procedures after, 48–51
vaginal delivery, 44–46
VBAC, 48
Birthmarks, 135–37, 831–34
Birthweight. *See* Newborns
Bisphenol A (BPA), 714–15
Bites
  animal, 686–88
  human, 688
  insects, 571–74
  PTSD following, 688
  when to call the doctor, 687
Biting, 575–80, 586
Black eye, 730
Blood. *See also* Anemia; Sickle cell diseases
  bleeding, stopping, 693–94
  hemophilia, 646
  in stool, 114, 140, 522, 528, 534, 625
  in urine, 625, 771–72
Blood pressure, 799–802
  drop in, anaphylactic shock and, 564
  hematuria and, 772
  high, xxxv, 799–802
  glomerulonephritis and, 841, 851
  proteinuria and, 773
  scarlet fever and, 851
  sodium in foods, 800
  UTIs and, 779
Blood tests, 370, 718. *See also specific diseases*
Blue baby, 151
Body mass index (BMI), 320
Bonding, 44, 50, 53, 143
Bones, broken, 699–701
  "toddler," 826–27
Bottle-feeding, 84, 115–25. *See also* Weaning
  amount of, 124–25, 177
  bowel movements and,
  BPA in bottles, warning, 714–15
  breastfeeding and/or, 25–27, 95, 104–5

breast milk, 105, 107–9
burping and, 128, *129*
formula, 115–19, 221
formula preparation, 119–22, *120–22*
formula storage, 121
hypoallergenic formulas, 117
juice, 126–27
milk allergy and, 567
nipples, 122
position for, 122–23, *123*
premature babies, 118
schedule for, 124–25
spitting up, 128–30
supplementation for, 125–28
tooth decay and, 287, 316
traveling and, 185–86
Botulism, 539
Bowel movements. *See also* Constipation; Diarrhea
  1 to 3 months, 216
  4 to 7 months, 244
  blood in stool, 114, 140, 179, 522, 528, 534, 625
  color of stool, 68, 244
  constipation and withholding of, 528, 530
  digestive disturbances and, 179
  newborns, 67–69, 103, 108, 138, 140, 179, 180, 193
  toilet training, 358
Bowlegs, 823–24
Boys. *See also* Circumcision
  autism and, 637
  divorce, response to, 743
  growth, weight, and BMI charts, 878, 880, 882, 884
  hydrocele, 138, 546–47, *547*
  hypospadias, 774
  inguinal hernia, 138, 545–46, 777
  meatal stenosis, 774
  middle ear infections in, 662
  sex-linked genetic abnormalities and, 646
  toilet training, 358, 390–92, *391*
  undescended testicles, 776–77, *776*
  urethral valves, 777–78, *777*

Brain. *See also* Meningitis
early development, 162–65, 272–74
stimulating growth, 218–19, 247–48, 273–74, 309–310, 365–66
surgery, meningitis and, 786
Breast(s), *88*, 88–90, *90*
areola, 88, 89, *95*, 114
cancer, 114
engorgement, 96–100, 105, 110
inverted nipples, *90*
lack of fullness, 178
lanolin/lotions on, 89, 109
mastitis, 110–11
plastic surgery, 114–15
Breastfeeding, 25–27, *26*, 85–115, 241
after delivery, 45, 48, 84, 90
amount of, 84, 103–4
attitude for, 130–31
benefits, *26*, 84–85
bottle-feeding vs., 25–27
bowel movements and, 67–68, 103, 108, 180, 216
burping, 86, 101, *101,* 128, *129*
constipation and, 529
correct vs. incorrect nursing checklist, 97
diarrhea and, 533
duration of, 84–85, 215–16
engorgement, easing, 97–100
expressing milk, 89, 97, 98, 105–9, *106, 107*
father's role, 86
feeding patterns, 102–3
frequency, 84, 100–105, *100,* 108, 177
guidelines for ensuring baby is getting enough nourishment, 108
growth spurts and, 112, 178
health benefits for babies, 86
infant fussiness, 112–14
lactation preparation, *88,* 88–90
lanolin/lotions, 89
latching on, 89–96, *91,* 177

let-down-process, 89, 91, 92, 95–96, 105, 113
medications and, 87, *96*
milk allergy and, 566–67
multiples and, *99, 99*
nipples, 88, 90, *90,* 97, 109–10
nursing bras, 89, *89*
nursing pads, 101, 105
overfeeding, 167
pain and, 87, 92, 95, 96, 97
plastic surgery and, 114–15
positions, 92, 92–94, *93, 94*
premature babies, 53–54
problems, 87, 109–15
recommended reading, 131
reflux and, 113
rooting reflex, 90–91, *93,* 123, 159, 177
secondhand smoke, 709–11
siblings' roles, 88
supplemental bottle, 105
supplemental nurser, 111–12 *111*
support for, 131
vitamin supplements and, 98
weight gain and, 103–4, 179, 180, 215–16
Breast milk, 96–100
colostrum, 45, 88, 89
DHA in, 10
diet and irritating foods, 167
drug warning, 96
hindmilk, 85
increase in, 96–100
jaundice and, 153
oversupply of, 113
storage of, 107
transitional, 96
volume of, 100
Breast pumps, 97, 102, 105, 106–7, *107*
Breath-holding, 330, 588, 591, 791
Breathing
Apgar score of, 48–49
newborn, 46
of premature babies, 53
shortness of breath, 800
Breathing difficulties. *See also* Bronchiolitis; Respiratory distress

anaphylactic reactions, 570, 571
anemia and, 622
asthma, 553–60
breastfeeding and, 85
chickenpox and, 835
first month, 192–93
hives and, 570
HIV infection and, 631
insect bites or stings and, 572
pneumonia and, 605
premature babies, 53, 55
Bronchiolitis, 85, 222–23, 255, 595–98, *595*
Bronchitis, 254, *595*
Bronchodilators, 556, 557–58, 600
Bronchopulmonary dysplasia, 55, 597
Burns, 684, 688–91
electrical or chemical, 689
precautions, 225, 257, 294, 371, 401, 480, 484, 490
when to call the doctor, 689
Burping, 86, 101, *101,* 128, *129*

Caffeine, 6, 113, 167
Campylobacter bacteria, *538*
Cancer
breast, 114
breastfeeding and rates, 86
chemotherapy, bronchitis and, 597
circumcision and, 25
pneumonia and, 605
skin (melanoma), 831
Capillary hemangiomas, 136, 833–34
Capillary malformations, 832–33
Carbon monoxide, 712
Cardiopulmonary resuscitation. *See* CPR
Carrying your baby, 180, *181*
Car safety, 334–35, 398, 430–31, 683
air bags, 499, 501
car pools and, 463

check-in routine before exiting vehicle, 498–99
grandparents and, 368–69
heatstroke, 766
kids around cars, 336, 501–2
rules for, 431
Car seats, 144, 186, 198, 398, 491–99, *492, 493,* 501
4 to 7 months, 256
8 to 12 months, 293
13 to 24 months, 334–35
booster, 401, *493,* 499
choosing, 492–94
grandparents' car, 517
installing, 495–97
LATCH system, 496
multiples and, 760
newborns and, 17
rear-facing-only, 186, *492, 493,* 494, 760
traveling tips, 186, 500–501
travel vests, 495
two-year-olds, 369, 372
types, *492, 493, 494*–95
use of, 186, 497–99
Cataracts, 80, 710, 725, 727, 732, 821
Celiac disease, 526–28
Centers for Disease Control and Prevention, 640, 642, 710
breastfeeding report card website, 85
Cereals, 216, 242
Cerebral palsy, 55, 642–46, 826
Cesarean section, 7, 11, 46–48, 135, 145
Chalazia, 731
Changing tables, 29, 199, 204, 262, 477–78, *478*
Cheesing, 549–50
Chest and lungs, *554,* 595–611. *See also* Colds/upper respiratory infections
asthma, 553–60, 595
bronchiolitis, 85, 222–23, 254, 595–98, *595*
bronchitis, 254, 595
coughs, 224, 598–600

croup, 255, 600–601, *601*
flu, 254, 595, 602–5
pneumonia, 255, 605–7
respiratory syncytial virus (RSV) infections, 222–23, 595–98, *595*
tuberculosis, 607–9
whooping cough, 609–11
Chickenpox, 6, 805–6, 834–36
Chickenpox (varicella) vaccine, 6, 81, 293, 331–32, 370, 810, 835–36
booster shots, 429, 835
newborns or preemies, 835
side effects, 810
two-year-olds, 370
who should not receive, 836
Child abuse and neglect, xxxiv, 739–43
Child care, 435–70. *See also* Preschools
accreditation, 443
caregivers, guidelines for choosing, 436–38, *437*
caregivers, relationship with, 452–55
car pool safety, 463
centers, 445–46
centers, napping in, 451
centers, for sick children, 458
checklist, 886–87
child abuse and, 742
child/staff ratios, 444, 447, *447*
choices for parents, 438–52
conflicts, resolving, 455–56, *455*
CPR and first aid, 691
family, 442–44, *443*
general facts, 435–36
grandparents and, 441–42
head lice and, 840
Head Start, 445
how to find, 440, 443, 446
infant-centered, 201–2
infectious diseases and, 458–59
in-home/nanny, 439–42
injuries, 462, 464
medication given by, 457

naps and, 867–68
for newborns, 183–85
questions to ask, 447–52
safety issues/references, 513
safety walk checklist, 466–68
separation anxiety, 278, 454
sick children care, 448, 456–58
sitters, 184–85, 211, 277, 514
special-needs children, 464–66, 468–70, *468*
transportation safety, 372, 462, 463, 464, 465
trial period, 440
Child Care Aware, 443, 446
Childhood disintegrative disorder, 637
Child Passenger Safety (CPS) Technicians, 497
Child-proofing home, 259–60, 475–91
Choking, 684
coughing and, 599, 600
emergency treatment, 691–92
foods to avoid, 283–84, 313, 352, 692
prevention, 225, 257, 294, 313, 352, 692
Chordee, 774
Chorionic villus sampling, 12–13
Chromosome abnormalities, 646–51
Chronic conditions and diseases, 613–34
anemia, 621–23
balancing the needs of family and child, 618–21
coping with 613, 614
cystic fibrosis, 548, 626–27
diabetes mellitus, 627–30
getting help for your child, 617–18
HIV/AIDS, 630–34
medical home model for, 616
navigating the health care system, 615–17
receiving the diagnosis, 614–15

Circumcision, 24–25, 26, 138–39, 773
Cleft lip or palate, 122, 647
Clostridium perfringens, 538
Clothing. *See also* Shoes
  dress-up play, 315
  dyes, dermatitis from, 561
  going outside, 182–83
  heatstroke and, 766
  infants, 30, 75, 78
  kindergarten preparation, 426
  newborn, 28, *28*, 72
  safety check, 199, 200
  toilet training and, 392
Clubfoot, 5, 828
Cognitive development
  4 to 7 months, 236–38, *237*
  8 to 12 months, 270–72, *271*, *272*
  four- to five-year-olds, 409–10
  one-year-olds, 302–4, *303*, 333
  three-year-olds, 382–83, *382*, *383*
  two-year-olds, 343–45, *344*
Colds/upper respiratory infections, 223–24, 596, 598, 599, 605, 659–662, 793, 819
  acetaminophen or ibuprofen for, 661
  asthma attacks and, 553
  child care and, 459
  congested nose, 153, 223–24, 661
  cough medicine, caution, 661
  coughs and, 598–600
  ear infection and, 662
  fever and, 660, 763
  fifth disease and, 837
  how spread, 459, 659–60
  prevention, 661–62
  RSV and, 595
  sinusitis and, 668–69
  symptoms, 459, 660
  treatment, 254
  when to call the doctor, 660
Cold sores, 460. *See also* Herpes simplex
Colic, 113, 166–68, 522

Color blindness, 646
Colostrum, 45, 88, 89
Communicating hydrocele, 546–47, *547*
Computers and Internet, xxxvi, xxxvii, 813–18. *See also* Media
  special-needs children and, 817
Conduct disorder, 577
Concussion, 702–3
Congenital abnormalities, 5, 6, 646–51
  cerebral palsy, 642–46
  chromosomes and, 646
  coping with, 647
  cystic fibrosis, 548, 626–27
  cytomegalovirus (CMV), 459–60
  detecting, 11–13
  Down syndrome, 12, 13, 646, 647–48
  fetal alcohol syndrome, 5, 584, 647
  genetic and environmental factors, 646
  hearing loss, 652–56
  homoglobinopathies, 13
  intellectual disability (ID), 656–58
  muscular torticollis, 792
  nevi, 831–32
  pregnancy and, 5–6, 626, 642, 646–47, 649, 651
  resources, 651
  rubella and, 6, 646–47, 849
  sickle cell diseases (SCD), 623–26
  single-gene, 646
  spina bifida, 10, 12, 647, 648–51
  Tay-Sachs disease, 13
  unknown causes, 647
Conjunctivitis (pink eye), 194, 255, 460, 728, 837, 842
Consoling techniques
  for crying, 59, 167–68, 246
  newborns, 160
  self-soothing, 212, 246, 591–92
  separation anxiety, 276–77, 278, 287–88

Constipation, 69, 117, 150, 521, 523, 528–30
  bed-wetting and, 780, 782
  lead poisoning and, 718
  newborns, 193
  prevention, 529–30
  treatment, 529
Consumer Product Safety Commission (CPSC), 477, 483, 485, 489, 491
  recalls, 468, 491, 524
Convulsions (seizures), 790–92
  febrile, 763–64, 768, 770
  Reye syndrome and, 835
  tonic-clonic, 786, 791
Cord blood, 27
Corticosteroids, 556–58
Cortisone, 562, 835
Coughing, 598–600. *See also* Croup; Pneumonia
  cystic fibrosis and, 626
  newborns, 151
  roseola infantum and 847
  sinusitis and, 668–69
Cough medicine, 600, 601, 611
Coxsackie virus, 674
CPAP (continued positive airway pressure), 53
CPR (cardiopulmonary resuscitation) and mouth-to mouth resuscitation, 15, 510, 691
  Choking/CPR instructions, 888, 889
  sitter requirement, 184, 185
Cradle cap, 196
Crawling, 262–63, *262*, 265, 270, 291–92, 472, 628
Crib bumpers, 29, 477
Crib death. *See* Sudden Infant Death Syndrome
Crib gyms, 32, 477
Crib mattresses, 29, 31, 476–77
Cribs, 29
  recalls, website for, 31
  safety, 31–33, 185, 199, 234, 475–77
  "side car" arrangement, 33

Croup, 255, 600–601, *601*
Crying, *58,* 58–61. *See also*
    Discipline
    colic and, 166–67
    consoling techniques, 59,
        167–68, 246, 287–88
    fussiness, 112–14
    hyperalert or high-needs
        infants, 113
    middle ear infection and, 663
    newborns, 142, 165–66, 177
    newborns, excessive, 151
    prolonged or peculiar, DTaP
        vaccine and, 809
    self-soothing, 212, 246, 288
    stranger anxiety, 228
    types, 58–59, 212, 228, 246,
        246, 287–88, 290
Cryptorchidism, 776–77, *776*
Cryptosporidiosis, 539
Cuts and scrapes, 693–96
    on eyelid, 730
Cystic fibrosis, 626–27, 646
    bronchiolitis and, 597
    malabsorption and, 548
    pneumonia and, 605
Cystic Fibrosis Foundation,
    627
Cystitis, 778
Cytomegalovirus (CMV),
    459–60, 652

Dactylitis or hand-foot
    syndrome, 624
*Dad to Dad: Parenting Like a
    Pro* (Hill), 189
Day care. *See* Child care
Death of a loved one, 582–83
    funeral service, 583, 750
    grief, 583, 748–51
    reassurance and behavior,
        583, 749–50
    telling a child, 582
DEET, 574, 821, 854–35
Dehydration
    diabetes and, 629
    diarrhea and, 531, 534
    electrolyte solution for, 532,
        533, 534, 535, 552
    fever and, 127, 770
    motion sickness and, 788–89

signs of, 193, 540, 551, 552,
    596
sunburn and, 852
vomiting and, 532, 552
Delirium, 767
Dental care, 355–56, 399
Depression, xxxiv, xxxvii,
    195, 320, 352, 615,
    739–40, 742, 743, 747,
    751
    postpartum, 146, 147–48,
        187
Dermatitis
    atopic, 221–22, 560–62
    causes, 561
    contact, 561, 845–46
    seborrheic, 196, 836–37
Dermoid cysts, 731
Developmental disabilities,
    635–58
    anemia and, 622
    autism spectrum disorder,
        349, 636–42
    brain development and, 164
    cerebral palsy, 635, 642–46
    congenital abnormalities,
        646–51
    general facts, 635–36
    hearing loss, 635, 652–56
    intellectual disability (ID),
        635, 656–58
    learning disorders, 635, 636
    preschool for, 396–97
    seizure disorders, 635–36
    vision loss, 635
Development health watch
    1 to 3 months, 213
    4 to 7 months, 239–40
    8 to 12 months, 280
    first month, 175
    four- to five-year-olds,
        413–14, *413*
    one-year-olds, 312
    three-year-olds, 388
    two-year-olds, 350
Developmental dysplasia of
    hip (DDH), 827
Diabetes, xxxv, 627–30
    bed-wetting and, 781
    breastfeeding and, 26, 86
    congenital abnormalities
        and, 646

gestational, 13
support groups for, 630
Diaper rash, 66–67, 197, 629
Diapers, 28, 63–67
    how to diaper, 64–65, *65*
Diarrhea, 219–20, 530–35
    bloody, 118, 179, 522, 534,
        539, 566, 563
    breastfeeding and, 85, 86
    causes of, 531
    child care and, 460
    dehydration, 68, 127, 531,
        533, 534, 540
    electrolyte solutions, 532,
        533, 534, 535, 552
    food poisoning and, 537–42
    foods or liquids to avoid,
        532, 533, 534
    Giardia lamblia, 523
    HIV infection and, 630
    infants, 66, 68, 84, 116, 118,
        127, 179, 193, 255
    milk allergy and, 116, 118,
        179, 566
    prevention, 535, 537,
        541–42
    probiotics to treat, 119,
        536–37
    roseola infantum and, 847
    solid foods and, 242
    toddler's 534
    treatment, 532–34
    viral or bacterial infections,
        523
    when to call the doctor,
        534
Diet. *See* Feeding
Diphtheria, 7–8, 81, 806,
    808–9. *See also* DTaP
    vaccine; Tdap vaccine
Discipline. *See also* Temper
    tantrums
    4 to 7 months, 248–49,
        251–52
    8 to 12 months, 288–90
    anger, biting, and
        aggression, 577–79
    behavior management
        program, 579–80
    effective, 586
    extinction technique,
        363–64

Discipline (*cont.*)
four- and five-year-old, 424–25
golden rules of toddler and preschool, 361–62
grandparents and, 250, 368–69
one-year-old, 295–96, 323–30
physical punishment, 289, 325–26, 329, 347, 587
preschools or child care programs, 397
single parents and, 324
in stepfamilies, 757
three-year-old, 394–95
time-out, 289, 326, 362–63, 394, 424–25, 578–79
two-year-old, 361–64
when to call the doctor, 579–80
Distractible children, 583–85, 587. *See also* ADHD; Hyperactivity
Divorce, 743–48
Docosahexaenoic acid (DHA), 117
Down syndrome, 646, 647–48
Drowning. *See also* CPR
bathing, 72, 256, 481
bathrooms, 480–81
child care programs, 397
non-fatal, 684
prevention, 696–97
safety precautions by age, 256, 294, 334, 402, 509–11
what to do, 696–97
DTaP vaccine, 7–8, 224, 255, 332, 370, 371
basic facts, 808–9
booster shots, 429
during pregnancy, 7

E. coli bacteria, 538
Ear infections
allergy and, 568
in babies, 220, 254, 255
bottle feeding and, 123, 287
breast feeding and, 85, 86
heredity and, 662
measles and, 843
middle ear infections (otitis media), 662–68, *663*, 667
prevention, 667–68
secondhand smoke and, 709–11
signs and symptoms, 651–52
swimmer's ear (external otitis), 664, 666, 677–79, *678*
treatment, 254, 664–67
Ears, *653, 667, 678. See also* Hearing loss
drops, how to administer, 679
earwax removal, 679
examination of, 80
fever and, 763
tubes, 654, 667, 667–68
tympanometer, 664
Ears, Nose, and Throat, 659–81
allergies, 567–68
antibiotic overuse, 665
colds/upper respiratory infections, 223–24, 596, 598, 599, 605, 659–62, 793, 819
epiglottitis, 669–70, *669*
herpes simplex, 670–71
middle ear infections (otitis media), 662–68, *663*, 667
nosebleeds, 671–73
sinusitis, 668–69, *668*
sore throat (strep throat, tonsillitis), 673–75, 851
swimmer's ear (external otitis), 664, 666, 677–79, *678*
swollen glands, 660, 680–81, *680*
tonsils and adenoids, 675–77, *675*
Eczema, 86, 221–22, 560–62. *See also* Dermatitus
chickenpox and, 835
swimmer's ear and, 667–68
Eggs, 242, 281, 562, 565, 692, 800
immunizations and allergy, 604, 810
salmonella and, 537–38
Eight to twelve months, 259–94
acquainting your baby with a sitter, 277
basic care, 280–90, 292
behavior, 288–90
bilingual babies, 268
brain development, 272–74
cognitive development, 270–72, *271, 272*
emotional/social development, 273, 274–80, *275*
feeding, 280–84
first steps, 263–66, *263*
general facts, 259–60
grandparents, 291–92
growth, appearance, and development, 260–80
hand and finger skills, 266–67, *267*, 292
health watch, 280
immunizations, 292–93
language skills, 267–69
meningitis, 786
movement, 261–66, *262, 263, 265*, 291–92
safety checks, 293–94
sample menu, 283–84
siblings, 290–91
sleeping, 287–88
transitional objects, 282, 287
toys for, 266, 273, 274, 279
weaning, 284–87
Elbow injuries, 824–25, *824*
Electric shock, 482, 490, 684, 697–98
Electrocardiograms (ECGs), 796–97, 798
Electrolyte solution, 220, 532, 533, 534, 552
amounts required by body weight, 535
Emergencies, 683–708
bites, 686–88
bleeding, 693–94
choking, 684, 691–92
CPR, 691

croup, 600–601, *601*
cuts and scrapes, 693–96
electric shock, 684, 697–98
eye injuries, 728–30
fingertip injuries, 698–99
first-aid supplies for home
    and car, 695
fractured bones, 699–701
head injuries, 702–3
heatstroke, 336, 766, 852
lead poisoning, 370, 524,
    716–18, 720
phone numbers, 684
plan for, 582
poisoning, 703–8
seizure, 685
symptoms to watch for,
    685
what to do, 685–86
Emotional development
1 to 3 months, 210–15
4 to 7 months, 238–41
8 to 12 months, 273,
    274–80, *275*
four- to five-year-olds, 412,
    414–15, 425
kindergarten and, 425–27,
    426
one-year-olds, 307–9, *307*,
    313, 334
three-year-olds, 387–89
transitional objects, 282, 287
two-year-olds, 349–52, *351*
Emotional upset. *See also*
    Death of a loved one;
    Divorce; Grief reactions
abdominal pain and,
    524–25, 581
autism and 639
bed-wetting and, 581, 780
coping with disasters and
    terrorism, 580–81
Encephalitis, 767, 843
Enteritis, 531. *See also*
    Diarrhea
Enuresis, 780–83
Environmental health,
    709–22
air pollution, 709–11
asbestos, 711–12
carbon monoxide, 712
contaminated fish, 712–13

drinking water, 713–16
lead poisoning, 370, 524,
    716–18, 720
organic foods, 719–20, 721
plastic bottles (BPA), 714–15
radon, 722
secondhand smoke, 709–11
Environmental Protection
    Agency
asbestos inspections and,
    711, 712
fish advisories, 713
Radon Hotline, 722
Safe Drinking Water
    Hotline, 715
Epiglottitus, 669–70, *669*,
    806
Epilepsy, 790–92
Epinephrine, 570, 571
Equipment. 485–91, 516. *See
    also* Furniture, Toys
activity center, 264
car safety seats, 144, 198,
    372
cribs and accessories, 29,
    475–77
diaper pails, 29
gate for stairs, 401, 482,
    485, 514
humidifiers, 34, 661, 673
infant seats, 486–87, *486*,
    504
mattresses, 29, 31
music boxes, tape, CD, or
    player, 34
stationary walker, 264
washtubs, 29–30
ERIC (Education Resources
    Information Center), 817
Erythema infectiosum,
    837–38
Erythema toxicum, 136
Erythromycin, 51
Exercise
four- to five-year-olds,
    416–17
games and sports, 417
hypertension and, 799, 801
JIA and, 823
pregnancy and, 10
screen time and, 816
Extinction technique, 363–64

Eyes, 723–35, *724. See also*
    Vision
amblyopia, 726–27, 732,
    734
astigmatism, 735
cataracts, 727
chemicals in, 728
conjunctivitis, 460
emergency guidelines,
    728–30
epicanthus and, 733
eyelid problems, 158,
    730–31
farsightedness, 734
general facts, 723–24
glaucoma, 731–32
infections, 193–94, 220,
    460, 728
injuries, 728–30
injury prevention, 729
JIA and, 822
Kawasaki disease, 802–3
light sensitivity, 240
nearsightedness, 734
newborn, 135, 142–43,
    733
newborn, examination
    of, 80
newborn, reflexes of, 159
particle in, 730
pseudostrabismus, 733
retinopathy of prematurity,
    55, 723–24
sickle cell diseases and, 626
strabismus, 645, 724,
    732–33, *732*, 734
tear production problems,
    193–94, 240, 733–34,
    734
when to call the doctor,
    725–26

Fainting, 330, 712, 796
breath-holding and, 588,
    589, 591, 791
Fallen arches, 825–26, *826*
Falls, 225, 293, 371, 401
cribs and, 31–32, *33*
prevention of, 257
toddling and, 297
walking and, 263–66

Family issues, 737–61. *See also* Chronic conditions and diseases; Death of a loved one; Discipline; Divorce; Parents/parenting
adoption, 737–39
child abuse/neglect, 739–43
divorce, 743–48
grief reactions, 583, 748–51
military parent, 755
multiples, 758–61
sibling rivalry, 751–54
single-parent families, 324, 754–56
stepfamilies, 756–58
Fantasy play, 387–88, 404, 414
Fathers. *See also* Parents/parenting
breastfeeding and, 86
newborns and, 148, 187–89, 180
preparation for newborn, 37
reading for, 189
Fatigue, illness and, 800, 820
Fears. *See also* Separation anxiety
the dark, thunder, loud appliances, 280
fantasy play and, 387–88
nightmares, 360, 362, 393–94
night terrors, 394, 421–23
Febrile convulsions (seizures), 763–64, 768, 770, 791
Feeding. *See also* Bottle-feeding; Breastfeeding; Food
4 to 7 months, 241–44
8 to 12 months, 280–84, 281, 283
calorie requirements, 116, 120, 177, 197–98, 280, 309, 311, 312, 419
demand, 100, 177–78
family mealtimes, 352
finger foods, 242, 282–83, 283, 692
four- to five-year-old, 418–21

healthy choices, importance of, 352, 390
one-year-old, 309–21
sample menus, 283–84, 318, 353–54, 416–17
self, 317, *317*, 319
sweets moderation, 311, 317, 390
television as obstacle to healthy, 421, 815–16
three-year-old, 389–90
two-year-old, 352–54
Feet
arch, 261, *261*
clubfoot, 5, 828
flat feet, 825–26, *826*
pigeon toes, 828–29, *828*
two-year-olds, 338
Fencing posture, 160, 161, 203
Fetal alcohol syndrome, 5, 647
Fever, 763–70. *See also* Thermometers
1 to 3 months, 224
4 to 8 months, 255
acetaminophen dosage chart, 767
appendicitis and, 526
chickenpox and, 835
diarrhea and, 531, 532, 534
DTaP vaccine and, 808
ear infections and, 663
eczema and, 562
epiglottitis and, 669
febrile convulsions, 763–64, 768, 770, 810
fifth disease and, 837
first month, 194
flu and, 602–5
general facts, 763–64
heat-related illness confused with, 766
HIV infection and, 630
ibuprofen dosage chart, 768
immunizations and, 810
JIA and, 822
Lyme disease and, 820–21
measles and, 842
medications for, 767–69
meningitis and, 786
MMR vaccine and, 810
newborns and, 60, 68, 194

pneumococcal vaccine, 812
pneumonia and, 605
poison ivy, oak or sumac and, 846
roseola infantum, 847–48
scarlet fever, 851
sore or strep throat and, 674
sunburn and, 852
swollen glands and, 680
treatment, 768–70
upper respiratory infections, 224
water or fluids for, 127, 770
when to call the doctor, 194, 224, 766–67
Fiber, dietary/supplements, 529, 530
Fifth disease, 837–38
Fingernails
chicken pox itch and, 834
infections, 197
poison ivy and, 845
trimming infants, 73, *73*, 135
Finger sucking, 282, 591–92
Fingertip injuries, 698–99
Fire
magical thinking and, 473
prevention, 199, 430, 480, 482
First-aid
courses, 691
supplies, home and car, 695
First Candle organization, 195
FIRST MONTH, 157–200
baby acne, 158–59
basic care, 176–86
bowlegged appearance, 158
brain development, 162–65
breathing difficulties, 192–93
carrying your baby, 180, *181*
child-care help, 183–85
colic, 166–68
consciousness states, 165–66
crying, 166–67, 177
diarrhea, 193
excessive sleepiness, 193, 224
eye infections, 193–94
defensive moves, 161

fathers and, 187–89, *188*
feeding and nutrition,
      176–80
fever, 194
first smile, 169, 201
floppiness, 194
going outside, 182–83
grandparents and, 189–90,
      189, 192
growth, appearance, and
      development, 157–76
hair loss, 158
head, 158
health issues, 192–98
health watch, 175
hearing, 173, 194
jaundice, 196, 624
jitters, 196
meningitis in, 786
mothers and, 186–87
movement, 169–71, *170*
pacifiers, 62, 95, 180–82,
      185, 186
rashes and infections,
      196–97
reflexes, 159–62, *160, 162*
safety checks, 198–200
siblings and, *191*, 191–92
skin, 158–59
sleep, 860–62
smell and touch, 174
temperament, 174–76
thrush, 197
toys for, 176
traveling with baby,
      185–86
umbilical cord, 159
vision, 171–73, *171, 172,*
      197
vomiting 197
weight gain/loss, 108,
      157–58, 197–98
Flat feet, 825–26, *826*
Floppiness, 175, 194, 239, 643
Flu (influenza), 459, 602–5
antiviral medication, 604–5
bronchiolitis and, *595*
fever and, 763
shot (vaccine), for, 81, 370,
      371, 603, 604, 810–11
when to call the doctor, 605

Fluoride supplements, 127–28
Folic acid supplements, 10,
      625, 649
Fontanelles. *See* Soft spots
Food and nutrition. *See also*
      Choking; Feeding; Milk
      (cow's)
diabetes and hypoglycemia,
      630
fiber-rich, *529*
finger, 242, 282–83, 353,
      692
fish warning, 5–6, 712–13
four basic nutrition groups,
      311, 352
how much is enough,
      418–19
juice, 126–27, 243
media and, 390, 815–16
nutrition during
      pregnancy, 10
organic foods, 719–20, 721
picky eaters, 390
sample lunch, 390
sample one-day menus,
      283–84, 318, 353–54,
      416–17
self-feeding, 281–83
snack foods, 431
sodium content, 800
solid foods, 216, 241–44
table foods, 243–44, 313
Food allergy, 86, 527, 531,
      562–66. *See also*
      Anaphylactic reactions
Food intolerance or sensitivity,
      563
Food poisoning, 531, 537–42
Forceps marks, 151
Formula. *See* Bottle-feeding
Four- to five-year-olds,
      403–33
basic care, 415–29
bullying, 428–29
cognitive development,
      409–10
developmental health watch,
      413–14
discipline, 424–25
emotional development, 412,
      414–15, 425

feeding and nutrition,
      418–21
general facts, 403–4
grandparents and, 432–33
hand and finger skills,
      405–6, *405*
healthy lifestyle, 415–18,
      420
immunizations, 852–53
language development,
      406–9
lying, 424–25
media use and, 816–17
menu, sample, 416–17
movement, 404–6
nightmares or night terrors,
      421–23
pediatrician visit, 429, *429*
preparing for kindergarten,
      425–26, *426, 427*
reading skills, 408
safety check, 429–30
siblings, 412
sleeping, 421–22, *422*, 860,
      866
social development, 410–12
table manners, 421
traveling, 430–31
Four to seven months,
      227–57
behavior, 248–49, 251–52
brain development, 247–48
cognitive development,
      236–38, *237*
common illnesses, 255
crying, 228
dietary supplements,
      244–45
discipline, 248–49, 251–52
emotional, 238–41
food recommendations,
      242–43
general facts, 227–28
grandparents and, 249–51
growth, appearance, and
      development, 229–41
health watch, 239–40,
      253–55
hearing, 235–36
illness symptoms, 254
immunizations, 255–56

Four to seven months
  (*cont.*)
  language development, *233,*
    235–36
  meningitis in, 786
  movement, 228–33, *230,*
    231, 232
  obesity, 244
  personality development,
    228–29, 238
  playpens, 246, 248
  safety checks, 251–52,
    256–57
  sleeping, 245–46, 862–63
  solid foods, 241–44
  stranger anxiety, 228
  swings, 246, 248
  teething, 246
  temperament, 238–39
  toys for, 232
  vision, 233–35
  weaning, 284–85
Fractures/broken bones,
    699–701
  "toddler," 826–27
Freckles, 832
Fruit juice, 126–27
Furniture
  bassinets/cradles, 29,
    33, 63
  bunk beds, 478–79
  changing table, 29, 477–78
  cribs, 29, 31–33, 199, 250,
    475–77
  high chairs, 243, 250,
    485–86, *486,* 516
  infant seats, 486–87, *486,*
    504
  for newborns, 29–34
  rocking chair or glider, 34

Galactosemia, 118
Gastrocolic reflex, 69, 216
Gastroenteritis, 523, 531, 551.
  See also Diarrhea;
    Vomiting
Gastroesophageal reflux, 113,
  220–21, 241, 554, 598
Gastroesophageal reflux
  disease (GERD), 550–51,
  559

Gates, stairs and room, 401,
  482, *485,* 514
Gender identification, 305,
  385–87
Genetic abnormalities, 12–13,
  647, 652. *See also*
    Congenital abnormalities
Genital and urinary systems,
  771–83, *772*
  blood in urine, 625, 771–72
  proteinuria, 772–73
  urethral valves, 777–78, *777*
  urinary tract infections, 393,
    778–80
  wetting problems, 780–83
Genitals, boys, 80, 138–40
  circumcision, 24–25,
    138–39, 773
  hydrocele, 138, 546–47, *547*
  hypospadias, 774
  inguinal hernia, 138,
    545–46, *546, 777*
  meatal stenosis, 774–75
  natural curiosity, 414–15
  penis care, newborns,
    138–39
  undescended testicles,
    776–77, *776*
  urethral valves, 777–78, *777*
Genitals, girls, 80
  labial adhesions, 775–76,
    775
  normal curiosity, 414–15
German measles. *See* MMR
  vaccine; Rubella
Giardia lamblia parasite, 523
Girls. *See also* Gender
    identification; Genitals
  divorce, response to, 743
  growth, weight, and BMI
    charts, 879, 881, 883, 885
  JIA and, 822
  labial adhesions, 775–76,
    775
  sex-linked genetic
    abnormalities and, 646
  toilet training, 358, 390–92
  urinary tract infections,
    778–80
Glands, swollen, 680–81, *680*
Glaucoma, 731–32, 822
Glomerulonephritis, 841, 851

Gluten sensitivity, 527. *See
    also* Celiac disease
Grand mal seizures, 791–92
Grandparents
  1 to 3 month babies and, 79,
    214
  4 to 7 month babies and,
    249–51
  8 to 12 month babies and,
    291–92
  child care and, 441–42
  four- to five-year-olds, 432–33
  newborns and, 79, 189–90,
    189, 192
  one-year-olds and, 333–34
  safety inside and outside the
    home, 514–17
  smiles for, 211
  SPEGOS (safety rules),
    514–15
  three-year-olds, 400
  toys, 516
  two-year-olds, 368–69
Grief reactions, 583, 748–51
Growth (physical)
  1 to 3 months, 202–3
  4 to 7 months, 229
  8 to 12 months, 260–61,
    261, 281
  charts, 878, 879, 880, 881,
    882, 883
  crying and, 112–13
  measuring, 79–80, 375, *375*
  newborns, 140–41, 155
  one-year-olds, 296–97
  spurts, 158, 178, 202
  three-year-olds, 374–75, *375*
  two-year-olds, 338–39
Gun safety, 335, 484, 684

*Haemophilus influenzae (*Hib)
    infections, 331, 459, 670,
    806. *See also* Flu; Hib
    vaccine; Meningitis
  epiglottitis and, 669, 806
Hair, 53, 135, 137
  care, 70, 72, 196
  loss, 158, 838
Hand and finger skills
  1 to 3 months, 205–6
  4 to 7 months, 229–32

8 to 12 months, 266–67, *267*
four- to five-year-olds,
405–6, *405*
grandparents and, 292, 333
one-year-olds, 299–300,
299, 300
three-year-olds, 377–79,
377, 378
two-year-olds, *341,* 341–42
Head
carrying baby and, 180, *181*
cradle cap, 196
first year growth, 261
infant, 80, 202
injuries/concussion, 702–3
lice, 460–61, 839–41
movement of, 169–71, *170*
newborn, 45, 137, 158
one-year-olds, 296–97
soft spots, 80, 137, 203, 836
three-year-olds, 375
Head, neck, and nervous
system, 785–94
head tilt (torticollis),
792–94, *794*
meningitis, 785–88
motion sickness, 788–89
mumps, 789–90, *790*
seizures, convulsions, and
epilepsy, 790–92
sinusitis, 668–69, *668*
Headaches
behavior issues and, 591
carbon monoxide and, 712
emergency and, 685
emotional stress or abuse
and, 428, 741
head injury and, 702–3
lead poisoning and, 718
motion sickness and, 788, 789
secondhand smoke and, 710
sunburn and, 852
as symptom of illness, 523,
669, 670, 674, 787, 800,
802, 820, 837, 851, 854
vision and, 726, 734
Head lice, 460–61, 839–41
Head Start, 445
Head tilt (torticollis), 792–94,
794
congenital muscular
torticollis, 793

Healthy Children.org, 580
Hearing
1 to 3 months, 208–10, *209*
4 to 7 months, *233,* 235–36
first month, 194
language development and,
235–36
newborns, 20, 142, 173
test, 144, 236, 429, *429,*
653–54
three-year-olds, 399
Hearing loss, 652–56
causes, 652
cerebral palsy and, 645
cochlear implants, 654–55,
656
language development lag
and, 235–36
lead poisoning and, 718
loud noises and, 491
middle ear infection, 663–64
sign language, 656
signs of, 235–36, 240, 655
speaking and, 655–56
treatment, 654–56
tubes, surgically implanted,
654, 667, 667–68
Heart, 795–803, *796*
Apgar scores of, 48, 49
arrhythmias, 795–97
blue baby and, 151
bradycardia, 55
disease, congenital, 597
examination, 80, 155
fetal rate, 11, 46
home monitor, 195
hypertension/high blood
pressure, 799–802
JIA and, 822
Kawasaki disease, 802–3
murmur, 55, 797–99
patent ductus arteriosus, 798
rate, normal, 795
skipping a beat, 795–96
Heartburn. *See*
Gastroesophageal
reflux disease
Heat-related illness or
heatstroke, 336, 766, 852
Hemangiomas, 136, 730–31,
833–34
Hematuria, 771–72

Hemophilia, 646, 672
Hepatitis, 542–45
Hepatitis A, 461, 542–43
vaccine, 370, 544, 545, 812
Hepatitis B, 461, 542,
543–44, 545
vaccine, 20, 81, 224, 255,
256, 293, 370, 544,
811–12
Hepatitis C, 542, 543–44
Hernia. *See also* Hydrocele
inguinal, 138, 545–46, *546,*
777
umbilical, 154–55
Hero worship, 367–69, *367*
Herpes simplex, 6–7, 670–71
Hib vaccine, 81, 811
1 to 3 months, 224
4 to 7 months, 255, 256
meningitis and, 787, 811
one-year-olds, 331, 332
two-year-olds, 370
Hiccups, 128, 142
Hide-and-seek, 303
High blood pressure. *See*
Blood pressure
High chairs, 243, 250,
485–86, *486*
Hips and legs. *See also* Feet
bacterial infection of the
joint, 819–20, 821
bowlegs and knock knees,
158, 823–24
DDH, 827
examination of, 81, 155
internal tibial torsion,
828–29, *828*
joint contractures and
scoliosis, 645
limp, 826–27
newborn, 155, 158
transient synovitis of hip, 819
HIV/AIDS, 461–62, 630–34
child care and, 461–62, 631,
632
flu vaccine and, 604
immunizations and, 632
pregnancy and, 14, 632
school and, 632, 633–34
screening tests for, 14
Hives, 114, 117, 564, 566,
570–71, 572, 665, 807

Hordeola, 731
Hot tub caution, 511
Human papillomavirus, 853
    vaccine, 812
Humidifiers, 34, 661, 673
Hunger, crying and, 58–59,
    112, 125, 177
Hydrocele, 138, 546–47, 547
Hydrocephalus, 649, 658
Hydrocortisone cream, 562
Hydrolysate formulas, 221
Hydrolyzed formulas, 117
Hyperactivity, 348, 583–85,
    587
Hypertension, 799–802
    sodium content of foods,
    800
Hypertrophic pyloric stenosis,
    197, 550, 550
Hypoglycemia, 630
Hypospadias, 774
Hypothyroidism, 658

Ibuprofen. See also treatment
    for specific illnesses
    dosage chart, 768
    first-aid, 695
Imaginary friends, 387–88
Imitation, 302–3, 306–7
Immunity, low. See also HIV/
    AIDS
    bronchiolitis and, 597
    chickenpox and, 835
    chickenpox vaccine and, 836
    MMR vaccine and, 810
    pneumonia and, 605
Immunizations, 805–12. See
    also specific vaccines or
    diseases
    1 to 3 months, 224
    4 to 7 months, 255–56
    8 to 12 months, 292–93
    AAP position on, 809
    child care and, 459
    during pregnancy, 7
    easing the hurt, 808
    HIV infection and, 632
    kindergarten and, 426,
    429
    newborns, 20

one-year-olds, 331–32
    safety of, 806–7
    schedule, 876, 877
    side effects and reactions,
    806, 810, 811, 812
    thimerosal and concerns
    about, 806–7
    three-year-olds, 400
    two-year-olds, 370–71
Impetigo, 460, 731, 841
Individuals with Disabilities
    Education Act (IDEA),
    465–66
Infant feeding device, 111–12,
    111
Infants. See also Eight to
    twelve months; First
    month; Four to seven
    months; Newborns; One
    to three months
    basic care, 57–81
    bathing, 69–72, 69, 70–71,
    198–99
    bowel movements, 67–69
    clothing, 75, 78
    cow's milk caution, 68
    crying, 58, 58–61, 177
    developmental
    milestones, 81
    diapers, 63–67, 65
    dressing and undressing,
    74–75, 74–75
    feeding, 62, 83–131,
    176–80
    grandparents' role, 79
    growth, 79–80
    growth chart, 878, 879
    hyperalert or high-needs,
    113
    immunizations, 81
    pediatrician visits, 79–81,
    141
    rectal temperature, 79
    skin and nails, 72–73, 73
    sleep, 61–63, 195, 196, 216,
    217, 860–61, 862
    swaddling, 76–77, 76–77,
    168
    urination, 67, 103, 108
Infant seats, 486–87, 486
    shopping cart caution, 504

Infections. See also Bacterial
    infections; Viruses/viral
    infections
    child care and, 458–59
    congenital abnormalities
    and, 650
    first month, 197
Insect bites and stings,
    571–74, 681
    anaphylactic reaction and,
    570, 572
    chart of, 573
    repellents, 574
Insulin, diabetes and, 628–30
Intellectual disability, 5,
    656–58, 718, 720. See
    also Cerebral palsy;
    Developmental
    disabilities; Down
    syndrome; Spina bifida
Internet. See Media use
Intoeing, 828–29, 828
Intussusception, 522–23
Iron. See also Anemia
    deficiency, 621–23
    poisoning by, 623
    sources of, 319
    supplements, 126, 245, 315,
    353, 623
Itching. See Insect bites and
    stings; Poison Ivy, oak, or
    sumac; Rashes; Scabies

Jaundice, 55, 151–53, 196
    anemia and, 622
    cerebral palsy and, 642, 645
    diarrhea and, 534
    phototherapy for, 55, 152, 153
    SCD and, 624
Jiggling a baby, 200
Joints. See also Arthritis; Hips
    and legs
    bacterial infection of,
    819–20
    cerebral palsy and, 645
    JIA and, 822
    Lyme disease and, 821
    pain, Kawasaki disease and,
    802
    rheumatic fever and, 851

Juvenile Diabetes Research Foundation, 630
Juvenile idiopathic arthritis (JIA), 821–23, 826

Kawasaki disease, 802–3
Kidnapping and abduction, 513–14
Kidneys
  glomerulonephritis, 841, 851
  stones, 772
Kindergarten, 395, 425–26, 426, 427
  bullying in, 428–29
  developmental testing, 427
  immunizations and, 426, 429
Knock knees, 823–24
Kohler's disease, 826

Labial adhesions, 775–76, 775
Lacrimal system, 733–34
Lactation, 84, 88, 88–90. See also Breastfeeding
La Leche League, 131
Language development
  1 to 3 months, 208–10, 209
  4 to 7 months, 233, 235–36
  8 to 12 months, 267–69, 273–74, 292
  autism spectrum disorders and, 638
  bilingual babies, 268, 273
  early brain development and, 165
  echolalia, 638
  four- to five-year-olds, 406–9
  hearing loss and, 655–56
  one-year-olds, 300–302, 301, 310
  picture books and, 268–69
  reading, 408
  sign language, 656
  stuttering, 379–80
  three-year-olds, 379–82
  two-year-olds, 342–43
Lanugo, 53, 135
Larynx (voice box), 598, 600. See also Coughing; Croup

Latex allergies, 649–50
Lazy eye, 726–27
Lead poisoning, 370, 524, 716–18, 720
Learning disorders, 635, 636
Left-handedness, 300
Legs. See Hips and legs
Lethargy, in newborns, 153
Light sensitivity, 240, 726
Limb shortening, 645
Limp, 826–27
Liver. See Hepatitis
Lumbar puncture. See Spinal tap
Lungs. See Chest and lungs
Lying, 424–25
Lyme disease, 820–21
Lymph glands, 680–81, 680

Magical thinking, 473
Magnets (refrigerator or in toys), 480, 490
Make-believe. See Fantasy play
Malabsorption, 547–49. See also Cystic fibrosis
Managed care plans (HMOs and PPOs), 23–24
Manners, table, 421
March of Dimes, 651
Mastitis, 110–11
Masturbation, 306
Measles, 842–43. See also MMR vaccine; Rubella
  immunization, 81, 809–10, 843
Meatal stenosis, 774
Meconium, 67–68, 140
Media use, xxxvi, 347, 813–18. See also television
  ages four and five, 816–17
  ages two and three, 814–16
  early years, 813–14
  guidelines for, 817–18
  obesity and, 321, 816
  sleep and, 816–17
Melanoma, 831
Melanosis, pustular, 136

Meloxicam, 823
Meningitis, 767, 785–88, 806
  breastfeeding and, 85
  prenatal testing for, 13
  vaccines for, 331, 332, 788, 811, 812
Meningococcal vaccine, 788
Meningoencephalitis, 822
Mental retardation. See Intellectual disability
Microwaving formula and/or milk, 107, 122, 480
Milia, 136
Miliaria, 136
Military parent(s), 755
Military Youth Deployment Support, 755
Milk (cow's) and dairy products
  allergy to, 26, 221, 524, 527, 531, 566–67
  anemia and, 621
  calcium recommendations and, 418, 420
  celiac disease and, 526
  constipation and, 68
  diarrhea and, 220
  four- to five-year-olds, 418, 420
  hives and, 563
  in infant formula, 116, 117
  iron and, 314, 353, 621
  one-year-olds, amount daily, 315
  two-year-olds, amount daily, 353, 354
  weaning and, 285, 316
  when to call the doctor, 566
Mirrors
  crib and as toys, 176, 206, 232, 279, 315
  separation, self-awareness and, 241, 278, 306
  vision of babies and, 234
MMR vaccine, 81, 292, 789, 809–10, 843
  autism and, 637, 809–10
  booster shots, 429
  one-year-olds, 331, 332
  two-year-olds, 370, 371
  who should not receive, 810

Mobile phones. *See* Media
Mobiles, for cribs, 32, 34, 176, 203, 206, 218, 234, 477
Moles (nevi), 731, 831–32
Mongolian spots, 136
Mononucleosis, 674, 681
Moro reflex, 160, *160*, 161, 203, 213
Mosquitoes, 573, 854–55
Mothers. *See also* Birth; Parents/parenting
   breastfeeding, psychological and emotional advantages for, 85–86
   concerns after new baby arrival, 144–48
   C-section and, 145
   newborns and, 186–87
   preparing for newborns, 38
   returning to work, 201–2
Motion sickness, 788–89
Motor skills. *See* Hand and finger skills; Walking
Movement
   1 to 3 months, 203–6, *203, 204, 205, 207*
   4 to 7 months, 229–33, *230, 231, 232*
   8 to 12 months, 261–66, *262, 263, 265*
   four- to five-year-olds, 404–6
   newborn, 169–71, *170*
   one-year-olds, 297–300, *297, 298*
   three-year-olds, 375–77, *375, 376*
   two-year-olds, 339–42, *340*
Multiples, 758–61
   breastfeeding, 99, *99*
   in vitro fertilization and, 758
   transporting newborn, 760
Mumps, 789–90, *790*. *See also* MMR vaccine
Muscle tone and strength
   Apgar scores of, 48–49
   floppiness, 194, 239, 643
   stiffness, 239, 643
   weakness or paralysis, 650
Muscular dystrophy, 646

Musculoskeletal system, 819–29, *820*
   arthritis, 819, 821–23
   bowlegs, 823–24
   elbow injuries, 824–25, *824*
   flat feet or fallen arches, 825–26, *826*
   knock knees, 823–24
   limp, 826–27
   pigeon toes, 828–29, *828*
   sprains, 829
Myocarditis, 822

Nails
   fingertip injuries, 698–99
   infections, 197
   trimming infants', 73, 135
Naproxen, 823
Naps, 60, 113, 202, 245, 421, 862–68
   in child care settings, 451, 867–68
National Association for Family Child Care, 443
National Center for Missing & Exploited Children, 514
National Down Syndrome Congress, 651
National Highway Traffic Safety Administration, 494
National Resource Center for Safe and Healthy Child Care, 442
Natural disasters, 580–82
   emergency plan for, 582
Neomycin ointment, 561
Neonatal intensive care unit (NICU), 53
Neonatologist, 54
Nephritis, 771–72
Neural tube defects (NTDs), 651. *See also* Spina bifida
Nevi (moles), 731, 831–32
Newborns, 43–56, 133–55. *See also* Bottle-feeding; Breastfeeding; First month; Infants; Premature birth
   abdomen, 137

   abdominal distention, 150
   anoxia, 645
   Apgar scores, 48–49
   appearance, 44–45, 48, 134–40
   bathing, 71–72
   behavior, 142–43, *142*
   birth injuries, 150–51
   birthweight and measurements, 140–41, 155
   blue baby, 151
   bonding, 44, 50, 53, 143
   bowel movements, 67–68, 138, 140
   breastfeeding, 20, 25–27, *26*, 45, 48, 51, 176–80
   bottle-feeding, 25–27, 44, 177–80
   car seat for, 17, 186
   Cesarean births, 46–48
   chickenpox vaccine and, 835
   clothing, 28, *28*
   cord blood of, 27
   coughing, 151
   crying excessively, 151
   discharge from the hospital, 24, 143–44
   dressing, 74–75, *74–75*
   DTaP vaccine, 7–8, 808–9
   examinations, 20, 21–22, 51, 53, 79–81, 141, 155, 178
   eye drops, 51, 194
   eyes and vision, 135, 142–43, 171–73, *171, 172*, 724, 733
   father's preparation for, 37
   first moments and warning against washing, 44
   forceps marks, 151
   furniture and equipment for, 29–34
   GBS infection, 13–14
   hair, 137
   head, 45, 137
   health watch, 150–55
   hearing, 20, 173
   hemolytic anemia, 621
   herpes and, 6–7
   hormones (baby's), 137

immune system of, 7
immunizations, 20
jaundice, 20, 55, 151–53, 152, 642, 645
lethargy and sleepiness, 153, 224
low birth weight, 5, 141, 176
meningitis, 785–88
nails, 72–73, 73, 135
penis, 138–39
respiratory distress, 153–54
screening tests, 20, 56, 144, 653, 657
siblings and, 34–37, 35, 36, 146, 149–50, 149, 150, 191, 191–92, 365–69
skin, 44–45, 72–73, 135
swaddling, 76–77, 76–77, 168
umbilical cord, 48, 50, 154
vaginal birth, 44–46
vitamin K injection, 51
Night-lights, 360
Nightmares and night terrors, 360, 362, 394, 421–23
Nipples. See Breastfeeding
Nonsteroidal anti-inflammatory drugs (NSAIDs), 823
Norovirus, 531
Nose
    congested, 223–24
    saline nose drops and suctioning, 153, 223–24, 661
Nosebleeds, 671–73
Nursemaid's elbow, 824–25, 824
Nursery, 4, 35, 36
    child-proofing, 475–79
    cleanliness, dust, and air quality, 30, 34
    furniture and equipment for, 29–34, 234
Nursery schools. See Preschool

Obesity, 244, 311, 319–21, 628
    BMI and, 320
    bottle-feeding and, 177
    breastfeeding and, 26, 86
    healthy lifestyle and, 416–17

high blood pressure and, 799, 801
media use and, 390, 417–18, 421, 815–16
Oedipal behavior, 415
One to three months, 201–25
    basic care, 215–19
    burns, 225
    cerebral palsy symptoms, 643
    choking, 225
    diarrhea, 219–20
    ear infections, 220
    emotional and social development, 210–15
    falls, 225
    feeding, 215–16 (see also Breastfeeding; Bottle-feeding)
    gastroesophageal reflux, 220–21
    grandparents and, 214
    growth, appearance, and development, 202–15
    hand movements, 205–6
    health watch, 213, 219–24
    hearing and making sounds, 208–10, 209
    immunizations, 224
    legs, 204
    meningitis, 785–88
    movement, 203–6, 203, 204, 205, 207
    neck strength, 203–4, 204, 205
    neediness levels, 212
    rashes and skin conditions, 221–22
    reaching, 206
    reflexes, 203–4
    rolling over, 204
    RSV infections, 222–23
    safety checks, 225
    self-esteem, 212
    siblings, 217–18, 217
    sleeping, 216–17, 217
    smiles, 210, 211, 213
    toys for, 218
    upper respiratory infections, 223–24
    vision, 206–8, 207, 208

when to call pediatrician, 224
One-year-olds, 295–336
    behavior, 323–31
    car safety, 334–35
    cognitive growth, 302–4, 303, 333
    dietary supplements, 313–5, 317
    discipline, 323–30
    discontinuing bottle, 316
    emotional growth, 307–9, 307, 334
    family relationships, 330–31
    feeding and nutrition, 309–21
    gender identification, 305
    general facts, 295–96
    grandparents and, 333–34
    growth, appearance and development, 296–309
    hand and finger skills, 299–300, 299, 300
    health watch for, 312
    immunizations, 331–32
    language, 300–302, 301, 310
    left- or right-handedness, 300
    masturbation, 306
    meningitis, 786
    menu, sample, 318
    movement, 297–300, 297, 298, 333
    safety checks, 332–36
    shyness, 307, 307
    sleeping, 322–23, 332
    social development, 304–7, 304, 307, 333–34
    temper tantrums, 326–30
    toilet training, 321–22, 322
    toys, 305, 309, 332, 334
Optimism, xxxvii
Organic foods, 719–20, 721
Organ transplants, 597
Oxytocin, 11, 41, 91

Pacifiers, 63, 180–82
    breastfeeding and, 62, 103, 125
    colic and, 168

Pacifiers (*cont.*)
  reducing SIDS risk, 62
  safety check, 200, 488–89
  traveling with baby and, 185, 186
Pain. *See specific parts of body*
Palivizumab (Synagis), 598
Palmar grasp reflex, 161
Parasites, 523, 531
Parainfluenza, 595, 600
Paralysis, 650
Parents/parenting, xxiii–xxxix. *See also* Behavior; Brain, stimulating growth of; Discipline; Fathers; Mothers; Pregnancy
  building resilience, xxxiv–xxxvii
  car exiting routine for, 498–99
  child's gifts to, xxiii–xxv
  child's temperament and, 238–39, 307, 308
  communication, hope and honest, xxx–xxxi
  coping strategies, providing, xxxiii, xxxviii
  demonstrative love toward child, xxx
  early brain development and, 163–65
  education and, xxix
  emotions, xxiii–xxv
  emotions after birth, 144–48
  enjoying a child as an individual, xxviii–xxix
  getting help, xxxviii–xxxix, 164, 169, 212, 619–21, 651
  gifts to child, xxv–xxviii
  health care, xxvii
  in-person, "face-time" with child, xxxvi
  joy in life, xxvi–xxvii
  media guidelines for child xxxvi, 817–18
  minimizing frustrations and maximizing success, xxxii–xxxiii
  modeling behavior, xxix–xxx, xxxvi, xxxvii, 321, 347
  nurturing growth and change, xxxii
  obesity prevention and, 321
  physical contact with child, xxx, 219, 247, 273, 309, 365
  secure surroundings, xxvii
  self-esteem, xxvi, 351
  sibling rivalry, 217–18, 290–91
  skills and abilities, xxvii–xxviii
  sleep deprivation, 861
  teaching optimism, xxxvii
  time spent together, xxxi, xxxvi
  unconditional love and, xxv–xxvi
  uniqueness of child and, 228–29
  values and traditions, xxvi
Parvovirus, 459–60, 837
Patent ductus arteriosus (PDA), 798
Pattycake, 274
Peanuts
  allergy, 562, 565, 570
  choking, 313, 352, 692
Pediatricians, 17–25
  checkup schedule, 21–22
  choosing, 17–19
  first examination, 20, 79–81
  four- to five-year olds and, 426, 429
  immunization schedule, 876, 877
  interviewing, 19–22
  issues to discuss with, 22, 24–25
  screening tests, 56, 427
  three-year-olds, 399
  training and board certification (FAAP), 18–19
  two-year-olds, 370
  weight and measurements by, 141
Peekaboo, 219, 237, 240, 262, *271*, 271, 274, 278
Penis
  care in newborns, 138–39
  chordee, 774
  circumcision, 24–25, 138–38, 773
  foreskin, 138, 139
  hypospadias, 774
  meatal stenosis, 774
Pericarditis, 822
Personality, development of, 228–29, 238
Pertussis (whooping cough), 7–8, 81, 609–11, 805, 806. *See also* DTaP vaccine; Tdap vaccine
Pervasive developmental disorders not otherwise specified (PDD-NOS), 637
Pesticides, 720–22
Pets. *See* Animals
Phenylketonuria (PKU), 657
Phototherapy, *152*, 153
Pigeon toes, 261, 828–29, *828*
  internal tibia torsion, 828–29, *828*
  medial femoral torsion, 828
  metatarsus adductus, 828–29, *828*
Pincer grasp, 231, 266, 267, *267*
Pink eye. *See* Conjunctivitis
Pinworms, 844–45
Plantar grasp reflex, 161
Plantar warts, 853
Playground safety, 506–8, *507*, 517
  trampolines, 507–8
Playpens, 246, 248, 487–88
  safety standard (ASTM F406), 487
Pleuritis, 822
Pneumococcal vaccines, 81, 224, 255, 256, 331, 332, 370, 606–7, 787, 812
  side effects, 812
  who should not receive, 607
Pneumonia, 85, 86, 222, 255, 605–7, 787, 844

cough suppressant warning, 606
MRSA infections and, 844
Pneumocystis jiroveci, 631
Pneumonitis, 822
Poisoning, 684, 703–8
  in eye, 707
  food, 537–39
  fumes, 707
  iron, 623
  lead, 370, 524, 716–18, 720
  mushrooms, 539
  plants, 482–83, 508–9, 517
  Poison Help Line, 482, 508, 541, 684, 685, 689, 704, 705, 706
  poison-proofing your home, 508–9, 705
  prevention, 294, 371, 479, 480, 707–8
  on skin, 707
  swallowed, 704, 706
Poison ivy, oak, or sumac, 845–46
Polio vaccines, 81, 811
  1 to 3 months, 224
  4 to 7 months, 255, 256
  booster shots, 429
  inactivated, 811
  one-year-olds, 332
  two-year-olds, 370, 371
Polyps, nasal, 672
Port wine stains, 137, 731, 832–33
Posture, 261, 338
  standing, 261, *265, 266*
Potty chairs, *322, 357, 358,* 452
Pregnancy, 3–41. *See also* Birth; Pediatricians; Rubella
  birthweight and, 5, 140–41
  chickenpox and, 6
  congenital abnormalities and, 5, 646–47
  family relationships and new babies, 34–37, *35,* 331
  fifth disease warning, 838
  fish warning, 5–6, 712–13
  gestational diabetes, 13
  healthy practices and nutrition, xxvii, 4–10, 140

herpes and, 6–7
HIV and, 14, 632
labor and birth, 38–41
prenatal care, 9–14, 164
preparing for delivery, 14–17
rubella and, 6
smoking, 9
Tdap vaccine, 7–8
tests during, 11–14
toxoplasmosis, 7, 513, 727
Prematurity, 52–55, *52,* 135
  apnea and, 195
  asthma and, 595
  backpack warning, 503
  breastfeeding, 53–54
  cerebral palsy and, 628
  chickenpox vaccine and, 835
  CPAP, 53
  delayed development, 175
  formulas for, 118
  health issues, 54–55
  retinopathy of prematurity, 55, 723–24
  RSV infections and, 222–23
  screening tests, 56
  stress (parents') and, 53
  supplemental nurser, 111–12, *111*
  vernix lacking, 53
Preschool
  child-to-staff ratio, 397
  evaluating the school, 396–98
  hygiene at, 398
  illness policy, 397–98
  preparation for, 395–98, *396*
  safety issues, 513
  special needs children and, 396–97
Probiotics, 119, 536–37
Prolactin, 91
Proteinuria, 772–73
Ptosis, 730
Pulmonary function testing (PFT), 555
Pustular melanosis, 136
Pyelonephritis, 778
Pyloric stenosis, 221

Rabies, 512, 513, 687
Radon, 722

Radon Hotline, 722
Raising Twins (Flais), 99, 758
Raking grasp, 231
Rashes. *See also* Eczema; Impetigo
  diaper, 66–67, 197, 629
  diarrhea and, 534
  feeding allergy and, 179
  fifth disease, 837–38
  hives, 570–71
  immunizations and, 810
  Kawasaki disease, 802–3
  measles, 842–43
  MMR vaccine and, 810
  newborn, 196–97, 221–22
  poison ivy, oak or sumac, 845–46
  roseola infantum, 847
  scabies, 849–51
  scarlet fever and, 851
  solid foods and, 242
Reading, 310, 333, 359, 363, 394, 400, 408
Reflexes
  Apgar scores of, 48–49
  gastrocolic, 69, 216
  Moro, 160, *160,* 161, 203, 213
  newborn, 80, 159–62, *160, 162*
  palmar or plantar grasp, 161
  rooting, 90–91, *93,* 123, 159, 177
  stepping, 161, *162,* 204–5, 213
  sucking, 159–60
  tongue-thrust, 216, 241
  tonic neck, 160, *160,* 161, 203, 213, 628
Resilience, xxxiv–xxxvii
  7 crucial Cs, xxxv–xxxvii
Respiratory allergy, 567–68
Respiratory distress, 55, 153–54
Respiratory syncytial virus (RSV) infections, 222–23, 253, 595–98. *See also* Croup
  palivizumab (Synagis) for, 598
Retinopathy of prematurity (ROP), 55

Reye syndrome, 549, 835
  aspirin warning, 220, 224, 549, 603, 803
Rheumatic fever, 675, 851
Rickets, 314, 354, 824
Right-handedness, 300
Ringworm, 462, 846–47
Rolling over, 204, 230, 240, 262
Roseola infantum, 847–48
Rotavirus (stomach flu)
  as diarrhea cause, 531, 535
  vaccine, 81, 255, 531–32, 535, 812
  as vomiting cause, 535, 551
Rubella (German measles), 848–49. See also MMR vaccine
  congenital abnormalities from, 6, 646–47, 849
  hearing loss and, 652
  pregnancy and, 6, 849

Safety, xxvii, 471–517. See also Car safety; Drowning; Emergencies; Environmental hazards
8 to 12 months, 293–94
air travel, 399
animals, 512–13
baby carriers, 502–3
baby equipment, 485–91, 516
baby walkers, 264, 488
backyard, 508–9, 517
bassinets and cradles, 29, 33, 63
bathrooms, 480–81, 516
burns, 225, 252, 257, 294, 371, 480, 484, 490, 684, 688–91
changing tables, 199, 204, 477–78, 478
child care programs, 466–68
child-proofing a home, 259–60, 475–91
choking, 225, 257, 283–84, 294, 313, 352, 480, 684, 691–92
community and neighborhood, 513–14

cribs, 31–33, 199, 475–77
cuts, 693–96
electric shock, 482, 490, 684, 697–98
eye injuries, 729
falls, 32, 33, 225, 371, 401
first month, 198–200
garage/basement, 481–82, 517
grandparents and, 251, 292, 514–17
home (all rooms), 335, 482–84, 514–17
household chemicals, 251–52
household water temperature, 252
kidnapping and abduction, 513
kids around cars, 501–2
kitchen, 479–80, 515–16
lead poisoning, 524
magnets, refrigerator or toy, 480, 490
medications, 294, 335, 371, 371
necklaces and cords, 32, 200
nursery, 475–79
outdoor, 335–36, 341, 491–17
playgrounds, 506–8, 507, 517
poisonings, 294, 371, 479, 480, 481, 484, 508–9
preschool programs, 466–68
reporting unsafe products, 491
school bus safety, 465
shopping carts, 504, 517
situations associated with injuries, 474
sleeping, 332
SPEGOS, 514–15
stair gate, 401, 482, 485, 514
statistics, 471–72
strollers, 503–4, 504, 517
three-year-olds, 376–77
toys, 332, 334, 516
trampolines, 507–8
two-year-olds, 371–72
water, 509–11

why children get injured, 472–75
Saline nasal drops, 153, 223–24, 661
Salmonella bacteria, 537–38
Salmon patches, 135–36, 832–33
Scabies, 460, 849–51
Scarlet fever, 851
School. See Kindergarten; Preschool
School bus safety, 465
Scoliosis, 645
Seborrheic dermatitis, 196, 677–78, 836–37
Security blankets or bottle, 282, 287, 360
Seizures, 644, 685, 790–92. See also Convulsions
Self-esteem, xxvi, 212, 248, 260, 351, 577, 644
Separation anxiety, 274, 265, 275, 276, 278, 308, 313
  consoling techniques, 276–77, 278, 287–88
  sitters and, 278
  sleeping and, 287–88, 360
  tips for transitioning, 454
Sexual abuse, xxxiv, 387, 739–43
Sexual identity, 305, 385–87
Sexuality
  normal curiosity, 414–15
  rules about, 415
Shaking a baby, 168–69, 200, 213–14
Shampoo, baby, 72
Sharing, 304–5
Shigella bacteria, 538
Shoes, 30, 264–66, 561, 823, 829
Shopping cart safety, 504, 517
Shy child, 239, 307, 307
Sibling(s)
  1- to 3-month baby and, 217–18, 217
  4- to 7-month baby and, 252
  8- to 12-month baby and, 290–91, 291
  breastfeeding and, 86
  death of, 748–49
  four- to five-year-olds, 412

hero worship and, 367–69, *367*

in multiples, 758–61

need for privacy, 290

newborns and, 149–50, *149, 150, 191,* 191–92, 365–69

preparing for new baby, 34–37, *35, 36,* 331, 365–67, *367*

one-year-olds and, 330–31

two-year-olds, 365–69, *367*

rivalry, 751–54

Sickle cell diseases (SCD), 623–26, 646

anemia, 621, 622

complications of, 624–25

crisis, 624–25

dactylitis or hand-foot syndrome, 624

detecting, prenatal, 13

eye involvement, 626

pain management, 625, 626

plane travel and splenic infarction, 625

Sickle cell trait, 624

SIDS. *See* Sudden Infant Death Syndrome

Single-gene abnormalities, 646

Single-parent families, 324, 754–56

Sinusitis or sinus infections, 254, 554, 559, 668–69, *668*

Sitting up, 230, *231*

Skin, 831–55. *See also* Rash

1 to 3 months, 221–22

Apgar scores on color of, 48–49

baby acne, 158–59

birthmarks, 135–37, 730–31, 831–34

chickenpox, 834–36

cradle cap, 836–37

eczema, 86, 221–22, 560–62, 677–78, 835

fifth disease, 837–38

hair loss, 838

head lice, 460–61, 839–41

hemangiomas, 730–31, 833–34

hives, 570–71

HIV infection and, 630

impetigo, 841

infants, 72–73

infections, 460

insect bites and stings, 571–74

Kawasaki disease and, 802–3

measles, 842–43

MRSA infections, 843–44

newborn, 44–45, 135–36, 151, 152, 182

poison ivy, oak, or sumac, 845–46

poison on, 707

ringworm, 846–47

roseola infantum, 847–48

scabies, 849–51

scarlet fever, 851

seborrheic dermatitis, 196, 667–68, 836–37

soap and, 222

sunburn, 182, 851–53

warts, 853

West Nile virus, 854–55

yeast infections, 837

Sleep/sleeping, 857–70

birth to six weeks, 60–63, 195, 196, 216, *217,* 860–61, 862

4 to 12 months, 245–46, 858, 862–64

10 to 12 months, 287–88, 864

13 to 23 months, 864–65

apnea, 55, 195, 596

bedtime routines, 861, 866, 847

breastfeeding and, 101, 102, 103

child care and naps, 867–68

clues to determining adequate amounts, 860

crying and sleep patterns, 858, 860–66

emotional upset and, 581

excessive, 193, 224

four- to five-year-olds, 421–22, *422,* 860, 866

getting the most out of sleep, 866–69

getting sleep in sync, 859–60, 866

health issues and, 869

implementing a sleep plan, 861–64

media use and, 816–17

naps, 60, 113, 202, 245, 421, 862–66, 867–68

newborns, 32, 60–63, 101, 102, 103, 153, 165–66

night terrors, 394, 421–23

one-year-olds, 322–23, 332, 843

perspective, keeping, 869–70

positioning for, 31, 63, 195, 196

safety, 332

separation anxiety and, 287–88

three-year-olds, 393–94, 866

transitioning to a bed, 360

two-year-olds, 359–63, 865–66

Smell, sense of, 142, 174

smile/smiling

1 to 3 months, 210, 211, 213

lack of, 240

newborn, 169, 201

vision and, 206

Smoking

AAP on, 9

asthma and, *559*

ear infections and, 663, 667

during pregnancy, 4–5, 9

help with quitting, 711

RSV infections and, 223

secondhand smoke, 9, 709–11

Social development

1 to 3 months, 210–15

4 to 7 months, 238–41

8 to 12 months, 274–80, *275*

autism and, 638

four- to five-year-olds, 410–12, *411*

friendships, 348, 384, 411

grandparents and, 333–34

one-year-olds, 304–7, *304, 307,* 333–34

preschool or early education programs and, 348, 366

three-year-olds, 384–87, *386*

two-year-olds, 345–48, *346*

Soft spots (fontanelles), 80, 137, 203, 836

Solid food. *See* Food

Sore throat, 673–75, 851. *See also* Strep throat
epiglottitis and, 669–70, 669
fever and, 763
head tilt and, 793
scarlet fever and, 851
treatment, 674–75

Soy formulas, 118

Spacer, 557–58, 557

Spanking, 289, 325, 329, 347, 587

Special-needs children. *See also specific conditions*
child care and, 464–66, 468–70, 468
computers and, 817
preschools and, 396–97
Starlight Foundation, 817

Special Olympics, 658

Speech. *See* Language development

Spina bifida, 10, 12, 647, 648–51

Spina Bifida Association of America, 651

Spinal tap (lumbar puncture), 786, 787

Spine, curvature of, 645

Spitting up, 178, 180. *See also* Vomiting
allergies and, 179, 180
bottle-feeding and, 128–30
cheesing, 549–50
reflux and, 113, 241

Sprains, 829

Stairs
climbing, 263
gate, 401, 482, *485*, 514

Staphylococcus aureus, 537
MRSA infections, 843–44

Starlight Foundation, 817

Stepfamilies, 756–58

Stepping reflex, 161, *162*, 204–5, 213

Sties, 731

Stomach virus. *See* Rotavirus

"Stork bites," 135–36, 832–33

Strabismus (crossed eyes), 645, 724, 732–33, *732*, 734
pseudostrabismus, 733

Stranger anxiety, 228, 275, *275*, 276, 278

Strawberry hemangiomas, 136, 730–31

Strep throat, 523–24, 673–75
measles and, 843
scarlet fever and, 851

Streptococcus, 331, 523, 673, 674
glomerulonephritis, 841, 851
Group B, (GBS), 13–14
impetigo and, 841

Stress, xxxv, xxvii, 219, 239, 320
accidents and injuries associated with, 474, 707
asthma and, 554
behavior and, 36, 149, 282, 288, 324, 331, 384, 392, 393, 740–41, 742, 780, 781, 838
building resilience for, xxxiv–xxxvii
chronic and brain development, 247, 274, 310
coping "toolbox," xxxvii
depression and, 352
divorce and, xxxiv, 393, 524, 743, 746
grief reactions and, 583, 749, 750
herpes and, 670
nightmares and, 360
parental, xxx, 4, 38, 53, 148, 186–89, 213–15, 409, 456, 474, 707, 742, 755, 761, 869
parental expectations and, xxxiii
postpartum blues and, 187
premature birth and, 53
step families, 756
thumb sucking and, 282, 591–92
unhealthy distractions and coping with, xxxvii

Strollers, 503–4, *504*, 517

Sturge-Weber syndrome, 833

Stuttering, 379–80

Substance abuse
mother's, during pregnancy, 141
parental, xxxiv
as risk for child, xxxiv

Sucking reflex, 159–60

Sudden infant death syndrome (SIDS), 61, 62, 63, 86, 195–96, 451, 488, 710
prevention, 196

Suffocation prevention, 199

Suicide attempts, xxxv, 577

Sunburn, 851–53

Sunscreens, 852–53

Supplementation, dietary
4 to 7 months, 244–45
AAP on, 124, 245
fluoride, 127–28
folic acid, 10, 625, 649, 651
for infants, 98, 125–26, 178
iron, 126, 245, 315
one-year-olds, 313–15, 317
prenatal, including DHA, 10
two-year-olds, 353–54
vitamins, 4, 10, 98, 125–26, 178, 244–45, 313–15, 317

Support services, parenting help, xxxviii–xxxix, xxxvii, 164, 169, 620–21, 651

Swaddling, 76–77, 76–77, 168

Swear words, 404, 407, 420

Sweat test, 548

Swimmer's ear, 664, 677–79, 678

Swimming, 430, 509–111
motion, 230
pool, 511, 517

Swings
infant, 246, 248
playground, 507

Swollen glands, 660, 680–81, *680*. *See also* Mumps
Kawasaki disease and, 802–3
Lyme disease and, 820
strep throat and, 674

Taste, sense of, 142

T & A surgery, 677

Tay-Sachs disease, 13, 646
TB tests, 370, 607–9
Tdap vaccine, 7–8
Tear production problems, 193–94, *734*, 733–34
Technology devices. *See* Media
Teeth
　cavities, 246, 355, 356, 399, 419, 645
　cerebral palsy and, 645
　cleaning, 246, 343–44, *343*
　dental visits, 356, 399
　first, 246
　fluoride, 127–28, 243
　nursing-bottle tooth decay, 122, 287, 316
　two-year-olds, 237
Teething, 246, 354–55
Television and videos, xxxvi, xxxvii, 321, 347, 362, 390, 411, 421, 813–18. *See also* Media
　AAP on, 417, 814, 815
Temperament, 174–76, 238–39, 307, 308
Temperature, 763, 766
　best way to take, 78–79, 765
　normal, 763
Temper tantrums, 587–91
　breath-holding and, 330, 588, 591
　coping with, 326–30
　how to respond, 586, 589–90
　management, 347, 586
　prevention, 327–28, 588–89
　when to call the doctor, 590–91
Terrorism, coping with, 580–82
Testicles, 138, 776–77, *776*
Tetanus, 7–8, 808–9. *See also* DTaP vaccine; Tdap vaccine
Thalassemia, 13, 622, 623
Thermometers, 78–79, 764, 765
　how to take a temperature, 765
　types of, 79, 764, 765

Three-year-olds, 373–402
　basic care, 389–99
　bed-wetting, 392–93
　cognitive growth, 382–83, *382, 383*
　discipline, 394–95
　divorce, reactions to, 743–44
　emotional development, 387–89
　family relationships, 34–37
　feeding and nutrition, 389–90
　general facts, 373–74
　grandparents, 400
　growth and appearance, 374–75, *375*
　hand and finger skills, 377–79, *377, 378*
　health watch for, 388
　immunizations, 400
　language, 379–82
　media use and, 814–16
　meningitis signs, 786–87
　menu, sample, 353–54
　movement, 375–77, *375, 376*
　pediatrician visits, 399
　preparing for school, 395–98
　safety checks, 401–2
　sleeping, 393–94
　social growth, 384–87, *386*
　stuttering, 379–70
　toilet training, 390–92, *391*
　traveling, 398–99
Thrush, 197, 630
Thumb sucking, 282, 591–92
Ticks, 573, 681
　arthritis and, 820–21
　how to remove, 573, 821
　Lyme disease and, 820–21
Tics, 592–93
Time-out technique, 289, 326, 362–63, 394, 424–25, 578–79
"Toddler" fracture, 826–27
Toddler's diarrhea, 534
Toenail infections, 197
Toilet training
　bed-wetting, 392–93, 780–83
　clothing for, 392
　constipation and

withholding bowel movements, 530
　excitement and "accidents," 392
　expecting new baby and, 331
　grandparents and, 369
　nighttime dryness, 358–59
　one-year-olds, 321–22, *322*
　potty chair, 322, *357, 358*
　pressuring child, 331
　public restrooms, 391
　three-year-olds, 390–92, *391*
　two-year-olds, 356–59, *357*
Tongue-thrust reflex, 216, 241
Tonic-clonic convulsions, 786–87, 791
Tonic neck reflex, 160, *160*, 161, 203, 213
Tonsillectomy, 675, 677
Tonsillitis, 673, 675–76
Tonsils, 675–77, *675*
　pus on, strep and, 674
Torticollis, 792–94, *794*
Touch, sense of, 143, 174
Toxoplasmosis, 7, 513, 727
Toys, xxvii, xxxiii
　1 to 3 months, 218
　4 to 7 months, 232, *232*
　8 to 12 months, 266, 273, 274, 279
　activity center, 264
　balloons, 490, 692
　balls, 232, 266, 279, 315
　bathtub, 72, 279, 314
　blocks, 266, 273, 279, 314, 342, 378
　books, 232, 268–69, 279, 314
　boxes and toy chests, 489, 516
　cars, trucks, trains, 279, 314
　connecting, 315
　crayons, 315, 342, 378
　digging toys, 314
　discipline and, 586
　dolls, 279, 314, 378, 490
　gender and, 305
　household objects, 232, 270, 274, 279, 315
　kiddie push cars, 264

Toys (*cont.*)
  mirror, 176, 206, 232, 234, 241, 278, 279, 306, 315
  mobiles, 32, 34, 176, 203, 206, 218, 234, 477
  musical toys, 232, 315
  music boxes, CDs, iPods, or tapes, 176, 218, 279
  nesting toys, 314
  for newborns, 176
  one-year-olds, 305, 309, 314–15, 332, 334
  push-pull, 266, 267, 279, 315
  puzzles, 314, 344, 378, 408
  rattles, 218, 229, 232, 490
  recalls of, lead content, 524
  safety, 332, 334, 489–91, 516
  squeeze toys, 279, 490
  stationary walker, 264
  stuffed animals, 273, 315, 490
  telephones, 279, 315
  wagon, 264
Trachea (windpipe), 598, 600
  epiglottitis and, 669–70, 669
Trampolines, 507–8
Transient synovitis of the hip, 819
Transitional objects, 282, 287, 360
Traumatic events, coping with 580–81
Traveling. *See also* Car safety; Motion sickness
  by car, 186, 398, 498–99
  four- to five-year-olds, 430–31
  infants, 185–86
  by plane, 186, 398–99, 625
  preschoolers, 398–99
  safety tips, 399, 625
  by train, 186
Tricycles, 315, 402, 430, 505–6, 517
Tripod movement, 230, 230
Tuberculosis, 370, 426, 607–9
Tumors
  bowlegs and, 824
  on eyelids, 731
  testicular, 777
Twins. *See* Multiples

two-year-olds, 337–72
  autism spectrum disorders, 349
  basic care, 352–64
  cognitive development, 343–45, 344
  dietary supplements, 353–54
  discipline, 361–64
  discipline, golden rules, 361–62
  emotional development, 349–52, 351
  family relationships, 365–69
  feeding and nutrition, 352–54
  general facts, 337–38
  grandparents and, 368–69
  growth and development, 338–52
  hand and finger skills, 341, 341–42
  health watch for, 350
  hyperactivity, 348
  immunizations, 370–71
  language, 342–43
  media use and, 814–16
  meningitis signs, 786–77
  menu, sample, 353–54
  movement, 339–42, 340
  new babies and, 34–37, 35, 36, 365–67, 367
  pediatrician visits, 370
  safety checks, 371–72
  siblings and, 365–69, 367
  sleeping, 359–63
  social growth, 345–48, 346
  stimulating brain growth, 365–66
  tantrums, 347, 350
  teething and dental hygiene, 354–56, 355
  toilet training, 356–59, 357
  transitioning to a bed, 360
Tympanometer, 664
Tympanostomy tube, 654, 667, 667–68

Ultrasound exam, 11
Umbilical cord, 48, 50, 71, 72, 137–38, 154–55, 159, 197
  saving blood from, 27

Umbilical granuloma, 154
Umbilical hernia, 154–55
United Cerebral Palsy Association, 644, 651
Upper respiratory infections (URIs), 86, 659–62. *See also* Bronchiolitis; Chest and lungs; Colds; Croup; Pneumonia
  1 to 3 months, 223–24
  head tilt and, 793
  RSV and, 222–23, 595–98
  sinusitis and, 668–69
Urethral valves, 777–78, 777
Urethritis, 778
Urinalysis, 370, 778
Urinary tract infections (UTIs), 393, 523, 778–80
  circumcision and, 25
  fever and, 763
  sickle cell disease and, 625
  wetting problems and, 393, 780, 781
Urination
  infants, 67, 103, 108
  newborns, 138
  toilet training, 358, 390–92, 391
Urine
  blood in, 625, 771–72
  color of, 67
  glomerulonephritis and, 841, 851
  protein in, 772–73

Vaccines. *See* Immunizations; *specific vaccines*
Vaporizers, 34, 569, 661
  when to use, 600, 601, 603, 611, 661, 673
Vegetarian diet, 98, 118, 314
Vehicle Safety Hot Line, 494, 497. *See also* Car safety
Vernix, 44, 53, 135
Viruses/viral infections, 255, 523, 604–5. *See also* Diarrhea; *Specific diseases*
Vision. *See also* Eyes
  1 to 3 months, 206–8, 207, 208, 213

4 to 7 months, 229, 233–35, 240
astigmatism, 735
cerebral palsy and, 645
difficulties requiring corrective lenses, 734–35
disturbances, high blood pressure and, 800
first month, 197
newborns, 142–43, 171–73, *171*, *172*, 724
problems, signs of, 240
testing and exams, 429, 724–25
three-year-olds, 399
Vitamin A, 5, 313
Vitamin B12, 98, 314
Vitamin C, 623
Vitamin D, 98, 178, 244–45, 313–15, 317, 353–54
Vitamin K, 51
Vitamin supplements, 4, 10, 98, 125–26, 178, 244–45, 313–15, 317
Vomiting, 255, 549–52, *550*. *See also* Food poisoning
allergies and, 179
appendicitis and, 525
blood, 534, 673
bottle-feeding and, 128–30
breastfeeding and, 85, 86
causes, infectious, 551
diabetes and, 629
diarrhea and, 534
first month, 197
meningitis and, 786
milk allergy and, 566
motion sickness and, 788–89

pyloric stenosis and, 221, 550, *550*
poisoning and, 706
Reye syndrome and, 549, 835
solid foods and, 241
treatment, 552
when to call the doctor, 551, 552

Walkers, 264
Walking
aids, 264
first steps, 263–66, *263*
one-year-olds, 297–300, *297*, *298*
shoes, 264–66
stepping reflex, 161, *162*, 204–5, 213
three-year-olds, 375
two-year-olds, 339–40
Walking reflex. *See* Stepping reflex
Warts, 853
Water
air travel and, 398–99
bisphenol A (BPA) in bottles warning, 714–15
bottle-feeding and, 126
safety of drinking, 713–16
Water safety, 256, 294, 334, 402, 430, 509–11
AAP on, 509, 510
bathrooms and, 481
Weaning, 284–87, *286*, 316
Weight. *See also* Obesity
1 to 3 months, 202
4 to 7 months, 244

8 to 12 months, 260–61
BMI and, 320
breastfeeding and, 26
first month, 197–98
healthy lifestyle and, 416–17
illness and, 254
loss, 104, 108, 254, 420, 527, 548, 608, 628, 629, 801
measuring and recording, 374, *375*
three-year-olds, 374
two-year-olds, 338–39
West Nile virus, 854–55
Wetting problems, 780–83
Wheezing, 85, 114, 599. *See also* Asthma
Whooping cough. *See* Pertussis; DTaP vaccines; Tdap vaccine
Wryneck. *See* Head tilt

X-ray
of bladder, 782
chest, 798
for coughs, 600
for flat feet/fallen arches, 825
for foreign objects, 692
for fracture, 827
for head tilt, 793, 794
hip and leg, for limp, 827
kidney, 800
for pneumonia, 606
for sprains, 700
for tuberculosis, 608, 609

Yeast infections, 66, 110, 837